NATIONAL GEOGRAPHIC SOCIETY

Research Reports

VOLUME 17

A fossil pirate perch, *Eristmatopterus*, found in the Green River Formation in Wyoming in association with fossil catfish. See Buchheim and Surdam, p. 245.

NATIONAL GEOGRAPHIC SOCIETY

Research Reports

VOLUME 17

On research and exploration projects supported by the National Geographic Society, for which an initial grant or continuing support was provided in the year

1976

Compiled and edited by
John S. Lea, Nancy Link Powars, and Winfield Swanson
under the direction of the
Committee for Research and Exploration

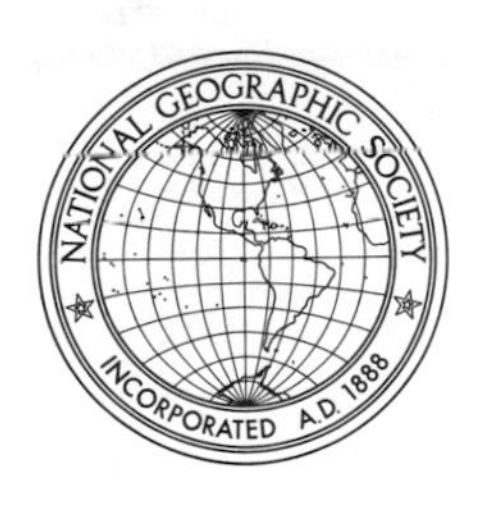

NATIONAL GEOGRAPHIC SOCIETY
WASHINGTON, D. C.

• • • •

International Standard Book No. ISBN 0-87044-558-8
Library of Congress Catalog Card No. 68-26794

This volume was prepared with the assistance of Cynthia Collins and Nancy Simson.

Statement by the Chairman

In 1888, a group, composed largely of Washington scientists, founded the National Geographic Society with two objectives in mind: to increase and diffuse geographic knowledge, in the broad sense—including geology, paleontology, astronomy, geophysics, oceanography, biology, anthropology, archeology, ethnology—and to promote research and exploration. The latter objective was first advanced in 1890 with a grant for the geographic and geologic exploration of the Mount St. Elias Range in Alaska. From this one grant the Society has come to give an average of 160 grants per year (a total of over 2900 for more than 2500 different projects), which represent some $3,800,000 of its 1984 budget.

This volume is the 17th in the series reporting summaries of the results of these projects. It contains 69 accounts covering work for which the initial grant was made in 1976; 7 grants made previously are reported in the beginning of the volume. In many cases more detailed accounts of the work have been published elsewhere. Occasionally they have been published in *National Geographic* or in book form. These accounts are listed among the references each author has been encouraged to submit.

Volumes 18 through 20 (projects funded in 1977, 1978, 1979) will be published within the year. Projects funded since then will be published in another format.

MELVIN M. PAYNE

Editor's Note

The accounts in this volume are arranged alphabetically under the name of the principal investigator, who is not necessarily the senior author named in the Table of Contents (p. xi). A list of the 1976 grants on which these are based appears in the Appendix (p. 612) of *National Geographic Society Research Reports 1970 Projects* (vol. 11), published in 1979.

Reports on the 1976 grants listed below have appeared in earlier volumes of *Research Reports* as noted; hence, no further treatment of them here is required.

1570: To Margaret A. Alexander, for a corpus of the mosaics of Tunis. (Vol. 14, 1973 Projects, pp. 9-22.)

1571, 1646: To Kenan T. Erim, for archeological excavations and investigations at Aphrodisias. (Vol. 12, 1971 Projects, pp. 185-204.)

1572: To Philip B. Tomlinson, for study of evolutionary mechanisms in *Rhizophora* and related Rhizophoracea (trees). (Vol. 14, 1973 Projects, pp. 669-677.)

1581: To Thomas B. Thorson, for study of the evolution of freshwater adaptation in stingrays (Colombia). (Vol. 15, 1974 Projects, pp. 663-694.)

1589: To Galen B. Rathbun, for study of territorial, pair bonding, and scent marking correlates in captive elephant shrews *(Elephantulus rufescens)*. (Vol. 15, 1974 Projects, pp. 549-555.)

1590: To Richard E. Leakey, for continued interdisciplinary studies of the prehistory of Lake Turkana. (Vol. 14, 1973 Projects, pp. 349-423.)

1591: To Mary D. Leakey, for further exploration of Laetolil beds. (Vol. 15, 1974 Projects, pp. 379-386.)

1593: To Richard L. Hay, for study of stratigraphy of the Laetolil beds, Tanzania. (Vol. 15, 1974 Projects, pp. 379-386.)

1594: To Marvin J. Allison, for study of pre-Columbian American disease (Peru). (Vol. 12, 1971 Projects, pp. 1-11.)

1595: To Paul F. Healey, for archeological study of cultural change on a pre-Columbian Mesoamerican frontier (northeastern Honduras). (Vol. 16, 1975 Projects, pp. 339-358.)

1599: To Walter R. Siegfried, for conservation of the jackass penguin (South Africa). (Vol. 14, 1973 Projects, pp. 597-600.)

1600: To Mary R. Dawson and Robert M. West, for study of paleogene terrestrial vertebrates, Canadian high arctic—their affinities and environment. (Vol. 14, 1973 Projects, pp. 143-148.)

1601: To Gary L. Neuchterlein, for study of breeding biology and social behavior of the Western Grebe. (Vol. 16, 1975 Projects, pp. 529-535.)

1606: To Gus Van Beek, for archeological investigations at Tell Jemmeh, Israel. (Vol. 16, 1975 Projects, pp. 675-696.)

1608: To David H. Thomas, for study of prehistoric demography and paleoecology of Gatecliff Shelter, Nevada. (Vol. 16, 1975 Projects, pp. 663-674.)

1610: To Masakazu Konishi, for study of the ecology and neuroethology of the oilbird. (Vol. 16, 1975 Projects, pp. 439-449.)

1624: To James A. Baldwin, for study of the pig complex of New Guinea—culture and ecology. (Vol. 14, 1973 Projects, pp. 31-43.)

1631: To Ralph M. Wetzel, for study of the mammals of Paraguay. (Vol. 14, 1973 Projects, pp. 679-684.)

1634: To David L. Pearson, for a pantropical comparison of lowland forest bird community structure in West Africa. (Vol. 15, 1974 Projects, pp. 505-511.)

1636: To Frank C. Craighead, Jr., for continued research toward tracking raptors by satellite. (Vol. 14, 1973 Projects, pp. 107-126.)

1637: To Patricia D. Moehlman, for study of the organization and ecology of jackals on the Serengeti Plain, Tanzania. (Vol. 16, 1975 Projects, pp. 511-518.)

1639: To John J. Craighead, for analysis of grizzly bear habitat using LANDSAT multispectral imagery and computer science. (Vol. 16, 1975 Projects, pp. 153-162.)

1643: To Anna K. Behrensmeyer, for study of the bones of Amboseli Park, Kenya, as a key to East African paleoecology. (Vol. 16, 1975 Projects, pp. 91-109.)

1645: To Biruté M. F. Galdikas, for study of orangutan adaptation in Tanjung Puting Reserve, Borneo. (Vol. 13, 1972 Projects, pp. 1-10.)

1646: To Kenan T. Erim, for his archeological program at Aphrodisias, Turkey. (Vol. 12, 1971 Projects, pp. 185-204.)

1647: To C. Vance Haynes, for study of the Quaternary geology of the Libyan Desert, 1977 project. (Vol. 15, 1974 Projects, pp. 257-293.)

1648: To Donald H. Menzel, for observation of total solar eclipse, October 23, 1976. (Vol. 13, 1972 Projects, pp. 435-441.)

1649: To Eldon E. Ball, for study of the biological colonization of a recently formed volcanic island. (Vol. 13, 1972 Projects, pp. 89-97.)

1650: To Harald A. Rehder, for study of the marine mollusks of the Tokelau Islands. (Vol. 14, 1973 Projects, pp. 541-548.)

1653: To Talbot H. Waterman, for study of the vision and orientation of marine animals. (Vol. 11, 1970 Projects, pp. 547-566.)

1659: To Charles Walcott, for study of the behavior of dusky and southern bottlenosed dolphins. (Vol. 16, 1975 Projects, pp. 759-769.)

1660: To Donald C. Johanson, for paleoanthropological research in Hadar, central Hafar, Ethiopia. (Vol. 16, 1975 Projects, pp. 383-403.)

1662: To Robert J. Sharer, for archeological investigations at Quirigua, Guatemala. (Vol. 15, 1974 Projects, pp. 85-112 [grant no. omitted in heading, p. 85].)

1667: To José F. Bonaparte, for study of Jurassic and Cretaceous vertebrates of South America. (Vol. 16, 1975 Projects, pp. 115-125.)

1669: To Frederick A. Urquhart, for study of the northward migration of the monarch butterfly from the overwintering site in Mexico. (Vol. 12, 1971 Projects, pp. 721-730.)

1676: To John M. Legler, for study of the biology of sympatry in eastern Australian chelid turtles. (Vol. 13, 1972 Projects, pp. 391-404.)

1683: To Krzysztof Serkowski, for a search for other planetary systems in the universe. (Vol. 15, 1974 Projects, pp. 221-231.)

1685: To Roger S. Payne, for study of singing and behavior in humpback whales. (Vol. 12, 1971 Projects, pp. 551-564.)

1694: To J. David Ligon, for study of the adaptive significance of communality in the Green Wood Hoopoe. (Vol. 16, 1975 Projects, pp. 451-461.)

1698: To Larry G. Marshall, for study of correlation and geomagnetic chronology of late Cenozoic South American land mammal age. (Vol. 15, 1974 Projects, pp. 403-415.)

1699: To James R. Karr, for study of turnover rates in tropical forest bird communities. (Vol. 16, 1975 Projects, pp. 421-425.)

Reports on the following grants made in 1976 will appear in later volumes:

1578: To Douglas M. Lay, for study of Plio-Pleistocene fossils in tar pits in southwestern Iran.

1597: To William R. Powers, for archeological and paleontological research at Dry Creek, central Alaska.

1598: To Alaska Early Man Project, for an interdisciplinary study to establish the archeological record of man's arrival and subsequent progress in the Western Hemisphere and to relate it to the geology, ecology, and climate of the region.

1604: To Ray A. Williamson and Florence H. Ellis, for a study of pre-Columbian towers in the "four-corners" area of the southwestern United States as to their possible astrological purposes.

1605: To Charles W. McNett, Jr., for archeological excavation at the Upper Delaware Valley Early Man Project.

1633: To Ronald A. Nussbaum, for studying the origin and evolution of amphibian fauna of the Seychelles.

1654: To Douglas W. Marshall, for study of military map sources of the American Revolution.

1673: To John A. Graham, for archeological investigation of Abaj Takalik, Guatemala.

1682: To Kenneth L. Brown, for archeological and ethnohistoric study of the development of central Quichean civilization.

1688: To Carl D. Hopkins, for study of electric communication of Gabon mormyroids.

The list below shows the volume in which grants given since 1890 were published, and when:

Grants	Year Made	Volume No.	Publication Date	Grants Lists*
1-224	1890-1954	(1)	1975	
225-314	1955-1960	(2)	1972	
315-378	1961-1962	(3)	1970	
379-425	1963	(4)	1968	
426-477	1964	(5)	1969	
478-549	1965	(6)	1971	
550-600	1966	(7)	1973	(4)
601-670	1967	(8)	1974	(5)
671-743	1968	(9)	1976	(5)
744-822	1969	(10)	1978	(6)
823-917	1970	(11)	1979	(6)
918-1035	1971	12	1980	(7)
1036-1136	1972	13	1981	(8)
1137-1285	1973	14	1982	(9)
1286-1421	1974	15	1983	(10)
1422-1568	1975	16	1984	(11)
1569-1731	1976	17	1984	(11)
1732-1844	1977	18		12
1845-1974	1978	19		12
1975-2130	1979	20		13
2131-2287	1980			14
2288-2420	1981			15
2421-2589	1982			16
2590-2768	1983			17

**The Appendix in these volumes lists each of the grants in the first column.*

Contents

Pre-1976 Projects

1976 Projects

Mapping the Radio Sky[1]

Grant Recipient: James N. Douglas, Department of Astronomy and the Radio Astronomy Observatory, University of Texas, Austin, Texas.[2]

Grants 1248, 1385, 1525: In support of a long-term, systematic study of discrete radio sources and their optical counterparts.

The University of Texas Radio Astronomy Observatory (UTRAO) and the McDonald Observatory have undertaken a long-term and systematic study of discrete radio sources and their optical counterparts. This program is being carried out in three interrelated parts:

(1) The Texas Survey is covering the entire sky north of -35° declination at various frequencies near 365 MHz and is intended to be essentially complete for sources stronger than 0.25 Jy and smaller than 1 arc-min. For each of the approximately 70,000 sources listed, the catalogue gives accurate (1 arc-sec rms) position, flux density, and a simple structure model, together with indications of spectrum slope and degree of variability for many of them. We hope that the survey will serve as a useful resource for astronomy in general, as well as being the foundation for the second part of our program.

(2) Optical identifications with objects on the red and blue Palomar Sky Survey plates are being sought in each radio source field, with identification based on coincidence of the accurate survey radio positions and equally accurate optical positions measured with the UTRAO computer-interactive laser measuring engine. Selection effects based on color or appearance may thereby be avoided; a reliable list of 15,000 to 25,000 identifications is expected.

(3) Utilization will be made in various ways of the greatly expanded information base provided by the survey and the identification program. Particular emphasis is being given to spectroscopic and photometric observations at McDonald Observatory of quasars and related objects and

---

[1] This report is condensed from the authors' *The Texas Survey: Preliminary +18° Strip,* University of Texas Publication in Astronomy no. 17, October 1980.

[2] Co-workers were Frank N. Bash, Geoffrey W. Torrence, and Chip Wolfe, also of the Department of Astronomy and the Radio Astronomy Observatory, University of Texas, Austin.

of galaxies in faint clusters, and to continued radio and optical investigation of the low frequency variable sources detected by the survey.

Survey observations using the Texas interferometer began in 1973 and was 90% complete in 1980. The optical identification program and various utilization programs are proceeding in parallel.

The preliminary version of the +18° strip of the Texas Survey lists 7250 sources covering a solid angle of 0.949 steradians, corresponding to a surface density of 7640 sources per steradian or 122 beams per source. Sources are listed to a lower cutoff flux density of 150 mJy at 365 MHz; however, the survey is expected to be reasonably complete only to 250 mJy. There are 6191 sources listed brighter than 250 mJy, corresponding to a surface density of about 6500 sources per steradian.

The Texas Interferometer

Original planning of the Texas Survey included three fundamental requirements: Whole sky coverage for general utility, listing of more than 50,000 sources for expansion of existing material by a factor of 10, and arcsec position accuracy to make optical identification possible on the basis of position coincidence alone. The interaction of these requirements with economic and technical capability, with a desire to maximize reliability and statistical describability of the catalogue, governed the design of the survey instrument.

We were aware that the Bologna (northern hemisphere) and Molonglo (southern hemisphere) pencil-beam surveys to a similar source density were just beginning. Therefore we decided to survey with interferometers which can yield far more accurate positions far more rapidly than either of the major pencil-beam systems, along with some information on angular size. In return it is necessary to accept some inevitable lobe shift problems and a more complicated set of angular size selection effects than those that afflict pencil-beam surveys. The interferometry of the Texas Survey in many ways complements the pencil-beam efforts, and provides unique depth over the much larger part of the sky so far mapped only to the 1-Jy level.

The listing of sources at a surface density of 5000 per steradian with accurate positions requires a system with greater than 500,000 antenna solid angles per steradian (i.e., equivalent to a dish 700 or more wavelengths in diameter) and a combination of system temperature, bandwidth, antenna area, and effective integration time (including redundancy) adequate to provide the required sensitivity. Furthermore, since this is a survey, the sampling theorem requires that $4 \times 500{,}000$ or $2(10)^6$ directions per steradian be inspected to the limiting sensitivity, thereby making speed a prime requirement.

These considerations, together with economics and technology, suggested an array-type system in the meter to decimeter range. RFI and ionospheric fluctuations important in this spectral region (and equipment downtime, important at any wavelength!) added a separate requirement of a high degree of redundancy, further exacerbating the speed requirement, and necessitating a large number of simultaneous beams or a very long time to survey, or both. And whatever the technique adopted, data handling on a large scale is involved, which is itself a major challenge.

Completeness

Completeness to flux density S is defined as that fraction of sources with flux density greater than S that appear in the catalogue. Three limitations to completeness were expected in advance: *Noise* (including confusion) means that sources fainter than about 250 mJy are increasingly likely to be missed by FINDER, the cataloguing program. *Obscuration* means that close (< 10 arc-min) pairs are generally counted as one (poorly modeled) source, and *angular structure* makes sources with large components appear weak or invisible on all sub-beams. We can investigate completeness by comparison of the differential source count-rate with the known behavior of the logN-logS curve, and to a limited extent by direct comparison with other surveys.

Let n(S) be the number of sources per steradian per Jansky with flux density S to S+dS, and write:

$$n(S)ds = K(S)S^{-(5/2)}dS$$

In a Euclidean universe, K will be constant; in the real universe it is a function of S whose shape is approximately known to small values of S through deep surveys of small selected areas of sky. We may estimate n(S) and K(S) from the +18° strip data, assuming it to be wholly complete; compare it with the approximately known shape, deducing thereby the differential completeness as a function of S. Table 1 has the results of this process.

Column (1) is the center of a logarithmic flux interval containing the number of sources entered in column (2); column (3) is the estimate of K(S) after correcting for the known effects of obscuration. Assuming that the sources have a spectral index of -0.8, we adapt the normalization K_O used in Robertson (1977) to 365 MHz; column (4) is the ratio of K(S) to that value. Column (4) should now be comparable to column (5), which represents the expected values based on Molonglo and Cambridge data, scaled to 365 MHz. Column (6) is the ratio of column (4) to column (5): an estimate of the completeness of the Texas Survey data, corrected for

TABLE 1. Texas Survey: +18° Strip

(1) S(365 MHz)	(2) N	(3) K(S)	(4) $K(S)/K_0$	(5) Expected*	(6) Completeness
0.178	335	149	0.10	0.48	0.21
0.224	686	432	0.28	0.56	0.50
0.282	1064	892	0.58	0.65	0.89
0.355	1130	1271	0.83	0.76	1.09
0.447	1013	1549	1.00	0.89	1.12
0.562	813	1691	1.09	1.03	1.06
0.708	627	1809	1.17	1.20	0.98
0.891	441	1760	1.14	1.20	0.95
1.122	338	1885	1.22	1.20	1.02
1.778	526	1828	1.17	1.20	0.98
4.469	227	1609	1.00	1.00	1.00

*Expected values interpolated and scaled from Robertson (1977).

obscuration. The survey appears to be essentially 90% complete in the interval centered on 0.282 Jy; this interval has a lower bound of 0.25 Jy. (Without the correction for obscuration, the completeness in this interval would have been 73%.) Differential completeness, whether corrected or uncorrected for obscuration, is essentially unity (within the 10 to 20% errors of the "expected" column) for sources brighter than 0.4 Jy. From Table 1 we may conclude that the survey is meeting its goal of useful completeness to 0.25 Jy.

A direct external comparison for completeness can be made with the third Molonglo (MC3) catalogue (Sutton et al., 1974) which is entirely contained within the +18° strip. This 408-MHz catalogue from Molonglo lists 657 sources in 0.142 steradians (4627 sources/steradian) down to 0.24 Jy; the catalogue is stated to be substantially complete for sources brighter than 0.4 Jy (519 sources). The +18° strip lists 559 of these 657 sources, or 85%; the number of MC3 sources not found is approximately consistent with the effect of resolution and obscuration in the survey. An additional 530 Texas sources are listed in the MC3 survey zone which are not in MC3. Assuming a spectral index of -0.8, 455 of these fall below the MC3 completeness limit of 0.4 Jy at 408 MHz; 40 of the remaining 75 are close to it. Some of the residual 35 sources may have significantly overestimated flux densities in the Texas Survey; some are doubtless part of the incompleteness of MC3 (if the MC3 were 95% complete for sources brighter than 0.4 Jy, 27 sources would have been missed by them). Thus, one may use this comparison with the Texas Survey to conclude that the MC3 catalogue is substantially (>90%) complete above 0.4 Jy, as claimed.

Direct checks of the completeness of the Texas Survey to 0.25 Jy are difficult: It is the only large survey now available going that deep. However, a number of Westerbork supersynthesis maps covering a total of 16 square degrees within the +18° strip have been published, at observing frequencies of 610 MHz (6 square degrees; Valentijn, 1980) and 1420 MHz (10 square degrees; Willis et al., 1976). These maps contain 326 sources to very faint flux limits; of this number 28 would be expected to be brighter than 0.25 Jy at 365 MHz if a spectral index of -0.8 is assumed. The Texas Survey lists 25 of these 28 sources, for a completeness of about 90% based on this small sample.

Reliability

Reliability is the probability that a listed source corresponds to a true source in the sky, having within listed error the parameters given. This may be further represented as the product of enumeration reliability (the probability that a source of approximately this flux density is approximately in this direction) and characterization reliability (the probability that a correctly enumerated source is correctly described, e.g., is at the right position lobe).

A general idea of enumeration reliability may be obtained from the comparison with MC3 and Westerbork data mentioned above. There are 75 Texas sources within the MC3 survey zone with extrapolated flux densities above the MC3 completeness limit but not found in the MC3 catalogue; 35 of these are sufficiently strong that they represent either incompleteness in MC3 or gross errors or spurious sources in the Texas survey. The ratio 519/(519+35) = 0.94 is the product of the reliability of the Texas Survey and the completeness of MC3; this comparison suggests an enumeration reliability better than 94% for these relatively strong sources. The Westerbork synthesis maps (except at their edges) go to a flux density far below the Texas Survey; all Texas sources within the region of these maps should appear on them, if they are not spurious. Of 34 Texas sources in the overlap region, 33 are found in the Westerbork maps, corresponding to an enumeration reliability of 97%; the one not found is on the very edge of a Westerbork map and might not in fact be spurious.

Of equal concern to users of the Texas Survey is characterization reliability: What is the probability that the error in the listed quantities will grossly exceed the quoted error due, e.g., to position or structure lobe-shifts?

The stronger sources in the Molonglo catalogue have sufficient position accuracy to permit assessment of lobe-shift incidence. About 1 to 2% of sources with no adverse flags (code +++) are lobe-shifted; sources whose final code character is W denoting lobe-shift warning have a lobe-shift incidence of about 40%; all other sources have an incidence of about 8%. The relative proportion of catalogue sources in these three categories, and thus the overall rate of lobe-shift incidence, is naturally a function of flux density. About two thirds of the sources brighter than 0.8 Jy are in the 2% category, with about a tenth in the 40% category. Sources between 0.25 and 0.40 Jy on the other hand fall half into the 40% category and three tenths into the 2% category.

The incidence of lobe-shifts for the various categories has only been reliably set by the above Molonglo comparisons for sources brighter than about 0.5 Jy. However, some limited data for the very faintest sources have been obtained from comparison with supersynthesis maps. Five of the 33 faint Texas sources appearing on Westerbork maps are lobe-shifted: All of them have a lobe-shift W flag. Predictions of an alternative lobe were made in four of these cases; three were correct and one wrong.

Checking the incidence of structure lobe-shifts in a systematic manner is more difficult due to a lack of data on all but the brighter sources (which are not always useful for comparisons since they are the very ones that are expected to be poorly modeled in the survey and flagged as such). Wills' (1979) observations of 4C sources with the National Radio Astronomy Observatory (NRAO) interferometer produced 16 source maps which overlap the +18° strip; 15 are consistent with the models listed in the survey. Based on this, and on comparison with a heterogeneous collection of models in the literature, we estimate that about 80% of the acceptable models are substantially correct.

Accuracy

Errors quoted are internal, based on the covariance matrix of the least-squares adjustment, using the appropriately propagated baseline noise or the observed standard deviation of unit weight obtained from the residuals to the overdetermined solution, whichever is larger. The correctness of the internal error calculation procedures for all parameters has been verified by extensive Monte Carlo testing. Table 2 summarizes the average accuracy of centroid right ascension and declination and model flux density as a function of model and of flux density. The right ascension error is systematically twice as great as the declination error—an expected result of the Texas interferometer antenna arrangements. The larger errors of D and particularly AD models reflect the larger number of parameters in these cases, but more importantly are a result of covariance of position and flux with the structure estimates themselves.

Determination of the external random and systematic position error is more difficult. Optical positions are measurable with accuracy comparable to these data, but contain an unknown deviation between the radio

TABLE 2. Average Internal Position and Flux Errors

Model	*Error*	$0.25<S<0.50$	$0.50<S<1.00$	$1.00<S$	*All S*
P	σ_α	1″.40	0″.76	0″.36	1″.07
	σ_δ	0″.59	0″.35	0″.19	0″.49
	σ_S	20.3 mJy	21.8 mJy	30.7 mJy	22.4 mJy
D	σ_α	1″.58	0″.94	0″.43	0″.98
	σ_δ	0″.74	0″.46	0″.23	0″.48
	σ_S	39.6 mJy	42.6 mJy	56.9 mJy	45.8 mJy
AD	σ_α	3″.40	1″.70	1″.01	1″.36
	σ_δ	2″.53	1″.45	0″.85	1″.13
	σ_S	42.1 mJy	45.1 mJy	69.3 mJy	59.3 mJy

and optical centroids. Some radio positions have been measured to significantly greater accuracy (about 0.01 arc-sec in each coordinate) by Wade and Johnston (1977) and by Elsmore and Ryle (1976). The position system of Wade and Johnston was adopted, and final corrections were applied to survey positions to adjust our system to theirs (this involved adding -0.015 to right ascensions, -0.335 to declinations). The residual scatter of Texas positions to these accurate calibrators was 0.53 arc-sec in right ascension and 0.29 arc-sec in declination; taking the Texas internal error into account, these residuals suggest an added external error of about 0.4 arc-sec in right ascension, 0.2 arc-sec in declination. The excess residuals to a group of 39 astrometrically determined optical positions in the strip were significantly higher: 0.8 by 0.8 arc-sec, presumably a result of radio-optical centroid variation.

Flux densities are on the system of B. Wills (1973). Well modeled sources exhibit a flux density scatter of about 4% referred to other observations of the sources on this system, which is about the limit of accuracy of the other measurements. Internally, variation of the flux density scale from cycle to cycle for strong constant sources is about 1.4%.

The external accuracy of the spectral index and the structure model parameters has not yet been systematically assessed. When supersynthesis maps show that a source is indeed a double or asymmetric double of the form we assume, the errors appear to be representative. The spectral index is poorly determined because of the restricted frequency baseline used, and can be confused with variability; generally speaking, the distinction between a flat and steep spectrum source appears to be reliable.

Conclusion

Analysis of the catalogue shows that basic survey goals are being met: The surface density of sources is about 7640 per steradian; the catalogue is usefully complete to about 0.25 Jy; point-source position accuracy averages 1 arc-sec in right ascension, 0.5 arc-sec in declination; simple but useful structure models are given, with indications of spectrum and flux density variability for many sources; and meaningful errors and quality flags are associated with each source.

Acknowledgments

The Texas Survey is the result of the combined efforts of all UTRAO staff members, past and present.

Dr. C. C. Brooks and Dr. Gerard F. Moseley proved the viability of the space-frequency synthesis technique through construction and use of the prototype 245-MHz interferometer during 1966-1969; Dr. Moseley later coordinated the construction of the Texas interferometer and UTRAO facilities in general. Many current survey analysis routines originated in their work.

The Texas interferometer was constructed in 1969-1971; this was particularly assisted by the efforts of Frederick L. Beckner, James A. Isbell, and UTRAO Superintendent Dino R. Parenti and his staff. Pre-survey observations and analysis carried out in 1971-1973 form the basis of current survey procedures; important contributions to this work were made by former graduate students Drs. William D. Cotton, Frank D. Ghigo, and Frazer N. Owen.

The Texas interferometer in its expanded and computer-controlled configuration came into operation in 1973, and the survey has occupied its time since then. The authors are grateful to those who have maintained and operated this instrument over the years, particularly to Dr. F. Arakel Bozyan (Deputy Director, UTRAO), to Grant C. Conant (UTRAO Superintendent) and to his predecessor Dino R. Parenti, and to the entire UTRAO Marfa staff, especially to those who have been with the project since its beginning: Eliberto S. Franco, Pablo R. Rubio, and Samuel Whatley. The data processing group in Austin is particularly important in this information-intensive project. We thank Ms. Diana B. Hearn and Mr. Kirk Webb and their co-workers for indispensable interest and assistance.

Our colleagues in the radio group, Drs. Paul D. Hemenway, Beverley J. Wills, and Derek Wills, have contributed broad-ranging advice and very particular assistance in areas too numerous to mention. We are grateful for their continued help.

REFERENCES

DOUGLAS, J. N.; BASH, F. N.; GHIGO, F. D.; MOSELEY, G. F.; and TORRENCE, G. W.
1973. First results from the Texas Interferometer: Positions of 605 discrete sources. Astron. Journ., vol. 78, pp. 1-17.

ELSMORE, B., and RYLE, M.
1976. Further astrometric observations with the 5-km radio telescope. Mon. Nat. Roy. Astron. Soc., vol. 174, pp. 411-423.

MOSELEY, G. F.; BROOKS, C. C.; and DOUGLAS, J. N.
1970. Precise declinations and optical identifications of selected discrete radio sources. Astron. Journ., vol. 75, pp. 1015-1026.

ROBERTSON, J. G.
1977. The Molonglo Deep Sky Survey of radio sources. III. Source counts. Aust. Journ. Phys., vol. 30, pp. 241-249.

SUTTON, J. M.; DAVIES, I. M.; LITTLE, A. G.; and MURDOCK, H. S.
1974. The Molonglo radio source catalogues 2 and 3. Aust. Journ. Phys. Astrophys. Suppl., vol. 33, pp. 1-44.

VALENTIJN, E. A.
1980. A Westerbork survey of clusters of galaxies. XIII. Deep 610 MHz source counts from the Cancer Cluster field. Astron. Astrophys. vol. 89, pp. 234-238.

WADE, C. M., and JOHNSTON, K. J.
1977. Precise positions of radio sources. V. Positions of 36 sources measured on a baseline of 35 km. Astron. Journ., vol. 82, pp. 791-795.

WILLIS, A. G.; OOSTERBAAN, C. E.; and DE RUITER, H. R.
1976. A Westerbork 1415 MHz survey of background radio sources. I. The catalogue. Astron. Astrophys. Suppl., vol. 25, pp. 453-505.

WILLIS, B.
1973. On the calibration of flux densities and the determination of spectra at radio frequencies. Astrophys. Journ., vol. 180, pp. 335-350.

WILLS, D.
1979. Radio studies of complete samples of QSOs from the 4C and Parkes catalogues. Astrophys. Journ. Suppl., vol. 39, pp. 291-315.

JAMES N. DOUGLAS

Settlement Patterns in Northwestern Yucatán

Grant Recipient: Edward B. Kurjack, Department of Anthropology, Western Illinois University, Macomb, Illinois.

Grant 1463: For study of archeological settlement patterns by means of air-photo interpretation and field reconnaissance.

A grant from the National Geographic Society in 1975 supported the first systematic attempt to take advantage of special circumstances facilitating study of archeological settlement patterns on the northwestern corner of the Yucatán Peninsula. A survey of 2000 km was carried out using a combination of air-photo interpretation and field reconnaissance. These investigations focused on the environs of the large site at Dzibilchaltún, where National Geographic Society—Tulane University research teams had worked for over 10 years (Andrews IV and Andrews V, 1980). Inspection of aerial photographs of the region surrounding the primary 2000-km study area and visits to locations with signs of human remains produced a more general overview of pre-Columbian communities. The project resulted in the development of information about the size, layout, and distribution of ancient settlements as well as conclusions concerning relationships between human geography and social organization.

Several conditions favor investigation of settlement patterns in northwestern Yucatán. The limestone bedrock that forms the coastal plain is covered by only a few centimeters of soil; therefore, archeological features, mostly the remains of masonry buildings or foundations, are not buried. Instead, collapsed structures form conspicuous heaps of rubble on the level landscape. Walls, corners, and doorways protrude from these piles of debris, so that reasonably accurate ground plans can be prepared without digging. The archeologists can examine entire communities without having to undertake the costly excavations needed in most other areas of the world.

Aerial Photography

The exceptional utility of aerial photography also facilitated fieldwork. The low vegetation that covers northwestern Yucatán, while heavy enough to obstruct the vision of surveyors at ground level, does not completely disguise archeological remains from the view of aerial cameras. Numerous photographs illustrate overall configurations and even many of the details of whole communities abandoned centuries ago. Features, such as walls surrounding some sites and causeways connecting others, are more efficiently studied through aerial images than in the field. On a regional level, the locations of important settlements, characterized by the presence of monumental architecture, can be compared with the distribution of lesser satellites. Of course, photographs of the rain forests that grow over most of the southern Maya lowlands contain relatively little data, so aerial views of the plantations and bush of northern Yucatán are unique sources of information for interpretations of Maya life and society.

Dzibilchaltún Environs

The method described above was first tried in the area surrounding Dzibilchaltún, a major pre-Columbian settlement situated a few kilometers north of Mérida, Yucatán, Mexico. E. Wyllys Andrews IV (1965), Director of the National Geographic Society—Tulane University Program of Research at the ruins, reported evidence of an exceptionally long period of occupation there, lasting from Formative through Colonial times. A map of the site (Stuart et al., 1979; Kurjack, 1974) shows the distribution of ancient buildings over an area of 19 km. Exploration of the region beyond the map to learn more about Dzibilchaltún was one goal of the present project (Kurjack, 1979).

Interpretation of the aerial imagery constituted the first phase of research. Photographs at a scale of 1:30,000 that had been taken in 1948 were purchased from the Compañía Mexicana Aerofoto, S.A. Additional views at a scale of 1:20,000 that had been prepared in 1962 were made available by the Centro Regional del Sureste, Instituto Nacional de Antropología y Historia. The photographs were inspected under binocular stereoscopes for signs of pre-Columbian buildings. Efforts were concentrated on the area covered by the "Progreso Sheet" of the *Carta Militar De La República Mexicana,* 1:100,000, prepared by the Secretaría de la Defensa Nacional.

All of the locations where ruins appeared in the photographs were checked in the field in order to verify the existence of pre-Hispanic architecture and provide feedback for further air-photo interpretation. Three months of reconnaissance resulted in the registration of 145 sites over an area of 2000 km^2. All of these ruin groups included numerous large platforms that once served as foundations for houses constructed of perishable materials. Most of the sites also contained pyramidal heaps of rubble that probably functioned as elevated shrines or adoratories. Causeways, called *sacbeob* in Maya, connected the more important buildings at several larger sites. Most of the sites, however, were small, covering areas less than 25 ha.

The sites encountered by the survey are not distributed evenly across the map. Approximately half the area, a strip of land 15 to 20 km wide that borders the Gulf of Mexico, is almost devoid of ruins. By comparison a 1000-km^2 zone on the interior portions of the chart averages approximately one settlement for every 7 km^2.

This striking contrast is almost certainly due to the lack of agricultural potential in areas approaching the coast. Despite the attraction of coastal resources, including salt, a commodity known to be important in pre-Columbian trade, the Maya situated the majority of their communities inland, where self-sufficiency in basic foodstuffs could be maintained. Dzibilchaltún and several other major sites seem to be located as close as possible to the coast while remaining on land where agriculture was at least possible.

The history of urban growth was a theme from earlier research that was expanded by the survey. The map of Dzibilchaltún showed that monumental construction activity became progressively more concentrated during late Classic times.

Determining the patterns formed by the distribution of "expensive" buildings in areas off the map was another research objective. Surface indications of buildings covered by masonry roofs, the most characteristic feature of Classic monumental construction, were observed at only 2 of the 145 locations. The carefully dressed and squared blocks from late Classic concrete-veneer masonry, so easily indentified on piles of debris formed when Florescent Period vaulted structures collapsed, were found at only one site. This evidence indicates that most monumental building at these smaller settlements took place during the late Preclassic Period. Monumental structures from the Preclassic, then, seem more dispersed than those of the Classic Period. This conclusion, however, is tentative for the data are based on surface observations rather than excavations.

The density of ruins in the region surrounding Dzibilchaltún constitutes the highest recorded number of sites per square kilometer found anywhere on the peninsula. South of our study zone, however, the usefulness of aerial photography is diminished because of heavier vegetation, and many of the lesser ruin groups are still uncharted. Still, the quantity of sites on the northern coastal plain recalls the words of Landa, the 16th century chronicler who wrote that ruins were found in every Yucatecan field. Obviously this is not true, at least for the coastal margins. But the frequency of small communities encountered by our survey suggests the need for future investigation comparing the study area with sample tracts in other parts of the Maya lowlands. Such research would indicate which environmental settings were most favored by pre-Columbian populations and which resources were considered crucial for their way of life.

Settlement Hierarchy

Problems concerning the size of pre-Columbian communities were a particular focus of interest for the project. Earlier research dealing with this question at Dzibilchaltún had excited considerable discussion. E. Wyllys Andrews IV (1965, 1968; Kurjack, 1974) described those ruins as a settlement of urban proportions, but other scholars insisted Dzibilchaltún consisted of several small sites rather than a single big one. Many specialists viewed the evidence of population concentration at Dzibilchaltún as a rare phenomenon contrasting with the more usual dispersed Classic Maya settlement patterns.

Judged from the amount of monumental architecture visible in aerial photographs, Dzibilchaltún is indeed a huge site. Collapsed buildings are spread over an area of at least 3 km^2 with causeways connecting the biggest ruin groups. The contrast between the size of Dzibilchaltún and that of the 145 other sites in the vicinity is obvious.

The presence of a settlement hierarchy is an important criterion of urbanism. The existence of a pre-Columbian system of ranking interrelated settlements in northern Yucatán is strongly supported by the differing quantities of monumental construction found at the cores of the sites. The volume of material used in the principal buildings and the area covered by the heaps of rubble can be estimated from the aerial photographs. If Dzibilchaltún is the standard for a large community, at least two smaller types of settlement occur in the surrounding 1000 km^2. The chief difference among these three ranks is in the amount of monumental architecture present.

How many sites in northern Yucatán as a whole are comparable to Dzibilchaltún on the basis of total effort expended in monumental construction? Rapid perusal of hundreds of aerial photographs from areas farther from Dzibilchaltún showed that important settlements were few in number. Of these, Izamal, which contains at least two pyramids that are enormous even by the standards of Dzibilchaltún, was the biggest. Uci, Muna, Ake, and Dzilam were also among the more significant sites (Garza and Kurjack, 1980).

Demographic parameters, however, are the customary criteria for estimating the rank of a community in a modern settlement hierarchy and the number of houses at an archeological site is a more direct measure of population than monumental architecture. Evidence for a large resident population had been encountered by tedious surveying and mapping at Dzibilchaltún, but information concerning similar population centers in northern Yucatán was lacking. Most of the large ruin groups nearest to Dzibilchaltún were too overgrown for a study of small structures by means of aerial photography.

Photographs of Yaxcopoil and Chunchucmil, however, provided the best evidence of population concentrations surrounding assemblages of monumental architecture. Both of these sites are situated in areas of exceptionally low vegetation, so numerous house remains were visible.

Chunchucmil proved to be of particular interest. Visits to that site verified the presence of a defensive wall enclosing the central buildings and causeways connecting the more important structures. Beyond the pyramids at the core of the settlement was a broad zone filled with low mounds. Boundary walls divided this area into a series of adjacent compounds. Narrow walkways were the only space left vacant between these dwelling complexes. The data from Chunchucmil are definitive; large population concentrations constituted at least one form of settlement in the northern lowlands during the Classic Period (Vlcek et al., 1978).

Conclusion

In summary, three characteristics of ancient Maya geography were documented by the survey. The first two, existence of a settlement hierarchy and the presence of communities that included large resident populations, suggest a highly structured and functionally interrelated urban society that is consistent with the quality of art and monumental architecture associated with Yucatecan ruins. But a third principle also seems to have influenced the distribution of archeological sites: Only locations where agricultural potential could ensure basic economic self-sufficiency developed as key centers. This indicates that ties between population centers were not necessarily vital except, perhaps, for the support of the highest ranking communities.

The techniques that evolved during the course of this research were later refined and used over a much larger area (Garza and Kurjack, 1980; Kurjack and Garza, 1981), so the general features of pre-Columbian community layout and distribution are now well known. Interpretation of these data, however, seems to require resolution of apparent contradictions, such as existence of a social system that included both settlement hierarchies and self-sufficient communities. This compatibility of what appear from the vantage point of a highly integrated contemporary society to be opposing tendencies in the case of the lowland Maya may have general implications for our understanding of the world before the industrial revolution. Therefore, rather than being conceptualized as the remains of a highly gifted, unique people, the patterns formed by the distribution of ruined architecture of the Yucatán Peninsula can be considered the result of universal adaptive strategies that still guide the survival of human groups in many parts of the world.

REFERENCES

ANDREWS, E. WYLLYS IV

1960. Excavations at Dzibilchaltún, northwestern Yucatán, Mexico. Proc. Amer. Phil. Soc., vol. 104, pp. 254-265.

1965. Archaeology and prehistory in the northern Maya lowlands; an introduction. Pp. 288-330 *in* vol. 2, "Handbook of Middle American Indians." University of Texas Press, Austin.

1968. Dzibilchaltún, a northern Maya metropolis. Archaeology, vol. 21, pp. 36-47.

ANDREWS, E. WYLLYS IV, and ANDREWS, E. WYLLYS V

1968. Excavations at Dzibilchaltún, Yucatán, Mexico. Publication 48, Middle American Research Institute. Tulane University, New Orleans.

GARZA, SILVIA, and KURJACK, EDWARD

1980. Atlas arqueológico del estado de Yucatán. Instituto Nacional de Antropología y Historia, Mexico, D.F.

KURJACK, EDWARD

1974. Prehistoric lowland Maya community and social organization: A case study at Dzibilchaltún, Yucatán, Mexico. Publication 38, Middle American Research Institute. Tulane University, New Orleans.

1979. Introduction. *In* "Map of the Ruins of Dzibilchaltún, Yucatán, Mexico." Publication 47, Tulane University, New Orleans.

KURJACK, EDWARD, and GARZA, SILVIA

1981. Pre-Columbian community form and distribution in the northern Maya area. Pp. 287-309 *in* "Lowland Maya Settlement Patterns," Wendy Ashmore, ed. University of New Mexico Press, Albuquerque.

STUART, GEORGE; SCHEFFLER, JOHN; KURJACK, EDWARD; and COTTIER, JOHN

1979. Map of the ruins of Dzibilchaltún, Yucatán, Mexico. Publication 47, Middle American Research Institute. Tulane University, New Orleans.

VLCEK, DAVID; GARZA, SILVIA; and KURJACK, EDWARD

1978. Contemporary farming and ancient Maya settlement; some disconcerting evidence. Pp. 211-223, *in* "Prehistoric Maya Agriculture," P.D. Harrison and B. L. Turner, eds. University of New Mexico Press, Albuquerque.

EDWARD B. KURJACK

Excavation of a Shipwreck in Mombasa Harbor, Kenya

Grant Recipients: Hamo Sassoon, National Museums of Kenya, Fort Jesus Museum, Kenya (Grant 1524); and Robin C. M. Piercy, Institute of Nautical Archaeology, College Station, Texas (Grant 2096).

Grants 1524, 2096: In support of the survey and excavation of a wooden shipwreck in Mombasa Harbor, Kenya, East Africa.

Preliminary Underwater Survey of Mombasa Wreck

During the last 3 weeks of January 1976, two staff members of the American Institute of Nautical Archaeology (INA), Dr. Donald Frey and Mr. Robin Piercy, were able to visit Mombasa (Fig. 1). This visit was made possible by a grant from the National Geographic Society, arranged by Hamo Sassoon of the National Museums of Kenya. The object was to evaluate for excavation a wreck site thought to be of a Portuguese frigate that sank in 1697 to the east of Fort Jesus.

The site had been known to local divers for some time. In 1971 it was surveyed by the finders, Conway Plough and Peter Phillips, with the help of a small team of volunteers. The work was done with the archeological guidance of the curator of Fort Jesus, Dr. James Kirkman.

A number of artifacts were raised and identified as being Portuguese from the late 17th century (Fig. 2). A plan was made and the objects suitably recorded. INA's survey was greatly helped by this previous work and by the fact that the graduated nylon baseline used in 1971 was still intact on the bottom.

The remains of a large wooden vessel lay diagonally down a steeply shelving 30° slope on the edge of a deep water shipping channel immediately below Fort Jesus. At its shallowest, the site is approximately 11 m below sea level and at its deepest nearly 20 m (Fig. 3).

Apart from wooden ship remains, an abundance of modern harbor debris littered the area. Much of this was removed during the survey with generous help from local divers.

Preliminary site work consisted of laying down 5 additional nylon lines parallel to the original baseline. These were graduated at 2-m intervals and set 3 m apart. Thus we had effectively gridded an area 15 by 44 m

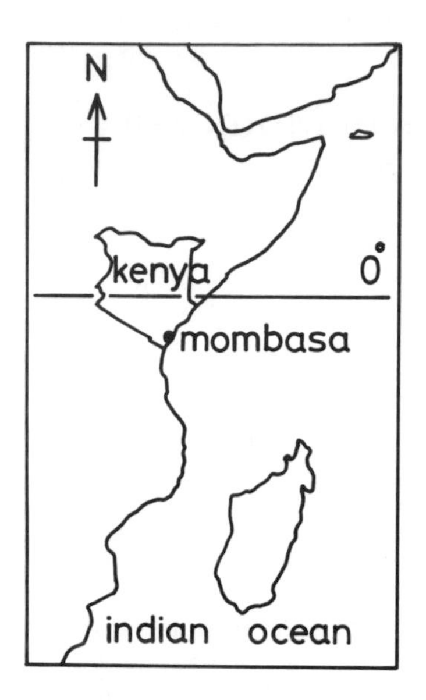

FIGURE 1. Kenya, in East Africa (left); and (below) Mombasa Harbor entrance, showing Mombasa Island and proximity of the wreck to Fort Jesus. (Maps by Robin Piercy.)

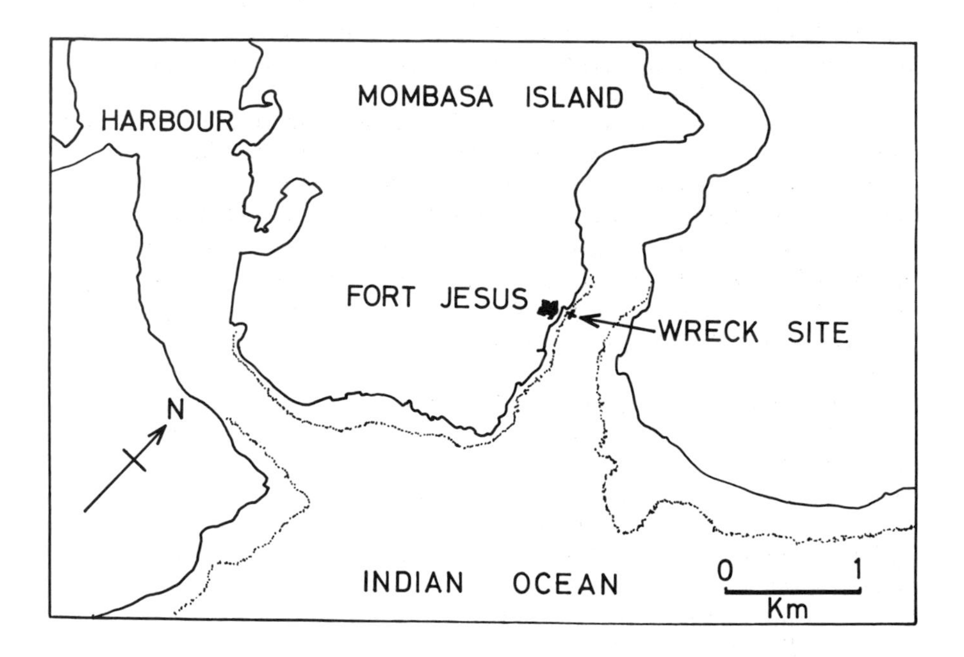

into 2- by 3-m rectangles (Fig. 3). The vertical numbers on the right side of the drawing indicate the grid lines, with 4 being the original baseline. We had hoped to cover the site photographically with at least one 2- by 3-m grid rectangle per exposure. This would have ensured good coverage and overlap for a simple photomosaic. Unfortunately, after several attempts at all stages of the tide, we were foiled by the unpredictable visibility—at worst, zero, while at best, 6 m. The nylon grid lines, however, proved invaluable in orienting ourselves during bad periods.

A careful visual search over an area covering 1200 m^2 revealed two distinct rows of massive frames curving in toward each other. They were easily followed along the seabed, often protruding above the silt by as much as 30 cm. The 1971 plan again proved useful and with a few additions it was possible to project the curves onto paper. From this information it was possible to estimate the ship to be in the region of 39 m in length by 8 m beam. Further verification of this was impossible owing to the absence of any recognizable stem or stern post. Careful inspection of some of the more exposed timbers indicated that little more than the bottom 1.5 m of hull remained. This was well covered in sand and fine broken coral, and appeared to be well preserved.

The 10-cm-thick strakes were spiked to 22- by 22-cm frames, set solidly side by side, with a 4- by 22-cm ceiling laid on the inside. According to a previous analysis the timber generally used in the construction has been identified as teak.

A select number of small trial trenches were opened to confirm the state of hull preservation beneath the seabed. These, in addition to the trenches of previous years, indicate that below the thin silt covering there lies a well-preserved hull structure. In one area just inside the hull amidships a layer of ballast stones 1 m thick was encountered. The entire extent was not determined but it is conceivable that the ballast covers a greater proportion of the ship's hull.

As the ship lay at a steep angle much of the upperworks and associated material would have rotted and tumbled down the slope as the ship slowly broke up. Heavy objects such as cannon would have been among the first to have broken free and fallen down the slope. Because of their weight they would have buried themselves quickly and deeply.

With this in mind, a local diving company was approached and arrangements made for the hire of their ELSEC metal detector. This proved to be of considerable value in the location of both ferrous and nonferrous targets beneath the sand. It was unfortunate that in the area of especial interest there were no fewer than 5 submarine power-and-telephone cables lying across the northern end of the site. These made almost all the

FIGURE 2. Left, bronze cannon with arms of Portugal and date 1678. Right, Siamese jar with dark brown glaze, height 90 cm. (Photos, Fort Jesus Museum.)

readings highly ambiguous and unreliable. Away from the cables the relative absence of signals or the smaller number of targets indicated that there was not much metal in evidence. A few cannonballs were found in conjunction with several large iron concretions downslope from the hull.

Use was also made of the photomosaic grid lines to take proton magnetometer readings at 140 different stations which covered an area of 650 m^2. This enabled us to complete a thorough investigation of the whole site.

The magnetometer's detecting head, having been designed for towing behind a boat, was extremely cumbersome when operated by hand. Eventually we mounted the sensor on a wooden pole with a float to achieve neutral buoyancy. A diver, wearing aluminum tanks and carrying a minimum of ferrous metal, was able to position the unit with relative ease. When the detector head was on station, the diver signaled with

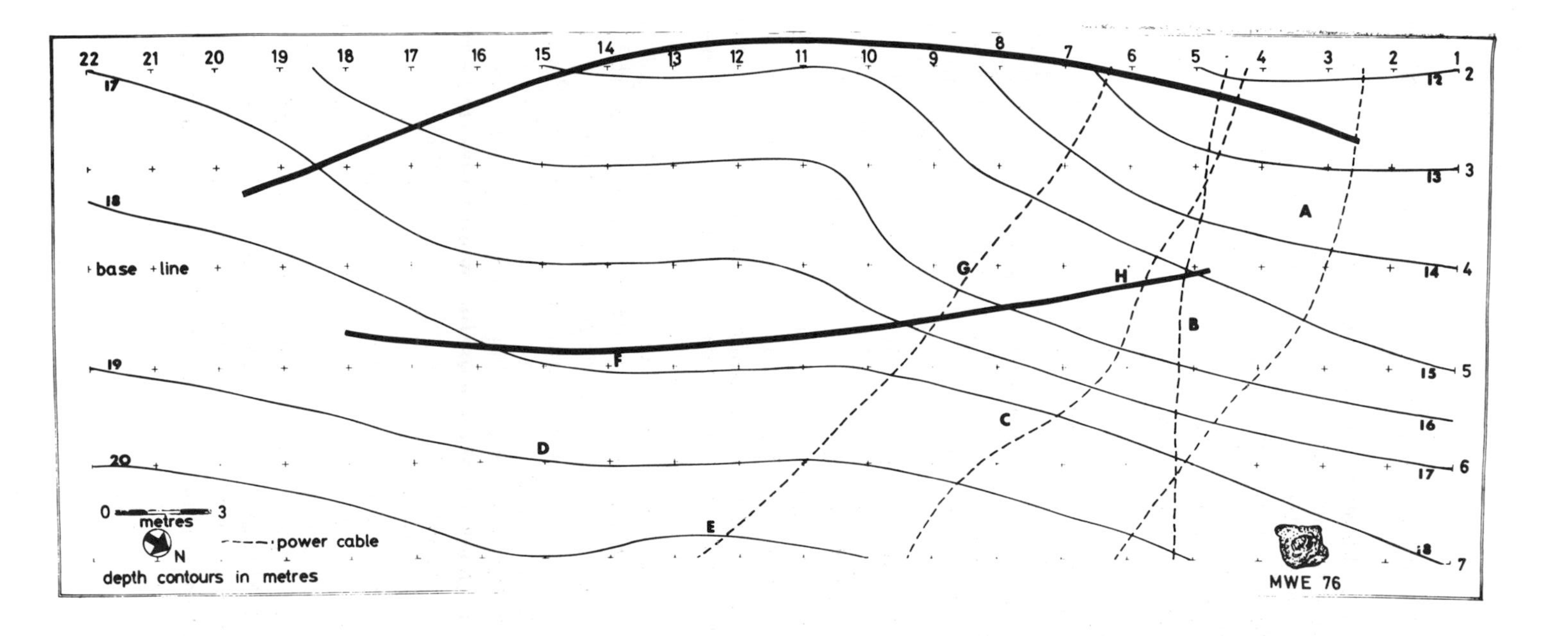

FIGURE 3. Site plan (by Robin Piercy) showing the outline of the hull. Key to small finds: A, 1971 excavation areas. B, bronze cannon; C, large glazed jars; D, copper bucket; E, large glazed jar; F, olive jar and chain mail; G, Chinese porcelain plates; H, half an hourglass.

a marker buoy to the surface operator to commence or finish readings (Fig. 4).

A proton magnetometer is unaffected by nonferrous metals, and measures minute variations in the earth's magnetic field with extreme accuracy. A cannon or similar large conglomeration of ferrous metal can be detected many feet away, as can an object as small as a cannonball buried several feet under the sand. It would show as a change in field on a magnetic contour map of the site. With the magnetometer, we were able to eliminate the interference caused by submarine cables on the earlier metal detector survey.

The data produced some interesting anomalies (Fig. 5). These targets were deep beneath the sand and covered by a chaotic jumble of ship's timbers. So substantial were the timbers in both size and quantity that we were unable to excavate farther in the time available.

While the 1976 survey was unable to prove beyond any doubt that the wreck was the Portuguese frigate *Santo Antonio de Tanna* sunk in 1697, the wealth of additional information collected strongly reinforces the theory that it is. From records it is known that the *Santo Antonio* was built in Portuguese Goa. Teak was plentiful in India and was used in shipbuilding at the time. The solid construction and size of the hull is consonant with a ship of the era armed with at least 40 guns. The lack of cannon on board can be explained by the fact that the ship did not sink immediately and there was plenty of time to salvage most or all of them before the ship went down. They would have been extremely useful in the defense of Fort Jesus, which was under intermittent siege at the time.

As a result, it is felt that an excavation of the site is both highly practicable and desirable. (In fact, excavation of the site was undertaken the following year, and many suppositions have been proven correct. See the following section of this report.) Little is known of early Portuguese shipboard life in the Indian Ocean, and excavation would shed new light on the topic. Although many interesting objects may be recovered, it is likely that a thorough investigation of the hull would prove to be of greater value. The well-preserved nature of the wood below the sand would yield considerable information concerning the techniques of Portuguese ship construction of the period. In the past INA has produced ships' lines and reconstructed hulls from considerably less evidence than that presented by the Mombasa wreck.

The discovery of this site, the earliest known preserved shipwreck found on the East African coast, has raised a good deal of local interest. Present goodwill and generous offers of help from the Mombasa community show that an excavation could be mounted at a reasonable cost and be assured of success.

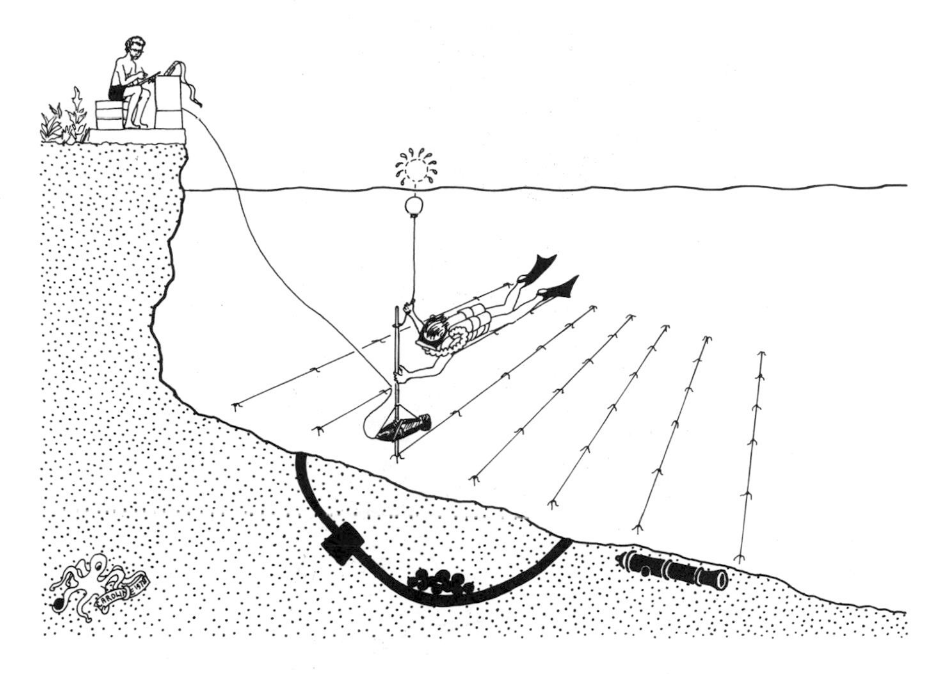

FIGURE 4. Diagram by Caroline Sassoon, to show method of magnetometer survey.

Excavation of the Mombasa Wreck

Subsequent to the underwater survey discussed above, excavation of the Mombasa wreck site was begun in 1977, under the direction of the Institute of Nautical Archaeology, and continued through 1978, 1979, and 1980.

For a report on the work of the 1977, 1978, 1979, and 1980 seasons, see *The International Journal of Nautical Archaeology* (vol. 6, pp. 331-347; vol. 7, pp. 301-319; vol. 8, pp. 303-309; and vol. 10, pp. 109-118). Also see the *Institute of Nautical Archaeology Newsletter* (no. 3, p. 3; no. 5, p. 4; and no. 6, p. 3).

1980 SEASON

The fourth excavation season of what is now believed to be the wreck of the Portuguese frigate *Santo Antonio da Tanna* ran from January 8 to April 13, 1980.

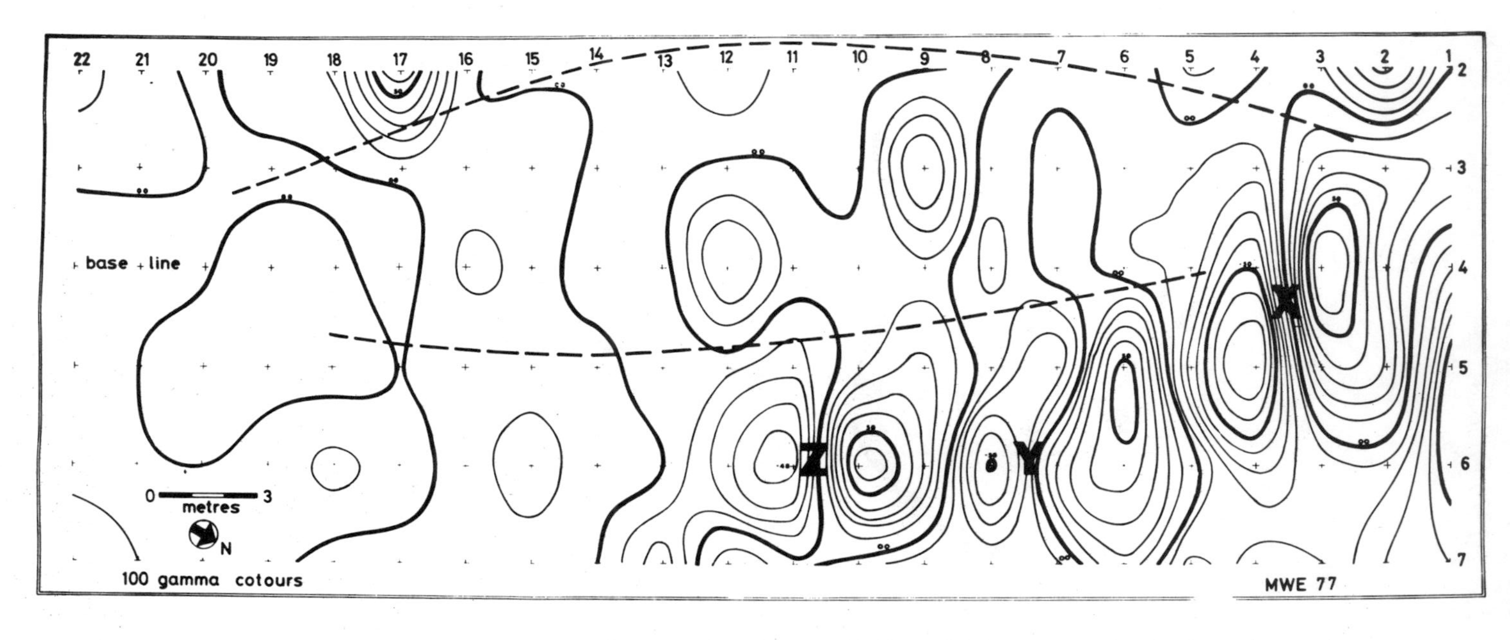

FIGURE 5. Magnetic contour map showing disturbances (X, Y, and Z) large enough to be buried cannon or a mass of iron shot. The contours are at 100-gamma intervals. (Map by Don Frey.)

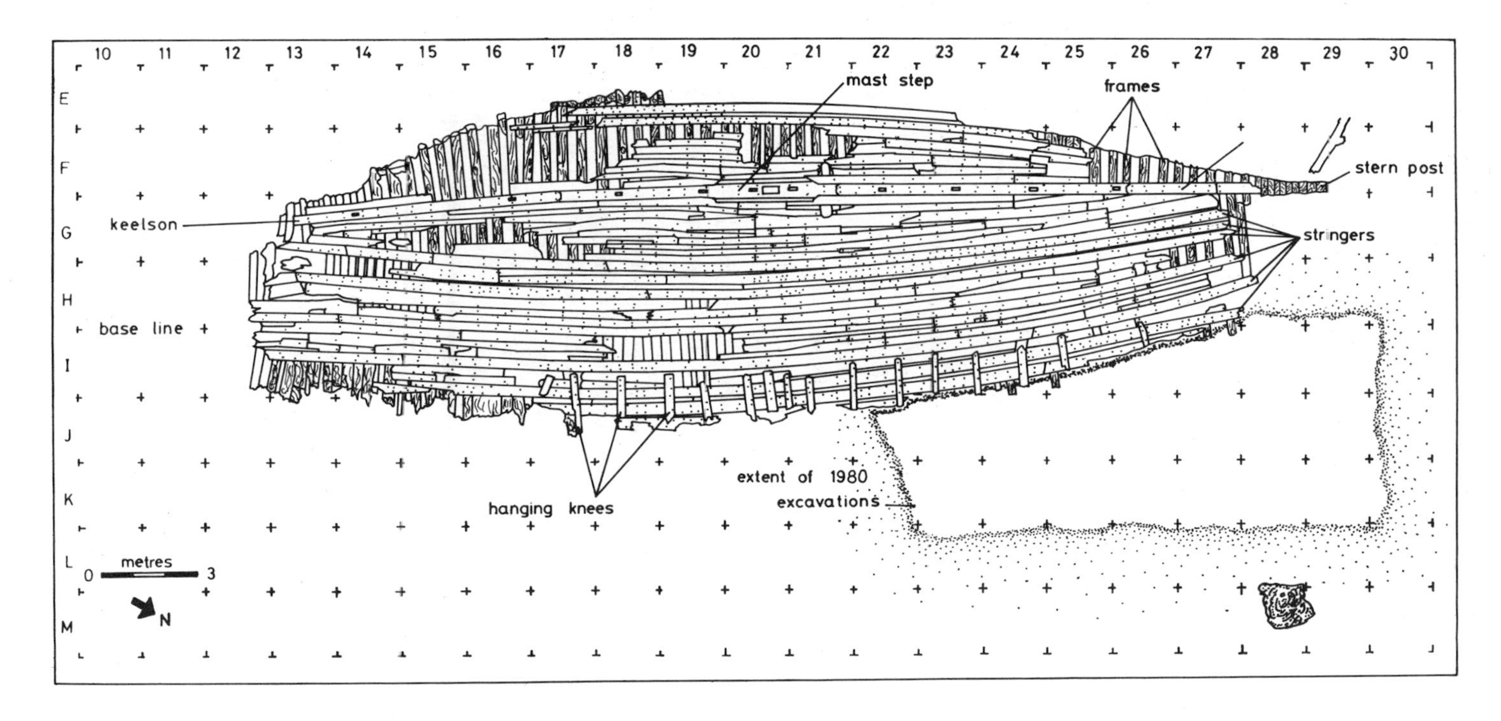

FIGURE 6. Site plan, showing extent of 1980 excavations. The hull was excavated and recorded in the 1977, 1978, and 1979 seasons. (Plan by Robin Piercy.)

The project was directed by the Institute of Nautical Archaeology under the auspices of the National Museums of Kenya. Considerable financial help was received from the National Geographic Society, the National Museums of Kenya, and the Institute of Nautical Archaeology. In addition, many gifts in kind were donated by local Kenyans.

Initially it had been intended to finish the project in the 1980 season. Only a 6-m-wide band immediately below the wreck and along her entire length remained to be excavated. By mid-season it was obvious that there was no chance of achieving this goal. The enormous number of objects encountered and the complexity of the collapsed wooden structure meant that barely a third of the proposed area was excavated (Fig. 6). In the 1980 season, the longest season to date, the team logged more than 1300 hours underwater in 74 days and in the process recorded nearly 3500 objects. The entire season's effort was concentrated below the stern third of the ship.

The normal pattern of excavation was followed, using 2-m-square metal grid frames to help orient the divers and provide reference for excavated objects. After an overburden of previous seasons' ballast stones and general harbor debris had been removed, large pieces of eroded frames and broken deck beams were found. The hull was further represented by an enormous quantity of concreted bolts and nails. As these were removed, excavation continued downward for nearly a meter before stopping against a layer of partitioning and lathe-turned wooden posts (Fig. 6). During previous seasons, a similar type of partitioning had been found within the hull nearby and, while it is not clear what the relationship with it is, it is felt that it must belong. After the partitioning was removed, no other objects were found and further excavation proved the seabed to be sterile. The large majority of the season's small finds were made in close proximity to the partitioning and consisted mainly of Chinese porcelain, fragments of thin-walled unglazed flasks, and Portuguese faience. Jet medallions and earrings, silver buttons, and brass buckles appeared to have a slightly wider distribution. Out of the same area, a small bronze breech-loading swivel gun complete with iron bracket was recovered; it bore the date 1677. Although it was complete, it had obviously received a direct hit at some stage during the engagement, as a section the size of a cannonball had been carried away (see Fig. 7).

In 1976 during the National Geographic Society's sponsored survey of the site, a number of large magnetic anomalies were recorded outside the hull. Until the 1980 season, in spite of earlier efforts, no metal objects had been found that would have registered such a large variation. Generally, magnetometer contour maps do not indicate exact positions of iron concentrations but only a general area in which to look. As a result, in previous seasons we had missed 2 large iron cannon by less than a meter

FIGURE 7. Bronze breach-loading swivel gun in situ. (Photo by Chip Vincent).

(Fig. 5, anomaly 2). Another iron cannon was found partially covered by the hull and by more than 2 m of debris. Attached to this cannon were parts of its gun carriage, including its wooden axle and a well-preserved wheel. The rest appears to have been destroyed by teredo worms.

As the excavation proceeded beyond the extent of the stern, a number of pieces of wooden decorative work were removed, including a small, carved wooden figure and part of a Portuguese coat of arms. The latter object was found in close proximity to a well-preserved gunport and a section of latticed leaded light and other fragments of turned and carved woodwork. These begin to suggest a well-decorated stern castle. The style in which the captain and officers of the vessel lived in the stern is well represented by the recovery of a silver candlestick, a decorated brass table bell, 2 pewter juglets with matching tray, a pewter porringer, and faience and porcelain plates (Fig. 8).

By the close of the season more than 44 people of 7 different nationalities had helped with the project. Diving equipment and procedure was supplied and maintained by a team of 8 Royal Engineers from the British army, who have consistently supported our project over the past 3 years.

FIGURE 8. Objects from the ship's stern indicate the style of living enjoyed by the officers. (Photo by Chip Vincent.)

The diving barge, a converted ammunition lighter, was anchored to one side of the site (Fig. 9).

Photographer Chip Vincent was present at all major events during the season and covered all aspects of the work in as much detail as time would allow. Nearly 30 rolls of color film were used and more than 80 rolls of black-and-white film were shot.

FUTURE SEASONS

With only a third of the intended area excavated there is promise for a further two seasons' underwater work. The quantity and variety of objects that have been recovered from the small area excavated was more than rewarding. A far better understanding of conditions and life in the stern of the ship is beginning to emerge. After consultations with the National Museums of Kenya, it has been decided to go ahead with the planned 1981 study season and to continue excavations in 1982 and 1983. It is hoped that with the completion of these two seasons the fullest possible picture of the vessel will be obtained.

FIGURE 9. Below the walls of Fort Jesus (extreme left), the diving barge lies anchored to the seaward of the wreck. (Photo by Chip Vincent.)

Acknowledgments

The writer and Dr. Frey wish to thank the following for their generous help and hospitality: National Museums of Kenya; Provincial Commissioner Eliud Mahihu; Mombasa Club; Bahari Club; Divecon; Neville Chittick, Alan Alder, Tony Dunne, Kevin Patience; Car and General Ltd.; the 1971 survey team for permission to reproduce in part their survey plan; and Mr. James Kirkman. Particular mention should be made of Mr. and Mrs. Hamo Sassoon, and Conway Plough, who gave us so much of their time.

Through the good offices of Dr. E. T. Hall, Research Laboratory for Archaeology, Oxford, Dr. Frey was able to spend several days at the Oxford Computer Centre. In 1971, he developed a computer program at Oxford to analyze magnetometer data from archeological land sites. This was adapted to accept underwater data and produced the overall picture of magnetic disturbance on the Mombasa site, as shown in Figure 5.

REFERENCES

SASSOON, HAMO

1978. Marine thoughts of a land archaeologist derived from the Mombasa wreck excavation. *In* "Beneath the Waters of Time: Proceedings of the 9th conference of Underwater Archaeology," J. Barto Arnold III, ed. Texas Antiquities Committee Publication no. 6.

1981. Ceramics from the wreck of a Portuguese ship at Mombasa. Azania, vol. 16, pp. 97-130.

1982. The sinking of the Santo António de Tanná in Mombasa Harbour. Paidenma, vol. 28, pp. 101-108.

——. Silver coins from the Portuguese shipwreck in Mombasa Harbour. Coin Hoards (British Museum). (In press.)

ROBIN C. M. PIERCY

An Analysis of Prehistoric Engravings on Boulders in Koonalda Cave, South Australia

Grant Recipient: Christine E. Sharpe, Auckland, New Zealand.

Grant 1523: In support of an expedition to the art sanctuary in Koonalda Cave, South Australia.

An investigation of engravings on boulders in the northwest passage of Koonalda Cave, South Australia, was undertaken in January 1976 on an expedition supported by the National Geographic Society and the South Australian Museum (Sharpe, 1977; Sharpe and Sharpe, n.d.[1] and n.d.[2]).

Background

During the summer of 1972-1973, my husband, Kevin Sharpe, and I were part of a group led by Alexander Gallus to examine evidence of a prehistoric people who utilized Koonalda Cave. There, we found carefully engraved boulders on the floor of the cave's Upper Chamber (Sharpe and Sharpe, 1976; see Figs. 1 and 2). Koonalda Cave has been known over many years for its prehistoric flint mining, stone constructions, and markings at least 20,000 years old made by human fingertips being stroked across the soft, powdery limestone surface of the cave walls (Wright, 1971).

Koonalda Cave, located 14 mi (23 km) from the coast—the Great Australian Bight—and 54 mi (87 km) from the Western Australian border (Fig. 3), is one of the largest of the 170 known caves on the Nullarbor Plain, part of a limestone karst of some 78,000 mi^2 (200,000 km^2) (Dunkley and Wigley, 1967; Lowry and Jennings, 1974). The land around Koonalda is fairly arid, with only about 8 in. (200 mm) of rain falling per year, and an evaporation rate that always exceeds rainfall (Leonard, 1980).

In 1957, Gallus had recognized Koonalda's archeological significance, and continued his investigations until 1976 (Gallus, 1968, 1971, 1977). Another archeologist to operate in Koonalda was Richard Wright of the University of Sydney (Wright, 1971). Robert Edwards and Leslie Maynard have described the cave's finger markings and wall engravings in a number of publications (Edwards and Maynard, 1967, 1969; Maynard and Edwards, 1971).

FIGURE 1. Engraved boulders fronting onto a deep "cavern," Upper Chamber, Koonalda Cave. The uppermost one resembles a snake's head, complete with eye. Scale is in centimeters.

The Upper Chamber

The floor of the Upper Chamber of Koonalda Cave comprises at least five rockfalls of different ages and degrees of weathering (which renders the rocks smooth and rounded) (Figs. 3, 4, and 5). The oldest collapse, rockfalls C and F, is engraved; engravings within the other areas are sparse if not absent altogether. Within rockfall C are individual engraved rocks and a number of human activity areas, some obviously intentionally constructed and flanked by engraved boulders. This part of the cave is a prehistoric ritual sanctuary of some magnitude.

The boulders in rockfall A are fairly smooth and rounded, and those in rockfall D are more rough and jagged. But the latter have been used significantly by humans in that there is an impressive series of activity areas constructed here, together with bone placements and a chalcedony flake, presumably an engraving tool. The remains of torches abound in all but rockfalls B and E, the most recent. In them is no evidence of human use, but underneath them—and under A and D as well—can be found the original smooth, rounded, and engraved boulder floor.

An important question to be answered is by what mechanism did the rockfalls become smooth and rounded. This process is active on rockfalls

FIGURE 2. Detail of the "snake's head" boulder in Figure 1. Note the streaming of the engraved lines.

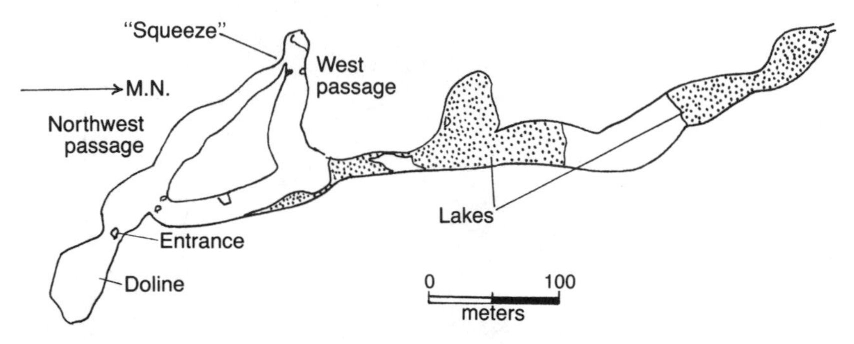

FIGURE 3. Koonalda Cave, location and floor plan (after J. B. Hinwood, 1960).

over already engraved smooth and rounded boulders, and difficulties obviously exist if the process is achieved by water flow as is often supposed. In fact, the most promising mechanism is that of exsudation or salt weathering, in which crystals form in the surface pores of the limestone, forcing off particles. There are, however, details to be settled with this proposal (Sharpe and Sharpe, n.d.[1]).

The above perspective on the Upper Chamber was a result of the 1976 investigation. At that time, also, a thorough survey was made of the cave, especially noting the exact positions of the engraved boulders.

Meanders and Engravings

During the last few years there has been a growing interest in the subject of cave meanders and line engravings, and more and more Australian caves containing them are coming to light. Cutta Cutta and Kintore Caves in the Northern Territory, published by W. P. Walsh in 1964,

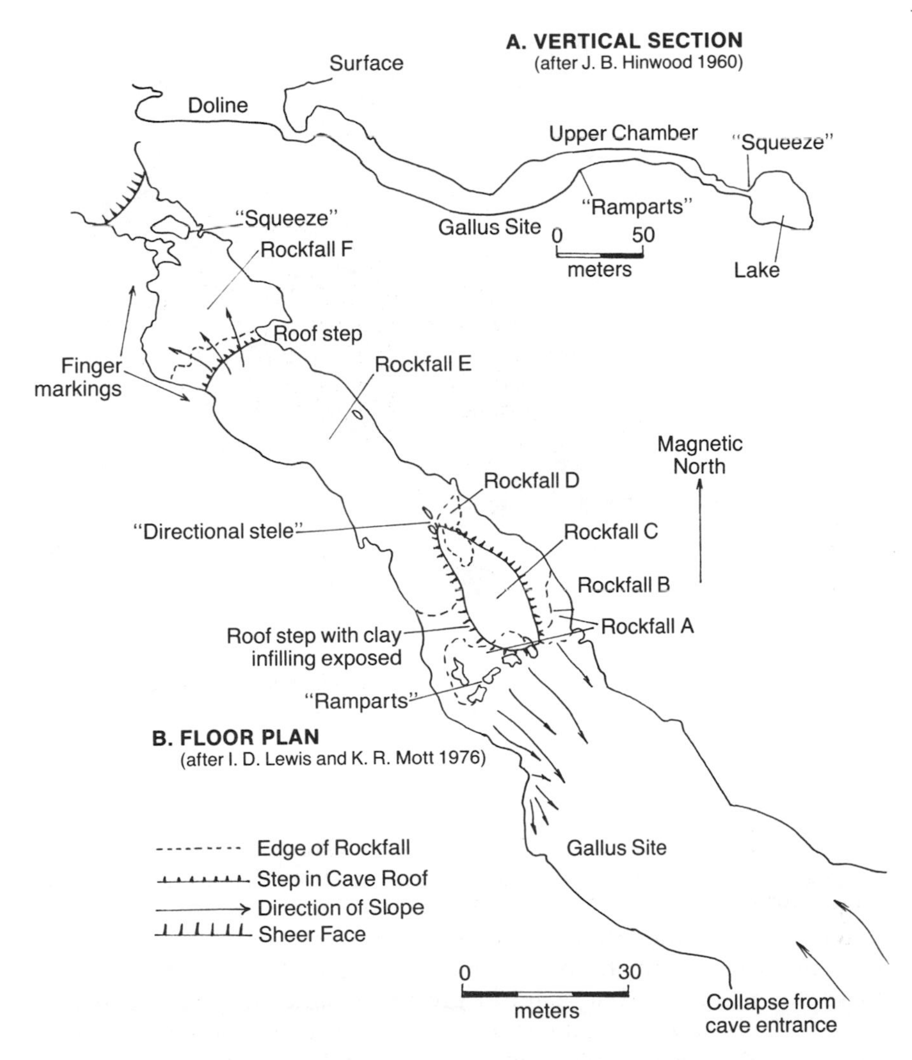

FIGURE 4. Northwest passage of Koonalda Cave.

contain Koonalda-type markings (Walsh, 1964). There are finger markings in the Orchestra Shell and Ross Caves north of Perth, Western Australia, and a little farther south in Morfitt's Cave (Hallam, 1971; Dortch, 1976). In the caves around Mount Gambier in South Australia, finger markings and engravings have been discovered, and we believe they also are to be found in a number of other Nullarbor caves. In Victoria, markings can be seen in Princess Margaret Rose Cave, McEachern's Cave, and in New Guinea 2 Cave (Walsh, 1964; Link, 1967; Stubbs, 1979).

FIGURE 5. Part of the Upper Chamber of Koonalda Cave, showing the contrast between rough boulders of recent rockfalls, and those smooth, rounded, and engraved.

Alexander Marshack is well known for his studies of prehistoric engravings on small portable pieces of stone and bone from Europe (Marshack, 1972a, b, c, 1975, 1977, 1979). His intention is to discover something of the thought patterns of prehistoric people. By careful microscopic observation, he has found that the tools used to incise the marks differ from mark to mark or group of marks to group of marks, which he feels proves that the marks were made over a period of time or perhaps by different people. The marks tend to form sets, each an obvious unit in itself, which Marshack describes as "mythic" rather than "arithmetic" (tally marks); that is, the line series brings to mind an idea that sparks off many associations relating to myths.

In relation to Koonalda Cave and the Australian meander tradition, Marshack provides us with specific tools to set about recording the lines in a way that may be helpful in their later interpretation. He personally suggested we investigate how the lines were made, how they were built up over time, and whether they were drawn with different tools.

Aim and Method

An aim during the 1976 expedition to Koonalda was to follow Marshack's suggestion of trying to discover something about the internal structure of the engraved lines on the boulders. By doing this, we hoped to see if there were any similarities between the engravings on boulders of the northwest passage of Koonalda Cave and those that Marshack had studied in Europe. We were especially interested in his claim that the work was participatory in nature, and wanted to see if the line series or streams were consistent in that all the lines of which they were composed had the same cross sections (i.e., were made with the same point) and that different streams had different cross sections. A stream can be defined at first **visually** as being a group of parallel lines which have a common direction and a consistent interval between lines, and which **appear** to have the same cross section and degree of wear.

First, a suitable sample of engravings was chosen, one relatively clear and easy to "read" (some areas are so heavily engraved that the lines are virtually impossible to sort out). The work was then undertaken with a strong side light (gas), and hand-held candle which could be moved across the streams until the light was thrown directly into each line. This eliminated the shadows thrown by the side light and, with the aid of a magnifying glass, allowed a look into the lines, to establish the contour of their cross sections.

It was possible to establish which groups superimpose others by examining the junction at which they crossed. These results can be seen in Figures 6-13. An important word of caution needs to be appended. The figures drawn are replications of those made in the cave and show the overlays and the cross sections; the visual discrimination between different streams has been (almost) ignored. The point was to test the hypothesis that a visually definable stream shows consistency in the cross sections of its constituent lines, and consistency in the way its lines overlay or are overlaid by lines of other streams. As can be seen from the drawings, this hypothesis is born out in most of the line sets examined, in that lines grouped by common cross sections and common overlayings do in general correspond with the visually discernable streams.

However, this is subject to a number of circumspections. Because the above hypothesis itself and the method of drawing the lines evolved during the examination of the lines themselves, there are inaccuracies in the figures and the method of representation that cannot be rectified without further examination of the lines in situ (the hypothesis, however, still seems well established). For instance, some lines are given the same level in the overlay structure, and so are represented by the same symbol, when this is not ascertainable since they have no crossing or touching with other lines. Some lines have been given the same level of overlay when they do meet or cross one another, meaning their relative overlaying was not looked for. And thirdly, some sets of lines have no crossings or meetings at all and yet an overlay structure has been given to them. Thus, the method of representation used has its drawbacks and in further investigations should be modified.

Results

(1) Two areas on one particular boulder were studied, one is the central section and the other directly above a hole in the foot of the boulder.

The central section (Fig. 6) lies to the left of a natural hole in the limestone that penetrates the boulder to the depth of 30 cm. For convenience, this grouping is described in four clusters physically separated from each other, but which contain different streams. Working from left to right we have the top cluster 1. In this, stream 1 slants from top left to bottom right, and comprises closely spaced parallel lines; there are four of these with a fifth farther to the right but still at roughly the same angle, though curved. The second line is broken. The cross section for these is a flat-bottomed U. Laying on top of these are the regularly spaced marks of stream 2. The first four of these slant to the right across the previous set, the fifth and broken seventh are vertical, and the sixth (lower down) slants back toward the left with a small line slanting from the left toward and meeting it (shallow cross section). Across the lower part of the first stream leaning to the left is a third stream, more deeply engraved than either the first or second. These have deep V cross sections.

Cluster 2 has two streams only, one overlaying the other (called 4 and 5 for convenience). Stream 4 slants from the top right to the bottom left, one long line and a group of four small lines, the first of which branches at the bottom to the left. The nine lines of stream 5 slant from the bottom right to the top left. The first of the 4 group has a shallow U cross section, and on the other three a deep V.

Cluster 3 has four distinctive levels, the lowest (stream 6) has an extremely low U cross section and arches almost horizontally upward toward the left where it intersects with cluster 2. The next layer (7) is composed of four vertical lines, overlapping 6. Stream 8 consists of three wavy lines, parallel and slanting toward the right-hand upper corner. Cutting over all of these, and deepest, is the curved line probably part of stream 5 in cluster 2.

Cluster 4 has four horizontal wavy lines (9) crossing the top; they are very faint and shallow and have a V-shaped cross section. Directly below and to the middle of these are seven parallel lines (10) which slope toward each other, the set of which seems to branch off one of two very deep lines (11). A tiny group to the right consists of three curved lines (12) overlaid by three straight vertical ones (13).

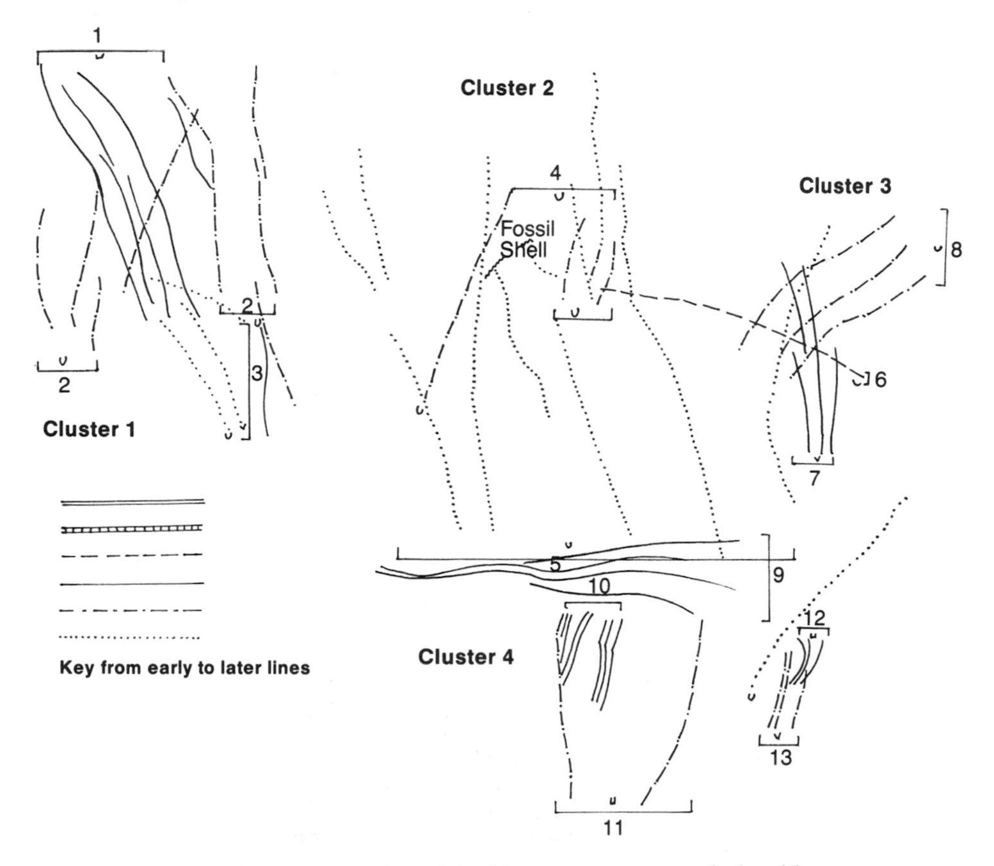

FIGURE 6. Linear plot of markings on two areas of a boulder.

(2) The lines from the lower portion of the above boulder are shown in Figure 7. They form an "arrow" pointing downward to a hole at the floor level of the boulder, reminiscent of a similar "arrow" in the "squeeze" area which points downward toward a mining hole (Gallus, 1968). It is a very simple grouping. Four lines (stream 1) slant toward the hole from above left and these are the deepest and have a squared-off U

cross section; two more of these lines join the stream at its base. From the right slant four short thin lines (deep and thin U cross section); there is a gap and two more similar lines at the same angle meet the hole (stream 2). In the center of the cluster are four deep lines (stream 3) slanting in toward each other and pointing downward to the junction of the left and right streams, and also pointing to the hole.

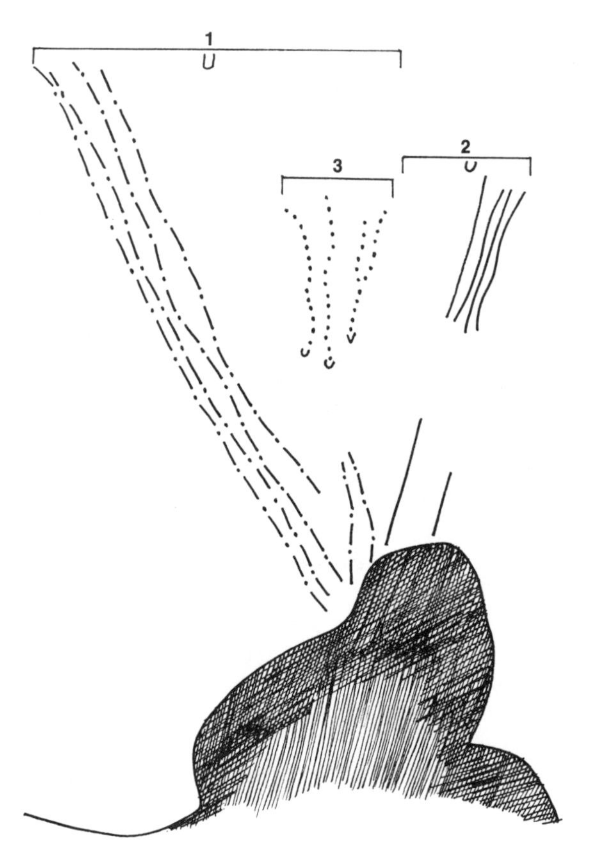

FIGURE 7. Lines from the lower portion of the boulder shown in Figure 6. For key, see Figure 6.

(3) The section selected to draw from another boulder shows interesting stream patterns which appear to link together natural holes in the limestone surface (Fig. 8). The lowest right-hand hole shown in the draw-

ing has lines (stream 1) drawn toward it and then going inside it. It was rather difficult to sort out superimpositions in this example owing to the great confusion of lines. Those drawn have been selected from this mass. There is little variation in cross section although we can still see that, like the first drawing, the cross sections are fairly consistent with the streams.

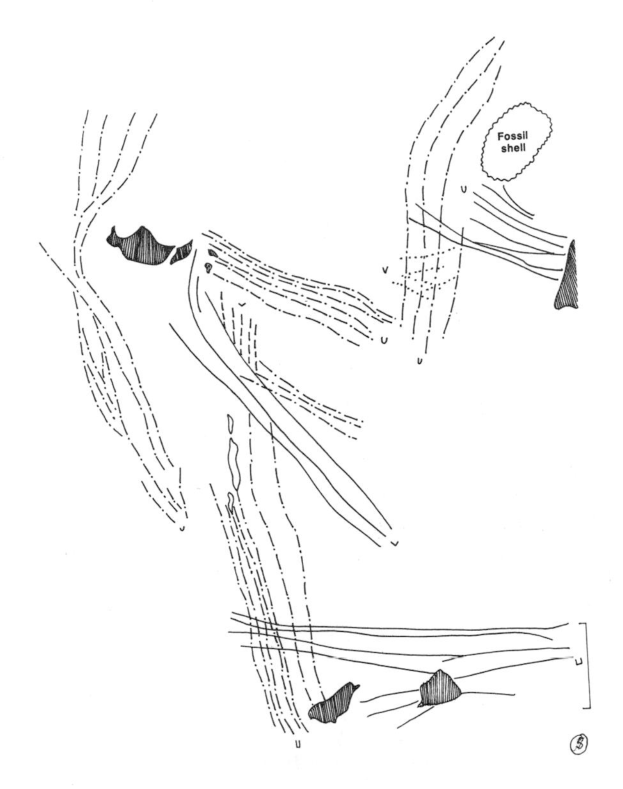

FIGURE 8. Stream patterns appear to link together natural holes in this limestone boulder. For key, see Figure 6.

(4) Two drawings have again been made from one boulder, which this time faces onto an activity area. The engraved surface is badly cracked and it may soon flake off.

Superimpositioning is obvious in the first example (Fig. 9). The form is basically tentlike, with two strong streams of parallel lines leaning toward each other. It appears that the left-hand side stream (1) overlays the right-hand side (2). A smaller stream of lines (3) is between the two sides and pointing toward their apex.

These three general aspects are similar to the lower cluster on example (2), except this "arrow"-type form points upward. Variation in cross section can again be observed.

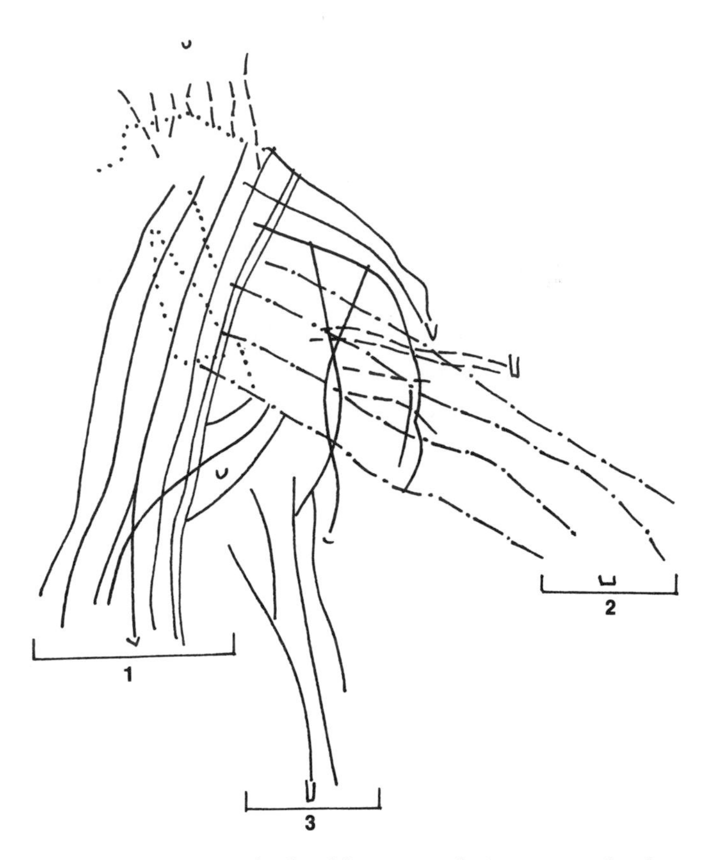

FIGURE 9. Lines on this boulder are an obvious example of superimpositioning. For key, see Figure 6.

(5) The second example from this boulder is a complex patterned surface immediately below the first (Fig. 10). It appears to contain two systems joined together, one large (upper) and one small (lower) with various short parallel streams scattered about.

A vague similarity exists between the two systems in that, in both, two separate streams slant from the lower-left to the upper-right and two more slant through these from the upper-left to the lower-right. Perhaps this shows some left/right symmetry.

FIGURE 10. The markings on this boulder are a complex patterned surface below the first markings. For key, see Figure 6.

(6) This is a single system consisting of seven separate streams (Fig. 11), four running roughly vertically (1, 2, 3, 4) and three crossing the upper section of these like an arrow pointing to the right (5, 6, 7). The three vertical streams incline slightly from lower-left to top-right. The "arrow"

portion consists of two sets of four parallel lines (5 and 7), and a further parallel group (6) joins these from behind like a tail.

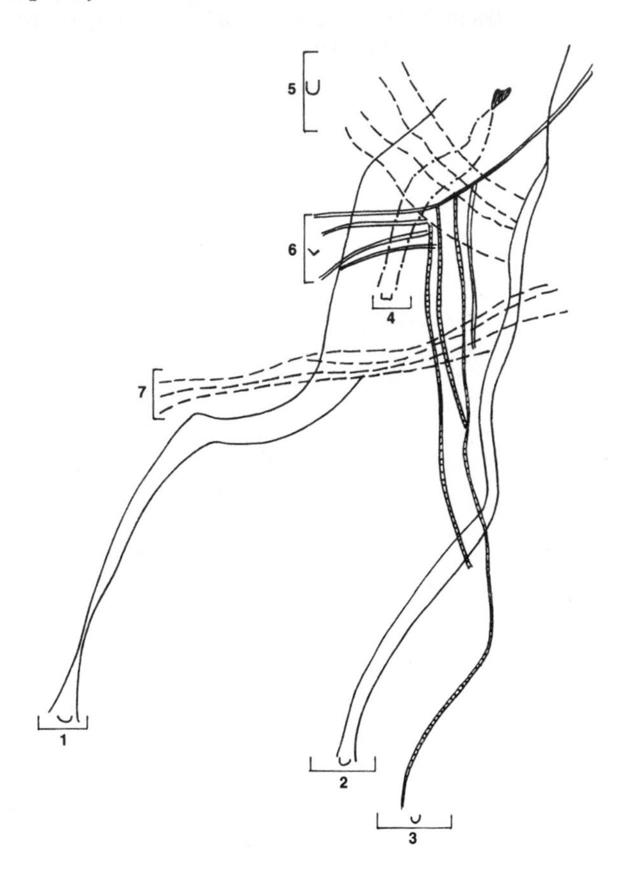

FIGURE 11. Markings showing a single system consisting of seven separate streams. For key, see Figure 6.

(7) The next engraving to be described was found on the "altar" stele (Fig. 12). Briefly, the engraving has two parts: a large and vertical V (apex at A) of streams 1, 7, and 8, and a small "fan" grouping of parallel-line streams at the upper-left. The large V is intersected at the top of its right arm by the base of a second and upturned V of streams 6 and 9. The "fan" consists of four streams of parallel lines, two of two (2 and 5), and two of four (3 and 4). Stream 2 is crossed by the other two-lined stream 5.

The most interesting aspect of this cluster is the intimate association of the engraved lines with the natural structure of the limestone. Streams

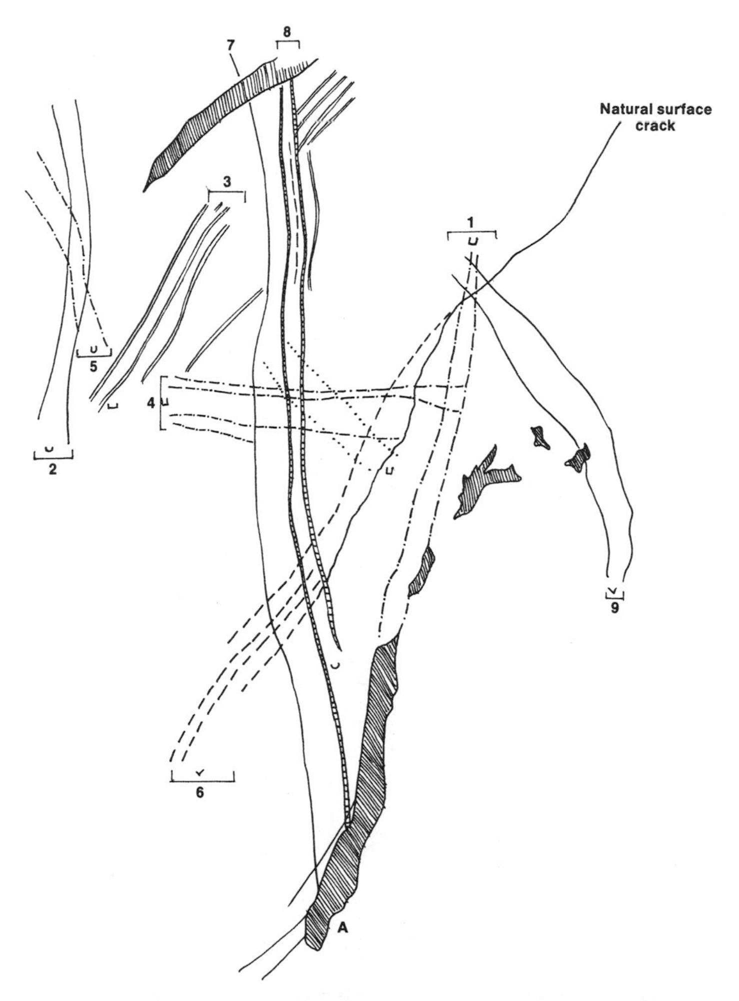

FIGURE 12. Engraving on the "altar" stele. For key, see Figure 6.

7 and 8 connect holes. A long hole sets the direction of the shorter arm (stream 1) of the first V mentioned, the lines being a continuation of the upper end of the hole. A natural surface crack is followed in contour by stream 6 forming the left-hand arm of the second and upside-down V. The longest line of this four-line stream meets the crack about halfway up, and the remaining three shorter lines lock into the end of the space formed like fingers into a hand.

(8) The final area of lines to be described is located on the lower stone of the two at the entrance to the "cavern" (Figs. 1, 2, and 13). The lines do

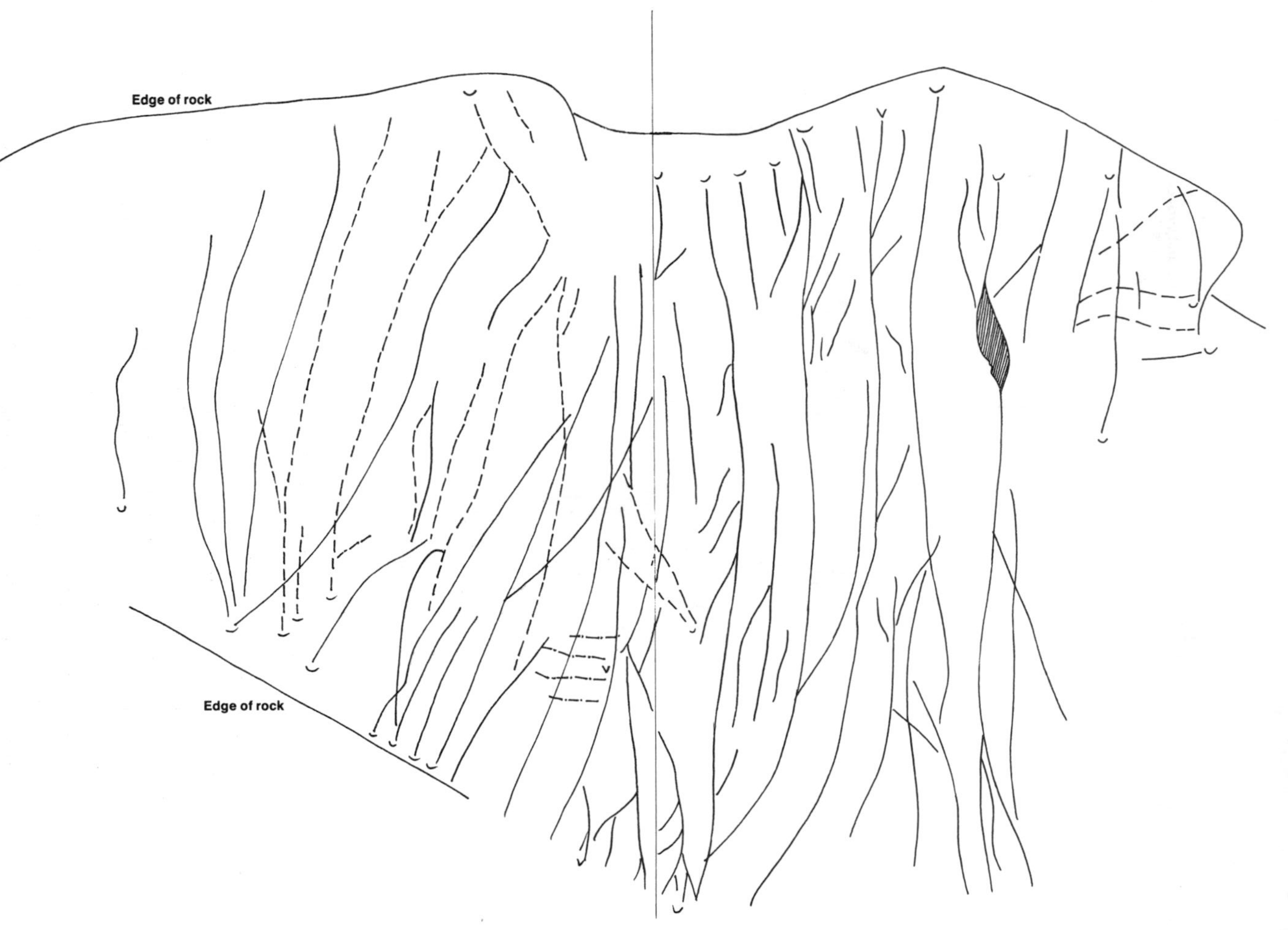

FIGURE 13. Engravings from the lower stone at the entrance to the "cavern" (Figs. 1 and 2). For key, see Figure 6.

not form clusters as do most of the others, but are, almost without exception, vertical; some intersect at their lower ends and there are a few small side-branches. As there are few places where lines cross, it is impossible to work out any real time sequence, but three levels have been sorted out. As in the previous example, a longish hole is incorporated into the design.

Conclusions

There are many aspects to be considered in analyzing the markings found in Koonalda Cave, which may well represent in Australia the earliest human artistic expression. Nine findings of our expedition, briefly listed below, will be of assistance in interpreting these markings aged in excess of 20,000 years.

1. Cross sections seem consistent across a stream of lines.
2. Cross sections range from a sharp V to a broad, shallow U.
3. There is a direct relationship between natural features of the boulder surface and some engraved lines. For instance, small pits or holes are joined by lines, or have lines passing through or coming out of them. Long cracks are imitated by lines engraved parallel to them. And large holes are often indicated by a complex of a number of streams converging on the holes.
4. Fine-line groups tend to underly thicker ones.
5. The majority of parallel lines are in groups of four. This is consistent with the finger markings (presumably executed with the four fingers).
6. Marshack (pers. comm.) mentions groups of parallel lines, overlapping each other and moving systematically down the rock face or wall. We noticed no structuring similar to this on Koonalda boulders.
7. The engravings on the lower boulders of the cavern are distinctly different from the others that were studied. They are mainly parallel and move uniformly up and down the face (see Figs. 1 and 13). They are also emphatically drawn and thus possibly related to the striking form of the "cavern." In general, it appears that engraving patterns associated with outstanding "hole" formations such as the "cavern" have a distinctly different form from other boulder engravings; they are clear, vertical lines with fairly even spacing and lack any underlying mesh of lines. Perhaps this definite change of style in engraving implies that different sets of lines have different purposes or meanings.
8. In some systems of streams there is rough left/right symmetry.
9. A number of clusters contain V-shapes of streams bisected at the apex by other streams.

Marshack's method can tell us a great deal about the (temporal) structure of the Koonalda markings. More, of course, must be done along this line. But the future task must also be to discover more of what they meant to their makers. This will require a number of techniques including anthropological, structural, psychological, and artistic approaches, each of which will tell something, perhaps, but no one of which will probably tell the whole story.

Acknowledgments

As principal investigator, I wish to express my thanks to the National Geographic Society and to the South Australian Museum for their financial and other support toward the 1976 expedition to Koonalda Cave. I am also grateful to the South Australian Aboriginal and Historic Relics Advisory Board (for permission to enter the cave), Mr. and Mrs. Cyril Gurney of Koonalda Station, Dr. Alexander Marshack, Professor Hallam Movius, Jr., and to the members of the expedition: Dr. Alexander Gallus (nominated by the South Australian Museum as field investigator), Dr. Kevin Sharpe (photographer), Messrs. Ian Lewis and Kevin Mott (surveyors), and Mr. Neil Chadwick (representing the South Australian Museum). Dr. Kevin Sharpe gave invaluable help in the preparation of this report.

REFERENCES

DORTCH, C. E.

1976. Two engraved stone plaques of late Pleistocene age from Devil's Lair, Western Australia. Arch. Phys. Anth. Oceania, vol. 11, no. 1, pp. 32-44.

DUNKLEY, J. R., and WIGLEY, T.M.L., eds.

1967. Caves of the Nullarbor, 61 pp., illus. Speleological Research Council, Sydney.

EDWARDS, R., and MAYNARD, L.

1967. Prehistoric art in Koonalda Cave. Proc. South. Aust. Br. Roy. Geogr. Soc. Australasia, vol. 68, pp. 11-17.

1969. Prehistoric art in Koonalda Cave (Australia). Bol. Cent. Cam. Stud. Preist., vol. 4, no. 4, pp. 117-130.

GALLUS, A.

1968. Parietal art in Koonalda Cave, Nullarbor Plain, South Australia. Helictite, vol. 6, no. 3, pp. 43-49.

1971. Results of the exploration of Koonalda Cave, 1956-1968. Pp. 87-133 *in* "Archaeology of the Gallus Site, Koonalda Cave," 133 pp., illus., R.V.S. Wright, ed. Australian Institute of Aboriginal Studies, Canberra.

1977. Schematisation and symboling. Pp. 370-386 *in* "Form in Indigenous Art," 486 pp., illus., P. J. Ucko, ed. Australian Institute of Aboriginal Studies, Canberra.

HALLAM, S. J.
1971. Roof markings in the "Orchestra Shell" Cave, Wanneroo, near Perth, Western Australia. Mankind, vol. 8, no. 2, pp. 90-103.
LEONARD, B. E.
1980. South Australian year book no. 15: 1980, 666 pp., illus. Australian Bureau of Statistics, South Australian Office, Adelaide.
LINK, A. G.
1967. Late Pleistocene-Holocene climatic fluctuations; possible solution pipe-foibe relationships; and the evolution of limestone cave morphology. Zeitschr. Geomorph., vol. 11, no. 2, pp. 117-145.
LOWRY, D. C., and JENNINGS, J. N.
1974. The Nullarbor karst, Australia. Zeitschr. Geomorph., vol. 18, no. 1, pp. 35-81.
MARSHACK, A.
1972a. Cognitive aspects of upper Paleolithic engraving. Curr. Anthr., vol. 13, nos. 3-4, pp. 445-477.
1972b. The roots of civilization, 413 pp., illus. McGraw-Hill Book Co., New York.
1972c. Upper Paleolithic notation and symbol. Science, vol. 178, no. 4063, pp. 817-828.
1975. Exploring the mind of ice-age man. Nat. Geogr., vol. 147, no. 1, pp. 62-89.
1977. The meander as a system: the analysis and recognition of iconographic units in upper Palaeolithic compositions. Pp. 286-317 *in* "Form in Indigenous Art," 486 pp., illus., P. J. Ucko, ed. Australian Institute of Aboriginal Studies, Canberra.
1979. Upper Paleolithic symbol systems of the Russian Plain: cognitive and comparative analysis. Curr. Anthr., vol. 20, no. 2, pp. 271-311.
MAYNARD, L., and EDWARDS, R.
1971. Wall markings. Pp. 59-80 *in* "Archaeology of the Gallus Site, Koonalda Cave," 133 pp., illus., R.V.S. Wright, ed. Australian Institute of Aboriginal Studies, Canberra.
SHARPE, C. E.
1977. Koonalda Cave—the beginning of artistic expression. New Quart. Cave, vol. 2, no. 3, pp. 226-234.
SHARPE, C. E., and SHARPE, K. J.
1976. A preliminary survey of engraved boulders in the art sanctuary of Koonalda Cave, South Australia. Mankind, vol. 10, no. 3, pp. 125-130.
SHARPE, K. J., and SHARPE, C. E.
n.d.(1). The Upper Chamber of Koonalda Cave, South Australia: A second report. Preprint.
n.d.(2). Koonalda in the Nullarbor: A prehistoric Australian heritage. Preprint.
STUBBS, D.
1979. Prehistoric art of Australia, abridged ed., 80 pp., illus. Sun Books, Melbourne.

Walsh, W. P.
1964. Unexplained markings in Kintore and Cutta Cutta Caves, Northern Territory, Australia. Helictite, vol. 2, pp. 83-91.
Wright, R.V.S., ed.
1971. Archaeology of the Gallus Site, Koonalda Cave, 133 pp., illus. Australian Institute of Aboriginal Studies, Canberra.

Christine E. Sharpe

Field Studies of the Insect Order Neuroptera in South America

Grant Recipient: Lionel A. Stange, Instituto-Fundación Miguel Lillo and Facultad de Ciencias Naturales, Universidad Nacional de Tucumán, Argentina.

Grants 1310, 1501, 1689: For field studies of the insect order Neuroptera in South America.

Principal objectives of the field studies of South American Neuroptera, conducted during the years 1974, 1975, and 1977, were: to obtain material for systematic studies, to study the distribution patterns of these insects, and to gather biological data concerning them.

Part I— Field Studies, 1974

The 1974 field studies of South American Neuroptera were given to the exploration of the western slopes of the Colombian Andes (Cauqueza, Villavicencio, and Restrepo), the dry (coastal) and wet slopes of the Peruvian Andes (Cupiche, Matucana, Simbal, Laredo, and Tingo María), and the Subandean Desert and Chaco of Argentina; and to the retrieval of malaise trap samples from near Santa Cruz, Bolivia. Special objectives of this fieldwork were to study distribution patterns along the Andes and to obtain data on seasonal flight periods. In all, 805 specimens of the families Coniopterygidae, Hemerobiidae, Chrysopidae, Mantispidae, Myrmeleontidae, and Ascalaphidae were collected, prepared, and identified.

The Coniopterygidae are represented by only 15 species in South America according to the monograph by Meinander (1972). These belong to 5 genera: *Neoconis* Enderlein, *Pampoconis* Meinander, *Coniopteryx* Curtis, *Incasemidalis* Meinander, and *Semidalis* Enderlein. During the 1974 studies 214 specimens representing all of these genera (except the Chilean-Patagonian *Pampoconis*) were collected in diverse Andean countries. Included in the material are about 10 new species. In addition a series of the poorly known, highly aberrant *Semidalis absurdiceps* (Enderlein) were collected in malaise traps in Bolivia. Also specimens of *Coniopteryx callangana* Enderlein, previously known from Peru, were found in Bolivia and Argentina. Most of the adults were collected by beating shrubs or trees.

The Chrysopidae is usually the most common group of Neuroptera in any ecological zone. About 315 specimens were collected. Most of the species appear to belong to the genera *Chrysopa* Leach and *Leucochrysa* McLachlan. This economic group is poorly known in South America because of the confused taxonomic state brought on by the inadequate descriptions of earlier workers.

The Hemerobiidae are best represented in cool, humid regions. Most of the tropical fauna consists of a few species of the cosmopolitan genera *Hemerobius* Linnaeus, *Sympherobius* Banks, and *Megalomus* Rambur. There is 1 endemic Neotropic genus, *Nusalala* Navás. There are also 2 species known of the pantropical genus *Notiobiella* Banks in South America. Species collected include specimens of *Hemerobius hageni* Navás from the Peruvian Coastal Desert, from Bolivia, and from Argentina. Two other species were collected at Tingo María in Peru and from Colombia. *Notiobiella callangana* Kimmins was found in Argentina (Horco Molle) and in Bolivia (Santa Cruz). An unidentified species was collected in Colombia (Restrepo). Several species of *Nusalala* were collected from Colombia (Cauqueza) and Argentina (Horco Molle). This Neotropical indicator genus does not occur in the deserts of Peru, Chile, or Argentina. Several species of *Megalomus* were taken from Colombia (Cauqueza), Peru (Tingo María), Bolivia (General Saavedra), and Argentina (Horco Molle). *Sympherobius maculipennis* Kimmins and *S. psychodoides* (Blanchard) were found in several localities in northern Argentina. An unidentified species was taken at Cupiche, Peru, and at Restrepo, Colombia. A total of 76 specimens of Hemerobiidae were collected during the 1974 fieldwork.

Only 6 specimens of Mantispidae were found. Five of these belong to the genus *Mantispa* (Restrepo, Colombia) and 1 species of the Neotropical genus *Trichoscelia* Westwood (Tingo María, Peru).

Of Myrmeleontidae, 189 larvae and adults were collected. In Colombia larvae of *Eremoleon* were found in caves at Cauqueza. In the sand dunes near Laredo, Peru, the larvae of *Vella assimilis*, of *Abatoleon camposi* (Banks), and of *Myrmeleon perpilosus* Banks were discovered by sifting the sand. The larvae of *Myrmeleon* were abundant in the Peruvian Coastal Desert. Another species of *Myrmeleon* was found at Tingo María, Peru. Specimens of *Myrmeleon argentinus* Banks were found in central and southern Bolivia as well as at diverse localities in Argentina. *Brachynemurus immitus* (Gerstaecker) was collected by a malaise trap at Santa Cruz, Bolivia.

Specimens of *Haploglenius* Burmeister (Ascalaphidae) were collected at Tingo María, Peru, and at Horco Molle, Argentina. One larva and several adults of this family were found in the Bolivian malaise trap samples.

Zoogeography

There are 24 distinct biogeographical provinces in South America, according to Cabrera and Willink, 1973 (Fig. 1). With a few changes based on Neuroptera distribution patterns (Fig. 1) the scheme presented by them is followed here. The subsequent discussion, based on the Neuroptera collected during the 1974 National Geographic Society explorations of Colombia, Peru, Bolivia, and Argentina, is concerned with the biotic provinces Yungas, Peruvian Coastal Desert, Subandean Desert, and Chaco.

Yungas Province

This province extends from Venezuela to Argentina and includes a series of mostly uninterrupted cloud forests which vary considerably with latitude. The altitude of the province also varies with latitude, and cloud forests can be found from as low as 500 m to as high as 3500 m. They occur along the eastern slopes of the Andes between the Andean Province to the west and a variety of biotic provinces to the east which include (north to south) the Venezuelan Province, Savanna Province, Amazon Province, and Chaco Province. These areas are very humid but are cooler than the lowland provinces, especially at night.

Fieldwork was conducted in the Yungas of Colombia (Cauqueza, Restrepo), in Peru (Tingo María), and in Argentina (Horco Molle). These localities differ greatly in plant composition. Horco Molle is situated near the southern limit of the Yungas Province whereas the Colombia localities are near the northern limit. All of these localities (except Cauqueza) are near their lowest altitudinal limits. Restrepo borders the Savanna Province, Tingo María is near the Amazon Province, and Horco Molle borders the Chaco Province.

All of these localities have about the same genera of Neuroptera but different species. The cosmopolitan genera *Coniopteryx, Semidalis, Hemerobius, Megalomus, Sympherobius, Chrysopa,* and *Myrmeleon* are present. The Neotropic genera *Nusalala, Leucochrysa, Trichoscelia, Navasoleon,* and *Haploglenius* are also represented in the Yungas. The only other widespread genus in this biotic province is the New World *Eremoleon* (Myrmeleontidae). This is a good indicator genus for this province because it only occurs in the Yungas and the Brasilian Provinces in South America. Two species are found throughout the province: *Eremoleon anomalus* (Rambur) and *Eremoleon punctipennis* (Banks). At least 2 other species of *Eremoleon* occur in Colombia. Since the genus is best developed in North America, it would appear that *Eremoleon* invaded South America from the north and this would explain why Colombia has the richest *Eremoleon* fauna in South America. Furthermore the genus is absent from Chile and from southern Argentina. This either means that the genus has not had time to

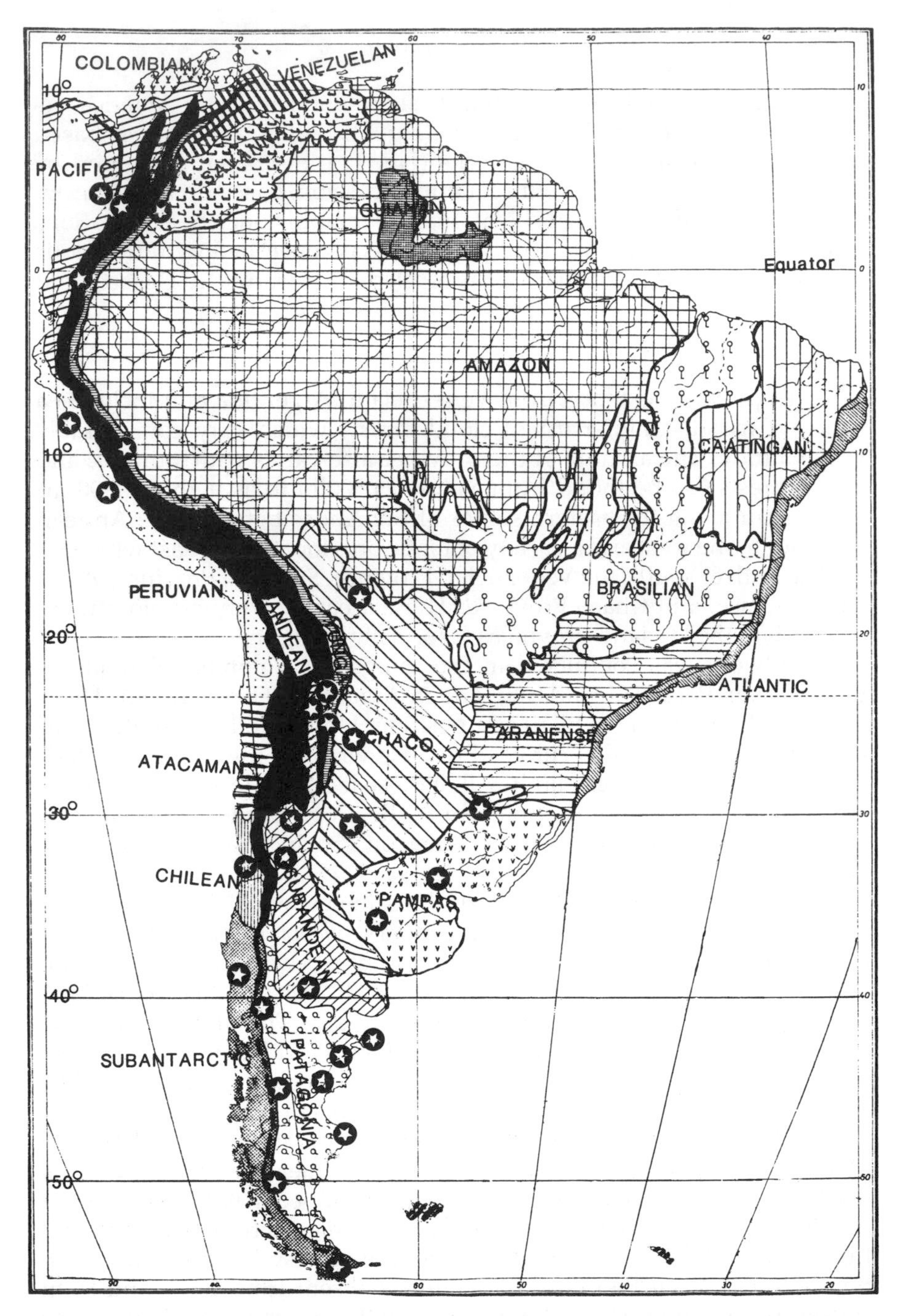

FIGURE 1. South America showing biogeographical provinces (modified from Cabrera and Willink, 1973). Important study sites are indicated by a circled star.

reach these areas or that the species have not been able to compete successfully with other cave-dwelling groups of antlions (*Eremoleon* is an obligatory cave dweller).

PERUVIAN COASTAL DESERT PROVINCE

This dry biotic province extends from about 5° S lat. in Ecuador to about 25° S lat. in northern Chile. It is sharply delimited to the west by the Pacific Ocean and to the east by the Andes. The northern limits are set by a tropical humid climate in Ecuador. However, the southern limits are set by the driest area in the world, the Atacamá Desert. This Chilean "super desert" separates the Peruvian Desert from the Coquimbo Desert.

The Peruvian Coastal Desert is not uniform, owing to differences in moisture. Although it is true that fog formed at sea regularly covers the lower part of this desert (to about 600 m), it is apparent that the lower elevations are the driest. Today most of the lower elevations are also quite bare owing to the activity of man. This can be appreciated by looking at the ancient mud city of Chan-Chan (near Trujillo) which was stripped of all wood for cook fires before being made a national monument. Most of the moisture is concentrated along more than 20 rivers which flow from the mountains to the sea, providing local wet conditions. Near these rivers may be found shrubs and small trees, such as *Prosopis, Acacia, Inga, Schinus,* and *Salex.* The slopes have a characteristic cacti flora including the large endemic species of *Neoraimondia* and *Lemaireocereus.*

The upper limits of this desert province are determined by two climatic factors, more moisture and winter frosts. This climatic change occurs at about 2000 m in the Rimac River valley, above which is grassland.

The Neuroptera of the Peruvian Coastal Desert are poorly known. The investigator sampled two river valleys between June 24 and July 8, 1974. The Rimac River valley above Lima provides a broad range of environments. At Cupiche there is considerable moisture in the river bottom, a condition that contrasts strikingly with the dry slopes, with their isolated cacti. The most notable feature at this locality is the great abundance of the antlion pitfall traps of *Myrmeleon perpilosus* Banks. The fact that these pitfalls are in the open indicates the low rainfall of the area. In the wetter grasslands above the desert (sampled at Matucana, 2389 m) these pitfalls are absent. Apparently this is a feature of the Peruvian Desert, since at all localities visited there were to be seen many antlion pitfalls, providing that there were also ants or other suitable prey. Several species of *Chrysopa* were common on the *Salex* trees, and an undescribed species of *Sympherobius* (Hemerobiidae) was found on the thorny *Prosopis* trees. No Coniopterygidae were found. *Hemerobius hageni* Navás is a common insect at this locality. At the grassland locality of Matucana, which is a few hundred meters above the Peruvian Desert, the only shared species of

Neuroptera is *Hemerobius hageni.* Other grassland species (*Incasemidalis* sp., *Chrysopa* sp.) are unknown from the lower desert.

At about 500 km to the north, near the city of Trujillo, further exploration of the Peruvian Desert river valleys was undertaken. At Simbal conditions were found to be similar to Cupiche, although judging from the cultivations it is a more "tropical" site. The antlion pitfalls of *Myrmeleon* were abundant, and several of the species of the genus *Chrysopa* also appear abundant. *Hemerobius hageni* was present, as well as a species of *Semidalis* (Coniopterygidae), on the shrubs of *Schinus.*

The sand dunes near Trujillo were found to harbor species of *Abatoleon, Myrmeleon perpilosus,* and *Vella assimilis* Banks. Some of the same species of *Chrysopa* recorded from Cupiche and Simbal were found.

On the basis of the fieldwork of the investigator, as well as previous data, tentative conclusions can be drawn as to the zoogeographical position of the Peruvian Coastal Desert. Although there appear to be no endemic genera in the desert, there is an endemic subgenus of *Dimares.* Other groups of Myrmeleontidae are represented by 2 species of the *Brachynemurus indiges* group, *Myrmeleon perpilosus* Banks (also found in the Galápagos Islands) and an endemic species of *Vella.* Many species of Chrysopidae are present but their taxonomic analysis is not possible, owing to the confused nomenclature. Hemerobiidae are represented by a few species, mostly of wide southern South American distribution. Only 1 species of Coniopterygidae *(Semidalis)* is known to date. Thus, on the basis of the still meager extant collections of Neuroptera, it is apparent that the fauna is poor (especially in comparison to their desert faunas), with a predominance of cosmopolitan genera *(Chrysopa, Hemerobius, Sympherobius, Semidalis, Myrmeleon)* and Neotropical groups *(Abatoleon, Vella, Dimares).* Although much more fieldwork remains to be done in this area before the Neuroptera fauna can be properly evaluated, it can be stated at this time that the fauna of this province is quite distinctive and is related to the Chilean Desert Province (Hemerobiidae) and to the Neotropic fauna (Myrmeleontidae).

Subandean Desert Province

This province lies completely within Argentina from about 27° to 44° S lat. A predominant group of plants is the Zygophyllaceae, with endemic species of *Larrea, Bulnesia,* and *Plectrocarpa.* Other plant indicators are discussed by Morello (1958). The investigator has been studying the Neuroptera fauna for several years. The 1974 fieldwork was done in the northern parts of this province (Cachi, Cafayate, Quebrada de los Toros).

The Neuroptera are richly represented in this desert province with the following genera: *Coniopteryx, Semidalis, Incasemidalis, Pampoconis,*

Hemerobius, Sympherobius, Spinomegalomus, Chrysopa, Chrysopiella, Myrmeleon, Vella, Dimares, Brachynemurus, Glenurus, Elachyleon, Navasoleon, Ululodes, Veurise, Pastranaia, and *Brucheiser.* There are many endemic species, and the last three genera mentioned are endemic. According to Stange (1969) 31% of the genera are endemic, 19% are cosmopolitan, 25% are Neotropical, and 25% are widespread New World genera. Recently 2 genera with Chilean affinities have been discovered *(Pampoconis* and *Spinomegalomus).*

Fieldwork was done in November 1974 and provided specimens of *Sympherobius psychodoides* (Blanchard) and several species of *Chrysopa* from the Quebrada de los Toros, the most northern locality of the Subandean Province. This Quebrada is of special zoogeographical interest because it is isolated from the rest of the Subandean Desert by mountains. The study of its Neuroptera is providing data on short-distance dispersal of Subandean species.

CHACO PROVINCE

This large biotic province is situated in western Paraguay, southern Bolivia, and north-central Argentina. Morello and Adamoli (1968) have provided a detailed description of the vegetation. There are numerous tree species, of which the most characteristic are *Schinopsis, Aspidosperma, Chorisia, Tabebuia, Ximenia, Cercidium, Caesalpinia,* and *Prosopis.* Cacti are also abundant, with the most typical species being *Opuntia quimilo* and *Cereus coryne.* There are several ecotypes included in this biotic province, with deciduous forest most common near the mountains and in wetter areas, isolated groups of low palm trees, and with more shrublike vegetation in the drier zones. There are also some salt flats. The Neuroptera fauna indicates that the Espinal Province of Cabrera and Willink (1973), centered in Córdoba, should also be considered a part of this province.

Coniopterygidae are well represented, with many species of the cosmopolitan genera *Coniopteryx* and *Semidalis.* The family Dilaridae is represented by the endemic *Nallachius bruchi* Navás. Hemerobiidae are fairly abundant, with species of *Hemerobius, Nusalala, Sympherobius,* and *Megalomus.* The genera of Chrysopidae in the Chaco are *Chrysopa, Leucochrysa,* and *Nacarina.* Several species of Hemerobiidae and Chrysopidae appear to be endemic, and there are several species of *Mantispa.* The Myrmeleontidae are represented by *Myrmeleon argentinus, Elachyleon punctipennis* Esben-Petersen, *Dimarella riparius* Navás, and several species of *Ameromyia, Abatoleon,* and *Brachynemurus.* The species of *Dimarella* may be endemic. *Elachyleon punctipennis* is found only in the Chaco in Argentina, but also occurs as far north as Mexico. There are several species of *Ululodes* Currie and of the endemic species *Fillus brethesi* Navás (Ascalaphidae).

Neuroptera were studied in 1974 at Tartagal, Salta (July), between Salta and Jujuy (November), and in the Sierras de Córdoba (January). Also the malaise trap samples from General Saavedra, Bolivia, contain important material of Chaco Neuroptera.

Based on the Neuroptera the zoogeographical affinities of this province can be described as follows: There are no endemic genera except possibly for the genus *Fillus* Navás, which, however, is known from only three localities; there are several endemic species of the cosmopolitan genera *Coniopteryx*, *Semidalis*, *Chrysopa*, and *Megalomus*; and there are also a few endemic species of widespread Neotropical genera *(Dimarella riparius* and *Nallachius bruchi)*.

Probably the most critical limiting climatic factor of the Chaco is the contrast between the cold, dry winters (when many of the trees and shrubs lack leaves) and the hot, humid summers. This may explain why there are not more of the genera found in bordering biotic provinces (Yungas, Amazon, Paranense) which are relatively warm and wet the year around. The rich Subandean Desert Province Neuroptera fauna is probably limited by the hot, humid summers. However in the drier parts of the Chaco a number of Subandean species are established (especially Myrmeleontidae). Thus the Chaco, one of the largest biotic provinces in area in South America, extending well north of the Tropic of Capricorn, with interdigitation with at least six other biotic provinces, is a relatively impoverished area in respect to the Neuroptera.

Biological Studies

Larvae of 5 genera of Myrmeleontidae *(Eremoleon, Myrmeleon, Vella, Abatoleon, Brachynemurus)* were discovered during the 1974 field studies in Colombia, Peru, Bolivia, and Argentina.

At Cauqueza, Colombia (Yungas Biotic Province) the larvae of a new species of *Eremoleon* were found in several small caves. Several full-grown larvae were present, in addition to other instars, indicating overlapping generations. Also, the large number of old cocoons present points to the continued use of the habitat by the species. Three larvae were successfully reared and the other material is preserved for anatomical and taxonomic studies now in progress. The species differs from other known *Eremoleon* in having very long tarsi, antennae, and abdomen. However, the structure of the larva agrees with the other known species (the investigator has reared 7 other species, including *Eremoleon anomalus* [Rambur] from Horco Molle, Argentina). This supports the broader taxonomic definition of the genus made by the investigator (Stange, 1970b). Also the genus can be defined by biological characteristics, as follows: obligatory cave dwellers; feed on a wide variety of insects, including members of their own species; larvae are creepers and climbers.

Larvae of *Myrmeleon perpilosus* Banks were found to be abundant in the Peruvian Coastal Desert. Specimens were collected at Cupiche, Laredo, and Simbal. Adults were reared to confirm the identification. This species is of special interest because it is the only continental antlion that has reached and colonized the Galápagos Islands. Studies of the variation between mainland and insular populations based on both larvae and adults are in progress. Also larvae of *Myrmeleon* sp. from the eastern slopes of the Andes (Tingo María, Peru) were located. These larvae were found only in protected areas (under rock ledges). Thus in contrast to the *Myrmeleon* larvae, which live in exposed areas in the desert, the *Myrmeleon* larvae which live in very rainy areas are restricted to limited habitats and consequently exist in smaller populations. The larvae of *Myrmeleon argentinus* Banks were found in Bolivia and Argentina. The larvae of *Myrmeleon* exhibit the same characteristics throughout the world. They dig and maintain pitfall traps, can only move backwards, throw out sand at insects that try to escape by climbing the steep slopes of the trap, and eventually make their silken cocoons underneath the sand.

Representatives of all 3 instars of *Vella assimilis* Banks were discovered in the extensive sand dune area near Laredo, Peru. This species of *Vella* was the most abundant of the 3 antlion species found in the sand dunes. They were collected by sifting the sand under plants on the lower slopes. The larval habits of *Vella* are very curious. They can only move backwards, but dig no pitfall traps like other larvae *(Myrmeleon)* which are obligatory retrograde animals. They must search for their prey under the sand, and they pursue it by going backwards. Information to date (see Stange 1970b, p. 20) suggests that the *Vella* antlions are predators of *Myrmeleon* larvae. Laboratory studies of the Peruvian *Vella* antlions revealed that they will readily attack not only *Myrmeleon* larvae but also other insects placed on the surface of the sand.

Also discovered in the sand dunes of Laredo was the larva of *Abatoleon camposi* (Banks). This larva was reared, providing the first larva/adult association of the genus. This larva showed behavior similar to *Brachynemurus* larvae. The species is very fast moving on the surface of the sand and also can bury itself quickly underneath the sand surface. The silken cocoon imbedded with sand grains agrees with all other cocoons that have been described in the family.

Seasonal Distribution in Central Bolivia

Data on seasonal flight periods of various families of Neuroptera were obtained by the use of malaise traps. Malaise traps represent a good method for sampling the fauna of certain groups of insects, but it is apparent that certain families of Neuroptera are collected much more than others. It is, for example, excellent for entrapping Coniopterygidae and

TABLE 1. Monthly Malaise Trap Captures of Neuroptera at General Saavedra, Bolivia (1974)

Family and Genus	*Jan.*	*Feb.*	*Mar.*	*Apr.*	*May*	*June*	*July*	*Aug.*	*Sep.*	*Oct.*	*Nov.*	*Dec.*
CONIOPTERYGIDAE (♂/♀)												
1. *Coniopteryx*	0	0	0	?	0	2/1	?	2/2	5/7	5/5	0	0
2. *Neoconis*	0	0	0	?	0	0	?	2/4	11/2	2/0	0	0
3. *Semidalis*	0	0	0	?	0	0/2	?	2/3	6/12	0/2	0	0
TOTAL	0	0	0	?	0	5	?	15	43	14	0	0
MANTISPIDAE												
4. *Trichoscelia*	0	0	0	?	0	0	?	0	1	0	0	0
HEMEROBIIDAE (♂/♀)												
5. *Megalomus*	0	0	0	?	0	0/1	?	1/0	0/1	1/5	0	0
6. *Notiobiella*	0	0	0	?	0	0	?	0	0/1	0	0	0
7. *Nusalala*	0	0	0	?	0/1	1/0	?	0	1/2	0	0	0
8. *Sympherobius*	0	0	0	?	0	0	?	0/1	0	0	0	0
TOTAL	0	0	0	?	1	2	?	2	5	6	0	0
CHRYSOPIDAE												
9. *Chrysopa*	0	0	0	?	0	1	?	0	3	5	0	1
MYRMELEONTIDAE												
10. *Brachynemurus*	0	0	0	?	0	0	?	0	1	0	0	0
11. *Myrmeleon*	0	0	0	?	0	0	?	0	0	1	0	0
ASCALAPHIDAE												
12. *Haploglenius*	2	0	0	?	0	0	?	0	0	1	1	0
TOTAL NEUROPTERA	2	0	0	?	1	8	?	17	53	27	1	1

Hemerobiidae, whereas the other families are less commonly collected. The Mantispinae have never been taken in the traps, although occasionally a few Platymantispinae are found. No doubt this is due to the fact the Mantispinae are relatively wary insects and poor fliers.

Two traps were installed in a Chaco forest at the experimental station near General Saavedra, Santa Cruz, Bolivia, a locality that is at the northern limits of the Chaco Province and shows some transition toward the Amazon biota. Samples from the traps were taken every month and kept in alcohol; those representing the months of April and July, however, were lost.

The results of the trap samples are given in Table 1. It is apparent that most Neuroptera are active in the months of August, September, and October. Only the family Ascalaphidae is relatively more active during the summer rainy season. This seasonal picture of the Neuroptera in central Bolivia is in close agreement with one obtained from malaise trap samples at Las Cejas, Tucumán, Argentina. That locality is also within the Chaco Biotic Province.

Part II—Field Studies, 1975

The second year of field studies (July to December 1975) of South American Neuroptera was given to the exploration of the western slopes of the Colombian Andes (Cali, Dagua), the Pacific Province rain forests (near Zabaletas; August 25 to September 5), the highlands of Ecuador (near Quito; September 5 to 10), the Peruvian Coastal Desert (Samne, Lambayeque, Laredo, Chongoyape, Río Chancay, Pacasmayo, and 50 km east of Zaña; July 10 to August 2), the Argentine Chaco (Santiago del Estero; December 26 to 30), and the Argentine Subandean Desert (November 20 to December 5). Special objectives of the fieldwork were to obtain material for systematic studies of the families Myrmeleontidae and Coniopterygidae, to study the biology of the Myrmeleontidae, and to study distribution patterns in the Subandean Province.

Collecting and Systematic Results

About 1200 specimens of diverse families of Neuroptera (Coniopterygidae, Hemerobiidae, Chrysopidae, Mantispidae, Myrmeleontidae, Ascalaphidae, Nemopteridae) were obtained through night and day collecting in Colombia, Ecuador, Peru, and Argentina.

Coniopterygidae

Collected were 314 specimens from Colombia (79), Peru (135), and Ecuador (100). All of the species belong either to the genus *Coniopteryx*

Curtis or to *Semidalis* Enderlein. Most of the species appear to be undescribed and are more closely related to the North American fauna than to the South American fauna found east of the Andes. Of special note was the finding of *Semidalis* in the Peruvian Coastal Desert. Although this genus is abundantly represented by species in Argentina, none occur in the Argentine Subandean Desert, a situation which contrasts with that on the western side of the Andes (and also that in North America). More details on the relationships of the species will have to await the completion of taxonomic studies now under way.

Chrysopidae

The collection of 512 specimens included 80 from Colombia, 14 from Ecuador (specimens of the widespread *Chrysopa externa* Hagen), 218 from Peru, and 200 from Argentina. Most of the species belong to *Suarius* Navás, *Leucochrysa* McLachlan, and *Chrysopiella* Banks. The latter genus occurs in the Sonoran Biotic Province of North America and in Argentina. This is the only known case of disjunct distribution in a genus of Neuroptera in the Western Hemisphere. Of special importance was the discovery of a species of *Meleoma* Fitch in the Peruvian Coastal Desert near Samne, La Libertad (see Fig. 2.). This genus is North American, with one species known from Venezuela. This Peruvian *Meleoma* is unique in the family in having the antenna strongly bent near the scape. All of the foregoing material belongs to the subfamily Chrysopinae.

Hemerobiidae

The collection of 125 specimens included 51 from Colombia, 18 from Ecuador, 36 from Peru, and 20 from Argentina. In Colombia species of *Notiobiella* Banks, *Hemerobius* Linnaeus, and *Anotiobiella* Kimmins were found on the following trees: *Nectandra* sp. (Lauraceae); *Trichanthera gigantea* (Humbolt and Bonpland) (Acanthaceae) and *Inga* (Leguminosae). *Anotiobiella withycombei* Kimmins was previously known only from Mexico. *Nusalala colombiensis* (Banks) was found near Cali, Colombia, and an unidentified species from Peru. A species of *Megalomus* (near *minor* Banks) was collected in Cali and another species of *Megalomus* was found on ferns in Peru. Also on the ferns was the widespread species *Hemerobius hageni* Navás. This species or a very similar one (according to the male genitalia) was found near Quito, Ecuador. In Argentina *Nusalala pallida* (Esben-Petersen), *Hemerobius hageni* Navás, and *Sympherobius maculipennis* Kimmins were collected at lights.

Mantispidae

The collection included 15 specimens. In Colombia a green *Mantispa* was found on shrubs. Also green *Mantispa* were discovered in the Peruvi-

FIGURE 2. Peruvian Coastal Desert Province near Samne, La Libertad. On the dry slopes above the desert proper are large rock overhangs where *Eremoleon* larvae are found.

an Coastal Desert on *Inga* trees. *Mantispa wagneri* Navás was found at lights at the salt flats at Río Saladillo, Santiago del Estero, Argentina. Several other *Mantispa* were found in the Chaco.

MYRMELEONTIDAE

The collection included 200 specimens (adults and larvae) from Colombia, Peru, and Argentina. In Colombia, larvae of *Myrmeleon perpilosus* Banks were located in a relatively dry area near Dagua. In Peru, the finding of larvae of a species of *Eremoleon* in a cave at Samne represents the first record of this genus from the Peruvian Coastal Desert; previously this tribe of antlions (Glenurini) was unknown from this area (Fig. 2). Also in Peru, larvae of *Vella assimilis* Banks, *Abatoleon* spp., and *Myrmeleon perpilosus* Banks were found in sand dunes at Laredo and also near Lambayeque, and adults of *Myrmeleon perpilosus* and *Abatoleon* spp. were found in the field. In Argentina, *Brachynemurus dispar* (Banks), *B. immitus* (Walker), *B. frontalis* (Banks), *B. verticalis* (Banks), *Ameromyia strigosus* (Banks), and *Navasoleon leptocera* (Navás) were collected in the Subandean Desert; and *Eremoleon punctipennis* (Banks) was found in a cloud forest near Tucumán.

Ascalaphidae

Several specimens of *Ululodes brachycera* Navás were found in the Chaco of Santiago del Estero, Argentina. An adult was observed resting in the typical *Ululodes* habitus with the head directed groundward (opposite to the resting position of Myrmeleontidae).

Nemopteridae

The crocine species *Veurise bruchi* Navás was found at lights near Belén, Catamarca, Argentina.

Zoogeography

The following discussion of the zoogeographic provinces of South America is based on the biotic definitions given by Cabrera and Willink (1973).

Pacific Province

This biotic province includes areas with the greatest precipitation known in the world (as much as 10,000 mm annually). There are a number of subprovinces, such as the lowlands with tropical rain forest, the cloud forests which are above 1000 m, and less lush vegetation at intermediate altitudes. There are some relatively arid areas (such as near Dagua, Valle) which are in rain shadows. This province covers most of Costa Rica and Panama, the western parts of Colombia and Ecuador, the interandean valleys of Colombia and probably also the cloud forests of northern Peru on the western slopes of the Andes. According to the zoogeographic studies of the wasp genus *Zethus* Fabricius (Hymenoptera; Eumenidae) by Bohart and Stange (1965) the entomofauna is more related to the North American Neotropics than to the South American Neotropics. They used the term "tropical transition area" to indicate that this province is faunistically an overlapping one between these two great Neotropical biotas and is logically the corridor of faunal exchange. With a scarcity of extant collections and published accounts, the Neuroptera are poorly known. Exploration in the state of Valle provided more data on this subject. There exists a diversity of ecological zones in this state from rain-forest lowlands to cloud-forest uplands. There are no known endemic genera of Neuroptera in this province, but there are endemic species and species groups. About 30% of the genera are cosmopolitan (*Coniopteryx, Semidalis, Chrysopa, Hemerobius, Megalomus, Sympherobius, Mantispa, Sisyra, Myrmeleon*). The genus *Notiobiella* (Hemerobiidae) is pantropical. The rest of the genera, including all of the Dilaridae, the Platymantispinae, and nearly all of the Myrmeleontidae, are restricted to the Western Hemisphere. Furthermore nearly all of these genera found in the Pacific Province have species in both North American Neotropics (roughly Mexico to Nicaragua) and South American Neotropics (east of the Andes). The only North American Neotropical endemic genus found in the Pacific Province is *Anotiobiella* (Hemerobiidae) known only from Vera Cruz, Mexico, and Valle, Colombia. Since little zoogeographic significance can be ascertained at the genus level at present, it is necessary to study species groups to appreciate the relationships of the Pacific Province entomofauna. Species or species groups of the Myrmeleontid genera *Glenurus, Psammoleon,* and *Abatoleon* are clearly allied with the North American Neotropics whereas those of the genus *Dimarella* Banks are related to the South American Neotropics. Other groups of Neuroptera are too poorly known taxonomically or geographically to provide even preliminary analysis. Nakahara (1965) indicates that the North American species *Sympherobius barberi* (Banks) and *Megalomus minor* Banks are present in the zone but the species I have seen are different.

PERUVIAN COASTAL DESERT PROVINCE

The following data supplement those given in Part 1. Stange (1978) has discussed features of this province based on these two trips. Several species of *Semidalis* Enderlein and *Coniopteryx* Curtis were discovered. Of special interest is the fact that *Semidalis* occurs in the Peruvian deserts as it does in the North American deserts. However, in the South American Neotropics (east of the Andes) *Semidalis* is absent from the Argentine Subandean Province (although this genus is common in other areas of Argentina). Many different species of Chrysopidae were found, including *Suarius* Navás and *Meleoma* Fitch. The latter genus was previously known only from North America and Venezuela. The genera *Megalomus* and *Nusalala* (Hemerobiidae) are new additions to the Peruvian Coastal Desert entomofauna. The latter genus is a Neotropical indicator group. Two species of the formerly unrecorded antlion tribe Glenurini were found. One species (from near Lima) belongs to the genus *Rovira* Navás and is closely related to a species found in the Coquimbo Desert of Chile. This genus is otherwise restricted to the South American Neotropics, except for 1 species that extends from Argentina to Mexico. The other glenurine species is *Eremoleon anomalus* (Rambur) which otherwise is recorded from various localities on the eastern slopes of the Andes from Colombia to northwestern Argentina. No Ascalaphidae have been found to date. The only other temperate to tropical zone in the Western Hemisphere where this family is absent is Chile. Information on the Neuroptera to date indicates that the Peruvian Coastal Desert has a predominant cosmopolitan generic fauna (46% of the genera), a decided Neotropical influence (27% of the genera), a small Chilean relationship (13% of the genera), a small endemic element (7%, namely a subgenus of *Dimares),* and a small special relationship with the North American Neotropics (7%, genus *Meleoma*).

SUBANDEAN DESERT PROVINCE

About 200 specimens were collected during the 1975 fieldwork but do not represent any new additions to the Subandean fauna. Neuroptera have been discussed by Stange et al. (1976).

CHACO PROVINCE

About 50 specimens were obtained from this province during 1975 but all belong to previously recognized groups.

Biological Studies

MYRMELEONTIDAE

Larvae of 4 genera (*Eremoleon* Banks, *Myrmeleon* Linnaeus, *Abatoleon* Banks, and *Vella* Navás) were discovered during the 1975 field studies in Colombia and Peru.

At Samne, Peru (1500 m) the larvae of a species near *Eremoleon peterseni* (Banks) were found in a large rock-overhang enclosure. Several specimens were reared. This area is in constant use as a latrine by the townspeople. Since the area is protected against rain, it is noteworthy that the larvae could survive in such an organic-waste–laden soil. However, it is likely a case of preadaptation since the caves selected by members of this genus are often full of bats that lay down great deposits of guano and urine in the soil or sand in which the larvae live. On the other hand the larvae succumb easily to any moisture and no larvae have ever been found in caves or cavelike environments that are moist.

In sand dune areas in Peru at Laredo (La Libertad) and at Lambayeque (Lambayeque), larvae of *Vella assimilis* Banks, and *Abatoleon* spp. were found (see Fig. 3). Very few of the pit-making *Myrmeleon perpilosus* Banks were present. It seems likely that *Vella* larvae could not possibly survive as predators of just *Myrmeleon* since they are by far the most common larvae present (at least 10 times as many *Vella* larvae as all other larvae together). Some data on antlion larvae were utilized in a paper on Florida antlions (Stange, 1980).

PART III—FIELD STUDIES, 1977

The third year of field studies (January to March 1977) of South American Neuroptera was given to the exploration of southern Argentina, which includes three principal biogeographical provinces: Subantarctic *Nothofagus* forests, the Patagonian steppes, and the Subandean Des-

FIGURE 3. Peruvian Coastal Desert Province near Mocupe, Lambayeque. *Abatoleon* larvae inhabit the tops of the dunes, whereas large *Vella* larvae are found in all fairly deep sand conditions. In 1982 *Dimares* larvae were found here near the bottom of the dunes.

ert. About 15,000 km were traversed by private vehicle. Special objectives of this year's fieldwork were: to obtain material for systematic studies of the families Myrmeleontidae and Coniopterygidae, to study the biology of the Myrmeleontidae, and to study distribution patterns in the circum-andean biotic provinces.

Collecting and Systematic Results

About 700 specimens of diverse families of Neuroptera (Osmylidae, Hemerobiidae, Coniopterygidae, Chrysopidae, Mantispidae, Myrmeleontidae) were obtained through night and day collecting as well as by malaise trapping.

CONIOPTERYGIDAE

Pampoconis latipennis Meinander and *Semidalis kolbei* Enderlein were found throughout the *Nothofagus* forests of the Subantarctic Province. Neither species occurs in other Argentine biotic regions although in Chile *Semidalis kolbei* is found in the Chilean Province. Only 1 species was found in Patagonia Province—a new species of *Incasemidalis*. The Subandean Desert Province has many species of *Coniopteryx* but no *Semidalis*. There are also species of *Incasemidalis* and of an undescribed genus.

HEMEROBIIDAE

The only species found in the beech forests of Tierra del Fuego (Subantarctic Province) is *Hemerobius hageni* Navás, which was one of the most common insects in the forest. Over 200 adults and some larvae were found on the trees. However, north of the Strait of Magellan (Los Glaciares Parque Nacional) species of *Megalomus* and *Gayomyia* were found in addition to the *Hemerobius* (which is widespread in the southern half of South America). Many specimens of the widespread *Sympherobius psychodoides* (Blanchard) were collected in several localities of the Patagonia Province. No other species are known from this zone. The Subandean Desert has 2 species each of *Sympherobius*, *Hemerobius*, and *Spinomegalomus* (also found in northern zones of the Subantarctic Province). No additional specimens of *Sympherobius cinereus* (Kimmins) were located in the southern beech zone.

CHRYSOPIDAE

Several species of *Suarius* were found in the northern part of the Subantarctic Province (Lanin Parque Nacional). No other genera of this family have been discovered in this area. *Chrysopiella argentina* (Banks) was collected in the Patagonia Province (first records) and also in the southern part of the Subandean Province. Many other species of other chrysopine genera are found in the Subandean Desert but their taxonomy is in a confused state. In January 1966, species of *Suarius* were common in the *Nothofagus* areas of Chile, but in 1977 few specimens were seen in the Argentine part.

MANTISPIDAE

Drepanicus gayi Blanchard and *Drepanicus schajovskoyi* Williner and Kermilov are endemic species in the *Nothofagus* forests (Subantarctic Province) and at least the latter species is in the Chilean Biotic Province. No further specimens were seen. Specimens of *Mantispa viridula* Erichson were collected in the Sierras de Cordoba (Chaco Province).

OSMYLIDAE

Two species of *Kempynus* and 1 species of the endemic genus *Phymatosmylus* Adams are found in the northern parts of the *Nothofagus* forests (Subantarctic Province). Apparently these species are not attracted to lights and material has been collected in malaise traps and also flying at dusk (in Chile). One larva of *Kempynus* found near a stream in Chile is being studied and compared with larvae known from Australia.

SISYRIDAE

Climacia chilena Parfin and Gurney has been known from 1 specimen from Llanquihué, Chile. A second specimen from Lanin Parque Nacional is on hand. Both localities are in the Subantarctic Province. Apparently no freshwater sponges are recorded from the area but undoubtedly they exist, since this family are ectoparasites of the Porifera.

MYRMELEONTIDAE

Lemolemus litigator (Navás) is the only antlion known from the *Nothofagus* forests (Subantarctic Province). Larvae were discovered in small caves near El Bolson, Río Negro. A second species of *Lemolemus* was discovered in the southern part of the Subandean Desert Province (Malargüe). The widespread species *Brachynemurus irrigatus* (Gerstaecker) (known from Venezuela to Chubut, Argentina) occurs in the Patagonian Biotic Province and shows some differences in coloration and body form from specimens taken farther north. The Peninsula Valdez is botanically an isolated (by the Subandean Desert) part of the Patagonian Biotic Province. Here were found *Abatoleon frontalis* (Banks), *Brachynemurus verticalis* (Banks), and the Patagonian form of *Brachynemurus irrigatus* (Gerstaecker). Additional specimens of widespread Subandean species *(Ameromyia strigosus, Brachynemurus dispar, Brachynemurus immitus, Myrmeleon argentinus, Dimares elegans)* were taken in southern parts of the Subandean Desert (Sierra Lihuel Calel, La Pampa).

Biology

Larvae of *Hemerobius hageni* (Navás) were collected in Tierra del Fuego. Larvae of *Lemolemus litigator* (Navás) were collected from small caves near El Bolson, Río Negro. One was reared. These larvae are now being studied and compared with *Lemolemus* larvae collected by Stange in 1966 in central Chile. Notes derived from larval studies made during the National Geographic Society–sponsored field trips were presented by Stange (1977) at the "Séptimo Congreso latinoamericano de Zoología," at Tucumán, Argentina.

Zoogeography

The following discussion of the zoogeographic provinces of South America is based on the biotic definitions given by Cabrera and Willink (1973).

SUBANTARCTIC (*NOTHOFAGUS* FOREST) PROVINCE

This province corresponds nearly exactly with the distribution of the tree genus *Nothofagus*. The most northern extreme of the province exists on the Chilean side of the Andes at about 35° S lat. (about 40° S lat. in Argentina) and its southern limits are found in the Isla Navarino just south of Tierra del Fuego (55° S lat.). There are about 25 species of trees in the Argentine part of this beech zone but most of them are restricted in distribution. Going from north to south there is a steady decrease in the number of species of plants and animals, as can be appreciated by comparing the tree diversity with Neuroptera diversity at different latitudes shown in Table 2. An interesting feature of this biotic province is that most genera have only 1 or 2 species and there is a decided relationship with Australia at the generic level. In the Neuroptera (Planipennia) this is best illustrated by the genus *Kempynus* Navás (Osmylidae). There are 2 species in the Subantarctic Province of Argentina and 4 species in Australia or New Zealand. There is 1 endemic, monobasic genus of Osmylidae *(Phymatosmylus)* in the area. The family Mantispidae is represented by 2 green species of *Drepanicus* Blanchard, which is considered one of the most primitive groups in the family, with vague relationships with Australian groups. On the other hand, 1 of the most common species of Neuroptera is *Semidalis kolbei* Enderlein which belongs to a genus found in all regions of the world except Australia and New Zealand. Other species of Coniopterygidae are 2 species of *Pampoconis* Meinander. All the known species of the ubiquitous family Chrysopidae belong to the genus *Suarius* Navás. The Hemerobiidae represent the most diverse family in the province, with 5 species in 5 different genera *(Megalomus, Spinomegalomus, Sympherobius, Hemerobius, Gayomyia). Spinomegalomus* and *Gayomyia* appear to be subantarctic elements, although the former is found in the Subandean Desert. The curious family of Spongilla-flies (Sisyridae) is represented by *Climacia chileana*. There are no Ascalaphidae or Nemopteridae, and the Myrmeleontidae are represented by 1 species of *Lemolemus*, a genus centered in Chile. The salient zoogeographic features of this highly interesting biotic province are the following: There is no apparent close relationship with the Neotropical Region (shared genera are also shared with other regions); there are 13 genera, with about 18 species, known from the area (1.5 species per genus); at the generic level there is a considerable relationship with the arid Chilean biota (about 75% of the genera are shared) and with Australia (30%, about 20% of the Neuroptera genera being endemic or nearly so to the area); all the species are found in the northern part of the biotic province, with a decline in the number of species toward the south (only 3 species are known from Tierra del Fuego).

TABLE 2. Relative Abundance of Trees and Neuroptera *(Planipennia)* in Southern Argentine National Parks

		Trees		*Neuroptera*	
National park	*Latitude*	*Genera*	*Species*	*Genera*	*Species*
Lanin	40° S	14	17	13	18
Los Alerces	41° S	9	11	7	7
Los Glaciares	50° S	4	6	5	5
Tierra del Fuego	55° S	3	5	3	3

PATAGONIAN PROVINCE

This is a vast biotic zone occurring from about the middle of Mendoza Province (35° S lat.) to northern Tierra del Fuego (54° S lat.) occupying lands west of the Subantarctic Biotic Province. The climate is arid and cold, with regular strong westerly winds. There is snow in winter and frosts can occur all year long. There are no native trees, the predominant vegetation being various species of clump grasses and usually yellow-flowered bushes, mostly Compositae. It is a poorly known area entomologically and almost no Neuroptera have been recorded (see Stange, 1969). Information obtained during the present studies indicates that there are only 4 species in the area, and that these exist in more northern areas, near the Subandean Desert. These are: *Brachynemurus irrigatus* (Gerstaecker) (Myrmeleontidae); *Sympherobius psychodoides* (Blanchard) (Hemerobiidae); *Chrysopiella argentina* (Banks) (Chrysopidae); and a new species of *Incasemidalis* Meinander (Coniopterygidae). The first 2 named species are widespread in South America whereas the *Chrysopiella* is characteristic of the Subandean Desert. The genus *Incasemidalis* is known from arid central Chile, from the high, arid Andean Province and also from the Subandean Desert. Thus it is apparent that Patagonia Province is poorly exploited by the Neuroptera. This is not surprising since in other cold (and especially treeless) areas of the world there are relatively few Neuroptera.

SUBANDEAN DESERT PROVINCE

The only additions to our knowledge of the Neuroptera of this biotic zone are records from more southern parts. *Lemolemus* Navás occurs at about 35° S lat., near the Andes, whereas 5 other antlion species are found in the southern (and coastal) limits in Chubut *(Brachynemurus irrigatus, B. verticalis, B. lizeri, Abatoleon frontalis,* and *Ameromyia strigosus).* The most southern record for *Dimares elegans* can now be extended to about 38° S lat. (Lihuel Calel), at which locality is a mixture of pampean *(Ameromyia longiventris)* and Subandean Province elements.

General Zoogeographical Conclusions

Information on the Neuroptera fauna has been obtained in 7 circumandean biogeographical provinces during a 3-year study period (1974-1977). Previous data on the Chilean Province, based on studies made by the author in 1966, is included for comparison. These 8 provinces are compared at the generic level (59 genera in 13 families) and this information is summarized in Tables 3 and 4.

TABLE 3. Comparison of Neuroptera in Circumandean Biotic Provinces

Family and Genus	*Pacific*	*Peruvian Coastal Desert*	*Yungas*	*Chaco*	*Subandean Desert*	*Patagonian*	*Chilean*	*Subantarctic*
CONIOPTERYGIDAE								
1. *Neoconis*	0	0	0	1	0	0	0	0
2. *Pampoconis*	0	0	0	0	1	0	1	2
3. *Coniopteryx*	1	1	1	3+	2+	0	0	0
4. *Incasemidalis*	0	0	0	0	1	1	1	0
5. *Semidalis*	2	1	1	3	0	0	1	1
6. Undescribed genus	0	0	0	0	1	0	0	0
7. *Brucheiser*	0	0	0	0	1	0	1	0
POLYSTOECHOTIDAE								
8. *Fontecilla*	0	0	0	0	0	0	1	0
DILARIDAE								
9. *Nallachius*	1	0	1	1	0	0	0	0
OSMYLIDAE								
10. *Kempynus*	0	0	0	0	0	0	0	2
11. *Phymatosmylus*	0	0	0	0	0	0	0	1
12. *Isostenosmylus*	0	0	1	0	0	0	0	0
SISYRIDAE								
13. *Climacia*	1	0	0	0	0	0	0	1
BEROTHIDAE								
14. *Cyrenoberotha*	0	0	0	0	0	0	1	0
15. *Lomamyia*	1	0	0	0	0	0	0	0
16. *Naizema*	0	0	0	1	1	0	0	0
MANTISPIDAE								
17. *Plega*	1	0	0	0	0	0	0	0
18. *Trichoscelia*	1	0	1	1	1	0	0	0
19. *Drepanicus*	0	0	0	0	0	0	1	2

20. *Gerstaeckerella*	0	0	0	0	0	0	1	0
21. *Nolima*	1	0	0	0	0	0	0	0
22. *Climaciella*	1	0	1	0	0	0	0	0
23. *Entanoneura*	1	0	1	1	0	0	0	0
24. *Mantispa*	2	0	2	3	1	0	0	0
25. *Paramantispa*	0	0	0	1	0	0	0	0
HEMEROBIIDAE								
26. *Notiobiella*	1	0	1	0	0	0	0	0
27. *Anotiobiella*	1	0	0	0	0	0	0	0
28. *Gayomyia*	0	0	0	0	0	0	1	1
29. *Megalomus*	1	1	1	2	0	0	1	1
30. *Nusalala*	1	1	2	2	0	0	0	0
31. *Hemerobius*	1	1	1	1	1	0	1	1
32. *Spinomegalomus*	0	0	0	0	1	0	1	1
33. *Sympherobius*	1	1	1	3	2	1	2	1
CHRYSOPIDAE								
34. *Chrysopiella*	0	0	0	0	2	1	1	0
35. *Leucochrysa*	5	1	5	0	1	0	0	0
36. *Meleoma*	2	1	0	0	0	0	0	0
37. *Suarius*	1+	1+	1+	1+	1+	0	4+	3+
38. *"Chrysopa"*	1+	1+	1+	1+	1+	0	0	0
MYRMELEONTIDAE								
39. *Dimares*	0	3	0	1	1	0	0	0
40. *Vella*	1	1	0	1	1	0	0	0
41. *Abatoleon*	1	1	1	2	3	0	0	0
42. *Ameromyia*	0	0	0	3	1	0	0	0
43. *Brachynemurus*	1	0	0	4	5	1	0	0
44. *Jaffuelia*	0	0	0	0	0	0	1	0
45. *Lemolemus*	0	0	0	0	1	0	4	1
46. *Dimarella*	1	0	1	1	0	0	0	0
47. *Eremoleon*	1	0	2	0	0	0	0	0
48. *Glenurus*	1	0	2	0	1	0	0	0
49. *Navasoleon*	1	0	1	0	1	0	0	0
50. *Psammoleon*	3	0	0	0	0	0	0	0
51. *Rovira*	1	1	1	1	1	0	1	0
52. *Myrmeleon*	1	1	1	1	1	0	0	0
ASCALAPHIDAE								
53. *Haploglenius*	1	0	2	0	0	0	0	0
54. *Fillus*	0	0	0	1	1	0	0	0
55. *Ululodes*	1+	0	1+	3	2	0	0	0
56. *Cordulecerus*	1	0	2	0	0	0	0	0
NEMOPTERIDAE								
57. *Pastranaia*	0	0	0	0	1	0	0	0
58. *Veurise*	0	0	0	0	1	0	0	0
59. *Stenorrachus*	0	0	0	0	0	0	1	0
TOTAL SPECIES	43	17	36	43	38	4	26	18
TOTAL GENERA	34	15	26	25	29	4	19	13

TABLE 4. Percentage of Shared Genera Between Circumandean Provinces (% = number of shared genera/total number of genera in both provinces)

Province	Pacific	Peruvian	Yungas	Chaco	Subandean	Patagonia	Chilean	Subantarctic
Pacific		44	74	59	33	6	11	15
Peruvian	44		40	48	33	6	21	22
Yungas	74	40		52	34	3	16	18
Chaco	59	48	52		37	3	14	15
Subandean	33	33	34	37		21	29	17
Patagonia	6	6	3	3	21		15	6
Chilean	11	21	16	14	29	15		45
Subantarctic	15	22	18	15	17	6	45	

In South America there are two major zoogeographical regions. The Neotropical Region which includes the circumandean provinces (Pacific, Peruvian, Yungas, Chaco, and Subandean) and the Neantarctic Region which includes the Chilean, Subantarctic, and Patagonia Provinces. The number of shared genera (expressed in percentages in Table 4) is in good agreement with this scheme. It is apparent that the Subandean Province is somewhat intermediate between these two major regions whereas the Patagonia Province is somewhat an anomaly, owing to the highly impoverished fauna adapted to the only treeless zone among the provinces being discussed.

The greatest endemism is found at the southern end of South America, with 4 endemic genera in the Chilean Province, 3 in the Subandean Province, and 2 (both Osmylidae) in the Subantarctic Province. The subfamily Brucheiserinae in all the world is found only in the deserts of central Chile and Argentina. There are at least 3 genera found in the Pacific Province that are not present in other regions of South America, but they also occur in North America.

There are few records of Neuroptera from the high Andean provinces. This is mainly because of the little collecting done in these areas, but it probably also reflects the impoverished Neuroptera fauna. In general, areas with cold weather and no trees (such as Patagonia) have few Neuroptera. The known Neuroptera of high Andean zones are 3 genera of Coniopterygidae *(Coniopteryx, Semidalis, Incasemidalis)* and several species of *Hemerobius* (probably derived from North America, since there is a decrease in species north to south). All these genera are cosmopolitan and, except for *Incasemidalis*, are widespread in nearly all zones in South America. This latter genus is adapted to cold, arid areas (with or without trees) since it is restricted to the Andean, Patagonia, Subandean Desert, and Chilean Provinces. Thus the Andes represent one of the most important natural barriers to faunal exchange in South America. However, the Cordillera is not a perfect barrier and considerable faunal exchange probably has occurred in the extreme north and south of South America.

The temperate deserts of southern South America (Chilean and Subandean) represent important refugia for the Neuroptera containing 8 endemic genera between them (*Brucheiser, Fontecilla, Cyrenoberotha, Naizema, Pastranaia, Veurise, Stenorrachus,* and an undescribed genus of Coniopterygidae). This is in agreement with other temperate deserts of the world, such as the Sonora Desert of southwestern United States (see Adams, 1967).

REFERENCES

Adams, P. A.

1967. A review of the Mesochrysinae and Nothochrysinae. Bull. Mus. Comp. Zool., vol. 135, pp. 215-238.

Bohart, R. N., and Stange, L. A.

1965. A revision of the genus *Zethus* Fabricius in the Western Hemisphere. Univ. Calif. Publ. Ent., vol. 40, pp. 1-208.

Cabrera, A. L., and Willink, A.

1973. Biogeografía de América Latina. Organización de Estados Americanos, Serie de Biología, Monografía, no. 13, 120 pp.

Meinander, M.

1972. A revision of the family Coniopterygidae (Planipennia). Acta Zoologica Fennica, vol. 136, pp. 1-357.

Morello, J.

1958. La provincia fitogeográfica del monte. Opera Lilloana, vol. 2, pp. 1-155.

Morello, J., and Adamoli, J.

1968. Las grandes unidades de vegetación y ambiente del chaco argentino. Primera parte: Objetivos y metodología. INTA, Buenos Aires, Serie Fitogeografía, no. 10, 125 pp.

Nakahara, W.

1965. Contributions to the knowledge of the Hemerobiidae of western North America. Proc. U. S. Nat. Mus., no. 116, pp. 205-222.

Stange, L. A.

1969. Tipos de distribución de Neuroptera: Planipennia en Argentina. Acta Zool. Lilloana, vol. 24, pp. 101-110.

1970a. Revision of the ant-lion tribe Brachynemurini of North America. Univ. Calif. Publ. Ent., vol. 55, pp. 1-192.

1970b. A generic revision and catalog of the western hemisphere Glenurini with the description of a new genus and species from Brazil. Contributions in Science, Los Angeles, vol. 186, pp. 1-28.

1977. Comportamiento larval de las hormigas leon (Neuroptera: Myrmeleontidae). Resúmenes del Séptimo Congreso Latinoamericano de Zoología. San Miguel de Tucumán, p. 80.

STANGE, L. A. *(continued)*
1978. Los *Zethus* del desierto de Peru. Acta Zool. Lilloana, no. 33, pp. 71-78.
1980. The antlions of Florida. II. Genera based on larvae. Florida Dept. Agric. & Consumer Serv., Div. Plant Industry, Ent. Circ., no. 215, pp. 1-4.

STANGE, L. A.; TERAN, A. L.; and WILLINK, A.
1976. Entomofauna de la provincia biogeografica del monte. Acta Zool. Lilloana, no. 73, pp. 73-120.

LIONEL A. STANGE

The Evolution and Systematics of Hispaniolan Urocoptid Land Snails

Grant Recipient: Fred G. Thompson, The Florida State Museum, University of Florida, Gainesville, Florida.

Grants 1541, 1946: In support of a study of the evolution and systematics of Hispaniolan urocoptid land snails in certain areas of Haiti and the Dominican Republic.

The Urocoptidae are a family of land snails endemic to the Greater Antilles and Mexico, with some species straggling onto adjacent islands in the West Indies and onto adjacent areas of the American continents. The family contains about 500 species. Most are obligate inhabitants of limestone substrates where they dwell among boulders, in crevices, or under leaf litter. A few are arboreal. The greatest species diversity occurs in xeric regions owing to the harsh ecologically isolating mechanisms of such an environment in combination with the snails' predilections for limestone outcrops. Urocoptids generally are cylindrical in shape, an adaptation favoring water conservation due to the reduced size of the shell aperture in proportion to the total shell surface. They vary in size from about 1 to 10 cm in length. Many species are brightly colored.

Two principal centers of evolution are recognized, Mexico and the Greater Antilles, and are characterized by different subfamilies. Among Antillean islands Hispaniola has the greatest diversity at higher taxonomic levels, although Cuba has a greater diversity in species. Urocoptid genera and species have been defined primarily on the basis of shell structures. Little attention has been given to characteristics of the soft anatomy. Therefore their earlier classification was based upon features that evolve relatively easily in response to changing environmental factors. Similar shell features have evolved independently in different regions due to similar environments. Other anatomical features that evolved due to physiological adaptation, reproductive selection, habitat selection, and feeding strategies have remained unstudied. Thus knowledge about the evolution and systematics of this large family of snails has been hampered by incomplete data on their biology.

An overview of the higher systematics of the Urocoptidae based on the soft anatomy was initiated several years ago. The study was divided into two segments, the Mexican fauna and the West Indian fauna. Hispaniola was selected as the center for the West Indian study because of its high diversity at the generic and suprageneric level, and because its fauna was the least known in the West Indies. Material from other West Indian islands supplements the Hispaniolan material. Studies on the Mexican fauna will be completed after the Hispaniolan fauna is reviewed.

I. Fieldwork in the Dominican Republic, 1976

Funds were obtained from the National Geographic Society to conduct fieldwork during January and February 1976, in the Dominican Republic in conjunction with a study of the systematics and evolution of the urocoptid mollusks of Hispaniola. The fauna of Hispaniola includes about 84 known species of Urocoptidae, which probably represents less than half of the species that occur on the island. The purpose of the fieldwork was to complete, as nearly as practicable, a field survey of the urocoptid fauna of the Dominican Republic. I had previously surveyed most of the country; further work, however, remained to be done in Puerto Plata Province and near the Haitian border in the Sierra de Neiba, Sierra de Baoruco, and the Sierra de Martin Garcia.

Puerto Plata Province has several small limestone mountain ranges which are isolated from each other by intervening igneous and metamorphic formations. Thus each of these ranges is an ecological island on which organisms that require a calcareous habitat are restricted. The two principal ranges explored on this trip are the Loma del Puerto and the Loma Martin Ocampo. The former range provided several remarkable undescribed species of snails.

The Sierra de Neiba was investigated from several points along its north, south, and west slopes. Generally, the molluscan fauna consists of species that are relatively widely distributed within this range. There was little indication of local endemism. Several new species were discovered which are widely distributed throughout the range and in adjacent foothills.

The Sierra de Baoruco was thoroughly worked along its northern, eastern, and southern slopes. Two distinct faunal units occur among the land snails. The central and western ends of the range have many species that are widely distributed in this area, and apparently their distributions continue west into the Sierra de la Selle in Haiti. The eastern end of the Sierra de Baoruco appears to be physiographically distinct and has a highly characteristic fauna with many endemic species that do not occur farther west.

The Sierra de Martin Garcia was entered at its west slope from various trails out of Puerto Alejandro and from the east at Barrera. The mountain range is most unusual faunistically. Its closest zoogeographic affinities are with the eastern Sierra de Baoruco, even though the Martin Garcia is closer to the Sierra de Neiba and is separated from the Sierra de Baoruco by the Cul-de-Sac Basin and Barahona Bay. Many endemic species were discovered in the Sierra de Martin Garcia. The biological affinities of most of these are with species occurring in the Sierra de Baoruco, and not with species from the Sierra de Neiba or other mountain ranges or hills nearby.

This expedition permitted the principal investigator to determine the geographic distributions of most of the Urocoptidae in the Dominican Republic and to conduct a nearly complete assay of the urocoptid fauna. Anatomical material was obtained for all species.

II. Fieldwork in Haiti, 1979

The objective of this project was to complete fieldwork in significant portions of Haiti as part of a comprehensive systematic study of the Urocoptidae of Hispaniola. Most regions in the Dominican Republic had been surveyed in 1974-1978. Some regions in central Haiti were also surveyed in 1978. Major areas of limestone in the north and south peninsulas of Haiti and the central plains remained to be investigated. The survey of these areas was accomplished during March-May 1979, and January 1980, as a result of support provided by the National Geographic Society.

Fieldwork in 1979 concentrated on the south peninsula and the central mountainous areas, with less time devoted to the northern part of the country. On the south peninsula, the Massif de La Selle was worked from the north slope and the south slope. Higher interior areas of the massif were not visited because of their very difficult accessibility. Farther to the west the Massif de La Hotte was worked at many localities. It is accessible in general, except at the far west end of the peninsula where the higher peaks such as Macaya and Grande Colline are located. These higher and remote areas still remain unworked. In January 1980, fieldwork was conducted on Ile de La Gonave, and again in the Massif de La Selle.

The results of the work to date show that in Haiti a major evolutionary radiation of the Urocoptidae occurred in the south peninsula. This radiation includes a large number of endemic genera and numerous species. Most of the taxa are undescribed, and those that have been named are classified incorrectly. The central and northern regions of Haiti are characterized by a few species of three widely distributed genera. Coincidental to the investigations on the Urocoptidae, it was found that other families of land snails also have evolved extensively on the south peninsula of Haiti. These include the Helicinidae, Proserpinidae, Annulariidae, and the Sagdidae. As with the Urocoptidae a far greater radiation of endemic genera and species was found than had been reported previously.

PUBLICATIONS

THOMPSON, FRED G.

1977. The polygyrid genus *McLeania* in Hispaniola. Nautilus, vol. 91, pp. 77-80.

1978. A new genus of operculate land snail from Hispaniola with comments on the status of the family Annulariidae. Nautilus, vol. 92, pp. 41-54.

1980. Proserpinoid land snails and their relationships within the Archeogastropoda. Malacologia, vol. 20, pp. 1-33.

1982. The *Helicina umbonata* complex in the West Indies (Gastropoda, Prosobranchia, Helicinidae). Bull. of the Florida State Museum, vol. 28, pp. 1-23.

_____. Dominican land snails of the genus *Brachypodella*. Bull. of the Florida State Museum. (In press.)

FRED G. THOMPSON

The Galápagos Land Iguana *(Conolophus)*: Natural History and Conservation Survey

Grant Recipient: Dagmar Werner, Lehrstuhl für Tierphysiologie, Universität Bayreuth, Bayreuth, West Germany.

Grants 1444, 1665, 1773, 1918, 1947, 2217: In support of a study of the general history and conservation of Galápagos land iguanas.

I. Survey of Field Research: 1976-1979

This report gives a survey of the field research carried out from 1976 through 1979 in the Galápagos Islands. The results presented are preliminary and are described in more detail elsewhere (Werner, 1982).

The fieldwork was carried out on the following schedule:

1976 (entire year) under Grant Nos. 1444 and 1665—Survey of the status of *Conolophus* on various islands. Conservation-oriented research, inauguration of the land iguana conservation program. Principal field assistant: Hanspeter Stutz (Zürich, Switzerland).

1977 (entire year) under Grant No. 1773—Beginning of thorough studies about social structure and ecology of iguanas on Fernandina Island. Continued surveys on other islands. Advising land iguana conservation program. Principal field assistants: Hanspeter Stutz; Monique Altenbach (Luzern, Switzerland).

1978 (January-July) under Grant No. 1918—Fieldwork on Fernandina Island. Thorough search for surviving land iguana populations in the southern part of Isabela Island. Continued advising of the conservation program.

1979 (January-August) under Grant No. 1947—Fieldwork only on Fernandina Island. Main field assistants: Fanny Rodriguez; Udo Hirsch; K. Lein.

1980 under Grant No. 2217—Field analysis study. Principal assistant: Fanny Rodriguez.

The land iguana, *Conolophus*, is a genus endemic to the Galápagos Islands, and its specific environment offers the rare opportunity to investigate a vertebrate with no or limited resource competition. Moreover, adult males and females have no natural enemies. Most of the land iguana populations are threatened by extinction through man-introduced mammals that either kill the iguanas or interfere by food competition. In view of this, my research had two main aspects: (1) To investigate the behavior, social structure, and ecology of the iguana and (2) to promote and give advice on a conservation program for the threatened populations, on the basis of the research carried out in the field.

Behavior, Social Structure, and Ecology of Conolophus

The main research on the behavior, social structure, and ecology of *Conolophus* was carried out on Fernandina Island, where the only population of land iguanas exists that is not disturbed by introduced feral mammals or tourists.

Fernandina is among the most active volcanoes of the world. Only about one third of the island's surface is covered with vegetation, which is distributed in a more or less patchy way, according to where the most recent lava flows and ash decays happened to cover the surface. Fernandina Island has a diameter of 32 km and an altitude of 1495 m and consists of a single shield volcano. Its flanks are covered with numerous parasitic cones. According to age and type of volcanic actions there are different soil types, and weather conditions vary depending on altitude and prevailing winds. As a consequence, the island offers a number of plant communities and types of vegetation that range from sparsely vegetated lava or ash fields to junglelike forests and pampa. Due to the lack of resource competitors, the land iguana is not restricted to specific habitats, rather it is distributed over the entire island as far as food requirements and thermoregulatory needs permit. The only areas where the land iguana does not occur are those where vegetation is absent or where it is so dense that the sun cannot heat the ground.

The weather conditions in the Galápagos are characterized by two seasons. The warm season normally lasts from December to May with daily maxima of around 32, 30, and 27°C at the shore, at altitudes of 300 m and 1230 m, respectively. During the rest of the year, in the cold season, the temperatures are several degrees below those measured in the warm season.

According to the two seasons two phases can be distinguished in the yearly cycle of *Conolophus*. The reproductive phase falls in the warm season, whereas the cold season corresponds to the nonreproductive phase.

The Reproductive Phase

The social structure is based on a female-choice system in which the males defend territories or occupy home ranges. The central part of a home range or territory consists of 1 to 7 burrows, which the males construct and defend against intruders. Territories are established in areas where soft soil is combined with an extensive feeding ground nearby; home ranges are established where food is sparse and scattered. A home range is twice the size of a territory and covers between 200 m^2 and about 900 m^2. The distance between the burrows of neighboring males is greater in home ranges than on territories, and fighting is much rarer in sparsely vegetated areas (home ranges). The combination of soft soil for burrow construction and food exists on only about 5% of the island's surface. Therefore, the entire adult population is concentrated in this small part of the island during reproduction.

A territory does not necessarily contain food. The males feed little or not at all during the entire reproductive phase (4 months), even if their territory has food. Females, on the other hand, feed extensively, and by means of an appeasing gesture have access to any territory, or they feed outside the territories.

The males do, or tend to, occupy the same territory or home range in subsequent years. They may start with its establishment as early as 3 months before the mating phase in May. Not all males attempt to defend a territory or home range. About one third of the male population in the F 270 study area are nonterritorial; at mating time there is forced copulation by these males with the females without regard to the female-choice system.

About 70% of the females return to the same general mating area they inhabited in the preceding mating season. A female may return to the same territory and remain with its owner, or she may roam through the territories, staying with one male for days or weeks before she joins another male.

Males arrive in the mating area before the females, and in the early stage of territory establishment the territorial boundaries are defined by ecological criteria (soil, bushes, food plants, location of existing burrows). The boundaries may be shifted without obvious reason or with the influence of newly arriving males. When the females arrive in the mating area their presence strongly influences the territorial limits. Males whose territory is devoid of females may attempt to approach the females of neighbors. In this way fights are instigated and the intruding male may conquer a neighbor's burrow together with the female who uses it. Such a situation led in one case to a fight between two males that produced about 6 weeks of daily fights. Due to the females' loose affiliation with the males whose territory they share, a male may have several females at one time and none shortly afterward. The females thus indirectly provoke the males' fights and cause a shifting of the territorial boundaries. A female's influence on the male's behavior becomes most obvious when she stays directly within a territorial limit, "feeding" where there is practically no food. Sometimes two respective males want to court the same female and immediately get involved in a fight, while the female stays nearby. Several females repeatedly showed this behavior and the fight between the males ended when she joined one of them or when she left the area.

Besides fighting, a male has a number of behavioral strategies to attract females: (1) He increases his activity level (display, burrow construction); (2) he directs precopulatory behavior patterns at females; (3) he steals a neighbor's female (the male enters a neighbor's territory, grabs the female by a neckfold, and carries her into his own territory where he copulates with her in front of one of his burrows); (4) he herds a female, i.e., he prevents her from leaving his territory; and (5) he sexually assaults females of other males (only a male whose territory is devoid of females does that).

A male may display one or more of these strategies, and there seems to be great individual differences as to which of the strategies a male employs. The maximum number of females a male fertilized was four. Females may seek multiple inseminations, a behavior also observed in *Cyclura stejnegeri* (Wiewandt, 1977). This iguana shows a degree of individual flexibility and complexity of social structure comparable to *Conolophus*.

Most surprising was the fact that the females in the 1979 season refused to mate. The premating activities were comparable to those observed in the preceding reproductive season, except that the activity level of the males was much lower in 1979. Presumably this is related to weather conditions. The last rain in 1978 occurred in mid-April. By June food abundance in a sample area had declined from 95% food plant coverage to 30%. By the end of October it had still not rained (at least at the crater rim: Tom Simkin, pers. comm.), and food must have been extremely scarce by then. The males, therefore, were most likely unable to restore the depleted fat bodies on which they must rely again in the following mating season. A low level of activity in that season (1979) was the consequence. I suspect that the females refused to mate in 1979 because they had too few behavioral criteria on which to base their choice of a male. In spite of not mating, the females migrated to the nesting areas, and the clutch of the only female we were able to locate during laying contained fertile eggs. The females probably fertilized their eggs with sperm stored from the previous mating season or by parthenogenesis.

In order to find out where the females go for egg deposition I needed to radio-track them. Long-distance tracking devices for reptiles are not available on the market. I was lucky that Mr. Udo Hirsch and Mr. Karl Wagener proposed to provide me with the tracking equipment I needed for my purpose. The transmitters they constructed enabled us to locate the females from a distance of 5 km by means of a radio with a directional antenna. From the mating area at 300-m altitude we followed the females to the crater rim to which all of them headed. This is an aerial distance of 6 km and an altitudinal difference of 1100 m. Depending on weather conditions, the females needed between 4 and 10 days to reach the rim. From there they all descended into the crater. The radio signals were reflected and bundled by the concave crater walls leading to a labyrinth effect. After several unsuccessful attempts to locate the females, even from inside the crater, we gave up our search. The nesting areas we discovered show the following characteristics: They are located along a fumarole crevice where there is soft earth of at least 40 cm depth and they are heated by hot vapor. The nest temperatures are almost constant during a day-night cycle and are as warm as 32 to 34°C, whereas temperatures measured in comparable areas lacking fumarole activity are below 30°C and fluctuate several degrees during 24 hours. A female lays between 8 and 23 eggs, which is one-fourth to one-third her own weight. Incubation lasts for 3 to 4 months. Competition for nesting places is very strong and completed nests are guarded. In an area of about 150 by 30 m^2 we counted 350 to 400 females on a single day. Probably more than 95% of the female population from the western side, where we made our observations, marched to the crater for laying. We counted several thousand females.

The Nonreproductive Phase

As soon as the females leave the mating area for nesting, the activity level of the males drops drastically. The territories are no longer defended, and the males maintain only one burrow now. Some males leave the mating area altogether, whereas others use it as a home base, going on feeding excursions lasting for days or weeks. The iguanas now avoid close contact with one another and fighting is extremely rare. After their feeding abstinence during the mating season males now have first access to feeding sites. They now chase away the females who no longer perform the appeasement gesture. After nesting, the females slowly return to the proximity of the mating area. A few females were observed there 2 months after their departure for nesting. Others were seen in the mating area only in the following mating season. They probably exploit feeding grounds distant from the mating area.

Conclusions and Discussion

Evidence for a high degree of flexibility in the social system of iguanines has recently been demonstrated by a number of workers (Berry, 1974; Dugan, 1980; Ryan, 1980; Werner, 1982; Wiewandt, 1977). The socioecological determinants of mating strategies in this group of lizards are discussed by Dugan and Wiewandt (1980). The studies on the Mona iguana *(Cyclura stejnegeri)* and my own studies show that these two iguanas have the most complex structure of the group, and individual differences in appearance as well as in behavior are pronounced. The land iguana shows the highest investment of behavioral energy (especially fighting) during the reproductive phase. This is probably related to the diversity of the habitats on Fernandina Island. Only about 10% of the available feeding areas is exploited during reproduction. During the nonreproductive phase the population distributes over a much wider range. The extended fights observed in the land iguanas are also a consequence of the lack of natural enemies, which in other populations select out those individuals that behave in a conspicuous way.

A land iguana male's mating success depends on his ability to monopolize resources (territory providing food, shelter, burrows, thermoregulation places); a male's behavior, however, is of such an importance that the defense of an ecologically good territory is no guarantee for his mating success.

The land iguana is the only vertebrate known to me that combines multiple inseminations in one year with female refusal to mate in another year. Although parthenogenesis may enable the females to reproduce without insemination, the more likely and common pattern is sperm storage by the females. The males obviously had sperm; they tried to rape females and ejaculated in inappropriate places, e.g., on the backs of the struggling females, or on the ground. It is likely that either territory or male quality failed to trigger female willingness to be inseminated in this year. Territory quality did not seem to differ between years, and, therefore, the more likely reason for the females' refusal is the low level of activity the males showed in the 1979 reproductive season.

The fact that females seek multiple inseminations may reflect an advantage of a diversified gene combination in the heterogeneous habitat Fernandina Island offers. This conflicts with the possibility of parthenogenetic reproduction in the population.

Comparison Between Land Iguana Populations from Different Islands and Conservation Survey

The genus *Conolophus* was last classified by Van Denburgh (1913), who distinguishes two species, *C. subcristatus* and *C. pallidus*. According to modern classification ecologically separated populations are incipient species. The land iguana populations on the various islands are isolated and there is indication that they have subdivided into several subspecies.

A thorough classification study has been carried out by H. Snell since 1977. Differences in scalation patterns and morphological criteria are used to determine the degree of differentiation between the various land iguana populations. My own studies show that the observed populations differ in three main aspects: (1) Size and degree of sexual dimorphism; (2) yearly cycle; and (3) behavior patterns such as head-bobbing sequences vary between populations.

On all islands, except for Fernandina, the populations are endangered by introduced mammals or are disturbed by interference of man. Table 1 gives a survey of the distribution of *Conolophus* and the status on the various islands.

Introduced herbivores are more effective in exploiting food resources, and food competition leads to a decline in the number of land iguanas. Moreover, donkeys, cattle, and horses destroy the burrows by trampling. Iguana males whose burrows are destroyed desert the territory. Females mate only with males who own a territory (burrow). If the burrows are destroyed, reproduction is either stopped altogether or to a large extent. I see the reason for the low number of iguanas on Alcedo (Isabela) in the high number of donkeys on this volcano.

Carnivores (dogs, cats) and an omnivore (pig) are the most immediate threat to the land iguanas. Due to the lack of natural enemies during the evolution of *Conolophus* the iguanas show no fear toward introduced predators. They are an easy kill for the dogs, who kill large numbers of iguanas without even eating them. The degree of damage dogs cause is best demonstrated by the events in Cerro Dragon (Santa Cruz Island); within less than one year they had eradicated almost the entire population of Conway Bay/Cerro Dragon, around 1000 individuals. My studies to the effect that the Santa Cruz iguana would disappear if nothing was done immediately came just in time. It was possible to save 56 iguanas from this island; these are now kept at the Charles Darwin Research Station. The same tragedy happend in Cartago Bay (Isabela); it was possible to save 37 individuals from there.

Cats concentrate in the nesting areas of the land iguanas at hatching time. I have seen cats, waiting at a hatching spot, killing one hatchling after another. They severely interfere with the expansion of the population.

Pigs most likely are responsible for the extinction of *Conolophus* on James Island. Pigs have easy access to adult land iguanas by digging them out of their burrows, the shelter where they flee when threatened. They also dig out nests to feed on the eggs. Skeletons of land iguanas were found in the highlands of Santa Cruz by Debby and David Clark. None of the settlers I asked has ever seen a land iguana there. Dogs became feral in Santa Cruz only in 1969; therefore, the pigs, which were introduced much earlier, must have eradicated the land iguanas in the highlands.

TABLE 1. Distribution and Status of *Conolophus subcristatus* and *C. pallidus*

First column indicates island or part of island on which subspecies differentiation is expected (Isabela). The second column indicates the source of disturbance or threat.

Island	*Threatened by*	*Endangered*	*Comments*
Conolophus subcristatus			
Fernandina	Undisturbed	No	Only undisturbed island where the land iguana occurs.
Isabela			The island consists of five main volcanoes: Darwin, Wolff, Alcedo, Sierra Negra, Cerro Azul. All volcanoes are, or were, populated by land iguanas that probably differ from each other on the subspecific level.
Darwin & Wolff	Cats	Not immediately	Large numbers of iguanas were seen by National Park wardens and by Tom Fritts, 1972-1977.
Alcedo	Donkeys, cats, goats	Yes	Very few individuals existing. Donkeys most likely are responsible for the low number and for destroying the burrows. Goats were first seen in 1976.
Sierra Negra	Dogs, cats	Severely	Only one of many populations survives in a vegetation oasis between the two volcanoes.
Cerro Azul	Cattle, horses		Population size is about 300 individuals. The Cartago Bay population became extinct in 1976 except for 37 individuals taken to the Charles Darwin Research Station (CDRS), a rescue measure from the attacks of dogs.
Santa Cruz	Dogs, cats, donkeys, goats, pigs	Severely	All populations extinct, except for 56 individuals that were taken to the CDRS or transferred to Venecia (small island close to Santa Cruz) in 1976, the only measure to protect the last survivors from the attacks of dogs.
S. Plaza	Tourists	No	Until 1972, tourists disturbed the population by feeding them. Tourists have negligible effect now.
N. Plaza			About eight individuals were seen on this small island in 1971-72. The population possibly was introduced from S. Plaza.
James	Pigs, goats	Probably extinct	One individual found on this island was taken to the CDRS. It is possibly introduced from S. Plaza.

Island	Threatened by	Endangered	Comments
Bartholomé			Four or five individuals live here. They are probably introduced from S. Plaza.
Baltra	Man	Yes	Population exterminated during World War II by people. In 1934 and 1936 about 140 individuals were transferred to North Seymour. Of these only 30 to 34 survive today.
North Seymour			See Baltra Island.
Conolophus pallidus			
Barrington	(goats)	No	The goats were exterminated in 1972.

In view of the alarming findings from my research studies, namely, that the Santa Cruz and Cartago Bay populations would become extinct within weeks or months if no measures were taken, the land iguana conservation program was initiated in 1976—in the early stages of my studies. On the basis of the results I obtained from the field it has been possible for the National Park, in cooperation with the Charles Darwin Research Station, to carry out an extremely successful and ongoing conservation program, which has been supervised by H. Snell since 1977.

II. Data Evaluation Period: 1980

In 1980 data concerning male and female reproduction were evaluated at the Max-Planck-Institut für Verhaltens-physiologie, West Germany.

Since males and females invest in reproduction differently, their reproductive success is determined by different parameters. In the promiscuous mating system of the land iguana, males not only should seek to fertilize a high-quality female but also to inseminate as many females as possible, as male investment in gamete production is low. Females expend a much higher amount of energy in the production of gametes, and their choice of a partner should be based only on male quality and/or the quality of the resources he defends.

Female Reproduction

The effect of environmental quality on clutch size was investigated in one study period (1979). Females were captured and measured at the caldera rim on their way to and from the nest sites in the caldera. Snout-vent-length (SVL) in relation to female weight correlations are low. For gravid females the correlation is $r = 0.59$ ($n = 102$, $p < .001$) while for nongravid females it is $r = 0.48$ ($n = 69$, $p < .001$). The low correlation is probably because (i) females from extremely different (good/bad) habitats intermingle on their way to and from the nest sites, and (ii) females ascend from different altitudes to the caldera rim and accordingly their investment in migration (fat deposits) varies.

Females from the two poor (little food) study areas F 20 and F 1230 are by 19 and 23%, respectively, lighter than females from the good (abundant food) study area F 270 ($p < .0001$, T-test). Heavy females produce a larger clutch than light ones ($r = 0.73$, $n = 14$, $p < .01$), and relative clutch mass (i.e., the percentage the clutch contributes to the combined weight of female and clutch) increases with size ($r = 0.73$, $n = 12$, $p < .01$, outliers omitted). Females that were relatively heavy (weight/SVL ratio) before laying remain so after laying ($p < .01$). These data are evidence that females from good habitats should have a higher reproductive success than those from poor habitats. They produce more offspring, and in addition are better equipped (are heavier and have fat reserves) for potential harsh conditions in the unpredictable environment the island offers.

On the other hand, differential selection should favor offspring from females living in poor habitats. This can be expected because the population can be assumed to share the same genetic background. Females from all habitats nest in a single area (the caldera) from which offspring disperse. Offspring from females living in poor conditions should have a higher chance of survival in all habitats than offspring from females living in favorable environmental conditions. Fernandina Island offers the extraordinary opportunity to study this aspect in detail, as well as the adaptive nature of the plastic response of a population to varying environmental conditions.

Females spent from their arduous migration have a mean SVL of 41.2 cm ($n = 69$, $SD = 1.7$, $min = 36.7$, $max = 44.6$) and weigh 2.9 kg on the average ($n = 69$, $SD = 34$, $min = 2.1$, $max = 3.8$). Clutch weight is 0.691 kg ($n = 15$). Migration costs are very high. Nine females equipped with transmitters needed a median of 9 days (range 4 to 14 days) to reach the island's summit from mating area F 270 (aerial distance is about 6 km and 1100 m difference in altitude). They took an additional 23 days to reach the final nest site, for nesting and returning to the rim. Weight loss per day during migration was measured in 7 females. The minimum weight loss per day was 3.08 g/kg/day and mean weight loss was 8.76 g/kg/day. Using these figures as the most likely range for investment in migration, a female uses between 352 g and 1009 g of her body weight for reaching the nest site and nesting. This is half to one-and-a-half times the clutch weight (51 to 146 %). These results strongly suggest that migration costs should be taken into account in studies and theories relating to reproductive effort in reptiles.

Areas suitable for nesting in other iguanine and land iguana populations, such as beaches, or nearest areas offering soft soil for burrow construction, are not used by the Fernandina population (see Wiewandt, 1982, for review). On Fernandina Island the caldera must offer advantages that compensate for the high effort and risks the females face to reach it. Although there is no conclusive evidence, there are several possibilities that could select for nesting in the caldera: (1) The funnel shape causes favorable (high) soil temperatures which may enable the population to place egg production and mating activities in the warm, and incubation in the cold, season. (2) Predator swamping comparable to the mass synchronous nesting behavior of sea turtles (Richards and Hughes, 1972). (3) Nests were found in fumarole-heated soil. This could be used to concentrate hatching in a much shorter period of time than laying, by early females laying in cooler soil than latecomers—an anti-predator mechanism. (4) If sex in *Conolophus* is determined by incubation temperature (see Bull, 1980, for review), the sex of *Conolophus* offspring could be determined by a female on the basis of the soil where the eggs were laid.

Further investigations are necessary to determine the selective forces responsible for the peculiar nesting phenomenon observed in the Fernandina land iguana.

Male Reproduction

In a female choice system a male's mating success depends on two main factors: His (genetic) quality and the quality of the resources he defends (if any).

In the studied land, iguana males defended territories in all years of observation (study area F 270) and females gathered there during the reproductive period. In one of the study periods, however, females refused to mate (1979). In order to test whether territory quality or other factors are responsible for male mating success, data from a year when matings took place were compared to those when females refused copulations.

The questions to be answered are the following:

- (i) Is there a difference in territory quality in the two study years (1978 when females mated, 1979 when females refused matings)?
- (ii) Do females show a preference for certain territories in one (1978) or in both years?
- (iii) Is there a difference in the criteria on which females base their choice in the compared years?

Male territory quality was described by the following list of 10 parameters.

1. Territory size (m^2).
2. Soft soil suitable for burrow construction (m^2).
3. Bush-covered area (m^2) (thermoregulation).
4. Area covered by food plants (m^2).
5. Distance (m) to feeding area outside the territory.
6. Area not covered by plants (m^2) (thermoregulation).
7. Number of different plant species.
8. Number of adjacent male territories.
9. Number of territories within less than 10 m distance from the periphery of respective territory.
10. Snout-vent-length of male.

The attractiveness of a male and his territory to females was measured by the frequency with which females spent the night in the burrow of a male during the mating period (May). In 1978 this measure reflected the probability of mating of the respective territory owner. I will use the term "female success" in the following for this measure.

(i) Difference in territory quality between the two years was tested by discriminant analysis using the 10 parameters listed above. In none of these parameters could a statistically significant difference be detected (all $p > .05$); the significance level of the canonical discriminant functions is $P = .63$. In other words, if there was a difference in territory quality between the two years the parameters used do not reflect it.

(ii) Female preference for male territories was tested by multiple regression analysis. Female success was used as dependent, the 10-mentioned territory criteria were used as independent variables.

In both years there is a highly significant correlation between certain territory parameters and female success. In 1978 two parameters, food and territory size, correlate significantly with female success ($p = .004$) and explain 77% of the variance. In 1979 soft soil and snout-vent-length are the main predictors for female success ($p = .03$) and explain 53% of the variance. If the data for both years are combined, soft soil, bush cover, and male size (SVL) correlate significantly with female success ($p = .05$) and explain 61% of the variance.

The fact that different parameters predict female success in the two years cannot be interpreted as difference between the two years. This is because most of these parameters correlate significantly with each other as can be seen from Table 2.

Also, if there was a strong difference in the two years a much lower percentage of variance should be explained by significant parameters in the combined sample.

TABLE 2. Correlations Between Parameters Predicting Female Success

Units in m², SVL (snout-vent-length) in cm. Asterisks indicate level of significance at the $p<.05$ (*), $p<.01$ (**), and $p<.001$ (***) level. See text for further explanations.

Parameters	*Soft soil*	*Bush cover*	*Food plants*	*SVL*
Territory size	.47**	.63***	.14	.35*
Soft soil		.48**	.40*	.13
Bush cover			.61***	.58***
Food plants				.36*

For field data the percentage of variance regarding female success explained by the 10 parameters used is extremely high: 92% of the variance is explained in 1978 and in 1979 it is 67%. This indicates that relevant parameters were recorded and that the lack of difference in territory quality between the years stated in (i) is likely to reflect reality. This step demonstrates that females made a choice in both years, but it remains unclear whether or not different criteria were used by the females.

(iii) For testing whether or not females chose males (territories) according to similar criteria in the two study years, the territories were classified according to the value obtained for female success. Territories with values above the median were ranked "good," those below the median were ranked "bad." The samples from both years were combined and subjected to discriminant analysis. The result shows that "good" and "bad" territories in both years can be distinguished on the basis of identical parameters, which are soft soil, bush cover, and territory size (all $p < .005$) with an overall significance of $p = .004$ (canonical discriminant functions).

These results show that females use definite parameters for territory (male) choice. However, as the females refused to mate in 1979 additional criteria are necessary if we are to determine what guarantees copulation. Males were much more active in 1978 compared to 1979. Analysis of the behavioral data will give evidence whether or not the observed difference is statistically significant and which of the behavioral criteria trigger female willingness to be fertilized.

REFERENCES

BERRY, K. H.
1974. The ecology and social behavior of the Chuckwalla, *Sauromalus obesus obesus* Baird. Univ. Calif. Publ. Zool., vol. 101, pp. 1-60.

BULL, J. J.
1980. Sex determination in reptiles. Quar. Rev. Biol., vol. 55, no. 1, pp. 3-21.

CASE, T. J.
1982. Aspects of the ecology and evolution of the incular gigantic *Sauromalus*. *In* "Iguanas of the World: Behavior, Ecology and Evolution," G. M. Burghardt and A. S. Rand, eds. Noyes Publ., Park Ridge.

DUGAN, B. A.
1982. The mating behavior of the green iguana *(Iguana iguana)*. *In* "Iguanas of the World: Behavior, Ecology and Evolution," G. M. Burghardt and A. S. Rand, eds. Noyes Publ., Park Ridge.

DUGAN, B. A., and WIEWANDT, T. A.
1982. Socio-ecological determinants of mating strategies in iguanine lizards. *In* "Iguanas of the World: Behavior, Ecology and Evolution," G. M. Burghardt and A. S. Rand, eds. Noyes Publ., Park Ridge.

RICHARDS, J. B., and HUGHES, D. A.
1972. Some observations on sea turtle nesting activity in Costa Rica. Marine Biol., vol. 16, pp. 297-309.

RYAN, M. J.
1982. Variation in iguanine social organization: Mating systems in the genus *Sauromalus*. *In* "Iguanas of the World: Behavior, Ecology and Evolution," G. M. Burghardt and A. S. Rand, eds. Noyes Publ., Park Ridge.

VAN DENBURGH, J.
1913. Expedition of the California Academy of Sciences to the Galápagos Islands, 1905-1906. Proc. California Acad. Sci., vol. 2, no. 1, pp. 133-202.

WERNER, D. I.
1982. Social organizations and ecology of land iguanas, *Conolophus subscristatus*, on Fernandina Island, Galápagos. *In* "Iguanas of the World: Behavior, Ecology and Evolution," G. M Burghardt and A. S. Rand, eds. Noyes Publ., Park Ridge.

WIEWANDT, T. A.
1977. Ecology, behavior, and management of the Mona Island iguana, *Cyclura stejnegeri*, 338 pp. Ph.D. dissertation, Cornell Univ., Ithaca, New York.
1982. Evolution of nesting patterns in iguanine lizards. *In* "Iguanas of the World: Ecology, Behavior and Evolution," G. M. Burhardt and A. S. Rand, eds. Noyes Publ., Park Ridge.

DAGMAR WERNER

Meadowcroft Rockshelter

Grant Recipient: J. M. Adovasio, Department of Anthropology, University of Pittsburgh, Pittsburgh, Pennsylvania.

Grants 1584, 1753: In support of archeological excavations in Meadowcroft Rockshelter and the Cross Creek drainage, Washington County, southwest Pennsylvania.

From June 1973 through August 1978, the University of Pittsburgh and a series of cooperating institutions conducted a detailed, multidisciplinary examination of Meadowcroft Rockshelter in Washington County, Pennsylvania, and the immediately contiguous Cross Creek drainage in Washington County, Pennsylvania, and Brooke County, West Virginia. Essentially, the central goal or theme of this research was empirical and involved the systematic acquisition, analysis, and integration of any and all data bearing on the archeology, history, paleoecology, geology, geomorphology, pedology, hydrology, climatology, and floral and faunal succession of the entire Cross Creek watershed. Generous support was made available by the National Geographic Society, the University of Pittsburgh, the Meadowcroft Foundation, the National Science Foundation, the Alcoa Foundation, the Buhl Foundation, the Leon Falk Family Trust, and Messrs. John and Edward Boyle of Oil City, Pennsylvania. It is significant that this research was carried out virtually without temporal or fiscal constraints, using state-of-the-art data gathering, analytical, and synthetic methods (Carlisle et al., 1982).

The data base generated by the Meadowcroft/Cross Creek Archaeological Project is truly enormous. In addition to Meadowcroft Rockshelter, some 235 other sites in the watershed were located and surface collected or tested. Cultural features abounded, with 276 recorded at Meadowcroft alone. Some 20,000 flaked and ground stone (Fitzgibbons, 1982), bone, and other perishable artifacts (Stile, 1982) constitute the so-called aboriginal artifactual record of the study area. Additionally, more than 965,000 unmodified animal bones (Guilday et al., 1980; Guilday and Parmalee, 1982) and 1.4 million individual plant remains (Volman, 1981; Cushman, 1982) were recovered. Literally thousands of geological, geochemical, hydrological, pedological, archeomagnetic, and other samples were collected. A substantial number of these geo-archeological samples are now analyzed (Beynon, 1981; Beynon and Donahue, 1982; Stuckenrath et al., 1982). While space precludes even a cursory synopsis of the results of the 1973-1978 field operations, the salient aspects of the Meadowcroft/Cross Creek research are set forth below, following a brief orientation to the study area. Details on the Meadowcroft/Cross Creek Archaeological Project are available in Carlisle and Adovasio (1982) and Adovasio et al. (1983).

General Setting

Meadowcroft Rockshelter (36WH297) is a stratified, multicomponent site located 48.27 air km (30 mi) (78.84 km; 49 mi via road) southwest of Pittsburgh and 4.02 surface km (2.5 mi) northwest of Avella in Washington County, Pennsylvania. The site is situated on the north bank of Cross Creek, a small tributary of the Ohio River which lies some 12.16 km (7.6 mi) to the west. The exact location of the site is 40° 17′ 12″N, 80° 29′ 0″ W (U.S.G.S. Avella, Pennsylvania, 7.5′ Quadrangle).

Meadowcroft Rockshelter is oriented roughly east-west, with a southern exposure, and stands some 15.06 m (49 ft) above Cross Creek and 259.9 m (853 ft) above sea level. The area protected by the extant overhang is some 65 m^2 (699 ft^2), while the overhang itself is some 13 m (42.6 ft) above the modern surface of the site. In addition to the water potentially available from Cross Creek, springs are locally abundant in the immediate vicinity of the shelter. The prevailing wind is west to east across the mouth of the shelter providing almost continuous ventilation and ready egress for smoke and insects.

Geologically, Meadowcroft is located in the unglaciated portion of the Appalachian or Allegheny Plateau west of the Valley and Ridge Province of the Appalachian mountains, and northwest of the Appalachian Basin. The surface rocks of this region are layered sedimentary rocks of Middle to Upper Pennsylvania age (Casselman Formation). The predominant lithologies are shale, quartz, sandstone, limestone, and coal in decreasing order of abundance. Deformation is very mild, with a regional dip of 3° to 5° to the southeast.

Meadowcroft Rockshelter is formed beneath a cliff of Morgantown-Connellsville sandstone; the Morgantown-Connellsville is a thick fluvial or channel sandstone within the Casselman Formation (Flint, 1955) of Pennsylvanian age. The cliff above the rockshleter is 22 m (72.2 ft) high; the sandstone was deposited as two superimposed point-bar or sandbar sequences. The rock within each sequence changes from cross-bedded, coarse-grained sandstone to laminated, fine-grained sandstone. The sandstone decreases in thickness along the Cross Creek Valley both to the east and west; it has its maximum thickness at the rockshelter site.

The Morgantown-Connellsville is an immature sandstone composed predominantly of quartz grains, with minor amounts of mica, feldspar, and rock fragments. A clay matrix is present between grains. Some zones within the cliff sequence are cemented by calcium carbonate. The rock ranges from subgraywacke to protoquartzite in composition (Pettijohn, 1975).

The rock unit immediately underlying the Morgantown-Connellsville sandstone was exposed during the 1975 field season. It consists of shale, a less resistant lithology that caused the development of a re-entrant or rockshelter beneath the sandstone cliff. The ceiling of this re-entrant is gradually migrating upward and cliffward as erosion occurs both on the rockshelter ceiling and cliff face. Within the rockshelter excavation, the recession of the drip-line, representing the cliff-edge position, can be seen plainly (Beynon and Donahue, 1982).

Topographically, the region within which Meadowcroft is located is maturely dissected. More than 50% of the 14,164.3-ha Cross Creek watershed is in valley slopes with upland and valley bottom areas in the minority. Maximum elevations in the Cross Creek drainage are generally above 396 m (1299 ft). At the divides on the east, elevations are above 426 m (1398 ft). Elevations at stream level are 310 m (1017 ft) at Rea on the South Fork, 276 m (905.5 ft) at Avella, and 193 m (633.2 ft) normal pool level at the confluence with the Ohio River.

Within the Cross Creek watershed, the main stem of Cross Creek flows for some 31.3 km (19.4 mi). The maximum north-south width of the watershed is approximately 15 km (9.3 mi). The prevailing stream pattern is dendritic, with numerous small creeks and runs supplying the main stem of Cross Creek. The steep gradient headwaters and tributaries of Cross Creek have their sources in the hills of central Washington County. Cross Creek and its major tributaries of North, Middle, and South Forks have an average gradient of 0.4%. Most of the gradient is in the upper portions of the watershed where the streams are small and of low volume. The drainage is northwestward to westward toward the West Virginia-Ohio border and the Ohio River.

Cross Creek exhibits a markedly asymmetric drainage pattern, with the northern tributaries significantly shorter than those on the south. Consequently, the drainage area to the south of Cross Creek is much larger than its counterpart to the north. This condition is probably the result of a drainage pattern superimposed on the 3° to 5° regional dip noted above.

Chronology and Technology

All presently available data indicate that a much larger version of Meadowcroft Rockshelter (and by inference a Cross Creek drainage topographically similar to that of today) was initially occupied or visited by aborigines as early as ca. 17,000 B.C. (ca. 18,950 B.P.) and certainly no later than ca. 14,000 B.C. (ca. 15,950 B.P.). The flaked-stone assemblage from the lower and middle portions of Stratum IIa at Meadowcroft as well as limited flaked-stone materials from the Mungai Farm site complex, the lithic reduction station at 36WH351, and several other open localities in the Cross Creek drainage (Fitzgibbons, 1982), suggest that the earliest human populations who used the study area possessed a relatively sophisticated lithic technology. At a very early time, this technology included the production of diminutive blades or conical cores via indirect percussion as well as the manufacture of distinctive flake unifaces (or knives) and bifaces. Though dominated by utilized flakes, the earliest lithic industries in the drainage are by no means crude or technologically "backward" (Adovasio et al., 1977, p. 87). Indeed, the reverse seems to be true.

Also included in the tool kits of the earliest Meadowcroft inhabitants are worked bone, modified wood, and basketry. Sites of this period are scarce, but it is clear that the entire length of the drainage was probably used. It is also apparent that in addition to a variety of exotic imported cherts, the earliest visitors to Cross Creek quickly began to exploit the local Monongahela chert resources (Vento and Donahue, 1982).

Despite the ephemeral and obviously transitory nature of the earliest occupation of the drainage as it is reflected in lower Stratum IIa and the lower portion of middle Stratum IIa at Meadowcroft (as well as elsewhere, see below), it is clear that these early and presumably highly mobile groups of hunters and foragers represent the chronological baseline not only for the occupation of the Upper Ohio River Valley but also for the lower reaches of the Northeast and eastern North America.

Later Paleo-Indian usage of both Meadowcroft Rockshelter and the Cross Creek drainage is evidenced in the upper levels of middle Stratum IIa at Meadowcroft; at the Mungai Farm site complex; 36WH351; 36WH520 (north of the Avella Mound, 36WH415); and at a series of fluted-point localities in the drainage. The occurrence of Clovis points in the Cross Creek drainage attests to the continuing use of the area in so-called "Classic" Paleo-Indian times. Despite the appearance of both Miller Lanceolate and Clovis points, the basic tool kit remained essentially unchanged. The perishable tool kit from the rockshelter continued to include basketry, modified bone, and wood.

The latest Paleo-Indian occupation of the drainage is signaled by the recovery of a series of Plano-like points from site 36WH351 and from site 36WH520. These points include McConnell Lanceolate, Stringtown Stemmed, and Sawmill Stemmed points, all of which are ascribable to the late Paleo-Indian period.

Despite the absence of diagnostic materials, the presence of lithic debitage, ash, charcoal, incinerated bone, and limited plant material indicate that Meadowcroft continued to be used intermittently during this time. If the data from site 36WH351 and upper Stratum IIa at Meadowcroft are representative, the lithic tool kit continued to feature utilized flakes with limited numbers of bifaces, unifaces, modified bone, and wood. Basketry also persisted.

Occupation of both the rockshelter and the Cross Creek drainage during the Early Archaic is evidenced by a single Dalton-like projectile point from site 36WH520 and by Palmer Corner-Notched-like, Big Sandy I-like, Kirk Corner-Notched, Kirk Serrated, Thebes, Lost Lake, Cache Diagnoal, St. Charles/Dovetail-like, Charleston Corner-Notched, and MacCorkle Stemmed points from a variety of open sites in the study area. Also recovered were a series of bifurcate base projectile points including St. Albans Side-Notched, Kanawha Stemmed, and LeCroy Bifurcate Base points.

Once again it should be noted, especially given the observations of Dincauze (1981), that Meadowcroft clearly was utilized during the Early Archaic despite the low number of flaked-stone diagnostics. Two radiocarbon dates in the 8th and 7th millennia B.C., as well as extensive incinerated bone, limited lithic debitage, a variety of non-fire-pit cultural features, and abundant plant remains all indicate that the site was not abandoned at this time. Indeed, as noted by Adovasio, et al. (1977, p. 88), the portions of the rockshelter that have produced both terminal Paleo-Indian and Early Archaic materials are co-extensive with the massive roof spalling event that separates Stratum IIa from Stratum IIb, and with a later series of less dramatic spalling episodes. It is strongly suggested that materials ascribable to the period ca. 9000-7000 B.C. (ca. 10,950-8950 B.P.) are much more likely to be abundant east of the epicenter of the collapse rather than *in* or *on* the piles of spalls and roof blocks themselves. Again, if Meadowcroft is any reflection, Early Archaic tool kits included utilized flakes and limited numbers of bifaces and unifaces, as well as modified bone, wood, and basketry. Significantly, the small blades with faceted and/or ground platforms so characteristic of the Paleo-Indian period at both the rockshelter and at 36WH351 disappear abruptly. The only "blades" recovered from any Archaic contexts are so dissimilar to the Paleo-Indian forms and so unstandardized as to suggest that most of them are "accidents." This is supported by the disappearance of conical cores as well.

The "beginning" of the early Middle Archaic utilization of Meadowcroft is marked by the appearance of Morrow Mountain-like and Kanawha Stemmed forms at the rockshelter, and by the occurrence of Stanly points at both the Mungai Farm site complex and site 36WH512. Kanawha points also occur at the Mungai Farm.

Other indications of Middle Archaic utilization of the drainage are

Big Sandy II-like points that occur at Meadowcroft, the Mungai Farm site complex, and at several other loci along Cross Creek. Despite the general scarcity of Middle Archaic materials, it appears that the composition of the tool kit remained basically unchanged from the Early Archaic—at least in terms of technomorphological variety or persistent emphasis on utilized flakes, bifaces, and unifaces. No change is evident in the perishable assemblage.

Utilization of Meadowcroft and the Cross Creek drainage throughout the duration of the Archaic is attested to by the recovery of a wide number of temporally-diagnostic points, including Lamoka and Lamoka-like, the entire Brewerton series (Brewerton Corner-Notched, Brewerton Side-Notched, Brewerton Eared-Notched), Normanskill-like, Hansford-Notched-like, Merom, and Trimble-like. Also present are several Late Archaic stemmed varieties including Buffalo Straight Stemmed, Buffalo Expanding Stemmed, Steubenville Stemmed, Cotaco-Creek-like, and Perkiomen-like. Other Late Archaic diagnostics include two types that span the terminal Archaic/Early Woodland boundary—Forest-Notched and Dry Brook-like.

It is of some interest to note that there is greater typological diversity to the non-projectile point flaked-stone assemblages at this time both at Meadowcroft and at other Late Archaic or terminal Archaic sites. This is paralleled by increased diversity among all the perishable "assemblages" except basketry.

The onset of Early Woodland occupation at Meadowcroft and/or other localities in the drainage is marked by the persistence of the aforementioned Forest-Notched and Dry Brook-like point types and by the appearance of Cresap Stemmed, Adena Ovate Base, and Robbins Stemmed point types. Early Woodland at Meadowcroft is also evidenced by the early appearance of Half-Moon Cord-Marked ceramics (Johnson, 1982) and cultigens (Adovasio and Johnson, 1981; Cushman, 1982). Lithics and the perishable tool kit are more diversified typologically than previously, but the basically utilitarian character of the flaked-stone assemblage persists, as reflected in the high numbers of recovered utilized flakes.

Diagnostic Middle Woodland points from Meadowcroft and from the study area in general include Snyders-like, Manker and Manker-like, and a new local type, Bennington Corner-Notched, the center of utilization of which at present appears to be the Cross Creek and adjacent Ten Mile Creek drainages. Other common Middle Woodland points include the Raccoon-Notched, Jack's Reef Corner-Notched, and Jack's Reef Pentagonal types, as well as Levanna Triangular points. Less common and apparently uncharacteristic *of* but temporally diagnostic *for* the late Middle Woodland of the study area are Klunk and Koster-like projectile points.

Late Woodland utilization of the drainage is marked by both Philo and Fort Ancient-like triangular points as well as the Madison Triangular form. In both the Middle and Late Woodland, the basic character of the non-projectile flaked stone does not change appreciably. The Middle and Late Woodland levels at Meadowcroft, however, are somewhat depauperate in all classes of artifacts for reasons to be discussed below.

Intensity of Rockshelter and Drainage Utilization

Many indices can be employed to gauge the spatial and temporal intensity of aboriginal utilization of Meadowcroft Rockshelter and the Cross Creek drainage. These include counts of sites per chronological period corrected for length of the period, numbers of temporally-diagnostic artifacts per period (again corrected for length of period), as well as quantification (both with and without correction factors) of the artifactual and ecofactual data by stratigraphic level at Meadowcroft. It is significant that whatever measure or combination of measures is employed, it is clear that a slow but steady increase in the use of the drainage is evidenced from the onset of occupation late in the Pleistocene through the end of the Middle Archaic. While there is apparently a dip or "regression" in the Middle Archaic, it is uncertain whether this is "real" or an artifact of sampling or identification.

The entire drainage shows a scattered, almost ephemeral Paleo-Indian occupation, generally at higher elevations (with the notable exception of Meadowcroft), and characterized by few if any real base camps. The Early Archaic materials are differentially distributed with a concentration in the headwater areas of the drainage, particularly near the Mungai Farm site complex. Scant representation is found elsewhere at this time period, but the reasons for this are imperfectly understood at best.

The Late Archaic in the drainage, the period from ca. 4000-1100 B.C. (ca. 5950-3050 B.P.), and especially the latter portion of that period, simultaneously witnessed a rise in numbers of sites and diagnostic projectile points as well as a dramatic increase in rockshelter utilization; this underscores the appearance of genuine base camps. Extensive reduction of local lithic resources also characterizes this period with the appearance of flimsy "surface structures" at one of the two major lithic reduction localities, Cross Creek Village (36WH293; Applegarth and Cowin, 1982). Additionally, the greatest range of topographic settings was employed at this time for site placement. The magnitude of the change in intensity of drainage utilization during the Late Archaic and terminal Archaic (especially if the preceding Middle Archaic actually should prove to be poorly represented) is sufficiently striking to suggest genuine population increase of a considerable magnitude.

Continued intensive use of the drainage is indicated during the Early Woodland, a time when Meadowcroft was still a base camp with other base camps located sporadically throughout the drainage. Thereafter, although there was a decline in rockshelter utilization due to massive rock fall, the drainage continued to be heavily utilized in the Middle Woodland but perhaps in a different fashion than previously.

During the Late Archaic, a tendency developed to place sites on or near tributaries that provided access to adjacent drainages and that collectively are both much larger and ecologically richer than Cross Creek. This pattern intensified through the Early Woodland, so that by the Middle Woodland, base camps for the aboriginal visitors to the Cross Creek drainage actually appear to be *outside* it in the "more attractive" contiguous drainages. A possible exception is the area near the Avella Mound (36WH415) which once may have had a Middle Woodland base camp of some size but which is now obliterated (Applegarth and Cowin, 1982).

By the Late Woodland, base camps were absent from Cross Creek, and the number of known sites is low. Utilization of both the rockshelter and the drainage persisted, however, and doubtless reflects an influx of hunting and foraging groups from permanent villages located outside the drainage.

It should be reiterated at this juncture that the horizontal or spatial distribution of occupational materials (and hence the loci of human utilization) at Meadowcroft Rockshelter has been determined by roof spalling events which dictate the amount of available dry floor space. The occupational record at this site consequently can deviate (as noted above) from that in the rest of the drainage due to site-specific geomorphic circumstances.

The general scarcity of late Paleo-Indian and Early Archaic materials at the site reflects very specifically the consequences of roof falls, while the apparent decrease in utilization of the rockshelter after ca. A.D. 285-660 (ca. 1665-1290 B.P.) likewise reflects the collapse of the huge New Roof Fall (Adovasio et al., 1977). Nevertheless, there are broad concurrences in the occupational history of Meadowcroft and in the adjacent Cross Creek drainage that can be taken to reflect the natural incidence and intensity of utilization of both settings.

Environment, Seasonality, Subsistence, and General Character of Site Utilization

Perhaps no subject exclusive of the lower and middle Stratum IIa radiocarbon dates has engendered more discussion than has the reconstruction of the early environment of Cross Creek as interpreted on the basis of the Meadowcroft Rockshelter data. The absence of Pleistocene big game and the presence of deciduous floral elements in very ancient levels have both been the subject of considerable debate and helpful criticism. The following summarizes the authors' environmental reconstruction for the Pleistocene/Holocene transition, as reflected by the data from the rockshelter.

All of the extant ecofactual information specifically including macrofloral, microfloral, macrofaunal, and microfaunal remains, as well as various categories of geological data suggest that from ca. 9300 or 9000 B.C. (ca. 11,250 or 10,950 B.P.) to the present the environment of Cross Creek was essentially *modern in aspect*. This is not to suggest that there have been no changes over the past 11,000 years, since the data presented by Cushman (1982), Guilday and Parmalee (1982), and Lord (1982) do indicate that cooler and/or moister as well as warmer and/or drier intervals can be detected in the environmental record. Specifically, the plant and invertebrate remains suggest some shift in forest species composition, with indications of fluctuating temperatures before, during, and after the so-called Altithermal episode.

Conditions seem to have been considerably warmer and perhaps drier during the Middle Archaic and early Late Archaic (4000-2000 B.C.; 5950-3950 B.P.) as well as immediately after the Middle Woodland. The magnitude of these changes is presently unknown, but clearly they should not be overstressed. No exception has been taken to the reconstruction of the latest Pleistocene or Holocene environmental history of the drainage. Rather, the focal point has been the lower and middle Stratum IIa deposits, with their deciduous forest elements and lack of Pleistocene fauna; these levels, however, which lie outside the modern drip-line, reflect poor preservation. The materials that are preserved are neither large nor numerous, but indicate the presence, within "striking distance" of the rockshelter, of both deciduous and coniferous trees with appropriate "modern" fauna. Although this picture differs with some reconstructions, it is not inconsistent with the mosaic character of late Pleistocene environments elsewhere in the Midwest or the Northeast (cf. Dincauze, 1981). Cross Creek not only lies relatively far south of the Wisconsinan glacial front, but it occurs in a topographical setting that in one recent year had 40 to 50 more frost-free days and a generally higher mean annual temperature than did areas of higher elevation directly east or north of it. Cross Creek, compared with other area drainages, exhibits a temperate regime that is appropriate to a more southerly setting. Both the faunal and floral data from the rockshelter indicate that the environment of the late Pleistocene in that portion of Cross Creek immediately adjacent to the rockshelter was *not* radically different from that at present.

The interpretation of the archeological data from Meadowcroft argues that throughout its history the site served as a temporary locus or station for hunting, collecting, and food-processing activities. The predominance of used flakes as well as projectile points that show multifunctional use coupled with limited numbers of bifaces and unifaces, the relative abundance of food bone, edible plant remains, and (at certain times) invertebrate resources, plus perishable artifacts used in the acquisition, transport, or processing of these remains, all support this conclusion. In marked distinction, the general absence of extensive *in situ* manufacture of lithic, ceramic, or shell artifacts militates against an interpretation of long-term or permanent occupation of the site.

Significantly, while the intensity of site use changes through time, ranging from what may well represent very sporadic "day trips" in the Paleo-Indian, Early Archaic, and Middle Archaic periods to longer visits of perhaps several weeks or more in the Late Archaic through Early Woodland, the basic function of the site did not change appreciably even after the appearance of domesticated plants. What is in evidence, however, are subtle changes in the apparent composition of human groups using the rockshelter. Despite the high incidence of projectile points and other flaked stone artifacts traditionally linked to hunting, it is basketry and the high incidence of modified bone (ethnohistorically associated with female activities) in the Late Archaic and Early Woodland levels at the site that strongly suggest utilization by groups composed of both males and females at this time. Likewise, the relatively high incidence of Late Woodland ceramics and the low incidence of Late Woodland points imply a somewhat different pattern of collecting than that practiced in the Paleo-Indian, Early Archaic, or Middle Archaic occupational horizons.

As directly reflected in the deposits, the primary subsistence modes, at least of the various post-9300 B.C. (ca. 11,250 B.P.) Meadowcroft populations, included the hunting of deer and elk augmented by the taking of smaller game and perhaps bird egg collecting. The intensive collection of hackberries, nuts, and other fruits and seeds and the exploitation of riverine fauna, notably mussels, are also known from the archeological record. While the data from the pre-9300 B.C. (ca. 11,250 B.P.) levels is rather limited in size and preservation (as noted above and in various Meadowcroft publications), the extant information does at least suggest that the first human visitors to the site also practiced a rather more diversified subsistence round than is normally associated with the Paleo-Indian period.

The hunting mode seems to have remained more or less constant throughout the post-middle Stratum IIa sequence, while the other subsistence modes mirror a number of potentially significant changes. Hackberry exploitation sharply diminished in frequency after Stratum VII, along with the collection of *Rubus* sp. and *Vaccinium* sp. Conversely, the gathering of other nuts and seeds remained more or less constant. Similarly, exploitation of riverine resources, relatively insignificant before the Late Archaic, became markedly important immediately thereafter and remained so until the onset of Stratum VI, ca. A.D. 285 (ca. 1665 B.P.) when it virtually ceased. Doubtless, these changes reflect both climatically-induced differential availability as well as specific food preferences. However, a full assessment of their significance is still under way. In recapitulation, the addition of cultigens toward the end of the long Meadowcroft sequence does appear to correlate with a diminution in the collection of certain wild plants though it does not seem to have changed the basic character of site use.

Examination of constituents of the dietary modes of the post-middle Stratum IIa Meadowcroft populations leads to the conclusion that the principal utilization of the site occurred during the fall of the year. While the hunting mode and to a lesser extent the riverine exploitation mode are seasonally independent, the nuts, berries, and seeds constituting the "staples" of the collecting mode would have been most abundant in the fall, thus dictating the time of site occupation. If, as the constant volume sample data suggest, egg collecting was pursued by some of the aboriginal visitors to the rockshelter, then some limited spring utilization of the site is also indicated.

Data on the seasonality of the earlier occupations of the rockshelter are so limited that they virtually preclude any cultural generalizations. However, if their apparently diversified subsistence strategy concentrated to any extent on plant resources, then the predominantly fall pattern of site utilization can be extended back into the late Pleistocene.

The data from all of the other sites in the drainage except Cross Creek Village (36WH293; Applegarth and Cowin, 1982), which could have been occupied in the spring, are not conducive to reconstructing any seasonal patterns of aboriginal use. However, with the exceptions of the Avella Mound (36WH415), Cross Creek Village (36WH293), the lithic reduction station at 36WH351, and perhaps the Mungai Farm site complex for some of its long occupational history, all of the open sites in the drainage appear to be short-term, limited-activity loci presumably associated with one or another aspect of seasonally-based hunting, collecting, and food processing.

Pending the completion of the data analysis, it nevertheless appears that it will be possible to link at least some of the aboriginal visitors to Meadowcroft with specific open sites and hence to "track" the movements of certain aboriginal groups within the drainage. One can hope that by extrapolation this will facilitate the generation of inferences on the seasonality of use of at least a number of these open loci.

External Correlations

The archeological assemblages from Meadowcroft Rockshelter and the Cross Creek drainage exhibit a number of basic affinities to complexes elsewhere in the Upper Ohio River Valley, the eastern United States, and, indeed, throughout North America. These affinities vary in time and space and are predicated on stylistic and morphological resemblances of one or another of the Meadowcroft artifact classes or their constituents to similar materials from elsewhere. Though detailed comparisons of the Meadowcroft/Cross Creek archeological materials are either complete or nearly so, space necessitates that external correlations be restricted to the following observations.

The lower and middle Stratum IIa assemblages at Meadowcroft share a number of technological and morphological features with other and generally somewhat later assemblages in both eastern and western North America. Although only one possible fluted point fragment is represented, certain items in the assemblage (notably the so-called Mungai "knives," the blades, and to a lesser extent the retouched flakes, bifaces, gravers, etc.), are more or less duplicated at Shoop (Witthoft, 1952), Debert (MacDonald, 1968), Williamson (McCary, 1951), Blackwater Draw (Hester, 1972), Lindenmeier (Wilmsen, 1974), and many other fluted-point localities. Moreover, some general resemblances can be seen both to the unfortunately scant basal assemblages from Fort Rock Cave, Oregon (Bedwell, 1973), and Wilson Butte Cave, Idaho (Gruhn, 1961).

The unfluted Miller lanceolate projectile point form is morphologically similar to points recovered in the basal strata at Fort Rock Cave, Oregon (Bedwell, 1973); Ventana Cave, Arizona (Haury, 1950); Levi Rockshelter, Texas (Alexander, 1963); and Bonfire Shelter, Texas (Dibble and Lorrain, 1968). In general, the point is also superficially similar to the Plainview and Milnesand types of the Great Plains region. The Plenge site in New Jersey (Kraft, 1973), the St. Albans site in West Virginia (Broyles, 1971), and numerous surface finds attest to the presence of unfluted lanceolate points in the eastern United States. However, the Miller Lanceolate form appears to antedate all of these specimens based on its associated radiocarbon dates. Given the fact that fluting is the only thing necessary to transform a Miller Lanceolate into a small Clovis point and further, given the occurrence of two unifacially-fluted "Miller Lanceolate" points at 36WH351, it may be that this form is *locally* ancestral to the Clovis fluted type. Whatever the case, the basal assemblages from Meadowcroft with their evidence of sophisticated bifacial thinning, and core and blade production resemble what an industry ancestral to Clovis "ought to look like." At the same time they are not markedly dissimilar to even earlier tool kits from Siberia (Mochanov, 1978, 1980).

The basic affinites of the Early Archaic and the Middle Archaic materials from both the rockshelter and the Cross Creek drainage lie to the south or are essentially pan-Appalachian. Specifically, the stylistic affinities of the various Early Archaic and Middle Archaic diagnostics are either to the Carolina Piedmont or toward the Kanawha River and points south and west. The Late Archaic materials suggest a broad overlap in "directional relationships" with the Early Archaic/Middle Archaic and a marked tendency toward more regionally-specific connections in terminal Archaic times. Similarities in projectile point styles can be seen to the Appalachians in the immediate south as well as progressively westward to the Middle Ohio Valley and even beyond to the Illinois and Middle Mississippi valleys. Unlike the previous periods, however, there are also ties evidenced to the east and northeast typified by a variety of essentially New York/Northeast point types.

The various Woodland assemblages from the Cross Creek area appear to be part of the "Woodland milieu" typical of the Middle and Upper Ohio valleys, though connections rather far afield also are suggested by limited Illinois Valley diagnostics.

While the "meaning" of any or all of these "directional connections" remains to be assessed, we are reasonably confident that the posited stylistic relationships are more or less accurate.

Conclusion

The single most noteworthy aspect of the entire Meadowcroft/Cross Creek Archaeological Project is the unparalleled opportunity which it has provided to examine an incredibly long and exceptionally well-dated archeological and environmental record from multiple perspectives. The data from this drainage afford one of the best available perspectives from which to examine the "reaction" or adjustment of human populations to their subtly-changing climatic, geological, floral, and faunal milieux. Remaining research on the Meadowcroft/Cross Creek Archaeological Project will focus on the articulation and integration of the various data sets derived from the finished or soon to be finished, archeological, geological, floral, and faunal analyses. This massive correlation will involve both synchronic and diachronic study aimed at elucidating not only long-term interaction between humans and their environment in the broadest sense of that term, but also specific, short-term interrelationships. These can reveal phenomena as diverse as specific Late Woodland activities within the rockshelter or Late Archaic spatial utilization of Cross Creek Village (36WH293), to name but two cases.

REFERENCES

ADOVASIO, J. M.; DONAHUE, J.; CUSHMAN, K.; CARLISLE, R. C.; STUCKENRATH, R.; GUNN, J. D.; and JOHNSON, W. C.

1983. Evidence from Meadowcroft Rockshelter. Pp. 163-190 *in* "Early Man in the New World," R. Shutler, Jr., ed. Sage Press, Beverly Hills, California.

ADOVASIO, J. M.; GUNN, J. D.; DONAHUE, J.; and STUCKENRATH, R.

1975. Excavations at Meadowcroft Rockshelter, 1973-1974: A progress report. Pennsylvania Archaeologist, vol. 45, no. 3, pp. 1-30.

1977. Meadowcroft Rockshelter: Retrospect 1976. Pennsylvania Archaeologist, vol. 47, no. 2-3, pp. 1-93.

ADOVASIO, J. M., and JOHNSON, W. C.

1981. The appearance of cultigens in the Upper Ohio Valley: A view from Meadowcroft Rockshelter. Pennsylvania Archaeologist, vol. 51, no. 1-2, pp. 68-80.

ALEXANDER, H. L., JR.

1963. The Levi Site: A Paleo-Indian campsite in central Texas. American Antiquity, vol. 28, no. 4, pp. 510-528.

APPLEGARTH, J. D., and COWIN, V. L.

1982. Excavations at Cross Creek Village (36WH293) and the Avella Mound (36WH415), Washington County, southwestern Pennsylvania. Pp. 241-256 *in* "Meadowcroft: Collected Papers on the Archaeology of Meadowcroft Rockshelter and the Cross Creek Drainage," R. C. Carlisle and J. M. Adovasio, eds. Department of Anthropology, University of Pittsburgh.

BEDWELL, S. L.

1973. Fort Rock Basin: Prehistory and environment. University of Oregon Books, Eugene.

BEYNON, D.

1981. The geoarchaeology of Meadowcroft Rockshelter. Unpublished Ph.D. dissertation, University of Pittsburgh, Pittsburgh, Pennsylvania.

BEYNON, D., and DONAHUE, J.

1982. The geology and geomorphology of Meadowcroft Rockshelter and the Cross Creek Drainage. Pp. 31-52 *in* "Meadowcroft: Collected Papers on the Archaeology of Meadowcroft Rockshelter and the Cross Creek Drainage," R. C. Carlisle and J. M. Adovasio, eds. Department of Anthropology, University of Pittsburgh.

BROYLES, B.

1971. The St. Albans Site, Kanawha County, West Virginia: Second preliminary report. West Virginia Geological and Economic Survey. Morgantown, West Virginia.

CARLISLE, R. C., and ADOVASIO, J. M., eds.

1982. Meadowcroft: Collected papers on the archaeology of Meadowcroft Rockshelter and the Cross Creek Drainage, 270 pp. Department of Anthropology, University of Pittsburgh.

CARLISLE, R. C.; ADOVASIO, J. M.; DONAHUE, J.; WIEGMAN, P.; and GUILDAY, J. E.
1982. An introduction to the Meadowcroft/Cross Creek Archaeological Project: 1973-1982. Pp. 1-30 *in* "Meadowcroft: Collected Papers on the Archaeology of Meadowcroft Rockshelter and the Cross Creek Drainage," R. C. Carlisle and J. M. Adovasio, eds. Department of Anthropology, University of Pittsburgh.

CUSHMAN, K. A.
1982. Floral remains from Meadowcroft Rockshelter, Washington County, Southwestern Pennsylvania. Pp. 207-220 *in* "Meadowcroft: Collected Papers on the Archaeology of Meadowcroft Rockshelter and the Cross Creek Drainage," R. C. Carlisle and J. M. Adovasio, eds. Department of Anthropology, University of Pittsburgh.

DIBBLE, D. S., and LORRAIN, D.
1968. Bonfire Shelter: A stratified bison kill site, Val Verde County, Texas. Texas Memorial Museum Miscellaneous Papers, no. 1.

DINCAUZE, D.
1981. The Meadowcroft papers. Quarterly Review of Archaeology, vol. 2, pp. 3-5.

FITZGIBBONS, P. T.
1982. Lithic artifacts from Meadowcroft Rockshelter and the Cross Creek Drainage. Pp. 91-111 *in* "Meadowcroft: Collected Papers on the Archaeology of Meadowcroft Rockshelter and the Cross Creek Drainage," R. C. Carlisle and J. M. Adovasio, eds. Department of Anthropology, University of Pittsburgh.

FLINT, N. K.
1955. Geology and mineral resources of Somerset County, Pennsylvania. Pennsylvania Geological Survey County Report, no. C56A.

GRUHN, R.
1961. The archaeology of Wilson Butte Cave, south-central Idaho. Occasional Papers of the Idaho State College Museum, no. 6.

GUILDAY, J. E., and PARMALEE, P. W.
1982. Vertebrate faunal remains from Meadowcroft Rockshelter, Washington County, Pennsylvania: Summary and interpretation. Pp. 163-174 *in* "Meadowcroft: Collected Papers on the Archaeology of Meadowcroft Rockshelter and the Cross Creek Drainage," R. C. Carlisle and J. M. Adovasio, eds. Department of Anthropology, University of Pittsburgh.

GUILDAY, J. E.; PARMALEE, P. W.; and WILSON, R. C.
1980. Vertebrate faunal remains from Meadowcroft Rockshelter (36WH297), Washington County, Pennsylvania. Ms. on file, Department of Anthropology, University of Pittsburgh.

GUNN, J. D.
1975. An envirotechnological system for Hogup Cave. American Antiquity, vol. 40, no, 1, pp. 3-21.
1977. Analysis of occupation floors. Pp. 223-345 *in* "Hop Hill: Culture and Climatic Change in Central Texas," J. Gunn and R. Mahula, eds. Center for Archaeological Research Special Report, no. 5.

Haury, E. W.
1950. The stratigraphy and archaeology of Ventana Cave, Arizona. The University of New Mexico and University of Arizona Presses, Albuquerque and Tucson.

Hester, J. J.
1972. Blackwater, Locality No. 1. Publications of the Fort Burgwin Research Center, no. 8, Southern Methodist University, Dallas.

Johnson, W. C.
1981. Archaeological review activities in Survey Region IV, northwestern Pennsylvania: Year end report of the regional archaeologist for the period September 1979 through August 1980. A report prepared for the Pennsylvania Historical and Museum Commission by the Cultural Resource Management Program, University of Pittsburgh, Pittsburgh, Pennsylvania, under the supervision of J. M. Adovasio, Ph.D. in accordance with provisions of Service Purchase Contract 645987.
1982. Ceramics from Meadowcroft Rockshelter: A re-evaluation and interpretation. Pp. 142-162 *in* "Meadowcroft: Collected Papers on the Archaeology of Meadowcroft Rockshelter and the Cross Creek Drainage," R. C. Carlisle and J. M. Adovasio, eds. Department of Anthropology, University of Pittsburgh.

Kraft, H. C.
1973. The Plenge Site: A Paleo-Indian occupation site in New Jersey. Archaeology of Eastern North America, vol. 1, no. 1, pp. 56-117.

Lord, K.
1982. Invertebrate faunal remains from Meadowcroft Rockshelter, Washington County, southwestern Pennsylvania. Pp. 186-206 *in* "Meadowcroft: Collected Papers on the Archaeology of Meadowcroft Rockshelter and the Cross Creek Drainage," R. C. Carlisle and J. M. Adovasio, eds. Department of Anthropology, University of Pittsburgh.

MacDonald, G. F.
1968. Debert: A Paleo-Indian site in central Nova Scotia. National Museum of Canada Anthropolgical Papers, no. 16. Ottawa, Canada.

McCary, B. C.
1951. A workshop of Early Man in Dinwiddie County, Virginia. American Antiquity, vol. 17, no. 1, pp. 9-17.

Mochanov, J. A.
1978. Stratigraphy and absolute chronology of the Paleolithic of Northeast Asia, according to the work of 1963-1973. Pp. 54-66 *in* "Early Man in America from a Circum-Pacific Perspective," A. L. Bryan, ed. Occasional Papers of the Department of Anthropology, University of Alberta, no. 1.
1980. Early migrations to America in the light of a study of the Dyuktai Paleolithic culture in Northeast Asia. Pp. 119-131 *in* "Early Native Americans," D. L. Browman, ed. Mouton, The Hague.

Pettijohn, F. J.
1975. Sedimentary rocks. Harper and Row, New York.

STILE, T. E.
1982. Perishable artifacts from Meadowcroft Rockshelter, Washington County, southwestern Pennsylvania. Pp. 130-141 *in* "Meadowcroft: Collected Papers on the Archaeology of Meadowcroft Rockshelter and the Cross Creek Drainage," R. C. Carlisle and J. M. Adovasio, eds. Department of Anthropology, University of Pittsburgh.

STUCKENRATH, R.; ADOVASIO, J. M.; DONAHUE, J.; and CARLISLE, R. C.
1982. The stratigraphy, cultural features and chronology at Meadowcroft Rockshelter, Washington County, southwestern Pennsylvania. Pp. 69-90 *in* "Meadowcroft: Collected Papers on the Archaeology of Meadowcroft Rockshelter and the Cross Creek Drainage," R. C. Carlisle and J. M. Adovasio, eds. Department of Anthropology, University of Pittsburgh.

VENTO, F. J., and Donahue, J.
1982. Lithic raw material utilization at Meadowcroft Rockshelter and in the Cross Creek Drainage. Pp. 112-129 *in* "Meadowcroft: Collected Papers on the Archaeology of Meadowcroft Rockshelter and the Cross Creek Drainage," R. C. Carlisle and J. M. Adovasio, eds. Department of Anthropology, University of Pittsburgh.

VOLMAN, K. C.
1981. Paleoenvironmental implications of botanical data from Meadowcroft Rockshelter, Pennsylvania. Unpublished Ph.D. dissertation, Texas A&M University.

WILMSEN, E. N.
1974. Lindenmeier: A Pleistocene hunting society. Harper and Row, New York, Evanston, San Francisco.

WITTHOFT, J.
1952. A Paleo-Indian site in eastern Pennsylvania: An early hunting culture. Proceedings of the American Philosophical Society, vol. 96, pp. 464-495.

J. M. ADOVASIO
J. DONAHUE
R. C. CARLISLE
J. D. GUNN
R. STUCKENRATH

Reproductive Interactions Within Bisexual/Unisexual Complexes of *Poecilia* from the Río Purificación in Northeastern Mexico

Grant Recipients: Joseph S. Balsano, Biomedical Research Institute, University of Wisconsin-Parkside, Kenosha, Wisconsin; and Ellen M. Rasch, Department of Biology, Marquette University, Milwaukee, Wisconsin.[1]

Grant 1674: For study of the competitive interaction in bisexual/unisexual complexes of *Poecilia* in northeastern Mexico.

Introduction

Competition is one of the most fundamental concepts of evolutionary biology. The competitive exclusion principle of Gause states that no two species can share the same ecological niche without one of them eliminating the other through competition. Niche overlap, however, need not necessarily lead to competition unless resources are in short supply. Indeed, Pianka (1974) has reasoned that extensive overlap might actually be correlated with reduced competition that resulted from nonoverlapping patterns of resource utilization. The bisexual-unisexual complexes of *Poecilia* in northeastern Mexico, because of the genetic and reproductive relationships among the members of these complexes, offer a unique opportunity for study of the application of this exclusion principle.

Each complex includes four members: females and males of a gonochoristic (bisexual) diploid species, *Poecilia mexicana;* and a diploid all-female species, *P. formosa,* and its triploid all-female associate. The two unisexuals reproduce asexually by gynogenesis (Rasch and Balsano, 1974), i.e., the eggs require a stimulus from sperm of a congener to initiate development, but inheritance is entirely maternal. Hence, the two types of unisexual females must at least potentially compete with the bisexual females for the services of the males. Genetically, the three types

[1] Co-author with the grantees was Paul J. Monaco, Quillen-Dishner College of Medicine, East Tennessee State University, Johnson City, Tennessee.

of females are very closely related: *P. formosa* arose as a diploid hybrid between two bisexual species, *P. mexicana* and *P. latipinna* (Hubbs and Hubbs, 1946; Abramoff et al., 1968; Monaco et al., 1982); the triploid unisexual is a hybrid that orginates when a sperm from a male of *P. mexicana* actually fertilizes a diploid egg of *P. formosa* (Rasch and Balsano, 1974). Since these three types of females are so closely related, they probably have quite similar niche dimensions and, therefore, are potential competitors.

Although the frequencies of unisexuals varied quite widely from season to season and from site to site, there appeared to be a distributional pattern and a microgeographic pattern to the variations in the frequencies of these three types of females. The bisexuals were most abundant in more headwater localities whereas the unisexuals increased in the downstream localities; within a single locality the bisexuals were more abundant in the shallows of the main river whereas the unisexuals were more abundant in cul-de-sacs and backwater pools; and the triploid unisexuals typically outnumbered the diploid unisexuals (Balsano et al., 1981). Two objectives of this study were to examine field collections (1) to determine if there was indeed a sequential change in the relative frequencies of three types of females from headwaters to downstream localities within the same tributary for various seasons of the year; and (2) to compare the reproductive success of each type of female for different seasons. To carry out these objectives, it was important to determine if there was competition or some dynamic equilibrium between bisexual and unisexual females for sperm from males of *P. mexicana*. Three factors were examined to indicate which alternative was operating in nature: (1) relationship of sex ratio to bisexual/unisexual ratio, (2) mating preferences of males for different types of females, and (3) the role of male dominance hierarchies in the reproductive interactions within bisexual/unisexual complexes. Both field and laboratory studies were conducted.

Materials and Methods

The data reported here were based upon collections taken with a 0.6-cm seine during 12 field trips to various localities in the Soto la Marina drainage of northeastern Mexico (Fig. 1). Since most of our field data came from the Río Purificación, this river was selected as the best tributary to test our hypothesis that the frequencies of unisexuals increased in downstream localities. Funds provided by the National Geographic Society were used to obtain one to three samples from four new locations as well as more samples from five old locations along the Río Purificación during 1977 and 1978. These collections were combined with those taken during 1970 to 1975. Sampling details are specified in the legends of each

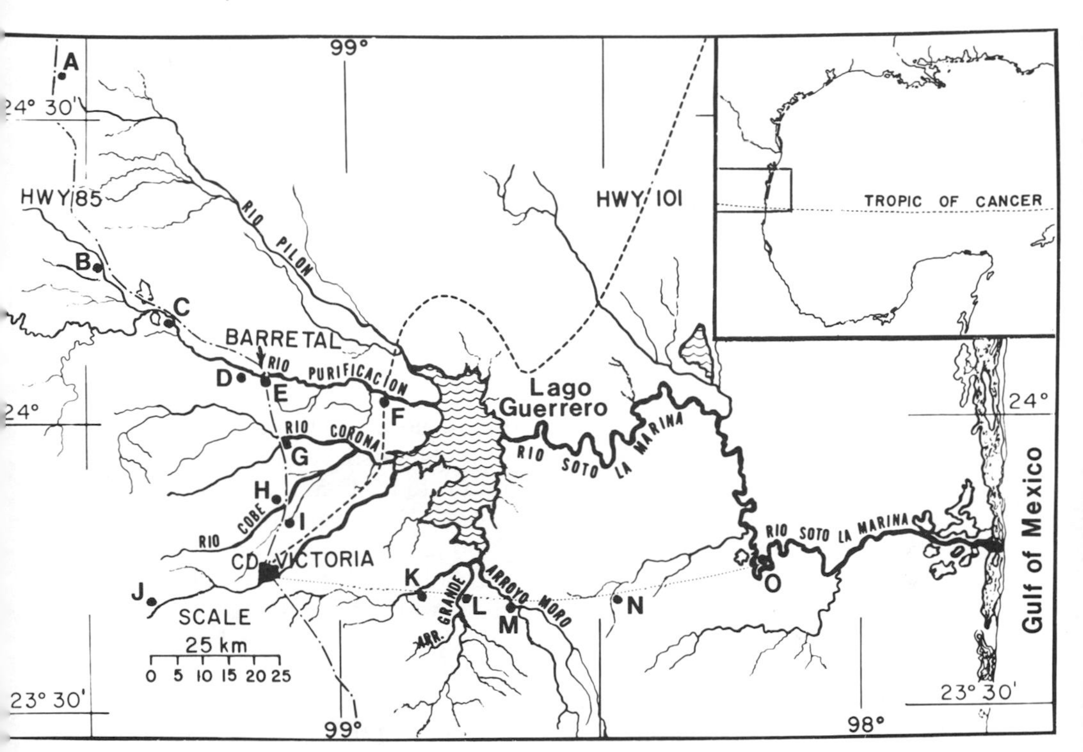

FIGURE 1. Tributaries of the Soto la Marina drainage in northeastern Mexico. Females of *Poecilia* spp. collected from headwater sites A, B, C, and J include less than 5% unisexuals; whereas sites D, G, H, I, K, and M, which are ecologically more downstream habitats, have 7 to 20% unisexuals; and sites E, F, and L, which are even farther downstream, have over 50% unisexuals (from Balsano et al., 1981).

figure and table. Winter collections were made between January 4 and 15; spring collections between March 10 and April 15; summer ones between June 15 and July 26. The identification of all specimens was based upon three criteria as described previously (Rasch and Balsano, 1974): body morphology, amount of DNA/blood cell nucleus, and plasma albumin phenotype.

Behavioral studies were initially conducted in the laboratory and then in the field. Nine 85-L aquaria were set up with gravel and vegetation and maintained at 28°C under a 12-hr light/12-hr dark cycle from June 1 to August 26, 1977. Eight aquaria had four females of *Poecilia mexicana;* the ninth had four unisexuals of *P. formosa*. The first three aquaria had one, two, or three males respectively whereas all other aquaria had four males of *P. mexicana*. Fish were fed tetramin staple food twice daily—usually in the early morning an hour or more before observations would start and in the late afternoon after observations were done for the day. The frequency data reported here were based upon 160 15-min. observations taken between June 10 and August 8, 1977, for a total of 40 hr of laboratory observations. Data were transcribed from tape recordings.

Field observations were carried out at eight different locations (March 15-19, 1978) including both isolated pools and semi-isolated segments of the Arroyo Moro, Río Cobe, and Río Purificación. Data were recorded on tape and on film. Each river provided different microhabitats in which to observe behavior in nature. Since all microhabitats yielded the same behavioral interactions, frequency data for various activities were obtained only from one isolated pool along the Río Cobe upstream from the Highway 85 bridge. A grid was set up using stakes and twine to divide this 8-m × 4-m pool into 12 sections to facilitate observations and data recording done on the following day. There were about 250 adult fish in this pool that morphologically looked like *Poecilia mexicana;* very few, if any, were unisexuals. After observations of the resident fish were completed, 30 tagged females of *P. formosa* were added to this pool to determine the males' behavior towards unisexuals. These observations could have been biased because the unisexuals were also "foreigners." Consequently, another pool experiment was conducted from May 26 to June 2, 1980, using all tagged fish that were originally collected from the Río Purificación at Barretal. The pool used in this experiment was smaller (3 m × 1.5 m) and much shallower than the previous one. All resident fish were removed; then nine of each type of female plus three males were added. Since the fish tags were individually numbered and colored differently for each type of female, male reactions to specific females could be observed. Three days later another sample of tagged fish was added to double the density of fish in this pool; and after three more days another sample was added to bring the total fish population to four times its initial size. This experiment was terminated on June 2 because some local children found the pool and apparently tried to catch the fish; only 65 of the total 120 fish were left in the pool.

Specific Results and Discussion

Frequencies of Bisexuals and Unisexuals

The seasonal variation in the frequencies of bisexuals and unisexuals from nine localities along the Río Purificación is shown in Figure 2. The frequencies of males show no significant seasonal differences except at Barretal and Nuevo Padilla. Typically only 10% of the *Poecilia* populations are males, even at locations where there are less than 15% unisexuals.

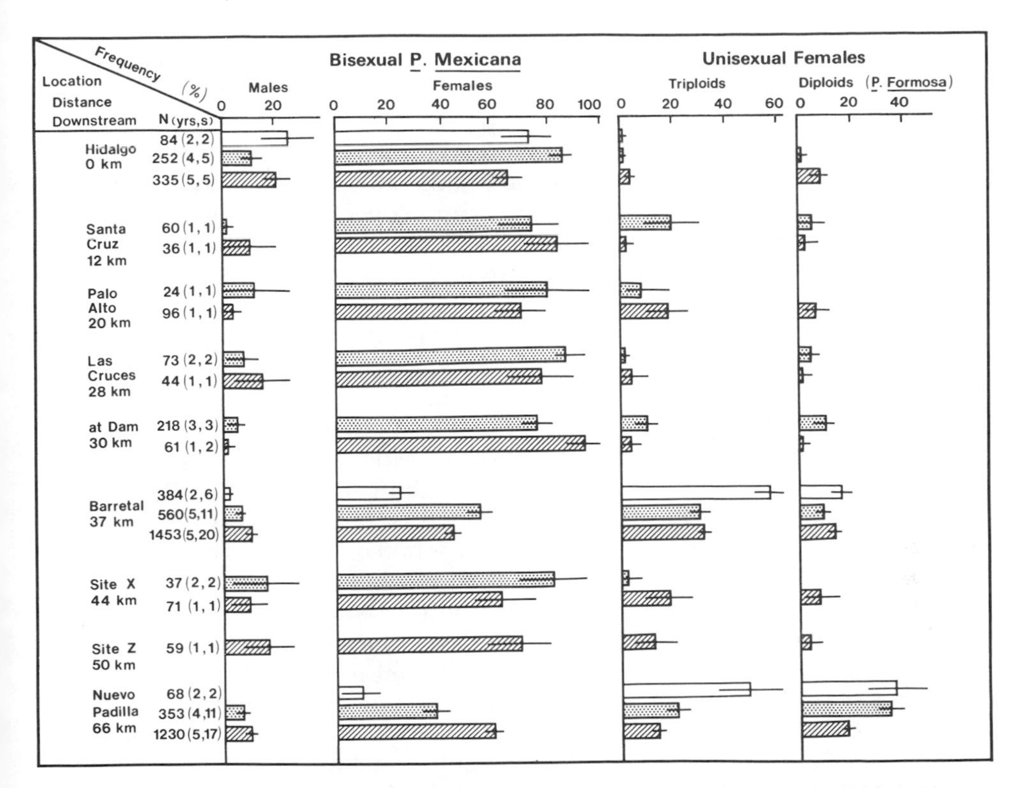

FIGURE 2. Seasonal frequencies of *Poecilia* spp. collected from 1970 to 1978 from nine localities along the Río Purificación in northeastern Mexico (see Fig. 1 for location). The village of Hildalgo corresponds to site B in Figure 1, site C is at Palo Alto, site D is at the earthen dam, site E is at Barretal, and site F is located at the village of Nuevo Padilla. Sampling details are listed after each locality: N refers to the total number of *Poecilia* spp. collected for each season at a given locality, yrs. refers to the number of years in which collections were made, and s indicates the total number of different samples collected from various stations at one locality. Open bars are used for all winter frequencies, stippled bars for spring frequencies, and cross-hatched bars for summer frequencies. The horizontal line at the end of each bar indicates the 95% confidence interval for each percentage.

Attempts to find correlations between either the frequencies of males or the sex ratio and various other parameters during the same season, such as frequency of bisexual females or frequencies of unisexuals or the bisexual/unisexual ratio, all yielded non-significant results ($-0.37<r<0.19$); this was also true for comparisons made between successive seasons and between two successive years ($-0.24<r<0.38$). Since no significant correlations could be found, we infer that the frequency of males is not affected by the presence of unisexuals at the frequencies found in the Río Purificación.

The frequencies of the three types of females exhibited no significant seasonal differences. There were a few exceptions, but they are probably due to sampling bias or random fluctuations rather than any systematic difference. To verify this interpretation, some collections which were taken from sites throughout the Soto la Marina drainage during two or more seasons of the same year were compared. One set of these data is illustrated in Figure 3, which clearly shows that the percentage of triploids fluctuates randomly between any two seasons of the same year: triploid frequencies were significantly higher in spring (April) than in winter (January) collections from two localities, i.e., Arroyo la Presa and Río Corona, whereas the reverse was true for three other localities, i.e., Río Cobe, Río Purificación at Padilla, and Arroyo Moro; but there was no significant seasonal difference for the two remaining localities, i.e., Arroyo Grande and Río Purificación at Barretal. Arroyo la Presa, Río Cobe, and Arroyo Moro have similar microhabitats, whereas the Río Corona, the two Río Purificación localities, and the Arroyo Grande localities all have different microhabitats. Consequently, these seasonal fluctuations cannot be correlated with specific microhabitats. Other sets of data for two or more seasons in one year show similar random fluctuations in the frequency of triploids. Furthermore, collections taken from the same isolated pool over two seasons also provide evidence for random fluctuations. For example, a 100-m long, narrow pool at Barretal which yielded 80 fish including 35.2 ± 4.2% triploids in January 1974 was dried down to two separate pools by April of the same year; a collection of 60 fish from the one pool included 91.7 ± 3.6% triploids, whereas 40 fish from the other pool included no triploids! Although we recently reported that the frequencies of unisexuals increased along a tributary as the distance downstream increased (Balsano et al., 1981), this pattern is not readily evident when the frequencies are analyzed by season. Apparently, random fluctuations between seasons are so high that any pattern, if present, is obscured.

Relative Reproductive Output

Three previous reports provide a basis for trying to determine if there are any differences among the three types of females in their reproductive outputs. First of all, Monaco et al. (1981) showed that wild-caught males of *Poecilia mexicana* maintain essentially similar levels of reproductive competence throughout the year. Furthermore, there were no significant differences in testicular maturation values associated with body size, hierarchical rank, or collecting localities within the Río Purificación.

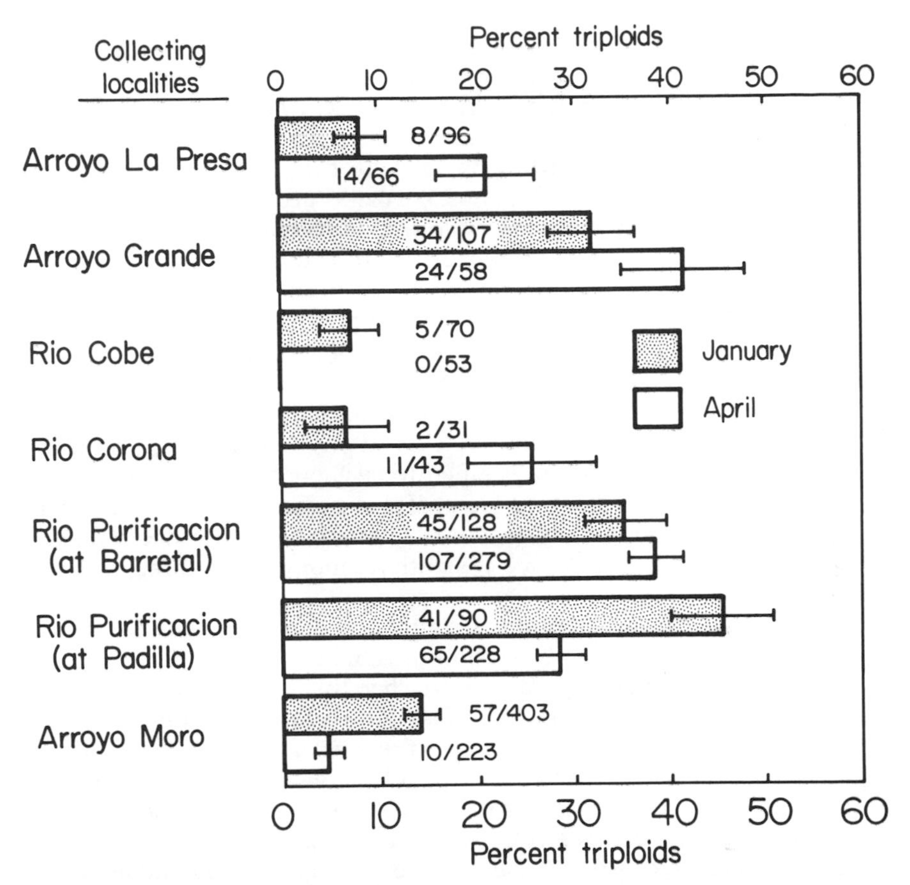

FIGURE 3. Variation in the frequency of triploids among females of *Poecilia* spp. collected in January and April 1974 from seven localities throughout the Soto la Marina drainage of northeastern Mexico. Arroyo la Presa is at Site I shown in Figure 1; all other localities are indicated by name in Figure 1. The fraction by each percentage represents the number of triploids in the numerator and the total number of all females in the denominator. The horizontal line at the end of each bar indicates the 95% confidence interval for each percentage. Multiple seine hauls were taken from the same microhabitats on April 9 as were made on January 4, 1974.

Previously, Monaco et al. (1978) had reported that egg development in females of *P. mexicana* collected in winter and in summer seasons both showed significantly higher incidences of vitellogenic oocytes than either unisexual. The summer samples of females of the diploid unisexual showed significantly higher incidences of vitellogenic oocytes than the triploid unisexuals, but in the spring samples all three females were indistinguishable. When presence of mature eggs was used as the sole criterion to assess reproductive capacity, all three types were also indistinguishable. In the third study Balsano et al. (1981) reported that no significant differences existed in the 1970 or 1971 collections between the proportion of pregnant bisexual and unisexual females. In 1972, however, there were significant differences: more unisexuals than bisexuals were found pregnant in spring samples, whereas in July samples more bisexuals and diploid unisexuals were pregnant than triploids. Although the differences in mean number of embryos per female were not significant, they tended to be higher for females of *P. mexicana* collected in the spring and higher for *P. formosa* females collected in the summer. Since males appeared to be continuously "turned on," whereas egg development and reproductive output seemed to be asynchronous for the three types of females, we wanted to know if there were any seasonal differences in relative reproductive output to suggest the occurrence of a non-overlapping pattern of resource utilization among these three types of females.

The relative reproductive output (RRO) of the three types of females is summarized by locality and by season in Table 1. The summary by locality shows that females of *Poecilia mexicana* had the highest RRO in six of the nine localities; at two localities, i.e., Palo Alto and Site Z, the RROs were relatively high, whereas at Las Cruces the RRO of *mexicana* females was significantly lower than the RROs of both unisexuals. The unisexuals of *P. formosa* exhibited the highest RRO at two localities and had RROs almost equal to those of *P. mexicana* at three other localities; their RROs were significantly less than those of *P. mexicana* females at the dam and at Barretal; and no diploid unisexuals were even collected at Santa Cruz and at Site X. The triploid females showed the highest RRO only at Las Cruces and they typically had an RRO that was significantly smaller than those of *P. mexicana* and *P. formosa*.

When the data were summarized by season, the winter collections exhibited the greatest difference. All three types of females showed similar RROs during the spring but during the summer the RRO of the bisexual species was significantly higher than those of both unisexuals. The totals for the entire year showed that the triploids were only 56% as productive as the bisexual females, and diploid unisexuals were 71% as productive as the bisexuals. Such a statement, however, conceals a tremendous amount of variation in both the proportion of females that had embryonated eggs (as shown in Table 2) and the number of embryos per female (as illustrated in Fig. 4).

The percentages of all three types of females that had embryonated eggs typically varied from zero in some samples to 100% in other samples

TABLE 1. Relative Reproductive Output for Females of *Poecilia* spp. Collected from Nine Localities Along the Río Purificación

Note: Data are summarized from collections made during 1970 to 1978; details of samples from each locality are given in Figure 2. PEmb: proportion of a given type of female that had embryos; x̄ Emb: mean number of embryos for females with embryos; RRO: relative reproductive output which is the product of PEmb times x̄ Emb divided by the highest value for this product from among the three females at a given locality. Entire year totals are weighted by the corresponding sample sizes for each season.

	P. mexicana			Triploids			*P. formosa*		
Locality	PEmb	x̄Emb	RRO	PEmb	x̄Emb	RRO	PEmb	x̄Emb	RRO
Hidalgo	0.31	22.35	1.00	0.20	18.00	0.52	0.30	21.70	0.94
Santa Cruz	0.50	23.16	1.00	0.46	9.33	0.37	0.		
Palo Alto	0.42	37.33	0.86	0.55	22.55	0.68	0.43	42.33	1.00
Las Cruces	0.22	14.86	0.58	0.33	17.00	1.00	0.50	10.50	0.94
at Dam	0.35	23.72	1.00	0.21	13.80	0.35	0.27	15.00	0.49
Barretal	0.37	16.76	1.00	0.24	15.19	0.59	0.21	15.18	0.52
Site X	0.21	19.31	1.00	0.07	1.00	0.02	0.		
Site Z	0.33	30.85	0.78	0.14	14.00	0.15	0.50	26.00	1.00
Nuevo Padilla	0.32	22.78	1.00	0.30	16.52	0.68	0.33	19.45	0.88
Season Totals:									
Winter	0.19	20.87	1.00	0.01	7.33	0.02	0.06	14.2	0.21
Spring	0.41	19.51	1.00	0.52	13.66	0.89	0.48	15.53	0.93
Summer	0.32	21.88	1.00	0.23	17.66	0.59	0.22	21.25	0.69
Entire Year	0.34	20.85	1.00	0.25	15.65	0.56	0.28	18.34	0.71

from the same locality regardless of season (Table 2). There were no significant differences in these proportions among the three types of females collected during the winter, spring, or summer seasons at Barretal or at Nuevo Padilla. During the spring season, however, these proportions were approximately twice as large as they were in summer for all three types of females.

Females with embryos collected from Barretal and Nuevo Padilla typically had an average of 15 to 20 embryos per female with a range from 3 to 42 (Fig. 4). The triploid unisexuals collected in the spring, however, had a significantly smaller number of embryos than the bisexual females ($t = 2.48$ for Barretal comparisons, $t = 3.00$ for Nuevo Padilla). Part of the variation in the number of embryos per female is due to the variation in the size of the females. There is a significant correlation between the number of embryonated eggs and the standard body length for both the bisexual and unisexual females (Fig. 5). But there still was considerable variation within fish of equal lengths, especially for triploids. Although females of *Poecilia mexicana* tend to have more embryos than triploid

TABLE 2. Seasonal Comparison of Proportion of Females of *Poecilia* spp. with Embryonated Eggs Collected from 1970 to 1978 from the Río Purificación

Note: M=females of *P. mexicana;* T=triploid unisexuals; F=females of diploid unisexuals, *P. formosa.*

Season, locality, & No. of samples	*Type of female*	*Total No.*	*Proportion with embryonated eggs* ($\bar{x} \pm tse$)	*Range of proportions among collected samples*	
				Minimum	*Maximum*
Winter, Barretal (6)	M	94	0.31 ± 0.39	0	1.0
	T	220	0.02 ± 0.04	0	0.1
	F	62	0.28 ± 0.46	0	1.0
Winter, Nuevo Padilla (2)	M	6	0	0	0
	T	33	0.03	0	0.03
	F	25	0.08	0	0.1
Spring, Barretal (11)	M	302	0.47 ± 0.20	0	0.9
	T	169	0.64 ± 0.25	0	1.0
	F	53	0.55 ± 0.22	0	1.0
Spring, Nuevo Padilla (11)	M	130	0.58 ± 0.24	0	1.0
	T	75	0.56 + 0.27	0	1.0
	F	123	0.45 ± 0.21	0	0.7
Summer, Barretal (20)	M	634	0.30 ± 0.11	0	0.8
	T	464	0.27 ± 0.15	0	1.0
	F	193	0.17 ± 0.10	0	0.6
Summer, Nuevo Padilla (17)	M	712	0.28 ± 0.08	0.1	0.6
	T	169	0.29 ± 0.14	0	1.0
	F	217	0.35 ± 0.17	0	1.0

females of the same size, these differences were not significant ($t_{slope} = 0.0486$, $t_{intercept} = 1.5591$). When individual females were monitored for number of offspring per brood in the laboratory, there were 9.38 ± 2.54 (mean ± 95% confidence interval) offspring per brood. Although the range went from 1 to 44 offspring, the vast majority of broods (33 out of 55) had less than 9 offspring. Since pregnant females typically had 15 to 20 embryos per female, this suggested that such females had two or more broods of embryos of different developmental stages, i.e., they exhibited superfetation. Data were presented elsewhere to document that this phenomenon occurred in all three types of females regardless of size (Monaco et al., 1983), and it is simply illustrated in this report (Fig. 6). Superfetation can occur in these fish in part because maturation of oocytes is asynchronous (Monaco et al., 1978) and viable sperm can be retained within the ovary for long periods of time. For example, wild-caught females routinely deliver broods in the laboratory for 5 to 6

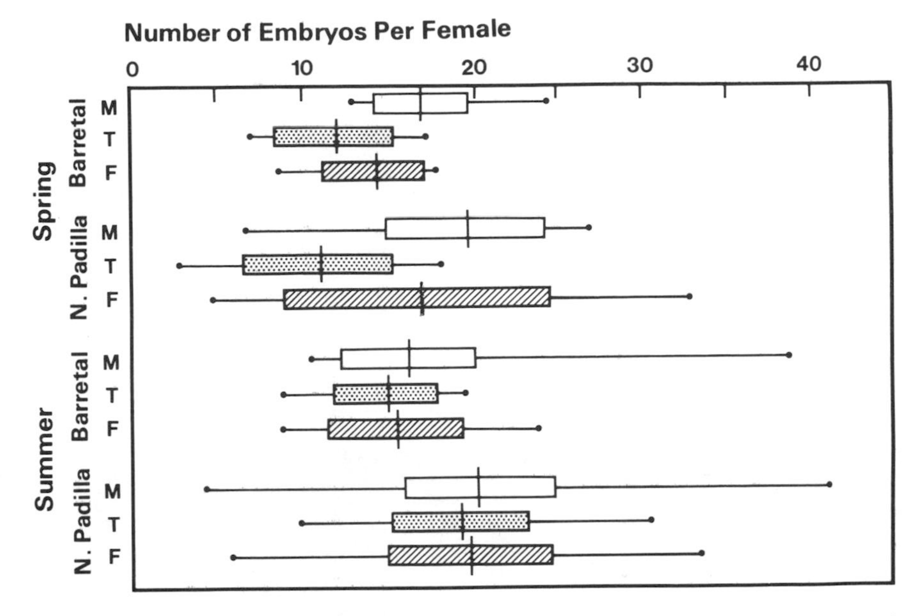

FIGURE 4. Variation in the number of embryos per female with embryonated eggs collected during spring and summer seasons from the Río Purificación at Barretal and at Nuevo Padilla. Bars represent the 95% confidence interval for the observed mean (vertical line).

months after their isolation from males and a few females delivered broods after more than a year of isolation from any male.

REPRODUCTIVE BEHAVIOR OF MALES

Since all three types of females depend upon males of *Poecilia mexicana* for sperm and since males typically account for less than 20% of the total sample of *Poecilia* spp. from a given locality, we wanted to elucidate the role male behavior played in the maintenance of these bisexual/unisexual complexes. Previous laboratory studies of two other groups of poeciliid fish had shown that males preferred conspecific females and that either subordinate males inseminated the unisexual females because they had limited access to conspecific females (McKay, 1970; 1971) or allopatric males were indiscriminate as to which females they inseminated because they were inexperienced in differentiating between bisexual and unisexual females (Hubbs, 1964). Furthermore, Moore and McKay (1971) and Moore (1976) had reasoned that a dynamic equilibrium maintained these bisexual/unisexual complexes: when the density of the bisexual species was high and unisexuals was low, the unisexual females were

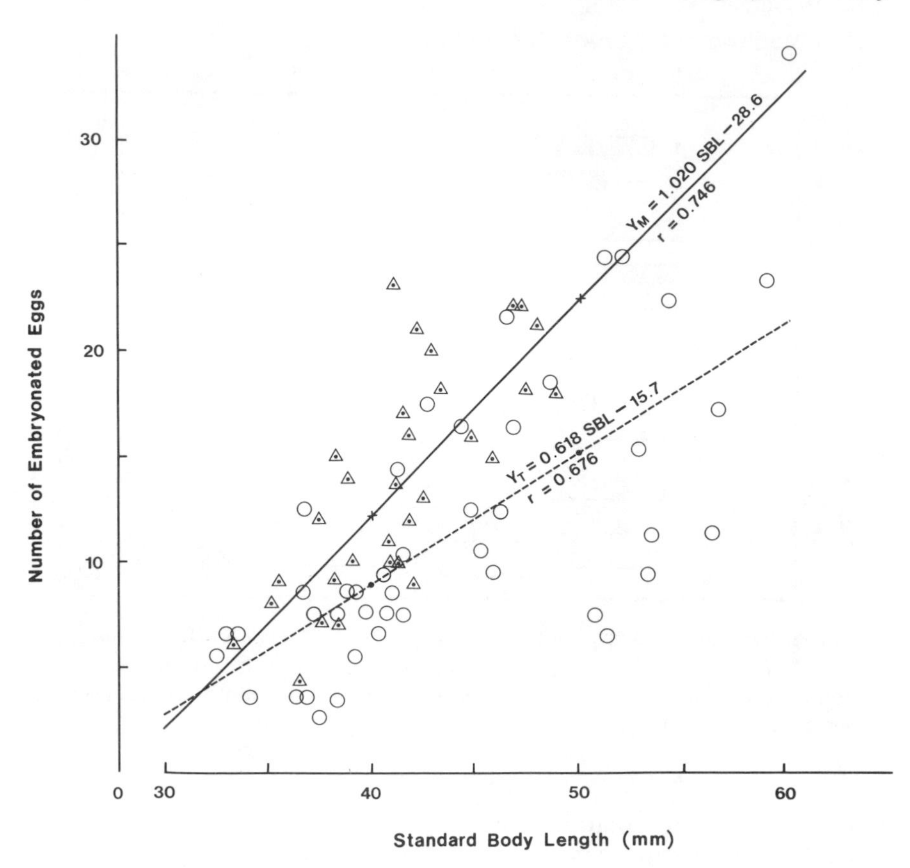

FIGURE 5. Relationship of the number of embryonated eggs to standard body length in 31 females of *Poecila mexicana* (△) and in 44 triploid unisexuals (o) collected from the same microhabitat in Río Purificación at Barretal. There is no significant difference between these two relationships $t_{slopes} = 0.049$, $t_{intercepts} = 1.559$).

inseminated by subordinate males; when the densities were reversed, almost all the bisexual females were pregnant whereas over 90% of the unisexuals were not. This latter situation leads to the demise of the unisexual population and an increase in the bisexuals.

When four males and four females of *Poecilia mexicana* were introduced into laboratory aquaria, behavioral interactions were very common, but they gradually tapered off over a 3-month period. Males initiated the interactions by following and actively courting the females. As males went from one female to another, they encountered other courting males. Such encounters would be followed by one of several

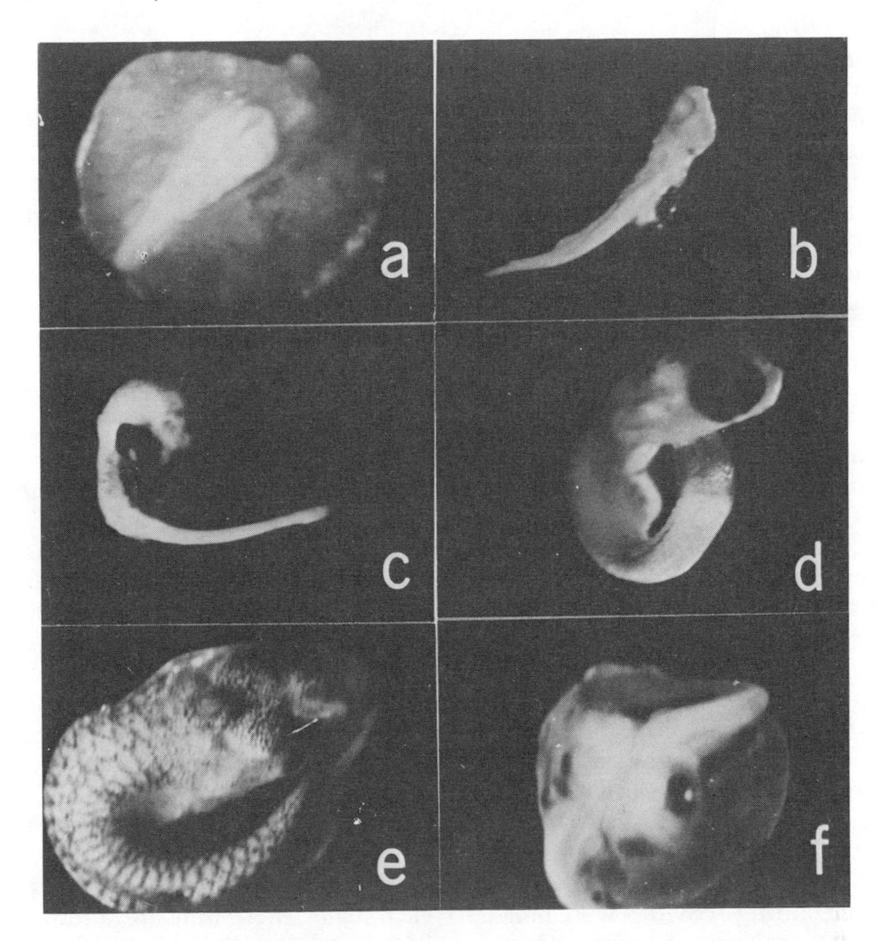

FIGURE 6. Representative stages of embryonic development to illustrate the occurrence of superfetation in *Poecilia formosa*. (a)-(d) are from the same ovary. (a) Embryo at neural fold/optic vesicle stage shown at 10x. (b) Embryo at early lens formation stage, removed from its egg, is shown at 11x. (c) Eye spot and tail fin bud are the dominant features of this embryo, at 6x. Melanophores are first seen in the head region at this stage. (d) Embryo shown at 5x with elongated tail fin-containing rays; numerous melanophores spread over the body at this stage, the opercula are well developed, and organogenesis is nearly completed. (e) Full-term embryo at parturition, shown at 5x; all fins are fully formed and the pigment pattern is that of a fully developed fish. (f) Example of twin embryos at Stage c from a wild-caught specimen of *P. formosa*, at 5x.

alternatives: One male would stop courting but remain near the female; or he would maneuver with the other courter(s) for a position closer to the female; or he would display to the other male(s) which would lead to fighting or limited aggression. Males that retreated from fights were permanently lower on the resulting male hierarchy than the winning male. As male encounters continued, a linear hierarchy was established in each aquarium. Braddock (1945) described such hierarchies as those in which an individual dominates all other individuals whose ranks are lower than its own. Similar hierarchies were observed in the field.

The frequencies of all social interactions observed in the laboratory are summarized in Table 3. Most male/male interactions were aggressive, i.e., either chase, nip, lunge, or display. The dominant male (D♂) directed most of his activity to the highest ranking subordinate male (S_1) who directed most of his activity to the S_2 male, etc. The amount of aggression that a male displayed was correlated with his rank in the hierarchy. The D♂, however, received the least amount of activity whereas the S_1 male received the most. The D♂ directed about two thirds of his activities towards other males whereas the S_3 male directed two thirds of his activities towards females. Furthermore, the D♂ directed a significantly greater proportion of his activities towards other males than did the S_1 male ($d = 3.079$, $p < 0.01$), but the proportion of S_1 male's activities towards other males was significantly greater than those of the S_2 male ($d = 6.066$, $p < 0.001$). The differences in these proportions between the S_2 and S_3 males were not significant ($d = 1.1613$, $p = 0.1$). The amount of fighting among males decreased after a hierarchy was established. A higher ranking male could stop a subordinate male's activities by the use of display or some other single aggressive act.

Once a male hierarchy was established, the frequencies of four different courting activities were tallied for each male. These data are summarized in Table 4. Since D♂♂ exhibited more activity than S♂♂, comparisons between these two classes of males were based upon the d-test for proportions. S♂♂ more frequently followed females than did D♂♂, whereas the D♂♂ more frequently touched the genital area of the females with their mouths or top of their heads. The most significant differences between the two classes of males occurred in fin displays and thrusting the gonopodium towards the female to inseminate her. Fin displays were relatively more frequent among D♂♂ than S♂♂, whereas the S♂♂ thrust their gonopodia more often at the females than did D♂♂. It is pertinent to mention here that the sequence of events involved in courting behavior is quite short. D♂♂ showed 1.99 ± 0.12 courting events whereas subordinates exhibited 1.79 ± 0.12 steps ($\bar{x} \pm SE$ based on 244 and 63 events, respectively, tallied from 19 15-min. observations of

TABLE 3. Frequency of Social Interactions Within Groups of *Poecilia mexicana* Relative to Male Rank

Note: Data summarized from laboratory observations of 4 replicate aquaria containing 4 males and 4 females in each tank. Male-to-male interactions were tallied from 47 15-min. observation periods; male-to-female interactions were tallied from 46 15-min. periods. Values in the body of the table represent the total number of all behavioral activities received by each male from every other male in the aquarium. D=dominant male; S=subordinate male, with subscript to indicate his rank in hierarchy.

Initiator	*Recipient of activity*				*Frequency of all activities from initiator received by:*			
of activity	D	S_1	S_2	S_3	*males (proportion)*		*females (proportion)*	
D		721	457	337	1515	(0.632)	882	(0.368)
S_1	197		235	94	526	(0.574)	391	(0.426)
S_2	26	27		94	147	(0.389)	231	(0.611)
S_3	24	16	18		58	(0.319)	124	(0.681)
	Total activities received							
	247	764	710	525				

TABLE 4. Frequencies and Proportions of Courting and Aggressive Activities Directed Towards Females of *Poecilia mexicana* by Dominant and Subordinate Males

Note: Data summarized from 52 15-min. observation periods of 5 replicate aquaria, each of which included 4 females, 1 dominant male, and 2 or 3 subordinate males. The d-test for proportions was used to compare the differences between the two classes of males. Aggressive activities include nipping, chasing, lunging at, and aggressively approaching the female. F=frequency, P=proportion.

	Dominant males		*Subordinate males*		*Comparison*	
Courting activities	*F*	*P*	*F*	*P*	*d-test*	*p-level*
Following	228	0.235	177	0.291	2.495	<0.02
Nosing genital area	297	0.306	143	0.235	3.082	<0.001
Erect fin displays	247	0.254	80	0.131	5.907	<0.001
Gonopodial thrusts	132	0.136	153	0.251	5.819	<0.001
Aggressive activities	67	0.069	56	0.092	1.670	~0.10
Total of all activities	971	1.000	677	1.000		

five aquaria). Consequently, both types of males tried to inseminate females after one or two courting steps. The absence of an elaborate courting sequence in these fish may account for the observation that male dominance hierarchies do not prevent subordinate males from inseminating any receptive females. Occasionally a female would display to attract the attention of a particular male, but she allowed other males to court and inseminate her as well as the male to whom she initially displayed. Such behavior was observed in both bisexual and unisexual females; the unisexuals, however, appeared to facilitate insemination by tilting their ventral surface towards the male.

When frequency of courting activity was used as an indicator of female preference, 19 out of the 23 males (6 of the 7 D♂♂ and 13 of the 16 S♂♂) used in the laboratory studies showed a significant preference for a particular bisexual female over a 3-month period of time. These males, however, routinely courted and inseminated other bisexual females in addition to their preferred female. In aquaria that had both bisexual and unisexual females the males did not consistently show any significant preference for conspecific females. Previous experiments in which a male was given a choice of only two females had shown that sometimes a male spent more time courting and trying to inseminate a conspecific female whereas other times he courted and tried to inseminate a unisexual female more often than his own type of female (Balsano et al., 1981).

The laboratory data described above were confirmed and clarified by two field experiments: an isolated pool (8 m x 4 m) containing about 250 bisexuals and possibly a few unisexuals was observed for 2½ days; another smaller pool (3 m x 1.5 m) had all natural inhabitants removed and was stocked with tagged fish to permit observation of particular fish over an 8-day period. Dominance hierarchies were routinely observed in all microhabitats that contained several males. All the activities observed in the laboratory experiments were observed in the field, but the frequencies were different. The D♂ spent most of his time in a single area; usually the site was most preferred by many other fish. Large males occupied deeper areas or more shaded areas, whereas the smaller males were more often seen in the shallows or more open areas of a pool or stream. For example, the largest D♂ used the two deepest parts of the pool shown in Figure 7 as his home range. The D♂ chased S♂♂ out of his home range, but these S♂♂ were able to move freely in other areas of the pool and would regularly court and mate with any females in these areas. S♂♂ did mate with females in the D♂'s home range when the D♂ was chasing some other male away or when he was resting after an extended chase. Large D♂♂ usually showed no aggression towards small males who were courting females in the D♂'s home range. The frequencies and corresponding

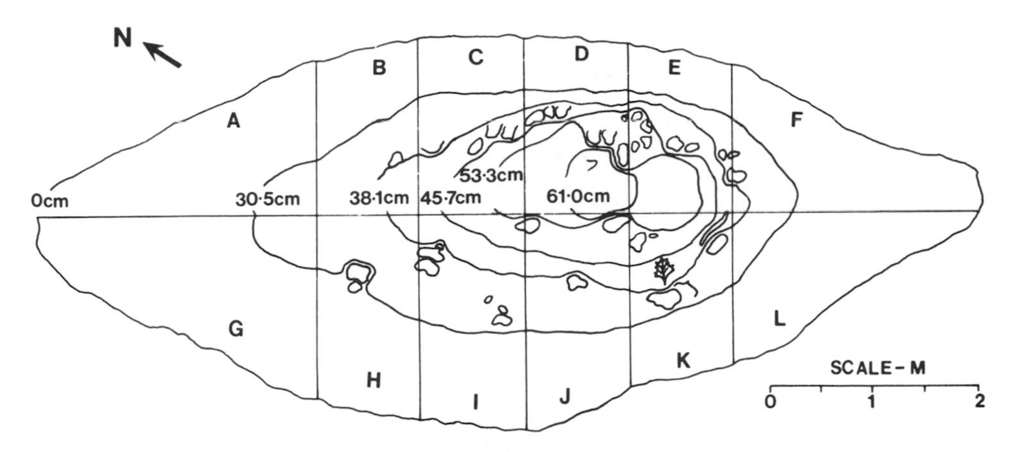

FIGURE 7. Contours of an isolated pool along the Río Cobe that was used to observe dominance hierarchies and behavioral interactions among males and females of *Poecilia mexicana* in March 1978. Locations of several large rocks are shown since they provided boundaries for home ranges defended by males.

proportions of aggressive activities exhibited by males of *Poecilia mexicana* in the pool illustrated in Figure 7 are summarized in Table 5. Three dominant males occupied the deep end of section D, with usually one or more large rocks to provide a border for their home ranges; the fourth D♂ occupied the deep part of section K. There were 16 subordinates comprising at least four different hierarchies, but it was not possible to determine which subordinate males belonged to each hierarchy. Although these subordinate males moved routinely throughout all parts of the pool, they preferred some areas and were observed more often in them (Table 6). As far as aggressive activities were concerned, the D♂ exhibited significantly more approach and display but less lunging than did the subordinate males (Table 5). Although the frequencies of different courting activities shown in Table 5 were too few to show any significant differences between D♂♂ and subordinates, the D♂♂ directed a significantly smaller proportion of their activities towards females than did the S♂♂, which was similar to what had been observed in the laboratory experiments. When any male followed and courted a female, she sometimes tilted her ventral side towards the male. At such times as many as seven other males including dominants and subordinates would try to inseminate this female; the males did not appear to be aggressive towards each other, but rather seemed to take turns thrusting at this receptively posturing female. These mating frenzies were observed whenever courting activity

TABLE 5. Frequencies and Proportions of Behavioral Activities Exhibited by Dominant and Subordinate Males Towards Males and Females

Note: Observed in a small (8-m x 4-m) field pool. Data were summarized from 6 different observations made on March 18, 1978, for a total of 75 min. The d-test for proportions was used to compare the differences between the two classes of males. F = frequency, P = proportion.

Behavioral	Dominant males		Subordinate males		Comparisons	
activity	*F*	*P*	*F*	*P*	*d-test*	*p-level*
Aggression toward males:						
Approach	39	0.684	55	0.524	1.971	< 0.05
Chase	0	0	3	0.029	1.309	~ 0.20
Display	14	0.246	11	0.105	2.375	< 0.02
Lunge	2	0.035	35	0.333	4.320	< 0.001
Nip	2	0.035	1	0.010	1.129	~ 0.25
TOTAL	57	1.000	105	1.001		
Activities towards females:						
Following	2	0.182	28	0.418	1.491	~ 0.15
Nosing genital area	1	0.091	8	0.119	0.269	~ 0.80
Erect fin display	6	0.545	22	0.328	1.391	~ 0.17
Gonopodial thrust	0	0	2	0.030	0.583	~ 0.60
Aggressive activities	2	0.182	7	0.104	0.750	~ 0.45
TOTAL	11	1.000	67	0.999		
Proportion of all activities directed to female	11/68	0.162	67/172	0.390	3.400	< 0.001

was prevalent in the field, but it was only rarely observed in laboratory aquaria. On 10 occasions females were observed lunging at or nipping a courting male who quickly retreated; this happened equally to dominant males as well as subordinate ones.

When 30 tagged unisexual females of *Poecilia formosa* were added to this pool, they dispersed throughout the pool and exhibited similar preferences for some sections as shown by the resident fish (Table 6). There were no significant differences between the mean frequencies of the two groups of fish. Furthermore, 12 schools of fish varying in size from 14 to 37 fish (with $\bar{x} \pm SD$ of 25.5 ± 7.82) were seen over a 2-day period; they contained 13.7 ± 9.0 foreign unisexuals and 13.5 ± 9.6 resident fish. Not only were these foreign females incorporated into schools of resident fish, but resident males courted and mated with them.

The second behavioral experiment using all tagged fish conducted in the field confirmed the above results. There was a definite preference for

TABLE 6. Mean Densities ($\bar{x} \pm SE$) of *Poecilia* spp. in Various Sections of an Isolated Pool Along the Río Cobe After Addition of 30 Tagged Females of *P. formosa*

Note: Sections of the pool are identified by letters shown in Figure 7. Data are based upon 16 observations made during March 19, 20, 1978.

Section of pool	*Males of* P. mexicana	*Resident females*	*Tagged females of* P. formosa
A	0.13 ± 0.13	1.25 ± 0.39	1.33 ± 0.56
B	0.81 ± 0.14	10.81 ± 1.68	2.94 ± 0.47
C	3.89 ± 0.68	21.38 ± 2.81	3.88 ± 0.89
D	4.75 ± 0.34	25.44 ± 2.58	2.00 ± 0.54
E	1.80 ± 0.26	20.60 ± 1.96	3.31 ± 0.80
F	0.30 ± 0.10	7.40 ± 1.40	1.60 ± 0.42
G	0	0.80 ± 0.49	0.47 ± 0.34
H	1.06 ± 0.19	12.38 ± 1.92	4.00 ± 0.94
I	2.00 ± 0.27	22.63 ± 2.32	4.88 ± 1.66
J	2.63 ± 0.34	17.88 ± 1.70	1.75 ± 0.30
K	1.50 ± 0.24	13.75 ± 1.79	1.87 ± 0.65
L	0.07 ± 0.07	1.20 ± 0.40	0.19 ± 0.10

three of the eight sections of this 3-m x 1.5-m pool. These areas were shaded by overhanging weeds, whereas the two avoided sections were at the opposite end of the pool, which was fully exposed. Linear dominance hierarchies were initially established among the first group of males and then reestablished each time another group of males was added. These hierarchies related to the defense of a home range and did not pertain to courting activity except for the D♂'s preference for bisexual female no. 21 (described below). Schools of 8 to 12 fish including mostly bisexual and triploid females plus fewer females of *Poecilia formosa* and males were seen periodically swimming around the entire pool. Newly introduced fish were quickly integrated into existing schools. There was an increased amount of aggressive activity as well as courting on both occasions when more fish were added to the pool; the activity subsided by the next day. The males became increasingly more aggressive towards each other as the density of fish increased, but the females were never observed to be involved in these aggressive male interactions. The D♂ spent most of his time following bisexual female no. 21, but for the first 4 days he rarely tried to mate with her. On the 5th day he mated with her several times, but so did S♂♂ who were chased away by the D♂. On that day female no. 21 was also involved in several mating frenzies which the D♂ tried to break up, but the S♂♂ persisted until the female took shelter under a rock. During the 8 days of observations 13 females were involved in mating frenzies: 5 bisexuals, 3 triploids, 1 diploid unisexual, and 4 females whose tags were not visible at the time of the frenzy. Courting activity, however, was definitely more biased in favor of the bisexual females, i.e., 13 times versus only 3 times for a unisexual female. Generally the S♂♂ as well as the D♂ mated with any receptive female regardless of whether she was a bisexual or unisexual. Consequently, these male dominance hierarchies observed in the field did not limit the access of S♂♂ to any receptive female as had been observed in laboratory aquaria. Presumably the D♂ was defending access to his home range in the aquarium, which was typically smaller than the size of a home area defended in the field.

General Discussion

The bisexual/unisexual complexes of *Poecilia* spp. from the Soto la Marina drainage are routinely characterized by a highly skewed sex ratio in favor of females. Two predictions were based on this observation: females would compete for the services of males; and the frequency of males would be inversely correlated with the frequency of unisexuals. Since this report invalidates both predictions, some explanation seems warranted.

Both the field and laboratory data indicate there are very few females simultaneously receptive to courting males. The mating frenzies provide field evidence that there are many males ready to inseminate females when they are receptive. These behavioral data are consistent with cytological data that indicated that ovarian maturation was asynchronous among the three types of females (Monaco et al., 1978) and that a constant sperm supply was available throughout the year (Monaco et al., 1981). We infer that females do not compete for the services of males, but rather they exhibit non-overlapping patterns of resource utilization.

Hubbs (1974) reported that populations of *Poecilia latipinna* from southeastern Texas had a low, genetically determined proportion of males; we also observed this in laboratory broods of *P. mexicana* and in commerical stocks of *Poecilia* spp. These observations, coupled with the ability of females to retain viable sperm for extended time periods and with the large, sample-to-sample variations in the frequencies of the three types of females, may be responsible for obscuring any relationship between the sex ratio and bisexual/unisexual ratio, if one does exist. The possibility of such a relationship is currently under laboratory study.

Male dominance hierarchies were observed in both laboratory and field experiments. Dominant males preferred to court particular females, which were usually conspecifics but not always. Attempted matings, however, occurred with any receptive female, regardless of type. Since

TABLE 7. Seasonal Differences in the Frequencies of Adult and Juvenile Triploids

Note: Percent triploids (% ± 95% confidence interval) are based upon the total number of all females of *Poecilia* spp. collected from localities where both adults (SL ≥ 35.0 mm) and juveniles (SL ≤ 25.0 mm) were obtained. The localities included for each season are indicated by letters which are identified in Figure 1.

Season and year	*Localities*	*Samples*	*Adults*	*Juveniles*	*Percent triploids*	
					Adults	*Juveniles*
Winter 1974	B,E,F,G,H,I,L,M	12	628	290	22.8 ± 3.4	11.4 ± 3.7
Winter 1975	B,E,F,G,H,I,M	14	747	656	28.9 ± 3.3	8.8 ± 2.2
Spring 1974	E,L,M	5	193	71	39.4 ± 7.0	5.6 ± 5.5
Summer 1974	B,E,F,G,M	14	1051	472	14.7 ± 2.2	6.1 ± 2.2
Summer 1975	B,E,F,G,M	14	943	744	14.2 ± 2.3	9.5 ± 2.2
TOTALS		59	3,562	2,223	20.3 ± 1.3	8.7 ± 1.2

the proportion of gonopodial thrusting was significantly higher in S♂♂ than in D♂♂ observed in aquaria, the S♂♂ may inseminate as many females as do the D♂♂ despite the reduced activity of the S♂♂. In nature the S♂'s access to the home range of the D♂ is restricted, but the S♂'s position in the hierarchy does not determine his access to receptive females. All males appear to have equal access to any receptive female; some restriction of this access can occur if a receptive female is in the home range of the D♂. Consequently, we infer that what was observed in laboratory aquaria was biased by the fact that all the fish were confined to a relatively small area. The field observations clearly indicate that competition among the three types of females for the services of males does not exist.

On the basis of previous work, we had predicted that relative reproductive output (RRO) among the three females would be seasonally asynchronous, i.e., highest for females of *Poecilia mexicana* in early spring, highest for triploids in May, and highest for diploid unisexuals in June and July. Instead we observed that the three types of females had the same proportion of pregnant individuals in spring, which was about twice as high as in the summer samples. The mean number of embryonated eggs per female was about the same for the bisexual and unisexual diploids, but the triploids had significantly fewer embryonated eggs per female than the bisexual females. If 10 to 30% of the RRO of *P. mexicana* represents males, then the RRO of *P. formosa* is comparable to the female portion of the RRO of *P. mexicana*. The RRO of the triploids, however, is lower than that for the other two types of females for all seasons. But adult triploids are typically more abundant than diploid unisexuals and sometimes more abundant than bisexual females. When the frequencies of adult vs. juvenile triploids are compared, the adult samples have typically two to three times more triploids than do the juvenile samples for all seasons (Table 7). This suggests that natural selection favors the triploid juveniles over the diploid juveniles. Since there are collections from three seasons over 2 consecutive years included in Table 7, one can rule out random fluctuations and the possibility that these differences are due to asynchrony of reproduction. Consequently, it appears that the lower reproductive output of the triploids is balanced out by a higher survivorship among their offspring. This interpretation leads us to postulate that the fluctuations in the frequencies of the three types of females may be the result of a dynamic equilibrium between reproductive output and survival rather than the male dominance hierarchies.

Acknowledgments

The cooperation of the Mexican Department of Fisheries in granting collecting permits (no. 2858 for 1977 to J. S. Balsano and no. 5512 for 1978 to E. M. Rasch) is gratefully acknowledged. This research was also supported in part by the National Science Foundation (most recently DEB 78-07758 to E. M. Rasch and DEB 80-23277 to J. S. Balsano), the University of Wisconsin-Parkside Committee on Research and Creative Activity, and the National Geographic Society's Committee for Research and Exploration (grant 1674, for the period January 1, 1977 through June 1, 1978.).

REFERENCES

ABRAMOFF, PETER; DARNELL, REZNEAT; and BALSANO, JOSEPH
1968. Electrophoretic demonstration of the hybrid origin of the gynogenetic teleost *Poecilia formosa*. Amer. Naturalist, vol. 102, pp. 555-558.

BALSANO, JOSEPH; KUCHARSKI, KRISTINE; RANDLE, EDWARD; RASCH, ELLEN; and MONACO, PAUL
1981. Reduction of competition between bisexual and unisexual females of *Poecilia* in northeastern Mexico. Env. Biol. Fish., vol. 6, no. 1, pp. 39-48.

BRADDOCK, JAMES C.
1945. Some aspects of the dominant-subordination relationship in the fish *Platypoecilius maculatus*. Physiol. Zool., vol. 18, pp. 176-195.

HUBBS, CARL, and HUBBS, LAURA
1946. Experimental breeding of the Amazon molly. Aquarium Journ., vol. 17, pp. 4-6.

HUBBS, CLARK
1964. Interaction between a bisexual fish species and its gynogenetic sexual parasite. Bull. Texas Mem. Museum, vol. 8, pp. 1-72.

McKay, Francis
1970. Behavioral aspects of population dynamics in unisexual-bisexual *Poeciliopsis* (Pisces: Poeciliidae). Ph.D. thesis, Univ. of Connecticut, 92 pp.
1971. Behavioral aspects of population dynamics in unisexual-bisexual *Poeciliopsis* (Pisces: Poeciliidae). Ecol., vol. 52, pp. 778-798.

Monaco, Paul; Rasch, Ellen; and Balsano, Joseph
1978. Cytological evidence for temporal differences during the asynchronous ovarian maturation of bisexual and unisexual fishes of the genus *Poecilia*. Journ. Fish. Biol., vol. 13, pp. 33-44.
1981. Sperm availability in naturally occurring bisexual-unisexual breeding complexes involving *Poecilia mexicana* and the gynogenetic teleost, *Poecilia formosa*. Env. Biol. Fish., vol. 6, no. 2, pp. 159-166.
——. The occurrence of superfetation in the Amazon molly, *Poecilia formosa,* and its related sexual species. Copeia, no. 4. (In press.)

Monaco, Paul; Rasch, Ellen; Balsano, Joseph; and Turner, Bruce
1982. Muscle protein phenotypes and the probable evolutionary origin of a unisexual fish, *Poecilia formosa,* and its triploid derivatives. Journ. Exp. Zool., vol. 221, pp. 265-274.

Moore, William
1976. Components of fitness in the unisexual fish *Poeciliopsis monacha-occidentalis*. Evolution, vol. 30, pp. 564-578.

Moore, William, and McKay, Francis
1971. Coexistence in the unisexual-bisexual species complexes of *Poeciliopsis* (Pisces: Poeciliidae). Ecology, vol. 52, pp. 791-799.

Pianka, Eric
1974. Niche overlap and diffuse competition. Proc. Nat. Acad. Sci., vol. 71, pp. 2141-2145.

Rasch, Ellen, and Balsano, Joseph
1974. Biochemical and cytogenetic studies of *Poecilia* from eastern Mexico. II. Frequency, perpetuation, and probable origin of triploid genomes in females associated with *Poecilia formosa*. Rev. Biol. Trop., vol. 21, pp. 351-381.

Joseph S. Balsano
Ellen M. Rasch
Paul J. Monaco

Volcanic Rocks of Micronesia

Grant Recipient: Fred Barker, U. S. Geological Survey, Anchorage, Alaska.[1]

Grant 1613: To collect and study Tertiary volcanic rocks of Saipan, Guam, Truk, and Ponape: generation of island-arc andesite and low-K rhyolite.

The major objective of this project was to collect Tertiary volcanic rocks of Saipan and Guam, Mariana Islands, Micronesia. These rocks formed in the early stages of an oceanic island arc, where the oceanic Pacific plate was subducted or thrust many hundreds of kilometers under the oceanic Philippine plate. Complex interaction of the two converging plates led to melting in the mantle and to development of a volcanic ridge along the leading edge of the Philippine plate (see, e.g., Nat. Geog. Soc., "Atlas of the World," ed. 5, 1981, pp. 20-34). This volcanic ridge, which is arcuate in plan and is exposed above sea level in scattered islands, thus is termed an "island arc." From Saipan 16 relatively fresh samples of 2 to 5 kg weight were collected, and from Guam 13. These 29 samples now form a reference collection to replace the now-exhausted suite collected in the 1950's by R. G. Schmidt, J. T. Stark, and J. I. Tracey, Jr., in their detailed mapping of the Mariana Islands (Schmidt, 1957; Stark, 1963). The new samples have been analyzed in the laboratories of the Geological Survey for major elements, rare earth elements (REE's) and other minor elements such as Rb, Sr, Ni, Cr, and Co.

Drs. Carl Hedge and M. Tatsumoto of the Geological Survey requested that I sample for volcanic rocks of Truk and Ponape, Caroline Islands. These two island groups consist largely of volcanic rocks of ocean-island type (e.g., those of the Hawaiian Islands). Ocean-island volcanism probably occurs as a tectonic plate—in this case the Pacific plate—moves over an upwelling mass of partially molten mantle material, which is termed a "mantle plume" or "hot spot." This plume consists of a mush of rock-forming mineral grains such as pyroxene and olivine and of an interstitial melt or magma. The melt tends to collect as the buoyant plume moves upward, and magma bodies are formed. Most of this magma is ejected at

[1] Co-investigators were Joseph G. Arth, U. S. Geological Survey, Reston, Virginia, and Carl E. Hedge, U. S. Geological Survey, Denver, Colorado.

the surface to form volcanoes, submarine lava flows, or other constructional features. Mantle plumes are generated from relatively stationary sources in the intermediate mantle, and they emit magma spasmodically. So the passage of a plate over a plume gives a linear or elongate chain of islands or submarine seamounts (e.g., the Hawaii-Emperor chain). My collecting on the islands Moen and Tol in Truk Lagoon, however, met with poor success because much of the land is posted and permission to collect could not be obtained. Only six samples were taken. Ponape was not restricted in this way and 11 excellent samples were collected; these have been turned over to Dr. Hedge.

This project is investigating two different groups of island-arc volcanic rocks. The first is the distinctive low-K, very high-SiO_2, dacitic or rhyolitic volcanic flows and air-fall tuffs of Saipan; the second is the andesitic rocks of Guam, which are partly common, low-magnesian varieties, and partly the recently recognized high-magnesian type.

The low-K, high-SiO_2 rocks of Saipan were called "dacite" by Schmidt (1957) in his comprehensive monograph, and many later workers also have used this term. However, the recent terminology of Ewart (1979), using K_2O-SiO_2 relations, defines "dacites" at 63 to 69% of SiO_2 and "rhyolites" at SiO_2 greater than 69%. In addition, increasing proportions of K_2O give low-K, middle-K, and high-K varieties of dacite and rhyolite. Thus the Saipan "dacite" now should be termed low-K rhyolite.

The Saipan rhyolite is found at the lowest exposed part of the island's stratigraphic column. To the author's knowledge there are no deep drill holes on Saipan, hence the nature of the underlying rocks is not known. However, like other island arcs, Saipan probably is built on a foundation of basaltic and andesitic rocks that were erupted before the rhyolite. The rhyolite forms the bulk of the Sankakuyama Formation, and was emplaced as massive flows, explosive breccia, glassy tuff, and air-fall lapilli tuff (Schmidt, 1957). Phenocrysts of oligoclase, quartz, and magnetite form from a few to about 10% of most Saipan rhyolite.

Only four samples of the rhyolite were analyzed for major elements in previous studies: three by Schmidt (1957) and one—of sample S299 collected by Schmidt—by Barker et al. (1976). Sample S299 also was analyzed for REE's (Rb, Sr, and Ba). These four rocks show the characteristic low K_2O contents of oceanic island-arc–type rhyolite—typically 1.0 to 1.6%. Their SiO_2 contents, however, do not represent primary magmatic values, because secondary silica minerals have been deposited in the interstices of all samples. These minerals are tridymite, opal, and chalcedony; they occur as linings of vugs and other tiny cavities and as fillings of small (0.1 to about 5 mm thick) veinlets. Much of this silicification took place as groundwater percolated through the rocks, probably at temperatures below 100°C. The four analyses (like all others in this report, as cal-

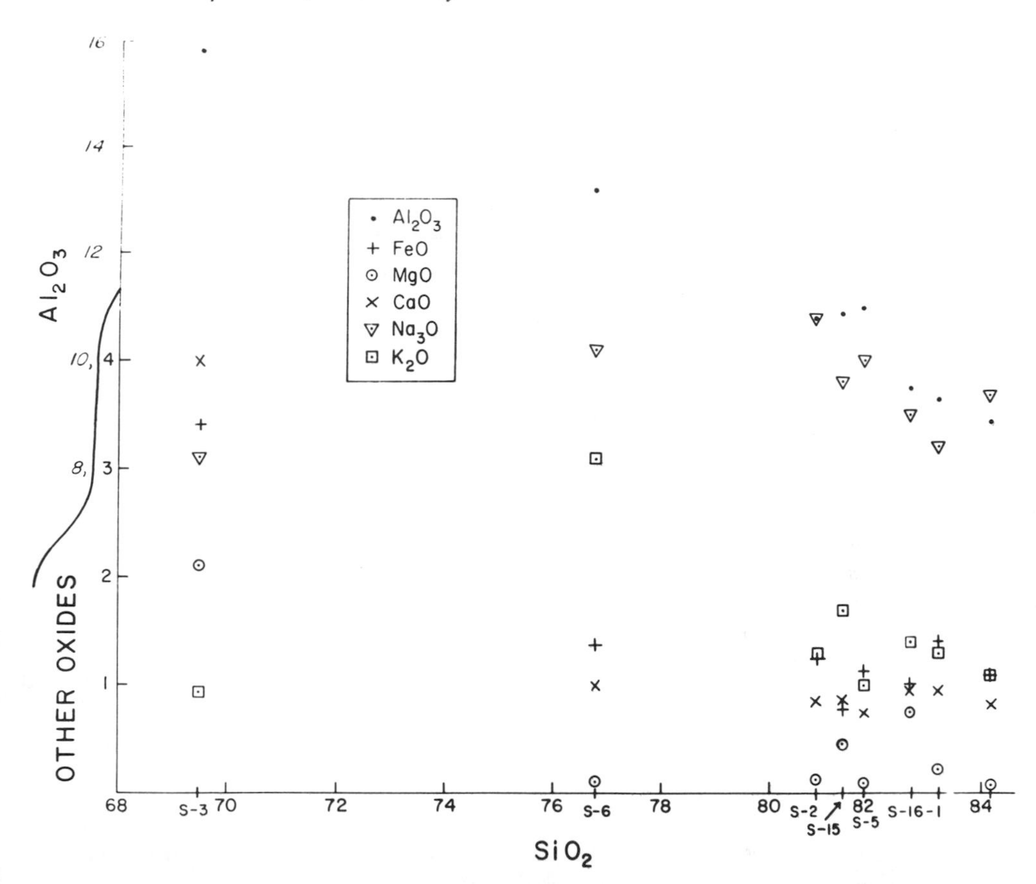

FIGURE 1. Silica variation diagram of rocks of the Sankakuyama Formation, Saipan.

culated H_2O- and CO_2-free) range in SiO_2 content from 79.61 to 82.00%. These rocks thus may well be termed "hypersiliceous." The problem of such high SiO_2 contents is discussed further on in this report.

Eight new samples of Saipan rhyolite were collected. Six of these are of the hypersiliceous type, containing 80.9 to 84.1% SiO_2, and they show other major elements like those of the four published analyses. My other two samples are: S-3, a hydrated (total H_2O=12%), very friable, light gray tuff containing 69.5% SiO_2, and S-6, a perlitic flow of 76.8% SiO_2. This perlitic rhyolite, which is largely glass, contains only 4 to 5% phenocrysts of plagioclase (the sodic variety, oligoclase) and quartz. It is virtually free of secondary silica minerals and probably represents a lease-altered igneous composition. However, the K_2O content of S-6 at 3.1% is about twice its expected value, and its MgO content of 0.1% is lower than normal.

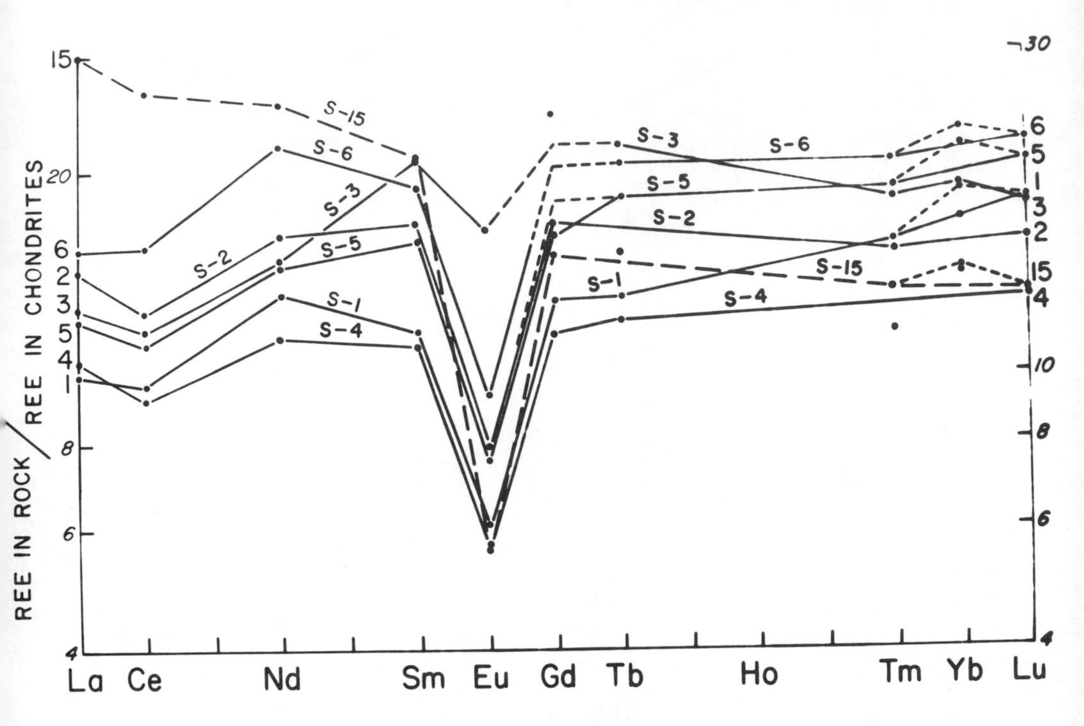

FIGURE 2. Rare-earth–element plots of some low-K rhyolites, Sankakuyama Formation, Saipan.

Both of these components are known for their mobility in volcanic rocks and such anomalous values probably are not primary.

Major elements of the eight new samples of low-K rhyolite from the Sankakuyama Formation are shown in Figure 1 on a silica-variation diagram. These new data, in conjunction with the published analyses, give us a rather good characterization of the Saipan rhyolite. Notable features include: high Na_2O and low K_2O, moderate FeO* (FeO*=FeO + 0.9 Fe_2O_3), low MgO, and CaO that is relatively invariant with SiO_2.

Plots of REE's, as determined by the instrumental neutron activation technique and as normalized to REE abundances of average chondritic meteorites, of seven of the new samples are plotted in Figure 2. The pattern for sample S-16 is not included in this figure because for unknown reasons its Ce, Nd, Sm, and Eu are anomalously low relative to the other REE's. Six of the plotted samples show depletion of the light REE's, whereas that of S-15 shows enrichment in light REE's. All samples show negative Eu anomalies: that of S-3 is small, but those of the remaining six samples are pronounced. Heavy REE's give flat plots at 12 to 20 times chondrites. The published analysis of Saipan rhyolite S299 by Dr. J. G. Arth (Barker et al., 1976), made by the precise isotope dilution-mass spectrometry method, shows flat light REE's, a moderate negative Eu anomaly, and heavy REE's gently concave upward. Thus the new analyses show a slight variability but a more general depletion of light REE's and more pronounced Eu anomalies than was previously known.

Genesis of these hypersiliceous, low-K rhyolites of oceanic island arcs is an outstanding problem. The very high SiO_2 contents of these rocks, as Schmidt pointed out (1957), may be partly or wholly the result of silicification after emplacement. The maximum amount of secondary silica minerals visible in thin sections of the new samples is about 20% in S-16. The other samples show only a few to about 10% by volume. There is poor correlation between the amount of secondary silica minerals and the SiO_2 of the rock.

The 76.8% SiO_2 of S-6 *could* be close to the primary igneous maximum—determined either by differentiation of less siliceous parental magma or by partial melting of a less siliceous parental-rock deep in the crust. But many unaltered samples would be required to establish such a maximum SiO_2 value. The four published and six new analyses of Saipan rhyolite that show very high SiO_2 contents, from 79.6 to 84.1%, are of silicified rocks. We can assess the process of silicification of primary, unsilicified rhyolite in terms of a silica-perturbation diagram. One can assume rhyolite as extruded to contain 78% SiO_2. One can then calculate the SiO_2 content of silicified rhyolite as a function of secondary silica added to this primary rock of 78% SiO_2. This is done in Figure 3, where the addition of secondary silica is given as grams of silica added per 100 g of starting rock, with all values given as H_2O-free. This diagram shows that rather large amounts of silica are needed to produce moderate increases of the SiO_2 content of silicified rhyolite. For instance, addition of 20% of anhydrous silica minerals (tridymite and chalcedony are anhydrous, whereas opal contains about 6 to 10% H_2O), as perhaps in S-16, would raise the SiO_2 content of a 78%-SiO_2 rhyolite to 81.7%—or a net increase of only 3.7%. If S-16 before silicification contained 78% SiO_2 it would have had 27.5% silica minerals added to give its analyzed value of 82.7% SiO_2. Sample S-4, which shows the highest SiO_2 content of any silicified rhyolite known to the author, would require addition of 38.5% (or 38.5 weight units per 100 weight units of primary rock). Yet in microscopic examination this sample shows only about 10% of secondary silica minerals.

Another means of adding SiO_2 to the rhyolite is needed. A possible mechanism involves the fact that the quartz phenocrysts of low-K rhyolites invariably are embayed. In the process of embayment or resorption SiO_2 must enter the liquid part of the magma. So I suggest the following scheme: (1) oligoclase and quartz crystallize from "rhyolitic" liquid in a

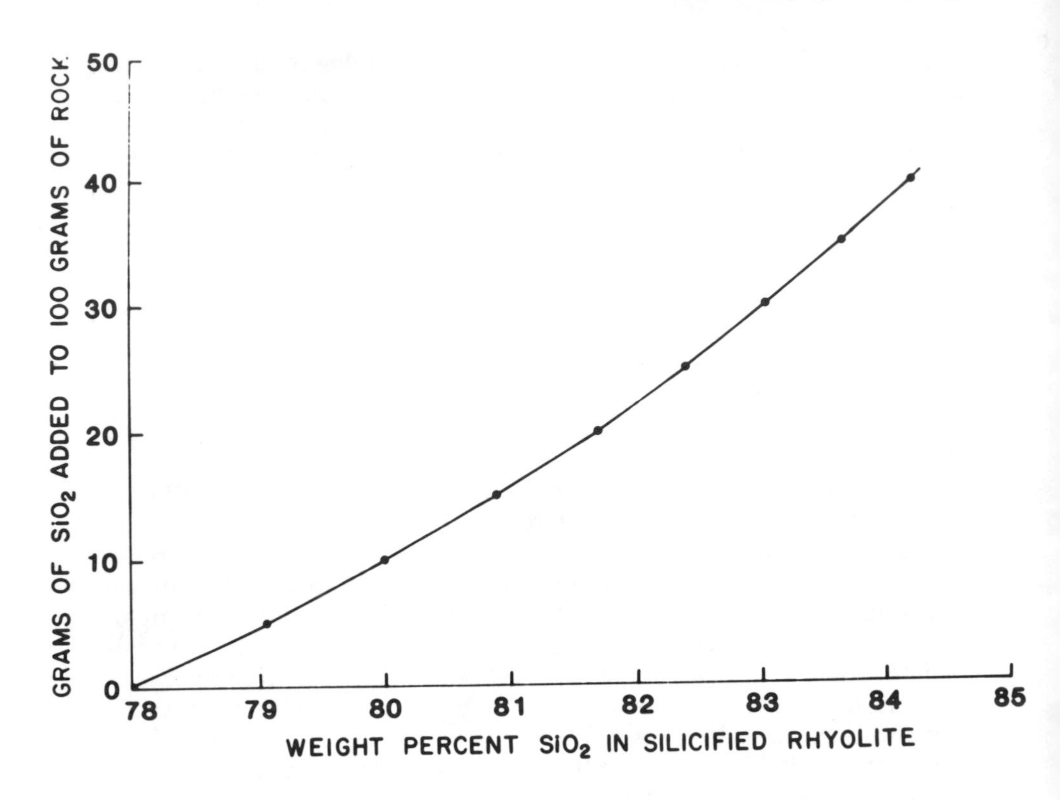

FIGURE 3. Silica perturbation diagram for a rock containing 78% of SiO_2.

chamber some 5 to 15 km below the surface, in proportions of about 60:40 (Tuttle and Bowen, 1958); (2) during ascent of the magma toward the surface, quartz becomes unstable and is resorbed, raising the SiO_2 content of the liquid; and (3) the phenocrysts also tend to settle out during ascent of the magma, but because quartz is dissolving and decreasing both in amount and grain size it does not settle out nearly as effectively as oligoclase. Loss of oligoclase causes the liquid to become further enriched in SiO_2 but depleted in Na_2O, CaO, Al_2O_3, and Eu. Thus, the primary liquid or glassy phase of the magma may become hypersiliceous by resorption of quartz and also by loss of oligoclase phenocrysts. These processes and the low-temperature deposition of silica minerals in voids in the rock thus in toto may give the 80-plus percentages of SiO_2 in the Saipan rhyolite.

The other aspect of the generation of these island-arc rhyolitic magmas involves formation of a primary magma of some 76 to 78% SiO_2 content. Most petrologists consider that these magmas are formed in the crust, because such compositions in the mantle would react with olivine to produce pyroxene. Two general processes could produce rhyolitic liquid: (1) Fractional crystallization of andesitic liquid, in which plagioclase, pyroxene, magnetite, hornblende, or other mineral phases are precipitated from the liquid and thereby make it more siliceous; or (2) partial melting of a basaltic or andesitic rock, where the heat of melting would be supplied by a nearby intrusive mass of mantle-derived gabbroic or dioritic magma. At the present time our knowledge of fractionation and melting processes in the lower and intermediate crust of oceanic island arcs is very sketchy, and the calculation of quantitative models of generation would be premature. However, knowledge of the various types of island-arc magmatic rocks—ranging from basalt to rhyolite and including such varieties as the highly magnesian boninite-series rocks—is increasing at a gratifying rate. In the next several years we may have reasonable schemes of origin of the low-K rhyolite of island arcs.

The volcanic rocks of Guam range in composition from basalt to low-K rhyolite, but—as in most sequences of island-arc volcanic rocks—andesite and dacite are predominant. These rocks are of Eocene, Oligocene, and Miocene age, ranging in age from slightly more than 40 to about 10 m.y. The geologic history of the Mariana Islands is complex, involving seafloor spreading of back-arc type. The account by Crawford et al. (1981) presents the present state of understanding of this history. Prior to about 45 m.y. ago the Pacific plate moved in a north-northwest direction in the west-central Pacific Ocean, and the Mariana Islands, Palau, and the other island chains along the eastern and southeastern margins of the Philippine Sea did not exist. About or just after 45 m.y. ago, however, the Pacific plate changed its direction of motion, or spreading direction, to its present westward one. Old, cool oceanic crust was subducted westward under younger, warm oceanic crust. A great island arc, the ancestral Palau-Kyushu arc, and the associated back-arc basin, the Philippine Sea, were formed. Volcanism in this Palau-Kyushu arc occurred from about 42 to 34 m.y. ago. The arc then was fractured along its crest and spread apart in an east-west direction, as deduced by Karig (1971, 1975). The western fragment is preserved as the Palau-Kyushu Ridge, which is volcanically inactive. The eastern segment experienced further volcanism from about 20 to 11 m.y. ago, in late Oligocene and Miocene time, and rocks of this age are preserved both on Guam and in the submarine West Mariana Ridge. In a second rifting event this late Oligocene-Miocene volcanic ridge broke apart, forming the Mariana Trough. The low-K rhyolite of the Sankakuyama Formation of Saipan formed in the ancestral Palau-Kyushu island arc. Rocks of this early arc are represented on Guam by the Alutom Formation (Tracey et al., 1964; Stark, 1963). This unit consists mostly of marine pyroclastic flows and volcanigenic mudstone, sandstone, and conglomerate. The younger, late Oligocene-Miocene volcanism produced the Umatac Formation of Guam, which consists of interbedded massive volcanic flows, pyroclastic rocks, limestone, mudstone, sandstone, and conglomerate. Rocks of the Alutom Formation are intensely faulted and show mild folding—largely as a result of the splitting apart of the ancestral Palau-Kyushu island arc, whereas rocks of the Umatac Formation are cut by only a few faults and are not folded (Tracey et al., 1964).

The volcanic rocks of Guam are largely of submarine emplacement and they were subjected to chemical alteration by hot seawater. Since then, they have been at or close to sea level, and so have been affected by submarine and subaerial weathering and by groundwaters passing through them. Thus, samples sufficiently fresh for geochemical studies are rare. Both Stark (1963) and I were forced to collect samples of boulders found in pyroclastic breccia of the Alutom Formation. I obtained 10 samples of these clasts, so my suite consists of dense, strong flow rocks and one diabasic dike from the walls of a volcanic conduit. Position of individual samples in the volcanic stratigraphy, of course, is not known, but such a suite is valuable for geochemical analysis. These clasts are not weathered, but they may have been affected by seawater alteration. Such alteration cannot be determined unequivocally because the samples range from 50.1 to 73.8% SiO_2. In such a range elemental abundances also undergo changes by crystal-liquid fractionation, mixing of magmas of differing compositions, or other mechanisms. I also collected two wave-washed and fresh samples of feeder dikes of the Facpi Volcanic Member of the Umatac Formation from Facpi Point. The flow member of the Dandan Formation of the Umatac Formation also was sampled; like many other basaltic flows subjected to tropical weathering, this rock is much fresher than associated, more siliceous rocks.

Of the 10 Alutom samples 3 are of andesitic to allied dacitic compositions (SiO_2 at 60.7 to 64.2%); these contain 5.6 to 5.9% MgO and 255 to 380 ppm Cr; such abundances indicate affinity to the boninite series or magnesian andesites. The 1 sample of basalt in this suite, G-7, contains 7.5% MgO and 355 ppm Cr, which are typical of normal arc rocks. The remaining 6 samples show anomalously high Cr but normal MgO concentrations. There is a possibility that mixing of two types of magma was involved in the Alutom rocks: a normal suite of basaltic-andesitic-dacitic magmas and a boninitic (or high-magnesian), andesitic magma contains Cr-rich phenocrysts of orthopyroxene and/or chromian spinel. Further petrologic and chemical studies of the Alutom samples are needed.

The two new samples of the Facpi Volcanic Member of the Umatac Formation are basaltic andesites: G-8 contains 52.8% SiO_2 and G-9 54.5%. G-8 shows 6.0% MgO and 160 ppm Cr, whereas G-9 shows 7.9% MgO and 430 ppm Cr. Thus, G-9 exhibits affinity with boninite-series rocks, whereas G-8 is of normal calc-alkaline type. The major-element analyses by Stark (1963) of andesites of the Facpi Member also show a dichotomy; 4 samples are highly magnesian (MgO = 7.5 to 10%), 4 are of much lower MgO content (3 to 5%), and 1 is intermediate. Thus we apparently have an example here of essentially simultaneous eruption of both normal and boninitic magmas. Well-documented examples of such magmatism have appeared recently in the literature—e.g., at Shido-Shima Island, southwestern Japan, these contrasting types of magma were extruded almost simultaneously about 11 m.y. ago (Tatsumi and Ishizaka, 1982). Most workers now agree that the boninitic or magnesian andesites are primary melts of relatively wet mantle, whereas the normal basalts and andesites of island arcs are generated in two steps—partial melting of relatively dry mantle to produce basaltic liquid, followed by fractionation to andesite and often dacite and tryolite.

The timing and location of boninite-series magmas in oceanic island arcs remains a matter of controversy. Crawford et al. (1981), on the one hand, contend that early arc magmatism is strictly of normal (low MgO) type, and that magnesian andesite forms only at a late stage, when the arc is breaking apart and ocean-ridge–type basalts are about to erupt. Further work on Guam, however, may show that boninitic andesites were erupted in the early or ancestral Palau-Kyushu island arc.

REFERENCES

Barker, Fred; Arth, Joseph G.; Peterman, Zell E.; and Friedman, Irving
1976. The 1.7- to 1.8-b.y.-old trondhjemites of southwestern Colorado and northern New Mexico: Geochemistry and depths of genesis. Bull. Geol. Soc. Amer., vol. 87, pp. 189-198.

Crawford, Anthony J.; Beccaluva, L.; and Serri, G.
1981. Tectono-magmatic evolution of the West Philippine-Mariana region and the origin of boninites. Earth Planet. Sci. Lett., vol. 54, pp. 346-356.

Ewart, Anthony
1979. A review of the mineralogy and chemistry of Tertiary-Recent dacitic, latitic, rhyolitic, and related salic volcanic rocks. Pp. 13-121 *in* "Trondhjemites, Dacites, and Related Rocks," F. Barker, Ed. Elsevier, Amsterdam.

Karig, Daniel E.
1971. Origin and development of marginal basins in the western Pacific. Journ. Geophys. Res., vol. 76, pp. 2542-2561.
1975. Basin genesis in the Philippine Sea. Pp. 857-879 *in* "Initial Reports of the Deep Sea Drilling Project," vol. 31.

National Geographic Society
1981. Atlas of the World, Fifth Ed. National Geographic Society, Washington, D. C.

Schmidt, Robert G.
1957. Geology of Saipan, Mariana Islands. Part 2. Petrology and Soils, Chapter B. Petrology of the Volcanic Rocks. U. S. Geol. Survey Prof. Pap. 280-B, pp. 127-206.

Stark, John T.
1963. Petrology of the volcanic rocks of Guam. U. S. Geol. Survey Prof. Pap. 403-C, 32 pp.

Tatsumi, Yoshiyuki, and Ishizaka, Kyoichi
1982. Magnesian andesite and basalt from Shodo-Shima Island, southwest Japan, and their bearing on the genesis of calc-alkaline andesites. Lithos, vol. 15, pp. 161-172.

Tracey, Joshua I., Jr.; Schlanger, Seymour O.; Stark, John T.; Doan, David G.; and May, Harold G.
1964. General geology of Guam. U. S. Geol. Survey Prof. Pap. 403-A, 104 pp.

Tuttle, Orville F., and Bowen, Norman L.
1958. Origin of granite in light of experimental studies in the system $NaAlSi_3O_8$-$KAlSi_3O_8$-SiO_2-H_2O. Geol. Soc. Amer. Mem. 74, 153 pp.

Fred Barker

Early Nomads in Southern Sinai

Grant Recipient: Ofer Bar-Yosef, Institute of Archaeology, Hebrew University, Jerusalem, Israel.

Grant 1671: In support of a study of the origins of pastoralism in southern Sinai.

Introduction

Many scholars have dealt with the problem of the origins of farming societies in the Levant. In their constant efforts to give an answer to the question of "where" and "how," they have conducted their fieldwork mainly in the Mediterranean valleys and the hilly flanks of the northern Levant (Braidwood, 1972; Cauvin, 1978). Little attention was paid to the arid zones. The documented observation that during historic periods the desertic areas were inhabited by pastoralists—as they are today—has brought up the question, in recent years, as to the origins of these pastoralists as well as to their relationship with contemporary agricultural societies.

The rapidly accumulating data in the Near East concerning the origins of the farming societies can be summarized briefly in a schematic framework as follows (Flannery, 1972; Braidwood, 1972, 1975; Redman, 1978; Cauvin 1978; Bar-Yosef, in press).

PHASE A (17,000-10,000 B.C.)

During the Late Pleistocene, micro-bands of hunter-gatherers occupied most of the regions of the Levant and expanded during 12,500-10,000 B.C. into the deserts, following a climatic amelioration. Their sites were small and the material culture was characterized by microlithic flint industries, scarce bone tools, and pounding tools.

PHASE B (10,000-8300 B.C.)

Formation of macro-bands took place in both the hilly and valley terrains of the Levant. Their economy was based on hunting and intensive vegetal food collection, evidenced archeologically by the large assemblages of animal bone, numerous pounding tools, and sickle blades. Rounded houses, burials, bone industry, art objects, shell beads, etc., are common in base-camps. Several of these campsites are considered as year-round settlements.

Contemporary micro-bands of hunter-gatherers exploited adjacent semiarid and arid regions.

PHASE C (8300-7300 B.C.)

Early Neolithic settlements were established in the favorable habitats of the Levant, continuing the previously started process of sedentation. Within large sites (1 to 2 ha in size) rounded structures, burials, grinding stones, sickle blades, arrowheads, and axes are among the commonest attributes of material culture. Goats and sheep were domesticated in the northern Levant. Scarce botanical remains indicate incipient agriculture.

Contemporary micro-bands in both the semiarid regions and the mountainous areas carried on basically the same way of life as their predecessors in these habitats.

PHASE D (7300-6000 B.C.)

During this time unit, known in the southern Levant as Pre-Pottery Neolithic B, large settlements provide evidence of the presence of domesticated goats and sheep, wheat, barley, and legumes. The architectural innovations are expressed in the appearance of rectangular houses with plaster floors. Common attributes are burials, plastered skulls, flint axes and adzes, arrowheads shaped by pressure flaking, increase in obsidian trade, etc.

Within the arid zones micro-bands of hunter-gatherers continued their nomadic way of life while adopting the grinding stones from the contemporary farming societies. The nature of the vegetal food resource for which they used the grinding stones is yet unknown. Moreover, the question of whether they adopted the domesticated goat was one of our research goals in the project reported here.

This was more or less the current state of research in early 1976, when the project to focus on the early nomads of southern Sinai was formulated. The understanding of the nature of desertic human adaptations during the Late Pleistocene and the very early Holocene was just emerging from intensive fieldwork carried out in the Negev and northern Sinai (Marks, 1976, 1977; Phillips and Bar-Yosef, 1974; Bar-Yosef and Phillips, 1977).

The aims of our newborn project in 1976 can, therefore, be summarized as follows: (1) To investigate the remains of Neolithic societies, to recognize and define their economic basis, and to uncover their archeological aspects that may be interpreted as expressions of seasonal movements. (2) To study briefly the remains of later populations and especially of those who had left the built-up tombs known as *nawamis.* (3) To collect comparative data concerning the organization of Bedouin campsites in the higher mountains of Sinai, and the arrangements within the tents of both summer and winter camps.

The choice of southern Sinai as a research area was a consequence of the following two factors: (1) This is a geographic region with special topo-climatic features; and (2) there was an urgent necessity in conducting emergency excavations in sites endangered by civil development and building activities of the local inhabitants.

Fieldwork lasted from April 1976 to May 1979, for 21 weeks, and in many instances under unfavorable weather conditions. No surveys were carried out because the main intention was to collect the maximum amount of information concerning each excavated or tested site. Four Neolithic sites were fully excavated, amounting to about 850 m^2, and four others were partially tested. Two other later sites were intensively exposed and about 15 *nawamis* and other tombs were dug up; 400 Bedouin deserted tents were recorded, mostly in the higher mountains of Sinai. The following pages describe briefly the major results of the project, following a short summary of the special geographical features of southern Sinai.

The Study Area

Southern Sinai represents only a portion of the whole peninsula, but it possesses its own special characteristics. Although Sinai is a planetaric desert, the climate in the northern part is influenced and ameliorated by the Mediterranean. There, limestone anticlines emerge from sandy areas and Mediterranean plant relicts indicate a wetter climate during the Late Pleistocene.

The central part of Sinai is basically a flat plateau, drained by the many tributaries of Wad el-Arish and dominated by a dry desertic climate. Isolated *Pistacia atlantica* trees indicate a past connection with the Irano-Turanian vegetation of the higher Negev. The sedimentary escarpment of Gebel El-Tih, Gebel Igma, and Gebel Gunna delineates the border with southern Sinai.

The southern portion of the peninsula, triangular in shape, is 17,000 km^2 in area and is composed of a strip of Nubian sandstone plateau and magmatic rocky terrain. Topographically the crystalline area reaches elevations in excess of 2000 m, such as Gebel Katherina (2642 m) and Gebel Umm Shumar (2586 m). The valley floors of this region lie at 1000 to 1600 m above sea level. To the east the mountains drop sharply into the Gulf of Eilath and to the west into a low lying basin known as El-Qa'a, forming the coastal plain of the Gulf of Suez.

The climate of southern Sinai is basically cold and dry in winter, with infrequent rain and snow. The summer is hot and dry. Precipitation is erratic and never exceeds 75 mm per annum though variations occur, with greater quantities in the higher mountainous areas. Apart from general extreme diurnal and seasonal differences in temperature, elevation is also an important factor.

The vegetation of the region is represented by Sudanese elements in the coastal portions of the Rift Valley, Saharo-Arabian associations in the Nubian Sandstone strip, and Irano-Turanian vegetation up to 1300 m above sea level in the central region. The high mountains above 1600 m are vegetated with steppic and relict Alpine-Tragacantic elements.

The fauna of southern Sinai forms an even more variegated mosaic than the vegetation. Mammals are of desertic, tropical, steppic, or Palearctic origins. Common are the gerbil, hystrix, dormouse, fox, and hare. The ibex and the wolf are rare today, the result of intensive hunting. Leopards were more frequent in the past, as attested by stone-built traps that are often found around passes.

Birds and reptiles are mainly of desertic and tropical origins although two Mediterranean species, the partridge and a spotted lizard, are also found.

The Neolithic Sites

The excavated Neolithic sites (Fig. 1) can be divided into two categories: (1) sites with small closed structures made of built-up walls which are reminiscent of the winter Bedouin tents (Wadi Jibba I and II, Wadi Tbeik); (2) sites with either flimsy large structures, accompanied by silos and numerous grinding stones, or small sites in natural shelters with the same tool kit (Ujrat el Mehed, Abu Madi I and III).

Brief reports of each of the major excavations are given below.

Wadi Jibba I and II

These two sites are located at the foothills of Gebel Sirbal (2070 m) on an alluvial fan, about 300 to 350 m above sea level, 25 km from the shores of the Gulf of Suez, on the edges of the El-Qa'a.

Wadi Jibba I (Fig. 2) is a small site comprised of six built-up structures (2.5 to 3.5 m in diameter) attached to each other, forming a linear campsite. It was totally excavated and only in one structure was evidence for architectural modification uncovered. All the visible entrances lead to an open space which provided numerous lithics. Each structure has a wall 0.60 to 1.00 m wide built up to 0.50 to 0.80 m high but the collapsed stones indicated an original height of 1.00 to 1.30 m. Besides several dozens of arrowheads, denticulated blades, and very few grinding stones *(manos),*

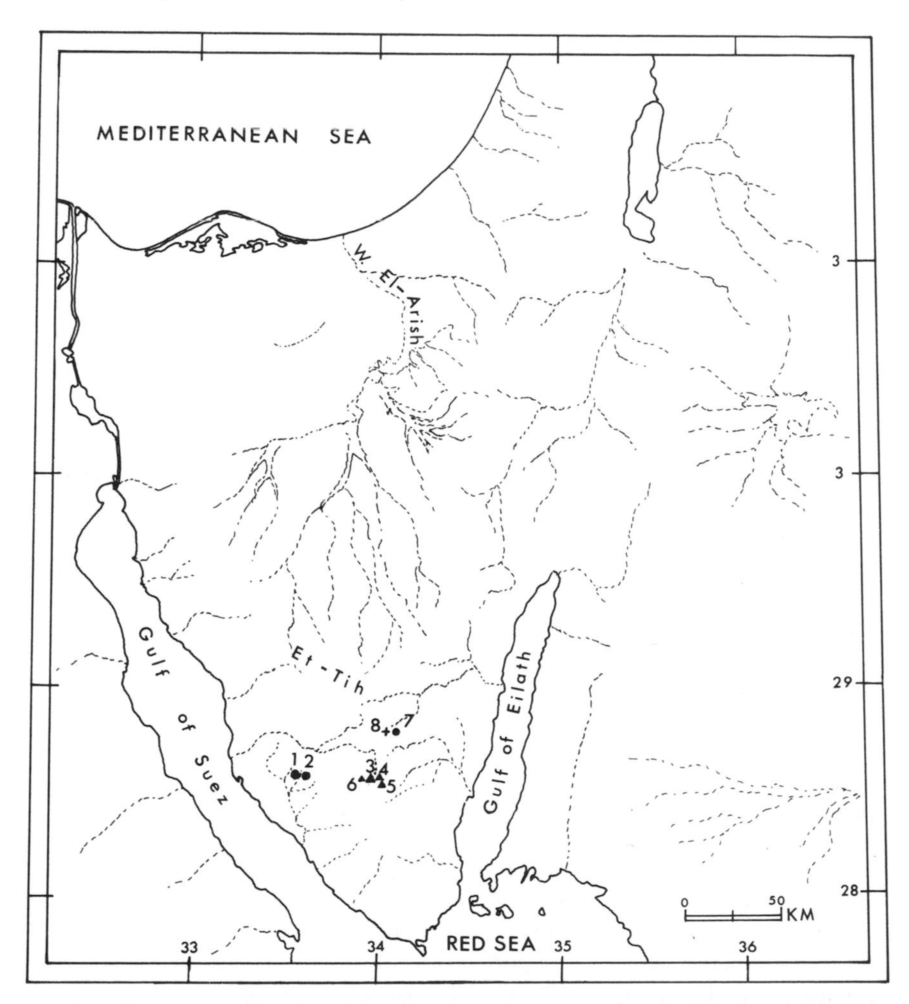

FIGURE 1. Location map of Sinai showing the sites excavated by the expedition: 1. Wadi Jibba I. 2. Wadi Jibba II. 3. Ujrat el Mehed. 4. Abu Madi I. 5. Abu Madi III. 6. "Bananah II." 7. Wadi Tbeik. 8. nawamis near Gebel Gunna.

the assemblage was rich in debitage, the waste of flint workshops. No bones were preserved.

The neighboring site, Wadi Jibba II, is larger than the former. The few excavated structures are similar to those of Wadi Jibba I, both in the way they were built and in their contents (numerous lithic artifacts, scarce grinding stones, badly preserved bones).

The lithic industry of these sites is dominated by arrowheads, mostly of leaf-shaped form made by pressure flaking. The relatively scarce seashells were brought from the Red Sea. Both sites might be interpreted as winter camps owing to their size of structures, thickness of walls, scarcity of grinding tools, and lack of silos.

Wadi Tbeik

This site is located on the left bank of a small gully of a tributary of Wadi Tbeik. The area of the site encompasses ca. 250 m^2 and its structures were built up on an east-facing moderate slope from the gully bed upslope, without reaching the highest portion of the topographic spur. A few isolated structures were found on the other bank of the gully and are of special interest.

The Neolithic people dug the lower parts of their structures into the deteriorated, fragmented metamorphic bedrock and used adjacent sandstone slabs as building material.

The site has a beehive plane and it appears as if each living unit comprised a small open court, built of upright sandstone slabs, and a closed room with walls 40 to 60 cm thick. The interior faces of these walls were constructed of similarly placed upright slabs, while the outer faces were built with horizontally laid smaller stones. Stratigraphic analysis indicates that, although the site was occupied for a long duration, no more than 4 to 5 units were inhabited during each phase.

All the structures were filled with ashes mixed with sand, creating a soft sediment that apparently was comfortable for sleeping. Only 4 stone-lined hearths were uncovered, but many burnt stones were noticed elsewhere.

The lithic industry is characterized by bipolar cores and the production of blades. The selected blades were shaped into a limited repertoire of arrowhead types, mainly with retouched tang and shoulders. Other blades were used as saws or perforators. A few end-scrapers were also encountered. The proportion between the debitage and the shaped tools indicates that flint knapping was one of the activities that took place in Wadi Tbeik. The flint nodules originate from the top of the Gebel Gunna escarpment about 3 km away.

Grinding stones are rare at this site and comprise only a few *manos* and flat grinding bowls. Preliminary identification of the bones indicates a dominance of ibex and hare with rare gazelle, wild ass, and birds. Many seashells were brought from the Red Sea for the manufacture of beads and pendants.

Ujrat el-Mehed

The site is situated on top of an elongated shallow hill at the wide-opening junction of Wadi ed-Deir and the flat valley known as Sahel er-Rahha (the Biblical "Plain of the Encampment"). Located about 1600 m

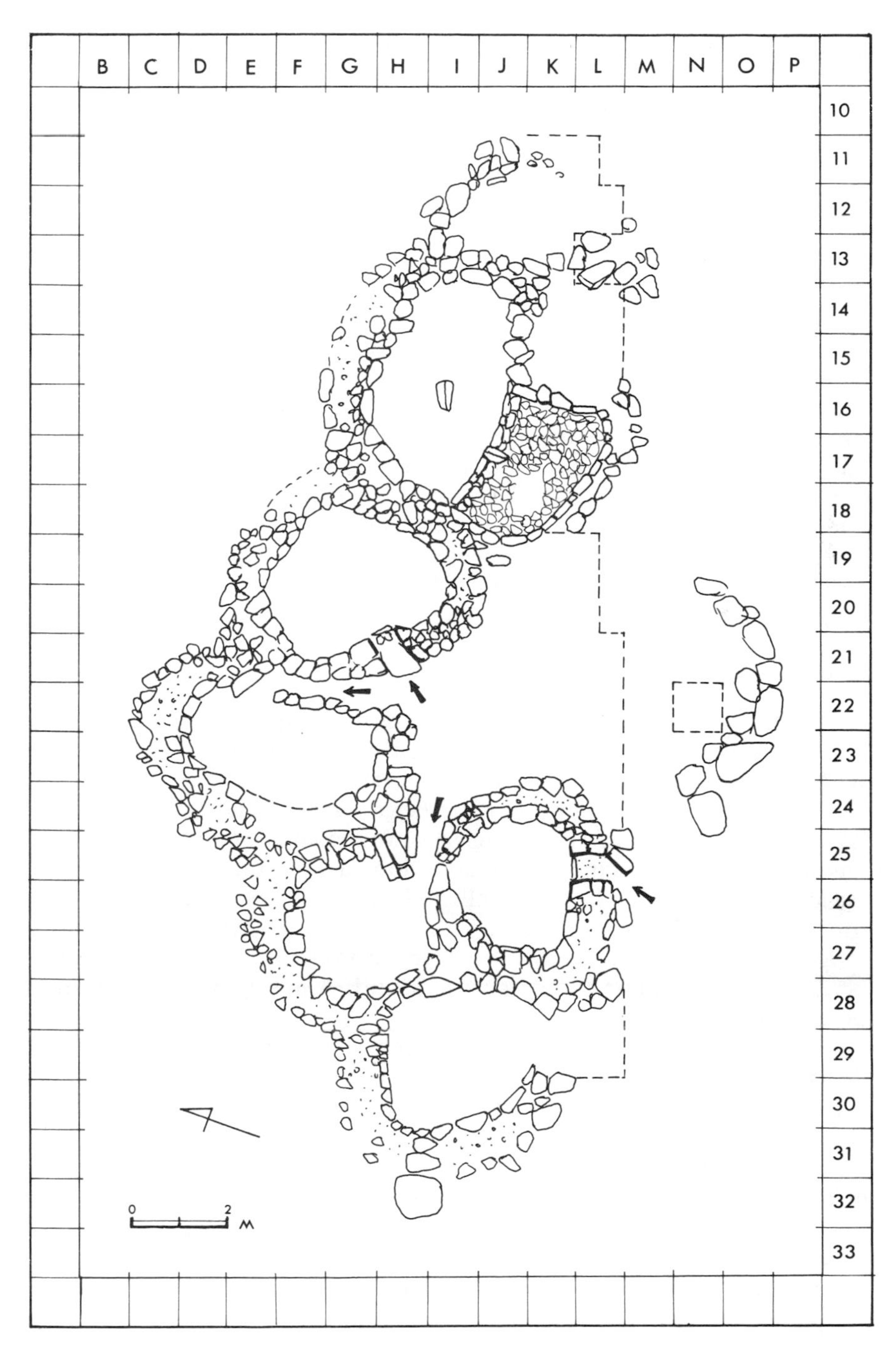

FIGURE 2. Plan of the excavations at Wadi Jibba I, showing the different loci and their entrances.

above sea level, winter habitation would have been impossible, since even today, harsh freezing winds blow through the valley.

The excavation presently extending over an area of 160 m^2 has uncovered the remains of three complete double semicircular structures, 4.5 and 6 m in diameter. Each structure was dug into the ground (20 to 50 cm deep) and then a single course of upright flat granite cobbles collected in the vicinity was laid, forming the wall. Seven silos were exposed, each about 1.0 to 1.2 m in diameter.

The structures contained the deposit of sand mixed with ashes and small burnt stones. The lithic industry was rather poor in debitage, and cores, especially, are extremely rare. It appears that most of the flint blades were brought as final products from the closest source (perhaps Gebel Gunna which lies ca. 30 km away). The tools mostly comprise arrowheads, dominated by leaf-shaped pressure-flaked forms. Denticulated blades, a few scrapers, and burins are also present. Numerous grinding stones were found within the excavated area. The *manos* were mainly made of local metamorphic rock as were the grinding bowls.

Animal bones were mainly of ibex, and Red Sea shells were used for making beads and pendants. One Mediterranean shell indicates long-range exchange, as yet not fully understood.

Abu Madi I and III

About 6 km north of Santa Katherina, in Wadi Sba'iyah, three Neolithic sites were found following their partial distribution by a Bedouin, who used their deposits as building material.

Two sites could have been a subject for systematic excavations. At Abu Madi I the Neolithic people used a broken large granite boulder as a major support for erecting their habitation. It was comprised of an oval structure (4 m in diameter), a small enclosure (between the two parts of the boulder), a kitchen area, and a silo. Arrowheads with shoulders and a tang and denticulated blades were the dominant tool type. Unused blades were scarce and no cores were found. A few grinding tools completed the small tool kit.

Abu Madi III was a small rock shelter created by a huge granite boulder, used by the local people in recent years as a summer habitation. The excavated 18 m^2 provided more than 100 arrowheads (mainly of the leaf-shaped form made by pressure flaking), denticulated blades, and scarce debitage. Numerous Red Sea shells and a relatively large number of grinding stones were collected at the site.

These two sites, as well as another small site, yet only partially excavated (near Ujrat el Mehed), are considered to be small family summer camps containing basically the same elements as Ujrat el Mehed.

The Nawamis *Near Gebel Gunna*

A group of 15 *nawamis* was located by us during a preliminary survey, some 6 km west of the Neolithic site of Wadi Tbeik. The *nawamis* are clustered at the foot of Ras el-Gunna on a dissected Nubian sandstone terrain.

With the exception of minor variations they are almost identical in all respects to the *nawamis* previously excavated by us at Ein Huderah (Bar-Yosef et al., 1977). Thus they are all constructed of locally available sandstone slabs and the entrances all face west. Construction is perhaps less well executed overall than at Ein Huderah and on occasion circular foundation platforms were built prior to construction of the *nawamis* itself. Entrances were identical in technique to those at Ein Huderah.

Unfortunately, the problem of the burial technique employed remains unresolved, in part due to poor bone preservation. Secondary interment appears to be well documented, as at Ein Huderah, but the possibility of primary burial is still unclear.

The grave goods placed with the burials present an almost identical repertoire to those recovered from Ein Huderah, although variations in quantity occur from *nawamis* to *nawamis*. These include transverse arrowheads and fan scrapers on flint, quartz flakes, copper pins, and bone tools. Beads were made of faience, carnelian, bone, ostrich eggshell, and various Red Sea shells. But shell bracelets and mother-of-pearl spacers were missing. The overall impression thus gained from the Gebel Gunna group is identical to that at Ein Huderah, similarly located on a major path leading to central Sinai or the Gulf of Eilath.

The habitation site Gunna 25 is of great significance. Situated ca. 2 km to the east of the *nawamis*, it consists of a large courtyard with several circular structures attached, two isolated stone circles, and a square construction containing four small silos, each ca. 1 m in diameter. Limited excavations brought to light transverse arrowheads, fan scrapers, seashell beads, and pottery, permitting correlation with the same general culture of the *nawamis*. Radiocarbon dates from Gunna 25 and a similar habitation structure placed on top of the Neolithic site of Wadi Tbeik were as follows: Gunna 25, 2106 ± 72 B.C. SMU-658; Wadi Tbeik, structure 100, 2423 ± 64 B.C. SMU-659.

The preliminary conclusions are that the local pastoralists of southern Sinai lasted probably from the 5th through the 3rd millennia B.C. and during a certain phase of their history built up the *nawamis* as burial places. Mortuary practices might change quite rapidly (Ucko, 1969) and it seems that some other burial sites, like the tumuli might represent the graves of these nomads. Their material culture, studied from habitation sites in central Sinai and the southern Negev, was given the name of Timnaian (Kosloff, 1972-1973).

The Bedouin Camps

Among the Bedouin tribes of southern Sinai it is the Gebeliyah who inhabit the higher mountains.

The Gebeliyah have both winter and summer camps, each composed of a small group of families. During winter they camp in a sheltered gully or a topographic depression seeking locations protected from the harsh, cold winds (Fig. 3). Inside their tents they build a low wall made of local undressed stones in order to insulate the tent for the sake of both the goats and the occupants. Additional higher walls protect the entrance and also veil activities conducted inside the tent. In mid-May they move to their summer camp, frequently located only 100 to 300 m away in the open valley. The summer camp is a cluster of simple shelters, commonly erected with wooden poles and covered with branches and canvas. The goats are kept outside in a small attached enclosure. Some families go up to the higher, narrower valleys (sometimes to a small flat vale known as *farsh* in Arabic) where they own small tree-gardens *(bustans)*. In early or mid-October, after the harvest season and when temperatures begin to drop, they return to the protected wadis and erect their winter camps, either in the same place as previously, or in a new, cleaner spot.

This kind of transhumance is also common to several other tribes in southern Sinai, although only the Gebeliyah leave behind numerous built-up structures.

Summary

While laboratory work is still in progress it seems to be too early to present detailed results. A general résumé of the project should stress the following points:

a. A number of important Neolithic sites and *nawamis* were salvaged from further damage.

b. The archeological potentials of the Neolithic sites in southern Sinai, to be interpreted in terms of seasonal campsites, were demonstrated. Further work should enable the delineation of certain social territories, indicating the seasonal move of more accurately defined micro-bands.

c. The earliest pastoralists, or Bedouins, as a social phenomenon in Sinai emerged only in post–Pre-Pottery Neolithic times, i.e., during the 5th millennium. The adoption of grinding tools in the Neolithic and the goat at a later date indicates the rate of diffusion from the favorable regions to the marginal ones at that part of the Levant.

d. There is an interesting correlation in the process of adaptation expressed in building walls inside tents for winter time, between the Gebeliyah Bedouins who are limited in their territory to the higher mountains,

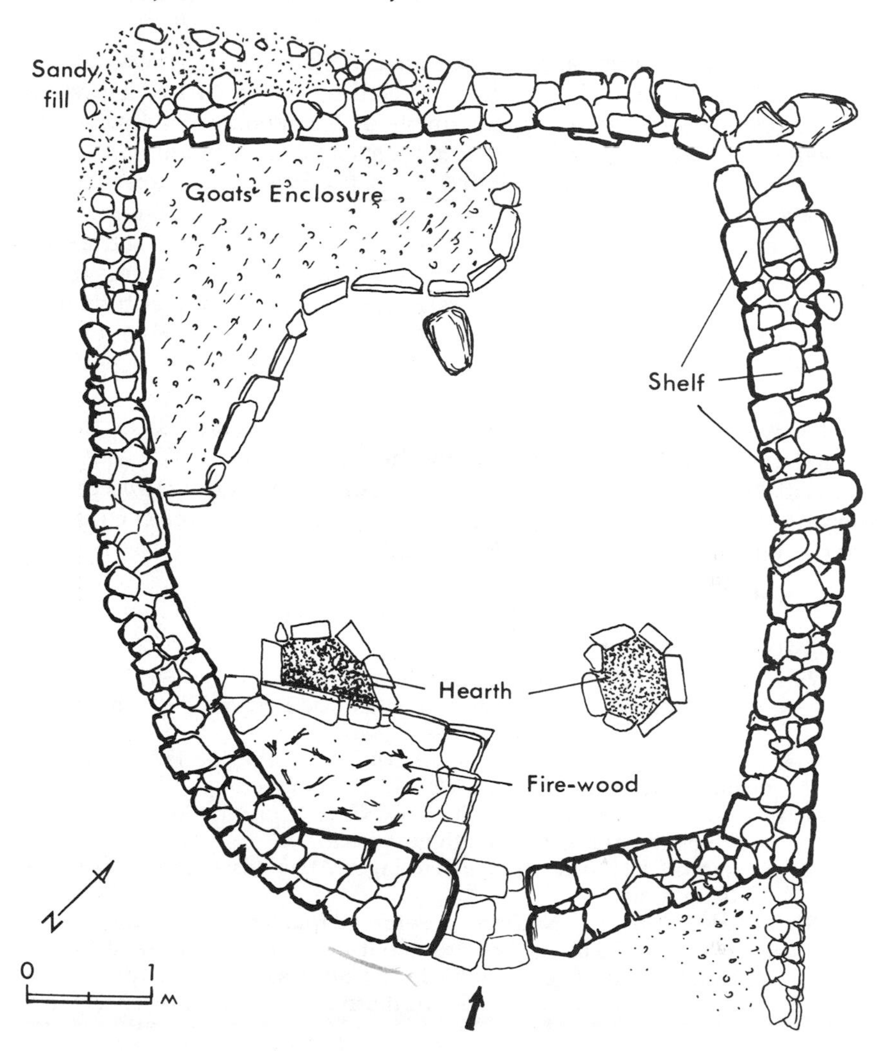

FIGURE 3. A plan of a Bedouin winter tent.

and the Neolithic micro-bands who had larger territories that were open for seasonal movement.

Acknowledgments

I am grateful to the following organizations and people who made the fieldwork of this project possible: The National Geographic Society, Washington, D. C.; The Civil Administration for the Development of

Southern Sinai (Haminhal Lepituh Merhav Shlomo); Earthwatch, Belmont, Massachusetts; Mr. J. Feldman, Dallas, Texas; Mr. N. Dreyffus, Los Angeles, California; and the Institute of Archaeology of the Hebrew University, Jerusalem. Without the enthusiasm and constant help of Mr. A. Goren, the Archaeological Staff Officer for Sinai, this project would not have been carried out. Mr. N. Goring-Morris, Mrs. A. Belfer, Mr. U. Baruch, and Mr. A. Goldberg helped enormously in conducting the excavations; Miss N. Goren and Mr. I. Herskovitz were my partners in the survey of Bedouin camps. Mr. I. Herskovitz is in charge of the study of all human remains; Prof. E. Tchernov and Dr. S. Davis, of the bone studies; Mr. H. Mienis, of the shells; and Mr. U. Baruch, of the palynological analyses.

I would like to thank the Israel Commission for Basic Research, who sponsored the laboratory work during the past 4 years.

Without the devotion and the enthusiasm of my students and the numerous volunteers who helped with the fieldwork, this project could not have been accomplished. I thank them all.

REFERENCES

Bar-Yosef, O.

1975. The Epi-Palaeolithic in Palestine and Sinai. Pp. 363-378 *in* "Problems in Prehistory: North Africa and the Levant," F. Wendorf and A. E. Marks, eds. SMU Press, Dallas.

1981a. From hunter to herder in southern Sinai. Pp. 156-157 *in* "Temples and High Places in Biblical Times," A. Biran, ed.

1981b. Neolithic sites in Sinai. Pp. 217-235, *in* "Contributions to the Environmental History of Southwest Asia," W. Frey and H. P. Uerpmann, eds. Beihette zum Tubinger Atlas des Vorderen Orientes, Reihe A, no. 8.

1981c. Palaeolithic and Neolithic desertic adaptations in the Sinai Peninsula. Pp. 35-61, *in* "Environment and Culture of Fossil Man in Asia," A. Ghosh, ed. 10th UISPP Congress, Mexico City.

1982. Pre-pottery Neolithic sites in southern Sinai. Biblical Archaeologist, vol. 45, pp. 9-12.

____. The Mediterranean Levantine Epi-Palaeolithic as the background to the "Neolithic Revolution." *In* "Origins of Agriculture and Technology: West or East Asia ?" P. Sorensen and P. Mortensen, eds. (In press.)

Bar-Yosef, O., and Phillips, J. L.

1977. Prehistoric investigations in Gebel Maghara, northern Sinai. "Qedem" 7, Monographs of the Institute of Archaeology, Hebrew University, Jerusalem, 269 pp.

Bar-Yosef, O.; Belfer, A.; Goren, A.; and Smith, P.

1977. The *nawamis* near Ein-Huderah (eastern Sinai). Israel Exploration Journ., vol. 27, pp. 65-88.

BRAIDWOOD, R.
1972. Prehistoric investigations in southwestern Asia. Proc. Amer. Phil. Soc., vol. 116, pp. 310-320.
1975. Prehistoric men, 213 pp. Eighth ed. Scott, Foresman & Co., Chicago, Illinois.
CAUVIN, J.
1978. Les premièrs villages de Syria-Palestine du IXéme au VIIème Millenaire avant J. C. Coll. de la Maison de l'Orient Mediterraneén Ancien, Lyon.
FLANNERY, K. V.
1972. The origins of the village as a settlement type in Mesoamerica and the Near East: A comparative study. Pp. 23-53 *in* "Man, Settlement and Urbanism," P. J. Ucko, R. Tringham, and G. W. Dimbleby, eds. Duckworth, London.
1973. The origins of agriculture. Annual Rev. Anthrop., vol. 2, pp. 271-310.
KOZLOFF, B.
1972-1973. A brief note on the lithic industries of Sinai. Museum Ha'aretz Yearbook, vol. 15/16, pp. 35-49.
MARKS, A. E., ed.
1976. Prehistory and paleoenvironments in the central Negev, Israel, vol. I, 383 pp. SMU Press, Dallas.
1977. Prehistory and paleoenvironments in the central Negev, Israel, vol. II, 356 pp. SMU Press, Dallas.
PHILLIPS, J. L. and BAR-JOSEF, O.
1974. Prehistoric sites near Nahal Lavan, western Negev, Israel. Paléorient, vol. 2, pp. 477-482.
REDMAN, C.
1978. The rise of civilization, 367 pp. Freeman, San Francisco.
UCKO, P. J.
1969. Ethnographical and archaeological interpretation of funerary remains. World Archaeol. vol. 1, pp. 262-280.

OFER BAR-YOSEF

Excavation of an 11th-Century Shipwreck at Serçe Liman, Turkey

Grant Recipient: George F. Bass, American Institute of Nautical Archaeology, and Texas A&M University, College Station, Texas.[1]

Grants 1607, 1897, 2066: For investigation, excavation, and restoration of a shipwreck with a cargo of glass located in Serçe Liman in 1973.

During the summers of 1977 through 1979 the Institute of Nautical Archaeology, again in collaboration with the National Geographic Society, excavated a shipwreck discovered in the course of its joint 1973 survey of the southwest Turkish coast (Bass, 1982).

The site had been described to the 1973 survey team by Mehmet Aşkin of Bozburun, a retired sponge diver who recalled seeing other divers bringing pieces of glass from the water about 75 m from the northeast shore of a small bay called Serçe Liman (Sparrow Harbor). An amphora and several glass fragments brought to the surface by the survey team suggested that the ship was Late Byzantine; Virginia Grace of the American School of Classical Studies at Athens identified the amphora as being probably from the 11th century A.D.

A wreck of the suspected date was important for the institute's study of the development of wooden hulls, especially if it could show whether by that date the change from ancient Greco-Roman "shell-first" construction techniques to modern "skeletal" construction had been completed. The Serçe Liman wreck was chosen for excavation also by the promise of what seemed to be at least a partial cargo of medieval glass.

Diving in 1977 began at the end of June, after a camp of tents and concrete-block buildings had been established on the nearest shore, and a 15-m wooden barge had been moored directly over the site, which lay at a depth of about 33 m. The barge held necessary compressors, air banks, diving equipment, and a double-lock recompression chamber. The excavation, additionally sponsored by Texas A&M University and the Corning Glass Works Foundation, continued through the first week of September.

[1] Co-authors are J. Richard Steffy and Dr. Frederick H. van Doorninck, Jr., both of the Institute (in 1978 its name was changed to "Institute of Nautical Archaeology") and of Texas A&M University.

Techniques of excavation were those developed during earlier National Geographic Society-sponsored projects in the eastern Mediterranean, mostly in the 1960s (Bass, 1963, 1966, 1968a, 1968b, 1970, 1974; Bass and van Doorninck, 1969; Katzev, 1970, 1980): polyvinyl chloride airlifts were used to remove sand overburden, an "underwater telephone booth" acted as a communications center and safety refuge near the site, and a rigid metal grid constructed over the wreck aided mapping. The use of the relatively new 15-mm underwater lens, however, allowed photomapping of the site without the use of tall photographic towers on the gridwork.

The ancient ship had landed at the base of a rocky slope and settled on her port bottom in sand, save for the after end of the keel, which came to rest on a rock outcropping (Fig. 1). The bottom of the hull, including the keel, was well preserved to the turn of the bilge. The port stern area survived from the waterline to the main wale, along with half of the sternpost. The stem was missing, only 2 m of keelson and ceiling remained, and surviving hull members above the turn of the bilge were limited to a few fragments. While the excavation yielded less than one fourth of the original hull mass, the distribution of surviving hull timbers was such that we were able to make an extensive study of the construction.

The hull had a keel made of elm, but was otherwise built of softwoods. The rocker-shaped keel was only 11 cm thick and 16 cm high. Most frames were 11 to 12 cm wide, and the center-to-center frame spacing varied from 25 cm to about 40 cm. Hull planking had a thickness of only 3.7 cm, while the wales were relatively heavy strakes whose thickness was nearly 15 cm. The keelson, which was the true backbone of the vessel, had a cross-sectional area which was twice that of the keel.

In 1977 the Serçe Liman hull was seen to have relied more heavily on its framing for strength than had earlier Mediterranean hulls which have been brought to light. It did not have the independently strong shell of Greco-Roman hulls with their many mortise-and-tenon joints, but its framing system was considerably stronger.

Anchors, cargo, and shipboard utensils mapped and raised in 1977 are described below, with those found in 1978.

A longer campaign in 1978, between early June and early October, was financed by the original sponsors and by the National Science Foundation and F. Alex Nason. The diving procedures and excavation techniques employed during the 1977 season were continued. Special techniques, however, were used in mapping and raising the hull remains, a primary objective of the second campaign. In preparing the hull remnants for photomapping, each hull member was labeled with a large, white plastic tag. Since much of the wood, particularly planking, was in a

FIGURE 1. Plan of site.

very fragile state and clearly would break into smaller pieces when removed, each potential fragment was tagged with a smaller, Dymo label legible in close-up photographs. Hull members, once mapped, were removed and placed in wooden trays that were constructed in various modular sizes at the camp as needed. The trays with their contents were transported in a large lifting box to shallow water and there repacked so that each would contain as much wood as possible. The hull remnants were then transported by ship to the Bodrum Museum within roughly 150 trays sealed in plastic tubing.

Conservation and eventual restoration of the hull are being conducted largely with the assistance of grants from the National Endowment for the Humanities. Over the period of a year following diving in 1978, the hull remnants were cleaned, catalogued, and drawn and photographed in detail. Volunteers Michael van Doorninck, Bülent Erdemoglu, John Frey, Nergis Günsenin, and Thomas Goedicke assisted in the preliminary study and conservation of wood and artifacts during the months immediately following excavation. Cleaning wood proved to be a major task, since much of it was heavily concreted with iron oxide from nails and anchors. Tiny air hammers were the most effective tools in removing these deposits and did not damage the underlying wood. Plans call for a reassembly of the hull remains for museum display after completion of their chemical conservation in polyethylene glycol, now completed.

Excavation was completed during a few weeks in July and August of 1979, when we dived from land rather than from a barge. The few remaining fragments of wood and glass, plotted and raised to the surface, filled out our picture of the wreck but did not change any of our tentative ideas about its construction or cargo.

The remainder of the academic year 1979-1980 was devoted to the study of the ship's cargo and other artifacts, undertaken with grants from the National Geographic Society, National Science Foundation, and Ashland Oil, Inc. For this work, Oguz Alpözen, director of the Bodrum Museum of Underwater Archaeology, assigned to us the largest of the towers of the castle of the Knights of St. John which houses the museum; mending and study of glass were on the bottom floor, and pottery was conserved and studied on the top. We also were allowed use of the museum's darkroom, conservation laboratory, and drafting rooms. Artifacts were conserved by Robyn Woodward, drawn by Netia Piercy and Sema Pulak, and photographed by Donald A. Frey.

A major task throughout the year was the sorting and preliminary mending of broken glass. Those involved in this were Dorothy Slane, Robert Adams, Lynn Waters, Ann Bass, Gordon Bass, Alan Bass, Bill Collins, Suzanne Biehl, Cemal Pulak, and Jay Rosloff.

After building necessary worktables and storage shelves, we

weighed and then emptied separately the contents from each of nearly 2000 plastic bags in which the glass had been collected on the seabed. Each bag had been labeled with a code that told which 50-cm square on the wreck had yielded the fragments inside. These code numbers were written on most glass fragments with pen and then covered with a thin coating of polyvinyl acetate to prevent the numbers from being worn off during subsequent handling.

We did not know how many, if any, joins we might find between shards. At first we were discouraged when we laid out on tables all fragments from one 50-cm square of the wreck and found virtually no joins. Then we decided on a different approach and divided all fragments from the wreck into 19 basic groups such as plain green, purple, amber, dimpled, purple dimpled, green-threaded, engraved, blue, and the like. Workspace was always a problem, as we were dealing with between half a million and a million fragments, but the acquisition later in the year of 30 chests of drawers from United States government excess property in Turkey provided 120 drawers which, lined with thin sheets of white foam rubber, allowed us to lay out in labeled drawers many of the basic categories and subcategories. Purple glass, for example, was divided into darker purple and lighter purple subcategories. Then the darker purple was divided into darker and lighter shades, with the resultant darkest subsubcategory divided into still darker and lighter groups. After many such divisions of tens of thousands of fragments of purple glass, we eventually would have 10 or 15 shards of exactly the same color and thickness, and these, coming originally from the same glass vessel, could be fitted together to form a nearly complete bowl, jar, bottle, or other shape.

During the course of the year we worked mainly with 3 categories of glass: green-threaded, plain dimpled, and purple dimpled. We were surprised to find that most of the fragments could be joined to one another, so that at the end of the year we had, for example, only a handful of purple dimpled shards remaining unmended on the tables. We had, by then, restored complete profiles of nearly a hundred vessels, almost all differing from one another. Joining shards from any one vessel often came from areas of the wreck separated by several meters, indicating that the broken glass cargo was thoroughly mixed before being put on board; we also learned, beyond any doubt, that few if any of the vessels had been complete when added to the cargo.

While glass sorting and mending continued in the spring, Cynthia J. Eiseman began a study of ceramic finds, assisted by Margaret Morden.

Continued conservation and recording of the ship and its contents will take many years before their full interpretation can be attempted, but we have reached some tentative conclusions about the merchantman and her final voyage.

A preliminary study of the hull remnants has already generated considerable information about the ship's dimensions, design, and construction. The hull had an overall length of ca. 15 m and a beam of ca. 5.2 m. It possessed a very flat bottom with no deadrise amidships and abruptly up-curving sides, bow, and stern. The lines were relatively simple throughout; the hold was extremely boxlike (Fig. 2).

The hull's construction is of considerable historical interest. Although essentially skeletal-built, only a few of its frames were initially erected before belts of planking were installed on the bottom and sides to determine the rest of the hull form. The rest of the framework was then fitted to this standing planking and the remainder of the planking added to it. The shipwright was still essentially shaping his hull with planks, although the framework was now the primary structure. The Serçe Liman ship is presently the earliest extant seagoing ship so constructed. Nautical archeological research in the Mediterranean in recent years, including National Geographic Society-sponsored work at Yassi Ada, Turkey, has yielded considerable evidence indicating that skeletal hull construction gradually evolved into being within the Mediterranean world out of the earlier Greco-Roman shell construction method, in which framing was installed within an already assembled shell of hull planking (van Doorninck, 1976, pp. 130-131). The emergence of skeletal building was to have important historical consequences, for it helped produce the ships that enabled Europe to explore and colonize other parts of the world.

The hull's framing pattern is noteworthy. It was reported initially that frames with short floors alternated with frames with long floors (Bass and van Doorninck, 1978, p. 122). This is not quite the case. Rather, all the floors had a short and a long arm. The short arm extended out almost to the turn of the bilge, while the long arm continued on through the bilge turn. Floors with their short arm on the port side alternated with floors with their long arm on the port side. The frames were completed by at least one futtock on either side of the hull. Futtocks overlapped floors or were scarfed to them. These joins frequently were left unfastened; the frames were not solidly fabricated units as were frames of later periods. Floors were only nailed and not in some instances bolted to the keel, as was earlier reported.

Remnants of the ship's rigging include two or three partially preserved pulley blocks and over a dozen pulley sheaves of several different sizes. A surviving halyard block and evidence provided by the keelson, floor timbers, and hull design presently suggest that the vessel sported two lateen-rigged masts.

It will be convenient at this early stage in the study of the ship's layout and the disposition of her contents to distinguish five general areas

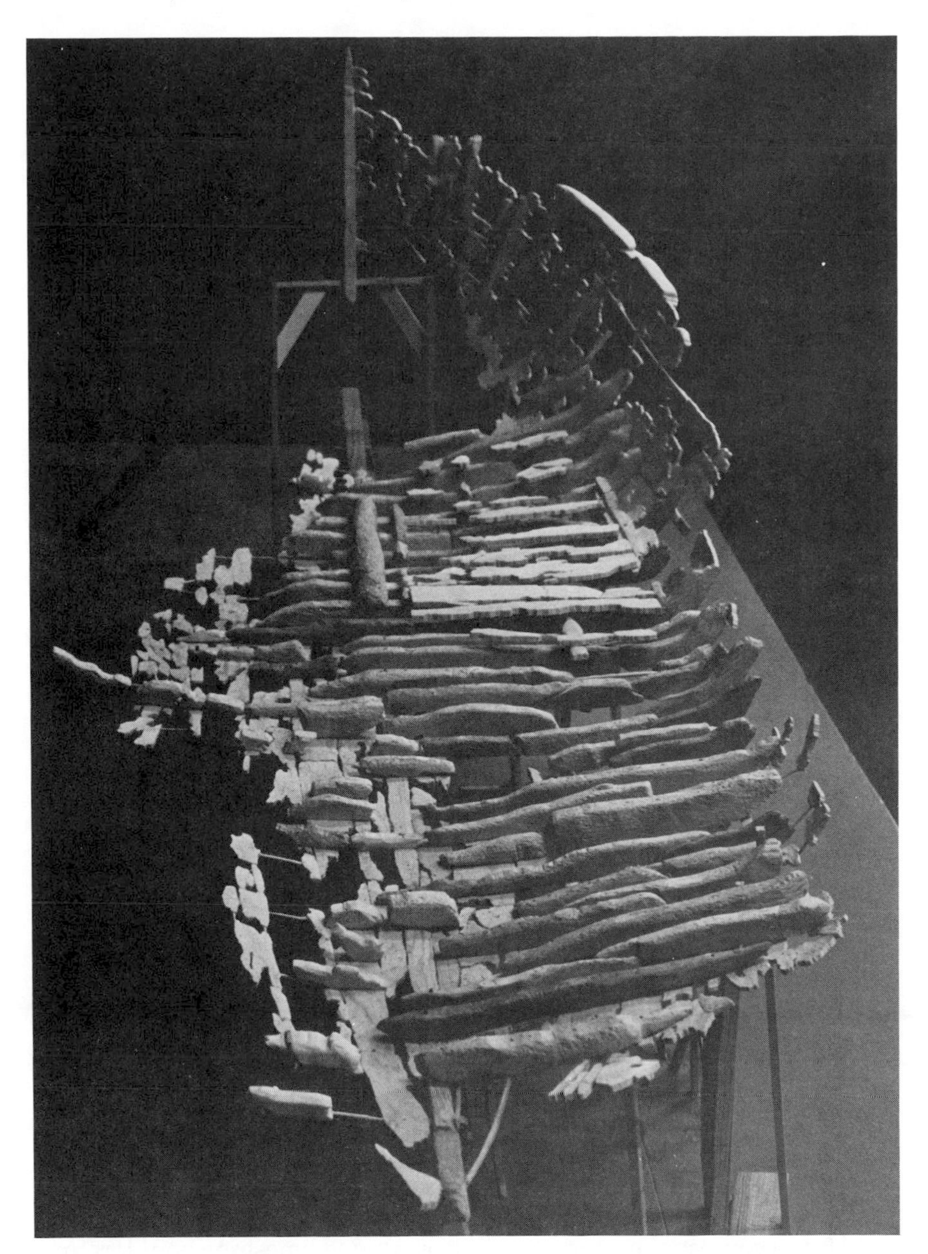

FIGURE 2. Reconstruction model of hull.

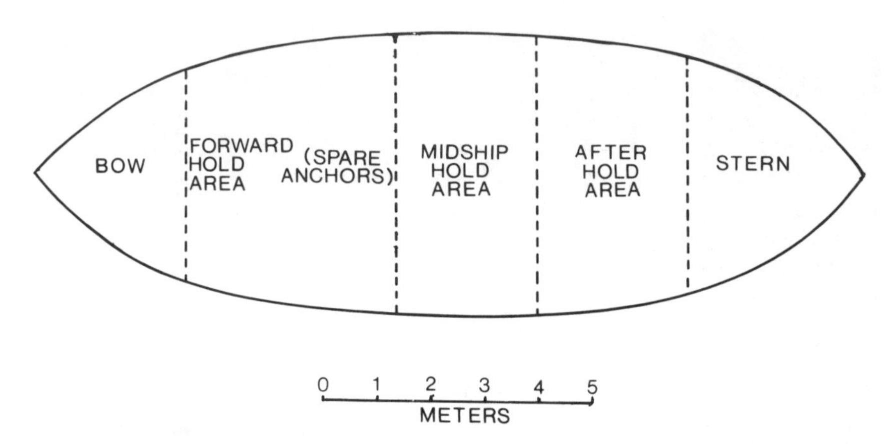

FIGURE 3. Schematic plan showing general disposition of artifacts within the hull.

within the hull: bow, stern, and forward, midship and after hold areas. The approximate extent of each area is schematically indicated in Figure 3. No evidence for decking has as yet been detected, but the integrity of the surviving hull structure seems to demand the longitudinal and lateral strength provided by decks and deck beams. At least one beam knee suggests decking in the stern. The bottom of the hold between midships and the stern was lined with transverse planking extending out to the turn of the bilge on either side of the keelson. Ceiling remnants found elsewhere were standard longitudinal planks, clamps, and footwales.

This hull is a monument to mechanical simplicity. Using straight lines and a few natural curvatures, the builder achieved a design that appears to be smooth and round throughout. The vessel was light, strong, spacious, and probably sea-kindly. It hints at the design flexibility that was later to become available to advanced forms of skeletal construction. Most importantly, this is the earliest example we have studied in which construction was controlled by a proper architectural discipline, such as the use of centerlines, baselines, and controlled mensuration. Clearly, this sparsely preserved hull will make many contributions to the study of shipbuilding technology and our research is now being directed to that end.

The ship carried approximately 2½ metric tons of stone ballast. Two tons of this ballast took the form of just over 100 boulders carefully laid on the transverse ceiling planking within the midship hold area so as to form as low and compact a mass as possible. Rounded limestone boulders and angular blocks of beach rock in similar numbers constituted about 90% of this ballast; the rest consisted mainly of rounded boulders of friable chalk. The ship was ballasted further with around 400 kg of cobbles, roughly three quarters of them of rounded limestone. About 90% of these cobbles had been laid between the floors throughout the forward hold area. Some substantial portion of several hundred kilograms of pebbles recovered from the wreck site appears also to have been ship's ballast.

Eight iron anchors of a peculiar Y shape, known previously only from a few isolated finds off Cyprus and Italy, were uncovered in 1977 and 1978. They are quite small: shank lengths do not appear to exceed ca. 1.4 m; the span between flukes, ca. 1.3 m. The locations of 3 anchors suggest that the ship was carrying 2 port and 1 starboard bower when she sank. (An anchor located some distance forward of the wreck and initially reported as a possible bower anchor proved to be cruciform and does not belong to the ship.) The 5 spare anchors were carried just forward of midships, but it is not yet clear whether they were stowed on the deck or in the forward part of the hold.

The anchors' removable stocks apparently were all wooden; no remnants of iron stocks were found. Inspection of the anchors' heads has revealed that each was equipped with an iron ring. Substantial portions of 4 of the anchors remain in an unoxidized state and will yield considerable information concerning how the anchors were made.

The ship was carrying a cargo of approximately 3 metric tons of glass in the after hold area. Roughly 2 tons of this was comprised of blocks of raw glass ranging in size from tiny chips to large chunks some 30 cm across. Most of the remaining glass consisted of broken glassware that had been purposely smashed so as to take up as little space as possible within the hold (Fig. 4). This glassware appears to represent more than 200 different vessel types. Major categories include lamps, tumblers, cups, saucers, plates, bowls, jugs, pitchers, bottles, and jars in a great variety of shapes, sizes, and hues, many bearing either engraved or molded designs. Some of the vessels clearly had been defective, suggesting that they had to do with waste material from one or more glass factories; other fragments, however, showed signs of wear on their bases, suggesting long household use. Over 11,000 various-sized, rimmed disks with central holes, included in the glass cargo, must also represent glass waste (Fig. 5). This mixed cargo of glass undoubtedly will yield a wealth of new information on medieval glassware and its manufacture and trade.

The ship also carried over 80 intact glass vessels, including a variety of bottles, jars, tumblers, cups, and bowls (see Figs. 6 and 7). Almost all of these were found in the bow or stern. In the bow these included a yellow-green globular vase with inverted conical neck (Fig. 6a), a matching bottle and tumbler with lions engraved on them (Figs. 7a, b), and a pitcher and jug (Fig. 6b) with thumbpieces on their handles. Among the intact vessels from the stern were bottles (Figs. 6c, d), tumblers (Fig. 7c), bowls, and cups (Fig. 6e), in a variety of shapes and designs. Most of the types of

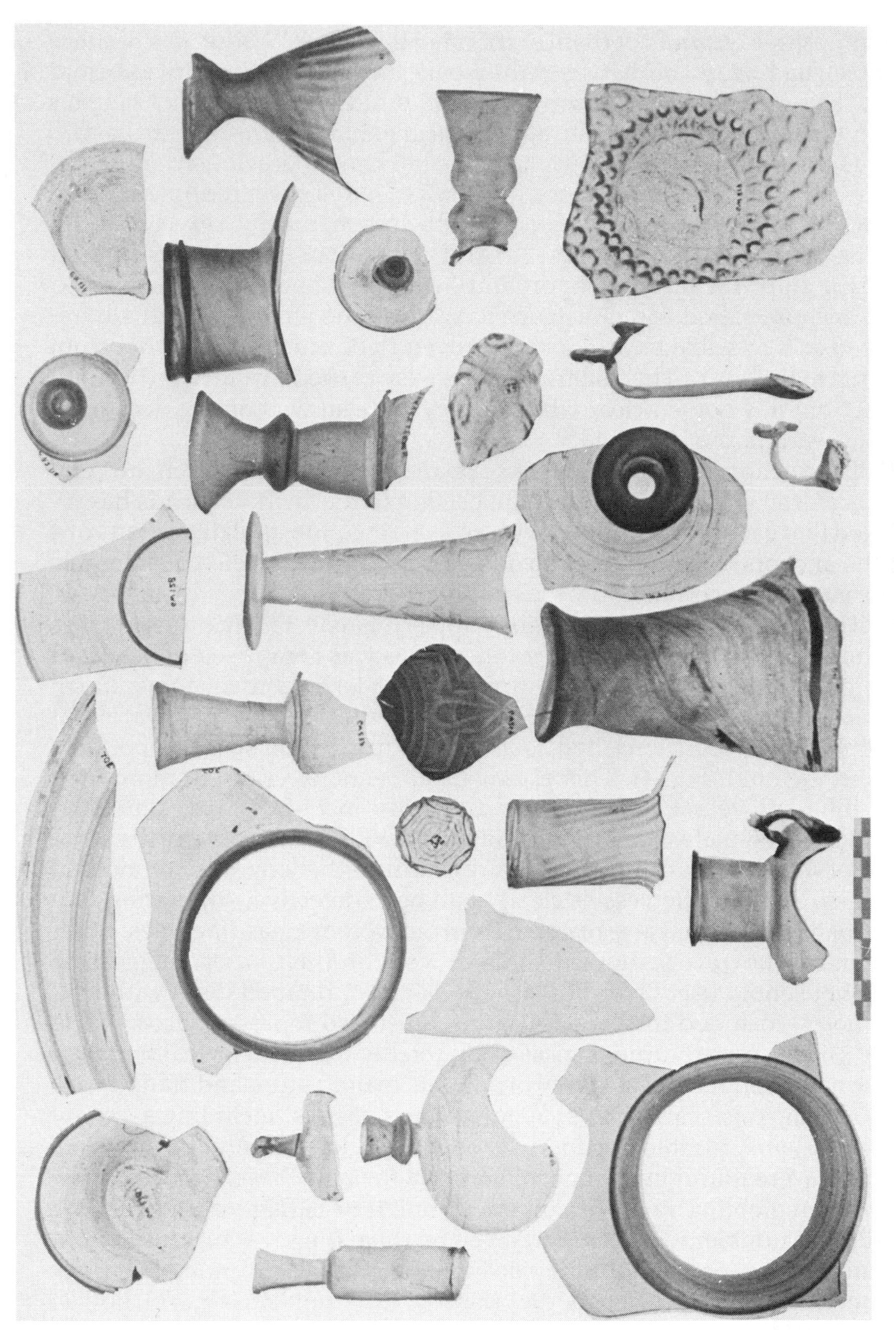

FIGURE 4. Glass cargo: examples of broken glassware.

FIGURE 5. Glass cargo: rimmed disks with central holes.

intact glassware have excellent Islamic parallels, especially from Egypt and/or Persia. As these vessel types are also represented by fragments in the cargo of broken glass, it appears that both the intact and broken vessels are Islamic in origin. The intact glassware may have been a secondary cargo.

Nearly 90 complete or fragmentary pyriform amphoras, in 3 basic sizes, were recovered from the wreck. Of these, 21 have a capacity of ca. 5 L; 10, a capacity of ca. 21 L; the others, capacities ranging from ca. 8 to 14 L. Flotation recovery of organic remains from a number of the amphoras did not produce evidence as to their contents; it appears likely that they were carrying wine. Their interiors are lined with pitch, and pitch also was used to seal stoppers made of a tree bark that has not yet been identified. The total weight of the amphoras when full of wine would have been ca. 1.6 metric tons; their total capacity ca. 1000 L. Approximately 50 of the amphoras were carried in the stern; some 30 in the midship hold area; only a few in the bow. They had the same general distribution on the wreck that storage jars and other amphoras did, raising the possibility that they had belonged to ship's stores. However, it seems likely in view of their number and total capacity that at least a substantial portion of them constituted secondary cargo.

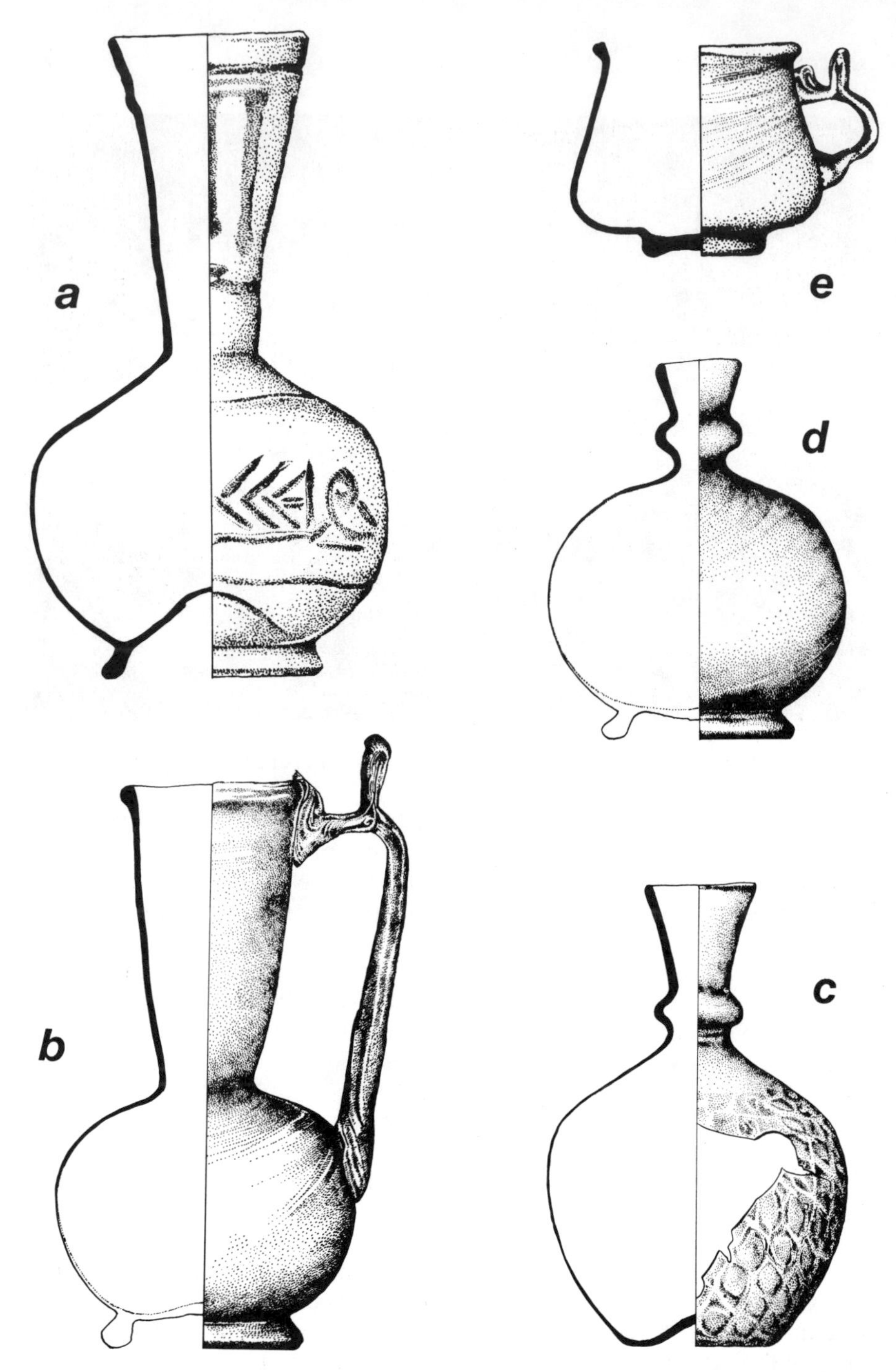

FIGURE 6. a, Engraved glass bottle; b, glass jug with thumbpiece on handle; c, d, glass bottles; e, glass cup.

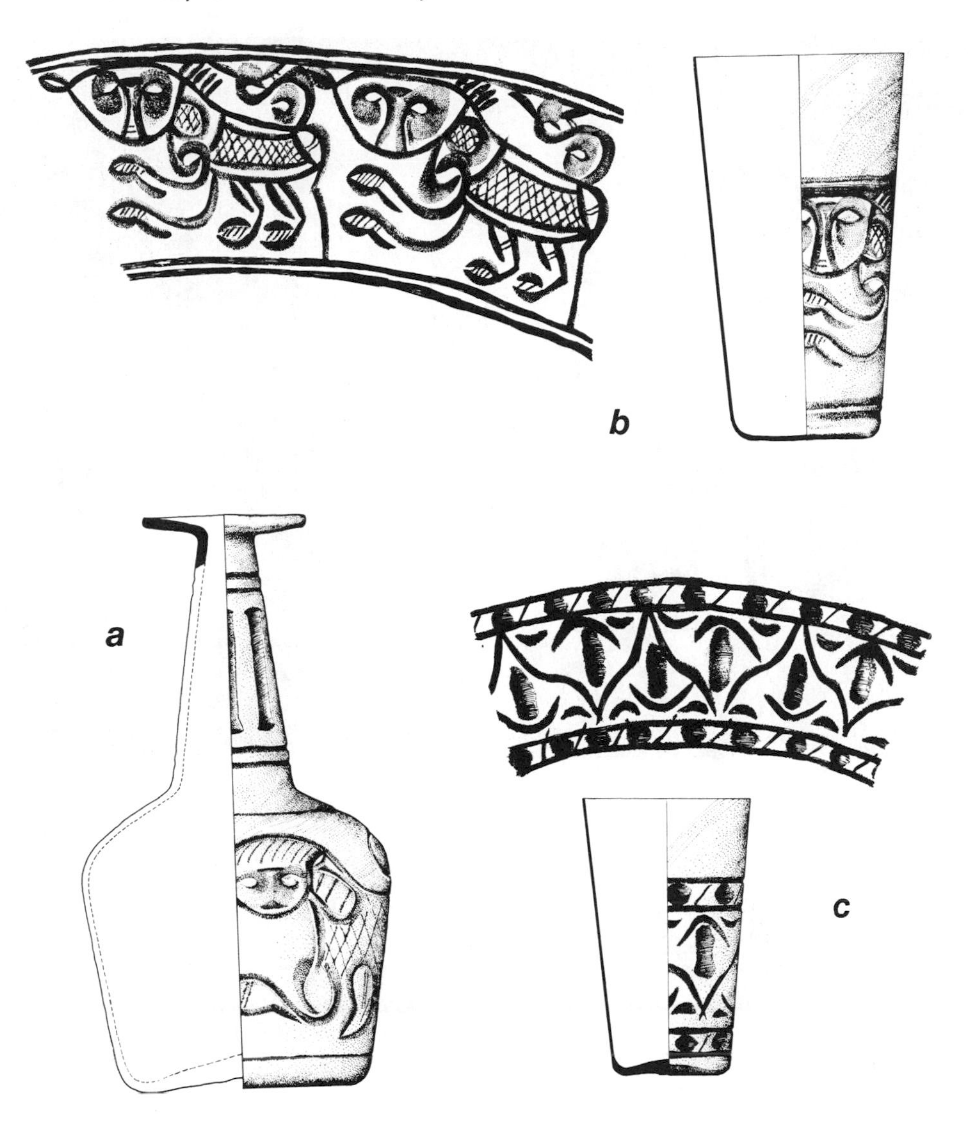

FIGURE 7. a, b, Matching bottle and tumbler with engraved lions; c, glass tumbler.

Graffiti, inscribed before firing, appear on the shoulders of all but about 20 of the pyriform amphoras. With the exception of a 5-pointed star on 2 of the amphoras, all of the graffiti appear to consist of Greek letters or monograms. At least 8 different names, including Leon, occur.

FIGURE 8. Terra-cotta storage jars.

Storage vessels on the ship included a variety of amphoras and jars, over 40 vessels in all (Figs. 8 and 9). Roughly half had been stowed in the stern; most of the others were in the midship hold area, with only a few in the bow. The shipboard diet seems to have been quite varied, apparently including lentils (stored in amphoras), olives, at least two varieties of nuts, perhaps half a dozen different fruits, meat, and fish.

Over 150 animal and fish bones have been recovered, the fish bones and roughly four fifths of the animal bones from the stern and most of the remaining animal bones from the midship hold area. A preliminary study of the animal bones by Gail Carlson indicates that they may be from joints of meat rather than from animals carried alive on board. There appear to be at least 8 joints involved, from at least 3 individual sheep or goats and 2 pigs.

Fishing nets, kept both in the stern and the midship hold area, are represented by over 900 lead net weights and 3 types of net floats. Around 100 of the weights bear geometric patterns in relief. Fishing-net

FIGURE 9. Terra-cotta storage amphoras.

strands are still preserved within several of the weights. A multi-tined fish spear was also recovered (Fig. 10).

Cooking utensils, found mainly in the stern and the midship hold area, include over 40 cooking pots, some with fire-blackened bottoms, several dozen pieces of charcoal, and what appear to be remains of an iron gridiron. No evidence for hearth or firebox installations was found, but gridirons would have been ideal for shipboard use.

Four disk-shaped millstones recovered from the wreck belong to 2 rotary querns of different size. Initially thought to have been part of the ship's ballast amidships, they in fact had been situated at some higher level within the hull. Such millstones were an item of maritime trade in the Mediterranean during the medieval period. However, Curtis N. Runnels, a student of medieval millstones, has examined photographs of the stones and detected signs of wear on the opposing faces of either quern. Thus, the possibility that they were being used on board must be considered.

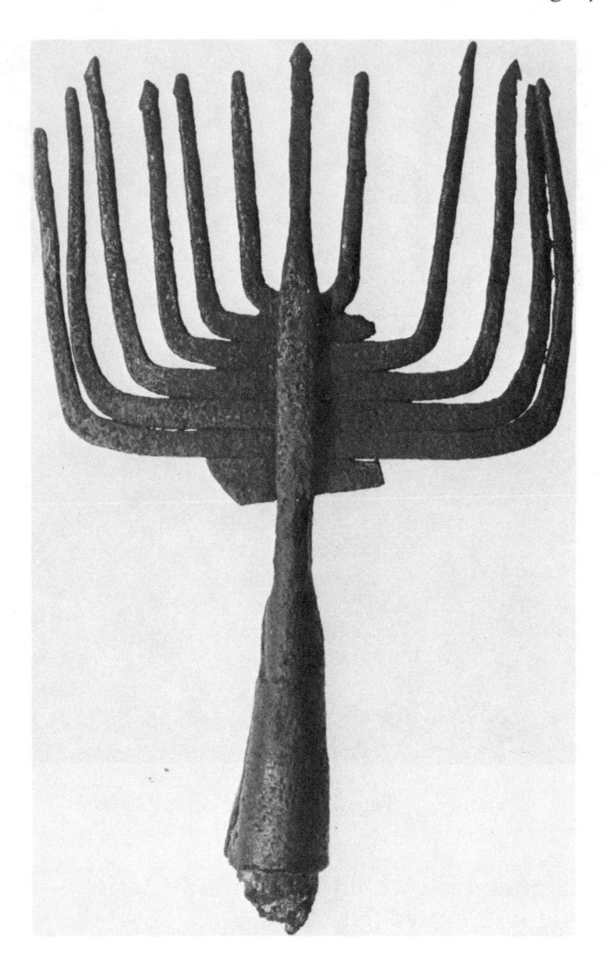

FIGURE 10. Fish spear.

Ceramic tableware included some 40 glazed bowls, a dozen *gargoulettes* (one-handled jugs with decorative strainers in their necks), and a variety of jugs and pitchers (Fig. 11). Nearly two thirds of these vessels had been kept in the midship hold area; the rest were in both the bow and stern. Ten of the glazed bowls found have *sgraffito* decoration; all but 2 were recovered from the midship hold area. Others, found in all 3 areas, are imitations of T'ang dynasty imports from China, then popular in the Moslem world. *Gargoulettes* from the stern, 5 or 6 in number and possibly Egyptian in origin, are of a finer quality than the others, which were kept amidships.

FIGURE 11. Ceramic vessels: cooking pots, jugs, pitcher, and (center) *gargoulettes*.

The presence of fish bones within one glazed bowl indicates that these bowls were to some extent utilized on board. However, an absence of ceramic drinking cups suggests that wooden vessels probably were being used as well; fragments of several wooden vessels, including a tray and a possible drinking cup, were recovered. Mention should also be made of a one-handled bronze cup found amidships.

The stern and, to a lesser degree, the midship area produced a large number of weapons, including 2 or 3 swords (one with an ornate bronze hilt illustrated by Fig. 12), 7 or 8 spears, and some 60 javelins. One of the spears had been sheathed in a wooden scabbard.

Other finds of particular interest include just under 500 g of orpiment ($As_2 S_3$), a yellow pigment, from the bow; 2 wooden combs, 1 from the bow and the other from the midship area; 8 decorated spindle whorls of bone, from midships; jewelry, from the stern; 3 bronze buckets (Fig. 13); and gaming pieces, from both midships and the stern. The jewelry includes a dozen finger rings and a gold earring of exceptionally fine work-

FIGURE 12. Bronze sword hilt.

manship; gaming equipment includes 1 backgammon and 8 chess pieces of wood (Fig. 14). Chess apparently was played in the stern; backgammon, amidships.

Money and commercial equipment were with few exceptions kept in the stern and are, like the cargo, of both Islamic and Byzantine origin.

Three gold coins and 15 clippings from other gold coins were recovered. All are Islamic. The gold coins, identified by Michael L. Bates of the American Numismatic Society, are quarter dinars of the Fatimid Caliph al-Hākim (996-1020) and were most probably struck between ca. 1000 and 1009. About half of some 40 copper coins found are legible; all appear to be later "anonymous" issues of Basil II (976-1025). Several of the copper coins were found in the bow, and 1 amidships.

FIGURE 13. Bronze bucket.

Four metal disks recovered from the stern, at first thought to be silver coins, proved to be lead sealings. Three of the sealings had been used, perhaps to secure bags of coins or clippings, but the other remains a blank. At least 2 of the used sealings are Byzantine, both carrying partially legible Greek inscriptions on the reverse. The ecstatic meeting of the Apostles Peter and Paul is shown on the obverse of one; the Virgin holding the infant Christ is on the obverse of the other.

Weighing equipment included 3 balance scales, a steelyard, 2 sets of balance-pan weights apparently based on Islamic units of weight, and glass weights for weighing coins and the like. A total of 16 glass weights

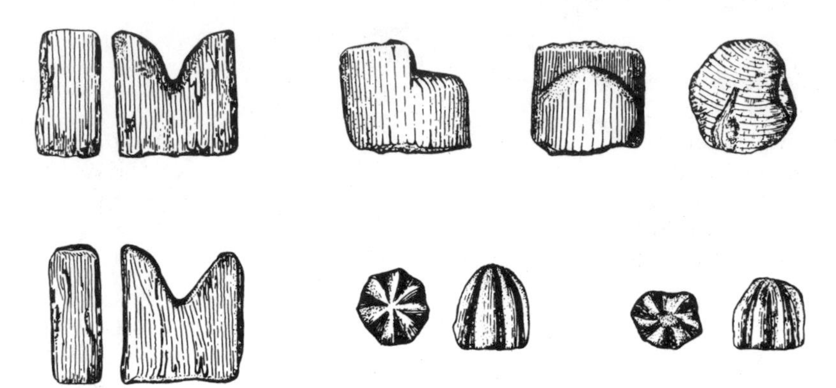

FIGURE 14. Wooden chess pieces: two rooks, a king or queen, and two pawns.

was found, including 2 from the bow and 1 from amidships. Fourteen are legible and bear Arabic inscriptions. They have been identified by Michael Bates as being of the Fatimid caliphs al-'Azīz (975-996), al-Hākim, and al-Zāhir (1020-1035). Four of the al-Hākim weights are dated to 411 AH (1020/21), a new date for al-Hākim, who died that year. Three of the al-Zāhir weights are dated to 415 (1024/25) or possibly 412 (1021/22). The denominations of a majority of the weights are presently uncertain due to weight loss. Five may be 1-dinar weights; the others may all belong to the dirham series and include 1/8-, 1/4-, 1/2-, 1-, and 2-dirham weights.

The coins and glass weights point to a date of around A.D. 1025 for the ship's sinking. A determination of the nationality or nationalities of the ship and those who sailed with her, still uncertain due to the mixed Islamic and Byzantine origins of items on board, will be a major aim of future research.

Staff

The permanent staff (1977-1979) consisted of George F. Bass, Frederick H. van Doorninck, Jr., Donald A. Frey, Robin C. M. Piercy, and Tufan Turanli of the Institute of Nautical Archaeology (INA); artist Netia Piercy; darkroom assistant Suzanne Biehl; and students Faith Hentschel, Hasan Inciroglu, Cemal Pulak, and Lisa Shuey.

Serving in 1977 were Cynthia Eiseman and Jack W. Kelley of INA; artist Gündüz Gölünü; physician John Cassils; students Barlas Çaglayan, Paul Johnston, Donald H. Keith, Sina Mandalinci, Ali Manisali, and Osman Pekin; engineer Ömer Zeki Elbi; cataloguer Jean Kelley; photographer Ayhan Sicimoglu; and diving instructors Wade Hahn and Tom Dickenson.

Serving in 1978 were Henry B. Graham, Donald H. Keith, Jack W. Kelley, and J. Richard Steffy of INA; William P. Fife of Texas A&M University; students Christian Buys, Necat Cinar, Deniz Ergener, Ahmet Igdirligil, Mehmet Inhan, Paul Johnston, Jay Kaufman, Sheila Matthews, Yavuz Onaran, Cynthia Orr, Osman Pekin, Joseph Schwarzer, Feyyaz Subay, Rhys Townsend, and Oguz Tameroglu; artists Gündüz Gölünü, Peter Hentschel, and Helen Townsend; physician Timothy L. Williamson; and Cengiz Celep, Betty Jean van Doorninck, Omer Zeki Elbi, Haluk Yalçinkaya, and Yaşar Yildiz.

Serving in 1979 were Don L. Hamilton of Texas A&M University and INA; Pilar Luna of Federación Mexicana de Actividades Subacuáticas, A.C.; artists Sema Pulak and Helen Townsend; conservators Robyn Woodward and Ann Singletary Bass; physician T. L. Williamson; and students Robert Adams, Kenneth Cassavoy, Nejat Çinar, Sheila Matthews, Dorothy Slane, Feyyaz Subay, and Rhys Townsend.

Oguz Alpözen served as commissioner from the Turkish Ministry of Culture each year, assisted in 1977 by Yüksel Egdemir, in 1978 by Sirri Özenir, and in 1979 by Yaşar Yildiz. A documentary film was produced for Turkish Radio and Television in 1978 by Arsal Soley.

REFERENCES

Bass, George F.

1963. Underwater archaeology: Key to history's warehouse. Nat. Geogr. Mag., vol. 124, no. 1, pp. 138-146, illus.

1966. Archaeology under water, 224 pp., illus. Frederick A. Praeger, New York and London.

1968a. New tools for undersea archaeology. Nat. Geogr. Mag., vol. 134, no. 3, pp. 402-423, illus.

1968b. Underwater archeological expedition to Turkey. Nat. Geogr. Soc. Res. Rep., 1963 Projects, pp. 21-34, illus.

1970. Underwater archeological expedition to Turkey, 1961-1962. Nat. Geogr. Soc. Res. Rep., 1961-1962 Projects, pp. 11-20, illus.

1974. Underwater archeological expedition to Turkey, 1967. Nat. Geogr. Soc. Res. Rep., 1967 Projects, pp. 11-19, illus.

1978. Glass treasure from the Aegean. Nat. Geogr. Mag., vol. 153, no. 6, pp. 768-793, illus.

1982. Survey of ancient shipwrecks in the Mediterranean. Nat. Geogr. Soc. Res. Rep., vol. 14, pp. 45-48.

Bass, George F., and van Doorninck, Frederick H., Jr.

1969. Excavations of a Byzantine shipwreck at Yassi Ada, Turkey. Nat. Geogr. Soc. Res. Rep., 1964 Projects, pp. 9-20, illus.

1978. An 11th century shipwreck at Serçe Liman, Turkey. Internat. Journ. Nautical Archaeol. and Underwater Exploration, vol. 7, no. 2, pp. 119-132, illus.

KATZEV, MICHAEL L.
1970. Resurrecting the oldest known Greek ship. Nat. Geogr. Mag., vol. 137, no. 1, pp. 840-857, illus.
1980. Assessing a chance find near Kyrenia. A cargo from the age of Alexander the Great. The study and conservation of an ancient hull. Pp. 40-45 *in* "Archeology Under Water, an Atlas of the World's Submerged Sites," illus., Keith Muckelroy, ed. McGraw-Hill, New York and London.

STEFFY, J. RICHARD
1982. The reconstruction of the 11th century Serçe Liman vessel. A preliminary report. Internat. Journ. Nautical Archaeol. and Underwater Exploration, vol. 11, no. 1, pp. 13-34, illus.

VAN DOORNINCK, FREDERICK H., JR.
1972. Byzantium, mistress of the sea: 330-641. Pp. 134-146 *in* "A History of Seafaring Based on Underwater Archaeology," illus., George F. Bass, ed. Walker and Company, New York.
1976. The 4th century wreck at Yassi Ada: An interim report on the hull. Internat. Journ. Nautical Archaeol. and Underwater Exploration, vol. 5, no. 2, pp. 115-131, illus.
1982. An 11th century shipwreck at Serçe Liman, Turkey: 1978-81. Internat. Journ. Nautical Archaeol. and Underwater Exploration, vol. 11, no. 1, pp. 7-11.

GEORGE F. BASS,
J. RICHARD STEFFY
FREDERICK H. VAN DOORNINCK, JR.

Taxonomy of Certain Species of Birds from Rio Grande do Sul, Brazil

Grant Recipient: William Belton, Rocky Hollow, Great Cacapon, West Virginia.

Grant 1668: In support of a survey of the birds of Rio Grande do Sul, Brazil.

During a survey of the birds of Rio Grande do Sul, Brazil, I found three separate situations where the accepted taxonomy appeared open to question. A National Geographic Society grant supported travel during which I gathered strong indications that the Olive Spinetail, *Certhiaxis (Cranioleuca) obsoleta,* and the Stripe-crowned Spinetail, *C. pyrrhophia,* may be only extreme color phases of a single species; and that two subspecies of the Fuscous Flycatcher, *Cnemotriccus f. fuscatus* and *C. f. bimaculatus,* may be separate species. On the third problem, where two very distinct songs of the Small-billed Elaenia, *Elaenia parvirostris,* had led me to suspect the existence of two separate but morphologically similar populations within this species, I was able to satisfy myself that the same individual birds sing both songs.

Results

Rio Grande do Sul is the southernmost state in Brazil. Broadly speaking, the northern half of the state contains the southern end of the Brazilian coastal range and significant forested areas, whereas the southern half has extensive grasslands, often studded with scattered trees, and more gentle, rolling topography similar to that of neighboring Uruguay. In the northeast corner the narrow coastal plain contains remnants of dense rain forest, while in the northwest in the vicinity of the Uruguay River there are areas of subtropical forest similar to those of the continental interior farther north. At the western tip of the state *chaco*-like vegetation and terrain intrude slightly across the Uruguay into Rio Grande do Sul.

CERTHIAXIS (CRANIOLEUCA) OBSOLETA and *C. (C.) PYRRHOPHIA*

C. obsoleta occupies a range extending across most of southeastern Brazil and through Misiones, Argentina, well into southern Paraguay. *C.*

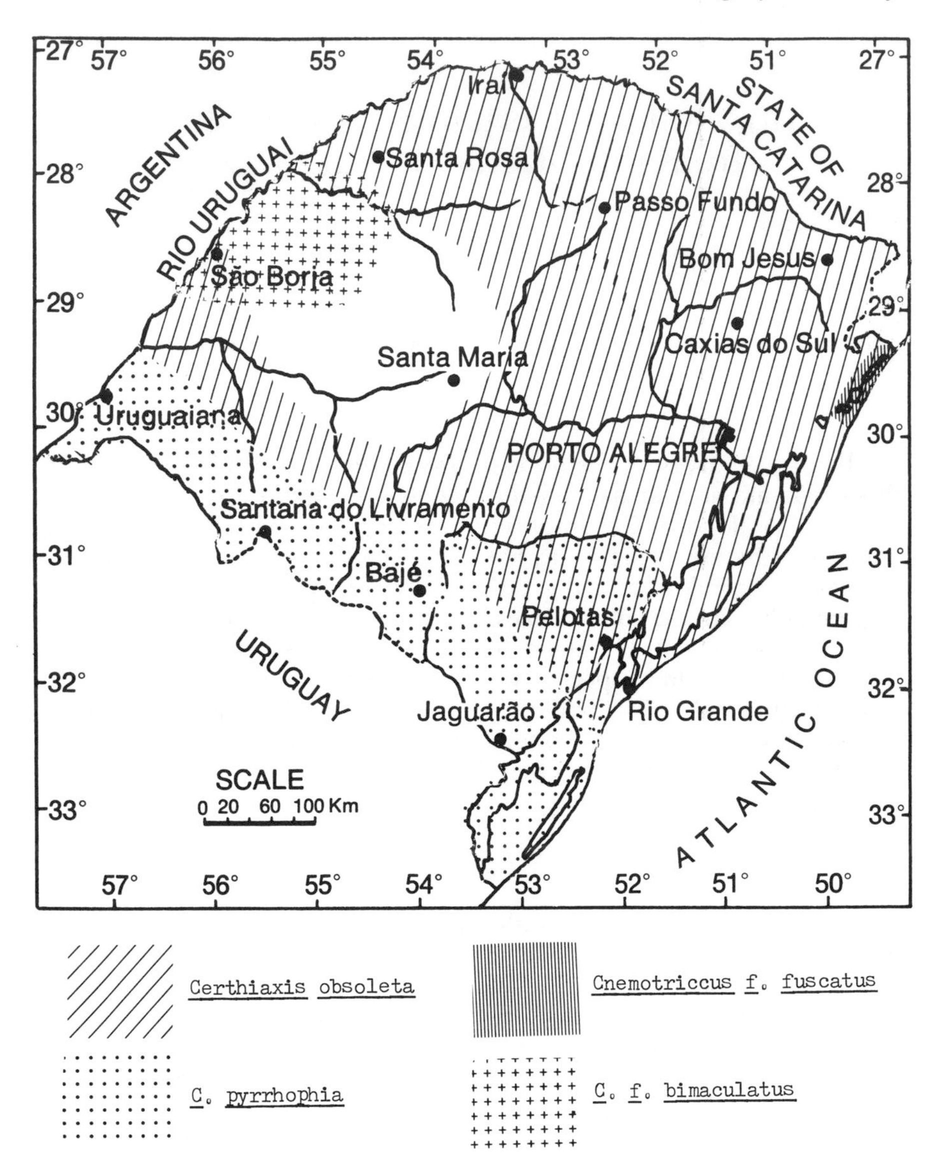

FIGURE 1. Distribution of *Certhiaxis obsoleta, C. pyrrhophia, Cnemotriccus f. fuscatus* and *C. f. bimaculatus* in Rio Grande do Sul, Brazil.

pyrrhophia occurs in immediately adjacent areas to the south and west of *obsoleta*, as well as farther south and west in Uruguay and Argentina and farther north in northern Paraguay and central Bolivia (Vaurie, 1980, pp.

133-134). In Rio Grande do Sul, *obsoleta* is found in most of the state except a strip within approximately 60 km of the Uruguayan border and a small sector between the Ijuí and Ibicuí Rivers. The border strip from which *obsoleta* is absent is occupied by *pyrrhophia*. Individuals identifiable as *pyrrhophia* are also found north of the east end of this strip as far as the Camaquã River in terrain where specimens identifiable as *obsoleta* have been taken.

Study of a series of more than 70 specimens of these 2 species from Rio Grande do Sul shows some intergradation of plumage characteristics, both in color of the underparts and amount of striping on the frontal area. Intergradation is most noticeable in some of the specimens from the area of overlap south of the Camaquã River.

Extensive recordings of voices of the two forms have been made. Sonograms are still lacking for detailed study, but no obvious difference between the voices of the two species are distinguishable by ear. The birds themselves apparently do not distinguish either. Taped voices of typical *pyrrhophia* individuals from the western tip of Rio Grande do Sul have been played near Gramado in the highlands of the northeastern corner (29°23′ S, 50°53′ W) and have produced the same strong reaction among *obsoleta* individuals as playback of their own voices produced. Similarly, taped *obsoleta* voices have been played at the western tip and aroused the same agitated response among resident *pyrrhophia* as playback of their own voices did.

Confirmation of these preliminary indications that the two forms may not be specifically distinct requires additional study of nests and nesting behavior, comparison of voice sonograms, and more detailed analysis of the apparent plumage cline.

ELAENIA PARVIROSTRIS

The typical song of the Small-billed Elaenia can be rendered as "wee-dable-wee." It is usually the first song of any diurnal species to be heard at dawn during spring in Rio Grande do Sul. It is also sung during the remainder of the day, especially later in the breeding season. Another song, "p-weer" is common during the early stages of the nesting process. It is also heard before daylight and can be understood as a dawn song but also continues to be sung during the day. Having frequently heard both of these songs originating with what were apparently *E. parvirostris* individuals, and being aware of the notorious similarity of various species within this genus, I speculated that a morphologically identical species with a different voice might be masquerading as *parvirostris*. Using methods developed by Stein (1963) in his study of the Alder Flycatcher, I attempted to distinguish between individuals using one song and the other; only confusion resulted. I then undertook to prove that both songs originated with the same individuals. This was more productive, for by color-banding I was able to identify one individual as it switched from singing "weedable-wee" to "p-weer." Because "p-weer" is commonly heard early in the breeding season and rarely in mid and late season, it may be an advertising and mate-soliciting song, whereas "weedable-wee" may be used to announce and confirm nesting and maintain the pair-bond.

CNEMOTRICCUS FUSCATUS

This species is widespread in northern and central South America but its range only touches the more temperate portions of the continent (Meyer de Schauensee, 1966). It has been recorded for the two Brazilian states immediately to the north of Rio Grande do Sul, Santa Catarina (Sick et al., 1981), and Paraná (Scherer, 1980), but details on the subspecies found there and their precise locations are not available. In Rio Grande do Sul *C. f. fuscatus* occurs in remnant patches of rain forest in the narrow coastal plain at the foot of the escarpment in the northeastern corner of the state. *C. f. bimaculatus* has been found in a limited area on the other side of the state, from the Uruguay River east to about 54°30′ W latitude between 28° and 29° S longitude.

Early during my investigations in Rio Grande do Sul I noticed a clear difference between the vocalizations of these two subspecies. The song of *C. f. fuscatus* is a short, wavering, slightly down-scale whistle, while there is an extensive variety of notes: an insect-like abrupt "bzt bzt bzt"; "bewíck bewíck bewíck"; "chuwee chuwit"; "wheeo wheeo"; and a trilled "wheety-oo." These are mostly delivered in an intense, forceful fashion and are frequently all mingled together with a very short, cracked, single-noted whistle. In contrast *C. f. bimaculatus* sings a clear, single whistle, uptrending at the end with a quick stop: "oooooooooEE," and the only other vocalization I have heard is a low "meal-chuk" or "meal-chuck-chuk."

On January 5 and 6, 1977, at Fazenda do Pontal, municipality of Osorio (29°48′ S, 50°09′ W), where *C. f. fuscatus* is common, I played recordings of *C. f. bimaculatus* voices taped at Rincão do Faxinal, near Garruchos, municipality of São Borja (28°10′ S, 55°34′ W) without any perceptible response from local *fuscatus*. As soon as taped *fuscatus* voices were played, a pair of *fuscatus* appeared and reacted with tail flips and wing lifts in an agitated fashion near the loudspeaker.

Similar tests were conducted at Rincão do Faxinal during the period November 19-22, 1977, using *C. f. bimaculatus* voices taped in the area and *C. f. fuscatus* voices from the northeast coastal region. Of 19 occasions when *bimaculatus* voices were played at 11 different sites, 13 tests at 8 of these places resulted in a positive response, either by voice or close approach, from *bimaculatus* individuals in the vicinity. On the other hand, *fuscatus* voices played at the 8 positive sites did not attract any *bimaculatus* individuals, and in 3 of the places where *bimaculatus* was already observed to be present when the tests began, the birds ignored the recordings and eventually departed.

On October 17-18, 1978, tests were again run at Fazenda do Pontal. Approach, vocalization, or both by *C. f. fuscatus* individuals was induced in 9 of 10 trys at 6 sites by playing taped *fuscatus* voices. Several other sites produced no response. Less extensive use of *C. f. bimaculatus* taped voices produced no noticeable reaction in any case.

On October 21 and 22, 1978, at a forest patch near the southwest corner of the Lagoa do Jacaré, municipality of Torres (29°20′ S, 49°49′ W), *fuscatus* tapes obtained positive reactions in three *fuscatus* territories, while *bimaculatus* recordings produced no response.

At Fazenda do Pontal, November 16-18, 1978, with nesting in progress, tape test results were less clear-cut, as the birds were much less inclined to vocalize than on previous occasions. Near an active nest, one *C. f. fuscatus* adult, immediately after feeding a nestling, was alert and interested, and approached within about 10 m when I played a *C. f. bimaculatus* tape, but displayed no agitation. Subsequently when the pair was at the nest, I played a *fuscatus* tape. Both birds immediately approached to within 2 m and agitatedly flew around me.

Two *C. f. fuscatus* nests were found on this occasion. Each was about 10 m up in a tree within the forest. One, under construction, was supported by a bromeliad and slightly protected by the overhang of a branch above, but essentially in the open. The other, with a single nestling close to fledging, was about 2 m below the treetop and placed between a green bromeliad and the trunk. The nest was a simple, cup-shaped structure of dried bromeliad leaves and a few fine, fibrous stems and vines, sparsely lined with hyphae of *Marasmius* sp. fungus.

At Rincão do Faxinal on November 21, 1977, a *C. f. bimaculatus* nest with a single nestling was found in a small patch of trees surrounded by grasslands, placed in a rotted hole in the side of a tree about 40 cm above ground. The bottom of the hole was poorly lined with leaves and also contained a few large wood chips, while the outer side was almost totally exposed.

Further investigation of the relationship between *C. f. bimaculatus* and *C. f. fuscatus* is called for given the following: the sharp difference in vocalizations of the two subspecies; the fact that they do not react to each others' voices; the apparent difference in nest location and construction (assuming that the one *bimaculatus* nest observed is typical); and my additional observation that *bimaculatus* is usually found lower in its habitat, from 1 to 4 m above ground, than *fuscatus*, which ranges from 1 to 12 m up. This relationship will have to be pursued north of Rio Grande do Sul, perhaps by tracing their ranges to a point where they abut or coincide so that whether they hybridize or are sympatric can be determined.

Acknowledgments

In addition to the National Geographic Society, I am obliged to the Frank M. Chapman Memorial Fund, the Museu Nacional, Rio de Janeiro, and the Smithsonian Institution for support of much of my research in Rio Grande do Sul, and to Philip S. Humphrey for editorial suggestions on this paper.

REFERENCES

BELTON, WILLIAM
____. Birds of Rio Grande do Sul, Brazil. American Museum of Natural History, New York. (In press.)
MEYER DE SCHAUENSEE, RUDOLPH
1966. The species of birds of South America with their distribution, 577 p. Academy of Natural Sciences of Philadelphia.
SCHERER NETO, PEDRO
1980. Aves do Paraná, 32 p. Zôo-botânica Mário Nardelli, Rio de Janeiro.
SICK, H.; ROSÁRIO, L. A. DO; and AZEVEDO, T. R.
1981. Aves do Estado de Santa Catarina, 51 p. Sellówia, ser. zool., no. 1, FATMA, Florianópolis.
STEIN, ROBERT C.
1963. Isolating mechanisms between populations of Traill's Flycatcher. Proc. Amer. Philos. Soc., vol. 107, no. 1, pp. 21-50.
VAURIE, CHARLES
1980. Taxonomy and geographical distribution of the Furnariidae. Bull. Amer. Mus. Nat. Hist., vol. 166, pp. 133-134.

WILLIAM BELTON

Paleobiogeography and Evolution of the Late Cretaceous Crabs of North America, 1976-1978

Grant Recipient: Gale A. Bishop, Georgia Southern College, Statesboro, Georgia.

Grant 1629: In support of a study of the paleobiogeography and evolution of Late Cretaceous crabs of North America.

On May 15, 1976, I was informed by the National Geographic Society of the funding of my proposal to study the fossil Cretaceous crabs of North America. The goal of the proposed study was "to compare decapod faunas from three paleobiogeographic provinces (Atlantic Coastal Plain, Gulf Coastal Plain, and Western Interior) that existed in North America during the Late Cretaceous. . . ."

The goal of the one-year proposal was to be accomplished by summarizing the literature, examining existing collections of fossil crabs, and making additional collections in each of the three provinces. This ambitious project has carried over into a second year because of scheduling conflicts caused by illnesses in my family. (As luck would have it, this factor delayed a trip to the Mississippi Embayment and allowed me to discover a new locality!)

Introduction

In spite of a real or apparent paucity of crab fossils (Schopf, 1978, p. 266), I had in my possession at the beginning of this study two large collections of fossil Cretaceous crabs. Some 4000 crabs had been collected during and since my graduate school days at various Cretaceous localities in the Western Interior and on the western Gulf Coastal Plain. A collection of about 2000 Cretaceous crabs from the Chesapeake and Delaware Canal, Delaware, had been placed in my hands for study by Mr. Harry Mendryk of Harrison, New Jersey. Literature citations (Rathbun *in* Wade, 1926; Rathbun, 1935; and Sohl, 1960) indicated an abundance of crabs in the Cretaceous rocks of the Mississippi Embayment. Because of deteriorating national energy conditions I deemed it wise (and still do) to concentrate efforts on acquiring new specimens from new localities in case such travel becomes severely limited (by economics or government decree).

Field trips were planned to each of the regions mentioned. I hoped to extend stratigraphic control in the Western Interior by finding additional crab specimens at different stratigraphic levels, and I also wanted to visit several localities which had been recently discovered by amateur paleontologists Mr. Larry Eichhorn and Mrs. Delores Baresch. I wanted to meet the collector of the fine collection from the Chesapeake and Delaware Canal, Mr. Harry Mendryk, and accompany him to examine the collecting sites. At the same time I hoped to be able to examine fossil crab collections in the National Museum of Natural History (Smithsonian Institution). I then wanted to spend time collecting crabs in the Mississippi Embayment and particularly search for and collect specimens of *Avitelmessus grapsoideus* Rathbun, 1923, to help in my study of the paleobiogeography of the Dakoticroidea.

Collections

In carrying out this research project a total of 52 days was spent in the field, including 33 field days collecting in the Western Interior (3 separate trips), 8 days spent collecting on the Northern Atlantic Coastal Plain, and 11 days spent collecting in the Mississippi Embayment. These efforts resulted in the addition to my collection of 913 fossil crabs, 101 fossil lobsters, 132 mud shrimp, and numerous associated fossils (Table 1) from 19 localities.

New Localities

During this study four new decapod localities were discovered or collected for the first time. Three of the localities are in the Western Interior.

The Bitter Creek locality in north-central Montana was discovered by Mr. Larry Eichhorn and has been collected by both of us. This new locality is especially significant because, although the crab assemblage is nearly contemporaneous with the *Dakoticancer* Assemblage (Bishop, 1981) of South Dakota, this assemblage consists of 2 crabs not found in the *Dakoticancer* Assemblages and which are both currently being described for publication (Bishop, 1983d) as 2 new species, *Notopocorystes (Eucorystes)* n. sp. and *Zygastrocarcinus* n.g., n.sp. This *Notopocorystes* will extend the geographic range of the subgenus from the Gulf Coastal Plain into the Western Interior and from the Coniacian Stage into the Campanian Stage. *Zygastrocarcinus* n.g., n.sp. is the second species-level taxon of this genus to be described from the Western Interior.

The Baresch Locality, Butte County, South Dakota, was discovered by Delores Baresch and her husband who held its location a tight secret until 1976, when she guided me to the exposure. The locality is extremely important for two reasons: (1) the *Dakoticancer overanus* (Fig. 10) from the

TABLE 1. List of Fossil Crabs Collected During Research Under National Geographic Society Grant

Locality	*Stratigraphy*	*Date(s) visited*	*Specimens collected*	*Remarks*
		WESTERN INTERIOR		
Mobridge, S.D. (GAB 4)	Pierre Shale Zone of *B. grandis*	8/25 - 26/76	300 crabs	Possibly new *Raninella*, second and confirming specimen of new species of *Zygastrocarcinus* (found by Harry Mendryk), and second *Dakoticancer* intersex (different than described by Bishop, 1974, 1983a, d).
		8/13/76	197 crabs	
Baker, Mont. (GAB 43)	Fox Hills Ss.	8/27/76	13 burrows	Search of burrow fills *(Ophiomorpha nodosa)* for decapod inhabitants not successful.
Ft. Peck, Mont. (GAB 22,29)	Bearpaw Sh. Zone of *Baculites rugosus*	8/29 - 30/76	10 lobsters	Lobster locality did not yield any crabs (Feldmann, Bishop, and Kammer, 1977).
		7/9/77	16 of 30 lobsters collected	
Bitter Creek (GAB 31)	Bearpaw Sh. Zone of *Didymoceras nebrascense*	8/28/76	8 crabs	*Notopocorystes* and *Zygastrocarcinus* are each represented by a new species (Bishop, 1983d).
		11/1/76	15 crabs on loan from Eichhorn	
Fost Locality Baker, Mont.	Bearpaw Sh.	9/1/76	0	Not found. Specimens in U. S. Nat. Mus. and Carter County Mus. (Ekalaka, Mont.)
Oliver Ranch Albion, Mont. (GAB 23)	Pierre Sh. Gammon Ferruginеous member Zone of *Scaphites hippicrepis* III	9/2/76	3 crabs 25 lobsters	*Zygastrocarcinus* represented either by new species or by same species as at Bitter Creek. Second *Necrocarcinus* and one *Raninella* also collected. These 4 crabs only ones known from this lobster assemblage.

TABLE 1. *(continued)*

Locality	*Stratigraphy*	*Date(s) visited*	*Specimens collected*	*Remarks*
Heart Tail Ranch Belle Fourche, S.D. (GAB 36)	Pierre Sh. Gammon Ferruginous member Zone of *Baculites* sp. (smooth)	9/2/76 9/10/76 9/12/77	1 lobster 1 *Callianassa* 3 crabs 3 lobsters 23 *Callianassa* 10 crabs 1 lobster 12 *Callianassa*	This new locality has yielded a total of 53 fossil decapods including 13 fossil crabs belonging to three new species. The decapod assemblage antedates the migration of *Dakoticancer* into the Western Interior.
Baresch Locality Butte Co., S.D. (GAB 35)	Pierre Sh. Zone of *Exiteloceras jenneyi*	9/3/76 7/12/77	6 crabs 1 crab	This is the earliest known occurrence of *Dakoticancer overanus* in the Western Interior. Unlike most crab assemblages preserved by apatite, these crabs are preserved in calcite concretions.
Wasta, S.D. (GAB 5, 7, & 12)	Pierre Sh. Zone of *Baculites compressus*	9/11/76	15 crabs	This locality adds stratigraphic control even though it has not yielded many crabs.
		NORTHERN ATLANTIC COASTAL PLAIN		
Chesapeake and Delaware Canal (GAB 42)	Merchantville Fm. (Canal spoil banks)	8/27/77	21 crabs	Recent dredging on the C & D Canal yielded Mendryk's collection of 2000 crabs and lobsters. Some are excellently preserved.
Biddle Point (GAB 38)	Merchantville Fm. (Canal spoil banks)	8/27/78	34? crabs	The 34 specimens collected are hematite concretions that contain pyritized crabs. The unusual preservation has led to questionable identification as *Tetracarcinus subquadratus* in the past.

TABLE 1. *(continued)*

Locality	*Stratigraphy*	*Date(s) visited*	*Specimens collected*	*Remarks*
Maple Shade Claypit (GAB 41)	Merchantville	8/28/77	3? crabs	Site of previous collections in Mendryk collection
Bellmawr Sanitary Landfill (GAB 39)	Upper Merchantville	8/28/77	53 crabs	Site of previous collections in Mendryk collections
		GULF COASTAL PLAIN—MISSISSIPPI EMBAYMENT		
Troy, Miss.	Ripley Fm.	6/7/78	0	U. S. Geol. Surv. Locality has yielded numerous crabs in the past.
Aberdeen Rd.	Ripley Fm.	6/8/78	0	Underwater. U. S. Geol. Surv. Locality has yielded numerous crabs in the past.
Blue Springs, Miss. (GAB 37)	Ripley Fm.	6/7/78 8/22 - 25/78	107 crabs 24 lobsters 43 *Callianassa* 139 crabs 21 lobsters 43 *Callianassa*	This new locality has yielded crabs, lobsters, and *Callianassa*. It is one of the most diverse crab faunas from the Mississippi Embayment. Added significance is the abundance of *Dakoticancer australis* which until now was relatively uncommon. A fine molluscan fauna is also presently under study by Robert Mitchell (Bishop, 1981a, 1983c).
Graham, Miss. (GAB 40)	Ripley Fm.	8/25/78	11 crabs	Poorly preserved *Avitelmessus*.
Pleasant Ridge Lake Union Co. Miss. (GAB 44)	Ripley Fm.	8/25/78 8/26/78	leg frags. 2 crabs	Famous *Avitelmessus* locality; could produce again.

TABLE 1. *(continued)*

MUSEUM COLLECTIONS

Collection	*Host*	*Number of specimens*	*Remarks*
Nat. Mus. Nat. Hist. (Smithsonian Institution)	Warren C. Blow	12 crabs borrowed and examined	Two days were spent examining Nat. Mus. collections. A catalog of specimens of Dakoticancroidea was compiled. Eleven type specimens or critical specimens were borrowed, measured, and photographed. Numerous other specimens were "tagged" for future loans.
U. S. Geol. Survey (Denver)	W. A. "Bill" Cobban	53+ crabs	Two days were spent examining collections in Denver. Fifty-three specimens were borrowed for description and photographing. Several new taxa are represented as are extensions in geographic and stratigraphic range.
Wagner Free Institute of Science (Philadelphia)	(corresponding)	9 crabs	Four suites of type specimens were borrowed to be examined and rephotographed.
Carter County Museum (Ekalaka)	Marshall Lambert	5 crabs	A one-day visit resulted in the loan of 5 specimens for study, photography, and casting.

locality are the oldest now known from the Western Interior, and (2) the crabs are preserved in calcite concretions in contrast to the normal preservation of the *Dakoticancer* Assemblage in apatite concretions. These crabs apparently represent the first migration of *Dakoticancer* into the Western Interior.

The Heart Tail Ranch Locality, Butte County, South Dakota, is older yet than the Baresch Locality, and the crab assemblage is apparently quite diverse, yielding 13 specimens belonging to *Necrocarcinus ef. pierrensis* Rathbun, 1917 (Fig. 8), *Glaesnerella* n.sp. (Fig. 7), and *Xanthosia* n.sp. along with the mud shrimp *Protocallianassa* and lobster *Hoploparia*. The assemblage will, when adequately collected, provide a comparison for the *Dakoticancer* Assemblage (e. g., compare *Necrocarcinus pierrensis* in Fig. 8, 13) and, being ancestral to it, may allow some inferences about decapod community evolution in the Western Interior.

The fourth new locality, the Blue Springs Locality, was discovered in June 1978, in Union County, Mississippi. The small road cut exposure has yielded 246 crabs, 45 lobsters, and 86 mud shrimp during 2 collecting trips. Preliminary examination of the collections indicates this abundant fauna consists of the crabs *Dakoticancer australis* Rathbun, 1935, *Tetracarcinus subquadratus* Weller, 1905, *Avitelmessus grapsoideus* Rathbun, 1923, *Paguristes whitteni, Raninella tridens, Prehepatus* sp., *Notopocorystes* sp., *Raninella testacea* Rathbun, 1926; the lobsters *Linuparus canadensis* (Whiteaves), 1885, and *Hoploparia tennesseensis* Rathbun, 1926; and the mud shrimp *Protocallianassa mortoni*. Also included are numerous yet unidentified claws. This fauna is one of the most abundant and diverse decapod assemblages ever discovered. Continued collection of the fauna is guaranteed by a Georgia Southern College Faculty Research grant in the amount of $1385.10 to cover the interim between the termination of current National Geographic funding and possible future funding. Besides the diversity and abundance of decapod remains, this locality is important because it provides a contemporaneous analog for comparison with the Western Interior *Dakoticancer* record of *Paguristes* from the Gulf Coastal Plain, and the first assemblage to contain all 3 taxa of the Dakoticancroidea, *Avitelmessus, Dakoticancer,* and *Tetracarcinus*. One specimen collected by Mr. Robert Mitchell, then a graduate student at the University of Mississippi at Blue Springs, is the only fossil specimen out of about 5000 specimens of *Dakoticancer* with evidence of any attached organisms living commensually. The specimen (Fig. 6) exhibits a small oyster attached to the posterior of the carapace. Continued study of this locality is currently being carried on by myself and Mr. Robert Mitchell. It is anticipated that the complete molluscan and decapod fauna will be tied into a regional analysis of depositional environments in the Ripley Formation in the Mississippi Embayment. The specimens at the Blue Springs Locality are collected as float specimens as well as in situ specimens. The in situ specimens will allow a taphonomic analysis of the fauna (Bishop, 1983c).

Re-collection of Old Localities

Re-collection of known localities is an important facet of this continuing research as new taxa and new data on preservation and paleoecology invariably turn up with additional work.

Visits to the well-collected Mobridge Locality yielded the anterior of a carapace of a new species of *Homolopsis mendryki* Bishop, 1982 that was previously known only from the posterior of the carapace. Oddly enough, the specimen (Fig. 11) was discovered by Mr. Harry Mendryk on a 1-day visit to the outcrop during 1977, not by my numerous visits to the outcrops over the past several years. A new example of a *Dakoticancer* intersex was discovered in 1976, represented by a specimen (Fig. 12) with female gonopore at the base of the fourth leg and male gonopore at the base of the fifth leg which thus differs from that previously described (Bishop, 1974, 1983a.).

Re-collecting the Oliver Ranch Locality in Carter County, Montana, yielded the heretofore uncollected crabs *Zygastrocarcinus* sp. and *Raninella* sp.

The 2000± specimens placed in my hands for study by Harry Mendryk from the Chesapeake and Delaware Canal include many specimens with exoskeleton preserved. For the first time we know what the North Atlantic crabs including *Tetracarcinus subquadratus* Weller, 1905, looked

---

FIGURES 1-13. Fossil Cretaceous crabs from various localities.

1-5. Crabs from Merchantville Formation, Chesapeake and Delaware Canal, Delaware: 1, Steinkern of *Tetracarcinus subquadratus* cf. *Dakoticancer overanus* in hematite concretion (carapace broken out along shear cone controlled by sternum), (x 1.0); 2, Carapace of *Tetracarcinus subquadratus,* (x 1.0); 3, Carapace of *Homolopsis atlantica*(?) with right branchial chamber inflated due to isopod parasite, (x 1.0); 4, Carapace and legs of *Raninella tridens,* (x 1.0); 5, Carapace of *Paranecrocarcinus gamma* showing fine preservation, (x 1.0).

6. Steinkern of *Dakoticancer overanus australis* with commensal oyster attached to posterior of carapace, Ripley Formation, Mississippi, (x 1.0).

7-8. Crabs from the Heart Tail Ranch Locality, Pierre Shale, South Dakota: 7, Carapace and legs of *Glaessnerella* n. sp., in concretion, (x 1.5); 8, Carapace of *Necrocarcinus pierrensis* broken free of concretion, (x 1.5).

10. *Dakoticancer overanus* from the Baresch Locality, Butte Co., South Dakota in calcite concretion, (x 1.0).

9, 11-13. Crabs from the *Dakoticancer* Assemblage, Mobridge Locality, Pierre Shale, South Dakota: 9, Carapace of *Dakoticancer Overanus;* 11, Anterior part of carapace of *Homolopsis* n. sp. found by Harry Mendryk, (x 1.5); 12, Ventral view of intersex of *Dakoticancer overanus* (anterior downward) showing female gonopore on left (arrow) and male gonopore on right (arrow), (x 2.0); 13, Carapace of *Necrocarcinus pierrensis* showing excellence of preservation, (x 1.5).

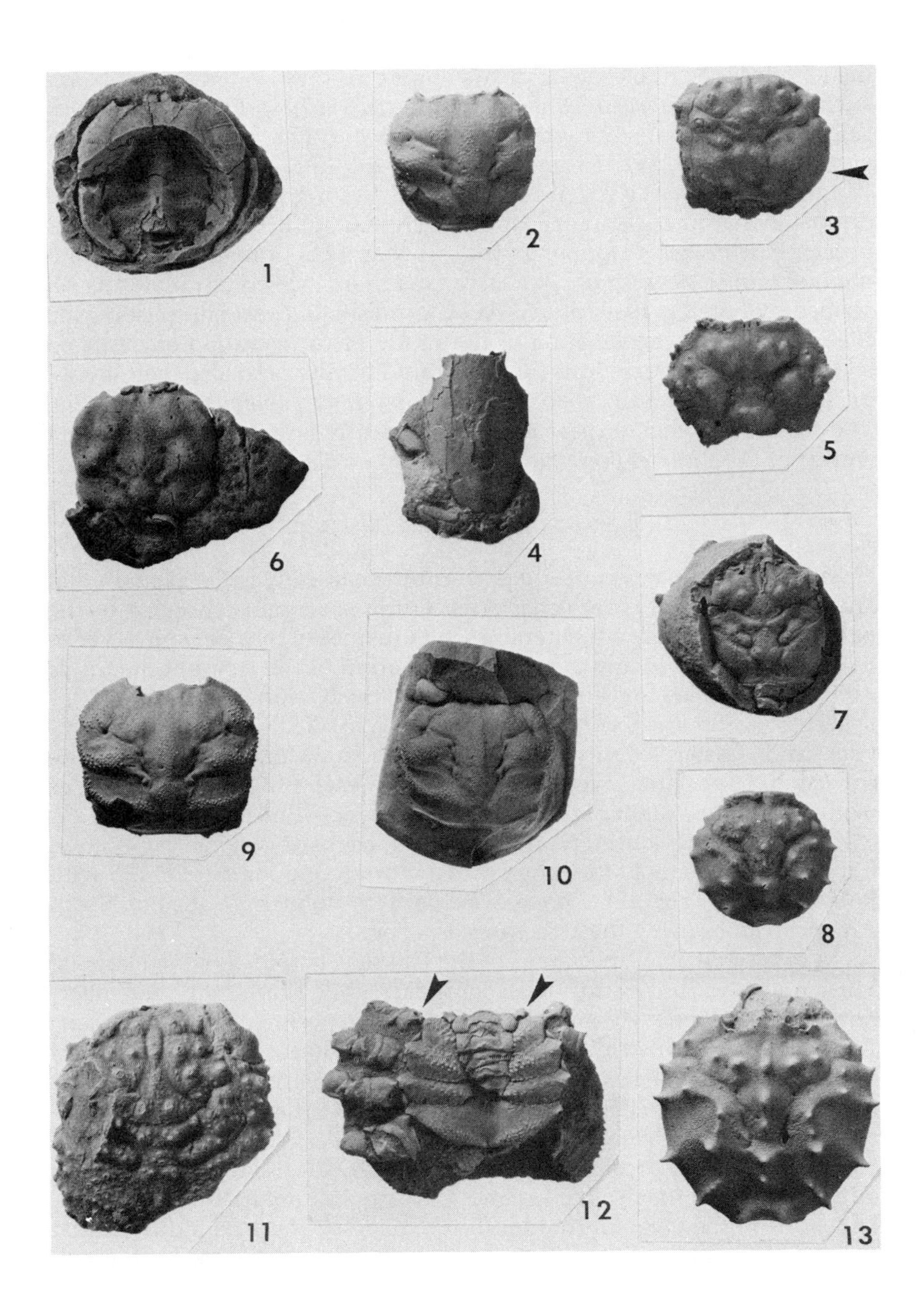
1
2
3
4
5
6
7
8
9
10
11
12
13

like (Fig. 2). The fine preservation of those specimens (Fig. 2-5) will allow me to redescribe numerous taxa and should resolve systematic problems such as whether *Homolopsis atlantica* Roberts, 1962, and *Homolopsis dispar* Roberts, 1962, are synonymous with one another or with *Homolopsis punctata* Rathbun, 1917 (from the Western Interior) as was suggested by Wright and Collins (1972, p. 44). Other interesting relationships will undoubtedly become apparent as the collection is studied in detail (e.g., the presence of parasitic isopods in the gill chambers of many of the specimens of *Homolopsis atlantica* [Fig. 3] caused them to become inflated as described by Förster, 1969, p. 51). Another problem presenting itself from the locality is the explanation of the mode of preservation of pyritized crab in hematite concretions (Biddle Point Locality) and also their identity. They have classically been identified as *Tetracarcinus subquadratus* (Fig. 1) even though they appear to be significantly larger and disturbingly similar to *Dakoticancer overanus* (Fig. 9).

Reevaluation of Old Collections

An important aspect of any paleontological study is the examination and reevaluation of older collections. Often specimens collected in the past can be extremely enlightening when restudied by a new observer or by new methods. In any case the examination of the type specimens of each taxon is called for. Visits were made to the National Museum of Natural History (Smithsonian Institution), the U. S. Geological Survey (Denver), and Carter County Museum (Ekalaka, Montana) to examine collections. Specimens were borrowed from each of these collections as well as from the Wagner Free Institute of Science (Philadelphia).

Specimens have been rephotographed, as many original publication figures are inadequate for comparative work (e.g., compare Fig. 5 with Roberts, Pl. 85, Fig. 12). I hope eventually to publish an atlas of North American crabs using these pictures as a base.

A catalogue of all specimens of the Dakoticancroidea in the National Museum of Natural History was compiled while examining that collection. This catalogue will provide basic data on specimens of *Dakoticancer, Tetracarcinus,* and *Avitelmessus* in the National Museum that are currently available for study; it has already provided the basis for additional collecting of the Mississippi Embayment which, consequently, led to the discovery of the Blue Springs Locality.

The U. S. Geological Survey collections in Denver have been given an initial screening that yielded many exciting specimens previously unknown from the Western Interior (e.g., *Eomunidopsis*) and indicates that many additional localities rich in decapods are available for further collecting and many undescribed crabs are available for study.

Collections of the National Museum of Natural History and the Carter County Museum (Montana) indicate the existence of a rich crab fauna in the Bearpaw Shale near Baker, Montana. Time spent in the field searching for this locality has thus far been unsuccessful.

New Techniques

This study resulted in the funding (Faculty Research Committee, Georgia Southern College, $408.65) of a proposal in 1977 to purchase a $2\frac{1}{4}$ x $3\frac{1}{4}$ Galvin View camera; the camera was subsequently built into a macrophotographic system which I designed. This primary imaging system was augmented during the summer of 1978 by an International Scientific Instruments scanning electron microscope (Model SMS 2-2, Super II). These two systems allow whole-specimen imaging from 0.5 to about 100,000 magnifications.

Summary

The pursuit of this study has led to the collection of more than 1000 fossil decapods from 19 localities in Delaware, New Jersey, Mississippi, South Dakota, and Montana. Examination of these collections is still under way but it is already obvious that numerous new species are represented by the material. New paleoecological relationships (e.g., oyster commensals on *Dakoticancer*, intersex of *Dakoticancer*, parasitic deformation of *Homolopsis*) have been discovered and are being described. Many type specimens have been examined and rephotographed, which will facilitate future systematic work. Two new crab localities were discovered and 4 new localities collected. Each holds great promise of producing exciting scientific results in testing hypothesized relationships.

The synthesis of the data as of June 1977 was presented to the Second North American Paleontological Convention and that in turn resulted in invitations to publish two papers in symposia volumes. Three papers have been published during the duration of this grant. The National Geographic Society grant has acted as a stimulus; already our research has yielded significant results in our understanding of Cretaceous crab history in North America.

Acknowledgments

Direct financial aid for this study has been received from the National Geographic Society and the Faculty Research Committee of Georgia Southern College. Direct personal assistance has been received from Mr. Harry Mendryk, Mr. Larry Eichhorn, Dr. W. A. Cobbon, Mr. Warren C.

Blow, Mrs. Delores Baresch, Dr. and Mrs. J. Paul Gries, Mr. Robert Mitchell, Dr. Norman Sohl, and Dr. Richard Petkewich. Special thanks are extended to students who served as unpaid field assistants: Mr. H. C. "Card" Smith, Mr. R. L. "Rob" Priestley, and Mr. Tony Hemphill. As always, this scientist owes a great debt to his wife, Nelda, and children, Kim and Eric, for their understanding, as I spent too much time away from home completing this work. Specimens have been graciously loaned by the National Museum of Natural History, the U. S. Geological Survey (Denver), the Carter County Museum (Ekalaka, Montana), and the Wagner Free Institute of Science (Philadelphia).

REFERENCES

Bishop, Gale A.

1974. A sexually aberrant crab (*Dakoticancer overanus* Rathbun, 1917) from the Upper Cretaceous Pierre Shale of South Dakota. Crustaceana, vol. 26, pp. 212-219.

1977. Pierre feces: A scatological study of the *Dakoticancer* Assemblage, Pierre Shale (Upper Cretaceous) of South Dakota. Journ. Sedimentary Petrol., vol. 27, pp. 129-136.

1978. Two new crabs, *Sodakus tatankayotankaensis* n. gen., n. sp. and *Raninella oaheensis* n. sp. (Crustacea, Decapoda) from the Upper Cretaceous Pierre Shale of South Dakota. Journ. Paleont., vol. 52, pp. 608-617.

——. Fossil decapods from the Heart Tail Ranch Locality and the Baresch Locality, Butte Co., South Dakota. Bureau of Land Management (Belle Fourche Office), April 1, 1978. (Unpublished report).

1981a. The lobster *Linuparus* preserved as an attachment scar on the oyster *Exogyra costata*, Ripley Formation, Late Cretaceous, Union County, Mississippi. Miss. Geol., vol. 2, pp. 2-5.

1981b. Occurrence and fossilization of the *Dakoticancer* Assemblage from the Upper Cretaceous Pierre Shale of South Dakota. Pp. 383-413 *in* "Communities of the Past," Jane Gray, A. J. Bouct, and W.B.N. Berry, eds., Hutchinson and Ross Pub. Co.

1982. *Homolopsis mendryki:* A new fossil crab (Crustacea, Decapoda) from the Late Cretaceous *Dakoticancer* Assemblage, Pierre Shale (Maastrichtian) of South Dakota. Journ. Paleont., vol. 56, pp. 221-225.

1983a. A second sexually aberrant specimen of *Dakoticancer overanus* Rathbun, 1917 from the Upper Cretaceous *Dakoticancer* Assemblage, Pierre Shale, South Dakota. Crustaceana, vol. 44, pp. 23-26.

1983b. Fossil decapod crustaceans from the Lower Cretaceous, Glen Rose Limestone of Central Texas. Trans. San Diego Soc. Nat. Hist., vol. 20, pp. 27-55.

1983c. Fossil decapod crustacea from the Late Cretaceous Coon Creek Formation. Journ. Crustacean Biol., vol. 3, pp. 417-430.

1983d. Two new species of crabs, *Notopocoryste (Eucorystes) eichhorni* and *Zygastrocarcinus griesi* (Decapoda, Brachyura) from the Bearpaw Shale (Campanian) of north-central Montana. Journ. Paleont., vol. 57, pp. 900-910.

BISHOP, GALE A. *(continued)*

____. A preliminary report on the Cretaceous crabs of North America. *In* "The North Temperate Cretaceous (Symposium)," Earle Kauffman, and Don Hattin, eds. Dowden, Hutchinson, and Ross, Inc. (Ms. 43 pp., 2 figs., 2 pls., 1 table.) In press.

FÖRSTER, REINHART

1969. Epökie, Entökie, Parsitismus und Regeneration bei fossilen Dekapoden: Mitteilungen der Bayerischen Staassammlung für Palaontologie und Historie. Geologie, Heft 9, p. 45-59, Tafel 2-3.

GILL, JAMES R., and COBBAN, WILLIAM A.

1966. The Red Bird Section of the Upper Cretaceous Pierre Shale in Wyoming. U. S. Geol. Survey Prof. Paper 393-A, 73 pp.

RATHBUN, MARY J.

1917. New species of South Dakota Cretaceous crabs. U. S. Nat. Mus. Proc., vol. 52, pp. 385-391.

1923. Decapod crustaceans from the Upper Cretaceous of North Carolina. N.C. Geol. Survey, vol. 5, pp. 407.

1926. *In* Wade, Bruce, "The fauna of the Ripley Formation on Coon Creek, Tennessee." U. S. Geol. Survey Prof. Paper 137, 272 pp.

1935. Fossil Crustacea of the Atlantic and Gulf Coastal Plain. Geol. Soc. Amer. Spec. Paper 2, pp. 1-160, 26 pls., 2 figs.

ROBERTS, HENRY B.

1962. The Upper Cretaceous decapod crustaceans of New Jersey and Delaware. Pp. 163-191 *in* "The Cretaceous fossils of New Jersey," H. G. Richards, ed. N.J. Bur. Geol. and Topo., Bull. 61.

SCHOPF, THOMAS J. M.

1978. Fossilization potential of an intertidal fauna: Friday Harbor, Washington. Paleobiology, vol. 4, pp. 261-270.

SOHL, NORMAN F.

1960. Archeogastropoda, Mesogastropoda, and stratigraphy of the Ripley, Owl Creek, and Prairie Bluff Formations. U. S. Geol. Surv. Prof. Paper 331-A, pp. 1-151, 18 pls., 11 figs.

WELLER, STUART

1905. The fauna of the Cliffwood, New Jersey clays. N.J. Geol. Surv., Ann. Rept. for 1904, pp. 136-141.

WRIGHT, C. W., and COLLINS, JOSEPH S. H.

1972. British Cretaceous crabs. Palaeontographical Society Monograph, publ. 533, 114 pp.

GALE A. BISHOP

A Preliminary Estimate of the Reduction of the Western Arctic Bowhead Whale (*Balaena mysticetus*) Population by the Pelagic Whaling Industry: 1848-1915

Grant Recipient: John Bockstoce, New Bedford Whaling Museum, New Bedford, Massachusetts.

Grant 1652: In support of a study of the bowhead whale population of the western Arctic.

Introduction

Today the bowhead whale (*Balaena mysticetus*) population of the Bering, Chukchi, and Beaufort Seas is at the center of a controversy about the effect of the Alaskan Eskimo hunt on its numbers. Although many observers believe the population has not recovered significantly from the low level at which it probably stood in 1915, hitherto no thorough attempt has been made to estimate the number of bowheads that were taken by the pelagic whaling industry. Based on primary resources (logbooks and maritime newspapers), this report presents the results of the first systematic endeavor to reach an estimate of the annual bowhead kill.

Although a few bowheads may have been taken between 1843 and 1847, these whales were not deliberately sought until 1848. In that year Captain Thomas Roys sailed into seas unknown to whalemen and discovered the great whaling grounds beyond Bering Strait where the bowheads, oil-rich, baleen-laden, and docile, were found in numbers. Roys quickly filled his ship and returned to Honolulu to broadcast his success. Word of these new whaling grounds spread quickly, and in the following year more than 40 vessels sailed north and enjoyed equally successful cruises. In succeeding years the news of the 1849 season increasingly lured other vessels, and in 1852 more than 200 whaleships operated in the Bering Strait region. (For the purposes of this report I defined the Bering Strait region as the waters of the Bering and Chukchi Seas between approximately lat. 60° and 72° N.)

The whalers quickly established a routine that they would vary only slightly for the next 60 years. Leaving New England in the autumn and rounding Cape Horn in the southern summer, they would fit out at Hawaiian ports or San Francisco, sailing for the Arctic in late March to reach the pack ice of the central Bering Sea a month later. They took a few whales as they worked their way north toward Bering Strait through the melting floes, but by early June most of the whales had passed them and gone deep into the safety of the ice on the migration to their summer feeding grounds in the Arctic Ocean. The whalemen would not see their quarry again until late July when the ice allowed the ships to approach the north coast of Alaska and intercept the whales traveling from the Beaufort Sea to their autumn feeding grounds near Herald Island in the Chukchi Sea. The ships often cruised near Herald Island until the violent weather and encroaching ice of early October drove them back to ports in the Pacific Ocean.

The whalemen usually repeated these summer voyages once or twice more before returning to their home ports. Some alternated their summer hunts among cruises to the Arctic, the Okhotsk Sea, or the Gulf of Alaska, depending on where the best catches were being made; nevertheless, they rarely visited more than one of these areas per year.

The intensity of the hunting in the early years of the fishery quickly reduced the bowhead population, and it is possible that the whales themselves responded to the threat, for the catches of 1853 and 1854 were poor enough in comparison with previous years that the fleet virtually abandoned the Bering Strait region in 1855, 1856, and 1857, and turned its attention to the bowheads of the Okhotsk Sea. It too was soon overhunted, and the whalemen returned to Bering Strait in 1858 to cruise there regularly for the following half century.

In spring, once the ships reached lat. 57° or 58° N, the whalemen began to watch for bowheads; for the next 5 or 6 months they generally kept themselves in constant readiness to lower their boats. When they saw whales, if the seas were not too rough, 4 or 5 boats usually went after them. If the men were lucky, a boat got close enough to strike a whale with a harpoon. The whale would then run, towing the line and boat after it and eventually becoming sufficiently exhausted so that it could be killed with a lance. But frequently whales escaped into the ice, towing lines and gear. In response to these losses the whalemen, after about 1860, increasingly used darting guns (which were fixed to the harpoon shaft and fired a small bomb into the whale at the moment of striking) and shoulder guns (28-lb, brass smooth bores that fired a similar bomb from a distance and, thus, generally replaced the lance).

Once the whale was dead, or if a dead whale were found, the carcass was towed to the ship, where the crew took the baleen aboard and stripped off and "tryed out" (rendered into oil) the blubber. As a rough average, a moderate-sized bowhead yielded 100 bbl of oil (a barrel was 31½ U. S. gal) and 1500 lb of baleen.

By 1866 the hunting pressure had put the bowhead population in steep decline, and to offset poor catches the whalemen began taking walrus and gray whales *(Eschrichtius robustus)* in the "middle season" between their spring and autumn encounters with the bowheads. A decline in oil prices soon ended this; by 1800 oil prices were so low that profits could only be made by taking baleen, the great flexible plates that hang from a bowhead's upper jaw and are used to filter food from the water. As the price of oil sank, forced down by petroleum products, the price of baleen began to rise dramatically, driven by the call of the fashion industry for, among other uses, "whalebone" corset stays and skirt hoops.

In 1880 the western Arctic remained the major profitable whaling ground for the American fleet (vessels of other nations had ceased whaling there in the 1870s), and the rising price of baleen stimulated the development of steam-auxiliary whaling vessels. These immediately proved successful in pursuing the whales to the least accessible corners of the Arctic Ocean. In 1889 steamers reached the bowheads' summer feeding grounds off the Mackenzie River delta in Canada's Northwest Territories, and from then until 1915 the focus on the industry was concentrated largely on those waters. Changes in fashion and the introduction of flexible spring steel as a cheap substitute for baleen caused the market to collapse in 1908, dragging the industry with it. After 1915, although a few vessels cleared port as whaleships, they were in fact primarily as fur trading and freighting voyages, and only a few whales were taken by ships thereafter.

Resources and Methods

The basic source for this study was the *Whalemen's Shipping List and Merchants' Transcript*. Published in New Bedford from 1843 to 1914, it contains the most comprehensive documentation of the American whaling industry; its weekly issues posted the latest information on all American whaling vessels throughout the world (Fig. 1). The *Shipping List* was of particular use to this project because whaling vessels usually touched at a major port to refit, to take on fresh provisions, and to report their cargoes immediately before and after their half-year Arctic cruise; thus, their Arctic catch can usually be determined (expressed in barrels of oil and pounds of baleen) by subtracting the cumulative cargo listed in the spring from that listed in the autumn. Once in the Arctic, ships passing one another frequently reported their "season's catch" (usually expressed in the number of whales they had taken); this information, carried by ships

287 **WHALEMEN'S SHIPPING LIST AND MERCHANTS**

VESSELS' NAMES	ton	MASTERS	AGENTS	SAILED	BOUND	LAST REPORT.	OIL.
NEW BEDFORD.							
Abigail	310	Drew	Wm G E Pope	Aug 24, 52	N Pacific	Sept 18, 52, at Fayal	clean
A H Howland	414	Pease	Abraham H Howland	Aug 18, 51	N Pacific	Mch 29, 52, at Maui	90 sp
Ab'm Barker	400	Norton	Abraham Barker	Sept 10, 50	N Pacific	Aug 52, in Bherings sts wanting 1 wh	
Active, bark	333	Morrison	Cook & Snow	June 1, 52	Indian Ocean	Aug 11, 52, at Fayal	landed 84 sp
Adeline	329	Carr	I Howland jr & Co	Sept 21, 50	N Pacific	June, 52, off Cape Thadeus	unk
Addison	426	Cash	Isaac B Richmond	Sept 20, 52	Pacific		
Alexander	421	Ryan	John A Parker	June 11, 51	N Pacific	Aug 1. 52, off Bh'ngs sts 8 whs this sea	
Alex Coffin	381	Purrington	Jonathan Bourne jr	Nov 13, 51	N Pacific	June 1, 52, in Bherins sts 1 wh this sea	
Alice Frazier, bk	406	Taber	Lemuel Kollock	Sept 10, 51	N Pacific	No date in Bherings sts	5 whs
Alice Mandell	413	Wing	C R Tucker & Co	Sept 10, 51	N Pacific	Apl 10, 52, at Oahu for Arctic	50 sp
Alto, bark	236	Carr	Richmond & Wood	Sept 3, 51	Atlantic & Ind	Abt Jan 4, 52, off River Platte	150 sp
Alfred, sch	184	Gifford	Wm. G. E. Pope	June 12, 52	Atlantic	Sept 10, 52, at Fayal	landed 35 sp
Alfred Gibbs	425	Jenney	Wood & Nye	Nov 13 51	N Pacific	Apl 3, 52, off Oahu, bd N.	25 sp on bd
America	418	Fisher	I Howland jr & Co	June 25, 51	N Pacific	Aug 1, 52, off Bh'ngs sts 6 whs this sea	
America, bark	257		Joseph A Beauvais	In port		Arrived Oct 2, 52, 450 sp	
Amethyst	349	Howes	John A Parker & Son	Sept 28, 50	Pacific	Aug 23, 52, at Tombez	750 sp
Anaconda, bark	383		Isaac B Richmond	In port			
Anadir, bark	615	Swift	Swift & Perry	Jan 2, 51	N Pacific	Aug 21, 52, off Bh'ngs sts 8 wh this sea	
Andrews, bark	393	Nye	Wm P Howland	June 3, 50	Pacific	Sept 20, 52, at Tombez	900 sp
Antarctic	319	Bradbury	Wm P Howland	May 3, 52	Pacific	Sept 2, 52, at Fayal	landed 15 sp
Archer	322	Macomber	Edward W Howland	Oct 5, 52	Pacific		
Arnolda	360	Harding	James B Wood & Co	July 19, 52	Pacific	Sept 3, [illegible] at Fayal	landed 22 sp
Atlantic, bark	367	Lane	Hathaway & Luce	Oct 31, 51	Atlantic &c	Sept 25, 52, sld fm Fayal 440 sp landed	
Balaena	301	Dexter	J & J Howland	Sept 1, 49	Pacific	Sept 20, 52, at Tumbez	1300 sp
Baltic, bark	395	Brooks	Alexander Gibbs	Nov 16, 51	N Pacific	June 21, 52, lat 56 N. lon 172 w	unk
Barnstable	373	Coon	William F Dow	May 6, 51	Pacific	Apl 9, 52, at Paita	200 sp on board
Barclay	261	Taber	Henry Taber & Co	July 7, '52	Atlantic	Aug 17, 52, at Fayal	landed 150 sp
Bart Gosnold	356	Heustis	I Howland jr & Co	July 15, 51	Pacific	Aug 20, 52, off Bh'ngs sts 12 whs this sea	
Benj. Tucker	349	Sands	C R Tucker & Co	Nov 5, 51	N Pacific	Early in season in Arctic had done well	
Bevis, bark	214	Snell	Benjamin B Howard	June 4, 50	Indian Ocean	June 12, 52, off Johanna	640 sp
Brandt	310		Alexander Gibbs	In port		Arrived Sept 12, 52, 1000 sp 140 wh	
Brighton	364	Weaver	James D Thompson	Oct 9, 50	N Pacific	Aug, 52, in Bherings sts	clean
Braganza	470	Devoll	Wm G E Pope	Sept 10, 50	N Pacific	Aug 1, 52, off Bh'ngs sts 10 whs this sea	
Bramin	345	Childs	Gideon Allen	Sept 9, 51	N Pacific	Mch 14, 52, at Hilo	clean
Callao	324	Baker	Henry Taber & Co	July 27, 52	N Pacific	Sept, 52, at Fayal	clean
Cambria	362	Cotte	James B Wood & Co	Sept 3, 51	N Pacific	Mch 28, 52, at Maui	clean
California	398	Wood	I Howland jr & Co	Oct 22, 51	N Pacific	Last of July heard from	7 whs
Caroline	364	Gifford	William Gifford	Aug 3, 52,	N Pacific		
Carolina	395		S Thomas & Co	In port			
Catalpa, bark	260	Hamblin	I Howland jr & Co	Aug 12, 52	Atlantic & Ind	Sept 17, 52, lat 31 N. lon 42 w	clean
Canada	545	Ths West	Barton Ricketson	Oct 1, 51	N Pacific	Aug 1, 52, off Bh'ngs sts 6 whs this sea	
Canton	409	Wing	E Perry & W C N Swift	Aug 10, 52	N Pacific	Sept 14, 52, at Fayal	clean
Canton, 2d	280	Folger	C R Tucker & Co	July 31, 51	Pacific	Jan 7, 52, off Juan Fernandez	clean
Canton Packet	274	Howland	I H Bartlett & Son	Dec 28, 49	New Zealand	Dec 29, 51, cld at Oahu 20 sp	550 wh
Chas W Morgan	351	Sampson	Edward M Robinson	June 5, 49	Pacific	April 20, 52. off French Rock	900 sp
Chandler Price	441	Taber	Wm G E Pope	July 25, 51	N Pacific	First of season heard from	unk
Charles	290	Manchestr	Lemuel Kollock	July 25, 49	Pacific	May 27, 52, at Gallipagos Is 500 sp	700 w
Champion	336	Waterman	James D Thompson	June 18, 50	N Pacific	Mch 20, 52, sld fm Hong Kong	240 wh
Ch'n Packet, bk	184	Lewis	Tho's Knowles & Co	Apl 19, 51	Indian Ocean	June 1, 52, off Seychelle Is	clean
Chas Frederick	317	Haskins	John A Parker & Son	Aug 22, 50	Pacific	Aug 28, 52, off Ceros Island	900 sp
Cherokee, bark	261	Smith	Hathaway & Luce	Aug 19, 51	N Pacific	Mch 28, 52, at Maui	clean
China	370	Howes	William Phillips	June 22, 52	N Pacific	July 19, 52, at Fayal	clean
[illegible]	[illegible]	Anderson	Benjamin B Howard	July 13, 52	Pacific		

VESSELS' NAMES	ton	MASTERS	AGENTS
NEW BEDFORD.			
Ja's Andrews, b	275	Beetie	Charles Hitch
James Arnold	393		Henry Taber
James Edward	434	R Luce, jr	George F Bar
Java	278	Lawrence	Geo & Math H
Janus	321	Cornell	T & A R Nye
James Maury	395	Whelden	C R Tucker &
Jasper, bark	223	Rotch	Alexander Gil
Jeannette	340	West	Isaac B Richm
Jireh Perry	435	Lawrence	E Perry & W C
John	308	Tilton	Frederick Par
John A Parker b	342	Taber	Henry F Thor
John Howland	377	Taylor	James H How
John & Edward	318	Cathcart	Wilcox & Ric
John Wells	366	Cross	Tho's Knowle
Joseph Butler, b	193	Mayhew	I Howland jr
Joseph Meigs	356	G Allen	George Husse
Julian	356	Cleveland	Hathaway &
Junior	378	Hammond	David R Green
J E Donnell, bk	343	Earl	Swift & Allen
Kathleen, bark	312	Allen	James H Sloc
Kensington	357	Clark	David B Kem
Kutusoff	415	Pierce	Henry F Thor
Lafayette, bark	341		I H Bartlett &
Lætitia, bark	275	Alden	F & G R Tabe
Lagoda	341	Tobey	Jonathan Bou
Lalla Rookh	323	Gardner	John A Parke
Lancaster	383	Almy	T & A R Nye
Lancer	395	Lakeman	Richmond &
Leonidas	231	Clark	Russell Maxfi
Levi Starbuck	376	Ellison	Edward W H
Lewis	308	Clement	I H Bartlett &
Lexington, bark	201		Benjamin B H
Liverpool	306	Barker	Abraham Bark
Liverpool 2d	428	Swift	Thomas Wilco
Logan	302	Tucker	I Howland jr &
Louisiana	297	Taber	T & A R Nye
Louisa, bark	316	Wyatt	Swift & Allen
L C Richmond	341	Cochran	James B Woo
Magnolia	396	G L Cox	Wm G E Pope
Malta, bark	151	Smith	Benjamin B H
Manuel Ortez, b	351	C H Cole	Weston Howla
Majestic	297	Percival	S Thomas & C
Marengo	426	Devoll	Jonathan Bou
Marcella, bark	210	Rounds	C R Tucker &
Massachusetts	364	Bennett	William F Do
March, brig	89	Reynolds	William P Ho
Marcia	315	Wing	Edward W H
Margaret Scott	307	Eldridge	Rodney Frenc
Maria, bark	202		Samuel W Ro
Maria Theresa	330	Taylor	T & A R Nye
Mars, bark	270	Harrison	C R Tucker &
Martha, bark	271	Chase	Swift & Allen
Martha, bark, 2d	400	Tooker	William O Br

FIGURE 1. Detail of page from *Whalemen's Shipping List and Merchant's Transcript* 1852 (courtesy of New Bedford Whaling Museum).

leaving the Arctic, would also find its way to the pages of the *Shipping List*. To organize these data we constructed a ledger sheet (Fig. 2), listing information gathered for each year and subdivided by home port.

The data from the *Shipping List* were augmented and corrected by adding information from other newspapers (principally from Honolulu's *Friend* and *Pacific Commercial Advertiser* and several San Francisco papers) as well as from scattered data in more than 500 printed books, magazine articles, manuscripts, government documents, and logbooks. This body of data was then spot-checked for accuracy against information compiled in the 19th century by Dennis Wood, a New Bedford insurance broker (Wood's records are held by the New Bedford Free Public Library). These resources allowed us to expand our purview beyond the American whaling industry to include vessels of the other nations operating in the western Arctic: Hawaii, Germany, France, and Great Britain (Australia). In all, more than 14,000 reports were tabulated.

Of particular value was the information from logbooks and private journals (Fig. 3). After we had constructed the basic list of Arctic voyages from newspaper sources, we turned to the published checklists of the logbooks and journals that are now held in public collections. Using our list of Arctic voyages, we were thus able to identify the manuscript materials from this fishery. Of the more than 2600 seasonal cruises, we found records of more than 600 in public collections. We then tried to examine a number of records equal to 5 to 10% of the Arctic cruises for each year. We extracted the following data from the logbooks and journals for each Arctic cruise: the number of lowerings for whales, the number of whales struck and lost, the number found dead, and the number taken, as well as the names of ships seen in the Arctic and their reported catches. These data allowed us to expand and correct our list of Arctic voyages and to appraise a number of other aspects of the whale kill that varied from year to year throughout the duration of the fishery (see Results section).

The logbook data also provided us with information on both the total number of bowheads taken during a vessel's Arctic season and on those whales' combined yield of oil and baleen. From this information we derived a crude average for the size of the whales captured (expressed in barrels of oil and pounds of baleen); and, using this average as a rough guideline, we then applied it to the figure for the products of each ship's seasonal catch to estimate the number of bowheads taken by that ship.

When coupled with an understanding of the changing tactics and economics of the whaling industry, these averages proved to be a useful analytical tool for exposing spurious additions of oil or baleen. For instance, once the figures for a ship's oil and baleen had been divided by

WHALEMEN'S SHIPPING LIST

YEAR 1852 PAGE 2 N.B.

			SEASON REPORT			SEASON REPORT			SEASON REPORT			POST SEASON REPORT			PRE SEASON REPORT			WHALES			
			DATE OF EDITION: Nov. 16			DATE OF EDITION: Nov. 23			DATE OF EDITION: Dec. 7			DATE OF EDITION: Jan. 18, 1853			DATE OF EDITION: Sept. 7						
HOME PORT	VESSEL/RIG	MASTER	DATE OF REPORT	LOCATION	CATCH/CARGO	DATE OF REPORT	LOCATION	CATCH/CARGO	DATE OF REPORT	LOCATION	CATCH/CARGO	DATE OF REPORT	LOCATION	CATCH/CARGO	DATE OF REPORT	LOCATION	CATCH/CARGO			PROBABLE NUMBER	
N.B	BARTHOLOMEW GOSNOLD		Aug 28	B.S.	12 whales	[MILO log] Aug. 22	Arctic	14 whales	Sept. 6	Arctic	16 whales		MAUI	1850 bbls.	March 16	MAUI	no whale oil				
	SHIP	HEUESTIS				[CONDOR log] Aug. 14	Arctic	19 whales	[NIAGARA log] Sept. 7	Arctic	16 whales	Dec. 17		1850 30,000					1850 30,000	16.51 18.24	17
N.B	BENJAMIN TUCKER		[B. WILLIAMS log] May 26 N. Bering	Arctic no whale oil	"had done well"	[NIAGARA log] July 5	B.S.	2 whales	Sept. 1	Arctic	8 or 9 whales	[B. TUCKER log] 7 whales Arctic	OAHU	800 bbls.	April 12	LAHAINA	clean				
	SHIP	SANDS	[Oct. 8]	June 15	Boiling	[Oct. 8]	Aug. 18	6 whales	[MONTREAL log] Sept. 1	Arctic	8 whales	[Dec. 17]	HONOL. Oct. 23	800 12,000	11 Mos.				800 12000	7.13 7.29	8
N.B.	BRIGHTON		[CONDOR log] June 27 Aug?	B.S.	clean clean	[MILO log] Aug 31	Arctic	4 whales	Sept. 12	Arctic	1100 bbls.		OAHU	1000 bbls.	March 30	At sea	Un-known				
	SHIP	WEAVER	[NIAGARA log] June 14	B.S.	Clean														1000	8.92	9
N.B.	BRAGANZA		Aug. 1	B.S.	10 whales	[MONTREAL log] Aug 14	Arctic	11 whales	Sept. 1	Arctic	2200 bbls.		HILO	2250 bbls.	Jan. 15	MOMANGUI	480 bbls.				
	SHIP	DEVOLL	[MONTREAL log] June 16	NAV.	2 whales	[Oct. 8]	Aug. 15	11 whales	[Montreal log] Sept. 8	Arctic	13 whales	[Dec. 17]		2250 30,000					1770 30000	15.79 18.24	16
N.B	CALIFONIA		"Late" July	N.R	7 whales	[MILO log] Aug. 16	Arctic	7 whales	Sept. 9	Arctic	8 whales		OAHU	1650 bbls.	April 1	Honol.	no whale oil				
	SHIP	WOOD	[Oct. 8]	July 20	1000 bbls.	[MONTREAL log] July 30	B.S.	7 whales	[CONDOR log] Aug 16	Arctic	8 whales	[Dec. 17]		1650 25,000	12 Mos.				1650 25000	14.72 15.20	15
N.B	CANADA		Aug. 1	B.S.	6 whales	[HARVEST log] Aug. 12	Arctic	6 1/2 whales	Sept. 16	Arctic	9 whales		OAHU	1000 bbls.	April 13	OAHU	clean				
	SHIP	THOMAS WEST	[Sept. 17]	July 4	3 1/2 whales	Oct. 8	July 25	6 1/2 whales				[Dec. 17]		1000 10,000	13 Mos.				1000 10000	8.92 6.08	8 1/2
N.B	CITIZEN		July 10	B.S.	8 whales	[B. WILLIAMS log] Aug. 29	Arctic	11 whales	Sept. 20	Arctic	1700 bbls.	Wrecked in Arctic	Sept. 25		April 23	HONOL.	clean				
	SHIP	NORTON	[MONTREAL log] July 8	B.S.	9 whales	[HARVEST log] July 10	B.S.	8 whales + 1 dead											1700	15.17	15
N.B	CORNELIUS HOWLAND		Aug. ?	B.S.	10 whales	[NIAGARA log] July 5	B.S.	5 whales	Sept. 29	Arctic	1850 bbls.		OAHU	1800 bbls.	March 6	GUAM	N.R.				
	SHIP	CROSBY	[NIAGARA log] April 24 Oct. 8	N. BERING	clean 12 whales	[MILO log] July 12	B.S.	5 whales	[B. TUCKER log] Sept. 8	Arctic	12 whales	[Dec. 17]		1800 30,000	14 Mos.				1800 30000	16.06 18.24	12
N.B.	COWPER		[MILO log] May 24 N. Bering	clean	July 10 B.S. 2 whales				July 19	B.S.	4 whales		OAHU	1600 bbls.	March 10	MAUI	N.R.				
	SHIP	FISHER	[Oct. 8]	June 25	2 whales	[HARVEST log] July 5	B.S.	2 whales				[Dec. 17]		1600 25,000					1600 25000	14.27 15.20	14

FIGURE 2. *Whalemen's Shipping List*, one of the project's ledger sheets for New Bedford vessels, 1852 (courtesy of New Bedford Whaling Museum).

the appropriate year's average, if a wide discrepancy were found between the number of whales indicated by each (Fig. 2, right column), then a high oil figure from a voyage in the 1870s might indicate the presence of walrus oil or gray whale oil in the cargo; similarly in the 1890s (when the price of oil was very low) a high baleen figure frequently indicated that little oil was being saved.

A note should be made about the sources that we intentionally did not consult. A number of compendia of data about whaling voyages exist, but an examination of each revealed serious deficiencies for our needs. Although Starbuck's (1964) and Hegarty's (1959) important works were based on the information in the *Shipping List,* these authors included only the cumulative results of the entire whaling voyage and hence are of little value for determining the annual bowhead catch; furthermore there are some omissions and errors in each. Townsend (1935) devoted a section of his report to the bowhead whales of the North Pacific, but he segregated them neither geographically nor chronologically; consequently bowheads from the Okhotsk Sea and the western Arctic are listed together under the total number taken on an entire whaling voyage, not for each season. In addition, a spot-check of his data revealed that occasionally gray whales and right whales were counted as bowheads and that some bowhead captures were overlooked. Although Clark (1887) listed seasonal reports for voyages to the western Arctic from 1868 to 1884, he omitted some vessels that operated there and included others that did not; his figures for each vessel's seasonal products frequently include walrus oil, gray whale oil, right whale oil and baleen, or bowhead baleen that was obtained in trade from the natives. Estimates of the bowhead kill that are based on these sources should be treated with skepticism.

Results

The results of this project are summarized below.

Preliminary Information: Average Size of Whales Taken (Table 1)

If the number of whales that a ship took in the Arctic was not recorded, then it was necessary to determine the average size of the whales taken in that year (expressed in barrels of oil and pounds of baleen) and then to apply this average to the ship's cargo of oil and baleen. The averages were computed from information that was extracted from logbooks, from journals, and from those newspaper reports that included both the total number of whales taken on an Arctic cruise and the amount of oil and baleen they yielded. Because these averages were obtained from a relatively small sample, we restricted their use to that of a rough guide and coupled

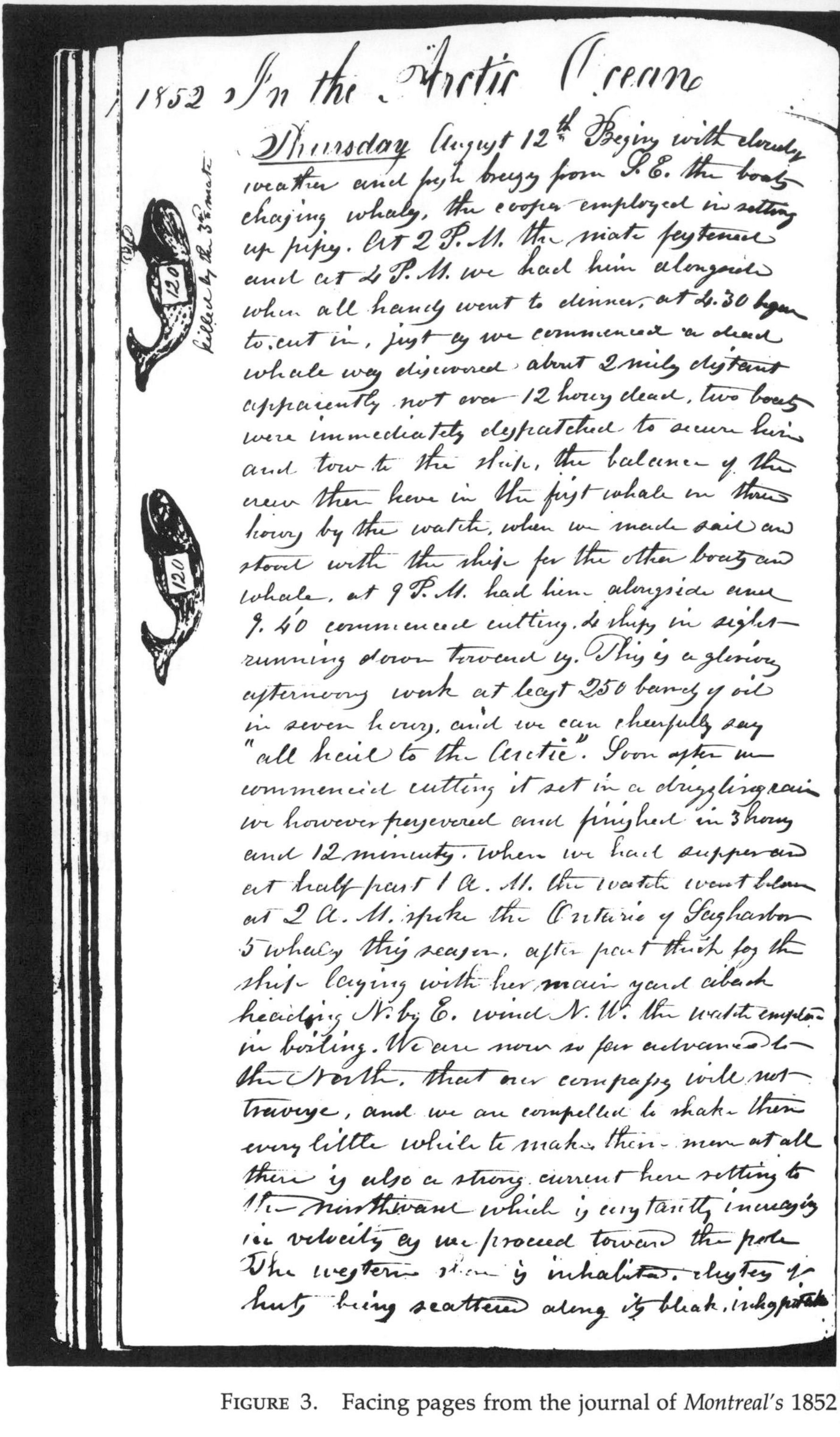

1852 In the Arctic Ocean

120

killed by the 3d mate

120

Thursday August 12th Begins with cloudy weather and fresh breeze from S.E. the boats chasing whales, the cooper employed in setting up pipes. At 2 P.M. the mate fastened and at 4 P.M. we had him alongside when all hands went to dinner, at 4.30 began to cut in, just as we commenced a dead whale was discovered about 2 miles distant apparently not over 12 hours dead, two boats were immediately despatched to secure him and tow to the ship, the balance of the crew then hove in the first whale in three hours by the watch, when we made sail and stood with the ship for the other boats and whale. at 9 P.M. had him alongside and 9.40 commenced cutting. 4 ships in sight running down toward us. This is a glorious afternoons work at least 250 barrels of oil in seven hours, and we can cheerfully say "all hail to the Arctic". Soon after we commenced cutting it set in a drizzling rain we however persevered and finished in 3 hours and 12 minutes. when we had supper and at half past 1 A.M. the watch went below at 2 A.M. spoke the Ontario of Sagharbor 5 whales this season. after part thick fog the ship laying with her main yard aback heading N. by E. wind N.W. the watch employed in boiling. We are now so far advanced to the North, that our compasses will not traverse, and we are compelled to shake them every little while to make them move at all there is also a strong current here setting to the northward which is constantly increasing in velocity as we proceed toward the pole The western shore is inhabited. clusters of huts being scattered along its bleak, inhospitable

FIGURE 3. Facing pages from the journal of *Montreal's* 1852

1852 In the Arctic Ocean

shore as far up as 70 North: the location of the North Pole, according to the experiments of the different exploring expeditions in search of the N.W. passage. the current here however we do not think extends 30 miles from land! as we found ourselves at noon about 30 miles from land and had not been currented at all

No current these 24 hours | Lat. by Obs. 67.28 N.
Long. " Chron 171.25 W

Friday August 13th Begins with foggy weather and light breezes from N.W. the ship heading N.N.E. and laying with main yard aback, the crew employed in boiling and setting up pipes. At 4 P.M. lights up for a short time, saw 4 ships two of them boiling also braced forward and wore ship heading S.W. by W. middle part occasional fog squalls, saw a whale the mate lowered and just as his boatsteerer stood up the whale settled, at an early saw upwards of 20 ships 14 of them boiling 2 cutting and the others whaling, after part mild clear beautiful weather, and whales in sight – lowered 1st 2nd and 3rd boats, did not take at 9 the boats were called to the ship a light breeze on from the Eastward, the ship running for more whales in sight from mast heads in half an hour they lowered again. remainder of the day employed in boiling

Lat. by Obs. 67.36 N.
No current these 24 hours | Long. " Chron. 170.58 W

Saturday August 14th Begins with fine weather and light breezes from the Eastward. plenty of whales in sight, and boats chasing in every direction, each chasing their own whales

cruise (courtesy of New Bedford Whaling Museum).

TABLE 1. Preliminary Information: Average Size of Whales Taken, 1848-1915

a = 1849 average used
b = 1852 average used
c = 1853 average used
d = 1858 average used
e = 1872 average used
f = 1875 average used
g = 1879 average used
h = 1883 average used
j = 1885 average used
k = no average needed

Year	*No. ship's returns*	*Avg. size of whales taken*[1]		*Year*	*No. ship's returns*	*Avg. size of whales taken*[1]	
		Bbl[2] *oil*	*Lb baleen*			*Bbl*[2] *oil*	*Lb baleen*
1848	a	a	a	1882	h	h	h
1849	12	132.43	b	1883	7	110.00	1543.75
1850	6	119.87	b	1884	j	j	j
1851	9	117.04	b	1885	11	96.98	1149.31
1852	24	112.05	1644.06	1886	7	95.11	1546.51
1853	11	113.07	1509.61	1887	9	91.70	1403.25
1854	c	c	c	1888	17	89.23	1548.35
1855	c	c	c	1889	13	83.17	1403.57
1856	d	d	d	1890	27	75.73	1413.37
1857	d	d	d	1891	20	88.97	1212.02
1858	6	97.74	1516.12	1892	11	88.54	1556.36
1859	16	111.21	1469.69	1893	8	86.95	1521.73
1860	8	93.58	1597.22	1894	4	93.33	1690.47
1861	5	113.33	1733.33	1895	3	92.50	1260.00
1862	2	106.25	1562.50	1896	3	87.50	1425.00
1863	6	106.17	1419.75	1897	3	122.33	1461.11
1864	13	93.22	1388.88	1898	k	k	k
1865	13	98.13	1526.08	1899	5	102.08	1503.21
1866	26	90.07	1616.93	1900	k	k	k
1867	30	86.95	1383.06	1901	k	k	k
1868	6	82.85	1385.71	1902	k	k	k
1869	22	88.20	1464.00	1903	k	k	k
1870	7	77.84	1150.53	1904	3	82.45	1390.36
1871	e	e	e	1905	k	k	k
1872	10	102.61	1488.37	1906	k	k	k
1873	4	95.90	1568.18	1907	k	k	k
1874	2	86.36	1590.90	1908	k	k	k
1875	6	97.09	1327.27	1909	k	k	k
1876	f	f	f	1910	k	k	k
1877	2	125.00	1568.18	1911	k	k	k
1878	g	g	g	1912	k	k	k
1879	5	118.05	1527.77	1913	k	k	k
1880	g	g	g	1914	k	k	k
1881	h	h	h	1915	k	k	k

[1] If data are insufficient, another year's average is used for further computations.
[2] 1 bbl = 31½ U. S. gal.

them with other information (see Resources and Methods section and Fig. 2) to estimate the number of whales taken by each vessel in a particular year. For those years in which insufficient data were available the average we used for computations was drawn from another year, close in time, with a reliable data base. For the years after 1897, when the total number of whales taken by each ship was frequently reported, it was often unnecessary to construct averages.

AVERAGE CATCH AND EFFORT PER VESSEL (TABLE 2)

To determine the average annual catch and effort per vessel the following information was extracted from the logbooks: the number of times a ship lowered its boats to chase whales, the number of whales struck and lost, the number found dead, and the number taken alive.

TABLE 2. Average Catch and Effort per Vessel, 1848-1915

Averages used where data were insufficient: a = 1849, b = 1858, c = 1911.

	Logs consulted	*Lowerings per vessel*	*Whales struck and lost per vessel*	*Whales found dead per vessel*	*Whales taken alive per vessel*	*Whales taken alive and dead per vessel*[1]	*Live whales as % total catch*	*Effort: lowerings per whale taken alive*
Year	A	B	C	D	E	F	G	H
1848	0	a	a	-	-	-	-	a
1849	1	30	1	0	11	11	100	2.72
1850	5	31	1	0	5	5	100	6.20
1851	11	22	3	1	7	8	87	3.14
1852	13	39	4	1	14	15	93	2.78
1853	7	34	3	2	5	7	71	6.80
1854	4	18	3	0	2	2	100	9.00
1855	2	41	3	0	4	4	100	10.00
1856	1	16	2	0	3	3	100	5.33
1857	1	b	0	1	b	3	66	8.00
1858	6	18	2	0	2	2	100	9.00
1859	5	19	2	0	3	3	100	6.33
1860	6	13	2	1	4	5	80	3.25
1861	3	15	1	0	6	6	100	2.50
1862	2	20	3	0	7	7	100	2.85
1863	5	27	2	0	14	14	100	1.92
1864	5	20	1	1	5	6	83	4.00
1865	6	24	2	1	7	8	87	3.42
1866	4	26	2	0	5	5	100	5.20
1867	4	27	1	0	8	8	100	3.37
1868	3	20	0	1	5	6	83	4.00

TABLE 2. *(continued)*

1869	7	21	1	1	9	10	90	2.33
1870	9	24	1	0	12	12	100	2.00
1871	6	11	1	0	3	3	100	3.66
1872	6	16	1	1	3	4	75	5.33
1873	4	14	1	0	3	3	100	4.66
1874	2	46	2	0	5	5	100	9.20
1875	4	15	1	0	9	9	100	1.66
1876	1	4	0	0	2	2	100	2.00
1877	3	23	2	0	9	9	100	2.55
1878	2	11	2	1	2	3	66	5.50
1879	1	27	9	2	7	9	77	3.85
1880	3	36	2	0	20	20	100	1.80
1881	1	33	0	0	17	17	100	1.94
1882	2	8	1	0	4	4	100	2.00
1883	2	7	0	0	2	2	100	3.50
1884	2	15	1	0	4	4	100	3.75
1885	4	20	2	0	6	6	100	3.33
1886	1	6	1	0	2	2	100	3.00
1887	2	30	1	0	6	6	100	5.00
1888	4	17	1	0	1	1	100	17.00
1889	3	8	0	0	1	1	100	8.00
1890	4	13	0	0	5	5	100	2.60
1891	5	16	1	0	6	6	100	2.66
1892	3	15	1	0	5	5	100	3.00
1893	4	11	0	0	5	5	100	2.20
1894	4	15	1	1	4	5	80	3.75
1895	4	17	1	0	4	4	100	4.25
1896	3	2	0	0	2	2	100	1.00
1897	3	19	1	0	5	5	100	3.80
1898	4	20	3	0	8	8	100	2.50
1899	3	24	0	0	15	15	100	1.60
1900	3	16	1	0	8	8	100	2.00
1901	3	6	0	1	3	4	75	2.00
1902	2	30	2	0	10	10	100	3.00
1903	2	19	1	0	5	5	100	3.80
1904	1	4	0	0	2	2	100	2.00
1905	2	18	2	1	8	9	88	2.25
1906	1	1	0	0	1	1	100	1.00
1907	1	16	1	0	5	5	100	3.20
1908	0	c	c	c	c	c	c	c
1909	1	5	0	0	2	2	100	2.50
1910	1	14	0	0	4	4	100	3.50
1911	2	18	1	0	7	7	100	2.57
1912	0	c	c	c	c	c	c	c
1913	0	c	c	c	c	c	c	c
1914	0	c	c	c	c	c	c	c
1915	0	c	c	c	c	c	c	c

[1] Total of columns D and E, this table.

For the purposes of this report we have defined a struck-and-lost whale as one that could not be processed after being wounded; that is, any live whale struck by a harpoon, darting gun, or bomb lance shoulder gun. Hence, any whale that was struck and lost and later found dead by a ship would be counted under the dead whale category. The very few whales that died of natural causes and were found by ships are also included in the dead whale category. These data, in turn, allow an estimate of the effort expanded per caught whale by computing the average number of lowerings per live whale taken. Because the technology of the fishery was altered somewhat with the introduction of steam auxiliary vessels, it would have been interesting to segregate these data into sail and steam categories; unfortunately the size of our data base would not allow us to do this with confidence. We plan to carry out such an analysis in a future project (see Future Research section).

Similarly, although it would have been desirable to collect information on the number of boats that were lowered during each encounter with whales (thus providing a better estimate of the effort per caught whale), this information rarely appears systematically in logbooks. It is likely that a larger body of data, collected with greater refinement, will allow this analysis (see Future Research section).

Estimated Number of Whales Taken and Struck and Lost by Known Vessels (Table 3)

The information compiled in our ledgers (Fig. 2) yielded evidence of more than 2600 whaling cruises to the Arctic. For the vast majority of these we were able to determine the amount of oil and baleen collected there and then to estimate the number of bowheads taken (see Resources and Methods section). The results of these computations appear in columns B and C of this table. We were, however, unable to determine the Arctic products of some of the ships; consequently we estimated their catches by using the figure for the average catch per vessel that we had established from logbooks and other reliable data (see Resources and Methods section and Table 2, column F). We estimated the annual total catch of whales (both alive and dead) taken by all known vessels (Table 3, column F) by combining the figures in columns C and E of this table. The estimated number of whales that were annually struck and lost (as defined for Table 2) was computed by applying the annual average (Table 2, column C) to the total number of known cruises in column A of this table.

A note must be made about the "half" whales listed in columns C and F of this table. Occasionally whaleboats from two ships would assist one another in capturing a whale; in such a case the products would be shared, and, correspondingly, a midseason report might list "7½ whales." If, in column F of this table, a year's total for the estimated number of whales taken by known vessels included a "half" whale, this fraction was rounded off to the next whole number for use in further computations because, of course, it represented one whale kill.

TABLE 3. Estimated Number of Whales Taken and Struck-and-Lost by Known Vessels, 1848-1915

	Total known vessels cruising Arctic	*Known vessels with recorded products*	*Est. of whales taken[1] by known vessels with recorded products*	*Known vessels without recorded products*	*Est. of whales taken[1] by known vessels without recorded products[2]*	*Est. of whales taken[1] by all known vessels[3]*	*Est. of whales struck and lost[4]*
Year	A	B	C	D	E	F	G
1848	1	1	15	0	0	15	1
1849	46	38	454	8	88	542	46
1850	110	94	1358	16	80	1438	110
1851	150	111	562½	39	312	874½	450
1852	220	211	2585½	9	135	2720½	880
1853	161	148	852½	13	91	943½	483
1854	42	35	78	7	14	92	126
1855	5	5	21	0	0	21	15
1856	13	13	49	0	0	49	26
1857	8	7	49	1	3	52	0
1858	101	99	442½	2	4	446½	202
1859	82	79	331	3	9	340	164
1860	47	46	267	1	5	272	94
1861	45	41	211	4	24	235	45
1862	17	16	111	1	7	118	51
1863	35	34	331	1	14	345	70
1864	80	77	373½	3	18	391½	80
1865	84	70	415	14	112	527	168
1866	78	77	660	1	5	665	156
1867	81	79	597	2	16	613	82
1868	59	58	458½	1	6	464½	0
1869	42	42	436	0	0	436	42
1870	54	53	601	1	12	613	54
1871	43	38	105	5	15	120	43
1872	34	31	196	3	12	208	34
1873	32	32	111½	0	0	111½	32
1874	17	16	134	1	5	139	34
1875	20	20	190	0	0	190	20
1876	19	18	140	1	2	142	0
1877	22	21	116½	1	9	125½	44
1878	24	13	43	11	33	76	48
1879	29	23	93	6	54	147	261
1880	23	20	252	3	60	312	46
1881	22	15	186½	7	119	305½	0

1882	34	31	177	3	12	189	33
1883	36	35	85	1	2	87	0
1884	38	35	174½	3	12	186½	38
1885	41	36	234	5	30	264	82
1886	33	32	161	1	2	163	33
1887	37	37	300	0	0	300	37
1888	39	36	147	3	3	150	39
1889	42	40	72	2	2	74	0
1890	39	37	133	2	10	143	0
1891	35	35	126½	0	0	126½	35
1892	45	44	243½	1	6	249½	45
1893	45	43	303	2	10	313	0
1894	33	32	111	1	5	116	33
1895	30	29	39	1	4	43	30
1896	26	25	91	1	2	93	0
1897	24	24	81	0	0	81	24
1898	20	20	152½	0	0	152½	60
1899	16	16	109	0	0	109	0
1900	16	11	81	5	40	121	16
1901	13	12	38	1	4	42	0
1902	12	12	68	0	0	68	24
1903	14	14	25	0	0	25	14
1904	17	17	57	0	0	57	0
1905	15	15	59	0	0	59	30
1906	14	14	25	0	0	25	0
1907	11	10	58	1	5	63	11
1908	10	10	25	0	0	25	10
1909	5	4	14	1	2	16	0
1910	4	4	8	0	0	18	0
1911	5	5	43	0	0	43	5
1912	4	1	2	3	24	26	4
1913	5	0	0	5	40	40	5
1914	4	2	11	2	14	25	4
1915	1	0	0	1	7	7	1

[1] Whales taken both alive and dead.
[2] Based on average from Table 2, column F.
[3] Total of columns C and E, this Table.
[4] Based on Table 2, column C.

Estimated Number of Whales Killed by Known Vessels (Table 4)

It is obvious that more whales were killed than merely those that were captured: some wounded whales escaped and died; others were killed, sank, and could not be recovered; others were killed, taken to the ship, and then lost during gales before they could be processed. It is reasonable to assume that 50% of the whales that were struck and lost (as defined for Table 2) died of their wounds.

TABLE 4. Estimated Number of Whales Killed by Known Vessels, 1848-1915

Year	*Logs consulted* A	*Est. number of whales taken alive and dead*[1] B	*Pct. of live whales taken to total taken*[2] C	*Est. number of whales taken alive*[3] D	*Est. number of whales struck and lost*[4] E	*Est. mortality of whales struck and lost*[5] F	*Est. total mortality of whales by known vessels*[6] G
1848-1859	56	7536	91	6858	2503	1252	8110
1860-1869	45	4068	94	3824	788	394	4218
1870-1879	37	1873	95	1779	570	285	2064
1880-1889	24	2032	99	2012	308	154	2166
1890-1899	37	1428	97	1385	227	114	1499
1900-1915	19	660	97	640	124	62	702

[1] From Table 3, column F.
[2] From logbook data.
[3] From columns B and C, this table.
[4] From Table 3, column G.
[5] 50% of column E, this Table.
[6] Total of columns D and F, this table.

But because our estimate of the number of whales taken by known vessels (Table 3, column F) included both whales captured alive and those found dead, in order to reach an estimate of the total mortality it was necessary to reduce this figure to an estimate of the number of whales taken alive (Table 4, column D) before adding to it the estimated number of whales that died after being struck and lost. It was necessary to group our data into six periods of time to allow a more reliable data base for computing the percentage of alive whales taken to the total number taken (Table 4, column C).

Estimated Number of Whales Taken and Killed by all Pelagic Whaling Vessels

I estimate that we have identified 98% of all pelagic whaling cruises to the Bering Strait region and western Arctic from 1848 to 1915. In this estimate I am excluding vessels used solely for trading, shore whaling, freighting, walrusing, or wrecking, although some of these vessels cleared port as whalers. Thus, with 2609 known cruises (Table 3, column A), it is likely that 2662 cruises were actually made (assuming column A = 98% of all cruises). If 17,597 whales were taken by those known vessels (Table 3, column F), it is likely that 17,956 whales were taken by all vessels (assuming column F = 98% of total no.); and if 18,759 whales were killed by known vessels (Table 4, column G), it is likely that 19,142 were killed by all vessels (assuming column G = 98% of total kills). Although further research may well refine these estimates, it is probable that they fall within 15% of the actual number.

Future Research

This work should be considered a reconnaissance. In order to assess quickly the reduction of the western Arctic bowhead population we restricted ourselves to using those resources that were both convenient and accurate. Out of the strictures of time and budget we limited our logbook research to a representative sample, extracting data on a relatively coarse level.

This study provided the basis for a more far-reaching assessment of the western Arctic bowhead population. (See "The Historical Status and Reduction of the Western Arctic Bowhead Whale [*Balaena mysticetus*] Population by the Pelagic Whaling Industry, 1848-1914," by John R. Bockstoce and Daniel B. Botkin, appearing in *Reports of the International Whaling Commission*, Special Issue 5, International Whaling Commission, Cambridge, U.K., 1983, pp. 107-141.)

In the future we plan to expand greatly our data base and to refine our methods of data extraction through a project to be carried out in association with the Marine Biological Laboratory (Dr. Daniel B. Botkin, co-principal investigator) of Woods Hole, Massachusetts. We plan to build on the research we have begun here, using logbooks as our primary resource, extracting daily information and storing it in a computer-based retrieval system, and organizing the information under a number of topics (including date, latitude and longitude, weather conditions, number of whales seen, and their size, if they were captured).

Coupled with modern mathematical and ecological techniques and theories, these records can provide estimates of former stocks, relative changes in populations, population distribution, migration patterns, and the depletion of the whales. These data will allow development and verification of mathematical models of the bowhead present and future population trends and into the requirements for the successful protection of this and other species.

Acknowledgments

I am grateful to Mr. Richard Kugler, director of the New Bedford Whaling Museum, and to Mr. Philip F. Purrington, senior curator, for their support and advice. I wish to thank Dr. David Henderson, research associate of the Whaling Museum and Professor of Geography, California State University at Northridge, and Dr. Daniel Botkin, Associate Professor, Marine Biological Laboratory, Woods Hole, Massachusetts, for their helpful criticisms. Several other people have generously given valuable assistance to the project: Miss Judith Downey, Mr. Bruce Barnes, and Mr. Bruce Brigell of the New Bedford Free Public Library; Mrs. Virginia Adams of the Providence Public Library; Mr. Douglass Fonda and Dr. Adam Weir Craig of the International Marine Archives; and the Research Assistants of the Whaling Museum, Mrs. Rosalie Baker, Mr. Homer Langlois, and Mrs. Judith Oliviera. I am particularly indebted to Miss Susan Cohen whose diligence and care have greatly contributed to the success of the project.

Funding for the project was contributed by the Old Dartmouth Historical Society, Marine Mammal Commission, National Geographic Society, and American Philosophical Society. Logistical support at Point Barrow, Alaska, was provided by the U. S. Naval Arctic Research Laboratory.

REFERENCES

Clark, A. Howard
1887. The whale fishery. The history and present condition of the fishery. Pp. 86-95, sec. 5, vol. 2 *in* "The Fisheries and Fishery Industries of the United States," George Brown Goode, ed. Government Printing Office, Washington, D. C.

Hegarty, Reginald B.
1959. Returns of whaling vessels sailing from American ports, 1876-1928, 58 pp. Old Dartmouth Historical Society, New Bedford, Massachusetts.

Starbuck, Alexander
1964. History of the American whale fishery from its earliest inception to the year 1876, 779 pp. Argosy Antiquarian Ltd., New York.

Townsend, Charles Haskins
1935. The distribution of certain whales as shown by logbook records of American whaleships. Zoologica, vol. 19, no. 1, pp. 3-52.

John Bockstoce

Fish Collecting and Exploration of the Río Nichare, Venezuela

Grant Recipient: James E. Böhlke, Department of Ichthyology, Academy of Natural Sciences, Philadelphia, Pennsylvania.[1]

Grant 1615: Fish collecting and exploration of Río Nichare, Venezuela.[2]

The freshwater fish fauna of South America is the richest and most diverse in the world but remains relatively poorly known compared with those elsewhere. Although it has been collected and studied since the 17th century, the literature dealing with it is vast and widely scattered and usually deals with limited regions. Large and ecologically important areas have remained uncollected. Current progress in the economic growth of many areas, resulting in alteration of habitats by deforestation, agriculture, and industrialization, makes it imperative that fishes be sampled and faunal studies initiated before the habitats and the fish are lost (Böhlke et al., 1978). Such studies can provide valuable additional information on the geographical distribution of neotropical freshwater fishes.

South American faunistic regions were defined in a 1969 publication by Jacques Géry, in which eight regions were outlined and described based on the distribution of freshwater fishes. They have been generally and largely uncritically followed by subsequent workers, although doubted in various aspects by ichthyologists working with South American fishes. One such proposed regional line, demarcating the Orinoco-Venezuelan region from the Guianean-Amazonian area, was questioned

[1] Deceased March 1982. His wife, Eugenia B. Böhlke, prepared this report "from departmental records on the collection, from my husband's notes on the trip, and on discussions he had with colleagues both before and after the trip, in particular with Stanley H. Weitzman of the Smithsonian Institution. He had also kept a day-to-day journal, basically a narrative of the journey, from which I obtained a few items included in the report."

[2] Additional support for this study was provided by the T.F.H. Fund administered through Dr. Victor G. Springer of the Smithsonian Institution, Washington, D. C.

by James E. Böhlke and a Venezuelan colleague, Agustín Fernández-Yépez,[3] in discussions between them in 1972. The area in question had remained untested by any study of the fauna of that region at that time.

This expedition was planned primarily as a biogeographical study to sample the fish fauna of a small north-flowing stream in southern Venezuela, to obtain a concept of the species there, and to compare them with those in the black waters of the upper Río Negro and Río Orinoco and, when collections eventually become available, the upper Río Branco. Such comparisons would serve to test the validity of Géry's hypothetical line.

The Río Nichare, a tributary of the Río Caura, which flows into the Río Orinoco in the central Venezuelan state of Bolívar, was selected as the area of study. An untouched stream near the middle of the course of the Caura, it appeared to be an ideal collecting site; upper tributaries with isolated populations would be expected to exhibit greater differentiation and a high degree of endemism; lower areas would be likely to have similar faunas throughout the two regions. The Nichare is in the area separating Géry's two faunistic regions and, while the river had been explored and the general topography and forest of the region described (Williams, 1941), it had not previously been collected. Fernández-Yépez was familiar with the region and agreed to participate in the expedition and assist with preparations, and a joint collecting trip was proposed.

The expedition was delayed for several months by unusual flooding and high water which precluded access to the area, but was finally undertaken January 13 to February 13, 1977. Participants were James E. Böhlke and William G. Saul of Philadelphia, and Agustín Fernández-Yépez and assistants Edilberto Ferrer-Veliz and José Moreno of Barquisimeto, Venezuela. Supplies and vehicles (a station wagon and pickup truck) obtained in Barquisimeto were driven to the small settlement of Jabillal (La Prisión), located on the Río Caura about 20 minutes upstream from the Nichare-Caura junction, which served as the base camp for the trip. From there, travel was by dugout boat and by foot on trips of one to several days' duration to various collecting sites; one plane trip allowed a collection farther upriver about halfway into the Río Caura drainage. Collecting was carried out during the day and at night using ichthyocides, seines, dip-nets, hook and line, and any other means available. Life color of fishes was recorded by photography in addition to field notes. All specimens were preserved in formalin for shipment to the Academy of Natural Sciences in Philadelphia for further study.

The Río Nichare proved impossible to collect as planned. "Heading upriver through several series of rapids, we soon were stopped abruptly

[3] Deceased May 1977.

FIGURE 1. Looking into the Nichare rapids at the junction of the Río Nichare and the Río Caura in central Venezuela, state of Bolívar.

by impenetrable rapids—swift water at a low water level (Fig. 1). Our stated goal of collection and exploration of the Nichare clearly was beyond us, there not even being good trails through the jungle paralleling the river, so we turned back to the parent stream, the Caura, for collecting emphasis" (Böhlke field journal). The Río Caura was explored and collected as far as its impassable rapids and falls at Salto de Para. One collection was obtained at the head of the falls, a 7-km hike up the almost vertical western face of the mountain, where pools were collected by dip net and by hand (using cheese sandwiches as chum). Collections were made in the Río Nichare as far as the impenetrable rapids.

Collections were obtained from the following sites (listed north to south): Río Cuchivero at Cuchivero; Caño Morichal Zambrai between Río Tauca and Río Tiquire; Río Urbana at the Maripa-Las Trincheres road; Río Mato at Quebrada Cuchivero and at other tributary streams; Caño Puerto Cabello at Puerto Cabello; Río Caura at Jabillal and environs (many collections) and at Caño Chuapo, Caño Barranca, Surapire Rapids, and at various small unnamed caños and pools; Río Nichare at its junction with the Caura and upstream and various sites up to and at La Raya Rapids; Río Cusime at Caño Cuchime (this the farthest upriver and reached by plane).

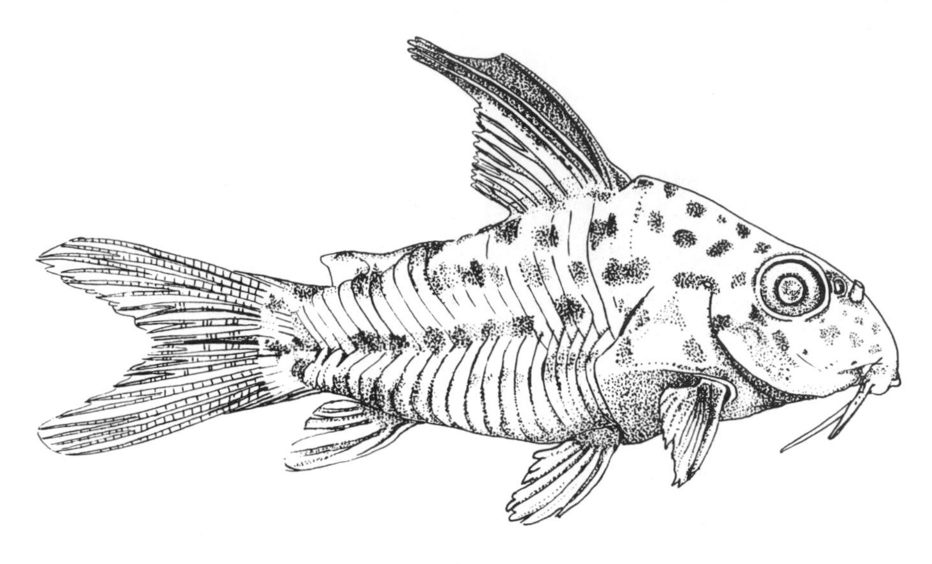

FIGURE 2. *Corydoras boehlkei* Nijssen and Isbrücker, paratype, ANSP 149257. Illustration by Mary H. Fuges.

The resulting collection of some 463 lots including more than 6300 specimens has been identified (some to genus only) and catalogued into the collection at the Academy. Included are 3624+ characoids, 1917+ catfishes, 379 gymnotoids, 322 cichlids, 17 hemirhamphids, 3 synbranchoids, 3 stingrays, and 1 anchovy. The comprehensive faunal study envisioned has not been completed owing to the deaths of both Böhlke and Fernández-Yépez. Some results of the study to date are available at this time. The discovery of two new species from the locality farthest upstream on the Caura (at Río Cusime) supports previous observations and predictions of a high degree of endemism at high elevations; additional new species will likely be found through continued collecting of these remote areas. A new species of catfish, *Corydoras boehlkei* (Fig. 2), has been described by Nijssen and Isbrücker (1982), and the description of a new species of the characid genus *Aphyocharax* will be completed by Stanley H. Weitzman of the Smithsonian Institution. The collection of many specimens of *Poecilocharax weitzmani,* described by Géry from Peru, extended the range of that species north and east into the Orinoco drainage. Preliminary comparison of the fauna of this area of the Río Caura with those from other river systems indicates some relationships with the Río Negro.

This collection is now available for study by other workers. Selected families and groups of taxa are currently on loan to specialists working on them. Although this expedition should be considered a preliminary exploration with future collecting in additional areas desirable, the collection at the Academy provides a basis for a faunal study of this area of Venezuela. It will serve as a valuable sourcc of material for comparison of species of the upper and lower parts of a river system. Eventually, when the fauna of this area can be adequately compared with those of the upper parts of the Río Negro, Río Orinoco, and Río Branco, Géry's concept of faunistic regions for freshwater fishes in northern South America can be further tested.

REFERENCES

Böhlke, J. E.; Weitzman, S. H.; and Menezes, N. A.
1978. Estado atual da sistemática dos peixes de água doce da América do Sul. Acta Amazonica, vol. 8, no. 4; pp. 657-677.

Géry, J.
1969. The freshwater fishes of South America. Pp. 828-848 *in* "Biogeography and Ecology in South America," vol. 2, E. J. Fittkau et al., eds. Dr. W. Junk, The Hague.

Nijssen, H., and Isbrücker, I. J. H.
1982. *Corydoras boehlkei*, a new catfish from the Río Caura system in Venezuela (Pisces: Siluriformes: Callichthyidae). Proc. Acad. Nat. Sci. Philadelphia, vol. 134, pp. 139-142.

Williams, L.
1941. The Caura valley and its forests. Geographical Review, vol. 31, pp. 414-429.

Eugenia B. Böhlke

Palynological Research at Olduvai Gorge

Grant Recipient: Raymonde Bonnefille, Laboratoire de Géologie du Quaternaire Centre National de la Recherche Scientifique, Faculté des Sciences du Luminy, Marseille, France.

Grant 1592: Palynological studies related to paleoecology and evolution of early hominids at Olduvai Gorge.[1]

Palynological investigations on the Omo-East Turkana Basin have proved useful for the reconstruction of the paleoenvironment of early hominids in east Africa (Bonnefille, 1976a, b). Fieldwork at Olduvai Gorge was coming to an end; geological and archeological studies were ready to be published (Hay, 1976; L.S.B. Leakey, 1965; M. D. Leakey, 1971). G. Riollet and the author began a search for fossil pollen grains in the Olduvai beds in order to complete the paleoenvironmental picture at Olduvai Gorge (Jaeger, 1976).

Analytical pollen data obtained from lake sediments provide information directly relevant to the reconstruction of the flora and vegetation during the time of occupation by early hominids. Such information can be useful in order to answer two questions. The first deals with the kind of vegetation—how the environment looked: Was it forest, steppe, or grassland or was it a mosaic of forest and grassland? This is a paleoecological reconstruction (Bonnefille and Riollet, 1980). The second question regards what kind of plant food was available in the environment occupied by early hominids. This depends on the taxonomical composition of the flora. However, since fossil pollen grains can rarely be identified to the species level, information on plant resources must be sought indirectly (Peters and O'Brien, 1981).

Modern flora and vegetation are both related, broadly speaking, to the modern climate. Another function of pollen analysis is to provide indirect information relevant to the reconstruction of past climate. This is based on the assumption of the principle of uniformity and on the modern character of the flora that has been established since the mid-Miocene (Chesters, 1957; Hamilton, 1968; Axelrod and Raven, 1978).

---

[1] G. Riollet served as co-leader for this study; J. Raynal, G. Buchet, and N. Buchet were scientific personnel.

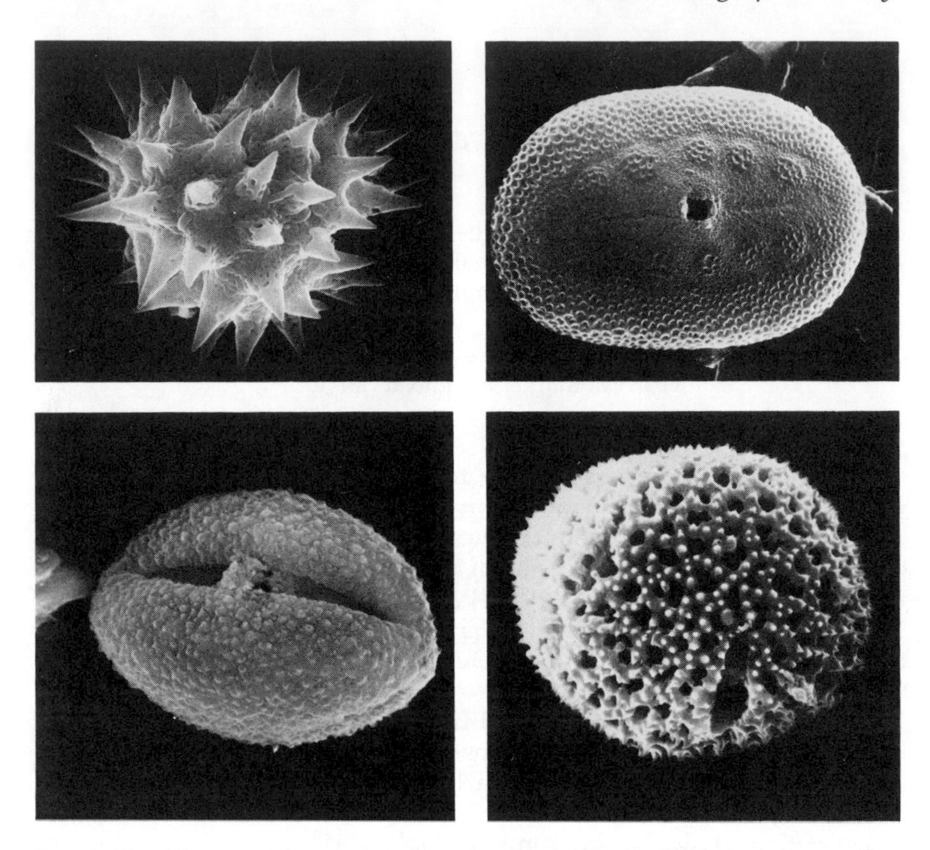

FIGURE 1. Electron microscope photographs (by G. Riollet) of modern pollen from Olduvai. Upper left: *Delamerea procumbens* (Compositae), x1500. Upper right: *Justicia fischeri* (Acanthaceae), x1300. Lower left: *Boscia angustifolia* (Capparidaceae), x2000. Lower right: *Commiphora madagascariensis* (Burseraceae), x1700.

Method of Investigation

FIELDWORK

Plio-Pleistocene palynology has shown that preservation of fossil pollen grains is very poor in east Africa. Sampling at Olduvai Gorge was almost exclusively restricted to the lacustrine deposits in Beds I and II. This was performed by digging deep trenches to obtain fresh uncontaminated, unweathered sediments. On the basis of preliminary fieldwork conducted in 1973, sections were selected. Extensive Pleistocene sampling during the 1975 fieldwork revealed the following:

Stratigraphic levels	*No. collected*	*No. pollen spectra*
Divers	4	0
Ndutu	2	0
Bed III	3	0
Bed II	68	7
Bed I	36	4
Total	113	11

This program was completed by collecting modern plants to build up the reference collection of pollen. In 1973, 137 plants were collected by Bonnefille and Riollet, mainly in the Olduvai-Serengeti area (cf. Herlocker and Dirschl, 1972). They were identified by the East African Herbarium in Nairobi (Gillett and Kayu, 1974). During the 1977 field season more plants were collected by J. Raynal and Bonnefille, and over 400 specimens deposited at the National Museum in Paris (Raynal's "Liste des récoltes botaniques effectuées en Tanzanie, region de Laetoli, Olduvai, Ngorongoro, Mt. Meru," *in* Bonnefille and Riollet, in press). N. Buchet prepared a pollen reference collection of 380 species from this collection and from herbarium specimens. In order to pursue the modern pollen rain studies, 58 soil samples were collected from various natural plant communities selected at various altitudes in the Olduvai-Serengeti-Ngorongoro area (Table 1 and Fig. 2).

TABLE 1. Altitudinal Location of Surface Samples Collected for Modern Pollen Rain Study

Altitude (m)	*Vegetation Communities*	*Eyasi*	*Laetoli*	*Olduvai-Serengeti*	*Endulen-Lemagrut-Karatu*	*Ngorongoro Crater*	*Satiman*	*Empakai*	TOTAL
3000-3500	Moorland above tree line							2	2
1500-3000	Upland juniper forest						6	3	9
2000-2500	Upland forest					8	2		10
1500-2000	Wooded grassland + *Sporobolus-Kyllinga* grasslands		10	11	7	3			31
1000-1500	Bushland and thicket	6							6

TOTAL: 58

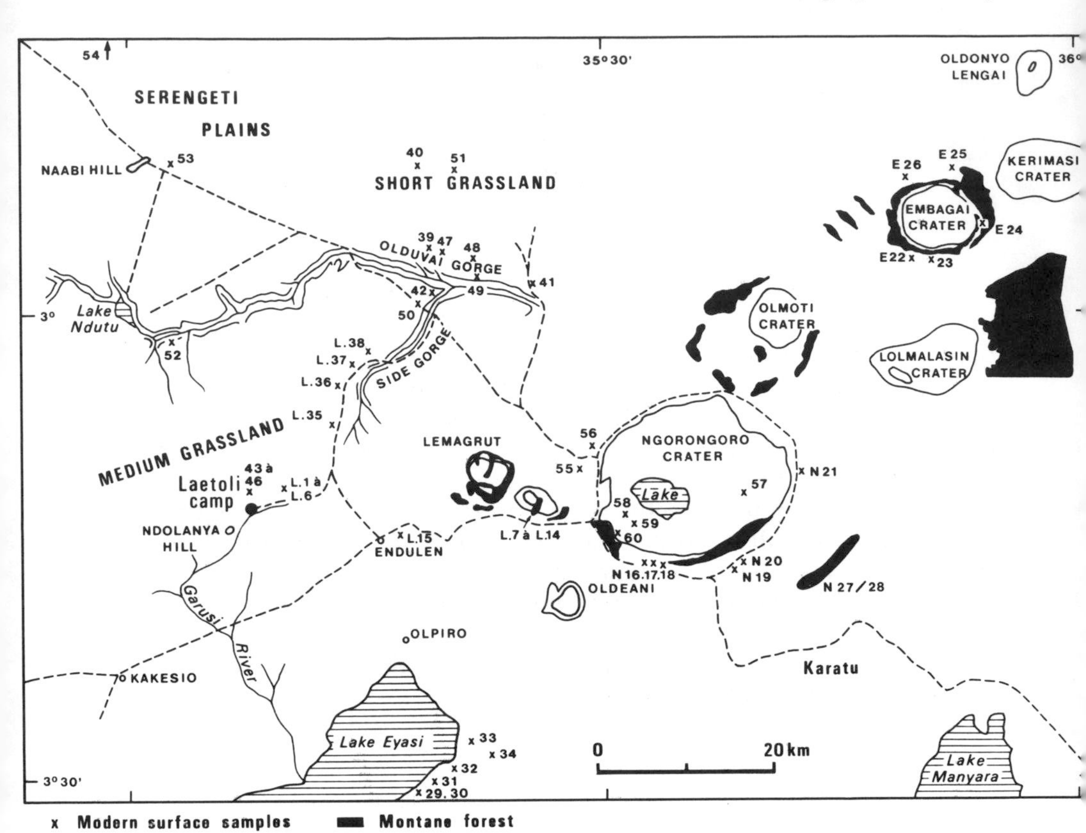

FIGURE 2. Olduvai Gorge area. Numbers refer to samples for modern pollen rain (Fig. 5).

LABORATORY WORK

The 113 Pleistocene and the 58 modern soil samples were processed in Marseille at the Faculté des Sciences de Luminy. The chemical treatment was carried out by G. Buchet in an uncontaminated, pressurized room. As the above tabulation shows, only 10% of the samples contained preserved fossil pollen grains. This is not caused by a reduced atmospheric pollen rain in tropical areas. We have shown that $\simeq$ 1000 grains/cm^2/yr were trapped in gauze filters in the Olduvai area in 1974-1975. Conditions of sedimentation are most likely to be responsible for the lack of pollen fossilization. High sedimentation rates for lakes surrounded by volcanic tephra, in the Rift Valley (Yuretich, 1982) imply that organic content is very low. Nonfossilization may also be due to intense biological activities within shallow alkaline lakes with high temperatures.

Palynological Results

Palynological fossil pollen assemblages were obtained for 11 stratigraphic layers, 4 within Bed I, and 7 within Bed II as shown in Figure 3 and in the tabulation below (small letters refer to the palynological sampling):

	Site location	Sediment	Pollen count
BED II	FCWc	Top of Tuff IIB	667
	FCWd	Clay with chert nodules just below Tuff IIB	237
	LEMUTA MEMBER		
	HWKEEi	Green clay 20 cm below the vitric tuff, 2 m above Tuff IF	390
	VEKb	Siliceous earth 80 cm above Tuff IF	707
	VEKg	Olive clay 60 cm above Tuff IF	406
	FLKc	Olive clay 40 cm above Tuff IF	846
	VEKa	Olive clay 10 cm above Tuff IF	724
TUFF IF			
BED I	FLKa	Grey clay 10 cm above Tuff IF	247
	FLKN1i	Grey clay 20 cm below Tuff IF	633
	RHCg	Lacustrine clay 30 cm below Tuff ID	502
	FLKNNc	Lacustrine green clay just below Tuff IB	453

Pollen data provide information on vegetation and environment for a 200,000-year period starting slightly before Tuff IB deposition, that is, beginning 1.8 million years ago and ending exactly with Tuff IIB deposition approximately 1.6 million years ago (Hay, 1976). Although sampling was performed at regular intervals, the best results came from sediments close to Tuff IF at the limit between Bed I and Bed II.

At the laboratory, pollen was identified by microscopy based on comparison with a 6000-species reference collection of pollen from herbarium specimens of plants from east Africa. In all, 6800 fossil pollen grains were counted. They were attributed to 113 botanical angiosperm taxa identified to the family or generic level, and more exceptionally to the species level; 46 of them can be related to arboreal plants (arboreal pollen = AP); 44 to herbaceous plants (nonarboreal pollen = NAP); 23 uncertain cases belong to genera known to be herbaceous plants, trees, or shrubs. Only 1 to 9% were not identified.

Detailed pollen counts for each stratigraphic level are presented in Table 2. Some results have been refined since the previous publications (Bonnefille and Riollet, 1980, Bonnefille et al., 1982). The polliniferous

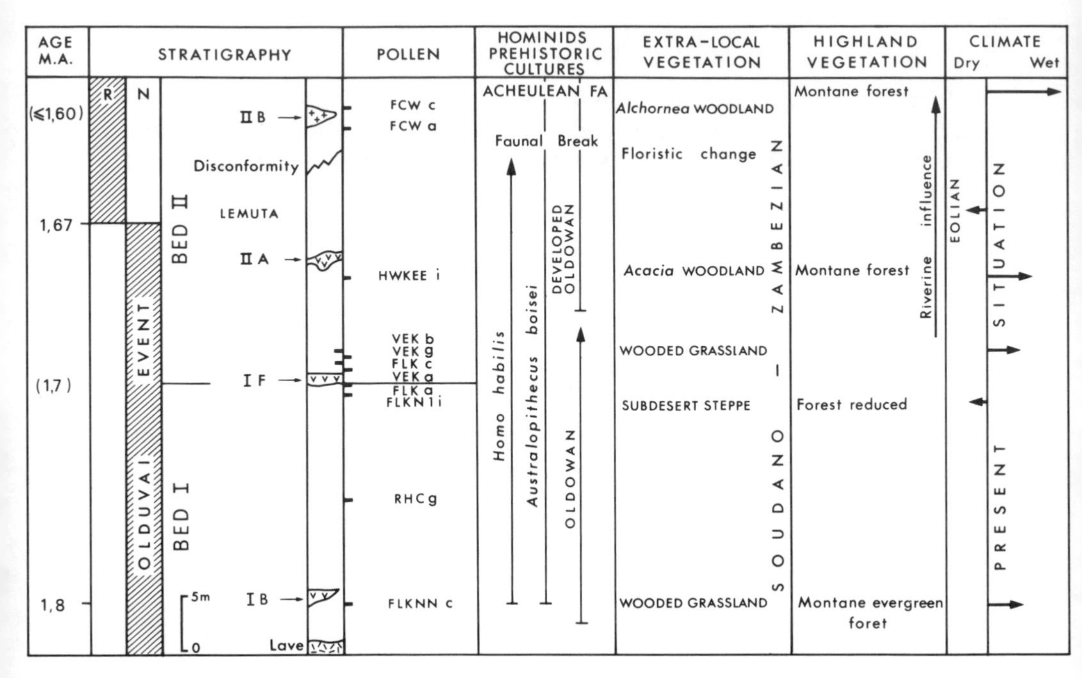

FIGURE 3. Stratigraphic position of pollen data and paleoenvironmental reconstructions at Olduvai.

samples contain a rich and internally consistent pollen assemblage of well preserved pollen grains, with only 5 to 8% unrecognizable except for FLKN1i (18%) and FCWa (30%).

Paleoenvironmental Interpretation

Unlike biocenotic plant communities in which the various elements are highly interrelated in a concrete ecosystem, the pollen assemblage is essentially thanatocenotic, consisting of an autochthonous local component and an allochthonous regional component that arrives in the deposit after transportation from the source of dispersal (Janssen, 1981). Therefore in handling palynological data for the reconstruction of past vegetation, it is important to distinguish among local, extra-local, regional, and extra-regional components.

For vegetation of Olduvai, we can use the geologists' paleogeographical reconstruction (Hay, 1976). Pollen was deposited in a medium-sized lake (17 to 25 km in diameter); fluviatile drainage into the lake is documented in the upper Bed II after deposition of the Lemuta Member.

In these fossil pollen assemblages several components can be distinguished.

Local and Extra-local Component

The ubiquitous Gramineae and Cyperaceae may belong either to the local environment (grass and sedge belts around the lakeshore) or to the extra-local environment such as grasslands to be found nowadays on the Serengeti Plain.

The relative abundance of Cyperaceae (10 to 20% in pollen samples from upper Bed I and lower Bed II) (Fig. 4) can be correlated with fluctuating lake levels and new swampy areas developed around the lake. *Typha* (cattail) is an aquatic freshwater plant which can tolerate some degree of salinity. Its pollen percentages increase in samples from middle Bed II (FCWa and c) when stronger freshwater drainage was indicated, after deposition of the Lemuta Member. The pollen data agree in full with Hay's (1976) paleogeographical reconstruction.

Regional Component

According to their phytogeographical affinities, two groups of arboreal taxa can be distinguished. The first group can be attributed to trees distributed today in the so-called Sudano-Zambezian phytogeographical region which occupies savannah surrounding the equatorial rain forest to the north and south (Keay, 1959; White, 1965). The second group is related to trees common to montane forests from highlands of east and central Africa, called the Afro-montane phytogeographical element (Chapman and White, 1970). Other pollen taxa having species present in each group are left in an undifferentiated AP category (APi).

Variations in pollen percentages from taxa of each group are shown in Figure 4. From K/Ar dating we know that volcanos such as Satiman and Ngorongoro have been erupting for 3.7 or 2.45 million years. We assume that montane forest occupied a relief zone of about 2000 m. The arboreal Afro-montane pollen group can be considered to form a regional component, its source being 30 to 50 km away from the Olduvai Pleistocene lake. The Sudano-Zambezian arboreal pollen group represents the extra-local component of wooded grassland or woodland between the volcanos and the lake. Plants can thus be assumed a priori to have been associated in the past just as they are at present. This assumption may need to be tested by appropriate statistical methods. The distinction between the Afro-montane and the Sudano-Zambezian groups cannot be made among the NAP pollen taxa which belong to very diverse botanical families. Some other pollen taxa cannot even be attributed to arboreal or nonarboreal categories. Therefore the separation between regional and extra-local components is not possible for the NAP category.

TABLE 2. Counts of Plio-Pleistocene Pollen by Stratigraphic Level, Olduvai Gorge

NAP	AP and NAP	AP: I	AP: SZ	AP: AfrM	Pollen Taxa	STRATIGRAPHIC LEVELS — BED I: IB FLKNNc	ID RHCg	FLKNIi	IF FLKa	BED II: VEKa	FLKc	VEKg	VEKb	IIA HWKEEi	IIB FCWa	FCWc
+	?				Acanthaceae					3	5	2				
+					type *Asystasia*									2		
+					type *Dyschoriste*									1		
+					type *Hypoestes*					1	1	2				
	+				type *Justicia anselliana*		2				2	2		1		1
	+				type *J. odora*				2		7			21		1
+					Amaranthaceae type *Achyranthes*				18		91	2		157	1	
+					type *Aerva persica*							1				
+					type *Celosia trigyna*	1						2				
+					type *Digera muricata*							2				
+					type *Pupalia*						1			1		
+					type *Sericocomopsis*									3		
+					type *Volkensinia prostrata*				1			2		1	1	5
+	?				Amaranthaceae/Chenopodiaceae	3	6	11	8	8		1	8		1	7
			+		Anacardiaceae type *Rhus*	2	1			1		1				2
			+		Apocynaceae type *Adenium*											1
	+				type *Ancylobotrys*						1					
			+		type *Carissa*					2						
		+			Apocynaceae								1			
			+		Bombacaceae *Adansonia* type *digitata*										1	
+					Boraginaceae *Heliotropium*											
					type *steudneri*						4				1	
			+		Burseraceae *Commiphora*		1		2		3	1		16		4

		+			Caesalpinioideae							2				
			+		Capparidaceae type *Boscia*	2				1						1
+					type *Gynandropsis gynandra*			2								
			+		Capparidaceae			242				1				1
+					Caryophyllaceae						1					
+					Chenopodiaceae type *Suaeda monoica*	1			5		5					
+					Chenopodiaceae	1						95		12	2	3
			+		Combretaceae	1		20	1	1		1	1		2	2
+					Commelinaceae											
+					type *Commelina benghalensis*				2				1			
+					type *C. forskalaei*										3	
+					Commelinaceae						4	1		5		
	?				Compositae *Artemisia*				1	6	1	4		1	1	1
+					type *Crepis*	1							3			
+					*Hirpicium* type *diffusum*				8		22			30		
+	?				liguliflorae		3	1	2	4	2	7		3	1	1
				+	type *Stoebe kilimandscharica*						1					
+	?				tubuliflorae	12	5	1	14	10	31	24	21	35	2	3
	+				type *Vernonia*	1										
				+	Cupressaceae *Juniperus*	9	10	8	1	4	7		7	19	4	19
+					Cyperaceae	30	32	37	38	36	137	9	59	185	10	69
			+		Ebenaceae *Euclea*	4		1								
		+			Ebenaceae					1					1	
				+	Ericaceae					1	1		1	3		1
	+		?		Euphorbiaceae *Acalypha*			3			5	1				
			+		*Alchornea*										19	2
	+		?		type *Clutia*						2			2		1
	+		?		type *Croton*									2	1	
	+				type *Euphorbia hirta*							3				
	+				type *E. hypericifolia*				5		6			6	1	
	+				type *Euphorbia*			2	1	1	2	1	4	5	3	19
			+	?	type *Macaranga*											1
	+				type *Monadenium*									1		
+	?				*Ricinus*											5
				+	type *Sapium*						1			1		
	+				Euphorbiaceae											2
		+			Flacourtiaceae											1
+					Gentianaceae type *Enicostema*									1		
+					Gentianaceae							1				

TABLE 2. Counts of Plio-Pleistocene Pollen by Stratigraphic Level, Olduvai Gorge *(continued)*

NAP	AP and NAP	AP			Pollen Taxa	STRATIGRAPHIC LEVELS										
						BED I							BED II			
						IB	ID		IF					IIA	IIB	
		I	SZ	AfrM		*FLKNNc*	*RHCg*	*FLKNli*	*FLKa*	*VEKa*	*FLKc*	*VEKg*	*VEKb*	*HWKEEi*	*FCWa*	*FCWc*
+					Gramineae	306	357	235	110	517	317	206	478	186	91	260
	+			?	Guttiferae *Hypericum*										1	1
+					Labiatae type *Leucas*				1		12	2		8		
+					type *Plectranthus*						1					
		+			Loganiaceae/Salvadoraceae								1			9
	+				Menispermaceae											1
			+		Mimosoideae *Acacia albida*									1		1
			+		*Acacia* Gr. I			3	2		20			45		2
			+		*Acacia* Gr. III									48		5
			+		*Acacia*		1			1	3		1	5		
		+			type *Dichrostachys*					3	1					1
+	?				Monocotyledoneae		9	1			2		2		1	1
			?	+	Myricaceae *Myrica*											2
				+	Myrsinaceae *Myrsine*								1			
			+	?	Myrtaceae type *Syzygium*		5			8		3				
		+			Myrtaceae	10							9			
+					Nyctaginaceae type *Boerhavia*									3		
			+		Olacaceae *Ximenia*				15		55			157	1	
				+	Oleaceae *Olea*	1	1									1
				+	*Olea* type *africana*	5	1			5	1		3	8		2
				+	*Olea* type *hochstetteri*						1		1	1		4
		+	?		Palmae type *Phoenix*			1								
	+		+		Papilionoideae type *Ormocarpum*			1							1	1
	+				type *Rhynchosia*					1						
	+				type *Vigna*											1

	+				Papilionoideae		1				1	1	2	2	1	2
+					Plantaginaceae *Plantago*	18	4		1	42		4	29		2	
				+	Podocarpaceae *Podocarpus*	17	17	1	1	32	8		43	12	3	15
+					Polygonaceae *Rumex*			1								
+	?				Portulacaceae			14				2				
	+		?		Ranunculaceae type *Clematis*					1				1		
			+		Rhamnaceae										1	1
				+	Rosaceae *Hagenia abyssinica*		1							3	10	6
			?	+	*Prunus* type *africana*			1			3					1
+					Rubiaceae *Anthospermum*		10				1			6		
	+				type *Oldenlandia*									5		
	+				type *Pavetta*									35		
	+				Rubiaceae		1				23		1			
			+		Salvadoraceae *Salvadora*			5								
		+			Sapindaceae type *Dodonaea*	21	4			21	1		16		2	3
		+			Sapindaceae										1	
	+				Solanaceae type *Solanum*			1			2	1				1
	+				Solanaceae				1					4		
			+	?	Sterculiaceae type *Dombeya*									2		
			+		Tiliaceae type *Grewia*											1
+					Typhaceae *Typha*	1	5	15	1	2	2	3	4	4	16	133
		+	?		Ulmaceae *Celtis*											8
		+			*Trema*											1
+	?				Umbelliferae	1							1			
+	?				Urticaceae	2	1	3						2	3	2
?	+				Verbenaceae type *Clerodendron*											1
+	?				Vitaceae type *Cissus quadrangularis*											2
+					Zygophyllaceae *Tribulus*		1				5	1		3	1	1
					Bryophyta Anthocerotaceae		2									
					Pteridophyta monolete	1									13	
					trilete						2				12	
					Pteridophyta		6			4			2			12
					Unidentified	2	15	23	6	7	42	15	7	35	22	32
					Total	453	502	633	247	724	846	406	707	1390	237	667
					Unrecognizable	38	37	117	23	51	49	23	61	8	100	62

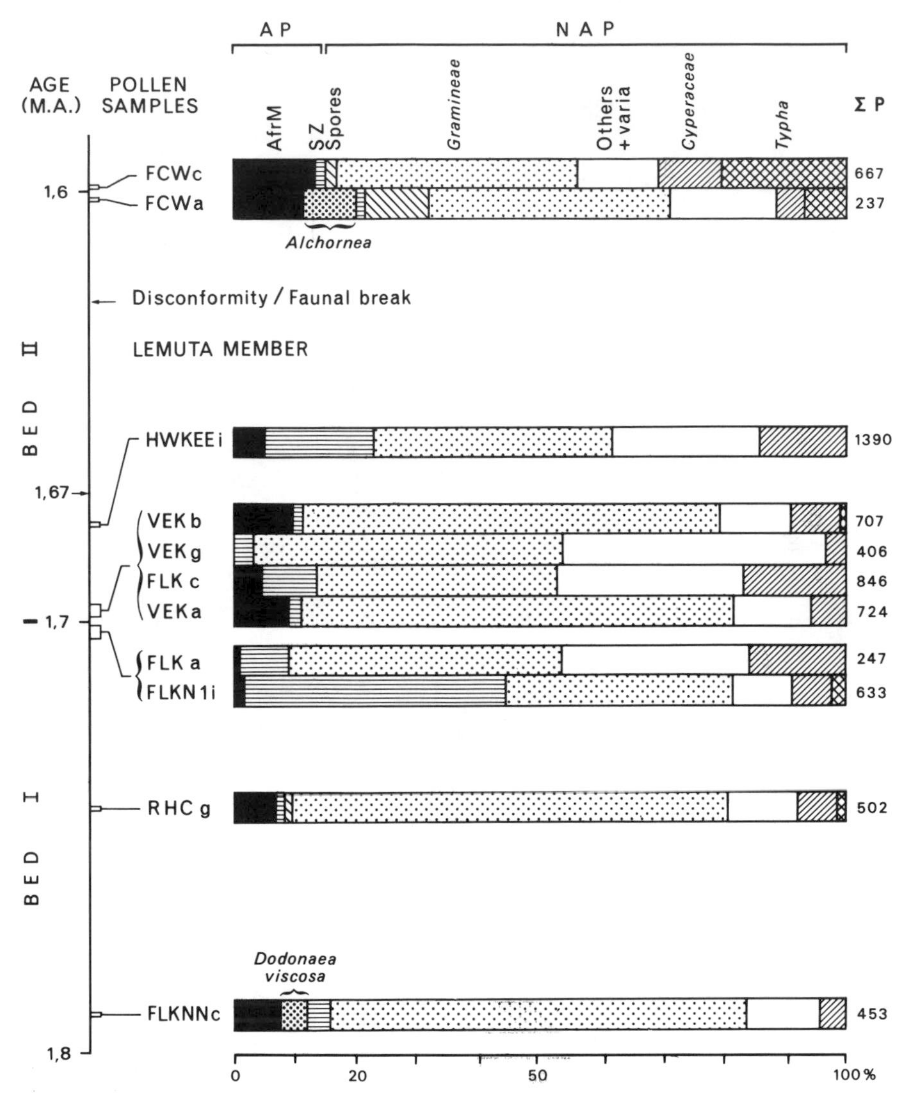

FIGURE 4. Pollen diagram based on findings from Olduvai Bed I and lower Bed II. The relative percentages of the two AP groups on the left side indicate abundance and composition of past tree cover.

Variations in the arboreal Sudano-Zambezian pollen frequencies reflect the density of the tree cover in the extra-local wooded grassland. Variations in the Afro-montane pollen frequencies are related to extension of the forest among the regional vegetation. Such variations are not totally synchronous (Fig. 4). This distinction changes the view of the paleoenvironmental interpretation (Bonnefille and Riollet, 1980), a change also based on a comparison with modern pollen analyses of 24 samples including more than 8000 pollen counts from the Laetoli-Serengeti transect (Fig. 5).

PALEOENVIRONMENT OF BED I

The oldest pollen assemblage, FLKNNc from lower Bed I, documents a vegetation contemporaneous with *Homo habilis* and *Australopithecus boisei,* first recorded at Olduvai. The Afro-montane arboreal pollen taxa reach percentages higher than 12%, including *Dodonaea viscosa,* a shrub abundant on volcanic soil and disturbed forestland. This value is almost three times higher than those recorded among the 24 modern samples from the Olduvai-Serengeti area which average 2.5%. The difference indicates that the area occupied by montane forest was much greater than it is now.

Sampling the middle of the lake, the pollen assemblage RHCg, just below Tuff ID, gives a similar picture, with a tendency to a reduction in forest pollen such as *Olea* (olive), while the appearance of *Acacia* and *Commiphora* indicates more steppe-like conditions. This trend is well expressed in the two assemblages from upper Bed I, just below Tuff IF, which show considerable reduction in the percentages of forest pollen (less than 2%), that is, less than in most of the modern samples. This reduction correlates with a decrease in rainfall at least in the mountains. Simultaneously there is an increase in Sudano-Zambezian pollen frequencies registered, among which the Capparidaceae are the most abundant. Together with the Amaranthaceae *(Volkensinia prostrata),* Combretaceae, and Portulacaceae, they indicate a more arid, steppe vegetation close to the lake, and most probably under higher temperatures. The Capparidaceae are insect-pollinated trees and shrubs. Their high percentage ($\simeq$ 37%) can be explained by local sampling near the trees themselves, or by particular taphonomic conditions such as those suggested by the abundance of rodent remains from owl pellets which occur exactly in the same level.

PALEOENVIRONMENT OF BED II

Immediately above Tuff IF, in the first meter of the olive clay, the four assemblages at VEK and FLK show pollen compositions very similar to those of the lower Bed I assemblages. Except for the VEKg sample, the frequencies of two groups of arboreal taxa are of the same order. Sedges (Cyperaceae) and reeds *(Typha),* as well as nonarboreal pollen frequencies exhibit the greatest variations in response to rapid fluctuations in the lake when new land becomes available for local herbaceous vegetation as the water retreats.

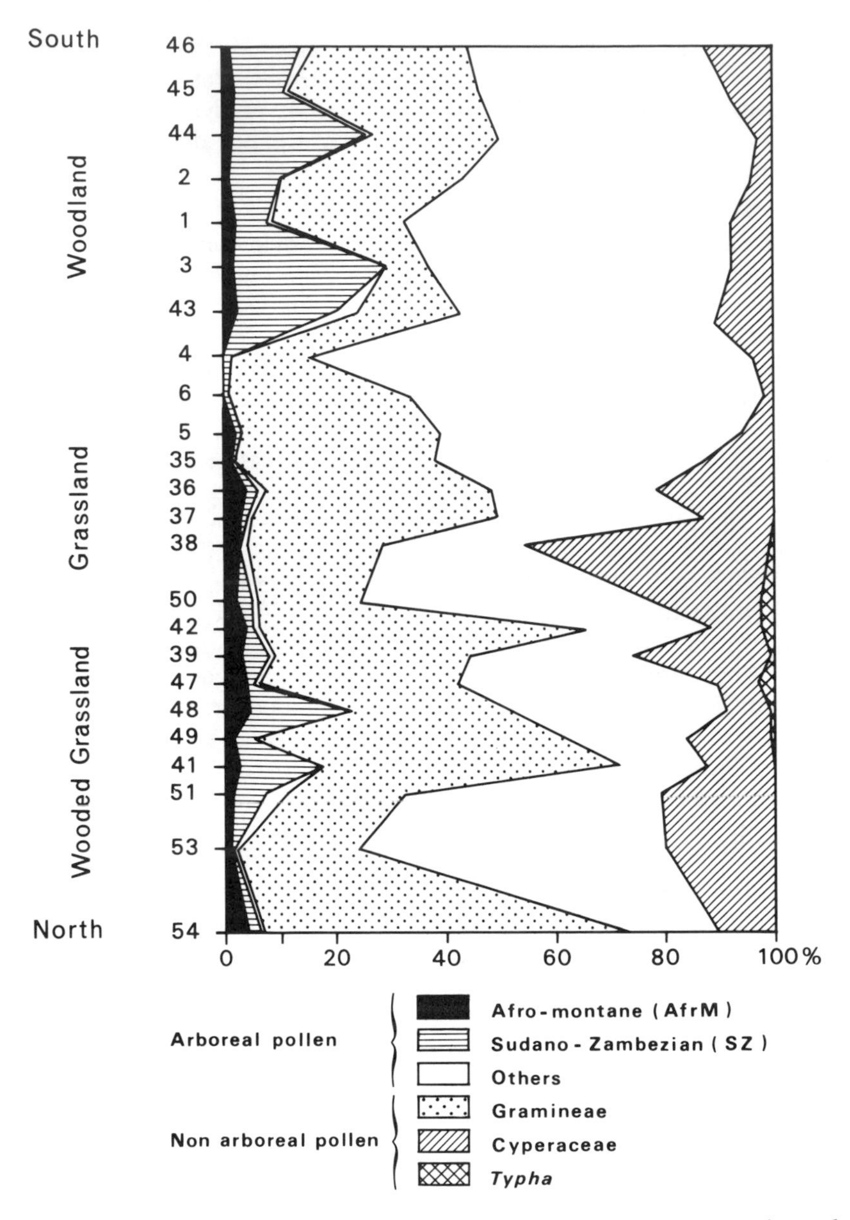

FIGURE 5. Pollen diagram based on modern pollen samples taken along the Laetoli-Serengeti transect.

The particular sample VEKg from the "siliceous earth" may represent a local community of Chenopodiaceae herbaceous plants, for example, *Suaeda,* which grows on saline soil such as that resulting from extreme evaporation of groundwater. Such a community can be in places on Lake Eyasi's southern shore. The pollen assemblage from HWKEE which again registers an increase in the arboreal Sudano-Zambezian pollen group is well documented. Because of the very high pollen content, 46 taxa have been listed. Among them, the high number of polyade from *Acacia* and pollen from Olacaceae, both known to be local pollen producers, attests to a dense woodland in the local and extra-local vegetation. This is also confirmed by the abundance of pollen from the shade-loving *Achyranthes.*

Regarding the floristic pollen composition, the greatest modification is registered in samples FCWa and FCWc from above the Lemuta Member. Indicating more mesic conditions are the higher proportion of arboreal pollen (close to 10%) together with the first appearance of new taxa such as *Asystasia, Alchornea, Macaranga, Hypericum, Myrica,* Rhamnaceae, Menispermaceae, *Acacia albida,* and *Ricinus;* the increase in *Hagenia* and *Clerodendron;* and the decrease in Chenopodiaceae and Amaranthaceae. A Sudanian woodland such as that found today under much higher rainfall conditions (≃ 800 mm) is then documented in the surroundings of the lake, that is, the extra-local vegetation. It is consistent with more freshwater, shown by the great increase in the aquatic reed *(Typha).* This is just after the eolian deposits of the Lemuta Member, which suggests an arid episode of a 20,000-year duration (Hay, 1976) before the first occurrence of Acheulean man just after Tuff IIB.

Conclusion

In agreement with other paleoenvironmental information provided by the geological, geochemical, and paleontological studies, the pollen analysis indicates an arid or semiarid environment for the Olduvai Bed I and lower Bed II time deposition. Comparing these pollen data with the modern situation provides new information. The conditions have been more arid than now only once: just before Tuff IF at the limit between Bed I and Bed II. At other times the tree cover was more dense and suggests a climate with increased or more regular rainfall. The local environment is a mosaic in which tree-cover density oscillates among grasslands such as the Serengeti Plain today, wooded grassland such as exits near Olduvai Gorge or Laetoli, and woodland such as is found near Endulen or in the Serengeti National Park. The conclusions are summarized in Figure 3. By the time of Tuff IIB deposition, a dense woodland of *Alchornea* (Christmas bush) occupied the area just before the appearance of Acheulean man. The montane forest has always been present on the highlands. Except just before Tuff IF where it was very much reduced, its extent must have been two or three times what it is today. Since nothing is known of the pre-deforestation stage, we cannot conclude that during Bed I and lower

Bed II time the temperature was lower than now. When forest areas were more extensive, they were also closer to the Olduvai archeological site. This may be of some importance for hominids exploiting plant resources.

The seasonal variations in the climate in the Olduvai area have been well established through the permanent Sudano-Zambezian affinities of the pollen flora (Bonnefille et al., 1982). More information on climate can be obtained from comparison with more data on modern environments in Africa.

The pollen data corroborates the coexistence of two ecological systems that do not register synchronous fluctuations. Could it be that the two hominids occupied two distinct ecological niches: *Homo habilis* in the low and medium grassland or woodland environment and *Australopithecus* in the montane forest? At one time or another they were somehow sharing the edges of the Olduvai Lake.

REFERENCES

Axelrod, D. I., and Raven, P. H.

1978. Late Cretaceous and Tertiary vegetation history of Africa. Pp. 77-130 *in* "Biogeography and Ecology of Southern Africa," M.J.A. Werger, ed., 1440 pp. (Monographiae Biologicae, 31.) Junk, The Hague.

Bonnefille, R.

1976a. Palynological evidence for an important change in the vegetation of the Omo Basin between 2.5 and 2 million years ago. Pp. 421-431 *in* "Earliest Man and Environment in the Lake Rudolf Basin," Y. Coppens, F. Clark Howell, G. L. Isaac, R.E.F. Reakey, eds., 615 pp. (Prehistoric archeology and ecology series.) University of Chicago, Chicago, London.

1976b. Paleoenvironmental implications of a pollen assemblage from the Koobi Fora Formation ("East Rudolf"). Nature, vol. 264, pp. 403-407.

Bonnefille, R., and Riollet, G.

1980. Palynologie, végétation et climats de Bed I et Bed II à Olduvai, Tanzanie. Pp. 123-127 *in* "Actes du 8° Congrès Panafricain de Préhistoire et d'Études du Quaternaire," R. E. Leakey, B. A. Ogot, eds., 400 pp. Tillmiap, Nairobi.

Bonnefille, R.; Lobreau, D.; and Riollet, G.

1982. Pollen fossile de *Ximenia* (Olacaceae) dans le Pléistocène inférieur d'Olduvai en Tanzanie: Implications paléoécologiques. Journ. Biogeogr., vol. 9, pp. 469-486.

Bonnefille, R., and Riollet, G.

——. Palynological spectra from the upper Laetolil beds. *In* "Laetoli: Geology, Fossils and Footprints," M. D. Leakey and J. M. Harris, eds. University of California. (In press.)

Chapman, J. D., and White, F.

1970. The evergreen forests of Malawi, 190 pp. Commonwealth Forestry Institute, University of Oxford.

CHESTERS, K.I.M.
1957. The Miocene flora of Rusinga Island, Lake Victoria, Kenya. Paleontographica, ser. B, vol. 101, pp. 30-71.

GILLETT, J. B., and KAYU, E.P.K.
1974. List of specimens collected from Serengeti National Park, Tanzania T2 by Dr. R. Bonnefille, 5 pp. Unpublished, East African Herbarium Library, Nairobi.

HAMILTON, A. C.
1968. Some plant fossils from Bukwa. Uganda Journ., vol. 32, pp. 157-164.

HAY, R. L.
1976. Geology of the Olduvai Gorge: A study of sedimentation in a semiarid basin, 203 pp. University of California Press, Berkeley.

HERLOCKER, D. J., and Dirschl, H. J.
1972. Vegetation of the Ngorongoro conservation area, Tanzania, 39 pp. (Rep. Ser, 19). Canadian Wildlife Service, Ottawa.

JAEGER, J.-J.
1976. Les Rongeurs (Mammalia, Rodentia) du Pléistocène inférieur d'Olduvai Bed I (Tanzanie). 1ère partie: les Muridés. Pp. 57-120 *in* "Fossil Vertebrates of Africa," R.J.G. Savage, S. C. Coryndon, eds., vol. 4, 338 pp. Academic Press, London.

JANSSEN, C. R.
1981. On the reconstruction of past vegetation by pollen analysis: A review. Pp. 163-172 *in* "Proceedings of the 4th International Palynological Conference, Lucknow, India, 1976-1977," vol. 3

KEAY, R.W.J.
1959. Vegetation map of Africa south of the Tropic of Cancer. Explanatory notes. 24 pp., 1 map. Oxford University Press.

LEAKEY, L.S.B.
1965. Olduvai Gorge. Vol. 1: Fauna and background. Cambridge University Press.

LEAKEY, M. D.
1971. Olduvai Gorge. Vol. 3: Excavations in Bed I and Bed II, 1960-1963, 306 pp. Cambridge University Press.

PETERS, C., and O'BRIEN, M.
1981. The early hominid plant-food niche: Insights from an analysis of plant exploitation by *Homo, Pan, Papio* in eastern and southern Africa. Curr. Anthrop., vol. 22, no. 2, pp. 127-140.

WHITE, F.
1965. The savanna woodlands of the Zambezian and Sudanian domains: An ecological and phytogeographical comparison. Webbia, vol. 19, no. 2, pp. 651-681.

YURETICH, R. F.
1982. Possible influences upon lake development in the east African Rift Valley. Journ. Geol., vol. 90, pp. 329-337.

RAYMONDE BONNEFILLE

Fossil Catfish in the Green River Formation, Wyoming: New Discoveries and Implications to Depositional Models

Grant Recipients: H. Paul Buchheim, Department of Geological Sciences, Loma Linda University, Riverside, California; and Ronald C. Surdam, Department of Geology and Geophysics, University of Wyoming, Laramie, Wyoming.

Grant 1642: For a paleoecological study of new fossil catfish localities in the Green River Formation, in Wyoming.

Introduction

This study seeks to meet the following objectives:

1. To document the paleogeographic occurrence (localities) of fossil catfish within the Laney Member of the Green River Formation (ancient Lake Gosiute), in southwestern Wyoming.
2. To document the vertical (stratigraphic) distribution of fossil catfish within the Laney Member.
3. To study and document the preservation of fossil catfish, with the goal of better understanding the taphonomy (process of burial and preservation) of fossil catfish.
4. To study the associated fossils, rock types, minerals, and sedimentary structures, so as to better understand the paleoecology and paleoenvironments of ancient Lake Gosiute.
5. To apply the data obtained from the above objectives to evaluating models for the deposition of the Green River Formation.

The Eocene Green River Formation of Wyoming (ancient Lake Gosiute) has become famous for its oil shale, unusual minerals, sedimentological features, and, above all, for its well-preserved fossil fishes.

Since Leidy (1856) first recorded the discovery of a fossil fish in the Green River Formation of Wyoming, numerous workers (Hayden, 1871; Cope, 1884 a, b; Eastman, 1917; Thorpe, 1938; Bradley, 1948, 1963, 1964; Shaeffer and Mangus, 1965; Baer, 1969; Lundberg and Case, 1970; Perkins, 1970; Lundberg, 1975; McGrew, 1975; and McGrew and Casilliamo, 1975) have studied the Green River Formation and its fossil fish fauna. Most recently, Grande (1980) has completed a thorough compilation that includes figures and plates of nearly all known species and occurrences of fossil fishes to date.

Studies specifically dealing with fossil catfish in the Green River Formation include Lundberg (1975), Lundberg and Case (1970), Buchheim and Surdam (1977), and Grande (1980).

Previous to the initiation of this study, fossil catfish were thought to be rare in the Green River Formation. Except for one locality near the town of Farson (Lundberg and Case, 1970) in the northern part of the Green River Basin, none had been reported. However, the discovery of abundant catfish in a rich oil-shale unit 7 miles north of the town of Green River in 1976 resulted in a short paper (Buchheim and Surdam, 1977), and that study was broadened and continued under the support of the National Geographic Society. Since then, numerous localities and spectacular fossils have been discovered. This study reports these discoveries and their significance. Significant amounts of the data collected during this study were published in a report by Buchheim and Surdam (1981) and in an additional paper in press (Buchheim and Surdam, in press).

Methods

The study involved an area of 43,000 km^2 (Fig. 1) within the Green River and associated basins of southwestern Wyoming. The study was restricted to the Laney Member of the Green River Formation because this member is exposed over a wide area, contains an abundant fish fauna, and, most importantly, includes abundant fossil catfish.

The Laney Member was studied at over 80 localities. In these, 24 stratigraphic sections (see Fig. 1) were measured and sampled for both fossils and minerals. When fossil fish were encountered, detailed quarrying was conducted to determine their state of preservation, abundance, and associated fossils. Also sedimentological, mineralogical, geochemical, and stratigraphic data were collected by both field and laboratory studies.

Laboratory studies consisted of chemical, X-ray defraction, and thin-section studies of rock samples containing fossil fish. Slabs of rock were photographed, using medical X-ray equipment, to determine the structure, size, and abundance of the fossil catfish they contained. This part of the study specifically led to the discovery of perhaps the largest known articulated fossil catfish.

Results

Throughout this section reference will be made to Figures 1 (the locality map) and 2 (the composite stratigraphic section and accompanying

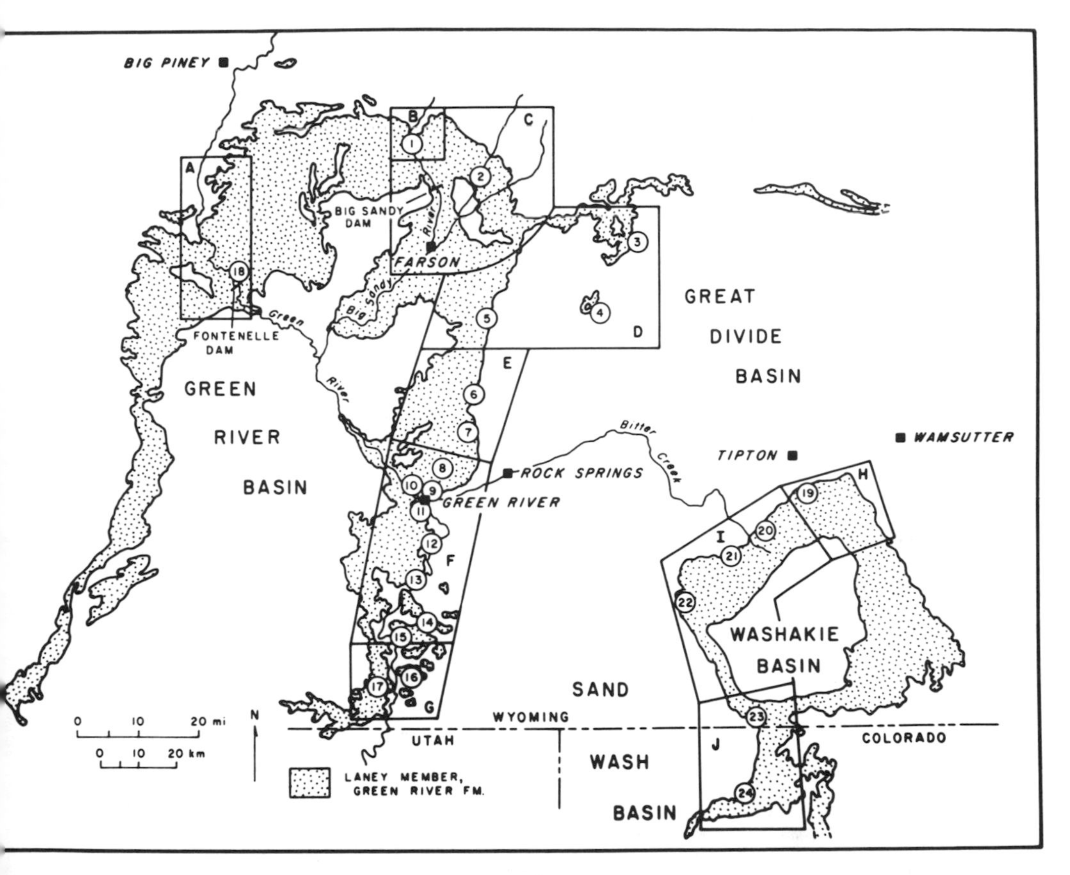

FIGURE 1. The study area includes 43,000 km^2 and is restricted to outcrops of the Laney Member of the Green River Formation. Boxed-in areas have distinct and differing paleontology and sedimentology. Circled numbers locate measured stratigraphic sections.

explanation), and the data will be discussed in a locality and stratigraphic context. Other localities geographically between those marked with circled numbers in Figure 1 were also studied, but discussion here will be limited to only a few of the localities indicated.

AREA F, LOCALITIES 8 to 15

Within area F fossil catfish were found to occur most abundantly, particularly at locality 8, where the initial discovery that led to this study was made while a stratigraphic section was being measured. Unit FG 47 (Fig. 2) was found to contain the fossil catfish *Astephus antiquus* (Fig. 3) ranging in length from 11 to 24 cm with a mean of 18 cm. It is estimated

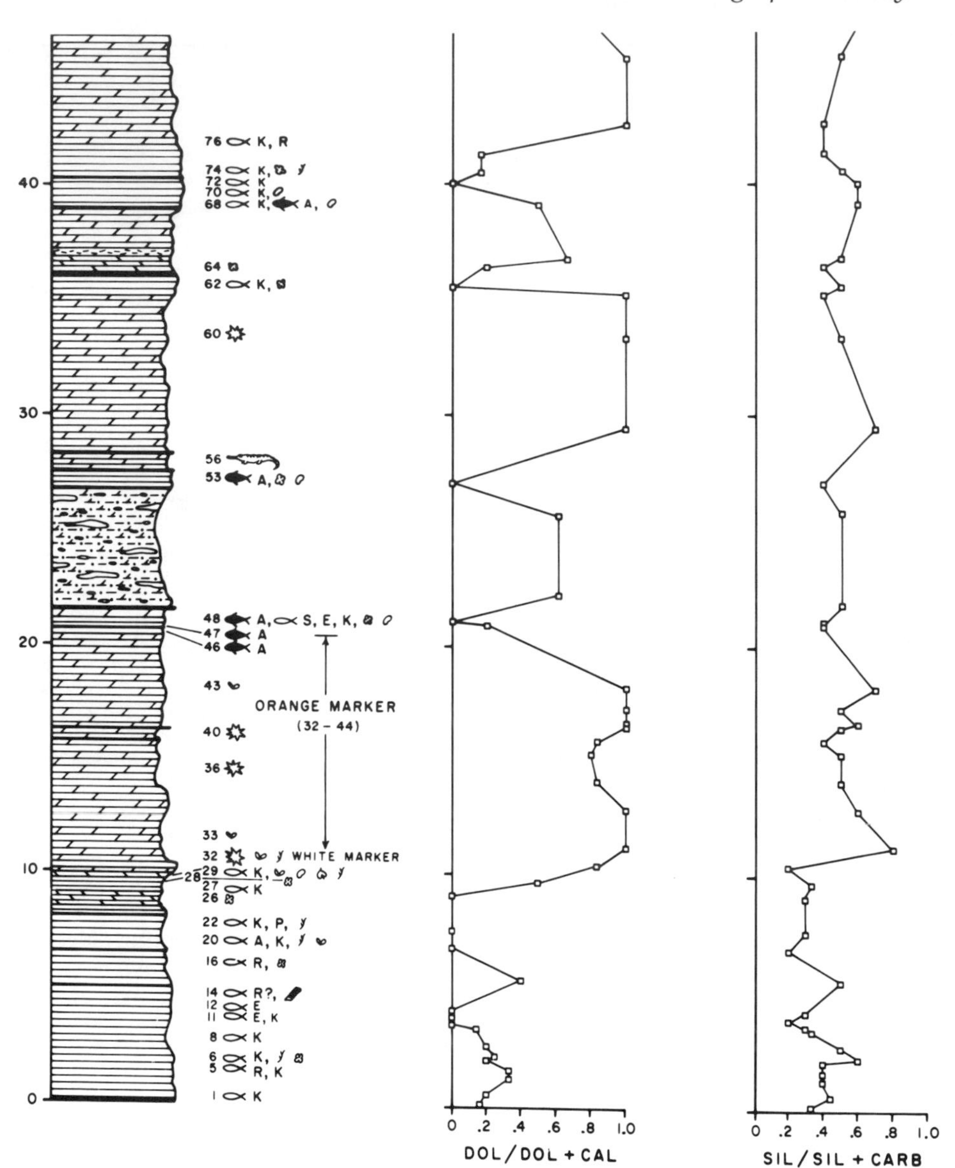

FIGURE 2. Composite stratigraphic section representing sections measured and studied within area F. See opposite for explanation of lithologies and fossils. Dolomite-calcite (DOL/DOL + CAL) ratios are directly related to the occurrence of fossil fish. Silicate-carbonate ratios (SIL/SIL + CARB) show similar trends. Vertical scale is in meters.

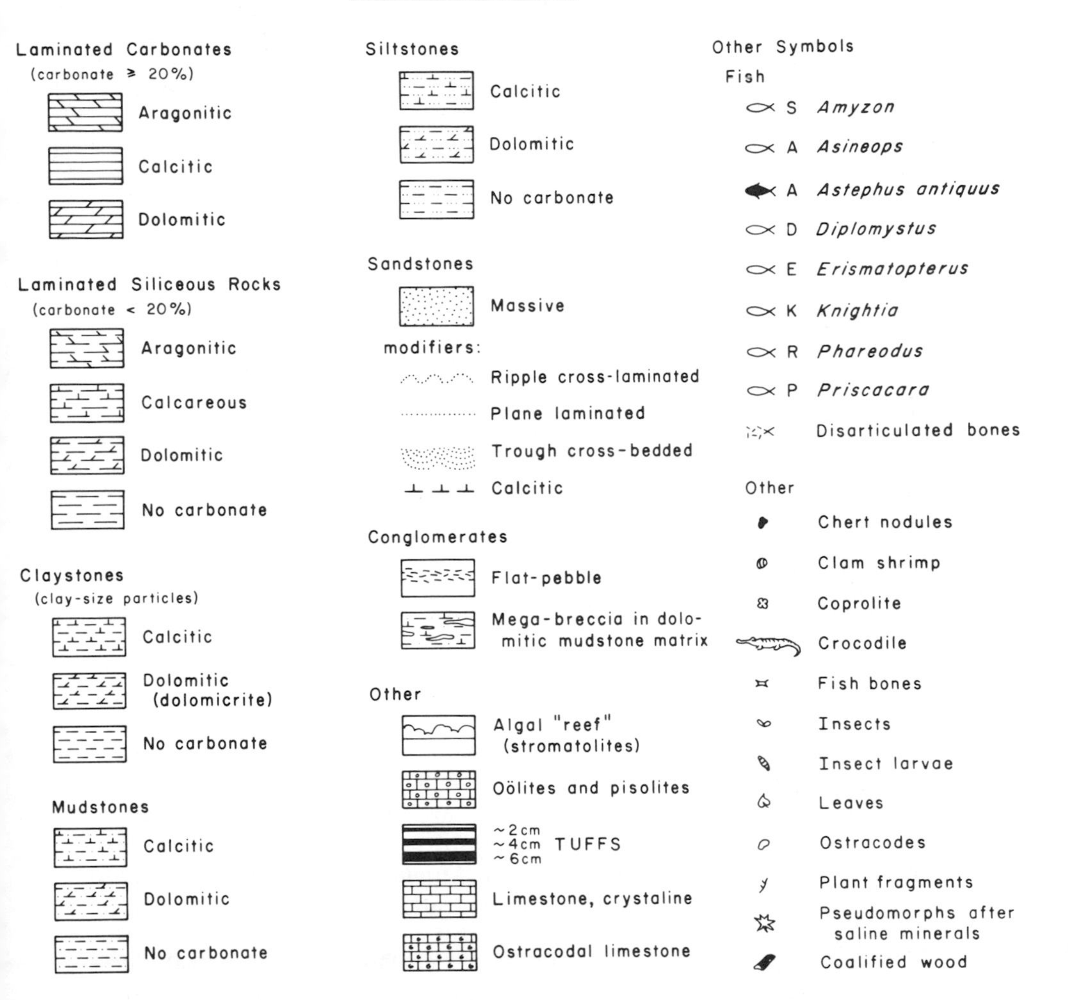

that about one million *Astephus* per square kilometer occur within FG 47 in this area. This is based on estimates of about 2 catfish/m^2 of exposed shale surface. Outward from this locality the numbers decrease substantially, until at locality 12 only 1 catfish was found in FG 47. Farther south in locality 13 no catfish were found. *Astephus* also appears to decrease in localities in other directions from locality 8, but well-exposed outcrops are not as abundant there, making estimates of abundance more difficult. At locality 7, no fossil catfish were found.

FIGURE 3. Apatitic (a calcium phosphate bone mineral) coprolites are found associated (just to the right of the fin, for example) with fossil catfish.

Abundant (commonly 100 to 350 m^2) apatitic fish coprolites (Fig. 3) are found associated with the fossil catfish. The coprolites, ranging in length from a few millimeters to 2.5 cm, are nearly identical to fecal pellets produced by live catfish in the laboratory. Other associated fossils include large numbers of *Erismatopterus*, *Knightia*, and *Amyzon* (a type of hump-backed sucker). It is of no small significance that the suckers *(Amyzon)* are found associated with the catfish.

The sedimentary features of FG 47 are dominated by well-defined organic and calcite laminae (Fig. 4) that average 4 to 5 μ in thickness. It forms a resistant, bluish, slab-shaped ledge that can be traced for at least 10 km. It exudes a petroliferous odor when struck with a hammer, and can be justly described as an oil shale (tests indicate that it would yield oil at the rate of about 15 gal./ton), and is jet black in color when freshly broken.

The most amazing discovery in this study was the excavation of an *Astephus* with all the skin intact, including the soft adipose fin and barbels. No catfish had been discovered previously with the skin preserved in such a marvelous condition. Several specimens were collected from FG

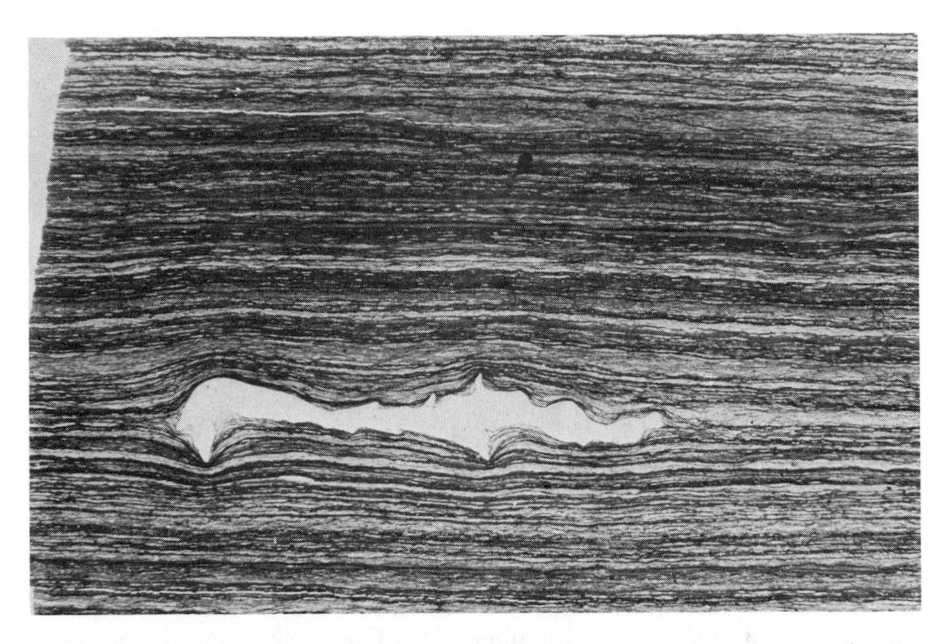

FIGURE 4. FG 47 is a well-laminated oil shale. This thin section contains a fossil catfish bone. The dark laminae are composed mostly of organics while the light laminae are primarily calcite. A thin section is about 2 cm thick.

48, just above FG 47 at locality 8. This unit contains half as much organic matter as FG 47, is light brown in color, and is very fissile.

At locality 12 two additional units containing fossil catfish were discovered; units FG 53 and FG 68 (see Fig. 2). This established the fact that fossil catfish were not restricted to just one period of time in Lake Gosiute's history.

AREA B, LOCALITY 1

This locality is unique in that excavation of a unit here (BSR 21) provided a prolific assemblage of fossils that are well preserved and represent a shallow, near-shore (littoral) paleoenvironment. Although only one individual catfish fossil has been found here, it does provide evidence that catfish inhabited a wide range of habitats in ancient Lake Gosiute. Associated fossils include abundant fish fry, insects, ostracodes, horsetails *(Equisetum)*, cattails *(Typha)*, and willow leaves.

BSR 21 is a fissile, well-laminated siliciclastic shale that is dramatically different from the laminated, calcite-rich oil shale from the lake's depocenter (Area F). It is typical, however, of sediments found in the near-shore areas of ancient Lake Gosiute.

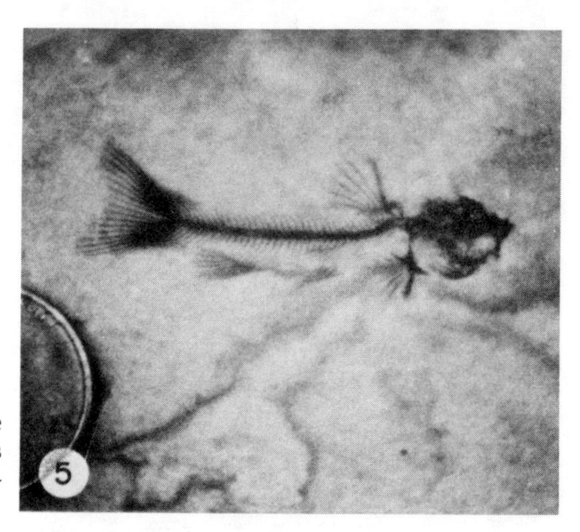

FIGURE 5. A rare juvenile catfish specimen identified as belonging to the genus *Hypsidoris* (Grande, 1980).

AREA B, LOCALITY 2

Lundberg and Case (1970) first described a fossil catfish *(Hypsideris farsonersis)* from the Laney Member of the Green River Formation near this locality. Recently Grande (1980) reported on a juvenile catfish *(Hypsidoris)* (Fig. 5) as well as *Astephus antiquus.*

Like locality 1, this locality represents a near-shore paleoenvironment. Associated fossils include herring *(Knightia)*, stromatolites, and silicified upright tree trunks. The fossils occur in a feldspathic siltstone that is poorly laminated.

OTHER LOCALITIES

Area I, locality 20, has yielded *Astephus antiquus*, but not commonly. They occur in a well-laminated calcimicrite that is kerogen-poor. In area L, locality 23, a unit (SCR 33) was discovered to contain extremely abundant disarticulated catfish remains, including large numbers of skulls and spines. Coprolites are also very abundant in this unit. The only other fossils observed were ostracodes (about 120 cm^2). This unit is a massive siliciclastic mudstone with only about 20% calcite.

In Area F, locality 15, a thickly laminated dolomicrite overlain by thinly laminated claystone (units MMS 16 and 17) was found to contain well-preserved *Astephus* in the claystone. Associated fossils include *Knightia* and *Diplomystus* (a herring). In the 2 m of sediment below this unit abundant beetle larvae, well preserved beetles, plant fragments, leaves, and masses of fossil wood fragments were found.

Area A, locality 18, has yielded uncommon, but well-preserved fossil catfish in near-shore siliciclastics.

Interpretations

Although by 1970 only 1 locality in the Green River Formation of southwestern Wyoming had yielded fossil catfish (Lundberg and Case, 1970), they are now known from at least 13 localities and they occur in the millions at ancient Lake Gosiute's depo-center near the town of Green River, Wyoming. The state of preservation and size of these is rivaled by no other fossil catfish locality in the world.

Implications with Respect to Depositional Models

The occurrence of abundant fossil catfish as well as the sucker *Amyzon* in a rich oil-shale unit provides some constraints to postulated depositional models for the Green River Formation. The stratified-lake model (Bradley, 1948) requires a relatively deep lake with an anaerobic, H_2S-rich hypolimnion. The presence of catfish and suckers, both bottom dwellers and feeders, suggests that the lake bottom was oxygenated, contrary to the anaerobic conditions postulated by the stratified-lake model. The great abundance of the catfish along with catfish coprolites at the lake's depo-center, as well as numerous localities in near-shore areas, precludes the possibility of a fluke situation where the fish may have drifted in as carcasses. This does not mean, however, that temporary stratification could not have developed, causing deaths of fossil catfish en masse. It must be kept in mind that fossil catfish are also found in a well-preserved state in near-shore areas that would be oxygenated even in the stratified-lake situation. The stratified-lake model was partly invoked, however, to explain the excellent preservation of the fossil fish (Bradley, 1948). Thus, it does not explain well-preserved fish or well-laminated sediments in near-shore oxygenated zones. The playa-lake model of Eugster and Surdam (1973) allows oxygenated conditions throughout the lake, as well as temporary stratification. The excellent preservation could be ensured by rapid burial before decomposition could take place.

Carbonates, Saline Cycles, and Fossil Catfish

The dolomite-calcite ratios (see mineralogic plots in Fig. 2) are directly related to occurrence of fossil fishes, including catfish. The silicate-carbonate ratios mimic these trends, but are more subtle. These variations are interpreted as cyclic changes in salinity and alkalinity (Buchheim and Surdam, 1983). During periods of hypersalinity, catfish retreated to surrounding freshwater ponds and streams. The nearly complete absence of fishes in highly dolomitic rocks with saline minerals is evidence of the hypersaline conditions that existed during cyclic intervals of time.

The discovery of abundant fossil catfish in the Green River Formation has added to a better understanding of conditions existing in ancient

Lake Gosiute, and has provided a priceless and important record of ancient life. Further study of these fossils and their entombing sediments will surely provide more insights into the paleoecology, paleoenvironments, and processes operating in ancient lake deposits.

Acknowledgments

Financial support from the National Geographic Society, the National Science Foundation (EAR 77-08636), Marathon Oil Company, the Geological Society of America (two Penrose grants), and the National Sigma Xi and University of Wyoming Chapter of Sigma Xi is gratefully acknowledged.

Individuals who contributed to the accomplishment of this research include Carole Buchheim (drafting) and Ray Kablanow (field assistant through three field seasons).

Data collected in this study has been published in several papers (Buchheim and Surdam, 1983, 1981, 1977), and as a Ph.D. dissertation (Buchheim, 1978).

REFERENCES

BAER, J. L.
1969. Paleoecology of cyclic sediments of the Lower Green River Formation, central Utah. Brigham Young Univ. Geol. Studies, no. 16, pp. 3-95.

BRADLEY, W. H.
1948. Limnology and the Eocene lakes of the Rocky Mountain Region. Geol. Soc. Amer. Bull. vol. 59, pp. 635-648.
1963. Paleolimnology. Pp. 621-648 *in* "Limnology in North America," D. G. Frey, ed. The University of Wisconsin Press, Madison.
1964. Geology of the Green River Formation and associated Eocene rocks in southwestern Wyoming and adjacent parts of Colorado and Utah. U. S. Geol. Survey Prof. Pap. 469-A, 86 pp.

BUCHHEIM, H. P.
1978. Paleolimnology of the Laney Member of the Eocene Green River Formation. Ph.D. Dissertation, University of Wyoming, Laramie, Wyoming.

BUCHHEIM, H. P., and SURDAM, R. C.
1977. Fossil catfish and the depositional environment of the Green River Formation, Wyoming. Geology, vol. 5, pp. 196-198.
1981. Paleoenvironments and fossil fishes of the Laney Member, Green River Formation, Wyoming. *In* "Communities of the Past," Jane Gray, et al., eds. Hutchinson Ross Publishing Company, Stroudsburg, Pennsylvania.
——. Carbonate cycles of the Laney Member of the Eocene Green River Formation. Journ. Sediment. Petr. (In press.)

COPE, E. D.
1884a. The vertebrata of the Tertiary Formations of the West, Book 1 (test). Geological Survey of the Territories, Rept. Washington, D. C.: U. S. Government Printing Office, no. 3, pp. 1-1009.
1884b. The vertebrata of the Tertiary Formations of the West, Book 2 (plates). Geological Survey of the Territories, Rept. Washington, D. C.: U. S. Government Printing Office, 350 plates.

EASTMAN, D. R.
1917. Fossil fishes in the collection of the United States Museum. U. S. Nat. Mus. Proc., no. 2177, pp. 235-304.

EUGSTER, H. P., and SURDAM, R. C.
1973. Depositional environment of the Green River Formation of Wyoming: A preliminary report. Geol. Soc. America Bull., vol. 84, pp. 115-120.

GRANDE, LANCE L.
1980. Paleontology of the Green River Formation with a review of the fish fauna. Bull. 63, Geol. Surv. of Wyoming, Laramie, Wyoming.

HAYDEN, F. V.
1871. Preliminary report of the U. S. Geological Survey of Wyoming and portions of contiguous territories. U. S. Geol. and Geog. Surv. Terr., 4th Ann Rept., 511p.

LEIDY, J.
1856. Notice of some remains of fishes discovered by Dr. John E. Evans. Acad. Nat. Sci. Philadelphia Proc., vol. 8, pp. 356-357.

LUNDBERG, J. G., and CASE, G. R.
1970. A new catfish from the Eocene Green River Formation, Wyoming. Journ. Paleont., vol. 44, pp. 451-457.

MCGREW, P. O.
1975. Taphonomy of Eocene fish from Fossil Basin, Wyoming. Fieldiana-Geology, vol. 33, pp. 257-270.

MCGREW, P. O., and CASILLIANO, M.
1975. The geological history of Fossil Butte National Monument and Fossil Basin. Nat. Park Serv. Occ. Pap., no. 3, pp. 37.

PERKINS, P. L.
1970. Equitability and tropic levels in an Eocene fish population. Lethaia, vol. 3, pp. 301-310.

SCHAEFFER, B., and MANGUS, M.
1965. Fossil lakes from the Eocene. Amer. Mus. Nat. Hist. Bull., no. 74, pp. 11-21.

THORPE, M. R.
1938. Wyoming Eocene fishes in the Marsh Collection. Amer. Journ. Sci., vol. 36, pp. 279-295.

H. PAUL BUCHHEIM
RONALD C. SURDAM

Reproductive Ecology and Behavior of the Green Turtle *(Chelonia mydas)* at Ascension Island

Grant Recipient: Archie Carr, Department of Zoology, University of Florida, Gainesville, Florida.[1]

Grant 1690: For study of nest-site selection in the green turtle *(Chelonia mydas)* at Ascension Island.

Ascension Island is an isolated volcanic peak in the central equatorial Atlantic Ocean midway between Brazil and Africa. It is a true oceanic island, with no littoral platform to support marine vegetation, on which green turtles *(Chelonia mydas)* normally feed. Yet each year thousands of green turtles migrate to Ascension to deposit their eggs on the beaches. Because these beaches differ greatly from one another, they provide a superb natural laboratory in which to study the effects of various environmental parameters on the nesting behavior and reproductive success of green turtles. The 32 cove-head beaches strewn along the western and northern coastline of the island vary strongly in size and shape, in offshore configuration and approach, and in sand characteristics. A central effort of the present study was to determine what effect these variables may have on nesting density and beach preferences, on reproductive homing, on the process of nest construction, and on hatching success.

The Ascension green turtle colony has other features that make it an attractive subject for research. Since 1926 it has been completely protected from human depredation on the nesting beach (Hart-Davis, 1972). It is the sole breeding place for the turtles nesting there, and it is small enough that nesting activity can be effectively monitored. Moreover, the results of previous basic research into the biology of the population have both posed many unanswered biological problems and provided useful background for the present study.

The turtle colony became well known after Carr initiated a turtle-tagging program there in 1960 and demonstrated that the foraging grounds for the turtles are more than 2200 km west of Ascension, off the eastern

[1] Senior author of this report is Jeanne A. Mortimer, Department of Zoology, University of Florida, Gainesville, Florida.

coast of Brazil (Carr, 1962, 1964, 1967, 1972, 1975; Koch et al., 1969; Carr and Coleman, 1974). Intermittently, during the years between 1960 and 1976, turtles were tagged by collaborators from the University of Florida, by personnel of the Mariculture Ltd. turtle farm, and by local residents who tagged during their spare time. Morphometric data on the adult turtles and descriptions of the nesting behavior of the population have been published (Carr and Hirth, 1962; Simon and Parkes, 1976); and Carr and Hirth (1962) and Carr (1975) reported on nesting periodicity. Carr et al. (1974) discussed internesting behavior of the females, and Stancyk and Ross (1978) made a preliminary analysis of the beach sand at Ascension.

Not until the National Geographic Society financed the present study was it possible to gather data in a consistent fashion throughout the duration of an entire nesting season. During 1976-1977 and 1977-1978 seasons Mortimer conducted 16 months of intensive fieldwork at Ascension Island. In addition to fulfilling the above-described primary objectives of the study, the data obtained materially supplemented the meager information previously gathered on within-season nesting periodicity and remigration intervals. The Ascension Island green turtle colony is now the best-documented insular sea turtle population in the world.

Nesting, Renesting, Migration, and Remigration

The beaches were patrolled nightly, and each turtle encountered was tagged, on the trailing edge of its right front flipper, with cow eartags of Monel metal. Because of the long distances between beaches, equal attention could not be given to all 32 of them. Tagging effort was most intensive on those beaches where nesting activity was heaviest. When previously tagged turtles were encountered, tag numbers were recorded. Turtles were routinely checked for old tag scars. The point along a beach where a turtle was observed was also recorded, and an effort was made to count or estimate the number of trial nest pits she had excavated before depositing her eggs.

During the 1976-1977 and 1977-1978 nesting seasons at Ascension 1100 turtles were tagged. Of these, 371 were observed nesting at later dates, and were involved in a total of 973 multiple emergences, ranging from 2 to 10 per turtle. From these data, estimates could be made of the average number of times a turtle emerged before successfully laying a clutch of eggs, the number of egg clutches laid by the average turtle in a given season, and the time that elapsed between these renestings and between remigrations to the nesting grounds in subsequent seasons. The degree to which turtles show site fidelity in their choice of nesting beach was also investigated.

It was found that the turtles dug more trial nest pits in beach sands with larger mean particle diameters than in finer sand, probably because the coarser beach sand was more prone to cave-ins. Presumably for the same reason, turtles also made more emergences on coarse-grained beaches ($\bar{x} = 3.3$) than on finer grained ones ($\bar{x} = 2.2$) prior to successfully laying a clutch of eggs.

Successive egg clutches are laid at intervals of about 14 days (range 7 to 20 days). Although females may lay as many as 7 clutches in a season, the average number recorded was between 2 and 3. There was a higher total number of observed within-season nestings by turtles bearing tags from previous seasons (remigrants) than by turtles that arrived tagless (recruits). For the 68 remigrant turtles observed on shore since 1960, 4 years is the predominant remigratory interval recorded, with 3 years next in frequency.

Moving clockwise around the island from South West Bay beach, four clusters of beaches are easily identified. These are the South West Bay cluster, the Long Beach cluster, the English Bay cluster, and the North East Bay cluster (Fig. 1). The degree of nest site tenacity evinced by Ascension turtles was defined in terms of whether the turtles returned to the same cluster of beaches, to the same beach within a cluster, or to the same point within the boundaries of a given beach. In analyzing the data on reproductive homing, 2 types of emergences were considered separately: those separated by fewer than 7 days, which were assumed to involve returns after aborted nesting attempts were distinguished from those separated by intervals of 7 or more days, which were considered to involve 2 separate egg clutches.

For emergences separated by less than 7 days, site tenacity at the level of the beach cluster is nearly perfect, but when time intervals greater than 7 days separate the emergences it is lessened. A Chi-square test showed no significant difference in cluster site fidelity among turtles from the three major beach clusters—South West Bay, Long Beach, and North East Bay. In cases in which a turtle did stray among beach clusters during successive emergences, she was more likely to go to an adjacent beach cluster than to one farther away.

The Ascension turtles also showed a tendency to nest repeatedly on the same beach within a cluster, especially when the emergences were separated by less than 7 days. As might be expected, however, the data suggest that within the boundaries of a beach cluster it may be easier for a turtle to home in on a longer beach than on a shorter one. Site fidelity was stronger on beaches within the South West Bay cluster than on beaches within the North East Bay cluster. The mean length of beaches within the South West Bay cluster, 255 m (range 123 to 480 m), is longer than that of those within the North East Bay cluster, 87 m (range 10 to 340 m).

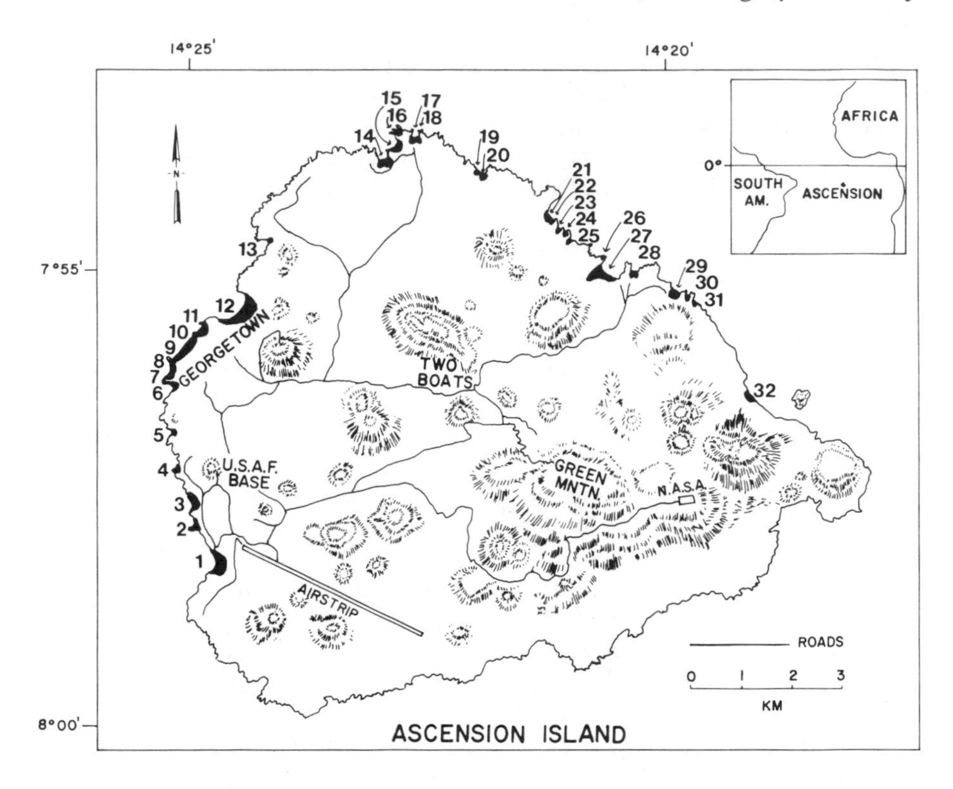

FIGURE 1. Nesting beaches of Ascension Island. The beach clusters referred to in the text are the following: South West Bay cluster (beaches 1-4); Long Beach cluster (beaches 6-12); English Bay cluster (beaches 14-18); North East Bay cluster (beaches 21-31). Turtles were monitored in the internesting habitat after leaving South West Bay (beach 1) and North East Bay (beach 27).

Internesting Behavior

The travel of 12 female turtles in the sea after they had left the nesting beach was monitored. The movements of each turtle were recorded by visually tracking a float attached by a 20-m nylon line to the posterior margin of the carapace. Simultaneous compass bearings were taken, at intervals of about 3 min, from 2 points on the shore. Successive positions of the float were determined by triangulation.

The purpose of this exercise was threefold. One aim was to learn how the turtles respond to the extreme conditions in the internesting habitat at Ascension. Having no continental shelf, the island is surrounded on all sides by very deep water; there is no forage for the turtles to eat. We also wanted to compare the behavior and movements of females that had successfully constructed nests and laid eggs with those of turtles that had been forced to abort their nesting attempt. Finally, we looked for clues to sensory mechanisms employed in locating an appropriate nesting beach.

Four turtles were tracked after successfully laying eggs—3 from South West Bay beach and 1 from North East Bay beach (Fig. 1). Eight other turtles that had not been permitted to lay eggs before returning to the sea were also tracked. Six of these were from South West Bay beach and 2 from North East Bay beach. The latter 2 turtles included an individual that was rigged with a float after abandoning her nest and then was tracked through a successful laying the next night and for 2 additional days—making a total contact period of 60 hr.

The post-nesting travel patterns of the turtles that had laid eggs were consistently different from those of turtles that had abandoned a nesting attempt. All the turtles that had laid eggs moved into water 12 to 16 m deep, and traveled parallel to the shoreline for distances of up to 7 km, and did not venture into water less than 8 m deep during the first 3 to 11 hr (Figs. 2 and 6). The frustrated nesters, on the other hand, stayed in the vicinity of the beach from which they had been frightened, and traveled back and forth in near-shore waters (Figs. 3-5). Both patterns of behavior were clearly shown by the individual (number 15206) that was tracked under both circumstances (Figs. 5 and 6).

These differences in observed behavior may account for the higher levels of site tenacity observed when nesting emergences were separated by less than 7 days (see above). Similarly, there were higher levels of site fidelity in turtles nesting at South West Bay beach than at North East Bay beach (see above). The movements of turtles tracked after frustrated nesting attempts at South West Bay beach were more restricted (Figs. 4 and 5) than those of turtles that had abandoned nesting attempts at North East Bay beach (Fig. 3).

Effects of Beach Characteristics on Nesting Density and Hatching Success

The entire coastline of Ascension Island was surveyed on foot, and every patch of sandy shoreline was evaluated as to its suitability for turtle nesting. The 32 nesting beaches, which ranged in length from 10 to 915 m and in area from 110 to 63,064 m^2, were mapped. The locations of horizontal beds of rock or strewn boulders, either submerged or on the foreshore, that partially obstructed emergences were recorded. The percentage of the total length of each beach on which the approach of a turtle would be inhibited by each type of obstacle was measured. The amount of artificial light visible on the shore was also noted.

Nesting density on each of 26 beaches was determined by counting turtle tracks at least once a week. From these data the total number of

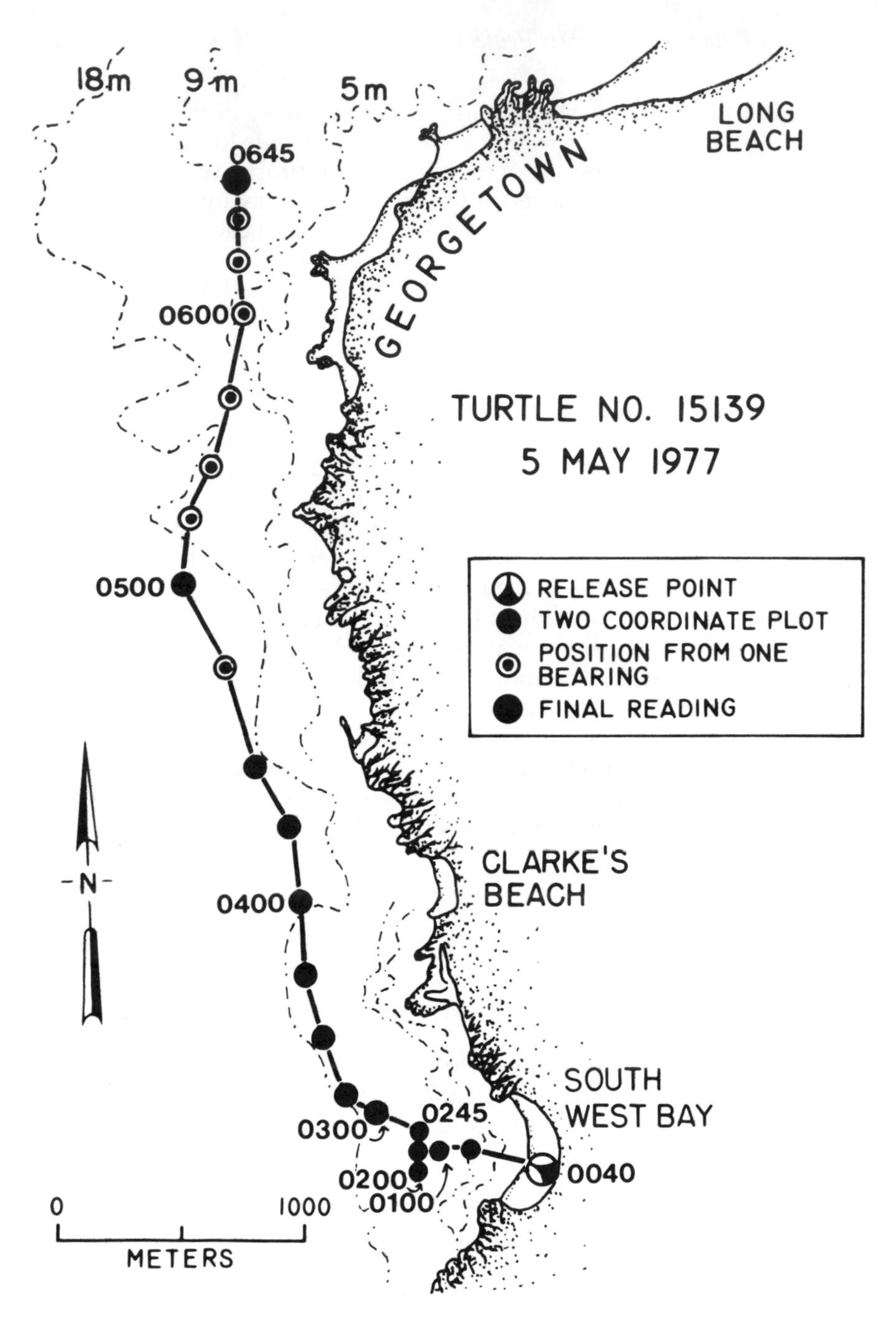

FIGURE 2. Movements of turtle 15139 during the first 6 hr after laying eggs on South West Bay beach.

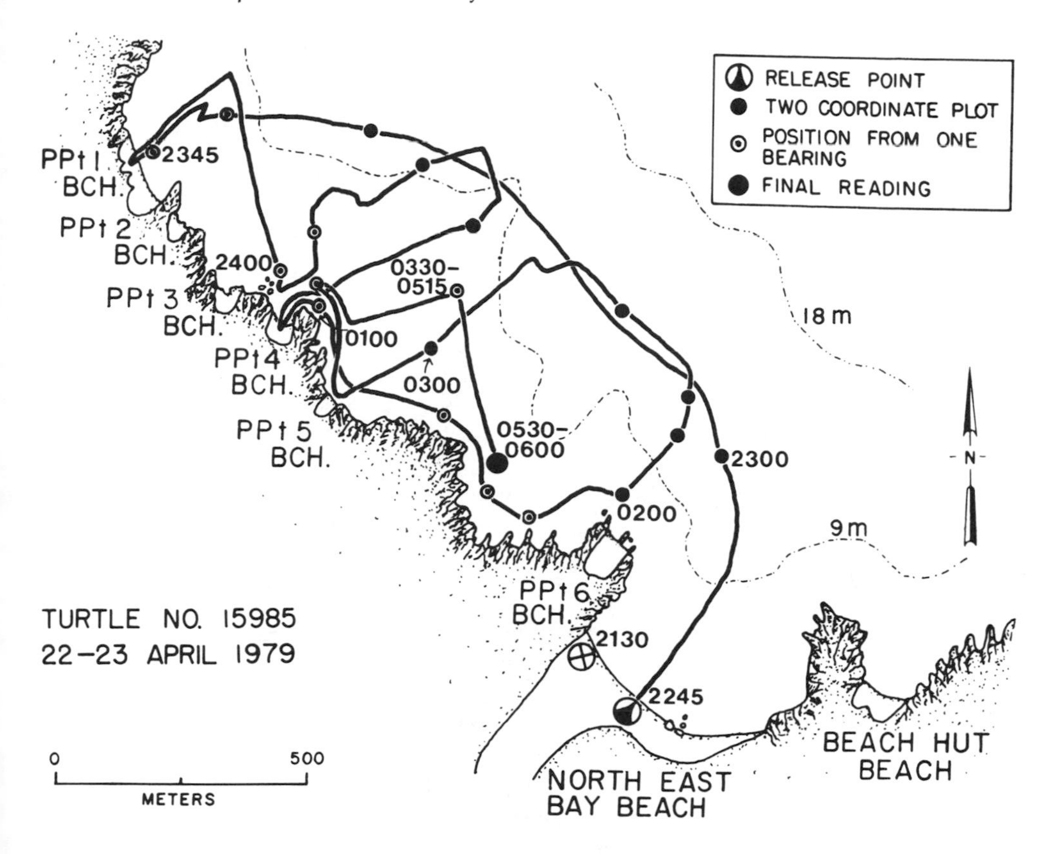

FIGURE 3. Movements of turtle 15985 during the first 7.2 hr after having been frightened away from her second nest hole at North East Bay beach. Eggs were not laid.

turtle emergences during the season was estimated. The number of egg clutches laid on each beach could then be determined by dividing the total number of emergences by the average number of times each female emerged before successfully laying a clutch of eggs.

Relative hatching and emergence success was determined by examining the contents of nests from which young had hatched and emerged from the sand. By the same examination the viability of clutches laid on different beaches was compared. An attempt was made to determine whether hatching success was correlated with depth of the nest, position of the nest on the beach, and several physical and chemical characteristics of the sand in which the clutch was incubated. These parameters were particle size distribution, salinity, moisture content, hydraulic conductivity, pH, percent organic carbon, and percent calcium carbonate.

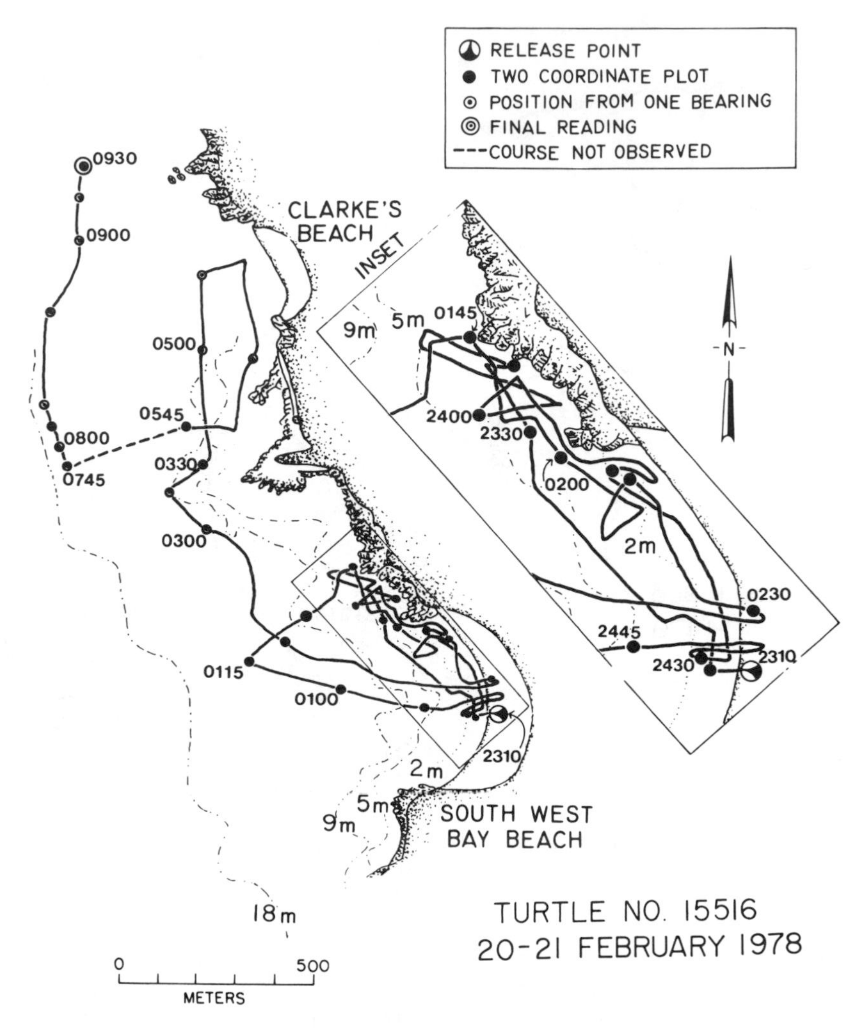

FIGURE 4. Movements of turtle 15516 during the first 10.3 hr after having been frightened away from her third nest hole on South West Bay beach.

The effect of predators on eggs and hatchlings was also investigated.

Figure 7 shows the relationship between beach length and estimated total number of clutches laid at each beach during the season. The symbols differentiate among beaches with respect to the presence or absence of adverse factors, such as submerged rocks offshore, artificial lighting, and obstruction by exposed slabs of rock on the foreshore. Submerged rocks and artificial lighting seem to be the greatest hindrances to nesting,

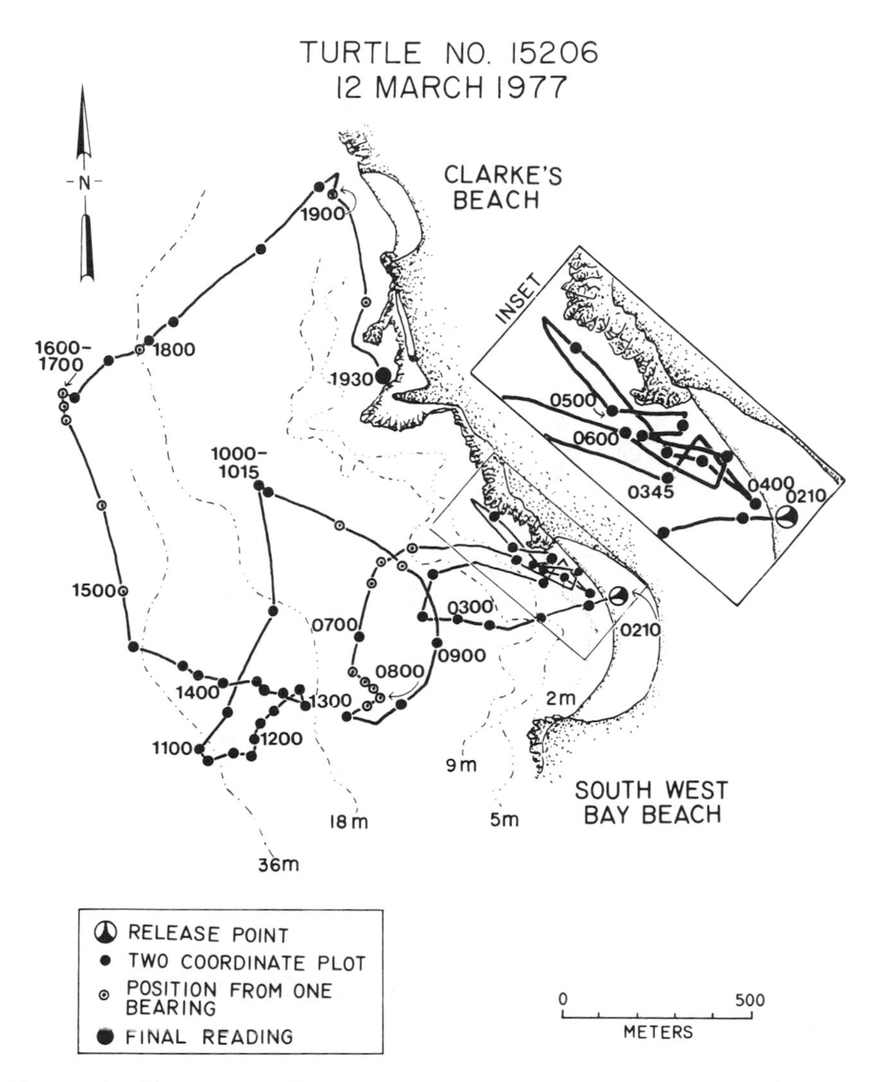

FIGURE 5. Movements of turtle 15206 during the first 17.3 hr after she abandoned a nesting attempt at South West Bay beach. Eggs were not laid. Tracking ended at sundown (1930 hr), because the light on the float had been smashed. At 2115 hr, 1.8 hr later, the turtle emerged from the surf towing the float, and nested at approximately the same point on South West Bay where she had come out the previous night. Figure 6 illustrates her movements after nesting.

followed by the presence of low slabs of beachrock alon~ the foreshore of the beach.

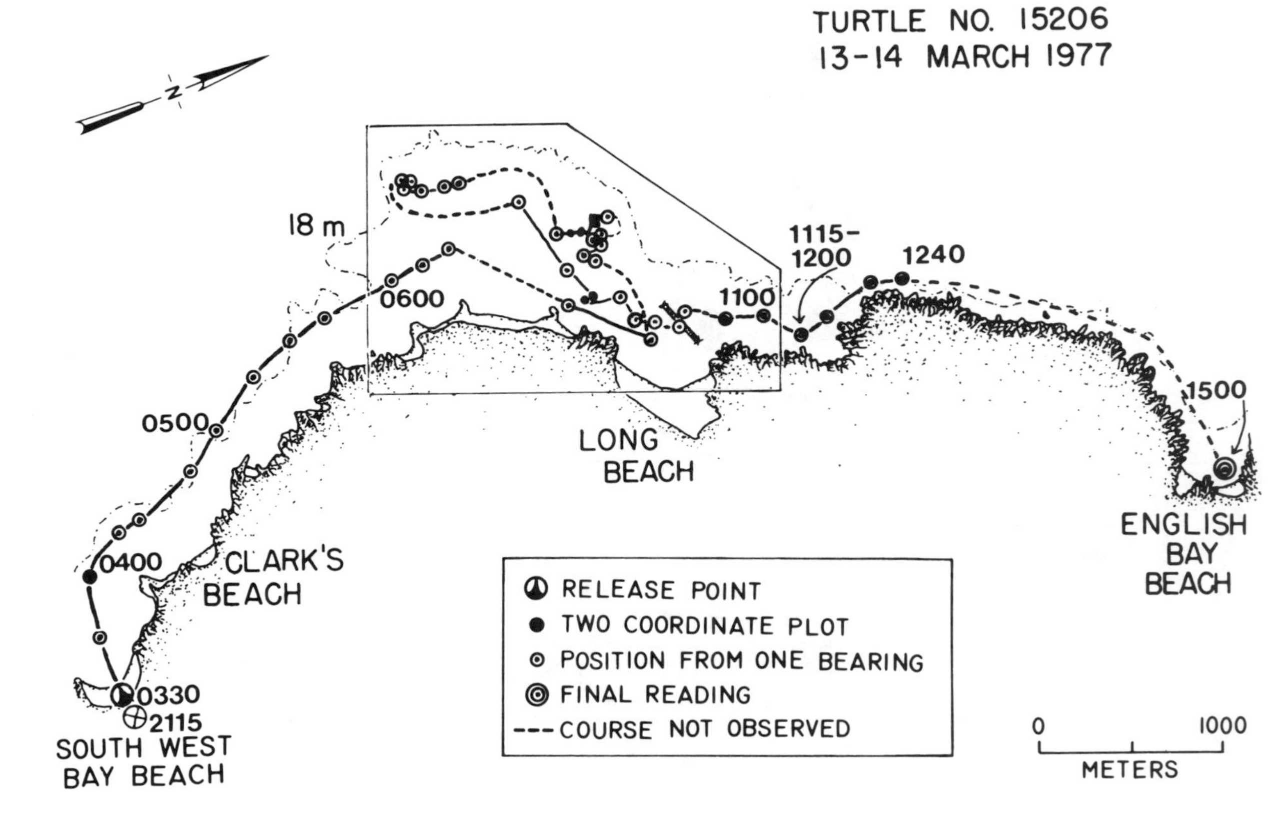

FIGURE 6. Movements of turtle 15206 during the first 36.3 hr after laying eggs at South West Bay beach (0330 hr), in her sixth egg chamber.

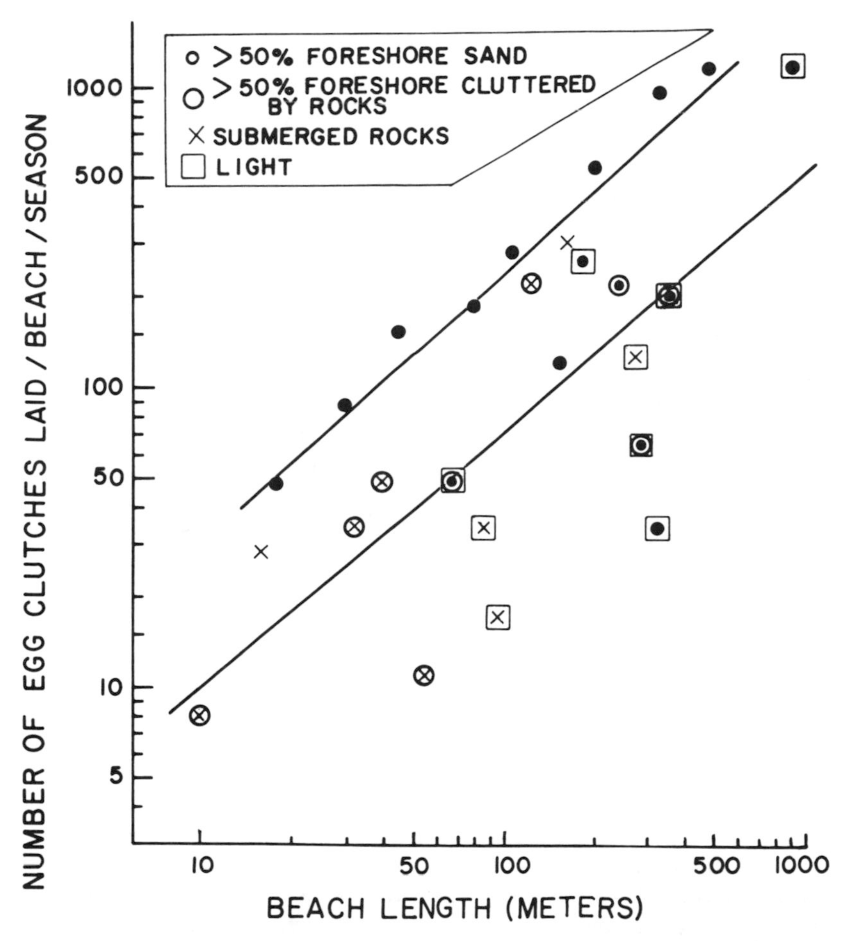

FIGURE 7. Relationship between estimated number of egg clutches laid on each beach during a season, and beach length, for 26 beaches at Ascension Island. The three symbols (×, ○, and □) indicating different obstacles to nesting are used in combination for some beaches. The upper line is a regression based on the 9 beaches without obstacles ($r = 0.92$; $p < 0.001$). The lower line is from the remaining 17 beaches, where one or more obstacles occur ($r = 0.76$; $p < 0.001$).

The relationship between the distribution of nesting activity on each of the three major Ascension Island beaches and offshore contour lines is shown in Figure 8. The heaviest nesting occurs on stretches of beach where the offshore approach is deepest.

The hatching and emergence success of egg clutches varies from beach to beach at Ascension. Most of the variation measured appears to

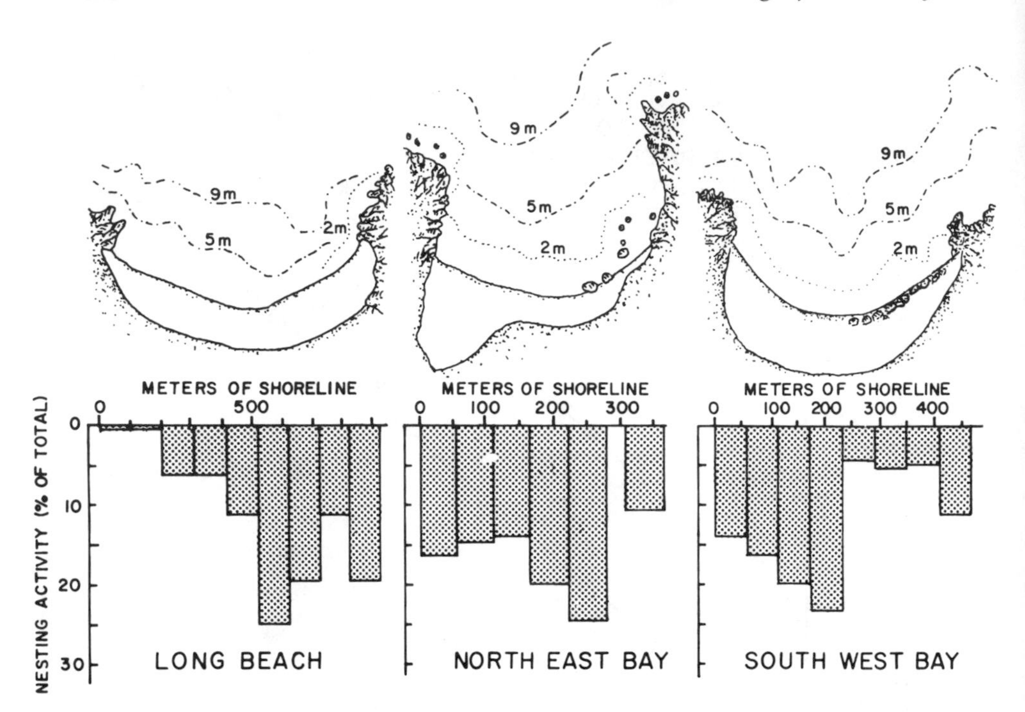

FIGURE 8. Relationship between nesting density along the shoreline, and the position of the offshore contour lines, at the three major Ascension beaches. Data were gathered by counting tracks during the 1977-1978 nesting season.

be attributable to differences in the composition of the sand in which the eggs are incubated. Particle size distribution seems to be the most important single physical parameter involved. Clutch viability is very low in poorly sorted sand (i.e., in sand that has little uniformity in particle size), or in very fine sand—probably because the rate of gas diffusion is impeded. Coarse sand encourages cave-ins and may be responsible for high levels of mortality observed between the time the hatchlings emerge from their eggs and when they make their way to the surface of the sand.

There is evidence that desiccation also reduces hatching success at Ascension. Positive correlation between hatching success and depth of nest was observed, probably because higher moisture levels occur at greater depths. Elevated levels of salinity, most frequently seen in poorly sorted sand, may induce desiccation through osmotic stress. Hatching success and distance from the sea were positively correlated, which may be related to inundation by rollers.

There is a relative dearth of both terrestrial and offshore predation upon the eggs and hatchlings. Heavy mortality is caused by beach erosion and inundation. Density-dependent mortality occurs when females destroy previously laid clutches while digging multiple trial nest holes.

Paradoxically, the turtles do not show any clear preference for beaches with the higher levels of clutch viability. In fact, percent hatchling emergence and nesting density on the beaches were negatively correlated. Although reproductive success (i.e., clutch viability) is correlated with characteristics of the beach sand, the levels of nesting density are not. The nature of the offshore approach exerts more influence on beach selection by nesting turtles than do features above the high-tide line.

REFERENCES

CARR, ARCHIE

1962. Orientation problems in the high seas travel and terrestrial movements of marine turtles. Amer. Sci., vol. 50, no. 3, pp. 359-374.

1964. Transoceanic migrations of the green turtle. Bioscience, vol. 14, no. 8, pp. 49-52.

1967. Adaptive aspects of the scheduled travel of *Chelonia*. Pp. 35-55 *in* "Animal Orientation and Navigation," R. M. Storm, ed. Oregon State University Press.

1972. The case for long-range chemoreceptive piloting in *Chelonia*. NASA SP-262, pp. 469-483.

1975. The Ascension Island green turtle colony. Copeia, vol. 1975, no. 3, pp. 547-555.

CARR, ARCHIE, and COLEMAN, PATRICK J.

1974. Seafloor spreading theory and the odyssey of the green turtle. Nature, vol. 249, no. 5453, pp. 128-130.

CARR, ARCHIE, and HIRTH, HAROLD

1962. The ecology and migrations of sea turtles, 5. Comparative features of isolated green turtle colonies. Amer. Mus. Nov., no. 2091, 42 pp.

CARR, ARCHIE; ROSS, PERRAN; and CARR, STEPHEN

1974. Internesting behavior of the green turtle, *Chelonia mydas,* at a mid-ocean island breeding ground. Copeia, vol. 1974, no. 3, pp. 703-706.

HART-DAVIS, DUFF

1972. Ascension—the story of a South Atlantic island, 244 pp. Constable and Co., Ltd., London.

KOCH, A. L.; CARR, A.; and EHRENFELD, D. W.

1969. The problem of open-sea navigation: The migration of the green turtle to Ascension Island. Journ. Theoret. Biol., vol. 22, pp. 163-179.

MORTIMER, JEANNE A.

1979. Influence of beach characteristics on nesting density, site fixity and hatching success of green turtles at Ascension Island. Amer. Zool., vol. 19, no. 3, pp. 954. (Abstract of paper presented at Annual Meeting of American Society of Zoologists, 1979).

Mortimer, Jeanne A. (*continued*)
1981. Reproductive ecology of the green turtle, *Chelonia mydas,* at Ascension Island. Ph.D. thesis, University of Florida, 163 pp.
1982. Factors influencing beach selection by nesting sea turtles. Pp. 45-51 *in* "Biology and Conservation of Sea Turtles," K. A. Bjorndal, ed. Smithsonian Institution Press, Washington, D. C.

Simon, Marlin H., and Parkes, Alan S.
1976. The green sea turtle *(Chelonia mydas)*: Nesting on Ascension Island, 1973-1974. Journ. Zool., Lond., vol. 179, pp. 153-163.

Stancyk, S. E., and Ross, J. P.
1978. An analysis of sand from green turtle nesting beaches on Ascension Island. Copeia, vol. 1978, no. 1, pp. 93-99.

Jeanne A. Mortimer
Archie F. Carr

The History of American Exploration in Africa

Grant Recipient: James A. Casada, Winthrop College, Rock Hill, South Carolina.

Grant 1640: In support of a study of the history of American exploration in Africa.

The support provided by the National Geographic Society enabled me to pursue research on the contributions which American explorers, or those with American connections, made to the geographical reconnaissance of Africa. My work focused primarily on the careers of five individuals: Henry Morton Stanley, Charles Chaillé-Long, Henry S. Sanford, Paul Belloni du Chaillu, and Mary French Sheldon. Other less prominent individuals, however, who figured in the American part in the discovery of Africa, were also considered.

The basic purpose of the research was to provide a historical evaluation of the largely unappreciated role that Americans had in African discovery. The monograph that will be the final result of my work should provide a full overview of American participation in unveiling the geographical mysteries of the vast region that long was known as the "dark continent." In conducting my research under the grant, I visited a number of major libraries and archives in the United States and in Europe. The grant also enabled me to acquire microfilm copies of portions of the extant papers of several of the explorers studied, most notably those of Sanford and Sheldon.

The basic research connected with the proposal has now been completed, and in the course of my ongoing studies has contributed to a number of publications. These include biographical pieces; longer narrative articles that appeared in *The Discoverers: An Encyclopedia of Explorers and Exploration* (1980); a book-length bibliographical treatment of Stanley—this work was in progress at the time the grant was received, and the grant not only facilitated research on the project but also contributed to the comprehensiveness of the work (Casada, 1977a); and various articles (Casada, 1979). These publications, however, should be viewed as interim work leading to the book-length treatment that will be the ultimate outgrowth of my research. This study is now in the process of being written and when finished will constitute the completion of the project.

REFERENCES

CASADA, JAMES A.

1977a. Dr. David Livingstone and Sir Henry Morton Stanley: An annotated bibliography with commentary, 224 pp. Garland Publishing, New York.

1977b. Sir Henry M. Stanley: The explorer as journalist. Southern Quarterly, vol. 15, pp. 357-369.

1980. Royal Geographical Society, pp. 359-361. Exploration of Africa pp. 6-24. Charles Chaillé-Long, pp. 115-116. Paul Belloni du Chaillu, p. 146. Literature and exploration, pp. 209-217. Nile River: Search for its source, pp. 283-287. Henry Morton Stanley, pp. 407-409. *In* "The Discoverers: An Encyclopedia of Explorers and Exploration," Helen Delpar, ed. McGraw-Hill, New York.

CASADA, JAMES A., ed.

1979. African and Afro-American history: A review of recent trends, 137 pp. Conch Publishing, New York. Of particular note is the editor's article "Exploration in Africa" (pp. 113-124).

JAMES A. CASADA

A Buried Site Reconnaissance in the Tellico Reservoir, Eastern Tennessee

Grant Recipient: Jefferson Chapman, Department of Anthropology, University of Tennessee, Knoxville, Tennessee.

Grant 1661: For early site location and testing in the proposed Tellico Reservoir.[1]

The Little Tennessee River and its tributaries drain portions of western North Carolina, northeastern Georgia, and eastern Tennessee. In the last 35 mi of flow to its confluence with the Tennessee River, the river leaves the foothills of the Blue Ridge Province and flows west to northwest, bisecting several ridges that constitute a portion of the Ridge and Valley Province. The lower valley is bounded by dissected hills rising 100 to 200 ft above a relatively narrow floodplain composed of recent alluvium. Formations of limestone, dolomite, sandstone, and shale form the geologic base for the area. The region is characterized by a temperate deciduous forest with a humid, mesothermal-type climate. Precipitation averages 51 to 59 in./yr and the valley has average winter temperatures of 39.3°F and average summer temperatures of 78.9°F.

In 1967, the Tennessee Valley Authority (TVA) began construction of the Tellico Dam at the confluence of the Little Tennessee River and the Tennessee River (Fig. 1). The proposed reservoir would inundate the last 33 mi of the river valley and would cover over 14,000 acres. In the same year the University of Tennessee Department of Anthropology began, under contract, a series of archeological investigations. These efforts continued in annual field seasons until the reservoir was filled in fall 1979.

Between 1973 and 1976, investigations had located and sampled six deeply stratified archeological sites; these excavations produced an unprecedented in situ collection of lithic assemblages and feature data spanning 3000 yr (7500 B.C. to 4500 B.C.) (Chapman, 1975, 1977, 1979). Additional buried site exploration, however, was warranted. First, there were other locales within the proposed reservoir that had strong potential for containing buried sites. Exploration of these could strengthen a

[1] A detailed report of these investigations was published in 1978 by Jefferson Chapman (see References).

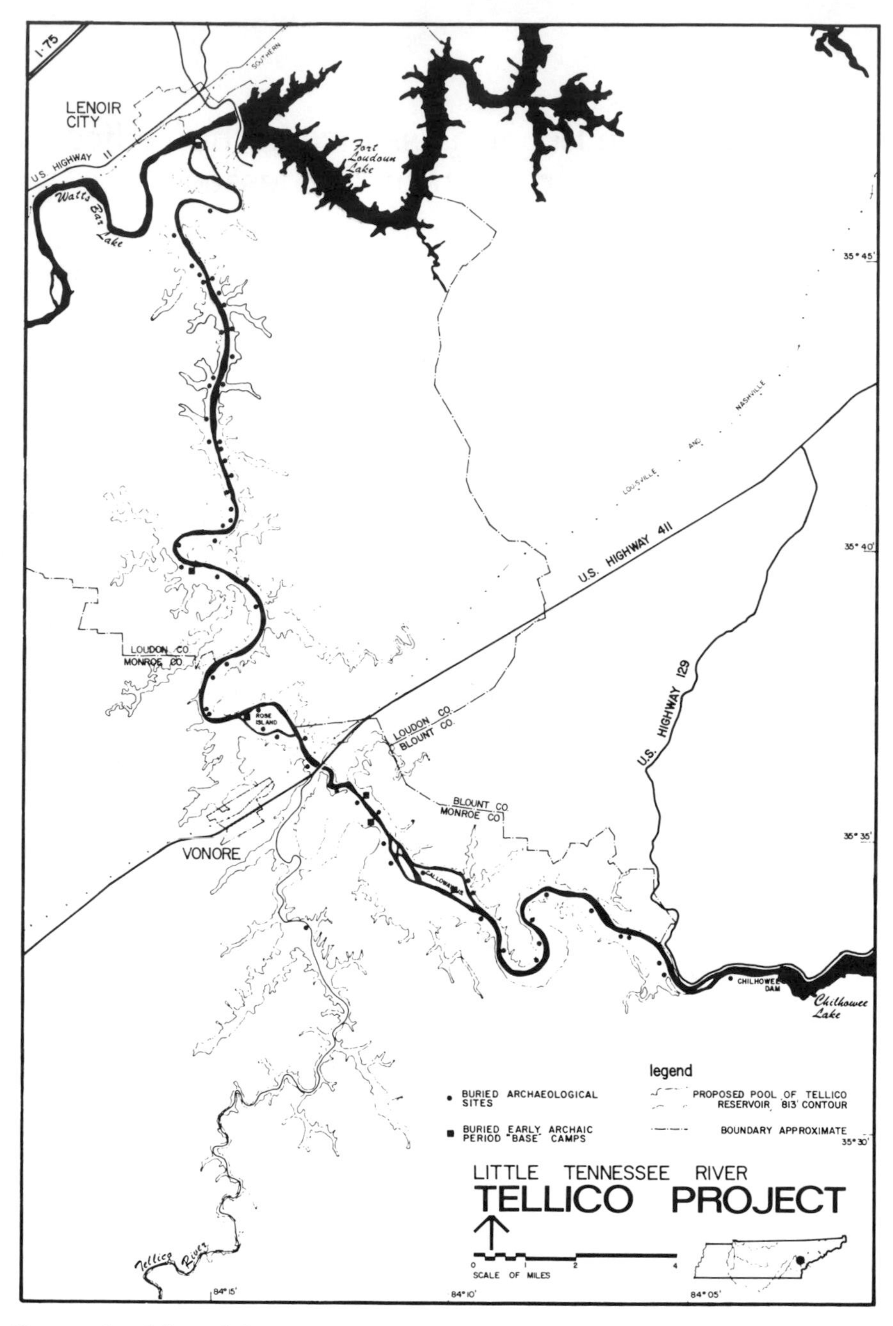

FIGURE 1. Map of the Tellico Project area showing buried archeological sites identified during the reconnaissance.

previously employed intuitive predictive model for site location and potential for burial, while further investigation of low probability areas could confirm or modify the model. Second, such an extensive survey had never been done before and would certainly serve as an important model in any future research efforts concerning the investigation of alluvial terraces. The time was also appropriate, since TVA owned all of the land; and crops, once harvested, were not scheduled to be replanted. This situation would make all of the land accessible to testing by backhoe without the usual concern for crop damage and fences.

Third, it was obvious that no statements or interpretations concerning Archaic period settlement patterns could be generated unless a subsurface survey of the valley was undertaken. Traditional surface reconnaissance had already been demonstrated as inadequate for identifying all of the prehistoric cultural resources; for example, none of the buried sites located to date in the valley would have been recorded from their surface manifestations.

The research procedure of the deep testing program was to test by means of backhoe trenches all of the first terraces along the Little Tennessee River and lower Tellico River that had not been previously tested (Fig. 2). Timing and location were dependent upon the harvest of row crops. Testing was limited to the first terraces since previous investigations had shown the second terraces to be too old to contain buried cultural remains. The principal piece of equipment was a tractor backhoe with a 14-ft reach, equipped with a 3-ft-wide toothless bucket and front-end loader. Over 350 backhoe trenches were excavated in locations throughout the study area. Trenches were spaced anywhere from several hundred feet apart to less than 10 ft apart, depending upon the stratigraphy and questions concerning the strata. Optimum trench size was that excavated by a single arc of the backhoe—approximately 13 ft long at the top and tapering to a length of 3 to 4 ft at the bottom. A sketch or description of one profile was made of each backhoe trench; the locations of trenches were recorded on land acquisition maps prepared by TVA.

There were 45 new subsurface sites recorded during the survey (Fig. 1); on an additional 15 sites that had already been assigned site numbers based on surface manifestations, deep testing revealed buried zones as well.

The largest and one of the most significant sites located and tested during the reconnaissance was the Bacon Farm site (40LD35). Backhoe testing at this location revealed a large site with stratified Early Archaic period deposits similar to the sequence at Icehouse Bottom (40MR23) (Chapman, 1977) (Fig. 3). Test pits exposing over 2100 ft^2 were excavated to determine the cultural affiliation of the various strata. The backhoe was used to remove the sediments overlaying strata to be tested. Hand

FIGURE 2. Typical backhoe trench employed in the reconnaissance. Two buried cultural horizons can be seen above the hands of the archeologist.

excavations focused on Stratum IX, a 1.8- to 2.6-ft-thick layer of fine sandy loam that contained several occupational surfaces associated with the Early Archaic Kirk Corner Notched phase (ca. 7500 B.C. to 6800 B.C.). Over 14,000 in situ artifacts (94% of this total is debitage) were recovered

FIGURE 3. South profile of Test Pit 7 at the Bacon Farm site (40LD35).

and 34 features recorded from this stratum. A radiocarbon assay of 9105 ± 190 C^{14} yr B.P. (GX4707) was obtained from carbonized wood and nutshell from Stratum IX; this date is consistent with other dates for the Kirk Corner Notched phase in the valley (Chapman, 1980a). Flotation samples from this stratum produced abundant carbonized plant remains which have been used in subsequent paleoenvironmental and subsistence reconstructions (Chapman and Shea, 1981; Chapman et al., 1982).

Backhoe testing below the Early Archaic period strata at Bacon Farm exposed no evidence of occupation. At approximately 10 ft below the deepest cultural horizon, a layer of waterlogged leaves and wood fragments was encountered; radiocarbon assays produced dates of 8760 ± 210 C^{14} yr B.P. (GX4708), 9070±210 C^{14} yr B.P. (6X4709), and 9420±200 C^{14} yr B.P. (A2591). A similar layer with a comparable date was found below the deepest Early Archaic stratum at Icehouse Bottom; the overlap in these dates and those on the earliest cultural components suggests that during the early Holocene increased sediment load resulted in rapid terrace aggradation (cf. Delcourt, 1980). Deep testing on the second terrace adjacent to the site failed to yield any organic material for dating; however, a date elsewhere in the valley suggests that these sediments may have been deposited as early as 27,000 yr ago.

Limited excavations were conducted at 20 sites; at 17 of these, excavations were restricted to 1 to 3 test pits placed adjacent to backhoe trenches in order to sample one or more buried cultural horizons. At 2 sites, the plow zone was stripped from areas to sample features; at the Negro Hollow site (40LD42) 1285 ft^2 were exposed and 10 Mississippian and Woodland period features were excavated. At the Jones Ferry site (40MR76) 300 ft^2 were exposed and 12 features excavated. Middle Woodland and Early Mississippian period components were identified and additional work was conducted at Jones Ferry in 1979 (Chapman, 1980b). At the Iddins site (40LD38) a buried Late Archaic period component was encountered. A total of 587 ft^2 of the stratum was excavated and 25 features recorded; radiocarbon assays of 3205 ± 145 C^{14} yr B.P. (GX4706) and 3655 ± 135 C^{14} yr B.P. (GX4705) were obtained from carbonized wood in 2 fire pits. The density of artifacts and features within Stratum III suggested that additional excavations were warranted; these occurred in 1977 (Chapman, 1981).

Conclusions

1. The deep testing reconnaissance suggests that the distribution of buried sites is not restricted to areas below river constrictions, the lower ends of islands, and the inside of the lower ends of river bends, but that sites occur within most of the first terraces within the Little Tennessee River valley.

2. This preservation and stratification is a product of late Glacial/early Holocene sediment influx and rapid terrace aggradation from 15,000 to 8000 yr B.P.

3. The absence of earlier sites (PaleoIndian, Dalton) is probably a function of this same geomorphological process. The T2 is too old for buried in situ occupation and the T1 may be too young. While earlier channel bars containing PaleoIndian remains may be buried within the T1, they will be difficult to locate, and a greater possibility exists that the dynamics of the late Glacial sediment influx destroyed these earlier occupations.

4. The preceding three conclusions are probably applicable throughout much of the southern Ridge and Valley Province except in areas of narrow valley and steep river gradients. Consequently, similar stratified sites can be expected to occur.

5. Larger buried Early Archaic period sites in the Little Tennessee River valley such as Bussell Island, Bacon Farm, Rose Island, Patrick, Icehouse Bottom, and Calloway Island are situated in areas that offered access to a diversity of aquatic, floodplain, and upland habitats; these sites functioned as residential bases within a hunter/gatherer settlement subsistence system. Smaller buried sites probably represent field camps or

resource extraction loci within the system. The number of sites occupied at any one time or articulating within a single annual settlement system are cultural questions as yet too fine-grained to extract from the archeological record. Subsequent studies and surveys (Davis et al., 1982) have concluded that early aboriginal land use within the study area was clearly dichotomized between valley and upland zones. Residential bases are strongly associated with first- and second-terrace land forms, whereas resource extraction loci dominate the upland zone. Field camps occur within both valley and upland zones but tend to be more prevalent on valley land forms.

6. Finally, the buried site reconnaissance clearly demonstrated the potential for significant cultural resources deep within alluvial terraces. That these resources should be considered in plans for future work in alluvial valleys appears obvious.

Acknowledgments

In addition to the grant from the National Geographic Society, the Tennessee Valley Authority continued to pay the salary of the grantee and provided field equipment. Several local businesses assisted with the loan of backhoes, bulldozers, a truck and trailer, and diesel fuel. Several individuals donated money to help defray wage costs. Concurrently with this funding, the National Park Service provided additional money for the continued investigations at the Toqua site (40MR6), a situation that enabled us to share field camp facilities.

REFERENCES

CHAPMAN, JEFFERSON

1975. The Rose Island site and the bifurcate point tradition. University of Tennessee, Department of Anthropology, Report of Investigations 14.

1977. Archaic period research in the lower Little Tennessee River valley—1975: Icehouse Bottom, Harrison Branch, Thirty Acre Island, Calloway Island. University of Tennessee, Department of Anthropology, Report of Investigations 18.

1978. The Bacon farm site a buried site reconnaissance. University of Tennessee, Department of Anthropology, Report of Investigations 23 and Tennessee Valley Authority, Publications in Anthropology 21.

1979. The Howard and Calloway Island sites. University of Tennessee, Department of Anthropology, Report of Investigations 27, and Tennessee Valley Authority, Publications in Anthropology 23.

1980a. The Early and Middle Archaic periods: A perspective from eastern Tennessee. Pp. 123-132 *in* "Proceedings of the Conference on Northeastern Archaeology," James A. Moore, ed. University of Massachusetts, Department of Anthropology, Research Reports 19.

CHAPMAN, JEFFERSON *(continued)*

1980b. The Jones Ferry site (40MR76). Pp. 43-58 *in* "The 1979 Archaeological and Geological Investigations in the Tellico Reservoir," Jefferson Chapman, ed. University of Tennessee, Department of Anthropology, Report of Investigations 29, and Tennessee Valley Authority, Publications in Anthropology 24.

1981. The Bacon Bend and Iddins sites: The Late Archaic period in the lower Little Tennessee River valley. University of Tennessee, Department of Anthropology, Report of Investigations 31, and Tennessee Valley Authority Publications in Anthropology 25.

CHAPMAN, JEFFERSON and SHEA, ANDREA BREWER

1981. The archaeobotanical record: Early Archaic period to contact in the lower Little Tennessee River valley. Tennessee Anthropologist, vol. 6, no. 1, pp. 61-84.

CHAPMAN, JEFFERSON; DELCOURT, PAUL A.; CRIDLEBAUGH, PATRICIA A.; SHEA, ANDREA B.; and DELCOURT, HAZEL

1982. Man-land interaction: 10,000 years of American Indian impact on native ecosystems in the lower Little Tennessee River valley, eastern Tennessee. Southeastern Archaeology, vol. 1, no. 2, pp. 115-121.

DAVIS, R. P. STEPHEN, JR.; KIMBALL, LARRY R.; and BADEN, WILLIAM W.

1982. An archeological survey and assessment of aboriginal settlement within the lower Little Tennessee River valley. Report submitted to the Tennessee Valley Authority in accordance with contract TV-56255A.

DELCOURT, PAUL A.

1980. Quaternary alluvial terraces of the Little Tennessee River, east Tennessee. Pp. 110-121 *in* "The 1979 Archaeological and Geological Investigations in the Tellico Reservoir," Jefferson Chapman, ed. The University of Tennessee, Department of Anthropology, Report of Investigations 29, and Tennessee Valley Authority, Publications in Anthropology 24.

JEFFERSON CHAPMAN

Evaluating Portions of Three Late 18th-Century Maps by Core-Boring Analysis

Grant Recipient: Roland E. Chardon, Department of Geography and Anthropology, Louisiana State University, Baton Rouge, Louisiana.

Grant 1695: In support of the scientific testing of the accuracy of early historical maps.

This report summarizes the results of efforts to determine, using core techniques and boring log data, the accuracy of three late 18th-century maps of the northern Biscayne Bay region, in the presently urbanized Miami area of southeastern Florida. The maps, two of which are so similar that they may be considered stages of the same map, were drawn in the 1770s by William Gerard De Brahm, then Surveyor-General for the Southern District of (British) North America, and for the (British) province of East Florida (Figs. 1 and 2). These maps have been cartographically analyzed (Chardon, 1975a, 1975b, 1982). While in some areas they exhibit a very high degree of geographic correspondence with later and modern charts, other portions of the maps are incompatible with the vegetation or shoreline patterns depicted on later U. S. Coast Survey and other charts, or on modern aerial photographs (Chardon, 1975b, 1982; Teas et al., 1976).

It was proposed, therefore, that probing and coring be undertaken in the discrepant areas, to try to obtain physical evidence corroborating the patterns shown on the De Brahm maps or, failing this, to determine whether the physical evidence indicated local environmental change over the past 200 years. If neither resulted from core sample examination, it could reasonably be concluded, pending further evidence, that the De Brahm maps were at least in part inaccurate.

The original proposal called for the selection of at least 18 probing and coring sites. Four of these were to be concentrated on the mainland (western) side of the bay area. A second set of sites was to sample the western portion of Key Biscayne, and at least 6 cores were to be taken from the barrier complex of northeastern Biscayne Bay. These 3 areas contained the greatest apparent discrepancies between the De Brahm maps and modern topographic charts. As fieldwork progressed, it

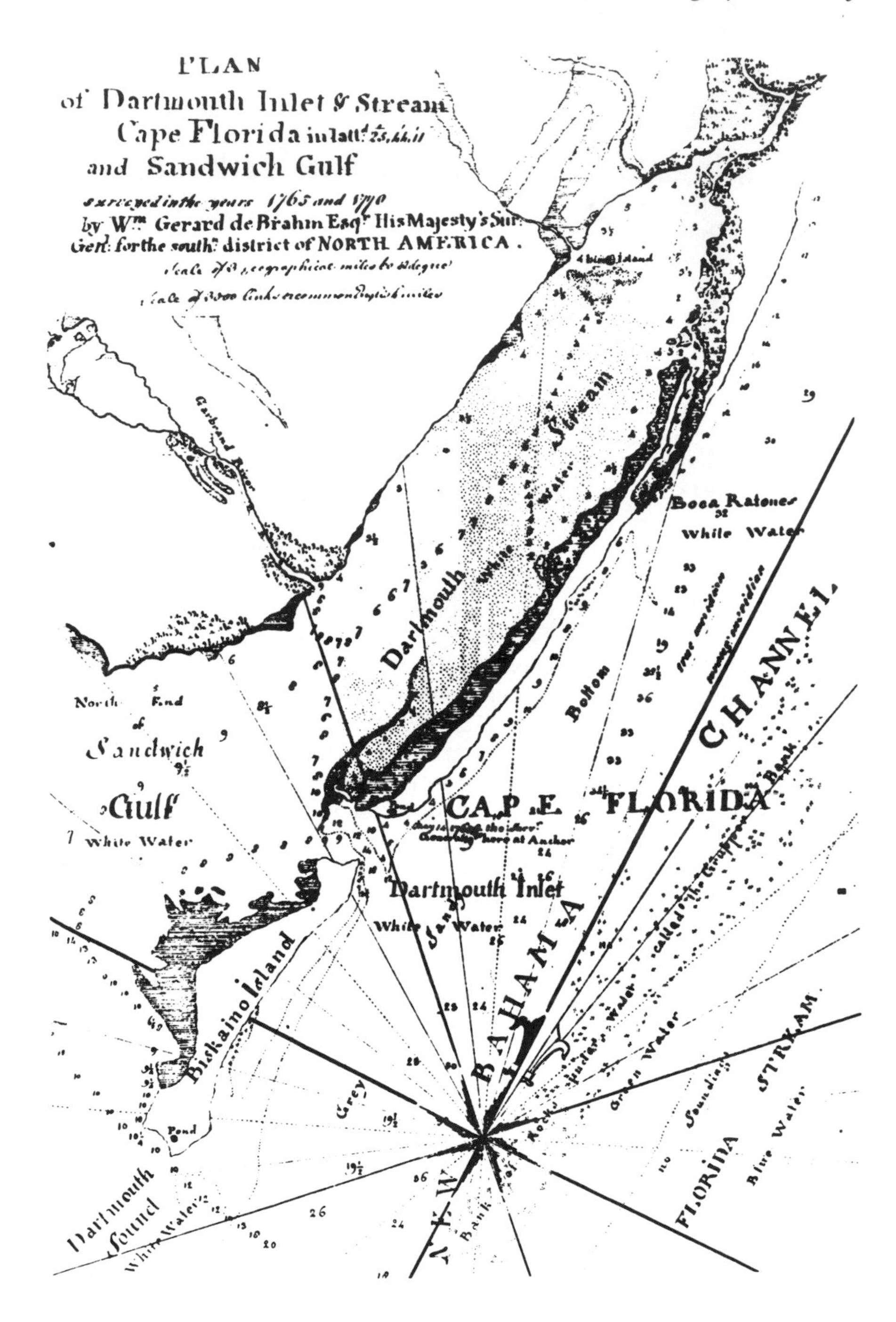
PLAN
of Dartmouth Inlet & Stream
Cape Florida in latt. 25.44.11
and Sandwich Gulf
surveyed in the years 1765 and 1770
by Wm. Gerard de Brahm Esqr. His Majesty's Sur. Genl. for the southn. district of NORTH AMERICA.
Garbrand River
Stream
White Water
Dartmouth
Boca Ratones
White Water
Bottom
CHANNEL
North End of Sandwich Gulf
White Water
CAPE FLORIDA
Dartmouth Inlet
White Water
Biskaino Island
BAHAMA
Grey
Pond
Dartmouth Sound
White Water
Green Water
Soundings
FLORIDA STREAM
Blue Water

turned out that probing and coring in the urbanized parts of Miami Beach was impractical, so copies of more than 120 boring logs were acquired from local engineering firms. The logs are records of cores taken when the firms tested foundations for the erection of various buildings.

All the sites are shown in Figure 3, which also indicates the 1770 and 1974 shorelines of the 3 discrepant areas mentioned. The drilling and analyses of the mainland and Key Biscayne cores were carried out by Dr. Harold R. Wanless and Peter Harlem, of the University of Miami's Rosenstiel School of Marine and Atmospheric Sciences (RSMAS). The engineering boring logs were interpreted both in Miami by some of the firms' personnel, and by the principal investigator at the Department of Geography and Anthropology, School of Geoscience, Louisiana State University. Since detailed reports of the results of this investigation will be published later, the following represents a summary of our findings to date. The evaluation is organized regionally; for illustrative purposes, 1 or 2 representative cores are included for each of the 3 areas covered.

The Western Mainland Shore of Central Biscayne Bay

In this area several major discrepancies appear between the De Brahm chart drawn in 1773 (Fig. 2) and the earliest U. S. Coast Survey charts drawn in the mid-1850s. There are also points of similarity, however. In other papers (Chardon, 1975a, 1975b) the difficulties involved in evaluating this map as an accurate cartographic document are discussed at some length, and it was concluded that De Brahm's mainland shore configuration cannot be described as an accurate portrayal of the true 1770 shoreline along its entire length. But it was also noted that certain features, especially vegetation types, were quite similar in character and geographic distribution to those shown on later Coast Survey charts (e.g., U. S. Coast Survey, 1858). This suggested that some vegetative and perhaps even shoreline changes might have occurred between 1770 and the 1850s. Specifically, De Brahm's map (Fig. 2) showed a large freshwater marsh extending to the bay's edge, while an 1858 Coast Survey map

---

FIGURE 1. "Plan of Dartmouth Inlet & Stream, Cape Florida, . . . & Sandwich Gulf. Surveyed in the Years 1765 and 1770, by Wm. Gerard de Brahm Esqr." This map of northern Biscayne Bay is a preliminary version of the map submitted by De Brahm in a lengthy report of a 6-year survey of the Florida east coast; the finalized map is in the British Museum and was published by DeVorsey (1971, p. 209). The working map reproduced here is published with the permission of the Houghton Library, Harvard University.

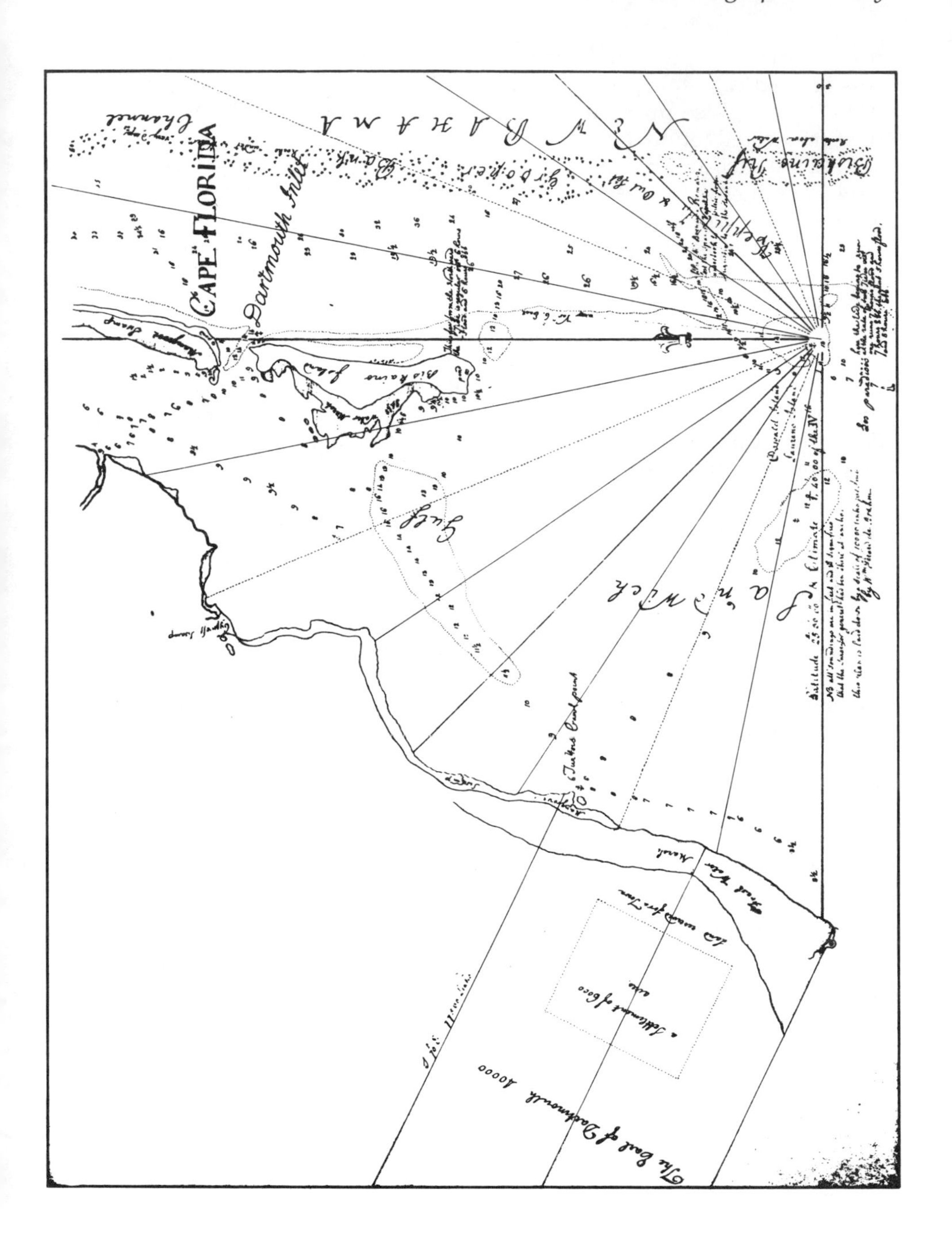
CAPE FLORIDA
Dartmouth Inlet

(not reproduced here) identified the same freshwater marsh, but it was separated from the bay waters by a narrow coastal mangrove fringe.

To assess the accuracy of De Brahm's map, and at the same time evaluate this possible change in coastal environment, vertical core samples were taken at three locations north of Black Point (Fig. 3); these cores are identified as RC-1, RC-2, and RC-3. At each of the sites there was less than 1 m of soft sediment accumulation over Pleistocene limestone bedrock. Fibrous red mangrove (*Rhizophora mangle*) peat dominated each of the samples below a surficial zone of incompletely decomposed leaf litter and incompletely dissolved calcium carbonate sand laminae washed in during storms. The great abundance of living mangrove root and rhizome material most certainly has obliterated precursor organic and carbonate sediment from these sites, with the possible exception of Core RC-3, where the pervasive fibrous and rooted mangrove detritus is intermixed somewhat with carbonate sands. Figure 4 represents Core RC-1 and its materials down to bedrock.

The processes leading to the red mangrove dominance in these cores, where bedrock is not very deep, can be compared with the growth of new roots in a flower pot. They will quickly concentrate toward the bottom of the pot, consuming or dominating precursor material. If the pot is shallow, or given sufficient time, the new roots will dominate the entire pot. The release of tannic acid by the mangrove permits root growth not only to consume the preexisting organic debris, but also to dissolve calcium carbonate contained in the sediment.

That this "flower pot" effect is important has been verified by Meeder and Wanless (1977), who took a core boring through the paralic (i.e., between marine and continental sediments) red mangrove swamp along the mainland of Card Sound, in southern Biscayne Bay. Here, about 2.5 m of sediment overlie Pleistocene limestone. The vertical sedimentary sequence consists of: (1) a gravelly zone overlying limestone containing fresh red mangrove rootlets; (2) a reddish mangrove peat with fresh rootlets and rhizomes; overlain by (3) a freshwater calcitic marl; overlain by (4) marly red mangrove peat becoming purer peat upward to

---

FIGURE 2. Untitled map drawn by William Gerard De Brahm for the Earl of Dartmouth in 1773. It is based on De Brahm's survey map of 1770 and indicates the site for a proposed but unsuccessful European settlement near present-day Cutler Ridge, about 16 km southwest of Miami. The map covers part of central Biscayne Bay to the south of Figure 1. A slightly modified version of this map was first published in 1975 (Chardon, 1975a), but this is the first time it has been reproduced in its original form. With the permission of the Earl of Dartmouth, the Staffordshire County Record Office, and the Historical Association of Southern Florida.

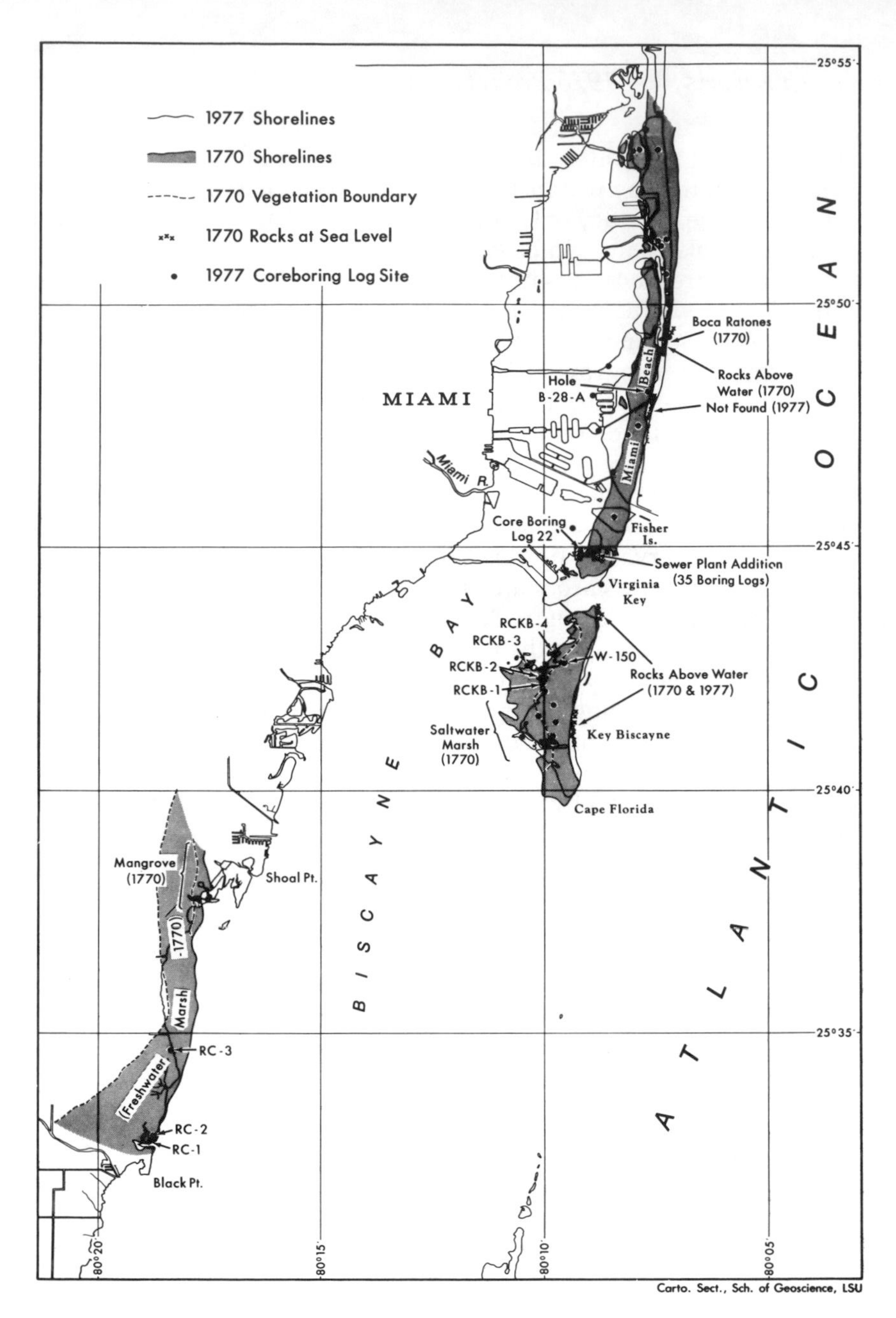

FIGURE 3. Location map of the northern Biscayne Bay area. Specific sites mentioned in the text are identified, as well as the sites of the cores and boring logs obtained in 1977. The 1770 shorelines as drawn by De Brahm have been superimposed on a modern chart based on "best-fit" wherever possible (Chardon, 1982). The base map is derived from National Ocean Survey Nautical Charts 11451 and 11467 (1974 editions).

surface. C^{14} dating of peat samples from this core showed a gradual increase in age downward through the upper peat zone to an age of 3900 B.P. (Before Present) at a depth of about 2 m below mean low water (MLW). This corresponds well with the sea level history of south Florida. Surprisingly, however, the lower peat just above bedrock dated at 1300 to 1400 B.P.! Recent mangrove growth has clearly penetrated the soft sediment sequence and formed a contaminating and obliterating rootlet mat in a 50-cm zone just above the less penetrable limestone surface.

In view of these results, and considering the similarity of the area we were coring to that cored by Meeder and Wanless, we decided not to submit the samples taken in our area (Fig. 3) to C^{14} analysis (and its expense), and they have not been dated. The 3 cores (RC-1, RC-2, and RC-3) are in an area of even shallower bedrock limestone than the one analyzed by Meeder and Wanless, and come from a very similar coastal environment only a few kilometers away. The results obtained by Meeder and Wanless provide supporting evidence that mangrove growth can quickly obliterate preexisting sediment in the zone above the limestone surface. Where the limestone surface is only slightly above sea level, as in the sites of the 3 core samples taken for the De Brahm investigation (Fig. 3), the mangrove peat growth may well have consumed and replaced the entire precursor sedimentary deposit.

For this reason also, it was decided to abandon further coring along this part of the mainland shore of central Biscayne Bay, since the limestone surface underlying the shore is generally quite shallow along the entire shoreline (Wanless, 1969), and we would not have been able to establish—due to the flower pot effect—whether a freshwater marsh ever existed at bayside. In this case, core techniques cannot help us determine whether this portion of De Brahm's map accurately portrays the vegetation of 1770 at bayside, for the cores neither confirm nor deny the existence, at that time, of marsh in the localities sampled.

The Western, or Bayside, Portion of Key Biscayne

De Brahm's western third of Key Biscayne (Figs. 1 and 2) is more or less accurately outlined in that the major coastal features found today are identifiable on his maps. Along with many later surveyors, De Brahm "thickened" the key, enlarging its width by almost a third. But unlike his successors, De Brahm showed the dominant vegetation as comprising saltwater marsh in this part of the key (Fig. 2). Coast Survey maps of the key, drawn after 1849, indicate that this portion of the island exhibited dominant mangrove vegetation, though some of the survey maps describe the vegetation as mixed mangrove and marsh, with mangrove clearly dominant by midcentury. It would seem either that De Brahm was totally wrong in his portrayal of the vegetation in this area, or that a major transformation occurred in the vegetative cover of western Key Biscayne between 1770 and the 1850s.

There seems no way, at present, to measure scientifically the lateral extent of Key Biscayne from east to west, as it is shown on De Brahm's maps (Figs. 1 and 2). If a greater width than at present did exist, erosion would have removed most of the evidence of former shorelines (i.e., west of the present one) in the intervening 200 years. What may be determined, however, are the vegetation layers underlying the present mangrove forest, for in this area the limestone bedrock surface is far beneath present water levels (Wanless, 1969). It appears that a marsh-type vegetation may well have existed in this area two centuries ago; certainly substantial environmental changes have occurred over the past 800 years. To find out, early aerial photographs of western Key Biscayne were analyzed in detail, along with the De Brahm maps. Then, 4 core sites were selected, and cores taken, along the present western shore of the key; these sites are shown as RCKB-1 through RCKB-4 in Figure 3.

The first indication, aside from De Brahm's maps, that the present mangrove swamp complex bordering the bay side of Key Biscayne may have recently changed, or fluctuated historically, is provided by aerial photographs of the area taken in 1932 and 1972. The earlier photographs show portions of the present paralic mangrove swamp to have had a patchy geographic distribution, inland from a very narrow coastal mangrove fringe. The 1972 photos, by contrast, show these same locations covered entirely by mangrove with no evidence of other vegetation. The 4 core boring sites were chosen specifically from areas that were marsh in 1932, but mangrove in 1972. The cores show considerable diversity, and are individually summarized as follows.

Core RCKB-1 was taken at a locality about 30 m inland from the present (and 1932) shoreline (Fig. 3). Like the other cores, this one was designed to be a short core, and was sunk to a depth of only 60 cm; bedrock in this area is about 20 m below MLW. The sample is characterized throughout by alternating red mangrove peat and sandy red mangrove peat, with a 1-cm layer of some quartz sand at 19 cm below the surface (i.e., a few cm above MLW). This sample shows no specific evidence of a dominant marsh environment and was consequently not C^{14} dated.

Core RCKB-2 was taken from about 200 m north of RCKB-1 (Fig. 3), at a spot about 15 m inland from the western shoreline of Key Biscayne. This core indicates a 14-cm layer of calcareous quartz sand with some shell fragments, fine root hairs, and very decayed roots. Below this upper layer is a 3-cm-thick, very sandy red mangrove peat mixed with calcareous quartz sand. Below this second layer, the sample is represented primarily by red mangrove peat, turning into a sandy red mangrove peat at

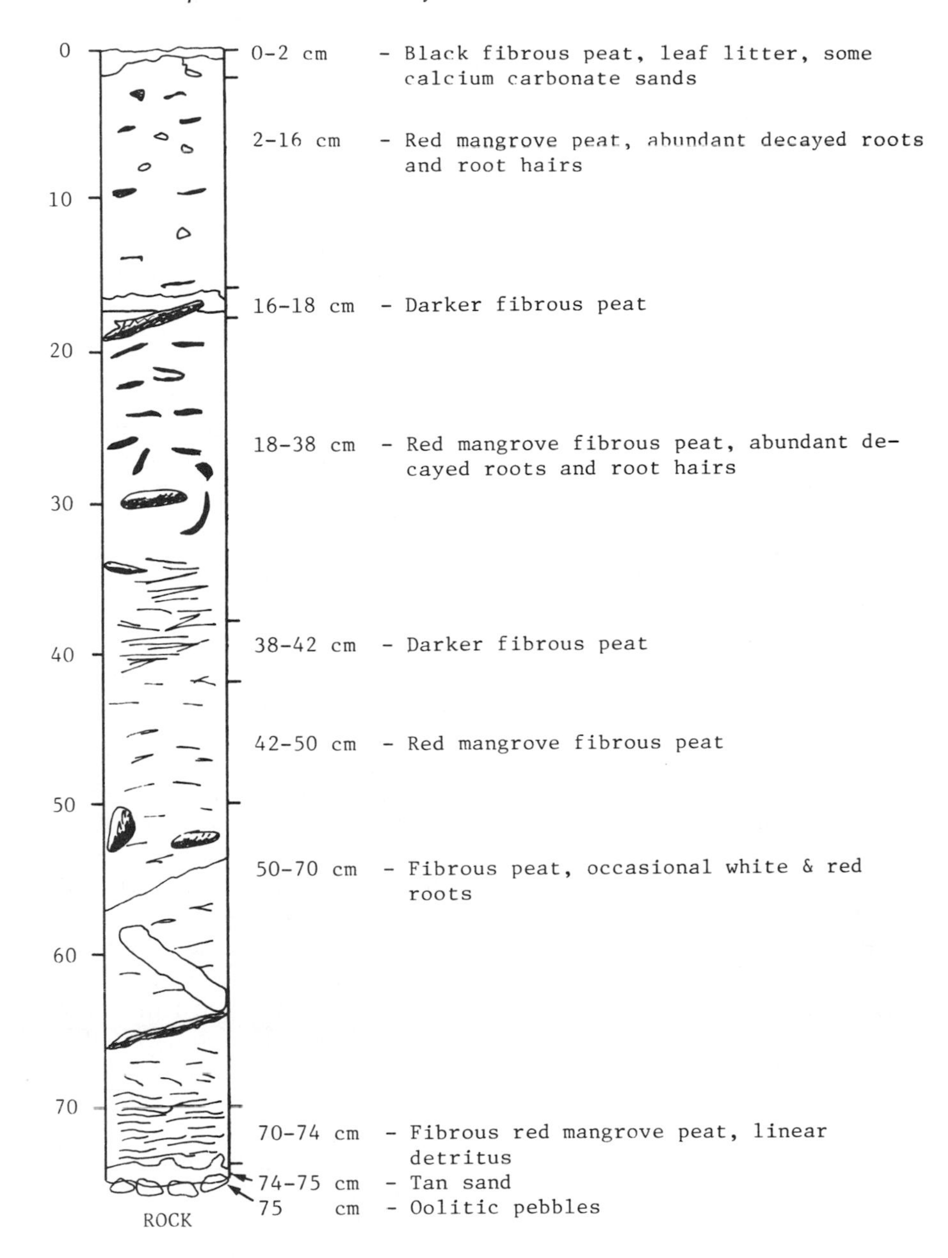

FIGURE 4. Core RC-1, taken from the mainland shore of central Biscayne Bay. See Figure 3.

about -50 cm. Since the upper 14 cm may have been the result of a single storm's washover and of very recent deposition, a sample from the red mangrove peat at about the 24- to 25-cm level was analyzed for C^{14} dating; the date was estimated at 330 ± 60 years B.P. Aside from the top layer, there is nothing to indicate that this site was covered by marshic vegetation.

RCKB-3 was taken at the center of a small island just north of West Point (Fig. 3) and presents a rather different stratigraphy. The top layer is clearly dominated by red mangrove peat for the first 19 cm, below which is a layer of brown calcareous quartz sand with large mangrove roots, root hairs, and shell fragments. At the 42-cm level, these are replaced by a calcareous quartz sand with shells, gastropods, and some horizontal mangrove roots. This core seems to indicate that its site was not characterized by a monotonous or continuous red mangrove history, particularly if one takes into account the remnants of calcareous sands which have not been leached by the mangrove's tannic acid.

RCKB-4 was taken at the southwestern edge of another island just off the northwest shore of Key Biscayne (Fig. 3) and is presented here as Figure 5. This is perhaps the most interesting of the samples taken for the purposes of this investigation, for there are clear indications of carbonate muds, muddy peats, quartz sands, and other biota, rather than a somewhat overwhelming red mangrove sequence. Two samples from this core were analyzed for C^{14} dating (Fig. 5) and, though the dates obtained are by no means meant to be precise, it appears that the materials at about 44 cm in depth are somewhat younger than those above them, at about 38 to 39 cm. Once again, we are confronted by a reversal from expectation, in that the younger dating is found stratigraphically below an older one. In this case, the superposition probably reflects, as previously discussed for the mainland, partial leaching of some calcareous materials, but it may also reflect the broad statistical range of C^{14} analysis of the samples from core RCKB-4. Material from the muddy peat layer at 15 to 19 cm (Fig. 5) was not subjected to C^{14} analysis, for we felt this particular core sample, like other muds in similar circumstances, would not be sufficiently reliable for our purposes in this investigation.

What seems evident is that the 30-cm accumulation since the RCKB-4 C^{14} date of about 800 years ago indicates a fairly rapid and complex history of sedimentation, and a far from continuous red mangrove history. Three types of layers appear in the core; mangrove peat and detritus, sand (due to storms), and calcareous muds and muddy peats. This core boring shows vertical change from mangrove peat down to peritidal mud, as well as a downward alternation of peat to shell-mud to peat. Once again, this core does not specifically prove that there was saltwater

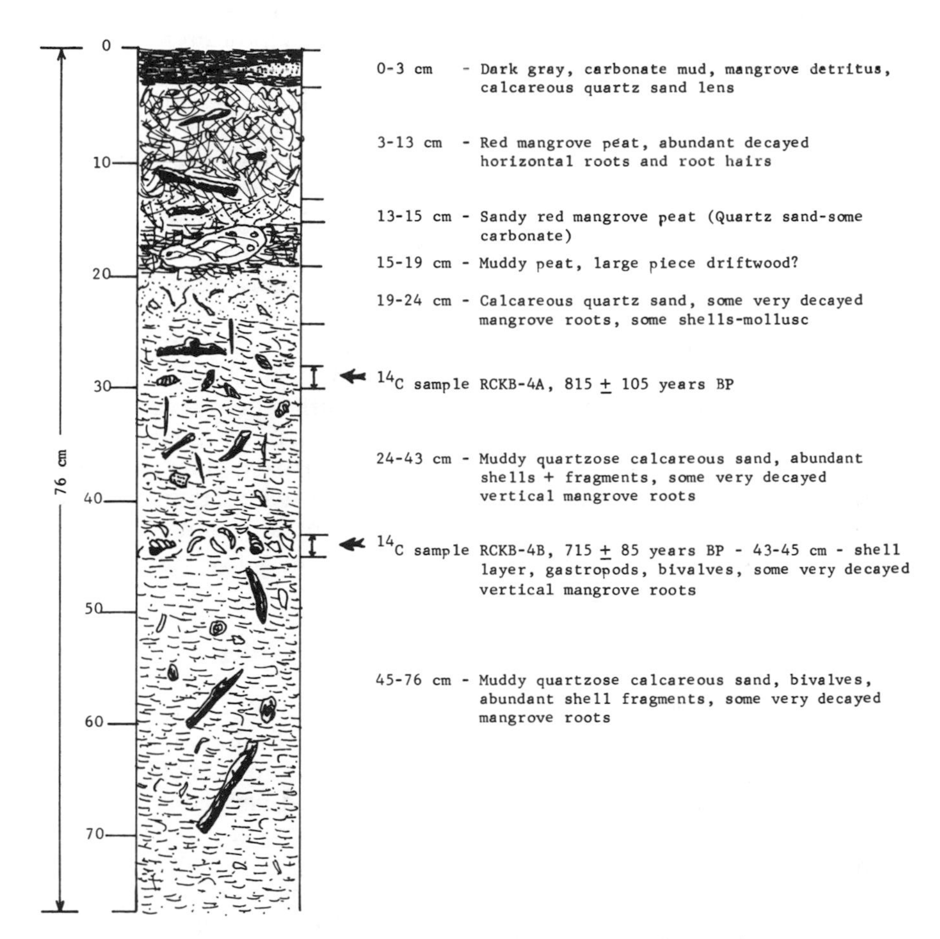

FIGURE 5. Core RCKB-4, derived from the western shore of Key Biscayne. See Figure 3.

marsh in the western Key Biscayne area in 1770, but it at least is not inconsistent with the possibility that such a marsh existed at this locality.

A core boring taken several years ago, along the northwestern margin of Key Biscayne, displays a similar sequence, containing three alternations of red mangrove peat and shell-mud (Wanless, 1969). C^{14} dating of this sample (W-150 in Fig. 3) showed that these alternations all occurred within the past 2000 years, with the layers dating progressively older as core depth increased. Boring logs obtained from the files of Nutting Engineers, Inc., show (Fig. 3) predominant greyish sands throughout these cores down to 7 to 10 m. Two of these logs indicate mangrove root fragments 1 to 2 m below MLW, while some of the others record only organic materials in general at present surface levels. However, the boring logs available indicate materials described in general terms, and are not comparable in detail or accuracy with the core samples taken directly for this investigation. Nonetheless, the evidence they provide also suggests some alternations between red mangrove and other layers, though the logs indicate that the mangrove layers exist at levels lower than the ones observed in our cores, aside, of course, from the organic layers noted at or very near present surface levels.

In brief, the physical evidence so far indicates historical fluctuations in the environments along the bay side of Key Biscayne, and that these fluctuations are compatible with the indicated differences recorded on the De Brahm maps. On the other hand, the general pattern of the cores also suggests that, if a saltwater marsh environment existed on the western side of Key Biscayne in 1770, it probably was more local than general. The evidence points more to a mixed mangrove-marsh vegetation complex, with red mangrove quite probably dominant in many, if not most, of these coastal areas.

The Northern Biscayne Bay Barrier Complex

Though this portion of the northern Biscayne Bay area contains several discrepancies between what is shown on the De Brahm map of 1770 (Fig. 1) and on the first U. S. Coast Survey charts, the availability of a number of reference areas that remained unchanged between 1770 and the 1850s (and for that matter well into the 20th century) greatly facilitates the problem of determining De Brahm's cartographic reliability. One evaluation of his map of this part of the bay area has been made (Chardon, 1982) and the conclusions are that, so far as the barrier is concerned, De Brahm was quite accurate in his portrayal of most of its features. Furthermore, those changes observed between the De Brahm and later Coast Survey charts can readily be explained on theoretical grounds by referring to well-known coastal geomorphic processes; a brief summary of some of these coastal changes has been published (Chardon, 1978).

Nevertheless, several minor discrepancies still remain which, could they be resolved, would place the final seal of approval on De Brahm's map as a very accurate one of the barrier complex, aside from Key Biscayne's western shore, in 1770. The present project called for several cores and probes in the discrepant areas, but the complexities of obtaining the necessary permits for probing and coring within the Miami Beach urban area proved overwhelming, and precluded this type of activity. A few preliminary probes were made at tidewater, but since the Miami Beach shoreline is now in many places several meters seaward of its original position due to the location of the present bulkhead line, probings in the present intertidal zone of the beach are not very meaningful as checks of the De Brahm map.

The solution to the problem of obtaining subsurface descriptions of the barrier complex was to some extent resolved by searching the files of several cooperative engineering firms for their exploratory boring logs and reports along the barrier. These logs are derived from core borings made prior to construction of a particular building and, though not nearly as detailed nor as standardized as borings undertaken specifically for environmental research purposes, are often useful for describing the subsurface stratigraphy of a given locality in general terms.

While searches of office files were quite time consuming, especially in those cases where boring records were filed by client name only, rather than by street address at the construction site, the results have been fruitful. The locations of those logs pertaining to the barrier are shown in Figure 3; frequently several holes were cored at one site. Also, two examples of individual logs are presented as Figures 6 and 7.

The complexity of the subterranean and submarine depositional layers and bedrock structures precludes a detailed examination here. The records indicate a generally level though undulating surface of soft tan sandy limerock or calcareous sandstone, depending on location and interpretation of the core, about 4 to 6 m below MLW. This surface is also characterized by solution holes and possibly former tidal channels, but other features are also found. Notable among these is an apparent series of rock ridges trending more or less north-south, whose elevations in some cases rise to only 1 or 2 m below MLW, but whose troughs may reach depths of 10 to 12 m or even more below MLW. The linearity and positions of several of these ridges, some of which are found not only under the barrier complex but off its Atlantic shore as well, have not yet been mapped precisely. Some of the ridges or troughs may well have influenced the depositional trend and configuration of the Miami Beach sand barrier, as suggested by Wanless (1969). When the mapping of the preexisting Pleistocene bedrock is completed, the resultant patterns and their influence on the barrier's geography and depositional history will be examined in detail.

So far as the De Brahm map is concerned, there is as yet no evidence of the rocks he shows at about sea level, at Boca Ratones and just south of it (Fig. 1). It should be noted, however, that I have so far located only a few boring logs for these precise areas (Fig. 3). It is of course possible that no rocks existed in the localities where De Brahm places them on his

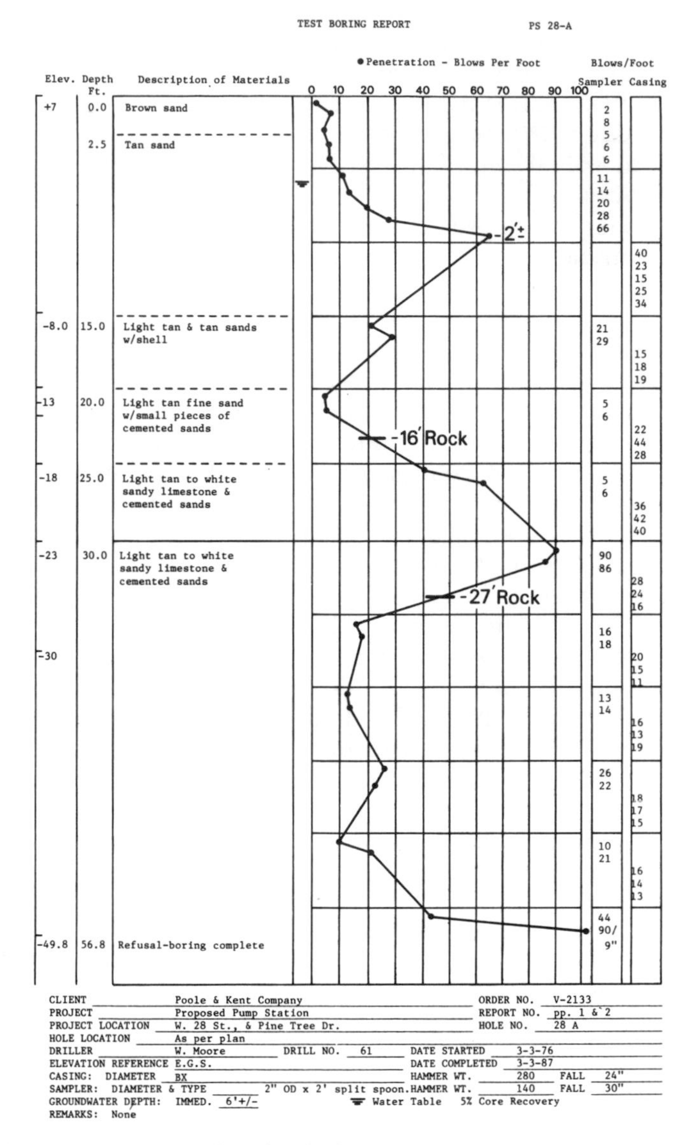

FIGURE 6. Boring log for hole 28-A (see Fig. 3), courtesy of Nutting Engineers, Inc., and Bunnell Foundation, Inc.

map, but this seems unlikely. Not only did he identify and locate them on a map which, for the barrier complex, seems remarkably accurate in other respects, but the Spaniards named the inlet found here Boca Ratones, which translates as "mouth of sharp, submerged rocks," and not "mouth of rats" as is sometimes believed. These two independent sources strongly support the existence of rocks at or near sea level in this vicinity during at least the 18th century.

At the same time, it is quite possible that the rocks may have been eroded away, or that the record of their existence was destroyed during the building booms of the 1920s and 1960s in these areas. Rocks such as those De Brahm's map indicates could have resulted from three processes. First, they may have been upward protrusions of the Key Largo Limestone Ridge (i.e., bedrock surface) to just below MLW; a similar underwater bedrock ridge can easily be observed on aerial photographs just off present Fisher Island and Virginia Key, and its surface rises to about 1 m below MLW. Second, the rocks could have formed under conditions similar to those that formed the fossil mangrove root reef, also shown by De Brahm on his map (Fig. 1), at the northeastern tip of Key Biscayne (Hoffmeister, 1974). If this was the case, the rocks may well have been eroded completely under natural conditions prior to Miami Beach's urbanization. Third, the rocks could have been created by sabellariid worm action of the type described by Kirtley and Tanner (1968). Sabellariid accretions have been located at more than one point along the barrier by Wanless (1969).

Thus the boring logs and our inability to core and probe in those areas critical for determining the reliability of De Brahm's map of this part of the barrier do not prove or disprove the existence of the rocks he shows at Boca Ratones and along the beach south of this inlet. But the physical record indicates nothing to negate his portrayal of the barrier's other features, or its configuration, for 1770. The barrier complex developed by southward accretion of sand transported by net north-to-south longshore currents and deposited in a general line from the head of Biscayne Bay to Cape Florida, at southern Key Biscayne, as indicated by Wanless (1969). Behind the sand barrier a parallel mangrove swamp developed, but it seems to have done so only within the past few hundred years for, unlike western Key Biscayne, there is little physical evidence of mangrove at lower levels, judging from the boring logs so far examined. This evidence supports De Brahm's cartographic evidence with no apparent contradiction so far as the year 1770 is concerned.

Conclusions

The scientific testing of the accuracy of the De Brahm maps of northern Biscayne Bay has proved to be more difficult than anticipated, largely due to the unique nature of the coastal environments along the shores of the bay. Along the mainland shore, the processes by which mangrove

Sample & Type	Depth	SOIL DESCRIPTION	Penetration Blows For 6"		"N"
		6.0' Gray sand & rock fragments (fill)	6	13	
SS1	2		19	23	32
			26	23	
	4		21	13	44
SS2			11	15	
	6		7	6	22
		5.0' Firm to loose gray silica sand	6	7	
SS3	8		7	6	14
			5	4	
	10		4	3	8
			4	2	
	12	6.5' Very loose gray silt with some layers of sand & organic peat	1	2	3
			2	2	
	14		1	1	3
			1	1	
SS4	16		2	2	3
			3	2	
	18		3	2	5
		12.0' Firm gray sand with some broken shells	3	6	
SS5	20		4	6	10
	22				
	24		6	6	
SS6			6		12
	26				
	28				
			2	2	
SS7	30		16		18
		8.5' Firm tan sandy limerock			
	32				
	34		6	6	
SS8			6		12
	36				
	38				
		3.0' Very loose gray silica sand	1	1	
SS9	40		1		2
	42	3.0' Very loose gray silica sand			
	44		1	0	
		4.5' Open cavity	0		0
	46				
	48				
			21	20	
SS10	50	16.5 Moderately hard to hard gray sandy limerock	7		27
	52				
	54		9	18	
SS11			20		38
	56				
	58				
			24	44	
SS12	60		52		96
	62				
	64		36	51	
SS13			49		100
	66	End of Boring: 65.0'			

SOIL BORING NO. 22
SURFACE ELEV. 14.8
GROUND WATER AFTER COMPLETION ELEV. 6.6

FIGURE 7. Sitework Core Boring Log. No. 22, Miami-Dade Water and Sewer Authority (see Fig. 3), courtesy the Authority and David Volkert & Associates. This log represents one of 35 borings sunk in connection with the construction of an addition to the Virginia Key sewer facility.

acidity affects the preexisting vegetative matter in an environment characterized by shallow limestone bedrock precludes definitive conclusions as to the accuracy of De Brahm's map of this area where vegetative cover is concerned; it had previously been determined (Chardon, 1975a, 1975b) that De Brahm's portrayal of this part of the shoreline configuration was quite faulty. A different set of circumstances leads us to similar conclusions regarding the western shore of Key Biscayne: The physical evidence from local cores indicates that there were historical fluctuations in the vegetation cover, but we lack the necessary precision to establish definitely whether, in 1770, there was a salt marsh throughout the western third of the island. The predominant cover appears to have been mangrove in this area, though some marsh may well have been present locally. Here, as on the mainland across the bay, we know that De Brahm's depiction of the shoreline was only generally accurate and that in detail, as well as in the width of the key, De Brahm erred considerably.

With regard to the barrier complex from Key Biscayne north, we were unable to undertake our own probing and coring in those areas that showed greatest discrepancy, or in those areas characterized by rocks in 1770, within the built-up area of Miami Beach. Taking the next best course, we obtained and analyzed over 120 boring logs, and the evidence they provide suggests, though it does not prove, that De Brahm was quite reliable with reference to his map of the barrier. This supports other evidence that, for this area, De Brahm's map appears to have been remarkably accurate (Chardon, 1982).

The determination of early map reliability, insofar as it can be tested solely by probing and coring, remains obscure at this time. In theory, there seems to be no reason why at least some physical evidence could not be used to help establish an early map's accuracy. In fact, when the physical evidence is durable and has been observed and mapped at the surface, and when it remains unaltered from the time the map was drawn to the time when that evidence can be accurately recorded using modern techniques, this is the best evidence possible for the purpose outlined here. But it would seem that coring techniques and the materials thereby obtained are, at least in some cases, not sufficiently refined to permit reliable testing of early maps on that basis alone. Aside from the problems of obtaining cores in areas now overlain by pavement or buildings, C^{14} dating and other indices derived from coring samples are not yet able to pinpoint certain types of environments at given dates in recent historic times.

This, at least, is our conclusion for the northern Biscayne Bay area as evidenced by De Brahm's maps in 1770. Though he specifically labeled the environments for which we tried to obtain corroborating cores, the materials we acquired were usually insufficient to confirm or deny his portrayals in detail. Taken with other, largely cartographic evidence, De Brahm appears not to have been very accurate in mapping along the mainland of Biscayne Bay between Shoal Point and Black Point, nor was he more than generally accurate concerning the western portion of Key Biscayne. And yet we cannot be sure. On the other hand, he appears—but again, largely on other evidence—to have been very reliable in his mapping of the barrier complex north of Key Biscayne. These conflicting conclusions suggest that there may have been more than one surveying party involved in the charting of Biscayne Bay in 1770, but again this conclusion can be reached without recourse to coring techniques (Chardon, 1982).

If coring techniques have been somewhat disappointing in terms of providing specific questions about De Brahm's cartographic reliability regarding northern Biscayne Bay in 1770, they do yield intriguing data about past natural environments in this region. It was noted in the original proposal that, should the cores fail to confirm De Brahm's maps, they would nonetheless be valuable for insights into the natural environment as it developed in recent years. The lessons learned here are also useful; we now know not to trust core materials for dating purposes, where there are presently mangrove forests, since the tannic acid produced by mangrove tends to obliterate at least some—and quite possibly all—of the evidence of other, previous environments. This is especially true in areas where mangrove exists in a shallow soil environment. For western Key Biscayne, the same problem exists to a lesser degree, but the cores taken from this shore suggest that a number of rapid environmental changes have taken place there over the past 800 years, and probably over the past 300 years.

The boring logs obtained for the barrier complex to the north of the key indicate a bedrock pattern which, when it is finally mapped, may yield clues as to specific processes by which sand movement, deposition, and erosion, along with mangrove development, are related to the preexisting bedrock topography. Wanless (1969) followed this theme consistently for the bay area, and his conclusions in this regard may be further supported in considerable detail for the area now under Miami Beach. There may, for example, be a real possibility that the natural tidal inlets of this barrier were created at least partially due to slight depressions in the bay's bedrock floor just to the west of the inlets' bay entrances. The north-south bedrock ridges may have played a role in the migration of the channel of Boca Ratones (Chardon, 1978) before it was closed naturally in 1822. Thus, the use of cores, boring logs, and other physical evidence coupled with judicious use of documentary evidence, such as early maps, can be a powerful means of reconstructing past environments, especially in presently urbanized areas. The questions raised by examining both the cores taken as a result of this investigation and the De Brahm maps are significant, but it will be some time before answers to such questions can be formulated with any certainty. The maps, cores, and boring logs indicate that, if nothing else, northern Biscayne Bay's recent environmental history is complex and anything but static.

REFERENCES

CHARDON, ROLAND
1975a. The Cape Florida Society of 1773. Tequesta, no. 35, pp. 1-36.
1975b. Northern Biscayne in 1776. Tequesta, no. 35, pp. 37-74.
1978. Coastal barrier changes, 1770-1867, Biscayne Bay area, Florida. Geology, vol. 6, no. 6, pp. 333-336.
1982. A best-fit evaluation of De Brahm's 1770 chart of northern Biscayne Bay, Florida. The American Cartographer, vol. 9, no. 1, pp. 47-67.

DEVORSEY, LOUIS, JR., ed.
1971. De Brahm's report on the general survey in the Southern District of North America, xvi + 325 pp., illus. University of South Carolina Press, Columbia.

HOFFMEISTER, JOHN E.
1974. Land from the sea: The geologic story of south Florida, 143 pp., illus. University of Miami Press, Coral Gables, Fla.

KIRTLEY, DAVID W., and TANNER, WILLIAM S.
1968. Sabellariid worms: Builders of a major reef type. Journ. Sedimentary Petrology, vol. 38, no. 1, pp. 73-78.

MEEDER, JACK, and WANLESS, HAROLD R.
1977. Inverted stratigraphic sequences generated by mangrove swamps. Ms., 20 pp. Dept. of Marine Geology, Rosenstiel School of Marine and Atmospheric Sciences, University of Miami, Miami, Fla.

TEAS, HOWARD J.; WANLESS, HAROLD R.; and CHARDON, ROLAND E.
1976. Effects of man on the shore vegetation of Biscayne Bay. Pp. 133-156 *in* "Biscayne Bay: Past/Present/Future," A. Thorhaug, ed. University of Miami Sea Grant Special Report no. 5, Coral Gables, Fla.

UNITED STATES COAST SURVEY
1858. Coast Chart No. 166, 1st ed. Cartographic Archives Division, National Archives and Records Service, Washington, D. C.

WANLESS, HAROLD R.
1969. Sediments of Biscayne Bay—distribution and depositional history, 260 pp., illus. University of Miami Institute of Marine Sciences Technical Report 69-2, Miami, Fla.

ROLAND E. CHARDON

Near Infrared Photographic Sky Survey: A Summary Report

Grant Recipient: Eric R. Craine, Steward Observatory, University of Arizona, Tucson, Arizona, and Bell Technical Operations, Bell Aerospace Corporation, Tucson, Arizona.

Grant 1619: In support of a deep near infrared sky survey.

Continuing strides in the development of astronomically useful detectors that operate in increasingly diverse regions of the electromagnetic spectrum have opened new vistas in the collection of astronomical data. In particular, large areas of the sky are now subject to sensitive surveys in a variety of wavelengths to which the human eye is totally oblivious. These studies have contributed dramatically to the store of data and new array of questions with which we must address the nature of the celestial universe. In spite of the ever more accessible extremes of the electromagnetic spectrum, much of modern astronomy still relies heavily upon making an optical identification of these invisible sources of radiation. Such identification enables the optical astronomer to pursue a wide range of follow-up or post-discovery observations which may ultimately be important in yielding an understanding of the nature and behavior of the object. The optical identification problem is often complex and frequently relies on bootstrapping through several complementary sets of data, observations, or surveys.

An important and largely unsurveyed spectral region is the near infrared, variously known as the optical or photoelectric infrared. Located between wavelengths of 0.8 and 1.1 μ, this region lies just redward of light visible to the unaided eye, and just blueward of the infrared radiation peaks characteristic of very cool or highly obscured celestial objects. Thus, this spectral region is an important and interesting bridge between visible light and the invisible infrared. The near infrared region is also of interest because of the absence of bright hydrogen radiation which so heavily obscures photographs taken in the blue or visible regions of the spectrum, thus obliterating any possible information on the stellar content of large areas of the sky.

With the assistance of the National Geographic Society, we have conducted an unusual photographic program to provide a two-band Near

Infrared Photographic Sky Survey (NIPSS) of the northern celestial hemisphere. In this report we summarize the salient features of this survey, briefly describe the nature of the results obtained to date, and outline plans for this immense and valuable data base.

Project Parameters

The NIPSS project consisted of photography in two bands: the visual (V) at 5200 to 6400 Å and the near infrared (I) at 8000 to 9000 Å. The visual band was chosen in such a fashion as to avoid inclusion of the bright hydrogen line at 6563 Å, resulting in two unobscured photographs of each field.

Each program field has a diameter of 4.5° on the sky, and is recorded on film at an image plane scale of 110 arc sec mm^{-1}. The survey fields are packed hexagonally on the sky, giving a substantial overlap of adjacent fields and resulting in 1900 program fields for coverage of the northern celestial hemisphere. In practice, the north celestial polar cap was not accessible from our observing site and hence the survey consists of 1885 fields. During the 3 years we devoted to observational photography we obtained approximately 5500 photographs, from which the requisite 3770 photographs were finally chosen.

The survey photographs in each field were obtained one after another, insofar as was possible, to minimize the effects of variable or moving objects recorded on the film. This practice also aided in establishing a more nearly constant relative sky background between photographs of the same fields. Exposure times were 6 and 15 min in the V and I bands, respectively, giving limiting magnitudes of about 19 mag in V and 16.5 mag in I. These exposures thus assured that a stellar image which appeared neutral on the two photographs of a given field had a V-I color of approximately 2.5 mag. This characteristic of the photographs makes it extremely easy to identify very red stars, one of the prime motivations of conducting the survey.

Survey Instrumentation

Historically, near infrared photography has been a very difficult endeavor owing to the very low sensitivity of photographic emulsions available for this type of work. Progress has been made in the area of hypersensitization of photographic plates, but the process remains painstakingly slow. The NIPSS project successfully applied to this problem the alternative approach of utilizing a very large format electronic image intensifier tube. This fact alone makes the project unique and interesting, and certainly deserving of a place in the history of significant astronomical projects.

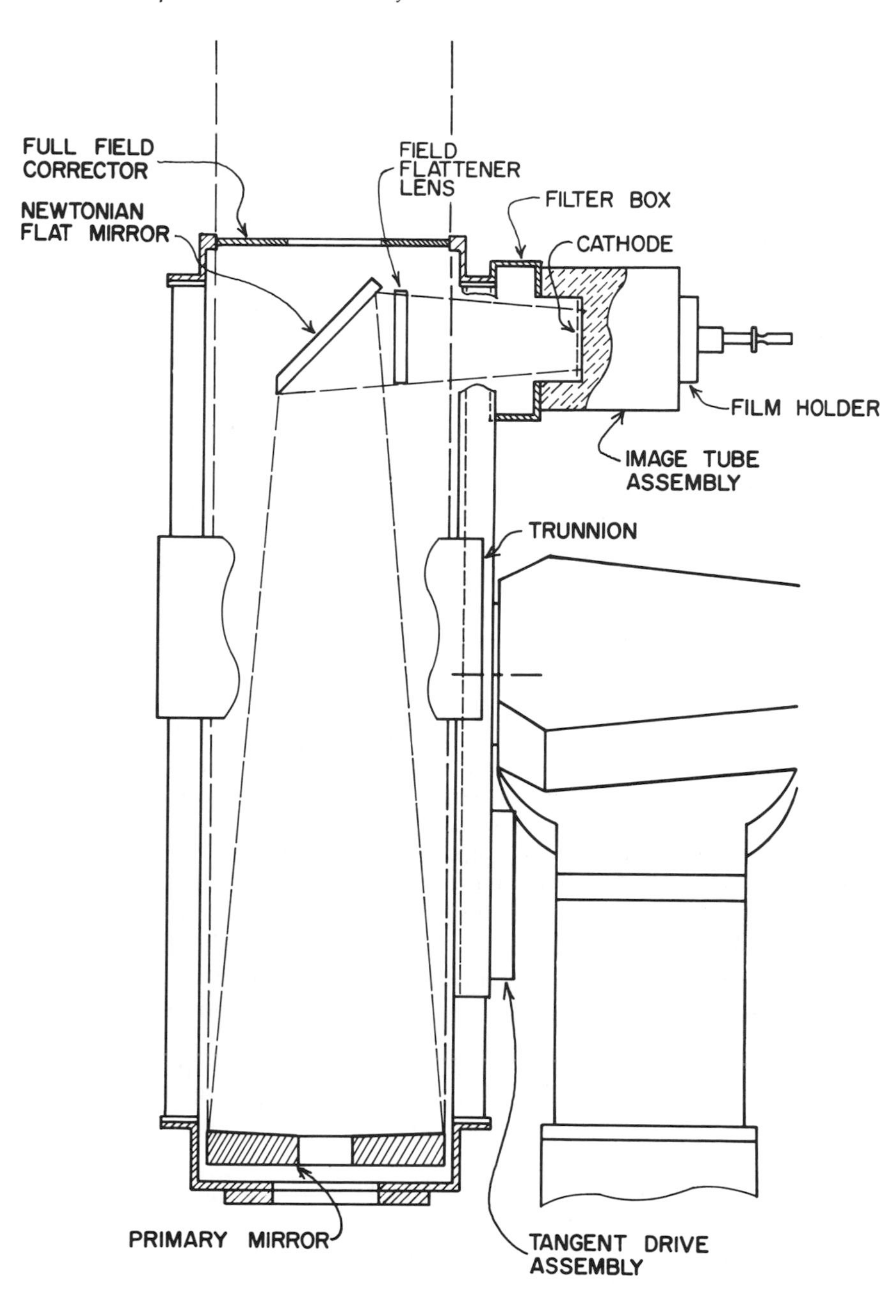

FIGURE 1. Diagrammatic layout of the survey telescope, showing the modified optical path which imbues the Newtonian focus with the optical characteristics of the prime focus. The location of the image intensifier camera is also shown.

The image intensifier we have used is a single-stage, magnetically focused device with a multialkalai photocathode sensitive to 9000 Å. The intensifier is very large, with a photocathode diameter of 146 mm. The output of the camera is a green (visible) phosphor which presents an image that is transferred through a fiber-optic faceplate to the photographic emulsion. We have utilized a special Kodak emulsion, (SFT061-04) which approximates the astronomical IIa-D emulsion, with a film rather than glass substrate. Justification for this choice is discussed in Craine (1978); the initial film requirements were met by the National Geographic Society.

The image tube camera served the dual function of increasing our sensitivity to low light levels and converting the near infrared radiation to a wavelength that could be easily recorded by more conventional photographic emulsions.

The "lens" for our image tube camera was a highly modified 20-in. aperture telescope which we located near the summit of Kitt Peak, approximately 50 mi west of Tucson, Arizona, on the Papago Indian reservation. This telescope had been purchased from U. S. Navy surplus for the sum of $1.00, and was subsequently modified to provide a wide, flat field at a quasi-Newtonian focus, thus accommodating the optical and mechanical requirements of the large image tube camera (see Fig. 1 and 2 and Craine, 1979, 1980).

The construction of the telescope modifications, the installation of the system at the mountain peak, and the subsequent testing program consumed the first full year of this project, but provided valuable information regarding the many unique aspects of our enterprise. For example, we performed extensive laboratory tests on the behavior of the largest image intensifier actively used in astronomical applications (Tifft and Craine, 1976; Craine and Cromwell, 1978, 1979), we developed a system for collimating a unique optical system, and we solved a number of problems characteristic of handling large format film with image intensifier cameras.

In addition to the mountaintop facility, we established a project presence on the University of Arizona campus at the photographic laboratory of the Lunar and Planetary Laboratory. It was here that all of the exposed film was processed (by machine) and subsequently evaluated and cataloged.

The completion of the Kitt Peak and Tucson facilities allowed us to begin a period of observational testing, followed by numerous modifications to improve the performance of the system, including refiguring of the corrector plate, installation of a new electrically activated shutter, and design and construction of an improved image tube mounting device. A number of problems arose and were dealt with during the first half of

FIGURE 2. The survey telescope as installed at Kitt Peak, Arizona. Note the large size of the image intensifier camera.

1977, including malfunctions in the cooling system for the image tube solenoid and imaging problems that were a function of telescope position angle. With the most serious problems in the system under control, we were able to begin the active observational phases of the program in 1978.

The Observing Program

The observing program involved photography of 1885 program fields in each of the two bands, using target field centers generated by a computer program. The field center program was written to maximize the efficiency of the field packing scheme, and to allow us to compute the offset positions of a single guide star in each field.

A concerted effort was made to make the photographs of each field in sequence, with the appropriate filter change and refocus after each photograph. Although this was less efficient than using a single filter in any given night, it had the aforementioned effect of minimizing temporal problems that complicate the comparison of the resultant two-band images. In practice this goal was not always attainable and when using the survey for research projects the astute investigator will always determine the epoch of the photographs.

Notwithstanding the minor problems that always accrue to an observational project of this magnitude, the observing program was basically very simple. The greatest initial difficulty was to attain the dull but desirable routine so crucial to the success of a long-term scientific data-gathering program. With this goal accomplished by the winter of 1978-1979 we began to accumulate completed fields at the rate of about 60 per month. The last field was photographed in July 1981, approximately 2½ yr after initiation of the photographic phase of the project.

Survey Applications

A data base as unique and as extensive as that comprising the NIPSS collection of photographs is necessarily imbued with at least as many potential applications as there are users. Further, as the data continue to be used, it is certain that additional applications will come to light. For the present we may categorize some of the applications in the following areas: optical identifications, discovery of interesting objects, and statistical studies.

In order to use the survey data most effectively, we have attempted to organize a coherent program that, while limited in scope by funds and manpower, is structured sufficiently cleverly to provide a foundation and impetus for support of further analysis. To this end we have undertaken several ancillary programs, including photoelectric photometry of an extensive network of bright stars for brightness calibration of the photographs; construction of a catalog of the most red stars contained in a selected set of the survey photographs; analysis of this catalog as a source of optical identifications of previously observed infrared sources; use of the survey in the analysis of interstellar molecular clouds (related to star formation activity); use of the survey data to study the nature of particular dark nebulae; and study of particular examples of interesting stars, including (but not limited to) carbon stars, S stars, extremely late-type dwarfs, and cometary nebulae. This list represents only a fraction of the types of programs that can benefit from the NIPSS data. In the following sections we briefly discuss those projects already initiated; in the next section we discuss what the future may hold for the survey data.

Calibration Photometry

In order to maximize the usefulness of the survey photographs, it is desirable to be able to extract magnitudes, or brightness information, from the photographs for each star in a given field. This process ideally requires that both visual and near infrared brightnesses be known for several comparison stars in each field, and further, that a large range of brightnesses be represented in these calibration data. Visual magnitudes have been measured for so many stars over the years that most of our survey fields contain some V photometry; the near infrared band is another story, these observations being relatively much rarer and existing for only about 10 percent of our fields. In most instances those fields have I-band photometry for only one or two potential calibration stars.

The problem is further aggravated by the fact that even in the instances of availability of both V- and I-calibration magnitudes in a particular field, a range of brightnesses will almost certainly not be represented. As a consequence, it is impossible to construct for the field a calibration curve that will relate image size or density to actual brightness.

We have addressed this problem by determining the shape of a mean calibration curve using extensive V- and I-band photometry in the vicinity of the galactic star cluster NGC 2264. A large number of V and I photographic pairs of this region of the sky were obtained in order to form the mean calibration curve. In principle, these calibration curves can now be used for any of the survey photographs if only the proper scale factor can be introduced. This task can be performed if we have only a few calibration stars in the field, regardless of the brightness range represented.

In order to assist in setting the zero point of the calibration curve for a statistically significant sample of survey fields, we have initiated a program of photoelectric photometry to measure the V and I brightnesses of a large number of potential calibration stars in a uniformly distributed sample of survey fields. The photometry project was started while survey photography was still under way, and continues as time and resources allow. The observations have been made using the 0.5-m telescopes of Kitt Peak National Observatory and have resulted in several lists of V and I magnitudes for approximately 500 stars (Scharlach and Craine, 1980, submitted; Craine and Scharlach, 1982).

Not only has this program proven useful for the NIPSS project, it also has provided a useful pool of photometric data for application to a number of other astronomical purposes.

Red Star Catalog

With calibration curves and scaling photometry in hand, it was possible to create a catalog of the most red stars in a selected set of survey fields. These data were useful as a preliminary determination of the content of the survey photographs and as a source of astronomically interesting objects worthy of further observation and study.

The first of these catalogs (Craine et al., 1979) was extracted from 23 survey fields, located at a range of galactic latitudes and including 1183 stellar-appearing objects with a V-I color more red than 2.5 mag. The stars were identified by means of a blink comparator technique that involved the manual examination of every star on the photographs, looking alternately at the image in one spectral band and then the other to determine on which photograph the image was brighter.

The Red Star Catalog contains finding charts, positions, V magnitudes, and color information for each of the 1183 stars cataloged. This catalog has served as a very productive starting point for further observation of interesting objects, as discussed below.

An important question that arises upon construction of such a catalog addresses the state of our knowledge of the nature of each of the catalog entries. This has proven to be a significant problem, since it is poor practice to consume expensive telescope time investigating an interesting-looking catalog entry, only to discover later that the literature contains ample discussion of that very object. To help alleviate this problem, Rossano and Craine (1980) have published a field index that lists the contents of each NIPSS program field as derived from several previously published catalogs of diverse types of objects or region descriptors. In practice, of course, we cross-correlate positions of interesting NIPSS objects with a series of catalogs of celestial objects in an effort to establish the existence of any prior observations.

Infrared Source Identification

The use of the NIPSS data as a tool for infrared source identification was one of the driving motivations for the survey, and as such could be discussed at greater length than is feasible for this forum. Alternatively, we shall indicate one way in which we have explored the applicability of the survey data to this particular problem.

Horner and Craine (1980) have used the data compiled in the first Red Star Catalog (see above) in a cross-correlation comparison with several extant infrared source catalogs, including the California Institute of Technology Infrared Catalog (IRC), the Air Force Geophysical Laboratory (AFGL), and the Equatorial Infrared Catalog (EIC) compilations. In each event the object was to establish correlations between known celestial infrared sources and the very red stars contained in the NIPSS catalog.

These were the conclusions reached in this study:

1. In regions otherwise obscured by hydrogen emission, the NIPSS photographs offered a clear advantage in resolving and providing color information for stars located in the field.
2. Optical identification of near infrared sources, using NIPSS data, is a strong function of galactic latitude of the sources.
3. At high galactic latitudes approximately 50 percent of the IRC sources can be optically identified, using colors as a supplement to position data.
4. The optical identification of near infrared sources, using NIPSS data, can be extended profitably to surveys four orders of magnitude more sensitive than the Cal Tech IRC survey.
5. The NIPSS photographs may prove to be particularly valuable for identification of exceedingly red objects by searching for those stars that appear only on the infrared photograph, and that lie below the threshold of detectability on the visual photograph.

Though this work represents only a very preliminary attack on the problem of infrared source identification, it clearly demonstrates the applicability of the data base to this particular problem.

That the NIPSS data can often serve as a dramatic aid in the optical identification of infrared sources is indicated by comparison of V- and I-band photographs as shown in Figure 3. Figure 3 (top pair) shows the visual and near infrared appearance of the star, which is optically identified with the infrared source known as AFGL2609; near the threshold of the visual photograph, this star is quite bright in the near infrared and is readily distinguishable on the near infrared photograph. A similar comparison appears in Figure 3 (bottom pair) for the previously unidentified infrared source EIC260.

POST-SURVEY OBSERVATIONS: INDIVIDUAL STARS

While the survey photography was still under way we initiated a program of follow-up observations of a number of individual red stars contained in the Red Star Catalog. The observations were of a variety of types, including spectroscopy, polarimetry, and high-resolution image tube photography.

Because the survey stars we are most interested in are extremely red, it is most efficient to make spectroscopic observations of them in the red region of the spectrum. These observations were made with a red-sensitive Reticon array producing spectral scans in the region 5500 to 8500 Å. Because of the dearth of good comparison spectra in this region usable for classification purposes, we undertook to create a comprehensive catalog of red scanner spectra of standard stars. This catalog is composed of spectra of 75 late-type stars, representing a range of temperature and luminosity types (Turnshek et al., in prep.).

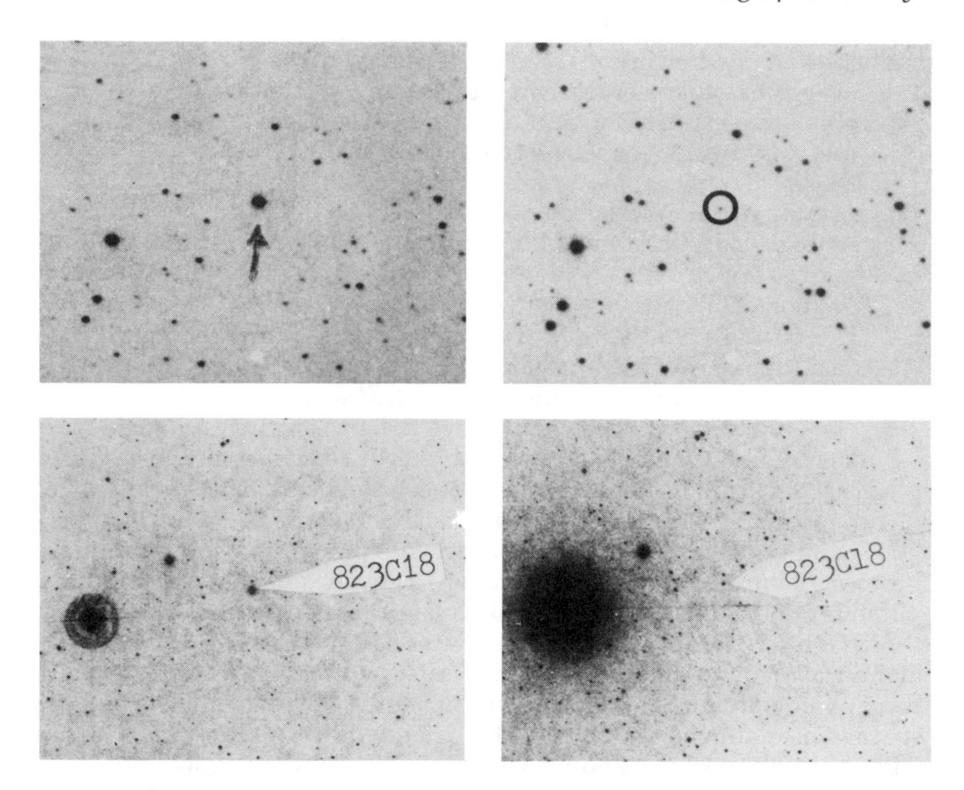

FIGURE 3. (Photographs on the left are from the NIPSS near infrared, on the right, from the NIPSS visual; north up, east left; the field is approximately 5 arc min.) Top: An example of an extremely red star which may be identified with a galactic infrared source. In the case shown here, the infrared source is AFGL2609, detected at 4, 11, and 20 μ (0.3, -2.0, and -2.7 mag, respectively) by rocket-borne telescope. This infrared source was also detected at 2 μ in the IRC survey (1.14 and 8.43 mag, respectively, at K and I). The source is unidentified in the IRC listing; the AFGL suggests, through catalog cross-correlation, that it may be the star DO 38592, however, we note from our data that the brightness of this star is not consistent with a correct identification. The (apparently uncataloged) star in these photographs is very faint visually (about 17 mag) and extremely bright in the near infrared.

Bottom: Example of an extremely red star which may be identified with a previously unidentified infrared source. In this case the infrared source was detected at 2.7 μ and listed in the Interim Equatorial Catalog as EIC260. The original detection was made by an infrared sensor on board a U. S. Air Force satellite. The EIC source listing also has optical identifications based on catalog cross-correlations; in the case of EIC260 there is no suggested identification. This object lies within 2 arc sec of the very red star 823C18 listed in our NIPSS Catalog of Red Stellar Objects. We take this star to be the new optical identification of EIC260.

Using the Red Star Catalog and our atlas of spectral types as a reference, we have obtained spectroscopic observations of about 200 of our red survey stars. Included in this list have been previously undiscovered carbon stars and examples of the more rare S stars (characterized by strong bands of La0 and Zr0). The S stars we have discovered (Craine et al., 1983) represent the visually faintest examples known of these stars, and they are located in a part of our galaxy previously thought to be largely devoid of such stars.

In addition, we have discovered an interesting member of a class known as the cometary nebulae (see Fig. 4), stars with compact surrounding nebulae of very characteristic morphology. This is a group of objects with a very small population, hence any addition to the class membership is significant to the understanding of the evolutionary status of these stars. Further observation of this star, both photographic (Craine et al., 1981) and spectroscopic (Craine et al., submitted) indicates that it possesses an unusual hydrogen light jet and that its spectral appearance is temporal in nature, suggesting that variations in morphological appearance may also occur.

Optical Observations of Molecular Clouds

Star formation is a process now known to be intimately related to interstellar molecular clouds. These clouds are characterized in part by aligned dust particles in the clouds that obscure and redden the light of embedded and distant stars in a very well-defined way. Observations of the linear polarization of the starlight that has passed through the cloud can be used to map the magnetic field alignments in the clouds and thus provide additional information on the extent, structure, and, to some degree, dynamic state of the clouds.

We have used the NIPSS photographs to generate a list of very red stars near NGC 1333, a reflection nebula surrounded by a molecular cloud. We have made spectroscopic and polarimetric observations of the stars in this list to determine which may be associated with the cloud as well as the position angles and magnitudes of the electric vectors arising from the cloud (Turnshek et al., 1980).

These data allowed us to map the region containing the molecular cloud and to determine new (larger) limits on the angular extent of the cloud, as well as to strengthen the case for a previous suggestion of the existence of two molecular clouds in the region. In addition, we refined the quantitative description of the dual-cloud structure and geometry and made determinations of the particle size distribution in the cloud.

This application of NIPSS data will surely be continued and expanded in the future, as it offers a powerful and unusual tool for studying molecular clouds.

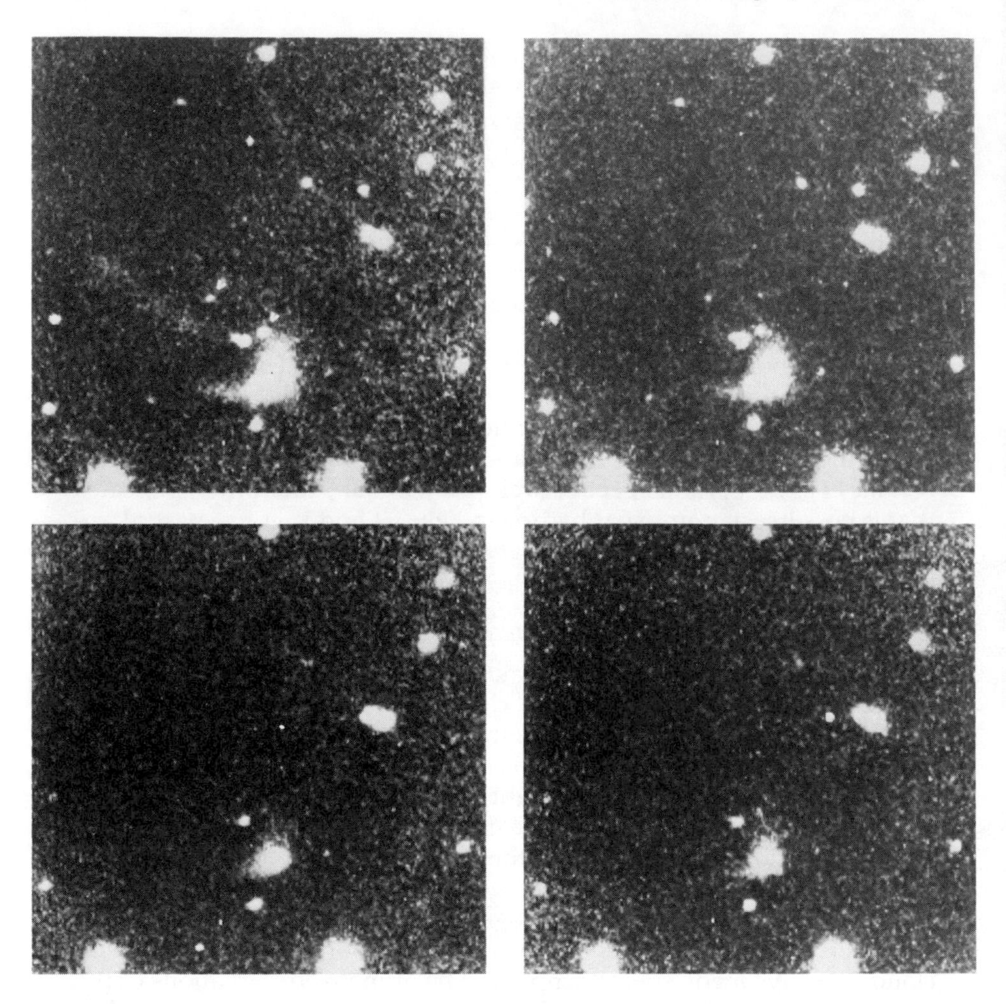

FIGURE 4. Four images of the cometary nebula 1548C27 obtained with the KPNO video camera on the 2.1-m telescope (north is up, east is left, image size is 110 x 110 arc sec). Upper left, an Hα image, with red continuum at the upper right. Lower left is an Hβ image, with blue continuum at the lower right.

OBSERVATIONS IN DARK CLOUDS

Another useful application of the NIPSS data may be illustrated by our studies of the dark nebula L1454 (Duerr and Craine, 1982a, b). In this case we used a scanning microdensitometer to digitize a pair of NIPSS photographs containing the regions of the dark cloud. Star counts were then made using a computerized routine that suggested the existence of two clouds along the line of sight. These data allowed estimation of the distances, extinctions, and masses of the clouds. In addition, maps of the region as a function of redness of the constituent stars were generated (see Fig. 5). These, when compared with the extinction maps, allow a discussion of the star formation properties of the dark cloud. This is a potentially very powerful application of the survey data and will also likely be continued in the future.

This section on survey applications has dealt with only a small number of the possible uses of the NIPSS data. We have already made a number of interesting and worthwhile discoveries, but what is most apparent to those who have worked with the NIPSS program is that it represents a huge quantity of raw data with almost unlimited potential for further discovery and exploitation.

The Future for the Survey

We have already noted several areas in which the NIPSS data will be used to amplify our knowledge of astronomical phenomena. The cataloging of very red stars recorded by the survey photographs will continue, and these catalogs will stimulate further observations of several varieties. The subsequent observations will be particularly relevant to the characteristics of clouds of dust and molecules in regions that may harbor star formation. The process of making detailed observations of these individual stars will, as it has in the past, generate a shorter list of stars that are intrinsically interesting because of their own peculiar properties.

Sophisticated tools will be applied to our survey data, which will accelerate the process of discovery related to the study of the near infrared photographic observations. Particularly exciting is the use of digitizing facilities that will convert the photographs to digital records which can be stored on tape or disk in anticipation of computer processing. Our work on the L1454 dark cloud was predicated upon this approach, and serves as a modest indication of the benefits to be derived from machine processing of the data.

We have conducted a feasibility study of the efficacy of a digitized survey, and find that the techniques are available and quite workable. The astronomical benefits of such an undertaking are enormous and could revolutionize some areas of astronomical research.

The first large-scale beneficiary of a digitized NIPSS data base would be the Infrared Astronomy Satellite (IRAS) program. Launched in January 1983, this satellite is expected to survey the sky systematically in four wavelength bands from 8 to 120 μ. It is anticipated that as many as 10^6 celestial infrared emitters, of a wide variety of different types, may be detected. The majority of the detections will be in the short-wavelength band at about 10 μ.

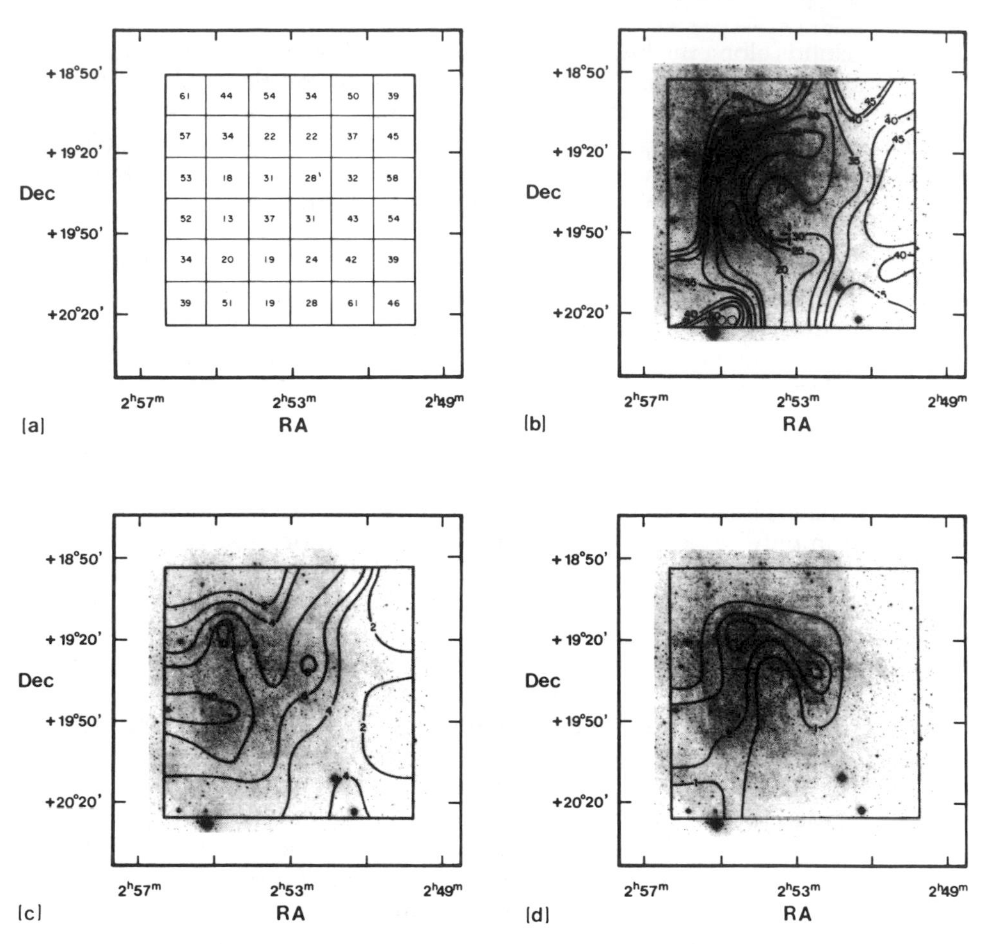

FIGURE 5. (a) Number of stars counted in each 0.26° square of the region studied (north is down, east is left). (b) Distribution of stars within the region (crosses denote positions of known T Tauri/Hα emission stars). (c) Distribution of stars with V-I$\geqslant 2^m5$. (d) Distribution of stars with V-I$\geqslant 4^m5$.

The Scientific Data Analysis System (SDAS) of the Jet Propulsion Laboratory will process IRAS data and produce an Infrared Source Catalog, the principal content of which will be source sky position, flux in each of four IRAS wavelength bands, estimated errors, an estimate of the source classification and correlation with known celestial objects where possible or practicable.

Even allowing for the cross-correlation of IRAS detections with existing catalogs of celestial objects, a staggering number of new detections will remain which will not yield to identification through these catalog searches. Yet, for the infrared detections to attain their full potential it is imperative that optical counterparts be identified, where possible, particularly in the shorter wavelength bands. Failure to adequately address this problem denies or complicates the application of powerful optical techniques to the study of these objects.

Historically, the techniques for identifying infrared sources in surveys such as the Cal Tech Two Micron Survey and the AFGL rocket survey have involved two stages: the aforementioned cross-correlation of IR positions with catalogs of celestial objects (position coincidence perhaps supported by complementary photometric or broad-band spectroscopic characteristics); and source-by-source reobservation at higher spatial resolution to assist in subsequent optical identification.

It is of considerable interest to note the analogy between infrared survey source identifications and the optical identification problems encountered by existing radio surveys. The Ohio State University Radio Observatory (OSURO) Sky Survey of the 1960s and early 1970s generated 2×10^4 source detections accessible from Lat. 40 N (hence quite comparable to expected number densities of IRAS detections). Just as one expects considerable interest in the optical counterparts of IRAS sources, there was great interest in the OSURO sources, since many were expected to be exciting extragalactic objects, perhaps (as hoped in the case of IRAS) representing new classes of objects. Indeed, the most distant known quasi-stellar objects (QSOs) were among the many important objects to emerge from a study of the optical counterparts of the OSURO radio sources.

With this sort of stimulus as a driver, tremendous effort has been expended on the optical identification of these radio sources. The basic techniques were precisely those discussed above for infrared surveys; catalog cross-correlations and reobservation for refinement of the positions. The analogy is further strengthened by noting that the positional errors in the radio data were in general of the same order of magnitude as those expected in the IRAS 10-μ band, i.e., about 30 arc sec.

In spite of the compelling arguments supporting the optical identification of these radio sources, and the incredible resources of time, equipment, and money devoted to the task, only about 2.5 percent of the sources have been identified during the past decade! The major contributor to this situation is the inadequacy of the optical identification techniques described above when applied to a large quantity of data.

IRAS will very significantly compound the problem set forth in this example by virtue of detecting 10^2 more objects than were cataloged in the OSURO survey (the OSURO program having less sky coverage). It seems apparent that the optical identification of the IRAS sources is a difficult and significant problem.

This application is a powerful driver for the digitization of the NIPSS photographs. It is important to note, however, that no matter how urgent the need of IRAS for these data, the digitized survey will be of far broader application to astronomical problems. Such a data base will result in by far the most comprehensive catalog of stellar positions, magnitudes, and colors ever compiled. Statistical studies of stellar distributions will be possible on a much grander scale than anything presently attempted, and, further, the data will exist in the absence of hydrogen emission obscuration which hampers other surveys in selected regions of the sky. Thus, in our view the most important development in the future of the NIPSS program is the digitization of these data.

The NIPSS program, if used for its intended purpose following a successful launch and deployment of the IRAS, will become a major contributor to the list of optical identifications of newly discovered infrared sources. Another large-scale, potential application of NIPSS data supports an important, planned space mission by providing a source of information on guide stars for the Space Telescope. Digitization of the NIPSS photographs would provide a slightly greater spatial density of stars for use as guide stars than is presently required by the Space Telescope. The color bands of the survey are ideal for selection of guide stars; moreover, the photographs have been recently obtained, thus minimizing the problems of unknown proper motions of most of the stars. In addition, recent measurements of digitized survey data (obtained using the Kibblewhite APM digitizer at the Institute of Astronomy, Cambridge, England) have shown that we can measure positions of stars on our photographs to better than 1 arc sec.

On a less sweeping scale, we expect the survey data to be analyzed for a number of purposes, one of the most interesting at the moment involving a search for very cool, red, nearby stars. This project could be important to characterize the distribution of very faint, high proper motion stars within 10 parsecs of the sun, and to allow a determination of the possible contribution of such stars to the mass of our galaxy. This project would take advantage of our ability to detect visually faint, but extremely red stars at high galactic latitudes. We are also using the temporal data provided by the survey, in the form of the substantial regions of overlap of the photographs obtained at different epochs, to search for stars exhibiting large proper motions (thus indicating that the stars are very near the sun).

These temporal data are also being used at the present time to search for previously undiscovered variable stars. The techniques can be manual, using the blink comparator, or automated, using a digitized pair of photographs.

Most of the scientific programs described in this summary are being carried out at Steward Observatory in collaboration with the author, using the data that are now directly available to him. As the task of digitizing the survey photographs progresses, the magnetic tapes will be made available to other interested scientists. In the meantime, plans have been made to reproduce the survey data in the form of an atlas of continuous tone prints for distribution to the scientific community. Work on this project will commence in early 1983 and, because of the large volume of data represented, will continue through most of that year.

We are confident that these data represent a valuable new source of information that may be applied to a large range of astronomical projects. The enormity of the data base is difficult to appreciate without active participation in its use. We hope that an open invitation to the astronomical community to avail itself of this resource will increase awareness of its existence and lead to an expansion of the types of projects for which it is being used.

Acknowledgments

Chief among the many individuals who have contributed to the success of this project are R. Duerr, M. Fugate, V. Horner, C. Imhoff, G. McLaughlin, W. Scharlach, T. Swihart, D. A. Turnshek, and D. E. Turnshek. Special thanks go to the Turnsheks for their continuing devotion to various phases of the program. I also gratefully acknowledge support from the National Aeronautics and Space Administration, the National Geographic Society, the National Science Foundation, the Kitt Peak National Observatory, and the University of Arizona. I am particularly grateful to Drs. N. Boggess and J. Wright for their support and interest in the NIPSS.

REFERENCES

CRAINE, E. R.

1978. Optical infrared sky survey. Astronomical Journal, vol. 83, pp. 1598-1606.

1979. Optical infrared sky survey instrumentation. Proceedings of the Society of Photo-Optical Instrumentation Engineers, vol. 172, pp. 169-177.

1980. Optical infrared sky survey instrumentation. Optical Engineering, vol. 19, pp. 397-403.

CRAINE, E. R., and CROMWELL, R.

1978. Testing and astronomical applications of an image intensifier with a 146-mm diameter photocathode. Proceedings of the Seventh Symposium on Photoelectronic Image Devices, pp. 271-276.

CRAINE, E. R., and CROMWELL, R. *(continued)*
1979. Testing and astronomical applications of an image intensifier with a 146-mm diameter photocathode. Advances of Electronics and Electron Physics, vol. 52, pp. 339-346.
CRAINE, E. R., and SCHARLACH, W. W. G.
1982. VI photometry of selected SAO stars. Publications of the Astronomical Society of the Pacific, vol. 94, pp. 67-72.
CRAINE, E. R.; DUERR, R. E.; HORNER, V. M.; ROUTSIS, D. E.; SWIHART, D. L.; and TURNSHEK, D. A.
1979. Near infrared photographic sky survey: Catalog of red stellar objects. NIPSS Contribution no. 3, Steward Observatory, Tucson, pp. 1-74.
CRAINE, E. R.; BOESHAAR, G. O.; and BYARD, P. L.
1981. 1548C27: An interesting new cometary nebula. Astronomical Journal, vol. 86, pp. 751-754.
CRAINE, E. R.; TURNSHEK, D. E.; TURNSHEK, D. A.; and BOESHAAR, P.
1983. Two newly discovered S stars in a list of faint red objects. Publications of the Astronomical Society of the Pacific, vol. 95, pp. 185-191.
CRAINE, E. R.; TURNSHEK, D. E.; TURNSHEK, D. A.; and LYNDS, B. T.
——. The spectrum of 1548C27. Publications of the Astronomical Society of the Pacific. (Submitted.)
DUERR, R. E., and CRAINE, E. R.
1982a. Automated star counts in the dark cloud L1454. Astronomical Journal, vol. 87, pp. 408-418.
1982b. A catalog of red stars in L1454. Publications of the Astronomical Society of the Pacific, vol. 94, pp. 567-573.
HORNER, V. M., and CRAINE, E. R.
1980. Cataloged infrared sources in NIPSS data I. The RS01 catalog. Publications of the Astronomical Society of the Pacific, vol. 92, pp. 209-214.
ROSSANO, G., and CRAINE, E. R.
1980. Near infrared photographic sky survey: A field index, 202 pp., Pachart Publishing House, Tucson.
SCHARLACH, W.W.G., and CRAINE, E. R.
1980. VRI photometry of selected SAO stars. Publications of the Astronomical Society of the Pacific, vol. 92, pp. 845-853.
——. VRI photometry of SAO stars. Publications of the Astronomical Society of the Pacific. (Submitted.)
TIFFT, W. G., and CRAINE, E. R.
1976. Evaluation of a large format image tube camera for the shuttle sortie missions. Steward Observatory Space Sciences Contribution, Series A76-11, pp. 1-42.
TURNSHEK, D. A.; TURNSHEK, D. E.; and CRAINE, E. R.
1980. Spectroscopic and polarimetric observations of NGC 1333 and the surrounding dark cloud complex. Astronomical Journal, vol. 85, pp. 1683-1643.
——. An atlas of late type scanner spectra. (In preparation.)

ERIC R. CRAINE

Distributional Patchiness in Birds of Tropical Pacific Islands

Grant Recipient: Jared M. Diamond, School of Medicine, University of California, Los Angeles, California.

Grant 1635: In support of an ornithological expedition to study distributional patchiness in birds of the Solomon Islands and Papua New Guinea.

Biologists in the temperate zones take for granted that the distribution of a species can be predicted from knowledge of its habitat requirements: Wherever and only wherever these are fulfilled, the species will be locally present. So well does this principle usually work that apparent absence of a species in what seems to be suitable habitat is usually taken to mean incompetence of the observer, rather than a breakdown of the principle.

In the tropics this principle does break down: Many species are patchily distributed with respect to suitable habitat. For a long time temperate-zone biologists resisted this conclusion in the belief that populations of tropical species are too easy to overlook or have undiscernably subtle habitat requirements. However, increasing numbers of tropical ecologists in recent years have documented puzzling gaps in the distributions of conspicuous species, and have concluded that patchiness is a real and important characteristic of tropical communities. Such patchiness raises theoretical as well as practical problems. What is (are) the explanation(s) for patchiness? Why is it much commoner in the tropics than in the temperate zones? What are its practical implications for conservation strategy? For example, are the patches stable with time, or do they shift such that a national park located to contain populations of endangered species today may lose these populations as the patches shift?

The field studies summarized in this report were focused on the distributional patchiness that had struck me in previous expeditions to study tropical rain forest birds of the Solomon Islands and New Guinea. I had three objectives: to examine patchiness in an archipelago, the island-dotted lagoons near New Georgia in the Solomon Islands; to examine patchiness on the species-rich New Guinea mainland itself; and to provide the governments of the Solomon Islands and Papua New Guinea with practical suggestions for conservation strategies that would be useful in the face of this distributional patchiness.

On the night of September 3, 1976, I flew from Los Angeles via Fiji across the international date line and arrived the following afternoon (September 5), 23 hours of real time later, in the capital of the Solomon Islands, Honiara. Here I spent 2 days in discussions with government officers (Central Planning Office, Ministry of Natural Resources, Ministry of Education and Cultural Affairs), as background to the conservation studies that I had been requested to undertake on Rennell Island. When I flew to Munda on the island of New Georgia on September 8, the obliging Solair pilot made a detour to circle Gatukai submarine volcano, then in eruption and hurling glowing rocks from a black cone that had recently emerged above the sea. At Munda I was met by two friends, Mr. Alisasa Bisili and Mr. Teu Zinghite, who had worked with me during my 1974 expedition and whom I had learned to admire as walking encyclopedias of natural history, masters of bird identification, and also masters of all practical expeditionary problems. That same day we set up camp on the beach of an islet 6 mi down the lagoon from Munda and commenced fieldwork.

Our study areas were Vona Vona lagoon and Roviana lagoon, sheltered lagoons dotted with dozens of coral islands ranging in size from a single mangrove tree to several square miles. Highlights in the recent histories of these lagoons had been the activities of feared headhunters in the 19th century, battles between Japanese and American forces in the Second World War, and the well-known wreck nearby of president-to-be Kennedy's PT boat. The clear lagoon waters harbored lobsters, beautiful and diverse corals and small fish, and also stingrays, sharks, and mantas. The islets were covered with rain forest interrupted by some coconut plantations and often fringed by mangrove, a three-dimensional maze of aerial roots and branching trunks. During the next 3 weeks we visited 80 islets by a canoe with outboard motor and attempted to survey their bird species as completely as possible.

Our procedure was to approach each island by canoe, spend a few minutes offshore listening for species that were calling, then jump or wade ashore and fan out in three directions to cover the island. As most of the terrain lacked trails, we simply forced our way through the forest, with me constantly waving a small stick in front of my face to brush away the spiders' webs that crisscrossed the forest. Usually the weather was hot and sunny, and dried us out quickly whenever we got soaked by brief rainstorms. The chief discomfort arose from an almost invisibly tiny red mite, the "mini," that infested a few islands, crawled into one's socks and up one's legs, and bit. The bites raised welts and caused an itching that became unbearable for me after an hour and forced me to rush clothed into the ocean to kill the minis. On mini-less islands Alisasa, Teu, and I met back at the canoe after a period ranging from 15 minutes for a tiny islet to most of a day for an island of several square miles, and we assembled a list of the bird species and estimated numbers we had encountered. If there were people living on the islands, I quizzed them exhaustively about species that visited the island occasionally. Ornithologists would be astonished by the observational powers of many Solomon Islanders, who correctly identified small birds seen without binoculars in silhouette at hundreds of feet, and who accurately described birds seen on a single occasion 30 years previously.

In surveying these 80 islands, we soon found that although distributional patchiness prevented firm predictions of which species would be found on a particular island, we could nevertheless estimate the probability that a given species would occur on an island of a given size. Some species, such as the sunbird *Nectarinia jugularis,* were present on virtually all islands, even ones as small as a fraction of an acre. At the opposite extreme, the cuckoo-shrikes *Coracina holopolia* and *C. caledonica* were confined to the three largest islands of the lagoon, with areas of 210, 272, and 789 mi^2, and did not even occur on an island of 147 mi^2. Other species constituted intermediate cases: present on all or most large islands, patchily distributed on islands in a medium-area range characteristic of the particular species, and absent on all or most smaller islands. For most Solomon bird species, this characteristic island area at which the species' distribution becomes patchy exceeds a square mile.

How can this dependence of bird distributions on island area be explained? The answers emerged from observations of bird behavior and abundance, which suggest three types of distributional "strategies":

1. During our many trips across the lagoon by canoe, we observed some species flying over water between islands every day, other species rarely or never. On very small islands the daily "water-crossers" constituted most of the species present: e.g., the parrots *Eos cardinalis* and *Trichoglossus haematodus,* pigeon *Ducula pistrinaria,* hawk *Haliastur indus,* heron *Egretta sacra,* and kingfisher *Halcyon saurophaga.* These species can use small islands because their water-crossing ability frees them from restriction to islands large enough to fulfill their food needs for a long time.

2. The next category after the water-crossers consists of territorial species present on most islands large enough to hold at least one pair of the species: e.g., the kingfisher *Halcyon chloris,* flycatcher *Monarcha richardsii,* and starling *Aplonis grandis.* These species certainly do not cross water daily, but my field associates Teu and Alisasa occasionally had seen individuals or pairs flying between islands. Probably some juveniles of these species fly from their island of birth to seek an empty territory on another island, but if successful then spend their adult lives on the island

where they settle. On islands only large enough to hold a single pair, the species may occasionally die out, but the island is soon recolonized by a dispersing juvenile. Thus, most islands exceeding one territory size will be found to be occupied at any given moment.

3. The remaining species are confined to islands large enough to hold dozens or even hundreds of pair territories: for example, the cuckoo *Centropus ateralbus*, flycatchers *Rhipidura cockerelli* and *Pachycephala pectoralis*, and cuckoo-shrikes *Coracina holopolia* and *C. caledonica*. Not even Teu or Alisasa, in their 40 or 50 years on the lagoons, had seen these species cross water. These species colonize so rarely that, if a local population becomes extinct, years or even millennia may pass before the island is recolonized. Hence the species are confined to large islands, on which their populations are large, and rarely become extinct.

On October 2, I returned to Honiara for further discussions with the government before flying to Rennell. This remarkable island, isolated in the ocean 100 mi from Guadalcanal, is the largest uplifted coral atoll in the world, a former coral reef of 264 mi^2 that is now a plateau standing on cliffs that plunge vertically 500 ft into the sea, with almost no beaches. The former lagoon of 40 mi^2 is now the largest freshwater lake of the tropical Pacific. In this strange, isolated environment evolved one of the strangest avifaunas of the Pacific, including five endemic species and numerous endemic subspecies. The people of Rennell are not Melanesians, as are other Solomon Islanders, but instead are the westernmost population of Polynesians. Recently bauxite was discovered on Rennell, and a Japanese firm is evaluating the feasibility of mining. Faced with a classic problem in possible adverse effects of industrial development on a unique and fragile environment, the Solomons government requested me to visit Rennell and recommend ways of minimizing risks to the biological environment.

Although I had read extensively about Rennell, my first view of the island was still a shock. In a chartered airplane we had been flying for an hour from Guadalcanal over empty ocean, when I saw ahead what seemed to be a long line of breakers in the middle of the sea. On closer view this proved to be the coast of Rennell! In contrast to other Solomon islands, whose forest is interrupted by rivers and occasional clearings, the unbroken forest of Rennell is so homogeneous that at a distance it showed no texture and resembled the sea. As we flew over the forest, this initial impression yielded to the impression of an African savanna on a nearly level plain with scattered trees and occasional mysterious deep holes in the ground. In fact, the "plain" was not the ground at all but the homogeneous, 100-ft-high canopy of the forest; the "scattered trees" were crowns of giant strangling figs, towering above the canopy; and the "holes" were small clearings in the canopy where forest on the occasional pockets of cultivatable soil had been cut to plant gardens.

I spent October 5-12 on Rennell, walking from the airstrip to the lake and back, examining the lake and its small islets by dugout canoe, censusing birds, studying the regrowth of vegetation on trial-mined sites, and determining the plants whose fruit and seeds each species of bird ate. In all these activities I received much help from Rennell people, especially Mr. Kasipa Baigo and Mr. Charles Tetuha, who matched Alisasa and Teu in their knowledge of each bird species' diet, nest, and status for the past several decades. The main obstacle to bird studies on Rennell is the terrain, which consists of little soil and no rocks—just sharp coral like an unbroken expanse of broken bottles, pitted with deep holes concealed by forest litter and tree roots. In walking from the coast to the lake my pace averaged 100 yd in 4 min. (A Rennell story relates that, before God made other islands, He practiced by making Rennell. He later became angry at the Rennell people and punished them by scraping off all the soil and dumping it on another much more fertile island, Bellona.) But Rennell is still very rewarding and satisfying to an ornithologist, because of the abundance and conspicuousness of its native birds. These include the white ibis ("taghóa", Rennell name) that feeds in gardens along with the chickens, flocks of pygmy cormorants ("manukitáe") on the lake, beautiful green and orange doves ("higi") with a jazzy song, thrushes ("gagángo") like American robins but hopping on the ground among the coral, tiny warblers ("lóke-lóke") that sing duets, and the large white-eye ("ghagha") that calls incessantly like a soft machine gun. After a brief visit to the smaller raised coral atoll of Bellona, I returned to Honiara to present to the government my suggestions for reducing environmental effects of mining, and to give talks on conservation at the National Museum, Teacher's Training College, and Betikama High School.

On October 15 I flew to Port Moresby, capital of Papua New Guinea, for the remaining 6 weeks of fieldwork. A few hours after landing, I met with members of the government's Forestry Office and Wildlife Branch to plan an itinerary. Together with Mick Raga (head of Wildlife Research), Daink Kuro, and several other members of Wildlife Branch, and one or two botanists and foresters, I was to compare the avifauna of four different sites in lowland rain forest. One of these was at Vanimo on the zoogeographically distinct north coast; a second at Oriomo on the south coast, where there had been a broad land bridge to Australia during the Pleistocene and where populations of 21 species, otherwise confined in New Guinea to the mountains, occur as isolated lowland populations, stranded as relicts on the old ice-age invasion route to Australia; and two others at Kiunga and Nomad River on the upper Fly River and a tributary of the upper Strickland River, respectively, in possibly the largest expanse of relatively undisturbed tropical rain forest surviving outside South America. This itinerary gave me an excellent opportunity to study distributional patchiness within a single landmass, while providing the Papua New Guinea government with bird surveys of two areas proposed for major economic development (Vanimo Timber Area and the area downstream of the proposed Ok Tedi copper mines).

After a weekend "crash review course" in New Guinea birding with Harry Bell, I flew with Mick and Daink to Vanimo on October 19. We promptly had our first shared experience of the creative approach that Air Niugini, the national airline, devised to cope with the problem of unequal distribution of wealth. At the end of each flight, each passenger receives on the average only two thirds of the pieces of luggage that he or she checked. The remaining one third is either distributed to other passengers in other cities en route in exchange for pieces of still other passengers', or else returned to the owner between 3 days and 6 months later. On this particular flight we lost our formaldehyde and part of our collecting equipment in exchange for forestry supplies, while subsequent flights claimed my two tents and all of Mick's field notes and personal papers, which trickled back to us in various cities at varying intervals. Mick proved a genius at solving these and all other obstacles, thereby sparing me ulcers.

In the Vanimo area we surveyed coastal forest at Ningera and Waterstone, and hill forest on the Vanimo-Bewani road. Flights on October 27-30, 1976, brought us via Daru to Oriomo, where we explored both forest and savanna. The flight to Kiunga on November 5 was memorable for taking us over an uninterrupted expanse of tropical rain forest on completely flat terrain, where in an hour's flying time we saw no sign at all of man, not even a clearing or a hut. Birding at Kiunga involved two nuisances: land leeches that could not be scraped off our clothes and legs but had to be burnt off with matches; and clouds of mosquitoes that hovered around our heads and in front of our eyes despite copious use of insect repellent, so that I was constantly waving a piece of cardboard in front of my face and listening to the crunch of mosquito bodies swatted at each stroke. Pleasures of Kiunga included mixed foraging flocks of a dozen or more bird species, providing concentrated bouts of beauty and excitement; the beauty of traversing the meandering Fly River in a motorboat under the warm sun; and the even more magical beauty of paddling silently back to Kiunga at night in a canoe, after our motorboat had broken down on an oxbow of the Fly. On November 12, we flew on to Nomad River; on November 16, to Daru again, to examine the mangrove avifauna; and, on November 19, back to Port Moresby. At each of these study sites local guides gave us detailed pidgin-English accounts of over 100 bird species that they distinguished. Naturally, these accounts did not identify birds by Latin or English names but by local names: for example, i, di, kwok, wo, screw, screw-screw, hihi, dudu, pis-pis, kedídirik, yorbíchul-bíchul, i-bróchit-káuli, kúntry-kúntry-knai, wai-squírty-squírty, dumánigenhióbe, binkyaruankyanémi, dinigahawasogeri, etc., the length of the name apparently varying inversely with the size of the bird. Matching up these names with the correct bird posed delightful puzzles as well as provided the key to a gold mine of knowledge.

These comparisons of New Guinea sites, as well as the surveys of Solomon Islands in the first half of the expedition, suggested that at least four different mechanisms contribute to tropical patchiness:

Fine habitat sorting. In some cases we found patches of ecologically similar species predictably replacing each other. For instance, two similar-sized fruit doves, *Ptilinopus pulchellus* and *P. coronulatus,* were found to sort along a rainfall gradient, the former occurring in forest receiving higher rainfall than the latter.

Immigration-extinction equilibria. If local populations occasionally become extinct but can be reestablished by immigrations, the distribution at any instant will be patchy, but the locations of occupied patches will change with time. This is probably the main explanation for patchiness on the set of Solomon Islands surveyed, where the ratio of extinction rates to immigration rates produces for each species a characteristic dependence of percent patches occupied on island area.

Historical effect. An environment that is homogeneous today may have been patchy in the past. If bird distributions equilibrate more slowly than environmental structure, present bird distributions may continue to reflect past patches. A clear example is provided by the 21 montane bird species represented by lowland populations in the Oriomo forests but not at our other study sites. If we did not realize that these Oriomo forests had been joined to cooler subtropical forests of Australia during the Pleistocene and that these isolated montane populations are relicts, their presence would have been mysterious.

Lockouts. A species may be permanently excluded from an area with suitable habitat by established populations of competitors. We found two sets of examples. The grass-finches *Lonchura spectabilis, L. grandis,* and *L. castaneothorax,* which are widespread throughout New Guinea, are nevertheless absent in the Fly River area, correlated with the presence of three endemic finch species there (*L. nevermanni, L. leucostita,* and *L. stygia*). Correlated with the presence of the montane relicts, the Oriomo forests lack some otherwise widespread species, such as *Ailuroedus buccoides, Rhipidura rufidorsa, Reinwardtoena reinwardtsi,* and *Psittaculirostris desmarestii.*

In light of these interpretations, why is patchiness so much more marked in the tropics than in the temperate zones? I think that a major reason is the higher species diversity of the tropics, leading to finer habitat sorting, higher extinction rates because of lower population densities per species, and more lockouts because of more competing species. A contributing factor may be the greater sedentariness of tropical birds, leading to lower immigration rates and more vacant patches at any instant.

While the main focus of this expedition was on patchiness, opportunity for preliminary study of two other problems presented itself in the field:

Visual mimicry in birds. While vocal mimicry is well known in birds (cf. mockingbirds, lyrebirds, and some parrots and mynahs), visual mimicry is not, despite its frequency in other groups such as butterflies. Previously I had concluded that the New Guinea oriole *Oriolus szalayi* mimics a pugnacious larger honeyeater, *Philemon novaeguineae,* in plumage. At Nomad River I discovered that a rare smaller honeyeater, *Pycnopygius stictocephalus,* whose plumage as judged from specimens had always struck me as peculiar, apparently mimics *Oriolus szalayi* both in voice and in plumage. Another possible case involves mixed flocks centered on drongos and pitohuis, in which all flock members are either black (*Dicrurus hottentottus,* male *Coracina melaena*) or else rusty-brown (*Garritornis isidori,* female *Coracina melaena,* female *Cicinnurus regius, Pitohui ferrugineus, P. incertus, P. kirhocephalus*). Having been thus sensitized to the existence of visual mimicry in birds, I now suspect that the New Guinea avifauna may present other examples involving *Lophorina superba* and *"Parotia," Pachycephalopsis hattamensis* and *Pachycephala rufinucha, Toxorhamphus novaeguineae* and *Oedistoma iliolophum, Philemon meyeri* and *Meliphaga flaviventer,* and *Entomyzon cyanotis* and *Melithreptus lunatus.*

Fruit consumption by birds. Many tropical birds eat exclusively fruit, and many tropical plants depend exclusively on birds for dispersal of their seeds. How are resources matched to consumers, so that some birds do not starve and some fruit does not rot? At all my study sites (Solomon lagoon islands, Rennell, New Guinea mainland) I observed what bird species ate what fruit species and how. It turned out that there are many different sets of matched bird-fruit strategies: fruits with soft flesh surrounding large hard pits, eaten at a single gulp by pigeons, starlings, and hornbills that have weak stomachs and expel the undigested pits; hard nuts and seeds, taken by pigeons that have strong stomachs and swallow pebbles and grind up the nuts and seeds; large fruits, that are either bitten by strong-billed parrots, pecked by white-eyes, or (if very tough and fibrous) gnawed by bats; soft, seedy, raspberrylike fruits, that are gulped by honeyeaters; and grapelike firm-skinned soft berries, that are twirled, skinned, and gulped by dicaeids. We encountered a charming example of double use: fruits with soft flesh and hard pits, carried to a nesting tree by colonial starlings *Aplonis metallica*, which swallowed the fruits and defecated the pits, whereupon pebble-swallowing pigeons *Chalcophaps stephani* picked up the fallen pits and ground them up in their stomachs.

During my final few days in Port Moresby before flying back to Los Angeles on November 22, I had discussions with members of the National Parks Board and Office of Environment and Conservation about a national park plan for Papua New Guinea, which I drew up in more detail after my return. On this visit, my first to Papua New Guinea since it became independent, I was greatly encouraged to see the progress that had been made in government planning for conservation, compared with the situation during the Australian mandated administration that ended a few years ago. More than most other people in the world, the people of Papua New Guinea have their cultural identity and economic future tied to their fauna and flora. There is now a fine national park near the capital, and others planned; government review of all major development projects for their potential environmental impact; a program of wildlife management areas, which gives responsibility for conservation to local people while providing them advice and motivation; and a well-staffed, well-equipped Wildlife Branch with active programs in wildlife research. While future pressure on land, forest, and birds in Papua New Guinea will be great, the prospects for survival of its fauna and flora seem to me much more encouraging than on other Pacific islands.

PUBLICATIONS

DIAMOND, J. M.
1980a. Why are many tropical bird species distributed patchily with respect to available habitat? Pp. 777-782 *in* Proceedings of the 19th International Congress.
1980b. Patchy distributions of tropical birds. Pp. 57-74 *in* "Conservation Biology," M. Soulé and B. Wilcox, eds. Sinauer, Sunderland, Mass.
——. The avifaunas of Rennell and Bellona Islands. Copenhagen Zoological Museum. (In press.)

DIAMOND, J. M., and GILPIN, M. E.
1980. Contribution of turnover noise to variance in species number. Amer. Nat., vol. 115, pp. 884-889.

DIAMOND, J. M., and RAGA, M. N.
1980. The lowland avifauna of the Fly River region. Papua New Guinea Wildlife Publication 77/11.
1978. The Mottled-breasted Pitohui, *Pitohui incertus*. Emu, vol. 78, pp. 49-53.

DIAMOND, J. M.; RAGA, M. N.; and WIAKABU J.
1977. Report on bird survey in the proposed Vanimo Timber Area. Papua New Guinea Wildlife Publication 77/10.

DIAMOND, J. M.; RAGA, M. N.; WIAKABU, J.; MARU, T.; and FENI, S.
1977. Fruit consumption and seed dispersal by New Guinea birds. Papua New Guinea Wildlife Publication 77/10.

JARED M. DIAMOND

Status and Ecology of the Giant Otter in Suriname

Grant Recipient: Nicole Duplaix-Hall, Otter Specialist Group, Species Survival Commission, International Union for Conservation of Nature and Natural Resources, Gland, Switzerland.[1]

Grants 1678, 1836: For field study of the giant Brazilian otter in Suriname.

During a survey of the giant otter *Pteronura brasiliensis* conducted in Suriname from mid-July 1976 through March 28, 1978, 188 sightings were made, totaling 252 individuals, of which 97 were seen more than once. Total direct observation time was 108 hr, 54 min during 297 days in the field. Surveyed were 6/15 large tributaries, major rivers, 41 creeks, and 1 lake, some of them several times (Fig. 1). Kaboeri Creek, a tributary of the Corantijn River above Washabo, was especially emphasized. The activities of the 23 resident otters were monitored every 6 weeks from January to November 1977 and full-time from January 13 to March 11, 1978. During the rainy season (May to July), the otters desert the creeks and retreat into adjacent flooded forest, savannah swamps, and hidden oxbow lakes, where they are difficult to follow and observe: Only 16 sightings of 34 otters for 52 min were made from April to the end of July, versus 139 sightings of 56 otters for 100 hr, 46 min from August to April.

It has been determined that the giant otter is diurnal, with activity peaks in the morning and afternoon. None was seen or heard from 1800 to 0747 hr. A pair or family group usually swims with the tide during the morning hours, fishes along the way, and returns to the campsite or den to groom and to rest before the afternoon patrol and fishing sessions. Fish are chased and ambushed in shallow water or under floating vegetation and eaten in the shallows or on a log. It was possible to make 202 direct observations of prey capture by four individuals (two pairs). Eleven species of fish were taken belonging to four orders (characoid, siluroid, percoid, gymnotoid, in order of preference). Size of prey varies from 10 to 45 cm in length, 25 cm being the norm. Crabs are also taken. Prey items are not shared or stored but consumed entirely on the spot of capture.

[1] The author's present address is: Environmental Service Center, Tallahassee, Florida.

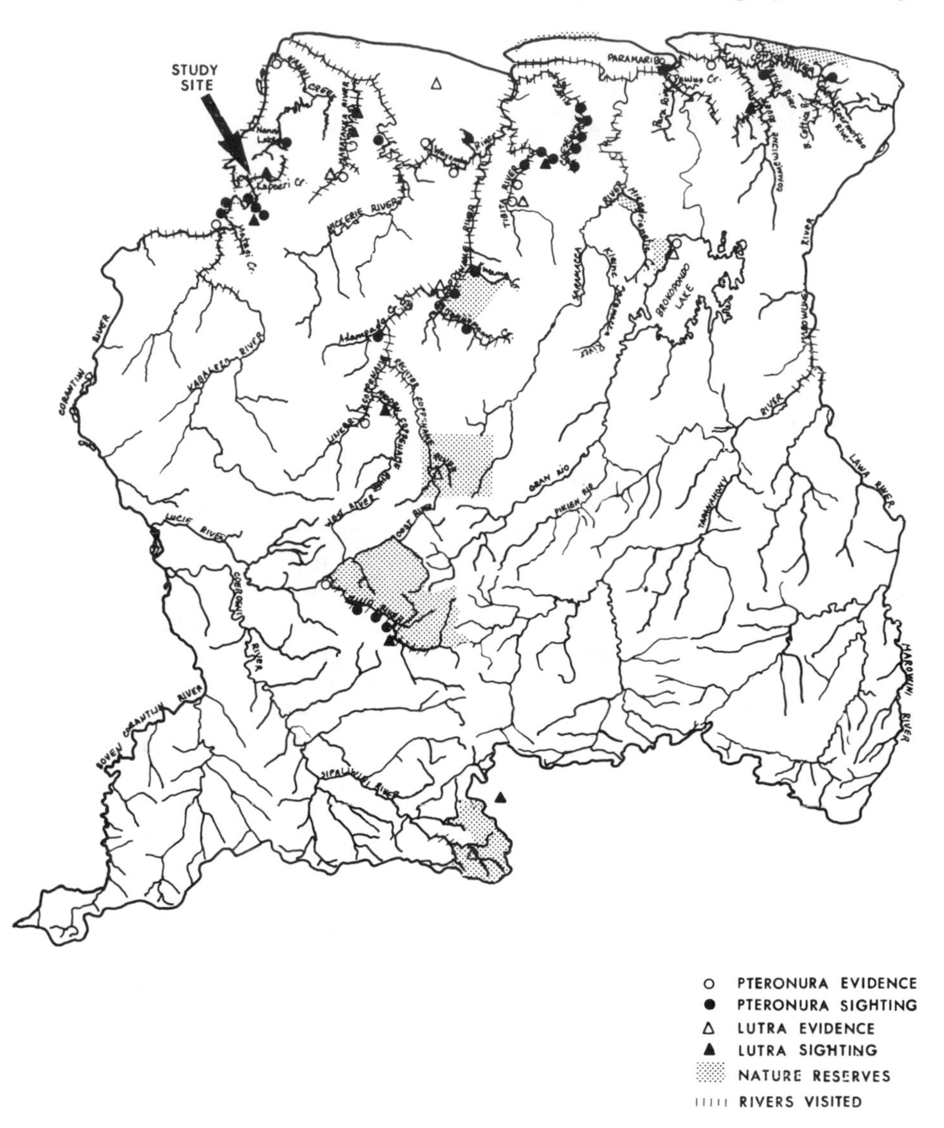

FIGURE 1. Suriname, showing the rivers visited during the giant otter survey 1976-1978.

Territorial Behavior

The otters clear the vegetation along portions of the riverbank; these areas are called campsites (8.2 x 5.7 m average for 227 measured). They are used for marking, grooming, and resting during the dry season on black-water creeks. Smaller campsites (2.5 to 5 m diameter) may be partially cleared and used overnight and then abandoned, while others, usually larger, are core areas in the territory and are maintained regularly. Several may be used simultaneously, the otters spending the night at one of them with no fixed pattern. On Kaboeri Creek, 53 of the 77 campsites were used to various extents during the dry season, whereas only 8 were sporadically visited during the rainy months.

Two forms of territorial marking have been observed: Scats or spraints are left on sloping logs or large boulders near or above the water (225 scats were collected for analysis); on campsites, both sexes spread feces over a specific and usually circular area (1.5 m diameter, average) set off to one side. It is used for a varying length of time, then abandoned when another spot is selected. Scent and urine are spread by both sexes over the whole campsite during the course of clearing the vegetation and kneading the substrate. The first type of marking seems to be used on forest creeks where the Guyana otter *Lutra enudris* is also present, and on larger rivers near waterfalls and rapids where clusters of boulders and small islands predominate. These two forms of marking do not usually overlap in one area.

Territory size appears to be correlated with the number of otters in residence. Normally a pair of otters will actively mark and defend 2 km of riverbank, sometimes as much as 4.2 km, even though they may wander beyond their boundaries as far as 6 km on either side. When a family group of two adults and their subadult offspring had three more cubs in 1977, they enlarged their territory upstream by 2.3 km, displacing a pair that had lost their two cubs to an Indian poacher. The pair's female subsequently disappeared and the solitary male's territory was reduced to a 600-m core area and his marking activities virtually ceased. A subadult pair set up a new territory of 2.1 km in a relatively poor fishing area at the entrance to the creek. These 11 individuals' three territories covered 7 km of creek and included several smaller forest creeks on both sides. These sizes apply only to the dry season, as it was impossible to establish these parameters in the rainy season when the forest was flooded. Territories appear to be perennial; the same pair returned to the same portion of the creek in 1977 and 1978. *Pteronura* spaces itself by sight, scent, and hearing.

Parental and Social Behavior

In Suriname the giant otter's birth season spreads over several months. In 1976, 2-month-old cubs were seen at the end of August, while in 1977 very young cubs were seen on October 2. A pair of habituated otters on Kaboeri Creek had one cub in 1976 and two in 1977, indicating that pairs can be monogamous for several years at least and breed every year. The 1976 cub remained in its parents' territory during the rearing of the new litter and then moved 6 km upstream where it was sighted in March, living alone. Subadults usually remain with the parents, however, as evidenced by another group on the creek mentioned above. Litter size, based on 19 sightings, appears to be one to three cubs. The male is as attentive to the cubs as the female, and both exit and enter the den together; cubs may remain alone up to 4 hr while the parents forage or rest elsewhere. Pairs and family groups swim parallel or in close proximity, with the cubs in the middle, diving and surfacing together. Dives during normal swimming last 20 sec on average but are much shorter during rapid chasing while hunting. Cubs that become separated are immediately sought by sight and calls and are retrieved by both parents. Family groups hunt as a group but there appears to be no cooperation or sharing. Giant otters are particularly noisy and conspicuous during hunting and investigating. They show little fear in undisturbed areas, "charging" the boat with loud cries when their vocalizations are imitated by the human observer. Nine separate vocalizations were identified and recorded. Lengths of continuous observation ranged from a glimpse to 5 hr, 7 min. Large groups of 7 otters were seen 7 times and a group of 16, once. Groups usually include three age classes and are most often seen toward the end of the dry season, when the subadults join their parents again. The female is dominant over the male as evidenced by the following: The male grooms the female in a mated pair for much longer bouts than vice versa; the female initiates departures and landings; the female is usually the first to mark or spraint on a campsite although thereafter the male spends longer clearing and marking. When cubs are present, the female and her subadult female offspring remain close to the cubs and the males defend the group. Both sexes are equally aggressive in intraspecific encounters. When invading a neighboring territory, the resident otters often flee into the forest when they hear a large group approaching. When humans approach they dive into the water or swim up a smaller branch of the creek. The otters were able to recognize and ignore the human observer, differentiating her from Indians in canoes, whom they feared.

The Guyana Otter

This smaller species, the Guyana otter *Lutra enudris,* was seen only 11 times (13 individuals), with no repeats, for a total of 23 min of observation time. It is solitary and much shyer than the giant otter. It uses logs and boulders for depositing scats like other *Lutra* species and does not clear campsites. In all, 27 scats were collected on 5 occasions within sight of

Pteronura scats. Both species are known to be sympatric on at least five major river systems. *Lutra* favors a wide variety of habitats, particularly small creeks in the forest and savannah swamps. Size of prey and more crepuscular habits appear to minimize competition or encounters between the two species. Cubs were seen in late October and December. Anacondas are known to prey on this species.

Conservation Recommendations

Both species of otter are well represented in Suriname. As far as can be ascertained, killing otters for their pelts has never been widespread except perhaps near the French Guiana border where *Pteronura* is less common. The highest density of *Pteronura*—Kaboeri Creek, Tibiti River, and upper Coesewijne River—coincides with a low floodable forest habitat with access to savannah swamps. This prime otter habitat occurs roughly on a band across Suriname between 5°30′ and 5° N lat. Two reserves were proposed for the upper Coesewijne and the Kaboeri areas but the local Indian populations opposed the idea, stating that this would jeopardize their ancestral hunting and fishing grounds. Compensation in the form of hunting and logging rights to adjacent forest areas have been rejected by the village leaders and matters are at a standstill. A more direct and permanent threat to the giant otters of Kaboeri Creek is the Western Suriname Development Project. Based in Apoera, 10 km upstream, a building site is under way to create a city of 60,000 people. Already a sawmill and a highway, 64 km long, with an adjacent railroad tract are functioning or well on the way to completion. The railway will be used in the exploitation of a bauxite mine farther inland. Plans for a major hydroelectric dam 50 km to the south will also have a major impact on the water level of Kaboeri Creek should they be implemented. The resident human population in Apoera tripled between January and October 1977 as workers from Guyana and eastern Suriname came to settle. The construction firms prohibit hunting during working hours and there are strict controls of firearms. Kaboeri Creek is accessible only by boat, and its narrow course is littered with fallen logs that impede progress. So far only Indians and a few European fishermen visit the creek regularly, but it can only be a matter of months before the situation changes. The resident otters are particularly vulnerable during the months of September to April when they are rearing cubs and the flooded forest, to the safety of which they can no longer retreat, is dry. Cubs are sometimes taken by the Indians to rear as pets; this occurred in December 1977 and, although released by police order soon thereafter, they were never seen again.

Conclusions

Suriname remains one of the few countries in the range of *Pteronura* where its numbers are stable and where, in the uninhabited interior at least, the outlook for its future is bright. The effective existing conservation laws and reserves are a guarantee that this situation will not dramatically reverse itself, with the one exception of Kaboeri Creek. In 1980, however, contrary to the wishes of the local Indians, plans to create a reserve in that area were realized, and adequate patrolling was organized. The threat to the giant otter, therefore, was removed.

A detailed report of this project appears in Duplaix (1980a).

REFERENCES

DUPLAIX, N.

1980a. Observations on the ecology and behavior of the giant river otter *Pteronura brasiliensis* in Suriname. Rev. Ecol. (Terre Vie), vol. 34, pp. 495-620.

1980b. Giant otters: "Big water dog" in peril. Nat. Geogr. Mag., vol. 158, pp. 130-142.

1982. Im Kielwasser der scheuen Riesenotter. Tier, no. 2, pp. 4-9.

NICOLE DUPLAIX

Excavations at Tal-e Malyan, Iran

Grant Recipient: R. H. Dyson, Jr., University Museum, University of Pennsylvania, Philadelphia, Pennsylvania.

Grants 1616, 1895: In support of archeological excavations at Tal-e Malyan, Fars Province, Iran.

The University of Pennsylvania excavations at Tal-e Malyan were undertaken during five field seasons, 1971-1978 (Sumner, 1974, 1976). This research was partially supported by National Geographic grants during the 1976 and 1978 seasons.[1] The project is under the general supervision of the grantee, R. H. Dyson, Jr., with William M. Sumner, Ohio State University, as Field Director, Research Coordinator, and editor of the projected monograph series to be published by the University Museum. The monographs will include contributions from some 14 associated scholars.[2]

Tal-e Malyan is located in the Kur River Basin, Fars Province, Iran, about 50 km west-northwest of Persepolis. The site, which encompasses 200 ha (Fig. 1), is identified as the city of Anshan (Reiner, 1973) which, along with Susa, was one of the political centers of the Elamite realm. The objectives of the Malyan Project, conceived as a preliminary exploration of the site, are to establish a chronological framework, to investigate cultural change during the early urban period, and to investigate the internal organization of production and other activities during several phases in the history of the city. The following summary of findings is presented in chronological order.

---

[1] Funds for the 1976 season were provided by the Metropolitan Museum of Art, by the University Museum (University of Pennsylvania), the National Geographic Society, the National Science Foundation (BNS 76—0645), and the Ohio State University. Funds for the 1978 season were provided by the Metropolitan Museum of Art, the University Museum (University of Pennsylvania), the National Geographic Society, and travel grants from Harvard and the University of California at Los Angeles.

[2] Malyan staff, in 1976, or 1978, or both seasons: J. Alden, J. Balcer, C. Beeman, M. J. Blackman, E. Carter, H. Eqbal, B. Hill, L. Jacobs, B. Kole, J. Kole, R. Liggett, M. Mavedat, K. MacLean, S. Mild, N. Miller, I. Nicholas, J. L. Nickerson, J. W. Nickerson, H. Pittman, P. Rissman, M. Rosenberg, M. Rothman, V. Sarkosh, M. Solper, W. Sumner, R. Wright, H. Youzan, and M. Zeder.

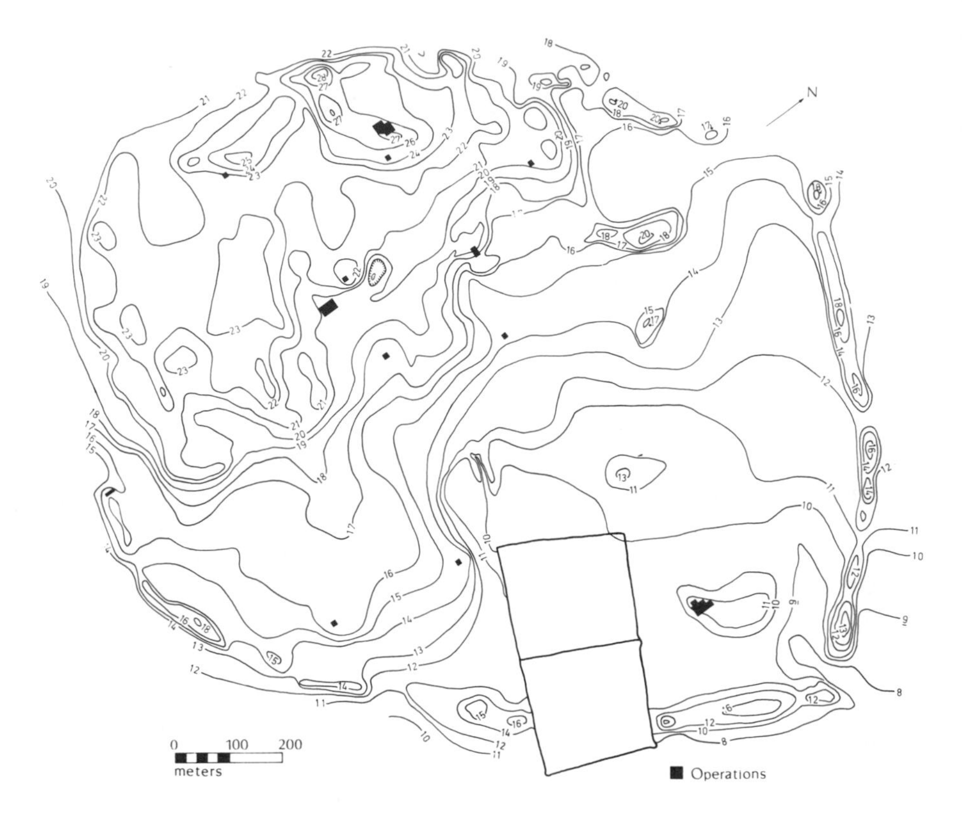

FIGURE. 1. Tal-e Malyan, a 200-ha site identified as the city of Anshan.

The city grew in size and acquired the properties of an urban center during the Banesh Phase, now dated to the period ca. 3400-2800 B.C. by a series of 15 radiocarbon determinations corrected according to the current calibration curve (Klein et al., 1982). These dates are earlier than expected and require reconsideration of the accepted Mesopotamian and Iranian chronology for the period of early urban states.

During 1976 and 1978, excavations in three separate operations revealed Banesh levels. Building Level 3 in operation TUV is a complex of rooms and open spaces producing domestic trash deposits and features such as hearths and ovens. This level also produced smelting scoria, copper prills, and smelting furnace fragments indicating small-scale metallurgical production. Other craft activities include flint knapping and shell working. Administrative activities are evidenced by seals, sealed jar stoppers, door sealings, bale tag sealings, and clay tablets bearing Proto-Elamite pictographs and numerical notations (Nicholas, 1981).

Excavation in operation ABC reached virgin soil some 8 m below the mound surface. Building Level 5, the earliest structure excavated, is a domestic building featuring a double entryway and several ovens. This building did not contain evidence of administrative activities comparable to the later painted Level-3 building (Nickerson, 1977) or the Level-2 warehouse but the regularities of plan and the care exercised in construction suggest that ABC Level 5, like the levels above, is qualitatively or functionally different from the Banesh buildings excavated in operation TUV. The great variation in plans, construction quality, and contents of buildings in the various Banesh operations provides a clear indication of the urban character of Malyan in Banesh times.

The third Banesh operation (By 8) was opened to investigate the city wall. This wall, originally constructed of unfired bricks late in the Banesh Phase, was later reinforced, then abandoned, and finally reconstructed during the subsequent Kaftari Phase. The construction of a city fortification wall at such an early date, probably around 2800 B.C., must have been a consequence of unsettled political conditions, possibly related to the growing strength of pastoral nomads in the region. The interaction of settled and nomadic peoples is a major topic in our study of the site and the region.

The excavation of a deep sounding in operation H5 during the 1978 season provided some evidence of continued occupation at Malyan during the third millennium B.C. It is not clear when the Kaftari Phase began but a consistent set of 10 calibrated radiocarbon determinations indicates that it began no later than 2300 B.C. and lasted until about 1600 B.C. These dates are consistent with the currently accepted Iranian and Mesopotamian chronology.

In 1976 and 1978 several large Kaftari buildings and a stretch of street were excavated in operation GHI. Deposits in these buildings produced a large faunal collection, a fine corpus of Kaftari- and Qale-style ceramics, seals, sealings, copper door studs, human and animal figurines, clay tablets inscribed in Sumerian, and evidence that a scribal school was in operation nearby.

Two additional Kaftari operations excavated in 1976 and 1978 (FX 106 and GGX 98) revealed domestic buildings with evidence of craft production and evidence of administrative activities in the form of clay sealings. The building in operation FX 106 showed signs of major structural repairs and appears to have been occupied for a considerable length of time. Finds of travelers' water flasks and sealings at operation GGX 98, located near a presumed gate in the city wall, suggest that this area of the site may have functioned as a receiving depot for items transported to the site. Operation GGX 98 was also notable for the discovery of an abandoned Kaftari-period brickyard and the articulated skeletons of several dogs in a well.

Malyan flourished during the Kaftari Phase. Craft and administrative specialization are clearly indicated, even within our limited excavations, by the spatial segregation of a number of productive activities. Trade with Susiana, Mesopotamia, and regions to the east was an important element in the local economy. Although the Kaftari ceramic style is quite distinctive and local in distribution, stylistic parallels in glyptique, figurines, and other small finds demonstrate close cultural ties with Susiana.

Three operations excavated in 1976 revealed deposits of the Qale-Middle Elamite Phase. The Qale style ceramics found throughout this phase first appear in late Kaftari levels indicating continuous occupation at the site during the second millennium. Excavations in the large burned building (operation EDD), located on the citadel, revealed either a portico or a second courtyard similar to the one excavated in earlier seasons (Carter and Stolper, 1976). A group of ceramic kilns was discovered above the ash stratum created in this area by the fire which previously damaged the building. These kilns produced a variety of Qale ware and show that at least some parts of the building continued in use after the fire. Excavations in 1972 and 1974 (Sumner, 1974 and 1976) produced two groups of Elamite texts recording transfers of various materials and animals. The animal bones found in this building include the usual sheep, goats, and cattle, but also a relatively high density of equids and camels. The texts and the animal bones suggest that the building was a warehouse or trade depot operated by royal or temple officials.

Operation BB 33 was opened to investigate a strong magnetic anomaly discovered during the proton-magnetometer survey conducted by Dr. Elizabeth Ralph in 1972. Excavation revealed remains of five large kilns used to produce Qale-style ceramics. Dung cakes fueled one of these kilns, which had reached such a high temperature that some pots were warped and partly vitrified.

Operation XX produced a large stone-paved courtyard and badly eroded walls dating to the Qale-Middle Elamite Phase or perhaps slightly later. This operation was abandoned when ancient inverted landfill strata were discovered below the paved courtyard.

Malyan was no more than an outpost of Elamite power by the end of Middle Elamite times (ca. 1000 B.C.), when large quantities of Susiana Middle Elamite plain wares were in use along with the local Qale-style ceramics. The Middle Elamite plain wares are confined to Malyan and only a small part of the site was occupied at that time. Elsewhere in the valley a few sites were occupied by people who used Qale-style ceramics and, farther to the east, a group of sites was occupied by people who produced an entirely different style of pottery. This striking cultural diversity at about 1000 to 800 B.C. is apparently related to the arrival of tribal peoples who may have been the precursors of the Achaemenids.

Since the 1978 season we have continued our stratigraphic, architectural, and distributional analysis. The first draft manuscripts of three monograph volumes are near completion; several Ph.D. dissertations on Malyan topics are in progress or completed; and technical studies of floral (Miller, 1982) and faunal remains (Zeder, in press), clays, obsidian, plasters (Blackman, in press), scoria, and metal objects are in process.

Finally, I would like to mention that members of the National Geographic Society Board of Trustees and Research Committee visited the site in 1978 and later entertained the staff at Persepolis. This visit provided a memorable Fourth of July holiday for which we are all grateful.

REFERENCES

Blackman, M. James

____. Obsidian exchange in the Iranian highlands after 3500 B.C. Archaeol. Chem., vol. 3. (In press.)

1981. The mineralogical and chemical analysis of Banesh Period ceramics from Tal-e Malyan, Iran. *In* "Scientific Studies in Ancient Ceramics," M. J. Hughes, ed. British Museum (Natural History) Occasional Papers 19.

Carter, Elizabeth, and Stolper, Matthew

1976. Middle Elamite Elam. Expedition, vol. 18, no. 2, pp. 33-42.

Klein, J; Lerman, J. C.; Damon, P. E.; and Ralph, E. K.

1982. Calibration of radiocarbon dates: Tables based on the consensus data of the workshop of calibrating the radiocarbon time scale. Radiocarbon, vol. 24, no. 2, pp. 103-150.

Miller, Naomi Frances

1982. Economy and environment of Malyan, a third millennium B.C. urban center in southern Iran. Ph.D. dissertation, Department of Anthropology, University of Michigan. University Microfilms.

Nicholas, Ilene M.

1981. Investigating an ancient suburb: Excavations at the TUV mound, Tal-e Malyan, Iran. Expedition, vol. 23, no. 3, pp. 39-47.

Nickerson, Janet W.

1977. Malyan wall paintings. Expedition, vol. 19, no. 3, pp. 2-6.

Reiner, Erica

1973. The Location of Arshan. Revue d'Assyriologie, vol. 67, pp. 57-62.

Sumner, William M.

1974. Excavations at Tall-i Malyan, 1971-72. Iran, vol. 12, pp. 155-180.

1976. Excavations at Tall-i Malyan (Anshan) 1974. Iran, vol. 14, pp. 103-115.

Zeder, M. A.

____. Meat distribution at the highland Iranian urban center of Tal-e Malyan. *In* "Animals and Archaeology. Vol. 3: Herding in Western Asia and the Mediterranean Region, British Archaeological Reports," J. Cluttan-Brock and C. Grigsan, eds. (In press.)

W. M. Sumner

Seabird Ecology and Tick Distribution in the Western Indian Ocean

Grant Recipient: Christopher J. Feare, Ministry of Agriculture, Fisheries and Food (M.A.F.F.), Worplesdon Laboratory, Worplesdon, Surrey, England.

Grant 1638: In support of a study of seabird ecology and tick distribution in the Indian Ocean.

During a study of the breeding biology of Sooty Terns *Sterna fuscata* Linnaeus in the Seychelles in 1972-1973 fewer late-reared young survived to fledging, and they fledged at a lower weight, than chicks hatched from eggs laid at the peak of the highly synchronized laying season (Feare, 1976a). The poorer survival of these late-reared chicks was due in part to competition with and interference from older neighbors, and it was thought that after commerical exploitation (Feare, 1976b), when all late-reared chicks would be the same age and would not suffer interference from older neighbors, late chicks may survive better than in an undisturbed colony.

During the 1973 study on Bird Island about 5000 pairs of Sooty Terns deserted their eggs and chicks. This desertion was associated with a heavy infestation of ticks, *Ornithodoros capensis*, which were infected with Soldado virus. At the same time, a high incidence of developmental abnormalities was found in Bird Island Sooty Terns, and in other birds elsewhere in the Seychelles (Feare, 1976c; Bourne et al., 1977). Similar abnormalities in Common Terns *S. hirundo* Linnaeus and Roseate Terns *S. dougallii* Montagu in the eastern United States were attributed to high concentrations of pollutants (Hays and Risebrough, 1972; Gochfeld, 1971), but a sample of Desnoeufs Sooty Terns and Masked Boobies, *Sula dactylatra* Lesson, showed only low levels of DDE and PCB in 1974, although the birds were infested with Soldado virus-infected ticks.

The present expedition was planned to answer two basic questions: (1) Do late-reared chicks from exploited Sooty Tern colonies fledge heavier and survive better than late-reared chicks from unexploited colonies? (2) Are abnormalities that have been observed in seabird colonies related to the presence of tick-borne viruses or to the presence of pollutants? Answers to these two questions were sought by visiting seabird colonies in the Seychelles, Amirantes, and Farquhar Atoll in October-November

1976; this was timed to coincide with the end of the Sooty Tern breeding season, when differences between exploited and unexploited colonies should have been most visible, and when the incidence of abnormalities should have been highest (assuming that the 1973 pattern was followed).

Fledging of Late Sooty Tern Chicks

Nisbet and Drury (1972) forced Herring Gulls, *Larus argentatus* Pontoppidan, to lay late in some colonies by breaking all of those eggs that were laid early. The chicks that hatched from these late eggs survived to fledging better than did chicks reared at the same late stage in the breeding cycle in undisturbed colonies, where most chicks were much older. During commercial harvesting of Sooty Tern eggs entire colonies or parts of colonies are cleared daily of eggs, so that eggs laid after the cessation of exploitation are laid at approximately the same time, paralleling the Herring Gull situation. In this case the late-reared young from exploited tern colonies may contribute to future generations, while chicks reared late in unexploited colonies do not (Feare, 1976a). The aim of this investigation was to visit exploited and unexploited Sooty Tern colonies toward the end of their breeding season in order to establish whether there were differences between their chicks that might indicate differential survival. Comparative data collected in 1972 and 1973 were also incorporated in the analysis.

A single visit to a colony cannot provide data on chick survival, but Perrins (1966) demonstrated a relationship between early hatching and subsequent survival in Manx Shearwaters, *Puffinus puffinus* Linnaeus. Feare (1976a) found that weight at fledging and chick survival decreased seasonally in Bird Island Sooty Terns in 1973, and considered that chick weights could provide an indication of future survival. In this study, therefore, chicks from the colonies visited were weighed and those weights were used as an index of potential survival.

In order that chick weights within and between colonies, and between different years, were comparable, the chicks were assigned to age categories based on their stage of plumage development, as described and illustrated by Feare (1976a). The rate of plumage development in the Seychelles was not affected by periods of food shortage in 1973 (Feare, 1976a but cf. Ashmole, 1963) and could, therefore, be regarded as a reasonably reliable indicator of age. These plumage stages, with approximate ages in days, were: downy (D), hatching to 10 days; small wings (SW), 10-20 days; head moulting (HM), 20-32 days; down on face (DF), 32-40 days; tail cocked (TC), 40-45 days; short tail (ST), 45-55 days; tail forked (TF), 55 days to fledging. Samples of chicks from each of the plumage categories present in the colonies were weighed using a 300-g Pesola balance. Table 1 shows the colonies that were visited in 1976: Weight data were obtained only from Bird Island and Desnoeufs because only weak chicks remained on Goelette and Aride and the colonies on African Banks and Étoile were deserted. In the analysis these data are compared with weights of chicks whose growth was measured in the Bird Island colony in 1972 and 1973 (Feare, 1976a).

TABLE 1. The State of Development of the Sooty Tern Colonies Visited in 1976

Colony	*Date visited*	*State of colony*
Bird Is.	Oct. 7	Colony occupied approx. 1/3 of the area occupied in 1972 and 1973 following exploitation of peripheral areas in June. Chicks well developed with some flying.
Desnoeufs Is.	Oct. 15-16	Chicks in unexploited half of island well developed but none flying. All chicks in exploited half of island small.
Goelette, Farquhar Is.	Oct. 24	All chicks (<10,000) present fledged but most very light and too weak to fly. Presumably most chicks from this colony had left.
Étoile Is.	Nov. 2	No Sooty Terns had bred due to erosion of the island.
African Banks Is.	Nov. 5	No Sooty Terns present: All eggs had apparently been taken by fishermen and others earlier in the year.
Aride Is.	Nov. 15	Few Sooty Terns left: all fledged but many weak and unable to fly.

In 1976, assessments were made of the proportions of birds in the different plumage categories by scanning areas of each colony with binoculars and assigning each bird seen to one of the categories. This enabled birds that could fly (and could, therefore, not be caught for weighing) to be included. The 25-m^2 squares that provided the weight data for 1972 and 1973 provided samples ranging from 111 to 207 birds whose plumage categories were also recorded, and in 1976 two areas of each colony were selected at random and scanned until at least 50 birds had been recorded. In the exploited part of Desnoeufs Island, however, chick density was low and the plumage categories of only one sample of 52 chicks were recorded. Owing to the uniformity of chick development in this part of the

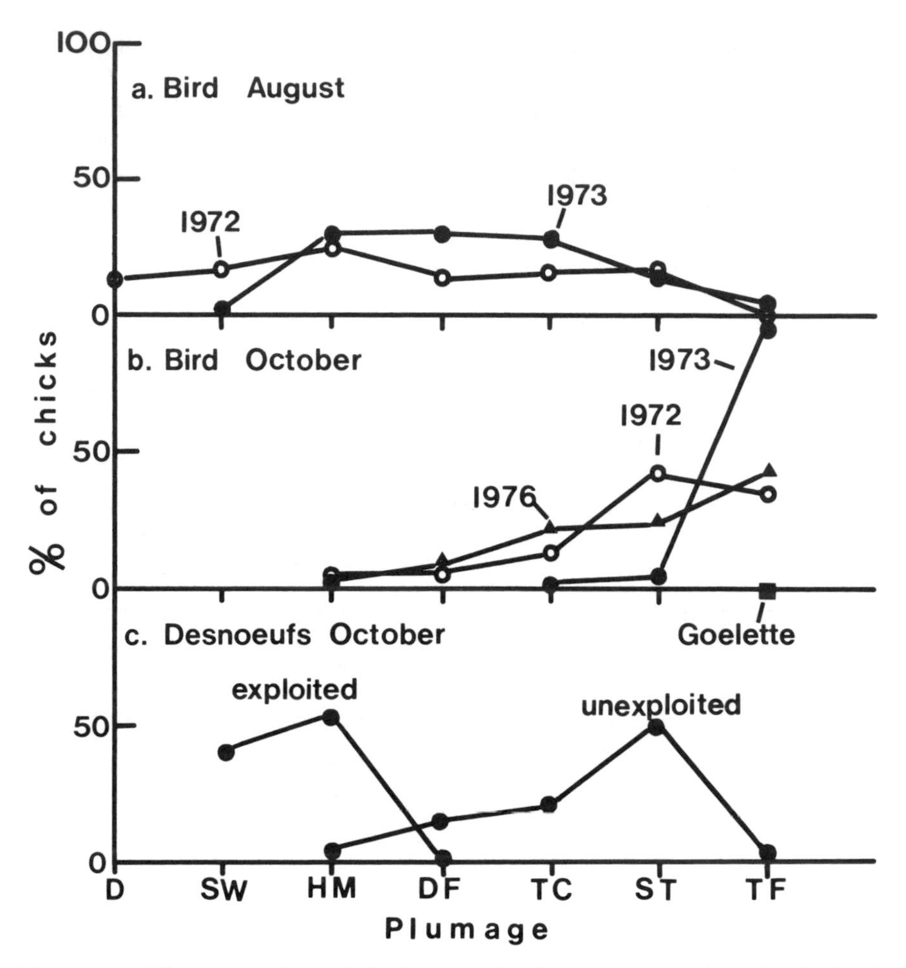

FIGURE 1. The proportion of chicks in each plumage category on Bird Island (August 1972, 1973, October 1972, 1973, 1976), on Goelette Island (October 1976) and in the exploited and unexploited halves of Desnoeufs (October 1976).

colony this small sample appeared representative of the entire exploited area.

The proportions of the various plumage (equivalent to age) categories provide a simple basis for comparing the states of development of different colonies at approximately the same time of year, and also allow comparisons of the differences in development between years in a single colony. In Figure 1a the data for Bird Island on August 17-18, 1972 and 1973 are presented graphically, and show that in 1973 the colony was more advanced than in 1972: The difference between the proportions of the plumage categories in the two years was significant ($X^2 = 32.8$, df = 6, $p<0.005$). This significant difference was maintained on October 7-8 of these two years, with most of the birds in 1973 approaching fledging or being able to fly (category TF, Fig. 1b: $X^2 = 83.3$, df = 4, $p<0.001$). Although the Bird Island colony on October 7, 1976, was less well developed than in 1973 ($X^2 = 70.2$, df = 4, $p<0.001$), there was no significant difference between colony development in 1976 and 1972 ($X^2 = 9.3$, df = 4, $p<0.05$).

All inter-island comparisons in October 1976 (Fig. 1b) showed significant differences, with Goelette Island, Farquhar Atoll, being well in advance of Bird Island ($X^2 = 71.9$, df = 4, $p<0.001$), and Bird Island in advance of the undisturbed half of Desnoeufs ($X^2 = 42.6$, df = 4, $p<0.001$). The difference between the exploited and unexploited halves of the Desnoeufs colony was highly significant ($X^2 = 170.7$, df = 5, $p<0.001$).

Figure 2 and Table 2 show the weights of chicks in the different plumage categories for Bird Island in 1972, 1973, and 1976 and for the exploited and unexploited halves of Desnoeufs in 1976. The weights of chicks from Bird Island in August 1972 and August 1973 were not significantly different, but the weights of chicks in all plumage categories available for comparison were significantly lower in October than in August in both years. Weights in October 1976 were significantly lower than in October 1972 (no comparison with October 1973 was made, as many 1973 chicks and some 1976 chicks had fledged and could not be caught, leaving only the lighter chicks). The weights of HM chicks in the exploited and unexploited parts of Desnoeufs were not significantly different.

Discussion

Following Feare's (1976b) recommendations, only Îlot Fregate (an island, predominantly of Brown Noddies, *Anous stolidus* Linnaeus, which was not visited in 1976) and Desnoeufs were commercially exploited for eggs in 1976. The considerable difference between the age structures of the exploited and unexploited halves of Desnoeufs on the October 15, 1976 visit indicated that egg collection had ceased before the end of the Sooty Tern laying season. In the exploited area eggs had all been laid at about the same time, and plumage categories were unifom (Fig. 1).

Significant differences in the age structures of the Bird Island colony in August 1972 and 1973 and in October 1972, 1973, and 1976 indicate that peak laying occurred at different times in each of these years. Ridley and Percy (1958) showed that the date of initiation of laying varied annually, and they suggested that it was related to the onset of the southeast trade winds which blow from May to October, with annual variations, in the Seychelles. However, at latitude 10°S the southeast trades blow for most

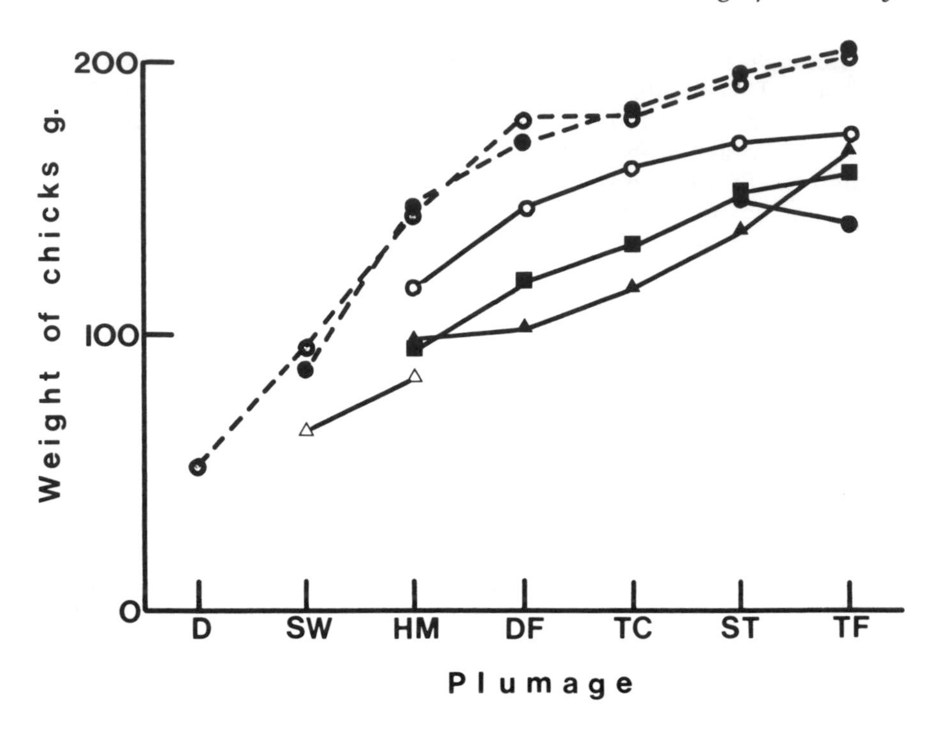

FIGURE 2. Mean weights of chicks in the plumage categories on Bird Island in August 1972 (●----●), August 1973 (○----○), October 1972 (●——●), October 1973 (○——○), October 1976 (■——■), and on Desnoeufs, exploited (△——△) and unexploited (▲——▲) in October 1976.

of the year and yet Sooty Terns breed annually at this latitude on Goelette Island, Farquhar Atoll, at approximately the same time that they breed in the Seychelles and Amirantes colonies. Although the age structure of the Goelette Island colony in October 1976 showed this colony to be well in advance of more northerly colonies, the Bird Island colony was more advanced than the undisturbed part of Desnoeufs, 300 km to the south. This suggests that there is no simple relationship between the onset of breeding and the northerly advance of the southeast trade winds across the western Indian Ocean in April, May, and June. Furthermore, Ridley and Percy (1958) reported that laying on African Banks began earlier than on other islands in the Seychelles and Amirantes, and this was confirmed by Feare (1979) who found that in July 1974 hatching had begun and laying ceased on African Banks while on Bird Island laying had only just begun. Thus, although laying does occur during the southeast-trade-wind period on all islands, variations in the laying periods on different islands suggest that on each island the onset of laying is linked to unknown local factors, which presumably include food availability.

Despite differences in the age structures of the Bird Island colony in August 1972 and 1973, there were no significant differences in the weights of chicks in the plumage categories (Fig. 2 and Table 2). The significant differences between the weights of chicks in all plumage categories in October 1972 and October 1976 indicate annual variations in the abilities of late chicks to attain high fledging weights. However, the similarity between October 1976 weights on Bird Island and Desnoeufs (unexploited half) suggest that, in this year at least, colonies in the Seychelles and Amirantes were subject to similar feeding conditions.

TABLE 2. Mean Weights of Chicks in the Plumage Categories on Bird Island
The t-test significance levels are shown with degrees of freedom in parentheses.

Years and months compared	*Plumage categories*					
	SW	*HM*	*DF*	*TC*	*ST*	*TF*
Aug. 1972, 1973[a]	NS(20)	NS(79)	NS(62)	NS(63)	NS(40)	NS(2)
Aug. and Oct. 1972[a]		<0.001(29)	<0.02(19)	<0.05(29)	<0.001(65)	<0.05(39)
Aug. and Oct. 1973[a]					<0.001(28)	<0.001(61)
Oct. 1972, 1976[a]		<0.01(13)	<0.01(22)	<0.01(19)	<0.02(54)	<0.001(52)
Oct. 1976[b]		NS(13)	<0.05(28)	NS(20)	NS(19)	<0.02(18)
Oct. 1976[c]		NS(28)				

[a] Bird Island.
[b] Bird and Desnoeufs Islands, unexploited.
[c] Desnoeufs Island, exploited and unexploited.

Chick weights in October were lower than those of chicks in August, suggesting that in October food was scarcer or adults were less able to locate it (Feare, 1981) and the October chicks, therefore, may survive less well (Feare, 1976a). After leaving their colonies in the Dry Tortugas, Florida, juvenile Sooty Terns migrate across the Atlantic to the Gulf of Guinea, and Robertson (1969) thought that the route they took had evolved in order to reduce the likelihood of their encountering cyclones. The recovery of a banded Bird Island juvenile Sooty Tern in northern Australia suggests that western Indian Ocean birds also undertake a long post-fledging migration, and it must be equally important for these birds to avoid the cyclone tracks that lie generally to the south of Seychelles and that usually begin in October. Birds leaving the colonies early may, therefore, stand a better chance of post-fledging survival than those leaving late, and low-weight birds from late eggs will be at a disadvantage.

The weights of chicks from the exploited part of the Desnoeufs colony were similar to the October weights of chicks from the unexploited part and from Bird Island. They appeared, therefore, to derive no benefit from all being at approximately the same stage of development. Assuming that these chicks developed at the same rate as earlier chicks they would not have fledged until mid-November, about two months later than chicks from main season eggs. It is unlikely that such late chicks would have a high fledging or post-fledging success, and they probably contribute no more to future generations than the late chicks from undisturbed colonies.

Tick Infestations of Seabird Colonies

Two species of tick, the ixodid *Amblyomma loculosum* Neumann and the argasid *Ornithodoros capensis* Neumann, occur in seabird colonies in the Seychelles and Amirantes (Hoogstraal et al., 1976; Converse et al., 1975). Aride virus, an agent new to science, was discovered in *A. loculosum* taken from dead and dying adult Roseate Terns, *Sterna dougallii* Montague, found on Bird Island in 1973 (Converse et al., 1976) and presumed to have come from the nearest breeding colony on Aride Island. *A. loculosum* also bites humans and has a wide distribution in the Indo-Pacific Oceans (Hoogstraal et al., 1976). On Bird Island in 1973 a heavy infestation of *O. capensis,* which appeared to be responsible for the desertion of their eggs and chicks of about 5000 pairs of Sooty Terns, was found to be infected with Soldado virus. The deserted area of the Sooty Tern colony was not reoccupied in 1974, when the tick infestation was still heavy (Feare, 1976c). Humans working in the deserted area were frequently bitten and experienced pruritus which lasted for several days.

Several abnormal Sooty Tern chicks were seen in 1973, especially late in the season, the most common abnormality being loss of growing remiges and rectrices. This kind of abnormality has been reported in tern colonies on the east coast of the United States, where Hays and Risebrough (1972) and Gochfeld (1971) attributed it to high concentrations of pollutants. However, low pollutant concentrations in Sooty Tern and Masked Booby eggs from Desnoeufs suggested to Bourne et al. (1977) that the observed abnormalities may have been associated with the tick-borne virus.

O. capensis has been found on islands throughout the tropical oceans and from East African lakes, and Soldado virus has been isolated from ticks collected in the Indian, Pacific, and Atlantic Oceans (Hoogstraal and Feare, 1984). In Europe, Soldado virus has also been isolated from the closely related *O. maritimus* Vermeil et Marguet. On islands in the Persian Gulf and off southern Arabia, however, seabird colonies are infested with another closely related tick, *O. muesebecki* Hoogstraal (Hoogstraal et al., 1970) from which a closely related Hughes serogroup virus, Zirqa, has been isolated (Varma et al., 1973). A seabird host common to both *O. muesebecki* in Arabian waters and *O. capensis* in the Amirantes is the Masked Booby, of which a distinct subspecies, *Sula dactylatra melanops* Heuglin, is endemic to the western Indian Ocean, but it is likely that other seabird species common to these two areas will be found to be host to the two tick species.

The aims of this part of the expedition were to (1) establish the distribution of ticks and virus infections in seabird colonies, (2) collect livers of small samples of seabirds from various colonies for subsequent pollutant analysis, (3) assess the incidence of abnormally-developed seabirds in different colonies, and (4) band Masked Boobies in an attempt to initiate a banding program that would eventually establish whether there was any overlap in the dispersal of the *O. capensis*- and *O. muesebecki*-infested populations.

On all seabird islands visited (Fig. 3), ticks were searched for in nests or scrapes, and under stones, litter, or vegetation in and near breeding colonies. Where young birds were present they were examined for ticks especially on the feet, head, and in the skin folds under the wings. All ticks found (except on Goelette Island where they were too numerous) were collected and kept alive for subsequent identification and virological examination.

Livers were collected from small samples of birds, mainly Sooty Terns, on Bird Island, Desnoeufs, and Goelette Island and preserved in 10% formalin in glass jars for subsequent pollutant analysis. The Sooty Tern livers included one from the only chick found with feather abnormalities (on Bird Island); in addition, the livers of two Crab Plovers, *Dromas ardeola* Paykull, found unable to stand, were collected. Feather and other abnormalities were looked for while birds were being handled during banding. Sooty Tern and Masked Booby pulli were caught by day, but fledged young and adult Masked Boobies were caught at night by dazzling them with a torch.

Table 3 shows the islands that were searched for ticks, the seabird species examined, the ticks found, and those from which Soldado virus was isolated. Ticks and Soldado virus were found on five islands, associated with three species of bird.

In the Bird Island Sooty Tern colony chicks were well grown and some had fledged (Fig. 1). Although broken eggshells indicated that in 1976 eggs had been laid in the area deserted in 1973, the absence of chicks suggested that the area had not been successfully recolonized. This deserted area was more vegetated, especially with *Suriana maritima* Linnaeus, than in 1973 and 1974, and *O. capensis* appeared to be much less abundant than in those years, although in no year was tick density measured.

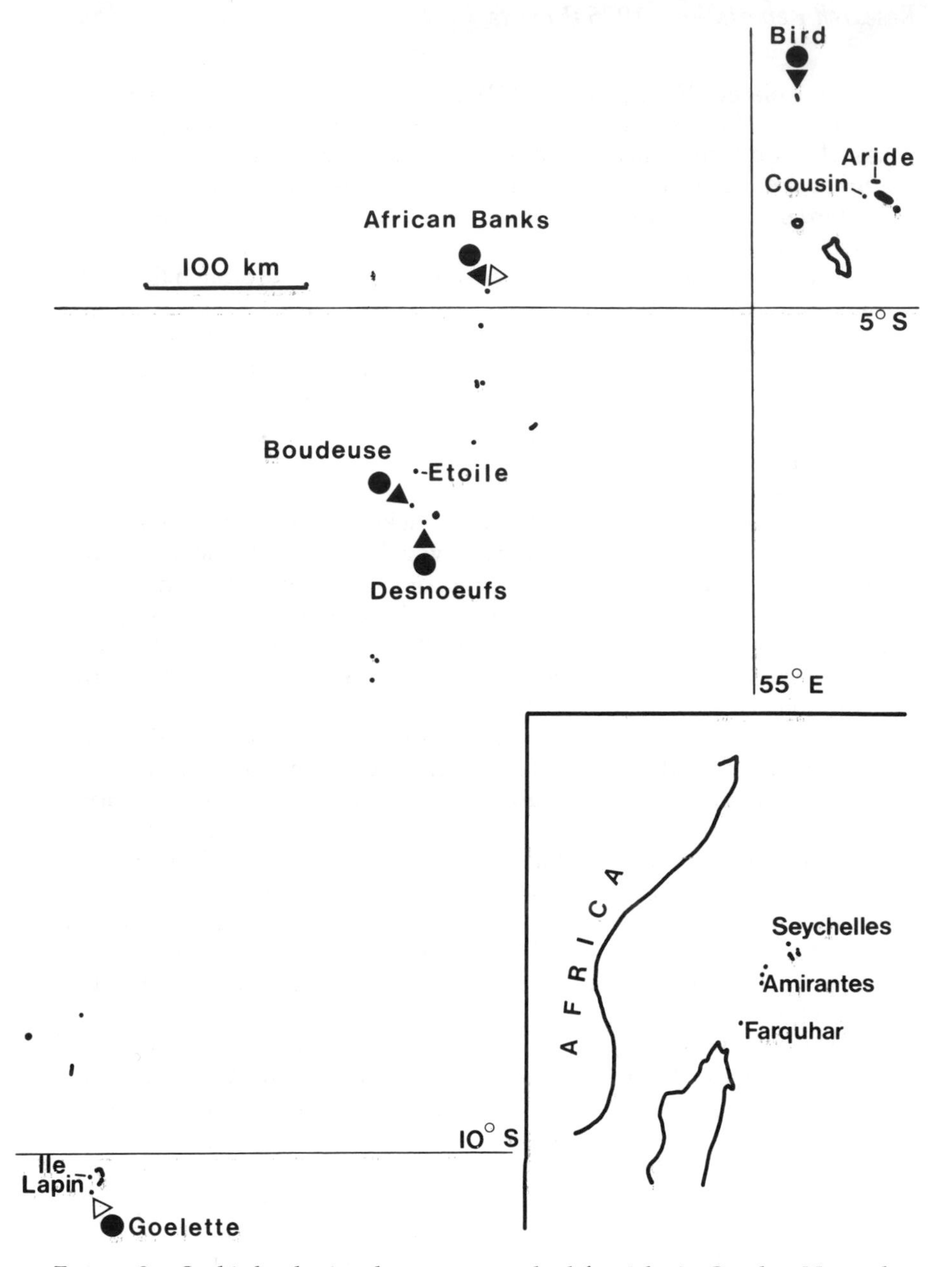

FIGURE 3. Seabird colonies that were searched for ticks in October-November 1976. Solid triangles = *Ornithodoros capensis* found; open triangles = *Amblyomma loculosum* found; solid circles = Soldado virus isolated. In addition to these collections, *O. capensis* is known from Cousin and *A. loculosum* from Cousin and Desnoeufs. *A. loculosum* has been collected on Mahe and Mamelles (Seychelles) and both species probably occur on Aride (see Hoogstraal and Feare, 1984).

On Aride most Sooty Terns and all Roseate Terns had left and searches of the ground and vegetation in nesting areas revealed no ticks despite reports of heavy infestations at the peak of breeding (A. W. Diamond and S. Warman, pers. comm.). Ticks were not found in nest sites or on chicks of all ages of White-tailed Tropic Birds, *Phaethon lepturus* Daudin, on Aride or Cousin.

No ticks were found in the deserted Sooty Tern nesting area on African Banks. However, *O. capensis* was found in two small colonies of Black-naped Terns, *Sterna sumatrana* Raffles, in the area usually occupied by Sooty Terns. In addition, adult *O. capensis* were found under stones and wood around the edge of the abandoned Sooty Tern breeding area and also under the leaf sheaths of a coconut tree, *Cocos nucifera* Linnaeus, where an adult *A. loculosum* was also found.

Although ticks were not found in occupied Sooty Tern, Brown Noddy, or Wedge-tailed Shearwater, *Puffinus pacificus* Gmelin, colonies on Desnoeufs, *O. capensis* was found in Masked Booby nests. On Boudeuse *O. capensis* was found in Masked Booby nests and on chicks, and one or more of the adults collected oviposited in the collecting tubes so that many larvae were present at the time of identification (November 29, 1976).

Goelette Island, Farquhar Atoll, was infested with *A. loculosum*, especially in areas of the plant *Achyranthes aspera* Linnaeus. In different clumps of this plant, tick development appeared to be localized: From some clumps observers emerged with legs covered in larvae, while from other clumps nymphs and adults were found on observers' legs. Bites sustained by humans (4 in the groin, 2 on shin, 1 on neck, and 1 on wrist) did not itch or produce inflammation. Under one area of *A. aspera* a large number of broken Sooty Tern eggs, but with no dead or living chicks, were reminiscent of the 1973 hatching failure on Bird Island. All Sooty Tern chicks present were well developed (Fig. 1) and many had presumably left the island. The weak and underweight chicks that remained, and the many recently dead chicks, were heavily infested with *A. loculosum*. Ticks were found on the nape, crown, forehead, chin, and feet, but the majority were attached in the feathered part of the tibia, under the wing (48 under one wing of one chick), and on the blood-filled bases of growing primaries (these bled profusely when ticks were removed).

Livers were analyzed for DDE, PCB, and total mercury, and the results of these analyses are given in Table 4. Both DDE and PCB were present in all birds but only at low levels. Similarly, mercury was present at low levels in the terns examined, but at higher levels in the two Crab Plovers.

None of the many Sooty Tern chicks found recently dead on Goelette Island showed signs of abnormal development, and no abnormally-developed birds were seen on Desnoeufs or Aride. On Bird Island one

TABLE 3. Bird Species Examined and Ticks Found on the Islands Visited in October-November 1976

Location; date; bird species	*Tick species*	*No. of ticks collected* ♂	♀	*N*	*L*	*Soldado virus*[1]
Bird Is., Oct. 7						
Sterna fuscata-ground in deserted area	*Ornithodoros capensis*	12	15	10	–	+
Sterna fuscata-ground in occupied colony	"	40	23	2	–	+
Aride Is., Nov. 15						
Sterna fuscata-20 weak chicks and ground in colony	–	–	–	–	–	
Sterna dougallii-unoccupied colony	–	–	–	–	–	
Phaethon lepturus-nests and chicks	–	–	–	–	–	
Cousin Is., Nov. 16						
Phaethon lepturus-nests and chicks	–	–	–	–	–	
African Banks Is., Nov. 4-5						
Sterna fuscata-unoccupied colony	–	–	–	–	–	
Sterna fuscata-ground at edge of colony	*Ornithodoros capensis*	9	3	–	–	+
Sterna fuscata-coconut leaf sheaths	"	17	14	–	–	–
Sterna fuscata-coconut leaf sheaths	*Amblyomma loculosum*	–	1	–	–	Not examined
Sterna sumatrana-nests	*Ornithodoros capensis*	11	1	–	25	+
Sterna sumatrana-chicks	"	–	–	3	–	–

Étoile Is., Nov. 2						
Anous stolidus-old nests	–	–	–	–	–	
Boudeuse Is., Nov. 1						
Sula dactylatra-nests	*Ornithodoros capensis*	14	12	6	c.400	+
Sula dactylatra-2 chicks	"	–	–	9	–	–
Desnoeufs Is., Oct. 15-16						
Sterna fuscata-ground + 230 chicks	–	–	–	–	–	
Anous stolidus-25 occupied nest (eggs)	–	–	–	–	–	
Puffinus pacificus-10 occupied burrows	–	–	–	–	–	
Sula dactylatra-12 nests with chicks	*Ornithodoros capensis*	35	6	3	–	+
Goelette and Farquhar Is., Oct. 24						
Sterna fuscata-chicks	*Amblyomma loculosum*	10	9	8	–	–
Sterna fuscata-dead chicks	"	8	11	12	–	+
Sterna fuscata-walking on and biting humans	"	–	–	11	–	–
Île Lapin and Farquhar Is., Oct. 25						
Sula leucogaster-4 nests (eggs)	–	–	–	–	–	
Ardea cinerea-6 nests (unoccupied + chicks)	–	–	–	–	–	

[1] A "+" means the virus was isolated from ticks.

TABLE 4. DDE, PCB, and Total Mercury Residues in the Livers of Seabirds from Three Western Indian Ocean Islands, and of Two Weak Crab Plovers

Species	Collecting site	Percent lipid	Residues		
			DDE ppm wet wt (ppm lipid)	PCB ppm	Mercury ppm wet wt
Sterna fuscata adult	Bird Is.	1.39	0.32(23.0)	<0.05	NA
" chick[1]	"	1.54	0.12(8.0)	<0.05	0.09
" chick[2]	"	2.73	0.11(4.0)	<0.05	0.15
Anous stolidus adult	"	2.21	0.17(8.0)	<0.05	NA
Sterna fuscata chicks	Desnoeufs Is.	1.89	0.17(9.0)	<0.05	0.12
"	"	1.88	0.04(2.3)	<0.05	0.20
"	"	3.33	0.03(0.9)	<0.05	0.13
"	Goelette, Farquhar Is.	2.70	0.10(3.0)	<0.05	0.20
" (dead)	"	2.48	0.25(10.2)	<0.05	0.23
"	"	1.45	0.28(19.2)	<0.05	0.33
" (dead)	"	2.49	0.05(2.2)	<0.05	0.32
Dromas ardeola[3]	Marie Louise Is.	2.14	0.14(6.0)	<0.05	1.99
"	"	3.04	0.10(3.0)	<0.05	3.08

[1] Chick with wings drooping (see Gochfeld, 1971).
[2] Chick which had lost remiges and rectrices, new pins showing.
[3] The two juvenile *Dromas ardeola* were found weak and unable to stand. Other juveniles and adults on the island apparently were healthy.

chick out of 55 examined had lost remiges and rectrices, and a second was trailing its wings on the ground. However, as many chicks had fledged and had either left the colony, or were still present but uncatchable, this represents a very small proportion of abnormalities compared with the 4.5% found in 1973 (Feare, 1976c).

None of the 186 Sooty Tern chicks banded in 1976 (19 on Bird Island, 131 on Desnoeufs, 20 on Goelette, and 16 on Aride) has so far been recovered; 35 Masked Boobies (12 pulli, 23 adults) were banded on Desnoeufs, and 365 (183 pulli, 154 fledglings, 28 adults) were banded on Boudeuse. One of the Boudeuse fledglings was recovered at Porbandar, India, on June 9, 1977.

Discussion

The discovery of *O. capensis* on Boudeuse represents a new distribution record for western Indian Ocean islands, and *S. sumatrana* has not previously been recorded as a host for this tick. Soldado virus has not previously been recorded from *O. capensis* on African Banks or Boudeuse, and the infection of *A. loculosum* on Goelette Island with Soldado virus is the first record of this agent from an ixodid tick. These data, together with previous information (Hoogstraal et al., 1976; Converse et al., 1975) from these islands, have been reviewed by Hoogstraal and Feare (1984). In addition, a new species of *Babesia*, probably transmitted by *A. loculosum*, was discovered in the blood smears of two Masked Booby chicks on Desnoeufs in 1976 (Peirce and Feare, 1978).

O. capensis and Soldado virus are now known to be widely distributed in seabird colonies in these islands. On Bird Island the annual cycle of the tick is closely tied to that of the Sooty Tern, and a similar situation appears to prevail on African Banks where in July 1974, when Sooty Tern eggs were beginning to hatch, ticks were readily found in scrapes in the colony, but were only found hidden in debris and vegetation around the periphery of the Sooty Tern breeding area in November 1976. That this annual cycle can apparently be modified, however, was shown by tick activity in the small parts of the deserted Sooty Tern colony occupied by small numbers of Black-naped Terns. The annual cycle of *O. capensis* is less clear on islands where seabirds breed aseasonally. For example, nymphs and larvae were found on White-tailed Tropic Bird chicks on Cousin Island in July 1974, but were not found on chicks present here and on Aride in November 1976, suggesting an annual cycle similar to that observed on Bird Island, although more supporting data are required. In the Masked Booby colony on Desnoeufs, on the other hand, active ticks were found both in July 1974 and in October 1976: Ticks on the Boudeuse Masked Booby colony were also actively feeding in November

1976. Normally, however, there seems to be a single generation each year with nymphs moulting to adults in the middle of the host's breeding season (H. Hoogstraal, pers. comm.).

The data currently available suggest that the annual cycle of *A. loculosum* may also vary on different islands. On African Banks in July 1974, at the height of the Sooty Tern breeding season, *A. loculosum* was extremely abundant, but in November 1976 only one aestivating individual was found, suggesting an annual cycle synchronized with that of the terns. On Goelette Island, on the other hand, all stages of the *A. loculosum* life cycle were present at the end of the Sooty Tern breeding season. Reasons for the remarkable abundance of *A. loculosum* on Goelette and its abundance on African Banks, in comparison with its scarcity on Bird Island (? and Desnoeufs), are not understood. Insufficient data are available for an assessment of tick status on Cousin and Aride.

The desertion of part of the Bird Island Sooty Tern breeding colony and subsequent death of chicks (Feare, 1976c) and the isolation of Soldado virus from ticks removed from dead chicks on Goelette (Table 3) strongly suggests that this virus may produce lethal effects. The absence of significant pollutant residues in Masked Boobies and Sooty Terns from western Indian Ocean islands (Table 4 and Bourne et al., 1977), and especially from the Bird Island Sooty Tern chick that had shed growing remiges and rectrices (Table 4), leaves tick-borne arboviruses as possible candidates responsible for developmental abnormalities but this requires experimental investigations.

Acknowledgments

This expedition was financed entirely by the National Geographic Society. Tick identifications and virus isolations were undertaken by Drs. Harry Hoogstraal and James D. Converse, U. S. Naval Medical Research Unit No. 3, Cairo. Pollutant residues were analyzed by Dr. James A. Bogan, Department of Veterinary Pharmacology, Glasgow University (DDE and PCB), and by Dr. Peter I. Stanley and the Biochemistry Department of the M.A.F.F. Pest Infestation Control Laboratory, Tolworth (mercury). Dr. Ian R. Inglis suggested improvements to a draft of this report. This project has benefited from the constant encouragement and assistance given by Harry Hoogstraal, and we are grateful to him and to all of the other people and organizations mentioned above for their help.

REFERENCES

Ashmole, N. P.
1963. The biology of the Wideawake or Sooty Tern *Sterna fuscata* on Ascension. Ibis, vol. 103b, pp. 297-364.

BOURNE, W.R.P.; BOGAN, J. A.; BULLOCK, D.; DIAMOND, A. W.; and FEARE, C. J.
1977. Abnormal terns, sick sea and shore birds, organochlorines and arboviruses in the Indian Ocean. Mar. Pollut. Bull., vol. 8, pp. 154-158.

CONVERSE, J. D.; HOOGSTRAAL, H.; MOUSSA, M. I.; FEARE, C. J.; and KAISER, M. N.
1975. Soldado virus (Hughes Group) from *Ornithodoros (Alectorobius) capensis* (Ixodoidae : Argasidae) infesting Sooty Tern colonies in the Seychelles, Indian Ocean. Amer. Journ. Trop. Med. Hyg., vol. 24, pp. 1010-1018.

CONVERSE, J. D.; HOOGSTRAAL, H.; MOUSSA, M. I.; KAISER, M. N.; CASALS, J.; and FEARE, C. J.
1976. Aride virus, a new ungrouped arbovirus infecting *Amblyomma loculosum* ticks from Roseate Terns in the Seychelles. Arch. Virol., vol. 50, pp. 237-240

FEARE, C. J.
1976a. The breeding of the Sooty Tern *Sterna fuscata* in the Seychelles and the effects of experimental removal of its eggs. Journ. Zool. London vol. 179, pp. 317-360.
1976b. The exploitation of Sooty Tern eggs in the Seychelles. Biol. Conserv., vol. 10, pp. 169-182.
1976c. Desertion and abnormal development in a colony of Sooty Terns infested by virus-infected ticks. Ibis, vol. 118, pp. 112-115.
1979. Ecological observations on African Banks, Amirantes. Atoll Res. Bull., no. 227, pp. 1-7.
1981. Breeding schedules and feeding strategies of Seychelles seabirds. Ostrich, vol. 52, pp. 179-185.

GOCHFELD, M.
1971. Premature feather-loss—a "new disease" of Common Terns on Long Island, New York. King bird, vol. 21, pp. 206-211.

HAYS, H., and RISEBROUGH, R. W.
1972. Pollutant concentrations in abnormal terns from Long Island Sound. Auk, vol. 89, pp. 19-35.

HOOGSTRAAL, H.; OLIVER, R. M.; and GUIRGIS, S. S.
1970. Larva, nymph and life cycle of *Ornithodoros (Alectorobius) muesebecki* (Ixodoidae, Argasidae), a virus-infected parasite of birds and petroleum industry employees in the Arabian Gulf. Ann. Entomol. Soc. Am., vol. 63, pp. 1762-1768.

HOOGSTRAAL, H.; WASSEF, H. Y.; CONVERSE, J. D.; KEIRANS, J. E.; CLIFFORD, C. M.; and FEARE, C. J.
1976. *Amblyomma loculosum* (Ixodoidea:Ixodidae) identity, marine bird and human hosts, virus infection and distribution in the southern oceans. Ann. Entomol. Soc. Am., vol. 69, pp. 3-14.

HOOGSTRAAL, H., and FEARE, C. J.
1984. Ticks and tickborne viruses. Pp. 267-280 *in* "Biogeography and Ecology of the Seychelles Islands," D. R. Stoddart, ed. The Hague: W. Junk.

NISBET, I.C.T., and DRURY, W. H.
1972. Post fledging survival in Herring Gulls in relation to brood-size and date of hatching. Bird-Banding, vol. 43, pp. 161-172.

PERRINS, C. M.
1966. Survival of young Manx Shearwaters *Puffinus puffinus* in relation to their presumed date of hatching. Ibis, vol. 108, pp. 132-135.
PEIRCE, M. A., and FEARE, C. J.
1978. Piroplasmosis in the Masked Booby. Bull. Br. Orn. Club., vol. 98, no. 2, pp. 38-40.
RIDLEY, M. W., and PERCY, R.
1958. The exploitation of sea birds' eggs in the Seychelles. Col. Res. Stud., no. 25, pp. 1-78.
ROBERTSON, W. B., JR.
1969. Transatlantic migration of juvenile Sooty Terns. Nature, vol. 223, pp. 632-634.
VARMA, M.G.R.; BOWEN, E.T.W.; SIMPSON, D.I.H.; and CASALS, J.
1973. Zirqa virus, a new arbovirus isolated from bird-infesting ticks. Nature, vol. 244, p. 452.

CHRISTOPHER J. FEARE
F. CHRISTINE FEARE

Field Study and Collection of Rattan Palms in Asian Rain Forests

Grant Recipient: Jack B. Fisher, Fairchild Tropical Garden, Miami, Florida.

Grant 1686: For field study and collection of anatomical samples of rattan palms in Asian rain forests.

Rattans, the climbing palms of the Old World, form a conspicuous element in the rain forests of southeast Asia. Many of the more than 500 species of rattans are of economic importance. They have a wide range of local uses and are important internationally in the cane trade. However, since all of these palms are very spiny and difficult to collect and to study, we have only a superficial knowledge of their biology. Recently, the field biology and classification of rattans have been undertaken by Dr. John Dransfield of the Royal Botanic Garden, Kew, England. My own interest in the development of form in tropical plants led me to study rattans, since they exhibit two very unusual features of organization. First, the barbed, whiplike inflorescence in many species of *Calamus* and the stouter inflorescences of *Ceratolobus* and *Daemonorops* arise from the top of the leaf sheath instead of from the stem directly above the leaf which is the typical position. Second, the vegetative or sucker buds of some species of *Daemonorops* arise 180° away from the normal site of such buds, that is, they are leaf-opposed. The evolutionary and biological significance of these features can only be understood by carefully studying the microscopic initiation and early development of the organs involved. To do this, the growing points of the palms must be carefully dissected and immediately preserved (fixed) in the field. John Dransfield and I had previously collaborated on rattan studies (Fisher and Dransfield, 1977), and we joined forces again in Malaysia while he was writing a forester's manual on rattans at the Forest Research Institute, Kepong. We collected together in the rain forests of the Malay Peninsula, and I proceeded to Java, where the staff of the Kebun Raya (Botanic Garden) at Bogor assisted me in field collecting. While there, I met botanist Johanis Mogea and began a collaborative study with him of unusual bud development in the salak palm, *Salacca* (Fisher and Mogea, 1980).

We have discovered that the rattans have a wide range in sucker development, including the presence of leaf-opposed buds, that is of taxonomic significance in two sections of *Daemonorops* (Fisher and Dransfield,

1979). The new information should be especially useful to horticulturists interested in propagating the commercial rattans. The continued destruction of primary forests is making it necessary to cultivate rattans to supply the cane market. A study of rattan shoot development was also made for the first time (Fisher, 1978a). The relationship between leaf and stem growth was quantitatively described and will serve as a foundation for future physiological or developmental studies of rattans and other palms.

While I was traveling in Malaysia, Indonesia, the Philippines, and Hawaii, I was able to collect data and specimens related to several other research projects. The branching angles of selected tropical trees were taken from many individuals growing in the botanical gardens in Bogor (Java), Singapore, University of the Philippines, and the University of Hawaii. This information was combined with a theoretical study of branching patterns in tropical trees based upon simulations of theoretical trees by computer (Fisher and Honda, 1979). In addition, material was collected for a survey of bud development in the banana and its botanical relatives. Wild and cultivated bananas and a rare banana relative, *Orchidantha* (Loweaceae), known only from Malaya, were collected. The completed study has shown that all species of the banana genus, *Musa,* have unusual leaf-opposed buds (Fisher, 1978b). The typical axillary buds are present in all the relatives of *Musa,* indicating that this group is a very natural one. Samples of wood from branches and buttress roots of forest trees were also collected and used as part of two extensive surveys of wood structure in tropical trees (Fisher, 1982; Fisher and Stevenson, 1981).

A popular account of a botanist's travels has been given to the members of Fairchild Tropical Garden (Fisher, 1978c). Altogether anatomical material of 96 species of plants was collected, including 34 species of rattans in 10 genera. In addition, 32 species of living plants or seed were brought back for growing in the Fairchild Tropical Garden. The results of this six-week field trip demonstrate how much is still to be learned about tropical plants and emphasize the need for continued field studies in the tropics.

REFERENCES

FISHER, J. B.

1978a. A quantitative description of shoot development in three rattan palms. Malaysian Forester, vol. 41, pp. 280-293.

1978b. Leaf-opposed buds in *Musa:* Their development and a comparison with allied monocotyledons. Amer. Journ. Bot., vol. 65, pp. 784-791.

1978c. Thorns and ants: A Malaysian expedition. Fairchild Tropical Garden Bull., vol. 33, no. 3, pp. 10-14.

1982. A survey of buttress and aerial roots of tropical trees for the presence of reaction wood. Biotropica, vol. 14, pp. 56-61.

FISHER, J. B., and DRANSFIELD, J.

1977. Comparative morphology and development of inflorescence adnation in rattan palms. Bot. Journ. Linnean Soc., vol. 75, pp. 119-140.

1979. Development of axillary and leaf-opposed vegetative buds in rattan palms. Ann. Bot., vol. 44, pp. 57-66.

FISHER, J. B., and HONDA, H.

1979. Branch geometry and effective leaf area: A study of *Terminalia*-branching. 1. Theoretical trees. 2. Survey of real trees. Amer. Journ. Bot., vol. 66, pp. 633-644, 645-655.

FISHER, J. B., and MOGEA, J. P.

1980. Intrapetiolar buds in *Salacca* (Palmae): Development and significance. Bot. Journ. Linn. Soc., vol. 81, pp. 47-59.

FISHER, J. B., and STEVENSON, J. W.

1981. Occurrence of reaction wood in branches of dicotyledons and its role in tree architecture. Bot. Gaz., vol. 142, pp. 82-95.

JACK B. FISHER

Mountain Gorilla Research, 1977-1979

Grant Recipient: Dian Fossey, Karisoke Research Centre, Ruhengeri, Rwanda.

Grants 1701, 1818, 1974: Further support of long-term field observations of the behavior and ecology of the mountain gorilla *(Gorilla gorilla beringei).*

The Karisoke Research Centre was established in September 1967 by the author for the purposes of long-term investigation into the behavior of the endangered mountain gorilla *(Gorilla gorilla beringei),* which exists only within the Virunga Volcanoes of Uganda, Zaire, and Rwanda. Census work conducted from Karisoke in 1976 accounted for 205 gorillas remaining within the 375-km^2 area set aside for their protection in 1925. The Karisoke Research Centre has been generously supported by the National Geographic Society since its commencement in 1967. Now in its 10th year of operation, the Centre continues to maintain a consistency of behavioral observations with gorillas whose achieved habituation greatly facilitates data accumulation.

Part I—Research 1977

Throughout 1977 the Karisoke Research Centre maintained near daily observations among 33 habituated gorillas of the 3 main study groups and 40 lesser habituated gorillas of 6 fringe groups, groups whose ranges overlap or abut ranges of the main study groups. Demographic changes and observational records from these groups are summarized. In 1977 research was also concentrated upon infant development and parturition. These topics are presented here, as is the observation by Kelly Stewart of a birth in the wild.

During 1977 the author was assisted for varying periods of time by Kelly Stewart, Ian Redmond, and Mr. and Mrs. Warren Garst.

Demography

By the end of 1977, among the 73 gorillas under observation from Karisoke, there was an adult male-to-female ratio of 1:1.8, an immature male-to-female ratio of 1:1.2, and an overall adult-to-immature ratio of 1:0.66 (see Table 1). For the second consecutive year there was a slight improvement in the female-to-male ratios for both adults and immatures, while the overall adult-to-immature ratio remained exactly as it was in 1976, a trend that, hopefully, should improve with the higher female counts within the study population. Also, in contrast to 1976, the number of individuals either permanently in residence or temporarily visiting the Karisoke study area increased by 15, which represents 14% of the entire Virunga population. Despite the slaying of 1 of the study-group silverbacks in 1977, it is strongly believed that the ultimate survival of the species will depend upon the remainder of the Virungas gaining at least as much security as is offered within the Karisoke study area.

Study and Fringe Group Observations

Group 4

During 1977 Group 4 added 3 km^2 to its previous range of 4.25 km^2. The additional land was first "surveyed" by Group 4 in a series of exploratory sallies into the far southwestern saddle region, most of which lies in Zaire and leads toward Mts. Mikeno and Karisimbi. Group 4, never known to use this area before, indicated its lack of familiarity with it by the use of circuitous trails, many in areas of extremely poor food resources. On several occasions the group appeared lost, and once directly retraced its own trail back to more familiar terrain. The gorillas then used the same night nests for 2 nights in succession, something never before known to have occurred. In unknown terrain they tended to travel in a "musical chair" style, settling for longer periods than usual when finding small plots of suitable vegetation. On Visoke's slopes the majority of time was spent in their old core region in the west, above the nettle slopes; in March however, they traveled to the alpine zone above 11,600 ft for the rare fruiting *Pygeum* tree and *Senecio* roots.

Elephants affected Group 4's saddle travel during April and November in its newly acquired portion of the southwestern saddle and, since gorillas prefer fresh, untrampled vegetation, Group 4 returned to Visoke's slopes. One correlation between elephant-and-gorilla-shared terrain, never fully realized until 1977, is that in the dry months (May-July, December), elephants need areas of permanent water availability; these are found only in small lakes on Karisimbi's high alpine meadows or about 12,000-13,000 ft in scrubbrush and bamboo regions lying around 8000-9000 ft in the Zairoise sector of the Virungas. The absence of elephants prompts gorillas to explore the saddle region more frequently during the months elephants and, to a lesser extent, buffalo are ranging within dependable water sources.

TABLE 1. Composition of Study and Fringe Groups at End of 1977 within Karisoke Study Area (25 km²)
Group names: N=Nunkie's, B=Basher's, W=Wageni's, C=Chui, B&R=Batman and Robin

Age/Sex Classifi-cation	*Age (yrs)*	*Study groups* 4	5	*N*	*Lone*	*Fringe groups* *B*	*W*	*C*	*Grp of 13*	*Grp 6*	*B&R*	*Total*
Silverback	13 - 15+	1	2	1	1	1	1	2	1	1	1	12
Blackback	8 - 13	2	0	0		0	1	0	0	1	1	5
Adult ?	8+	0	0	0		0	0	4	3	0	0	7
Adult ♀	8+	3	5	4		1	1	0	3	3	0	20
Young adult ?	6 - 8	0	0	0		0	0	1	2	1	0	4
Young adult ♂	6 - 8	0	1	0		1	0	0	0	0	0	2
Young adult ♀	6 - 8	2	1	0		1	0	0	0	0	0	4
Juvenile ?	3 - 6	0	0	0		0	0	0	1	1	0	2
Juvenile ♂	3 - 6	1	1	0		0	0	0	0	0	0	2
Juvenile ♀	3 - 6	1	1	0		0	0	0	0	0	0	2
Infant ?	0 - 3	0	0	0		0	1	0	3	3	0	7
Infant ♂	0 - 3	1	1	1		0	0	0	0	0	0	3
Infant ♀	0 - 3	0	2	1		0	0	0	0	0	0	3
TOTALS		11	14	7	1	4	4	7	13	10	2	73

Another influence on Group 4's range was the presence of poachers. In June, when exploring high-altitude sections along the northwestern Karisimbi foothills, the group encountered numerous new wire traps and Zairoise poachers accompanied by dogs. Within an 8-hour period the group fled 4½ km back to the security of Visoke's slopes. In December, of course, following Digit's slaying, they fled 3 km from the western saddle to Mt. Visoke.

The third explanation for speed or direction of travel movement was the presence of Nunkie's Group. In March Group 4 had auditory and visual interactions with Nunkie within their own western Visoke slope area and fluctuated between the slopes and saddle to avoid direct confrontation. In August the group again encountered Nunkie around the core area of its western slopes and proceeded to consistently follow him around to Visoke's southern-facing slopes as Uncle Bert appeared to literally chase him out of their range. Once Nunkie's retreat was obvious, Group 4 moved into the old core area until Nunkie returned in December. This time Group 4 moved to the saddle and the fateful interaction with poachers that resulted in the slaying of Digit on December 31. Following the killing of Digit, Group 4 fled back to Visoke and once again met Nunkie. It cannot be known if his group was the reason for Group 4's immediate flight back to the saddle and directly to Digit's death site. One may hypothesize that the gorillas were looking for Digit, since they had not seen him killed, but it is more likely that they were simply fleeing Nunkie. Uncle Bert no longer had the back-up support of Digit, thus was probably wary of interactions; secondly, the night following Digit's killing, 3 Group 4 members (Simba, Augustus, and Cleo) actually left Group 4 to sleep with Nunkie's Group. By staying near Nunkie, Uncle Bert might have lost these 3 females.

Except in May when Uncle Bert had intestinal problems, as evidenced by his diarrhetic dung deposits, foul body odor, and cantankerous mood, the silverback leader of Group 4 was in consistently good spirits throughout 1977 and led his group skillfully. Part of his newfound security as the group's leader was indicated by his prolonged explorations in the saddle area as he sought to increase the quality and variety of his group's food resources. Another indication of his capability was shown by his pursuit of Nunkie when the latter was encountered within Group 4's core area. Uncle Bert is probably not yet sufficiently experienced to seek an interaction with Nunkie's Group in order to obtain females, despite the fact that he only has 2 mates. Of the two, Flossie was impregnated sometime in September or October, her third offspring sired by Uncle Bert. The older female solicited him regularly for copulation throughout the first 9 months of 1977; however, he responded to her advances rather apathetically. Macho, his second mate, was only ready to return to cyclicity toward the end of 1977 when her infant, sired by Uncle Bert, was nearly 2½ years old.

All 4 of Uncle Bert's offspring are strongly attracted to him and his tolerance of their proximity is typical of all mature silverback leaders. His strongest association is with 10-year-old Tiger, thought to be Uncle Bert's half-brother. Only a mutual tolerance existed between Flossie and Macho during 1977, at least an improvement over the previous year, when a high degree of antagonism was exhibited between the two.

Part of the reason for the change was attributed to Flossie's return to regular estrous cycles throughout the first 9 months of 1977. There are generally higher degrees of affinitive social interactions among females when one is cycling. Flossie's maternal behavior and her permissiveness with Titus, 3 years old as of August 1977, also increased. Titus was observed suckling until August, or about 6 weeks before Flossie conceived. The weaning trauma was not as evident with Titus as it is for many infants, possibly because of her previous strictness with him. In addition he has been the recipient of growing amounts of maternal behavior from his sister Cleo, 6 years old in August, and the immigrant blackback male, Beetsme. The latter was very protective of Titus, was one of the infant's most frequent play partners, and was also observed mounting him on days when either Flossie or Simba was in estrus. Titus was also mounted by his mother and his father, Uncle Bert, following a copulation between the two of them. Cleo began irregular cycling during 1977 and, as is typical for young adolescent females, received a great deal of attention on the days her mother or Simba were receptive. She was awkwardly mounted by Tiger in January; in February she solicited Beetsme for a mounting; in September and November she was mounted by Digit, and in December by Tiger, who then refused to allow Beetsme access to her.

It is interesting to note the pattern of timing of the females. Flossie conceived just as Macho was entering her estrous cycling, and the next generation—that of Cleo and Simba—showed the same scheduling. Simba conceived an infant with Digit just about the same time as Flossie conceived with Uncle Bert. Thus, the first generation male, Uncle Bert, had Macho yet to impregnate and the second males, Digit, Beetsme, and Tiger had Cleo as a potential mate. There is also an absolute correlation between the time a female conceives and the time her infant is weaned. Macho exhibited behavioral signs of returning to estrus toward the end of September, when Kweli was 26 months old. Shortly thereafter Kweli evidenced the beginnings of intense weaning, and by December his whimpering and prolonged suckling sessions indicated that he was not obtaining as much milk as previously.

Macho's period of bond formation within Group 4 has been difficult, however, she became more assertive in 1977 because her infant son,

Kweli, was totally successful in establishing close rapport with all group members. Macho no longer needed to be as protective of him and as obsequious to others in the group. Kweli's development was exceptional, considering the low status of his mother. At the age of 18 months he was able to remain at long distances for prolonged periods of up to 5 hours in the company of other group members who cuddled, carried, groomed, and played with him before he would return to Macho for suckling. In April he was first observed chin-slapping, creating the clattering noise caused by the upper and lower teeth hitting together. This idiosyncratic type of play behavior was first seen with Titus, 1 year older than Kweli. It cannot be determined whether the younger infant picked up the activity from Titus or whether it is innate among gorillas, as it has been observed with 2 infants in another group. However, the hand-clapping ability of 7-year-old Augustus has never been observed among free-living gorillas. Augustus, a year older than Cleo, was still considered a male in 1977, an impression based upon her physical appearance and absence of any indication of cyclicity. Like Cleo, she was very playful on the days Simba was in estrus. Her play with Beetsme had sexual overtures though she was never observed being mounted by any of the group's males. Her main feminine traits were her adamancy about not allowing others, including Uncle Bert, to share her proximity when feeding on choice food or in restricted feeding sites, and the gradual replacement of play behavior for social grooming activities.

Simba was about 8½ years old when she conceived an infant with Digit, a year younger than the average age of 9 females for whom equivalent data are available. The regularity of Simba's estrous cycles, itself an indication of sexual maturity, was evident throughout the first 9 months of 1977, when she showed both behavioral and physical signs of receptivity between day 27 and 31 of each month. These were the only times Digit expressed keen interest in her. When Digit was at the edge of the group or at some distance, sexually immature Tiger and Beetsme also mounted Simba on her receptive days, as well as randomly throughout the month. The young female solicited all copulations with Digit and, to a lesser extent, with the younger males who were highly attracted to her. The extent of her flirtatious behavior created a number of pig-grunting squabbles in the group until she conceived, as did Flossie, either in September or October. Then, as is the tendency for primiparous females, her behavior altered markedly, for she withdrew from social interactions with others to spend the majority of her time at the edge of or apart from the group for prolonged feeding sessions.

While Simba was in estrus, Tiger's behavior became rather braggadocian; this, however, was not seen with Beetsme, who did not have Tiger's security within the group. Both Tiger and Beetsme were submissive to

Digit, as shown by their bowing down with their rumps up in the air or simply retreating when the older male purposely entered the group on the days Simba's swelling was at its maximum. Throughout 1977 Tiger was consistently groomed by Uncle Bert and enjoyed good relations with all group members, particularly Cleo, for whom he assumed a proprietary interest once Simba was impregnated.

Beetsme appeared to have improved his status by the gentle and protective behavior he directed toward younger animals, especially Titus, son of the group's dominant female. He did remain wary of Uncle Bert, who occasionally disciplined him by charges, mock bites, or whacks. When he was within the main body of the group, it was obvious that Beetsme sought Uncle Bert's proximity, but approached him only with caution to avoid being rebuffed. Thirty percent of Beetsme's play with the immatures had sexual overtures, and the frequency increased on Simba's days of receptivity. The blackback had immigrated to Group 4 in January 1976 from an area of poor quality north of Group 4's range. Since this immigration his physical appearance changed considerably from that of a scruffy and gaunt individual to one now resembling other Group 4 members. He still gave the impression of being an outsider and had not contributed toward sentry duty along with Tiger and Digit.

Digit was unrelenting when it came to placing himself at the edge of the group, or up to 100 m away, so that he could more advantageously survey the group's surroundings for other gorillas, poachers, or traps. It was in this role that Digit was killed on December 31, 1977. In January of that year Digit was found in his usual sentry position some 40 m from the group on the day that Nyiragongo, one of the active volcanoes located about 15 km from Visoke, erupted. Observers felt strong tremors while approaching and even after contacting Group 4, who were feeding calmly on contact, apparently taking no notice of the vibrations. Exactly 1 minute before Nyiragongo erupted Digit stopped feeding, began screaming loudly, and fled toward his group, who were also fleeing and screaming. Their outbreak lasted throughout the eruption, ceased, then began anew when a second violent tremor was felt following the unseen eruption. Simultaneously Nunkie's Group, located about 2 km farther away from the eruption, were also under observation. Although the observer, situated some 20 m from Nunkie's Group, felt the violent tremors, the gorillas continued feeding normally throughout, giving no indication that anything was amiss. Reputedly, chimpanzees maintained at the Stanford Research Facility in California were able to "predict" accurately earthquakes by the same type of behavior as seen with Group 4 before the earthquakes occurred. A similar characteristic is also shared by the mammals inhabiting the two active Virungas, for they leave the mountains 1 or 2 weeks preceding eruptions.

As previously mentioned, Digit could be attracted into the midst of the group on the days Simba's estrus was at its peak, and he also continued, for the second year, strutting, chest-beating, or whacking only male observers, never females. Digit was heard for the first time giving a weak hoot series in January when another group was within auditory distance of Group 4. On one occasion when Nunkie's Group was being "herded" from the core of their range area, Digit was in the lead ahead of Uncle Bert. It also seems possible that he was responsible for deflecting his group's direction of travel from a line of freshly set wire snares which only he could see from his lead position. Following Digit's sighting of the traps he emitted a strong fear odor, changed course, and headed downhill rather than in the western direction the group had been pursuing for several days. Hours later, after a prolonged sunbathing session, the group followed Digit's route though, unbeknownst to all of them, hidden in thick vegetation below were more traps. Group 4 had just reached them when a duiker was snared. A tremendous outbreak was heard from the group, as the author and a guest rushed toward the source of the noise. Once there they found the young duiker frantically struggling to free itself and the members of Group 4 some 30 m beyond. Seeing them, Nunkie's Group stopped and Digit, Beetsme, and Tiger immediately climbed into a large *Hagenia* tree to watch curiously as the author and guest freed the duiker, which fled unharmed. Once the rescue was completed the males all chest-beat and only then did they leave. It was very near this area some 6 months later that Digit gave his life so that his family, including his unborn offspring that was to be born to Simba in April 1978, might survive.

On January 1, 1978, a tracker had been unable to locate Group 4 in this portion of their saddle range because of numerous buffalo, elephant, poacher, and dog trails, but had found a great deal of diarrhetic gorilla dung. The following day a colleague, Ian Redmond, the author, and 2 trackers began searching the saddle area for Group 4. Digit's mutilated corpse was found lying in an area of blood-soaked vegetation some 10 x 15 m in diameter. His head and hands had been hacked off, and his body bore multiple spear wounds, 5 of which were considered lethal. Intensive trail investigation showed that 6 poachers and dogs had been following a trap line, exactly like that which Digit had spotted 6 months previously, when they unexpectedly encountered Group 4 in the saddle area. Group 4 had been in the wrong place at the wrong time. By the end of 1978, however, all but 1 of the poachers responsible for Digit's death had been captured.

Group 5

Throughout 1977 Group 5's range had grown to 8.45 km^2. The range was strongly affected by poachers in the far southwestern saddle region on Mt. Karisimbi, by other gorilla groups on Visoke's slopes and in the southeastern region, and by tourists on Visoke's southern-facing slopes. In March the first "herding" of a gorilla group was undertaken by 4 Karisoke trackers and 1 colleague, after Group 5 had moved up to 11,600 ft in the upper plateaus of Mt. Karisimbi, a heavily encroached poacher area and one totally unfamiliar to Group 5. The disoriented group found themselves confined to narrow forest strips containing dozens of freshly set wire snares. The forested sections were separated from one another by vast alpine meadows, favorite poacher hunting regions.

Because of the potential danger in the area, the author decided to herd the group back to their normally used range that lay at lower altitudes to the east. Herding is accomplished by Karisoke workers who simulate poachers by the use of dog bells and hunting calls, yet who stay out of sight of the gorillas being directed toward safer areas. This movement began at 10:10 a.m. at 11,380 ft and ended at 2:15 p.m. at 10,860 ft, roughly 1 km farther east. As have all subsequent herdings, the day's efforts succeeded in returning the group to familiar territory from which they continued to move even farther toward their core area. Within a 2-week period Group 5 was ranging 2½ km farther east in secure terrain. In April both poachers and other gorilla groups created many range fluctuations, but none as serious as those of March.

In May, when Group 5 sought prolonged periods within the bamboo zone that lies adjacent to the Parc des Volcans eastern boundary, they encountered many traps 2¼ km southeast of Visoke. Of interest was their deviation around most wire snares, an action that suggested "trap knowledge." They detoured the freshly set traps but tripped old hemp-snare traps (as did the author), resulting in a 3-km flight route containing much diarrhetic dung and night nests that, judging by their lack of structure, had been made after dark. The following day, while still headed toward the relative security of Visoke, 6½-year-old Ziz was caught in a wire snare. As determined by partially obscured observations through the bamboo and subsequent sightings of arm and hand injuries, Ziz had been released from the wire noose by the teeth of Beethoven, who then rapidly led the group back to Visoke. Group 5 did not venture into the saddle again until August when the gorillas once again met poachers and dogs that caused them to flee to the series of five hills, long a part of their core area in the saddle. The hills offer a relatively good variety of food resources and, more importantly, the opportunity to gain height when surveilling adjacent terrain.

Group 5 had 18 auditory and 9 physical interactions during 1977. They were only free from encounters with other social units when in their far southwestern range in the months of January, June, and August. In February Group 5 was contacted regularly in its old core area around the hills south of camp when the gorillas had an auditory interaction with the

Wageni Group from Karisimbi. Icarus had gone toward Wageni's Group and was separated from Group 5 by a kilometer while Beethoven remained behind with the group's females and immatures. Just before dusk a heavy hail storm appeared to have terminated the interaction between the two groups. The following morning, however, tracking evidence showed that the small Wageni Group had pursued Group 5 for 2527 m in a westerly direction during and after the hail storm. Group 5 ended up in an unknown region and built their night nests after dark, while Wageni's Group headed back toward the favored eastern hill area. This particular interaction, unlike most, probably occurred for the purposes of range, rather than female, acquisition and Wageni's Group succeeded in chasing Group 5 from the same region of their core area on two other occasions during the year. Other groups that Group 5 encountered on the slopes of Visoke were Basher's Group (see under Basher), Batman and Robin (under Batman and Robin), from whom Group 5 also fled, and Group 6, with whom they held their ground.

Unfortunately 1977 marked the beginning of an extremely heavy wave of tourists insistent upon seeing the habituated gorillas, particularly Group 5, whose range was the most accessible. Tourists were as directly responsible for shifting the group's movements into insecure saddle regions as were poachers. At the end of the year, during the holiday season when human influx into the park is most pronounced, Group 5 fled to Visoke's alpine zone as if to get away from it all. Beethoven received several deep bite wounds from the interactions with Wageni's Group and also from one interaction with the huge silverback, Batman, and his blackback, Robin.

Following the near simultaneous births by Beethoven's mate, Marchessa, and Icarus's mate, Pantsy, there was a decided shift among the females able to obtain his proximity. Beethoven's allegiances also switched, at least during the 3 months surrounding the birth of his new son Shinda, to Marchessa. His manner toward Effie became antagonistic whenever she expressed even the slightest interest in Marchessa's newborn. An unusual rapport developed during this time between himself and Marchessa, one that was only gradually redirected to his first acquired mate, Effie. Despite solicitations throughout 1977 when her son, Pablo, became 3 years old in August, Liza received little sexual attention from Beethoven, and by the year's end was rebuffed by him whenever she sought his proximity. Beethoven's other sexual behavior occurred twice with his 9-year-old daughter, Puck, and he usually prevented Icarus from copulating with Puck during her regular estrous periods throughout the year, though Icarus managed to mount her once in October. Icarus's one other copulatory episode was a mild mounting of Quince in December and both young females had solicited him.

FIGURE 1. Between 1967 and 1977 Beethoven, the aged patriarch and silverback leader of Group 5, had produced 11 offspring. As all silverback group leaders, Beethoven is the center of attention from his mates and progeny.

As was noted for most of 1976, Icarus could usually be found bringing up the rear of the group as his outside position enhanced his ability to determine whether another social unit was in the vicinity of Group 5. Icarus's reaction to the Wageni Group differed from that toward Batman and Robin. This might have been attributed to individual threats posed by the respective groups, or to which portion of range Group 5 was in when the encounters occurred. During the interactions with the Wageni Group, and in their own core area, Icarus first approached the Wageni Group before returning to flee along with the rest of Group 5. The meetings with Batman and Robin took place on the very fringe of Group 5's range and Icarus did not assist Beethoven during several observed confrontations.

Whether it was absolute knowledge of paternity or simply a result of pair bonding cannot be known, but Icarus's protectiveness and attachment to Pantsy, after the birth of his first-sired offspring Muraha, was exceptional. During the period before he resumed more distant travel, several months after the birth, he was consistently found within or very near the main cluster of group members and expressed irritability at either observers or young group members seeking to get near the new mother. Tracking Icarus's lone travel trails revealed that he spent a great deal of time feeding on these lone routes, thus suggesting that he could not afford to maintain the same activity pattern as the individuals of the group because his feeding requirements as a young silverback surpassed theirs.

Before the respective parturitions, on February 27 and March 1, of Marchessa and her daughter Pantsy, they were equally responsible for seeking one another's proximity and for the first time often expressed maternal interest in 3-year-old Pablo. Marchessa, as is typical for multiparous mothers, gave birth in 1 night nest and ate the placenta. Her male infant, Shinda, was first seen with about 8 in. of umbilical cord still attached the morning following his birth. He was considered extremely puny, particularly in comparison with Pantsy's female infant, Muraha, born 3 days later. Pantsy, as is typical of primaparous females, used 5 nests spread over an area of 100 ft before giving birth during the night.

In the first month following the births Marchessa was observed nursing and grooming Shinda 7 times more frequently than Pantsy tended to Muraha, a situation that reversed during subsequent months. Pantsy was seen playing with her infant when it was 2 months old and commonly dangled the baby over her head to stimulate the release of its feces. In contrast, Marchessa's abdominal area became stained by the urine and feces deposits of Shinda. Marchessa pushed Shinda into a dorsal travel position when he was 3 months of age while Pantsy continued to carry Muraha ventrally until slowly prompting her to ride dorsally at the normal age of 4 months. By the time both infants were 5 months old, Shinda had not yet been out of arm's reach of his mother, yet Muraha was walking up to 9 m away from Pantsy and interacting in gentle play with Group 5's immatures, all very attracted to her.

Locomotion among very young infants typically consists of more control and coordination in the forearms and hands, which are used from birth to cling to the mothers' ventral surface, and relatively awkward, pushing movements of the hind legs. Shinda was nearly 8 months old before attempting to play or locomote small distances from Marchessa. The near simultaneous births provided both mothers and their respective offspring with the optimal protection of the group's two silverbacks, a situation neither female had enjoyed with the births of their previous infants, neither of which survived because of intragroup violence, most likely between matrilines.

Marchessa's oldest son, Ziz, 6 years old in January 1977, rapidly withdrew from his "mamma's-boy" behavior upon acquiring a younger brother and a niece in the space of only a few days. Signs of his new maturity were seen in the significant increase of play interactions, an attachment to Beethoven and Icarus, whom he supported with struts and chest-beats during some of their interactions with other groups, and a new interest in sex. His practice mounting partners included Poppy, Tuck, Pablo, and Quince in that order. He evidenced no interest in the 2 newborns; their birth, however, prompted a significant increase in the maternal behavior among Group 5's young females, Quince, Puck, and Tuck. The only other infant in the group was Poppy, 2 years old in April 1977. She served as a substitute infant for her sisters, Puck and Tuck, and her half-sister, Quince, to practice their maternal attentions on until they were allowed access to the newborns.

Effie's overt expressions of interest in Shinda and Muraha lasted only a month, during which time she was strongly curtailed by Beethoven's protection of Marchessa. Just before the births Effie was seen with extremely serious head, neck, and shoulder wounds which possibly could have been inflicted during an intragroup squabble. Tension between the matrilines of Effie and Marchessa was then as high as it had been a year earlier, when Effie was nearing parturition and Pantsy's 6-month-old, Banjo, mysteriously disappeared during a series of intragroup quarrels. Effie's 8-year-old daughter, Puck, a sexually maturing female, assumed her mother's animosity toward the members of Marchessa's clan. She was observed strutting and running at Marchessa in a threatening manner the day following the birth of Shinda and also chest-beating and running at Pantsy the day following the birth of Muraha. Pantsy showed extreme fear of Puck's behavior. Puck and Effie were the only members of Group 5 whose dung deposits contained minute pieces of bone, teeth, and hair following the disappearance of Pantsy's first infant and might well have been responsible for its death. Because of the consistency of Effie's maternal attentions, her youngest daughter, Poppy, received optimal grooming and nursing attention and indicated no signs of weaning trauma even at the end of 1977 when 21 months of age.

One example of Effie's capabilities occurred in January 1977 when Poppy, then only 11 months old, was solo-playing in a giant *Senecio* tree some 20 ft behind her mother. Suddenly Poppy lost her balance, slipped and hung by her neck in a narrow fork of the tree. Her frantic struggles only wedged her tighter and, within a minute, it became obvious that she was about to strangle to death. Just as the observer was ready to run to her rescue, Effie quickly turned around, immediately took the situation in and ran to her daughter wearing a horrified expression. Standing bipedally, Effie, with considerable difficulty, was able to free the infant who gave a few weak whimpers before suckling for 4 minutes. Effie's instant perception of the danger Poppy was in and her level-headed reaction to the infant's actions were remarkable.

Effie's 2 older daughters, Puck and Tuck, were adolescent during 1977, thus their play records dropped significantly, being replaced by grooming, feeding, and maternal behavior. Though both were extremely interested in the 2 new infants, they were not allowed access to them and substituted Poppy and Pablo, who was 3 years old in August. Tuck was unusually solicitous of Pablo, whose traumatic weaning period lasted throughout the year, though Liza nursed him occasionally until July. The deformity of her breasts was even more marked by the end of the year with the left swollen and lumpy and the right hanging flat. As previously mentioned, her sexual attention from Beethoven was virtually nil and she occupied very much of a lone position at the group's edge until her daughter Quince, 7 years old in July, began showing estrous periods. Quince, possibly because of her tendency to groom nearly all group members, was better accepted by others than Liza, and her estrous periods made her even more attractive. Liza began seeking her daughter's proximity on the days she was in estrus and was, therefore, able to mix in the group by the end of the year. Her flirtatious and assertive behavior were tolerated while Quince evoked numerous social interactions and mountings from both males and females including Icarus, Beethoven, Puck, and Tuck. Quince was also the first Group 5 individual whom Pantsy allowed to carry, groom, and cuddle Muraha when the infant was only 4 months old.

NUNKIE'S GROUP

Nunkie's 4-km^2 range was distributed in essentially the same areas along Visoke's south- and southeastern-facing slopes, usually at high altitudes. He crossed over the summit twice to reach Visoke's northern slopes and probably gained another square kilometer in that area outside the Karisoke study area. In March his high-altitude treks were attributed to the fruit resource, *Pygeum*, which grows on only a few northwestern ridges on Visoke. At no time did his group enter the saddle area, thus his was the least affected of all the study groups by the presence of poachers. Nunkie's most notable interaction was a violent one that occurred in January when he lost the young female adult, Wizard, to a group of 3 individuals named Basher's Group. The 3-day interaction left numerous large display areas containing blood deposits, diarrhetic dung, hair tufts, and even skin. Nunkie and his supportive female, Pandora, were both severely wounded by the mammoth silverback Basher, who then chased them from the area on Visoke's southeastern slopes.

Throughout the remainder of 1977 Nunkie's Group had 19 auditory interactions and, quite unlike Nunkie, did not seek physical interactions with other social units. Nunkie's behavior was affected by the deep bite wounds he had received around his head and legs, and one that exposed the bone of his thumb. For some 6 weeks after the interaction with Basher he moved very slowly, bringing up the rear of his group by as much as 60 m. During January and February he was heard copulating with a female thought to have been Fuddle, and in November he copulated with Petula and the crippled female, Pandora.

Pandora lost part of an ear during January's violent interaction, in addition to suffering severe puncture wounds all over her body and around her eyes. Because of her hand deformities (missing and atrophied fingers), she was less able to groom herself effectively and no one was seen grooming her. It was also wondered to what extent her handicap might affect her diet. She seemed to feed primarily on galium, a vine growth that only requires plucking and wadding, not the more involved stripping and peeling needed for thistle and celery stalks. During 1977 she and Fuddle, both originally from Group 6, tended to travel and rest together while Petula and Papoose, originally from Group 4, also clung together. Petula's daughter, Lee, 2 years old in July, was remarkably well coordinated and sociable for an infant with no siblings and only 1 peer, 10 months younger than she. In February Lee developed the ability to hit the underside of her chin and produce the unique clattering noise also heard from Titus and Kweli in Group 4. In April, the only other infant in the group, N'Gee, at the early age of 11 months, also picked up the behavior. It has been suggested that infants without much social stimulation are more inclined to develop idiosyncratic behavior as a means of self-entertainment.

Basher's Group

In 1976 a group of 2 individuals, an extraordinarily large silverback and a young adult, was encountered several times in the southern region of the Karisoke study area around the foothills of Karisimbi. It seemed most likely that increased poaching pressure on Karisimbi was responsible for their movement into the Karisoke study area, as might also have been the case for Nunkie and other small groups. Nunkie's Wizard was the fourth addition to the new group which, other than herself, consisted of the silverback Basher, an older adult female (Broadnose), and a young adult male (Deepnose). Basher's footprint measurements were 30 cm from the heel to the longest toe; 14 cm in width at the widest point; and 7 cm in the width of 4 knuckles with the length of the longest knuckle 8 cm. He was estimated as about Uncle Bert's age and gave vigorous displays accompanied by a great deal of ground thumping. Like Nunkie, following his arrival in the study area, no precise range could be defined for Basher's Group. Throughout 1977 they were usually found on the eastern Visoke slopes or the eastern saddle adjacent to the bamboo zone, where they had 6 auditory interactions with Group 5. By December Wizard was no longer with them, and she was thought to have transferred to Group 6, which also ranged in that area.

WAGENI'S GROUP

This small group consisted only of the silverback, Wageni, a large blackback, Aladdin, an older female, Baby Jane, and her infant of about 22 months. The unit was first encountered in 1975, and was thought also to have come from Karisimbi. Throughout 1977 the gorillas wandered around the southern saddle terrain and, as previously mentioned, were successful on several occasions in forcing Group 5 out of the latter's long-established core area. The presence of poachers in this region frequently forced Wageni's Group to flee back to the higher slopes on Karisimbi. The group's knowledge of the saddle region was shown by its direct and unswerving routes toward large log crossings over the Suza River which enabled it to elude the poachers and dogs they encountered.

PEANUTS'S GROUP

Peanuts was last seen traveling alone in January 1976, after he lost Beetsme to Group 4. It was surprising, therefore, when he was found in March 1977 on Visoke's northwestern slopes traveling with 5 other individuals—1 blackback, 2 females, and 2 younger adults. The group was relatively calm and it was determined that 3 of the animals were Tynker, Maidenform, and Chamnel, all formerly of Group 9. This finding substantiated the death of Geronimo, the ailing silverback leader of Group 9 last seen in March 1972. Peanuts's health still appeared afflicted by a severe bite wound near the eye, received during an interaction with Group 4 in 1971. It was possible that his poor physical condition was responsible for his losing the newly acquired animals to another fringe group that also ranged northwest of Visoke, for in November he was found again traveling alone.

CHUI GROUP

The above animals with Peanuts were simultaneously observed when a group of 7 individuals interacted with Peanuts in March 1977. This clarified the existence of 2 groups, similar in size and sharing the same range area on Visoke. The Chui group consisted of 2 silverbacks, 4 adults, and 1 young adult. They had lost a juvenile since being first observed in 1976. The presence of 2 silverbacks and their lack of habituation made them difficult to observe for the purpose of obtaining noseprint sketches for identification.

GROUP OF 13

This large fringe group also ranged outside the study area on Visoke's eastern and northern slopes and down into the vast bamboo zone surrounding the mountain to the north. A group of 13 individuals was first found during census work in May 1973 in the same area. In 1977 these gorillas were sighted twice, but only 6 noseprints were obtained due to their lack of habituation and the density of the bamboo cover. The group consists of 1 silverback, 3 adults of unknown sex, 3 females with infants, 2 young adults, and 1 juvenile. The size of the group was quite surprising, considering that it ranged in an elephant-poaching area and one of inferior food resources. Tracking indicated that the gorillas were also inclined to frequent Visoke's subalpine zone which, on the eastern side of the mountain contained an unusual amount of herbaceous foliage and, more importantly, was subject to very little human encroachment.

Group of 18

The finding of this group in April on Visoke's northern slopes stressed the importance of simultaneous sightings, noseprint sketches, and accurate nest counts. It is highly unlikely that a fifth fringe group, particularly one of this size, could have ranged within an area of some 11 km^2 (Visoke's northern slopes and adjacent saddle) yet never be contacted during previous census work. Because of simultaneous observations in March, it was shown that the Group of 13, Peanuts' Group, and the Chui Group, all of which ranged in the same terrain, were definitely 3 distinct units. Tracking in that area, however, did not reveal any sign of a large group of 18 members. In addition to the tracking evidence not supporting the existence of this group, it was noted that 3 noseprint sketches obtained from them were very similar to noseprints obtained from the Chui Group. When the 7 members of the Chui Group are combined with the 11 members of Group 6 (see below) a total of 18 individuals may be accounted for with only minimal compositional differences. In the author's opinion, therefore, the Group of 18, which has never been subsequently observed, was more likely a sighting based upon a close interaction between the above 2 units which, for unexplained reasons, chanced to build their night nests in proximity for several days. For this reason the group is not listed in Table 1.

Group 6

Fringe Group 6 has been known to range around Visoke's eastern and northern slopes and adjacent saddle area since 1969. It is distinguished by an adult female named Yaws because of a facial disfigurement giving her the appearance of having 3 nares. This is also the group that Fuddle and Pandora emigrated from in 1976 to join Nunkie. When encountered in July 1977 Group 6 consisted of 1 silverback (Brutus), 1 blackback, 3 females with infants, 1 young adult, and 2 juveniles, giving a total of 8 nest builders and 3 dependents. By the year's end, 1 juvenile had disappeared.

BATMAN AND ROBIN

In July a third small unit consisting of a silverback, Batman, and a blackback, Robin, came into the study area from Mt. Karisimbi. They went directly to Group 5's core area along the series of small hills south of camp and pursued Group 5 for 4 km along the main porters' trail to the eastern boundary of the park. The entire flight took place during the night, the second time Group 5 underwent this type of interaction. In September the 2 new males followed Group 5 for 4 days in the eastern saddle before they returned to Karisimbi.

Infant Development and Parturition

The development of the gorilla infant is of special interest because of the organization of the unit in which it matures. Gorilla populations are basically divided into small family groups, the composition of which remains essentially constant for prolonged periods. The infant, therefore, is able to form relatively stable, consistent, and even long-term associations with his peers, siblings, parents, and other group members. It is suggested that such long-term cohesion, and, in particular, the permanency of the attachment of the dominant male to several older, high-ranking females, offers a unique social environment among all great apes.

By the end of 1977 a total of 27 infants had been born within the main study groups, membership in which has varied during the past 10 years from 33 to 69 individuals. Of the 27 infants, as of 1977, 41% (n = 11) had died; of these, 4 died from either intra- or intergroup violence (infanticide) and 2 were nonviable issues. The cause of death of the remaining 5 was not determined; but since all were between the ages of 2 and 17 months when they disappeared, infanticide is a likely explanation for death. Of the 16 surviving by the end of 1977, 6 remained classified as infants (0-3 years), 4 were classified as juveniles (3-6 years), 4 as young adults (6-8 years), and 3 as adults (8+ years).

The stages of development throughout the first 36 months of the gorilla infant's life are defined by the two separate criteria of physical characteristics and behavioral patterns (Fossey, 1979). The stages obviously intergrade; of equal importance are individual variations, a factor apparent even in zoo records (Gijzen and Tijskens, 1971). The physical characteristics described for each stage are those most outstanding during any one period. Since considerable change takes place during the first 6 months, that age period has been divided bimonthly. Subsequent physical changes are of a longer transitional period. Body weights are estimates based on actual weights of newly deceased infants and zoo records.

FIGURE 2. The maturation process of a gorilla infant is strongly shaped by the cohesiveness of its family group in which kinship ties normally guarantee the infant's security and protection.

PHYSICAL DEVELOPMENT

Newborn. The skin is pinkish-gray in tone and may have pink concentrations on the palms, soles, and tongue. Body hair is medium brown to black and sparsely distributed. Head hair is usually jet black and the white tail tuft is as yet undefined. The face is wizened, with a pronounced protrusion of the nasal region giving the infant a pig-snout appearance. The ears are prominent and the eyes are either squinted or closed. The limbs are thin and spidery, with digits usually tightly flexed. A portion of the umbilical cord, up to 8 in., may remain intact throughout the first 24 hours. The body weight is approximately 3½ lb. Schultz (1969) has estimated the birth weight of gorillas as 2.6% of the nongravid maternal weight. Groves (1970) gave an average birth weight, based primarily upon records of captive gorillas, as between 3½ and 5¼ lb.

1-2 Months. The body skin is pinkish-gray and the infant may retain pink concentrations on the palms, soles, and tongue. The body hair is black, short, and sparsely distributed on the ventral surface and inside of legs and arms. The head hair is usually black, short, and wavy and there is a faint definition of a white tail tuft. The face retains a wizened appearance, with the nose protrusion gradually receding while the ears are still prominent and the eyes small. The limbs and digits remain thin and spidery. The body weight is approximately 5 lb. Schaller (1963) also noted pink pigmentation spots on the soles of the feet of several infants.

2-4 Months. The body skin is gray, with pinkish-gray concentrations on face, ears, palms, and soles. The body hair is beginning to fluff and lighten in color with a thicker distribution on the dorsal surface. The head hair is long, wavy, and reddish brown. The white tail tuft is defined. The ears are now partially obscured by hair growth. Although gradually flattening, the nasal section is wide and remains the predominant feature of the face with very faint beginnings of indentations above the nostrils. The eyes are small and rounded. The limbs and digits still remain thin and spidery. The body weight is approximately 7 lb. Schaller (1963) also mentioned the brown crown hair at the age of 2½ months.

4-6 Months. The body skin is gray; the facial skin and ears are gray-black; the palms and soles are pinkish-gray, and the tongue is mottled pink. The body hair is long and fluffy and reddish-brown to black in color, but sparsely distributed on the ventral surface and insides of legs and arms. The head hair is nearing maximum length with a cap of reddish-colored hair growing out in tufts. The white tail tuft is clearly defined in color but not yet in size. The ears are obscured by hair growth; the nasal region is flattened and rounded. The eyes are larger, rounded, and becoming the predominant feature of the face. The limbs and digits are somewhat spindly in appearance. The body weight is approximately 11 lb. Schaller (1963) also noted a "wild fringe of brown hair" between the ages of 17 and 30 weeks.

6-12 Months. The body and facial skin is gray to gray-black; the palms and soles are grayish. The body hair is fluffy and reddish-brown to black in color, and the reddish-brown head hair is at maximum length, growing in straggly tufts. The white tail tuft is clearly defined in color and nearing maximum size. The head appears exceptionally large in proportion to the rest of the body. The large rounded eyes are the predominant feature of the face, with the nasal wings thickening and beginning to take a definite shape. The limbs show evidence of roundness and musculature. The body weight is approximately 18 lb. By the eighth month, the visible teeth (incisors), gums, and back surface of the tongue show traces of tartar deposits accumulated from foliage eaten. Groves (1970) listed the average weight at 1 year as being 15 lb and Schaller (1963) lists it as between 15 and 20 lb, both referring to zoo infants.

12-24 Months. The body and facial skin appears gray-black to black; the palms and soles are gray-black. Reddish-brown to black body hair is becoming thicker, shorter, and straighter as is the head hair. The white tail tuft is clearly defined in color and of maximum size (diameter up to 4 in.). The head-to-body proportions are beginning to approach those of an adult. The eyes have obtained their maximum roundness and are the predominant feature of the face with eyelashes long and abundant. The nasal region is well defined. The musculature development of the limbs is becoming much more pronounced. The body weight is approximately 30 lb. From zoo records Groves has estimated the body weight at 2 years as 30 lb while Schaller estimates it as 35 lb.

24-36 Months. The body skin is gray-black to black. The reddish-brown to black body hair is much thicker and becoming noticeable on the ventral surface. The head hair is thick and losing its fluffy appearance. The white tail tuft is diminishing in brightness of color and size. Rounded eyes remain the predominant facial feature, while the nasal region becomes less outstanding in size with strong wrinkles forming along the nasal bridge. The musculature is well-developed, and the protrusion of the abdomen is noticeably apparent for the first time. The body weight is approximately 45 lb. Based upon zoo records, Groves listed the average 3-year-old weight as between 55 and 60 lb, and Schaller lists it as 60 lb. Schaller notes that the tail tuft was present on the rumps of infants at birth and persisted at least until the age of 4 years. By that age, however, this study has noted the tuft appearing only as a faint, nearly imperceptible lightening of the hair around the rump region.

Behavioral Development

The stages of behavioral development indicate the maintenance activities and capabilities of the infant, the general nature of the interactions with its mother, and some aspects of its social awareness of others within the group. Again, it should be stated that there were intergradations in all stages of behavioral development as well as individual variations which were more pronounced in the behavior category than in the physical stages.

Newborn (First 24 Hours). The infant is capable of clinging to the ventral surface of the mother, unsupported, for at least 3 minutes, and can hold its head upright when the body is vertically supported. The limbs sometimes exhibit a spastic type of involuntary thrusting movement, especially when rooting for the nipple. Most of the time the baby appears asleep, and it is always carried in a ventral position when the mother travels. Vocalizations consist of weak, puppy-type whines. Schaller (1963) thought that newborns appeared to lack the strength to clasp the mother's hair securely and that mothers had to support them continuously with at least one arm. Land (1960a, as cited by Schaller) noted that the grasping reflex in one newborn infant was weaker than that of a chimpanzee or an orangutan, which was not the impression received in this study. In a zoo-born female, Hess (1973) noted considerable interest in genital inspection of a newborn male infant, which has not been observed in this study.

1-2 Months. The infant is capable of clinging unsupported to its mother's ventral surface for longer periods. Its limbs may exhibit random, flailing movements when being groomed or searching for the nipple, still accompanied by rooting and nuzzling head motions. Finger and precise arm movements remain uncoordinated. Eye-focusing ability appears limited to stationary objects within 10 ft of the mother. The infant flinches in response to loud noises or those made by other animals within the group. Solid food intake is limited to mouthing or prolonged chewing of vegetation debris deposited on the mother's body. Roughly 75% of the time the infant appears asleep and always travels in a ventral position. When in its mother's lap, the baby is supported about 50% of the time. Vocalizations consist of whines and loud, high-pitched wails. Groves (1970) said that the 8-week-old infant could not hold its head up for any length of time, a condition not confirmed by the results of this study.

2-4 Months. The infant clings unsupported ventrally for prolonged periods of time and with increased grasping strength which may possibly bother the mother. It may kick, whack, or push at its mother's body when being groomed. It is able to obtain the nipple without a preliminary period of rooting, and it will strongly pursue efforts to get the nipple when thwarted by its mother. Exploratory play activities with surrounding vegetation and on the mother's body are begun. Arm movements toward nearby foliage are gross and jerky with fingers widely spread before the object is contacted. Play on the mother's body consists mainly of unbalanced crawling, sliding, patting, and hair pulling. There is a high degree of individual variation in the mother's response. The infant can focus its eyes on objects at least as far as 40 ft and is able to follow moving objects. It flinches visibly at loud noises. Solid food intake consists of bits of vegetation, seeds, and wood remnants picked from the mother's lap. The infant is able to ride dorsally for brief periods, usually in a sideways, sprawled position when pushed on by the mother. Distressed and play facial expressions are now clearly defined and vocalizations consist of whines, wails, screeches, and panting play chuckles. Groves, citing observations of captive gorillas, stated that infants can crawl regularly by their 9th week and by the 15th week can push themselves into sitting positions for brief periods of time.

4-6 Months. An infant may now travel either ventrally or dorsally on its mother with the ventral position used about 60% of the time. If in a dorsal position, it rides high on the mother's neck or shoulder and with its body stretched out prone along the top of her back. Grooming is less objected to; prolonged sessions, however, usually result in the infant pulling out of the mother's grasp. Suckling bouts are of shorter duration; play behavior is expanded from solo exploration and manipulation of vegetation to play on the mother and mock-wrestling with her extremities. Social interactions with other peers consist of mild whacking or patting but usually within body contact or arm's reach of the mother. Focusing ability extends beyond 40 ft and head movement is noticeably more coordinated. The first quadrupedal walking is attempted but is clumsy and uncoordinated. Vocalizations consist of whines, wails, panting chuckles, screeches, and screams.

6-12 Months. The infant still continues to travel, both ventrally and dorsally, using the dorsal position about 80% of the time. Suckling efforts continue but are more frequently checked forcibly by the mother. Solo play now includes tree climbing, and locomotor patterns advance more rapidly than in any other period. Social play with other infants and juveniles increases greatly but is still not as frequent as solo play. There is still no preparation of food items, which are either plucked or gnawed on. Vocalizations consist of whines, wails, panting chuckles, screeches, hoot cries, and shrieks.

12-24 Months. The infant nearly always travels in a dorsal position when long distances are covered, but otherwise usually follows its mother independently or clings to her rump hair. Suckling efforts continue, but the infant is becoming more responsive to the restrictive measures taken by the mother when she wishes to terminate a bout. Play interactions with other infants and juveniles are much more vigorous and begin to outnumber solo play sessions. Obtaining food items now involves awkward attempts at preparation such as stripping leaves from central stalks or wadding of vines. Social responses toward adults now include grooming the mother and attraction toward the silverback. Vocalizations consist of whines, wails, panting chuckles, screeches, hoot cries, shrieks, temper tantrum screams, howls, and pig-grunts.

Five of 11 observations made by Schaller (1963) of suckling behavior occurred with infants between the ages of 1 and $1\frac{1}{2}$. Because it was easier to observe older infants suckling, such a low count suggested to him that partial weaning had taken place by that age. However, the author has observed suckling frequently during the second year, and it seems likely that intensive weaning occurs after that age.

24-36 Months. The infant may ride dorsally during prolonged travel but is more often seen following independently. Suckling efforts continue, but the mother may rebuff the infant severely if the attempts continue for too long. Plucking of food items decreases, as nearly all leaves and vines are eaten following a brief period of preparation. Awareness of other animals within the group is indicated, not only by grooming of the mother, but also by grooming of siblings, peers, and silverbacks; much more time is sought near the silverback; curiosity is expressed in copulation of adults. Vocalizations consist of whines, wails, panting chuckles, screeches, hoot cries, shrieks, temper tantrum screams, howls, and pig-grunts. Throughout all these periods, the infant continues to night-nest with its mother and may continue to do so until the age of 5 years.

Pregnancy

Napier and Napier (1967) have included the fetal phase as one of the life periods of primates and a process that is continuous with postnatal growth. The period is ended "when the size of the head is consonant with a safe delivery."

Eleven records of gestation periods of captive gorillas vary between 238 and 295 days (mean = 263; median = 258). During this study copulations have been observed from a minimum period of 212 days prior to parturition to a maximum of 284 days. Observations were not consistent enough during the assumed estrous cycles, however, to draw any positive conclusions about gestation periods except that they appeared grouped around the 260th day.

Parturition

Observations of a gorilla birth in the wild were made by Kelly Stewart and the following summarizes her findings (Stewart, 1977).

The observations were made on December 3, 1975, of a birth to a multiparous female, Marchessa, of Group 5. It was presumed that Marchessa had conceived sometime during the first part of March 1975, though the last time she was seen to mate was on February 18, 1975. She was also seen mating with Beethoven twice while pregnant, which is typical of impregnated gorilla females.

Three hours before parturition all of the group's animals were behaving normally and Marchessa was seen sitting some 8 m from the resting group during a heavy rain. When the rain stopped the group moved off to feed and Marchessa moved along with them with no sign of lagging behind nor any indication of being in pain. The group was next seen at 11:54 at the beginning of a day-resting period, and the closest animal to Marchessa was 6-year-and-11-month-old Puck. It was thought that Marchessa had begun labor. For 18 minutes she was restless and changed position often. At 11:54 she stood and made a nest upon which she sat or lay on her side until 11:57. "She then stood, touched her perineal region with her fingertips, and licked them tentatively." Later blood was found in the nest along with some fluid and mucus. "This possibly meant complete dilation of the cervix, indicating that the infant's head had entered the vagina (Nadler, 1974)." At 11:59 Marchessa moved 2 m and made another nest. From 12:01 to 12:09 she appeared restless, occasionally touched her perineal region and (after Nadler, 1974), was probably touching the emerging head of the infant. At approximately 12:10 Marchessa sat up again, squatted, reached back to the perineal region, grunted twice, and moved her hand in front of her. At 12:11 she put her head to her perineal area and grunted. At 12:12, still squatting, Marchessa reached both hands down behind her legs, she remained like that for a few seconds and the infant emerged. Marchessa sat up and began to chew vigorously. At about 12:12½ Marchessa faced the observer holding the infant in a low, ventro-ventral position. The infant was completely covered in a thick, greenish-brown mucus that showed its facial features. Several gorillas began approaching her. Marchessa moved off and was not seen again until 12:54. At this time there was no noticeable blood, fluid, or tissue around her lips, nor was the umbilical cord seen. Mucus was gone from the infant's hair which was wet and in "curly tufts." The infant's eyes were opened and it gripped the hair on Marchessa's arm, occasionally flexed its fingers and opened and closed its mouth. For 32 minutes Marchessa held the baby belly-down on her arm in wet and cold weather. Marchessa groomed her infant both orally and manually and also rocked it back and forth several times. At 13:23 the baby opened and closed its mouth more frequently and Marchessa twice held it slightly away from her body. The infant's whimpers grew into squeals and Marchessa gave a belch vocalization. She then positioned it with its head at her left breast. For the next 5 minutes the infant's head moved back and forth slightly suggesting suckling at 1 hour 14 minutes after parturition. In Marchessa's second nest there was later seen a great deal of blood along with fluid and globs of mucus. On her trail from the nest were several places where leaves smeared with blood were found. Roughly 12-15 m farther on were two pieces of pink tissue about 5 and 8 in. long, respectively.

Puck was the only animal showing overt interest in the parturition. She moved into Marchessa's first nest, touched the area where the blood was, sniffed her fingers and lay down in the nest. As the infant was being born, Puck moved toward Marchessa to look intently at the newborn. Marchessa's daughter, Pantsy, and Icarus began to approach when Marchessa left, followed by these three out of sight. Within 2 minutes sounds of a skirmish came from the spot where the animals had disappeared. Marchessa returned into view about 7 m below the others and Icarus returned to the nest site.

Discussion

Three stages of delivery behavior were modified by Stewart (1977), after Bowden et al., (1967):

> (1) Onset of contractions to the first appearance of the infant; (2) from the infant's first appearance to its complete emergence; (3) from the delivery of the infant to the complete emergence of the placenta. Marchessa's behavior was typical of that described for captive gorillas in labor. Stages 1 and 2 normally last 30-150 minutes, during which time most females appear restless and uncomfortable (Mallinson et al., 1973; Fisher, 1972; Nadler, 1974).
>
> Stage 2, during a normal delivery in gorillas, rarely lasts more than half an hour and usually only a few minutes.
>
> Stage 3 in gorillas usually lasts 10-30 minutes (Mallinson et al., 1973; Fisher, 1972). There is doubt as to whether or not Marchessa delivered the placenta in the presence of the observer (Stewart). When she was "chewing vigorously" right after the infant's delivery, she might have been eating the placenta.

During the author's study (1979), of 11 examinations of birth sites and adjacent trails, only 1 intact placenta was ever found in a nest and this followed a nonviable birth. Smaller bits and pieces of tissue were found in 8 birth nests, and blood deposits of varying quantities were found in all. In other parturitions, observers found group members interested in smelling or licking fecal material deposited in or around the birth site as well as expressing curiosity in the newborn. The group members showing the most interest in the neonate were juveniles, young adult females, and the group's silverback, in that order—individuals with whom the infant would interact throughout its formative years.

The social unit in which the infant matures is sufficiently small to allow individual relationships of varying degrees of intensity to be formed, and also large and complex enough to demonstrate the infant's ability to discriminate toward specific attachments. The gorilla's social structure is believed to be unique among all the great apes because of the nexus of associations involving recognition of familial ties.

FIGURE 3. Digit, a member of Group 4 and a young silverback in his prime, was senselessly killed on December 31, 1977 by poachers. He had stationed himself about 100 m from the group, a position he usually assumed in order to warn the others of approaching danger. It was in this role of sentry that he was killed, giving up his life so that his family, including his unborn offspring that was to be born to Simba in April 1978, might survive. His murder left an unforgettable void among researchers in the Karisoke area.

Part II—Research 1978

Throughout 1978 the Karisoke Research Centre maintained near daily observations among 28 habituated gorillas (number at end of year) of the 3 main study groups and 44 relatively unhabituated gorillas of 6 fringe groups, groups whose ranges overlap or abut with those of the main study groups. Demographic changes and observational records from these groups are summarized. Reasons for the disintegration of a gorilla group following the poacher slaying of its silverback leader are presented and data pertaining to the influence and relevance of gorilla kinship bonds, female emigrations, and infanticide are included. The author was assisted for varying periods of time by Ian Redmond, Amy Vedder, Bill Weber, Craig Sholley, and David Watts. Their research pursuits were concerned with parasitology and gorilla foraging strategies while the author continued behavioral observations. The Karisoke Research Centre was generously supported by the National Geographic Society for the 11th year and the author remains deeply indebted to the Society for its long-term support and encouragement.

Demography

By the end of 1978 among the 72 gorillas under observation from Karisoke, there was an adult male-to-female ratio of 1:1.1, an immature male-to-female ratio of 1.2:1, and an overall adult-to-immature ratio of 1.4:1 (see Table 2). During the course of the year 6 animals died and 3 were born. Two of the 6 lost were adult females; therefore, given the projected average of 1 female contributing 4 individuals to the population during the course of her reproductive lifetime, the Visoke population theoretically suffered almost a 10% loss (Fossey, 1982). Two of the deceased immatures were also female (3 and 9 months of age, respectively); however, because of a 45% mortality rate for infants during their first year, their projected contribution to the gene pool cannot be significantly determined.

Study and Fringe Group Observations

Group 4

Until July 24, 1978, Group 4 could be considered an average gorilla group despite the death of the young silverback Digit on December 31, 1977. The group remained with a dominant silverback leader, Uncle Bert, 3 sexually mature females, 2 young adult females approaching sexual maturity, 2 blackbacks, and 2 juvenile males. Following Digit's killing the animals returned to the death site to wander circuitously, as though looking for him. Their ranging in the distant western saddle soon became so

TABLE 2. Composition of Study and Fringe Groups at End of 1978 within Karisoke Study Area (25 km²)
Group names: N=Nunkie's, S=Suza, K=Kimbia, B=Basher's, W=Wageni's

Age/Sex Classification	*Age (yrs)*	*Study groups*			*Lone*	*Fringe groups*				*Grp of 13*	*Grp 6*	*Total*
		4	*5*	*N*		*S*	*K*	*B*	*W*			
Silverback	13 - 15+	0	2	1	1	2	2	1	1	2	1	13
Blackback	8 - 13	2	0	0		1	0	0	0	1	0	4
Adult ♀	8+	0	4	6		2	0	0	1	2	4	19
Adult ?	8+	0	0	0		0	2	1	1	2	0	6
Young adult ♂	6 - 8	0	1	0		0	0	0	0	0	1	2
Young adult ♀	6 - 8	0	1	0		1	0	0	0	0	1	3
Young adult ?	6 - 8	0	0	0		0	2	1	0	4	0	7
Juvenile ♂	3 - 6	1	1	0		0	0	0	0	0	0	2
Juvenile ♀	3 - 6	0	0	1		0	0	0	0	0	0	1
Juvenile ?	3 - 6	0	0	0		0	1	0	0	0	2	3
Infant ♂	0 - 3	0	2	3		0	0	0	0	0	0	5
Infant ♀	0 - 3	0	2	0		0	0	0	0	0	0	2
Infant ?	0 - 3	0	0	0		0	0	0	1	2	2	5
TOTALS		3	13	11	1	6	7	3	4	13	11	72

erratic that the author and camp assistants had to herd the animals back to Visoke's slopes to get them out of an area heavily infested with poachers. Between February and the first part of July they remained on Visoke where, on April 6, Simba gave birth to her first infant, a female named Mwelu, sired by Digit. Simba had, herself, been the first infant born into a group following her father's death. As a youngster she had been protected by Uncle Bert, possibly her half-brother, and it was Uncle Bert who also protected Simba and her newborn against the boisterousness of other group members. On June 22 Uncle Bert's mate, Flossie, gave birth to their third offspring, a female named Frito. It seemed likely that the two impending parturitions were the reason the group leader did not venture back into the saddle until July 16 where once again they ranged near the area of Digit's killing.

On the morning of July 24, after arising from their night nests, Uncle Bert and Macho were each killed by a single bullet during a planned capture attempt. The intended captive, 3-year-old Kweli, was shot in the clavicle as a means by the poachers of impeding his ability to escape, but he managed to flee with the rest of the group back to the safety of Visoke's slopes. Neither Uncle Bert nor Macho was the intended victim; however, gorilla parents will die in defense of their offspring, and both were killed as they rushed to Kweli's assistance.

Tiger, 10 years and 8 months old, took over Uncle Bert's lead position on the flight back to Visoke, where they met a group of 13 individuals, including 2 silverbacks. Tiger succeeded in repulsing the intervention of the group's 2 silverbacks and led his natal group into the core of their own range area. During the first week following the killings, Tiger and the dominant female, Flossie, alternated in leading the direction of travel while Tiger night-nested with Kweli and groomed the bullet wound of the 3-year-old orphan who was evidencing distress from the injury and the loss of maternal care. Tiger also was obligated to check the rambunctious and bully-type behavior from the 11½-year-old male immigrant, Beetsme, who increasingly threatened the harmony of the group. Initially, Beetsme's agonistic behavior was undirected toward any specific individual, but, 2 weeks after the death of Uncle Bert, Beetsme narrowed his aggressive actions to Flossie and her 2-month-old infant, sired by Uncle Bert.

Flossie had been strongly bonded to Uncle Bert who, because of his leadership role, was directly responsible for the maintenance of group cohesiveness, a responsibility that involved enforcement of near-constant discipline over Beetsme. Now, without such restraint, Beetsme was able to challenge Tiger's authority. As the violence of Beetsme's attacks against Flossie increased, Tiger's defense of the older female became more intense, despite the physical risk to himself, but 21 days after

FIGURE 4. In July 1978, months after Digit's slaying, Uncle Bert, the majestic leader of Group 4, was shot through the heart and decapitated by poachers. As no gorilla group can exist without its silverback leader, Group 4 disintegrated: The females emigrated to other males, subjecting their infants to infanticide.

Uncle Bert's death Beetsme succeeded in killing 3-month-old Frito, Uncle Bert's last offspring. The fatal wound, inflicted by Beetsme, was a 3-cm bite in Frito's brachial plexus that splintered the humerus and severed the right brachial artery and vein. Flossie carried Frito's body for 2 days, and was repeatedly attacked by Beetsme while Tiger consistently came to her aid. During the seventh attack Flossie dropped Frito's body and did not attempt to retrieve it because she was still being pursued by Beetsme but did look back to where the body lay for a full minute following the attack. Later the same day, Beetsme strutted and directed running attacks toward Flossie an additional 4 times. Three days following the infanticide, Flossie presented and copulated with Beetsme twice as a means of appeasement. Between the 2 copulations Beetsme directed 13 separate incidents of aggression toward the old female in the forms of chasing, strutting, and hitting. Following the second copulation, he aggressively displayed 18 times toward Flossie.

Seven days following Frito's death Flossie transferred to Nunkie's Group at the first opportunity she could get. (Because females do not travel alone, she had to wait until another group sought an interaction with Group 4.) Flossie remained in Nunkie's Group only 18 days before she transferred to the Suza Group, a small group of 4 members including 1 nulliparous female. By this move Flossie enhanced both her reproductive status as well as her rank. It was obvious that she could not remain with the remnants of Group 4 as there were no sexually mature males with whom she could breed. Flossie's immigration into Nunkie's Group might well have guaranteed her reproductive success but not her status, as Nunkie already had a well-established harem of 4 females. Because female dominance order depends upon acquisition order by the silverback, Flossie would have been the lowest ranking female in Nunkie's Group. This explained her near-immediate transfer to the small Suza Group, in which she was the only breeding female. In both transfers Flossie was accompanied by her 7-year-old daughter, Cleo, who, as a sexually maturing female, would eventually share her mother's advantages. Flossie's 4-year-old son, Titus, who would have gained no benefits by leaving with his mother, was left behind in Group 4. The 8-year-old female Augustus also left Group 4 with Flossie, but remained in Nunkie's Group since her mother, Petula, 4 years previously had become Nunkie's first acquired female, hence Augustus was able eventually to increase her rank above that bequeathed in Group 4. Flossie gave birth to her sixth infant 11 months following her transfer to the Suza Group, and since her time in the group was greater than gestation, it may be assumed that the infant was sired by the group's dominant silverback. She became a grandmother 27 months later, when her daughter Cleo gave birth in the same group.

Following the emigrations of the 3 females, Group 4 consisted only of 4 sexually immature males—Beetsme, Tiger, Titus, Kweli—plus Simba and her 5-month-old daughter, Mwelu, sired by Digit. Unlike Flossie, Simba was seldom the recipient of aggression from Beetsme. Possibly this was because Mwelu had been sired by Digit, not Uncle Bert, and Simba also had had a number of "appeasement copulations" with Beetsme *prior* to giving birth. In many nonhuman primate species such copulatory behavior appears to be practiced for the purpose of confusing paternity (Tutin, 1980). In this instance, however, because of Beetsme's sexual immaturity, the mountings seemed to function only toward reinforcement of social bonds. Tiger, the young, inexperienced group leader, now had a second orphan, 4-year-old Titus, to console by grooming, increased exchanges of belch vocalizations, play, and the sharing of night nests along with Kweli. Beetsme, having lost his scapegoat, Flossie, resorted to mounting Titus and the injured Kweli. By the end of September he began directing agonistic behavior toward Tiger and Simba in the form of chasing and whacking. Simba increased her distance from other group members in travel, feeding, and resting periods to avoid belligerence from Beetsme and for the protection of her infant.

Despite Tiger's paternal efforts toward Kweli, the 3-year-old died from complications of the bullet wound on October 26, 3 months after the slayings of his mother and father.

On December 6, 1978, the group was further reduced in membership when Simba transferred to Nunkie's Group. The transfer, of course, resulted in the infanticide by Nunkie of 8-month-old Mwelu, Digit's only progeny. The presumed fatal bite was to the skull, and another deep wound was evident in the groin region—both wounds typical of infanticide victims. Simba's emigration was necessary for her reproductive success, but it did not benefit her from the standpoint of status. Unlike Augustus, Simba had no mother in the group and, as Nunkie's last acquired female, her rank in the female hierarchy was the lowest of the 5 females who had preceded her. Subsequently there were no further interactions between Nunkie's Group and others such as had benefited Flossie and Cleo, thus Simba remained to give birth 32 months later to a female infant (Jenny) sired by Nunkie.

On January 21, 1979, Peanuts, the lone silverback of what was formerly known as Group 8, took over the leadership of the 3 Group 4 male remnants and eventually led them into distant range areas in pursuit of females from other fringe groups.

Group 5

There were no significant changes in Group 5's range area throughout 1978 except for their tendency to rely more heavily upon the bamboo zone even outside of prime shooting months. Past core areas on Visoke's southern slopes and also along the series of hills in the saddle south of Karisoke were seldom used. A heavy influx of tourists on the slopes was probably the reason the group infrequently visited that region, but why they spent so little time in the hill sector cannot be understood, unless they were deterred by the increasing presence of the Wageni Group in that area.

Group 5 had 16 interactions with 3 different social units during 1978, most of which were auditory, thus avoiding physical proximity. The only interaction of any consequence occurred on July 14 with Group 6 on Visoke's southeastern slopes, when Liza emigrated from Group 5. Liza, who had been in Group 5 for at least 13 years, had bred 3 offspring with Beethoven, but left her 8-year-old daughter, Quince, and her 4-year-old son, Pablo, behind when she transferred to Group 6. Her oldest daughter, Nikki, had emigrated 5 years previously from Group 5. Liza's departure from a group where she appeared to have developed permanent bonds with the dominant silverback was a reproductive strategy that enhanced her breeding capabilities. As was the case of Group 4's Petula 4 years previously, Liza had been coming into regular estrous cycles for over a year, that is, when her youngest offspring was nearly 3 years of age. Like Petula, she had continued to nurse her juvenile, a fact suggesting that prolonged lactation inhibits conception. Also, as in the case of Petula, Liza's solicitations for copulations with her long-term mate were largely ignored. Eleven months after the transfers of the 2 females, they gave birth to infants sired by their respective new mates. The advantages of the transfers would have been lost had the females taken their offspring with them and thus not completely terminated nursing. After his mother's transfer Pablo managed to build his own night nests very near to those of Beethoven, and also traveled and fed with his father rather than his sister, Quince.

For the past 6 years, Quince, even as an older infant, had shown strong grooming tendencies, particularly toward Beethoven, and keen maternal inclinations toward all newborn infants in Group 5. Quince was always the first individual in the group to be trusted with handling young infants, and gave every promise of becoming a highly skilled primiparous mother. On September 26 unusual blood and mucus deposits were recovered from Quince's night nest but no trace of a nonviable birth was found despite intensive searching. From that date until October 20, when Quince died, the depth of the mutual attraction between herself and her father, Beethoven, was profoundly illustrated. Occasionally, her weakening physical condition showed signs of remission; however, during most of this period she could locomote only by crawling on her elbows and knees until collapsing. Beethoven reduced the group's pace of travel so that she might keep up with them and he also intervened when immatures ran at, kicked, or hit at Quince. Such behavior, subsequently seen only once during the course of the study—Group 5's reaction to Marchessa in 1980 (Fossey, 1981)—is most likely an expression of the animals' reaction to abnormal responses from a weakened individual and perhaps represents "attackers' " efforts to evoke reactions to their stimuli which, to a human, mistakenly appear as aggression. Until the time of her illness Quince maintained excellent relationships with all group members, especially Beethoven, thus there is no reason to believe that she would suddenly become an object of hostility. Quince, as did others, showed unusual interest in both the liquid and solid contents of her anus. Despite her increasing weakness and prolonged periods of shaking, she continued trying to groom Beethoven and her brother, Pablo, until the very end, when it was no longer possible. Her body was taken to the Ruhengeri Hospital for an autopsy within an hour following her death. Her ovaries were found normal and inactive; however, her mammae when squeezed produced large quantities of thick white milk. The Ruhengeri surgeon assumed that Quince had been poisoned, but later examination of organ samples sent to France revealed a negative response. The author conducted a more detailed autopsy at Karisoke to collect additional specimens which, when examined in America, revealed malaria as the cause of death, the first known among gorillas.

Following his sister's death Pablo adhered closely to Beethoven and also sought proximity with the group's dominant female Effie. Effie's clan consisted of 4 offspring, including Icarus, while the subordinate Marchessa's line consisted of 2 sons and a daughter sired by Beethoven, and a granddaughter sired by Icarus. The breeding cross between matrilines (Pantsy with Icarus) was the most likely reason for the increase in intragroup discontent during 1978. Although there is always some degree of friction between gorilla matrilines, it usually is settled by a group's dominant silverback, who is inclined to come to the aid of his first acquired mate and progeny more consistently than of females and offspring acquired later. Because Icarus now had an offspring, Muraha, his defense was directed toward its mother, Pantsy, rather than to his mother, Effie, and his 3 full sisters. Subsequently, commonplace female squabbles resulted in physical clashes between father (Beethoven) and son (Icarus), each protective of his first acquired mate and progeny. An increasing number of such altercations occurred around the estrous cycles of the group's sexually mature and maturing females. For the first time since the study began, biting was observed between the 2 silverbacks though it was obvious that both used constraint.

Group 5 provided an excellent example of the way in which 2 closely related silverbacks may remain within a single group for the dual purposes of procreation and mutually advantageous protection of their respective females and young. Of necessity, such a situation must allow both father and son breeding opportunities, even though some degree of inbreeding may result, as it did in Group 5. By way of comparison, in 1968, Group 4's silverback father and son (Whinny and Uncle Bert) were far more widely spread in age, thus when Whinny died of natural causes, Uncle Bert took over breeding opportunities with some of the remaining females while others emigrated to interacting silverbacks.

NUNKIE'S GROUP

Throughout 1978 Nunkie's Group did not leave Visoke's slopes. Because of the frequent and prolonged travel of Group 4 and Group 5 in the saddle, Nunkie was able to use their respective ranges on the slopes as well as the less desirable higher subalpine region he appropriated after arriving in the study area in October 1972. Following the decimation of Group 4 Nunkie moved from Visoke's southeastern slopes, long an integral part of Group 5's range, and usurped Group 4's section on the western slopes. By the end of the year, and despite having had complete access to Uncle Bert's range for 5 months, Nunkie had not ventured into the western saddle which offered higher quality vegetation. Possibly, because of previous experience with poachers, Nunkie was a far more wary silverback than Uncle Bert and appeared to have been forfeiting resource gain for group security.

Until August, when he acquired Flossie, Cleo, and Augustus, Nunkie's encounters with other groups were either auditory or visual. With a harem of 4, he was no longer intent upon acquiring additional females. His temporary acquisition of Flossie and Cleo occurred primarily because of their willingness to transfer to him, and he did not strongly contest their departure to the small Suza Group 18 days later. The movements of the 2 females well illustrate the "domino effect" of one social unit upon another. Nunkie's Group served as an intermediary making it possible for Flossie and Cleo to transfer not only to another social unit, but also to another mountain (Karisimbi) where the core area of the Suza Group lay. The movements of the 2 females show how effectively the transfer process functions for the purposes of exogamy.

By the end of 1978 Nunkie's Group had grown to include 6 breeding females with whom he had sired 4 offspring over a 4½-year period. Of particular interest, and possibly contributory to Nunkie's breeding success, is that his females had been acquired in near-pairs from the same groups. He gained Papoose and Petula from Group 4, lost them for several weeks to Samson but reacquired them together in 1974. In 1976 he gained Fuddle and 5 months later Pandora from Group 6. Precisely the same spacing occurred in 1978 when he acquired Augustus and 5 months later, Simba, from Group 4. Whether his was an intentional or an accidental strategy cannot be known, but the attainment of mates in near-pairs from the same group appears to have optimized his reproductive abilities far more than that of other silverbacks, who usually obtain only 1 female at a time and, thus far, from random groups. Females obtained in such a manner are prone to transfer several times as they have difficulties integrating themselves into a well-established female hierarchy. Indeed, Nunkie himself lost 2 females who were taken singly and from different groups. There was a decided pairing among the 6 females of Nunkie's harem which was equivalent to mother and daughter pairing seen in long-established groups and contributes toward the overall cohesiveness of what is essentially a paternally-oriented familial unit.

SUZA GROUP

This group of 2 silverbacks (J. P. Suza and Jiwe), 1 large blackback (Hano), and 1 nulliparous female (Saba) were only identified as a distinct social unit in 1978 when they began visiting Visoke's slopes from their normally used range south of Visoke. Before acquiring Flossie and Cleo in September 1978 the group was nonviable, which possibly explains their efforts to seek interactions with Visoke groups to obtain females. As mentioned under Group 4, Flossie gave birth to an infant (Anjin) of unknown sex 11 months after her immigration; her daughter, Cleo, gave birth to her first offspring (Safari) in December 1981, at the age of 10 years and 4 months.

KIMBIA GROUP (CHUI GROUP)

This group was first seen in 1976. With the exception of the loss of 1 juvenile since that time, its composition has remained stable which is surprising considering its poacher-infested range. The 2 silverbacks are quite high-strung, and attempts at contacting the group usually result in each silverback splitting from the other, taking several group members with him.

BASHER'S AND WAGENI'S GROUP

There is nothing to add about these small groups except that they were accounted for again in 1978 for the third consecutive year along Karisimbi's foothills in the southern section of the study area.

GROUP OF 13

A group of comparable size has been known to frequent Visoke's northeastern slopes and adjacent saddle area since 1973. Of interest is that Peanuts, who had been traveling in the same area with 5 animals in March 1977 was found alone in October 1977. In February 1978 the same 5 animals were found in the large Group of 13. It was this group that Group 4 encountered on July 26 following the killings. When the Group of 13 was again contacted in September it was seen that Purser had just given birth and that a second female also had an infant of only several months.

Group 6

This fringe group of 11 members ranged on Visoke's northern and eastern slopes, and it was to this group that Liza of Group 5 transferred in July 1978. Since 1969 the group had been led by a dominant silverback Brutus; it is easily distinguished by the presence of an adult female named Yaws, whose facial disfigurement gives her the appearance of having three nares. Numerous noseprints have been made of the group's 3 immatures, Ringo, Josey, and Fluff.

Infanticide

In discussing the underlying causation and function of infanticide among gorillas it is first necessary to examine their reliance upon the resources of their habitat as well as the modes of their social structure. Mountain gorillas are essentially herbivorous, though meat eating has been incidentally observed when gorillas have found invertebrates in dead tree bark, foliage stalks, leaves, and galls. Exploitation of an infant victim as a food resource—cannibalism—may be disregarded as a motivation among gorillas though it has occurred in 83% of all chimpanzee episodes (Goodall, 1978).

Gorillas live in a cohesive, often uni-male group structure in which ordinarily the female, and not the male, emigrates. Female movements appear to be prompted for the purpose of exogamy and individual advancement of status. In five of six (83%) well-documented cases of gorilla infanticide the victim's mother exchanged breeding partners as a direct consequence of the event. By forming new bonds with the usually unrelated infanticidal male, the female functions toward exogamy (Fossey, 1983).

The sex of the victims killed by male gorillas appears to be insignificant, for it is the female who is considered the resource, and the victim only an entity to be disposed of in order to gain immediate access to the resource. Among gorillas there has been only one case in which the killer was suspected to have been a female. In this instance also, the infant's sex seemed of little consequence. The killing was an effective means of eliminating the subordinate matriline's progeny who would eventually become a competitor against the aggressor's own progeny for food resources, breeding opportunities, and paternal protection (Pusey, 1980). In the above case, the presumed female-inflicted infanticide also worked toward elimination of an incestuous infant, however it may only be speculated that the side-result influenced the motivation for the killing (Kawanaka, 1981).

Among the great apes, gorillas have the highest degree of sexual dimorphism, with adult females being half the size of silverback males. For this reason gorilla females cannot risk much retaliation in defense of their infants as they would be severely penalized by the infanticidal males. It is also possible that sexual dimorphism contributes to the manner in which infants are killed. Of 8 gorilla infanticide victims recovered during the course of the study, 63% were killed by fatal skull bites, "ritualized biting" (Angst and Thommen, 1977), and none were known to have been subjected to bizarre behavior from their attackers.

To conclude, the polygynous mating system of the gorilla imposes a penalty of sorts upon the female because of her total dependence upon a single mate for her protection as well as for that of the offspring she has conceived with that male. Additionally, there exists competition between matrilines of a gorilla group for the protection and the attention of a single group leader. The strong linear dominance hierarchy among females obviously becomes more marked as clans within any one group increase in size. There must be a balance at some level when genetic homogeneity, coupled by intragroup competition, prompts female dispersal and, subsequently, may result in infanticide (Fossey, 1983).

In general there appear to be at least five distinct situations in which infanticide occurred among mountain gorillas:

(1) The death of the silverback leader of the infant victim's natal group.

(2) Competition between sexually mature males to obtain permanent breeding access to nonestrous females so as to enhance their own reproductive success at the expense of competitor males.

(3) The existence within the basically one-male-structured familial gorilla group of a female linear dominance hierarchy, which prompts female emigrations for the advancement of their status and that of their subsequent offspring, even at the risk of losing current offspring.

(4) Intragroup competition between matrilineal lines that may provoke kin-bonded clans to infanticide of nonrelated young on occasions when their access to the dominant silverback's support, consanguinity, or even food resources are threatened by offspring of non-clan group members.

(5) Extensive range overlaps resulting in increased intergroup interactions, particularly when a disproportionate ratio of males to females exists.

Part III—Research 1979

Throughout 1979 the Karisoke Research Centre maintained near daily observations among 30 habituated gorillas (number at end of year) of the 3 main study groups and 38 relatively unhabituated gorillas of 4 fringe groups, groups whose ranges overlap or abut with those of the main study groups. Demographic changes and observational records from these groups are summarized as are the findings of a 17-month parasitology research study accomplished at Karisoke during 1976 and 1977.

During 1979 the author was assisted for varying periods of time by Peter Veit, Amy Vedder, Bill Weber, Craig Sholley, and David Watts. The Karisoke Research Centre was generously supported by the National Geographic Society for the 12th year, and the author remains deeply indebted to the Society for its long-term support and encouragement.

Demography

By the end of 1979, among all 68 gorillas under observation, there was a mature-to-immature ratio of 1:0.94. Among the study group individuals only, there was a mature-to-immature ratio of 1:0.81, an adult male-to-female ratio of 1:1.67, and an immature male-to-female ratio of 1:0.44. Among the 3 study groups, only 2 (Group 5 and Nunkie's) contained adult females (4 and 6, respectively) while the third group (Peanuts') contained none. Such unequal distribution of breeding combinations leaves the propagation of the species within the study area, at least, to only 3 males as compared with 5 adult males the previous year prior to the poachers' slayings. Given that a male's reproductive life is some 8 years shorter than that of a female because of the necessity of having to acquire his harem from other established groups, a male's potential reproductive output is between three to four times as high as that of a female because of the harem structure of any group. As of the end of 1979, 1 aged silverback (Beethoven) was known to have sired 13 offspring, thus the loss of 2 silverbacks in their prime represents a theoretical loss of at least 26 additions to the gene pool. Elsewhere within the Virungas the reproductive rate appears to be lower, particularly in the eastern section, where the gorillas are not as well protected and do not have access to prime vegetation. Here, groups show a median of slightly less than 2 females per unit and a lower birth rate than in the study area.

During the course of the year, among the main study groups, 2 deaths occurred, both immatures killed by poachers, and only 1 birth was recorded. Among the fringe groups, 2 births were known to have occurred, both to females (Liza and Flossie) who had transferred out of the study groups.

Study and Fringe Group Observations

Group 4

On January 21, 1979, the lone silverback Peanuts, formerly of Group 8, joined with the 3 male remnants of Group 4 (Beetsme, Tiger, and Titus), a merger considered as a means of providing a foundation for the expansion of a new and viable group unit. By the end of the year, however, only 2 additional animals had joined Peanuts's Group, and both of these were males obtained from a fringe group on Visoke's northern slopes in April. The all-male group of 6 ranged errantly in the saddle area far to the west of Visoke where they occasionally encountered 1 large group from Mt. Mikeno. They spent 70% of their time on Visoke's northern slopes in a region occupied by 2 fringe groups; thus, greater opportunities for intergroup interactions were available because of extensive range overlap. Less than 7% of their time was spent in areas unshared by other groups.

Characteristic of Peanuts's Group during the first half of 1979 was a high degree of intragroup friction as Peanuts, the eldest by at least 7 years, established his dominancy over the next in age, Beetsme. Tiger, 12 years old, became involved in skirmishes only when coming to the defense of 5-year-old Titus, also a natal member of Group 4. The degree of relatedness between the 2 young male immigrants from the fringe group (Stilgar's) is not known; it is assumed, however, that they share no kinship bonds with the other members of Peanuts's Group, thus they form the fourth division within the unit. Records of affinitive behavior show that young Titus exerted a cohesive effect between the oddly sorted group members by eliciting play and grooming bouts that prompted interactions. Beetsme was responsible for the highest frequency of aggressive behavior, particularly when attempting to mount the 4 group members, all younger than himself. Peanuts, though never observed mounting others, objected strenuously to Beetsme's sexual activities, and this resulted in severe fights between the 2 older males.

Group 5

Three major factors seemed obviously responsible for Group 5's range movements for a second consecutive year. From January through April the group ranged within very familiar terrain on Visoke's southeastern-facing slopes, where prime food resources included dirt (for its magnesium, calcium, and potassium content), *Vernonia* trees, celery, thistle, and other herbaceous slope foliage. In May, when tourists again frequently attempted contacts with the group, the animals left Visoke's slopes to travel up to 4 km away in the southwestern saddle area toward

Mounts Karisimbi and Mikeno, where they climbed into the subalpine and alpine zones. Food resources available in this region included giant *Senecio* and heather trees, blackberries, and numerous high-altitude plants sought for their roots.

This region has been used by the Suza Group longer than by Group 5, and from May through October, 18 known interactions occurred between the 2 groups, resulting in Group 5's fleeing back to its usual range on Visoke's slopes, with the Suza Group usually following over most of the 4-km distance. Once on Visoke, Group 5 seldom had more than a week's rest before tourists, particularly heavy during the summer months, forced the gorillas to retreat into the southern saddle region, where the Suza Group encountered Group 5 within a week's time. Much like a Ping-Pong match, Group 5's range fluctuated between these two specific regions until November, when the third factor responsible for range movements, bamboo shooting, shifted the group to the narrow, 3.75-km bamboo strip concentrated along the eastern boundary of the Parc des Volcans. Group 5 has been successful in slowly monopolizing this prime resource area only over the past 6 years.

It seems significant that, over a period of 11 consecutive years, 1979 was one of two in which no births occurred in Group 5. During 1973, the second year in which no births occurred, the intrusion of the lone silverback Nunkie was believed to have exerted the same type of pressure upon Group 5's range and daily movement pattern. It is also interesting to note that the group's dominant female Effie, prior to Nunkie's arrival into the study area, had a mean interbirth interval of 41 months (spans=2). Following the disturbance caused by Nunkie's persistent harassment of the group as he sought to obtain females, Effie's interbirth interval increased to 43 months (spans=3); and following the disruptions in 1979, her interbirth interval increased to 45 months (spans=4) when in early March she aborted a fetus, estimated as 2½ months' development, after an intense 3-week hounding of the group by a French ciné team.

Intergroup interactions between Group 5 and the Suza Group resulted in mild wounding of both Beethoven and Icarus on only two occasions and none to the 9-year-old blackback, Ziz, who, because of his invulnerable status as a sexually immature male, was able to mingle more closely with the 3 adult Suza Group males than could Beethoven and Icarus, thereby gaining considerable experience in interactions with extraneous males.

Icarus evidenced considerable curiosity about the Suza Group, but because he was sexually bonded to 2 Group 5 females, he was obligated to remain with his natal group, whose 12 members continued under Beethoven's influence with respect to both direction and speed of movement.

In 1979, 125 instances of sexual behavior were observed among Group 5 members, and 78% of these occurred during days when the Suza Group was within auditory distance of Group 5. The majority of those mountings were between animals of the same sex or were age-discrepant mountings of mature to immature animals. Four of Group 5's adult females—Effie, Puck, Tuck, and Pantsy—were consistently mounted when in estrus, as indicated by obviously swollen vulvas; among the 4, however, only Effie was ovulating, though she cycled for 4 months prior to conception by Beethoven. Beethoven's other mate, Marchessa, was only mounted in June, August, and September, less frequently than any other adult female in the group. Because her son, Shinda, was 34 months of age at the end of 1979, Marchessa should have evidenced more regularity in cycling. That she did not suggests the possibility of the beginnings of a menopausal condition.

By the end of the year, Shinda had not yet been observed undergoing any weaning restrictions, and Marchessa appeared to have plenty of milk. So did her daughter Pantsy for her 33-month-old daughter Muraha, although, toward the last 2 months in 1979, Pantsy began mild disciplinary tactics consisting of shielding her breasts with her arms or diverting Muraha's interest in suckling by grooming the infant. In contrast, Effie's daughter Poppy, 44 months old at the end of 1979, evidenced weaning distress throughout the year, with the most crucial period beginning in October, the same month in which her mother was thought to have been impregnated.

Friction between the clans of Effie and Marchessa diminished somewhat during 1979 for two possible reasons: (1) Icarus had "crossed" genetic barriers by breeding with Pantsy (of Marchessa) and with his own sister, Puck (of Effie). By so doing, he had taken on paternal responsibilities for both females and their respective offspring. Because his bonding with Pantsy was of longer duration than that with Puck, Pantsy and not his full sister Puck became his highest ranking female, as demonstrated by frequencies of defensive behavior on his part toward Pantsy and their daughter Muraha. (2) If Marchessa were commencing menopause, as suspected, she certainly represented less of a competitor to Effie, whose tolerance of Marchessa's proximity greatly increased as the year wore on. No similar tolerance was shown by Effie's daughters—Puck, Tuck, Poppy—toward Marchessa's daughter Pantsy and the latter's offspring Muraha. Friction between the younger females was settled either jointly or singly by Beethoven and Icarus.

NUNKIE'S GROUP

Throughout 1978 Nunkie's Group ranged exclusively on Visoke's slopes though, following the decimation of Group 4 in July 1978, the group had the opportunity of taking over that group's high quality vegetation zone in the saddle west of Visoke. In February 1979 Nunkie's Group left Visoke's slopes for the first time in 14 months and, within a month, on March 3, encountered a trap line which cost the life of Nunkie's first-sired offspring, Lee (of Petula), who was 46 months old when she died 3 months later, on May 9, from the effects of the wire snare. Nunkie's Group returned to the security of Visoke's slopes for only a month before returning to the saddle area because of consistent pressure from Peanuts's Group. Thus, in many respects, Nunkie's pattern of travel greatly resembled that of Group 5, whose routing was related to the presence or absence of other groups, as well as to human encroachment in 1979. Upon losing his second sired offspring, N'Gee (of Papoose), 43 months old when she disappeared after an unobserved encounter with poachers, Nunkie's Group returned to Visoke, where they remained for more than a year before again venturing into the saddle.

Some of the basic reasons for Nunkie's success as a group leader have been detailed (Fossey, 1983), though as of the end of 1978, he had not yet evidenced certain behavioral patterns seen in 1979. The addition of 2 females elevated the number in Nunkie's harem to 6, the largest known to have been acquired and maintained by any single silverback since the study began. Nunkie's quest for females was satisfied, and his need for a range of good quality vegetation was met after the decimation of Group 4 by poachers in mid-1978. With both of these essential requirements fulfilled by the beginning of 1979, Nunkie became more assertive in defense of his assets by increasingly resorting to prolonged auditory displays of chest-beats and hoot series whenever other groups infringed upon his appropriated terrain. Previously, he, not the silverbacks of Visoke's main study groups, had been the interloper and seldom advertised his proximity to other groups.

Although younger than Nunkie by 15-20 years, the lone silverback Peanuts had been expected to acquire females from Karisoke's study groups before Nunkie, because Peanuts had "inherited" the range of his natal group, Group 8, following the natural death of his father Rafiki. Youth, coupled with consequent inexperience in interactions, is suggested as one reason why Peanuts was unsuccessful in obtaining females, but an equally strong reason might be attributed to systematic pathology resulting from a bite wound Peanuts received in 1971 during an intergroup interaction. The injury impeded the young male's physical development and apparently reduced his previous inclinations for physical interactions with extraneous males, particularly Nunkie.

Fringe Groups

Suza Group. This group ranges in the extreme southern section of the study area on and adjacent to Mt. Karisimbi. It consists of 7 members, including Flossie and Cleo, formerly of Group 4. Flossie gave birth to an infant conceived by the Suza Group's dominant silverback, J. P. Suza, in August 1979. The group interacted with Group 5 fairly consistently when encounters occurred in the southern section of the study area.

Group 6. This group ranges on Visoke's northern and eastern slopes and consists of 10 members including Liza, formerly of Group 5. Liza gave birth to an infant conceived by Group 6's dominant silverback, Brutus, in June 1979. Group 6 interacted with Group 5 occasionally on Visoke's eastern slopes.

Group of 13. This group ranged on Visoke's northwestern and western slopes and adjacent saddle terrain. It consisted of 13 members, though this count is based primarily upon nest counts, thus infant dung may have been missed. It contained Purser and Maidenform, 2 females formerly of Group 9. The group interacted frequently with Peanuts's and occasionally with Nunkie's Group, and it is possible that 2 members acquired by Peanuts in 1979 came from the Group of 13.

Stilgar's Group. This group also ranged on Visoke's northwestern and northern slopes and adjacent saddle area, and it consists of 8 members, as judged from brief visual observations and dung contents of nests. They interacted frequently with Peanuts's Group though usually seeking to avoid encounters.

Though little in the way of behavioral observations may be gained from relatively unhabituated fringe groups, it is exceedingly important to contact them regularly so as to more fully comprehend demographic parameters within the Visoke population, which constitutes about half of the western distribution of the Virunga species. Eventually, a detailed comparison of the habitat in the eastern and western sections of the Virungas in relation to the differences that exist between the gorilla populations in the two areas could be very important toward understanding the environmental factors that control group size and composition.

Part IV—Parasitology Research 1976-1978

At Karisoke, between November 1976 and April 1978, research assistant Ian Redmond accomplished the first long-term parasitology study ever undertaken there. Working with an old microscope which he himself assembled, Redmond examined countless samples of gorilla feces to obtain specimens of endoparasites, and he made freehand drawings of his findings. Most of the samples were analyzed fresh at Karisoke, but some were preserved in 10% formalin for later study at the British Museum (Natural History). In England, assistance with facilities and identifications was received from Mrs. E. Harris, Dr. David Gibson, and Mr.

Charles Hussey of the Parasitic Worms Section of that institution. Specimens of ectoparasites, recovered from the bodies of deceased gorillas, were identified in the Entomology Department by Dr. C. Lyal. To the above people, the Karisoke Research Centre and Ian Redmond remain most grateful. Redmond's report follows.

Methods

Endoparasites were studied by fecal analysis and, on one occasion, by dissecting a juvenile (Kweli) who had died from a gunshot wound. Ectoparasites were never observed on healthy, free-living gorillas but were collected from deceased animals. Two kinds of ectoparasites were found, the gorilla louse *Pthirus gorillae* and a tiny, soft-bodied mite *Pangorillalges gorillae.*

Fecal samples were collected either when defecation was seen during behavioral observations, or by collecting from identified night nests. Samples were analyzed fresh at Karisoke or were preserved in 10 g of 10% formalin for later analysis in England.

The quantitative techniques which evolved over the first few weeks were as follows:

1. Samples were collected in polyethylene bags and weighed whole.
2. Direct smears were made by emulsifying 20 mg in 2 drops of 0.8% NaCl solution on a glass slide, then examined under a coverslip at 66 × magnification.
3. From the bulk of the sample 10 g were separated and washed through a sieve (1-mm × 1-mm mesh size) into a bucket using filtered stream water. This was left to settle. The sediment was then rinsed through a fine cloth sieve and closely examined in a black tray against which the white nematodes were visible. These were counted and examined, wet-mounted, under the microscope.
4. The remainder of the sample was washed through the large sieve, but this time the residue was searched for larger helminths, such as cestode proglottids.

Results

Nematodes (Roundworms)

Type A (a viviparous nematode to 4 mm in length, with a truncate head end). Adult females and larvae were recovered in varying numbers (0.1-10/g) but no males have yet been found. The specific characteristics of nematodes are often restricted to the shape of the male reproductive organs, so identification of Type A is not yet certain. It has obvious affinities to the genus *Probstmayria,* but the shape of certain structures differs from the generic description. Either the genus must be redescribed to include Type A or a new genus must be created.

Type B (similar to Type A but only 2 mm in length, more slender, and with a much more pointed head end). This is almost certainly *Probstmayria gorillae* Kreiss 1955, but, as with Type A, no males have been located to enable positive identification. The size and shape of females is exactly that of *P. gorillae*. Members of the genus *Probstmayria* are unusual for parasitic nematodes in that they exhibit continuity of generations within the same host. They live and reproduce within the gut of several diverse herbivores, including horses, pigs, apes, and tortoises. Larvae passed in the feces seem able to survive for several days in warm, damp soil or water, and from there may be accidentally ingested by a new host to begin an infection. Surprisingly, even in samples less than 1 hour old, none of the Type A or B nematodes was found alive. Possibly the ambient temperature at the altitude was too low for them to survive outside the host.

Types C,D,E,F,G, and H (found to be free-living or plant-parasitic nematodes). Collection of feces without environmental contamination is not possible in the wild; nematodes can get into a sample from leaves or soil, or even be carried on the bodies of flies feeding or egg-laying on dung. Types C, D, and E were identified, respectively, as *Rhabditis (Cephaloboides)* sp., possibly *R. curvicandata; Laimydorus* and *Aporcelaimus* sp.; and *Rhabditis* sp.

Strongyloid Eggs. These resemble eggs of the human hookworm, *Ancylostoma duodenale*, and were found in most samples examined by direct smear. Identification of species from eggs alone is not possible, and no adults were found.

Nematodes of the genus *Impalai* were collected from Kweli's small intestine during the postmortem. Members of this genus are normally found in giraffes and antelopes and have never been previously recorded from a primate host, or from this geographical area. All the specimens found were immature. This tends to suggest that they had accidentally infected the wrong host and were unable to develop fully as a consequence. Without adults it is not possible to determine the exact species, but it is likely that in the Virungas they would normally parasitize bushbuck or duiker.

Cestodes (Tapeworms)

Anopolcephala gorillae Nybelin 1927 is the only cestode recorded from mountain gorillas. No complete worms were collected, but proglottids (tapeworm segments) were visible in the feces of infected animals. The adult cestode is attached to the gut wall by its hooked head (scolex) and the tapelike body (strobila) lies freely along the length of the intestine absorbing nutrients from the gut contents. As each segment matures it is released, full of eggs, into the feces. Cestode life cycles are often complex; that of *A. gorillae* is not known, but it may involve soil mites (often found around dung) as intermediate hosts.

TREMATODES (FLUKES)

No trematodes were collected by Redmond, but a single large specimen was collected from the left lung of Digit during the postmortem 6 days after his death. It is likely that it was not parasitizing the lung, but had moved there after Digit was killed. It measured 32 mm × 19 mm and had a median ventral sucker 14 mm × 6 mm.

PROTOZOANS (SINGLE-CELLED ANIMALS)

When examining fresh feces by direct smear, one would expect to find ciliates (such as *Troglodytella*, which are found in chimpanzees) swimming around on the slide. No motile protozoa were seen during this study, even in samples less than 1 hour old on examination. Particles resembling protozoans, two or three times the size of the strongyloid eggs, were seen in most smears (32 of the 34 animals examined for them).

Coprophagy and Parasites

In many herbivores, digestion of cellulose is aided by microbes living in the gut; young of the species establish this "gut flora" (or more correctly, fauna) by ingesting some of their parents' or other adults' feces, or, in the ruminants, eructate from the fore-stomach. The exact role played by microbes in the gorilla's digestion has yet to be demonstrated, but coprophagy (eating feces) has been observed on many occasions. Usually an individual eats some of his or her own feces immediately on excretion, but sometimes an infant will eat that of an older animal, or vice versa. This is clearly the most direct means for a young gorilla to establish an active gut fauna; it may also explain why Types A and B nematodes were always, like the "protozoans," dead on examination.

If infection and reinfection of the host is achieved by coprophagy, these parasites (perhaps "symbionts" would be a better term if the gorilla benefits by their presence) would continue for generation after generation in host after host without ever experiencing anything other than body temperature. This is providing that the feces are always eaten warm, which observations show to be the case.

Infants begin passing viviparous nematodes and "protozoanlike objects" in their first year or 18 months of life. By this time they have begun taking solid foods, including occasional pieces of warm dung from their mother or peers. Once established in this way, populations of direct developers, such as *Probstmayria*, would continue in that host for life, perhaps being further supplemented if coprophagy becomes a habit.

Probstmayria viviparous larvae remain viable in the pasture for days, and horses, their host, have ample opportunity to ingest them. Gorillas seldom feed in one location for more than a few hours, so opportunities for such accidental ingestion are minimal and would not explain the very high percentage of animals infected. Coprophagy would have the advantage of ensuring the parasite's transmission to a new host, but the drawback appears to be that larvae have lost any resistance they might have had to low temperatures.

REFERENCES

AMBERSON, J. M., and SCHWARTZ, E.
1952. *Ternidens diminutus* Railliet et Henry, a nematode parasitic of man and primates. Ann. Trop. Med. Parsit., vol. 46, no. 3, pp. 227-237.

ANGST, W., and THOMMEN, D.
1977. New data and a discussion of infant killing in Old World monkeys and apes. Folia Primatol., vol. 27, pp. 198-229.

BOWDEN, D.; WINTER, P.; and PLOOG, D.
1967. Pregnancy and delivery behavior in the squirrel monkey *(Saimiri sciureus).* Folia Primatol., vol. 5, pp. 1-42.

CHABAUD, A. G., and ROUSSELOT, R.
1956. Un nouveau Spiruride parasite du gorilla, *Chitwoodspirura wehri* n.g.n. sp. Bull Soc. Path. Exot., vol. 49, no. 3, pp. 467-472.

FISHER, L. E.
1972. The birth of a lowland gorilla at Lincoln Park Zoo, Chicago. Int. Zoo Yearb., vol. 12, pp. 106-108.

FOSSEY, D.
1974. Observations on the home range of one group of mountain gorillas *(Gorilla gorilla beringei).* Animal Behavior, vol. 22, pp. 568-581.
1979. Development of the mountain gorilla *(Gorilla gorilla beringei)* through the first thirty-six months. Pp. 139-184, vol. 5, *in* "The Behavior of Great Apes," D. Hamburg, E. McCown, and J. Goodall, eds. Addison-Wesley, Menlo Park.
1981. The imperiled mountain gorilla. National Geographic, vol. 159, no. 4, pp. 501-523.
1982. Reproduction among free-living mountain gorillas. Amer. Journ. Primatol., Suppl. vol. 1, pp. 97-104.
1983. Mountain gorilla research, 1974. Nat. Geogr. Soc. Res. Rpts., 1974 Projects, vol. 14, pp. 243-258, illus.
____. Infanticide among mountain gorillas *(Gorilla gorilla beringei).* In "Infanticide Among Human and Nonhuman Primates," G. Hausfater and S. B. Hardy, eds. Aldine Publishing Company. (In press.)

FOSSEY, D., and HARCOURT, A. H.
1977. Feeding ecology of free-ranging mountain gorilla *(Gorilla gorilla beringei).* Pp. 415-447 *in* "Primate Ecology: Studies of Feeding and Ranging Behavior in Lemurs, Monkeys and Apes," T. H. Clutton-Brock, ed. Academic Press, London, New York.

GIJZEN, A., and TIJSJENS, J.
1971. Growth in weight of the lowland gorilla *(Gorilla gorilla gorilla)* and of the mountain gorilla. Int. Zool. Yearb., London, vol. 2, pp. 183-193.

GOODALL, JANE
1978. Infant killing and cannibalism in free-living chimpanzees. Folia Primatol., vol. 28, pp. 259-282.

GROVES, C. P.
1970. Gorillas, 96 pp. Arthur Barker, London.

HARCOURT, A. H., and FOSSEY, D.
1981. The Virunga gorillas: Decline of an "island" population. Afr. Journ. Ecol., vol. 19, pp. 83-97.

HESS, J. P.
1973. Some observations on the sexual behavior of captive lowland gorillas. Pp. 507-581 *in* "Comparative Ecology and Behavior of Primates," R. P. and J. H. Crook, eds. Academic Press, London.

KAWANAKA, K.
1981. Infanticide and cannibalism in chimpanzees, with special reference to the newly observed case in the Mahale Mountains. African Study Monographs, vol. 1, pp. 69-99.

MALLINSON, J.; COFFEY, P.; and USHER-SMITH, J.
1973. Maintenance and hand-rearing of lowland gorilla *Gorilla g. gorilla* (Savage and Wyman 1847), at the Jersey Zoological Park. Pp. 5-28 *in* "The Jersey Wildlife Preservation Trust, Tenth Annual Report." Trinity, Jersey, Channel Islands.

NADLER, R. D.
1974. Periparturitional behavior of a primiparous lowland gorilla. Primates, vol. 15, pp. 55-73.

NAPIER, J. R., and NAPIER, P. H.
1967. A handbook of the living primates. Academic Press, New York.

PUSEY, A. E.
1980. Inbreeding avoidance in chimpanzees. Animal Behavior, vol. 28, pp. 543-552.

SCHALLER, G.
1963. The mountain gorilla: Ecology and behavior, 431 pp. University of Chicago Press, Chicago and London.

SCHULTZ, A. H.
1969. The life of primates, 281 pp. The Universe Natural History Series, New York.

STEWART, K. J.
1977. The birth of a wild mountain gorilla. Primates, vol. 18, no. 4, pp. 965-976.

TUTIN, C.E.G.
1980. Reproductive behaviour of wild chimpanzees in the Gombe National Park, Tanzania. Journ. Reproductive Fertility, Suppl., vol. 28, pp. 43-57.

DIAN FOSSEY

Limnology and Ecology of the Dead Sea

Grant Recipient: Joel R. Gat, Isotope Department, Weizmann Institute of Science, Rehovot, Israel.[1]

Grants 1656, 1840: For a study of the limnology and ecology of the Dead Sea system.

The Dead Sea occupies the deepest part of the Jordan–Dead Sea–Arava Rift Valley, and with its surface at around -400 m (-1350 ft) below mean sea level it represents the lowermost naturally exposed surface on the face of the earth.

The Dead Sea has been a focal point of scientific interest for over 2300 years. The most thorough investigation of the Dead Sea was made by Neev and Emery from 1959 to 1963. At that time the Dead Sea had been a permanently stratified lake with the pycnocline at a depth of about 40 m. The pycnocline separated a micro-aerobic upper water mass (0 to 40 m) from an anoxic lower water mass (80 to 320 m) with a transition layer at depths of 40 to 80 m. It is believed that this physical structure of the lake was maintained for at least 200 years, and very probably for a longer period by a balance between incoming fresh water (mainly through the Jordan River and surface runoff), evaporation, and a countercurrent of saline brines flowing from the shallow southern basin to the pycnocline level in the northern basin.

In the years since the survey by Neev and Emery (which due to political reasons, was limited to the southwestern sector of the lake), the lake water level has been dropping gradually, primarily as the result of the diversion of Jordan River water for agricultural uses. Thus, the amount of fresh water introduced by the Jordan River dropped to about 50% as compared with its discharge 15 years ago. During 1975 the lake reached a low water stand of less than -400 m below mean sea level for the first time in 150 years. In September 1977 the level had dropped as low as -402 m, resulting in the interruption of free water transport between the southern and northern basins.

The present study was initiated in order to achieve two major goals. The first was to obtain some necessary data, not measured before, relating to the biological and chemical properties of the lake. The second was

[1] Arie Nissenbaum, also of the Weizmann Institute, was co-investigator.

to document the hydrographic and chemical properties of the present transient stage of the lake and to provide information on the mechanism of mixing in such a highly saline environment.

Operational Program

Eleven cruises were conducted on the Dead Sea for the purpose of establishing hydrographic stations for water sampling, bottom dredging, and sediment coring. These cruises were made during October and December, 1975; January, June, and December, 1976; March, July, November, and December, 1977; and January, 1978. Each cruise lasted 2 to 6 days. Sampling sites were located throughout the length of the lake, from the shallowest part to the deepest (about 1100 ft).

Temperatures were measured in situ with a bathythermograph. Water samples were collected in Nansen bottles and analyzed in our laboratory.

Results

Physical Limnology. The temperature and salinity profiles indicated that the salinity difference between the upper layers and the lower, "fossil" water, which had maintained stratification for more than 200 years, had almost completely disappeared by the end of 1977. The average water density at 25°C of 1.230 g/cm^3 was higher than in the 1960s and was uniform throughout the lake. It is, therefore, mostly water temperature that has controlled the structure of the water column.

The development of the water column can be demonstrated by the depth of the pycnocline which was about 40 m in 1960, 80 m in 1963-1965, 100 to 120 m in 1976, and 150 to 160 m in 1977. The instability of the situation could also be noted from the temperature inhomogeneities of the top half of the water column.

Two factors seem to be largely responsible for the change in the physical structure of the water column. The first was the decrease in lake volume due to withdrawal of water from the Jordan River—the main water supply to the lake—and also because of the drop in lake level which resulted in drying up of the Southern Basin, and, hence, interferences in the hydrological regime.

Major Element Geochemistry. The chemical composition of the Dead Sea has responded to the drop in lake level. The salinities reached values of 333 g/L in the lower water mass and 310 g/L in the upper water mass. The increase in total salt content was not accompanied by change in composition. Therefore, no significant amounts of minerals precipitated from the water column. The degree of saturation of the brine in respect to halite (NaCl, rock salt), however, increased markedly.

Minor Element Geochemistry. Analysis for strontium, lithium, and manganese showed that their concentration in the water column increased in the same manner as the major constituents, again indicating that no major process for removal of those elements was operative.

Analysis of Pore Water. Chemical analysis of water extracted from the Dead Sea sediments showed that the sediments are highly reducing, through the activity of sulfate-reducing bacteria. Calcium showed a decrease by precipitation of carbonates; iron and manganese are greatly enriched due to water-rock interaction; and the bottom sediments are potentially suppliers of manganese to the overlying water column.

Nutrients. Dissolved oxygen (Table 1) in the lake was found to be very low, even under saturation. The observed values are five times lower than those of ocean water. The concentration in the lower water mass was much smaller than in the upper, mixed layer.

TABLE 1. Dissolved Oxygen (mL/L) in Dead Sea Water (March 1977)

Sample	*Depth (m)*	*Dissolved O_2 (mL/L)*
Station 3		
M - 24	10	1.73
M - 25	35	1.01
M - 26	110	0.53
M - 27	210	0.46
M - 28	310	0.32
Station 4		
M - 37	surface	1.02
M - 38	80	0.81
M - 39	130	0.69
M - 40	180	0.35
M - 41	230	0.18

Concentration of ammonia (Table 2) in the water column was very high, on the order of 5 to 8 mg/L. No nitrate was detected. There was slightly more ammonia in the lower water mass as compared with the upper waters. The pore water was only slightly enriched in ammonia (Table 3).

Dissolved phosphate (Table 4) levels in the Dead Sea are very low and average around 30 μg/L. Particulate phosphate (Table 4) is of the same order of magnitude. Interstitial water phosphate was higher by a factor of 100 than that of the water column.

TABLE 2. Ammonia Concentration (in mg/L of N-NH_3) in Dead Sea Water (1977)

Sample	*Water depth (m)*	*N-NH_3 (mg/L)*
S - 46	25	6.13
S - 47	50	5.51
S - 48	100	6.18
S - 49	150	6.70
S - 51	155	7.22
S - 52	187	7.28
S - 50	200	7.22
S - 53	237	7.48
S - 54	287	7.38
S - 55	290	7.38
S - 56	300	7.64

Discussion

An Overture to Overturn. The investigation of the Dead Sea between 1976 and 1978 occurred during a critical period in the development of the lake. A water column that had been stable for many years began during this period to show a strong degree of instability.

In February 1979 the Dead Sea finally overturned. The detailed study between 1976 and 1978 allowed us to forecast this event, and the data collected were instrumental in deciphering the process, mechanism, and time scale involved in this unique event. The present investigation was also of extreme importance in collection of data before the overturn which could then be compared with the chemical changes resulting from the overturn.

Biological Investigation. The Dead Sea represents a unique ecological niche. The extreme salinity combined with peculiar chemical composition results in a food chain composed of only one stage: the primary producers (algae) and, in addition, consumers (bacteria). Although the variety of species is small, an important and interesting problem is what factor prevents the population explosion that could theoretically occur in the absence of predators. The present investigation indicates that ammonia is abundant enough in the lake. On the other hand, phosphate levels are very low. Since the input of phosphate is fairly high, there must be an efficient mechanism for phosphate removal. We presume that phosphate is probably removed by precipitation as apatite or perhaps even magnesium-ammonium-phosphate.

Although oxygen and carbonate are low enough to limit algal growth, and the turbidity of the lake is high, so that algal growth would be limited to the top 20 to 30 m, we believe that the two major constraints

TABLE 3. Phosphate and Ammonia in Pore Waters from Dead Sea Sediments

Station	*Depth in core (cm)*	*Phosphate (mg/L of P)*	*Ammonia (mg/L of N)*
Core 2EG, 30-m depth	overlying water	0.040	6.0
	0.0 - 0.5	-	-
	0.5 - 3.0	0.200	7.8
	3.0 - 6.5	-	8.8
	6.5 - 9.0	0.170	9.9
	9.0 - 11.2	0.270	10.1
	11.2 - 13.0	0.200	9.8
	13.0 - 15.5	0.180	10.0
	15.5 - 18.3	0.240	8.5
	18.3 - 22.2	0.170	9.5
	22.2 - 25.6	0.230	10.0
	25.6 - 28.6	0.240	8.5
	28.6 - 29.4	-	10.0
	29.4 - 31.6	0.160	8.4
	32.0 - 35.5	-	10.5
Core 1EG, 25-m depth	overlying water		
	0 - 1.7	-	8.0
	1.7 - 4.7	-	9.2
	4.7 - 9.4	0.240	13.1
	9.4 - 10.7	-	16.6
	10.7 - 16.2	0.260	15.8
	16.2 - 20.9	0.260	17.0
	20.9 - 27.9	0.340	17.5
	27.9 - 30.5	0.350	18.5
	30.5 - 33.0	-	18.7
	33.0 - 35.8	0.220	18.0
	35.8 - 39.9	-	18.0
Core GF, 318-m depth	overlying water	0.040	21.6
	0.7 - 7.0	0.130	24.5
	7.0 - 8.0	-	26.5
	8.0 - 12.5	0.530	35.5
	12.5 - 14.8	-	39.0
	14.8 - 17.0	0.260	36.5
	17.0 - 20.4	0.210	40.0
	20.4 - 26.2	0.250	41.5
	26.2 - 30.0	-	45.0
	30.0 - 41.0	0.330	50.0
	41.0 - 49.2	0.280	58.5

on growth are the salinity and phosphate concentration. If this is indeed the case, then biological blooms could be mainly restricted to an ephemeral, thin upper layer which can be produced by floods. Such a layer may

TABLE 4. Dissolved and Particulate Phosphate (as $P\text{-}PO_4$) in Dead Sea Water (March 1977)

Water depth (m)	*Particulate P-PO$_4$* (μg/L)	*Soluble P-PO$_4$* (μg/L)
surface	35.7	29.1 ± 0.6
30	54.6	27.6 ± 0.4
80	(-)	35.5 ± 1.8
130	9.4	32.3 ± 4.5
170	42.7	36.0 ± 4.4
180	(-)	32.0 ± 2.0
219	42.3	36.2 ± 4.0
230	(-)	32.4 ± 2.1
270	50.8	32.2 ± 1.9

be too transient to sustain a long-lasting bloom. We expect, therefore, that unless drastic changes in chemical composition occur, the life activity in the lake will remain at a fairly low level.

REFERENCES

ELAZARI-VOLCANI, B.
1936. Life in the Dead Sea. Nature, vol. 138, p. 467.

NEEV, D., and EMERY, K. O.
1967. The Dead Sea: Depositional processes and environments of evaporites. Bull. No. 41, 147 pp. Geological Survey of Israel, Jerusalem.

NISSENBAUM, A.
1975. The microbiology and biogeochemistry of the Dead Sea. Microb. Ecology, vol. 2, pp. 139-151.

STEINHORN, I.
1981. A physical and hydrographical study of the Dead Sea during the destruction of its long term meromictic stratification, 320 pp. PhD. thesis, Feinberg Graduate School at the Weizmann Institute of Science.

STEINHORN, I., et al.
1979. The Dead Sea: Deepening of the mixolimnion signifies the overture to overturn of the water column. Science, vol. 206, pp. 55-57.

JOEL R. GAT
ARIE NISSENBAUM

Taphonomic Specimens, Lake Turkana

Grant Recipient: Diane P. Gifford, University of California, Santa Cruz, California.

Grant 1657: In support of checking and permanently marking taphonomic specimens at Koobi Fora, Lake Turkana, Kenya.

In August and early September of 1976, I undertook a follow-up study of large ungulate carcasses on the northeastern side of Lake Turkana, Kenya. Beginning in late 1973, I had monitored these carcasses, and the effects of postmortem processes on them, from the day of each animal's death through the first 4 to 6 months of their postmortem histories.

This kind of study may be placed in the paleontological subdiscipline of taphonomy, which is concerned with the study of processes involved in the transition of parts of animals from their life contexts to fossil contexts. Over the last two decades, both vertebrate and invertebrate paleontologists, as well as paleoanthropologists, have sought to reconstruct and study the structure and workings of ancient ecosystems with data derived from fossil samples. At the same time they have become increasingly concerned with the effects that postmortem processes may have on the ultimate structure of the assemblages they study. It is clear that fossil assemblages do derive from ancient ecosystems, but how accurately their composition reflects the taxonomic composition, relative species abundances, and other aspects of prehistoric communities is open to debate.

Researchers interested in this problem have often turned to observations of modern situations in which animal remains are undergoing various processes of modification. The aims of such contemporary studies are two: to distinguish regularities in the operation of these processes on animal remains, and to discern, if possible, distinctive traces of the operation of the processes on these remains. These findings may then be used in elucidating the postmortem histories of fossils.

In 1973-1974, while conducting ethnoarcheological research with the Dassanetch people along the northeastern shore of Lake Turkana, Kenya, I had the opportunity to study the earliest phases of this transition from life to fossil contexts. Over a period of about 5 months, some 48 wild ungulates—mainly Burchell's zebra *(Equus burchelli)* and topi *(Damaliscus lunatus),* with some Beisa oryx *(Oryx gazella beisa)* and Grant's gazelle *(Gazella granti)*—died along a strip of grassy flats along the lakeshore or in the nearby hills, in a zone between Allia Bay and the Koobi Fora sand spit. (See Fig. 1.) The region as a whole is semidesert, receiving an average of 300 mm of rain annually, but for the years preceding 1974 the region had been in the grip of a prolonged drought. Many of the deaths observed in this study doubtlessly were due to starvation or to disease associated with poor nutritional state. Water-dependent species such as the zebra and topi suffered most, since they could not range far enough away from the lake to find forage and were restricted to the heavily grazed flats. Other animals, especially zebras, were victims of predation by lions.

Lake Turkana is a nonoutlet, alkaline lake that can vary in level as much as 6 m over 20 years. Transgressive phases of the lake may cover extensive areas, and a constant supply of sediments is washed down into the lake from its ever-flowing feeder river, the Omo, and from numerous ephemeral streams and rivers that flow during the region's sporadic rains. The modern lakeshore environment provides a suite of good analogies for the prehistoric sedimentary regimes in the same region, which have preserved numerous hominid and nonhominid fossils, as well as stone tools, dating from the Plio-Pleistocene epoch (Behrensmeyer, 1975). The modern Lake Turkana situation also provides a rough parallel to the ancient lake that existed in the Olduvai Basin in the same time span. A study of the fate of modern animal remains in such an environment was, therefore, of considerable interest to those concerned with early Quaternary studies in East Africa. Results of such a study, however, have a wider temporal and geographic application, in that they may help researchers elsewhere to isolate key processes affecting vertebrate remains and to describe the responses of bone to the action of these processes.

With these considerations in mind, I undertook documentation and repeated checking of every dead animal I encountered in the study area over a period of about 5 months in late 1973 and early 1974. By the end of this period, I had documented 48 animals: 33 zebra, 13 topi, 1 oryx, and 1 Grant's gazelle. By August of the same year, when I returned to the United States, I had been able to continue monitoring 31 of these (22 zebra, 9 topi). A substantial number of the animals not monitored disappeared from their death sites on the second night after death, while others lay in less accessible areas. Information recorded on each specimen included cause of death, damage to bone, disarticulation, dispersal, exposure of bone to elements, sedimentary environment, and potential for burial. As segments of carcasses became more and more dispersed, photographic records were supplemented by bone distribution plots.

In 1976, funded by a combination of grants from the L.S.B. Leakey Foundation, the National Geographic Society, and the Wenner-Gren

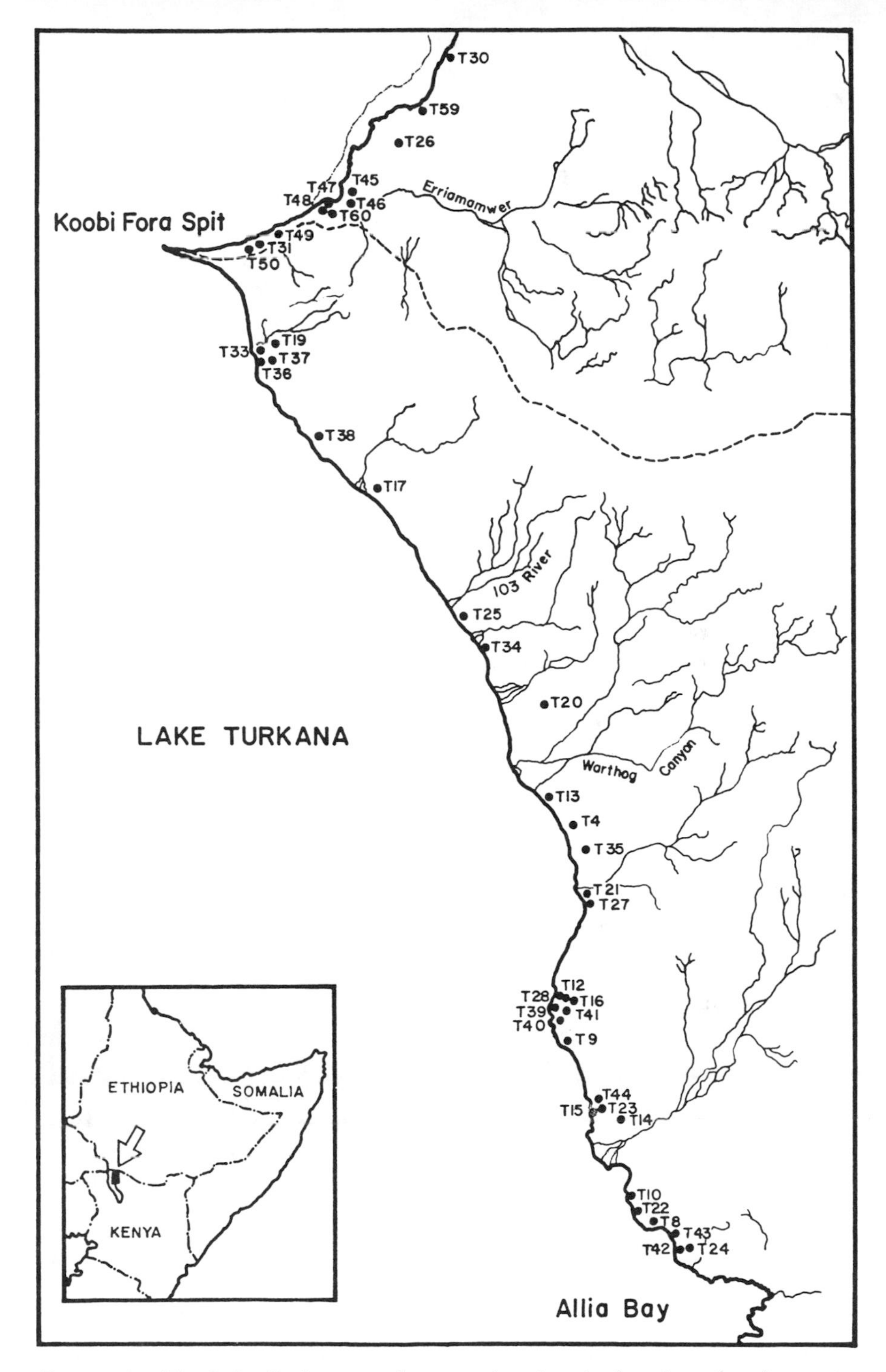

FIGURE 1. The Lake Turkana study area, showing the location of taphonomic specimens (marked with "T") in the Koobi Fora-Allia Bay region.

Foundation for Anthropological Research, I returned to the study area with the aim of locating, checking, and permanently marking the sites of the taphonomic specimens. I did the fieldwork in August 1976, 30 to 34 months after the deaths of the specimens. I was able to locate 28 of those monitored through August 1974 (20 zebra, 8 topi). Once again I surveyed the presence or absence of elements, damage to elements, and their disarticulation and dispersal, replotting a number of the bone scatters. In this check I also noted the degree to which individual bones had weathered, using a then-unpublished system developed by A. K. Behrensmeyer (1978). Additionally, I noted cases of burial of bone, excavating one scatter that was partly covered in windblown sediments.

Results of the 1976 Check

One of the unanticipated benefits of the follow-up check was the opportunity to see the same area after 2 years of abundant rains, which affected many aspects of the environment related to the formation of fossil bone assemblages. First, far fewer animals were dying in the area, a factor that contributed elements to the land surface assemblage at a much slower rate than at the peak of the drought, illustrating the "pulses" of mortalities that may go into forming a time-averaged fossil assemblage. Second, sediments carried down to the deltas of numerous ephemeral streams during the rainy years were being reworked by the high winds typical of the region, contributing to the burial of several specimens. Third, the slight transgression of the lake over the grassy flats had inundated a few elements of taphonomic specimens, illustrating in microcosm the process that led to preservation of many vertebrate remains in the local fossil record. Specific results of the check are discussed below.

Damage

Although primary carnivore damage, inflicted at the time of a kill or soon after the death of an ungulate, was relatively rare among the specimens, some evidence was found for subsequent gnawing of the bones, most probably by hyenas. The following tabulation shows gnawing associated with time of death, and death + 30-34 months (1976), expressed as the number of observed instances of gnawing over the total number of specimens examined (N°G/IND):

	Death	*Death + 30-40 mos.*
Zebras-N°G/IND	37/32	90/21
Bovids-N°G/IND	36/16	15/8

A much more significant source of damage to bones of the specimens checked was trampling by herbivores, which findings agree with Behrensmeyer's observations in Amboseli National Park, Kenya (Behrensmeyer, 1978). Fractures caused by trampling are distinct in form from those caused by carnivore gnawing; they include "wishbone" fractures of the mandible, snapping of scapula blades, and the splintering of long bones along deep longitudinal weathering cracks. Zebra bones, being more sturdily constructed than those of topi, appeared to resist this type of damage better. Fracture caused by trampling at death + 30-34 months (1976), expressed as the number of observed instances of trample fracture over the total number of specimens examined (N°T/IND), was 2/20 for zebras and 20/8 for bovids.

The same process that was breaking down bones with a high surface area to volume ratio was fostering preservation of bones with low ratios, since trampling appeared to be responsible for driving small, dense bones, such as podials and phalanges, into the substrate. This was especially true of bones lying in the zone just adjacent to the rising lake waters, since the sediments were soft and wet, and were repeatedly trodden by ungulates coming down to drink and graze.

Dispersion of Elements

Animal traffic also seemed to have a major effect on the "stability" of bone scatters, once they had been created through the disarticulation of the carcass by scavengers and more "passive" processes, such as the decay of connective tissue. Re-plotting of scatters showed that those lying close to the lake were substantially altered in configuration from the last plots made in the summer of 1974, while specimens well away from the lake were in essentially the same distribution in which they rested even earlier in 1974, in plots made during the spring rains of that year. Since no additional evidence of carnivore action was noted on the specimens near the lake, I have inferred that the continued "motion" of these scatters is due to the nearly constant traffic of ungulates through the lakeshore zone.

Disarticulation of Elements

By the summer of 1976, with only 2 exceptions among 28 animals, the only skeletal elements still in articulation were segments of the vertebral column plus the pelvis. The 2 exceptions were limb units still in articulation. The general sequence of detachments of cranium and appendicular skeleton from axial skeleton is given in Figure 2.

Presence or Absence of Elements

If one treats all the skeletal elements present at all individual specimen scatters as a lumped assemblage and compares the element frequencies in this assemblage with those in the original constitution of an "average

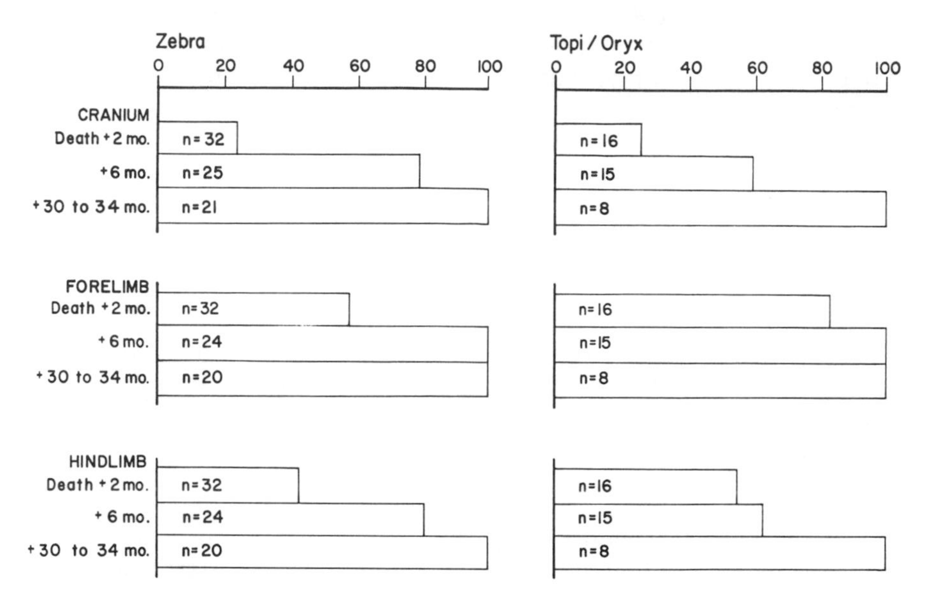

FIGURE 2. Percentage of cranium and limb detachments from axial skeleton at specified months after death.

ungulate" (equid + bovid body part frequencies, see Behrensmeyer and Dechant-Boaz, 1980) the 1976 check reveals some deviations from the original constitution of the animals involved. Table 1 shows that vertebrae are relatively more numerous, while podial bones and phalanges are less so. Limb bone frequencies are more or less the same. The absence of smaller podials and phalanges may be partially due to their complete burial in the substrate, as discussed earlier, and partially due to wholesale consumption by carnivores. Only more extensive excavations than time permitted would have answered this question (see below).

WEATHERING

I was able to assess weathering as it developed during the first 6 months after death by examining photographs of bones taken during that time in light of Behrensmeyer's weathering stage descriptions. Figure 3 presents weathering stage data, indicating that most bone of these large ungulates was at Weathering Stage 1 (hairline cracks, no exfoliation) within 6 months of exposure. By 30-34 months after death, no bone remaining on the surface was at Weathering Stage 0, and some were at

TABLE 1. Absolute and Relative Proportions of Elements Remaining at Death Sites (1976 check) Compared with Numbers and Proportions in "Average Ungulate"

Element	*Average ungulate*		*1976 Zebra*		*1976 Topi*	
	No.	%	No.	%	No.	%
Cranium	1	1.1	18	2.1	6	2.1
Mandible	2	2.3	34	3.9	15	5.3
Vertebra	28	32.2	448	51.3	154	54.4
Scapula	2	2.3	25	2.9	11	3.9
Humerus	2	2.3	24	2.7	9	3.2
Radioulna	4	4.6	44	5.0	17	6.0
Metacarpal	2	2.3	14	1.6	8	2.8
Pelvis	2	2.3	36	4.1	10	3.5
Femur	2	2.3	26	3.0	9	3.2
Tibia	2	2.3	12	1.3	10	3.5
Metatarsal	2	2.3	13	1.5	7	2.5
Podials	20	23.0	109	12.5	18	6.4
Phalanges	18	20.7	71	8.1	9	3.2
TOTAL	87	100.0	874	100.0	283	100.0

Weathering Stages 2 and 3. In all cases of bone at Weathering Stage 3, the bones lay in areas clearly subject to repeated inundation. I have previously observed different weathering rates for bones of the same animal in similar situations at Lake Turkana (Gifford, 1977, 1980), with elements in repeatedly inundated areas being one to two weathering stages ahead of counterparts on well-drained substrates. These observations fit well with P. E. Hare's (1980) experimental findings that the rate of disintegration of bone is affected by the relative amount of water and alkalinity in an element's immediate environment. Generally speaking, the rate at which the taphonomic sample bones are weathering accords well with my findings on bone at dated Dassanetch habitations in the area (Gifford, 1977, 1980), and with weathering rates in the somewhat moister Amboseli region, some 900 km to the south (Behrensmeyer, 1978). Bones that are buried before they develop evidences of weathering, or which are inundated completely by water, do not develop weathering stage features.

MAKING OF SPECIMENS

Each specimen was spotted on a set of aerial photographs taken of the region, and the site of each scatter was marked with a low stone and cement cairn, to be used as a datum in any future plotting of the specimens.

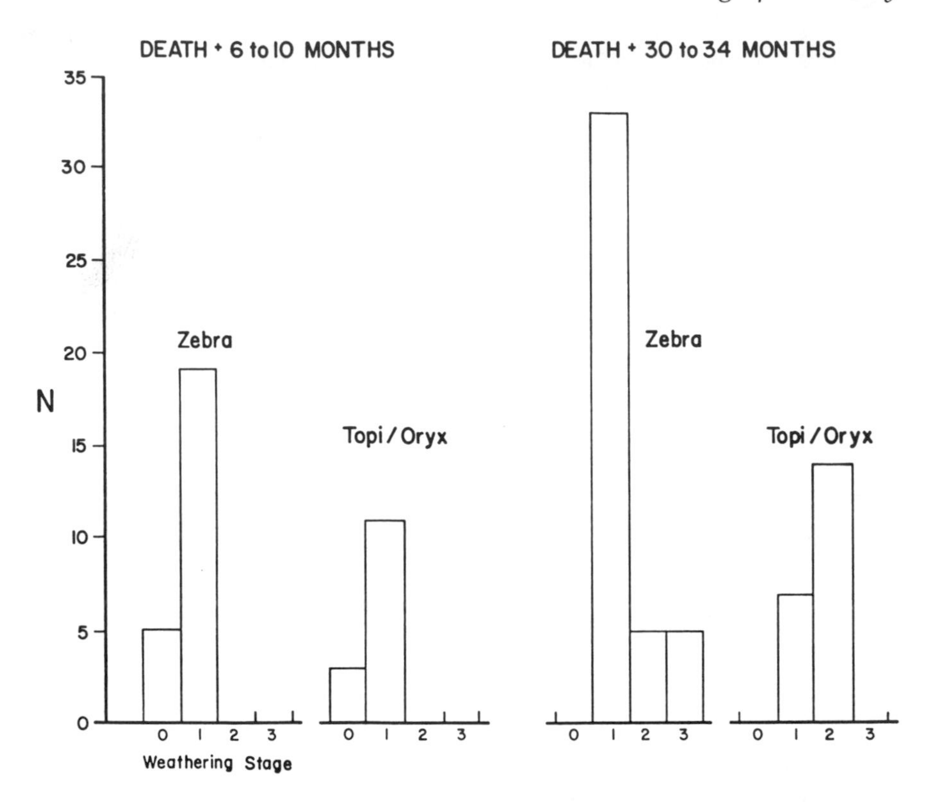

FIGURE 3. Weathering stages tabulated for individual bones at death plus 6-10 months (summer 1974) and death plus 30-34 months (summer 1976).

Further Research

In view of the relative ease in relocating specimens, and the rather slow rate at which some of the processes affecting the bones are operating, I revisited the study area in the summer of 1978 and again in 1983, to check the various attributes noted here.

During my 1978 field season, with the help of a pair of students from the University of California, Santa Cruz, I excavated a number of half-buried specimens. True to my earlier speculation, some of the smaller, denser podial and toe bones were recovered from below the surface. However, not all missing small bones were recovered, suggesting that the influence of carnivores cannot be ruled out. Fragmentation of long bones and bones of the axial skeleton had again increased among specimen scatters lying on the surface, and trampling was the most common apparent agent for this breakage. Again, bovid bones were more liable to breakage than were equid elements. Elements in scatters near the lake had again shifted substantially from their 1976 positions, while those in scatters farther away from this zone of heavy animal traffic were virtually unchanged. Nearly all elements were disarticulated, with the exception of some cervical, thoracic, and lumbar vertebrae units. Bovid bones were found to be weathering faster than equid bones, with most of the former at Behrensmeyer's Weathering Stages 3 and 4 while the latter were at Stages 2 and 3.

Five years later, in August 1983, I revisited the area to make a final check of the specimens. Major changes in the shoreline and heavy waterborne deposition of sediments in the littoral zone made it very difficult to locate many of my specimens. I found only 15—mostly zebra—after several days of intensive search for cairns and bones. These data have not been fully analyzed, but the most striking and useful finding of this field season is the fact that most equid bones on the surface were in the most extreme stages of weathering (Behrensmeyer's Weathering Stages 4 and 5), and many bore evidence of recent trampling damage to their weakened structures. The few bovid bones located were all disintegrating, although teeth were still relatively well preserved. Bones in such condition would not survive any but the gentlest of waterborne deposition events. Thus, it would seem that bones on the surface of the present-day Lake Turkana shore pass the stage of "viability" as potential fossils within 10 years of their initial exposure to the elements.

This longitudinal study is one of two carried out in Africa on the long-term effects of natural processes on vertebrate remains. My study complements ongoing monitoring of large ungulate carcasses by A. K. Behrensmeyer in Amboseli National Park.

REFERENCES

BEHRENSMEYER, ANNA K.

1975. The taphonomy and paleoecology of Plio-Pleistocene vertebrate assemblages east of Lake Rudolf, Kenya. Bull. Mus. Comp. Zool., Harvard University, vol. 146, pp. 473-578.

1978. Taphonomic and ecologic information from bone weathering. Paleobiology, vol. 4, pp. 150-162.

BEHRENSMEYER, ANNA K., and DECHANT-BOAZ, D. E.

1980. The recent bones of Amboseli Park, Kenya, in relation to East African paleoecology. *In* "Fossils in the Making," A. K. Behrensmeyer and A. P. Hill, eds. University of Chicago Press.

GIFFORD, DIANE P.

1977. Observations of contemporary human settlements as an aid to archaeological interpretation. Ph.D. thesis, University of California, Berkeley, 484 pp., illus.

GIFFORD, DIANE P. *(continued)*

1980. Ethnoarcheological contributions to the taphonomy of human sites. *In* "Fossils in the Making," A. K. Behrensmeyer and A. P. Hill, eds. University of Chicago Press.

HARE, P. E.

1980. Organic geochemistry of bone and its relation to the survival of bone in the natural environment. *In* "Fossils in the Making," A. K. Behrensmeyer and A. P. Hill, eds. University of Chicago Press.

DIANE P. GIFFORD-GONZALEZ

Landscape Change in the Canyons of the Green River, Utah and Colorado

Grant Recipient: William L. Graf, Department of Geography, Arizona State University, Tempe, Arizona.

Grants 1576, 1687: To study landscape changes on the Green River.

Introduction

In 1869, John Wesley Powell, an early trustee of the National Geographic Society, and 9 men explored for the first time the Green and Colorado River systems. Their observations began the process of filling in the last major blank spaces on maps of the territories of the United States, and publicized scientific exploration of the region (Powell, 1875). In 1871, with financial support from Congress, a second expedition with 10 men repeated a substantial portion of the first voyage but at a much slower pace to permit surveys and scientific observations on the terrain near the rivers. The second voyage included a professional photographer, E. O. Beaman, whose photographs provide a unique record of the environment of the Canyonlands region over a century ago (Sarles, 1968).

Although many reaches of the Green and Colorado systems remain remote in the late 20th century, numerous expeditions have repeated Powell's journey and have published photographs, providing periodic records of landscape changes. In 1889, Frank M. Brown and 16 men traveled the lower Green River and began a potential railroad survey along the Colorado River (Stanton, 1965). In 1909, Julius F. Stone retraced the Powell route for the express purpose of making photographs (Stone, 1932), and in 1911 the Kolb brothers completed a second photographic trip (Kolb, 1927). The U. S. Bureau of Reclamation, interested in the rivers for potential water development, sponsored surveys from 1916 to 1921 of the channels and near-channel areas that included photography (Wooley, 1930). A group of adventurers led by Clyde Eddy ran the rivers in 1927, providing additional photographs (Eddy, 1929), and Barry M. Goldwater has published photographs of the same areas from 1940 (Goldwater, 1970). After World War II, aerial photographs by the National Park Service and the U. S. Geological Survey provide images that bring the record to the present. Finally, the U. S. Geological Survey sponsored efforts to relocate the original 1871 camera stations, and photographs made in 1968 are directly comparable to those made almost a century before (Shoemaker and Stevens, 1969, 1975).

The most useful sources of data to achieve the research objectives are historical photographs and modern field data. Written historical accounts of the study area are interesting but imprecise, and early maps of the region lack details required for the research of geomorphic changes. Photographs, however, are reliable renditions of the landscape as it appeared in the past century, and details are faithfully retained. Photogrammetric measurement techniques originally designed for aerial photographs provide a means of extracting quantitative data from the historical ground photographs (American Society of Photogrammetry, 1960; Faig, 1976; Malde, 1973). Sites of the photos can be revisited and resurveyed for analysis of comparative modern conditions.

The National Geographic Society has sponsored two research expeditions to revisit portions of Powell's original itinerary in order to assess the nature and degree of landscape change that has occurred in the river canyons over the past century. Part I of this report reviews research efforts in Canyonlands National Park, where the Green River empties into the Colorado River. Part II of this report reviews research activities in Dinosaur National Monument, about 480 km (300 mi) upstream from the junction with the Colorado.

Part I—Canyonlands

In its lower reaches, the Green River meanders through canyons etched into sandstone and shale beds ranging from Pennsylvania to Jurassic in age (Hintze, 1973). Massive sandstone cliffs dominate the landscape, but the river flows slowly without rapids through the canyon bottoms that include numerous beaches, sandbars, and benches a short distance above river level.

A brief examination of the historic photographs of the Green River in Canyonlands National Park shows that, except for a few flash flood deposits and rock falls, the landscape of the Green and Colorado Rivers appears much the same now as it did in 1871. A remarkable change, however, has occurred in the vegetation community along the rivers with the introduction of saltcedar *(Tamarix pentandra* and *T. gallicia)*, an ornamental shrub or low tree imported from the Mediterranean area in the mid-1800s. The plant escaped domestication and colonized islands and sandbars along the southwestern rivers, choking small channels and causing great loss of water through transpiration (Robinson, 1965). In canyons, the photographs show that saltcedar has stabilized sandbars, beaches, and islands, resulting in a substantial reduction in the channel area available for floods.

The purpose of the research project sponsored by the National Geographic Society was to examine the lower Green River (including Labyrinth and Stillwater Canyons) in Canyonlands National Park and nearby areas to determine precisely the effect saltcedar has had on the channel and near-channel landforms (Fig. 1). The river between Green River City, Utah, and the confluence of the Green and Colorado Rivers (referred to hereafter as the Confluence) provides a useful study area because of the large number of historical photographs available from the region. No analysis had previously attempted to measure channel and landform changes resulting from the influx of saltcedar. An understanding of landscape changes resulting from the artificially introduced vegetation is significant because the southwestern canyons represent a valuable scenic resource and because the experiences of these areas may be useful in predicting the probable effects of saltcedar on areas yet to be invaded.

Methods

Although previous researchers have rejected historical photography as a source of quantitative data (Leopold et al., 1964, p. 392), photogrammetric techniques are available that permit measurement of features displayed on the images (American Society of Photogrammetry, 1960), despite the lack of metric cameras (Faig, 1976; Kolb, 1927). Methods designed for analysis of oblique aerial photographs are useful for many historical photographs that were taken from cliff tops and other points above the surrounding terrain. Measurements of reference distances in the photographs can be compared with measurements made in the field, on modern maps, or on aerial photos. The reference distances serve as checks on photogrammetric measurements, and in some cases they provide correction factors.

Field observations and measurements in 1976 provided quantitative data on the present condition of the river channel as well as the nearby landforms and vegetation. Several significant reference measurements were made for comparison with measurements of the same distances in the historical photographs. Photographs from the original 1871 camera stations provided useful updates at key localities. Ground surveys revealed the sizes and shapes of islands and bars, and confirmed the expansion of these features since the introduction of saltcedar. Channel widths were also surveyed in a number of locations.

Analysis of tree-ring data (reviewed by Fritts, 1965), obtained with a Swedish increment borer by permission of the National Park Service, showed that cottonwood trees located on the pre-saltcedar river banks (but now located well back from the river and screened from the river by dense saltcedar thickets) are the same woods that were growing along

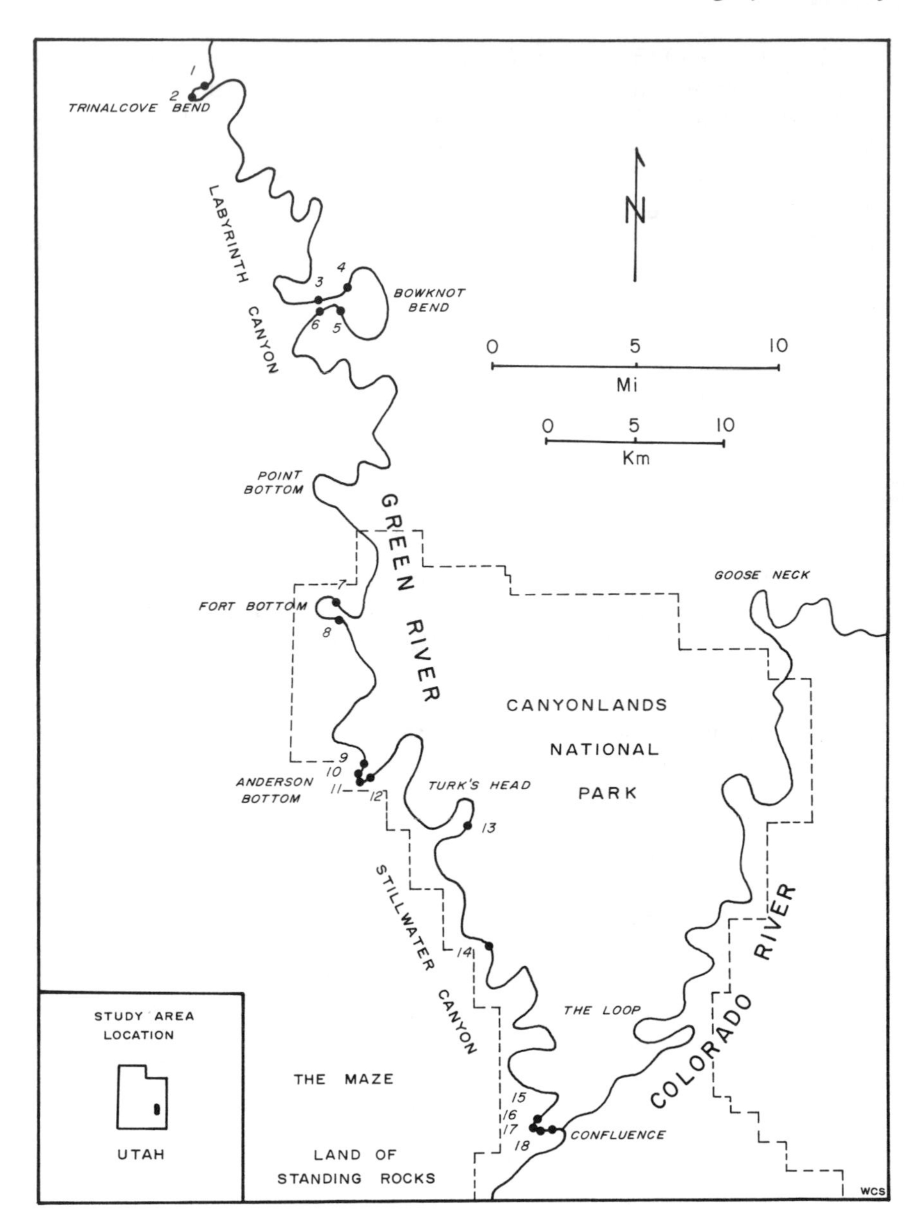

FIGURE 1. Green and Colorado River Confluence, Canyonlands National Park.

the river and that were photographed by Beaman in 1871. Their location some distance from the present river bank demonstrates the amount of bar growth since the introduction of saltcedar.

Sediment samples collected on bars and islands reveal that sediment deposited after the saltcedar invasion is very similar to sediment deposited before that time, so that the expansion to sandbars and islands is not a product of changes in river sediment characteristics. Most of the sediments consist of sand derived from local Navajo, Keyenta, Wingate, and White Rim Sandstones, but Precambrian debris from the Uinta Mountains occurs in some samples (Mutchler, 1969, noted similar materials from the Uinta Mountains in terrace gravels 20 to 30 ft above the present river level in the study area).

Stream-flow characteristics of the lower Green River have also been consistent before and after the invasion of saltcedar, so that river-level fluctuation is not a viable explanation for the observed landscape changes. The mean annual discharge of the lower Green River is slightly more than 6000 ft^3/sec, with large annual fluctuations related to snow melt and intense summer evaporation.

Changes in Channel Landforms

The role of saltcedar in landscape change near rivers is critical because the plant colonizes previously barren islands and bars, stabilizing the features by anchoring sediments and trapping new particles in extensive root systems (Horton, 1962; Horton et al., 1960; Robinson, 1958, 1965). The bars and islands that once were parts of the floodway for high discharges become very stable components of the landform system near the river, and their sediments and surfaces cannot adjust to extreme flows. As a result, floodwaters flow over the banks more frequently after the introduction of saltcedar than in previous periods when the sand deposits could be arranged to accommodate the maximum flows within the channels. The problem of channel restriction and floodplain expansion as a result of saltcedar growth has been examined in some areas (Hadley, 1961; Robinson, 1965), but the responses of canyon rivers to saltcedar have heretofore not been studied.

The photographic record shows that saltcedar invaded the confluence of the Green and Colorado Rivers between 1921 and 1927, and Christensen (1962) stated that it had been reported in Emery County (presumably near Green River City), Utah in 1931, indicating that the lower Green River in Canyonlands National Park was colonized by the plant during the 1920s. Photographs from numerous sources show that in previous decades the plant spread up the Colorado River system at a rate of about 12 mi/year. The source of saltcedar is unclear, but apparently the spread through uncultivated environments began in western Arizona or southern California, perhaps augmented by intentional plantings for erosion control in eastern Arizona and New Mexico. At present, the plant continues to expand its range; in 1976 it extended along the Green River into southern Wyoming.

In the half century since saltcedar colonized the lower Green River, profound changes have occurred in the river channel and the near-channel landforms. Field and photographic measurements at 18 sites between Green River City and the Confluence demonstrate that in some cases the low water channel has expanded, while in others it has narrowed, but at every measurement site the saltcedar and associated landforms have restricted the floodway (channel plus bars and islands, or the width between banks). Although the river varies in width from place to place, the average reduction in width between pre- and postsaltcedar conditions at 18 study sites is 27%. Over-bank flows, therefore, during peak discharges are much more likely now than before the invasion of the plant.

Islands and bars have greatly expanded since the arrival of saltcedar, accounting for almost all the floodway restriction. Changes in shapes of the features have not been common, but on the insides of many meanders, point bar deposits have a different morphology now than before the saltcedar began stabilizing materials. In some cases, smoothly curving point bars have been replaced by angular bars forming corners at the meanders. Colonization of exposed sand deposits during low-flow periods when the river did not fill the gently sweeping floodway accounts for the change. Once established, the plants have been able to trap enough sediment to stabilize the angular form and to prevent its destruction during maximum flows (Fig. 2).

Alluvial deposits in the forms of floodplains (locally known as bottoms) occur in many sections of Labyrinth and Stillwater Canyons. A river survey accomplished for the Bureau of Reclamation in 1916 (before the arrival of the saltcedar) shows that these bottoms are permanent features of the canyon landscape under present climatic and hydrologic conditions, but field surveys in 1976 and aerial photography from 1975 show that the invasions of saltcedar have had a remarkable effect on the bottoms in addition to mere expansion. Two entirely new bottoms have developed at miles 66.8 and 72.0, as sediment has been trapped by the plants (miles indicate distance upriver from the confluence of the Green and Colorado Rivers, with measures keyed to the original river survey by Herron, 1917). New islands have been stabilized by the plants at miles 106.0, 100.0, 61.8, and 31.3. The invasion of saltcedar also caused the conversion of some islands into bottoms by eliminating the narrow chutelike

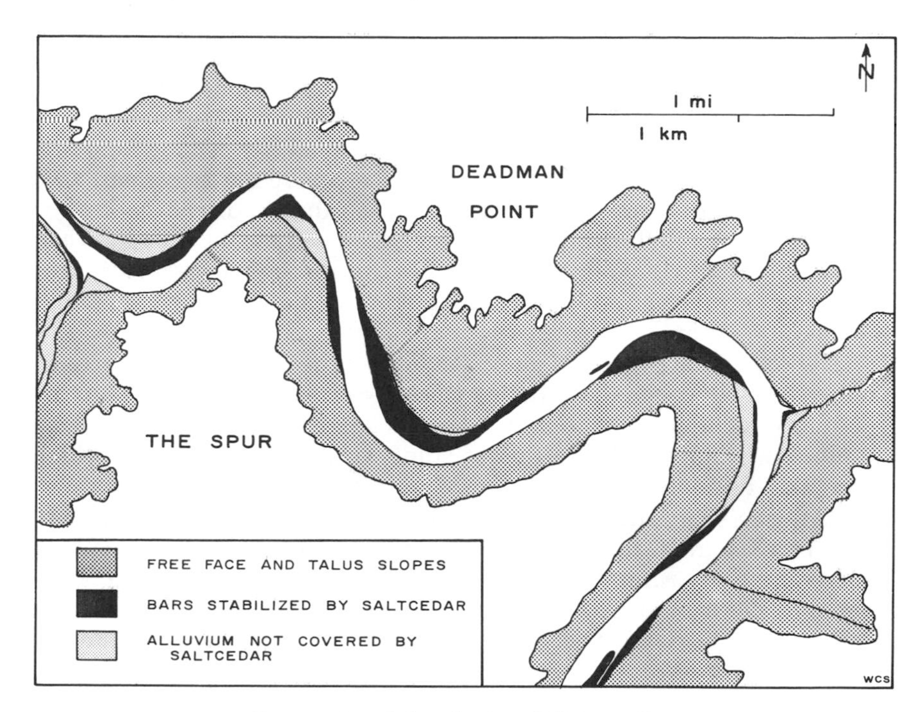

FIGURE 2. Saltcedar's stabilizing effects.

channels that separated the islands from the channel banks. Comparison of evidence from the pre- and postinvasion periods shows that the following developed in this fashion: Ruby Ranch Bottom opposite the mouth of the San Rafael River (mile 95.0), an unnamed bottom (mile 90.2), Saddle Horse Bottom (mile 45.5), and Valentine Bottom (mile 27.2). Junes Bottom (mile 87.0) was an island in 1951, but soon thereafter it was attached to the river bank. The process of island expansion and chute filling continues at present, and may be observed at an unnamed island just above the mouth of the San Rafael River (mile 96.5) and at Fort Bottom (mile 39.5).

The lengths and widths of the 143 islands and bars in the study area demonstrate that, although these features have been substantially enlarged by the incursion of saltcedar, the shapes have remained nearly constant. The quantitative data for length *(L)* and width *(W)* from aerial photos and field measurements show that the shapes of the depositional features may be accurately described by the function $W = a L^b$ where *a* and *b* are constants. The value of *b* is always less than 1.0 for islands and bars in Labyrinth and Stillwater Canyons, indicating that as they become larger, length increases more rapidly than width.

Field examination reveals that many of the islands and bars consist of a series of layers that are exposed at the perimeters in ledges or benches. A small beach usually occurs at the present waterline as a dynamic environment where sand is constantly being deposited, shifted, and eroded. The first bench frequently is located a few feet above the low waterline—it is covered with water during the annual maximum discharge (during spring snowmelt in the mountains), but is exposed for much of the year. Saltcedar seedlings colonize the surface of this low bench each year, only to be swept away by the annual flood and then replaced by new seedlings the following year.

A second bench, located a few feet above the first, is not frequently flooded and is covered by dense thickets of saltcedar, with varying amounts of willow. In some cases saltcedar is exclusive, in others, willow dominates. Debris indicates that at some times the river stage is high enough to inundate the second bench, but only infrequently.

Almost all bars and islands contain evidence of the two benches, but above most channel-side bars a third bench is also common. These high benches are rarely inundated by floodwaters and may not be genetically related to the bars nearby. They are composed of debris from riverside slopes, some alluvial deposits, and occasionally eolian sand. Cultural evidence in the forms of Anasazi Indian ruins, rare structures built by white settlers, and hearth sites remain undisturbed by flood activity, so that the highest bench is probably not the product of environmental processes active in the last 1000 years.

Analysis of tree-ring data demonstrates that climatic change probably did not play a large role in the spread of saltcedar into the Canyonlands region. Fluctuations in tree-ring widths suggest that dry periods occurred during the 1930s and 1950s, but year-to-year changes in moisture availability were relatively large throughout the late 1800s and all of the 1900s. The most useful tree-ring cores are those from oak trees growing on slopes above the riverbanks, but cottonwoods were also helpful for short-term records. Saltcedar trees were difficult to core, though some rare specimens approached 50 years in age. In most cases, saltcedar forms even-aged stands on fluvial deposits, and the plant ages do not show a marked progression in age that might differentiate older from younger parts of islands and bars.

In addition to providing a means of stabilizing islands and bars, the saltcedar shrubs and trees have a significant effect on the hydrologic environment by transpiration. Dense thickets of saltcedar withdraw large quantities of water from the subsurface (and thus indirectly from the nearby river) through normal plant processes (Campbell and Dick-Peddie, 1964; Horton, 1960; 1962). Saltcedar, with taproots over 10 ft in length, withdraws so much water from the ground that in some areas the plant has a substantial impact on local hydrologic cycles (Robinson, 1958). The total surface area covered by saltcedar between Green River City and the Confluence is 2442 acres as measured from the aerial photography and in the field. Assuming that previous research indicating that average annual water use by saltcedar is 4 acre-ft per acre of saltcedar growth (Gatewood et al., 1950) is correct, the saltcedar growing along the Green River between Green River City and the confluence of the Green and Colorado Rivers transpires more than 9600 acre-ft of water per year, or about 2% of the total discharge of the Green River through Canyonlands National Park.

Research in broad alluvial valleys of Arizona, New Mexico, and Colorado has suggested that, once established as a dominant species, saltcedar does not give way to other plant types (Robinson, 1965). This exclusiveness is not the case in the canyons of Canyonlands National Park and vicinity, and completely pure stands of saltcedar are unusual. Saltcedar is almost always mixed with dwarf willow, and occasionally with cottonwood or oak. In highly dynamic environments it appears that saltcedar alone colonizes new sand accumulations, and that after several years of stability, willow competes, sometimes successfully, with the saltcedar. New islands and bars are rarely colonized by cottonwood or oak because of dense stands of saltcedar and willow.

Conclusions

After more than 50 years of growth in the Canyonlands area, the artificially introduced saltcedar growing near the Green River has had a significant effect on the river landscape. A unique series of historical photographs and field investigations show that the width of the floodway of the river (the distance between the two banks) has been reduced by an average of 27%, and new landforms have been created by the stabilizing effects of the saltcedar growth. Old islands and bars have become larger, and new islands and bottoms have developed as a direct result of the invasion of the plant. Over-bank flooding is necessarily a more common occurrence now than before the plant colonized the area. A small though significant amount of water is transpired by the plants, a fact that must be considered an important component of the hydrologic cycle in the arid Canyonlands region.

The growth of saltcedar in the Canyonlands area poses several considerations from the standpoint of land management. Clearly the plant is undesirable from the hydrologic perspective because it uses vast quantities of precious water and draws down the water table, robbing more desirable plants of the means of existence. If the lower Green River is considered a wilderness area, it does not meet statutory requirements for inclusion in the national wilderness system because of the artificially introduced vegetation that dominates the riverside ecosystems (similar considerations have been encountered with upland vegetation in Grand Canyon National Park; National Park Service, 1975). Most of the saltcedar thickets along the river are so dense that travel through them is impossible, limiting embarkation and debarkation points for river runners (see Mutchler, 1969, for example). It might be argued, however, that the dense green vegetation in the canyon bottoms provides a scenic counterpoint to the red, brown, and buff shades of the bare rock surfaces that dominate vistas in the national park. Whatever value the plant has, the expense and unavoidable environmental damage required by a removal program seem to dictate that the saltcedar will remain as a permanent fixture of the landscape along with the substantial geomorphic changes it has fostered.

Part II—Dinosaur

In Dinosaur National Monument, the Green River and its tributaries have eroded into the eastern flank of the Uinta Mountains, and have carved four major canyons: Lodore; Whirlpool; Split Mountain; and the Yampa River flows through the fourth to join the Green in the center of the monument (Fig. 3). The canyons are etched into sandstones and limestones ranging generally in age from Precambrian to Permian (Hintze, 1973; Hansen, 1975), with walls soaring as high as 1100 m (3600 ft) from water level to plateau surfaces above (Fig. 4). Separated by open areas called parks, the canyons are focal points for surficial change because of steep slopes and the restriction of flowing water. The spectacular scenery attracts thousands of visitors each year who use the region as a primary recreation resource (McCool et al., 1977). Analysis of landscape processes has significance as applied and as basic research. Geomorphic (or landscape) changes represent hazards to visitors, but they are also components of a delicately balanced environmental system that may be disturbed by unwise management. In addition, modern landscape processes may be valuable indicators of how landscapes develop and change over periods of several million years. At present, however, our understanding of natural forces and rates of change in the canyons of the arid and semiarid regions of the United States is severely limited by the lack of field measurements (Lustig, 1968).

The purpose of the National Geographic Society-sponsored research was to determine the nature of changes in the canyons in the past century, to assess rates of change, and to evaluate the impact of Flaming Gorge Dam, located 64 km (40 mi) upstream. Because of limited resources, it

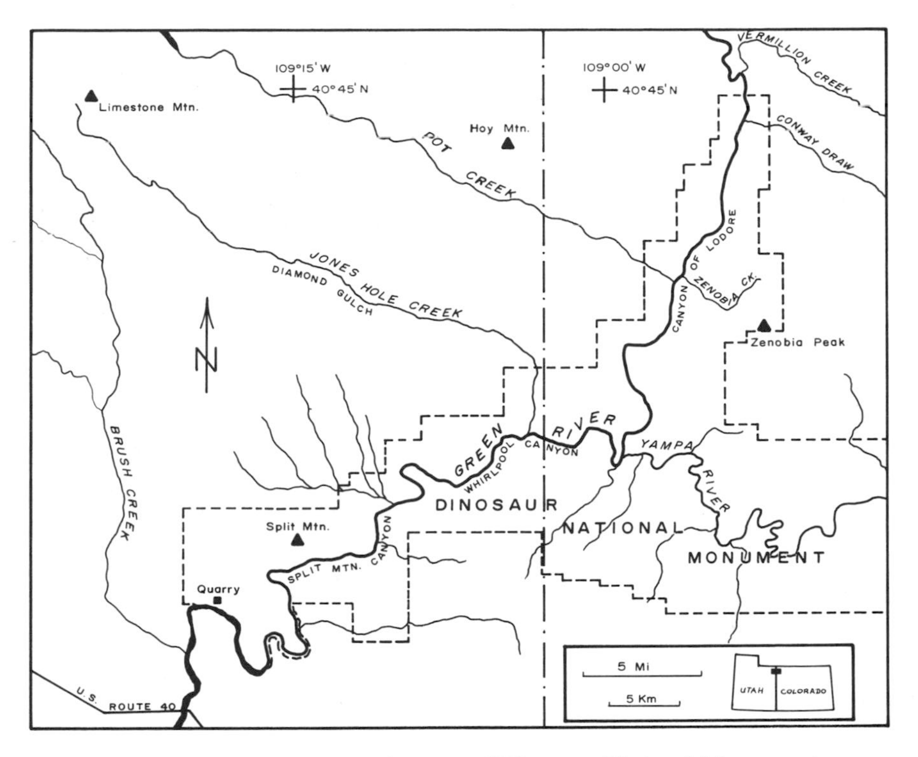

FIGURE 3. Green River in the area of Dinosaur National Monument.

was not possible to investigate fully all types of geomorphic change, but the following sections discuss the most significant landscape processes presently active.

Changes Since Powell

Comparison of modern and historical data shows four major types of landscape in the Green River canyons of Dinosaur National Monument: vegetation changes, effects of annual floods on the main stream, effects of sporadic floods on tributary streams, and rockfalls on the canyon walls.

Vegetation changes have not been as great in the Dinosaur canyons as in canyons south of the monument. In the Colorado Plateau region generally, and in the canyons of the lower Green River specifically, dramatic changes in near-channel landforms have resulted from the invasion of tamarisk. Tamarisk *(Tamarix chinensis)*, a tree artificially

FIGURE 4. General view of the Canyon of Lodore near the junction of the Green River and Pot Creek. The vertical distance from river level to plateaus at the top of the canyon wall is about 700 m (2300 ft).

introduced to the southwestern United States in the 1800s, has spread throughout western river systems, colonizing the previously empty ecological niche of moist sandbars and beaches. In many areas, dense growth of the plant has resulted in the stabilization of previously mobile sediments, and in the restriction of open channels. In the Dinosaur canyons, however, tamarisk grows only as widely spaced shrubs, and does not appear to be a dominant component of the botanic community. Its growth does not result in any geomorphic changes.

In addition to tamarisk, vegetation changes are limited to declining numbers of cottonwood *(Populus angustifolio* and *P. fremontii).* Cottonwoods shown on the Powell photographs are still present in 1977, but frequently only as dead trunks. New cottonwoods have not replaced the older trees which have been destroyed by fires accidentally set by river travelers. Powell's group was responsible for one such fire at Alcove Brook.

Besides vegetation changes, floods on the Green River have caused landscape changes near the channel. Floods on the trunk stream are related to large amounts of spring snowmelt from high elevations (Fig. 5), or to rare storm events that cause dramatic but short-lived increases in

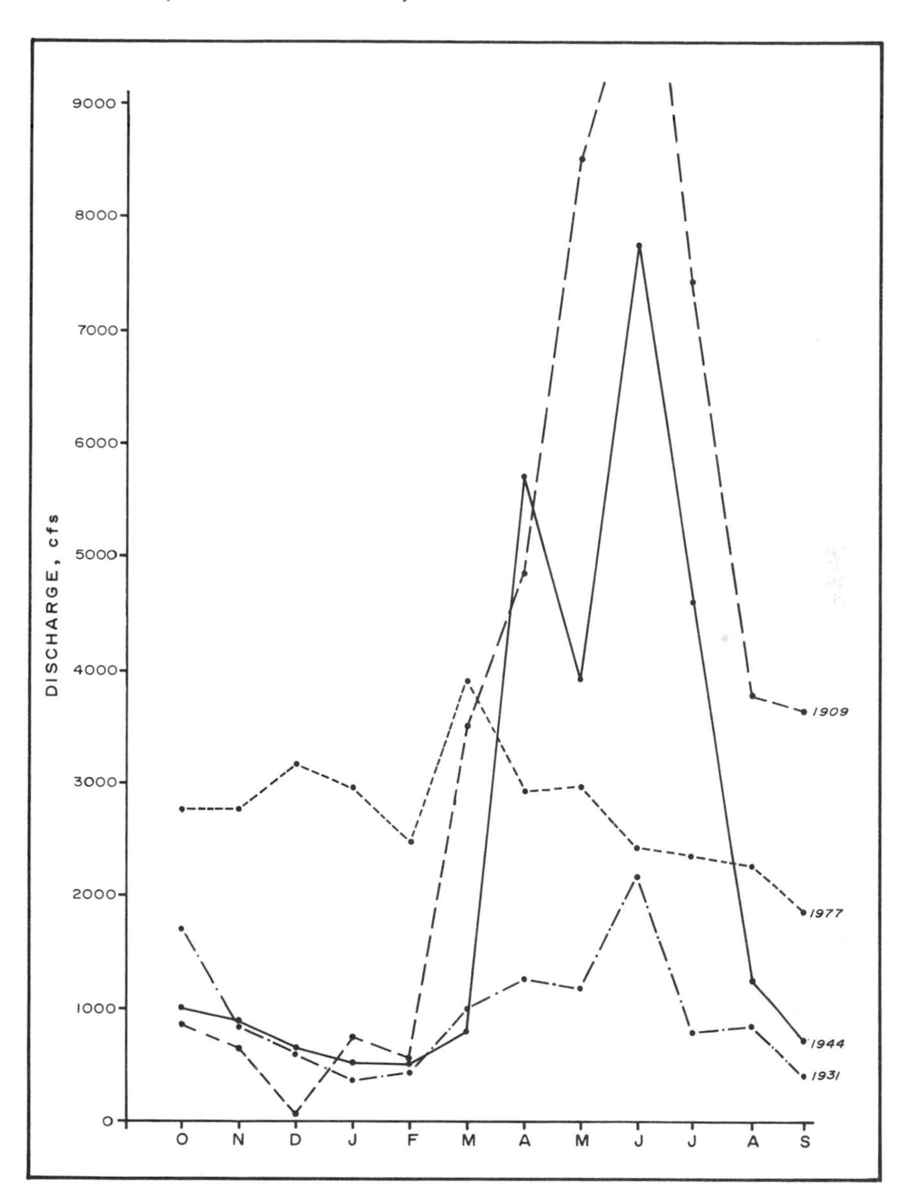

FIGURE 5. Mean monthly discharge for the Green River in the Dinosaur area, as determined from Bureau of Reclamation data at the Flaming Gorge Dam site. Months are indicated on the bottom scale. The years shown are 1909, one of the highest mean annual discharge years; 1931, one of the lowest; and two years near the mean discharge for the entire record, 1944 and 1977. Note the effect of the dam as shown by the 1977 data, the only post-dam period shown. High and low values are eliminated, with intermediate values maintained year-round. An average flow was maintained despite drought conditions in the region.

discharge. The maximum instantaneous discharge in Lodore Canyon, based on stream-gauge records for the river near Linwood (within the Flaming Gorge area), occurred in 1957 and was more than 18,000 ft^3/sec. Floods that are more than six times the mean discharge bring about radical geomorphic changes, especially in the islands and bars in the channel.

Three examples of flood-related changes are the landforms a few miles downstream from the Gates of Lodore, at the junction of the Green and Yampa Rivers, and at Tree Island. In the first case, the Powell photographs show a hook-shaped accumulation of sand and gravel on the canyon floor, partly submerged by the river's waters. In 1977, however, the channel had been straightened and the bar had been eliminated. Floods have changed the channel cross-section from an irregular shape to a smooth parabola.

At the junction of the Green and Yampa Rivers, floods on both streams have resulted in adjustments in the position of the mouth of the Yampa, and in the growth of an island near the junction. Powell's 1871 photographs show that at that time the junction contained a small island just downstream from the mouth of the Yampa. By 1977, floods on the Green River had flushed sediment from the lower reaches of Lodore Canyon and had choked the junction area. The island had grown to twice its 1871 size, and the major channel of the Yampa had been split into two lesser channels. Under natural conditions, future floods would remobilize the sediments and further alter the junction area, but the operation of Flaming Gorge Dam precludes such floods.

Tree Island is located between Whirlpool and Split Mountain Canyons. In the early 1920s, when it was mapped by river surveyors, it divided the channel of the Green River, with the main channel on the east side (Herron, 1917). In 1977 the east channel was no longer part of the river, and the island was attached to the bank. Floodwaters had realigned the river permanently into the west channel, leaving the east channel and ground that once was an island to be colonized by nonriverine vegetation.

Tributaries to the Green River are short streams draining small, very steep basins that are dominated by bare rock, conditions that produce flash floods. The tributary floods are difficult to observe and document, but their work is obvious. Many rapids in the main channel owe their existence to floods in the tributaries that wash rock debris down to the main channel. In 1965 Warm Springs Rapid on the Yampa River (about 6 km, or 4 mi, above its junction with the Green) was altered by a flash flood on a tributary. Large boulders were deposited in the main stream, and debris was added from the vertical wall opposite the entry point of the tributary. Photographs taken in 1871 and 1968 show changes involving hundreds of tons of rock. Observations along the Green show that this sequence of events and suite of landforms (tributary fan, boulder rapids, and vertical channel wall on the canyon side opposite the fan) are common, and that they represent major components of landscape change on the canyon floors.

Rockfalls above river level are also common in the canyons. No documented rockfall sites have been active in historic times, but during rainstorms, saturated material collapses on cliff faces and talus accumulations grow in the present climatic regime. Kolb (1927) reported such falls in progress during a storm in the Canyon of Lodore in 1911, and on August 25, 1977, I observed evidence of a rockslide in Whirlpool Canyon that occurred during a storm the previous night. Rockfalls near water level frequently occur as the stream undercuts cliff faces, with resulting debris falling into the channel and forming rapids.

Freshly fractured rock faces and smooth, polished talus chutes attest to the recent activity of the rockfall process. Many rock faces in the canyons are coated with desert varnish, a layer of iron and manganese compounds deposited rapidly in climatic periods more moist than at present (Hooke et al., 1969). General deposition of the varnish ceased about 2000 years ago (Hunt, 1961), so that those rockfalls that have created broken varnish surfaces without staining in the scar areas must have occurred within the last two millennia. Such scars are especially numerous in the slightly metamorphosed sandstones of the Uinta Mountain Group. They are less common in the Weber Sandstone. The scars show that rockfalls have occurred within the past 2000 years on almost every major cliff in the canyons.

From the foregoing qualitative discussion of general landscape changes, it is clear that the rapids of the main stream are focal points of geomorphic processes of the Dinosaur canyons. The rapids represent the joining of forces in tributaries and the main channel, they are related to rockfalls in many cases, and they represent the significant resistance to fluvial processes. A quantitative analysis of processes, then, must focus on the relationship between hydraulic forces and material resistance in the rapids zones.

Characteristics of Rapids

The rapids of the Green River in Dinosaur National Monument consist of angular boulders up to 3 m (10 ft) in diameter that accumulate at various sites across the main channel (Fig. 6). During extreme high discharges, all of the boulders may be submerged, but at average annual discharge a few are exposed above the water surface. Sections of the stream with such rapids have turbulent flows and steep gradients. Over 90% of the fall of the river through the canyons is in rapids reaches, producing a stepped longitudinal profile with steep rapids between relatively flat pools. Similar conditions exist in the Grand Canyon, Arizona

FIGURE 6. A typical rapid in the Green River—boulder accumulation at the junction of Rippling Brook where the Green has been displaced into the rock wall opposite the tributary. View across the stream from the tributary alluvial fan.

(Leopold, 1969). Rapids are usually colocated with rockfall sites, tributaries that have built alluvial or colluvial fans onto the canyon floor, or gravel bars in otherwise unrestricted sections of the canyons.

Because geographers are much concerned with the spatial characteristics of features on the earth's surface, the spacing of rapids along the main stream is of interest. Hamblin and Rigby (1968) suggested that in the Grand Canyon, rapids spacing is totally controlled by tributaries, because they are always colocated. Leopold (1969) suggested that rapids in the Grand Canyon are regularly spaced in order to maintain equilibrium. If equal spacing prevails, energy expended by the main stream is equalized along its length. Neither of these hypotheses explains the condition in Dinosaur National Monument.

Although rapids are usually located near sources of debris, 25% of the rapids in the Canyon of Lodore, 20% in Whirlpool Canyon, and 28% in Split Mountain Canyon are not located at debris sources. They are associated with gravel bars that, like their accompanying rapids boulders, have been transported and then redeposited by the main stream. Thus, the Hamblin/Rigby hypothesis fails to explain the locations of more than a quarter of all the rapids in the Dinosaur canyons.

Leopold's equal-spacing hypothesis also fails to provide a workable explanation. In some limited reaches, the rapids appear to be regularly spaced, but taken as a whole, regular spacing appears to be the exception rather than the rule (Fig. 7). If the distances between rapids are compiled into frequency distributions, they may be compared with model distributions to assess the degrees of randomness, regularity, or clustering in the spacing. The frequency distributions for inter-rapids distances do not closely approach any of the model distributions for spatial analysis. The distribution of rapids in Lodore Canyon may be described as more random than regular, in Whirlpool Canyon the rapids spacing approaches regularity, and in Split Mountain Canyon they are irregularly spaced.

An alternative to the two previously examined hypotheses is an appeal to dynamics—that is, the balance between force and resistance in rapids. Rapids occur where the resistance of the boulders cannot be overcome by the force of flow in the main stream. Analysis of forces in tributaries as well as main channels is required, since both systems affect the rapids at tributary/main channel junctions.

Force and Resistance in Rapids

The tractive force exerted by flowing water on the channel bed is given by the DuBoys equation, which includes components of density of the fluid, depth of flow, and channel slope (Chow, 1964). In determining the tractive forces of maximum flows in tributaries, slopes were measured in the field by a Brunton compass and from topographic maps. Depth of flow was calculated by a series of steps: (1) the discharge was determined by regional generalizations (Crippen and Bue, 1977); (2) the width of flow was measured in the field or determined by hydraulic geometry (Leopold et al., 1964); and (3) the depth of flow was calculated with a modified version of the Manning equation (Chow, 1964). The density of water in the floods was assumed to be 1.15, slightly more than the normal value of unity to account for flood debris.

The tractive force exerted by the maximum flood of record for the main channel was calculated in the same manner as above, except that gauging records were used to determine the discharge, and field surveys plus river survey records yielded slope data. Tractive force of the mean annual discharge was calculated for comparative purposes.

The resistance to movement of the boulders was determined by two processes, the Komar method and the White method (Komar, 1970; Leliavsky, 1966). Results of the two methods were usually within 10 to 15% of each other, and the results of the White method are arbitrarily used in the following discussion. Both methods relied on field measurements of boulder sizes.

Force and resistance under present climatic and hydrologic conditions dictate that the boulder rapids in the canyons of Dinosaur National Monument are slowly building features. The force available in tributary streams is much greater than the force available in the main channel, so that materials readily carried by tributaries cannot be removed by the Green River (Fig. 8). As a result, materials accumulate at source areas along the main stream. The largest particles in the accumulations were moved during floods larger than those observed since records were begun (about 1900), and they are not likely to be moved again by flows less than that of the 50-year flood.

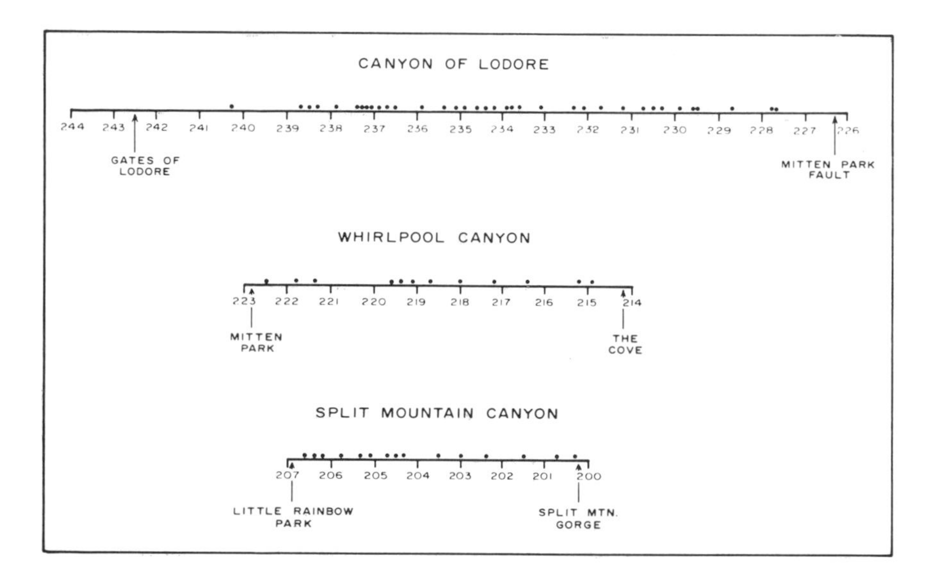

FIGURE 7. The spacing characteristics of rapids along the Green River in the Dinosaur area. Dots represent rapids locations, numbers are river mile marks measured upstream from the town of Green River and taken from Bureau of Reclamation surveys.

Mean annual depths of flow accomplish little work in the rapids. Rapids will be reduced in size and boulders will be transported by the Green River when climatic and hydrologic conditions change, or during a catastrophic flood with flows that occur once in several hundred years. With powerful tributaries (because of their steep gradients) and a relatively weak trunk stream, rapids at boulder sources will continue to grow in the foreseeable future, and those rapids not located at sources will remain stable.

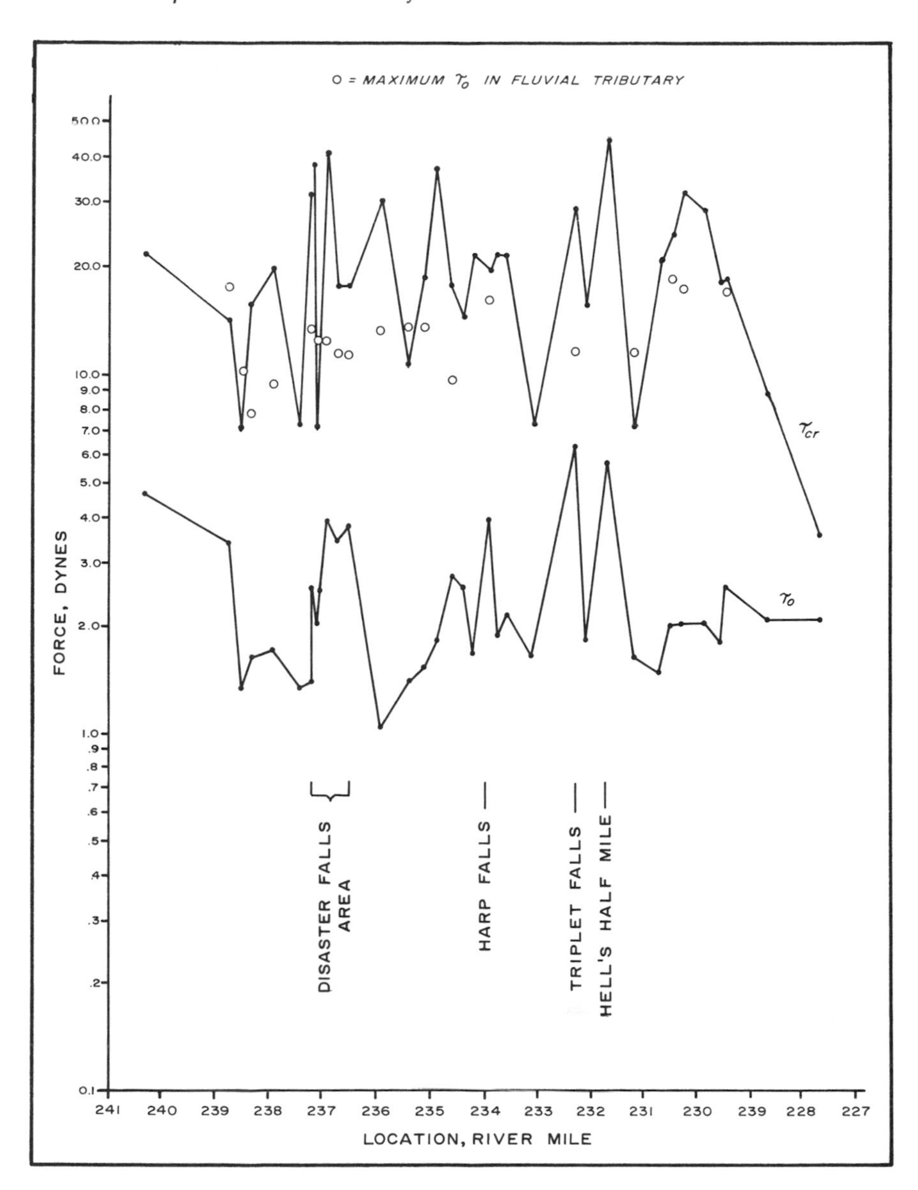

FIGURE 8. Maximum force levels in rapids of the Canyon of Lodore, based on field evidence. Note that the force applied by the Green River at its maximum known flood of 18,000 ft^3/sec, tractive force (τ_0) is well below the force required to move the largest boulders in the rapids (τ_c). In only a few cases is force in tributaries high enough to move the largest boulders, which therefore must have been moved under conditions much different than those at present.

Conclusions

The analysis of force and resistance suggests some generalizations about landscape change in arid and semiarid river canyons. First, the movement of materials is a discontinuous process that occurs only during extreme hydrologic events. Rockfalls are triggered by major storm events, and catastrophic floods play a dominant role in the movement of large particles through the fluvial system. The frequency of events that drives the landscape change processes is probably once in several hundred years for the rapids, but perhaps once every few years for rockfalls. This situation is much different than the case for small particles, which owe most of their movement to events of small magnitude that occur frequently (Leopold et al., 1964).

A second generalization is that the general terrain features—canyons, valleys, and cliffs—owe their overall form to processes that are effective under climatic and hydrologic conditions much different than those at present. Maximum discharge of the Green River would have to be two or three times the highest flow on record to accomplish effective down-cutting. The canyons, then, are products inherited from previous periods when geomorphic processes were more intense than at present, when the fluvial system is barely maintaining the movement of materials through the system. Glacial and pluvial climates have occurred frequently in the Green River basin in the past million years, and it is most likely that they represent the periods of effective flows of the river. That the canyons are inherited from previous climatic episodes is well known, but the required magnitude of events is now apparent, based on the measurements given in Figure 8.

The third generalization suggested by the force analysis is that human manipulation of the flow of the Green River at Flaming Gorge Dam is not likely to affect the stability of the rapids. In the Grand Canyon, river runners and administrators have expressed the fear that closure of Glen Canyon Dam would reduce flood flows and thus permit a dangerous buildup of the rapids (Dolan et al., 1974). In the Dinosaur canyons such a buildup was in progress before Flaming Gorge Dam was installed, and, in general, the river was not able to remove boulders in rapids even at naturally high flood flows. Although it is true that the dam reduces flood peaks by over 60%, such a reduction does not appear to be of significance under present climatic and hydrologic conditions.

Finally, the calculated volumes and depths of flash floods in tributary streams demonstrate the true dimensions of these natural hazards. Administrators and recreationists using the canyons must take into account the fact that approximately once every 50 years a wall of water 1 to 3 m (3 to 10 ft) high comes rushing out of each tributary gorge, a circumstance made doubly hazardous by the distribution of campsites which favors the junctions of tributaries with the main stream.

Since John Wesley Powell's journey over a century ago, landscape change has continued in the canyons of Dinosaur National Monument as a product of infrequent hydrologic events. The rapids that posed obstacles to his travel are slowly building accumulations of debris in a fluvial system that is spatially unbalanced: tributaries are more powerful than the main stream. Because of the dependence of geomorphic processes on climatic systems as sources of energy, a change in the geomorphic processes is unlikely until a shift in climatic conditions alters the magnitude and frequency of floods in the region.

REFERENCES

American Society of Photogrammetry
1960. Manual of photogrammetry, 2 vols, 1220 pp. Amer. Soc. Photogram., Falls Church, Virginia.

Campbell, C. J., and Dick-Peddie, W. A.
1964. Comparison of phreatophyte communities on the Rio Grande in New Mexico. Ecology, vol. 45, pp. 492-502.

Christensen, E. M.
1962. The rate of naturalization of *Tamarix* in Utah. Amer. Midlands Naturalist, vol. 68, pp. 51-57.

Chow, V. T.
1964. Handbook of applied hydrology. McGraw-Hill Book Co., New York.

Crippen, J. R., and Bue, C. D.
1977. Maximum floodflows in the conterminous United States. U. S. Geol. Surv. Water Supply Paper 1887, 52 pp.

Dolan, R.; Howard, A.; and Gallenson, A.
1974. Man's impact on the Colorado River in the Grand Canyon. Amer. Scientist, vol. 62, pp. 392-401.

Eddy, C.
1929. Down the world's most dangerous river, 293 pp. F. A. Stokes Company, New York.

Faig, I. W.
1976. Photogrammetric potentials of non-metric cameras. Photogram. Engineering and Rem. Sens., vol. 42, pp. 47-49.

Fritts, H. C.
1965. Dendrochronology. Pp. 871-879 *in* "The Quaternary of the United States," H. E. Wright Jr. and D. G. Frey, eds., 922 pp. Princeton University.

Graf, W. L.
1978a. The wild canyon of Ladore. Nat. Parks Conserv., vol. 13, pp. 459-463.
1978b. Fluvial adjustments to the spread of tamarisk in the Colorado Plateau region. Bull. Geol. Soc. Amer., vol. 86, pp. 1491-1501.

GRAF, W. L. *(continued)*
1979. Rapids in canyon rivers. Journ. Geol., vol. 87, pp. 533-551.
1980a. The effect of dam closure on downstream rapids. Water Resources Res., vol. 16, pp. 129-136.
1980b. On the rivers of Canyonlands. Sierra, vol. 65, no. 6, pp. 60-64.

GOLDWATER, B. M.
1970. Delightful journey, 209 pp. Arizona Historical Foundation.

HADLEY, R. F.
1961. Influence of riparian vegetation on channel shape, northeastern Arizona. U. S. Geol. Surv. Prof. Pap. 424-c, pp. 30-31.

HAMBLIN, W. K., and RIGBY, J. K.
1969. Guidebook to the Colorado River, Part 2, 126 pp. Brigham Young University Geology Studies, Provo, Utah.

HANSEN, W. R.
1975. The geologic story of the Uinta Mountains. U. S. Geol. Surv. Bull. 1291, 144 pp.

HERRON, W. H.
1917. Profile surveys in the Colorado River basin in Wyoming, Utah, Colorado, and New Mexico. U. S. Geol. Surv. Water Supply Paper 396, 6 pp.

HINTZE, L. F.
1973. Geologic history of Utah. Brigham Young University Geology Studies, vol. 20, pt. 3, 181 pp.

HOOKE, R. LeB.; YANG, H-Y; and WEIBLEN, P. W.
1969. Desert varnish: An election probe study. Journ. Geol., vol. 77, pp. 275-288.

HORTON, J. S.
1960. Ecology of saltcedar. Arizona Watershed Symposium, September 21, 1960, Proceedings, vol. 4, pp. 19-21.
1962. Taxonomic notes on *Tamarix pentandra* in Arizona. Southwestern Naturalist, vol. 7, pp. 22-28.

HORTON, J. S.; MOUNTS, F. C.; and KRAFT, J. M.
1960. Seed germination and seedling establishment of phreatophyte species. U. S. Dept. of Agric., Forest Serv. Research Note RM-48, 16 pp.

HUNT, C. B.
1961. Stratigraphy of desert varnish. U. S. Geol. Surv. Prof. Pap. 424-B, pp. 194-195.

KOLB, E. L.
1927. Through the Grand Canyon from Wyoming to Mexico, 344 pp., 2nd ed. Macmillan, New York.

KOMAR, P. D.
1970. The competence of turbidity current flow. Bull. Geol. Soc. Amer., vol. 81, pp. 1555-1562.

LELIAVSKY, S.
1966. An introduction to fluvial hydraulics, 257 pp. Dover, New York

LEOPOLD, L. B.
1969. The rapids and pools—Grand Canyon, the Colorado River Region and John Wesley Powell. U. S. Geol. Surv. Prof. Pap. 669-D.

LEOPOLD, L. B.; WOLMAN, M. G.; and MILLER, J. P.
1964. Fluvial processes in geomorphology, 522 pp. Freeman, San Francisco.

LUSTIG, L. K.
1968. Appraisal of research on geomorphology and surface hydrology of desert environments. Vol. 3, pp. 95-283, *in* "Deserts of the World," W. G. McGinnies, J. Goldman, and P. Paylore, eds. University of Arizona Press, Tucson, Arizona.

MALDE, H. E.
1973. Geologic benchmarks by terrestrial photography. Journ. Res. U. S. Geol. Surv., vol. 1, pp. 193-206.

MCCOOL, S. F.; LIME, D. W.; and ANDERSON, D. H.
1977. Simulation modeling as a tool for managing river recreation. Pp. 304-311 *in* "Proceedings of Symposium on River Recreation Management and Research." U. S. Forest Service Gen. Tech. Rept. NC-28, Minneapolis.

MUTSCHLER, F. E.
1969. River runner's guide to the canyons of the Green and Colorado Rivers with emphasis on geologic features. Vol. II, Labyrinth, Stillwater, and Cataract Canyons. 76 pp. Powell Society Ltd.

NATIONAL PARK SERVICE
1975. Final environmental statement, proposed master plan, Grand Canyon Complex, Arizona. U. S. Dept. of Interior, Denver.

POWELL, J. W.
1875. Exploration of the Colorado River of the West and its tributaries, 291 pp. Washington, D. C.

ROBINSON, T. W.
1958. Phreatophytes, Pp. 70-75 *in* U. S. Geol. Surv. Water-Supply Pap. 1423.
1965. Introduction, spread, and areal extent of saltcedard *(Tamarix)* in the western United States, 20 pp. U. S. Geol. Surv. Prof. Pap. 491-A.

SARLES, F. B.
1968. John Wesley Powell and the Colorado River, 212 pp. U. S. Dept. of Interior, National Park Service.

SHOEMAKER, E. M., and STEPHENS, H. G.
1969. The Green and Colorado River canyons observed from the footsteps of Beaman and Hillers 97 years after Powell. Geol. Soc. of Amer. Abstracts, Rocky Mountain Section, p. 73.
1975. First photographs of the Canyonlands. Pp. 111-122 *in* "Canyonlands Country," Four Corners Geological Society Guidebook, J. E. Tasset, ed., Four Corners Geological Society, 8th Field Conference, Moab, Utah.

STANTON, R. B.
1965. Down the Colorado, D. C. Smith, ed., 237 pp. University of Oklahoma Press, Norman, Oklahoma.

STONE, J. F.
1932. Canyon country, 442 pp. Putnam, New York.

WOODLEY, R. R.
1930. The Green River and its utilization. U. S. Geol. Surv. Prof. Pap. 618.

WILLIAM L. GRAF

Preliminary Archeological Survey of Lakeba, Lau Group, Fiji

Grant Recipient: Roger C. Green, University of Auckland, Auckland, New Zealand.

Grants 1569, 1702: In support of a study of the archeology of the Lau Islands, Fiji.

A program to study the cultural history of the Lau Islands in Fiji was initiated in 1974 by Dr. John M. R. Young, a historian at the University of Adelaide (Young, 1975).

Research, focused on the historical records and the traditional oral history of the whole Lau Group, was undertaken by Young (1975) and Mr. A. C. Reid (1977), a research assistant in history. In 1975 Dr. G. A. Rogers (1976) joined the project as a research assistant, and concentrated his initial efforts in the northern Lau Group, recording both archeological sites and oral traditions.

From Reid's research into the oral and traditional history of the island of Lakeba, about halfway down the north-south chain of 100 islands, which comprise the Lau Group, it was evident that this island not only constituted a central place in the traditional history of the group, but was also an island where archeological investigation of the traditional sites would provide further insights.

To this end archeological research was undertaken by research students from the University of Auckland.

Lakeba

Lakeba, the largest of the Lau Islands, is centrally located within that group. It is also situated almost midway between the main Fijian islands and those of the Tongan group. The island, roughly oval in shape, is 5463 ha (54.63 km^2) in area; inland, volcanic hills reach up to 200 m above sea level, while on the coast, outcrops of limestone up to 100 m high occur. Around the coast are alluvial flats up to 700 m wide, and valley floors run back toward the center of the island along the main rivers. Geologically, the island appears to have been tilted to the east, so that raised coral limestone bluffs predominate on the west side, and drowned flats choked with mangroves border the east coast. Here the fringing reef reaches its farthest point, some 9 km from land.

The island's vegetation is varied. On the limestone outcrops a typical rain forest occurs. Inland, only the hill on which Kedekede is situated and some of the valley heads are in bush. The rest is either in bracken or a tall reed, with the occasional pandanus or casuarina; this area is being planted in Caribbean pines. Except where villages occur at the mouths of rivers, the coastal flats are taken up with coconut plantations and gardens. These gardens and plantations extend inland along the bottoms and lower flanks of the valleys.

The last census figures show Lakeba to hold slightly over 2000 people. An all-weather road circles the island, which has Forestry, Agricultural, and Public Works Departments. An airstrip permits at least three flights a week from Nausori Airport, Suva.

Two seasons of archeological research have been spent on Lakeba: November 1975 to March 1976, and December 1976 to September 1977. In the first season the area was surveyed, and test excavations were carried out at five sites: a sixth, the fortified site of Kedekede, was examined more thoroughly and mapped. Four of these sites feature in the oral traditions of the island as being either the initial or early settlements of migrants, and the excavations were conducted to determine whether any evidence of cultural change could be found. The other, a large coastal rock-shelter, was excavated with the expectation of recovering a comprehensive stratigraphic sample of the pottery sequence for the island. In this way it was hoped to provide a key to the chronological ordering of all the recorded sites through their surface collections, especially of those prior to the period covered by traditions. Analysis of the pottery recovered from this rock-shelter, together with associated C^{14} dates, showed that the island had been occupied for approximately 2300 years. However, the pottery, and evidence that the sea had been washing into the shelter at the time, indicated a greater time depth for the island.

A major aim of the second season's research was to fill in the early stages of the sequence. It was with this in mind that a concentrated search was made along the base of the limestone bluffs in the northwest coast area of Lakeba, where they were farthest from the beach. Five dentate-stamped sherds, synonymous with the earliest settlements found in Fiji, Tonga, and Samoa, were found hard up against the cliffs, some 100 m from another rock-shelter. It was at this shelter site, and to a lesser extent, the rock-shelter test-excavated in 1976-1977, that most of the second season's excavations were carried out.

In addition, the limestone forts of Lakeba were further investigated. These were three in all: two known prior to this work and one discovered this season. A single charcoal sample obtained from a test square excavated in 1976 on the largest of the forts indicated an age of about 1000 years. The three sites appear to be similar, both in their manner of construction and in the pottery obtained from them, and are likely to represent an important period in Lakeba's prehistory. It was, therefore, decided to carry out plane-table surveys of all three sites, to make extensive surface collections of potsherds, flakes, etc., and to conduct more excavations on the largest site, Ulunikoro.

The final part of this season's work consisted of making plane-table surveys of selected sites. These included several inland hilltop sites where pottery of the later period had been found, a coastal ring-ditch site, perimeter maps of the two old villages of Yadrana and Nasaqalau, and a detailed map of the old village of Tubou.

Contemporary dwelling sizes were recorded, and the activity areas of single families living away from the villages mapped. A comparative collection of the 30 most frequently caught reef-fish was made and the 28 most common trees in the vicinity of the main rock-shelter were double cored with an increment borer, as aids to identifying the fish and charcoal remains in these sites.

As an aid to understanding the numerous earth ovens uncovered archeologically, the construction and use of modern ovens was studied. Features recorded included the dimensions; the number, type, and weight of oven stones; the type of fuel used; the type and amount of food cooked and for how long; and the number of adults and juveniles who were fed.

SITE SURVEY

The site survey was accomplished in one month using guides or local information on the coast, and by walking every ridge inland. It is considered likely that a high percentage of the inland sites have been recorded; however, a thorough coverage of the coast would probably take many months or even years, as sites only come to light when the thick scrub is cleared for gardening or other activities. Nevertheless, all known sites were located in this area, and as much of the country searched as was feasible, namely stream banks, cleared plantations, and gardens.

Oral traditions concerning the ownership of known sites and the sequence in which they were occupied were collected, and a part of the project will be to compare these with the archeological record.

Over 200 sites were located, and surface collections made of sherds, flakes, shells, etc. Initially, 17 types of sites have been recognized, based on topographical and cultural criteria. These are as follows:

1. Inland hilltop sites, with both man-made and natural defenses, of such large size that a communal purpose must be assigned to them.

2. Similar but much smaller sites.
3. Inland hilltop sites with no natural or apparent man-made defenses.
4. Similar sites but of very small area and very few remains.
5. Inland saddle sites, usually consisting of a very small group of sherds or the occasional flake.
6. Inland valley-bottom sites.
7. Spur-end sites, directly above coastal flats.
8. Coastal limestone ridge forts, with extensive stonework both for defense and habitation purposes.
9. Coastal limestone peaks, with no defenses.
10. Coastal limestone peaks, with earthworks.
11. Small isolated, rounded hills rising some 10 m above the coastal flats.
12. Coastal flatland sites, surrounded by a circular or subcircular ditch or watercourse or combination. No internal bank and no access bridges.
13. Similar sites but with internal bank and/or bridges.
14. Apparently undefended flatland sites, usually exposed by crabs or cultivation.
15. Coastal rock-shelters.
16. Caves: (a) habitation, both defended and undefended; (b) burial only.
17. Specialized sites: (1) dart-throwing pitch; (b) graves; (c) clay sources; (d) beach rock quarry; (e) tracks.

EXCAVATION UNITS AND METHODS

In the two rock-shelters, units were 2- × 2-m squares (in one of the sites enlarged to 2 × 5.5 m).

Excavation was by stratigraphic layers, and by 5-cm units within layers when necessary. All material was troweled, dry-sieved through a 5-mm mesh, and then wet-sieved through a 1.5-mm mesh in a set of three water drums. All material was retained from occupation floors (save for oven stones and the soil matrix), including pottery, stone, bone, and shell artifacts, wood charcoal, and bone and shell food remains. All carbonized seeds and husks were floated out in the first of the three drums and collected. All oven stones were weighed by layer and quadrant, identified as to whether volcanic, limestone, or coral, and the volcanic specimens sampled.

From disturbed midden deposits the procedure was the same, save for shell, which was retained from a 1-m^2 quadrant only.

Bone, shell, and charcoal samples were collected for C^{14} dating, and potsherds for thermoluminescence.

In open sites, due to the clay nature of the soil, the material was placed on a 5-mm mesh, partially sieved (dry), and then sorted. Otherwise, methods were the same as those used in rock-shelters.

RESULTS

Both rock-shelters contained occupation deposit over 4 m deep. The most productive in terms of occupation surfaces and artifacts was the site discovered during the second season.

Here the deposits were 4.7 m deep; the top 2.5 m consisting of occupation layers and midden; under this were eight occupation layers each separated by sterile sand. Half the area was then excavated 20 cm farther, and evidence of four apparently sterile beach surfaces encountered. Below this the sand was unsorted and strongly cemented.

The first occupation in this shelter occurred on a beach that was some 75 cm higher than that of the present day. Among the pottery used by these occupants are vessels decorated by the dentate stamp method and also vessels with strongly everted rims and notched lips, almost certainly from flat-based dishes. Both of these are typical of the Lapita tradition, which occurs throughout central and east Melanesia and west Polynesia, in the latter two areas marking the arrival of the first inhabitants.

Faunal material from this layer consisted of fish, turtles, molluscs, rats, and a large amount of bird bone. This and the next highest layer were the only ones at the site to contain bird bone in any quantity; initial analysis has indicated that these may include some extinct species.

Of the identifiable charcoal in this layer, carbonized coconut shell is the most common.

The next highest layer also contained pottery with dentate stamp decoration, but with this was a plain ware with gently everted and expanded rims, and with wipe-marks around the neck and sometimes upper shoulder. Over the next 2 m of deposit only this pottery is present; in the lowest layers occasional dentate stamping does occur, but is restricted to simple half-circles on rims, and executed with a shell, not a manufactured tool as previously.

Flat-based dishes disappear, the dominant vessels are large mouthed, slightly restricted pots with simple ovoid form, or with carinated shoulders and everted rims.

The class of temper used in the pots also changes, from the Lithic-Feldspathic and Feldspathic variants of the Lakeba Volcanic Sand Temper Group (with some examples of the Lakeba Calcareous Placer Temper Group) to a class composed almost entirely of the Lithic variant (Dickinson, 1978). That is to say, the addition to the clay of shell fragments and feldspar minerals ceases, and the temper consists mainly of rock fragments.

The faunal material is broadly similar to that of the lower layers, although the molluscs have not been analyzed in any detail as yet. Flying foxes are now represented, as are humans; burnt fragmented bones, mainly skull and limbs, occur in some quantity. These are also present in all younger deposits of the site.

A single C^{14} date for this pottery was obtained from the first season's work of 2300 ± 170 B.P.

At some time after this a new decorative technique appears, the vessel and rim shapes change, as does the temper. The technique is paddle impressing, the decorations being mainly vertical rib, with some cross-hatch. The vessel shapes tend to become more restricted, with the rims more everted. The rims are now parallel or very slightly expanded, with rounded lips. The temper is predominately shell.

The appearance of these ceramic changes in the rock-shelter is clear-cut; similar pottery occurs around the coast of Viti Levu at a time not yet fully determined, but in the region of 700 to 0 B.C. (Birks, 1978). The impetus for the changes may be internal; however, since similar decorative techniques are recorded from New Caledonia at approximately the same time depth (Frimagacci, n.d.), it is reasonable to suppose that the influence originated from that area.

At some time before 1000 B.P. the ceramic sequence again indicates external influence. Six new decorative techniques occur within a 5-cm band of living floors, accompanied by new vessel shapes. Flake tool material, mainly chert, increases from some 30 flakes in the previous 2 m to 149 in the living floors. Seven flakes of obsidian, the first recorded in Fiji, also occur at this time. Initial X-ray fluorescence tests on these show that of the known sources, that of the northern New Hebrides is similar, in proportions of rubidium, strontium, and zirconium. Further tests are in hand.

Above these layers in the rock-shelter the function of the site changes from one that produced discrete occupation surfaces to one where few such layers occur, but where earth ovens are numerous. These are of considerable size, up to 2 m across and with almost a ton of oven stones.

The sequence in the other rock-shelter parallels the above, in pottery, flakes, obsidian, and ovens.

Open Sites

Of these only the two large forts—the coastal limestone site of Ulunikoro and the inland volcanic hill site of Kedekede—were excavated to any extent.

Ulunikoro

The site is covered by dense rain forest and a close-growing scrub which covers the man-made stonework. Tracks were cut through these and the site surveyed. A surface collection resulted in over 11,000 sherds, about 1000 flakes and 12 adzes or adze fragments.

Two main areas were selected for excavation. On the top of the main ridge, one 1- × 1-m and five 2- × 1-m units were excavated, while on a lower terrace and on a flat living area at the base of the ridge, one 1- × 1-m and six 2- × 1-m units were excavated. Evidence from these excavations indicates that the site experienced several stages of buildup; both the ridge top and the base flats had been extensively modified and enlarged during the course of occupation.

Oral traditions place Ulunikoro as one of the earliest sites on the island that was settled in the general movement inland.

The pottery from this site, while indicating continuity with the earlier sequence, including all except one of the six new decorative techniques and the new vessel forms, also shows, in the latest stages of occupation, continuity with inland hilltop sites, including Kedekede.

Kedekede

This hill fort is situated on the highest point of the island, almost dead center. It consists of three terraced ditched ridges running up to a top platform of about 3000 m^2, on which five stone-faced house mounds occur.

Sixteen 2- × 1-m units were excavated. The earliest pottery on the site, contained in the fill of a large pit under the second highest house mound, included sherds similar to those from Ulunikoro, and also a few sherds belonging to the early period—that of the plain ware with expanded rims of about 2300 years ago. A burial in the pit, with triton trumpet, gave a C^{14} date of 670 ± 70 B.P. Subsequently a house mound was formed above this, with three or four stages of enlarging, the final stage including the addition of a markedly different subsoil, with quantities of andesitic rock fragments, possibly from one of the defensive ditches.

The other units produced evidence of terrace rebuilding and enlarging, and possibly indicate the sequence of occupation of the three ridges.

Artifacts

Shell artifacts formed the main part of those recovered by excavation. These included 40 sections of armbands and over 200 shell beads, covering some 2000 years. Also recovered was part of a possible breast ornament, shell "gouges," and small smoothed points or "awls."

Sections of 6 pearl shell fishhooks and 12 sawn fragments of pearl shell occurred in the layers containing the plain expanded-rim ware. Coral files were also present at this level.

The bulk of the stone artifacts was provided by more than 2000 chert flakes, recovered from excavations and from the surface of the large limestone fort. Seven adzes or large portions were excavated, and a further 20 found while surface collecting.

Bone artifacts were uncommon. They included a pendant of human bone, three bird or flying fox bone needles, and a turtle bone (?) "breadfruit splitter."

Conclusions

Excavations such as have been completed can only be of an exploratory nature, but they do allow some conclusions to be drawn at a basic level.

The excavation of a stratified rock-shelter containing samples of some 3000 years of occupation, probably covering the entire span of the island's occupation, has enabled some observations to be made. An idea of how the people interacted with their own immediate environment can be gained from the material collected. Moreover marked cultural changes occurred and can be dated.

The growing body of work from adjacent areas—Tonga, Samoa, Viti Levu and Taveuni, New Caledonia, and the New Hebrides—has enabled the suggestion of some external connections.

Situated halfway between Fiji and Tonga, Lakeba and the Lau Group may document the emergence of that intangible boundary separating the two great areas of the Central Pacific—Melanesia and Polynesia.

REFERENCES

Birks, L.
1978. Archaeological excavations at site V/L 16/81, Yanuca Island, Fiji. Oceanic Prehistory Records, no. 6. University of Auckland.

Dickinson, W. R.
1978. Petrographic Report WRD-72. Stanford University.

Frimagacci, D.
n.d. La Poterie Imprimee au battoir en Nouvelle-Caledonie ses rapports avec le Lapita.

Reid, A. C.
1977. The fruit of the Rewa: Oral traditions and the growth of the pre-Christian Lakeba state. Journ. Pacific History, vol. 12, no. 1, pp. 2-24.

Rogers, G. A.
1976. Preliminary report on an archaeological survey of Northern Lau, Fiji. Unpublished report, University of Auckland.

Young, J.M.R.
1975. The Lau Group; a progress report of an interdisciplinary research project. Journ. South Australian Anthrop. Soc., vol. 13, no. 4, pp. 3-17.

Simon Best

Electrolocation and Electrical Communication by Gymnotoid Fishes from Coastal Suriname

Grant Recipient: Walter F. Heiligenberg, Scripps Institution of Oceanography, La Jolla, California.[1]

Grant 1579: For field studies of electrolocation and communication in electric fishes.

Freshwater electric fishes evolved independently in the African mormyriformes and in the South American gymnotoids (Bennett, 1971); but all known representatives from either group can be readily classified with respect to their electric-organ discharges (EODs) as *wave*-species, in which the electric organ fires regularly in a nearly sinusoidal manner, or as *pulse*-species, in which the EOD impulses are short and are repeated less regularly (Lissmann, 1961; Hopkins, 1974a). The clear dichotomy between these two modes of electrical behavior and its presumed convergent evolution in Africa and South America suggests two alternate but incompatible strategies for electrolocation and communication. While one strategy may be better suited for one behavior function than it is for another, or for one ecological niche than another, the divergence of types among species suggests that an individual cannot adopt both adaptive strategies simultaneously. Comparative studies of African and South American electric fishes in their natural environments should help our understanding of this dichotomy and how it evolved. We wished to understand not only how wave- and pulse-species electrolocate and communicate but also how each type's EODs are adapted to these functions.

Laboratory studies have already indicated ways in which pulse- or wave-species differ in coping with electrical jamming, for example. Wave species appear to require a private EOD-frequency band to electrolocate accurately; pulse-species instead require private time intervals. Accordingly, wave-species will shift their EOD frequency away from the frequency of an interfering sinusoidal signal (Bullock et al., 1972; Watanabe and Takeda, 1963), whereas pulse-species will alter the phase (timing) of

[1] Co-author of this report is Carl D. Hopkins, Department of Biology, Cornell University, Ithaca, New York.

their EOD to minimize the chance of a coincident discharge (Heiligenberg, 1973, 1974, 1975, 1976). Behavioral studies on other species are required to establish the validity of this principle. Electric fish also use their EODs in communication. While invariant properties of both wave- and pulse-species appear to encode identifying signals such as those used for species- or sex-identity, temporal patterns of discharges (frequency modulation or discharge cessation) are most important for social display (Black-Cleworth, 1970; Hopkins, 1972, 1974a, 1974b, 1974c).

To learn more about the respective advantages of wave and pulse discharges, we thought it was essential to study electric fish in their natural habitat. We planned to examine different habitats with regard to their electrical characteristics, vegetation, bottom structure, etc. By studying the spacing patterns of each species, and by making recordings of EODs and of background noise, we hoped to learn about potential problems associated with temporal and spectral overlap of signals among sympatric species.

Methods and Approach

We worked in the coastal Guianas and northeastern Suriname from March 23 until April 6, 1976, and explored approximately 50 different creeks, swamps, flooded forests, and small rivers. The areas visited were Zandery, Coesewijne Savanna, Coesewijne River, Goliath River, Bigi Poika, Rikenau River, and Brownsberg. By monitoring the presence of electric fish with an electronic detector, which amplified the electric organ discharges, we could identify most species acoustically. We captured many specimens with hand nets. Their EODs were displayed on a battery-powered oscilloscope and were recorded at 38 cm on a Nagra SJ tape recorder (frequency response ± 3 dB from 20 Hz to 35 kHz) for subsequent spectral analysis. Approximately 100 specimens were shipped home for later behavioral and electrophysiological studies. We measured pH values and water resistivities of all habitats and recorded the type of bottom structure and vegetation and the presence and distribution of electric fish species. Our main concern was to relate different types of EODs to particular habitat features.

Electrophysiological recordings from electroreceptive neurons were begun upon return from Suriname.

Results

We found 11 species of electric fishes in various creeks, swamps, and flooded forests (see Fig. 1, col. 1). With the possible exception of *Parapygus savannensis*, all these species are common throughout South America,

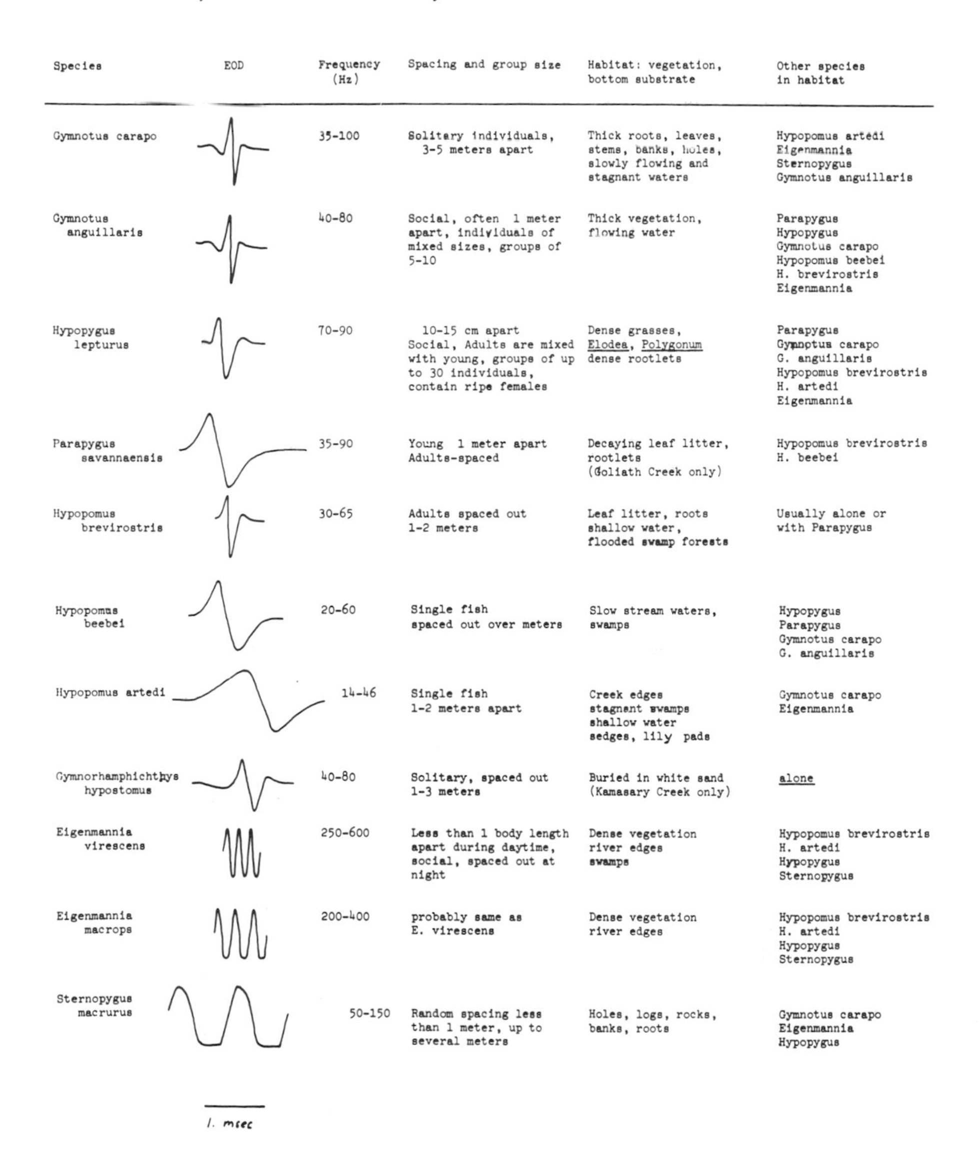

Species	EOD	Frequency (Hz)	Spacing and group size	Habitat: vegetation, bottom substrate	Other species in habitat
Gymnotus carapo		35-100	Solitary individuals, 3-5 meters apart	Thick roots, leaves, stems, banks, holes, slowly flowing and stagnant waters	Hypopomus artedi Eigenmannia Sternopygus Gymnotus anguillaris
Gymnotus anguillaris		40-80	Social, often 1 meter apart, individuals of mixed sizes, groups of 5-10	Thick vegetation, flowing water	Parapygus Hypopygus Gymnotus carapo Hypopomus beebei H. brevirostris Eigenmannia
Hypopygus lepturus		70-90	10-15 cm apart Social, Adults are mixed with young, groups of up to 30 individuals, contain ripe females	Dense grasses, <u>Elodea</u>, <u>Polygonum</u> dense rootlets	Parapygus Gymnotus carapo G. anguillaris Hypopomus brevirostris H. artedi Eigenmannia
Parapygus savannaensis		35-90	Young 1 meter apart Adults-spaced	Decaying leaf litter, rootlets (Goliath Creek only)	Hypopomus brevirostris H. beebei
Hypopomus brevirostris		30-65	Adults spaced out 1-2 meters	Leaf litter, roots shallow water, flooded swamp forests	Usually alone or with Parapygus
Hypopomus beebei		20-60	Single fish spaced out over meters	Slow stream waters, swamps	Hypopygus Parapygus Gymnotus carapo G. anguillaris
Hypopomus artedi		14-46	Single fish 1-2 meters apart	Creek edges stagnant swamps shallow water sedges, lily pads	Gymnotus carapo Eigenmannia
Gymnorhamphichthys hypostomus		40-80	Solitary, spaced out 1-3 meters	Buried in white sand (Kamasary Creek only)	<u>alone</u>
Eigenmannia virescens		250-600	Less than 1 body length apart during daytime, social, spaced out at night	Dense vegetation river edges swamps	Hypopomus brevirostris H. artedi Hypopygus Sternopygus
Eigenmannia macrops		200-400	probably same as E. virescens	Dense vegetation river edges	Hypopomus brevirostris H. artedi Hypopygus Sternopygus
Sternopygus macrurus		50-150	Random spacing less than 1 meter, up to several meters	Holes, logs, rocks, banks, roots	Gymnotus carapo Eigenmannia Hypopygus

FIGURE 1. EOD, (5/16 in. = 1 msec) and other data on 11 species of electric fishes found in coastal Suriname: EOD shape, EOD rate, individual distribution, habitat, and other species in same habitat are listed for each species. The identification of the three *Hypopomus* species is provisional, as type specimens could not be studied. Black water characterized all habitats, with pH values between 4 and 6, resistivities between 20 and 40 kΩcm.

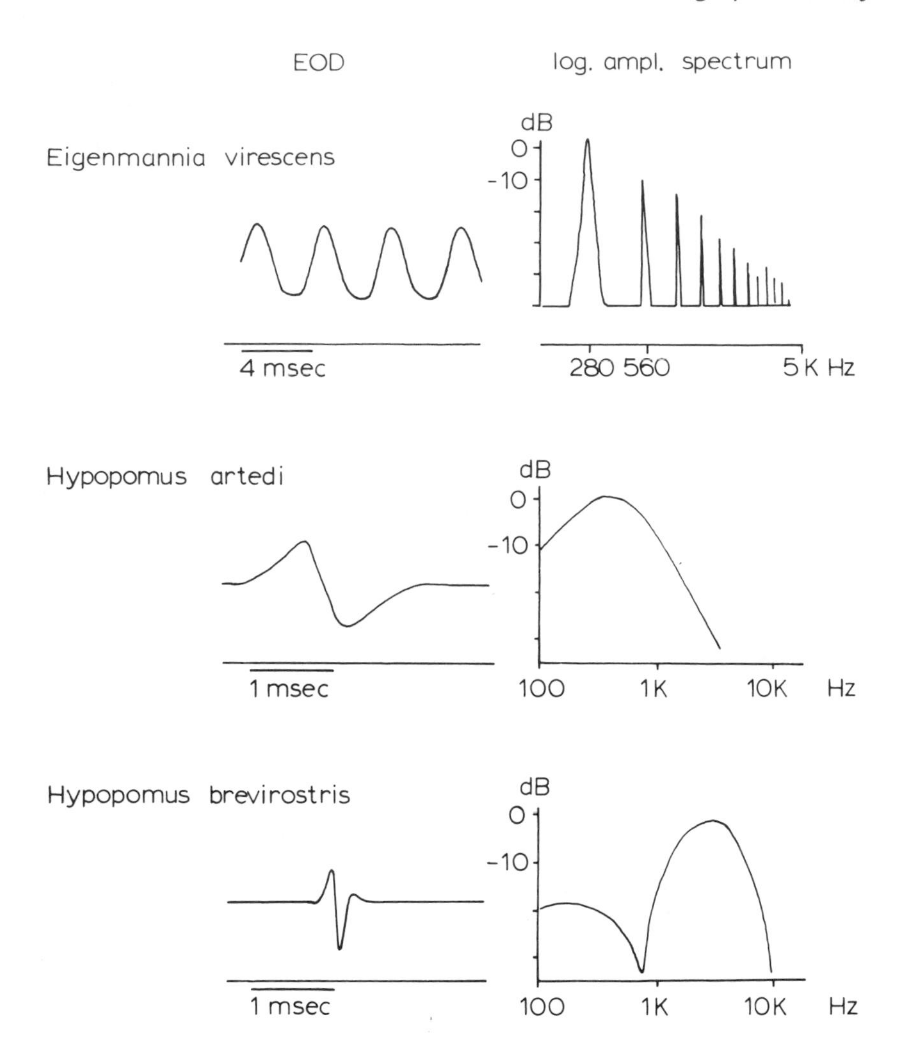

FIGURE 2. EODs could be classified as wave-types (top); biphasic (center) or multiphasic (bottom) pulse-type for all species. Amplitude spectra showing the frequency distribution of EOD energy were obtained using a Spectral Dynamics Corporation Real Time Analyzer, Model SD301D. EOD spectra were obtained as indicated in Figure 4.

including the Amazon Basin and the Orinoco. *Parapygus* may be endemic to Suriname (Hoedeman, 1962). While some species were ubiquitous in the coastal zone, others such as *Gymnorhamphichthys* and *Parapygus* showed a patchy distribution and were found in only one or two locations.

EODs of all species were recorded, in several cases for the first time. All EODs could be classified unambiguously as either wave or pulse discharges. The pulse-species could be further classified as having biphasic or multiphasic (more than two) discharges. Examples of each are given in Figure 2. Discharge waveforms of all Suriname species are shown in Figure 1, col. 2. The amplitude spectra of species with biphasic pulses are usually monomodal—energy is typically concentrated in a single peak; spectra from multiphasic pulse species frequently show a tendency to be bimodal—indicating that a two-component physiological process underlies the discharge. Wave species differ in that spectral energy is concentrated in distinct lines: a strong fundamental with multiple overtones at odd and even harmonics (Fig. 2).

Whereas wave-species discharge at remarkably stable frequencies, pulse-species modulate their EOD rate. Sudden rises are most commonly observed in novel situations, and at night when the gymnotoids are active, EOD rates are always higher than during the day. As a general rule, the duration of discharges is shorter for those species with higher mean repetition rates (see Fig. 3). Since electrolocation in pulse-species is most vulnerable to coincidental discharges, and since the probability of coincidences is proportional to the product of EOD rate and EOD duration, an inverse relation between these parameters should be expected.

Three genera of Suriname gymnotoids were represented by more than a single species: *Hypopomus (H. artedi, H. beebei,* and *H. brevirostris); Gymnotus (G. carapo* and *G. anguillaris);* and *Eigenmannia (E. virescens* and *E. macrops).* Sympatric congeners are especially interesting because differences in behavior between species may be important in preventing hybridization. Electrical signaling would be particularly interesting if shown to act in reproductive isolation.

The three species of *Hypopomus* differed clearly in their EODs. Individual variations in EODs were negligible in comparison to differences among species. Figure 4a shows the amplitude spectra for the three species. Because of differences in the tuning of the electroreceptors in these three species, we assume that each species may be far less sensitive to the EODs of other species than to those of its own. Species differences in waveform may thus serve the function of species recognition or reproductive isolation. This evidence, although preliminary, represents the first evidence, to our knowledge, for a communicative value in discharge *waveform* among pulse fish. Behavioral experiments are needed to confirm this hypothesis.

No consistent differences were found between the EOD spectra or waveforms of the two *Gymnotus* species (Fig. 4); but we did observe slight differences in the pulse repetition rates (Fig. 1). There may be significant differences in patterning of frequency modulation as well, but as yet

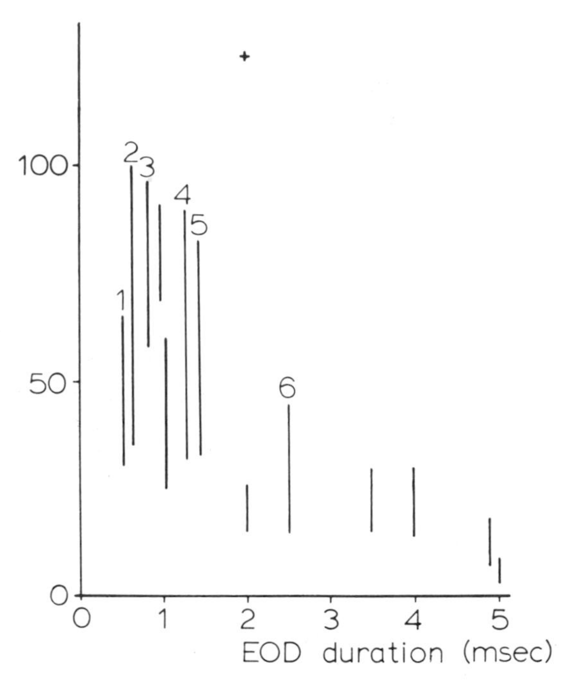

FIGURE 3. Gymnotoid pulse-species with higher EOD rates have shorter EOD pulses. Vertical bars indicate range of EOD rate, which is low while the animal is resting and high and more regular while the animal is active. Each bar represents one species: 1, *Hypopomus brevirostris;* 2, *Gymnotus carapo;* 3, *Hypopygus lepturus;* 4, *Parapygus savannaensis;* 5, *Gymnorhamphichthys hypopomus;* 6, *Hypopomus artedi.* Unlabeled bars represent unidentified species of *Hypopomus.* The + represents particular species of, presumably, *Hypopomus,* which fires broad and smooth sinusoidal pulses at highly stable frequency near 125 Hz. It is intermediate between pulse- and wave-species, and analysis of its jamming avoidance response (JAR) should give essential clues to the evolution of wave-species.

these possibilities have not been studied. The same situation may apply to *Eigenmannia* in which we did not find differences in waveforms or spectra between the two species. Behavioral studies of these two groups of fish undoubtedly will shed light on the mechanism of species recognition and reproductive isolation.

After sampling 50 different localities we were able to characterize each species in terms of its preferred habitat structure and vegetation and its typical social environment and pattern of spacing (Fig. 1). We did not confirm Lissmann's (1961) observation that wave- and pulse-species differ in habitat selection. Wave- and pulse-species occurred everywhere together in Suriname, and one species in particular, *Eigenmannia virescens,* was found in virtually every habitat studied.

Because the EODs we measured were composed of spectral energies with frequencies ranging widely from 0 to 20 kHz, we hypothesized that different frequency bands might propagate differentially in certain habitats, and that for this reason natural selection might favor certain electric fishes whose EODs had certain spectral properties optimal for long-range electrolocation or communication. To test this hypothesis, electronic-fish models—sinusoidal voltage sources with 100-Hz, 1-kHz, and 10-kHz "discharges"—were placed in open water, dense vegetation, or shallow creeks, and were compared. Attenuation of signal intensity was measured as a function of distance from each source, but in all cases we found no effect of frequency. We did find, however, consistent differences among habitats. The rate of decrease of the electric-field intensity with distance was less in shallow water (10 to 20 cm) over a sandy substrate than it was in deep water, as would be predicted from electrostatic theory.

We realize that our electronic-fish models were designed as constant voltage sources while electric fish, because of their high internal resistance, may be more comparable to a constant current source. For this reason the output voltage of the fish's EOD rises with the local resistance of its environment. One could now assume that certain habitats, such as a dense plant thicket with its high capacitive impedance, would represent a lower load resistance at higher spectral frequencies. Thus, higher frequencies might show lower output voltages and would be harder for other fish to "hear." New electronic models are being constructed to test this idea on the next occasion.

In fact, even this possibility may turn out to have a negligible significance. As mentioned above, we could not detect any systematic relationship between habitat features and EOD type. Neither wave- nor pulse-species seemed to prefer any habitat characteristics; both types occurred together regularly. We now think that EOD characteristics may not be selected so much for the way the EOD propagates through the environment as for the ways the EOD is adapted to particular behavioral functions of the fish. For example, some pulse-species, being more sluggish, may require less temporal resolution of the environment that they sense through electrolocation, than do the more mobile, wave-species. In particular, high-frequency species, such as species of *Apteronotus* (1000 Hz) or *Eigenmannia* (500 Hz), may have far greater sensitivity to rapidly moving objects than do low-frequency pulse-species, thus affording

a)

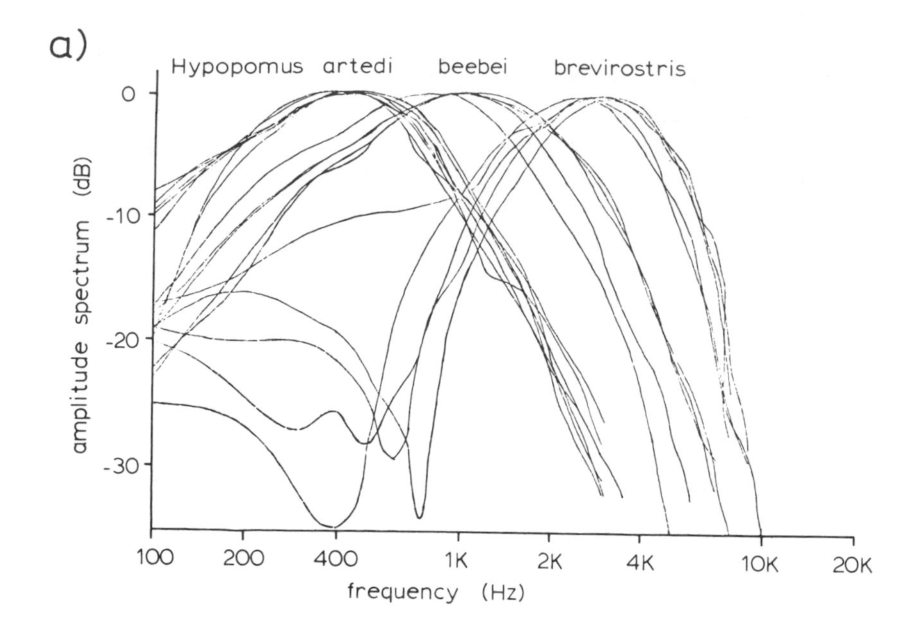

b)

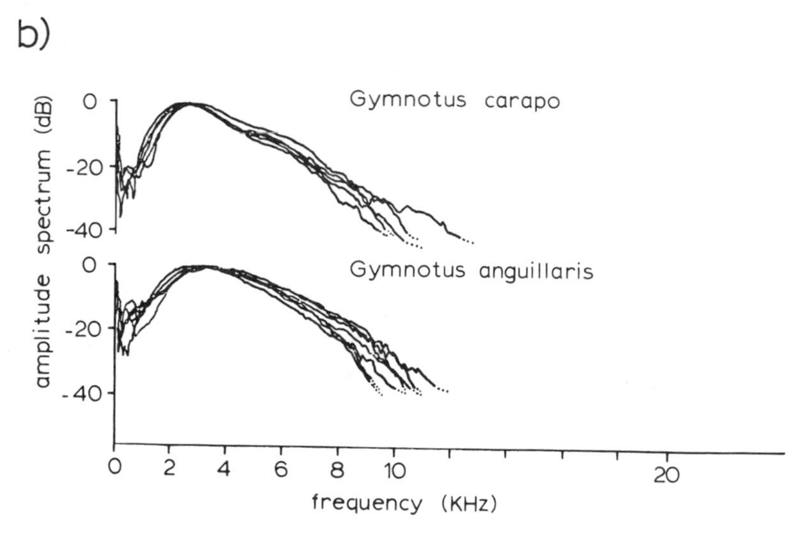

FIGURE 4a. Transient capture Fourier analysis of single EOD impulses from fish specimens belonging to the genus *Hypopomus* from Suriname. Figure illustrates how members of this genus have evolved divergent, yet species-specific, discharges. Each curve represents a single individual from which a single EOD was selected at random for analysis. The species were tentatively identified as: *Hypopomus artedi* (N=7), *H. beebei* (N=5), and *H. brevirostris* (N=5).

them greater mobility. Behavioral experiments are needed to test this hypothesis.

Because much of our understanding of the function of EOD signals in electrolocation and communication hinges on comprehension of the physiology of the receiving organs (electroreceptors), investigations into the filtering properties of tuberous electroreceptors in all three Suriname *Hypopomus* species began immediately when we returned from Suriname. We have completed studies of two individuals of each species; over 152 identified cells have been characterized electrophysiologically. Electrophysiological recordings were made in the posterior branch of the anterior lateral-line nerve (NLLa) in curarized (electrically silent) fish. Tone-burst stimuli were varied in frequency and amplitude and adjusted to evoke threshold responses. Resulting "tuning curves" are profiles of minimum sensitivity as a function of frequency. Earlier work on wave-species has shown that each species possesses electroreceptors that selectively filter the electrical environment for species-specific signals (Scheich et al., 1973; Hopkins, 1976).

Three distinct classes of electroreceptors have been identified from the posterior branch of NLLa: ampullary, pulse marker, and burst duration. Burst duration units can be subdivided into three types: low pass, wide band, and narrow band, thus making a total of five recognizable electroreceptor types. All three *Hypopomus* species had all five types of units, but differed dramatically in the frequency ranges to which each type was most sensitive. These differences in frequency correlate well with the differences in EOD waveform or spectrum.

Ampullary receptors are well known from other species of electric fish (Bennett, 1971). Low-frequency stimuli modulate a regular spontaneous discharge, but high-frequency (above 50 Hz) stimuli are ineffective. Thus, ampullary receptors do not play any role in active electrolocation or communication. Ampullary receptors are extremely sensitive: thresholds are as low as 0.05 mV/cm p-p for a 1-Hz stimulus.

Each individual was individually immersed in natural creek water (resistivity = 0.2 to 0.5 kΩm) in a rectangular plastic container for recording its EODs. The fish was oriented longitudinally between two Ag-AgCl electrodes facing the positive electrode; signals were amplified using a Princeton Applied Research 113 amplifier, and were recorded at 38 cm/sec using a Nagra SJ tape recorder. Fourier analysis was performed with a Spectral Dynamics 301C real time spectrum analyzer operating in the "transient capture" mode.

FIGURE 4b. Transient capture Fourier analysis of single EOD impulses of fish from the genus *Gymnotus* shows great similarity between the two species found in Surinam. Peak spectral energy for *Gymnotus carapo* (N=5) is between 2 and 3 kHz; there is a slight inflection in the curves at 6 kHz. Peak spectral energy for *G. anguillaris* (N=7) is at 2 to 3 kHz with no inflection. The peak for each curve is at 0 dB. Recording and analysis conditions as in Figure 4a.

Pulse-marker receptors are rather insensitive to electrical stimuli: thresholds typically range between 10 and 30 mV/cm p-p. In response to an EOD-like stimulus, these units fire only one spike per response. The latency is brief (0.6 msec) suggesting that an electronic synapse is probably involved. Bastian (1976) has suggested that these neurons act to mark the time of each EOD pulse for the fish's neural analysis networks. He has, therefore, termed the units pulse-marker (PM) units. PM units were sensitive only over a narrow frequency range—this frequency range corresponded to the peak spectral energy of the species-typical EOD (Fig. 4a) in each species. Thus, PM units are insensitive—and consequently are responsive to the animal's own pulses but not to those of other fish—and PM units are tuned to the species-specific EOD and thus are able to filter out extraneous electrical noise that might interfere.

Burst-duration units respond to EOD-like pulses by producing a burst of spikes. The duration of the burst codes changes in stimulus amplitude. Three different types of receptors are recognizable on the basis of tuning curves.

Low-pass (LP) units filter out high-frequency stimuli (above 500 Hz) but pass all low frequencies. Response sensitivity was between 1 and 10 mV/cm. All three *Hypopomus* species had LP units with similar tuning profiles. The function is presumably twofold: for sensing an individual's own EOD, and for sensing other electrical sources in the environment, i.e., conspecifics, competitors, predators, or prey.

Wide-band (WB) units showed broad responsiveness over the range between 40 and 500 Hz. All three species were approximately the same; these units differed from LP units in that they were insensitive to frequencies around 10 Hz or below. The function of these units is unknown.

Narrow-band (NB) units were unusually sensitive (0.7 mV/cm) and were highly frequency selective. Behaving as notch filters, the tuning curves matched the EOD spectral peaks for each *Hypopomus* species.

Electrophysiological work on electroreceptor stimulus-filtering will greatly help in our understanding of electrolocation and communication. Work on the remaining species of Suriname gymnotoids is continuing.

We now summarize our ideas into a general outline of the evolution of EOD types among electric fishes (Fig. 5). While our theory applies specifically to the gymnotoids, we expect general principles to apply to the mormyriformes as well.

The ancestral electric fish may have been a low-frequency pulser—much like the electric eel *(Electrophorus)* today. The principal use of the EOD might have been for electrolocation. As greater temporal resolution of objects in the environment is required this species will accelerate its discharge. All known species of pulse-fish accelerate their EOD when active (night) or when disturbed. If a population of individuals invaded a

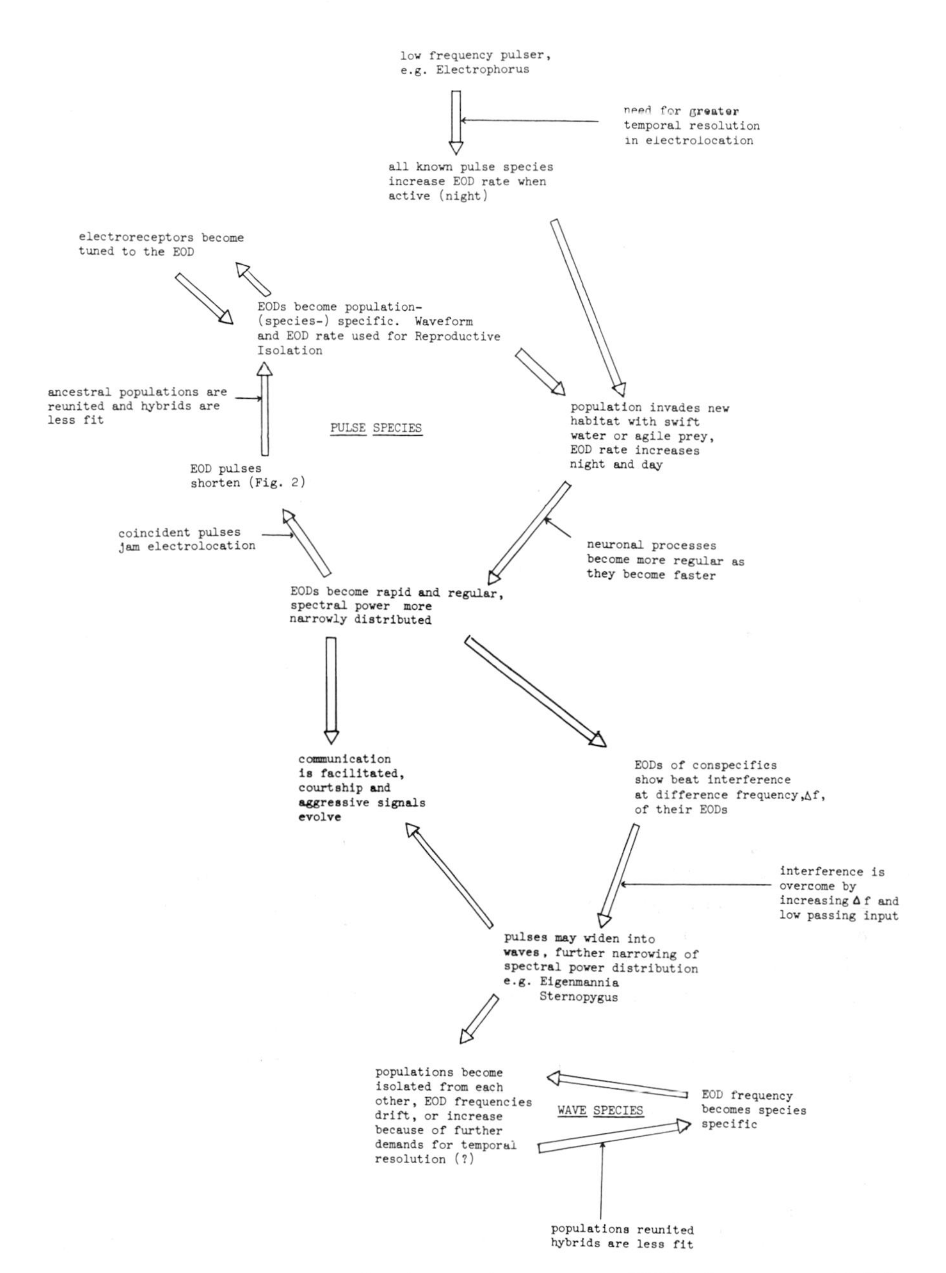

FIGURE 5. The evolution of pulse- and wave-type EODs in gymnotoid fish. Broad arrows indicate direction of evolution; thin arrows refer to its cause.

new habitat, however, where the water was swifter or the prey more agile, they too might require a tonic shift toward a higher EOD rate. As the EOD rate increased, the neuronal rhythmic process generating the EOD would become more regular, and simultaneously the pulses would tend to become shorter in order to minimize the probability of coincident discharges with other individuals. Regular discharges, then, being highly redundant, would have increased value for communication purposes, especially over a distance, and we might expect this population of fish to evolve courtship and agonistic signaling.

If at any time the two ancestral populations of fish were then to come back into contact with each other, each with its own characteristic EOD rate and pulse duration, and each with its own ecological requirements and adaptations, we might expect hybrids to be less fit than either parent population. In this case differences in EOD spectral energy or repetition rate could well serve for species recognition or for reproductive isolation. Fine tuning of electroreceptors (i.e., NB units) would enhance the sensitivity of an individual to its own population's signals even in the presence of noise from the other ancestral population—eventually EOD characteristics would become population specific and finally species specific as new species were formed. Increases in EOD rate may have occurred in several stages and *Hypopygus lepturus* with its 100-Hz, 0.7-msec pulse discharge may be a modern extreme in this cyclic process.

As the EOD rate increased in stages, fewer and fewer nerve spikes would be available for burst-duration coding of stimulus amplitude (Hagiwara and Morita, 1963). Ultimately, for very high EOD rates, local intensity changes had to be encoded as the probability of a single spike being triggered by an EOD pulse (probability coding). Especially, then, at high frequencies the electric fish began averaging the responses to many EOD cycles. Discharges of near conspecifics showed beat interference at the difference frequency, Δf, of their respective EODs. By sufficiently increasing the value of the Δf, i.e., by shifting EOD frequencies farther apart, two individuals could overcome beat interference by low-passing sensory input. This new mechanism of jamming-avoidance allowed sinusoidal EOD patterns; i.e., pulses could become wider. Wave-species thus began to evolve. Dramatic improvements in communication ability may have resulted from the adoption of narrowly tuned electroreceptive notch filters for receiving these sine-wave-like stimuli, and this may have further favored the evolution of wave EODs. Among wave-species, differences in frequency may have arisen for purposes of reproductive isolation—or if alternate means for isolation were already present, divergence in frequency may have been a response that lessens electrical jamming.

Wave-species, thus, may have evolved from pulse-species, in response to selection for efficient receptor mechanisms, for efficient communication, and for needs for increased temporal resolution in electrolocation. Other factors, such as the presence of electroreceptive predators or prey, or biogeographical considerations, would locally influence the pattern of evolution. These considerations may be important in explaining present-day differences between the types of EODs found in South America and in Africa. Further comparative field studies are planned to elucidate these mechanisms.

REFERENCES

BASTIAN, JOSEPH

1976. Frequency response characteristics of electroreceptors in weakly electric fish (Gymnotoidei) with a pulse discharge. Journ. Comp. Physiol., vol. 112, pp. 165-180.

BENNETT, MICHAEL L. V.

1971. Electric organs and electroperception. Pp. 347-574 *in* "Fish Physiology," vol. 5, W. S. Hoar and D. J. Randall, eds. Academic Press, New York.

BLACK-CLEWORTH, PATRICIA

1970. The role of electric discharges in the non-reproductive social behavior of *Gymnotus carapo*. Anim. Behav. Monogr., vol. 3, pp. 1-77.

BULLOCK, THEODORE H.; HAMSTRA, ROBERT H.; and SCHEICH, HENNING

1972. The jamming avoidance response of high frequency electric fish. Journ. Comp. Physiol., vol. 77, pp. 1-48.

HAGIWARA, SUSUMU, and MORITA, H.

1963. Coding mechanisms of electroreceptor fibers in some electric fish. Journ. Neurophysiol., vol. 26, pp. 551-567.

HEILIGENBERG, WALTER F.

1973. Electrolocation of objects in the electric fish, *Eigenmannia* (Rhamphichthyidae, Gymnotoidei). Journ. Comp. Physiol., vol. 87, pp. 137-164.

1974. Electrolocation and jamming avoidance in a *Hypopygus* (Rhamphichthyidae, Gymnotoidei), and electric fish with pulse-type discharges. Journ. Comp. Physiol., vol. 91, pp. 223-240.

1975. Electrolocation and jamming avoidance in the electric fish *Gymnarchus niloticus* (Gymnarchidae, Mormyriformes). Journ. Comp. Physiol., vol. 103, pp. 55-67.

1976. Electrolocation and jamming avoidance in the mormyrid fish *Brienomyrus*. Journ. Comp. Physiol., vol. 109, pp. 357-372.

HOEDEMAN, J. J.

1962. Notes on the ichthyology of Surinam and other Guianas, I, II. Bull. Aquatic Biol., vol. 3, pp. 53-60, 97-107.

HOPKINS, CARL D.

1972. Pattern of electrical communication among gymnotoid fish. Ph.D. thesis, Rockefeller University, New York City.

1974a. Electrical communication in fish. Amer. Sci., vol. 62, pp. 426-437.

1974b. Electric communication: Functions in the social behavior of *Eigenmannia virescens*. Behavior, vol. 50, no. 3-4. pp. 270-305.

HOPKINS, CARL D. *(continued)*
1974c. Electric communication in the reproductive behavior of *Sternopygus macrurus* (Gymnotoidei). Zeitschr. für Tierpsychol., vol. 35, pp. 518-535.
1976. Stimulus filtering and electroreception: Tuberous electroreceptors in three species of gymnotoid fish. Journ. Comp. Physiol., vol. 111, pp. 171-207.

LISSMANN, H. W.
1961. Ecological studies on gymnotid. Pp. 215-236 *in* "Bioelectrogenesis," C. Chagas and A. Paes de Carvalho, eds. Elsevier Publishing Co., Amsterdam, London.

SCHEICH, HENNING; BULLOCK, THEODORE H.; and HAMSTRA, RICHARD H.
1973. Coding properties of two classes of afferent nerve fibers: High frequency electroreceptors in the electric fish *Eigenmannia*. Journ. Neurophysiol., vol. 36, pp. 39-60.

WATANABE, A., and TAKEDA, K.
1963. The change of discharge frequency by A. C. stimulus in a weak electric fish. Journ. Exp. Biol., vol. 40, pp. 57-66.

WALTER F. HEILIGENBERG
CARL D. HOPKINS

Reproductive Adaptations of the Egyptian Plover, *Pluvianus aegyptius*

Grant Recipient: Thomas R. Howell, Department of Biology, University of California, Los Angeles, California.

Grant 1677: In support of a study on reproductive adaptations of the Egyptian Plover, *Pluvianus aegyptius.*

The Egyptian Plover *(Pluvianus aegyptius)* breeds only in Africa, primarily in the tropical zone but exclusive of heavily forested areas and most of the region east of the Rift Valley. It occurs most abundantly along rivers that run through sparsely wooded and open country, and it nests on the sandbars that are exposed at low water during the dry season; it does not nest around lakes or seacoasts. The species was described originally from specimens taken along the Nile in Egypt, but the great changes in the northern part of the river's condition in the past century have caused the bird's disappearance from that country. Furthermore, it is not a true plover (Charadriidae) but a courser (subfamily Cursoriinae; Glareolidae; Charadriiformes). It is nevertheless ploverlike in size and appearance; adult birds are about 22 cm long and weigh about 78 g during the nesting season.

The Egyptian Plover has been of special interest to naturalists for centuries for two principal reasons—first, it may be the bird said by Herodotus to pick the teeth of basking crocodiles, and second, it buries its eggs in the sand and allegedly leaves them to be incubated by solar heat. I did not see the birds pick crocodiles' teeth during two and a half months of observation and therefore cannot confirm the accounts of Herodotus and several subsequent authors. The primary purpose of my study, however, was to investigate the Egyptian Plover's remarkable and unique nesting habits. I conducted the study at Gambela, Ilubabor Province, Ethiopia, a village along the Baro River, which is a tributary of the Nile. The locality is in the southwest part of Ethiopia at lat. 8°15′N, long. 34°38′E. The duration of my stay was from January 24 to April 6, 1977.

The Egyptian Plover is a strikingly patterned bird (Fig. 1 and 2), and the sexes are identical in size, color, vocalizations, and virtually all aspects of behavior. The striking patterns seem to be used primarily in aggressive display, and pair formation appears to take place with little or no

FIGURE 1. A pair of Egyptian Plovers at their nest site with two newly hatched chicks.

overt courtship behavior. At the time of my arrival some pairs were already formed and territorial behavior was intense. Pairs of Egyptian Plovers are highly aggressive and attempt to defend an entire sandbar island as their territory even if the area is several thousand square meters; both sexes participate equally in this defense. Aggressive displays feature spreading of the black-and-white wings and the white-tipped tail, and vigorous fights result if threat is ineffective. The birds threaten and attack not only all other Egyptian Plovers but all potential predators and competitors, from large storks and raptors down to small sandpipers and wagtails that are winter residents from Eurasia. Insects and other arthropods are the principal food, and any other arthropod-eating bird on the territory will be driven off. Egyptian Plovers obtain food by diverse methods, including surface-picking, probing, scratching, turning stones, and snapping flying insects out of the air.

The nest is a simple scrape in the sand, and no materials are ever gathered around it. Both birds of a pair make many scrapes, for as long as 30 days before egg-laying. While one bird "scrapes," the mate may run up to it and continue the run in a tight half-circle (or two or three half-circles) around it; the latter bird may then start to make a scrape also. Either

FIGURE 2. Egyptian Plover giving interspecific threat display, in which the black-and-white patterned wings are spread and slowly waved up and down.

bird may "half-circle" the other. While not actively scraping, the birds often assume an exaggerated tilted posture, with the hindquarters much elevated. These displays and activities probably serve to secure and maintain the pair bond and do not seem to constitute preliminary courtship. There is no pre-copulatory display, and copulation is very quick, simple, and usually silent. Copulations are infrequent and seldom seen; they take place usually a few days before and during the period of egg-laying.

The usual clutch at Gambela was 2 or 3 eggs; I found a single 1-egg clutch. The first 2 eggs seem to be laid on successive days, but there may be a 1-day interval between the 2nd and 3rd eggs. The eggs have a light yellowish brown ground color with many superficial spots, varying in color from reddish brown to gray. If left uncovered, they would match well the appearance of coarse gravelly sand with some coloring from silt. Nests are always in fully exposed, unshaded sites, and sitting begins with the laying of the first egg, as it must be protected from solar heat. Eggs are kept largely or completely covered (generally the latter) with sand all during the daylight hours. The eggs are not deeply buried, with usually only 2 to 3 mm of sand over the tops. The adult birds cover them with sand only with an anteroposterior movement of the bill; they do not use the feet to kick sand over them. Egyptian Plovers may sit on fully covered eggs, or they may excavate with the feet while sitting during cooler parts of the day. Presumably this partly exposes the eggs to the incubation patch. Whenever the bird leaves, it quickly throws sand over the nest even if the eggs are already covered. The eggs are about two-thirds uncovered at night and are incubated throughout that time.

Chicks hatch while the eggs are partly or fully buried in the sand. They are very precocial and leave the nest permanently on the day of hatching. They may go to the river to drink and bathe when less than 1 day old.

The incubation behavior of the adults is complex. For the first 3 hr after sunrise (0700), the parents attend the nest only part-time, enough to maintain the buried eggs within the range of normal incubation temperature. A balance is achieved between body heat, solar heat, and heat retained by the sand. By about 1000 to 1030, solar heat becomes intense and temperatures soar. For approximately the next 6 hr, the eggs must be cooled to prevent overheating. Mere shading is not enough as shade temperature may exceed 45°C, which would be lethal for eggs. Burying the eggs and leaving the nest exposed to the sun would not work, as dry sand temperatures at buried-egg depth soon exceed 45°C. During these hot hours, the parent birds go to the river (water temperature 27 to 28°C) and soak their ventral feathers with a stereotyped rocking motion, ending with a quick dip of the bill. The wet bird then returns and settles on the buried eggs, soaking the sand around them and cooling them. As nest temperature gradually rises, the bird leaves and soaks again and returns. This goes on every few minutes, the mate often changing places. By about 1600 the heat begins to decline and the birds become much less attentive. The wet sand retains heat and keeps the eggs at normal temperatures while the parents forage. Dry sand is always tossed over the nest when a bird leaves, concealing the dark wet spot. On those rare days when clouds reduce the solar heat, the birds do not soak and wet the nest until and unless needed. They often poke the bill into the sand around the eggs as though testing the temperature.

Figure 3 summarizes environmental, nest, and egg temperatures and attentive behavior of the parent birds on a typically hot day. Egg temperatures were obtained by implanting a thermocouple into an Egyptian Plover egg and substituting this in a nest for one of the birds' own eggs. Other temperatures were recorded using probes of a thermistor thermometer. Instruments were battery operated, and by using long leads I could record temperatures at a distance sufficient not to disturb the birds. The removed egg was kept beside me, buried in the sand at progressively greater depths and wetted at intervals to keep the temperature within the

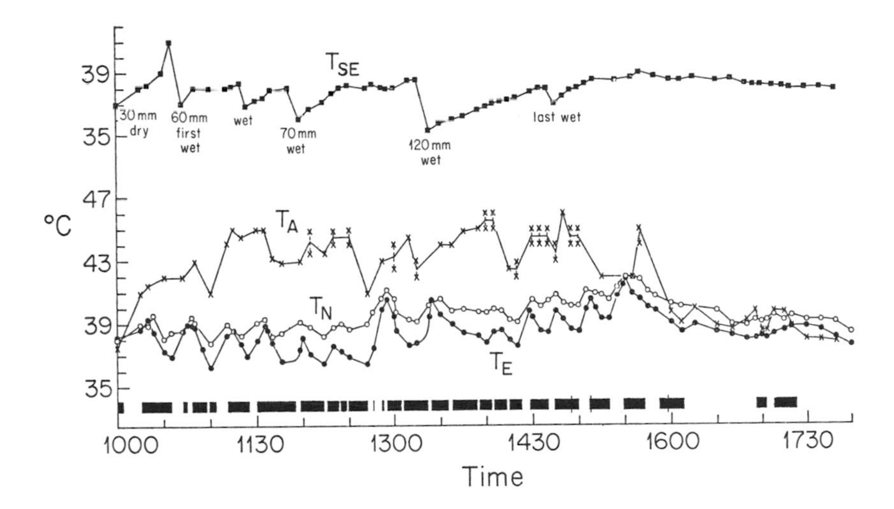

FIGURE 3. Record of temperatures at an Egyptian Plover nest site on March 19, 1977. T_E=temperature inside egg in nest, recorded by an implanted thermocouple; T_N=temperature of sand surrounding buried eggs, at about mid-egg level; T_A=shaded air temperature about 2 cm above ground; T_{SE}=temperature of removed egg, buried in sand by me to the depths indicated and wetted as indicated (this egg was returned to the nest and later hatched); dark bars along time axis indicate presence of attending parent. From 1016 to 1558, the parent bird soaked itself each time before coming to the eggs, and wetted them as it settled; hence, T_E rises as parent leaves, drops as parent returns.

normal limits of incubation. This egg was returned to the nest at the end of the experiment and the entire clutch hatched successfully, which indicates that the temperatures recorded approximated those regularly experienced at the nest.

One of my objectives was to measure the rate of daily weight loss of eggs during incubation, as this is known to be intricately involved in the duration of incubation and rate of embryonic development and is influenced by conditions immediately surrounding the eggs in the nest. Some background drawn from recent research, particularly by H. Rahn, A. Ar, and their associates, is required for discussion of these points (Ar et al., 1974; Rahn and Ar, 1974; Rahn et al., 1976). Greatly simplified, the relevant data are as follows:

An egg is heaviest at the time of laying and loses weight at a constant rate up to the time of pipping and subsequent hatching. Virtually all of this weight loss is the result of water vapor lost through microscopic pores in the eggshell. Most avian eggs lose 15 to 18% of their initial weight by the time of hatching. The amount of weight lost per unit time depends on the porosity of the shell and the difference in water vapor pressure between the egg contents and the outside medium. The greater this difference, the greater the rate of water loss. Water vapor pressure varies with temperature and degree of saturation, and as the contents of a normal egg are largely fluid the vapor pressure inside the shell is always at saturation. Among most birds, the surrounding medium (the nest) is usually not saturated. The temperature of the egg (incubation temperature) and the water vapor pressure of its immediate surroundings (the nest) will influence egg water loss (weight loss) and are, therefore, of great importance in the physiology of incubation.

The water vapor conductance of the shell is defined as the amount of water lost per 24 hr per torr (unit of atmospheric pressure $= 1/760$ atm $= 1$ mmHg). Conductance depends on the porosity of the shell and may differ among species. For example, eggs of about the same weight from different species may have quite different incubation periods; in those cases studied, the egg with the longer incubation period has the lower conductance. This means that it loses water less rapidly, and at the time of hatching has lost approximately the same percent of its initial weight as another egg with higher conductance but a shorter incubation period.

Rahn and Ar et al. have proposed various equations that predict incubation period, fraction of initial weight lost, and other parameters on the basis of empirically measured eggshell conductance, incubation temperature, and daily egg weight loss. These equations, based on data from a large number of species, are extremely useful to the field investigator, as any great variation from predicted values potentially indicates some unusual adaptation in the species under study. From measurements made in the field and in an improvised laboratory, I determined the following mean values for the Egyptian Plover egg (Howell, 1979):

Initial egg weight: 9.5 g
Daily egg weight loss in nest: 0.035 g
Conductance: 2.10 mg H_20/day/torr
Incubation period: 30 days
Fraction of initial weight lost: 11.4%
Incubation temperature: 37.5°C

The figure for conductance is not significantly different statistically from that predicted on the basis of egg weight, which suggests that the porosity of the shell is not modified in some unusual way. Incubation temperature varies throughout the day, but the 24-hr mean approximating 37.5°C is very similar to that of other charadriiform birds. All the other figures, however, are considerably different from those predicted or expected. Egg weight is less than predicted in relation to body weight of the adult bird of a species in which chicks are highly precocial. The incubation period is much longer than that predicted (19 to 20 days) on the basis of egg weight, and is the longest for an egg of its size outside the order Procellariiformes (in which some long-incubating Storm Petrels lay eggs of comparable size). The daily egg weight loss in the nest is only about half that predicted on the basis of initial weight, and the fraction of initial weight lost is the lowest recorded for any precocial species. The total data indicate that, although there is no evidence of reduced porosity of the eggshell (i.e., conductance is not low), daily water loss and fractional water loss are unusually low and incubation period is unusually long. If shell porosity is not reduced and incubation temperature is not low, the probable explanation for the low rate of water loss from the egg is that humidity in the nest must be unusually high. This is indeed the case, as the eggs are covered with sand throughout the day and kept soaking wet for the hottest hours. During that interval the water vapor pressure inside the egg and outside would be about the same (both saturated) and essentially no water would be lost from the egg. After active wetting of the nest stops in the late afternoon, the sand remains wet for some additional time. The wetting of the nest and eggs, which is necessary to keep the temperature down, is evidently responsible also for the low rate of water loss. The long incubation period would not be possible if water were lost from the eggs at the usual rate found in open-nesting charadriiform birds because the egg would lose more than 23% of its initial weight, a higher percentage than would be compatible with successful hatching.

Incubation periods in birds are species-specific, largely unmodifiable by environmental changes, and evidently genetically determined. I hypothesize that the long incubation period of the Egyptian Plover, made possible by the low rate of water loss, allows for maturation of the chick before hatching to a highly precocial condition. This, I believe, is necessary for probability of survival, since the chick hatches in a fully open nest site where it is exposed to extreme solar heat and constant threat of predation. It must be able on the day of hatching to respond to parental actions leading to its concealment (see below) and also to make its way to the river's edge for drinking and bathing, if necessary to recoup evaporative water loss and to relieve heat loading. A less precocial chick, without such well-developed capabilities, would probably have much poorer chances of survival in the critical first days after hatching.

While still in the nest, chicks are buried and wetted just like eggs. They can, however, easily raise their heads above the sand if necessary. More remarkably, chicks after they leave the nest are also completely covered with sand (Fig. 4) by the parents whenever danger threatens, which is usually many times a day. This practice continues until the young birds are at least 21 days old, when they are really juveniles with contour feathers. Buried chicks may also be wetted by the ventral feathers of adults if danger persists and temperatures get too high. I saw this type of wetting

many times but never saw chicks wetted by regurgitation. The latter allegation, which is widely quoted, is based on a unique observation by Butler (1931). I think he misinterpreted sand-testing with the bill for regurgitation of water. Buried chicks, although fully alert, remain immobile while being excavated out of the sand and may be gently handled, replaced, and reburied. If roughly handled, they may suddenly leap away and run off at high speed.

Chicks are brought small amounts of food in the nest by adults, as is typical of coursers. Some feeding may continue afterward, but mostly the chicks accompany the parents and feed on arthropods exposed by the adults. Adults flip over stones with the bill in the manner of turnstones *(Arenaria)*.

Young birds were not quite ready to fly at the age of 4 weeks, and I estimate the fledging period as about 35 days. Juveniles have the same plumage pattern as adults.

The Egyptian Plover is conspicuously marked and not at all cryptic, even while on its nest. The conspicuous markings are used importantly in driving away competitors and predators; presumably this provides greater selective advantages than would crypsis. To avoid revealing the location of the nest, the conspicuous parent must leave it when danger threatens. Like some other charadriiform birds, the Egyptian Plover quickly covers the eggs with sand as it leaves the nest. This was probably the original basis for its highly developed egg-burying habits.

As the sand substrate becomes dangerously hot, the birds have to cool the eggs by wetting them with the ventral feathers (as do many other charadriiform birds). The combination of burying eggs in the sand and also wetting them provides better and longer lasting protection against overheating than either one alone, and the Egyptian Plover is the only bird that does both. It can thus leave the nest repeatedly for at least a few minutes during the hottest part of the day, when forced to do so by approach of a predator. Kites *(Milvus migrans)* and Pied Crows *(Corvus albus)* forage constantly in the vicinity of Egyptian Plover nests. After the peak of the day's heat is past, the warm damp sand retains heat and essentially incubates the eggs for a period of 1 to 3 hr, providing the adult birds with free time for foraging.

Thus, the Egyptian Plover has the advantage of bold color pattern that helps it repel predators and competitors and thereby preserve the resources of the nesting island for itself; at the same time, it can conceal the

---

FIGURE 4. Recently hatched chick, away from the nest, concealed with a covering of sand by a parent (top); the same, partly exposed by the author for photographic purposes (center); the same, fully exposed (bottom). The chick remained immobile while being uncovered. The coin is 23 mm in diameter.

nest and safely leave it—not for long, but long enough—when danger approaches. This species is the only courser that has colonized the fluviatile environment; all the others are arid-country inhabitants. The adaptations discussed above have aided it in colonizing a habitat not occupied by other coursers, and it has been highly successful in its unique methods of incubating its eggs and caring for its chicks.

REFERENCES

AR, A.; PAGANELLI, C. V.; REEVES, R. B.; GREENE, D. G.; and RAHN, H.
1974. The avian egg: Water vapor conductance, shell thickness, and functional pore area. Condor, vol. 76, pp. 153-158.

BUTLER, A. L.
1931. The chicks of the Egyptian Plover. Ibis, series 13, vol. 1, pp. 345-347.

HOWELL, T. R.
1979. Breeding biology of the Egyptian Plover, *Pluvianus aegyptius*. Univ. Calif. Publ. Zool. vol. 113, pp. 1-76.

RAHN, H., and AR, A.
1974. The avian egg: Incubation time and water loss. Condor, vol. 76, pp. 147-152.

RAHN, H.; PAGANELLI, C. V.; NISBET, I.C.T.; and WHITTOW, G. C.
1976. Regulation of incubation water loss in eggs of seven species of terns. Physiol. Zool., vol. 49, pp. 245-259.

THOMAS R. HOWELL

Observation of the 1977 Uranus Occultation

Grant Recipient: W. B. Hubbard, University of Arizona, Tucson, Arizona.

Grant 1663: In support of expeditionary travel to observe a rare planetary occultation.

The purpose of this project was to make ground-based astronomical observations of the passage of the planet Uranus in front of a distant star, SAO158687. Such occultations of relatively bright stars are quite rare. They offer the chance to probe the atmosphere of the planet which occults the star, by observing the gradual decline of the starlight caused by differential refraction in the planetary atmosphere. We intended to use this technique to gain new information about Uranus by stationing special photometers at observatories in the eastern hemisphere, where the occultation was predicted to be observable. As sometimes occurs in scientific endeavors, we completed the project by measuring something quite different from that which we expected. Instead of studying the atmosphere of Uranus, we obtained independent measurements of one of the most exciting planetary discoveries in recent years: the rings of Uranus.

Our planning for this event was influenced by previous experience with the occultation of Beta Scorpii by the planet Jupiter in 1971 (Hubbard et al., 1972; Evans and Hubbard, 1971) where the expeditionary travel was also supported by the National Geographic Society. As before, the observations would have to be made from remote sites around the periphery of the Indian Ocean. Not all planetary occultations occur there; it is a curious circumstance, however, that the last three major events, involving Neptune (1968), Jupiter (1971), and now Uranus (1977), have all by chance involved this part of the earth. Thus, for the Uranus event we planned to use some of the same sites that were used in the 1971 Jupiter expeditions. We reserved telescopes at Perth, Australia, and at Naini Tal, Kodaikanal, and Hyderabad, India. Although the Uranus event would also be visible in South Africa, we thought that it would be a little low there and so relied on collaboration with the University of Cape Town to install an experiment on their 74-in. telescope at Sutherland.

The photometric apparatus was designed to be light and portable, as required by the need to transport it halfway around the world and back.

The basic photometers for the four sites were constructed identically. Each photometer had a red channel with an effective wavelength of about 8000 Å, and a blue channel with an effective wavelength of about 4500 Å. The red channel used an RCA C31034 photomultiplier as detector, cooled by means of a thermoelectric device because of the expected unavailability of dry ice. The blue channel used an uncooled EMI 9789-B tube. The photon counts on both channels were recorded at 10-msec intervals on the two channels of a portable high-fidelity cassette tape recorder. In addition, it was possible to use a rotating chopper mirror to scan to the adjacent sky at intervals of 20 msec to obtain background deflections. The observer was able to keep the star and planet centered on the diaphragm at all times by means of an uncoated pellicle mirror, which diverted a fraction of the incident light for guiding purposes. Despite its complexity, the occultation photometer was quite compact, and could be easily fitted into a standard-sized suitcase (Fig. 1).

We designed the photometer as a two-channel device because we expected some difficulty with the background during the observations. Even if the sky was perfectly transparent, it would be necessary to include the entire planet as well as the star in the field of view. Fluctuations in the brightness of Uranus would cause spurious signals in both channels, but since the star was a red giant, it would be largely invisible in the blue channel. Thus the blue channel could be used to correct variations in Uranus' light, caused either by clouds or by scintillation, in the red channel.

In January 1977, we received alarming news. Franz and Wasserman (1977) reported the results of improved measurements of the positions of Uranus and SAO158687, which showed that the positions adopted for the original prediction were in error. The effect of the changes was to move Uranus southward and the star northward in the sky. The predicted shadow zone for the occultation no longer covered the earth, but instead had a northern limit which ran roughly from Australia to equatorial Africa. There was almost no chance of observing the event from India. Fortunately, we were able to shift our stations to more favorable locations. According to plan, Dr. Benjamin Zellner of the University of Arizona proceeded to Perth, where an occultation was likely even with the revised prediction. Our other observers, all from the University of Arizona, shifted their experiments to more southerly locations. Dr. Tom Gehrels installed his photometer on the 40-in. telescope at Sutherland, South Africa. Dr. George Coyne located at the 36-in. telescope at Hartbeespoort, near Bloemfontein in South Africa. Dr. Bradford Smith took a portable 14-in. telescope to the island of Mauritius in the Indian Ocean, after failing to obtain diplomatic clearance to observe at the more southerly location of Madagascar.

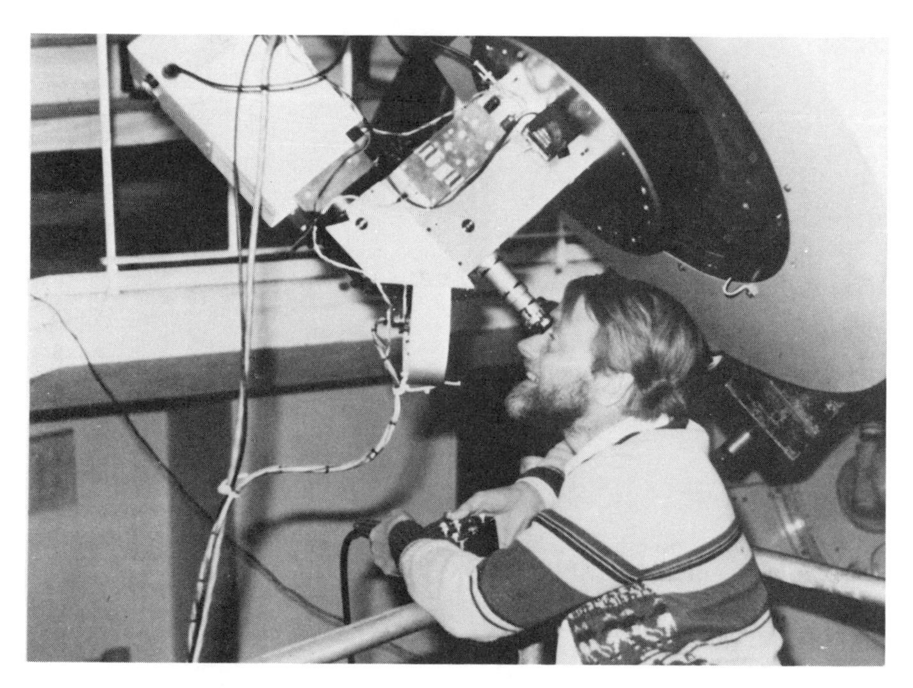

FIGURE 1. Dr. Tom Gehrels at the eyepiece of the two-channel occultation photometer, on site at Sutherland, South Africa. Photometers at the other sites were identical.

The occultation was predicted to occur on March 10. Our four observers met with varying degrees of success. At Hartbeespoort, it rained all night. At Sutherland, a heavy cloud bank moved in during the critical period of the night and thus incapacitated the only major observatory that was capable of observing the event. On Mauritius, the weather was also unsettled. Smith finally located his experiment at the base of a lighthouse on a tiny island to the north of Mauritius. He recorded the starlight through intermittent clouds, and finally had to terminate observations ahead of schedule owing to the onset of a rain shower.

At Perth, conditions were perfect. According to plan, Zellner began recording data at 20:20 Universal Time. Some seconds afterward, a brief dip in the starlight occurred, which caused no special interest at the time. There was no atmospheric occultation by Uranus observable, and with the onset of dawn at about 21:45, Zellner terminated observations.

Following the return of our observers to the United States, we received reports from other observers, who had used the airborne NASA telescope (Elliot et al., 1977), that Uranus apparently was surrounded by a ring system that had caused brief interruptions of the starlight. After

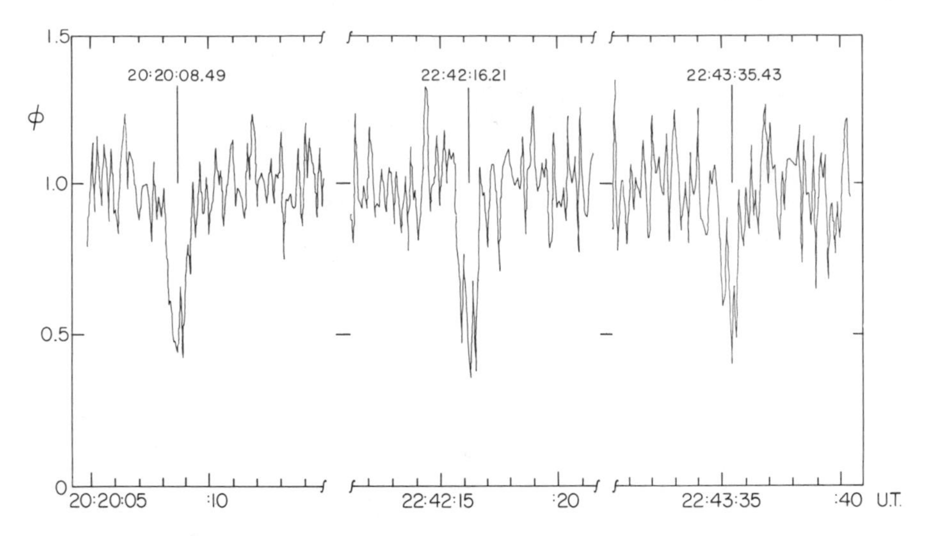

FIGURE 2. Three occultations by Uranian rings observed at Perth, Australia. Universal times of mid-event are shown. The deflection is measured in units of the unocculted stellar intensity. Events shown are (left to right): α (immersion), α (emersion), β (emersion).

our data and equipment were released by customs, we began examining the results to see if we could confirm the observations. The results of this initial investigation were published in *Nature* (Hubbard et al., 1977). In brief, we found that we were able to confirm the findings of other observers. The brief interruption observed by Zellner shortly after he began recording was produced by the so-called α-ring of Uranus, which is the innermost of the major Uranian rings. In addition to this event, a careful search of Zellner's data shows two other ring occultations (Fig. 2). Just before dawn, the latter two events were observed, and they correspond to a second crossing of the α-ring, as well as a crossing of the β-ring which lies exterior to the α-ring. From these observations, as well as others which have been reported (Millis et al., 1977; Bhattacharyya and Bappu, 1977), we have been able to deduce the approximate location of the center of the ring system and thus to fit our observations into the general picture of the Uranian ring system that has emerged.

Except for the NASA aircraft, no single observing station obtained an occultation measurement from all of the possible rings on both sides of the planet. Our Perth station was the only ground-based station to observe any of the rings on both sides of Uranus. The adjacent experiment of Millis at Perth observed three ring occultation events (ϵ,γ,β) but missed the α event during a recentering correction. They then terminated observations before any of the ring events on the other side of Uranus oc-

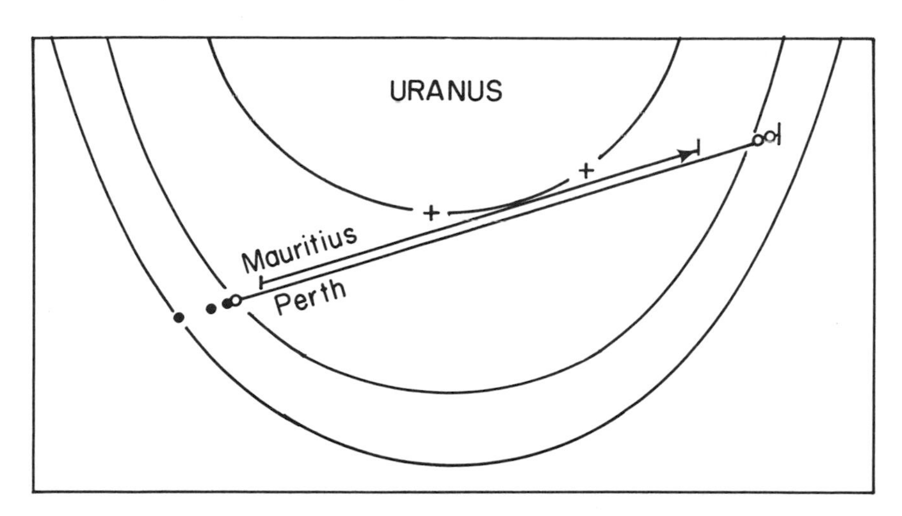

FIGURE 3. Geometry of occultation paths across the Uranian system. Rings shown are ϵ (outermost) and α (innermost). Between these rings are situated β, γ, and δ. Closed circles are ring events observed by Millis, open circles, by Zellner, both at Perth. Crosses show occultations by Uranus observed by the more southerly NASA aircraft (south is up in the figure).

curred. Zellner obtained three more events which nicely complement Millis' data (Fig. 3).

We have analyzed all reported timings, including our own data, those of Millis, those of Elliot et al., observations from Kavalur and Naini Tal in India, and observations from Cape Town in South Africa. Additional observations reported from China were not included in our solution but are consistent. There seem to be five well-defined rings of Uranus in all; the deduced radii of the rings are given below:

Ring	*km*
α	44,845
β	45,808
γ	47,701
δ	48,397
ϵ	51,039

Because of the geometry of the occultation, the absolute values of the radii are strongly correlated with the assumed position of Uranus. The figures given, however, should be valid to within 100 km.

A most interesting result has emerged from an analysis of our own data, combined with those of Millis from Perth. On immersion, the α-ring occultation occurred about 84 sec after the β-ring occultation. But on emersion, the α-ring occulted 79.5 sec before the β-ring. This discrepancy of a few seconds is quite significant, and means that the α-ring and β-ring cannot be concentric circles. All of the results given in the tabulation above assume that the rings are coplanar, but with different centers. This analysis also shows that α and β are off-center, as is the ϵ-ring. This result tells us something very important about the Uranian ring system. The only stable ring configuration in the absence of perturbations is a set of concentric circles, all in the equatorial plane of the planet. Since the occultation timings reveal that the rings are not in such a configuration, we conclude that they are not in a stable state, but instead are being driven by some sort of perturbation. This may be an important clue to the origin of the rings.

The centers of the rings do not coincide, but for the inner four rings the discrepancy is sufficiently small that one might identify their center with the center of mass of Uranus. When this is done, we find that the prediction of Franz and Wasserman was also in error, although not as seriously as the original prediction. The center of Uranus has to be moved another 2100 km south, and about 200 km west. Was there an occultation at Mauritius? We searched our data in great detail, using the blue channel to correct out the clouds, and the sky-chopped data to remove the intermittent lighthouse beam. The resulting data are constant to within less than 5% of the star's brightness, indicating that Uranus itself missed occultation at Mauritius. From this we conclude that the radius of Uranus is less than 26,300 km. From reported timings from the NASA aircraft (Elliot et al., 1977), we find that the radius of Uranus cannot be very much less than this; perhaps 26,200 km. Thus the shadow missed Smith near Mauritius by only about 100 km. Most frustrating!

Reports from the Indian observatory at Kavalur (Bhattacharyya and Bappu, 1977) indicate that their data show a peri-Uranian haze of obscuring material in addition to the discrete rings. This could be, if real, the background from which the rings themselves formed. We searched our data from Perth and Mauritius to see if we could confirm the existence of gradual changes in the star's light level. We have not been able to find any such variations. Apart from the three "glitches" due to the rings, our data are remarkably smooth. The Perth data show no systematic variations in excess of 1% of the unocculted signal. Our discrepancy with the Indians might be explained by a somewhat different instrumental system. The blue channel is remarkably useful for removing spurious "occultation events," which we might have otherwise thought real. Initially we were unable to confirm two other faint rings interior to α, which were reported by Millis et al., but have now done so.

We have carried out some calculations to investigate the sort of model that might explain the ring features that we observed. First, the rings are remarkably narrow. The width of the α-ring is about 10 km. The β-ring is probably about the same width or perhaps a little narrower. The stellar intensity never falls to zero (Fig. 2), indicating that the rings are partially transparent. Since the star occulted has a projected diameter at Uranus of 4.5 to 6 km, there can be no piece of ring material that is this large. Indeed, to produce a 50% residual intensity at midoccultation, the ring particles must be no bigger than about 1 km across. They could be much smaller. In any case, they must fill approximately 50% of the projected area of the ring. Because the stellar diameter is much greater than the Fresnel zone at Uranus, diffraction effects are not expected to be important, nor are they observed to within the noise limit in our data.

In summary, because of unfavorable weather we were unsuccessful in our attempt to observe an occultation by Uranus' atmosphere. However, we were among the discoverers of the rings of Uranus, which are clearly a remarkable phenomenon. Analysis of our data, in combination with results obtained from other observers, has helped to define the nature of the Uranian ring system. Comparison of results from various sites was still going on as of this writing. The results of further analysis of our data were published in 1980 (Hubbard and Zellner, 1980).

REFERENCES

BHATTACHARYYA, J. C., and BAPPU, M.K.V.
1977. Saturn-like ring system around Uranus. Nature, vol. 270, pp. 503-506.

ELLIOT, J. L.; DUNHAM, E.; and MINK, D.
1977. The rings of Uranus. Nature, vol. 267, pp. 328-330.

EVANS, D. S., and HUBBARD, W. B.
1971. Jupiter and Beta Scorpii. Sky and Telescope, vol. 42, pp. 337-341.

FRANZ, O., and WASSERMAN, L.
1977. Occultation of SAO158687 by Uranus on 1977 March 10. IAU Circular No. 3038.

HUBBARD, W. B.; COYNE, G. V.; GEHRELS, T.; SMITH, B. A.; and ZELLNER, B. H.
1977. Observations of Uranus occultation events. Nature, vol. 268, pp. 33-34.

HUBBARD, W. B.; NATHER, R. E.; EVANS, D. S.; TULL, R. G.; WELLS, D. C.; VAN CITTERS, G. W.; WARNER, B.; and VANDEN BOUT, P.
1972. The occultation of Beta Scorpii by Jupiter and Io. I. Jupiter. Astronomical Journ. vol. 77, pp. 41-59.

HUBBARD, W. B.; SMITH, B. A.; and ZELLNER, B. H.
1977. Observations of Uranus ring occultation events. Bull. Amer. Astron. Soc., vol. 9, p. 551.

HUBBARD, W. B., and ZELLNER, B. H.
1980. Results from the 10 March 1977 occulation by the Uranus system. Astron. Journ., vol. 85, pp. 1663-1669.
MILLIS, R. L.; WASSERMAN, L. H.; and BIRCH, P. V.
1977. Detection of rings around Uranus. Nature, vol. 267, pp. 330-331.

W. B. HUBBARD

Distribution and Medicinal Use of The Black-Boned and Black-Meated Chicken in Mexico, Guatemala, and South America

Grant Recipient: Carl L. Johannessen, Department of Geography, University of Oregon, Eugene, Oregon.[1]

Grants 1655, 1762: For study of the distribution and uses of black-boned chickens in Middle and South America.

The goal of our investigation (August and September 1976) was to determine the distribution of the black-boned and black-meated chicken in Mexico, Guatemala, and Belize and to identify its past and present uses.

Throughout most of the Maya and the Huasteca region, this chicken can be found associated with intricate and arbitrary beliefs in medicinally curative powers. There are several cases in Guatemala and Mexico of arbitrary use of feather, egg, whole live chicken, blood, both halves of just-killed chicken, or its meat and organs, for "medicinal" cures of fevers, evil eye, fright, ghost fright, evil winds, postpartum weakness, or general weakness. These uses and cures are very similar or identical to Chinese belief systems.

We found the use of melanotic chickens in full medicinal complexity among the Chortí, K'ekchí, Chol, and Maya, in the Petén and Campeche and among the Huasteca. Elsewhere, though full-blooded melanotic chickens are occasionally present, half-breeds or quarter-breeds are more numerous.

Away from the Maya center, very simplistic "medicinal" uses and fewer pure melanotic chicken uses indicate that the distribution started from a Mayan base. Mayan ties to Southeast Asia and China are therefore reinforced.

In 1977 these investigations were continued in Polynesia, Chile, Bolivia, Peru, and Ecuador where melanotic and other southeast Asian chickens are also present.

---

[1] Wayne Fogg, Eugene, Oregon, and May Chen Fogg, Lane Community College, Eugene, Oregon, served as team members during the 1976 fieldwork.

In Chile melanotic chickens and black-furred guinea pig, sheep, and llama are thought to be "sensitive" indicators of human ills. If the sick person can blow on the mouth of the animal, and a curer is able to incant properly, the curer can open the sacrificed animal to read the sympathetic response to the human illness in the respective organ of the animal.

In Peru and Bolivia the same sympathetic response is considered to be obtained by rubbing the guinea pig or chicken on the patient before sacrificing it in what is known as a *limpia*. This divining of the nature of the illness is not an activity encountered among Maya-speaking folk of Guatemala and Mexico when they use intricate curing systems involving the melanotic chicken. The Maya treatments are techniques of south China. The closest similarities are found among the Chipaya Indians of southwestern Bolivia who are said to have a Mayan-type language, though the corollaries are not definitive. The question to be resolved is whether divining is derivative of simply another culture in Southeast Asia or is autocthanous in South America.

Conclusions

A diffusion hypothesis of a pre-Columbian cultural transfer from Asia to the New World is supported once more as a result of this study on melanotic chickens. The black-boned, black-meated chicken is not European. It has an ancient context in southern China, Southeast Asia, and the Indian subcontinent.

The Chinese literature and modern practice described the ethnomedical treatments for specific maladies through the use of melanotic chickens. Among modern Maya of Mesoamerica (Chortí, K'ekchí, Chol) the same infirmities are cured with effectively the same application of feathers, blood, organs, meat, halves as poultices, etc. Six to seven hundred kilometers to the north of the Chol, the Huastecans (with a Maya language) utilize a large portion of the Mayan-Chinese ritual. The Chipaya 4000 km to the south are the most Maya-like of the South American groups I interviewed. Since they are said to have a proto-Maya–derived language, their use of the melanotic chicken fits a diffusion model. The additional filtering provided by another 2000 km has removed most Maya features from the ethnomedical system of the Mapuches (or Araucanians) of southern Chile, who also speak a proto-Maya–derived language.

The cultures intervening between the Chipaya, the Maya, and the Huastecans do not use this distinctive chicken in the Chinese–Maya medicinal mode. I postulate a long period during which the southern Chinese or at least southern Asian arts of folk medicine diffused. They were incorporated into the Maya tradition and maintained best near the zone of primary contact and reduced in intensity the farther Mayan speakers migrated from their culture hearth.

Because of the distributional similarities of Chinese-like medicinal folklore among groups who have a Mayan language connection, it is time to consider pre-Columbian Asiatic contacts with America in a more positive light than has been typical of traditional scholars.

This research is fully discussed in: Folk Medicine Uses of Melanotic Asiatic Chickens as Evidence of Early Diffusion to the New World; *Social Science and Medicine*, volume 15D, pages 427 to 434 (1981), and *Revista de Historia de America*, número 93, pages 73 to 89 (1982).

Carl L. Johannessen
Wayne Fogg
May Chen Fogg

The Lichen *Stereocaulon paschale* as Fodder in Caribou Winter Range

Grant Recipient: K. A. Kershaw, Department of Biology, McMaster University, Hamilton, Ontario, Canada.

Grant 1588: In support of a study of the lichen *Stereocaulon paschale* as fodder in caribou winter range.

The objectives of this research project were: to examine the growth rate of *Stereocaulon paschale* by photography of permanent quadrats, by photography of individual podetia, and by gravimetric methods (after the method of Kärenlampi, 1971); to monitor the net photosynthetic and respiration rates of the species in response to light, temperature, and moisture; and to analyze the major environmental variables of significance to the ecology of *S. paschale*, such as light, thallus temperature, thallus moisture, and interaction with winter snow conditions.

These objectives largely have been met successfully, and have been reported in depth (Kershaw and Smith, 1978; Crittenden and Kershaw, 1979). The following summarizes these results.

Thallus Growth Rates

Photographic Methods. Neither photography of permanent quadrats nor of individual podetia was successful and both have been abandoned. The permanent quadrats, intended to serve as a long-term experiment, in fact rapidly accumulated a large number of wind-borne fragments of *Stereocaulon*. This confirmed the importance of thallus fragments as a method of asexual reproduction but also effectively prevented the stripped quadrats from being used for controlled growth studies. Photography of individual podetia was similarly abandoned.

Gravimetric Field Study. The data for an experimental period running from June 8 to August 13 show some apparent weight losses, particularly in July, reflecting very dry conditions and low humidity during this period, but otherwise the growth increments are consistent for all duplicates. The average weight increase for all duplicates over the $2\frac{1}{2}$-month experimental period was 10.3 percent.

Physiological Ecology. The remaining objectives may be collectively discussed as the physiological ecology of *S. paschale*. As shown in Figure 1, the temperature optimum for net photosynthesis is about 20 to 30°C and not 0°C as has been previously reported in the literature. Maximal rates of net photosynthesis are only developed at low levels of thallus saturation (100% to 150% water content by weight), suggesting a good degree of adaptation to the xeric conditions normally found in spruce-lichen woodland. Increase in net photosynthesis is clearly related to increase in light intensity (Fig. 1). It seems that the species has not achieved

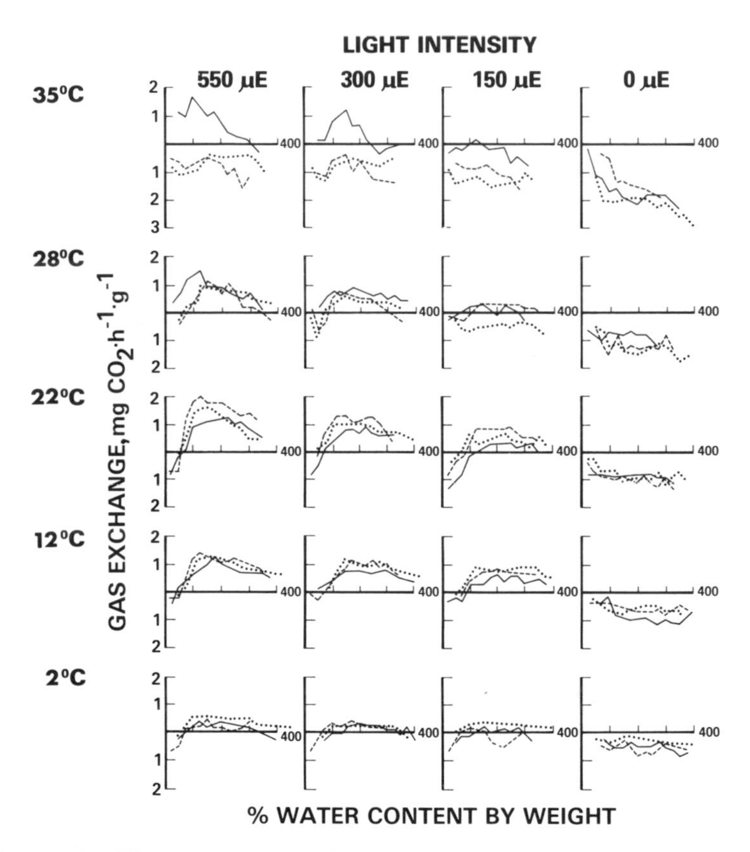

FIGURE 1. The respiration and net photosynthetic response matrix to 0, 150, 300, and 550 µE m^{-2} sec^{-1} illumination at 2, 12, 22, 28, 35°C temperatures and all levels of thallus water content during summer (—), fall (--), winter (.....) periods. Mean gas exchange is given in mg CO_2 per hour per gram with a maximum standard error of 0.6 mg CO_2 hr^{-1} g^{-1}. Thallus saturation is expressed as a percentage of the final oven dry weight of each duplicate. (Kershaw and Smith, 1978.)

light saturation at 550 μE m^{-2} sec^{-1} (E=Einstein)—the highest intensity routinely available experimentally. Other provisional data suggest that the optimum value for light intensity for this species is about 1000 μE, which would correlate well with the open nature of lichen woodland and especially with the disappearance of *S. paschale* in old woodland after the closure of the canopy.

The sensitivity of *S. paschale*, when dry, to prolonged thermal stress was examined in detail and even the moderate thallus temperature of 35°C was shown to be highly stressful to this species (Fig. 2 to 4). Surface temperatures in the low Arctic are often above 35°C and over recently burnt surfaces, temperatures above 45°C occur regularly. Thus the delayed entry of *S. paschale* into the successional sequence reflects its extreme sensitivity to thermal stress. With the gradual accumulation of an organic layer and an enhanced retention of soil moisture of the initial 60 years of succession, both the sensible heat flux and the surface temperatures are significantly reduced. At the same time, tree growth leads to a sharp decrease of full radiation (2000 μE). The combination of these two developments results in a much cooler surface and one that can be colonized by *Stereocaulon*.

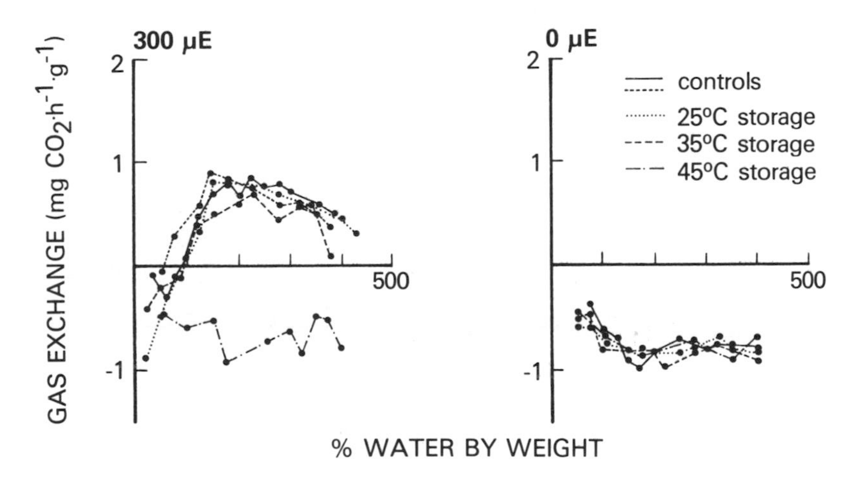

FIGURE 2. The respiration and net photosynthetic response at 25°C with 0 and 300 μE m^{-2} sec^{-1} illumination after the experimental duplicates had been stored air dry for 6 days at a range of temperature stress levels. Mean gas exchange rates are given as mg CO_2 per hour per gram with a maximum standard error of 0.6 mg CO_2 hr^{-1} g^{-1}. Thallus saturation is expressed as a percentage of the final oven dry weight of each duplicate. (Kershaw and Smith, 1978.)

This also suggests that thermal stress tolerance of lichens, in an air-dry state, to either high or low temperatures may be centrally important to their overall ecology. Furthermore, the net photosynthetic response pattern to temperature, moisture, light, and time of year, may, in fact, play a subordinate role in the ecology of a lichen.

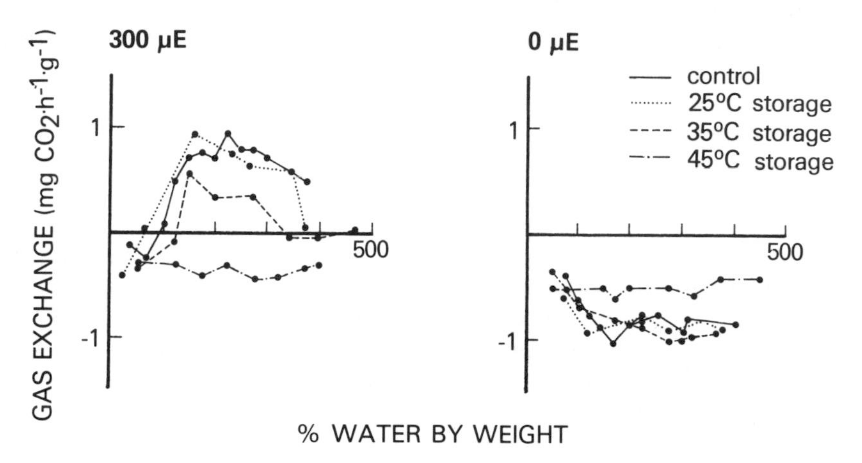

FIGURE 3. The respiration and net photosynthetic response at 25°C with 0 and 300 $\mu E\ m^{-2}\ sec^{-1}$ illumination after the experimental duplicates had been stored air dry for 14 days at a range of temperature stress levels. (Kershaw and Smith, 1978.)

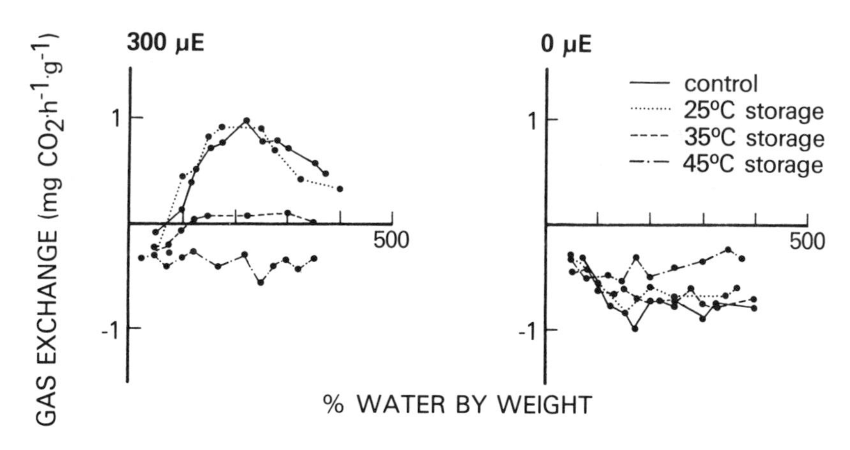

FIGURE 4. The respiration and net photosynthetic response at 25°C with 0 and 300 $\mu E\ m^{-2}\ sec^{-1}$ illumination after the experimental duplicates had been stored air dry for 21 days at a range of temperature stress levels. (Kershaw and Smith, 1978.)

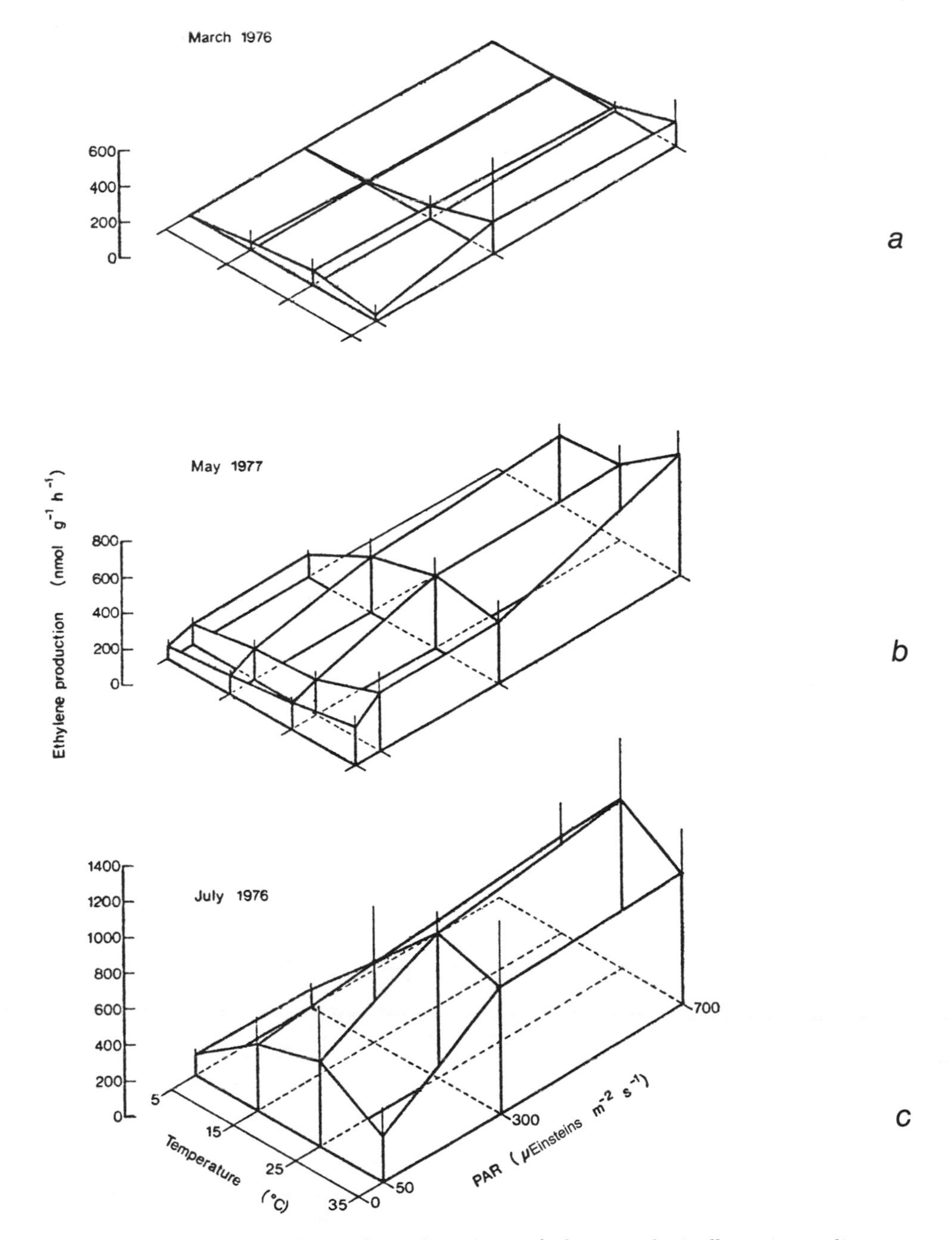

FIGURE 5. Effects of factorial combinations of photosynthetically active radiation (PAR) and thallus temperature on ethylene production (nitrogenase activity) in 3 collections of *S. paschale* made at different times of the year. Mean values are plotted together with 95% confidence limits (*n* ranges between 7 and 36). (Crittenden and Kershaw, 1979.)

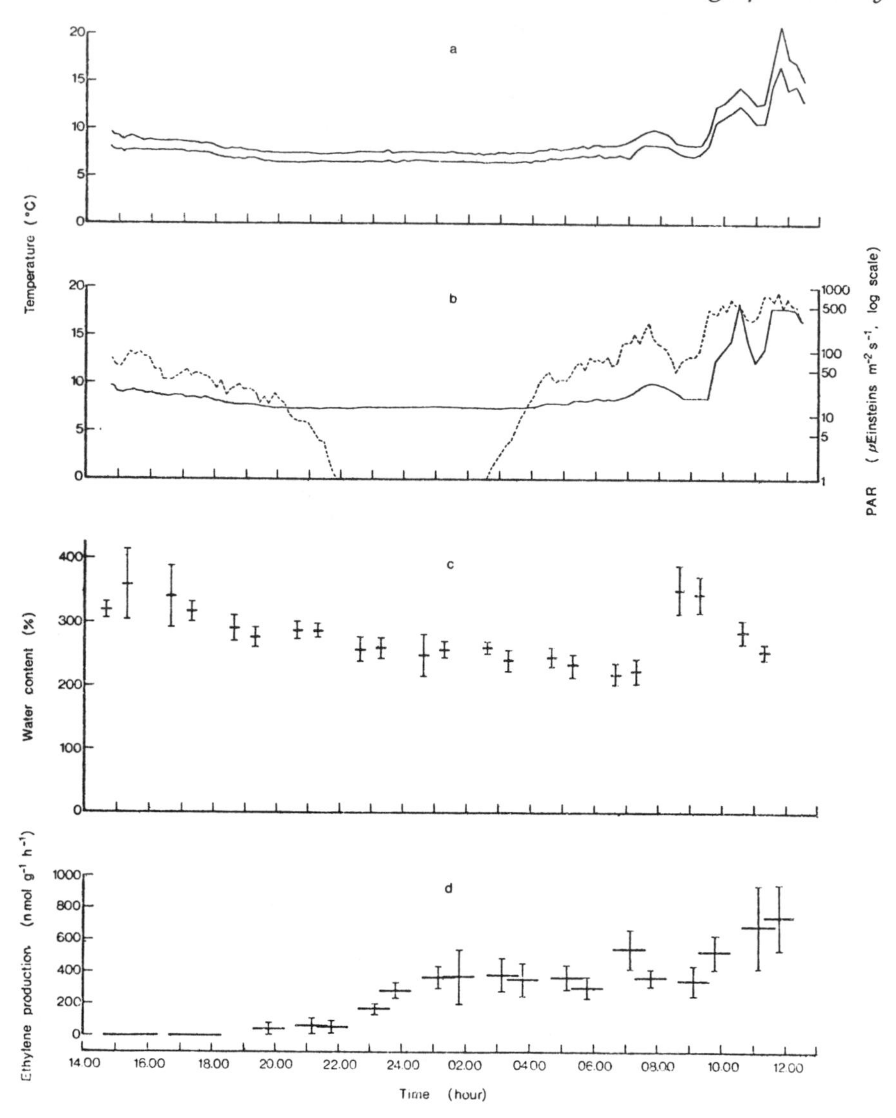

FIGURE 6. Microclimatic variables and nitrogenase activity in a mat of *S. paschale*, 24-25 June 1976 (solar time indicated). (a) Maximum and minimum thallus temperature within the lichen mat (range of 5 signals); (b) thallus temperature (—) and photosynthetically active radiation (PAR, note log scale) (-----) within the incubation bottles; (c) mean thallus water content within the lichen mat and of thalli prior to incubation for acetylene reduction assays (% of oven dry weight); (d) mean ethylene production (nitrogenase activity). Mean values (n=10) are plotted together with 95% confidence limits. Heavy rain commenced ca. 09.15 hr 24 June; measurements began at 14.30 hr. (Crittenden and Kershaw, 1979.)

The nitrogen fixation capabilities of this species have similarly been examined in depth (Fig. 5). Thus there is a strong light and temperature component (Fig. 5*c*), but we have now demonstrated two new phenomena: There is a very important seasonal effect with very low rates of nitrogenase-generated activity immediately following snow melt (Fig. 5*a*); and nitrogenase activity can be effectively maintained throughout the night although at a reduced level (Fig. 5*b*). The latter was very effectively shown in the field (Fig. 6) with rainfall commencing at 1500 hr and initiation of nitrogenase activity not occurring until 2000 hr (a normal lag-phase for thallus hydration and enzyme reactivation) with a marked rate increase actually occurring during total darkness.

REFERENCES

CRITTENDEN, P. D., and KERSHAW, K. A.
1979. Studies on lichen-dominated systems. XXII. The environmental control of nitrogenase activity of *Stereocaulon paschale* in spruce-lichened woodland. Can. Journ. Botany, vol. 57, pp. 236-254.

KÄRENLAMPI, L.
1971. Studies on the relative growth rate of some fruticose lichens. Reports from the Kevo Subarctic Research Station, no. 7, pp. 33-39.

KERSHAW, K. A.
——. Physiological Ecology of Lichens. Cambridge University Press. (In press).

KERSHAW, K. A., and SMITH, A. A.
1978. Studies on lichen-dominated systems. XXI. The control of seasonal rates of net photosynthesis by moisture, light, and temperature in *Stereocaulon paschale*. Can. Journ. Botany, vol. 56, pp. 2825-2830.

K. A. KERSHAW

Zoogeography of the Mammals of the Uinta Mountains Region

Grant Recipient: Gordon L. Kirkland, Jr., The Vertebrate Museum, Shippensburg University, Shippensburg, Pennsylvania.

Grants 1587, 1729: In support of a faunal survey of the mammals of the Uinta Mountains.

The Uinta Mountains in northeastern Utah are unique among the major mountain ranges of the conterminous United States in their east-west orientation. The Uintas are the highest mountains in Utah, with numerous peaks exceeding 12,000 ft. Extending eastward from the north-south oriented Wasatch Range for approximately 130 mi, the Uintas lie like a highland peninsula between two large, semidesert basins, the Bridger to the north and the Uinta to the south. To the east, the Uintas are bounded by the canyon of the Green River, which drains southward from the Bridger Basin (Fig. 1).

Because of their unusual east-west orientation, large size, and semi-isolated nature, the Uinta Mountains represent an ideal natural laboratory for studying the effects of mountains on the distribution and systematics of small mammals. The zoogeographic significance of the Uintas for mammals is revealed in the fact that they coincide with the boundary between two of the mammal faunal provinces of North America (Hagmaier, 1966). The distinctiveness of the mammal faunas of the Uinta Mountains and the adjacent Bridger and Uinta Basins was documented by Durrant (1952) who designated these areas as three of Utah's mammal provinces. Armstrong (1972) later classified the Uintas as a mammal subcenter and the two basins as mammal provinces. Both Durrant and Armstrong examined the mammals of the Uinta Mountains region as part of a zoogeographic analysis of the mammals of Utah, and therefore neither focused specifically on the region. In addition, several of the mammal surveys that have been carried out in the Uintas, such as those of Reynolds (1966), Dearden (1967), and Svihla (1931, 1932) have been limited to specific areas within the mountains. Thus, no study to date has provided a comprehensive analysis of the distribution and systematics of the small mammals of the Uinta Mountains and adjacent basins. Here, I summarize the results of a zoogeographic analysis of the

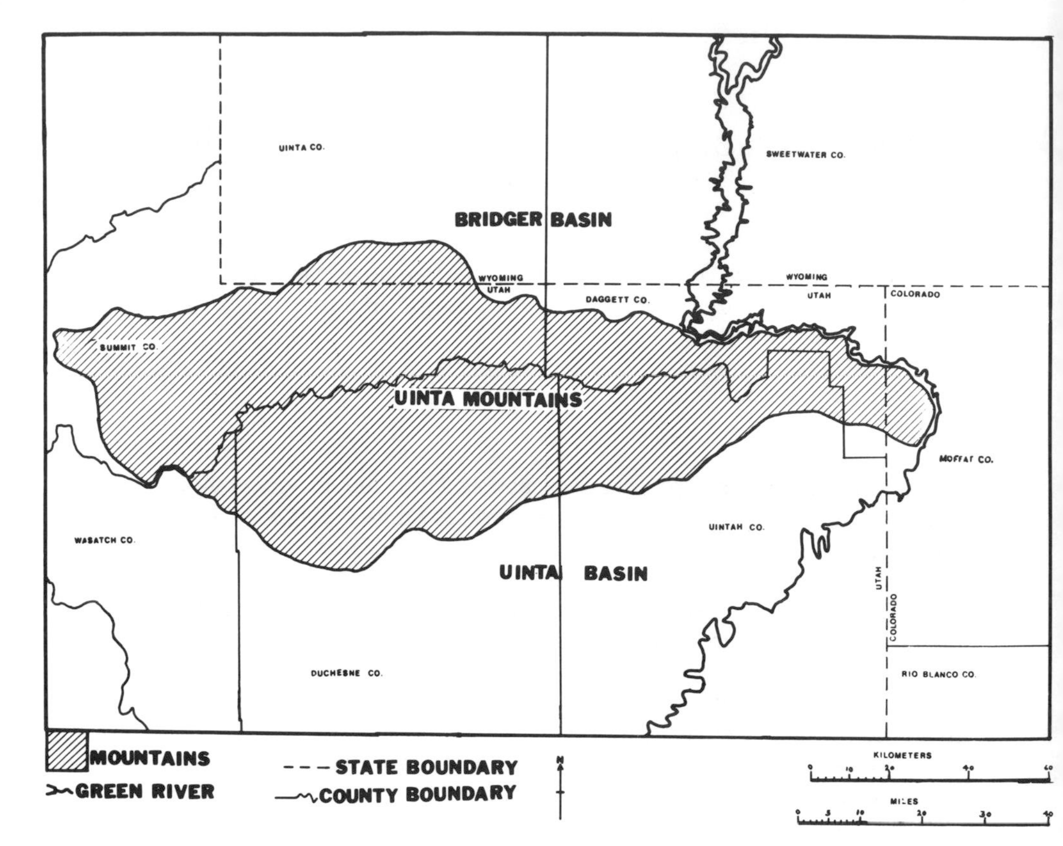

FIGURE 1. Uinta Mountains region.

mammals of the Uinta Mountains, which is based in part on data obtained during two summers of fieldwork in the Uintas (1976-1977) sponsored by the National Geographic Society. Additional data have been obtained from a review of the literature and an examination of mammal specimens from the Uintas housed at the University of Utah (UU); the Carnegie Museum of Natural History (CMNH); the Museum of Natural History, University of Kansas (KU); the Museum of Zoology, University of Michigan; and the National Museum of Natural History, Smithsonian Institution.

Methods and Materials

Fieldwork in the Uintas was carried out by personnel from the Vertebrate Museum, Shippensburg University (SU), during June and July 1976-1977 and September 1976. A total of 872 specimens of 27 species was collected at 23 localities in 6 counties: Daggett, Duchesne, Summit, Uintah, and Wasatch in Utah; and Uinta in Wyoming. Data from these specimens were supplemented by data obtained from specimens housed in the 5 mammal collections noted above.

Excluded from the analysis are 15 species of larger mammals (7 Artiodactyla, 2 Ursidae, 3 Felidae, 2 *Canis*, and *Gulo gulo)* because of the scarcity of specimens and records or the profound impact man has had on their current distribution. A majority of these species apparently are or were unaffected by the Uinta Mountains in their distributions or taxonomy. Exceptions would be the boreal species, such as *Felis canadensis* and *Gulo gulo,* that would have been confined to the Uintas (Hall and Kelson, 1959). Bats (Chiroptera), which are frequently deleted from faunal analyses due to their high powers of dispersal and/or the scarcity of records, will be included because the Uintas appear to play an important role in determining the distributional limits of several southwestern species.

The results of the analysis of the influence of the Uinta Mountains and surrounding areas on the zoogeography of the mammals of this region are presented in the context of Armstrong's (1977) analysis of the distributional patterns of mammals in Utah, and Armstrong's terminology for the mammal faunal elements is used throughout.

Results

As barriers, mountain ranges may affect the zoogeography of mammals at three different levels: They may limit the distribution of a species; they may limit gene flow to such an extent that recognizable subspecies are present on opposite sides; or they may disrupt gene flow to such a limited extent that populations on opposite sides are insufficiently differentiated to warrant subspecific designation. Whether or not distribution and gene flow are affected will be a function of the species' size, ecological characteristics, and dispersal capabilities, as well as the size, characteristics, and age of the mountain range. In addition, a mountain range may act as a dispersal corridor for montane and boreal species, or it may exclude nonmontane species.

Not counting the 15 species of larger mammals noted above, the Uinta Mountains and adjacent basins are included within the distributional limits of 82 of 109 species, or 75.2% of the mammals native to Utah (Durrant, 1952; Hall and Kelson, 1959; Armstrong, 1977). Of this number, 60 species, or 73.2%, are influenced in their distribution or taxonomy by the Uintas in the following ways: (1), for 20 species their boundary coincides with the Uintas; (2), 13 species have subspecies boundaries that fall within or coincide with the Uintas; (3), 7 species are excluded from the mountains but occur to the north and south; (4) 7 species use the Green River as

TABLE 1. Effects of the Uintas on the Distribution and Taxonomy of Mammals, Analysis by Family

Family	*No. species, Uinta Region*	*No. species, Utah*	*Species with boundary at Uintas*	*Species with subspecies boundaries at or in Uintas*	*Species excluded from Uintas*	*Boreo-montane species*	*Species using Green River as a dispersal route*	*Species not affected*
Soricidae	5	7	1			4		
Vespertilionidae	16	17	6	1				9
Molossidae	2	2	2					
Ochotonidae	1	1				1		
Leporidae	5	6	1		1	1		2
Sciuridae	16	21	6	3	2	4	1	1
Geomyidae	2	3	1	1				
Heteromyidae	4	13	1	2	2			
Castoridae	1	1		1				
Cricetidae	15	23	1	4	2	3	4	2
Zapodidae	1	1				1		
Erethizontidae	1	1						1
Canidae	2	3*					1	1
Procyonidae	2	2	1				1	
Mustelidae	9	10*		1	2			6
TOTALS	82	109	20	13	7	16	7	22

*Does not include larger species excluded from analysis.

a dispersal route; and (5), 15 boreo-montane species are excluded from the basins. The remaining 22 species are widespread throughout the region and do not appear to be affected by the Uintas (Table 1). This adds to a total of 85 because the red squirrel *(Tamiasciurus hudsonicus)* is a boreo-montane species that also has a subspecies boundary within the Uintas while the Great Basin pocket mouse *(Perognathus parvus)* and the northern grasshopper mouse *(Onychomys leucogaster)* are both excluded from the Uintas and represented in the Uinta and Bridger Basins by separate subspecies.

SPECIES WITH BOUNDARY AT THE UINTAS

Of the 20 species whose ranges are limited by the Uintas, 16 are

TABLE 2. Mammals Whose Ranges Are Limited by the Uintas
NOTE: Faunal elements represented by each are from Armstrong (1977).

Taxon	*Common Name*	*Faunal Element*
	SPECIES LIMITED SOUTH OF THE UINTAS	
Chiroptera : Vespertilionidae		
Myotis yumanensis	Yuma myotis	Chihuahuan
Myotis velifer	Cave myotis	Chihuahuan
Myotis californicus	California myotis	Chihuahuan
Pipistrellus hesperus	Western pipistrelle	Chihuahuan
Lasiurus borealis	Red bat	Widespread
Antrozous pallidus	Pallid bat	Chihuahuan
Chiroptera : Molossidae		
Tadarida brasiliensis	Brazilian free-tailed bat	Chihuahuan
Tadarida macrotis	Big free-tailed bat	Chihuahuan
Lagomorpha : Leporidae		
Lepus californicus	Black-tailed jackrabbit	Chihuahuan
Rodentia : Sciuridae		
Ammospermophilus leucurus	White-tailed antelope ground squirrel	Yuman
Spermophilus variegatus	Rock squirrel	Chihuahuan
Eutamias quadrivittatus	Colorado chipmunk	Arizonan
Spermophilus spilosoma	Spotted ground squirrel	Chihuahuan
Rodentia : Heteromyidae		
Perognathus apache	Apache pocket mouse	Arizonan
Rodentia : Cricetidae		
Neotoma lepida	Desert woodrat	Yuman
Carnivora : Procyonidae		
Bassariscus astutus	Ringtail	Chihuahuan
	SPECIES LIMITED NORTH OF THE UINTAS	
Rodentia : Sciuridae		
Eutamias amoenus	Yellow-pine chipmunk	Cordilleran
Spermophilus richardsoni	Richardson's ground squirrel	Bridgeran
Rodentia : Geomyidae		
Thomomys idahoensis	Idaho pocket gopher	Cordilleran
	SPECIES LIMITED WEST OF THE UINTAS	
Insectivora : Soricidae		
Sorex vagrans	Vagrant shrew	Cordilleran

southern species reaching their northernmost limits in the vicinity of the Uintas (Table 2). Three are northern species for which the Uintas mark the southern limits of their distributions. One species, the vagrant shrew *(Sorex vagrans)*, occurs in the Wasatch Mountains to the west but is not known to occur in the Uintas; in the Uintas, it is replaced by the montane shrew *(S. monticolus)*, a closely related sister species (Hennings and Hoffmann, 1977).

Of the 16 species limited south of the Uintas 8 are bats, of which all but the red bat *(Lasiurus borealis)* are members of Armstrong's (1977) Chihuahuan faunal element. *L. borealis* is widespread in the eastern two thirds of the United States, but in the west is largely restricted to the southwest (Barbour and Davis, 1969). Despite the difficulties of analyzing the distributional limits of bats because of their extensive powers of dispersal, there is good evidence that these 8 species are limited by the Uintas. None of these was reported by Long (1965) as occurring in southwestern Wyoming north of the Uintas. However, single specimens of the western pipistrelle *(Pipistrellus hesperus)* and the pallid bat *(Antrozous pallidus)* have been recorded for Daggett County, Utah, and Sweetwater County, Wyoming, respectively (Durrant and Dean, 1960). These records might correspond to extralimital occurrences frequently recorded for birds (Udvardy, 1969). Reynolds (1966) suggests that the *Pipistrellus* may have reached Daggett County by following the Green River northward. If this were the case, then this species might also be classed as one that uses the Green River as a dispersal route.

The 8 nonchiropteran species limited in their northward distribution by the Uintas are members of either Armstrong's Chihuahuan (4 species), Arizonan (2 species), or Yuman (2 species) faunal elements (Table 2). The northernmost records for these species occur at various localities in the Uinta Basin, with all known from at least central Duchesne or Uintah Counties (Durrant, 1952; specimens at UU, CMNH).

The species limited north of the Uintas consist of 2 Cordilleran and 1 Bridgeran species (Table 2). The yellow-pine chipmunk *(Eutamias amoenus)* whose range lies primarily north and west of the Uintas (Hall and Kelson, 1959) has recently been collected on the northwest slope of the Uintas in Summit County, Utah (R. S. Hoffmann, pers. comm.). Whether this represents dispersal of this species southward or is the result of previous sampling omissions is not clear at this time. The Idaho pocket gopher *(Thomomys idahoensis)* is a distinctive dwarf pocket gopher that has been taken at altitudes of up to 9000 ft in Daggett County (UU) but has not been reported from the south slope. We collected several specimens 9.6 km south of Manila, Daggett County, at 2400 m (7800 ft), but were unable to find any evidence of this species on the south slope in adjacent Uintah County. Richardson's ground squirrel *(Spermophilus richardsoni)* is a campestrian species that is very similar morphologically to the Uinta ground squirrel *(S. armatus)*. The ranges of the 2 species meet along the lower elevations of the north slope of the Uintas.

The net result of the isolation of 16 species to the south and 3 species to the north of the Uintas is to create distinctive mammal faunas in these regions. As previously noted, Hagmaier (1966) established the boundaries between 2 mammal faunal provinces in the region of the Uintas.

Species Having Subspecies Boundaries at or in the Uintas

Thirteen species of mammals have subspecies boundaries that fall within the Uinta Mountains region (Table 3). The distributional limits of the subspecies tend to vary somewhat with species, but several major patterns are evident. It should be remembered that these boundaries are not absolute, but generally represent zones of sharp character gradients among populations, suggesting a partial disruption of gene flow.

Table 3. Mammals with Subspecies Boundaries in the Uinta Mountains Region
Note: Faunal element designations from Armstrong (1977).

Taxon	*Common Name*	*Faunal Element*
Chiroptera : Vespertilionidae		
Myotis liebii	Small-footed myotis	Widespread
Rodentia : Sciuridae		
Eutamias minimus	Least chipmunk	Boreo-cordilleran
Spermophilus lateralis	Golden-mantled ground squirrel	Cordilleran
Tamiasciurus hudsonicus	Red squirrel	Boreo-cordilleran
Rodentia : Geomyidae		
Thomomys talpoides	Northern pocket gopher	Cordilleran
Rodentia : Heteromyidae		
Dipodomys ordii	Ord's kangaroo rat	Chihuahuan
Perognathus parvus	Great Basin pocket mouse	Nevadan
Rodentia : Castoridae		
Castor canadensis	Beaver	Widespread
Rodentia : Cricetidae		
Peromyscus maniculatus	Deer mouse	Widespread
Neotoma cinerea	Bushy-tailed woodrat	Cordilleran
Onychomys leucogaster	Northern grasshopper mouse	Nevadan
Microtus montanus	Montane vole	Cordilleran
Carnivora : Mustelidae		
Mephitis mephitis	Striped skunk	Widespread

In 4 species—the least chipmunk *(Eutamias minimus)*, Ord's kangaroo rat *(Dipodomys ordii)*, the bushy-tailed woodrat *(Neotoma cinerea)*, and the striped skunk *(Mephitis mephitis)*—the subspecies boundaries are coincident with (i.e., tend to follow) the Uintas such that specimens from the north slope are assigned to one subspecies and those from the south slope to another.

The situation in 2 other species is somewhat equivocal. In the small-footed myotis *(Myotis leibii)* specimens from the Bridger Basin, the Uinta and the Wasatch Mountains are assigned to *M.l. ciliolabrum;* those from the remainder of Utah are placed in *M.l. melanorhinus* (Durrant, 1952).

The only 2 specimens known from the Uinta Basin were identified as *M.l. melanorhinus* (Krutzsch and Heppenstall, 1955) as have been specimens from adjacent Moffat County, Colorado (Armstrong, 1972). In the montane vole *(Microtus montanus)*, populations from the Uinta Mountains are assigned to *M.m. nanus*, but specimens from the vicinity of Vernal, Uintah County have been placed in *M.m. amosus*, even though they retain some of the characteristics of *nanus* (Anderson, 1959).

The ranges of 3 subspecies of beaver *(Castor canadensis)* converge in the region of the Uintas. *C.c. duchesnei* occupies the area drained by the Duchesne and White Rivers in Utah and Colorado (Durrant and Crane, 1948). To the west is the range of *C.c. rostralis*, which includes the streams in the western Uintas draining into the Salt Lake Basin (Durrant and Crane, 1948). To the north in Wyoming is the range of *C.c. missouriensis* with localities as close to the Uintas as 9 mi south of Robertson, Uinta County, at 8000 ft (Long, 1965). Specimens from the north slopes of the Uintas appear to be intergrades among all 3 subspecies, depending on locality (Reynolds, 1966; Dearden, 1967).

The taxonomic situation in the northern pocket gopher *(Thomomys talpoides)* is even more confusing, with no less than 5 subspecies being recognized in the Uinta Mountains (Durrant, 1952; Hall and Kelson, 1959). *T.t. ravus*, a montane race, is confined to the higher elevations of the Uintas. *T.t ocius* is a resident of drier sagebrush areas, with a range that includes much of the eastern Bridger and Uinta Basins as well as adjacent western Colorado. The western Uinta Basin and southern slopes of the Uintas are included within the range of *T.t. uinta*. To the north, the western Bridger Basin and adjacent foothills of the Uintas are occupied by *T.t. bridgeri*. The fifth subspecies, *T.t. wasatchensis*, is found in the Wasatch Range and on the western flanks of the Uintas. The zoogeographic problems posed by *T. talpoides* have been lessened somewhat in recent years with the reclassification of *T.t. pygmaeus* to *T. idahoensis pygmaeus*. This revision resolved the questions previously raised by the presence of well-defined sympatric subspecies of *T. talpoides* on the northern slope of the Uintas.

The golden-mantled ground squirrel *(Spermophilus lateralis)* and the red squirrel *(Tamiasciurus hudsonicus)* each have subspecies in the Uintas that are different from subspecies occurring in the Wasatch Range to the west. In both species, intergrades between Uinta and Wasatch subspecies are found in Summit County on the northwest slopes of the Uintas.

In the deer mouse *(Peromyscus maniculatus)*, there is an altitudinal zonation of subspecies. *P.m. rufinus* is a darker montane race. It contrasts with the paler race, *P.m. nebrascensis*, which is primarily an inhabitant of drier communities at lower elevations of the Uintas and in the adjacent basins. Intergradation or possibly interdigitation of these races takes

TABLE 4. Mammals that Are Excluded from the Uintas
NOTE: Faunal element designations are those of Armstrong (1977).

Taxon	*Common Name*	*Faunal Element*
Lagormorpha : Leporidae		
Sylvilagus audubonii	Desert cottontail	Chihuahuan
Rodentia : Sciuridae		
Spermophilus tridecemlineatus	13-lined ground squirrel	Campestrian
Cynomys leucurus	White-tailed prairie dog	Bridgeran
Rodentia : Heteromyidae		
Perognathus fasciatus	Olive-backed pocket mouse	Campestrian
Perognathus parvus	Great Basin pocket mouse	Nevadan
Rodentia : Cricetidae		
*Onychomys leucogaster**	Northern grasshopper mouse	Nevadan
Lagurus curtatus	Sagebrush vole	Nevadan

*Separate subspecies to north and south *(0.1. arcticeps* to north and east; *0.1. pallescens* to south).

place throughout the Uintas, and specimens assignable to *P.m. nebrascensis* were taken in our study at altitudes of 2800 m (9200 ft). Durrant (1952) noted that specimens from Paradise Park (10,500 ft) were referable to *P.m. nebrascensis.*

Perognathus parvus and *Onychomys leucogster* are represented in the Bridger and Uinta Basins by different subspecies (Hall and Kelson, 1959). Both species are also excluded from the Uintas and are discussed in greater detail in the section on species excluded from the Uintas.

SPECIES EXCLUDED FROM THE UINTAS

Seven species of mammals found in both the Bridger and Uinta Basins are excluded from the Uinta Mountains (Table 4). Five of these also occur in central and western Moffat County, Colorado, and thus have a continuous distribution between the two basins (Armstrong, 1972). Although the northern grasshopper mouse *(Onychomys leucogaster)* is found in Moffat County, its range is apparently discontinuous, and it is represented by different subspecies on the north and south sides of the Uintas (Hall and Kelson, 1959; Armstrong, 1972). The Great Basin pocket mouse *(Perognathus parvus)* has not been recorded in western Colorado (Armstrong, 1972), but is also represented on the north and south slopes of the Uintas by different subspecies (Hall and Kelson, 1959). For a detailed discussion of the taxonomic status of populations for *P. parvus* in the Uinta Basin, see Kirkland (1981).

All of these species are inhabitants of steppe-desert habitats characteristic of the Bridger and Uinta Basins as well as western Colorado. With the exception of the sagebrush vole *(Lagurus curtatus)*, their distributions appear to be confined to the basins and do not extend into the montane regions. *Lagurus*, as its common name suggests, is a resident of communities dominated by sagebrush *(Artemesia)* and was taken by us at 2400 m (7900 ft) in Daggett County (9.5 km south of Manila) and at 2800 m (9200 ft) in Summit County (4.8 km east northeast of Bridger Lake). Five were trapped in a sagebrush flat in Daggett County, while the 7 Summit County specimens were taken on a sagebrush hillside.

Although *Onychomys leucogaster* and *Perognathus parvus* are the only species "excluded from the Uintas" for which separate southern and northern subspecies are recognized, 3 of the other species have Uinta and Bridger Basin populations that are noticeably different. Uinta Basin populations of the 13-lined ground squirrel *(Spermophilus tridecemlineatus)* are substantially browner than Bridger Basin specimens and have an ochraceous wash on the sides and belly. Bridger Basin specimens are pale brown, with no ochraceous wash. The distinctive Uinta Basin specimens have previously been noted by Armstrong (1971), who considered them to be typical of a pattern observed in isolated montane populations at the western margin of the range of *S. tridecemlineatus*, thus not warranting subspecific designation.

Lagurus and *Cynomys leucurus* exhibit less pronounced pelage difference between northern and southern populations. Specimens of *Lagurus* from Daggett County have a distinct buffish cast to the dorsum, whereas specimens from Uintah County are distinctly grayer (UU, CMNH, SU). In *Cynomys*, there is a tendency for Uintah Basin specimens to be darker and to have a more pinkish cast to the dorsum (UU, CMNH).

Insufficiently large samples of the desert cottontail *Sylvilagus audubonii)* and of the olive-backed pocket mouse *(Perognathus fasciatus)* have been examined to permit a meaningful comparison of northern and southern populations.

Boreo-montane Species

The 16 boreo-montane species of the Uinta Mountains region (Table 5) are all isolated in the Uintas proper, seldom being found at altitudes lower than 7000 ft, which marks the approximate transition between the lower piñon-juniper *(Pinus edulis-Juniperus* sp.) woodlands and the lodgepole pine *(Pinus contorta)*, Douglas fir *(Pseudotsuga menziesii)*, and ponderosa pine *(Pinus ponderosa)* forests of the higher elevations.

All 4 shrews known from the Uinta Mountains region are boreo-montane species (Table 5). To date, Merriam's shrew *(Sorex merriami)* has not been recorded from the Uinta Mountains region. This species is a resident of drier habitats of the west (Armstrong and Jones, 1971) and is known to occur in a number of areas surrounding the study area, includ-

TABLE 5. Boreo-montane Species of the Uinta Mountains
NOTE: Faunal element designations are those of Armstrong (1977).

Taxon	*Common Name*	*Faunal Element*
Insectivora : Soricidae		
Sorex cinereus	Masked shrew	Widespread
Sorex nanus	Dwarf shrew	Cordilleran
Sorex monticolus	Montane shrew	Cordilleran
Sorex palustris	Water shrew	Boreo-cordilleran
Lagomorpha : Cohotonidae		
Ochotona princeps	Pika	Cordilleran
Lagomorpha : Leporidae		
Lepus americanus	Varying hare	Boreo-cordilleran
Rodentia : Sciuridae		
Eutamias umbrinus	Uinta chipmunk	Cordilleran
Spermophilus armatus	Uinta ground squirrel	Cordilleran
Glaucomys sabrinus	Northern flying squirrel	Boreo-cordilleran
Tamiasciurus hudsonicus	Red squirrel	Boreo-cordilleran
Rodentia : Cricetidae		
Clethrionomys gapperi	Red-backed vole	Boreo-cordilleran
Phenacomys intermedius	Heather vole	Boreo-cordilleran
Arvicola richardsoni	Water vole	Cordilleran
Rodentia : Zapodidae		
Zapus princeps	Western jumping mouse	Cordilleran
Carnivora : Mustelidae		
Martes americana	Pine marten	Boreo-cordilleran
Martes pennanti	Fisher	Boreo-cordilleran

ing San Juan County in southeastern Utah (Durrant, 1952), Moffat and Rio Blanco Counties in northwestern Colorado (Armstrong, 1972), and central Wyoming, possibly including Sweetwater County (Long, 1965). Thus, it is possible that *S. merriami* may occur in the Uinta and Bridger Basins as well as the foothills of the Uintas, with its distribution being complementary to those of the other 4 species of *Sorex* in the study area.

When Durrant (1952) published his *Mammals of Utah*, only 2 species of shrews were known from the Uintas, *S. palustris* and *S. obscurus*, the latter subsequently renamed *S. monticolus* by Hennings and Hoffmann (1977). A single specimen of *S. vagrans* from Summit County, reported by Durrant, has been reidentified as *S. monticolus*. Thus, the ranges of the sister species *S. vagrans* and *S. monticolus* appear to be allopatric in the region of the Uintas, with only *S. monticolus* in the Uintas and *S. vagrans* (and possibly *S. monticolus*) occurring in the adjacent Wasatch Mountains to the west (Hennings and Hoffmann, 1977). In our work in the Uintas, we collected only *S. monticolus* and found it to be most abundant in riparian habitats adjacent to streams. *S. palustris* was even more restricted to moist habitats and was collected only at streamsides or in wet marshy areas adjacent to streams.

S. cinereus was added to the mammal fauna of the Uintas in the early 1960s when 3 specimens were collected during the mammal survey of Daggett County (Reynolds, 1966). Our sampling produced the first record of this species from Uintah County (SU 5435, 28 km north northeast of Vernal, altitude 2500 m). We also collected the first *S. cinereus* from the Uinta Mountains portion of Summit County, the previous county record being from Heiner's Canyon, northwest of the Uintas (Dearden, 1967). Our Summit County specimen was trapped in a marshy area, similar to the habitat reported for the 3 Daggett County specimens (Reynolds, 1966); however, the Uintah County specimen was trapped under a clump of common juniper *(Juniperus communis)* in a well-drained aspen *(Populus tremuloides)* park.

Possibly the most important specimen collected during our fieldwork in the Uintas was a dwarf shrew *(S. nanus)* (SU 6502), collected in Summit County (2.25 km south and 2.1 km west of Mirror Lake, altitude 3110 m). This is the first record of *S. nanus* from northeastern Utah and represents a considerable extension of the range of the species, based on the range map recently published by Hoffmann and Owen (1980). The Summit County specimen was caught among rocks on a talus slope at the transition zone between boreal coniferous forest and alpine tundra. Hoffmann and Owen (1980) note that *S. nanus* is most frequently captured in rocky habitats in the alpine tundra and subalpine coniferous forests.

The pika *(Ochotona princeps)* and the heather vole *(Phenacomys intermedius)* are 2 boreo-montane species typically associated with rocky habitats at the highest elevations in the Uintas. *Ochotona* is apparently fairly widely distributed and common in suitable habitats, being known from several localities in each of Daggett, Duchesne, Summit, and Uintah Counties (Durrant, 1952; Dearden, 1967; Reynolds, 1966; CMNH, SSC). In contrast, there are comparatively few *Phenacomys* from scattered localities extending from near Bald Peak, Summit County in the west to Paradise Park, Uintah County in the east (CMNH). With a single exception, these specimens were all taken at altitudes in excess of 10,000 ft. The single exception was from 9200 ft in Wyoming, Uinta County (11.5 mi south, 2 mi east of Robertson) (KU).

The red squirrel *(Tamiasciurus hudsonicus)*, varying hare *(Lepus americanus)*, northern flying squirrel *(Glaucomys sabrinus)*, red-backed vole *(Clethrionomys gapperi)*, pine marten *(Martes americana)*, and fisher *(Martes pennanti)* are all members of the boreo-cordilleran faunal element and are largely confined to the higher elevations of the Uintas. An exception is the red squirrel, which can be found throughout the montane and boreal forest regions.

TABLE 6. Mammals that Have Used the Green River as a Dispersal Route
NOTE: Faunal element designations are from Armstrong (1977).

Taxon	*Common Name*	*Faunal Element*
Rodentia : Sciuridae		
Eutamias dorsalis	Cliff chipmunk	Chihuahuan
Rodentia : Cricetidae		
Peromyscus crinitus	Canyon mouse	Yuman
Peromyscus boylii	Brush mouse	Chihuahuan
Peromyscus truei	Pinyon mouse	Chihuahuan
Reithrodontomys megalotis	Western harvest mouse	Chihuahuan
Carnivora : Canidae		
Urocyon cinereoargenteus	Gray fox	Chihuahuan
Carnivora : Procyonidae		
Procyon lotor	Raccoon	Widespread

In contrast, the Uinta ground squirrel *(Spermophilus armatus),* water vole *(Arvicola richardsoni),* montane vole *(Microtus montanus),* and western jumping mouse *(Zapus princeps)* are nonforest dwellers, confined primarily to herbaceous habitats associated with streams. Whereas *Arvicola* tends to be found at the high elevations, *Zapus* and *S. armatus* follow streams into the sagebrush zone at lower elevations.

The Uinta chipmunk *(Eutamias umbrinus),* a cordilleran species, is less confined to boreal forests and was captured by us in a variety of habitats within the boreal zone, including streamside areas.

All 16 boreo-montane species are restricted in their distributions by the Uintas. In addition to being excluded from the Uinta and Bridger Basins, none of the 16 occur in western Moffat County, Colorado, east of the Green River (Armstrong, 1972). Also, 4 of these species *(S. armatus, G. sabrinus, A. richardsoni,* and *M. pennanti)* are unknown from Colorado, while 12 occur farther eastward in the mountains of west-central Colorado, after a hiatus of at least 100 km. Of the 12, 4 *(O. princeps, E. umbrinus, Z. princeps,* and *C. gapperi)* are represented east of the disjunction by different subspecies than are present in the Uintas.

SPECIES USING THE GREEN RIVER AS A DISPERSAL ROUTE

Seven species apparently have used the Green River as a dispersal route to extend their ranges northward into the Bridger Basin and the north slope of the Uintas (Table 6). For all of these species, Daggett County, Utah, or adjacent southern Sweetwater County, Wyoming, represents the northernmost limits of their distribution in this portion of their geographic ranges. With the exception of the gray fox *(Urocyon cinereoargenteus),* all these species are associated either with rocky habitats or riparian zones in desert areas (Hall and Kelson, 1959; Schmidly, 1977; Findley et al., 1975). The Green River with its deep canyon at the eastern end of the Uintas would provide an ideal avenue for the dispersal of these species. A review of Armstrong (1972) indicates that these species, if present in northwestern Colorado, are restricted to the river valleys, thus strengthening the hypothesis that they have reached the Bridger Basin via the Green River. The case of the gray fox is more equivocal. The only specimen from north of the Uintas is a skull (UU 21408) obtained from Red Creek, Clay Basin, 6200 ft (Reynolds, 1966). Red Creek is a tributary of the Green River. However, Armstrong (1972) notes that in western Colorado, *Urocyon* is restricted to "rough country at moderate elevations." Thus, it is possible that *Urocyon* has reached the Bridger Basin by traveling overland rather than up the Green River.

Species not Affected by the Uintas

Classed as not being affected by the Uintas are 22 species of mammals placed in this category because they do not exhibit geographic variation in the region sufficient to warrant the recognition of subspeciation, and because they have ranges that extend throughout the Uinta Mountains region, including the adjacent basins (Table 7). It should be noted that not all the species are found in every habitat within the region. Nine of the 22 species (41%) are bats and should have sufficient dispersal capabilities to surmount or circumvent any barriers in the region. Seven of the species (32%) are carnivores and should not be trophically restricted to any particular plant community type as is sometimes the case with herbivores. The muskrat *(Ondatra zibethicus)* and otter *(Lutra canadensis)* are semiaquatic and can exploit the streams draining the Uintas as well as the numerous lakes at the higher elevations.

The porcupine *(Erethizon dorsatum)*, long-tailed vole *(Microtus longicaudus)*, and yellow-bellied marmot *(Marmota flaviventris)* have a considerable altitudinal distribution. Usually considered to be a boreo-montane species, the porcupine occasionally descends into the basins, possibly following riparian woodlands, and may be seen as road-killed specimens in sagebrush regions. *M. longicaudus* appears to be less restricted to mesic habitats than *M. montanus*. *Marmota* can be found wherever there are appropriate rocky habitats from the summit of the mountains to deep river canyons.

Although possessing less extensive altitudinal distributions than the preceeding species, Nuttall's cottontail *(Sylvilagus nuttalli)* and the white-tailed jackrabbit *(Lepus townsendii)* can be found in the sagebrush as well as montane regions.

TABLE 7. Species of Mammals not Affected by the Uintas
NOTE: Faunal element designations from Armstrong (1977).

Taxon	*Common Name*	*Faunal Element*
Chiroptera : Vespertilionidae		
Myotis lucifugus	Little brown bat	Widespread
Myotis evotis	Long-eared myotis	Chihuahuan
Myotis thysanodes	Fringed myotis	Chihuahuan
Lasionycteris noctovagans	Silver-haired bat	Widespread
Myotis volans	Long-legged myotis	Nevadan
Eptesicus fuscus	Big brown bat	Widespread
Lasiurus cinereus	Hoary bat	Widespread
Euderma maculatum	Spotted bat	Nevadan
Plecotus townsendii	Townsend's big-eared bat	Chihuahuan
Lagomorpha : Leporidae		
Sylvilagus nuttalli	Nuttall's cottontail	Nevadan
Lepus townsendii	White-tailed jackrabbit	Nevadan
Rodentia : Sciuridae		
Marmota flaviventris	Yellow-bellied marmot	Cordilleran
Rodentia : Cricetidae		
Microtus longicaudus	Long-tailed vole	Cordilleran
Ondatra zibethicus	Muskrat	Cordilleran
Rodentia : Erethizontidae		
Erethizon dorsatum	Porcupine	Cordilleran
Carnivora : Canidae		
Vulpes vulpes	Red fox	Widespread
Carnivora : Mustelidae		
Mustela erminea	Ermine	Boreo-cordilleran
Mustela frenata	Long-tailed weasel	Widespread
Mustela vison	Mink	Widespread
Taxidea taxus	Badger	Widespread
Spilogale putorius	Spotted skunk	Chihuahuan
Lutra canadensis	Otter	Widespread

Conclusion

The Uinta Mountains exert a considerable influence on the zoogeography of the mammals of this region of Utah. The effect is particularly noticeable upon the species comprising Armstrong's (1977) four semiarid and desert areographic faunal elements (Arizonan, Chihuahuan, Nevadan, and Yuman). For example, of the 27 species whose ranges are bounded by or excluded from the Uintas, 19 (70.4%) are members of these four faunal elements, which otherwise comprise only 41.5% (34 of 82) of the mammals of the Uinta Mountains region (Table 8). However, only 3 of 13 species having subspecies boundaries in the region are members of these four faunal elements (Table 8). This is attributable to the fact that many of the species have continuous distributions between the north and south sides of the Uintas via either the Green River or the desert/semidesert regions of western Colorado.

TABLE 8. Status of Species in Armstrong's (1977) Aerographic Faunal Elements Within the Uinta Mountains Region

	Zoogeographic Status in Uinta Mountains Region					
Faunal element	*Species w/ boundaries*	*Subspecies boundary*	*Excluded*	*Boreo-montane species*	*Green River*	*Not affected*
Cordilleran	3	4		7		4
Boreo-cordilleran		2		8		1
Chihuahuan	11	1	1		5	4
Arizonan	2					
Yuman	2				1	
Nevadan		2	3			4
Campestrian			2			
Bridgeran	1		1			
Widespread	1	4		1	1	9

As might be expected, members of the cordilleran and boreo-cordilleran faunal elements comprised the vast majority (94.1%) of the strictly boreo-montane species of the region (Table 8). Members of these two faunal elements are also well represented among the species having species or subspecies boundaries in the region, with 7 of 33 species so affected (Table 8).

The 16 species of widespread distributions were generally either not affected (9 species) or had species or subspecies boundaries (5 species) within the Uintas region (Table 8). Grassland species of the Bridgeran and Campestrian faunal regions were either excluded from (3 species) or bounded by (1 species) the Uintas (Table 8).

The fieldwork associated with this research added 1 new species, *Sorex nanus*, to the mammal fauna of the Uintas and added information on the distribution of 2 other species of shrews. The first *S. cinereus* from Uintah County, Utah, was taken during this study. Also, the failure to capture any *S. vagrans* helps to confirm that this species is excluded from the Uintas.

Acknowledgments

The following Shippensburg University students who worked as field technicians in the Uintas in 1976 and 1977 are acknowledged: Rick Bennett, Toni Bibb, Nancy Carpenter, John Hench, George Kirsch, Don Swigart, and Lynn Troutman. Andrew Langford, currently a graduate student at Utah State University, was the field technician during September 1976. Figure 1 was prepared by David Maxwell. My wife Carol, who was a member of the field crew in June 1976, has assisted in the analysis of data from the project. I also thank the personnel of the Utah Division of Wildlife Resources, the Wyoming Game and Fish Commission, and the U. S. Forest Service for their advice, assistance, and encouragement during our fieldwork in Utah and Wyoming. This research was supported by grants from the National Geographic Society.

REFERENCES

ANDERSON, S.
1959. Distribution, variation, and relationships of montane vole, *Microtus montanus.* Univ. Kansas Publ., Mus. Nat. Hist., vol. 9, pp. 415-511.

ARMSTRONG, D. M.
1971. Notes on variation in *Spermophilus tridecemlineatus* (Rodentia, Sciuridae) in Colorado and adjacent states, and description of a new subspecies. Journ. Mamm., vol. 52, pp. 528-536.
1972. Distribution of mammals in Colorado. Mono., Mus. Nat. Hist., Univ. Kansas, no. 3, pp. 1-415.
1977. Distributional patterns of mammals in Utah. Great Basin Nat., vol. 37, pp. 457-474.

ARMSTRONG, D. M., and JONES, J. K. JR.
1971. *Sorex merriami.* Mammalian Species, vol. 2, pp. 1-2.

BARBOUR, R. W., and DAVIS, W. H.
1969. Bats of America, 286 pp. Univ. Press of Kentucky, Lexington.

DEARDEN, B. L.
1967. Distribution and taxonomy of the mammals of Summit County, Utah, 175 pp. Unpublished Master's thesis, Univ. of Utah, Salt Lake City.

DURRANT, S. D.
1952. Mammals of Utah, taxonomy and distribution, 549 pp. Univ. Kansas Publ., Mus. Nat. Hist., vol. 6, pp. 1-549.

DURRANT, S. D., and CRANE, H. S.
1948. Three new beavers from Utah. Univ. Kansas Publ., Mus. Nat. Hist., vol. 1, pp. 407-417.

DURRANT, S. D., and DEAN, N. K.
1960. Mammals of Flaming Gorge Reservoir Basin. Pp. 210-243 *in* "Ecological Studies of the Flora and Fauna of the Flaming Gorge Reservoir Basin, Utah and Wyoming," S. Flowers et al., eds. Univ. Utah, Anthr. Pap. (Upper Colorado Series no. 3), no. 48, pp. 1-243.

FINDLEY, J. S.; HARRIS, A. H.; WILSON, D. E.; and JONES, C.
1975. Mammals of New Mexico, 360 pp. New Mexico Press, Albuquerque.
HAGMAIER, E. M.
1966. A numerical analysis of the distributional patterns of North American mammals. II. Re-evaluation of the provinces. Syst. Zool., vol. 15, pp. 279-299.
HALL, E. R., and KELSON, K. R.
1959. The mammals of North America. 2 vols., 1083 pp. Ronald Press, New York.
HENNINGS, D., and HOFFMANN, R. S.
1977. A review of the taxonomy of the *Sorex vagrans* species complex from western North America. Occ. Pap., Mus. Nat. Hist., Univ. Kansas, vol. 68, pp. 1-35.
HOFFMANN, R. S., and OWEN, J. G.
1980. *Sorex tenellus* and *Sorex nanus*. Mammalian Species, vol. 131, pp. 1-4.
KIRKLAND, G. L., Jr.
1981. The zoogeography of the mammals of the Uinta Mountains region. Southwestern Nat., vol. 26, pp. 325-339.
KRUTZSCH, P. H., and HEPPENSTALL, C. A.
1955. Additional distributional records of bats in Utah. Journ. Mamm., vol. 36, pp. 127-137.
LONG, C. A.
1965. The mammals of Wyoming. Univ. Kansas Publ., Mus. Nat. Hist., vol. 14, pp. 493-758.
REYNOLDS, R. N.
1966. Taxonomy and distribution of the mammals of Daggett County, Utah, 233 pp. Unpublished Master's Thesis, Univ. Utah, Salt Lake City.
SCHMIDLY, D. J.
1977. The mammals of Trans-Pecos Texas including Big Bend National Park and Guadalupe Mountains National Park, 225 pp. Texas A & M Univ. Press, College Station.
SVIHLA, R. D.
1931. Mammals of the Uinta Mountain region. Journ. Mamm., vol. 12, pp. 256-266.
1932. Ecological distribution of the mammals on the north slope of the Uinta Mountains. Ecol. Mongr., vol. 2, pp. 47-82.
UDVARDY, M.D.F.
1969. Dynamic zoogeography, 445 pp. Van Nostrand Reinhold Co., New York.

GORDON L. KIRKLAND, JR.

Atlas of Sky Overlay Maps (for the National Geographic Society–Palomar Observatory Sky Survey Photographs)

Grant Recipient: John D. Kraus, Department of Electrical Engineering, Ohio State University, Columbus, Ohio.[1]

Grant 1620: For preparing transparent overlay maps for the National Geographic Society–Palomar Observatory Sky Survey.

An atlas of transparent plastic overlay sky maps has been prepared for use with the sky photographs of the National Geographic Society–Palomar Observatory Sky Survey. The overlays provide the simplest and most comprehensive available means to identify the known astronomical objects appearing on the Sky Survey photographs. Approximately one-half million objects are shown, along with equatorial and galactic coordinates, precessional diagrams, and photograph defects.

Background

The series of astronomical photographs known as the National Geographic Society–Palomar Observatory Sky Survey Atlas (PSS) has become one of the most widely used basic references in astronomy. Use of the PSS to search for the optical counterparts of objects discovered at other than optical wavelengths (radio, x-ray, infrared, etc.) has become so widespread that the term "optical identification" is almost synonymous with inspecting the PSS at the position of the object. The PSS has also been used as source material for numerous surveys of objects of almost every type.

A summary of the background, techniques, and uses of the PSS is contained in *A User's Guide to the Palomar Sky Survey* (Lund and Dixon, 1973).

The major difficulty in using the PSS is that it is simply photographs. It contains no information to identify all the objects shown on the photographs. If one were to point to some small unusual object on a PSS print

[1] The grant was obtained by Professor Kraus to support a project organized and carried out by Dr. Robert S. Dixon, author of this report, who is Assistant Director, Ohio State University Radio Observatory, Columbus, Ohio.

and ask, "What is that?" it would be extremely difficult to answer. The PSS is analogous to an aerial photograph of the Earth. All the physical features are shown, but none of man's names, knowledge, or perspective are present. Just as aerial photographs are used most advantageously in conjunction with conventional maps that show place names, latitude and longitude, political boundaries, etc., so can the PSS be used most advantageously in conjunction with a similar means, such as overlay maps, indicating man's state of knowledge about the objects shown thereon.

The staff of the Ohio State University Radio Observatory had been optically identifying radio sources using the PSS for many years, by making small computer-drawn maps of the nearby Smithsonian Astrophysical Observatory Catalog (SAO) (Smithsonian Institution, 1966) stars and the desired radio source position on transparent plastic. This is bothersome, expensive, and good for only one object at a time. Even though we used the PSS many times, we found it difficult to obtain an intuitive perspective of the photographs' contents. Everyone has to figure out for himself where and what everything is on the prints. This is difficult, time-consuming, frustrating, and inefficient.

We decided to make a major effort to solve these problems once and for all by preparing a full-sized transparent overlay map for every NGS-Palomar print area. In the early 1970s, we began preparation of the *Master List of Non-Stellar Optical Astronomical Objects* (MOL, Dixon and Sonneborn, 1980)[2], a necessary prelude to the overlay map project. This reference work is an amalgamation of all 270 previously published catalogues of nonstellar objects of all types, including galaxies, clusters of galaxies, star clusters, nebulae of all types, supernova remnants, quasi-stellar objects, blue stellar objects, and others. It is the first complete listing of nonstellar objects since Dreyer (1962) completed his famous New General Catalog (NGC) and Index Catalog (IC) lists in 1908.

In 1974-1975 we sent letters to all owners of the PSS and to the directors of all observatories in the world inquiring as to their interest in having the overlays prepared. Hundreds of encouraging letters of support were received, so in 1975 funds were sought from the National Science Foundation and the National Geographic Society. Both agencies helped to support this project during the experimentation, computer program development, and prototype creation stages. Professor John Kraus also provided financial assistance. During the production, inspection, and publication stages, work was unpaid and done in the author's spare time.

Programs were written in Fortran to draw the overlays on a Versatec Electrostatic Plotter, having a resolution of 200 dots per inch. The plotter

[2] This reference work is commonly referred to by the acronym MOL (meaning Master Optical List, to distinguish it from the "Master List of Radio Sources" (Dixon, 1970) also prepared and maintained at our observatory).

FIGURE 1. Typical overlay being examined by the author.

is attached to an Amdahl 470 V6 computer (compatible with the IBM 370 series). Each facet of the overlays (e.g., stars, selected areas, right ascension/declination grids) was drawn by a separate Fortran subroutine. The entire program contains about 5000 statements and 35 subroutines. Great effort was expended to make the overlays easy to read and understand, at the cost of increased program complexity. The Versatec plotter output is 11 in. wide, so each overlay master had to be made in two pieces and later joined. The Versatec support software was modified to provide a 1-in. overlap between the two pieces to facilitate the joining operation. The joining was done very expertly by the printer, and the joint is invisible on the overlays. The printer then reproduced the master overlays very precisely onto transparent plastic sheets.

The plastic material used is dimensionally stable with temperature and humidity, and very resistant to mechanical stretching. All the printing is on the bottom surface, to avoid any parallax effects and to provide greater protection. The ink is tenacious and requires determined effort with a metal tool to scrape off. A user may add his private markings to the top surface of the maps, using water-soluble ink, and later wipe them off with a damp cloth, without damaging the overlay. The overall dimensions of the maps are the same as the NGS-Palomar prints (14 x 17 in.), so they may be stored directly with the prints, if desired.

A valuable feature of the overlays is that they are suitable for separate use as detailed sky maps. Since all published catalogues of nonstellar objects have been included, the overlays contain all of the different designations that have been assigned by various authors to the same objects. There are a total of 1037 overlays, one for each of the NGS-Palomar print areas, including the Whiteoak southern extension. When placed in a pile, a set of overlays is about 8 in. thick and weighs 80 lb.

The intended audience for these overlay maps is not only professional astronomers, but students, scientists, and engineers from any fields that have occasion to refer to the NGS-Palomar prints. Therefore, some things are shown on the maps that may be deemed elementary by some, but useful by others.

Since 1981 the overlay maps have been manufactured and distributed worldwide at a nonprofit cost of $725 per set; about 250 sets have been distributed. Figure 1 shows a typical overlay being examined by the author.

Major Contents of the Overlays

Stars

The quarter-million stars contained in the SAO are shown on the overlay maps as plus signs of varying size (Fig. 2). The height of the plus sign is proportional to the brightness of the star. The height of the plus sign is *not* intended to indicate the size of the star image on the print. Each star is labeled with its six-digit SAO number, with no alphabetical prefix. The lack of prefix serves to distinguish star labels from those used to designate nonstellar objects, all of which have alphabetical prefixes. Stars that have proper names (e.g., Polaris) are labeled with those names in addition to their SAO star numbers.

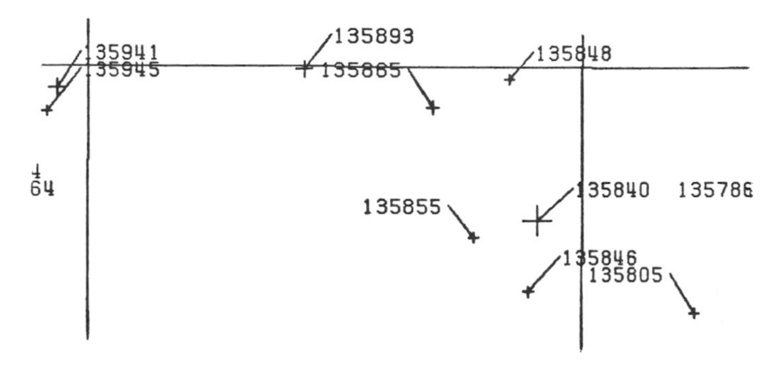

FIGURE 2. Method of showing SAO stars on overlay maps.

NONSTELLAR OBJECTS

The 200,000 nonstellar objects contained in the MOL are shown on the overlay maps by pictorial symbols representing the different types of objects. The symbols are designed to suggest the object they represent, yet be readable at a very small size. The marginal notes contain a customized table explaining the meaning of each of the symbols used on that specific overlay.

GALAXIES are depicted by the symbol shown in Figure 3a.

NEBULAE are depicted by a mnemonic alphabetical symbol (Fig. 3b) in those cases where the original catalogue did not specify what type of nebula the object is. When the nebula-type information is available, more illustrative symbols are used. *Reflection nebulae* are depicted by an open diamond symbol (Fig. 3c) suggestive of a reflecting mirror. *Dark nebulae* are depicted by a filled diamond symbol (Fig. 3d) suggestive of a foreground screen. *Planetary nebulae* are depicted by a circle with a dot at the center (Fig. 3e) suggestive of the actual star and shell components of the nebula. *Supernova remnants* are depicted as a series of lines radiating from a point (Fig. 3f) suggestive of their original explosion. *H II regions* are depicted by a mnemonic composite alphabetical symbol (Fig. 3g).

STARLIKE OBJECTS are depicted by mnemonic alphabetical symbols suggestive of their types, since their physical structures are not condu-

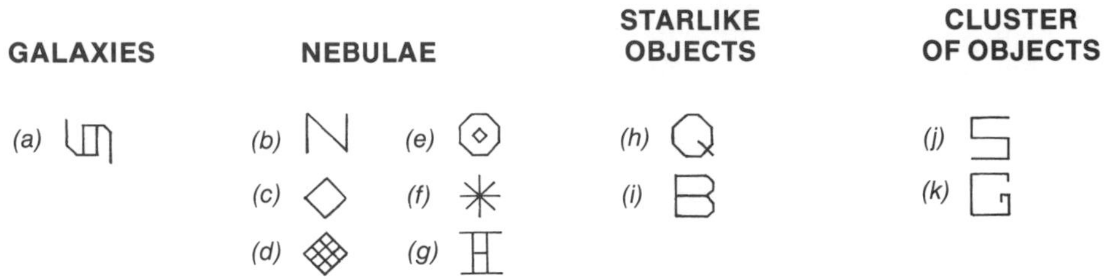

FIGURE 3. Symbols used to show galaxies (a), nebulae (b-g), starlike objects (h,i), and clusters of objects (j,k) on overlay map.

cive to pictorial representation. *Quasi-stellar objects* are shown by the symbol in Figure 3h, and *blue objects* are shown by the symbol in Figure 3i.

CLUSTERS OF OBJECTS are depicted by mnemonic alphabetical symbols suggestive of their types, since there is no obvious way to relate them symbolically to the symbols used to depict their individual components. *Star clusters* are shown by the symbol in Figure 3j, and *galaxy clusters* are shown by the symbol in Figure 3k. Since galaxy clusters are very numerous, large, and irregularly shaped, their extents cannot be totally portrayed by a simple symbol. The *Zwicky Catalog of Galaxies and Clusters of Galaxies* (Zwicky, 1961) provides maps of the actual boundaries of the galaxy clusters. These maps were converted to computer-readable form by us, using a Bendix digitizer, and transformed to the scale of the overlays. The Zwicky galaxy cluster boundaries are shown on the overlay maps as strings of caret symbols (Fig. 4). One of the carets of each cluster is labeled with its running cluster number as assigned by Zwicky.

POPULAR NAMES. A small number of nonstellar objects have popular names that are in common use (e.g., Andromeda Nebula). These names are shown on the overlay maps in addition to the astronomical names.

ANGULAR DIAMETERS. The size of the symbol used for each nonstellar object is the same as the catalogued angular diameter of that object, subject to the following conventions: (1) For objects whose linear diameter on the prints is less than 1.5 mm, a pictorial symbol of size 1.5 mm is shown, because smaller symbols would be unreadable. (2) For objects whose linear diameter lies between 1.5 and 25 mm, the size of the pictorial symbol is the same as the angular diameter of the object. (3) For objects whose linear diameter lies between 25 and 150 mm, a circle of the proper size centered on the object position is shown rather than a symbol, since very large pictorial symbols do not clearly encompass the sky coverage of the objects. An example of this is given in Figure 5.

It must be remembered that the size of the symbols for nonstellar objects indicates the size of the object, in contrast to stars where the size of

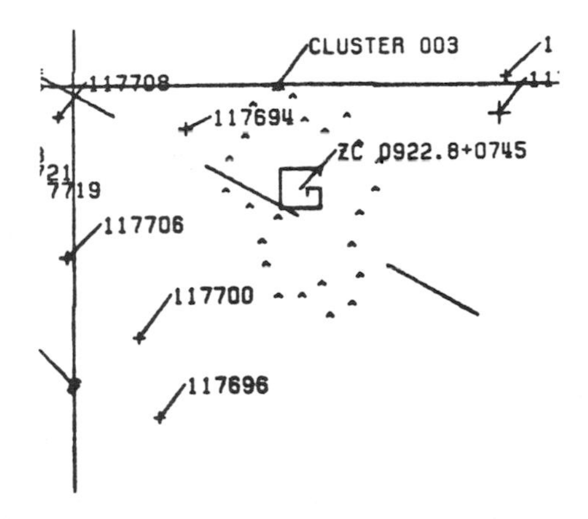

FIGURE 4. Method of showing Zwicky galaxy cluster boundaries.

the symbols indicates the brightness of the object. Since the MOL contains all of the original catalogues, many nonstellar objects are shown more than once, under different names. This allows one to learn all the aliases for a given object, and to obtain more information about it by tracking the names backward through the MOL to the original catalogues.

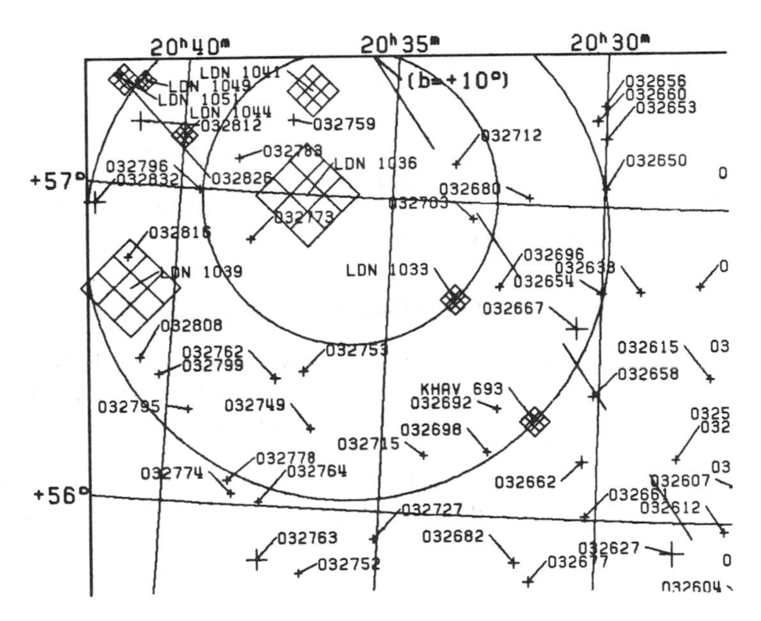

FIGURE 5. Method of showing angular diameter of nonstellar objects.

Omitted Nonstellar Objects. On a small fraction of the NGS-Palomar prints, the number of catalogued nonstellar objects is so large that it is impossible to include all of them on the overlay maps in any readable form. Such an example is shown in Figure 6. To avoid this overcrowding problem, several steps were taken under the guiding philosophy that it is better to have a reasonable amount of readable information rather than a lot of unreadable information. Each overcrowded map was considered individually. Each specific catalogue of nonstellar objects was evaluated for its contribution to the overcrowding. If the overcrowding could be eliminated by omitting the names of the objects in one or more catalogues, but leaving in the pictorial symbols, this was done. In more severe cases, the symbols themselves also had to be omitted. Each affected overlay map was made over and over, omitting progressively larger numbers of names and/or object symbols, until the level of readability was judged to be acceptable, as in Figure 7.

Solar-system Objects

The planets Neptune and Pluto and the recently discovered planet-like object Chiron appear on the NGS-Palomar prints. Neptune and Pluto are depicted on the overlays by their traditional symbols (Figs. 8a and b), and Chiron by the mnemonic symbol Chi (Fig. 8c).

Selected Areas

In 1906, J. C. Kapteyn issued his *Plan of Selected Areas* in which he delineated 252 small areas of the sky. His purpose in doing this was to concentrate the efforts of many astronomers on these specific areas, as opposed to the entire sky, and thereby enable the results of diverse types of observations to be combined and yield greater understanding of the structure of the universe. The selected areas are depicted on the overlays by dashed lines delineating their borders.

Coordinate Grids

A number of different coordinate grids and points are shown on the overlays. Each grid has a different line style, and each style is different from any other lines used on the overlays (such as the selected areas), so no confusion can result.

The 1950.0 right ascension/declination grid is shown as solid lines. The identifying labels for right ascension/declination grid are outside the overlay area.

The galactic coordinate grid lines are long dashes, and are labeled inside the overlay boundary at each intersection with the overlay boundary.

The 1950.0 ecliptic is shown on those overlays where it is present.

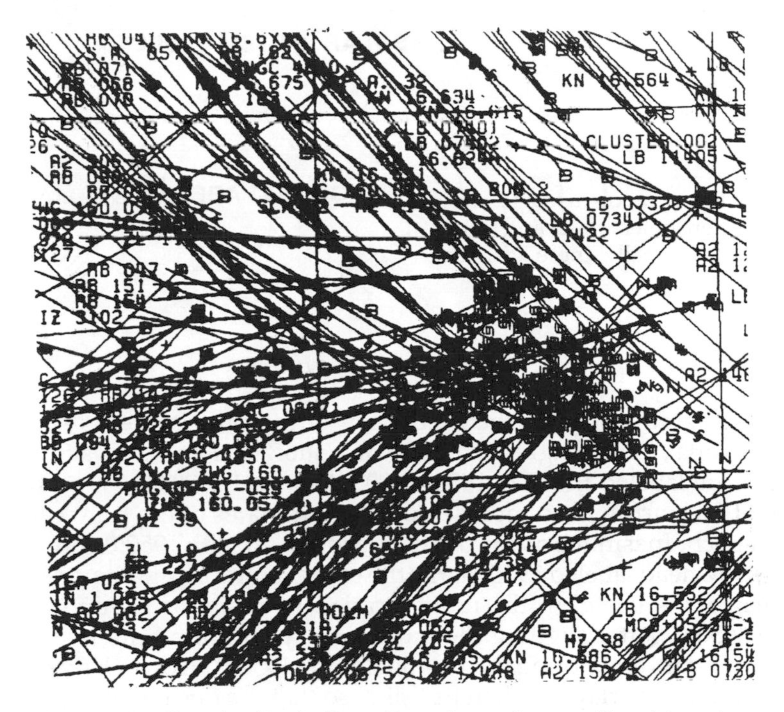

FIGURE 6. Result of including all catalogued nonstellar objects in a crowded region on overlay (compare with Fig. 7).

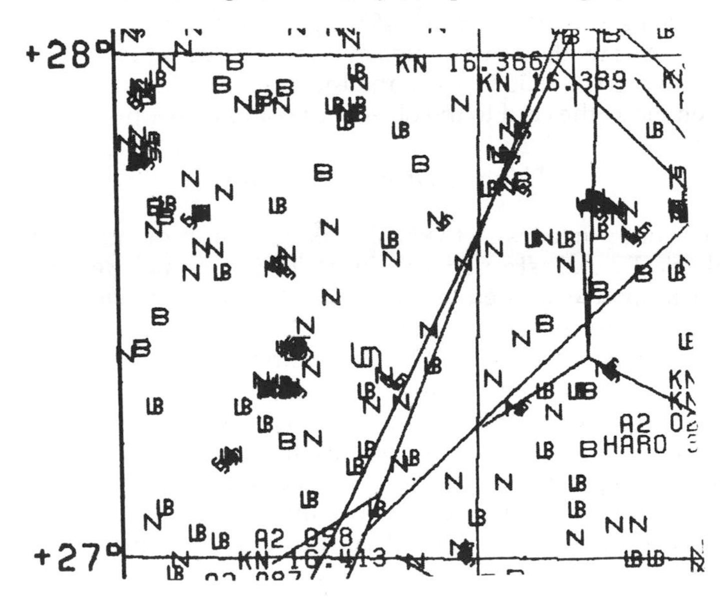

FIGURE 7. Typical result of selective omission of names and symbols to promote readability of the overlay.

SOLAR SYSTEM OBJECTS

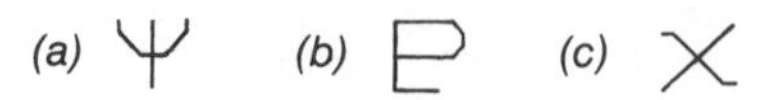

THINGS THAT ARE NOT REALLY THERE

(d) ╳ (e) + (f)

FIGURE 8. Symbols used to show solar system objects (a-c) and things that are not really there (d-f, see text).

Precessional Diagrams

A diagram showing the precession of the print center is shown on each overlay. The diagram consists of a short line and four arrowheads which are labeled EPOCH 1850, 1900, 1950, and 2000 (Fig. 9). The position of each arrowhead represents the coordinates of the print center for that epoch. Inasmuch as the overlays are drawn with 1950.0 coordinates, the arrowhead labeled 1950 marks the center of the print. The precessional diagram is useful in the rapid location of positions for epochs other than 1950.0. After aligning the transparency with the print by means of the SAO stars and noting the position of the 1950.0 arrow relative to nearby stars, the overlay can then be "slid" so that the desired epoch is above the point where the 1950.0 arrow previously was. The right ascension-/declination grid now closely approximates the grid for the desired epoch and can be used to plot or read off the positions of objects in that epoch. An alternative method that avoids moving the overlay is to transcribe the offset between the 1950.0 arrow and the desired epoch onto a small card, and then move the card to the object or position to be precessed.

Things That Are not Really There

Some of the images on the NGS-Palomar prints do not correspond to any physically real astronomical object. They are small defects resulting from basically two different mechanisms. One type of defect is caused by the optical design of the Schmidt telescope. This results in a spurious star image being recorded on the film symmetrically, opposite the plate center from the correct star image. These spurious images are called ghost images, and occur for virtually all bright stars. Each of the prints was manually inspected and all visible ghost images were catalogued.

Ghost images are depicted on the overlay maps by a symbol (Fig. 8d) to indicate that they are conceptually similar to stars, for which the similar symbol (Fig. 8e) is used, but that they are to be ignored or "crossed out."

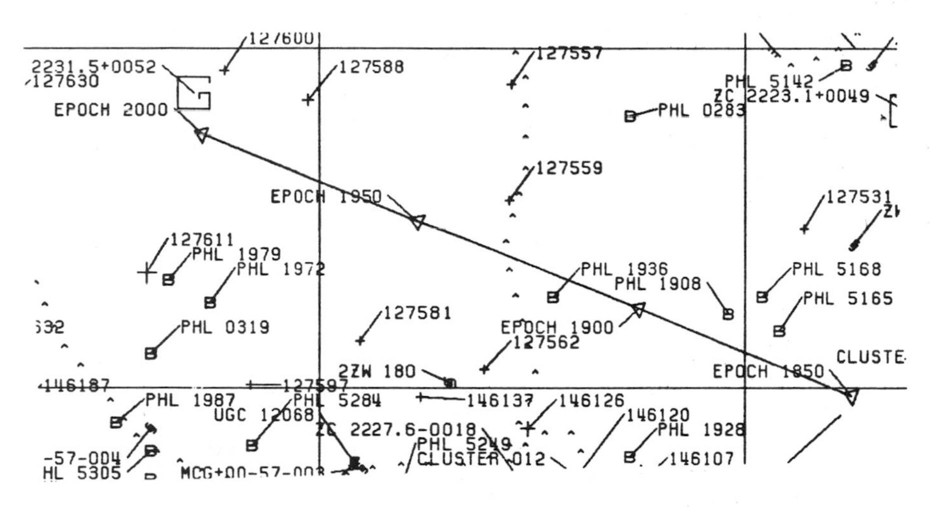

FIGURE 9. Method of showing precession of print center on overlay.

The second type of defect is caused by random imperfections in the film emulsion or by physical damage (scratches, etc.) that occurred in the development or duplication of the prints. These are referred to as print defects. As with the ghost images, each of the prints was manually inspected and all visible print defects catalogued. Print defects are depicted on the overlay maps by a symbol (Fig. 8f), to indicate that they are to be ignored, or "blanked out."

Marginal Notes

Each overlay contains a detailed set of customized marginal notes. Among other things, the following basic information is provided:

- PSS (or Whiteoak Extension) print number and the nominal coordinates of the print center.
- Published print center and actual print center positions.
- Galactic coordinates of the overlay center.
- Exposure data describing when and how the original photograph was taken.
- The number of unlabeled or omitted nonstellar objects.
- The names and positions of specially named objects.
- The names, positions, and sizes of Kapteyn's selected areas.
- The Zwicky field identification and the number of clusters of galaxies.
- The X-Y position (in mm from the lower left corner) of ghost images and plate defects on the print.

- A table summarizing the number of each type of symbol actually plotted on the overlay.
- A stellar magnitude symbol size table, at one- magnitude intervals.
- Detailed right ascension/declination interpolation scales with the right ascension scales customized to the declinations of the overlay center, top and bottom.

Scaling

An investigation was conducted to determine the appropriate mathematical transformation of the catalogued object positions into plotted X-Y coordinates on the overlays. The equations adopted are:

$$X = x + \frac{x\,(x^2 + y^2)}{6}\, S_x \qquad\qquad Y = y + \frac{y\,(x^2 + y^2)}{6}\, S_y$$

where—

$$\begin{aligned} x &= -\cos(\delta)\sin(\delta - A) \\ y &= \sin(\alpha - D) + \cos(\delta)\sin(D)\,(1 - \cos(\alpha - A) \\ \alpha, \delta &= \text{equatorial coordinates (radians) of object} \\ A, D &= \text{equatorial coordinates (radians) of overlay center} \\ S_x, S_y &= \text{scale factors} \end{aligned}$$

Second, a sample of about a dozen PSS prints was examined to determine the X and Y plate scales. The mean values are 67.53 arc sec/mm for X and 67.13 arc sec/mm for Y. The scaling used for the overlays generally maps the observed individual print scales to within 1 mm across the width of the print, i.e., about 0.3 percent. Shrinkage and expansion of the paper prints, even among samples of the same field from the same production batch, were found to be as much as 1 mm across the width of the print. Therefore, it is not necessary to map the coordinate field more accurately.

Labeling

Perhaps the most difficult aspect of this project was one not immediately obvious to a user of the overlays. This has to do with attaching a name label to each of the objects shown. The correct positions and symbols for the objects themselves can be computed in a straightforward way, since there is no choice as to position and there is generally not a great deal of overcrowding. The name labels, however, generally take up considerably more space than the objects themselves, and must be positioned so as to avoid obliterating other name labels or objects. While it is fairly easy for a human to position these labels so the names do not overlap, it is not easy to instruct a computer to do so. A very complex iterative algorithm had to be developed to ensure that nonoverlapping positions were chosen, and furthermore that the labels were positioned with maximum clarity and minimum clutter.

Future Projects

Several people have suggested that we prepare a similar set of overlay maps for the Southern Sky Survey. The computer programs and production techniques already developed could be used with only minor modifications. If a significant number of people write to us stating that they would be interested in obtaining such an overlay set, we will seriously consider doing so.

Acknowledgments

The author wishes to acknowledge the significant participation of Paul Schmidtke and Mirjana Gearhart during the initial preparation phase of this work. The true craftsmanship shown by the Ohio Printing Company in preparing the overlays is deserving of particular praise.

REFERENCES

DIXON, ROBERT S.
1970. A master list of radio sources. Astrophysical Journal, Supplement Series, vol. 20, nr. 180.

DIXON, ROBERT S., and SONNEBORN, George
1980. A master list of non-stellar optical astronomical objects. Book form by The Ohio State University Press, computer readable form by the Ohio State University Radio Observatory.

DREYER, J.L.E.
1962. New general catalog, 1888. Index catalog, 1895. Second index catalog, 1908. Royal Astronomical Society, London (reprinted).

KAPTEYN, J. C.
1906. Plan of selected areas. Astronomical Laboratory at Gronigen.

LUND, JAMES M., and DIXON, ROBERT S.
1973. A user's guide to the Palomar sky survey. Publications of the Astronomical Society of the Pacific, vol. 85, p. 230.

Smithsonian Institution
1966. Smithsonian Astrophysical Observatory catalog of stars. Smithsonian Institution Press, Washington, D. C.

ZWICKY, F.
1961-1968. Zwicky catalog of galaxies and clusters of galaxies. California Institute of Technology Press, 6 vol.

ROBERT S. DIXON

Geographical Variation in the Song of the Great Tit *(Parus major)* in Relation to Ecological Factors

Grant Recipients: John R. Krebs, Edward Grey Institute of Field Ornithology, Oxford, England, and Malcolm L. Hunter, Jr., School of Forest Resources, University of Maine, Orono, Maine.

Grants 1670, 1844: In support of research on geographical variation in bird song.

In this report we describe a study of large-scale geographical variations in the song of the Great Tit, in particular with the idea that the variation might be correlated with ecological factors such as habitat types and avian community. Chappius (1971) and Morton (1975) independently showed that species living below the canopy in tropical forests (in Africa and Central America, respectively) tend to have lower-pitched songs with more pure tones than species living in nearby open habitats such as savannah. Both authors suggested that forest birds sing lower-pitched songs because high-frequency sounds are more heavily attenuated in dense than in open habitats, and Morton went further in proposing on the basis of attenuation tests that low-frequency sounds of the type used by forest birds carry especially well in this habitat because of a "frequency window." This latter idea has been questioned by subsequent workers (Marten and Marler, 1977; Marten et al., 1977).

Nottebohm (1975) applied Morton's and Chappius's ideas to intraspecific song variation, showing that geographical variations in the song of the Chingolo *(Zonotrichia capensis)* throughout the South American subcontinent could in part be related to ecological factors. For example, Chingolos in forested habitats tend to have slower trills than those in open areas, and the maximum frequency of songs tended to be higher nearer the tropics. The exact reasons for these correlations are not clear, but they suggest that ecological factors somehow influence geographical variation in songs.

In our study we recorded the territorial songs (Krebs, 1977) of male Great Tits in two different habitat types, open woodland or parkland and dense forest. We visited five widely-separated places containing extensive forest habitat, and five places with extensive woodland or parkland areas. We chose study sites that contained relatively large and homogeneous tracts of habitat so that the possible complications arising from individuals moving between habitat types within a lifetime were minimized. Our prediction was that if habitat type influences song structure, perhaps through differences in acoustic transmission properties, birds living in dense forests should have similarities in song structure regardless of geographical location, and similarly woodland birds should converge on a different song pattern. We also measured in each habitat type a number of ecological factors we thought likely to be related to song structure.

Methods

Study Areas. Data were obtained from 10 areas which could be separated into two major habitats: dense forests in Sweden, Norway, Poland, New Forest in southern England, and the Middle Atlas Mountains of Morocco; and open woodlands and parks in Greece, Spain, Iran, Oxfordshire (England), and coastal Morocco.

Dense forests were characterized by a well-developed understory and an overstory that ranged from 10 to 26 m. The density of trees greater than 10 cm in diameter at breast height (dbh) varied from about 125 to 750/ha. Deciduous trees dominated the New Forest and Moroccan sites; the Norwegian and Swedish forests were primarily coniferous with a strong admixture of deciduous trees; the Polish sites ranged from nearly pure coniferous to nearly pure deciduous. Work was carried out before or just at the beginning of deciduous leaf emergence. All the forests were in a relatively natural state, having experienced little or no recent logging; one Swedish site and most of the Polish sites were virgin forest.

Most of the woodlands had virtually no understory and the largest trees, which ranged from 4 to 10 m, were usually too widely spaced to form an overstory canopy. The Oxfordshire sites were an exception to this generalization; they often contained quite large trees ($\bar{x}$ = 13 m) clumped into hedgerows with wide intervening spaces. Density varied from only 14 to 254 trees/ha. Oak trees dominated the Iranian, Spanish, and Moroccan sites, while in Greece olive trees were most common. Both the oak and olive are evergreen, and these were fully leaved during our studies. The Oxfordshire sites contained a variety of tree species, some of which were in leaf during the study. Most of the woodland sites were grazed by livestock, thus accounting for the scarcity of smaller trees and shrubs. Many of the olive groves were heavily managed for olive production; this often involved periodic ploughing.

Recording Songs. The songs of territorial male Great Tits were recorded in each study area between January and May in either 1976, 1977, or 1978. Almost all the recordings were made from within 25 m of the bird. Spain was visited in both 1976 and 1977 but different sites were used.

Often it proved expedient to stimulate the birds to sing by broadcasting a series of Great Tit songs recorded on a tape loop. The tapes were recorded in Wytham Woods, England; a different series was used each year and none was used in Spain in 1976. When a tit was recorded it was noted whether it had sung spontaneously or in response to a broadcast; approximately 55% of the songs were responses. Spontaneous songs were compared with response songs using the parameters described below (see Results). In only one case was there a significant difference between the spontaneous and response samples.[1] Because the overall differences were not significant and there was also no pattern to the differences, spontaneous and response songs were lumped in subsequent analyses. Broadcasting songs was a particularly useful method of stimulating a bird to sing more than one type of song.

Approximately a quarter of the birds sang more than one type of song; the maximum repertoire size recorded was four songs. We have considered different song types recorded from the same individual to be different observations. The validity of this assumption was supported by repeating the statistical analyses using just the first song recorded for each individual. The results were identical to those for the full sample except for minor differences involving a timing parameter. (The variation among locations for the inter-song–phrase interval became insignificant, thus causing the between-habitat variation to become significant.)

Neighboring birds often share song types, which raises the possibility that recordings of the same song type sung by different birds within the small locality should not be treated as independent observations. However, we do not know if neighbors all acquire their shared songs from a single common source, and our samples from each site involved large numbers of individuals spread over a wide area, so that we felt justified in treating each recording of a song type as an independent observation.

Song Analysis. The songs were analyzed with a Kay Electric Company Type 6061B sonograph using the FL-1 linear scale and narrow filter band settings. To eliminate excessive background noise they were first passed through a Kemo Type FOF/3 dual variable active filter set to filter out sounds below 2500 Hz. We were careful to standardize the reproduce and mark level settings on the sonograph to minimize variations in the

---

[1] In Spain the frequency range of spontaneous songs was lower than that of response songs.

production of sonograms, which could have affected our measurements of frequency.

Five main song parameters were measured: minimum frequency, maximum frequency, frequency range, duration of song phrase, and interval between phrases. A sixth parameter was calculated: the combined length of the song-phrase duration and inter-phrase pause. This parameter is a reciprocal expression of the repetition rate, i.e., the number of phrases per unit time.

Another set of parameters was derived from the notes by measuring their individual minimum, maximum, and range of frequency, their duration, and the interval between them and the following note.

Vegetation Sampling. Vegetation plots were selected at random or located on the recording point of attenuation tests (see below). The number, species, and height of all large (10-cm-dbh) trees were recorded in a 15-m radius. Small trees (dbh 2.5 x 10 cm) were identified and counted on an inner circle of 10-m radius. Mean large tree crown volume was estimated by assuming the trees to be cylinders with a radius equal to one quarter the measured mean height. Small tree crown volumes were estimated by assuming their height and radius to be half the respective values for large trees. An index of the total tree crown volume per hectare was constructed by multiplying the density of large trees and small trees by their respective volume estimates.

$$\text{Index} = h\,([\tfrac{1}{4}h]^2)d_L + \tfrac{1}{2}h([\tfrac{1}{8}h]^2)d_S$$

where h = mean height of large trees
d_L = large trees/ha
d_S = small trees/ha

Attenuation Tests. We attempted to measure the attenuation characteristics of forest and woodland habitats by broadcasting and recording a tape in each habitat. The tape was composed of three groups of sounds: the Great Tit song, pure electronic sounds, and modulated sounds.

The recordings were analyzed with a signal analysis computer, a Plurimat S. Large fluctuations in the signal power and technical difficulties made it infeasible to analyze the attenuation properties of the individual sounds on the recording as we had originally intended. Instead, we integrated the entire output of each tape into a single power-versus-frequency spectrum.

To compare the forest and woodland spectra we divided the raw woodland data by the raw forest data to get a power ratio.

Territory Size. We estimated the density of Great Tit territories while recording songs by judging the distance from one singing male to the next. On some sites this inter-bird interval was estimated by dividing the distance walked while recording by the number of birds recorded. On two sites both methods were used; the results were not significantly different. These data were not obtained for Norway, but because of the great similarity of the habitats and the geographic proximity, the data from Sweden were used for Norway.

Avian Song Community. We attempted to characterize the avian song community in each study area. In Spain, Greece, Morocco, and Poland, we gathered systematic data by listening to the bird community for several 6-min periods during the hour following sunrise. All the species heard during the first 10 sec of each of the 6 min were recorded. We eliminated those species whose frequency range did not overlap significantly with the Great Tit range, e.g., Hoopoe (*Upupa epops* L.) and Tree Creeper (*Certhia brachydactyla* Brehm.). From the remaining data the diversity of the song community was estimated by noting the number of different species heard during the 6 min. The abundance of song was estimated by totaling the number of species heard during each of the six 10-sec intervals. From these data, casual observations at other sites, listening to the background noise on the Great Tit recordings, and interviews with local ornithologists, we estimated the number of species of common singers for each of the eight areas. These numbers are an estimate of the number of species that sing frequently in the relevant habitat at the relevant time of day and year.

Other Measurements. The perch height of birds that sang spontaneously was recorded, as well as the height of the perch tree. Data on mean minimum and maximum temperature and relative humidity at dawn in April were obtained for each study area from records of nearby meteorological stations (Meteorological Office, 1958, 1972). The altitude to the nearest 100 m was obtained for each area from topographical maps. Data on the body size of male Great Tits from each area were taken from Snow (1953) and Garnett (1976).

Results

Song Parameters. A total of 759 different songs was recorded from 507 birds. We used nested analysis of variance to analyze the following parameters: maximum and minimum frequency, frequency range of songs, frequency range of notes, and number of notes per song phrase. We chose these parameters as the ones most likely to be relevant to the acoustic attenuation hypothesis. The data were structured as follows: 2 groups for the habitats; 10 subgroups, 1 for each area; and individual observations for each song phrase or note. We used countries instead of recording sites as subgroups because in some countries the recording sites were not dispersed enough to represent separate populations.

Three of the four song parameters show a clear dichotomy between the mean values obtained for populations living in woodlands and those in forests.

Table 1 shows the striking convergence of songs from widely separated countries into two groups: woodland and forest. The former group is characterized by songs with a higher maximum frequency, greater frequency range, and greater number of notes per song. The following sections describe some of the physical and biological features of these areas which may have led to this convergence, and to the differences between habitats.

Habitat Parameters. The most obvious difference between the environments inhabited by woodland and forest Great Tits is the vegetation itself. Small, sparsely distributed trees are characteristic of the woodland sites, and the closed canopy formed by many tall trees with an understory of smaller trees is typical in a forest habitat.

Woodlands tend to be farther south than forests, with the exceptions of English park and hedgerow and Moroccan forest, and this is reflected in warmer temperatures as measured by average daily minima and maxima for April. Data on altitude and relative humidity show no obvious trends separating the two habitat types.

Body Size. Great Tits from two of the southern woodland areas tend to be smaller, but there is no consistent difference in the size of forest and woodland Great Tits. There is also no pattern corresponding with the delineation of the Great Tits into subspecies. The British and Iranian samples are from *Parus Major newtoni* Prazak and *P. m. blandfordi* Prazak, respectively; all the others are from *P. m. major* L. (Snow, 1967).

Territory Size. Males hold larger territories in forests than in woodlands, suggesting that the overall density of Great Tits, including females and nonterritorial males, may be greater in woodlands.

Avian Song Community. For each of the study areas we directly estimated or recorded the number of other species of birds that could be heard singing regularly during the period of our observation. There is, on average, a greater diversity of songsters in the forests. Two particular points are noteworthy: With the exception of the Blue Tit, other tit species were found mainly in the forest sites, and there seem to be more thrushes (*Turdus* sp.) in the forests.

In three countries we made two quantitative measures of the amount of singing: the number of species and the number of songs heard per 6-min listening period (see Methods). These data confirm that there tend to be more species singing at any one time in forests than in woodlands; however, they do not indicate any differences in the total number of songs produced.

TABLE 1. Summary of Results of Measurements from Sonograms. Values Shown Are Means ± S.E. The ANOVA Refers to a One-way Nested Analysis of Variance.

	Woodland						Forest						ANOVA	
	Spain	*Iran*	*Greece*	*England*	*Morocco*	*Mean*	*Sweden*	*Norway*	*Poland*	*England*	*Morocco*	*Mean*	*Between habitats*	*Among locations*
No. songs	111	121	94	54	84	464	67	30	102	36	60	295		
Maximum frequency (kHz)	6.46 ±0.11	6.45 ±0.10	6.48 ±0.12	6.5 ±0.15	6.68 ±0.13	6.51 ±0.05	5.56 ±0.09	5.75 ±0.17	5.81 ±0.09	5.49 ±0.18	5.99 ±0.11	5.75 ±0.05	70.29 p<0.001	1.35 N.S.
Minimum frequency (kHz)	3.36 ±0.05	3.39 ±0.04	3.59 ±0.05	3.18 ±0.06	3.29 ±0.06	3.38 ±0.02	3.77 ±0.05	3.44 ±0.09	3.53 ±0.04	3.37 ±0.10	3.25 ±0.06	3.50 ±0.03	1.26 N.S.	8.98 p<0.001
Frequency range (KHz)	3.09 ±0.11	3.06 ±0.10	2.89 ±0.12	3.33 ±0.17	3.40 ±0.15	3.13 ±0.05	1.79 ±0.08	2.31 ±0.18	2.27 ±0.09	2.12 ±0.14	2.74 ±0.12	2.25 ±0.05	25.79 p<0.001	4.56 p<0.01
No. notes per song response	4.0 ±0.2	3.1 ±0.1	3.0 ±0.2	3.0 ±0.2	3.1 ±0.1	3.3 ±0.1	2.3 ±0.1	2.8 ±0.2	2.7 ±0.1	2.4 ±0.1	2.6 ±0.1	2.6 ±0.1	8.95 p<0.01	6.35 p<0.001
No. notes	446	379	283	162	260	1530	155	83	275	85	156	754		
Frequency range of notes (kHz)	0.78 ±0.04	0.78 ±0.04	0.85 ±0.04	0.97 ±0.04	0.76 ±0.05	0.81 ±0.02	0.60 ±0.05	0.69 ±0.07	0.73 ±0.04	0.70 ±0.08	0.98 ±0.05	0.74 ±0.03	1.19 N.S.	4.50 p<0.01

Perch Heights. The heights at which birds sing might be an important factor affecting acoustic attenuation (Marten and Marler, 1977). Forest Great Tits sing from much higher perches than woodland birds.

Attenuation Tests. The ratio of power spectra for the two habitats shows that throughout most of the frequency range used by Great Tits, the forest signal is slightly stronger, i.e., less attenuated. Above 5.6 kHz, however, the woodland spectrum is two or three times more powerful than the forest spectrum. This is the frequency zone in which woodland Great Tits sing about twice as often as forest birds.

Multiple Regression. We have shown that our woodland and forest sites differed with respect to a number of ecological variables. In order to try and assess the relative importance of each variable in predicting the differences between Great Tit songs in the two habitats, we did a stepwise multiple regression, using as dependent variables maximum frequency, frequency range, and number of notes per song. We used the following independent variables: latitude, longitude, tree-crown volume index (converted to log values twice because of the approximately hundredfold difference between forest and woodlands), wing length, number of other bird species commonly singing, average distance between singing males, altitude, temperature, and humidity. All the independent variables were average values for each study area and hence the regression is essentially based on just 10 points. Moreover, the independent variables were often closely correlated with one another, e.g., temperature was strongly correlated with latitude. Bearing in mind these reservations, the results were as follows. For maximum frequency the best three predictors (all significant) were, in order, temperature (positive correlation), tree density (negative correlation), and territory size (negative correlation). Territory size, temperature, and altitude were the best three predictors of frequency range (though only the first two were significant). Finally, the number of notes per phrase was best predicted by territory size, followed by tree density and relative humidity, the first two being statistically significant.

These results as a whole suggest that tree density and territory size are important in influencing the differences in song structure between habitats. The temperature differences between areas that we observed are sufficient to cause only a 1 or 2% change in the velocity of sound (sound travels 61 cm/sec slower for each degree Centigrade drop in temperature), so that if the birds were compensating for increases in temperature by increasing frequency to keep wavelength constant, the change in maximum frequency needed would be much smaller than that observed. Thus simple temperature effects on the velocity of sound could not account for the observed differences between habitats, and temperature is probably a good predictor in the multiple regressions because of its close correlation (about 0.7) with both tree density and territory size.

Discussion

Our results show a clear dichotomy between woodland and forest Great Tit songs: The woodland songs have a higher maximum frequency, a greater frequency range on song phrases (and perhaps notes), and more notes per song phrase. It is particularly striking that birds living in widely separated areas have converged on a similar song structure characteristic of their particular habitat: For example the Great Tits living in Oxfordshire have songs more similar in maximum frequency to those sung in Iran, 5000 km away, than to the songs used in the New Forest less than 100 km distant.

We suggest that the differences between forest and woodland songs can be at least partly explained by the idea that forest songs are better adapted for transmission through denser vegetation and over greater distances. If forest songs have better carrying properties, why are they not used also by woodland birds? It could conceivably be that the higher frequencies and greater number of notes per song phrase make woodland songs carry better in open areas, but this seems unlikely. Instead, we suggest a counteradvantage favoring higher frequencies or greater complexity in woodlands (these hypothetical advantages presumably operate in forests but are dominated by transmission needs). One possibility is that higher-frequency songs, because they do not carry so far, render the woodland birds less likely to be detected by predators. It seems unlikely that woodland songs are energetically cheaper to produce. They span a wider frequency range than forest songs and are thus more likely to diverge from the optimal reverberation frequency of the syringeal membrane. Finally it is possible that variability itself is advantageous, because it improves the effectiveness of song in mate attraction (Kroodsma, 1976) or territorial defense (Krebs et al., 1978) and that the wider frequency range and greater number of notes of woodland songs is an effect of this advantage.

Acknowledgments

We thank Jon Erichsen, Richard Cowie, Ruth Ashcroft, and Pete McGregor for help in recording songs, and Nick Davies, Martin Garnett, and Anders Kiessling for other help with fieldwork in England. The fieldwork in various countries was greatly facilitated by the generous help of the following people: Javier and Laura Castroviejo (Spain), Lindon and Rose Cornwallis (Iran), Luis Garcia Garrido (Spain), Etienne Edberg (Sweden), Anna Erichsen (Norway), Jan Pinowski (Poland), Derek Scott (Iran), and Ludwig Tomialojc (Poland). John R. Krebs's field trip to Iran was financed by a grant from The Royal Society; Malcolm L. Hunter was financed throughout by a Rhodes Scholarship.

Gary Green did much of the analysis of attenuation tests and the following read all or part of the manuscript: Chris Perrins, Alex Kacelnik, Nick Davies, Henry Bennet-Clark, Pete McGregor, and Peter Slater.

REFERENCES

CHAPPUIS, CLAUDE
1969. Un cline vocal chez les oiseaux palearctiques: Variation tonale des Vocalisations, sous differentes latitudes. Alauda, vol. 37, pp. 59-71.
1971. Un exemple de l'influence du milieu sur les emissions vocales des oiseaux: L'evolution des chants en forêt equitoriale. Terre Vie, vol. 25, pp. 183-203.

GARNETT, M. C.
1976. Some aspects of body size in the Great Tit. D. Phil. Thesis, Oxford University.

KREBS, JOHN
1977. Song and territory in the Great Tit *Parus major*. Pp. 47-62 *in* "Evolutionary Ecology," 310 pp., B. Stonehouse and C. M. Perrins, eds. Macmillan Press, London.

KREBS, JOHN; ASHCROFT, RUTH; and WEBBER, MIKE
1978. Song repertoires and territory defence in the Great Tit *(Parus major)*. Nature, vol. 271, pp. 539-542.

KROODSMA, DON
1976. Reproductive development in a female songbird: Differential stimulation by quality of male song. Science, vol. 192, pp. 574-575.

MARTEN, KEN, and MARLER, PETER
1977. Sound transmission and its significance for animal vocalization. I. Temperate habitats. Behav. Ecol. Sociobiol., vol. 2, pp. 271-290.

MARTEN, KEN; QUINE, DOUG; and MARLER, PETER
1977. Sound transmission and its significance for animal vocalization. II. Tropical forest habitats. Behav. Ecol. Sociobiol., vol. 2, pp. 291-302.

MORTON, EUGENE
1975. Ecological sources of selection on avian sounds. Amer. Natur., vol. 109, pp. 17-34.

NOTTEBOHM, FERNANDO
1975. Continental patterns of song variability in *Zonotrichia capensis:* Some possible ecological correlates. Amer. Natur., vol. 109, pp. 605-624.

SNOW, DAVID
1953. Systematics and comparative ecology of the genus *Parus* in the Palaearctic Region. D. Phil. Thesis, Oxford University.
1967. Family Paridue. Pp. 70-174 *in* "Check-list of Birds of the World," vol. 12, R. A. Paynter, Jr., ed. Museum of Comparative Zoology, Cambridge, Mass.

MALCOLM L. HUNTER, JR.
JOHN R. KREBS

Excavations at the Vidor and Ruiz Sites, Bay of Culebra, Costa Rica

Grant Recipient: Frederick W. Lange, Midwestern Archeological Research Center, Illinois State University, Normal, Illinois.[1]

Grant 1680: In support of archeological excavations at the Bay of Culebra, Costa Rica.

Excavations were carried out at the Vidor and Ruiz sites in northwestern Guanacaste Province, Costa Rica (Fig. 1). They are within the Greater Nicoya Archaeological Subarea as defined by Norweb (1964), and the known cultural chronology (first delineated by Baudez, 1967) ranges from 500 B.C. to A.D. 1550 (Lange and Abel-Vidor, 1980, Fig. 3). At the time of the field research the author was associate curator at the National Museum of Costa Rica.

The Vidor site is situated approximately 0.5 km from the coast, while the Ruiz site is behind a row of hills on the southern side of the bay. Both of these locations had been the sites of previous investigations, a fact that stimulated this research supported by the National Geographic Society. Earlier research had been supported by the Associated Colleges of the Midwest and by the National Museum of Costa Rica as part of its ongoing research program.

Interest in the Vidor site was stimulated by the possibility of obtaining extensive information on the earliest (Zoned Bichrome Period, ca. 500 B.C. to A.D. 500) ceramic-bearing cultural components in the region. Investigations there ultimately led to redefinition of the period.

The Bay of Culebra has been described as a pre-Columbian port of call, or trade enclave. Additional investigation at the Ruiz site was based on the surface recovery of a fragment of a lost-wax gold mold (Lange and Accola, 1979) and the possibility of locating further indications of either gold production or interregional trade during the last prehistoric period (Late Polychrome Period, A.D. 1200 to 1550) in the area.

In this way we would be able to approach both the beginning and ending periods in the regional cultural sequence, both of which were poorly known relative to the time span from A.D. 500 to 1200 (Early and Middle Polychrome periods).

[1] The author's present address is; Department of Anthropology, University of Colorado—Boulder, Boulder, Colorado.

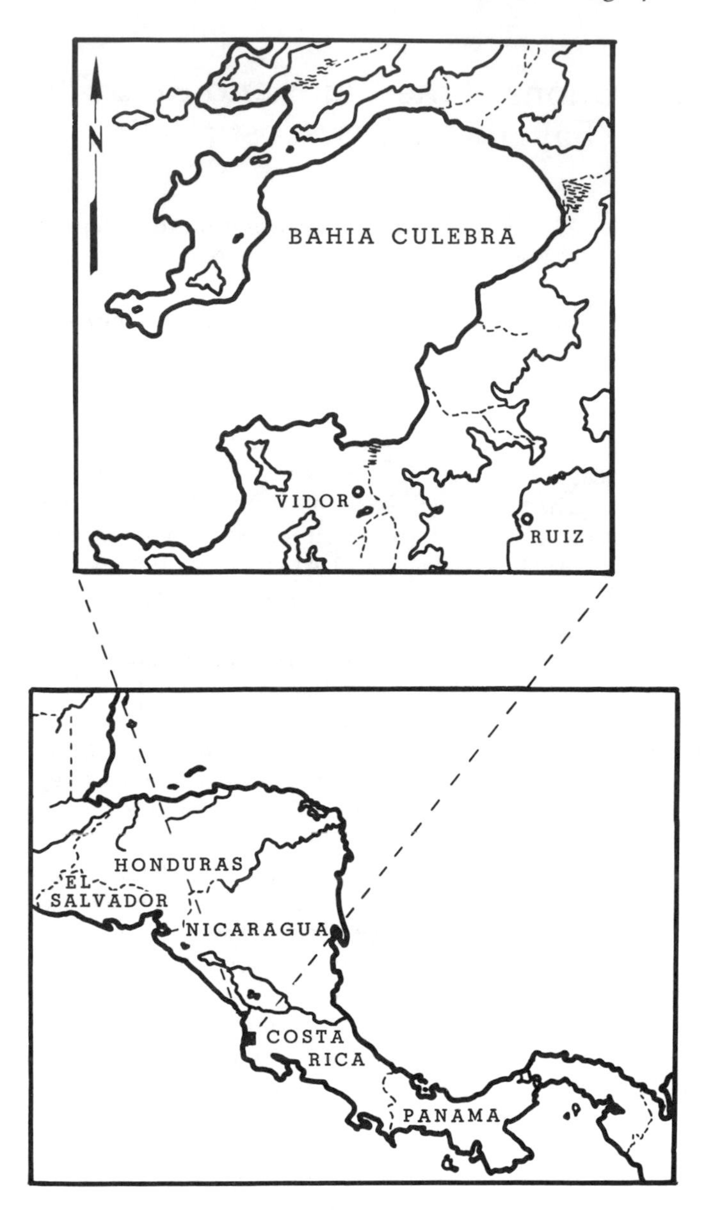

FIGURE 1. Location of Vidor and Ruiz sites within Central America, northwestern Costa Rica, and the Bay of Culebra.

The Vidor Site (30471-253-1)

The site designation system used for the Bay of Culebra survey was derived from systems previously applied to the Río Sapoa Valley and Bay of Salinas, to the north (Lange, 1971a), and to the Zapotitan Valley of El Salvador (Sheets, n.d.). The Bay of Culebra system used the 1: 50,000 geographical quadrangle number (30471) combined with a sequential square kilometer number within that quadrangle (253), with the final number indicating its rank within the number of sites identified within that square kilometer (1). Had the Universal Transverse Mercator (UTM) system of site location been more widely in use at the time we would have used it. It is the system I would recommend for all future surveys; Ichon (1980) provides an excellent example of its successful application in Panama. Survey efforts on the Bay of Culebra (Lange et al., 1980) intensively covered 88% of the bay area and resulted in the identification of 60 archeological sites.

The Vidor site originally consisted of 35 Middle and Late Polychrome shell middens overlying earlier Early Polychrome and Zoned Bichrome deposits. The majority of the mounds have been destroyed through agricultural practices, a mixed blessing making the earlier levels somewhat more accessible than they had been. This type of midden concentration is typical of the estuary systems around the Bay of Culebra and is indicative of the large (3000 to 5000) pre-Columbian populations that concentrated there to take advantage of the rich marine resources. There are marked settlement-pattern differences between the northern coast of the Nicoya Peninsula—where numerous embayments and a well-developed estuary system permitted exploitation of marine resources and concentrations of population—and the southern, straight coast of the peninsula—where such embayments are absent and large coastal sites are unknown (Lange et al., 1976).

The extensive middens forming the Vidor site were first called to my attention in 1972, although the area was well-known to pot-hunters and had been systematically exploited for many previous years. A brief reconnaissance was made in February 1973, and excavations were conducted from May to July of the same year. Additional work was carried out from January to July of 1976, January to August of 1977, January to August of 1978, and January to May of 1979, with work forces ranging from 5 to 25 persons. The overall results of this work have been summarized in Lange and Abel-Vidor (1980), and have also resulted in theses by Accola (1978a, b), Abel (1978), Kerbis (1979, 1980), and Bernstein (1979, 1980).

Through the end of the 1976 field season our sampling procedures at the site had been mainly vertical. This had resulted in basic confirmation of the regional sequence, but it was clear that we were getting only part of the interpretive picture. One deep cut (5 m) at the end of that season produced data indicative of earlier, buried cultural material. Work at the site, with the support of National Geographic Society funding, focused on opening a 5- × 5-m area that eventually reached a depth 7 m below the surface of the adjacent Late Polychrome and Middle Polychrome midden deposits.

Our research at Vidor in early 1977 was devoted entirely to the study of the earlier (Zoned Bichrome and Early Polychrome) components at the site. The excavations were gridded in 1- × 1-m, 1- × 2-m, or 2- × 2-m units, removed in either 10-cm or 20-cm artificial levels, and screened through 1/4-in. mesh. These tests were fully successful in opening a large area of the earliest Zoned Bichrome levels. To cross-check the results of the 5- × 5-m unit, we placed deep test pits in other parts of the site. These tests confirmed the results of the larger excavation and also revealed that the earliest occupation of the site had been much more extensive than we had supposed.

Many of the ceramic modes (broad- and fine-lined incised zoning of red and black on natural buff or red-slipped surfaces, and distinctive pastes and vessel shapes) seen in the early Vidor ceramics (Fig. 2 and Lange, 1980a) are similar to those found during the same field season on the Atlantic coast of Costa Rica (Snarskis, 1978). Such data are increasing our ability to compare patterns of development on both the Pacific and Atlantic watersheds and to be more aware of possible evidence of contact and exchange among peoples in the two areas. A structured attempt at such studies was made during the Guanacaste-San Carlos project in 1977 (Lange, n.d.) but such efforts need to be greatly increased.

These tests also revealed an extensive cemetery area that was pursued as a separate project (Vazquez and Weaver, 1980). The cemetery excavations revealed two cultural features associated with earlier levels at the site. Two large adobe and stone ovens were probably used to fire ceramics (Abel, 1978; Abel-Vidor, 1980); a radiocarbon sample (UCLA-2177A) from the deepest oven yielded a date of 880 ± 80 B.C. (MASCA corrected to 800 to 960 B.C.). This is but a single date and must be confirmed by additional dates from other contexts. Many similar ovens, but all from Early Polychrome contexts, have been encountered since in extensive National Museum of Costa Rica excavations at the site of Nacascolo on the north side of the Bay of Culebra (Vazquez, n.d.).

Summary

The 1977 excavations at the Vidor site produced the first clear-cut stratigraphic divisions in the earlier part of the Zoned Bichrome Period in northwestern Costa Rica. They also confirmed the impression, derived from previous, more limited deep excavations throughout the area, that

FIGURE 2. Zoned Bichrome ceramics from Vidor site: (a.) Rosales Zoned Incised (Orso phase, 300 B.C. to A.D. 300); (b.) Bocana Incised Bichrome, Bocana variety (Loma B phase, ca. 500 to 300 B.C.).

Zoned Bichrome Period subsistence practices placed little or no emphasis on the exploitation of marine fauna (Lange, 1976). These data have brought about revisions in the regional ceramic sequence, changed our ideas about the areal extent of Zoned Bichrome Period sites, and also changed our strategies toward excavation at similar sites elsewhere. It is clear that in many locations we must reach relatively deep levels to obtain Zoned Bichrome materials. This also indicates the potential value of restudying previously excavated sites in which adequate deep testing was not done.

Vidor is similar in general configuration and stratigraphy to other sites in coastal northwestern Costa Rica. Both Las Marias (Lange, 1971a) on the Bay of Salinas and Chahuite Escondido (Coe, 1962; Sweeney, 1975) on the Santa Elena Peninsula and Nacascolo (also on the Bay of Culebra) show the pattern of a loose arrangement of middens around central "plazas" or yards. In all these cases the middens appear to be almost entirely Middle and Late Polychrome in date, with the earlier two periods underneath. Zoned Bichrome components were not encountered at either Las Marias (Lange, 1971a) or at Nacascolo (Salgado and Vazquez, pers. comm.), but this may reflect the sampling strategies employed at the two sites.

A soil monolith (column) almost 4 m in length was fixed with a hardening agent, encased, and removed from the 5- × 5-m excavation as a permanent stratigraphic record covering almost 2500 years of northwestern Costa Rican prehistory. A portion of this column is now displayed in the archeological section of the National Museum of Costa Rica as a teaching device demonstrating cultural evolution and ecological change.

The Ruiz Site (30471-337-1)

The Ruiz site (Lange, 1980b) is located behind the foothills lining the south shore of the Bay of Culebra and was first surveyed in February 1976. By far the greatest percentage of material collected was from the Late Polychrome (A.D. 1200 to 1550) Period. Late Polychrome Period sites in northwestern Costa Rica appear to have been mostly concentrated in coastal areas or where they could participate in coastal systems via inland waterways.

Since this period was poorly represented in sites we had tested on the nearby Bay of Culebra, we decided that further studies at the Ruiz site would be very worthwhile. This interest was also stimulated by the surface recovery of a lost-wax gold mold fragment (Fig. 3). This was of particular interest because metallurgy was not previously known to have been practiced in this area in pre-Columbian times (Lange and Accola, 1979).

After the analysis of the initial survey results, a small field party returned to the site in May 1976, produced a topographic base map of the site, and made a carefully controlled surface collection. This work confirmed both the extensive nature of the site and the previous assessments of temporality. As a result of the systematic collection procedures, a small amount of Early Polychrome Period (A.D. 500 to 800) material was also found.

We then decided to conduct test excavations and to make phosphate tests of selected areas to determine more precisely the nature of the site and to uncover intact subsurface features related to the observed surface

FIGURE 3. Lost-wax gold mold fragment from Ruiz site, Late Polychrome Period (A.D. 1200 to 1550).

remains. These efforts began during a one-week period in July 1976 and were completed under the National Geographic Society grant during the first six weeks of 1977. In the meantime an extensive Late Polychrome cemetery had been pot-hunted at the site.

METHODS OF DATA COLLECTION

The site area was divided into 56 blocks of 1600 m^2 each and an additional 25 units of varying sizes (but all smaller than 1600 m^2) were demarcated around the uneven periphery of the property. Data were recovered through intensive survey and surface collection, vertical testing, extensive horizontal stripping, and selective phosphate sampling of different areas.

A total of 10 units was randomly selected for study from the combined total of 81 complete and partial units. One unit was eventually excluded because of severe surface erosion, 3 blocks were devoted to phosphate sampling at 5-m intervals, and 6 blocks were the location of test excavations or stripping operations. Phosphate samples were also collected at intervals of 10 m around the boundaries of blocks where excavations were conducted. Units of 1 × 1 m, 1 × 2 m, and 4 × 4 m were employed; all units were excavated in arbitrary 10-cm levels until natural stratigraphic levels were defined at 15 cm and 40 cm below surface.

Summary

The last phase (A.D. 300 to 500) of the Zoned Bichrome Period was represented by four sherds of Zelaya Bichrome. The Zoned Bichrome Period is better known in the Bay of Culebra area from deep levels at the Vidor site.

The Early Polychrome Period (A.D. 500 to 800) is represented at the site by only limited quantities of Carrillo Polychrome and Chavez White-on-Red. In the overall regional pattern this is the period during which substantial population growth took place in coastal areas (Lange, 1976) and it is generally better represented in coastal components than it was at the Ruiz site.

The Middle Polychrome Period (A.D. 800 to 1200) was poorly represented at the site, although components from this period usually dominate coastal shell middens. Papagayo Polychrome was the type most frequently associated with this period, although its presence was quite limited.

The Late Polychrome Period dominance of the site is seen in the ceramic statistics: Of the surface-collected data, 93.2% were from this period; of the temporally diagnostic sherds from excavation, 96% were also from this period. Decorated, and therefore temporally diagnostic, sherds constituted only 1.3% of the total excavated sample, a figure comparable to that calculated for other Late Polychrome deposits in Greater Nicoya.

The Late Polychrome ceramics from the site reflected cultural influences from both the north and the south: Vallejo Polychrome reflects Mexican influences, while Murrillo Applique reflects influences from the south. The exact nature of the transmission of these cultural contacts is not well known at this time, but is thought to have been largely overland rather than by sea from the north, while from the south the potential for seaborne contacts seems to have been somewhat greater. Recent research by Day and Abel-Vidor (Day, 1982; Day and Abel-Vidor, 1980, 1981; Abel-Vidor, 1980, 1981) has contributed significantly to our understanding of this later period, while a recent publication by Healy (1980) has presented a detailed summary of the regional ceramic sequence. In addition, ceramic analyses currently under way at the Brookhaven National Laboratory and the efforts of the Greater Nicoya Ceramic study group are refining the regional sequence and studying patterns of typological distribution and production and exchange.

In addition to stone celts, lithic materials associated with the late Polychrome Period at the Ruiz site included mano and metate fragments, many of which had been reworked into "nutting stones" (Lange, 1971b). One legless basin metate fragment, the first reported for Greater Nicoya, was also recovered. A single projectile point fragment was surface-collected, while other chipped stone materials were absent. Bernstein (1980) has completed a detailed analysis of celts from Greater Nicoya and concluded that they were used for a wide variety of activities, from felling trees to clearing brush and cutting out tree trunks for boats.

In location and cultural assemblage the Ruiz site is very similar to the Hunter-Robinson site (Moreau, 1980) from the same Bay of Culebra area and to sites in the vicinity of the Bay of Salinas to the north (Lange, 1971a).

We were disappointed not to find additional evidence of gold manufacturing at the site. However, a small gold frog (very similar in form to the one reflected in the Ruiz mold), surface-collected from a Late Polychrome midden at a site in an adjacent valley, further confirms the probability of pre-Columbian gold manufacture in the area, although on a limited scale.

Conclusions

The investigations carried out under the auspices of the National Geographic Society greatly enhanced our knowledge of early cultural development in the Pacific coastal area of lower Central America, contrasts between settlement and subsistence patterns in the Zoned Bichrome and Late Polychrome Periods, and cultural relationships between the Pacific and Atlantic watersheds of Costa Rica during the Late Formative.

Excavations at the Vidor and Ruiz sites met their objectives in providing data to refine various parts of the regional sequence and to better illuminate the nature of prehistoric occupation in northwestern Costa Rica between 500 B.C. and A.D. 1550. They also stimulated additional settlement pattern, subsistence, ceramic, lithic, human skeletal, and marine and terrestrial fauna research. We are still somewhat mystified by our inability to find earlier cultural remains in the area. Previously we had assumed our lack of success was in part owing to insufficient systematic survey; now it appears that there must be as yet undefined cultural ecological explanations.

The comparative data base in Greater Nicoya is presently still composed of little more than limited stratigraphic cuts designed to establish local and regional chronological sequences. They clearly pinpoint microregional differences within Pacific northwestern Costa Rica and the need for further studies designed to more thoroughly analyze the overall system of coastal-inland adaptation and exchange systems (Voorhies, 1978; Lange, 1978).

Acknowledgments

Research on the Bay of Culebra was carried out by the National Museum of Costa Rica. Luis Diego Gomez P. was director of the museum during that period and Hector Gamboa P. was head of the department of anthropology. Both of them greatly assisted the research efforts and gave valuable advice. The participation of many of the graduate and undergraduate students is partially recognized in the cited publications which they authored on related topics. My wife Holley was responsible for instigating the deep excavations in 1976 at the Vidor site, which first encountered the more deeply buried Zoned Bichrome materials. To the more than 30 others who helped with survey, excavation, and analysis, a sincere thanks as well. The JFM Foundation of Denver, Colorado, is making a substantial contribution to amplifying the results of this research by providing funding to carry out comprehensive studies of ceramic production and exchange networks in Greater Nicoya. Ceramics from the Vidor and Ruiz sites are a significant part of the analytical package.

REFERENCES

Abel, S.
1978. An interpretation of two burnt clay features in an early Central American village: Vidor site, Bay of Culebra, Guanacaste, Costa Rica. M. A. Thesis, Brown University.

Abel-Vidor, S.
1980. Dos hornos precolombinos en el sitio Vidor, Bahía Culebra, Guanacaste. Vinculos, vol. 6, no. 2, pp. 43-50.
1981. Ethnohistorical approaches to the archaeology of Greater Nicoya. Pp. 85-92 *in* "Between Continents/Between Seas: Precolumbian Art of Costa Rica." Abrams, New York.

Accola, R.
1978a. A decorative sequence of prehistoric ceramics from the Vidor Site, Guanacaste, Costa Rica. M. A. Thesis, University of Texas-Austin.
1978b. Revisión de los tipos de cerámica del Período Policromo Medio en Guanacaste. Vinculos, vol. 4, pp. 80-105.

Baudez, C.
1967. Recherches archeologiques dans la vallée du Tempisque, Guanacaste, Costa Rica. Travaux et Mémoires de l'Institut des Hautes Études de l'Amérique Latine, no.18 (Paris).

Bernstein, D.
1979. The Central American celt: Considerations of functional diversity. M.A. Thesis, Brown University.
1980. Artefactos de piedra pulida de Guanacaste, Costa Rica: Una perspectiva funcional. Vinculos, vol. 6, pp. 141-153.

Coe, M.
1962. Preliminary report on archaeological investigations in coastal Guanacaste, Costa Rica. "Acts of the 34th International Congress of Americanists," Vienna, vol. 1, pp. 350-365.

Day, J.
1982. Late Polychrome ceramics: Guanacaste Province, Costa Rica, A.D. 1200-1530. Paper presented at the 44th International Congress of Americanists, Manchester.

Day, J., and Abel-Vidor, S.
1980. The Late Polychrome Period: Guanacaste, Costa Rica. Paper presented in the symposium of Archaeology and Art History: Interdisciplinary Approaches for the 1980's, 79th annual meeting, American Anthropological Association, Washington, D. C.
1981. The complementary use of ethnohistory and archaeology for prehistoric research in the Guanacaste area of Costa Rica (and southwestern Nicaragua). Paper presented at the annual meeting of the American Society for Ethnohistory, Colorado Springs.

Healy, P.
1980. Archaeology of the Rivas Region, Nicaragua, 382 p. Sir Wilfred Laurier University Press, Waterloo, Ontario.

Ichon, A.
1980. Archéologie du sud de la peninsula d' Azuero, Panama. Études de Mesoamericaines, ser. 2, no. 3, 521 p. Mission Archéologique et Ethnologique Française au Mexique, Mexico.

Kerbis, J.
1979. An analysis of the vertebrate fauna from a Costa Rican shell midden. M.A. Thesis, University of Chicago.
1980. The analysis of faunal remains from the Vidor site. Vinculos, vol. 6, no. 2, pp. 125-140.

Lange, F.
1971a. Culture history of the Sapoa River Valley, Costa Rica. Occ. Pap. 4, Logan Museum of Anthropology, Beloit College, Wisconsin.
1971b. Northwestern Costa Rica: Precolumbian circum-Caribbean affiliations. Folk, vol. 13, pp. 43-64.
1976. Bahías y valles de la costa de Guanacaste. Vinculos, vol. 2, pp. 45-66.
1978. Coastal settlement in northwestern Costa Rica. Pp. 101-119. *in* "Prehistoric Coastal Adaptations," B. Stark and B. Voorhies, eds. Academic Press, New York.
1980a. The Formative Zoned Bichrome Period in northwestern Costa Rica (800 B.C. to A.D. 500), based on excavations at the Vidor site, Bay of Culebra. Vinculos, vol. 6, no. 2, pp. 33-42.
1980b. Una ocupación del Policromo Tardió en sitio Ruiz, cerca de Bahía Culebra. Vinculos, vol. 6, no. 2, pp. 81-96.

LANGE, F. *(continued)*

n.d. The Greater Nicoya Archaeological Subarea. Paper presented (1980) at the Advanced Seminar on the Archaeology of Lower Central America, School of American Research, Santa Fe, New Mexico.

LANGE, F. and ABEL-VIDOR, S.

1980. Investigaciones arqueológicas en la zona de Bahía Culebra, Costa Rica (1973-1979). Vinculos, vol. 6, no. 1-2, 186 p.

LANGE, F. and ACCOLA, R.

1979. Metallurgy in Costa Rica. Archaeology, vol. 32, pp. 26-33.

LANGE, F.; ACCOLA, R.; and RYDER, P.

1980. La administración de los recursos culturales en Bahía Culebra. Vinculos, vol. 6, no. 1, pp. 9-32.

LANGE, F., BERNSTEIN, D.; SIEGEL, M.; and TASE, D.

1976. Preliminary archaeological research in the Nosara Valley. Folk, vol. 18, pp. 47-60.

MOREAU, J.

1980. A report on the Hunter-Robinson and Sardinal sites. Vinculos, vol. 6, no. 2, pp. 107-124.

NORWEB, A.

1964. Ceramic stratigraphy in southwestern Nicaragua. Acts of the 35th International Congress of Americanists 1: 551-61, Mexico.

SHEETS, P.

n.d. Research of the protoclassic project in the Zapotitan Basin, El Salvador. Ms. on file, Department of Anthropology, University of Colorado, Boulder.

SNARSKIS, M.

1978. The archaeology of the central Atlantic watershed of Costa Rica. PhD. dissertation, Columbia University.

SWEENEY, J.

1975. Guanacaste, Costa Rica: An analysis of pre-Columbian ceramics from the northwest coast. PhD. dissertation, University of Pennsylvania.

VAZQUEZ, R.

——. Excavaciones de muestreo en el sitio Nacascolo. *In* Pre-Columbian Settlement Patterns in Costa Rica: Research Essays in Honor of Carlos Enrique Herra R. Journal of the Steward Anthropological Society, University of Illinois-Urbana. (In press.)

VAZQUEZ, R., and WEAVER, D.

1980. Un análisis osteológico para el reconocimiento de las condiciones de vida en sitio Vidor. Vinculos, vol. 6, no. 2, pp. 97-106.

VOORHIES, B.

1978. Previous research on nearshore coastal adaptations in Middle America. Pp. 5-21, *in* "Prehistoric Coastal Adaptations," B. Stark and B. Voorhies, eds. Academic Press, New York.

FREDERICK W. LANGE

Research Activities During the Second International Prochlorophyte Expedition, Singapore, April 4-25, 1977

Grant Recipient: Ralph A. Lewin, Scripps Institution of Oceanography, La Jolla, California.

Grant 1684: To collect prochlorophytic algae for biochemical and physiological study.

Prochlorophytes are phototropic prokaryotes that contain chlorophylls a and b and are capable of evolving oxygen when suitably illuminated. The class was first formally described by Lewin in 1976. It is of particular interest because ancestral algae of this kind may have given rise, by symbiogenesis, to the chloroplasts of green plants. This hypothesis is now being tested by comparative biochemistry and other analytical methods in a number of laboratories around the world.

Some of the accessible islets and reefs off the Singapore coasts were examined in three surveys, insofar as time and low-tide periods permitted, with particular attention to the presence of didemnids containing or bearing prochlorophytes. Extensive dredging and silting in the vicinity may soon render the area unfavorable for further studies, especially since the most suitable species for our work, *Lissoclinum patella,* seems to have narrow ecological tolerance limits.

About 7 kinds of didemnids were found to be invariably associated with endozoic algae; 4 other kinds sporadically bore patches of epizoic algae; more than 10 kinds were never found with algal symbionts. About 30 samples were preserved in 7% formalin in seawater buffered with calcium carbonate. Subsamples were sent to didemnid taxonomists and retained in our collection.

Some field observations on these and other didemnids were made, with records of location; substrate; color, area, and thickness of colony; and pH of crushed colony (range: 4.5 to 7.5).

Attempts to maintain various didemnids alive, on original substrates or detached, in small vessels or in aquaria with aeration, were generally unsuccessful. *Lissoclinum patella* died in 1 to 2 days, smaller forms such as *Diplosoma virens* and *Trididemnum cyclops* survived no more than 5 days.

(Obviously the effects of light, temperature, exposure, aeration, and nutrition factors should be studied in carefully controlled experiments, for which we had insufficient time in this expedition.)

Three kinds of prochlorophytes were distinguished on the basis of host species, cell diameter, and configuration of cell contents (as shown by light microscopy).

About 140 single algal cells from different host types were isolated and transferred to media prepared with natural or artificial seawater supplemented with various combinations and concentrations of bicarbonate, nitrate, and ammonium salts. Some were supplied with a carbon source (acetate, glucose, glycerol, or glycine). To some we added calcium carbonate or sodium thioglycollate, or both, respectively, to reduce the hydrogen-ion concentration or redox potential of the medium. Some were kept in partially anaerobic conditions; most were incubated in air. Some were incubated at 25°C; others at 28° or 30°C. Some tubes were left under observation in the Biochemistry Department of Singapore University; others were taken for further incubation at Scripps Institution of Oceanography at La Jolla. All such experiments were unsuccessful: No cultures were established.

For studies of translocation of CO_2-fixation products from alga to host, intact colonies of *Diplosoma virens*, with symbionts in situ, were supplied with C^{14}-labeled bicarbonate and illuminated for 2 hours. They were then washed and incubated for various periods in light or darkness, for later examination by radioautography.

For studies of photosynthetic products, algae expressed from *Lissoclinum patella* were incubated in light or darkness with C^{14}-labeled bicarbonate or acetate, and, at intervals, cells and medium were separated by centrifugation and each fraction was fixed with hot methanol for subsequent analyses in the University of California.

Experience gained in this expedition proved invaluable in planning subsequent expeditions to study prochlorophytes, both in their hosts and after the cells had been expressed in suspension. Much of the information thus obtained, published in some 15 articles, has been summarized by Lewin (1981).

REFERENCES

LEWIN, R. A.

1976. Prochlorophyta as a proposed new division of algae. Nature, vol. 261, pp. 697-698.

1981. The prochlorophytes. Pp. 257-266 *in* "The Prokaryota," M. P. Starr et al., eds. Springer-Verlag, Berlin, Heidelberg, and New York.

RALPH A. LEWIN

Quaternary History of Mount Kenya, East Africa

Grant Recipient: W. C. Mahaney, Geography Department, Atkinson College, York University, Downsview, Ontario, Canada.

Grant 1627: In support of a study of landform chronology, environmental reconstruction, and soil morphogenesis in the East African highlands.

Mount Kenya (Fig. 1) is distinctive in that some tills are related to volcanic rocks and organic materials that can be dated by radiometric methods. In addition, relative dating methods have been used to demonstrate age differences in the till sequence (Mahaney, 1972, 1979). Such relative dating methods include various rock-weathering parameters, loess thickness, vegetation cover (including lichen data), and soil properties. Recent reviews of these methods have been summarized by Mahaney (1979, pp. 166-167).

Valley-to-valley correlation of tills is not easy to achieve as a result of dense forest cover below 3200 m, and variations in climate between the west and north flanks of the mountain. This paper outlines the general distribution and dimensions of Quaternary glaciers in the Mount Kenya area and discusses the type section for each stratigraphic unit. Problems associated with the identification and differentiation of each unit and its age relationships are also discussed.

Diamictons in Interfluves

In a few localities, deposits considered to be tills are located in interfluves 25 to 125 m above existing drainages. The major deposits are above Lake Höhnel on the Höhnel/Teleki interfluve and along the west fork of the Kazita River (Baker, 1967; Mahaney, 1979). Correlation of these diamictons will have to be based on similar topographic positions and K/Ar dates. The diamicton in the Höhnel/Teleki interfluve (Fig. 2) is located 125 m above the Teleki Valley. It contains striated and polished material of boulder, cobble, and pebble sizes, indicating a probable glacial origin. This deposit, varying from 2 to 0.5 m in thickness, is discontinuous, thinning out laterally, toward the east. Underlying and overlying volcanic

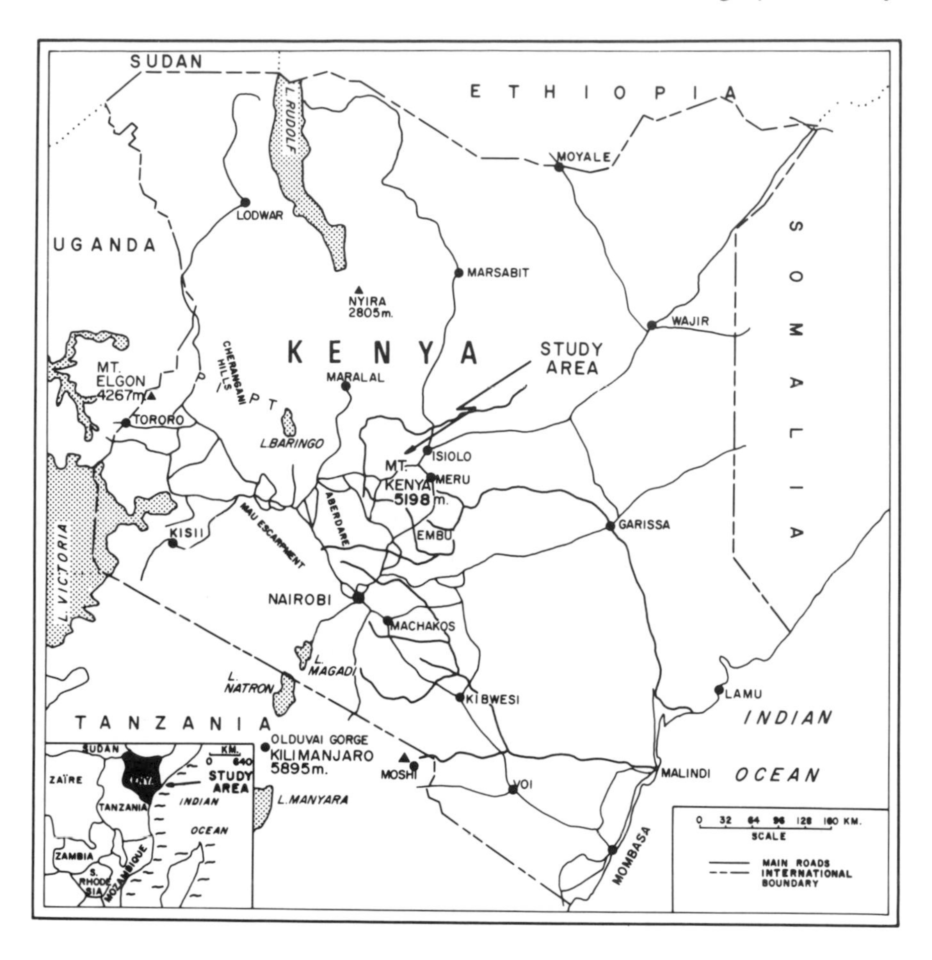

FIGURE 1. Map of Kenya showing the study area.

rocks are presently being dated to provide bracketing maximum and minimum ages. Additional fieldwork is required to determine if other diamicts are present on Mount Kenya or Ithanguni, a parasitic cone to the northeast.

Tills with Poorly Preserved Moraine Form

Unlike the older diamictons, tills deposited during the Teleki Glaciation are closely related to the valley floor over which the ice advanced. At

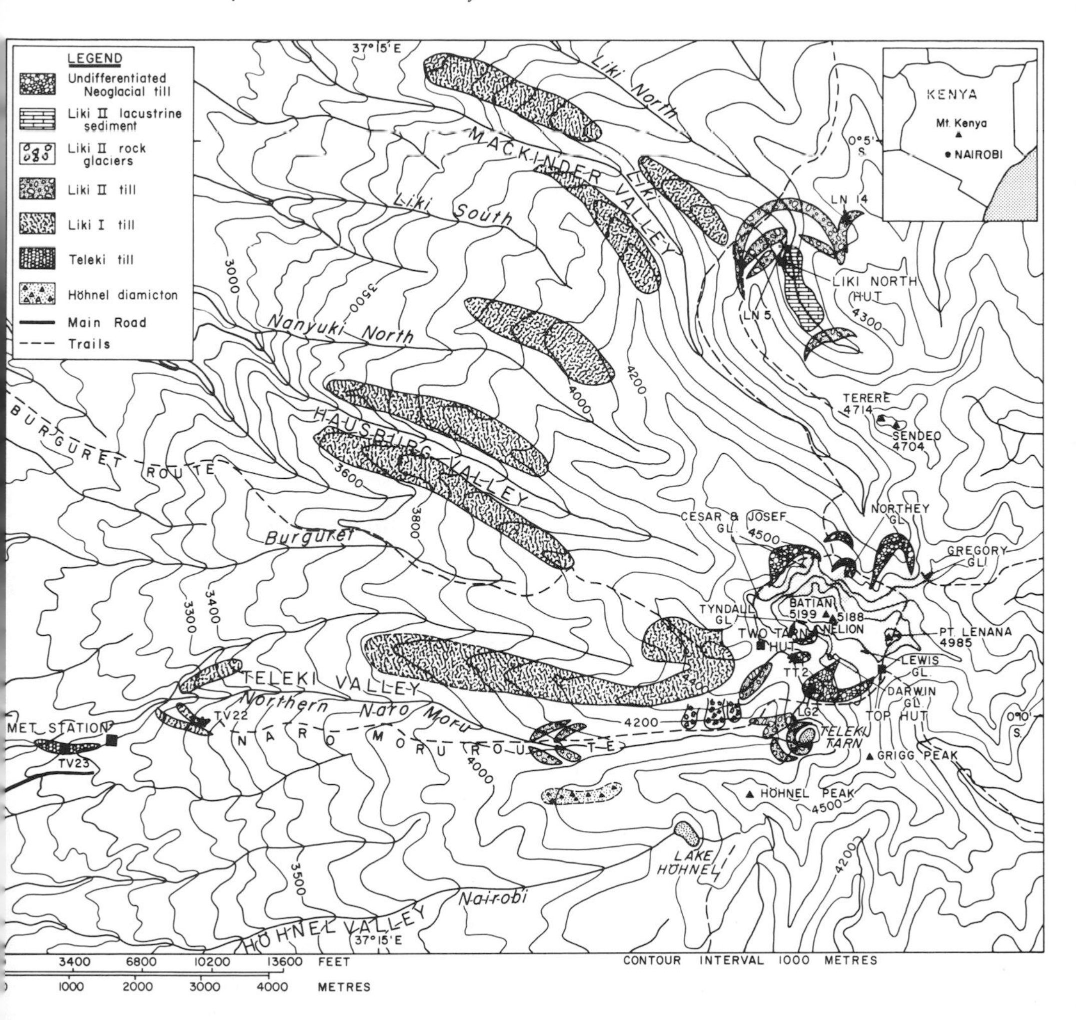

FIGURE 2. Mount Kenya, with location of principal glacial and periglacial deposits, and type sections described in text.

the type locality for Teleki till (site TV23; for location see Fig. 2) surface drift overlies older drift that may be coeval with the Höhnel Diamicton. Surface weathering data for Teleki till (Table 1) indicate an advanced state of weathering with a low boulder frequency, relatively high percentage of weathered stones, and fairly large rinds. Multi-story paleosols in site TV23 are described in the following list.

TV23: post-Teleki relict paleosol and pre-Teleki buried paleosol (for location see Fig. 2). Colors in the description are from Oyama and Takehara (1970) and are given as moist (m) and dry (d).

Horizon	*Depth (cm)*	*Description*
A11	0–18	Brownish black (10YR 2/3m; 3/3d) and dark brown (10YR 3/3d) silty clay loam, granular structure, friable, slightly plastic, and slightly sticky.
IIA12	18–38	Brownish black (10YR 3/2m) and dull yellowish brown (10YR 4/3d) clay, granular structure, firm, plastic, and sticky.
IIB21	38–91	Dark reddish brown (5YR 3/3m) and brown (7.5YR 4/4d) clay, blocky structure, firm, plastic, and sticky.
IIB22	91–104	Brown (7.5YR 4/4m) and dull brown (7.5YR 5/4d) clay, blocky structure, firm, plastic, and sticky.
IIC1ox	104–168	Reddish brown (5YR 4/6m), bright reddish brown (5YR 4/5m), and orange (7.5YR 6/6d) clay, massive structure, friable, plastic, and slightly sticky.
IIC2ox	168–176	Dull reddish brown (5YR 4/4m) and bright brown (7.5YR 5/6d) clay, massive structure, firm, plastic, and sticky.
Ab	176–186	Black (10YR 1.7/1m), yellowish brown (10YR 5/6m), and dull brown (7.5YR 5/3d) loam, massive structure, firm consistence, plastic, and sticky.
B21b	186–199	Yellowish brown (10YR 5/6m), black (10YR 1.7/1M), and dull yellow orange (10YR 6/4d) clay, massive structure, firm, plastic, and sticky.
IIB22b	199–217	(10YR 4/4m) and dull yellow orange (10YR 7/3m) clay, massive structure, firm, plastic, and very sticky.
IIB23b	217–247	Brown (7.5YR 4/4m) and dull yellow orange (10YR 6/4d) clay, massive structure, firm, plastic, and sticky.
IIC1oxb	247–277	Brown (10YR 4/6m) and bright yellowish brown (10YR 6/6d) clay, massive structure, firm, very plastic, and sticky.
IIC2oxb	277+	Brown (10YR 4/6m), some light gray (10YR 8/2m), and dull yellow orange (10YR 6/4d) clay, massive structure, very firm consistence, very plastic, and sticky.

Sola in buried and relict paleosols are distinctly different in particle-size content (Table 2). The buried soil is considerably heavier in texture, with greater amounts of clay and less sand when compared with the relict soil in Teleki till. Particle-size distributions (Fig. 3) show the clear differences between the two soils where the IIB22b, IIB23b, IIC1oxb, and IIC2oxb horizons have heavier textures. Calculations of the frequency

TABLE 1. Summary of Characteristics Useful in Subdividing and Correlating Deposits, Mount Kenya, East Africa

Deposit	*Elevation (m)*	*Vegetation*	*Boulders 10 m²*	*Weathering ratios*[a]			*Weathering rinds*[b]		
				% Fresh	*% Wx*	*n*	*Avg. Max. (mm)*	*Avg. Min. (mm)*	*n*
Lewis till	4550	Upper Afroalpine	120	100	0	100	1.0	nil	100
Tyndall till	4350	Upper Afroalpine	102	100	0	100	3.7	.02	100
Liki II till	3990	Upper Afroalpine	42	98	2	100	4.6	1.3	100
Liki I till	3260	Ericaceous zone	30	95	5	100	7.0	1.5	100
Teleki till	2990	Bamboo forest	6	52	48	100	15.6	2.9	100
Höhnel diamicton	4100	Upper Afroalpine	--	--	--	--	--	--	--

[a] Weathered-fresh differentiation based on surface state of the boulder as generally unweathered (e.g., fresh) or weathered (Wx), cavernous, and rotten.

[b] Oxidation rinds are developed to nonuniform depths in clasts found on moraine surfaces. The maximum rind is the maximum depth of discoloration measured on clasts split with a hammer. The minimum rind is the minimum depth.

TABLE 2. Selected Physical[a] and Mineral[b] Properties of Quaternary Type Sections Mount Kenya, East Africa

Site[c]	Soil horizon	Depth (cm)	Elevation (m)	Vegetation	Age	<2 mm			Mineralogy							
						% Sand (2 mm-63 μ)	% Silt (63-4 μ)	% Clay (<4 μ)	K	H	N	I	Q	F	M	G
LG2	C	0 - 10	4450	Upper Afro-alpine		75.0	19.2	5.8	-	-	-	-	xx	x	-	-
TT2	A1	0 - 20	4350	Upper Afro-alpine	post-Neoglacial soils	65.5	18.0	16.5	-	-	-	-	tr	tr	-	-
	Cox	20 - 41				64.1	24.4	11.5	-	-	-	-	tr	tr	tr	-
	Cn	41+				75.3	20.9	3.8	-	-	-	-	x	tr	tr	tr
LN14	02	8 - 0	3990	Upper Afro-alpine	post-Liki-II soil	8.6	48.4	43.0	-	-	-	-	xxx	x	x	-
	A1	0 - 10				30.5	28.5	41.0	-	-	-	-	tr	tr	-	-
	B2	10 - 20				33.8	30.2	36.0	-	-	-	-	-	tr	-	-
	IIClox	20 - 33				67.2	22.3	10.5	-	-	-	tr	x	x	x	-
	IIC2ox	33 - 58				82.3	8.2	9.5	-	-	-	-	xxx	x	x	-
	IICn	58+				89.5	3.5	7.0	-	-	-	-	xxx	x	x	-
TV22	A11	0 - 15	3260	Erica-ceous zone	post-Liki-I soil	7.4	62.6	30.0	-	-	-	-	xx	tr	tr	-
	A12	15 - 28				11.6	64.4	24.0	-	-	-	-	xx	x	tr	-
	IIA13	28 - 43				19.7	45.8	34.5	-	-	-	-	x	tr	tr	-
	IIB2	43 - 56				41.2	42.8	16.0	tr	-	-	-	tr	-	?	-
	IICox	56 - 82				56.5	27.5	16.0	tr	tr	-	-	tr	tr	-	-
	IICn	82+				38.9	45.1	16.0	-	-	-	-	tr	x	-	x

TV23	A11	0 - 18	2990	Bamboo	post-	12.3	62.7	25.0	-	-	-	-	xxx	x	x	-
	IIA12	18 - 38		forest	Teleki	11.9	21.6	66.5	-	-	-	-	tr	-	-	-
	IIB21	38 - 91			soil	15.5	16.5	68.0	-	-	-	tr	tr	-	-	-
	IIB22	91 - 104				11.1	7.9	81.0	-	-	tr	-	tr	-	-	-
	IIClox	104 - 168				24.6	14.4	61.0	tr	tr	tr	tr	tr	-	-	-
	IIC2ox	168 - 176				17.5	28.0	54.5	tr	-	tr	tr	tr	-	-	-
	Ab	176 - 186				45.5	33.5	21.0	tr	tr	x	tr	-	-	-	-
	B21b	186 - 199			pre-	5.9	28.1	66.0	tr	tr	x	tr	x	tr	tr	-
	IIB22b	199 - 217			Teleki	1.8	11.7	86.5	-	-	x	tr	tr	-	-	-
	IIB23b	217 - 247			soil	2.0	11.0	87.0	-	-	tr	tr	tr	-	-	-
	IICloxb	247 - 277				1.1	3.7	95.2	-	-	x	x	-	-	-	-
	IIC2oxb	277+				2.8	8.2	89.0	tr	tr	x	tr	x	tr	-	-

[a] Data are given in weight-percentages of sand, silt, and clay (<2 mm). Coarse particle sizes (2000-63 μ) determined by sieving; fine particle sizes (63-1.95 μ) determined by hydrometer.

[b] Mineral abundance is based on peak height: nil (-); minor amount (tr); small amount (x); moderate amount (xx); abundant (xxx). Minerals are kaolinite (K); halloysite (H); nacrite (N); illite (I); quartz (Q); feldspar (F); mica (M); gibbsite (G).

[c] Section locations are on Figure 2.

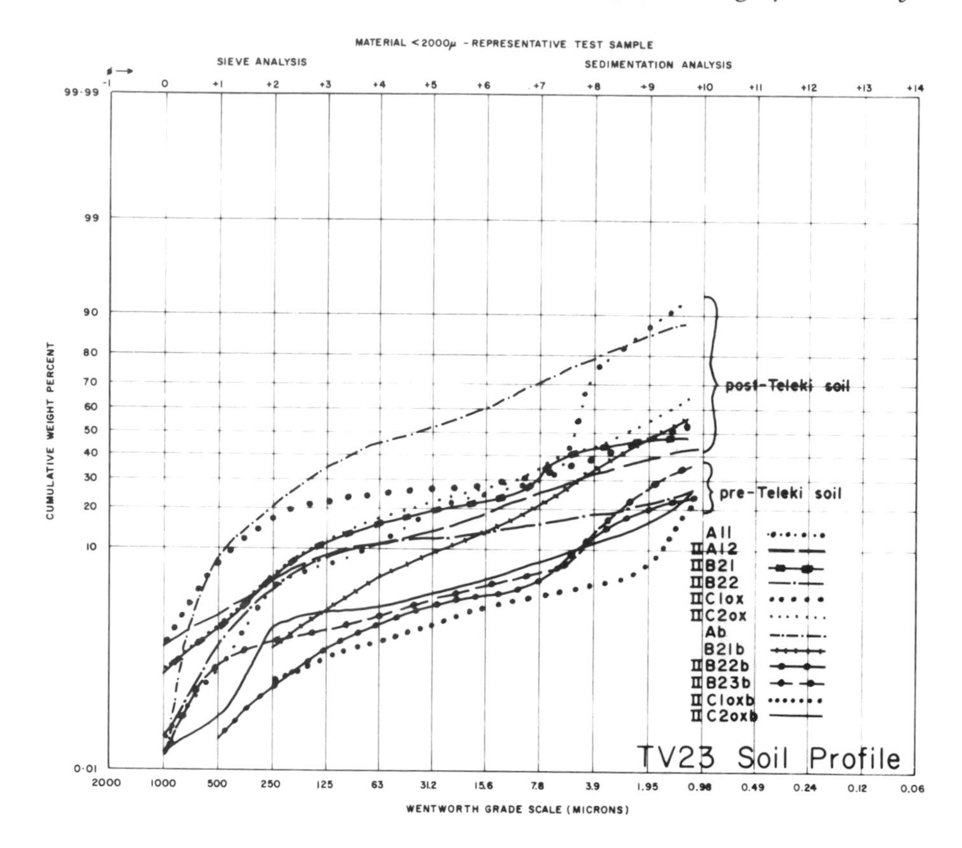

FIGURE 3. Particle-size distributions for soil horizons in TV23 profile formed in Teleki and pre-Teleki tills.

distribution center of gravity[1] for the sola in each profile yield values of 8.9 ($\bar{x}\,\Phi$) in the relict paleosol, and 12.0 ($\bar{x}\,\Phi$) in the buried paleosol. These data show a frequency distribution center of gravity shift of considerable magnitude suggesting considerable differences in time. High silt content in the A11 and Ab/B21b horizons may be of aeolian origin.

[1] The frequency distribution center of gravity ($\bar{x}\,\Phi$) is calculated from Figures 3, 4, 5, and 7 as follows:

$$\bar{x}\,\Phi = \frac{\text{25th + 50th + 75th percentiles}}{3}$$

Differences between the two paleosols are further supported by mineralogical data (Table 2). Within the clay mineral suites, kaolinite, nacrite, halloysite, and illite dominate in trace to small amounts. The presence of nacrite, a rare polytype of kaolinite with weak reflections at 3.58 Å (004) (Carroll, 1970), in the buried paleosol, and its absence in the relict paleosol, provides an important means of differentiation. Small amounts of quartz, feldspar, and mica in the buried paleosol suggest intense weathering over a long interval of time. The relatively low amount of clay minerals present reflects a lower Si content in Mount Kenya volcanic rocks, and a high rate of silica removal by leaching under a humid tropical mountain climate. In the A11 horizon relatively high amounts of quartz, feldspar, and mica are suggestive of aeolian influx. The absence of gibbsite may result from its incorporation into clay mineral lattices.

No attempt was made to date the Ab horizon in the buried paleosol, as it is considered beyond the range of radiocarbon. Moreover, organic matter and organic carbon distributions (Table 3) in the overlying relict profile suggest the possibility of contamination by leaching, which would make dating difficult. Dithionite-extractable iron oxide is slightly higher in the buried soil relative to the overlying relict soil. On the whole one might expect even greater values for free iron oxide, given the oxidizing potential of a strongly acid to very strongly acidic environment in the buried soil, and the apparent differences in age indicated by contrasting particle-size and clay-mineral distributions. The uniform pH in the buried soil indicates little leaching at depth; however, the increase in pH in the relict soil indicates moderate leaching, which is surprising given the high rainfall, luxuriant bamboo forest, and low quantities of common 2:1 clay minerals. In addition, the cation exchange capacity (CEC) should be sufficient to support larger amounts of illite and kaolinite. High Ca^{+2} in the A11 horizon may be due to the combination of aeolian influx and base recycling by plants, a phenomenon observed in the subalpine forests of western North America (Mahaney, 1973, 1974; Mahaney and Fahey, 1976).

Tills with Well-Preserved Morainal Form

End moraines deposited during the last glacial maximum (Liki I) are found as low as 3100 m, although ground moraine is found as high as 3600 m. These deposits carry significantly different weathering features indicating a younger age. Boulder frequency is higher than on the surface of Teleki till. Weathering ratios indicate substantial differences from older drift, and weathering rinds are considerably thinner. The type locality in Teleki Valley (Fig. 2) carries a soil with the description as given below.

TABLE 3. Selected Chemical Properties of the < 2-mm Fractions of the Soil Horizons in Table 1

Site[a]	Horizon	Depth (cm)	pH (1:1)	Extractable Cations (mEq/100g) Na $^{+}$	K $^{+}$	Ca $^{+2}$	Mg $^{+2}$	CEC (mEq/ 100 g)	Organic matter (%)	Organic C (%)	N (%)	Iron oxide (%)	C : N
LG2	C	0 - 10	6.8	2.68	0.39	1.20	0.35	5.0	0.7	0.4	nil	0.37	nil
TT2	A1	0 - 20	5.2	0.22	0.11	0.30	0.08	24.3	3.5	2.0	0.393	0.37	15.3
	Cox	20 - 41	5.8	0.22	0.05	0.35	0.05	19.3	3.4	1.9	0.188	0.47	10.5
	Cn	41+	6.4	0.74	0.25	0.74	0.10	9.6	0.4	0.3	0.011	0.15	23.6
LN14	02	8 - 0	5.1	0.23	1.24	0.76	0.90	65.3	38.9	22.6	1.620	0.84	14.0
	A1	0 - 10	5.0	0.16	0.20	0.10	0.17	57.1	24.4	14.2	0.718	1.10	19.8
	B2	10 - 20	5.2	0.15	0.19	0.09	0.05	37.7	5.8	3.4	0.279	1.15	12.2
	IIClox	20 - 33	5.5	0.16	0.45	0.80	0.08	18.7	0.7	0.4	0.019	0.34	22.1
	IIC2ox	33 - 58	5.6	0.20	0.70	1.30	0.12	17.0	0.6	0.3	0.009	0.28	35.6
	IICn	58+	5.6	0.32	1.25	2.40	0.18	18.7	0.5	0.3	0.003	0.22	86.7
TV22	A11	0 - 15	5.0	1.06	3.32	1.27	1.39	34.8	26.8	15.6	2.330	0.92	6.7
	A12	15 - 28	4.6	0.20	0.79	0.48	0.52	88.2	42.3	24.6	1.920	1.17	12.8
	IIA13	28 - 43	4.6	0.13	0.25	0.15	0.10	55.4	23.4	13.6	1.110	1.32	12.3
	IIB2	43 - 56	4.8	0.05	0.09	0.05	0.02	39.8	7.4	4.3	0.256	3.20	16.9
	IICox	56 - 82	5.2	0.05	0.12	0.08	0.02	26.4	2.0	1.2	0.089	1.27	12.9
	IICn	82+	5.3	0.10	0.25	0.15	0.02	25.0	0.6	0.3	0.025	1.15	13.2
TV23	A11	0 - 18	4.7	0.09	0.93	25.99	6.85	40.7	14.7	8.5	0.878	2.23	9.7
	IIA12	18 - 38	4.9	0.05	0.37	2.00	0.32	33.6	8.7	5.1	0.503	2.96	10.0
	IIB21	38 - 91	4.6	0.05	0.20	0.72	0.08	26.4	5.3	3.1	0.288	2.70	10.7
	IIB22	91 - 104	4.8	0.10	0.22	1.04	0.09	23.4	1.7	1.0	0.101	2.96	9.7
	IIClox	104 - 168	5.2	0.05	0.08	0.59	0.04	16.6	1.1	0.7	0.040	2.47	16.5
	IIC2ox	168 - 176	5.5	0.05	0.05	0.53	0.03	17.3	0.7	0.4	0.028	3.70	14.3
	Ab	176 - 186	5.3	0.10	0.09	1.04	0.07	25.0	0.1	<0.1	0.010	2.47	7.0
	B21b	186 - 199	5.0	0.10	0.19	1.20	0.09	27.8	0.1	<0.1	0.009	2.96	7.8
	IIB22b	199 - 217	5.3	0.10	0.20	1.04	0.09	33.9	0.3	0.2	0.011	3.20	15.5
	IIB23b	217 - 247	5.2	0.10	0.15	1.04	0.09	23.4	0.2	0.1	0.010	2.96	10.0
	IICloxb	247 - 277	5.1	0.05	0.25	0.98	0.09	30.2	0.4	0.2	0.003	2.96	66.7
	IIC2oxb	277+	5.0	0.05	0.20	0.95	0.10	26.4	0.1	<0.01	0.003	2.84	23.3

[a] Section sites are on Figure 2.

TV22: post-Liki-I soil (for location, see Fig. 2). Colors in the description are from Oyama and Takehara (1970) and are given as moist (m) and dry (d).

Horizon	*Depth (cm)*	*Description*
01	4-0	Black (10YR 2/1m).
A11	0-15	Black (10YR 1.7/1m) silty clay loam, granular structure, friable, plastic, and nonsticky.
A12	15-28	Brownish black (10YR 2/2m) silt loam, weak granular structure, friable, plastic, and slightly sticky.
IIA13	28-43	Black (10YR 2/1m) and dark brown (10YR 3/3d) silty clay loam, weak granular structure, friable, plastic, and slightly sticky.
IIB2	43-56	Dark brown (7.5YR 3/4m) and dull brown (10YR 5/4d) pebbly loam, weak blocky structure, firm, plastic, and sticky.
IICox	56-82	Brown (10YR 4/4m) and dull yellow orange (10YR 6/4d) pebbly sandy loam, massive structure, firm, plastic, and sticky.
IICn	82+	Light gray (2.5Y 8/1m), pale yellow (2.5Y 8/3m), and grayish yellow (2.5Y 7/2d) pebbly loam, massive structure, loose, nonplastic, and nonsticky.

This soil is moderately developed, and it contains a solum half the thickness of the TV23 solum, and a shallow depth. Granulometric data (Table 2, Fig. 4) indicate a lighter texture than in TV23; and the A horizons have significantly higher silt plus clay, suggesting an aeolian origin. The frequency distribution center of gravity ($\bar{x}\ \Phi$) is 4.8 for the B horizons and 6.7 for the A13. When compared with the granulometry for TV23 these data indicate a shift to the left, giving higher sand and lower silt plus clay in the lower solum. A $\bar{x}\ \Phi$ shift of this magnitude indicates a considerable difference in age.

X-ray reflections indicate that only minor amounts of kaolinite and halloysite are present in the post-Liki-I soil, together with moderate to trace amounts of quartz, feldspar, and mica. Within the primary mineral suites, a major break is seen at the A13/B2 boundary where quartz, feldspar, and mica diminish with depth. This may result from aeolian influx and tends to support the particle size data which indicate two parent materials (loess/till, i.e., I/II).

There is little indication of leaching in the TV22 profile, judging from the increase in pH with depth. CEC and extractable cation data suggest that 1:1 and 2:1 clay minerals are possible; their development may be inhibited by low amounts of Si. Organic matter and organic carbon are higher in the A horizon complex, suggesting that microbial activity is less intense at timberline in the Hagenia Woodland/Ericaceous Zone transition belt (Coe, 1967; Hedberg, 1964). This is further substantiated by the presence of an 01 horizon and a higher C:N ratio. Dithionite extractable

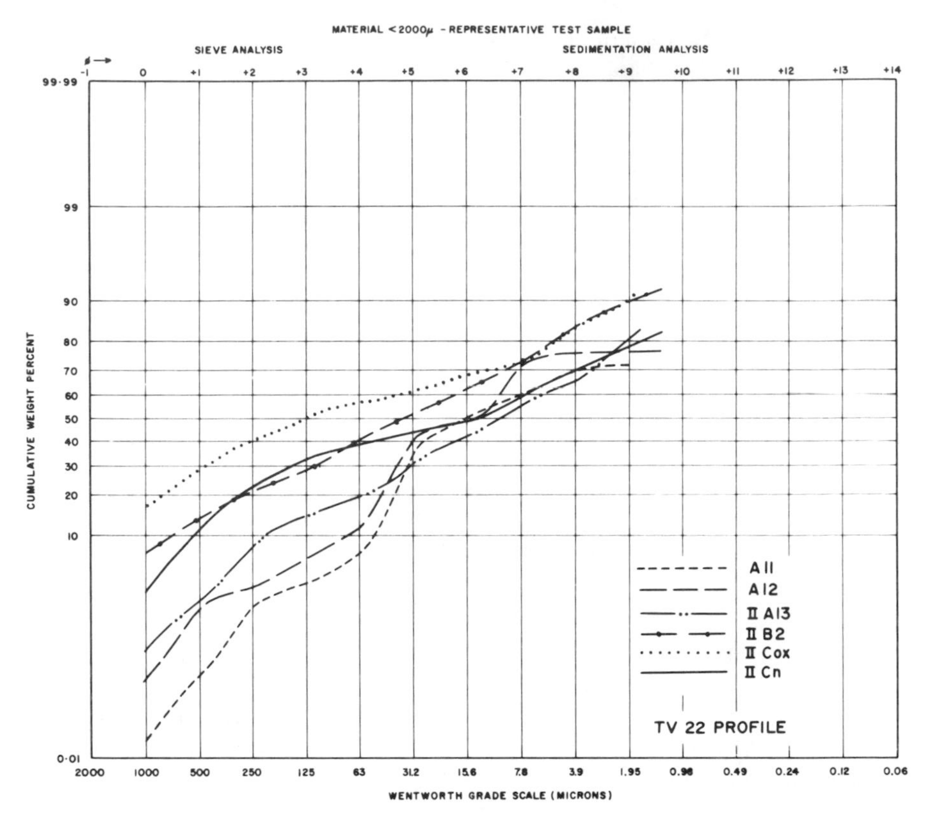

FIGURE 4. Particle-size distributions for soil horizons in TV22 profile formed in Liki-I till.

iron oxide is lower than in the TV23 soil, a factor attributed to less time for development.

Liki-II deposits, located above 3800 m in most drainages, form conspicuous and well preserved moraine and outwash systems. These systems are presumed to have formed when ice receded upvalley from its maximum extent during the last pleniglacial (Würm, Wisconsinan). The ice front halted at between 4000 and 4200 m and built up end and lateral moraines. A short core in outwash associated with these end moraines at site LN5 (Fig. 2) yielded basal organic matter dated at 12,590 ± 300 B.P. (GaK-8275). This date provides a minimum age for the Liki-II moraine complex, and a maximum age for the post-Liki-II soil. Cores from four other bogs on the Liki-II moraine complex are presently being analyzed for granulometry, clay mineral content, and radiometric age. Moreover, organic matter buried in lacustrine sediment behind the 4000-m moraine complex (Fig. 2) promises to provide at least two additional dates.

Weathering data indicate that boulder frequency is somewhat higher than for Liki-I deposits; weathering ratios are similar; and maximum and minimum rinds are slightly smaller. The data indicate that both Liki-I and -II deposits are closely related in age, and distinctly different from older deposits.

TV22: post-Liki-II soil. Described below, with colors in the description (from Oyama and Takahara 1970), given as moist (m) and dry (d).

Horizon	*Depth (cm)*	*Description*
02	8-0	Black (10YR 2/1m) silty clay, weak granular structure, friable, slightly plastic, and nonsticky.
A1	0-10	Brownish black (10YR 2/2m) clay, granular structure, firm, plastic, and sticky.
B2	10-20	Dull yellowish brown (10YR 5/4m), dark reddish brown (5YR 3/6m) and brown (7.5YR 4/6d) pebbly clay loam, weak blocky structure, firm, plastic, and sticky.
IIC1ox	20-33	Dull yellowish brown (10YR 4/3m) pebbly sandy loam, massive structure, loose, nonplastic, and slightly sticky.
IIC2ox	33-58	Grayish yellow brown (10YR 4/2m) pebbly loamy sand, massive structure, loose, nonplastic, nonsticky.
IICn	58+	Brownish black (2.5Y 3/2m) pebbly sand, massive structure, loose, nonplastic, and nonsticky.

The morphological data indicate that a B horizon 10 cm deep formed in 12,590 ± 300 years on the northwest flank of the mountain. The reddish brown (5YR) hue in this horizon suggests translocation of organic matter which is substantiated by the laboratory data (Table 3). The parent material and IIC1ox horizons have coarser textures and less clay, thus reducing plasticity and stickiness. Particle-size data (Table 2, Fig. 5) show increasing amounts of sand with depth, and a general fining sequence upward where silt and clay are highest in the solum. This mechanical mix of silt plus clay is considered to result from the combined effects of aeolian influx and pedogenesis. For the B horizon $\bar{x}\ \Phi$ values are 6.2 and for the A horizon, 6.6, which appear comparable to the post-Liki-I solum.

Clay minerals are largely absent from the LN14 profile with the exception of a trace occurrence of illite in the IIC1ox horizon. This phenomenon is seen elsewhere in post-Liki-II soils in the upper Afroalpine area, (especially at site TV1, Mahaney, 1980), and in soils containing basaltic and andesitic clasts on Mt. Adams in the Cascades of western North America (Mahaney and Fahey, in preparation). Insofar as the primary

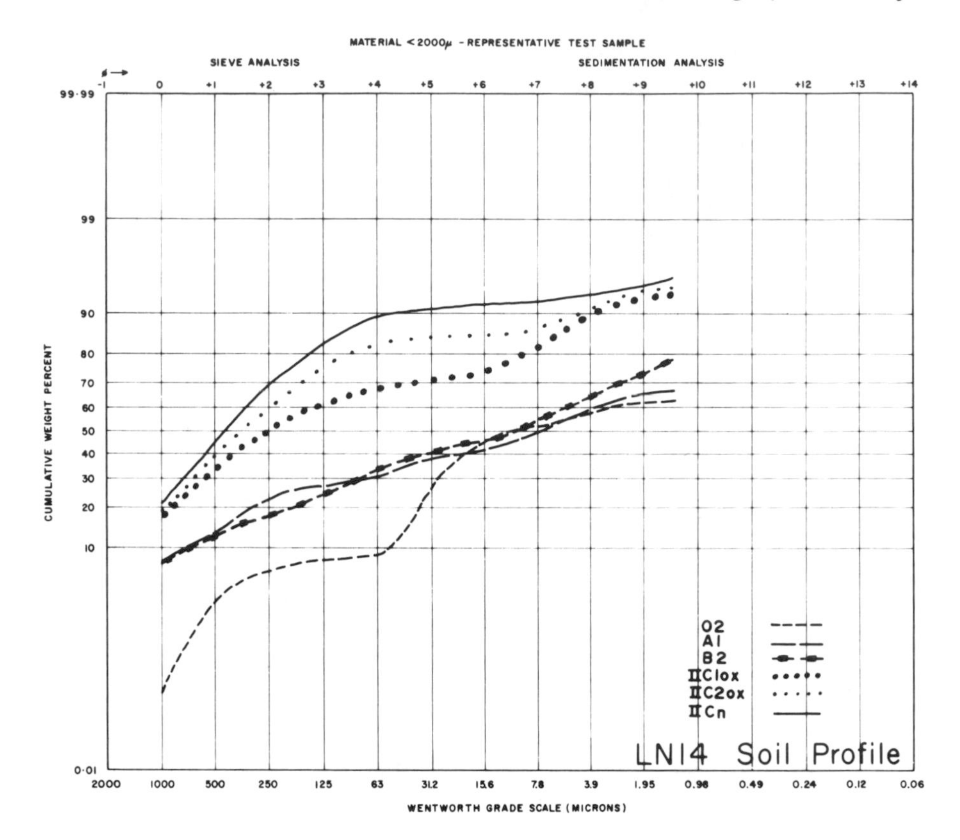

FIGURE 5. Particle-size distributions for soil horizons in LN14 profile formed in Liki-II till.

minerals are concerned, quartz dominates. It gives a pattern that suggests leaching is sufficiently powerful to translocate large quantities from the solum into the subsoil. The high amount of quartz in the 02 horizon may be due to aeolian influx. The distributions of feldspar and mica also suggest some aeolian contribution.

The post-Liki-II soil ranges from very strongly acid in the solum to medium acid in the subsoil and parent material. Dominant cations are K^+ and Ca^{+2}, and as with older soils, plant recycling probably accounts for high basic cation content in surface horizons. Organic matter, organic C, and N all diminish with depth suggesting that translocation of organic constituents is small. Free Fe is lower than in the post-Liki-I soil, probably a result of younger age and lower acidity.

Tills in High Valleys

Neoglacial deposits are divisible into two advances on the basis of topographic position, relative weathering features (Table 1), and presence of thin soils (Tables 2 and 3). The oldest deposits belong to the Tyndall advance (Fig. 2) and are here termed Tyndall till. Boulder frequency is high, stones have unpitted surfaces, and generally lack any surface discoloration. Weathering rinds are small (< 3.0 mm maximum rind) and 25 percent of all stones lack rinds. The minimum rind is nil. Soil at the type section (TT2; Figs. 2 and 6) is described below.

TT2: post-Tyndall soil. Colors in the description are from Oyama and Takehara (1970), given as moist (m) and dry (d).

Horizon	*Depth (cm)*	*Description*
01	2.5-0	Black (10YR 2/1m).
A1	0-20	Brownish black (10YR 3/2m) and grayish yellow brown (10YR 4/2d) pebbly sandy loam, friable, nonplastic, and sticky.
Cox	20-41	Dull yellowish brown (10YR 4/3m, 10YR 5/3d) pebbly sandy loam, friable, nonplastic, and slightly sticky.
Cn	41+	Light gray (2.5Y 7/2m, 7/1d) pebbly loamy sand, loose, nonplastic, and nonsticky.

This profile is thin and poorly developed to a depth of 41 cm. Particle-size data (Table 2, Fig. 7) confirm the downward movement of clay as suggested by the field data. The particle-size curve (Fig. 7) shows only minor changes in the soil relative to the parent material. For the Cox horizon $\bar{x}\ \Phi$ values amount to 3.1 and for the A horizon, 3.4, which are considerably smaller values when compared with older profiles. No clay minerals are present from the profile, but primary minerals such as quartz, feldspar, and mica are all present in minor amounts (Table 2). A surface pH of 5.2 (Table 3) indicates that this system is in disequilibrium with the environment (cf. LN14 profile, Table 3). Data for extractable cations and CEC show that the soil has a lower total exchange capacity, a condition attributed to insufficient time for development, and lower overall amounts of organic matter. This, combined with a smaller amount of N, produces a lower C:N ration. Free iron oxide development in the Cox horizon is less than half the amount in the A1, and only slightly higher than that reported for the LG2 weathering profile.

The Lewis advance laid down tills that consist largely of an open network of boulders lacking any appreciable soil cover. On the older moraine crests very thin weathering profiles cover perhaps 10 percent of the surface area to a depth of approximately 10 cm. Boulder counts are high, weathering ratios give 100 percent fresh stones with unpitted surfaces

FIGURE 6. Tyndall Glacier foreland and location of TT2 Section in background. Proximal slope of the Liki moraine is shown left of center, with Teleki Valley Ranger Station on the crest, and valley train of late-Pleistocene/Holocene age in foreground.

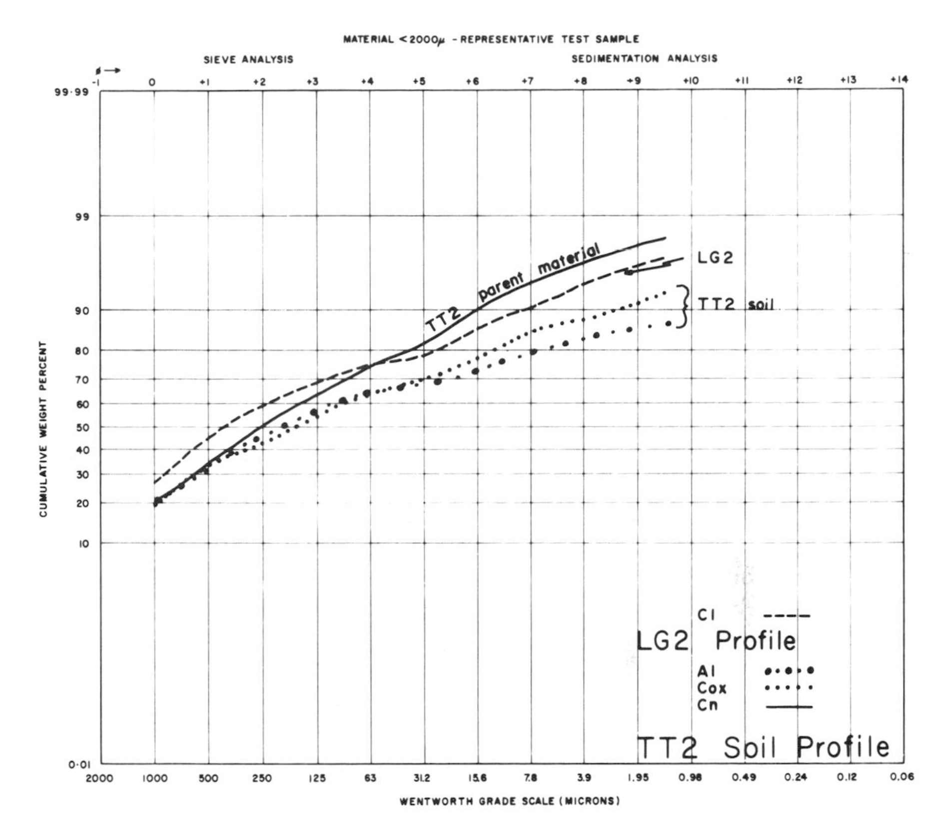

FIGURE 7. Particle-size distributions for soil and weathering profiles at TT2 and LG2 sites.

and weathering rinds are < 1.0 mm (Table 1). The LG2 profile is described as follows.

LG2: post-Lewis weathering profile.

Horizon	*Depth (cm)*	*Description*
C1	0-10	Dull yellow orange (10YR 7/3m; 7/2d) pebbly coarse loamy sand, massive structure, nonplastic, and nonsticky.

Particle-size distribution data (Fig. 7) correlate closely with the parent material curve for the TT2 profile. A $\bar{x}$ Φ of 1.9 indicates a light texture characteristic of relatively young soils formed in glacial drift (Mahaney, 1974, 1975). As with the older deposits of Tyndall age, no clay minerals are present. Somewhat larger amounts of quartz and minor amounts of feldspar appear common, which may indicate lithological differences between the two cirques.

Important differences between the youngest and oldest post-Neoglacial soils can be gleaned from the chemical data in Table 3. Soil reaction is close to neutral, and extractable cation data indicate high values for alkaline earths and alkali metals, presumably the result of fairly rapid hydrolysis in the tropical mountain environment. CEC is low and barely sufficient to support the development of 1:1 clay minerals. Low values for organic matter, organic C, N, and C:N ratio indicate the state of the system in the initial stage of development. Free iron oxide is nearly as high as in the TT2 profile (Tyndall age).

Chronology

The preceding sections describe the principal glacial units recognized in the Mt. Kenya area (Fig. 8), identify the criteria used in recognition and correlation, and summarize age relationships. Four units are recognized including deposits of pre-Teleki till (undifferentiated), deposits of Teleki till, deposits of Liki till, and deposits of Neoglaciation. Older units are exposed near the lower limit of glaciation or in interfluves in the Upper Afroalpine belt, the youngest being in the valley heads. Neoglacial and Liki deposits mantle four-fifths of nearly every glaciated valley, the remaining one-fifth being occupied by Teleki and pre-Teleki drifts. Stratigraphic names are taken from type localities along the north and west flanks of the mountain and these are extended to other drainages on the basis of morphology, weathering, and soil development.

In the correlation diagram (Fig. 8) most geologic-climatic unit boundaries are based either on maximum or minimum radiocarbon dates or on relative criteria. In most cases radiometric controls are lacking and most tentative (shown with a dashed line) boundaries will likely be shifted down the time column. Work in progress at this time may soon yield absolute ages for Liki-I drifts and for a multitude of alluvial fans of Holocene age (Mahaney, 1981). Boundaries for pre-Liki-I units are based on correlations with deposits for which radiometric ages have not been determined as yet. Liki interstades are omitted since no evidence for their definition has been found. Climatic optimum (van Zinderen Bakker and Maley, 1979) is considered to be the best term for an interval following the Liki glaciation when climate was presumably warmer than present. Time boundaries for the Climatic Optimum may be modified subsequently as new dates become available. Evidence from buried soils in alluvial fans built up during the mid-Holocene indicate at least one wet phase between 4000 and 6000 radiocarbon years ago (Mahaney, 1981). Neoglaciation and all Neoglacial advances are informal terms. Tyndall till is a local stratigraphic name for early Neoglacial deposits with indeterminate upper and lower boundaries. Termination of the Lewis advance

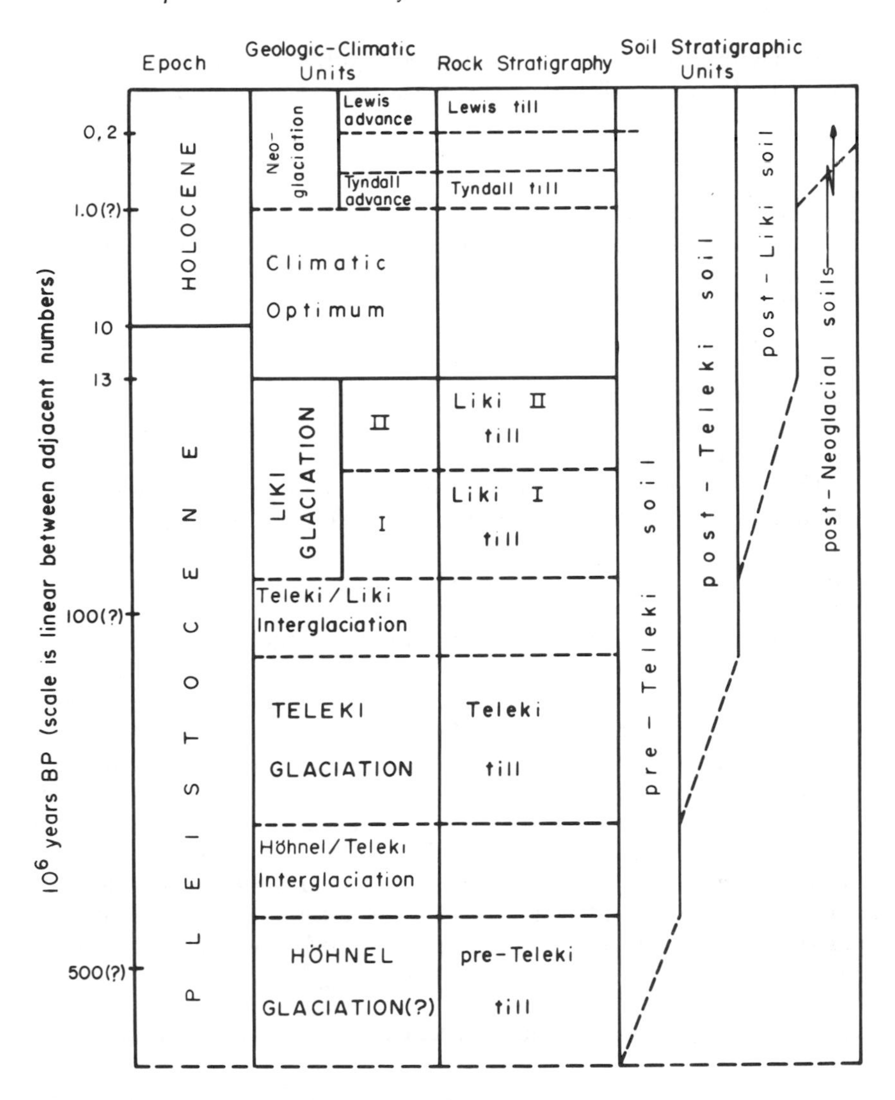

FIGURE 8. Correlation diagram. Geologic-climatic unit boundaries are based on maximum or minimum dates from nonglacial sediments. Dashes indicate boundaries for which there is no radiometric control. Liki interstades are omitted because there are no data for their definition. Climatic Optimum is considered to be the best term available for a warmer climatic interval following the Liki Glaciation. Neoglaciation refers to a resurgence of glaciation following the post-Climatic Optimum period.

coincides with glacial retreat documented in other mountainous areas of the world (Mahaney, 1974, 1978, 1979; Mahaney and Fahey, 1976).

Conclusions

Deposits belonging to four major glaciations are differentiated on the basis of radiocarbon ages, topographic position, weathering criteria, and soil development. Representative sections at the type localities are described in detail; and changes in horizon sequence, depth of weathering, color, structure, consistence, plasticity, stickiness, clay mineral assemblage, pH, and a variety of soil-chemical parameters are shown to have great utility in deposit differentiation. The greatest immediate need is to produce a large number of bracketing radiocarbon dates for late Pleistocene/Holocene deposits that mantle most major drainages on the mountain. This will allow more positive correlations to be made with adjoining areas, and permit the reconstruction of a detailed time stratigraphy.

Acknowledgments

Research was supported by grants from the National Geographic Society and York University. Fieldwork was authorized by the Office of the President, Geological Survey of Kenya, and Mountain National Parks, Republic of Kenya. I thank L. M. Mahaney, D. Halvorson, B. Blatherwick, R. Blatherwick, L. Gowland, and the students in my mountain geomorphology course (1976) for assistance in the field. In particular, I am indebted to W. D. and D. Curry, Naro Moru River Lodge, for logistical support, to P. M. Snyder (Assistant Warden) and F. W. Woodley (Warden), Mountain National Parks, Kenya, and their rangers for assistance during the course of fieldwork; to M. Bardecki for laboratory assistance; and to G. Berssenbrugge for preparing maps and diagrams. Bruno Messerli provided helpful comments in the field.

REFERENCES

Baker, B. H.
1967. Geology of the Mount Kenya area. Geol. Surv. of Kenya, Report 79, 78 pp.

Carroll, D.
1970. Clay minerals: A guide to their X-ray identification. Geol. Soc. Amer. Spec. Pap. 126, 80 pp.

Coe, M. J.
1967. The ecology of the Alpine Zone of Mt. Kenya, 136 pp. Junk, The Hague.

HEDBERG, O.
1964. Features of Afroalpine plant ecology. Acta Phytogeographica Suecica, Uppsala, vol. 49, 144 pp.
MAHANEY, W. C.
1972. Late Quaternary history of the Mount Kenya Afroalpine area, East Africa. Palaeoecol. of Af., vol. 6, pp. 139-141.
1973. Neoglacial chronology in the Fourth of July Cirque, Central Colorado Front Range. Bull. Geol. Soc. Amer., vol. 84, pp. 161-170.
1974. Soil stratigraphy and genesis of Neoglacial deposits in the Arapaho and Henderson cirques, Central Colorado Front Range. Pp. 197-240 *in* "Quaternary Environments: Proceedings of a Symposium," W. C. Mahaney, ed. Geographical Monographs, no. 5.
1975. Soils of post-Audubon age, Teton Glacier area, Wyo. Arctic and Alpine Res., vol. 7, no. 2, pp. 141-154.
1978. Late-Quaternary stratigraphy and soils in the Wind River Mountains, western Wyoming. Pp. 223-264 *in* "Quaternary Soils," W. C. Mahaney, ed. Geoabstracts Ltd., Norwich, U. K.
1979. Quaternary stratigraphy of Mt. Kenya: A reconnaissance. Palaeoecol. of Af., vol. 11, pp. 163-170.
1980. Late Quaternary rock glaciers, Mount Kenya, East Africa. Journ. Glaciol., vol. 25, no. 93, pp. 492-497.
1981. Paleoclimate reconstructed from paleosols: Evidence from the Rocky Mountains and East Africa. Pp. 227-247 *in* "Quaternary Paleoclimate," W. C. Mahaney, ed. Geoabstracts Ltd., Norwich, U. K.
MAHANEY, W. C., and FAHEY, B. D.
1976. Quaternary soil stratigraphy of the Front Range, Colorado. Pp. 319-352 *in* "Quaternary Stratigraphy of North America," W. C. Mahaney, ed. Dowden, Hutchinson and Ross, Stroudsburg, Pa.
OYAMA, M., and TAKEHARA, H.
1970. Standard soil color charts. Japan Research Council for Agriculture, Forestry and Fisheries.
VAN ZINDEREN BAKKER, E. M., and MALEY, J.
1979. Late Quaternary palaeoenvironments of the Sahara Region. Pp. 83-104 *in* "Palaeoecology of Africa," vol. 11. Balkema, Rotterdam.
ZEUNER, F. E.
1949. Frost soils on Mount Kenya and the relation of frost soils to aeolian deposits. Journ. Soil Science, vol. 1, pp. 20-30.

W. C. MAHANEY

Botanical Explorations in Celebes and Bali

Grant Recipient: Willem Meijer, School of Biological Sciences, University of Kentucky, Lexington, Kentucky.

Grants 1437, 1611: In support of botanical explorations for the establishment of Research Forests in Celebes, and botanical explorations in Bali.

As project leader of the two botanical expeditions—one to the Celebes and one to Bali—discussed in this report, I wish to thank the National Geographic Society for its support. I also am grateful to my field assistants: Noerta, a retired plant collector, Botanical Garden, Cibodas, of Java, for the 1975 expedition; and Mochtar, herbarium assistant and plant collector, Herbarium Bogoriense, for the 1976 expedition.

Nedi, retired technician of the Herbarium Bogoriense, was consultant for the identification of collections. During August 1981, Nedi suddenly died of a heart attack. There was nobody in the whole of Indonesia more experienced in long years of plant identification than Nedi. For the time being he might be irreplaceable (Jacobs, 1982). Without his assistance this report would not yet have been possible. The 1976 collections had still not arrived in the United States after this report was written (November 1982).

Dr. Marius Jacobs, editor of the *Flora Malesina Bulletin*, who was liaison at the Rijksherbarium, provided great assistance with typing and designing the labels of the collections. He suddenly died of a heart attack at the early age of 53 in April 1983.

Field assistance during the second expedition also was given as a work-study program by faculty and students of The Biological and Forestry groups of the Hasanuddin University in Udjung Pandang (Macassar) and by the Government Forestry staff in Palu, Udjung Pandang, and in Bali.

Research Aims and General Results

Indonesia with its burgeoning population, more or less trapped on the Island of Java—an area not larger than the state of Florida—is experiencing rapid conversion of its rain forests into shifting cultivation areas, depleted logged-over forests, and more permanent agricultural settlements (Goodland, 1981).

For rational land-use planning, especially to reach wise decisions concerning conservation of natural renewable resources, it is absolutely necessary to evaluate the botanical composition of different regions. This requires much detailed botanical exploration, using tree climbers and special techniques, good documentation with well-preserved herbarium specimens, and up-to-date preservation methods. A wide knowledge of plant genera and species, their affinities, distribution, ecology, and potential economic uses can be acquired with these collections in hand at botanical institutes, such as the Rijksherbarium at Leiden, Holland, and the Botanical Garden in Bogor, Indonesia, where the older collections and literature on the region are located (Jacobs, 1974).

Surprisingly little is known about the flora of Celebes and Bali compared with other regions in Indonesia, such as Java, Sumatra, and Borneo; even the large island of New Guinea was better known about 10 years ago than Celebes (van Steenis-Kruseman, 1973). After World War II, little botanical exploration was done in Celebes or Bali, although considerable activity was going on in east and North Borneo and New Guinea. Now 6 years after we started our explorations the tide has turned. Dr. Wirawan became a botanist of the Hasanuddin University. He has expanded the herbarium in Udjung Pandang, though it needs more funding. A number of follow-up expeditions went out to most of the localities visited by us, directed by Indonesian botanists from Bogor and Bandungs Technological Institute and a strong team of four Dutch botanists diverted from an expedition to Ceram. Our objective to stimulate local interest in the botanical exploration of central and south Celebes at the Hasanuddin University was at least partially successful, but still needs new infusions of manpower and enthusiasm.

In Bali, Dr. Tantra, a Balinese himself, carried out detailed forest surveys above the Bidugul Botanical Garden, after our visit. As a result of our survey and advice, the Indonesian forest service decided to give high priority to the preservation of the scenic beauty and botanical integrity of the remaining forests on Bali to make it even more attractive for tourism (Fig. 1). A West Bali National Park strongly recommended by me is now in the making (Robinson and Rustandi, 1982).

Our explorations of the Lindu-Lore National Park have helped in giving this park more of an international status and in formulating a World Wildlife Fund–International Union on Conservation of Nature and Natural Resources (WWF–IUCN) management plan (Effendy, 1981). This area was first explored by Bloembergen (1940) who collected 440 botanical specimens, 72 larger and 36 smaller trees included. Ours was the second botanical expedition in this area. We could compare the forest composi-

FIGURE 1. Tafel hoek-Tanjung Gagar, the southern point of Bali.

tion of this national park with the fast dwindling forests north of Palu in the neck of Celebes near a place called Kebon Kopi (coffee estate) and in logged-over forests along the west coast south of Donggala, and we were able to seek out the contrast with the savannas along the Palu Valley, known as the driest spot in Indonesia, with rainfall varying from 305 to 773 mm per year (average about 556 mm) rather evenly spread over the different monsoon seasons (Steup, 1929; Schmidt and Ferguson, 1951).

For the maintenance of the irrigated rice paddies in the valley near Palu it is essential to protect the water supply in the watershed north of Lindu Lake, which has a much higher rainfall than the valley itself. With the assistance of the head of the Irrigation Department, it was possible to make a strong case with the highest authorities of the country for absolute protection of the forests around Gunung Nokilalaki north of the lake, a mountain that is the habitat of the rare and endangered dwarf buffaloes (*Anoa*, 2 species) and *babirusa*—a botanical paradise. Unfortunately, after this conservation battle was settled, it appeared that greedy timber loggers had penetrated this area, felled the huge *Agathis* (kauri) trees, and had lifted them out by helicopter, according to field observations of the last Dutch expedition.

During the second expedition it was possible to make an accurate assessment of the flora on the limestone hills north of Maros in the newly established Karaenta Forest Reserve, only 40 to 60 mi from the capital. We established here a kind of "natural arboretum," where we collected about 215 species of trees, belonging to 100 genera and 44 families, besides 20 woody climbers. Arranging this arboretum was much more feasible than planting a whole new botanical garden around the new university campus. Our advice was to preserve as many species of trees as possible, and we assisted in identifying them, even as they were cut down under our eyes! Faculty, staff, and some well-selected students, who passed a field training course at the Karaenta site, joined in the assessment of the tree and herbaceous flora around the International Nickel Company's (INCO) mining sites near Lake Matano in the Malili region and along the Larona River near the Towuti Lake, where a new hydroelectric project, constructed by the Bechtel Company, was under way. Our advice was asked as to the use of native flora in erosion control. We also tried to give suggestions for the monitoring of the air pollution that might be caused by the new nickel smelter, but were assured that the same high standard would be used there as is used near Sudbury in Canada. The Indonesians, who were ignorant about the situation there, felt happy about the INCO's assurances. We even came up with a scheme on how to salvage the local flora that was logged and removed from the strip-mine sites, and on how to use successional tree species for reclamation. Apparently, however, we could not wean the local "experts" away from the idea of planting pines beside introduced *Eucalyptus* and of using horticultural strains of *Hibiscus* in erosion control. For the local golf course, sods of Bermuda grass and zoysia were flown in from the capital of South Celebes and the excellent local *Axonopus* was neglected.

After we considered our mission fulfilled we gave a special field trip around Matano Lake for the expatriate INCO ladies and a slide show pleading for the preservation and use of the local floristic beauties. We spent a weekend field trip on the Peak of Bonthain, where we could see all the exotic pine plantations replacing the original montane forest and not fulfilling any useful function for water catchment because these plantations are devoid of any undergrowth. Besides they have no value for local supplies of construction timbers. Those were illegally garnered in the remnants of the montane forest, using native species that no forester ever dreamed of using for mixed plantations.

The island of Bali is about 5770 km^2 with a population of 4 million people. Its flora has never yet been described in detail (Meijer, 1980 ms.). Only 3350 pre-war collections were made there (van Steenis-Kruseman, 1950) and some by Soepadmo more recently. We can also compare the area of this volcanic island with the state of Connecticut or with one third of the area of the Hawaiian Islands (Fig. 2). In 1975 we collected about 200 species and 348 collections were added to this in 1976. We collected all over the island except in the higher altitudes of Gunung Agung and only to a limited amount in the western mountains. On the basis of this preliminary survey we were able to make suggestions for more effective protection of the watersheds and for calling attention to the native flora, fauna, and vegetation types for the purpose of recreational nature study and tourism. It is now a firm policy in Indonesia to give in Bali the highest possible priority to watershed protection and nature conservation in land-use planning in accordance with the local Hindu culture to preserve sacred forests and sacred trees, which makes this place the most fascinating of all parts of Indonesia. My unpublished report, "Bali and its Neglected Flora," which also pays attention to remnants of original wild flora in the midst of the most cultivated parts of the island, was used in 1976 in a special conservation workshop organized by the Forestry Planning Division. There I suggested that the old neglected coffee gardens be replanted with local timber and firewood trees, such as *Altingia, Bischofia, Manglietia glauca, Weinmannia blumei, Toona surenii, Podocarpus imbricatus, Agathis, Palaquium javanicum, Albizia,* and *Erythrina,* instead of pure pine plantations, which serve little as water catchment and supply inferior wood for construction purposes. Renewed interest in agroforestry may assist in putting these ideas into practice. The Balinese with their great respect for living beings are the most ideal conservationists in southeast Asia.

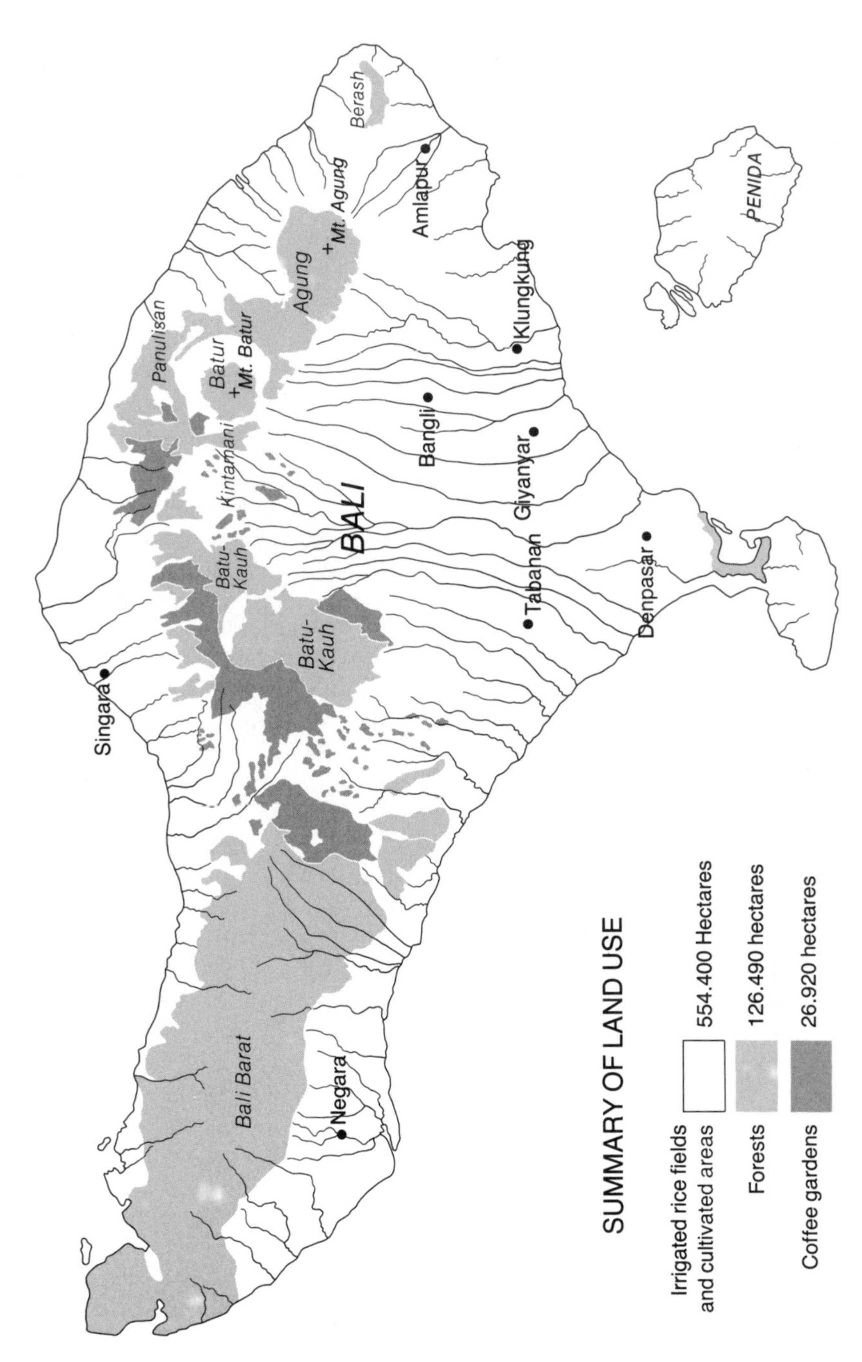

FIGURE 2. Land-use map of Bali.

Celebes

THE PALU VALLEY AND SURROUNDING HILLS

This area is known as the driest place of Indonesia (Fig. 3), with rainfall varying between 305 and 773 mm per year (average 556 mm) (Steup, 1929). However, the small amount of rain that falls here is rather evenly spread over the year. A number of decorative drought-resistant plants were seen by us and already listed by Steup (1929): *Acacia farnesiana* (Mimosaceae), *Calotropis gigantea* (Asclepidiaceae), *Cycas* (Cycadaceae), *Dracaena* (Liliaceae), and *Kalanchoe pinnata* (Crassulaceae; Fl. Males. i 4: 199) and also the introduced *Tamarindus indica* (Caesalpiniaceae). Noerta (Meijer 10154) found here *Capparis quiniflora* (Capparaceae: Blumea 12: 482, Fl. Males. i 6: 89). This is according to Dr. M. Jacobs, the monographer of this family—the second collection in Celebes—a drought plant of the Lesser Sunda Islands, Moluccas, New Guinea, and North Australia. Prof. van Steenis, the editor of *Flora Malesiana,* has pointed out the existence of a series of drought-tolerant species in the area around the wetter refugium of moist tropical rain forests of the Sundashelf through a corridor from the Asian mainland, including the seasonal drought areas of Celebes and other parts of east Malesia (van Steenis, 1979, and earlier publications cited there).

We collected in the Palu Valley the drought indicators *Crotalaria linifolia, Tephrosia pumila,* and *Rhynchosia minima*—all legumes that give some color to the monotonous grasslands and supply them with nitrogen. Our collection of *Rhynchosia minima* seems to be the first in Celebes and fills in a bit the disjunction between the Asiatic mainland and the Java-Australia-eastern New Guinea region of this species as illustrated in Figure 14 of van Steenis (1979).

Among the grasses also occurs the drought indicator *Heteropogon contortus* besides the less sensitive species, *Themeda triandra, Sorghum nitidum,* and *Cymbopogon flexuosus,* all identified by Jan Veldkamp of the Rijksherbarium. Also some very widespread grasses such as *Chloris inflata, Eragrostis amabilis,* and *Dactylotaenium aegypticum* make up the grass vegetation of this valley. The fact that nowhere in these grasslands is there a dominance of *Imperata cylindrica* but everywhere a rich assemblage of savanna grasses and legumes and some composites associated with them (in addition to the species mentioned there is also *Acanthospermum hispidus* [Compositae] and the legumes *Atylosia* [Cantharospermum], *Scarabacoides, Alysicarpus vaginalis, Indigofera linnaei, Indigofera hirsuta, Uvaria lagopodioides, Desmodium umbellatum,* and *Desmodium gangeticum*) points to the fact that these grasslands are not recent degradations of depleted tropical rain forests but more likely survivors of the Pleistocene arid flora of this part of east Malesia. The succession to shrub

FIGURE 3. South Celebes semi-arid zone south of Palu.

and forest vegetation is, of course, kept back by the grazing goats which make survival possible only for shrubs and climbers provided with spiny branches or thorns: *Harrisonia perforata, Capparis sepiaria, Capparis horrida, Azima sarmentosa,* and *Zizyphus oenoplia*. From a plant geographical point of view the most interesting woody shrub in these grasslands is *Santalum album,* the sandalwood. We found it in a small remnant population, about a 3- to 4-hr walk south of Palu. It is another drought-resistant plant of south and east Malesia. Against the slopes of the hills from 200 to 800 m secondary shrubby vegetation and forest invade the grasslands, mixed with woody and herbaceous climbers. Most likely this area has a moister climate and less competition from the goats that cover the area.

The species present here are not all ubiquitous secondary forest species. *Tristira triptera* (identified by Dr. Leenhouts, monographer of the family Sapindaceae, to which this tree belongs) is an eastern Malesian species known only from Celebes, the Philippines, and the Moluccas. Others to be analyzed are: *Erythroxoxylum cuneatum, Wikstroemia androsaemifolia,* and *Pittosporum pentandrum*.

The most simple form of reforestation in this area is fencing-in against cattle and goats and for fire protection. There is no way to find enough funds to catch up with the enormous backlog in any other way.

The Lowland Forests of Central Celebes West of the Malili Ultrabasics

These forests belong to the ever wet rain forests of central Celebes on paleogene and neogene sediments. The geology, soils, and topography are similar with parts of east Kalimantan and the distance across the Macassar Straits is only 50 to 100 mi; notwithstanding this, we find ourselves in a totally different world. While Borneo may have around 300 species of dipterocarps, Celebes harbors only about 12 species of this family. In the critically revised family Burseraceae (see Leenhouts, 1956), we find 16 species reported from Celebes and 32 from Borneo.

We studied the lowland forests inside the logging area: Sungai kaja, Sulwood Timber Company, 60 km south of Dongala, along the road between Palu and Parigi in the neck of the island and east of Kampong Toro, along the bridle path to the Lindu Lake, and north of the lake in the Lindu-Lore National Park. The same general area had been botanically explored by Bloembergen (1940) and, after our tours, by the American mammologist-ecologist Guy Musser of the American Museum of Natural History (Musser, unpublished). Pulling all the data on the tree flora together we can estimate that around 200 species of trees occur in these lowland forests with around 15 to 20 species really common. That would be about half of the species diversity of a similar area in Borneo. Apparently Pleistocene aridity has caused extinction of species here or the greater landmass of Borneo has been a richer center of evolution of new species, comparable with New Guinea. In the genus *Canarium*, for example, New Guinea has 17 species compared with only 10 in Celebes and 20 in Borneo (Leenhouts, 1956).

The coastal mangrove near Dongala and south of it does not differ from the east coast of Borneo. After all, all the mangrove species are dispersed by the sea. Also the strand flora with *Cerbera manghas, Terminalia catappan, Pongamia pinnata, Albizia saponaria, Ximenia americana,* and *Albizia lebbekoides,* besides *Hibiscus tiliaceus* and *Vitex trifolia,* are very widespread. Behind coastal mangroves or sandbars we saw some freshwater swamp flora which could have been transported straight with some floating islands out of the estuaries of some rivers in east Borneo: *Barringtomia racemosa, Samadera indica, Terminalia copelandii, Polyalthia lateriflora* (with its typical pneumatophores resembling those of *Sonneratia*), *Elaeocarpus littoralis,* and *Horsfieldia iriya.*

Some secondary dryland trees such as *Trema orientalis* and *Colona scabra* probably also could arrive here with easy dispersal from Borneo.

In the dryland forest flora we miss a rather long list of genera that find their boundary west of the Wallace line (Meijer, 1983), theories in long-distance dispersal notwithstanding.

For others this boundary does not seem to have played a great role. They went all the way between the land bridges from Borneo to the Philippines and from there to Celebes or had the ability to get dispersed over the Macassarstreet: *Canangium odoratum, Canarium hirsutum, Duabanga moluccana, Alstonia pneumatophora, Baccaurea lanceolata, Baccaurea racemosa, Dracontomelum mangiferum, Dysoxylum alliaceum, Engelhardia serrata, Grewia cinnamomifolia, Intsia bijuga, Koordersiodendron pinnatum, Lithocarpus havilandii, Mallotus ricinoides, Octomeles sumatrana, Mussaendopsis beccariana, Pangium edule, Pometia pinnata, Planchonia valida, Pterocarpus indicus, Siphonodon celastrinus, Terminalia copelandii, Symplocos fasciculata, Vernonia arborea, Turpinia pomifera, Buchanania arborescens, Cinnamomum parthenoxylon,* and many others. *Garuga floribunda,* very rare along the coast of Sabah, is a common tree here. Still this part of Celebes has also a number of species among some of the larger genera, such as *Calophyllum, Canarium, Palaquium, Dillenia, Dysoxylum, Celtis, Elaeocarpus, Eugenia, Ficus, Litsea* (and other Lauraceae), *Lithocarpus, Myristica,* and *Saurauia,* which are restricted to Celebes or the islands east of it.

The most famous is the Celebes ebony tree, *Diospyros celebica,* much sought after for its wood. *Elmerilla ovalis* often used by the local people has still not been discovered for its excellent properties by the foresters, as they were trained in Java, who never saw it. The timber companies have learned that the Sapotaceae have as good salable timber as the *Merantis* of Borneo and Sumatra. Probably they also log *Canarium, Duabanga, Dracontomelum, Planchonia,* and various larger sized Lauraceae. This forest is far less rich in genera, species, and biomass of trees that are centered in east Malesia: *Metrosideros, Eucalyptus,* only *E. deglupta* can be seen in small stands. *Himantandra belgraveana, Kibara coriacea, Macadamia, Lepiniopsis zernatensis, Casuarina rumphiana,* and *Weinmannia. Spiraeopsis, Trimenia,* and *Sycopsis philippinensis,* mentioned by Bloembergen (1940) and collected by Guy Musser (1976), are the main eastern elements, and nowhere are dominant in the forest composition.

The herbaceous flora—with its own genera and species in Zingiberaceae, some wild bamboos, *Musa,* Gesneriaceae, especially *Cyrtandra,* orchids, and pandans—shows that central Celebes has been long enough isolated from Borneo to evolve its own species among genera that are not so easily subjected to long-distance dispersal.

A case in point is also the palms with *Pigafetta* growing in majestic colonies in old landslides, *Licuala celebica,* many rotans, some *Areca* and *Pinanga.* For *Arenga pinnata* central Celebes seems to be the center of origin. Also *Averrhoa bilimbi, Gnetum gnemon,* and *Cordyline fruticosa,* all collected by us in the wild, might well take their origin from Celebes. The Bugis, great seafarers, possibly far into the Pacific, might have played a role in this. It is also possible that some of these plants were shared between Java and Celebes and became extinct in the wild in the central and eastern lowlands of Java. The almost complete absence of *Dipterocarps* in these forests is compensated by greater prominence of *Meliaceae, Sapotaceae,* and some *Burseraceae.* More accurate enumerations of sample plots will give a clearer picture of this.

THE LOWER AND UPPER MONTANE FORESTS ON MT. NOKILALAKI, 1500- TO 24,000-M ALTITUDE

On the lower slopes of this mountain a number of trees restricted to lowland rain forests, such as *Pometia, Duabanga, Emerillia,* a whole series of *Ficus, Koordersiodendron, Dillenia serrata,* and all sorts of Meliaceae, drop out of the picture. The slopes are taken over by some higher altitude Magnoliaceae, such as *Aromadendron elegans* and *A. nutans;* the local maple *Acer caesium;* some conifers, such as *Taxus baccata* (coll. Guy Musser); large *Agathis* trees; and two species of *Podocarpus (P. imbricatus* and *P. rumphii).*

Probably the most dominant tree in the lower zone is *Castanopsis acuminatissima,* mixed with all 4 species of oaks reported from Celebes: *Lithocarpus celebicus, L. elegans, L. glutinosus,* and *L. havilandii.* The latter was an old acquaintance from Mount Kinabalu in Sabah, and *L. glutinosus* is shared with the Philippines.

One species of *Tristania* and about 7 *Eugenias* and various Lauraceae and Theaceae with a scattering of *Evonymus, Tetractomia,* a few Myristicaceae, *Symplocos,* and *Pittosporum* remind one strongly of montane forests in Sumatra and Borneo. A special Celebes character is given to this forest by botanical curiosities, such as *Sphenostomum papuanum* (discovered by Guy Musser), *Macadamia hildebrandii,* and *Fagraea tacapana.*

At the higher regions some treasures are *Drimys piperita, Myrica javanica, Dacrydium elatum, Quintinia* and *Distylum stellare* (both coll. Musser), the latter species only once yet collected in Borneo on Kinabalu, at a site now destroyed, some species of *Symplocos* and *Rapanea, Trimenia papuana,* 4 species of *Astronia, Clethra,* besides shrubby *Rhododendron* (among others, we found the white flowering *R. bloembergii* and *Vaccinium*). The total montane tree flora might be about 100 species, based on our data and those of Musser (1976).

In the lower montane forest there are a number of peculiar ground herbs: wild gingers belonging to the genera *Hornstedtia, Alpinia* (a species with green flowers), and *Riedelia.*

We collected here also 2 *Aroids (Alocasia longiloba* and *Typhonium horsfieldii)* and the usual assortment of montane herbs: *Begonia, Peperomia candida, Rungia coerulea, Pilea, Nertera depressa, Burmannia longifolia,* and the less usual *Hedyosma orientale,* a giant herb, and the tiny saprophyte *Sciaphila javanica* and 3 species of *Carex (C. cruciata, C. breviscapa,* and *C. eymae).*

A rich harvest of mosses and hepatics was gathered in the cloud forest zone around the summit; the most spectacular was the giant moss *Spiridens* along with the somewhat less impressive *Dawsonia*.

Also some peat moss *(Sphagnum)* grew near the summit. One epiphytic *Nepenthes, N. maxima*, the legume climber *Strongylodon*, various species of the shrubby *Saurauia*, a climbing bamboo, and 2 bright red flowering Loranthaceae all disappeared into our plastic bags and presses, together with a good series of ferns that was well identified and analyzed by the Flora Malesiana botanists and reported upon by Dr. M. Jacobs as follows:

> Ferns deserve special mention because Meijer collected so many, probably far more than a posthumus fern specialist had done during a brief stay in 1930. The data below are based on those in the Leiden collection, and on identifications verified by Drs. R. E. Holttum and E. Hennipman; I looked them up for distribution and rarity. The most interesting ones follow here.

- *Antrophyum callifolium* (Meijer 9587): widespread but no material yet from Celebes.
- *A. reticulatum* (10036): one posthumus collection from Kulawi, and not known from outside the Lore Kalimanta area (name now changed to Lori Lindu).
- *Crypsinus enervis* (9479): all over Malesia except Celebes, this seems to be the first collection.
- *Didymochlaena lunulata* (10023): from Sumatra and Java, seems new for Celebes.
- *Diplazium porphyrorhachis* (9500): Borneo, Philippines, the second collection from Celebes.
- *D. whitfordii* (9491): Philippines, apparently new for Celebes.
- *Goniophlebium persicifolium* (9569): from Sumatra and Java, Lesser Sunda Islands, seems new for Celebes.
- *Gymnosphaera recommutata* (9477): Malaya, Sumatra, Borneo, seems new for Celebes.
- *Lomagramma lomarioides* (9590): Java, Lesser Sunda Islands, seems new for Celebes.
- *Monogramme paradoxa* (9459): Java, Lesser Sunda Islands, Philippines, New Guinea, seems new for Celebes.
- *Osmunda banksiifolia* (10 015): Philippines, Moluccas, the second collection from Celebes (the first one from Minahasa).
- *Prosaptia alata* (9553): Malaya, Sumatra, Borneo, New Guinea, seems new for Celebes.
- *Pyrrosia longifolia* (9566): Southeast Asia, Malaya, Sumatra, Borneo, Lesser Sunda Islands; Eyma collected it first in Celebes, this seems to be the second.
- *Thylacopteris papillosa* (9569): only a few specimens from Borneo.
- *Vaginularia paradoxa* (9568): widespread, second collection from Celebes.

In summary, 9 species of ferns collected were new for Celebes and 5 were new for the second collection for this island.

> All these cases point to the conclusion that Celebes in general and Lore Kalimanta in particular, is an important "stepping stone" in the distribution area of ferns.
>
> Palms were also given attention by Meijer, who noted 5 species of rattan, and the endemic *Pigafetta ciliaris*. Lore Kalimanta now called Linda-Lore National Park, however, is far richer in palms: Dr. Guy Musser collected in the course of time about 60 species, which he sent to Kew for study by Dr. J. Dransfield.

The one day we spent on our ascent to the summit of this mountain supplied us with a rich harvest of 153 specimens. Dr. Musser, who lived as a hermit in a shed at 1700-m altitude, more or less completed the inventory of trees, all studied in relation with seed dispersal, but never published the results.

THE FLORA IN THE MALILI REGION, SOUTH CELEBES

During July 1976, I spent 10 days in the Malili region with botanical collector Mochtar and faculty and 2 students from Hasanuddin University. We spent time especially at the INCO nickel-mining concession. We were flown over by INCO to their Soroaka town site where at that time 826 expatriate staff worked and stayed, together with 458 dependents. INCO had already spent 800 million dollars on developing the mining site and factory which would be in production by the end of the year. Part of the INCO concession and a large area of the surrounding region is being logged by the Japanese Zedsko timber firm. My advice was sought about fast replanting or chances for natural regrowth along a channel for a hydroelectrical plant along the Larona River, which receives water from the three magnificent scenic lakes in this large ultrabasic area of Celebes. The river ecosystem is already being destroyed without the slightest prior biological investigation.

The Forest Service has obliged the company by creating a large strict reserve (definitely not for another timber-concession) to prevent any future erosion in this area. A certain amount of damage is being done, of course, by all the excavation work, low roads, and three quarries. A lot of local ironwood, *Metrosideros*, poles are cut in the forest for use along the roads. The new reserve has *Agathis* in it and huge stands of *Metrosideros* forest mixed with a lot of *Calophyllum*, various Burseraceae, Sapotaceae, at least 2 dipterocarps (*Hopea celebica* and 1 *Vatica* species). It might differ from the nonserpentenized mining area south of Soroako, where *Metrosideros* is far less frequent, but Burseraceae (*Canarium* and *Santiria*) is rather dominant.

On rocky serpentenized hills near the Matano Lake, locally there is a lot of *Xanthostemon diversifolium*, some *Leptospermum flavescens* on formerly burnt off sites and on lakeside alluvium there is a lot of secondary savanna-like shrub with plenty of *Baeckia frutescens* and *Gleichenia-Nepenthes* thickets. *Macadamia hildebrandtii* is common there. We found in the Matano Lake still some *Ottelia mesenterica* (endemic) and even a small patch of swamp forest with *Elaeocarpus littoralis* and *Gonystylis* (new for Celebes). On islands and a peninsula in the eastern part of the lake, there is a lot of *Casuarina sumatrana* and some *Tristania*, a species without light-colored bark.

We made an almost complete inventory and collection of the flora near the guesthouse and the school in the western part of the Soroako town site and assisted the teaching staff and some local expatriate residents in plant recognition, especially such spectacular ornamental species as *Gardenia celebica, Deplancea glabra, Xanthostemum diversiflorum, Baeckia frutescens*, and some nice *Adinandra* (?), *Rapanea*, and the whole series of species of *Eugenia*—all suitable to be retained in local gardens. A nearby limestone hill south of the western half of the lake has interesting ponds with water plants along it, some *Gluta renghas* and some magnificent orchids and palms.

There are plenty of orchids to be collected from trees felled and burnt in the mining site and all sorts of plants including tree-ferns, *Bauhinia*, a beautiful flowering *Vitex*, and a pretty yellow flowering Goodeniaceae. *Scaevola oppositifolia* could also be collected there.

Special attention was paid to the anti-erosion potential of plants for the Larona area, and to a detailed report on that subject written for INCO.

Maros-Karaenta Forest Reserve, Natural Arboretum

This reserve is situated in the limestone hills, northeast of Udjung Pandang, the nearest place from the local Hasanuddin University in which to study native forest. We held here a workshop botanical exploration with 10 students. We collected about 350 numbers covering 215 species of trees, belonging to 100 genera and 44 families, besides 20 species of woody climbers. Here, the students learned how to make collections from permanent trees, how to annotate and dry collections, and above all how to tackle the treacherous terrain of the steep-creviced and honeycombed limestone cliffs. In this way the students gained a far better knowledge about trees and other plants than could have been possible in any classroom setting. Also 2 Forest Service staff members and 2 faculty members took part in this exercise. The first botanical explorations were made in these hills by Teysmann in 1877 (Teysmann, 1879).

FIGURE 4. A remnant of montane forest rich in *Acer laurinum* and *Podocarpus* with planted pine forest in background. Bonthain, south Celebes.

Mount Lompodatang-Peak of Bonthain

We spent one weekend with students and faculty of Hasanuddin University on this mountain. At the north side most of the montane forests have been converted into coffee gardens and pine plantations. We found a bit of natural forest with a lot of *Acer laurinum,* the native Malesian maple, and a dense undergrowth of shrubs and herbs above the pine plantations near the Forestry Resthouse (Fig. 4). The pines were heavily damaged by excessive tapping of the bark for resins. The natural forest was quite devastated by recent tree fellings for timber carted all the way to the capital. It was clear to us that in the montane region the natural forest has a far better function as a water catchment area than the pine forests that are practically devoid of undergrowth. Rainwater runs off along the slopes covered only by pine needles. We saw some interesting species of wild *Podocarpus* and were really amazed that apparently no forester had ever tried to plant those species and the local fast-growing *Acer* as well as other trees preferred by the locals instead of exotic pines.

Bali

Central and North Bali

The famous tourist island Bali has a flora that is more or less a microcosm of the flora of East Java. There is not yet a single paper written on the flora of this island in the English language. As a result, scientific tourists are left in the dark about the fascinating botanical aspects of this tropical paradise. With 2.5 million people living within 5770 km^2 there is of course not much left of the original lowland forests, nothing more than a 10-hectare sacred dipterocarp forest near Sangeh (Fig. 5) and a few remnants along the Bali West Forest Reserve, which, it is hoped will soon become a national park. It is, however, remarkable how many wild elements, sacred trees, and plants growing in the deep shady ravines carved out in the lava flows are still present. The cultural life of the Balinese roots in Stone Age periods when the seminomadic life of jungle-dwelling ancestors developed into the most sedentary type of agriculture, based on the terraced wet rice paddies with villages and homesites as holy ground and places of worship, with temples and surrounding trees respected as symbols of stability and long life, life full of rituals, in a landscape as colorful, with the magic of trees, shrubs, flowers, and birds as depicted in many Balinese paintings. Woodcarvings for the temples and houses were made from local timbers, the most favorite Sawo Ketik-*Manilkara kauki,* now almost extinct but still present in the western forests. Another timber tree used for carvings is satinwood-Pangal buaja belonging to *Fagara rhetsa*-Rutaceae. This tree is grown in the village gardens.

Local *Alstonia scholaris*-Pulai is in general used for masks. About 20 years ago ebony wood imported from Celebes replaced most of the local sources for woodcarving and a new cottage and atelier industry for the tourist market was developed. In the fertile triangle of Bali north of Den Pasar there still exists a flora of about 50 wild trees and shrubs, including majestic specimens of banyan figs, *Sterculia foetida, Cynometra ramiflora,* and *Engelhardia spicata.*

Forested areas around the volcanos and in the western mountains and a bit in the southern mangroves cover about 126,490 ha, about one fifth of the irrigated rice paddies and homestead gardens. The most luxurious montane rain forest can be found at 1200- to 2276-m altitude in the volcanic complex near the Bidugul Botanic garden with three scenic old crater lakes. Ornamental groups of the stilt-rooted *Pandanus faviger* still grow on the steep crater wall of Danau Bratan. The epiphyllous alga-like moss *Ephemeropsis tjibodensis* indicates the great humidity of the microclimate at this altitude. The mountains of Bali collect a lot more moisture than the rather dry coastal regions which have a savanna climate. The Bi-

FIGURE 5. Noerta, my field assistant, inspecting *Dipterocarpus hasseltii* in the Sacred Forest near Sangeh, south Bali.

FIGURE 6. Mount Agung from the air. This volcano is 10,308 ft high; it erupted in 1964. Mount Batur in the background has an altitude of 5636 ft. It last erupted in 1963. This photograph was taken in 1976.

dugul forest contains about 50 species of trees, with some giant specimens of *Podocarpus imbricatus* and *Casuarina junghuhniana* and some large banyan trees *(Ficus involucrata* and *F. sundaica).* The flora here is mostly west Malesian, but species of oaks and chestnuts are totally missing. This 1600-ha reserve deserves a much more detailed inventory. It is an ideal hydrological reserve and together with the Botanical Garden is screened off from the village coffee gardens with a marvelous mixed forest plantation, which is one of the few demonstrations in Indonesia that tree plantations may be far better than monocultures of pines. We noted here: *Altingia excelsa, Schimawallichii, Podocarpus imbricatus, Ehretia javanica, Erythrina* sp., *Mangietia glauca, Melia azedarachta, Agathis* sp., *Toona sureni, Glochidion glomeratum, Bischofia javanica, Crypteronia paniculata,* and *Cupressus goveniana.*

The more active volcanoes Gunung Batur (1717 m) and Gunung Agung (3142 m) which produced lava flows in 1926 and in 1964 (van Bemmelen, 1970) are more or less devoid of montane rain forest (Figs. 6, 7). Sleumer (1966, 1967) reports 10 species of shrubby Ericaceae from these mountains: 3 *Rhododendron,* 4 *Vaccinium,* 2 *Gaultheria,* and *Diplycosia heterophylla.* We were not able to climb the sacred Gunung Agung all the way

FIGURE 7. Vanda tricolor orchid growing on an old lava flow on Mount Batur. Photograph taken in 1976 by W. Meijer.

to the summit because it took us too long to make the round trip from Batur to Agung near the famous temple.

Only 13 species of trees could be found by us along the ravine we followed upwards, including *Myrica javanica, Weinmannia fraxinea, Saurauria distosoma, Engelhardia spicata, Viburnum coriaceum, V. lutescens,* and *Litsea cf. diversifolia;* all the others were more or less secondary shrub species like *Maoutia diversifolia, Claoxylon affine,* and *Antidesma tetrandum.*

Coastal Savanna and Montane Forest in West Bali

The monsoon climate of east Java and the Lesser Sunda Islands is most pronounced along the coasts. The daily movements of the clouds drives them away from the coast against the mountain range in west Bali.

The coastal vegetation is a kind of fire savanna with its spreading crowns of *Acacia* and its numerous Lontar *(Borassus)* palms (Fig. 8) almost reminding of parts of Africa and of the eastern coastal zone in Ceylon where *Lannea* and *Schleichera oleosa* are dominant among the trees. The spiny climber *Harrisonia perforata* is common here and an excellent example of the dry zone corridor around Malesia (van Steenis 1979). The grass

FIGURE 8. Coastal savanna with *Borassus* palms. Site of the proposed national park in west Bali.

fields are rich in small herbaceous legumes (*Crotalaria striata, C. acicularis, Indigofera hirsuta, I. linifolia, I. sumatrana, Uraria lagopodioides, Cantharospermum scarabaeoides*), about 10 different grasses, among others, *Heteropogon contortus* and *Sorghum amboinensis*, and all sorts of colorful herbs flowering during the wet season and well adapted to survive the dry, east monsoon. Among the trees we saw the very widespread *Albizia lebbeckoides, Zizyphus jujuba, Cordia obliqua*, and *Antidesma ghaesemblia. Erioglossum rubiginosum, Helicteres isora*, and *Schoutenia ovata* besides *Phyllanthus emblica* give this savanna a bit more local character.

Farther inland this savanna grades into a shrubby type of forest, now partly destroyed by plantations of teak, *Dalbergia*, mulberry, and *Leucaena glauca*, besides some of the more local *Fagara rhetsa, Manilkara kauki*, and *Santalum album*. No attention was paid here by diligent foresters to the local medicinal plant *Strychnos lucida*, disjunct between Thailand, east Malesia, and Australia.

We could only slightly explore the higher more moist forest. Farther southeast we found near Chandi Kusuma an interesting mixture of lowland moist forest elements with a real wild locality of *Dipterocarpus hasseltii* the last remnant of natural dipterocarp moist forest in Bali, now endangered by an irrigation dam project. We collected here and in the other parts of this reserve about 60 tree species.

The forest serves here as a source of local timber and firewood for the coastal population and becomes more and more devastated. A buffer zone of firewood species and local construction timber is absolutely needed.

In more eastern parts of Bali old abandoned coffee gardens would be the best sites for such agroforestry.

REFERENCES

Bemmelen, R. W. van
1949. The geology of Indonesia, vol. 1A, 732 pp., 3 vols. Government Printing Office, The Hague. (2nd edition, reprint of original, 1970, M. Nÿhoff, The Hague.)

Bloembergen, S.
1940. Verslag van een exploratie-tocht naar Midden Celebes (Lindoemeer en Goenoeng Nokilalaki ten Zuiden van Paloe) in Juli 1939. Tectona, vol. 33, pp. 377-417.

Effendy, A. Sumardja
1981. First fine national parks in Indonesia. Parks-IUCN, vol. 6, no. 2, pp. 1-4.

Goodland, Robert
1981. Indonesia's environmental progress in economic development. Pp. 215-276 *in* "Where Have All the Flowers Gone? Deforestation in the Third World." Studies in Third World Societies. Publ. 13, Dept. of Anthropology, College of William and Mary, Williamsburg, Virginia.

HAMILTON, WARREN

1979. Tectonics of the Indonesian region. Geol. Survey Prof. Paper 1078, pp. 1-345 and 1 map.

JACOBS, M.

1974. Botanical panorama of the Malesian Archipelago (vascular plants). UNESCO—Natural Resources in Humid Tropical Asia, pp. 263-294.

1982. Obituary, Nedi. (Bogor, 12 or 13, v. 1913-Bogor, 7, VIII. 1981). Flora Malesiana Bull., vol. 35, pp. 3712-3713.

LAM, H. J.

1945. Notes on the historical phytogeography of Celebes. Blumea, vol. 5, pp. 600-640.

LEENHOUTS

1956. Burseraceae. Flora Malesiana, series I, vol. 5, pp. 209-296.

MEIJER, W.

1974. Fieldguide for trees of west Malesia. Univ. of Kentucky Bookshop, pp. 1-328, 78 figs. and 26 plates.

1980. Bali and its neglected flora. Unpublished working paper for workshop on Nature Conservation in Bali. Directorate of Forestry, Division of Planning.

1982. Plant refuges in the Indo-Malesian region. Chapter 31, pp. 576-584, *in* "Biological Diversification in the Tropics," Ghillean T. Prance, ed. Columbia University Press.

——. The botanical significance of the line of Wallace. (In preparation.)

MUSSER, GUY

1976. Unpublished notes on flora of Mt. Nukilalaki.

ROBINSON, ALAN, AND RUSTANDI, JUS

1982. Bali Barat National Park. National Parks, IUCN vol. 7, no. 2, pp. 13-14.

SCHMIDT, F. H., and FERGUSON, J.H.A.

1951. Rainfall types based on wet and dry period ratios for Indonesia, with western New Guinea. Verhandelingen Kem. Perhub. Djawatan Meteorologi dan Geofisik, Kjakarta, no. 42, 2 clim. maps.

SLEUMER, H.

1966. Ericaceae. Flora Malesiana, series I, part 4, pp. 469-668.

1967. Ericaceae. Flora Malesiana, series I, part 5, pp. 669-914.

STEUP, F.K.M.

1929. Plantengeographische schets van het Paloedal. Tectona, vol. 22, pp. 576-596; and Trop. Natuur, vol. 25, pp. 29-31.

TEYSMANN, J. E.

1879. Beknopt verslag eener botanische dianstreis naar het Goevernement van Celebes en Onderhorigheden van 12 Juli tot en met 29 Dec. 1877. Pp. 54-125.

VAN STEENIS, M.

1979. Plantgeography of east Malesia. Botanical Journ. Linnean Soc., vol. 79, pp. 97-178.

VAN STEENIS-KRUSEMAN, M.

1950. Malaysian plant collectors and collections. Flora Malesiana, vol. 1, pp. i-clii + 3-639, 3 maps. Noordhoff–Kolff, Djakarta.

van Steenis-Kruseman, M. *(continued)*
1973. Malesian plant collectors and collections. Supplement II. Flora Malesiana, series I, vol. 8, no. 1, pp. i-cxu.

Whitmore, T. C.
1973. Plate tectonics and some aspects of Pacific plant geography. New Phytologist, vol. 72, pp. 1185-1190.
1981. Wallace's Line and plate tectonics. xii +91 pp., illus. Clarendon Press, Oxford.

Willem Meijer

Anthropological Studies on Sherpas: High Altitude Adaptation and Genetic Parameters

Grant Recipient: Giorgio Morpurgo, Instituto dell'Orto Botanico dell 'Università di Roma, Roma, Italy.[1]

Grant 1583: In support of anthropological studies on Sherpas, comprising high altitude adaptation and genetic parameters.

Oxygen Dissociation Curves

In a previous expedition (1976) we collected blood from the Sherpa population and a few days later measured (in Milan, Italy) the oxygen dissociation curves of the whole blood. The main result was a significant shift of the curves to the left in comparison with those obtained with blood of acclimatized Caucasians (Morpurgo et al., 1976). Such a shift, if effected by a higher oxygen affinity of the hemoglobin, would have represented one of the factors causing the special fitness of the Sherpa population to the high altitude. Similar results have been obtained for animals living at high altitude (Monge and Monge, 1968).

The aim of the second expedition was to control this result by constructing the dissociation curves from results on freshly collected blood. To do this, we set up a small experimental laboratory in the village of Kunde (Solo Khumbu, Nepal, 3900 m above sea level), tackling technical problems due to the shortage of electrical power as they arose.

Dissociation curves were determined, using blood collected from Sherpas who volunteered and who had remained for months at an altitude over 3000 m. The procedure was as follows: Specimens were deoxygenated at 37°C with N_2 containing CO_2 at concentrations of 5% or 8% (corresponding to a partial pressure of 27 and 44 mmHg at an atmospheric pressure of 550 mmHg). Blood was then gradually oxygenated with O_2

[1] Principal collaborators were: Guido Modiano, Full Professor of Human Genetics, University of Rome, Rome, Italy; Paolo Arese, Full Professor of Biochemistry, University of Torino, Torino, Italy; and Silvana Santachiara-Benerecetti, Researcher, Instituto di Genetica Biochimica ed Evoluzionistica Consiglio Nazionale delle Ricerche, Pavia, Italy.

TABLE 1. p50 Values in Sherpas and Acclimatized Caucasians at High Altitude

Sherpas		*Caucasians*	
8% CO_2	*5% CO_2*	*8% CO_2*	*5% CO_2*
35.0	21.5	37.1	25.5
37.2	28.5	37.8	–
34.1	27.5	30.9	25.7
37.4	23.0	30.9	27.1
32.4	27.4	–	26.5
38.5	–	–	–
37.1	30.9	–	–
30.0	–	–	–
34.5 avg.	26.5	34.7	26.2

containing CO_2 (5% and 8%) in the chamber of a Clark electrode (Rank and Brothers). At each value of pO_2 the percentages of reduced hemoglobin (Hb) was determined with the automatic hemoxymeter OSM2 (Radiometer); p50 was calculated directly on the curve obtained, by plotting the values of reduced hemoglobin vs. pO_2. It was also determined by mixing together a fully deoxygenated blood sample with an equal volume of fully oxygenated blood according to the technique introduced by Barry and Knight (1973).

The data obtained with both techniques were identical, but did not support the results of the 1977 expedition. That is, the dissociation curves for the Sherpa population compared with those for acclimatized Caucasians were not shifted to the left (Table 1). A similar result was obtained by Samaya et al. (1979). Figure 1 reports the average dissociation curve obtained with blood samples of 21 Sherpas. The venous percentage of HbO_2 varied between 75% and 22%. Plotting HbO_2 vs. pO_2 for the different samples resulted in a curve representing the average of the in vivo oxygen affinity of the Sherpa blood. In our opinion, these data reliably represent the most physiologically significant values of oxygen affinity determinations: p50 was 22.5, identical to that determined in vitro for the 1977 expedition. However, a comparable analysis for the Caucasian population is unfortunately lacking, so it is not known yet whether the two populations differ in this parameter.

The results of the 1976 expedition remain unexplained unless we admit the existence of unknown factors that can modulate the affinity of the hemoglobin for the oxygen. Since in the previous work all known factors were checked and curves normalized according to Musetti et al. (1975), the extreme variance of p50 values obtained by Samaya et al. (1979) and by us can only be explained by still unknown factors. The diminution of 2,3-dyphosphoglycerate (2,3-DPG) levels after storage, as suggested by

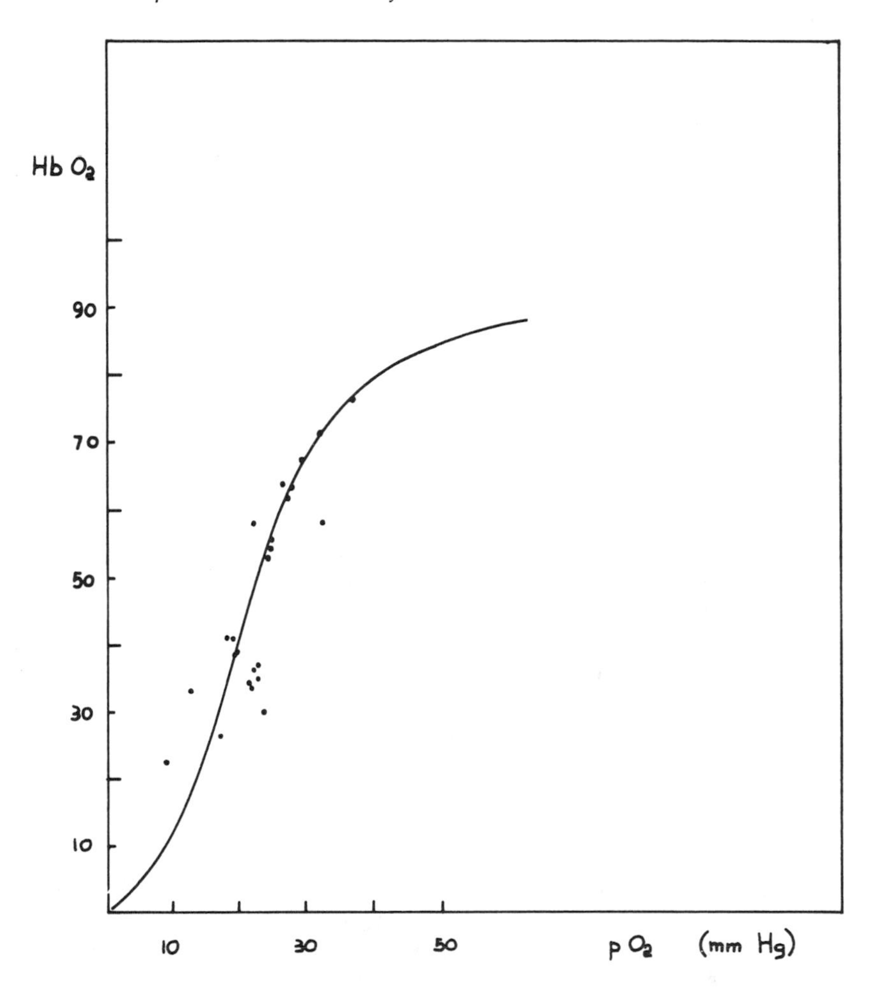

FIGURE 1. $HbO_2\%$ and pO_2 (mmHg) in the venous blood of different Sherpas. Each point represents an individual.

Samaya et al., cannot be responsible for these results because samples and controls were collected from individuals of the same age, concentration of the metabolite was measured, and the curves were normalized according to Musetti et al. (1975).

It is our opinion that the problem can be solved only by determining the oxygen dissociation curve of a rather large number of Sherpas and of acclimatized Caucasians. It would also be necessary to have a more precise idea of the factors that determine the variance of the oxygen dissociation curve in man.

Population Genetic Studies

The main purpose of these studies is to gain more information on the various world populations and to collect sufficient data for tracing a plausible genealogical tree of the various races and populations. Nepal, and more generally the Himalayas, is of special interest because of its uniqueness. The whole population (12 million, according to the 1980 census) is subdivided into 33 different groups, speaking mutually unintelligible languages. These populations are subdivided into many castes and into at least 4 religious groups, i.e., Buddhism, Hinduism, Bon-Po (a pre-Buddhist religion), and animism. Some Muslims are also present. Most of the populations are of Mongolic or Indo-European origin but some tribes are likely to be of Dravidian origin. The Himalayan situation, therefore, provides a worthwhile study area to determine whether the divisions among these different entities correspond to a real genetic separation.

In spite of the country's rugged terrain, the genetic separation, if real, is due almost entirely to cultural barriers and not to geographic separation; in fact different populations frequently live in the same village. We have therefore started a long-term project aimed at analyzing the genetic structure of the Himalayan populations. Here we report data gathered in expeditions supported by the National Geographic Society.

Kali Gandaki

In the first expedition, in the autumn of 1977, we studied the populations of the Kali Gandaki region and the valleys along its boundaries (Saglio et al., 1979, and Fig. 2). At that time we found only the ABO group as a genetic marker. Most of the blood specimens were obtained by pricking the fingers of schoolboys who volunteered (with the permission of the schoolmasters). Since most of the children attend school without any discrimination we assumed that these samples represent the ethnic composition of the villages.

Anthropological information on the populations examined can be found in the excellent book by Dor Bahadur Bista (1972). We would like to point out here that the Gurung, Magar, Thakali, and Tibetan are Mongolic populations speaking Tibeto-Burman languages, while the Chetri, Damai, and Kami are Indian castes. However, according to tradition, Chetris descend from the intermarriage of Brahman males (who were dislodged from India by Muslim invasion in the 12th century) with women of the local population, the Khas (Fig. 3). The main conclusion was that the populations examined are not only culturally but also genetically separate. Some groups, such as the Thakali, although represented by only a few thousand individuals, still maintain their identity. The fact

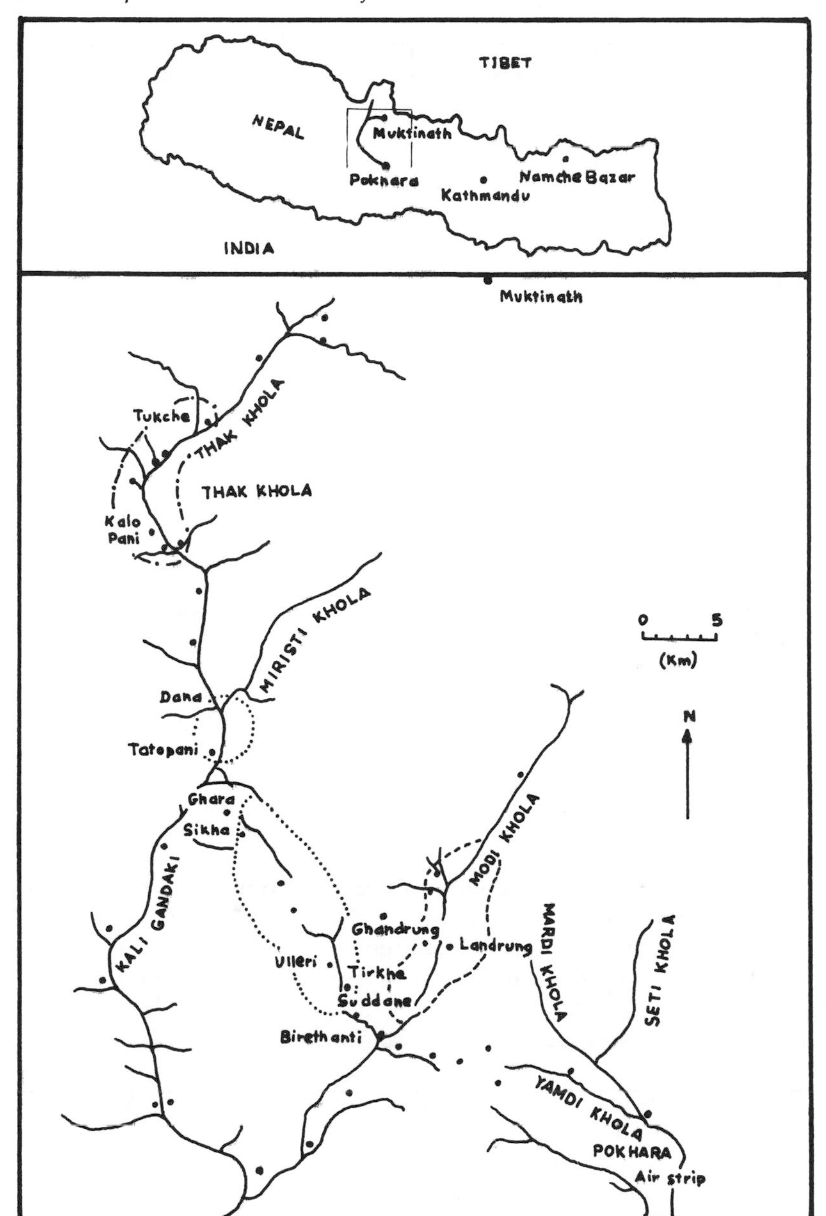

FIGURE 2. *Upper:* Nepal, the regions of the present study and the route followed by the expedition. *Lower:* the Kali Gandaki region in detail with the areas where each group is most represented. For the Namche Bazar (High Kumbu) area see Santachiara-Benerecetti et al. (1976). Villages:..... Magar;.... Gurung; -.- Thakali; - Chetri. (From Saglio et al., 1979).

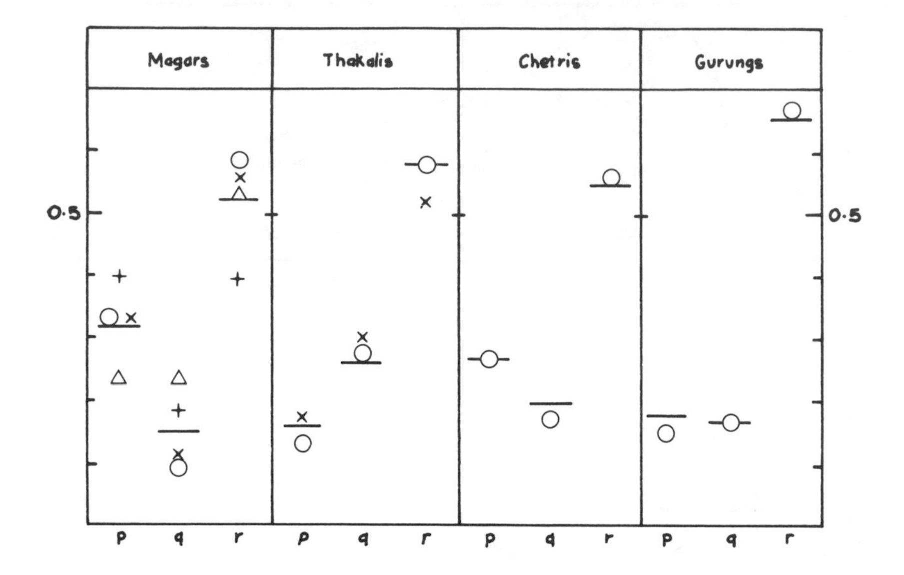

FIGURE 3. ABO gene frequencies of people living in different villages but belonging to the same population. Horizontal lines indicate the overall gene frequencies. Symbols of the villages: Magar: Ulleri, O; Sikna, X; Tatopani, +; Dana, Δ. Thakali: Kalo Pani, O; Tukche, X. Chetri: Ghara, O. Gurung: Ghandrung, O. Phenotype frequencies of the Magar were significantly different from both those of Thakalis ($x^2_{3df} = 26.53$; $P \leq 0.0001$) and the Gurung ($x^2_{3df} = 14.59$; $P \leq 0.005$). Differences in the remaining four comparisons were insignificant. (From Saglio et al., 1979).

that it is possible to show genetic isolation among them demonstrates that the cultural barriers have been effective as a mechanism of isolation for an extremely long period. In fact these populations live only in Nepal and have very likely lived in their present settlements for a very long time.

SIKKIM

The same type of research was done in Sikkim in 1978 (Morpurgo et al., 1983). Sikkim lies immediately east of Nepal. Before 1975, when it was annexed to India, its "traditional" population amounted to about 200,000 people and consisted of several still distinct ethnic groups of Mongolian or Hindu extraction. According to oral tradition they arrived in this country from Nepal during the last two centuries. The original people of Sikkim are the Lepcha, a frankly Mongolic group present only there. However Lepchas are at present one of the least represented ethnic groups. Since the annexation, numerous Indian immigrants have set-

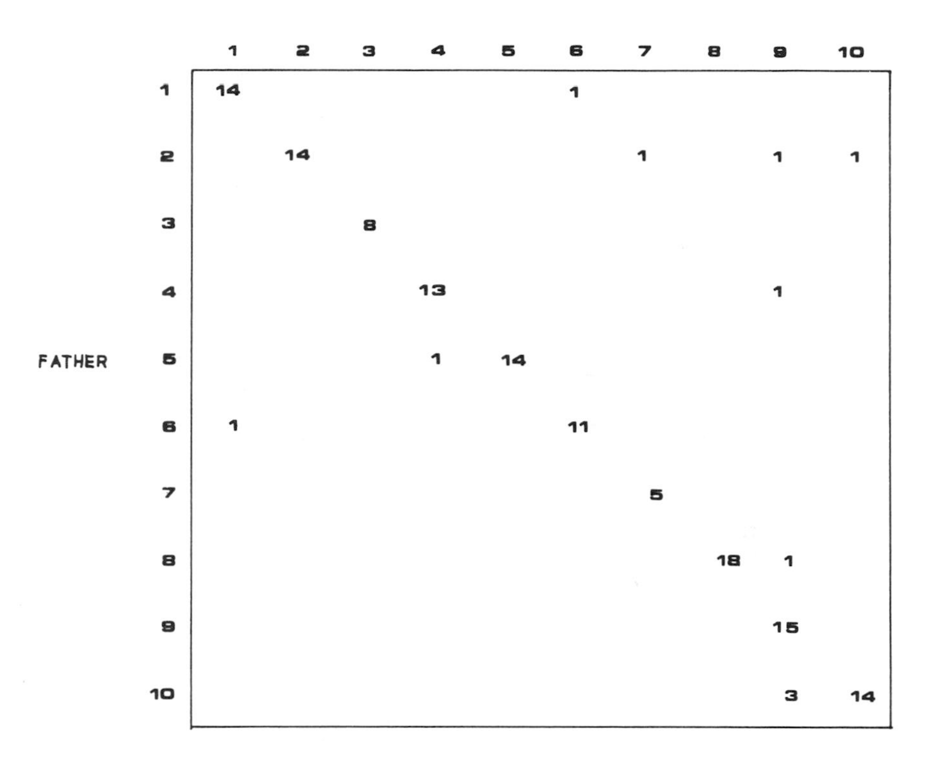

FATHER \ MOTHER	1	2	3	4	5	6	7	8	9	10
1	14					1				
2		14					1		1	1
3			8							
4				13					1	
5				1	14					
6	1					11				
7							5			
8								18	1	
9									15	
10									3	14

FIGURE 4. Mating migration matrix in a sample of 138 individuals of the study area. Key: 1=Bhotia; 2=Gurung; 3=Subba; 4=Rai; 5=Sherpa; 6=Lepcha; 7=Tamang; 8=Newar; 9=Chetri; 10=Hindu.

tled in the Sikkimese valleys; at the time of the study they represented about half the total population of Sikkim.

The present investigation was concerned with the "traditional" groups only. A preliminary evaluation of the extent of the interethnic marriages has shown that these groups still maintain their strong isolation (Fig. 4).

The genetic survey consisted of a study in some 500 individuals of the following markers: blood groups ABO and MN; phosphoglucomutase (PGM), locus 1 and 2; adenylate kinase (AK); phosphohexoseisomerase (PHI); glyoxylase (GLO); adenosinedeaminase (ADA); and hemoglobin (Hb).

Owing to the small size of each population, genetic data have been elaborated by subdividing them into three main groups: Mongolic (Tibet-

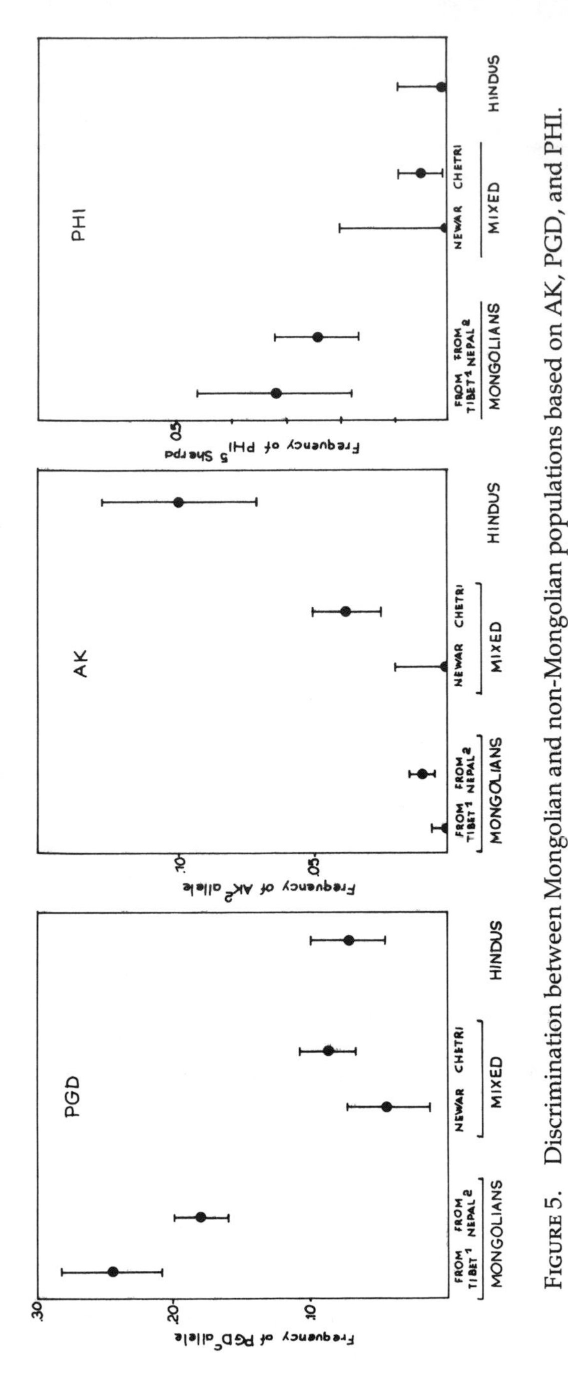

Figure 5. Discrimination between Mongolian and non-Mongolian populations based on AK, PGD, and PHI.

an, Tamang, Gurung, Lepcha, Sherpa, Subba, and Rai); mixed (Newar and Chetri); and Hindu. The relevant genetic findings appear to be: (1) the occurrence among Mongolics of a polymorphism for PHI, a gene usually found electrophoretically monomorphic; and (2) that three genetic markers—AK, PGD, and PHI—are particularly efficient in discriminating among ethnic groups (Fig. 5). This further confirms that the Himalayan populations may remain genetically separated even when sharing the same village.

SHERPAS

The results are shown in Table 2.

TABLE 2. Phenotypes and Gene Frequencies for ABO and Red Cell Enzyme Genetic Markers, Sherpa, High Khumbu

Genetic markers	*Phenotypes*	*Frequencies*		*Gene frequencies and standard errors*
		Obs.	*Exp.*	
	O	29	30.2	I^A =0.097±0.025
	A	11	9.6	I^B =0.251±0.039
ABO	B	29	27.7	i =0.652±0.043
	AB	2	3.5	X^2_{idf} =0.910 P>0.50
	Total	71	71.0	
	1	67	66.17	$UMPK^1$ =0.952
UMPK*	2-1	5	6.67	$UMPK^2$ =0.048±0.018
	2	1	0.17	
	Total	73	73.01	
	A	36	36.78	Pgd^A = 0.783
PGD**	AC	22	20.39	Pgd^C = 0.217±0.038
	C	2	2.83	X^2_{ldf} = 0.100 P>0.70 (Yates)
	Total	60	60.00	
	1	4	1.53	GLO^1 = 0.146±0.029
GLO†	2-1	13	17.93	GLO = 0.854
	2	55	52.54	X^2_{df} = 3.754 P~0.05 (Yates)
	Total	72	72.00	
LDH^A‡	Normal	68		
LDH^B	Normal	68		

* Uridine monophosphate kinase.
** 6-Phosphogluconate dehydrogenase; 3 specimens were not classified.
† Glyoxylase.
‡ Lactate dehydrogenase.

The ABO gene frequencies are in close agreement with those found by Heinrich (1966) on various groups of Sherpas (quoted by Mourant et al., 1976). A large survey concerning this system has also been carried out by Bingham and Sacherer (pers. comm.).

The PGD polymorphism among the Sherpas shows a particularly high frequency of the PDG allele. Few data concerning the neighboring populations are available (see Mourant et al., 1976): the PGD gene frequency among Indians was found to be low, falling within the European range; among the Chinese of Taiwan and a Nepalese sample it was about 0.1 whereas among Bhutanese it attained a value as high as 0.25, which is the highest value so far reported in the world.

The $UMPK^2$ gene frequency found in the present sample is comparable with that observed in the few populations so far examined, except for Blacks, who seem to lack this allele (for a review, see Ranzani et al., 1977).

The GLO^2 gene frequency is particularly high, but it should be pointed out that the same value has been found for the Chinese whereas Indians present frequencies around 0.25 (Ghosh, 1977).

REFERENCES

BARRY, W. L., and KNIGHT, V. A.
1973. A new method for demonstrating oxygen-hemoglobin dissociation curves. Journ. Physiol. (London), vol. 231, pp. 1-2.

DOR BAHADUR BISTA
1972. People of Nepal, 2d ed. Ratna Pustak Bhandar, Kathmandu.

GHOSH, A. K.
1977. Polymorphism of the red cell glyoxalase 1 with special reference to South and South East Asia and Oceania. Human Genet., vol. 39, pp. 91-95.

MONGE, M., and MONGE, C.
1968. Adaptation of domestic animals. Lea and Febinger, Philadelphia.

MORPURGO, G.; ARESE, P.; PESCARMONA, G. P.; LUZZANA, M.; MODIANO, G.; and KHRISHNA RANJIT, S.
1976. Sherpas living at high altitude: A new pattern of adaptation. Proc. Natl. Acad. Sci. U.S.A., vol. 73, pp. 747-751.

MORPURGO, G.; MODIANO, G.; ARESE, P.; RANZANI, G. N.; FELICETTI, L.; TOZZI, F.; MURA, G.; and SANTACHIARA-BENERECETTI, S. A.
1983. Population genetics studies in Sikkim. Journ. Human Evol., vol. 12, pp. 425-437.

MOURANT, A. E.; KOPEC, A. C.; and DOMANIEWSKA-SOBEZAK, K.
1976. The distribution of the human blood groups and other polymorphisms. Oxford Univ. Press, London, New York, Toronto.

MUSETTI, A.; ROSSI, F.; and ROSSI, BERNARDI L.
1975. The log P_{50} and oxygen dissociation curve nomogram for human blood at 37°C. Pp. 95-110 *in* "Physiological Basis of Anaesthesiology," W. W. Mushin et al., eds. Piccin Medical Books, Padova.

RANZANI, G.; BERTOLOTTI, E.; and SANTACHIARA-BENERECETTI, A. S.
1977. The polymorphism of the red cell uridine monophosphate kinase in two samples of the Italian population. Human Heredity, vol. 27, pp. 332-335.

SAGLIO, G.; ANTONINI, G.; ARESE, P.; BERRETTA, M.; MODIANO, G.; SANTACHIARA-BENERECETTI, A. S.; and MORPURGO, G.
1979. Genetic studies on some Nepalese populations. Journ. Human Evol., vol. 8, pp. 385-397.

SAMAYA, M.; VEICSTEINAS, A.; and CERRETELLI, P.
1979. Oxygen affinity of blood in altitude Sherpas. Journ. Appl. Physiol., vol. 47, pp. 337-341.

GIORGIO MORPURGO

Hybrids of *Dryopteris* in the Great Dismal Swamp

Grant Recipient: Lytton J. Musselman, Department of Biological Sciences, Old Dominion University, Norfolk, Virginia.

Grants 1675, 1827: For study of log fern hybrids and the biology of giant spores of *Dryopteris* hybrids in the Great Dismal Swamp.[1]

The Great Dismal Swamp has long been an area of great pteridological interest. Here occurs one of the richest assemblages of *Dryopteris* (log fern) anywhere in North America. Nine taxa are recorded from this area (Nickrent et al., 1978). Little research, however, has been conducted on these plants, especially the hybrids. No doubt this is due, in part, to the general inaccessibility of plants in the swamp. The establishment of the Great Dismal Swamp National Wildlife Refuge in 1973 led to an intensive survey of the biota of this wetland, including the ferns. This resulted in the discovery of several large populations of ferns, and a study of their biology was initiated. The objectives of the work supported by these grants were: to survey the swamp and adjoining areas for the distribution of *Dryopteris*, to hybridize several species, and to investigate the morphology, development, and viability of spores produced by the hybrids *D.* x *australis* and *D.* x *separabilis*. Results of the first objective are presented in Nickrent et al. (1978). The distribution and cytology of *D.* x *australis* is discussed in Wagner and Musselman (1982). Cytological work on the synthesized hybrids has not been completed because fronds are not yet mature. This paper summarizes work on the spores of two hybrids: *D.* x *australis* and *D.* x *separabilis*. Information on the motility of hybrid spores is presented elsewhere (Magraw and Musselman, 1979).

D. x *australis* (Wherry) Small (Fig. 1A) is a hybrid between *D. celsa* (Palmer) Small and *D. ludoviciana* (Kze.) Small. *D. ludoviciana* (Fig. 1L) is a diploid plant with southern affinities found only as far north as North Carolina, and does not occur in the swamp. *D. celsa* (Fig. 1C), first discovered in the Dismal Swamp, is a tetraploid species rare throughout its

[1] The valuable assistance of L. A. Pitchford in fieldwork and in cultivation of plants is acknowledged. The scanning electron microscope pictures were prepared by S. D. Rich and the drawings of spores by D. L. Nickrent.

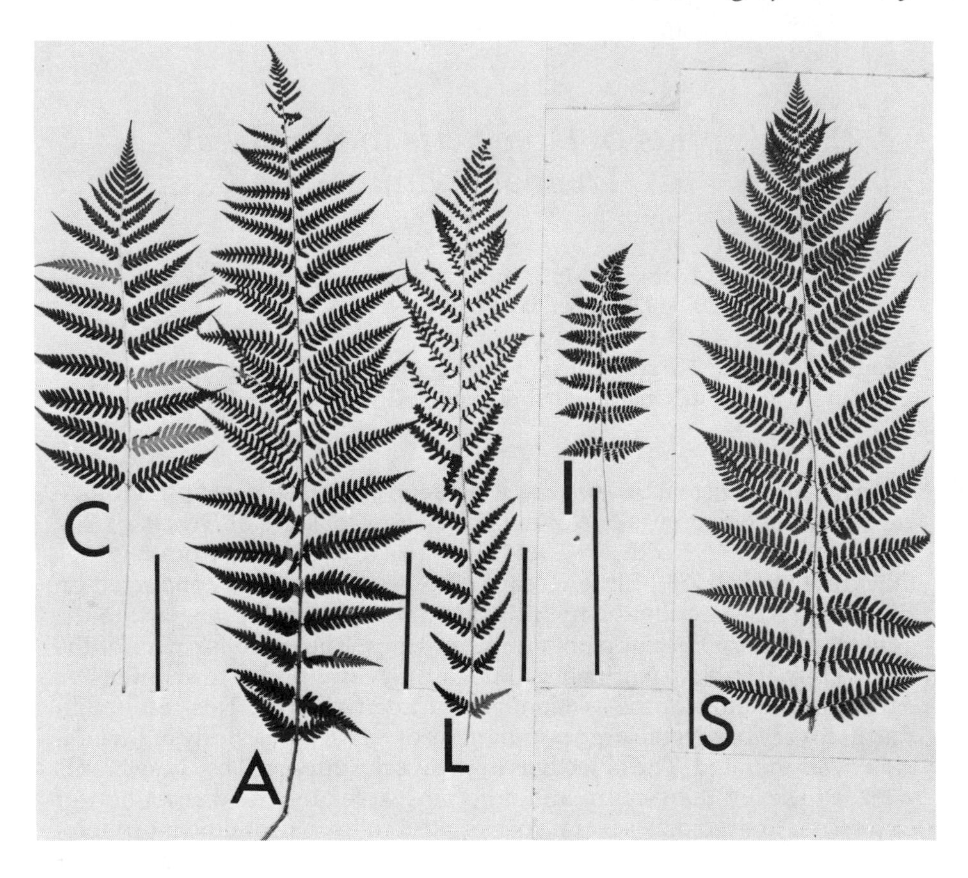

FIGURE 1. Fronds of *Dryopteris* hybrids discussed in this study and their parents. C—*D. celsa;* A—*D.* x *australis;* L—*D. ludoviciana;* I—*D. intermedia;* S—*D.* x *separabilis*. Scale equals 15 cm.

range except in the swamp, where several large populations occur. Thus, it is significant that the hybrid between these two, *D.* x *australis*, occurs in the swamp where only one parent is now present. This is the northernmost station for this fern (Wagner and Musselman, 1982).

First discovered in the Dismal Swamp, *D.* x *separabilis* (Palmer) Small is the hybrid between *D. celsa* (Fig. 1C) and the diploid *D. intermedia* (Muhl.) Gray (Fig. 1I). It is a strikingly beautiful fern (Fig. 1S) with erect, dark green, lacy fronds.

Like other *Dryopteris* hybrids (DeBenedictis, 1969) *D.* x *australis* and *D.* x *separabilis* produced an assortment of spore types. This paper deals with the morphology of these spores.

Materials and Methods

Spores were collected in early June 1976 and 1977 and stored in vials at 3°C. For germination tests they were sown on 10 percent agar in petri plates and kept in a growth chamber at 25°C with constant illumination. Permanent slides were made by mounting spores in Euparol. Drawings of spores were made from these slides. For scanning electron microscopy spores were plated with gold and examined at 10 kv.

Results

D. x *australis.* The range in spore types is presented in Figures 2 and 3. Considerable variation was evident in perispore morphology, especially in the "monospores" (Fig. 2, no. 1-7). The size of the monospores was likewise variable. Fewer than 1 percent of the monospores appeared viable; the remainder were clear with no apparent cellular content. No viable monospores are illustrated. Monospores (viable and nonviable) constituted about 42 percent of the total spore population. Approximately 20 percent of the total spores were diads (Fig. 2, no. 8, 9; Fig. 3, no. 1, 3). There was also considerable variation in the morphology of the diads. Two general types may be distinguished: those with equal-sized pairs (Fig. 2, no. 8, 9; Fig. 3, no. 2, 3); and those with unequal pairs (Fig. 3, no. 1). Some diads had a poorly developed perispore (Fig. 2, no. 8) and others a prominent perispore (Fig. 3, no. 3). Triads comprised about 20 percent of the total number of spores and usually had a well developed perispore (Fig. 3, no. 5). Lastly, occasional tetrads (ca. 10 percent of the total) were observed but none are illustrated for *D.* x *australis.* Giant spores accounted for about 8 percent of the total spore population.

D. x *separabilis.* The morphology and percentage of spore types represented is similar to that for *D.* x *australis*. The morphology of *D.* x *separabilis* spores is shown in Figure 4. Here a representative diad, tetrad, and giant spore are illustrated using the scanning electron microscope that provides a particularly critical view of the perispore. Two types of diads were again present: those with unequal pairs (Fig. 4, no. 1) and those with approximately equal members (Fig. 4, no. 6). The giant spore illustrated in Figure 4, no. 5, is somewhat atypical in that it lacks a well-developed perispore. The smooth exospore is evident in that figure.

Gametophytes. Both *D.* x *australis* and *D.* x *separabilis* will produce gametophytes when unsorted spores are sown on agar. However, the development of gametophytes is considerably retarded in time compared with that of sexual (nonhybrid) taxa. After one month numerous normal-looking gametophytes were present on the plates and also in pots. These produced normal-appearing motile sperm. After two months abundant

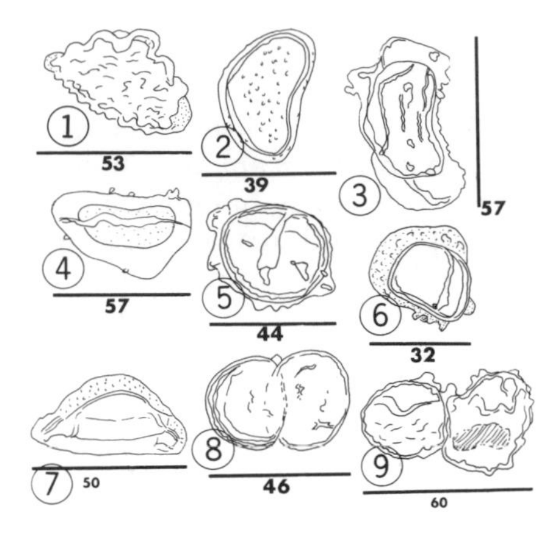

FIGURE 2. Spores of *D.* x *australis*. Black lines represent the longest measurement of each spore; heavy smaller numbers are microns. No. 1-7, monospores (note the variation in shape and degree of perispore development). No. 8-9, diads of spores.

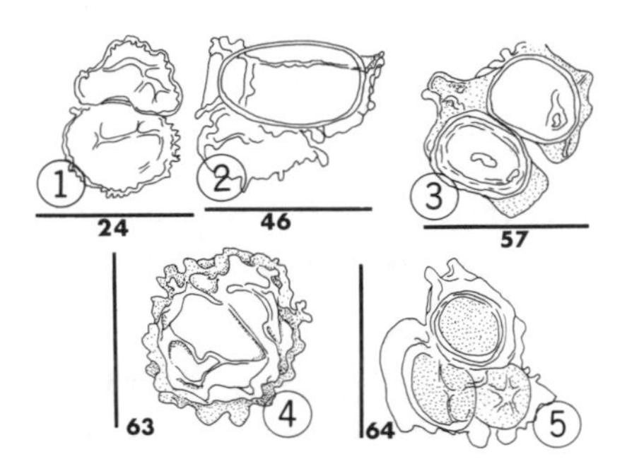

FIGURE 3. Spores of *D.* x *australis*. Black lines represent the longest measurement of each spore; heavy smaller numbers indicate microns. No. 1-3, diads. (In No. 2, the upper spore is clear while the lower is darkened). No. 4, a "giant," or unreduced, spore.

young sporophytes were present. Since no water had been added to the cultures, these sporophytes were considered to be the result of apogamy. Analysis of the genetic makeup of these sporophytes awaits their producing mature fronds.

Discussion

Spore production, viability, and structure have long been of interest to students of *Dryopteris*. In an extensive survey of apogamy in pteridophytes, DeBenedictis (1969) examined spores of *D.* x *separabilis*. Little information is available on other hybrids, however.

More recently, Hickok and Klekowski (1973) have outlined a mechanism for the production of the various spore types discussed for *D.* x *australis* and *D.* x *separabilis*. This involves two mechanisms, termed by Hickok and Klekowski (1973) nonreductional meiosis and abnormal reductional meiosis. The latter produces diad spores by omitting the first division of meiosis. In the second process, abnormal reductional meiosis, the first division takes place and the second division may or may not take place. Hickok and Klekowski (1973) suggest that a similar mechanism

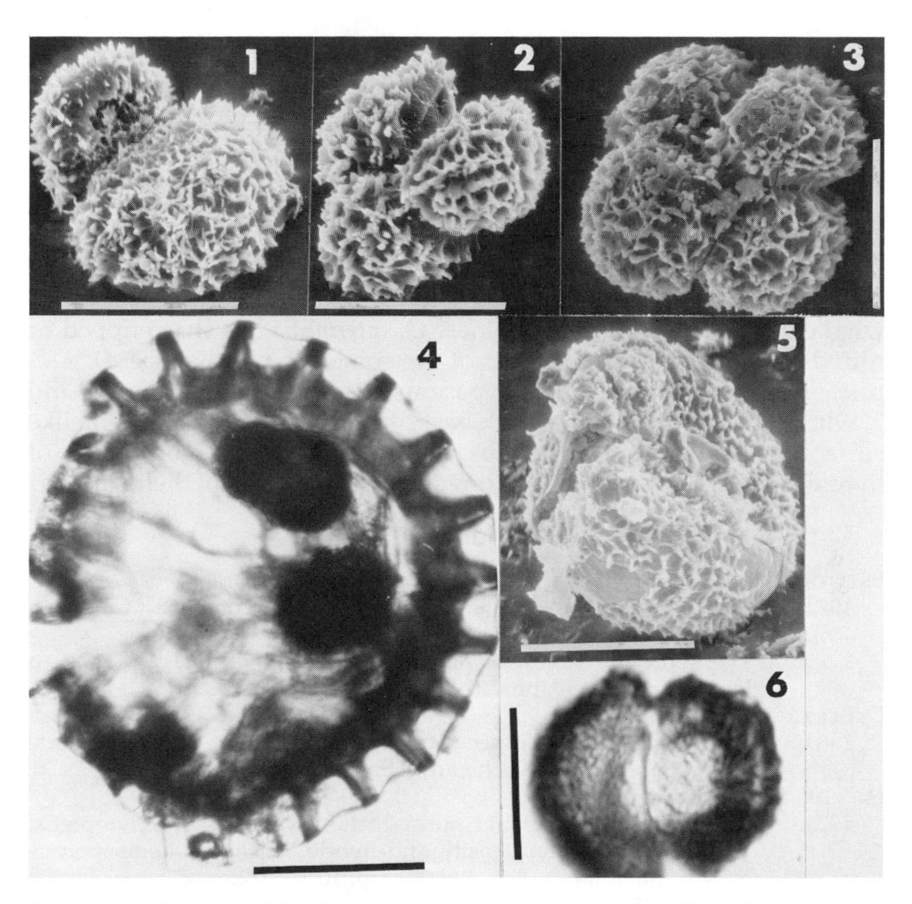

FIGURE 4. *D.* x *separabilis*. Scales equal approximately 25 μ. No. 1-3, a diad, triad, and tetrad of spores. No. 4, a just-opened sporangium with one giant spore, one triad, and one aborted spore (lower left); note darkened material within sporangium, a feature of these hybrids.

may be operative in *Dryopteris* hybrids and that "giant spores" may be produced in this way. The present work, while lacking cytological data, would not seem to support this, as the giant spores are much larger than any diads found in this study and are distinctive in morphology (cf. Fig. 3, no. 4 and Fig. 4, no. 5, with the diads in Figs. 2-4). Thus, it appears that the giant spores in these two hybrids may indeed be unreduced mother cells, a form of apogamy by means of spores. Many of the sporangia of these hybrids showed just 16 cells, supporting the concept of unreduced spore mother cell origin. Often all 16 cells were giant spores, but various degrees of mixing within one sporangium were seen (Fig. 4, no. 4). Tetrads (Fig. 4, no. 3) were only rarely observed. They are an example of postmeiotic abortion in which the spore apparently dies and does not separate into component spores soon after exospore material is laid down.

Although little information is available on the surface characteristics of hybrid *Dryopteris* spores, Britton illustrates the morphology of *D. celsa* (Britton, 1972b) and *D. intermedia* spores (Britton, 1972a), using the scanning electron microscope. According to his figures, *D. celsa* has a somewhat convoluted surface with spines. *D. intermedia* has sharp-tipped or round-tipped spines but the bases of the spines do not coalesce. *D.* x *separabilis* has characteristics of both parents as seen in Figure 4, no. 1-3 and 5, where sharp-tipped spines with bases fused to form a honeycomblike surface are evident. Britton (1972b) has found that spore morphology of hybrids (e.g., *D. celsa*) can be intermediate between that of their parents.

REFERENCES

Britton, D. M.

1972a. Spore ornamentation in the *Dryopteris spinulosa* complex. Canadian Journ. Bot., vol. 50, pp. 1617-1621.

1972b. The spores of *Dryopteris clintoniana* and its relatives. Canadian Journ. Bot., vol. 50, pp. 2027-2029.

DeBenedictis, V. M.

1969. Apomixis in ferns with special reference to sterile hybrids. Doctoral dissertation, Univ. of Michigan, Ann Arbor.

Hickok, L. C., and Klekowski, E. J. Jr.

1973. Abnormal reductional and nonreductional meiosis in Ceratopteris: Alternatives to homozygosity and hybrid sterility in homosporous ferns. Amer. Journ. Bot., vol. 60, pp. 1010-1022.

Magraw, T. W., and Musselman, L. J.

1979. Notes on motility of *Dryopteris* spores in the Dismal Swamp. Amer. Fern Journ., vol. 69, pp. 6-8.

Nickrent, D. L.; Musselman, L. J.; Pitchford, L. A.; and Sampson, D. W.

1978. The distribution and ecology of Dryopteris in southeastern Virginia and adjacent North Carolina. Amer. Fern Journ., vol. 68, pp. 45-51.

Wagner, and Musselman, L. J.

1982. The occurrence of the southern woodfern, *Dropteris* x *australis* (Wherry) Small. Castanea, vol. 47, pp. 182-190.

Lytton J. Musselman

Hunting and Ecology of Dugongs and Green Turtles, Torres Strait, Australia

Grant Recipient: Bernard Nietschmann, Department of Geography, University of California, Berkeley, California.

Grant 1626: In support of a study on exploitation and ecology of dugongs and green turtles in the Torres Strait.

A Place for Hunting

Many traditional seaside societies in the tropics were once highly adapted to and greatly dependent upon marine animals for subsistence. Along continental and insular margins, where the water was warm, shallow, and clear, and seagrasses and reefs were abundant, dugongs and green turtles commonly were the most important, sought-after, and culturally-esteemed large meat animals. Today, however, both traditional marine hunters and dugongs and green turtles have almost disappeared from tropical waters, having followed the pattern of so many other vanished societies and species that were overwhelmed by the spread of foreign colonization and commercialization of local faunal resources. Often they passed or were radically altered before much could be learned about the people's specialized cultural adaptation and their native knowledge of animal behavior, accumulated from generations of practical experience, or much about the natural history and ecology of the animals themselves. Largely extirpated from tropical coastal waters, seafaring and marine-resource–dependent peoples and the animals that provided both livelihood and a central cultural core are remembered almost solely from historical accounts. Yet in isolated corners of the tropics, small groups of marine hunters persist, as do the animals.

One such place is Torres Strait, where extensive shallow reefs support seagrass beds that are grazed almost exclusively by dugongs and green turtles; these animals are exploited solely by highly adapted marine hunters whose society, culture, and subsistence long have been intimately tied to these marine animals and environments.

The Torres Strait area is Australia's marine "outback" (Fig. 1). Starting in the 1860s, pearl shell, trochus, and bêche-de-mer attracted Europeans and others to the islands; in 1871, the London Missionary Society

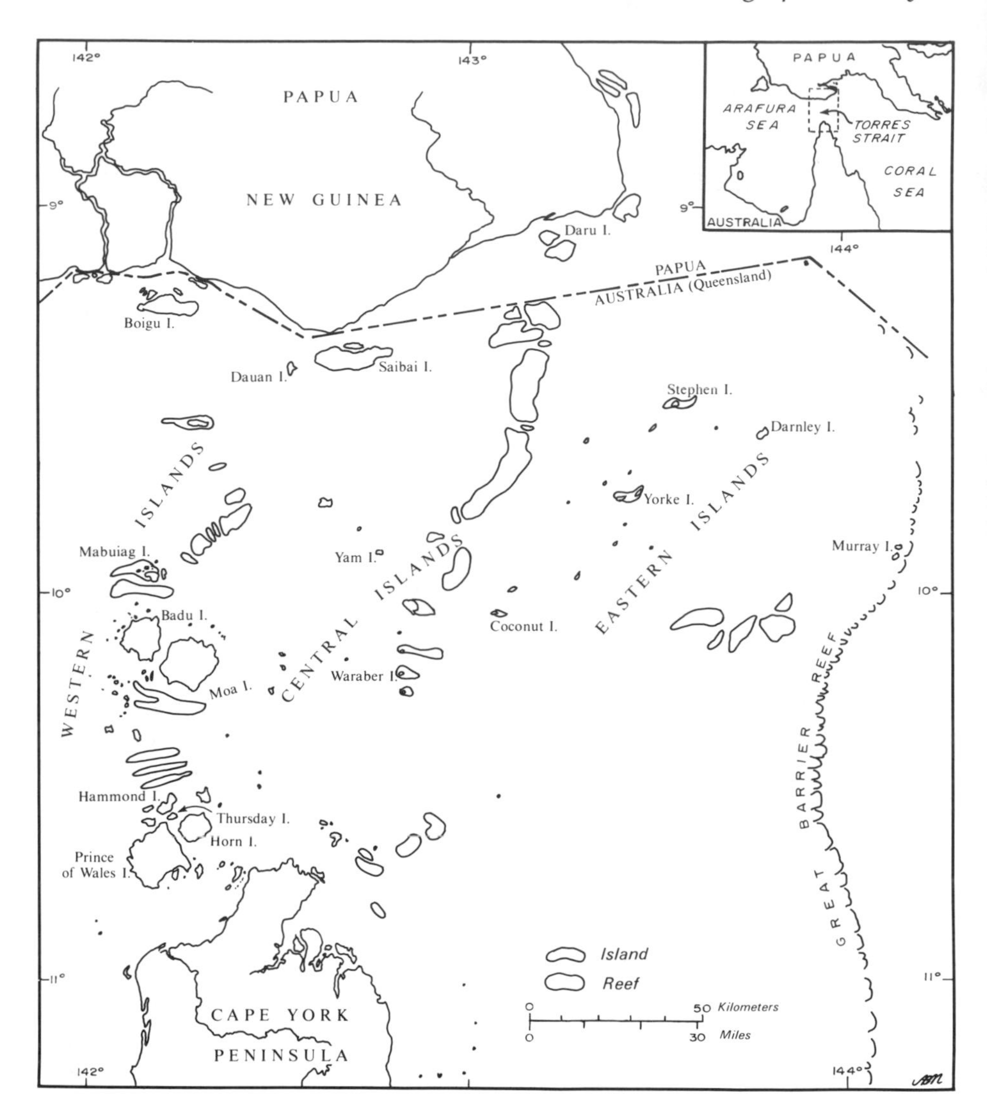

FIGURE 1. Torres Strait.

(LMS) began to Christianize the Islanders. The pearl shell beds became depleted, the LMS turned their missions over to the Anglican Church, most of the outsiders left what was turning into an economic backwater, and those who did not were excluded from residence when most of the islands were made reserves.

Australia's only indigenous Melanesian people live in Torres Strait. Overall, the Islanders share a distinct way of life with some linguistic and cultural variation among Eastern, Central, and Western Island groups.

Most of the island communities are politically and economically distinct from mainland Australia. Of the 17 inhabited islands, 14 are restricted reserves with a total resident population of about 2500 Torres Strait Islanders; the remaining three are "open," nonreserve islands, including tiny Thursday Island, the region's only commercial and administrative center, where live some 2000 Islanders and 1000 other people of multiethnic backgrounds. Queensland's Department of Aboriginal and Islander Advancement (DAIA) helps administer the reserve islands in cooperation with elected representatives from each community. Many of the Islanders receive social benefit payments from Queensland and commonwealth agencies with which they purchase some goods and foods from the small, state-supplied and -operated stores located on each island.

Reserve Islanders interact with the outside world through a one-way fence. They can travel between islands and to the mainland, but outsiders cannot visit the reserves without special permission from the elected island councils that administer community affairs, strictly limiting and controlling the intrusion of non-Islanders. To a large extent this has helped preserve a society and culture run by Islanders in their own way and with their own traditions.

Living on politically autonomous islands in the midst of extensive reefs, seagrass beds, and large numbers of dugongs and green turtles, and with most basic necessities taken care of through receipt of state and commonwealth benefits and occasional remittances from relatives who have emigrated to the mainland, the remaining Torres Strait Islanders have been able to maintain much of their traditional hunting way of life.

Research Objectives

The primary purpose of the research was to describe and analyze the pattern of relationships between a portion of the biotic and physical environment and culture and social organization; that is, between dugong and green turtle behavior and ecology and the marine environment, and Torres Strait Islander culture and society. The underlying approach and theory suggest that a fuller understanding of interactions of a human population, their culture, and their environment could be achieved by simultaneously considering each as part of a pattern that connects and reciprocally influences biological and cultural elements. Thus, to understand the behavior and ecology of a population of hunted animals, it is necessary to study the behavior and strategies of the hunters; so too, investigation of cultural adaptation and social relationships within a community of hunters should logically extend to consideration of the natural history and spatial and temporal behavior of the animals hunted.

Within this general research theme the project had four principal interrelated objectives:

(1) To describe dugong and green turtle natural history, behavior, and ecology, and seagrass availability;

(2) To assess the effects of hunting on these animal populations and to measure hunting intensity and productivity;

(3) To study Islander perception and knowledge of dugong and green turtle natural history and ecology and associated environmental factors that influence animal movements and availability; and

(4) To analyze the significance of these animals, hunting, and knowledge of natural history to the culture and society of the Islanders.

Previous Research in Torres Strait

Very little research had been done on Torres Strait Islanders or on dugongs, green turtles, and seagrasses in the area. Biological research by others most relevant to our work include studies by Anderson and Heinsohn (1978), Barnett and Johns (1976), Bertram and Bertram (1973), Bustard (1971, 1972), Carr and Main (1973), Heinsohn (1972), Heinsohn and Birch (1972), Heinsohn and Marsh (1977), Heinsohn and Spain (1974), Heinsohn, Spain, and Anderson (1976), Hudson (1976), Husar (1975), Spain and Heinsohn (1975), and Wake (1975). Most of the research on dugongs in Australian waters focused on physiology, feeding habits, general life history, estimates of population numbers, and general conservation status. Green turtles received even less attention. Prior to our project, no long-term, on-site research had been done on seasonal and spatial changes in dugong and green turtle populations or on the consequences of subsistence hunting on these populations.

In 1898, A. C. Haddon led a research team to Torres Strait to do the first interdisciplinary study of a primitive people. Much of the research was conducted on Murray and Mabuiag Islands. The results were published in six volumes between 1901 and 1935. These books contain a wealth of early post-European contact descriptions of Islander culture, society, hunting techniques, and rituals. Surprisingly, other than a study of political organization, no in-depth cultural and social research had been done after Haddon's ground-breaking investigations and before our project. It must be pointed out, however, that there are helpful studies of Torres Strait Islanders by Beckett (1963, 1965, 1967, 1972, 1977), Duncan (1974), Harris (1977, 1979), Laade (1971), Lawrie (1970), and Walker (1972).

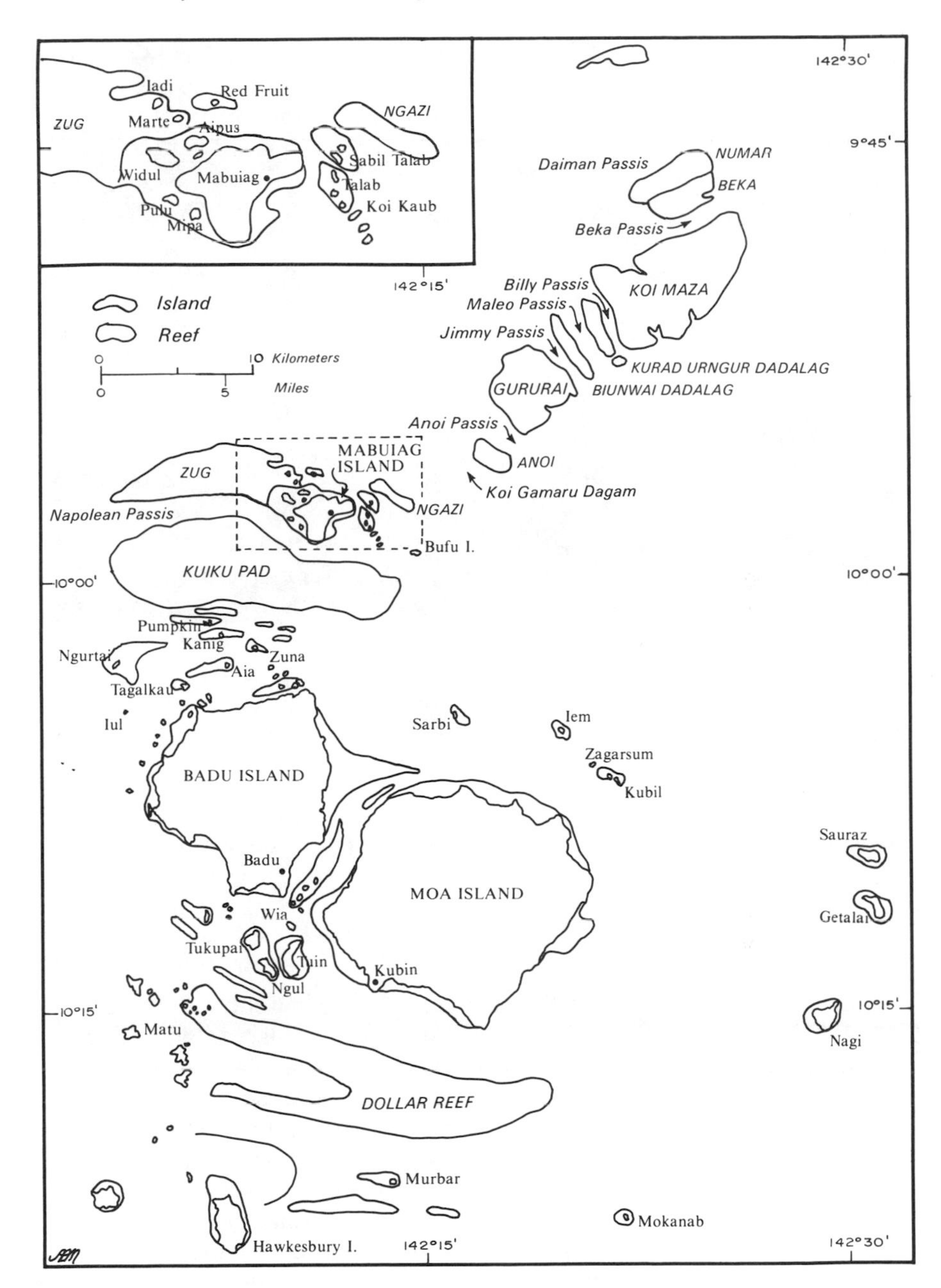

FIGURE 2. Study area.

FIGURE 3. A "Dinghy Blessing" for our inflatable and motor. Canon Amber of Mabuiag Island (Anglican Church) gives the blessing—standard operating procedure for a new dinghy and motor in Torres Strait, without which no Islander would accompany us. After the blessing, a feast is given for the entire community; this serves to socially distribute the good fortune of the individual who can afford such expensive purchases. In our case, the $200 feast was an unexpected deduction from the NGS-supported research budget. (Photograph by Judith Nietschmann.)

Research Methods

In July 1976, my wife Judith (co-investigator), our son, and I went to Torres Strait to spend a year living on a small reserve island. We selected Mabuiag Island and were granted permission by the Islanders to do our proposed research. In this we were fortunate because Haddon's 1898 Cambridge Expedition research centered on this same island and we were able to work with the descendants of his informants, and because Mabuiag was well known in the region for its hunters and large adjacent reefs. Mabuiag is a small, rugged island, 3 × 5 km in size, and has a population of some 125 people who live in 22 households. We made frequent trips to distant reefs, uninhabited small islands, and Islander communities on Badu and Moa Islands (Fig. 2).

Judith did most of the research on social and economic relationships

FIGURE 4. We traveled some 5000 mi (8045 km) in these two dinghies. The inflatable permitted quiet drifting for observations of feeding grounds and was convenient for scuba diving; the aluminum dinghy was faster and more seaworthy in rough weather. Styrofoam cases protected camera gear from spray, rain, sun, and wave shock. From left to right: Repu Sakawai, Barney Nietschmann, Jr., and Judith Nietschmann.

among the Islanders, while I worked with the hunters. Together with our son we made above-water and underwater observations of dugongs and green turtles. What to others might appear to have been esoteric research was to the Islanders a central part of their lives and thus they took it upon themselves to instruct us in kinship reckoning, social responsibilities, and hunting and environmental knowledge. To an Islander, one does not learn from observation alone, but through participating in "Island Custom" (Fig. 3).

Research methods included formal and informal discussions with hunters (interviews and questionnaires); observations made during some 50 hunts and butcherings; recording and measurement of the species, sex, size, quality, catch site, time spent, and distance traveled for each animal taken by hunters on three islands (Mabuiag, Moa, Badu); mapping of island and reef environments and distribution of seagrasses; collection of Islander natural history knowledge; several hundred hours of observation of dugong and green turtle behavior (from bamboo observation platforms, boats, and underwater with scuba equipment); collection of in situ and stomach content samples of seagrasses; two aerial surveys to count populations; small-scale tagging experiments with dugongs and green turtles; photographic recording (8000 frames) of hunting, of dugong and green turtle behavior, and of seagrasses and seasonal changes in environmental conditions; participant observation in kinship networks and distribution and receipt of meat from hunts (amounts measured and estimated); and collection of relevant historical materials from major libraries in Australia (University of Queensland, Australian National University, University of Sydney, the Mitchell Library, and the National Library).

Special equipment included two small boats (Fig. 4), two 25-hp outboards, air compressor and scuba equipment, 300 lb of camera gear, hydrophone and tape recorder, and observation platforms (which we constructed) over reef feeding grounds (Fig. 5).

After our departure, records of hunting returns were kept by an Islander in each of three communities (Mabuiag, Kubin, Badu), which greatly expanded the data range beyond our year-long collection period.

Research Results

The research project yielded a large quantity of biological and cultural information and many promising leads for further investigation. I present only a sketch here, since research results have been and will be published in detail elsewhere (B. Nietschmann, 1976, 1977a, 1977b, 1982, 1983, in press; J. Nietschmann, 1979, 1980, 1981; Nietschmann and Nietschmann, 1977, 1981).

Dugongs, Green Turtles, and Seagrasses

The dugong *(Dugong dugon)* and the green turtle *(Chelonia mydas)* are the world's only exclusively marine mammal and reptile which are herbivorous. These animals are unique in the sea because they convert the primary production of seagrasses and some algae into high-quality and good-tasting protein. Green turtles use more marine habitats, have greater dietary diversity, and tolerate rougher sea conditions than do dugongs, which prefer sheltered inshore and reef waters, largely consume only seagrasses, and move to leeside locations during rough weather. The green turtle's greater habitat and dietary range reduce its resource competition with the dugong.

Torres Strait is one of the world's most important remaining areas where can be found large, co-resident populations of dugongs and green turtles. These animals are abundant in the waters surrounding Mabuiag, Moa, and Badu Islands—the area we studied. Both these animals exert

FIGURE 5. A bamboo platform that we built on a seagrass reef-flat to observe dugongs. The structure is modeled after the hunting platforms *(nat)* that were once used for night harpooning. (Photograph by Barney Nietschmann, Jr.)

considerable grazing pressure on seagrass beds, and some green turtles eat large amounts of algae. Estimates of daily grazing consumption are 40 to 50 kg for an adult dugong and 5 to 8 kg for a large green turtle. Dugongs taken by hunters averaged 212.7 cm in length and 254.8 kg in weight; green turtles averaged 94.9 cm in carapace length and 131.1 kg in weight (Table 1). Dugongs yield approximately 35% of body weight in usable meat and fat, and green turtles provide about 50%.

These animals are difficult to study in Torres Strait because they are often hard to see in the frequently turbid and rough water, they are on the surface for very brief breathing periods (Fig. 6), and they have been hunted for so long that they readily flee from any unusual disturbance. We were able to reduce search time in looking for these animals by following environmental cues taught to us by the hunters (tidal movements, currents, winds, and so on), and by seeking the densest stands of seagrasses and then waiting for the animals.

Seagrasses, and thus dugongs and green turtles, are more abundant in the Western Island region than elsewhere in Torres Strait, because of shallower waters and extensive reefs and protected island-fringing reefs

TABLE 1. Sizes (cm) and Weights (kg) of a Sample of Dugongs and Green Turtles Taken by Mabuiag Island Hunters, 1976-1977

	Green Turtles (♂ 10, ♀ 44, N=54)			
	Mean	*Min.*	*Max.*	*Range*
Carapace length (cm)	94.9	72.0	114.0	42.0
Carapace width (cm)	73.1	57.5	87.0	29.5
Plastron length (cm)	76.2	61.0	87.0	26.0
Head width (cm)	11.8	9.5	13.0	3.5
Weight (kg)	131.1	52.2	205.0	152.8

	Dugongs (♂ 29, ♀ 11, N=40)			
	Mean	*Min.*	*Max.*	*Range*
Fluke width (cm)	68.6	51.0	88.0	37.0
Basal fluke girth (cm)	43.8	30.0	55.0	25.0
Maximum girth (cm)	148.5	112.0	178.0	66.0
Flipper length (cm)	35.7	27.0	46.0	19.0
Flipper width (cm)	15.4	12.0	18.0	6.0
Body length (cm)	212.7	174.0	256.5	82.5
Weight (kg)	254.8	159.0	351.0	192.0

and flats. Except for two species of *Halophila* (found in sheltered intertidal areas alongside fringing mangrove mud and silt flats), seagrasses do not occur in dense, single-species stands. Seagrass densities, distribution, and species composition vary depending on depth, exposure, type of bottom, and grazing selectivity. Seasonal variations in water turbidity, tidal range, and dominant wind direction also influence seagrass abundance and accessibility. Seagrass densities are generally low throughout the western Torres Strait due to environmental factors and grazing pressure. Thus, any one particular reef cannot support long-term grazing by sizable herds of dugongs and green turtles (Fig. 7). Due in part to environmental flux and ecological changes in seagrass, and, to a lesser extent, to algae availability, dugongs and green turtles exhibit frequent and wide-ranging patterns of local movement among dispersed feeding areas.

As determined from the analysis of a limited number of stomach samples and from underwater observations, dugongs are more discriminate seagrass grazers than green turtles, and also consume smaller quantities of algae (Table 2). Islanders claim that the more esteemed, fat dugongs and turtles feed on seagrasses *(damu)*, and that animals with less and poorer fat eat more algae *(pagar)*. This contention was generally confirmed by stomach content analysis and observations made during

FIGURE 6. A dugong surfacing for air. Diving times average 1½ to 2 min and range to an infrequent 9 min depending on activity and sea conditions. Dugongs only remain on the surface for a few seconds before diving again. To harpoon a dugong, hunters must accurately estimate breathing-diving intervals and current and dinghy drift speed in order to position the bow of the craft directly behind an ascending dugong.

butcherings. It appears that high grazing pressure from large herbivore populations on low-density seagrass beds may have resulted in differences in feeding behavior, animal condition, and fat abundance, and in the overgrazing of some areas. Several large pastures have been stripped of grass, primarily by dugongs. Overgrazed seagrass beds are especially noticeable around Hammond, Moa, Badu, and Mabuiag Islands. On all these islands people complain that the decrease in seagrasses has led to a parallel reduction in some species of fish.

TABLE 2. Seagrass Species and Percentages in Dugong Stomach Contents, Mabuiag Island, March-June, 1977

	Estimated percentages of seagrasses as portion of total leaf material (certain percentage not identifiable)															
Dugong number	*1*	*2*	*3*	*4*	*5*	*6*	*7*	*8*	*9*	*10*	*11*	*12*	*13*	*14*	*15*	*16*
Seagrass																
Thalassia hemprichii	50	20	30	40		60	45	50	50	30	35	45	60	25	50	40
Cymodocea sp.		5		5								5				
Halodule pirifolia		20														
Thallasodendron ciliatum					5	5			5	5	5	5		25		5
Enhalus acroides	30		60	35	60	10	25	40	30	40	35	20	10	20	15	40
Halophila sp.		40			10	5	5			10	5		10	20	15	5
Zostera sp.																

Identification and analysis done by Miss Judy Hart, Botany Department, James Cook University, Townsville, Queensland.

FIGURE 7. Dugong feeding trails *(nura)* on an exposed bed of *Halophila* seagrass. Each serpentine trail represents one continuous feeding dive. Daily tidal range can be as much as 3.5 m so that large shallow reefs are alternatingly opened and closed to grazing activity. During low tides hunters search for areas with fresh feeding trails to which the dugongs will return on the rising tide.

Stomach content analysis of 6 green turtles gave estimated percentages of 90 to 100% algae, 5 to 10% seagrass; but 16 dugong samples had estimated percentages of 90 to 100% seagrass, 10%, or less, algae. Based on this very small sample of dugong stomach contents, seagrass consumption by percentage rank is *Thalassia hemprichii* (47.7%), *Enhalus acroides* (35.6%), *Halophila* sp. (9.5%), *Thallasodendron ciliatum* (4.6%), *Halodule pirifolia* (1.5%), *Cymodocea* sp. (1.1%), and *Zostera* sp. (0.0%).

The Islanders distinguish between two general types of dugongs and green turtles, based on their behavior and appearance, and on the nature and condition of their fat. These differences were also apparent from our observations.

What the Islanders call *gatau waru* (bad, dry reef turtle) appear to be old green turtles, primarily algae-grazers, and semiresident on particular reefs (marker-tagged *gatau waru* confirmed site fidelity). They are slow and sluggish swimmers, easy to approach, do not move around much, and are frequently stranded on home reefs during low tides (Fig. 8). Although green turtles in the Pacific have been observed to haul out on a beach to "bask," *gatau waru* strandings are very different. Only old males

FIGURE 8. Stranded green turtles *(gatau waru)* on a Mabuiag fringe reef. This 17,500-m^2 reef was the home feeding ground for 30 to 40 *gatau waru*. Marine algae provided the bulk of these turtles' diet. *Gatau waru* are not exploited by Islanders except for an occasional kill to feed pigs.

and females are stranded. Their carapaces are heavily silted and barnacled and their plastrons are depressed. They are rarely seen in deep water; they have never been seen mating, nor have any eggs been found in butchered females (killed only for pig feed). Their fat is thin and tar-black in color. They weigh about 20% less than *kapu waru* (Table 3).

Kapu waru (good, reef, and open-water turtle) are fast and agile swimmers, wary and skittish, and difficult to catch; they have clean carapaces, filled-out plastrons, and are heavy; they feed more on seagrasses than on algae; move around a great deal from reef to reef, do not stay long on particular reefs, and are never stranded; they copulate during the mating season; butchered females are often gravid; and they have abundant green fat and savory meat.

The differences between these two types of turtles may be due to age, competition over scarce resources (seagrasses), or, perhaps, disease or parasites.

TABLE 3. Comparison of Sizes (cm) and Weights (kg) of *Gatau Waru* (Bad, Dry Reef Turtle) and *Kapu Waru* (Good, Open-Water, and Reef Turtle). Mabuiag Island Area, 1976-1977

	Gatau waru (♂ 32, ♀ 41, N=73)			
	Mean	*Min.*	*Max.*	*Range*
Carapace length (cm)	99.1	86.0	112.0	26.0
Carapace width (cm)	73.0	61.0	84.0	23.0
Plastron length (cm)	76.6	65.0	85.0	20.0
Head width (cm)	12.4	11.25	14.25	3.0
Weight (kg)	105.7	79.4	147.4	68.0

	Kapu waru (♂ 10, ♀ 44, N=54)			
	Mean	*Min.*	*Max.*	*Range*
Carapace length (cm)	94.9	72.0	114.0	42.0
Carapace width (cm)	73.1	57.5	87.0	29.5
Plastron length (cm)	76.2	61.0	87.0	26.0
Head width (cm)	11.8	9.5	13.0	3.5
Weight (kg)	131.1	52.2	205.0	152.8

In other areas of the world, the green turtle *Chelonia mydas* has been hunted so intensively and for so long that older turtles are rarely found, and have not been described in the literature. I believe that the *gatau waru* are old turtles, past breeding age.

Islanders distinguish *wati dangal* (bad, island dugong) from *malu dangal* (good, sea dugong). A *wati dangal* has thin, bad-tasting fat, and thin body shape; it frequents shallow, leeside island margins, and is a less selective grazer, consuming a higher proportion of algae. Islanders consider a *wati dangal,* like a *gatau waru,* to be inedible. *Malu dangal* have very different characteristics: thick and good-tasting fat, fuller, more rounded bodies; they are usually found on distant reefs and primarily consume seagrasses; and they are more difficult to catch. Differences between *wati* and *malu* dugong do not coincide with age or size but may result from competition over and adaptation to different food sources: seagrasses and algae. Dugongs have switched from their normal seagrass diet to algae because of environmental pressures. For example, Heinsohn and Spain (1974) found that with the destruction of near-shore seagrass beds off Townsville by the 1971 cyclone Althea, dugongs switched to feeding on brown algae, which have a faster recovery rate in disturbed areas than do seagrasses.

Along with the density and distribution of seagrasses, tides and general sea conditions are important environmental influences on the temporal and spatial occurrence of dugongs and green turtles. Many of the reef and island-margin feeding grounds are so shallow that they are dry during low tide. The animals move to near-shore and shallow reef areas to feed during high tides and then move during low tides to resting and feeding grounds in deeper water. Complicating this general pattern of high-low tide movement is a wide range of complex tidal conditions (Nietschmann, 1977b). Tidal changes in Torres Strait are among the most varied in the world. The area experiences two dominant weather patterns that affect tidal conditions and dugong and green turtle movements. During the southeast trade-wind season (May through September), gusting and strong winds and low tides during the day force the animals from the large and shallow windward reefs; they move to leeside reefs and island margins during the nighttime high tides. The northwest monsoon season (December through April) reverses the pattern: High tides occur during daylight hours, and there is a 180° shift between windward and leeward. Variations in tides and currents, wind direction, seagrass abundance, and sea conditions make up a kaleidoscope of environmental patterns that influence and determine dugong and green turtle movement, distribution, and herd size.

Dugongs are social animals, and group composition does not fluctuate as much as with green turtles. Yet, depending on environmental and ecological conditions, dugong herd size and composition do change. During the southeast trade-wind season, dugongs were commonly seen feeding and moving alone or in pairs during the day, but at night they formed small groups of 5 to 10 animals. In the northwest trade-wind season, larger groups of dugongs (10 to 30) gathered in the lee of reefs and islands during the day and spread out during nighttime low tides.

We made the first underwater recordings of dugong vocalizations in the wild (1 to 8 kHz). Most of the sounds were emitted when the animals first discovered our presence. These may be distress sounds and a signal for quick departure. Other distinct chirping sounds were heard and taped. Dugong vocalizations seemed to be important in social behavior between individual animals and in herd dynamics, especially during turbid water periods.

Estimates of dugong and green turtle populations proved far too problematical to be worthwhile at this stage of research. Aerial surveys produced counts that conflicted with surveys done the day before from hilltops and from boats. Based on year-after-year high hunting returns, the presence of overgrazed seagrass beds, and unanimous responses by Islanders, dugong and green turtle population numbers are high in the Torres Strait. Recruitment and migration from dugong and green turtle populations off southern Papua New Guinea and northern Queensland may maintain high local densities and balance losses from hunting and natural mortality.

FIGURE 9. Harpooning a dugong off Mabuiag Island. In order to pierce the animal's inch-thick skin and to hit the backbone area accurately, hunters jump with their 4.5-m-long harpoons. One of the crew will quickly help the hunter get back in before the harpoon line uncoils to the end and the dinghy is rapidly pulled away. The harpooned dugong will soon tire from swimming against the water drag of the dinghy and 70 fathoms of ½-in. nylon line.

CULTURAL AND SOCIAL CONTEXT OF HUNTING

Hunting is more than simply a means of getting meat to eat (Fig. 9). In the Torres Strait, marine hunting is the major activity of many males. It provides the majority of protein to households, it sets the context in which much cultural history and environmental knowledge are taught and reviewed, it is the source of the most favored item distributed among kin to satisfy social obligations, and it is based on a complex body of theory, logic, and technique that ensure high returns that reinforce traditional knowledge. Hunting is not a haphazard, catch-as-catch-can affair. Decisions of exactly when and where to go, which specific animal to try for, how to butcher it, and to whom to distribute the meat all follow a coherent, systematic pattern.

Torres Strait hunters share a body of knowledge that is detailed, complex, exacting, and productive. Islanders classify dugongs and green turtles by age, sex, location, type, size, and quality of fat and meat as named in the following list.

DUGONG *(Dangal)*

Age, Sex, Social Grouping	
garka dangal	male dugong
ipika dangal	female dugong
kazi dangal	young dugong
ngawaka dangal	adolescent female
kaukuik dangal	adolescent male
barakutau garka	adolescent male that stays with mother
sabi gudad	single male
puru dangalal	mating dugongs
kazilaig	pregnant dugong
nanaig	nursing mother
gilab	big, old dugong
tuarlaig	herd "leader"
ulakal	5 to 10 herd size
dangalal buai	"family" herd size, 10 or more
Location	
malu dangal	far reef, sea dugong
wati dangal	shallow water, island dugong
Type	
ubar dangal	black dugong
kaiad-gamul dangal	red-brown dugong
miakal dangal	white (albino) dugong, rare
kapu dangal	common, good dugong
wati dangal	bad dugong
Size	
gilab	a really big dugong
koi dangal	big dugong
nurai dangal	medium-sized dugong
mugi dangal	small dugong
Quality	
mina tupaial dangal	very fat
tupaial dangal	fat
tupigai dangal	"half-and-half," just edible
wati dangal	lean, bad fat, inedible

GREEN TURTLE *(Waru)*

Age and Sex	
garka waru	male green turtle
ipika waru	female green turtle
kazi waru	hatchling
sulal waru	mating turtles
gatau waru	old, dry reef turtle

Location	
kapu waru	open water and reef turtle
gatau waru	dry reef turtle
Type	
taupai kaubalnga	short-tailed male
naipie	long-tailed male
kapu waru	usually female
gatau waru	"bad" turtle, male or female
Size	
waiatan baba-sigmai waru	a really big turtle
koi waru	big
nurai	medium
mugi waru	small
Quality	
mina kapu waru	very fat
kapu waru	fat
gatau waru	lean, bad fat, inedible

Combinations of perceived characteristics exponentially expand the range of categories listed. The ability to recognize and predict tide and sea conditions involves determination of tidal cycle, moon phase, wind direction, island or reef exposure, and time of season. I was taught to distinguish some 50 different tide and sea conditions, and although this is but the basic repertoire of a novice hunter it goes well beyond textbook descriptions. A few examples should give an appreciation of the complexity of the Islanders' perception: *kukiau gi iabagar* is a northwest monsoon season daytime high tide; *mugi batainga ura,* an early morning strong clear-water west-to-east tide; *kadigat,* a long clear-water slack tide between two neap tides; and *kutau usalai,* a dirty-water afternoon west-to-east tide that occurs two to three days after new or full moons during the southeast trade-wind season. Large and small underwater features are all named. Reefs, passages, channels, sandbanks, feeding grounds, shallow- and deep-water places, coral heads, and various zones on reefs have both generic and specific names, many of which are important places in legends and myths.

Legends are the mnemonic means to recall mental maps and calendars which, in turn, determine the location and timing of hunting activity. Thus cultural history is intimately tied to natural history. For the Islanders, history has a spatial context and the present has an elaborate temporal dimension.

Dugongs and green turtles are extremely wary and elusive, yet the Islanders' skill is such that hunting is reliable and productive. Long-term

TABLE 4. Recorded Hunting Returns of Green Turtles and Dugongs for Mabuiag, Moa (Kubin Village), and Badu Islands, 1976-1979

	Mabuiag						*Kubin*						*Badu*						*Total*	
	Turtles			*Dugongs*			*Turtles*			*Dugongs*			*Turtles*			*Dugongs*			*Turtles*	*Dugongs*
	♂	♀	*Total*	♂	♀	*Total*	♂	♀	*Total*	♂	♀	*Total*	♂	♀	*Total*	♂	♀	*Total*		
1976 September	0	12	12	5	4	9													12	9
October	1	13	14	2	9	11													14	11
November	0	13	13	4	0	4							1	26	27	3	5	8	40	12
December	1	9	10	9	5	14							0	21	21	4	14	18	31	32
1977 January	0	16	16	10	2	12	0	10	10	4	2	6	0	12	12	6	3	9	38	27
February	1	4	5	4	2	6	0	17	17	3	0	3	0	18	18	9	7	16	40	25
March	0	9	9	4	3	7	0	5	5	3	1	4	1	10	11	8	9	17	25	28
April	6	10	16	2	0	2	0	17	17	1	1	2	2	21	23	4	1	5	56	9
May	1	8	9	7	5	12	1	9	10	2	2	4	0	28	28	3	1	4	47	20
June	0	10	10	11	2	13	1	11	12	2	1	3	0	19	19	6	3	9	41	25
July	0	8	8	5	6	11	0	9	9	2	1	3	0	12	12	5	7	12	29	26
August	0	9	9	5	3	8	0	6	6	3	1	4	0	15	15	5	4	9	30	21
September	0	11	11	6	7	13	0	27	27	2	7	9	0	15	15	8	6	14	53	36
October	0	14	14	2	3	5	0	20	20	0	5	5	0	16	16	6	5	11	50	21
November	0	19	19	2	5	7	0	12	12	0	3	3	0	19	19	3	3	6	50	16
December	0	16	16	4	3	7	0	20	20	0	4	4	0	20	20	5	4	9	56	20
1978 January	0	20	20	3	2	5							0	18	18	4	2	6	38	11
February	0	13	13	9	9	18							0	15	15	7	6	13	28	31
March	0	9	9	4	6	10							0	10	10	6	8	14	19	24
April	0	15	15	6	7	13							0	13	13	3	2	5	28	18
May	0	13	13	5	8	13							0	27	27	5	2	7	40	20
June	0	14	14	9	9	18							0	26	26	6	1	7	40	25
July	0	16	16	5	2	7							3	16	19	1	4	5	35	12
August	0	19	19	2	0	2							1	19	20	1	1	2	39	4
September													0	13	13	4	2	6	13	6
October													0	21	21	0	0	0	21	0
November													0	26	26	2	0	2	26	2
December													0	16	16	3	1	4	16	4
1979 January													1	13	14	2	1	3	14	3
February													0	14	14	1	2	3	14	3
March													0	12	12	0	3	3	12	3
	10	300	310	125	102	227	2	163	165	22	28	50	9	511	520	120	107	227	995	504

hunting records for Mabuiag, Moa, and Badu Islands show that monthly catches vary considerably, but collectively they are high (Table 4). For every hunting trip there was a 75% chance of getting an animal. Dugongs are more sought-after but are more difficult to harpoon; consequently, turtles made up a greater percentage (66%) of the total recorded catch, and of these, 98% were females, since the Islanders prefer their fat.

Animals are hunted for subsistence and thus hunting pressure is predicated on kin obligations and community population size and is spread fairly evenly throughout the year. Influencing hunting frequency are social and economic factors such as money available to buy gasoline and oil, desire for fresh meat, and the number and scheduling of feasts. Environmental flux also limits and encourages hunting activities.

Intervals between catches generally were no more than 2 to 3 days, although extreme weather periods often precluded hunting for a week or more. Butcherings are frequent and represent an important social activity. The manner and method used to cut up an animal follow traditional butchering patterns and social exchanges (Fig. 10).

During 1977, hunters from the three islands caught a total of 515 green turtles (almost all females) and 274 dugongs (152 males, 122 females). Amounts of meat obtained for this period averaged 0.31 kg (0.68 lb) per person per day for the combined three-community population. Additional meat from fishing and reef foraging increased the daily average to 0.35 kg (0.77 lb). Individual community meat returns varied from this composite average due to differences in location and availability of gasoline and working outboard motors (Table 5).

More dugongs and turtles are being taken for subsistence than have been previously reported. For example, in 1973, Bertram and Bertram noted that 24 dugongs were taken annually at Mabuiag. Estimates and recorded totals for 1976-1978 suggest that the annual Mabuiag catch is 100. Other underestimates are common. Increased catches could be the result of three possible factors: more hunters, more dugongs and turtles, or previous estimates that were too conservative. A very rough estimate of the average annual catch in Torres Strait is 2100 green turtles and 750 dugongs.

It costs money to hunt, yet meat is given to people free. Outboard motors and aluminum dinghies cost $1500 to $2500 and gasoline is $2.75 per gallon. The hunter and his household incur all these expenses. In what is a heavily monetized economy meat is given away freely and equally as it always has been. Continuation of traditional, socially based meat distribution reduces modern economic disequilibrium among households, maintains social solidarity, and ensures a more than adequate receipt of protein (Fig. 11). The receipt of meat is a social transaction, dependent upon kinship ties and independent of cash wealth.

FIGURE 10. In butchering a dugong a traditional pattern of cutting lines is followed to aid in systematic dismemberment into particular cuts, each of which has a species-specific name and is preference-classed for distribution to hunters, butchers, and kin. Dugongs are butchered into 45 meat and organ categories; green turtles into 30.

TABLE 5. Number of Dugongs and Green Turtles Taken in 1977 by Island Community, per Capita, and for Time and Distance

	Mabuiag (pop. 125)	*Kubin (Moa Is.) (pop. 65)*	*Badu (pop. 325)*
Hunting catch			
green turtles	142	165	208
dugongs	103	50	121
Per capita catch			
green turtles	1.13	2.54	.64
dugongs	.82	.77	.37
green turtles and dugongs	1.95	3.31	1.01

	Mean round-trip distance (km) traveled to catch animal			*Mean time spent (hr) to catch animal*	
	Dugong	*Green Turtle*		*Dugong*	*Green Turtle*
Male	18.6	17.5	Male	3:08	:57
Female	16.2	23.0	Female	3:41	2:03
Mean	17.4	22.9	Mean	3:20	1:56

Economic dependency and continuation of traditional social customs are not a contradiction in terms in Torres Strait Islander society.

Why has hunting persisted in the face of high operating expenses, access to imported foods and materials, and the availability of social benefit payments from state and commonwealth governments? Hunting continues to be an important cultural activity that preserves a way of life and a body of knowledge that gives meaning to livelihood and existence. To be a hunter is a cultural and perceptual affirmation of being an Islander. The persistence of hunting in the Torres Strait represents an extraordinary situation that involves isolation and acculturation, natural and cultural history, legislation and economics, and a remarkable adaptation by a seafaring people to the world's only two species of large marine herbivores.

Acknowledgments

Research was supported by National Geographic Society Grant 1626, in 1976, and by a visiting appointment as Senior Research Fellow in the Department of Human Geography, Research School of Pacific Studies, Australian National University (ANU), Canberra. Among the many people in this department who aided us, R. Gerard Ward, Diana Howlett, Elizabeth Lawrence, Shirley Halton, and Ken Lockwood provided tremendous help. Skip Rhodes and Alan McDonell of the Department of

FIGURE 11. Meat distribution is a social consequence of a hunt. Members of the hunting crew receive special cuts, as do the men who help butcher. A novice hunter is trained by his maternal uncle *(audi)*, and when he becomes a harpooner he will continue to honor that training by inviting his *audi* to help butcher. After the obligatory pieces are given out, the balance is distributed equally by type of cut into containers brought from specified households. Here, meat from two dugongs is sufficient for distribution to all 22 Mabuiag Island households.

Biogeography and Geomorphology at ANU lent us field equipment and provided sage advice. In Torres Strait, John Buchanan and Tom Bartlett of the DAIA helped arrange transport to the outer islands and channeled mail and supplies to us during the research period. Flo Kennedy always had a place for us on Thursday Island and kept us well fed on good food and island stories. Island Chairmen kindly provided accommodation and assistance: Naseli Nona, Mabuiag Island; Joey Nona, Badu Island; Wees Nawia, Kubin Village, Moa Island; and Tanu Nona and Getano Lui. Many Islanders helped us with our research, especially Repu Sakawai, James Eseli, Freddie Savage, Gib Gaulai, Kami Paipai, Young Bani, and Elliot Whop. Seagrass samples were analyzed in the Botany Department, James Cook University, Townsville, Queensland. A faculty grant from the University of California, Berkeley, funded assistance for computer analysis of the field data. I thank all these individuals, departments, and institutions.

REFERENCES

ANDERSON, PAUL K., and HEINSOHN, GEORGE E.
1978. The status of the dugong, and dugong hunting in Australian waters: A survey of local perceptions. Biological Conservation, vol. 13, pp. 13-26.

BARNETT, C., and JOHNS, D.
1976. Underwater observations of dugong in northern Queensland, Australia, with notes on dugong hunting and recommendations for future research. Advisory Committee on Marine Resources Research, Scientific Consultation on Marine Mammals. Paper 106, Mammals in the Seas Conference, Bergen, Norway.

BECKETT, JEREMY
1963. Politics in the Torres Strait Islands. Unpublished Ph.D. dissertation (Anthropology), Australian National University, Canberra.
1965. Australia's Melanesian minority: Political development in the Torres Strait Islands. Human Organization, vol. 5, pp. 152-158.
1967. Elections in a small Melanesian community. Ethnology, vol. 6, no. 3, pp. 332-344.
1972. The Torres Strait Islanders. Pp. 307-326 *in* "Bridge and Barrier: The Natural and Cultural History of Torres Strait," D. Walker, ed. ANU Press, Canberra.
1977. The Torres Strait Islanders and the pearling industry: A case of internal colonialism. Aboriginal History, vol. 1, no. 1, pp. 77-104.

BERTRAM, G.D.F., and BERTRAM, C.K.R.
1973. The modern Sirenia: Their distribution and status. Biol. Journ. Linnean Soc., vol. 5, pp. 297-338.

BUSTARD , ROBERT
1971. Marine turtles in Queensland, Australia. Marine Turtles, Proceedings of the 2nd Working Meeting of Marine Turtle Specialists, International Union for Conservation of Nature and Natural Resources, Supplementary Paper, no. 31, pp. 23-38.
1972. Sea turtles: Their natural history and conservation, 220 pp. Taplinger Publishing Company, New York.

CARR, A. F., and MAIN, A. R.
1973. Turtle farming project in Northern Australia: Report of an inquiry into ecological implications, 80 pp. Commonwealth of Australia, Canberra.

DUNCAN, HELEN
1974. Socio-economic conditions in the Torres Strait: A survey of four reserve islands. *In* "The Torres Strait Islanders, vol. I," 88 pp. E. K. Fisk, ed. Department of Economics, Australian National University, Canberra.

HADDON, A. C., ed.
1901-35. Reports of the Cambridge Anthropological Expedition to Torres Straits, vols. 1 (1935), 2 (1901-1903), 3 (1907), 4 (1912), 5 (1904), 6 (1908). Cambridge University Press, Cambridge.

HARRIS, DAVID R.
1977. Subsistence strategies across Torres Strait. Pp. 421-463 *in* "Sunda and Sahul: Prehistoric Studies in Southeast Asia, Melanesia and Australia," J. Allen, J. Golson, and R. Jones, eds. Academic Press, New York and London.
1979. Foragers and farmers in the Western Torres Strait Islands: An historical analysis of economic, demographic and spatial differentiation. Pp. 75-109 *in* "Social and Economic Systems," P. C. Burnham and R. F. Ellen, eds. Academic Press, London.

HEINSOHN, GEORGE E.
1972. A study of dugongs *(Dugong dugon)* in northern Queensland, Australia. Biological Conservation, vol. 4, no. 3, pp. 205-213.

HEINSOHN, GEORGE E., and BIRCH, W. R.
1972. Foods and feeding habits of the dugong *(Dugong dugon)* in northern Queensland, Australia. Mammalia, vol. 36, no. 2, pp. 414-422.

HEINSOHN, GEORGE E., and MARSH, HELENE
1977. Sirens of tropical Australia. Australian Nat. Hist., vol. 19, no. 4, pp. 106-111.

HEINSOHN, GEORGE E., and SPAIN, ALISTER V.
1974. Effects of a tropical cyclone on littoral and sub-littoral biotic communities and on a population of dugongs (*Dugong dugon* [Muller]). Biological Conservation, vol. 6, no. 2, pp. 143-152.

HEINSOHN, GEORGE E.; SPAIN, ALISTER V.; and ANDERSON, PAUL K.
1976. Populations of dugongs (Mammalia: Sirenia): Aerial survey over inshore waters of tropical Australia. Biological Conservation, vol. 9, pp. 21-23.

HUDSON, B.E.T.
1976. Dugongs: Distribution, hunting, protective legislation and cultural significance in Papua New Guinea. Advisory Committee on Marine Resources Research, Scientific Consultation on Marine Mammals, Paper 86, Mammals in the Seas Conference, Bergen, Norway.

HUSAR, SANDRA L.
1975. A review of the literature of the dugong *(Dugong dugon).* U. S. Fish and Wildlife Res. Rep., no. 4, pp. 1-30.

LAADE, WOLFGANG
1971. Oral traditions and written documents on the history and ethnography of the northern Torres Strait Islands, Saibai-Dauan-Boigu, 125 pp. Franz Steiner Verlag, Wiesbaden.

LAWRIE, MARGARET
1970. Myths and legends of Torres Strait, 372 pp. University of Queensland Press, Brisbane.

NIETSCHMANN, BERNARD
1976. The ecology of marine herbivores, seagrasses, and Torres Strait Islanders, 16 pp. Preliminary Research Report, Department of Human Geography, Research School of Pacific Studies, Australian National University.
1977a. Torres Strait Islander hunters and environment, 17 pp. Work-in-progress Research Report, Department of Human Geography, Research School of Pacific Studies, Australian National University.

1977b. The wind caller. Nat. Hist., vol. 86, no. 3, pp. 10-16. (Reprinted in Reader's Digest, Canadian Edition, October, 1977.)

1982. Indigenous island peoples, living resources and protected areas. Paper presented at the 3rd World National Parks Congress, Bali, Indonesia, October 10-22.

1983. Traditional societies and biosphere reserves. Paper for the Man and Biosphere Program, First International Meeting, Minsk, Soviet Union.

——. Torres Strait Islander sea resource management and sea rights. Paper presented at the UNESCO Workshop on Traditional Management of Coastal Systems, Jakarta, Indonesia, December 5-9. UNESCO. (In press.)

NIETSCHMANN, BERNARD, and NIETSCHMANN, JUDITH

1977. Eight decades on an island: Social and ecological relationships in the Torres Strait, 33 pp. Final Research Report, Department of Human Geography, Research School of Pacific Studies, Australian National University.

1981. Good dugong, bad dugong; bad turtle, good turtle. Nat. Hist., vol. 90, no. 5, pp. 54-63, 86-87.

NIETSCHMANN, JUDITH

1979. Haddon the headhunter. Paper at the 23rd Annual Meeting of The Kroeber Anthropological Society, University of California, Berkeley.

1980. Another way of dying: The social and cultural context of death in a Melanesian community, Torres Strait. Ph.D. dissertation, Anthropology, Univ. of Michigan, 382 pp.

1981. Tombstone openings, cultural change and death ceremonies in Torres Strait, Australia. Kabar Seberang, no. 8/9, pp. 1-15.

SPAIN, A. V., and HEINSOHN, G. E.

1975. Size and weight allometry in a North Queensland population of *Dugong dugon* (Muller) (Mammalia: Sirenia). Australian Journ. Zool., vol. 23, pp. 159-168.

WALKER, D. (ed.)

1972. Bridge and barrier: The natural and cultural history of Torres Strait, 437 pp. Department of Biogeography and Geomorphology, Australian National Univesity Press, Canberra.

WAKE, JUDITH

1975. A study of the habitat requirements and feeding biology of the dugong, *Dugong dugon* (Muller), 121 pp. B.S. Honors Thesis (School of Biological Sciences), James Cook University, Townsville, Queensland.

BERNARD NIETSCHMANN

Excavations at Carter's Grove Plantation, Virginia, 1976-1979

Grant Recipient: Ivor Noël Hume, Colonial Williamsburg Foundation, Williamsburg, Virginia.

Grants 1693, 1823, 1960: In support of an archeological investigation of 17th-century settlement sites at Carter's Grove, Virginia.

Carter's Grove, on the James River 7 miles east of Williamsburg, was deeded to the Colonial Williamsburg Foundation in 1969. Preliminary planning to develop this once important plantation into a working interpretation of rural life in colonial Virginia first called for an archeological survey (Fig. 1) of the more than 600 acres that represent what is left of the 1400 acres acquired by Robert Carter prior to his death in 1632. That survey, carried out in 1970 and 1971, unexpectedly led to the location of several areas of much earlier colonial occupation around the surviving 1755 mansion. Because those sites predated the house by a century or more—and could contribute nothing to the reconstruction of an 18th-century working plantation—their locations were only plotted, and the test trenches back-filled. One 2-acre area northeast of the mansion was not touched at all, the survey crew backing off when it encountered human burials on two sides, and 17th-century rubbish deposits on the others.

In April 1976, Colonial Williamsburg archeologists were asked to investigate the unexcavated area, designated Site A, to determine the age and extent of the cemetery, and to determine whether its presence would preclude the use of the adjacent ground as a location for 18th-century craft exhibits. The resulting excavations revealed evidence of the development and layout of the earliest plantation complex so far discovered in British America (Fig. 2). Dating between ca. 1625 and 1645, it included the posthole patterns for at least 9 structures, ranging from a 40-ft × 20-ft residence that had grown in at least two stages—to servants' quarters, and produce sheds. Fences of several styles outlined fields and yards, and a fence-flanked roadway marked the approach to the buildings—a roadway cut through by a group of 15 graves. Five more graves lay in a row behind one of its fences, and 3 others lay closer to the houses. All 23 graves could be attributed to the second quarter of the 17th century; their occupants ranged in age from infancy to 60, with average ages at death for males of 31.0 and 29.6 for females.

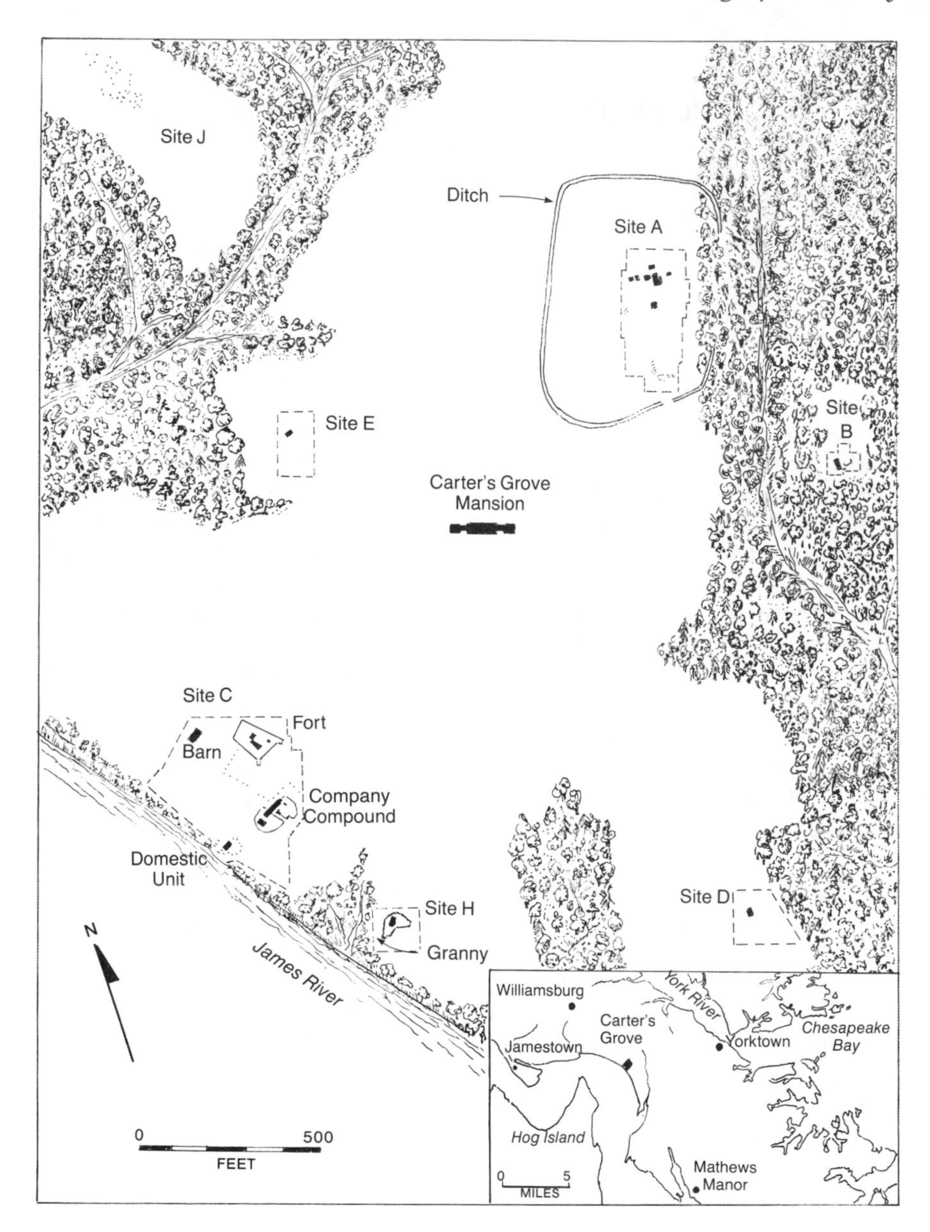

FIGURE 1. Site location map.

Scores of artifacts were retrieved from rubbish pits, tree holes, and a cellar, many pointing to a relatively high standard of living. But alongside imported, quality ceramics were larger numbers of vessels believed to be of Virginia manufacture, among them an almost complete alembic that can fairly claim to be the most sophisticated example of the earthenware potter's art yet discovered on a 17th-century colonial site. Spectrographic analysis of the alembic's clay, along with samples of clay dug at different points and at different depths on the Carter's Grove tract, left little doubt that the vessel was of Virginia manufacture. Furthermore, fragments of kiln "furniture" found in the same pit as the alembic suggested that the kiln site was located nearby.

Because hitherto little was known about the dating of early 17th-century artifacts, or indeed about the interpretation of post-supported domestic and farm buildings of that period, work on the cultural background began in tandem with the digging. Equally pressing, however, was the need to assemble the documentary evidence to reconstruct the history of the tract once known as Martin's Hundred.

The Society of Martin's Hundred was one of several joint-stock companies chartered between 1616 and 1618 to help underwrite new settlements in Virginia and to shore up the financially ailing Virginia Company of London. Although there were as many as 7 of these secondary companies, the Society of Martin's Hundred seems to have been the largest and to have possessed the most prestigious group of shareholders. Among these shareholders was Richard Martin, who gave his name to the enterprise and may have been the Martin who was recorder of the City of London and who died in 1617 before the venture could be launched. Another was Sir John Wolstenholme, a wealthy London merchant and backer of exploratory enterprises such as those of Henry Hudson and William Baffin, both of whom planted his name on the maps of the Arctic's frosted rim. The Martin's Hundred Society (as it alternatively was termed) gave Sir John's name to the Virginia settlement's administrative center, calling it Wolstenholme Towne. Early in 1619, the ship *Gift of God* arrived in the James River having left England with 220 settlers to carve a new life (and a profit for the London shareholders) out of a 20,000-acre tract on the north shore, about 10 miles downstream from Jamestown. During the next 3 years, the total number of dispatched settlers approached 280, but the death toll was high, and by the winter of 1622 the survivors were down to about 140 in a total colonial population of around 1400. In March of that year an Indian uprising left more than 300 dead, at least 58 of them in Martin's Hundred. The originally reported figures were 347 and 78, respectively. According to one report, nothing was left of Martin's Hundred but 2 houses and "a peece of a Church" (Kingsbury, 1935, p. 41). Nevertheless, the plantation was resettled, first by survivors and then by

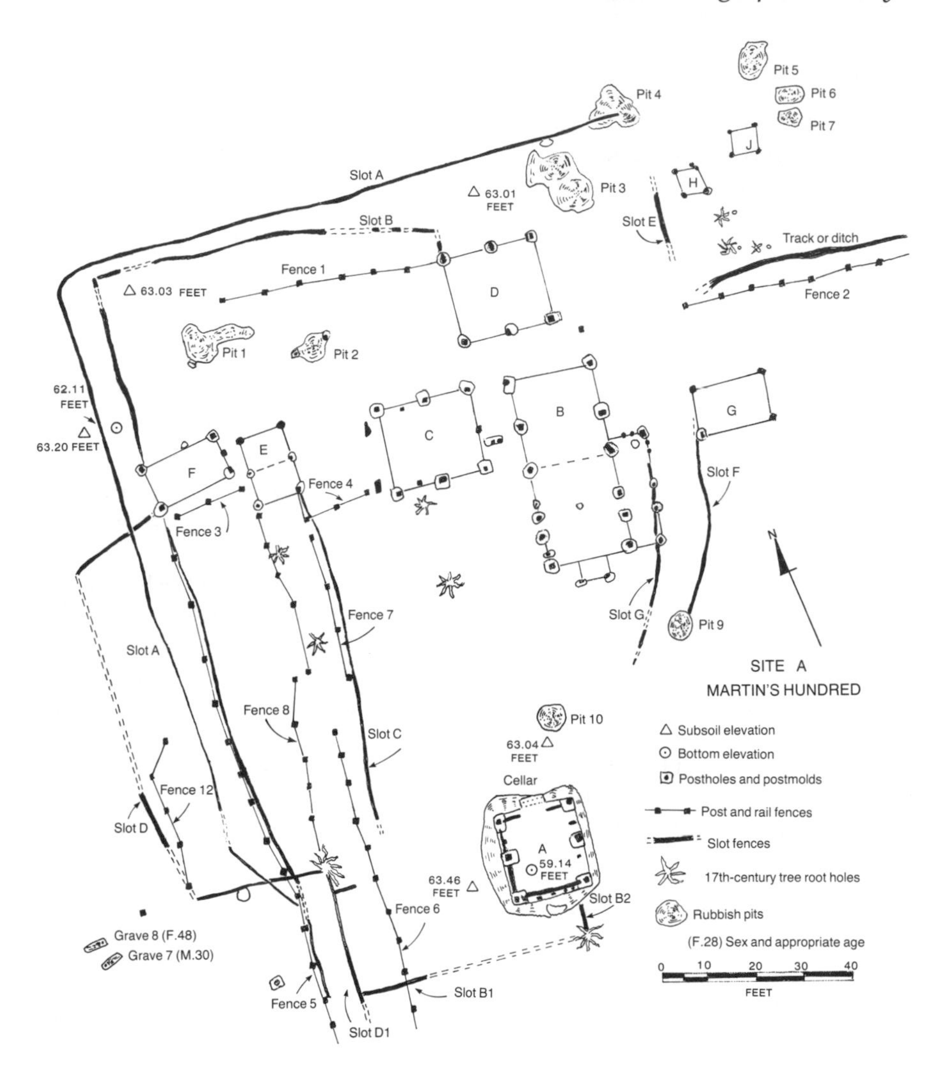

FIGURE 2a. Features at the northern end of Site A.

new immigrants, though by 1624 the Hundred's total population was no more than 30, grouped in only 7 households. Although the originally patented 20,000 acres was expanded to 21,500 in a 1622 re-patent (Kingsbury, 1933, pp. 592 f) and in 1625 was reported to embrace 800,000 acres "as is allegded" (Kingsbury, 1935, p. 556), the population never expanded to fill it. In 1624 Virginia became a Crown colony; the private companies were disbanded; and the issuing of land grants in what became

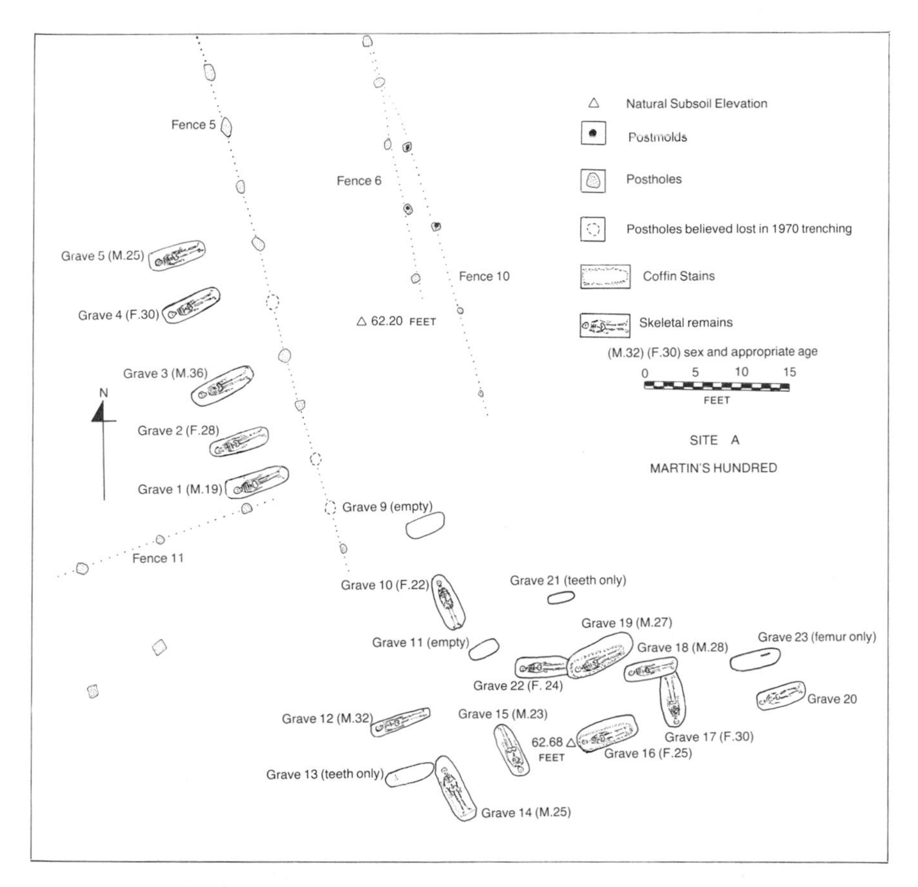

FIGURE 2b. Features at the southern end of Site A.

Martin's Hundred Parish became the business of the King's appointed governor at Jamestown.

These were the bare bones of Martin's Hundred's rise and fall, and it remained to the archeologists to build flesh upon them.[1] The records showed that in 1620 the Society had sent over William Harwood of Barnstaple to be the settlement's leader (Jester, 1956, p. 43), and accumulative archeological evidence would point to his having made his home on Site A.

In December 1976 the National Geographic Society awarded Colonial Williamsburg a grant to enable excavations to continue through a second year. These excavations were designed to explore a second site situated across a ravine to the east of Site A, where the principal investigator believed the potter's kiln might have stood. Although the discovery of large numbers of potsherds from locally made earthenwares (including several apparent "wasters") provided support for that belief, no kiln was found. Instead, Site B yielded the plan of another relatively large, post-built house, measuring 43 ft × 22 ft (Fig. 3), 1 shed, and the coffined remains of a small child. Unlike Site A, this one lay deep in the woods and had escaped mutilation by plowing; consequently, artifacts were scattered all through the soil layers, some even protruding from the surface once the overlying leaf mantle was swept away. Digging was slow but rewarding.

Site B evidently was occupied contemporaneously with its neighbor across the ravine, and the principal investigator's preliminary estimate of a date range between 1630 and 1640 was graphically supported by the discovery of a slipware dish dated 1631. This, too, was of local manufacture, and so lays claim to being the oldest recorded example of English (assuming Virginia to be an English province) slipware. Although Site B clearly was occupied after 1631, the question of a date for the dwelling's construction still remained open. A clay tobacco-pipe bowl found in the construction of its hearth pointed to a date potentially as early as the founding of Martin's Hundred, and thus to an existence prior to the 1622 Indian attack.

As artifact studies progressed, it became increasingly apparent that no yardstick existed to enable one to distinguish between household objects in use prior to 1625 and those made and used in the second quarter of the century. Indeed, most catalogues of museum parallels rarely offered anything more specific than attributions to the early, middle, or late 17th century. Consequently, if archeologists could not date their sites by their artifacts, sites having historically identified *termini ante quem* would have to be found to date the artifacts. The most obvious of such sites are shipwrecks, and as the Martin's Hundred excavations progressed, the evidence of wrecks ranging from the *Sea Venture* (1609) at Bermuda, to the *Wasa* (1628) at Stockholm, and the *Batavia* (1629) off the west coast of Australia was analyzed and incorporated. Greatest store, however, was placed in the hope of locating a Martin's Hundred site that had been destroyed in the 1622 attack, and never reoccupied.

Finding that Site B was small and its potential running out, in June 1977 the archeological crew moved to a site closer to the James River, another of those located but not explored in the 1970-1971 survey. Designated Site C, this one lay in an open field, and so, like Site A, had been subjected to centuries of plowing. Indeed, it quickly became apparent that the loam stratum was in places no more than 4 in. thick, and that any colonial stratigraphy had been totally destroyed. Nevertheless, also like

---

[1] It should be noted that the author of this report has written a book entitled *Martin's Hundred*, published by Alfred A. Knopf, New York, 1982, 343 pages.

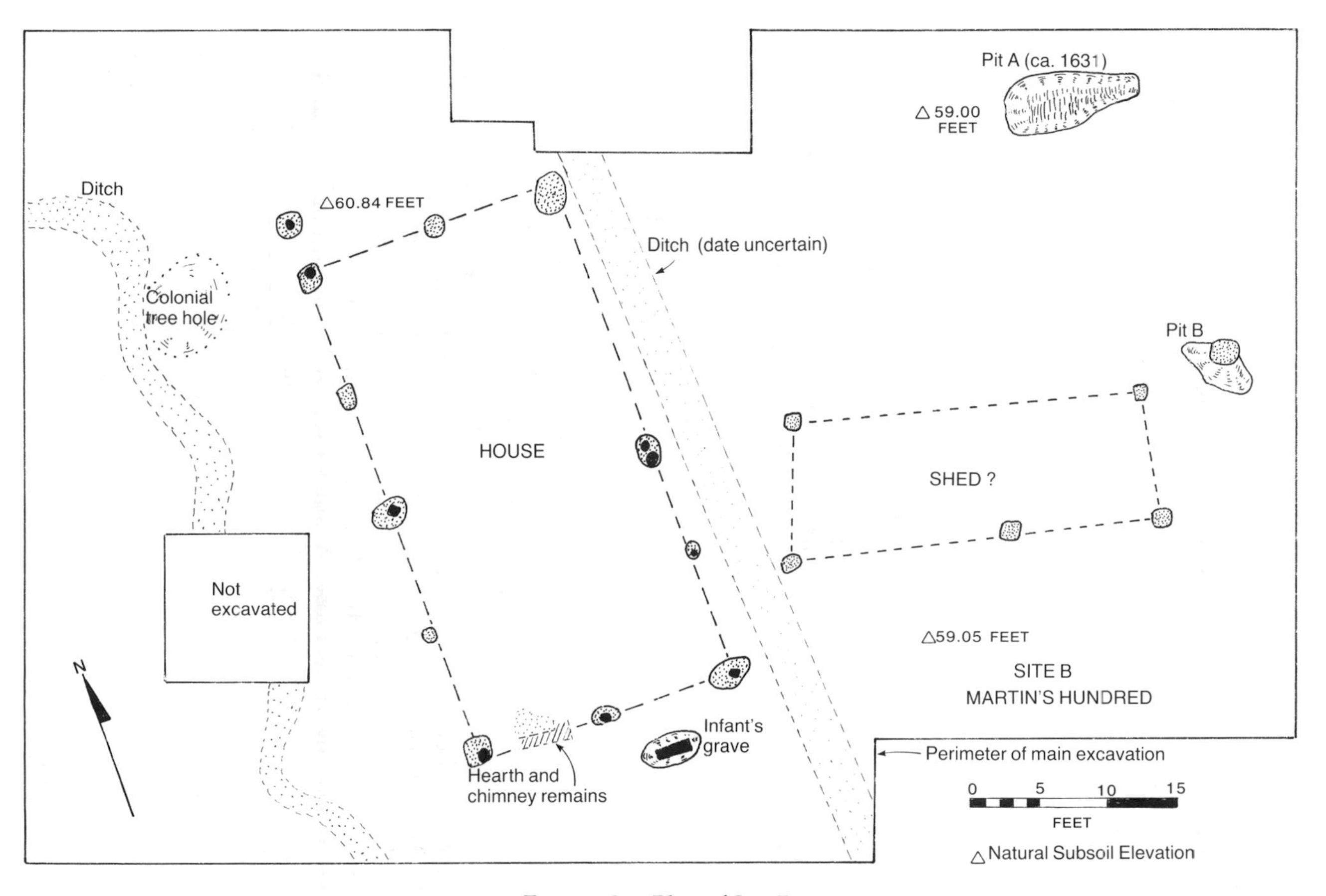

FIGURE 3. Plan of Site B.

Site A, this one retained large numbers of postholes. By the end of the summer they had sorted themselves out into what appeared to be the corner of a triangular fort. The spacing of the holes on 9-ft centers and a boxlike area at the corner fitted well Samuel Purchas's 1625 description of defenses at Jamestown, which were described as being built "with a Pallizado of Planckes and strong Posts," and having at every corner "where the lines meete, a Bulwarke or Watchtower" (Purchas, 1625, pp. 1752-1753).

A large pit within the fort proved to comprise both a cattle pond and a shallow well, the latter yielding, among other artifacts, an armor backplate and the first complete close helmet found in the New World. As for the fort, it was the oldest timber-built defense-work so far excavated on an Anglo-American site, and a major contribution to the interpretation of colonial life in Virginia. On the strength of that success, the National Geographic Society agreed to extend and increase its grant to enable excavations on Site C to be resumed in 1978. In the meantime, through the winter of 1977-1978, artifactual and historical studies progressed, and when the weather permitted, the field crew undertook renewed testing in the Carter's Grove woods. The excavation of Site B had been completed in the fall of 1977 without any major new discoveries being made, and hope that a kiln would be found, had long since faded.

Work resumed on Site C in April 1978 and led to the full excavation of the fort which proved not to be triangular but trapezoidal, with average interior measurements of 121 ft 6 in. × 85 ft 6 in. (Fig. 4). In addition to a watchtower and adjacent gate at the southeast corner, a flanker interpreted as a cannon platform was found at the southwest corner. Although slender subsoil disturbances hinted at another flanker at the northwest corner, the evidence was inconclusive. Clearly, however, there was none at the northeast which, being closest to a deep ravine up which attackers could approach unseen, rendered it the fort's most vulnerable corner.

The cannon platform could not have been intended for defense against Indians, but rather to discourage the approach of Spanish warships heading upriver toward Jamestown. A 3¾-in. cannonball found on Site A (and the knowledge that in 1625 Governor Harwood possessed "Peece of Ordnance, 1 with all things thereto belonging") (Jester, 1956, p. 43) suggested that this and the fort's only mounted gun were one and the same, and that the bore necessary to accommodate a 6¾-lb ball called for a gun of saker size and calibre. These guns normally had barrels 8 ft in length, and loading such a weapon on a platform as small as that suggested by the postholes would have been difficult. Nevertheless, the presence within and beneath the flanker of a slot for a substantial piece of timber indicated that the platform had been supported by a large, vertical

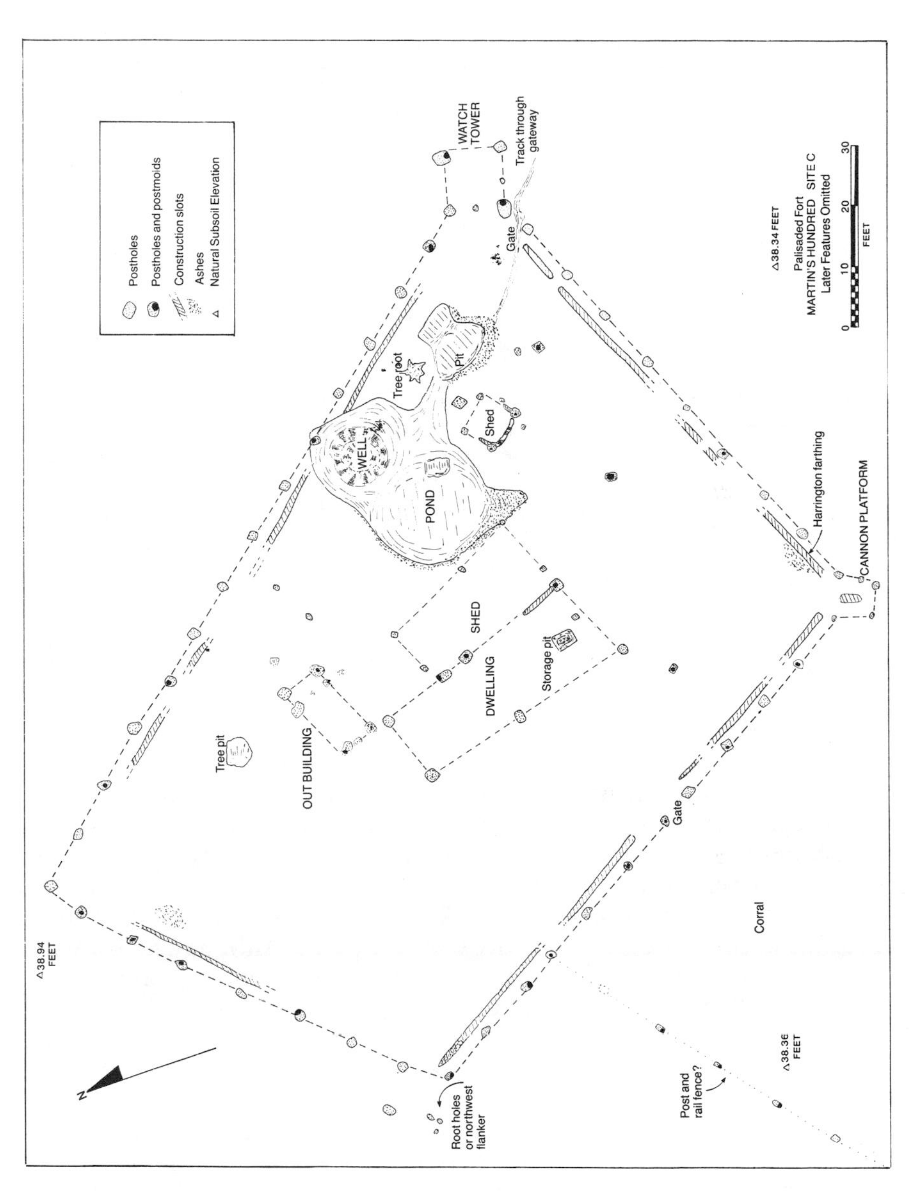

FIGURE 4. Plan of the fort at Site C.

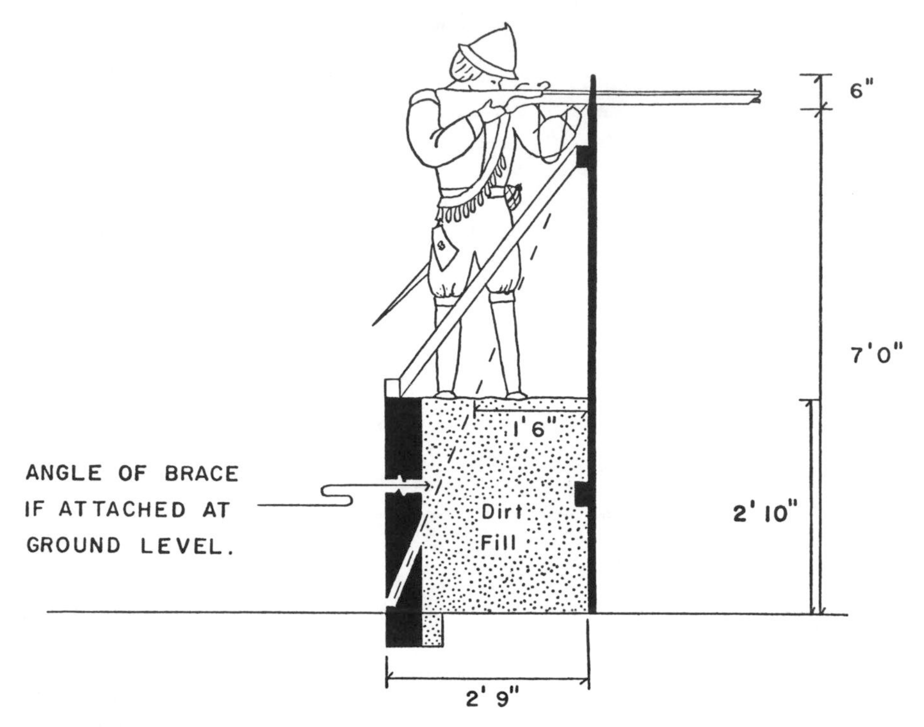

FIGURE 5. Conjectural elevation of the fort's parapet step and paling height.

block (probably a length of tree trunk) and had been intended to carry a considerable load. Saker barrels weighed as much as 1500 lb.

Estimates of the palisades' height were based in part on the evidence of archeology and in part on paralleling documentation. On a line 2 ft 9 in. behind the palisade planking and parallel to it ran a slot. Extending along all four sides, but absent at gates and corners, this slot is believed to have seated timbers forming the back of a dirt-compacted parapet step, upon which defenders stood to fire over the pales. Although no contemporary parallels for such construction have been found, a stone-backed and rubble-filled step designed to serve the same purpose survives at Southampton Fort in Bermuda, a fort whose origins go back to 1620, but whose gun platform (of which the step is part) is believed to date from the late 18th-century.

The presence of a relatively narrow, timber-supported step within the Martin's Hundred fort indicates that the walls were by no means as tall as those surrounding the Jamestown settlement, which were described as being 14 ft in height, and where defense relied entirely on infilade fire from massive flankers. Documentary evidence from Lord

Baltimore's Ferryland plantation in Newfoundland described how, in 1622, the settlement was protected by a palisade of vertical 7 ft-6 in.-high palings, which were pointed at the top—a wall intended to discourage marauders, both animal and human (Prowse, 1895, p. 129). Further evidence for the construction of palisades of comparable height (7 ft rather than 7 ft 6 in.) comes from a 1649 contract drawn up between the Duke of Ormond and two Irish carpenters to build a palisade around three Ulster villages. That document, now in the Bodleian Library at Oxford, described in precise detail how the posts, rails, and pales should be spaced, set, and supported (Bodleian, Ms. Carte 176). Assuming, therefore, that the 6-in. height difference was represented by the angular slicing of the Ferryland pales and was intended as much to provide rests for heavy matchlock muskets as it was to make the walls a little more difficult to scale, reconstructions of the Martin's Hundred fort (National Geographic, June 1979, p. 743) assumed a total height of 7 ft 6 in. for the pales, but otherwise followed the Ulster document's constructional directions.

Neither the Ferryland nor the Ulster documentary evidence said anything about a musketeer's step, and it is clear that the Duke of Ormond's palisade was not a military structure. The problem, therefore, was to estimate the height of the step. The answer was arrived at in the following manner: Assuming that a Martin's Hundred musketeer of average height would have stood no more than 5 ft 6 in. tall (this based on average measurements from male skeletons on all the Martin's Hundred sites), a staff member of that height stood holding a contemporary matchlock musket in the firing position, its barrel nestling in the crook of the U-shaped prop normally used in aiming these heavy guns. Measuring the distance from the underside of the stock to the soles of the marksman's feet revealed that in order to fire over a 7-ft palisade, he would have had to stand 3 ft above the land surface (Fig. 5).

Dating evidence for the fort was more circumstantial than specific. Ashes in the postholes of the ill-defined interior buildings indicated that all had burned, while the absence of comparable evidence from the palisade posts indicated that the defenses had not. This, coupled with the evidence of the armor discarded into the well, suggested that the fort had been overrun either during or after the Indian massacre in March 1622. That at least 68 settlers survived suggests that some were able to take refuge in the fort, and that the destruction came later. Four priming pans broken from matchlock muskets found on Site C suggest that guns were deliberately rendered inoperative by striking off their pans, a step that may have been taken by survivors intending to abandon the plantation, but who had to leave behind equipment they could not carry.

Additional dating evidence for the fort's construction was provided by the discovery of an English coin of considerable rarity in filling within the parapet step slot. This token farthing was issued under royal license to John Lord Harington in the spring of 1613, but was withdrawn within 3 months when a larger and more publicly acceptable farthing (Harington, Type 2) was issued (Peck, 1970, p. 26). In theory, therefore, the coin had no business to be found in a settlement established 6 years later. Taken at face value—which it cannot be—the farthing should indicate that the fort was built in 1613. More reasonable, however, is the as-yet-undocumented supposition that Harington's rejected coins were later sent to Virginia to satisfy the same need for small change that prompted Governor Sir John Harvey to petition the King in 1636 for the provision of farthing tokens (Sainsbury, 1860, p. 239).

Excavations southwest of the fort and closer to the river revealed another palisaded area, its posts again on 9-ft centers but with no parapet step to give it a military appearance (Fig. 6). These paled fences created 2 oval enclosures linked to each other through their attachment to a long and narrow building (60 ft × 15 ft) belonging to a well-known European form. The placement of the posts and associated interrupted sill remains seems to indicate that this was a row house divided into 2 dwelling units with a byre or stable at the west end akin to that shown in the Flemish artist Jan Siberecht's painting of a farmyard, now in the collection of the Musée des Beaux Arts at Brussels (Anon., 1977, p. 88). Within the oval fenced area that set the animal shelter apart from the rest of the house had stood a store building measuring 25 ft × 15 ft, apparently with large doors at its north and south ends. Two of its posts had burned so slowly that their charred remains survived at the bottoms of their respective postholes. Ashes found in postmolds from the longhouse combined with them to indicate that both buildings had burned.

The second paled area looped around the east end of the longhouse and enclosed not a building, but a large, silt-filled hole. At first thought to have been a basement for a third building, the hole proved to have been dug to obtain clay either for building the longhouse's wattle-and-daub walls or to provide a potter with his clay. The latter explanation was the more probable because the hole contained large quantities of locally made pottery, some unequivocally spoiled in the manufacturing process. Here was firm evidence for the presence of a Martin's Hundred potter, a skilled craftsman capable of throwing any vessel available in England or needed in Virginia, his genius limited only by the surliness of his clay and the vagaries of his kiln. Among the many metal artifacts found in the clay pit were a perforated paddle believed to be a blunger (the oldest recorded example of such a tool) and a part of a musket barrel, with its breach-block replaced by a bung, and its bore filled with fine lead shot which was probably intended for use in making lead glaze. The pit's treasures were not limited to evidence of the potter, however; other finds included a bill-hook, a frying pan, a brass cooking pot, plates from a brigandine vest, a broken armor backplate, and beneath it, a second complete close helmet.

The association of a backplate and a close helmet both in the fort's well and in the potter's pond has yet to be explained. Clearly, however, they demonstrate a paralleling of circumstances in the two locations, events which almost certainly were colored by the Indian attack in 1622.

Within the potter's pond enclosure and 10 ft from the door of the longhouse was the grave of an adult male; his skull had been cleft by a short, sharp instrument, and then battered both in the area of the right temporal bone and at the back, the latter blow driving and stacking fragments into the frontal region. A shallow groove running from the temporal suture to the left ear is believed to be the result of scalping. The evidence pointed to death at the hands of the Indians, though the felling blow is believed to have been administered with an iron-shod, European spade—an interpretation supported by the opinions of forensic pathologists both in Virginia and London. The identity of the murdered man has not been determined, though it is tempting to see the care with which he was buried as evidence of his importance in the community. Heading the list of Martin's Hundred settlers killed in the massacre is Lieutenant Richard Kean who was then responsible for the Hundred's military preparedness (Kingsbury, 1933a, p. 570).

The dead man's skull proved to possess an unusually powerful jaw, a feature that might point to a person of physical strength and resolve—though, in reality, bone structure has nothing to do with mental attitudes and capability. Nevertheless, in an effort to better appreciate the physiological evidence, a 3-dimensional facial reconstruction was made using a technique developed by the Forensic Anthropological unit of the Federal Aviation Administration's hospital at Norman, Oklahoma.

Identification of the massacre victim was closely linked to recognizing the use to which the longhouse and its related compounds had been put. Clearly a potter was part of it—but only a part of it. Unfortunately, few artifacts were found anywhere but in the pond, yet the presence there of an officer's helmet indicated a diversity of usage. Also recovered from the pond were parts of 5 lead bale seals bearing the emblem of the City of Augsburg in Germany. These are believed to have come from bales of fabric—i.e., supplies, and more of one item than a single family was likely to need. Thus, the seals, coupled with the proximity of longhouse to fort, and the similarity of artifacts associatd with them, pointed to an official relationship between the two. On this evidence, the longhouse and all features within its abutting fences, have collectively been identified as the "Company Compound," the place where the Martin's Hundred Society's stores were housed, and where a craftsman employed by it made pottery for sale to the settlers.

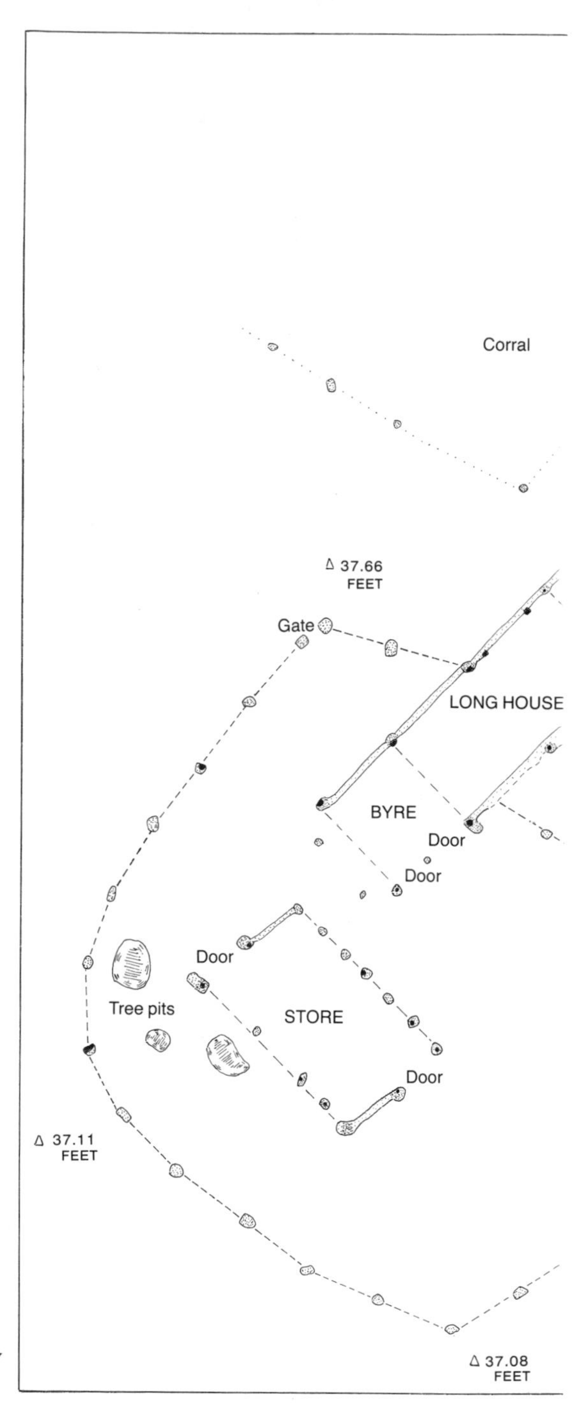

FIGURE 6. Plan of the Company Compound at Site C.

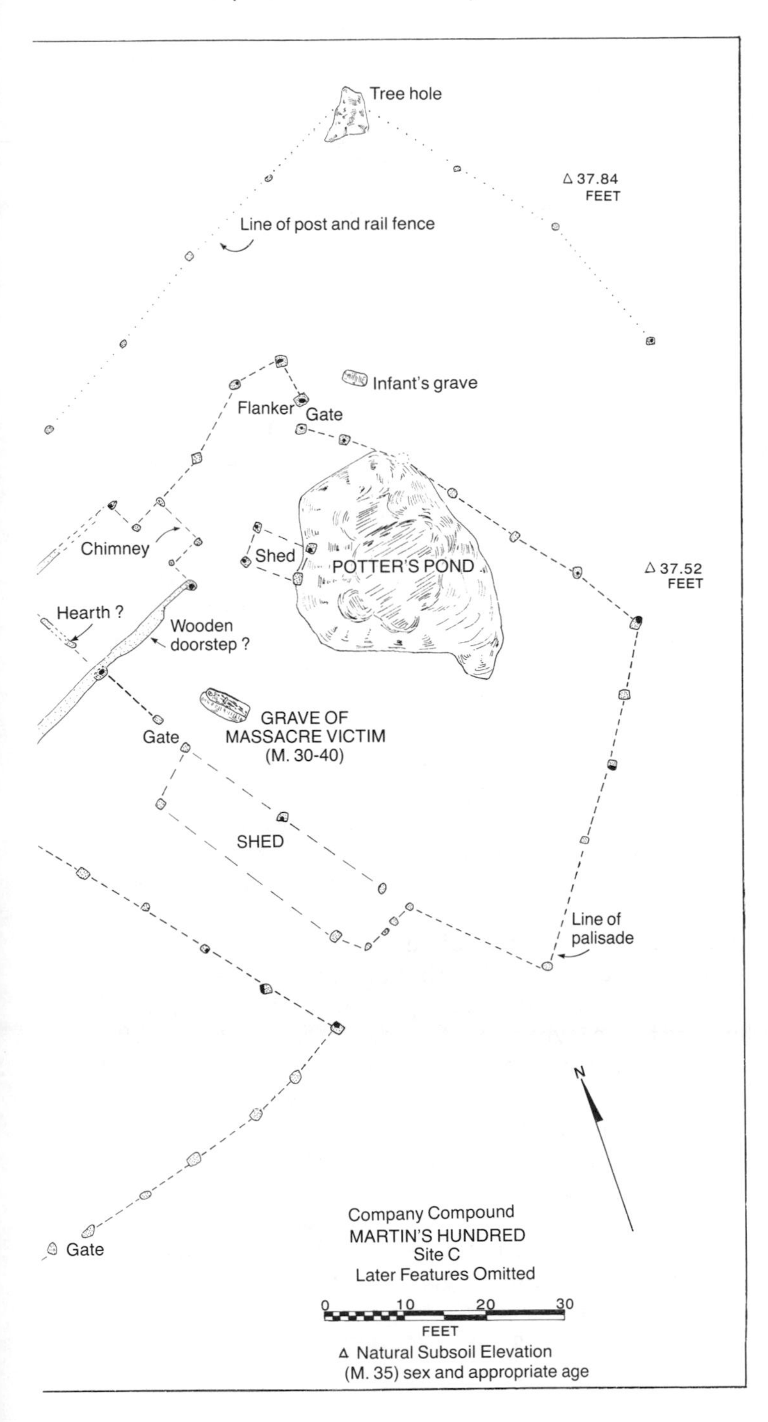
Tree hole
△ 37.84 FEET
Line of post and rail fence
Infant's grave
Flanker
Gate
Chimney
Shed
POTTER'S POND
△ 37.52 FEET
Hearth ?
Wooden doorstep ?
GRAVE OF MASSACRE VICTIM (M. 30-40)
Gate
SHED
Line of palisade
N
Gate
Company Compound
MARTIN'S HUNDRED
Site C
Later Features Omitted
0 10 20 30
FEET
△ Natural Subsoil Elevation
(M. 35) sex and appropriate age

Once again, no kiln foundations were found, yet in this instance its proximity should not be doubted. A narrow and lightly constructed shed of uncertain purpose had stood to the west of the potter's pond, a shed whose strange posthold pattern closely paralleled another such shed found near the dwelling on Site B—the place where previous evidence had pointed to a kiln's existence. Failure to discover a kiln on either site may have been occasioned by the fact that it had no foundations to find. The germ of this negative thesis was seeded on a visit to Yucatán where the principal investigator came upon a kiln wherein Mexican peasants were firing pseudo-antiquities for sale to tourists. That kiln had no below-ground flues, and was loaded and controlled by a door in one side of the clay-and-rock-built dome, and by a hole in the top of it capped by an all-controlling trashcan lid. The shape and size of the kiln is closely akin to one in a woodcut published in London in 1685 and purporting to show an English potter at work (Hudson, 1957, p. 51). As most of what archeologists think they know is based on what they find rather than on what they do not find, the possibility exists that many 17th-century kilns were of the Mexican type and had no flues or ash pits for excavators to expose.

A hundred feet west of the Company Compound lay another house having a fenced yard projecting behind it, and apparently arcing around a shade tree whose root hole survived (Fig. 7). The lightness of the postholes and curvature of their line suggested that this was a fence of wattles rather than of boards or posts and rails. The daub-walled house measured 25 ft × 15 ft, apparently had a hooded fireplace at one end, and had a lean-to roof projecting from its north side. Ashes in some of the postmolds pointed to this being another victim of the 1622 destruction in Martin's Hundred. Reaching to within 2 ft of the west wall was a group of 14 graves, their occupants in such poor condition that little could be learned from them.

The small dwelling, which has been dubbed the "domestic unit," extended to the present river's edge in a line that began at a tree (revealed by its root holes) 150 ft south of the fort's main gate, indicating a degree of orderliness and planning in the laying out of these structures. The careful study of contemporary colonial settlements in Northern Ireland showed a certain standardization of design among what are termed bawn villages—i.e., communities of undefended dwellings usually laid out on two sides of a central street or avenue, with a fortified enclosure at one end. The bawn originally was intended for the safe overnight housing of cattle but later became a fortification around the house or castle of the settlement leader. In some instances the main gates of the Irish bawns are located on the center line of the avenue or green—even when the gate is not set in the center of the bawn's wall.

The placement of postholes along the Martin's Hundred fort's west

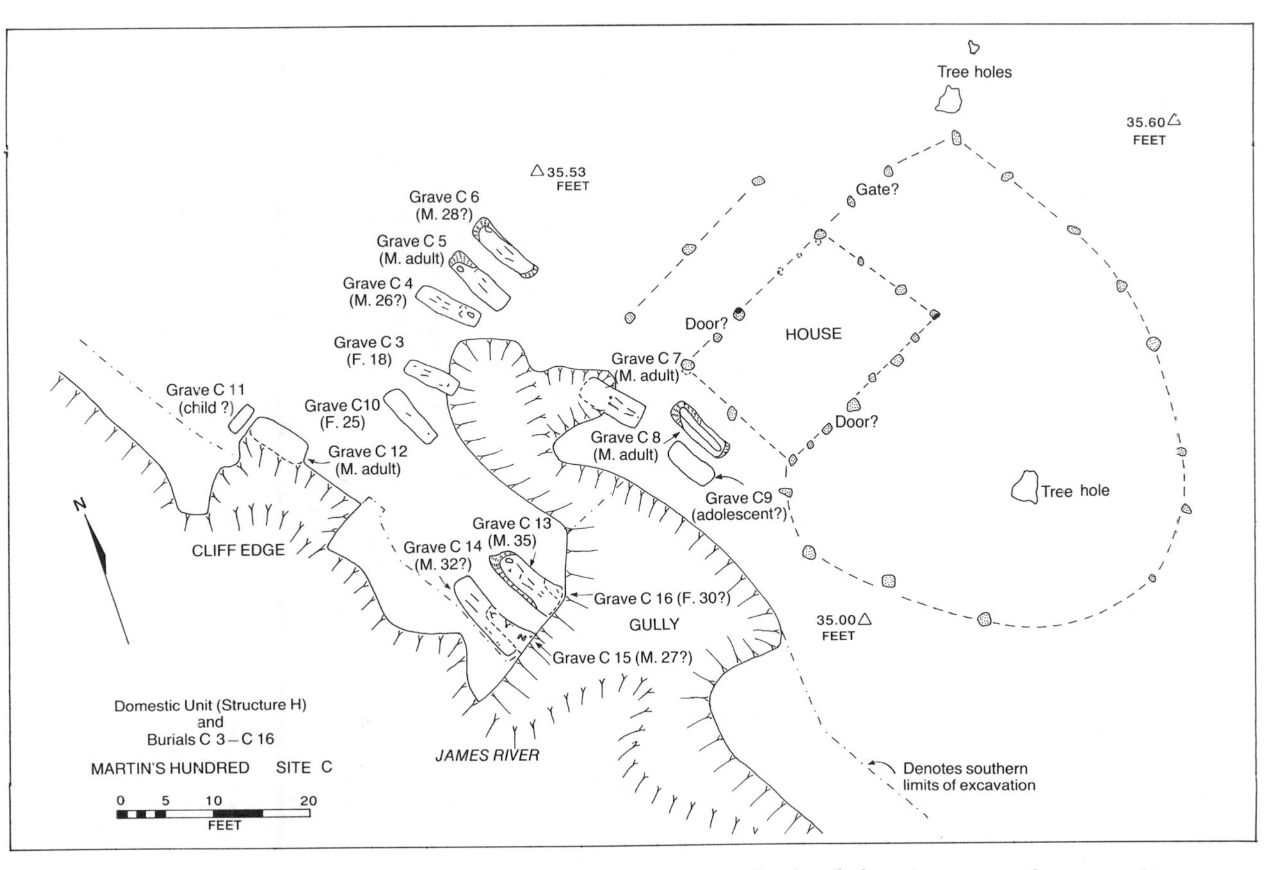

FIGURE 7. The Domestic Unit and adjacent graves at Site C: Δ, natural subsoil elevation; sex and age noted in parentheses below the grave number.

wall line indicated that its gate was not in the center. With the potential Irish plans in mind, test cuts were made to try to locate other structures 150 ft north of the gate. One was found; a barnlike structure measuring 45 ft × 29 ft, the largest building revealed on any of the Martin's Hundred sites and probably the place where the settlement's produce was stored. Three large postholes on the center line of the building (and only slight ones at the sides) pointed to this structure being less wall than roof, the latter's weight carried on the ridge pole (Fig. 8).

Most of the 1620 Ulster village plans showed their streets or avenues to be parallel sided. But this was not true in Martin's Hundred; there the angles created by the east, south, and north sides were set at 83°, suggesting that the village tapered toward the river. The presence of a ravine south of the Company Compound and the silted tail of another a few feet upstream from the barn indicated that the settlement site had once occupied a tapering promontory flanked by ravines. Estimates of river erosion at a rate of anything from a foot to a yard a year would mean a land loss since 1619 in excess of 350 ft. Similarly, conjecturing the maximum convergence of the settlement's two sides (no less than the width of the fort) suggested a riverside end between 350 and 400 ft beyond the extant shoreline.

Test pits dug into the riverbed by divers from the Virginia Research Center for Archaeology yielded no hoped-for traces of 17th-century riverside revetments, but at a distance of between 400 and 450 ft offshore redeposited shells from eroded marl beds under the Carter's Grove bluffs thinned out and disappeared. This hinted at the presence of an older river bed and a sloping downward of the headland at approximately the location whereat other indicators suggested the settlement terminated. A series of test pits dug on a right-angled traverse upstream from the first, revealed a similar absence of shells at a point that could well equate with the fall-off into the lost northerly ravine. Although the geological evidence is insufficient to be conclusive (there being neither time nor funds to pursue it further), the results of the underwater testing support rather than refute the conclusions reached through other means.

Assuming that the Martin's Hundred settlement was limited to 2 rows of buildings flanking a green 100 yd in width, the community was small, having no more than 6 or 8 tenant houses in addition to the fort, Company Compound, barn, and church. Based on Ulster parallels for villages of similar size, a total population of no more than 60 can be deduced, all living in small, post-constructed, wattle-and-daub buildings of no great durability. Although nothing has been found to prove archeologically that the settlement remains are those of Wolstenholme Towne, the circumstantial evidence is such that no other conclusion seems reasonable.

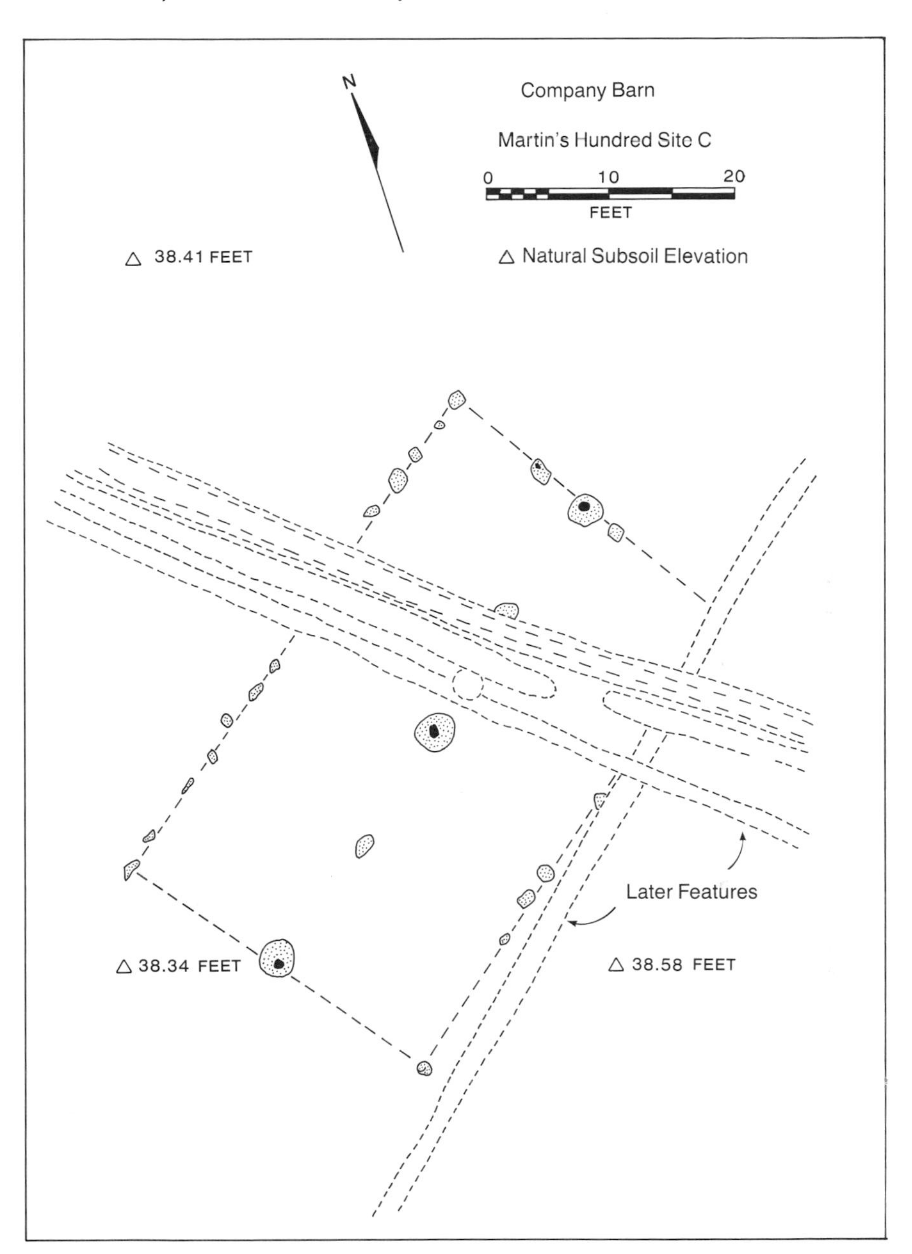

FIGURE 8. Plan of the Company Barn at Site C.

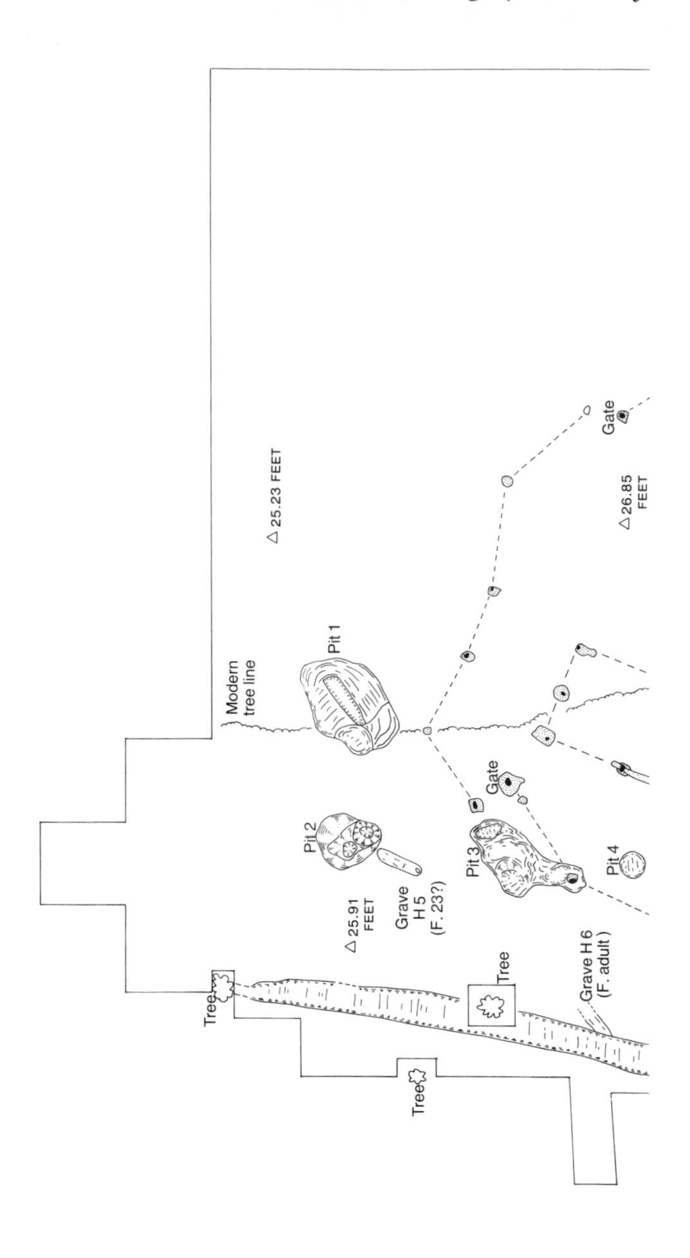

Δ 25.23 FEET
Gate
Δ 26.85 FEET
Modern tree line
Pit 1
Gate
Pit 2
Pit 3
Pit 4
Δ 25.91 FEET
Grave H 5 (F. 23?)
Tree
Tree
Tree
Grave H 6 (F. adult)

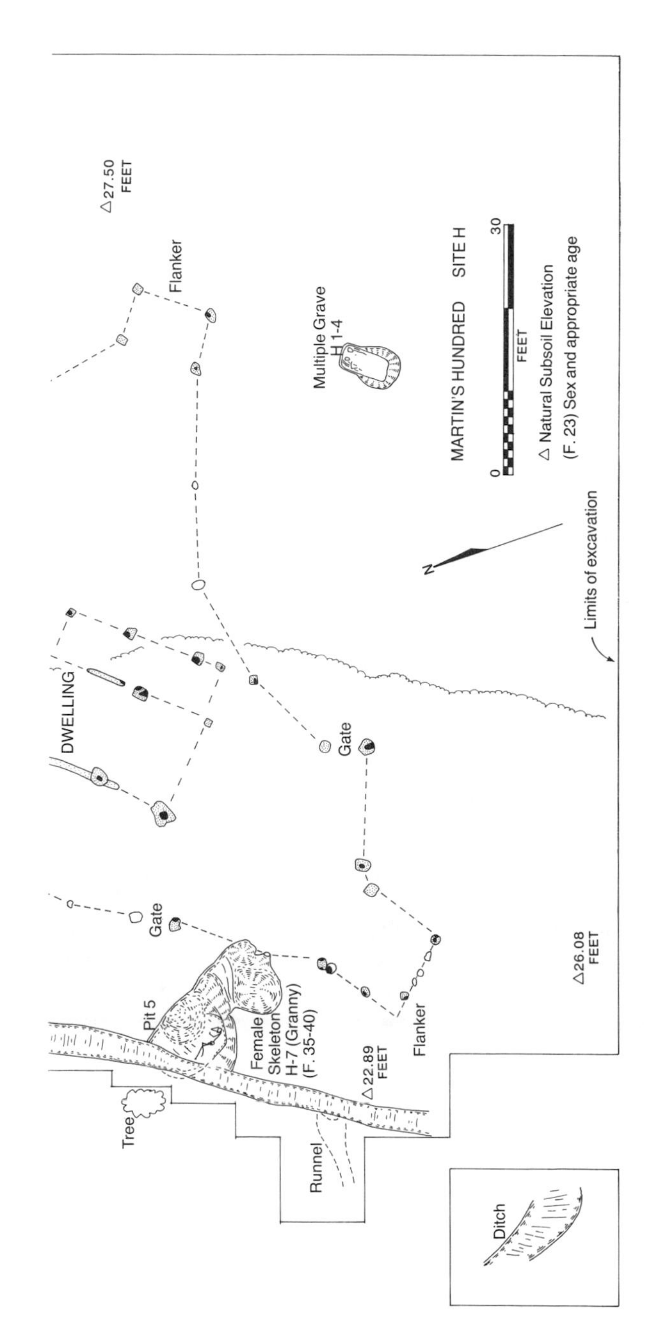

FIGURE 9. Plan of Site H or the "Wolstenholme Suburb."

Subsequent excavations south of the down-river ravine revealed another fenced or palisaded compound triangular in shape, with what may have been flankers at two corners, and containing a single dwelling whose core element measured 30 ft × 12 ft (Fig. 9). Here again, ashes in the postmolds and scorching of the back-filled holes around them pointed to destruction by fire. The skeletons of 3 people, all identified as women, were found outside the fenced area; one of them is believed to have been a victim of the 1622 Indian attack, who escaped only to die of exposure or loss of blood. Artifactual parallels and geographical proximity to Site C indicate that this one (Site H) was a "suburb" of Wolstenholme Towne.

The analysis of the artifacts and data from the first 4 years of excavations in Martin's Hundred, coupled with those from test excavations during 1980 to 1982, is expected to continue through 1985. Although interpretative modifications may yet result from it, the general conclusions are unlikely to be appreciably altered. Wolstenholme Towne seems to have been established in 1620 and no evidence has been found to indicate rebuilding after the Indian assault in 1622, though the fort walls may have survived for several years and have served as an enclosure for cattle—a bawn in the term's original sense. Thus, with the occupational time brackets embracing only 3 years, the artifactual evidence retrieved from the village site provides not only a hitherto unavailable picture of life in early colonial Virginia, but also contributes to a broader understanding of English material culture at the domestic level not to be drawn from any other British or American source.

Several more sites remain to be explored, one of them (Site J) seemingly spanning the years between ca. 1640 and 1700, would carry Martin's Hundred's archeological history forward to the time when part of it became one of Virginia's important 18th-century plantations (Fig. 1). No immediate plans exist to excavate the remaining 17th-century sites. The Carter's Grove lands owned by the Colonial Williamsburg Foundation are protected, and, therefore, the sites are in no way threatened. Indeed, the Wolstenholme Towne site has already been established as an educational tool, its house and plans defined and preserved.

Colonial Williamsburg is committed to publishing a two-volume report on the excavations, the first containing a history of Martin's Hundred and an analysis of the archeological evidence, and the second a catalogue of the artifacts, illustrated with more than a hundred pages of drawings. In addition, a popular book chronicling the excavations and the resulting research was published by Alfred A. Knopf, Inc. in 1982, and Colonial Williamsburg has completed a 58-minute film titled "Search for a Century" which is available for television and for education audiences. Notice, too, must be made of the National Geographic Society's own year-long exhibition of the Martin's Hundred discoveries which, between April 1980 and its closing on February 1981, attracted thousands of visitors.

REFERENCES

Anonymous
1977. Cour de Ferme, by Jan Siberecht, 1660. *In* "Art Ancien," 9th edition, no. 88. Ministry of Education and Culture and the Royal Museum of Fine Arts, Brussels.

Bodleian Library
——. Ms. Carte 176, ff. 170-171 v. Oxford.

Hudson, J. Paul
1957. A picture booklet on early Jamestown commodities and industries. (Reprinted from "Orbis Sensualium," by Johann Comenius, London, 1685.) Virginia 350th Anniversary Corporation, Williamsburg, Virginia.

Jester, Annie Lash
1956. Adventures of purse and person, Virginia, 1607-1625. Princeton University Press, Princeton, N.J.

Kingsbury, Susan Myra
1933a. List of persons slaine at Martins-Hundred on March 22, 1622. Vol. 3, p. 570 *in* "The Records of the Virginia Company of London," Library of Congress, Washington, D. C.
1933b. A repatenting and expansion of the Virginia lands granted to the Society of Martin's Hundred by the Virginia Company of London, January 30, 1622. Vol. 33, p. 592f *in* "The Records of the Virginia Company of London." Library of Congress, Washington, D. C.
1935. The Records of the Virginia Company of London, vol. 4 (Richard Frethorne to Mr. Bateman, March 5, 1623, p. 41; and "Extracts of all the titles and estates of land, sent home by Sir Francis Wyatt," May 1625, p. 556.) Library of Congress, Washington, D. C.

Peck, G. Wilson
1970. English copper, tin and bronze coins in the British Museum 1558-1958. The Trustees of the British Museum, London.

Prowse, D. W.
1895. A history of Newfoundland. Macmillan and Co., London and New York.

Purchas, Samuel
1625. Hakluytus postumus, or Puchas his pilgrims, contayning a history of the world in sea voyages and lande travells by Englishmen and others, bk. IX, p. 1752-1753. London.

Sainsbury, W. Noel, ed.
1860. Calendar of state papers. Colonial series, 1574-1660 (Sir John Harvey to Secretary of State Sir Francis Windebank, June 26, 1636, p. 239). Longman, Green, Longman and Roberts, London.

Ivor Noël Hume

Gorilla Language Acquisition

Grant Recipient: Francine G. Patterson, The Gorilla Foundation, Woodside, California and San Jose State University, San Jose, California.

Grants 1582, 1768, 1925, 2090, 2254: For a study of linguistic and behavioral development of a lowland gorilla.

Gorillas and chimpanzees are less than one percent different from humans both biochemically and genetically. Such discoveries render less surprising reports that these creatures possess capacities once thought unique to mankind: tool use and fabrication, self-concept, cross-modal perception, and language. Current research indicates that chimpanzees and gorillas clearly have the capacity to acquire certain visual language skills. The questions that remain relate to the nature and extent of this capacity.

Project Koko, now (1981) entering its 10th year, is the longest ongoing study of the language abilities of apes yet undertaken. The gorillas Koko (10 years old) and Michael (approximately 8 years old) have been exposed to a bimodal bilingual language environment (sign language and spoken English). Their progress has been documented and evaluated within the framework of the following objectives:

- To obtain a linguistic data base similar in nature and scope to that being compiled on human children and chimpanzees.
- To use this and other behavioral data to elucidate the role of cognition in language development and use.
- To use language as a probe to better understand the intellectual, emotional, and social development of the gorilla.

My research began in July 1972 with Koko, a one-year-old lowland gorilla. After 11 months, the project was moved from the San Francisco Children's Zoo nursery to a five-room, 10- × 50-ft house trailer. Relocation of the project permitted more intensive interaction between Koko and her signing companions—contact increased from 5 to 8 or 12 hr/day. Since August 1972, Koko's teachers have included fluent signers, that is, deaf individuals or persons with deaf parents, for 10 to 20 hr/week, or approximately one eighth to one quarter of her waking hours. In September 1976 the male gorilla Michael, then 3½ years old, was acquired and he too was immersed in an intensive language learning environment.

FIGURE 1. Koko signs "Sleep" in response to the question "Why want light off?" (Photo: Ronald H. Cohn)

The project has attempted not only to document vocabulary acquisition by the gorillas but also to investigate, in-depth, the uses to which these animals put language. This has involved tracing the development of linguistic strategies and behaviors that are innovative in some respects: the invention of new signs and compound words, simultaneous signing, self-directed signing, displacement, prevarication, reference to time and emotional states, gestural modulation, metaphorical and rhyming word use, humor, labeling of concrete and abstract representations (including self-generated ones), definition, argument, insult, threat, fantasy play, and moral judgment. In addition, we have given the gorillas empirical tests of comprehension as measures of their grasp and generalization of linguistic concepts which they may not yet have produced. Preliminary analyses indicate that linguistic innovation and generalization are a product of several factors including the subjects' biological heritage as gorillas, their cognitive abilities, and the structure and functioning of sign as a visual language.

By the end of 1979, after 78 months of training, Koko had acquired a

FIGURE 2. Koko comments to herself about a picture of a flower in a children's dictionary. (Photo: Ronald H. Cohn)

sign language vocabulary of 281 signs according to a strict criterion of spontaneous and appropriate use on more than half of the days of a given month (Fig. 1, 2). Her emitted vocabulary (those signs she used spontaneously and appropriately on one or more occasions) was 781 words. By the end of 1980, after 50 months of training, Michael had learned 150 signs, and had emitted 358.

Early in the project, signed communication between Koko and Michael became an everyday occurrence and Michael appears to have learned signs directly from Koko. Frequency of signing by Koko to Michael is much higher at present than the reverse. Signed communication addressed by Michael to Koko is interesting in that he uses forms of signs modeled by Koko but not by Michael's human companions. For example, he uses her version of *tickle,* and her invented signs for *obnoxious, girl* ("lip"), and *boy* ("foot").

Through the use of English in addition to sign language, it has been possible to make direct comparisons of three modes of communication: auditory, visual, and simultaneous. During the period of this report, data on Koko's language were analyzed in each of these modes through the use of a question-and-answer study and naturalistic language samples. In addition, a compilation of data on Koko's use of modulation and other innovative uses of language such as insult, rhyming, and displacement was assembled.

Naturalistic Samples

Analysis of Signed Utterances

Comparisons of the structure and meaning of the gorillas' utterances with those of human children can provide insight into the question of which aspects of human language are defining or unique and which are based on cognitive abilities man holds in common with other life forms.

One analysis of Koko's language used the computer facilities and programs at the Institute for Mathematical Studies in the Social Sciences (IMSSS) at Stanford University. IMSSS has been developing techniques for the analysis of the structure (syntax) and meaning (semantics) of children's speech (Suppes, 1971). From January 1974 to January 1979 samples of conversations with Koko were transcribed into IMSSS's PDP-10 computer system.

The preliminary analyses completed thus far cover 40 sample hours taken when Koko was between 2½ and 3½ years old (8 hr at each of five ages—30, 31, 35, 40, and 41 months). Comparisons are being made between Koko and Nina, a child who was studied between the ages of 2 and 3.

The total number of signs used by Koko in the 8 hr of recorded sessions each month almost tripled between ages 30 and 41 months (529 to 1577), with an increase in each monthly sample. She employed 62 different signs at 30 months and 140 at 41 months. During this time the number of signs in Koko's qualified vocabulary increased from 22 to 100.

Some quantitative data on the utterances of Koko and Nina available for comparison are presented in Table 1. Data from the first and last samples taken on each subject during the period under consideration (Koko at 30 and 41 months of age and Nina at 24 and 40 months) were selected for discussion here because they illustrate most clearly similarities and differences between the gorilla and the child. The first two lines give the number of utterance types and the number of tokens found in the samples taken at these ages. To understand the difference between type and token consider the following utterances: "chase me," "swing me," "tickle me," and "chase you." Each of these is of the type *verb, personal pronoun*. Thus they would be represented in the table as one type, but four tokens. Nina produced several times as many utterance types and tokens as Koko per sample hour. So a major difference between this gorilla and this child (and perhaps between apes and children in general) is one of

TABLE 1. Quantitative Comparisons between Language Samples of Koko and Nina

Measure	*Koko*		*Nina*	
	30 months	*42 months*	*24 months*	*40 months*
No. types/hr	8	36	215	404
No. tokens/hr	46	101	817	716
Type/token ratio	.17	.36	.26	.56
MLU*	1.37	1.82	1.75	3.04

*Mean length of utterance.

sheer volume of linguistic output. However, whereas the total number of utterances produced per hour by Nina had reached a plateau by 24 months of age (in fact there was a decline between 24 and 40 months), the total number of signed utterances produced by Koko more than doubled between the ages of 30 and 41 months. Also, although the number of types produced by both subjects increased, the rate of increase by Koko was more than double that of Nina.

The third line of Table 1 gives the type/token ratio, a measure of linguistic maturity. The higher the ratio, the greater the diversity of grammatical types in the utterances of the subject. Koko at 41 months is more advanced than Nina at 24 months but less advanced than Nina at 40 months. This same trend is reflected in another measure of linguistic maturity, the mean length of utterance (MLU).

Taken as a whole, the data presented in Table 1 suggest that on a number of measures of linguistic development, Koko at 41 months of age resembles Nina at slightly over 24 months.

WORD ORDER

The aspect of Project Koko that has perhaps the greatest relevance for recent discussions of the linguistic capabilities of apes is the gorilla's use of word (sign) order in a consistent way to express relational meanings. However, the issue of word order in sign language studies is complicated by the existence of certain simultaneous aspects of utterances that are possible in a visual but not in an auditory mode. In American Sign Language (Ameslan), word order is relatively free within the basic phrases but other mechanisms such as direction of hand movement and facial attitudes taken during signing may function grammatically.

Despite the flexibility allowed in sign language, the order of elements in Koko's signed utterances has never been totally random. Consistencies were apparent early in the study and have continued to be present, although over time certain patterns have changed. For example, in the 1974 data, the adjective in attributive constructions preceded the noun in

75% of all utterances of that type. In 1975 this pattern reversed and has continued to the present; utterances such as "lipstick red" and "baby new" are now the rule.

I looked at two types of constructions in which reversible actions were involved to see if Koko made use of word order appropriately to convey differences in meaning. Sign combinations of the forms Agent + Action and Action + Object drawn from records collected when Koko was between 42 and 54 months of age were analyzed. In 86% of the 160 cases sampled, the nonlinguistic context indicated that she had ordered her Agent + Action constructions correctly (e.g., "alligator chase" rather than "chase alligator" when she wanted to be chased by one). However, within the Action + Object category, there were two distinct types of utterances for which Koko seems to have separate ordering strategies. These two types corresponded to two different classes of verbs, those that have to do with feeding (e.g., eat, drink, taste, sip) and those involving social interaction (e.g., chase, tickle, sit, hug, pinch). In 90% of the 126 cases, utterances containing "social" verbs were ordered Action + Object (e.g., "Pinch shoulder" rather than "Shoulder pinch"). Utterances containing "feeding" verbs, however, consistently took the form Object + Action (73% of the 230 cases), an ordering that would be considered ungrammatical in English. For example, Koko characteristically signs "banana eat" and "medicine taste" despite the fact that such sequences are rarely modeled by her companions. This is of interest because it suggests that she may be inventing her own rules rather than passively imitating her human companions.

Language Production and Comprehension Testing

Ever since the horse Clever Hans was revealed to be a master not of mathematics but rather of subtle cues given by the humans around him, there has been a legitimate suspicion that animals credited with intellectual accomplishments approaching those of man might merely be accomplished observers of human behavior. To determine whether or not Koko's use of sign language is truly spontaneous, I have administered tests blind. If Koko could answer questions about objects and events that she alone could see, then the possibility that her performance was the result of cueing by her human companions could be ruled out. I employed the "box test" devised by Gardner and Gardner (1971) to test the gorilla's ability to produce language under these conditions (Fig. 3). One experimenter baited a plywood box with an object and a second experimenter who did not know its contents stood behind it and asked Koko what she saw. She responded correctly on 62% of the trials. This compares favorably with the level of performance reported for the chimpanzee Washoe (54%).

FIGURE 3. "Tiger" is a correct response given by Koko on a trial of the box vocabulary test. (Photo: Ronald H. Cohn)

Koko's responsiveness to spoken requests in our daily interaction with her suggests that she does indeed possess a considerable capacity for complex auditory analysis. She often surprises us by translating English words and phrases into signs during the course of the day. For instance, once a visitor asked Koko's companion what the sign for *good* was. Before an answer was given, Koko demonstrated the correct sign to the visitor. On another occasion, Koko's companion was making her a sandwich and asked if she wanted a taste of butter (in English only since her hands were occupied) and Koko responded "taste butter." She will also frequently respond to spoken suggestions to put refuse into the garbage, kiss a companion, find a towel, and so on.

In 1977, Professor Patrick Suppes and his colleagues at Stanford's Institute for Mathematical Studies in the Social Sciences designed a keyboard–computer link-up that permits Koko to produce English words through a speech synthesizer by pressing keys on a teletype. The 46 active keys bear the usual letters of the alphabet and numbers, but in addition each key is painted with a simple arbitrary geometric pattern in 1 of

10 different colors. Words on the keyboard represent objects, actions, pronouns, prepositions, and modifiers.

If I place, say, an apple before her, Koko may push the keys representing *want, apple, eat* and the computer-generated female voice speaks these words. Koko responds to hundreds of words independent of her auditory keyboard, but her vocabulary of spoken English is restricted to 46 words. A major objective of this study is to evaluate the gorilla's sense of spoken word order.

To assess Koko's ability to understand language under controlled conditions, I administered the Assessment of Children's Language Comprehension test (ACLC) (Foster et al., 1972). Because the gorilla has been exposed not only to sign language but also to spoken English, such a test allows an evaluation of claims such as the following: "Apparently it is the child's innate capacity for auditory analysis that distinguishes him from the chimpanzee" (Hebb et al., 1974, p. 153).

Naturalistic observations of auditory receptiveness were substantiated by Koko's performance on the ACLC test, administered early in 1976 when Koko was 4½ years old. The test consists of 40 large (6- × 4-in.) cards on which are printed four to five black-and-white line or silhouette drawings representing objects, attributes, or relationships between objects. The first 10 cards test 50 single vocabulary items, and the remaining 30 cards test comprehension of phrases consisting of two to four critical elements (e.g., little clown; little clown jumping; happy little clown jumping). Ten items at each of these three levels of difficulty were administered under three conditions: Instructions were given in sign only, English only, or sign and English simultaneously. All trials were recorded on videotape and administered blind.

Koko performed significantly better than chance under all three conditions and at each level of difficulty (Table 2). I had anticipated that comprehension might be enhanced under the simultaneous communication condition. Although there was a trend in this direction, it was not statistically significant. The data clearly show that Koko comprehends novel statements in sign language and spoken English with equal facility. An unexpected finding was that Koko's performance at all levels of difficulty was quite similar. She responded correctly to 43% of the 30 most difficult items (four critical elements), a level of performance that matched the norm for educationally handicapped children 4 to 5 years old. Her performance on the two critical element items was slightly better than her performance on items at the next two levels of difficulty, but not significantly so. This seems to indicate that some factor other than complexity of the phrase was operating to limit her performance. Evidence from her behavior during testing sessions indicated that motivation may have been the limiting factor.

TABLE 2. Koko's Performance on the Assessment of Children's Language Comprehension Test

No. of critical elements	*Percent Correct*				
	Chance	*Sign and voice*	*Sign*	*Voice*	*Total*
Vocabulary—one	20	72			
Two (e.g., happy lady)	25	70	50	50	56.7
Three (happy lady sleeping)	25	50	30	50	43.3
Four (happy little girl jumping)	20	50	50	30	43.3
	—	—	—	—	—
Totals (two, three, and four elements)	23.3	56.7	43.3	43.3	47.7

There has been very little research on auditory language comprehension in apes. Most other recent studies of language behavior have restricted language input to one mode only—the visual—and all have restricted language output to that mode. Koko's performance on the ACLC is one solid piece of evidence that, given a multimodal language environment, an ape's comprehension of auditory language is considerable, although inferior to that of a normal human child.

I also analyzed language samples gathered in a naturalistic communicative setting for possible mode-related differences in Koko's language production and comprehension. Samples from 1-hr sessions in which only sign, only spoken English, or only simultaneous communication were employed, were quantitatively and qualitatively compared for differences in Koko's comprehension of sign versus spoken English. Results of comparisons of direct imitation and appropriateness of responses to verbal requests in each of the modes (Patterson, 1979) substantiate Koko's ability to process and respond to spoken and signed language with equal facility. There were no significant differences between the three modes of communication. This corroborates the outcome of the ACLC test. The two results together I consider to be the first quantitative evidence for comprehension of complex auditory language by a nonhuman.

QUESTION-AND-ANSWER STUDY

Another way I assessed Koko's overall language ability by mode was to conduct a study of her answers to "Wh" questions. For one year data were collected daily on Koko's replies to 14 different question types in each of three modes of communication. The following represents the analysis of a subset of one month of the data:

Who + Action	Who see?	Know Mike there.
Whose + Demonstrative	Whose this berry?	For Koko red berry.
What Color	What color this?	Koko think orange.
What Happened	What happened?	Me break.
Where + Object	Where berry?	Do berry under.
How + State	How do you feel?	Fine.
Why + State	Why sorry?	Bad me.

Each day a random sample of 10 of 14 question types was asked (not all were equally represented) in an order and mode (sign, voice, sign and voice) which were also randomly determined. A total of 427 questions was recorded (on some days more than the 10 assigned questions were asked) and Koko used 125 different signs in response. A variety of questions was used, many of which related to novel objects and situations. A summary of the results of the 14 question types indicates that Koko replied to 91% of the 427 questions; her answers were correct (contained target sentence constituents) 83% of the time and were appropriate in context (true) 76% of the time. Koko's answers were both correct (on target) and appropriate (true) 70.3% of the time. Interestingly, these results indicate that Koko's replies were more often grammatically appropriate than they were truthful.

Additional analyses of the data were conducted in order to determine whether or not responsiveness, accuracy, and appropriateness in responding to "Wh" questions were related to the mode in which these questions were addressed. Koko answered questions addressed to her in the sign-only mode with greater accuracy than those in the voice-only mode ($X^2[4] = 13.71$, $p < .01$; $Z = 2.96$, $p < .01$). However, her accuracy in responding to voiced questions did not differ significantly from her accuracy in responding to questions that were both signed and voiced.

Elicited Imitation

Tests of elicited imitation of language are useful tools in the analysis of the gorilla's acquisition of grammatical structures. By focusing on the kinds of errors they make and the sentences they select to imitate we can begin to understand the conceptual processes underlying their performance and the areas of difficulty they experience in each of the three modes of communication. Several tests of elicited imitation have been administered, and although only a portion of the data has been analyzed, interesting trends are apparent. When requested to imitate two-word utterances, Koko produced an average of 1.7 signs and correctly reproduced an average of 1.02 of the words. When the modeled phrases were three signs long she produced 2.8 signs, correctly copying an average of 1.78. Thus Koko tended to correctly reproduce the length of the target utterance but only a portion of the exact content, adding her own new information.

Word Association

Free word association is a method allowing us to look at the development of the gorillas' linguistic and cognitive development as well as the relationship between the two. Two systems of conceptual organization are evidenced in free word associations made by humans: syntagmatic associations, which relate words according to their contiguity in a syntactic sequence, and paradigmatic associations, which relate words according to their relationship as members of the same grammatical form category. Adults tend to give more paradigmatic responses in a free association task (e.g., "eat"—"drink") whereas children respond more frequently with syntagmatic associations (e.g., "eat"—"apple"). One theoretical question our work with the gorillas may illuminate is whether the syntagmatic-paradigmatic shift reflects a restructuring of general cognitive organization at a particular time in development or whether linguistic organization itself contributes to restructuring in cognition.

A comparison of word associations given by Koko and Michael during the period of this report indicates that Koko made an average of 11% more paradigmatic associations than Michael—26% to his 15%. Continuing analysis of longitudinal association data should provide interesting developmental information which we plan to analyze qualitatively as well as quantitatively.

Modulation of Sign-gestures

The core meaning of signs can be altered intrinsically by changes in the articulation of one or more parameters (motion, location, configuration, facial expression, or body posture). By actively exploiting the possibilities for simultaneous expression afforded by sign as a visual language, Koko frequently alters the meaning of signs; in standard Ameslan this is labeled *modulation* (Bellugi, 1975). Modulations can serve grammatical functions which are performed by sequential devices such as word order and inflection in spoken languages. Most modulations in sign language are accomplished by variations in the movement of the hands.

Koko uses variations in motion to signal qualitative or quantitative differences in the referents of her signs. Alligator (clapping the palms, held horizontally, together) may be done with a small motion to indicate a tiny reptile, or with an exaggerated gesture to indicate a larger specimen. When she has been very bad, Koko enlarges the signing space and increases the speed and forcefulness of the motion of the hand down her face when executing the sign *bad*. She may vary the direction of the motion of a sign to indicate a specific actor. *Sip* turned from her own mouth to that of her companion can be translated *you sip*.

Like the human signer, Koko can provide emphatic stress through modulation. She may use two hands to execute a sign usually articulated with one hand. For example, Koko has signed *rotten* with two hands, with an English translation being *really rotten* or *very rotten*.

As shown in Table 3, Koko has used such modulational variations to mark relations of size, number, location, possession, manner (degree, intensity, or emphasis), agent or object of an action, negation (rejection or denial); to express questions; and as a form of word play akin to wit or humor. Furthermore, Koko seems to use changes in position as a modulation more often than human signers. It should be noted that most of these modulations are not mere imitations of sign use by others, but are created by Koko herself. The use of modulation has not been reported for chimpanzees learning sign language.

Simultaneous Signs

An aspect of sign language that has no parallel in spoken languages is simultaneity. Signers can literally say two things at once by executing different signs with each hand. Koko began signing simultaneously during the third month of the project, when she was just under 15 months old. Data drawn from five 1-hr sign samples at 6-month intervals from 1973 to the beginning of 1978 indicate that incidence of simultaneous signing was greatest early in 1973, with an average of 2.8 utterances per hour. In the following years this behavior decreased in frequency, ranging between 0.2 and 2.4 simultaneous combinations per sample hour. The number of signs Koko expressed in a given simultaneous combination averaged two or slightly above; she has used up to four different signs at the same time, for example, "Hurry-pour-there-drink." Koko uses three different methods to generate simultaneous expressions: executing one sign with each hand (e.g., "Drink-eat"; "You-tickle"), adding the motion or configuration of one sign to the place of articulation of another (e.g., "Koko-like"; "Hurry-pour") and adding a facial expression or head movement to a sign (e.g., "Fruit-frown"; "No-gorilla").

In some cases, two signs done simultaneously are merged to make a new composite or compound sign. For instance, Koko has made the sign for *Coke* with two hands while her arms are in the position of the sign for *love*. An English gloss might be *love-Coke*. Certain instances of simultaneous signing, which occurred early in the study, and some compound signs seem to be the result of excited or hurried signing and may be considered "slips of the hand"; other instances that appear consistently seem to be deliberate modulational forms.

TABLE 3. Gestural Modulations Used by Koko

Relation or function	*Modulation*	*Example*
Location	Variation in place of articulation of sign	Bite (on finger)
Size	Enlarge or decrease articulatory space.	Alligator (big) Alligator (little)
Number	Repetition of sign.	Bird(s)[a]
Manner:		
degree-intensity	Variation in force and/or rapidity of movement or size of sign.	(Very) bad
emphasis	Duplication or reduction (number of active hands) or simultaneous production of two versions of the same sign.	Tickle (2 hands) Yes (nod head and hand)
Agent-action	Change in direction of motion of sign.	Sip-you (sign moved from Koko's mouth toward that of companion)
Agent-object	Articulation of sign on other's body or object; direction of gaze.	Tickle (on Mike) Hungry (on doll)
Possession or modification[b]	Simultaneous production of signs; production of sign using object or other.	Baby-head Koko-good
Question	Facial expression, position of hands.	That pink?
Negation-rejection	Headshake or facial expression (frown).	No-gorilla Lemon-frown
Humor, word play	Variation in location of articulation	Drink (to ear) Black (on various body parts, persons, and objects)

[a] In Ameslan, only a few nouns are modulated in this way; verbs are most frequently modulated for plural subject or object in this way.

[b] This type of modulation has not been reported for Ameslan.

Insult, Swearing, Argument, and Threat

Koko appears to use diverse signs in her lexicon as insults. One sign, which I've transcribed as *darn* or *damn,* is a natural gorilla gesture identified by field researchers as a killing motion. Koko's own innovation (Fig. 4) appears to be the source of other insults such as *toilet* and *dirty.* In these instances she seems to be relating attributes of objects or characteristics she perceives negatively to the target of her invective. This may provide insight into those objects or traits Koko finds negative or aversive, as in the case of her use of the word *bird.* The use of *bird* as an insult was not to my knowledge modeled by her companions, although she may have been exposed to the expression "bird brain." More likely, Koko uses this sign as an insult because of her dislike of the incessant chatter of birds nesting near the trailer at Stanford.

Koko also imitates insults used by her companions such as *rotten, devil, stink,* and *nut.* As early as age 2.6 Koko may have used the word *nut* as an insult or expletive: She signed *nut* to herself after being locked in her room as a punishment for misbehavior. Her companions frequently used the English word in similar ways: "You nut!" when Koko would engage in silly behavior or "Nuts" when something went wrong. In some cases, Koko has used a slight modulation in the position of the sign to signal an insulting connotation.

We are able to obtain direct evidence that the gorillas understand the derogatory meaning of such words by asking them to define them. For example, when asked, "What does stupid mean to you?" Koko replied, "Koko lazy devil." In some cases we have found that the gorillas can express dual meanings for words employed as insults:

Penny: What is stink?
Koko: Rotten devil know.
Penny: What else does stink mean?
Koko: Nice all leaf. (Koko labels all flowers and leafy plants as "stinks.")
Barbara: What stink mean?
Mike: Pull-out-hair think bad.
Barbara: Can you tell me another meaning for stink?
Mike: Good flower Ann stink.

Koko often combines these signs to make compound insults. When Koko was 5 years old Kate, a research assistant, would not allow Koko to open the refrigerator. Koko responded by signing "Kate bird rotten." One such sequence was recorded on film with a motor-driven camera. Koko had ripped the leg off a rag doll (which had earlier lost its other leg when the gorilla Michael was playing with it) and I gathered the pieces (including both legs), sat Koko down in front of them, and scolded her for destroying the doll. She reacted by signing "You dirty bad toilet."

FIGURE 4. "Darn," Koko's invented expletive, is performed by hitting the back of a clenched fist onto a surface or object. Note the accompanying facial expression—lips drawn in, mouth compressed—a natural sign of annoyance in both gorillas and humans. (Photo: Ronald H. Cohn)

Koko has also used language to threaten and argue with her companions, as a means of obtaining their cooperation. The following conversation took place after Koko had been nagging Cindy Duggan for food and Cindy refused to comply:

Koko: Time nails nut.
Koko: Fruit . . . Key key time.

Cindy: No, not yet key time. (I.e., time to unlock the refrigerator and get food.)
Koko: Yes time come-on time, nut.
Cindy: No, not time!
Koko: Yes time.
Cindy: No time.
Koko: Nails.
Cindy: Why?
Koko: Time.

Signs Koko uses to threaten her human companions are diverse and explicit as evidenced in these exchanges with Marjie Iller.

Koko: Bite big-trouble bite big-trouble.
Marjie: What about bite big-trouble?
Koko: You do apple hurry.
Marjie: You don't do threats, no apple now, it's milk time.
Koko: Do milk hurry.

Marjie: Koko, yesterday you told me a few of your words you like best. Tell me words you don't like.
Koko: Big-trouble strangle you.
Koko: Smile.
Marjie: Oh you funny, ha ha.

Less volatile exchanges involving Koko's correcting companions have occurred more frequently. An example of a dinner time conversation with Barbara Hiller is illustrative:

Koko: Do that (pointing to squash which is on her dinner plate along with a variety of other foods).
Barbara: Potato.
Koko: Wrong squash.
Koko: Do hurry that (again pointing to squash).
Koko: Squash eat hurry.

Occasionally, since age 4½ Koko has corrected her human companions when they have labeled her with unfamiliar terms. The first incident, in December of 1975, involved the application of the spoken word *chicken* to Koko by a companion in an attempt to get her attention as she gazed out the window. Koko, still looking out the window signed, "No, gorilla." She has made similar responses when the terms *juvenile* and *genius* have been applied to her. In the case of the word *juvenile*, the conversation was not even directed to Koko, but was a discussion between Koko's companion and a visitor who had asked if Koko was an adolescent. Her companion had replied, "No, she's not an adolescent yet; she's still a juvenile." Koko resounded with, "No, gorilla." The discussion Koko overheard took place exclusively in English. On one occasion, a term was applied to Koko which she apparently thought was a mistaken color name: In a sign sample taken January 9, 1977, her companion, Ron, said "Well, dynamite?" to her in English during a pause in activity as she sat on her toy box with a red blanket. Koko signed "No, red."

Prevarication

Prevarication is a feature of the human communication system assumed by theorists to be unique in the natural world. Although it is difficult to empirically demonstrate intent, both Koko and Michael have made statements in response to questions about their misbehavior which appear to be lies. After ripping one of his companion's jackets, Michael was asked who had done it. He signed, "Koko," and after further interrogation, "Penny." Finally, after continued cross-examination, he signed, "Michael."

Koko has engaged in this kind of behavior more frequently. When asked who had bitten a hole in a new toy she signed, "Ron." Koko, asked to draw a picture had instead eaten the crayon. Her companion asked her where her drawing was and Koko signed, "Bird there," tapping the empty page.

Creation of Compound Names and Metaphor

Koko, like many young children, has, in the face of novel objects or situations and a limited vocabulary, generated new names, often composed of two or more words. Many of these names (especially single-word names) may be classified as errors in reference or overextensions; for example, Koko's labeling such diverse objects as bean sprouts, a dog's choke-chain, and a variety of green toys, "grass." Analyses of the contexts of such utterances and of Koko's lexical knowledge at the time of their occurrence indicate that Koko did not know the literal names of the objects or properties, and that she was not engaging in symbolic play with them. Other novel word uses by Koko and other young signers appear to be deliberate attempts to describe or request an unnamed object—for example, a deaf child's labeling of a mantelpiece as "fireplace wall-shelf"; Koko's labeling pomegranate kernels as "red corn drink"; or the chimpanzee Lucy's labeling of a watermelon as "drink fruit." Still other occasions seem to involve intentional nonliteral word use and may provide examples of early metaphor: "bottle match" for a cigarette lighter, "finger bracelet" for a ring, and "white tiger" for a toy zebra. In each case these new names referred to objects in her environment for which Koko had either just been given or earlier acquired a literal name. Perhaps more solid evidence of a metaphorical capacity can be found in those instances in which Koko has referred to feelings or emotional states. Koko has described herself as "red mad" or "red mad gorilla" when asked why she behaved aggressively, and spontaneously commented that a nose on a doll she had just labeled as red was "nose mad." Michael has used the phrase "red mad" when asked how he felt when Koko's visitors forgot to stop by to see him. Furthermore, the gorillas' responses to direct questioning have supported the linguistic and contextual evidence that they are engaging in deliberate verbal play with relationships between objects and states.

Koko's spontaneous ability to rhyme is one example of this verbal play. Once, after being offered a stalk of broccoli, she signed "Flower stink fruit pink . . . fruit pink stink." When I commented, "You're rhyming, neat!" Koko responded with "Love meat sweet!" Moreover, since mid-1978, Koko has generated rhymes when asked. In August 1980, for instance, I asked Koko, "Can you do a rhyme?" Her response: "Hair bear." I continued, "Another rhyme?" She answered, "All ball." We have tested her ability further with an animal game. Arranging toy animals in a row in front of Koko, we ask her questions about them: "Which animal rhymes with 'hat'?" "Which rhymes with 'hair'?" and so on. Koko has shown considerable facility in performing this task.

In order to obtain empirical evidence for the gorillas' metaphoric capacity I used a test devised by Howard Gardner (1974). For purposes of the test, metaphoric capacity was defined as "the ability to project in an appropriate manner sets of 'polar' or opposite adjectives onto a domain where they are not ordinarily employed." The polar adjectives used were light-dark, happy-sad, loud-quiet, hard-soft, and warm-cold. The corresponding modality was visual-color. In sessions administered under conditions in which Koko and Michael could see only the stimulus and not the experimenter, they had no difficulty identifying literal dark versus light (two shades of green), red (versus blue) as warm, brown (versus blue-gray) as hard, violet-blue (versus yellow-orange) as sad, and lemon-yellow (versus spring green) as loud. Koko indicated her answers either by pointing or verbal description (such as, "Orange that fine," when asked which was happy). Ninety percent of the gorillas' responses were metaphoric matches as determined by Gardner (1974) and by three adult research assistants on the project who took the same test.

Humor

Humor, like metaphor, requires a capacity to depart from what is strictly correct, normal, or expected. The gorillas' sense of humor has emerged in both modulated and unmodulated forms. I have found that, like human signers, they at times employ for witty effect techniques dependent on principles unique to sign language.

One is the overlapping of two signs which may be done by performing both simultaneously. For example, Koko has frequently responded to requests to "smile for the camera" by signing "sad-frown." Another technique is the blending of two signs by simultaneously expressing partial properties of both. Once I asked Koko, "Are devils smart or stupid?" Koko signed devil on the forehead, the location of the sign for smart, instead of at the side of the head where the devil sign is done. A third technique for humor is the substitution of one regular Ameslan prime for another sign. A human signer might jokingly make the sign *understand* backward to mean *un-understand.* In this way Koko has changed the movement of the attention sign to mean *unattention.* She used this sign with humorous effect when asked to rhyme with *book;* a possible answer was *look* but Koko instead covered her eyes. I told her that the sign *look* rhymed with *book,* and then started to play her game of opposites (a favorite of the gorillas who indeed do have a contrary streak), asking for the opposite of *look;* but she gave it one more twist and signed a new invention for the opposite of *listen,* covering her ears. (Michael has independently invented this gesture, translated *unlisten,* in which he covers his ears with his hands—used most frequently when he is being scolded. He modulates it at times by using his teacher's hands to execute the sign on his own ears.) Similarly, when asked to demonstrate her invented sign for *stethoscope* for the camera, Koko did it on her eyes instead of on her ears.

Appreciation of this kind of wit is dependent on recognizing the sign behind the distortion. A skeptic might see this as simple error but in the case of signs that the gorillas themselves invented this is not likely, and there are consistencies that run across the gorillas' humorous use of signs.

Michael appears to mark his humorous intent by signing *smile* either with or following a joking statement. In October of 1980, Barbara Weller asked Mike:

Barbara: Who you think stupid?
Michael: Think Barbara.
Barbara: Really or are you just joking?
Michael: Smile.
Barbara: Oh then you don't really think Barbara stupid?
Michael: Smile (Mike laughs).

Koko has at times simply and directly expressed an opinion that something is funny: One day in May of 1980, Barbara Hiller put on her glasses to read a magazine article and Koko laughed. Barbara signed:

Barbara: What?
Koko: That funny
Barbara: Thanks.
Koko: Eye eye.
Barbara: You've seen me in glasses before!

During the past several years we have noticed Koko chuckling at the results of her practical jokes and at our descrepant statements or actions. After blowing an insect onto me and observing the result (my shrieking and jumping), Koko repeated her prank, this time laughing. Michael laughed when his companion pointed to a small lizard sunning outside and said, "Oh, Mike there is a big alligator!"

Researchers in developmental psychology note that the earliest form of humor in young children, incongruity-based humor, relies on similar principles of discrepancy applied to objects, actions, and verbal statements. Children between the ages of 3 and 6 may laughingly apply different names to familiar objects or make statements about nonexistent things or properties. The following conversation is an example of Koko's incongruity-based humor. Koko had been nagging her companion, Barbara Hiller, for drinks all afternoon. After being told she could not have another she responded:

Koko: Sad elephant.
Barbara: What do you mean?
Koko: Elephant.
Barbara: Are you a sad elephant?
Koko: Sad . . . elephant me.
Koko: Elephant love thirsty.
Barbara: I thought you were a gorilla?
Koko: Elephant gorilla thirsty.
Barbara: Are you a gorilla or an elephant?
Koko: Elephant me me.
Koko: Elephant stink.
Koko: Time.
Barbara: Time for what?
Koko: Time know Coke elephant good me.
Barbara: You want a drink, good elephant?
Koko: Drink fruit.

Koko had not been talking about elephants previously that afternoon, however, she had been using a fat rubber tube to drink with, rather than her straw. Thinking that that might have reminded her of an elephant's trunk, it was shown to her.

Barbara: What's this?
Koko: That elephant stink.
Barbara: Is that why you're an elephant?
Koko: That there. (She pointed to the tube, then to her nose, and then wandered off laughing. She came back after a moment.)
Koko: That there. (Pointing to a can of soda, then to her glass.)
Barbara: Who are you?

Koko: Koko know elephant devil.
Barbara: You're a devilish elephant?
Koko: Good me thirsty.

Displacement

The gorillas have often made comments and responded to questions about past incidents, from moments to months after their occurrence, an indication that they are capable of displacement. The following examples of spontaneous conversations referring to past events are representative:

One morning in April 1979 I sneezed and noticed Koko signing something out of the corner of my eye.

Penny: What did you say?
Koko: Say nose me.

A day later, on October 8, 1980, Barbara Weller showed Mike a drawing he did the day before.

Barbara: What this?
Michael: Gorilla big-trouble mouth there. (Mike had tried to bite it immediately after drawing it because the pen was cinnamon-scented.)

An example of a longer delay—in November of 1980 Michael was having difficulty using the toilet properly at night. Barbara Weller exclaimed, "What are we going to do with you?"

Michael: Do visit garbage.

(We had in the preceding weeks often jokingly threatened to throw him into the garbage when he misbehaved.)

Over a month after Koko's sixth birthday, I brought a piece of birthday cake from the freezer.

Penny: What's this?
Koko: Six.

These naturalistic observations are supported by controlled tests of the gorillas' displacement ability. In a recent experiment, one teacher demonstrated an activity with an object such as a paper-towel tube. Later in the day, another teacher who did not know what had happened, asked Koko or Michael what was done with it. Although Koko did better than Michael, both were able to relate aspects of such past activities to persons who did not witness them. On one trial I put a plastic produce bag over my head at the same time cautioning Koko that this was a stupid thing to do, something she should not copy. When asked by a different teacher what I had done with the bag, she responded, "Head stupid."

Reference to Emotional States

If the gorillas have fallen from grace by virtue of their lying and insults, they may be partially redeemed by their capacity for empathy.

Once Michael, in the back of the trailer, was whining because he couldn't (refused to) sign *out* to be allowed out of his room. I asked Koko:

Penny: How feel?
Koko: Feel sorry out.

On another occasion, one of Koko's teachers had a stuffed bird pretend to eat a tiny toy bear.

Koko: Me sorry bear.
Maureen: Did you say you were sorry for the bear?
Koko: Love bear.

Spontaneous verbal expressions of emotion appeared relatively late in Koko and Michael (at approximately 4 years), as they do in children (approximately 2½ to 3 years). This contrasts with nonverbal vocal expressions of emotion which in both child and gorilla are either present at birth or appear within the first few months of life.

There is other evidence that the gorillas can reflect upon and report about their feelings. Koko has spontaneously informed her companions that she is happy or sad or tired, and regularly answers questions such as, "How are you?" and "How do you feel?" Usually Koko answers in a polite way, as do most people I know, by saying, "Fine." But on other occasions she may answer, "Thirsty," or "Hungry," or "Sad." When Koko was 5½ I asked her, "How are you this morning?" she signed, "Sad feel." Koko has signed "jealous" while watching Michael and his teacher walking outside or Michael and one of her friends playing together as well as in food-sharing situations with Michael. In January of 1980, a month after Nick, a volunteer, left the project, Mike was visited by a girl who was introduced as a friend of Nick's. When she left, Mike cried. His teacher asked him why he was crying and he replied, "Think cry Nick."

Both gorillas have made reference to past emotional states without actually experiencing them at the moment. This is an indication that they are able to separate affect from the context of their utterances, another important feature of displacement. In October of 1980, Barbara Weller asked Mike, "What happened to the black rabbit? Remember the rabbit you would chase outside?" (It had died a few days earlier and Mike watched Ron move it from beneath the back window of Mike's room with a shovel.) Michael's responses indicated that he was saddened by the death of the rabbit and that he thought Ron had eaten the rabbit:

Mike: Rabbit cry me like.
Mike: Rabbit rabbit Ron stupid rabbit eat.

(For a more detailed account of this conversation see *Gorilla*, Volume 4, Number 2, June 1980.)

The gorillas' responses to questions about their feelings are particularly revealing. In a study parallel to one with human children 5 to 13 years old by Wolman et al., (1971), Koko and Michael (each tested when they were $7\frac{1}{2}$) were asked a series of questions with these frames: (1) Do you ever have feelings of ______? (2) When do you feel ______? The target feeling states were anger, fear, happiness, sadness, hunger, thirst, sleepiness, and nervousness. Like the younger subjects mentioned by Wolman et al. the gorillas most frequently reported external events as conditions of emotional arousal. For example, when asked, "When do you feel hungry?" Koko answered, "Feel time." A possible explanation of this reply is that when it is time (to eat), she feels hungry. Michael replied, "Hungry when meat taste," to the same question.

Koko's replies to questions about anger and hunger seem to be related to the events of the preceding months. Koko had had great difficulty adjusting to a new teacher, Marjie, and was punished for her objectionable behavior in this woman's presence (aggressive ramming) by being left alone. This involved the lights being turned off and resulted in Koko's missing meals. Thus the outcome of Koko's anger in this circumstance was hunger.

Michael made an interesting reply to the question, "When do you feel angry?" He signed, "When thief visit," and "Cereal eat." That morning Mike had barked aggressively at a carpenter who came too close to Michael's breakfast cereal.

Conclusion

Project Koko has provided an opportunity to create a direct window into the mind of another species. Through language we have begun to examine and document the development of concepts by the gorillas. Using tests, spontaneous utterances, and questioning we have learned a great deal about their understanding of ideas ranging from dolls to dreams and death. Additionally, we have begun to gain insight into their emotional lives, their reasoning, sense of humor, fantasies, and creative abilities. Through language we are now better able than ever before to begin to understand and know another species.

REFERENCES

GORILLA FOUNDATION

____. Gorilla, a journal published biannually (1977-present) by the Gorilla Foundation, 17820 Skyline Blvd., Woodside, CA 94062.

MOSES, HARRY

____. Talk to the animals. A 12-minute 16-mm film produced for 60 Minutes, CBS. Available through CRM McGraw-Hill Films, 110 - 15th Street, Del Mar, CA 92014.

PATTERSON, FRANCINE G.

1978. The gestures of a gorilla: Language acquisition in another pongid. Brain and Language, vol. 5, pp. 72-97.

Patterson, Francine G. *(continued)*
1978. Linguistic capabilities of a young lowland gorilla. Pp. 161-201 *in* "Sign Language and Language Acquisition in Men and Ape: New Dimensions in Comparative Pedolinguistics," F. C. Peng, ed. Westview Press, Boulder. (Reprinted in R. L. Schiefelbusch and J. H. Hollis [eds.], Language intervention from ape to child. University Park Press, Baltimore, 1979.)
1978. Conversations with a gorilla. National Geographic, vol. 154, no. 4, pp. 438-465. (Condensed in Reader's Digest, vol. 114, no. 683, pp. 81-86, 1979.)
1978. Human communication with gorillas. Pp. 181-187 *in* "In the Spirit of Enterprise," G. B. Stone, ed. W. H. Freeman, San Francisco.
1979. Linguistic capabilities of a lowland gorilla. Dissertation, Stanford University, Psychology. University Microfilms International, Ann Arbor.
1980a. In search of man: Experiments in primate communication. The Michigan Quarterly Review, vol. 19, no. 1, pp. 95-114.
1980b. Comment on Terrace (letters). NYU Educational Quarterly, vol. 11, no. 3, p. 33.
1980c. Gorilla talk: Comment on "monkey business." The New York Review of Books, vol. 27, no. 15, pp. 45-46.
1980d. Creative and innovative uses of language by a gorilla: A case study. Pp. 497-561 *in* "Children's Language," K. E. Nelson, ed., vol. 2. Gardner Press, New York.
1981a. "Can an ape create a sentence?" Some affirmative evidence. Science, vol. 211, pp. 86-87.
1981b. Gorilla warfare. American Psychological Association Monitor, vol. 12, no. 1, pp. 16, 41.
1981c. More on ape talk. The New York Review of Books, vol. 28, no. 5, p. 43.
1981d. Generalized language ability in the gorilla. Paper presented at the annual meeting of the American Psychological Association, Los Angeles, August.

Patterson, F., and Linden, E.
1981. The education of Koko, 224 pp. Holt, Rinehart and Winston, New York.

Schroeder, Barbet
——. Koko, a talking gorilla. A 90-minute 16-mm film. New Yorker Films, 16 West 61st Street, New York, N.Y. 10023.

Francine G. Patterson

Biochemical Genetics of the Galápagos Giant Tortoises

Grant Recipient: James L. Patton, University of California, Berkeley, California.

Grant 1651: In support of studies of the evolutionary relationships of Galápagos tortoises.

The Galápagos Islands have captured the imagination of lay people and scientists alike for more than 400 years. A major reason for this has certainly been the giant land tortoises—in size and carapace shape so variable among the islands—to which the archipelago owes its name (*galápago* is Spanish for tortoise).

The most comprehensive treatment of the systematics and evolutionary relationships of the tortoises has been that of Van Denbergh (1914). More recently Hendrickson (1966) has summarized these relationships, treating all forms as endemic and belonging to the single species *Geochelone elephantopus,* but recognizing 15 subspecies or races. Of these, 10 are known, or have been known, to occur on separate islands, while the remaining 5 are each roughly restricted to one of the five principal volcanoes on the large island of Isabela. Of these 15 races, 3 are now certainly extinct (those from Islas Floreana, Santa Fé, and Rábida), while 1 is probably extinct (that on Isla Fernandina). Of the remaining 11 races, 1 is on the verge of extinction (that from Isla Pinta is known only from a single survivor; see Pritchard, 1977), and 2 others only recently have been brought back from the brink of extinction through careful management by personnel of the Ecuadorian Park Service and the Charles Darwin Foundation (MacFarland et al., 1974).

The present project was undertaken with two goals in mind. The first was to examine representatives of the surviving tortoise races for genetic markers that might be usable in the management and breeding programs which have been under way for the past decade at the Charles Darwin Research Station (CDRS), Academy Bay, Isla Santa Cruz. The second objective was to examine the relationships among the extant tortoise races by these same genetic criteria. Such genetic data, obtained from starch gel electrophoresis for the separation and identification of specific structural gene products (see Lewontin, 1974, for review), provide a means of assessing the evolutionary history of the group independent of that provided by the morphological criteria employed by Van Denbergh, Hendrickson, and other authors.

Materials and Methods

Blood samples from 244 specimens of Galápagos tortoises representing 7 races were collected by venous or cardiac puncture with heparinized syringes. Plasma and hemolysate fractions were separated by centrifugation and stored individually in liquid nitrogen for shipment to the laboratory. All specimens are maintained in the Frozen Tissue Collection of the Museum of Vertebrate Zoology and are available for loan to qualified investigators.

Samplings from subspecies were as follows: Specimens of *porteri*—from specimens collected from the tortoise reserve populations on Isla Santa Cruz (Cerro Chato, n=18; Casseta, n=11), and from 3 individuals housed in the CDRS breeding pens at Academy Bay; *chathamensis*—from individuals from populations at the eastern end of Isla San Cristóbal (Zona del Nidos, n=12; Pampas de los Burros, n=8) and from 10 juveniles in the CDRS pens that had been raised from eggs collected from Isla San Cristóbal.

The remaining samples came from individuals maintained in the breeding pens at the CDRS, as follows: *hoodensis*—from each of the 14 surviving adults taken from Isla Española and from 50 juveniles hatched from crosses of these adults at the CDRS during 1974, 1975, and 1976; *abingtoni*—from the single known survivor of this race from Isla Pinta; *ephippium*—from 14 juveniles raised from eggs collected on Isla Pinzón and hatched at the CDRS in 1974; *darwini*—from 30 juveniles raised from eggs collected on Isla Santiago during 1974, 1975, and 1976; *vicina*—from 42 juveniles raised from eggs collected on Cerro Azul, Isla Isabela, during 1974, 1975, and 1976.

Thirteen enzymes and 4 general proteins encoded by 21 presumptive gene loci were examined by starch gel electrophoresis. Protein type, tissue source, and buffer systems are as follows:

Tris HCl buffer (buffer no. 1 of Selander et al., 1971). Hemoglobin (Hb-1 and Hb-2, from hemolysate), general protein (Pt-3, a cathodal hemolysate protein), and esterase-D (Est-D, a fluorescent esterase from hemolysate).

Lithium hydroxide buffer (buffer no. 2 of Selander et al., 1971). Two general proteins from plasma (Pt-1 and Pt-2), peptidase on leucyl-alanine substrate from plasma (Pept), and guanine deaminase (GDA) from hemolysate.

Tris citrate I buffer (buffer no. 4 of Selander et al., 1971). Isocitrate dehydrogenase (ICD) from hemolysate, lactate dehydrogenase (LDH-1 and

LDH-2) from hemolysate, leucine aminopeptidase (LAP) from plasma, and glutathione reductase (GR) from hemolysate.

Tris citrate III buffer (Ayala et al., 1972). Manose phosphate isomerase (MPI) from hemolysate and acid phosphatase (ACP-1 and ACP-2) from hemolysate.

Phosphate-citrate buffer (buffer no. 8 of Selander et al., 1971). Malate dehydrogenase (MDH-1 and MDH-2) from hemolysate.

Tris-maleate buffer (buffer no. 9 of Selander et al., 1971). Phosphogluconate dehydrogenase (6PGD) from hemolysate, phosphoglucomutase (PGM) from hemolysate, and glucose phosphate isomerase (GPI) from plasma.

Results and Discussion

Inter-population Variation

Of the 21 enzymatic and other protein loci examined by starch gel electrophoresis, 16 were monomorphic for the same allele in all populations and races sampled (PGM, MDH-1, MDH-2, LDH-1, Pept, LAP, ICD, ACP-1, ACP-2, GR, GDA, MPI, Hb-1, Hb-2, Pt-1, and Pt-3); 1 locus showed a rare variant in one race (LDH-2, 1 *porteri* individual was heterozygous for an allele unknown elsewhere); and 4 loci were moderately variable in one or more races (see Table 1). The *chathamensis* samples contained alleles at the 6PGD, Est-D, and PT-2 loci not found in other races. One GPI allele found in low frequency in *chathamensis* is apparently fixed in *hoodensis* but not present elsewhere (GPI^a); for the remaining GPI alleles, *chathamensis* contained 2 that were unique (GPI^c and GPI^f) with 3 other alleles variously shared among the remaining taxa.

The overall genetic similarity among the sampled races of tortoises is quite high. The Rogers's genic similarity value (S-value; Rogers, 1972) ranges from a low of 0.9264 (*chathamensis* versus *porteri*, for example) to a high of 0.9978 (*ephippium* versus *darwini;* see Table 2). Not unexpectedly, intraracial S-values are quite high (0.9849 for within *chathamensis* and 0.9977 for within *porteri*), but these values are in fact lower than some between-race comparisons. Indeed, the population samples of *chathamensis* are as distinct as are the island populations representing *porteri, ephippium, darwini,* and *vicina.* In general, the Galápagos tortoises share an inordinately high level of overall genic similarity. The values recorded here are at the high end of the range usually seen for comparisons of conspecific populations among a variety of vertebrate taxa examined to date (see Selander and Johnson, 1973; Avise, 1974), and are much higher than those characteristically found between congeneric species. This low level of genic diversification is surprising considering the wide array of body sizes and carapace shapes characterizing the various races of tortoises

TABLE 1. Allele Frequencies for 4 Loci Assayed from Races of the Galápagos Tortoise *Geochelone elephantopus*

		chathamensis			*porteri**					
Locus	Allele	Zona del Nidos	Pampa de los Burros	*hoodensis*	Casseta	Cerro Chato	*ephippium*	*vicina*	*darwini*	*abingtoni*
6PGD	a	.084	.062	—	—	—	—	—	—	—
	b	.208	.188	—	—	—	—	—	—	—
	c	.708	.750	1.00	1.00	1.00	1.00	1.00	1.00	1.00
GPI	a	.083	.188	1.00	—	—	—	—	—	—
	b	—	—	—	.111	.059	—	—	—	—
	c	.625	.500	—	—	—	—	—	—	—
	d	—	—	—	.556	.559	.929	.794	.883	—
	e	—	—	—	.333	.382	.071	.206	.067	1.00
	f	.292	.312	—	—	—	—	—	—	—
Est-D	a	.833	1.00	1.00	1.00	1.00	1.00	1.00	1.00	1.00
	b	.167	—	—	—	—	—	—	—	—
Pt-2	a	.120	.120	—	—	—	—	—	—	—
	b	.880	.880	1.00	1.00	1.00	1.00	1.00	1.00	1.00
$\bar{H}$ for 21 loci		.079	.059	.000	.037	.042	.009	.014	.013	.000
$\bar{P}$ for 21 loci		19.0	14.3	0.0	4.8	4.8	4.8	4.8	4.8	0.0

*Two specimens of *porteri* from the CDRS pens contained alleles $6PGD^a$, $6PGD^b$, and GPI^g.

(Van Denbergh, 1914; Hendrickson, 1966) and the fact that some interracial crosses have produced subviable to inviable offspring (C. MacFarland, pers. comm.). The extremely high degree of genic similarity observed is at the same level as that recorded for species of *Anolis* lizards on Bimini (Webster et al., 1972) and genera of California minnows (Avise et al., 1975).

The genic similarity matrix was subjected to a clustering analysis to describe interpopulation relationships, using both an unweighted pair-group method with arithmetic means (UPGMA) and complete linkage (Sneath and Sokal, 1973). The results of only the former are presented here, since the two different techniques yielded identical results (Fig. 1). Three or four groupings of tortoises are recognizable by the analysis: *Chathamensis* is the most distinctive, followed in order by *hoodensis*, then *abingtoni*, and finally by the group of *porteri-ephippium-darwini-vicina*. The

TABLE 2. Matrix of Genic Similarity Values (Rogers's *S*-value) for Sampled Populations of *Geochelone elephantopus*, Based on 21 Genetic Loci

	chathamensis			*porteri*					
	Zona del Nidos	Pampa de los Burros	*hoodensis*	Casseta	Cerro Chato	*ephippium*	*vicina*	*darwini*	*abingtoni*
ZN	1.0000	.9849	.9353	.9264	.9264	.9264	.9264	.9264	.9264
PB		1.0000	.9498	.9360	.9360	.9360	.9360	.9360	.9360
H			1.0000	.9524	.9524	.9524	.9524	.9524	.9524
C				1.0000	.9977	.9843	.9902	.9857	.9706
CC					1.0000	.9837	.9900	.9848	.9719
E						1.0000	.9936	.9978	.9558
V							1.0000	.9943	.9622
D								1.0000	.9568
A									1.0000

results are indicated by a simple locus-by-locus comparison as well. *Chathamensis* is distinguished primarily by unique alleles at moderate to high frequency at each of the 4 polymorphic loci; *hoodensis* owes its distinctness to the fact that it is fixed for the GPI^a allele which also occurs in low frequency in *chathamensis* but is absent in other races; *abingtoni* is only separable from the *porteri* group of races because the single surviving individual is homozygous for the GPI^e allele which occurs in moderate frequency in *porteri* and *vicina* and in low frequency in *ephippium* and *darwini*. These last four races are virtually indistinguishable from one another, except for minor differences in allele frequencies at the GPI locus.

It is clear from these results that there is little correspondence between interracial relationships based on biochemical data and those based on carapace type. The extreme "saddle-backed" races, such as *hoodensis, ephippium,* and *abingtoni,* do not represent a single, closely related genetic unit relative to the "dome-shelled" races (e.g., *porteri*) or the intermediate carapace races (*vicina, darwini,* or *chathamensis*). Hence, these data support the suggestion that the saddle-backed carapace with other attendant morphological modifications (smaller size, longer legs, longer necks, and so forth) was derived independently several times, probably on each separate island where such morphological races occur today.

Unfortunately, in relation to one of the primary goals of the project, no biochemical markers unambiguously characterizing given races were found among the loci examined. It is not possible with this information, therefore, to assign individuals of unknown origin to a specific race or island population.

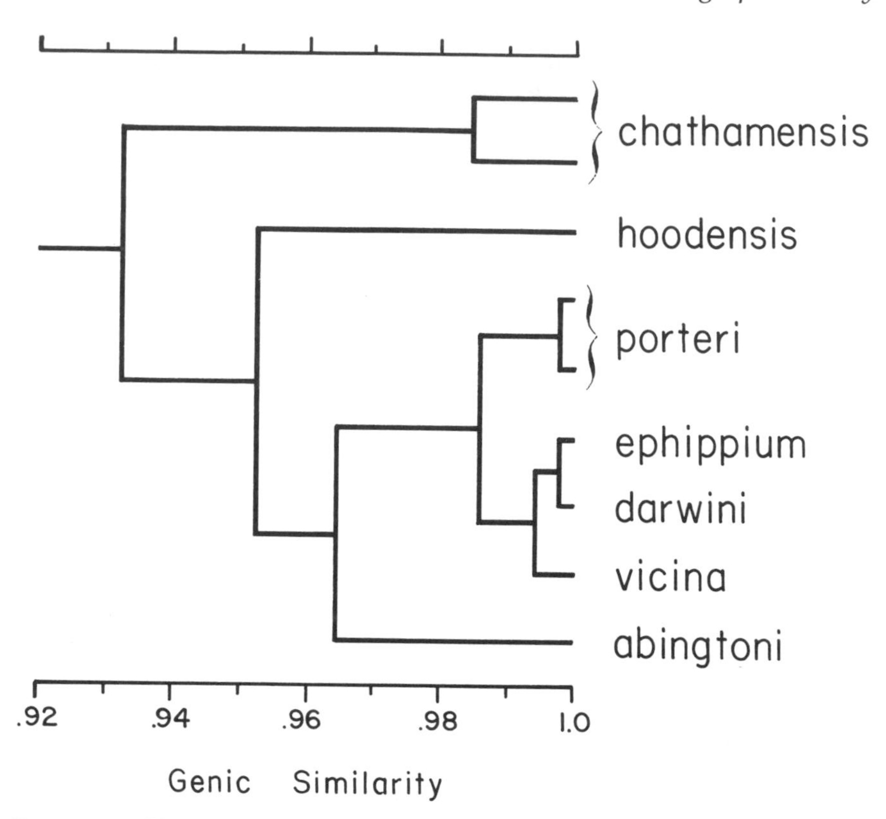

FIGURE 1. Phenogram of relationships of seven races of Galápagos tortoises based on overall genic similarity (Rogers's S-value), clustered by UPGMA.

INTRA-POPULATION VARIATION

Genic variation within and among individuals of single populations was measured by the percentage of loci found to be polymorphic (defined as where the frequency of the major allele is less than 0.95) per population (P) and by the percentage of loci heterozygous per individual per population (H). These data are given in Table 1. The range of individual heterozygosity values per population was 0.000 to 0.079 (unweighted mean H = 0.028) and that for percent polymorphic loci was 0.0 to 19.0 (unweighted mean P = 6.4). These values are low when compared with other vertebrates (mean H for a wide variety of vertebrate species is about 0.058; Selander and Johnson, 1973). This is not surprising, however, since most island populations are characterized by reduced variability (Selander et al., 1971; Avise et al., 1974), presumably as a result of founder effects associated with waif dispersal.

No data are available for any mainland population of *Geochelone,* however, so it is unknown whether the low level of variability observed in Galápagos populations is a result of their insular existence and evolution or a feature more broadly characterizing tortoises in general.

The range of observed heterozygosity in the Galápagos tortoises is rather great, and the geographic pattern of that variability is interesting. In general, intrapopulation variability is highest in the easternmost islands (e.g., San Cristóbal) and becomes regularly less in populations to the west (e.g., on Santa Cruz and then Isabela). The total or near lack of variability in *hoodensis, abingtoni,* and *ephippium* may possibly result from founder effects associated with original colonization. However, of the extant races these three have suffered the greatest deprivation by human activity during the past 100 years, and the populations are now reduced to only a remnant of their former sizes. Indeed, for both *hoodensis* (n=14) and *abingtoni* (n=1), our samples include all known living adults. The lack of genic variability in these races thus quite likely resulted from the severe population bottleneck each race has experienced in recent history. A similar explanation has been given to an absence of genetic variability in northern elephant seals *(Mirounga angustirostris)* which were nearly hunted to extinction in the 19th century (Bonnell and Selander, 1974).

Biogeographic and Evolutionary Implications

Several hypotheses regarding the origin and pattern of evolutionary divergence of the Galápagos tortoises are evident from the electrophoretic data. First of all, the very close overall genic similarity suggests that all tortoises developed from one initial mainland dispersal stock. The pattern of nonoverlapping alleles among groups of races at the GPI locus, however, suggests the possibility of two introductions, each from a different original source population. Distinctions between these possibilities cannot be made until mainland representatives of the genus are examined. Even then, conclusions are likely to remain ambiguous because the immediate ancestral stocks of the Galápagos races might now be extinct.

The geographic pattern of heterozygosity variation across populations does suggest a sequence of colonization events pertinent to the mode of origin and colonization of tortoises in the islands. As noted above, San Cristóbal, the easternmost island, contains populations of tortoises with the highest levels of genic variation recorded (*chathamensis,* H = .069). This level falls off rapidly in each race on successively more western islands (e.g., *porteri,* $\overline{H}$ = .040; *vicina,* $\overline{H}$ = .014; *darwini,* $\overline{H}$ = .013). This pattern of reduced variability across the archipelago most likely reflects a range-front phenomenon in small pioneering populations with a cumulative founder effect in each successive colonization event. Assuming a single initial colonization event from the mainland, the sequence of migration suggested from these data would be as follows: Arrival on San Cristóbal, with that island serving as the source for Española and Santa Cruz races; Santa Cruz would then have served as the source population for all other sampled populations, either directly or indirectly through other islands. A dual initial colonization from mainland source populations would only change the suggested sequence in the context that there would have been no San Cristóbal-to-Santa Cruz connection; mainland emigrants would have independently founded populations on both islands.

The fact that the heterozygosity pattern is best explained by successive island colonization events is a strong argument for the viewpoint that the archipelago is, and has been, at least since the arrival of tortoises, a series of independent islands. These data do not support the hypothesis that the present group of islands resulted from submergence of one large, continuous landmass (cf. Stewart, 1911; Van Denbergh and Slevin, 1913; Vinton, 1951).

Acknowledgments

This project was done in collaboration with Ronald W. Marlow. Assistance in the field was provided by Carol P. Patton and Kristine Tollestrup; laboratory assistance was provided by Dr. Richard D. Sage and Monica Frelow. Permission to sample the tortoise populations was kindly granted by personnel of the Ecuadoran Servicio Forestal and Parque Nacional Galápagos and the Charles Darwin Foundation. I am most grateful for the logistic and other support provided by Dr. Craig MacFarland, Director, Charles Darwin Research Station, and other personnel of the CDRS. Importation of samples of tortoise blood into the United States was made possible by Permit No. PRT 2-623 from the U. S. Fish and Wildlife Service, Department of the Interior. Supplemental financial assistance was provided by the Museum of Vertebrate Zoology, University of California, Berkeley.

REFERENCES

AVISE, J. C.
1974. Systematic value of electrophoretic data. Syst. Zool., vol. 23, pp. 465-481.

AVISE, J. C.; SMITH, J. J.; and AYALA, F. J.
1975. Adaptive differentiation with little genic change between two native California minnows. Evolution, vol. 29, pp. 411-426.

AVISE, J. C.; SMITH, M. H.; SELANDER, R. K.; LAWLOR, T. E.; and RAMSEY, P. R.
1974. Biochemical polymorphism and systematics in the genus *Peromyscus*. V. Insular and mainland species of the subgenus *Haplomylomys*. Syst. Zool., vol. 23, pp. 226-238.

AYALA, F. J.; POWELL, J. R.; TRACEY, M. L.; MOURAO, C. A.; and PERES-SALAS, S.
1972. Enzyme variability in the *Drosophila willistoni* group IV. Genic variation in natural populations of *Drosophila willistoni*. Genetics, vol. 70, pp. 113-139.

BONNELL, M. L., and SELANDER, R. K.
1974. Elephant seals: Genetic variation and near extinction. Science, vol. 184, pp. 908-909.

HENDRICKSON, J. R.
1966. The Galápagos tortoises, *Geochelone* Fitzinger 1835 (*Testudo* Linneaus 1758 in part). Pp. 252-257 *in* "The Galápagos," R. I. Bowman, ed. Univ. Calif. Press, Berkeley and Los Angeles.

LEWONTIN, R. C.
1974. The genetic basis for evolutionary change. Columbia University Press, New York.

MACFARLAND, C. G.; VILLA, J.; and TORO, B.
1974. The Galápagos giant tortoises *(Geochelone elephantopus)*. I: Status of the surviving populations. Biol. Conserv., vol. 6, pp. 118-133.

PRITCHARD, P. C. H.
1977. Three, two, one tortoise. Nat. Hist., vol. 84, no. 8, pp. 90-100.

ROGERS, J. S.
1972. Measures of genetic similarity and genetic distance. Univ. Texas Publ. no. 7213, pp. 145-153.

SELANDER, R. K., and JOHNSON, W. E.
1973. Genetic variation among vertebrate species. Ann. Rev. Ecol. Syst., vol. 4, pp. 75-91.

SELANDER, R. K.; SMITH, M. H.; YANG, S. Y.; JOHNSON, W. E.; and GENTRY, J. B.
1971. Biochemical polymorphism and systematics in the genus *Peromyscus*. I. Variation in the old-field mouse *(Peromyscus polionotus)*. Univ. Texas Publ. no. 7103, pp. 49-90.

SNEATH, P. H. A., and SOKAL, R. R.
1973. Numerical taxonomy. W. C. Freeman Co., San Francisco.

STEWART, A.
1911. A botanical survey of the Galápagos Islands. Proc. Calif. Acad. Sci., ser. 4, vol. 1, pp. 7-288.

VAN DENBERGH, J.
1914. The gigantic land tortoises of the Galápagos Archipelago. Proc. Calif. Acad. Sci., ser. 4, vol. 2, pp. 203-374.

VAN DENBERGH, J., and SLEVIN, J. R.
1913. The Galápagoan lizards of the genus *Tropidurus;* with notes on the iguanas of the genera *Conolophus* and *Amblyrhynchus*. Proc. Calif. Acad. Sci., ser. 4, vol. 2, pp. 133-202.

VINTON, K. W.
1951. Origin of life on the Galápagos Islands. Amer. Journ. Sci., vol. 249, pp. 356-376.

WEBSTER. T. P.; SELANDER, R. K.; and YANG, S. Y.
1972. Genetic variability and similarity in the *Anolis* lizards of Bimini. Evolution, vol. 26, pp. 523-535.

JAMES L. PATTON

Comparative Analysis of Coral Reef Community Structures in the Vicinity of Lizard Island (Australia)

Grant Recipient: Michel Pichon, Department of Marine Biology, James Cook University of North Queensland, Townsville, Australia.

Grant 1585: For a comparative analysis of coral reef community structures in the vicinity of Lizard Island, Australia.

A preliminary survey of the coral reefs around Lizard Island was undertaken in May and June 1976; sites were selected and the method and sampling strategies were tested.

Field data were collected yearly during expeditions which took place during the "calm weather" season (November through February), between 1977 and 1981. The sampling expeditions were either land based, at the Lizard Island Research Station, operated by the Australian Museum (Sydney), or shipborne, when the James Cook University Research Vessel, R. V. *James Kirby*, was chartered.

Aims and Objectives

The aim of the project was to study the benthic community structure and zonation of selected coral reefs belonging to markedly different morphological types (fringing reefs, platform reefs, barrier reefs) and situated in different environmental conditions, from the more sheltered terrigenous environment of inshore reefs to the very exposed offshore barrier reefs. In addition to the photophilic communities, special attention was paid to skiophilous reef communities, which remain very poorly known worldwide. A prerequisite for such a project was to remove the taxonomic impediment by a comprehensive study of the coral fauna of the Great Barrier Reef region.

Methods

Scleractinian coral taxonomy was carried out, using extensively the concept of "ecomorph" (Laborel, 1970; Wijsman-Best, 1972), in order to take into account the hitherto poorly documented, but nevertheless considerable intraspecific variability. This led to the collection of large series

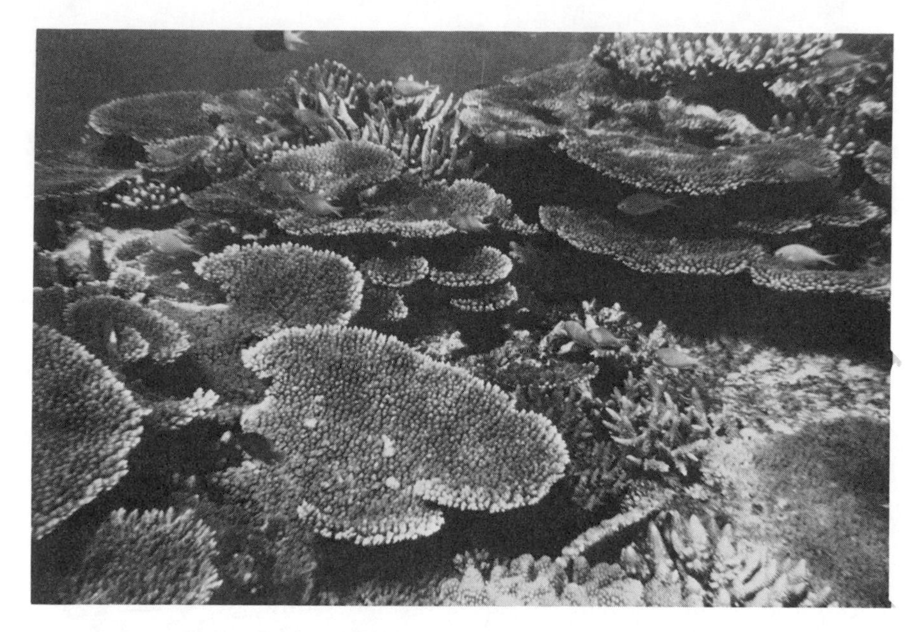

FIGURE 1. Coral community dominated by the genus *Acropora* in an exposed environment on the northeast side of Lizard Island. The family Acroporidae contains the largest number of species of reef builders and the genus *Acropora* in particular is dominant in many types of reef environment.

of specimens to assess both the intra-biotope and inter-biotope variability.

Methods for quantitative ecology in coral reefs are still under discussion, and no standard procedures have yet been adopted. One of the field techniques used in the present study is the "line transects" (Loya, 1972). Semiquantitative data have also been gathered by ranking species attributes (generally cover) with a six-point scale.

A number of procedures for numerical analysis have been tested, in particular agglomerative polythetic classifications. This includes the Lance and Williams flexible method, and the strongly clustering Ward's error sum of squares. The most commonly used similarity–dissimilarity indices are Bray-Curtis, Canberra Metric, and Squared Euclidean Distance.

Results

Results of the taxonomic studies have been incorporated in the four volumes of the scientific publication *Scleractinia of Eastern Australia* (Veron

FIGURE 2. On the mid-reef flat, diversity is generally high. A few of the more common mid-reef flat species are shown here, i.e., *Porites lutea* and several species of *Acropora*.

and Pichon, 1976, 1980, 1982; Veron et al., 1977). The family Acroporidae has been studied separately in cooperation with Dr. C. Wallace of James Cook University. A complete list including 292 species is now available for the coral reefs in the vicinity of Lizard Island.

Research on reef communities of skiophilous (shade-loving) corals involved the study of over 120 caves, with data on colony size, growth form, and irradiance levels recorded for more than 3000 individual specimens. Taxonomic studies arising from this work provided an opportunity to carry out a revision of the skiophilous coral genus *Leptoseris*.

Three groups of shade-dwelling corals are tentatively distinguished: generally skiophilous corals, found both in deep water and in shallow but shaded conditions; preferentially cavernicolous corals, growing mostly in shallow, cryptic habitats; and shade-tolerant corals, common also in better-illuminated parts of the reef, but tolerant of a wide range of conditions.

The growth form of hermatypic shade-dwelling corals is generally thin and flat, and coralla are generally of small size, suggesting that the low light intensity is restricting both the shape and size of colonies. Photoadaptation to low irradiance levels may be achieved by changes in zooxanthellar distribution and chlorophyll content, and small-polyped species may feed on suspended particulate matter by using mucous strands and nets.

Apart from an abundance of ahermatypic coral on the ceilings of some caves, particular zones or facies were not detected in different sectors of caves, or according to irradiance levels. This lack of zonation is attributed to the fact that the species concerned are all representative of a well shaded but not "obscure" aspect of skiophilous communities; and furthermore, that ahermatypic species were not found in conditions darker than those tolerated by some hermatypic corals.

Patterns within the skiophilous coral assemblages indicate definite regional differences in the skiophilous fauna, with caves in the Capricorn Group tending to have an impoverished scleractinian fauna compared with that recorded from caves in more northerly areas of the Barrier Reef. Observations of other skiophilous biota suggest that at higher latitudes, certain algal groups may be more successful than corals in cryptic habitats, and this suggestion is borne out by records from the southwest Indian Ocean.

In the study of scleractinian growth form distribution, 26 categories of growth form were recognized, and their cover and abundance were recorded in a variety of coral reef morphological types, exposed to differing conditions of swell, wave action, and sedimentation. Distribution patterns of the full range of growth forms were analyzed, using numerical classification and discriminant analysis. Growth forms were then reappraised and regrouped, to examine the distribution of the major forms.

The results confirm the view that hydrodynamic conditions play an important role in the distribution of coral growth forms. However, the principal pattern to emerge from the data is that reef flats support a limited range of growth forms, and that this can be attributed in part to conditions of water movement, but also to the rigors imposed by other physical factors, such as temperature, salinity, and emersion at low tide. Most semiexposed and sheltered reef slopes, which represent a more favorable environment, were found to support a wide variety of colony shapes, with few such slopes dominated by any particular growth form. It is suggested that the distribution of coral growth forms should be viewed not only in relation to hydrodynamic conditions, but also in the wider context of the severity and predictability of the environment.

With respect to photophilic reef communities, although inshore reefs have a depauperate coral fauna, when compared with outer shelf reefs, a number of genera are nevertheless highly characteristic of inshore reefs surrounded by predominantly murky waters with a high level of suspended particles. The genera *Duncanopsammia, Moseleya, Pseudosiderastrea, Palauastrea,* and *Catalaphyllia* are essentially restricted to the coastal

FIGURE 3. A typical example of lower slope community dominated by large, massive colonies of the genus *Porites*. Such colonies can often reach several meters in size.

FIGURE 4. A *Juncella* (whiplike gorgonacean) community on the lagoon slope. On the deeper part of the lagoon slopes scleractinian corals become scarce, and are often replaced by communities dominated by Gorgonacea.

and inner shelf reefs. Light and sedimentation limit the vertical development of coral communities on reef slopes and excess deposits of sediment also limit the development of coral communities on the reef flat.

Outer reefs, on the contrary, show a diversification of biotopes and of the scleractinian fauna. Sample sites were classified into 10 groups (Done and Pichon, in preparation), that fall into three major categories corresponding to slopes in low hydrodynamic energy areas, to high hydrodynamic energy areas, and to back reef areas. These site groups are as follows:

1. Slopes in low hydrodynamic energy areas: back reef slope, deep outer slope, deep channel slope, and sides of patch reef and knolls (back reef).
2. High hydrodynamic energy areas: mid-outer slope, upper outer slope, outer reef flat, and mid-reef flat.
3. Back reef areas: mid-inner reef flat, back reef flat (including top of patch reefs).

Five major types of distribution pattern were evidenced:

1. Species of the upper slopes (corresponding to high-energy conditions). These include six species of the genus *Acropora* (Fig. 1) plus *Pocillopora eydouxi*.
2. Species of the mid- or back reef flat (e.g., *Goniastrea favulus* and *Acropora millepora;* see Fig. 2).
3. Species with a broad spectrum of distribution, essentially r = strategists, such as *Stylophora pistillata* and *Pocillopora verrucosa*.
4. Species of the lower outer slope and back slopes, where low energy conditions prevail (see Fig. 3). This group of species is heterogeneous as far as its taxomonic composition is concerned.
5. Species restricted to pinnacle slopes, channel walls, and lagoon slope (see Fig. 4).

When considering all the reefs, from the coastal fringing reefs to the outer barrier (cross-shelf situation), it was possible to obtain a ranking of the scleractinian species, in terms of overall substratum cover, number of colonies, and frequency (number of times a given species is present in the sampling sites). These rankings for the 10 species scoring highest in each case are as follows:

Cover	Number of colonies	Frequency
Acropora formosa	*A. humilis*	*Porites lutea*
A. humilis	*A. palifera*	*A. humilis*
Porites cylindrica	*P. lutea*	*P. damiconis*
A. grandis	*A. formosa*	*P. lobata*
A. palifera	*P. lobata*	*Stylophora pistillata*
A. hyacinthus	*A. cuneata*	*Favis favus*
P. lutea	*A. hyacinthus*	*Montastrea curta*
Diploastrea heliopora	*Seriatopora hystrix*	*A. palifera*
A. cuneata	*P. cylindrica*	*P. verrucosa*
P. lobata	*Pocillopora verrucosa*	*Goniastrea pectinata*

To summarize, the major results obtained from the project are an updated taxonomic knowledge of the scleractinian fauna of the Great Barrier Reef, and in particular of the Lizard Island area; an accurate scheme of distribution of the major coral growth forms; a detailed scheme of zonation of coral communities established on various reefs, along a cross-shelf gradient, and a quantitative characterization of such communities; and a quantitative account of the hitherto poorly known skiophilous reef communities.

Acknowledgments

Assisting with this study were Dr. Terence Done, Department of Marine Biology, James Cook University; Dr. Mireille Pichon, Department of Marine Biology, James Cook University; and Ms. Zena Dinesen, Department of Marine Biology, James Cook University.

REFERENCES

DINESEN, ZENA
1980. A revision of the coral genus *Leptoseris* (Scleractinia: Fungiina: Agariciidae) Mem. Queensland Mus., vol. 20, no. 1, pp. 181-235.
1980. Some ecological aspects of coral assemblages in the Great Barrier Reef Province, 361 pp., illus. Ph.D. Thesis, James Cook University.

DONE, TERENCE
1977. A comparison of units of cover in ecological classifications of coral communities. Pp. 10-14 *in* "Proceedings 3rd International Coral Reef Symposium," Miami.

DONE, TERENCE, and PICHON, MICHEL
——. Coral communities of the Lizard Island area (Great Barrier Reef). I. The Outer Reefs. (In prep.)

LABOREL, JACQUES
1970. Madréporaires et Hydrocoralliarires récifaux des cotes bresiliennes. Systematique, écologie, repartition verticale et geographique. Ann. Inst. Oceanogr. vol. 47, no. 9, pp 171-229.

LOYA, YOSSEF
1972. Community structure and species diversity of hermatypic corals at Eilat, Red Sea. Mar. Biol., vol. 13, pp. 100-123.

PICHON, MICHEL, and BULL, GORDON
——. Coral reef community structure and zonation in the Lizard Island area (Great Barrier Reef). (In prep.)

VERON, JOHN, and PICHON, MICHEL
1976. Scleractinia of eastern Australia. Part I. vol. 1, Austr. Inst. Mar. Sci., 86 pp.
1980. Scleractinia of eastern Australia. Part III. vol. 4, Austr. Inst. Mar. Sci., 450 pp.

1982. Scleractinia of eastern Australia. Part IV. vol. 5, Austr. Inst. Mar. Sci., 159 pp.

VERON, JOHN; PICHON, MICHEL; and WIJSMAN-BEST, MAYA

1977. Scleractinia of eastern Australia. Part II. vol. 3, Austr. Inst. Mar. Sci., 233 pp.

WIJSMAN-BEST, MAYA

1972. Systematics and ecology of New Caledonian Faviinae (Coelenterata, Scleractinia). Bijdr. Dierk., vol. 42, no. 1, 76 pp.

MICHEL PICHON

Excavations at Abu Salabikh, a Sumerian City

Grant Recipient: John Nicholas Postgate, Faculty of Oriental Studies, University of Cambridge, Cambridge, England.

Grants 1632, 1894, 2143: In support of the archeological excavation of the Sumerian city at Abu Salabikh, Iraq.

Three seasons of excavations by the British Archaeological Expedition to Iraq at the site of Abu Salabikh in southern Iraq were substantially supported by the National Geographic Society (1976, 1978, and 1981). This composite report covers the results of those years as well as work in other years. The principal archeological results from the different parts of the site are briefly described, with some discussion of their implications for the history of the urbanization process in early Mesopotamia, to which Abu Salabikh is for various reasons uniquely qualified to contribute (cf. Adams, 1981, p. 63). This is obviously an interim report, since many detailed and general problems are still in need of solution, and it is hoped that excavations will continue in 1983.

Part I—Excavation in 1975 and 1976

The history of archeological excavation at Abu Salabikh goes back to 1963, when Prof. Donald Hansen and Dr. Vaughn Crawford began a small sounding at this group of low mounds not far north of the major Sumerian center of Nippur, where Prof. Hansen was working at the time. The original incentive to work here was the prospect of readily accessible levels of the Uruk period (ca. 4000-3000 B.C.), for although present at Nippur, there they were buried beneath many meters of deposits accumulated during later centuries of continuous occupation. Here at Abu Salabikh the potsherds littering the surface of one of the mounds indicated that it had hardly, if at all, been occupied after the late Uruk period, while the rest of the site seemed to have been abandoned in the last phase of the Sumerian Early Dynastic age (ca. 2400 B.C.). As so often happens in archeology, the site did not yield what had been expected of it: The Uruk mound proved disappointing, but in a test sounding on the main Early Dynastic mound the excavators came upon a severely burned building on a courtyard plan with inscribed clay cuneiform tablets scattered through its rooms. The size alone of some of these tablets showed at once that they were of great interest, and subsequent study of them and of others, excavated during a second season in 1965, revealed that they consist mainly of literary texts in the Sumerian language, which carry the history of Mesopotamian literature back some 500 years. The definitive publication of these tablets was undertaken by Prof. R. D. Biggs and appeared in 1974 (see References); many of the texts resist interpretation, largely because of the early stage of writing, but others can be identified with certainty as earlier versions of compositions known previously only from copies of about 1800 B.C.

When in 1975 the British expedition resumed work at the site, with the generous consent of Prof. J. A. Brinkman, then Director of the Oriental Institute at the University of Chicago, it was with two immediate objectives. We wanted to know more about the building in which these extremely important tablets had been found: As the earliest known library, it was obviously of interest to know where it had been housed—in a temple by priests, in a palace by scribes working for a secular authority, or in some other kind of institution. In fact, even after three additional seasons of work (see Part III of this report), this choice remains as difficult as before, although we do know that the building was of considerable size and complexity, and can hardly have been other than a temple or palace. Some clue may yet be discovered in the administrative documents found by us in 1975, which have been published by Prof. R. D. Biggs and the writer, but it is clear that more excavation will be needed to define the extent of the building and its character.

Our second, wider objective was to investigate the building's context within the city, and the nature of the city itself. Sumer fostered the earliest known fully urban society, with more than a score of important cities coexisting and sharing their distinctive south Mesopotamian culture. The identity of Abu Salabikh itself remains uncertain, although we have proposed ancient Eresh, the hometown of Nisaba, goddess of reeds and writing. The presence here, however, of a flourishing scribal tradition, the sheer area of the Early Dynastic settlement—perhaps as much as 50 ha—and the mention in the tablets of an *ensi* or "city-ruler" combine to show that Abu Salabikh was a city in its own right. Since the Early Dynastic levels lie directly beneath the surface, it seemed a good candidate for the investigation of the Sumerian city as a whole (Fig. 1). Previous work on Sumerian sites has understandably concentrated on the more spectacular features, such as royal cemeteries (especially at Ur) and major public buildings, so that little is known of the mundane details that are just as crucial to our knowledge of the city, such as housing, city layout, or the city walls.

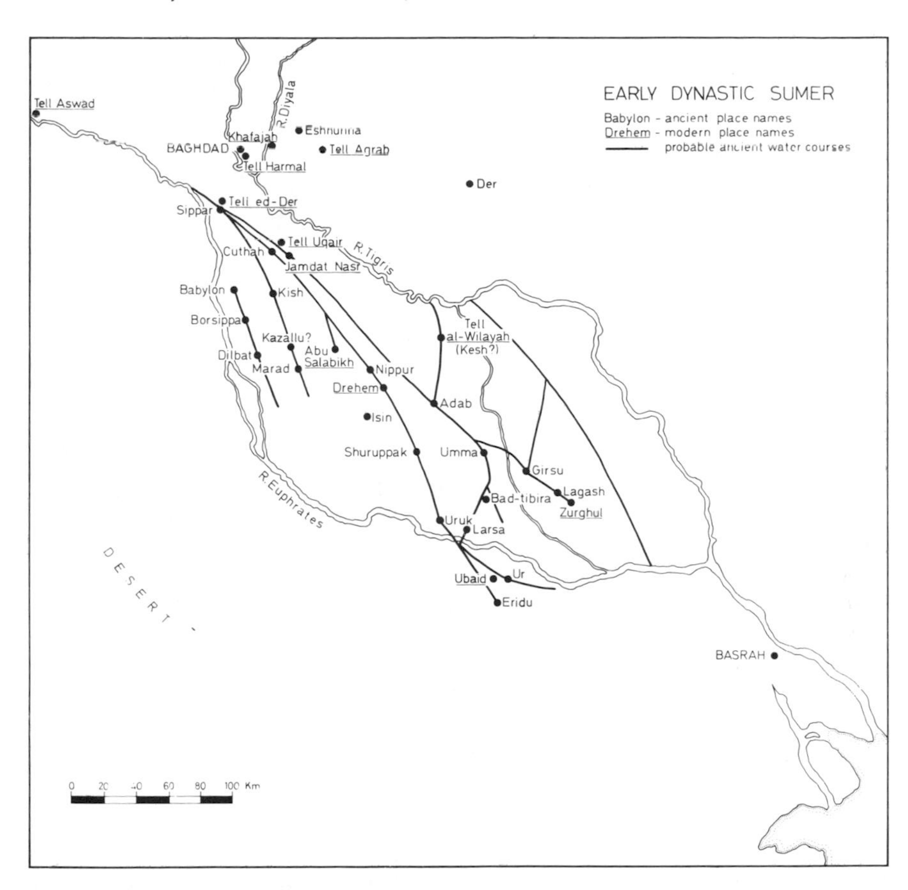

FIGURE 1. Early Dynastic Sumer.

Excavation in Area A

Our work in 1976 was largely a continuation of that begun in the preceding year, and was concentrated on Area E, from where the tablets had come, and on Area A, some 250 m to the north, where a well-constructed building had been located, occupying the highest surviving point of the mounds. The full extent of this building has yet to be established, and its purpose, too, remains uncertain. It seems to consist of long rooms (about 9 × 4 m), alternating with smaller ones and arranged around courtyards. At the north end of a room excavated in 1976 are the beginnings of a staircase rising to the roof or to a second story. Although the northern sector of this building had been burned, its rooms were surprisingly empty of objects, and virtually all that we found on the floor were charred pieces of roof-beams, and, behind the staircase, some remains of fish. At one side, probably in the open air, there was a large, ribbed pottery vessel set into the floor, with a small lid or ladle still inside it, and just next to it a small oven. This may have been a simple household breadmaking establishment, and the large jar may have held water or flour. As in virtually every other part of the site excavated (except the West Mound—see Part II of this report), there were graves cut down into the buildings. Here they were very close to the surface, and must have been dug from a much higher level, which is now completely eroded. As elsewhere, it is impossible to be certain whether these graves were dug when this part of the city had been abandoned and turned into a cemetery, or result from the practice of intramural burial, the burying of the dead beneath the floor of their lifetime houses, which is definitely attested for earlier phases at Abu Salabikh (see below) and elsewhere. In the main northern long room we came upon 2 graves, 1 of which yielded a typical group of Early Dynastic III grave goods, including the characteristic upright-handled jar and stemmed dish (sometimes called "fruit-stand"), a large unshaped stone slab, a cylinder seal with simple geometric design, a cockleshell of the kind frequently used at this date to hold cosmetic paints, a hair or dress pin of copper, and a copper knife.

Farther to the southeast the outline of the building becomes much less clear, principally because at least 6 graves had cut the original stratification of the area until little undisturbed soil remained. One of these graves was peculiar in that its grave furnishings consisted almost exclusively of 9 little undecorated pottery stemmed dishes, while in another we found the broken remnants of at least 8 ovoid pottery jars, with a unique pottery vessel of oblong shape with impressed knobbly decoration all over its underside, suggesting that it was intended, like a flower basket, for suspension by its pierced lugs. But perhaps the most interesting finds in this area were made on the floor of a room in the southern sector of the building: here, under a heavy layer of burnt debris, lay a varied collection of things, including 2 upright-handled jars, other pottery vessels, a shattered conch-shell bowl—which was restored from incredibly small fragments by Tamsen Fuller, our conservator—various utilitarian stone implements, and part of a primitive sickle made of saw-edged flint blades set in bitumen. All this combines to show that at least this part of the building was devoted to the everyday business of agricultural life, whether as a workshop or a storeroom. That we are dealing with a functional rather than a ceremonial establishment is proved also by a find in the southern courtyard: Here, in a circular shallow pit, we found several kilograms of flint, principally waste flakes. Nonetheless the collection included some finished blades, and some minute tools like borers, of a type

FIGURE 2. Grave 96 contained these five pots: In the large bowl stands a perforated clay cylinder, inside that, a tiny jar (extracted for the photograph); next to these stands the jar with a bowl in its mouth pierced to act as a strainer. Four similar sets have been found, but no convincing explanation of their use (AbS 1281-5).

known to have been used at contemporary sites farther east in the manufacture of objects in semiprecious stones, such as lapis lazuli. Like the flint blades of the sickle, this serves as a reminder that long after the introduction of copper tools, stone ones continued to be acceptable for many purposes, and it is of interest that the flint was actually worked on the site, not imported ready-made. Nearby, but presumably somewhat later in date, was part of another grave that contained a set of pottery vessels of a kind found farther north and west, as far as Mari on the middle Euphrates, emphasizing links as far west as Ebla (Tell Mardikh) in Syria, which are also hinted at by the script and language of the royal archives found there (Fig. 2).

In this same courtyard in 1963 the American expedition sank a shaft to virgin soil. Although this revealed not a trace of occupation before the Early Dynastic period, 4 interesting graves were found, apparently contemporary with one another, and well furnished with grave goods of the

Early Dynastic I period, including a handsome copper mirror. Wishing to tie this into our own stratification, we, therefore, in 1976, made a small cut to the east, the chief result of which was the discovery of a fifth grave. This grave of a child, one of the earliest we have yet excavated, belongs to the Early Dynastic II period. It was hardly a rich burial: Below a layer of reed matting, onto which two large pottery jars had been thrown down, and perhaps deliberately broken, was the simple inhumation, with a few pots by the head (Fig. 3). These included two very distinctive types: a round-based spouted jar and a little bottle in a black ware presumably imitating stone. Both these types can be exactly paralleled at the site of Kish, farther north, and are to be ascribed to the Early Dynastic II period.

Whether the buildings in Area A are part of a temple, a palace, or a large private establishment, it is impossible to say at present. There is nothing in the plan or character of the buildings to suggest a temple, but we know from the Temple Oval at Khafajah that purely domestic quarters could be incorporated within a temple complex. The buildings are well laid out, but their scale is by no means exceptional, and perhaps the only reason to suspect that they constitute more than a private house is their prominent position at the summit of the surviving mound. The only inscribed tablet found here seems to list personal names, but this too could point to a religious, governmental, or even large private establishment.

Area E: The Central Complex

A very similar problem confronts us still with Area E, where the tablets were found, principally in an awkward jumble of rooms. Our work in 1976 was aimed at extending the area of this complex, and concentrated on the southwest corner and on the south and especially east sides. At the southwest the Southern Unit was flanked by a corridor that led up toward the Burned Building in the north from the wide Southern Corridor that runs along the south side of the same Southern Unit. West of this we expected to find another component of the complex, now named by us the Central Complex, and, in fact, there seems to have been a range of domestic rooms, frequently rebuilt, and accommodating fireplaces and at least one bathroom with a bitumened floor. There was a noticeable contrast with the Southern Unit itself, as the floor deposits were dirtier, and the walls less well plastered. In the debris from the floors we recovered an unusually high proportion of stone vessels, fragments of a unique Early Dynastic III jar, of which the upright handle had been incised with the figure of a skirted man, and the shoulder with swimming fish, as well as other objects that looked as though they had been discarded from a more ceremonial part of the building.

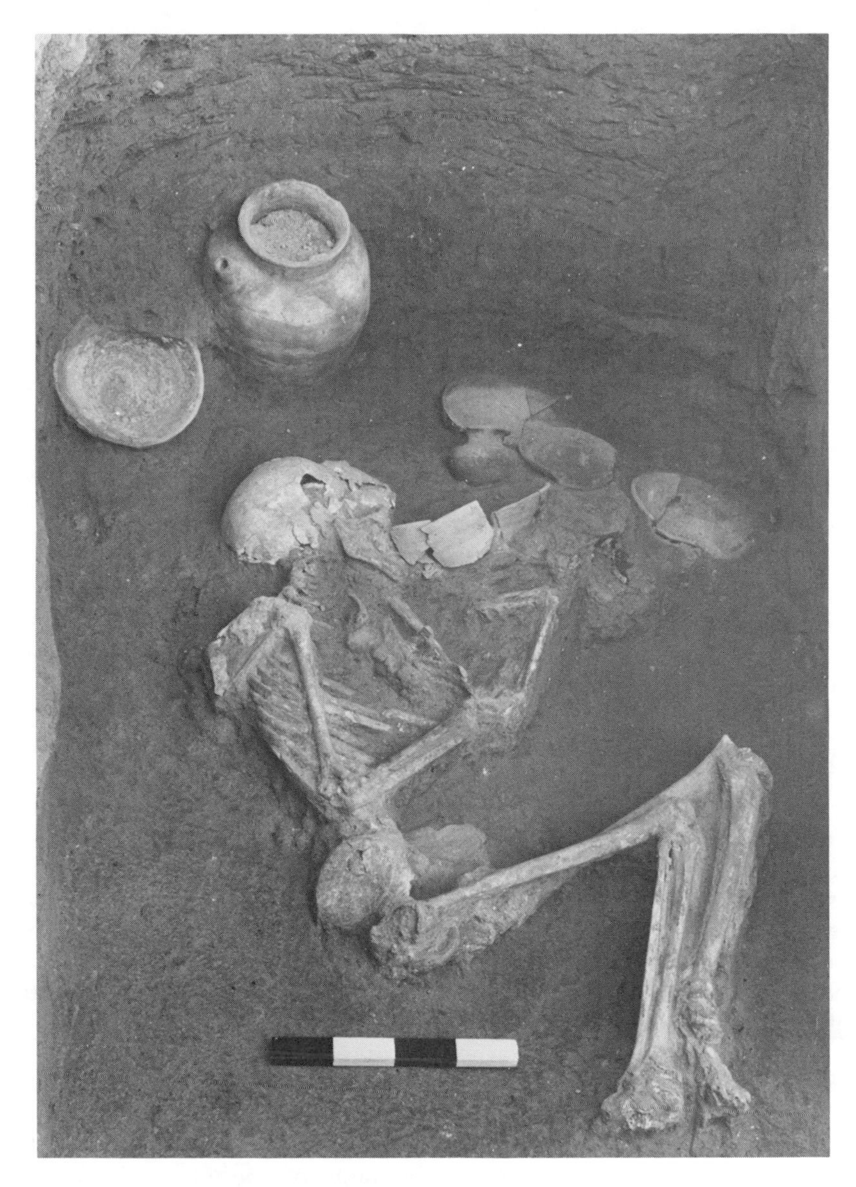

FIGURE 3. Grave 81 viewed from the east.

On the eastern side the results were satisfactory, in that we did succeed in locating at least one edge of the complex: The wall separating the Southern Unit from the corridor to its south turned to the northwest, and the corridor itself, while it may have continued eastward as well, also turned northwest, as a broad street with heavily striated dirty deposits, certainly pointing to an unroofed area. This is in distinct contrast to the deposits in the Southern Corridor itself, where there was, admittedly, a very long accumulation of markedly striated levels, but their color was a light, sandy pastel range, similar to the earths used to make the bricks of the walls. South of this corridor again there are rooms belonging to another whole complex; this part of the building, which we now call the Southeast Complex, was investigated in 1981 (see Part III, this report). The principal result of work in this area was to prove that during the Early Dynastic III period the rooms and other deposits to the south and east were cleared completely away, down to virgin soil in fact, so that on this side the complex must have stood as much as 6 m proud of the surrounding ground. This space was later filled in with deep piles of rubbish thrown out of the building; the contents of this rubbish-tip are discussed below, in Part II.

Area E: The Eastern Houses

Across the street from the Central Complex is an entirely separate establishment, structurally at least, which seems likely to be a well-to-do private house, or at least a residence. There may in fact be a second such house built back-to-back against its eastern wall, but as yet little can be said about it. Indeed, there is little enough to be said about the first house either, because although the walls and doors are present and can be readily identified, the floors of the rooms have almost all been dug out in antiquity to make space for intramural burials. Each of the 4 excavated rooms contained at least 1 grave, and the long room or court in the southeast has so far yielded no less than 5. Some of these were dug from a level now eroded, but in other cases we have been able to identify the exact floor from which the grave was dug, and the contents of the graves demonstrate quite clearly that they are earlier than the Central Complex, and date to the Early Dynastic II period.

One such grave is particularly intriguing: Our first warning of its existence was when a group of 3 copper arrowheads tumbled from the side of the pit we were excavating, where they had evidently been propped while their shafts still survived. Later another 3 were found in a similar position, and below this were the remains of roughly laid wooden planks, on one of which yet another arrowhead was lying. Under the planks the pit—now almost a shaft—continued down, until, a meter and a half on, we came on the main deposit, which consisted of 140 simple pottery bowls, 6 jars with spouts, a small pottery bottle, 2 cosmetic shells, and some sheep's bones, all laid under, around, and above a sadly crushed human skeleton. This grave, which from the pottery shapes is earlier than Grave 1 in the main Room 39 of the Southern Unit, is nevertheless similar to it in various ways. They are both unquestionably contemporary with the building under whose floors they were dug, which also applies to the 4 other graves associated with Grave 1. In Grave 1 there were 112 of the conical bowls, and although there was also jewelry, a stone bowl, a variety of pottery, etc., the contrast between the immense number of these simple cups and the remainder of the grave goods is almost as extreme. The spouted vessels in each case might have contained enough liquid—probably beer, of which the Sumerians, understandably in view of the climate, consumed quantities—to fill the bowls, but even if this be admitted, the problem remains of who, in the dead person's afterlife, was conceived to be going to use the bowls: not, surely, just the dead person alone? In the case of Grave 1, where the context, to the writer's mind, suggests a priestly occupant, we wondered whether there had not been some kind of graveside ritual in which all the mourners might each deposit a bowl. At present, however, I would incline to the alternative solution, that the number of bowls reflects the occupant's heavy social obligations in his or her lifetime, duties which might be expected to be mirrored in the afterlife. If this is right, it is surprising how spartan are the remainder of the grave goods. The location of the house next to what was evidently a major public building, the discovery of at least 4 cylinder seals in the area—and, indeed, of an inscribed tablet concerned with sheep—and the number of the bowls certainly point to a high social standing for the residents of the Eastern Houses, but it may be that social standing in Early Dynastic II Abu Salabikh did not automatically imply wealth, or, more simply, that there was not a tradition of enormously extravagant grave goods—such as we are accustomed to expect after the example of Ur, although not at Kish, which was quite as important politically.

Part II—Excavation in 1977 and 1978

Work continued at Abu Salabikh in 1977, and, with support from the National Geographic Society, in 1978. The results can be grouped in three main headings, which will be described in their chronological sequence: the West Mound, the Northeast Mound, and Area E.

The West Mound

When we began the renewed work at Abu Salabikh we had as our overriding general objective the reconstruction of as much of the life of the city as is archeologically recoverable. At the same time the site offered a good opportunity to establish a reliable stratified artifact sequence for central Sumer and, although we have made several traditional "deep soundings" to determine the sequence, we are also fortunate in that as work has proceeded it has become clear that different phases of the Early Dynastic and Uruk periods are lying at the surface on different parts of the site, so that we are able to concentrate on any period that engages our attention without necessarily having to clear a deep later overburden. Both these considerations came together in our work on the West Mound during 1977 and 1978. With the kind consent of the Iraqi Directorate-General of Antiquities we have been able to clear the surface soil from most of this mound to a depth of little more than 15 cm, and thus, without excavation, to plan a wide expanse of housing—something that would have taken years by normal methods of excavation. A total of 106 10-m squares was cleared during the two seasons, corresponding to almost all the mound above the 6.5-m contour. Only in the southeast are there a few untouched squares that might still yield useful information from a surface scrape; but, in spite of these, we have now enough to assess the composition of the entire mound. The plan that emerges from the operation is gratifyingly informative: In brief, we find a wide barren area on the southwest, which seems to be composed of deliberate fill, but contains no architectural remains and little pottery. This is bounded on the north by two parallel walls, each some 2 m thick, one in black and the other in yellowish bricks. Although this double wall vanishes off the western edge of the mound, and is obscured at its center by later deposits, it certainly ran for some 60 m from west to east. To its north the wall encloses a large area of buildings: We can readily make out a large rectangular courtyard on the west, with a pottery drainage channel leading into it from the northwest, and with relatively well-preserved rooms on its east side. From one of the rooms we recovered 2 very handsome large pottery jars in a style that dates the building unequivocally to the Early Dynastic I period. The summit of the mound conceals the eastward extension of this building, but beyond it, on the eastern slope, we meet a group of rooms (especially in squares 2G16-17 and 26-27) distinguished by a number of ovens and much burnt room fill, clearly indicating a domestic area. These rooms are separated from those farther east by a zig-zag alleyway, and where this emerges from between the buildings on the south side a thick wall takes off from the corner of the western house to join the eastern end of the double enclosure wall. This then marks the eastern limit of the enclosure, and here it seems to rub shoulders with other, similar, enclosures: Separated from it by a narrow street is a thick wall running north to south for at least 30 m, and must have enclosed the space to the east, which is now eroded to below the floors, while coming into the same point from the south is another thick double wall, forming the west side of the same street and enclosing an area to its west. We guess that the large area of building fill we observed here was designed to act as a platform for houses enclosed by this wall, which are now entirely lost through erosion. In sum, therefore, we can readily identify four contemporary enclosures or compounds occupying the major part of the site during the Early Dynastic I period.

This layout of part of our city at an early date is extremely suggestive. When in 1977 we had recovered only the plan of the northern rooms with the double enclosure-wall forming their limit, it seemed possible that we had to do with a public institution such as a palace or temple, despite the ordinary nature of the rooms. Now that it is clear that there were several, and perhaps even many, such compounds in the West Mound area—for we do not know how far the Early Dynastic I remains may stretch beyond the visible limits of the *tell*—that idea is untenable. Instead, one is forced to conclude that each compound housed a single "private" establishment, and if we seek to interpret our plan in human terms, we must visualize a city composed architecturally of large enclosures and socially of corresponding groups of persons, presumably extended families. This happens to coincide very closely with the current views of those who have sought to reconstruct the social conditions of early Sumer from the cuneiform sources. Thus I. M. Diakonoff has written that "The free community members are organized in extended patriarchal families or family communities" (Diakonoff, 1974, p. 8); while Gelb (1972, p. 90) writes that

> An *oikos*, or household, or manor is not simply a house or family, but a full socio-economic unit, largely self-contained and autarkic, which is needed to support the master of the household and its manifold activities. A household consists of the owners (or managers), labor personnel, and domestic animals, and it contains residential buildings, shelters for the labor force, storage buildings and animal pens, as well as fields, orchards, pastures and forests.

Although both writers base themselves primarily on written sources of a rather later date, the relevance of their reconstructions to the ground plan of our West Mound seems indisputable. Although it may be dangerous to generalize our conclusions on the evidence of a single, unexcavated mound, certain deductions seem inescapable. Large open compounds can hardly have sprung up in an already flourishing city; instead these enclosures, with their buildings occupying only a part of the space, seem typologically to be nothing other than single defended farmsteads brought next to one another for mutual protection, and that could indeed have been their origin. The emergence of many large urban centers in south Mesopotamia is accompanied by a startling drop in the number of small village sites, such that Adams can speak of "the collapse of rural settlement in ED I times" and can state that "the great Mesopotamian cities grew at the expense of smaller rural settlements in their hinterlands" (Adams and Nissen, 1972, pp. 17-19).

That this part of the city at Abu Salabikh may have been of quite recent origin could also be suspected from the very fact that it had retained this kind of layout. Over the years pressure of space in any thriving city would normally lead to the breakdown and eventual disappearance of such compounds, as each family group made optimum use of the space at its disposal. It would, therefore, be instructive to recover for comparison an area of Early Dynastic III housing at Abu Salabikh, to see what differences might have emerged in the course of the 500 years or so in question. To date, the only area of housing with which we could make a comparison is provided by the houses round the Temple Oval enclosure at Khafajah, and there at least we have a more familiar city layout.

Mention of the Temple Oval raises another aspect of town planning to which the West Mound may have something to contribute. The spectacle of a residential house standing independently within a large enclosure is very reminiscent of one of the most unusual features of Early Dynastic architecture, the temple ovals. Enclosures round a temple, similar to that at Khafajah, have been found at Al-Ubaid (near Ur), and at Al-Hiba (ancient Lagash) in southern Sumer, and yet no very satisfactory explanation of their design has been put forward. If, however, the normal private "house" at the beginning of the 3d millennium B.C. also consisted of a large enclosure-wall with buildings constructed independently inside it, these temple ovals would only be an exaggerated version of the same thing. The Sumerian temple was nothing more than the "house"—by which we mean the household or *oikos* as described above—of the god, and one would, therefore, have no cause for surprise if in architectural terms it turned out to be no other than a scaled up version of the ordinary mortal's house. If the temples retained this aspect longer than secular establishments (and that is not certain), it can easily be accounted for because ecclesiastical architecture is regularly more conservative, and the temples would have been less subject to the economic or social constraints that led to the dispersal of the Early Dynastic I private compounds.

If we seem to have pursued our results on the West Mound too far into the realm of theory, there is another aspect of the work that is more tangible and not uninstructive. During the clearance of the surface the artifacts lying on and just below the surface were gathered, and recorded square by square. In the narrower context, this has served the purpose of dating the buildings uncovered, but the procedure has wider implications because of the widespread use of surface collections by archeologists studying Mesopotamia to provide data on the dates, character, and size of the sites. For those who make use of such information to make deductions about what lies beneath, an intensive collection such as we have made will in itself be worth studying in detail, and when this is combined with a knowledge of what actually lay beneath—as revealed by eventual excavation (see Part III of this report)—the combination should supply welcome confirmation and/or cautionary lessons as to the validity and precision of the method. In the case of the West Mound, we have known since before we began clearance that it was predominantly of Early Dynastic I date, and this was confirmed by finds stratified within the buildings. However, as we moved toward the second high point of the mound, at its southeastern end, we met a much higher concentration of shards from the type-fossil of the Uruk period *par excellence*, the beveled-rim bowl. As emerges from their quantitative distribution, there was a significant absence of certain types (e.g., the conical bowl or the solid-footed goblet), which were regularly found on the Early Dynastic I parts of the *tell*, and a corresponding preponderance of the beveled-rim bowl. Moreover, "new" pottery types appeared or became much more common in this part of the mound, and it became clear that the pottery indicated that what lay beneath would date to the Uruk period. Fortunately, the clearance provided some support for this conclusion: Except for the very base of some walls there are no surviving structures here in the planoconvex bricks characteristic of the Early Dynastic period, which would have belonged with the enclosure walls. Instead, erosion has taken the surface down to a layer of ashy fill, and associated with this, on the extreme eastern edge of the area cleared, there are at least two walls built with rectangular bricks—a generally recognized indicator of Uruk date.

The Northeast Mound

Work at the Northeast Mound was wished upon us in 1977 when contractor's machinery cut through the west end of this small *tell*, revealing a settlement of the first half of the Early Dynastic period. Before then we had not known of the existence of this mound, since it was low and concealed by standing crops, but it clearly stands in a close relationship to the main site, together with the Northwest Mound nearby. During 1977 we were not able to do more than tidy up some of the disturbed areas and record some walls and graves, and although this gave us a rough idea of the site's date and nature, we thought it necessary to make a carefully recorded sounding to the bottom of the site, to determine the date of the first occupation. This we more or less achieved in 1978, showing that it began only in the Early Dynastic period, but the size of the sounding was much reduced because the work was arrested by the presence of no less than 4 contemporary burials, in successive levels. Although these were of some interest in their own right, and 2 were accompanied by handsome arrays of beads, they were unfortunately not provided with pottery for the afterlife, which would have been a welcome addition to our corpus of pottery for this period. In 1979, when we were not in fact supposed to be excavating, some compensation for this was provided by the accidental discovery of another Early Dynastic I grave, at the west side of the mound, in which were 3 solid-footed goblets and 4 jars, making a valuable associated group.

Area E

The excavations in Area E during 1978 had three main objectives: to make a deep sounding in the Southern Unit, to enlarge the plans of the Central Complex and the Eastern Houses, and to sieve a sample of the ash-tip to recover paleobotanical evidence. In 6G64b, just southeast of our earlier sounding in 6G54c, described above in Part I, we dug beneath the foundations of the Southern Unit and met an identical sequence: Resting on virgin soil are the thick walls of a brick building, which was rebuilt on at least three occasions. This we designated Level III, and it dates to the Early Dynastic I period. At about +5 m, or some 3 m above virgin soil, these walls were shaved flat as part of a major reconstruction, and the area then served, in Level II, as an open court, containing kilns from which there are many ashy layers. These deposits also contained an unusual double burial, in a shallow pit only 30 cm in depth (Fig. 4). Especially in 1978 we recovered a large number of potsherds from this level, which provide us with an excellent uncontaminated body of Early Dynastic II pottery. From elsewhere in the Central Complex it is apparent that Level II represents an earlier version of the Level I building, when the activities of the Southern Unit must have been housed somewhere else; but whether Level III is also an earlier incarnation of the same establishment must remain uncertain, since it lies too deep for any extensive investigation, at least at present.

Coming down (or rather, up) into the Early Dynastic III period and Level I, 4 new squares were opened to the north. These have added something to the overall layout of the building in Level I, and additions were also made to the northwest side of the Eastern Houses, which, although separated by a wide street, are probably closely connected with the Central Complex. Many graves and later intrusions had destroyed most of the walls in this area, and since the graves themselves were for the most part close to the surface, they too had suffered considerable disturbance.

While this necessary task of pursuing the plan of the building to its limits was inevitably rather unexciting, a compensation was provided by

FIGURE 4. Double inhumation of children in debris in Level II courtyard (Grave 149).

the unexpected result of our small sounding in 6G76, into the ash-tips falling away from the southeastern wall of the whole complex. We had selected this rubbish as a promising source of carbonized plant remains, especially seeds, in an attempt to recover evidence about the diet and agriculture of the population. Dr. Rosemary Ellison, from the Institute of Archaeology in London, nobly undertook the tedious task of supervising the sieving, water-sieving, and flotation of the soil from a specified area, but without recovering any significant quantity of seeds, since none were present. Fortunately, a much better sample of botanical material was recovered from the Eastern Houses, and the labor was not by any means lost, because the deposits contained other, more traditional items of archeological interest, many of which would probably have escaped the usual processes of excavation. Numerically the largest group was more than 150 pieces of clay sealings, many of which bear the impressions of seals. Some of them may have come from bales of cloth or other merchandise, but others have on their reverse the clear imprint of a wooden peg, with string wound round it, which results from a known method of securing doors by tying them to a peg in the wall, and which implies that these sealings had, in fact, been affixed to the doors of storerooms within the building from which they were thrown.

That the rooms in question, which are probably still unexcavated, did house commercial or administrative activities, is supported by the next most frequent category of object from the ash-tip, over 100 rough discs, formed by rubbing down a potsherd. These can hardly have been other than counters, which are known to have had a place in Mesopotamian accounting procedures even much later, in the 2d millennium B.C. The sealings themselves await detailed study, but apart from their undoubted interest to the art historian, a cursory look reveals that several of the sealings bear the feeling of the same stamp seal, showing a full-face lion's head. In each case this is stamped over a cylinder-seal rolling, and one has the impression that it may have been the "counter-signature" of an official who witnessed the sealing of the door (or other object) by the holder of the first seal.

Other finds from the ash-tip seem to have less of a commercial or administrative character: These are principally a relatively large number of human and animal clay figurines, many of them very schematic, but some of the human ones approaching the style of contemporary stone sculpture, while there are animals belonging to recognizable species, including pigs, rams, and equids (Fig. 5). There was also a large number of miniature clay vessels, small jars no more than 5 cm in height, and even smaller bowls made by pressing the finger into a lump of clay. These came in quantities unparalleled elsewhere on the site, and the concentration cannot be fortuitous. The only explanation which at present seems to us to fit the facts is that we have here the rubbish cast out from the anterooms of the temple: sealings from the storerooms, counters from the shrine's business quarters, and the miniature pots and figurines being ex-votos submitted by the worshipers and thrown away after the lapse of a suitable time. For this concentration of figurines and miniature pots in a temple we cannot quote any very close Mesopotamian parallels, but at a Palestinian site of the 2d millennium B.C., Nahariya, a large group of miniature vessels was found, and its excavator wrote: "It is clear that such small vessels could have had no practical use, and were, therefore, meant as models offered to the deity in lieu of full-sized vessels" (Ben-Dor, 1950, p. 19), an explanation which could also be transferred without difficulty to the presence of figurines. Whether or not the building is a temple, however, it is beyond doubt that we have as yet failed to locate the shrine that would have been its kernel. Although the rooms that would have been contemporary with the ash-tip are already eroded from the mound, the answer may lie in their forerunners, and this consideration directed our attention to the Southeast Complex, where the major work of 1981 took place.

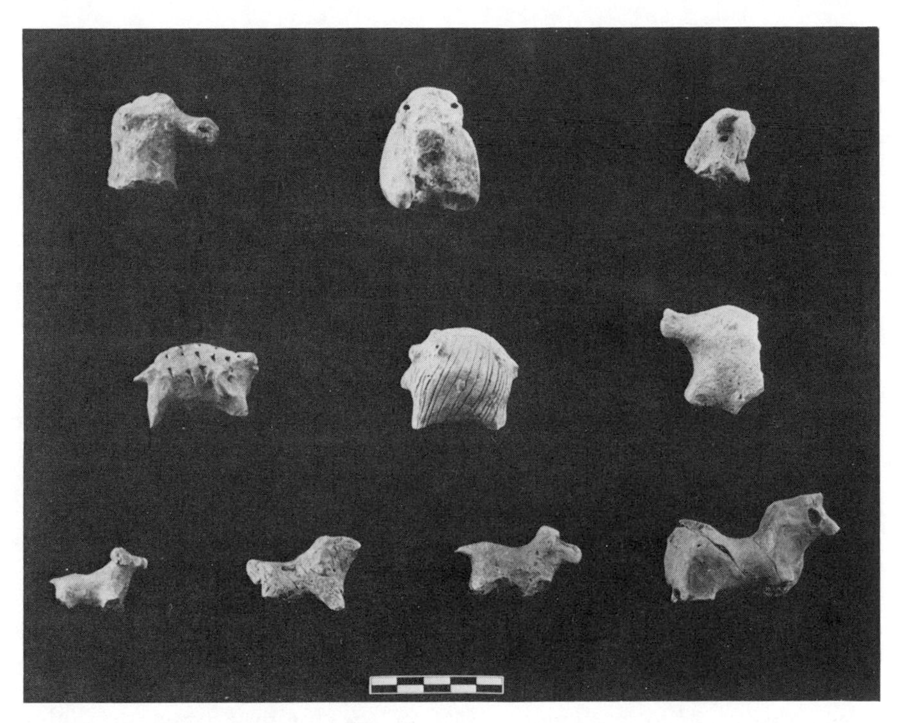

FIGURE 5. Selection of animal figurines, principally from ash-tip; note equids (bottom right and top left).

PART III—EXCAVATION IN 1981

When we began excavations in 1981—postponed unavoidably from 1980 as a result of the Gulf war—our operations in Area E were in the rooms south of the Southern Corridor, in an area now known as the Southeast Complex. Our objectives were to put to the test suspicions that a shrine might be found in this area, and to define the southern limit of the building. However, 40 m to the south of the 1978 excavation limit, there was still no sign of an end to this sprawling composite structure. Three more complexes of courtyards with related rooms were unearthed, and, although the details of the stratigraphy remain to be sorted out, they were certainly in use at the same time as the Southern Unit across the corridor.

The clearest group of newly excavated rooms is perhaps that grouped around Room 85, which was an open court with a bitumened threshold leading into it from Room 83. To the west lay a well-built and carefully plastered long room (Room 86) with rich intramural burials, rather like Room 39 in the Southern Unit. The same courtyard also gave access to Room 90 on the south, which was more than 13 m long, with a clay-plastered floor on which lay much burnt reed. Room 95, which lay to the southwest, was entirely floored and lined with bitumen, with a low sill between the western and eastern halves. Presumably it had some function connected with water. The shrine, or any other proof that the Area E building was a temple, still eludes us. However, the seemingly endless succession of rooms, corridors, and courtyards makes it more, rather than less likely that the temple is indeed where we are. As explained in Part II, the god's household was not different from anyone else's, merely larger and grander. And the more we dig, the larger and grander it turns out to be. Finding the outer walls becomes an even more pressing task, and in 1983 we hope we shall once again be able to devote ourselves to it.

As in previous seasons a number of graves were found dug into the floors and walls of the rooms. These are an inconvenience to the excavator, for it takes time to clear them carefully, and often the architecture he is trying to unravel is destroyed in the process. Nevertheless they are often a source of pottery and other objects surviving far better than under other conditions, and also light up a rather different aspect of Mesopotamian civilization from that revealed by the floors and walls of buildings.

The occupant of Grave 162 had been buried with a pair of equids, perhaps donkeys. They lay together, face to face, forelegs drawn up under their chins. Behind them was a tantalizingly empty space, and we are left guessing whether or not it contained a wooden chariot now completely disintegrated. Otherwise all the ancient robbers left us of this grave was a fragment of copper from over the eye of one of the animals, and some pottery bowls. The grave was dug into a courtyard floor, which had subsided and been relaid over the resulting shaft several times. Just to the south lies another burial with an equid, which awaits our attention next season. The royal tombs at Ur contained both chariots and oxcarts, with their draught animals. These were perhaps slightly later than our Grave 162, while cart and chariot burials at Kish were earlier (Early Dynastic I or II). More recently discovered sites in the Hamrin Basin, and at Usiyah on the Euphrates above Hadithah, have produced graves with teams but no chariots. These are probably of Akkadian date. At Usiyah at least there was not room in the stone-built chambers to fit a chariot too. So we cannot automatically assume that a pair of animals would have been accompanied by a wheeled vehicle.

Grave 176, dug into Room 86, had been unusually richly equipped, but this fact, unfortunately, was known to someone else, and it had been much disturbed by robbing. Much of interest to us, however, was recovered from the resultant large pit dug through it. The metal ornaments

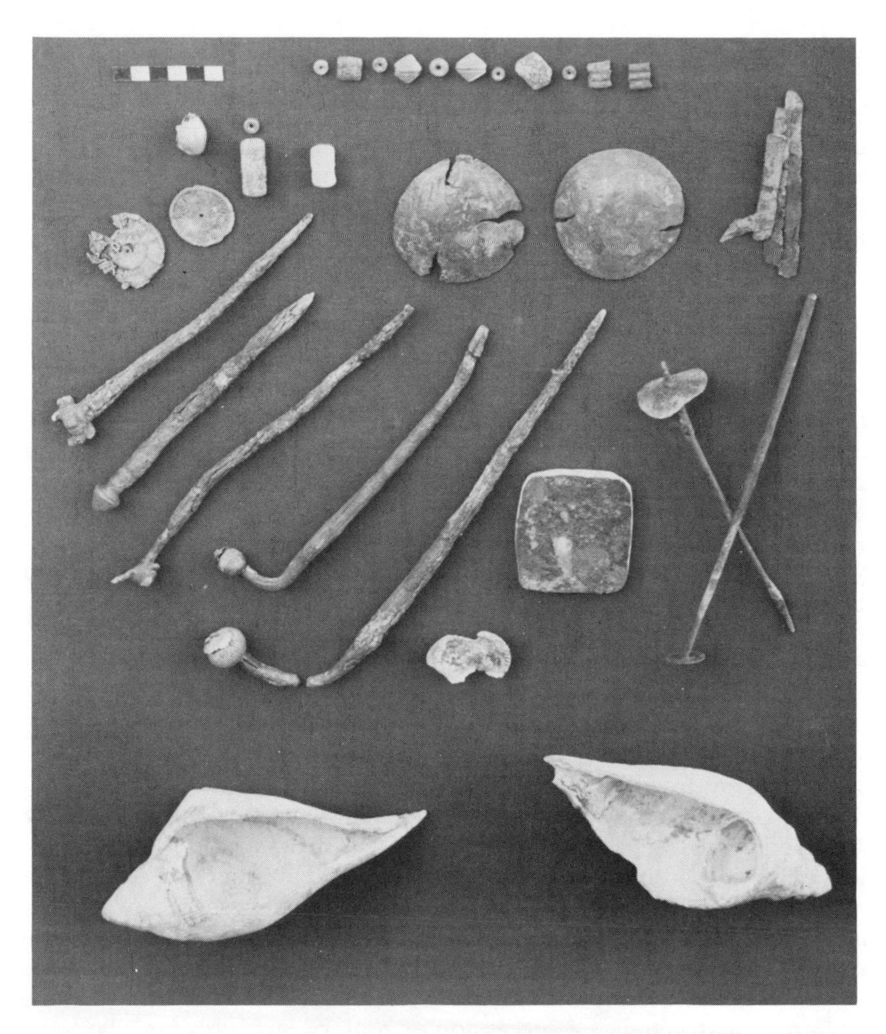

FIGURE 6. Grave goods from Grave 176: jewelry, metalwork, and shells.

from the small remaining undisturbed part of the grave were especially interesting (see Fig. 6). Two copper rods (20 and 24 cm long) were found crossed like swords, with disc heads and blunt ends, quite unlike the pins. Nearby were 2 copper discs, 7 cm across, lying back to back, their faces incised with stylized tree patterns, and accidentally bearing the marks of the cloth in which they had been wrapped. A plaster cast taken from the back of one of them shows what may have been a buckle (of leather?). Other finds from the undisturbed southern end included long pins with heads of different kinds: cast bull-man faces, one with a lapis lazuli head surmounted by a gilded silver cap; a pair of conch shells probably serving as lamps; silver hair ornaments; and a lapis lazuli seal. This last was carved in two registers with a banqueting scene in which figures are sitting on chairs drinking beer through drinking-straws from a communal pot. The copious pottery from the grave included a fragmentary painted bottle of a kind normally found in northern Syria.

Operations in 5I

Until 1981, investigation of the Early Dynastic III occupation of Abu Salabikh had concentrated on the two high points of the main mound, which, as we have seen, seem to represent two large single-building complexes. So this season, in order to find out something about ordinary domestic architecture of this date, it was decided to scrape an area to the southwest of Area A. This was chosen because it lies down, off the slope of the mound, and could, therefore, be expected to be part of the "lower town," while it could still be brought into relation with the excavated building in Area A.

In all, 36 squares, 10 × 10 m, were laid open in the way we had already practiced on the West Mound, revealing a collection of higgledy-piggledy house plans with relatively flimsy walls and irregular shapes, as well as many additions and changes that had been made during their period of use. The general irregularity is also, of course, accentuated in the plan by the nature of scraping, which indiscriminately shows up walls of different phases at the same time. It seems that every house had its own oven, built into the corner of the courtyard or into a specially screened-off alcove. We also found in five places the tops of large jars placed upside down in the ground and blackened on the inside: These, too, were presumably a cooking place of some kind, in two instances associated with a larger oven, and parallels have been found in the Hamrin Basin. In one house we found the top of a vertical drain, plugged with a small stone slab, and constructed of a succession of pottery jars with their bottoms knocked out.

In 5I47 an oven of a distinctly non-culinary nature was uncovered. It took the form of an oval brick-lined pit, filled with ash, clinker, and vitrified scraps of pottery. Clearly this was a pottery kiln. One corner had been cut by a later grave, which although still partly unexcavated has yielded a jar and a cylinder-seal of late Early Dynastic I style. This confirmed our impression from the surface shards that we were dealing not with Early Dynastic III houses, but with buildings some hundreds of years earlier. Further evidence for the earlier date emerged as the scraping operation extended into 5I31, where the ground rises sharply: The southeast corner of the Early Dynastic III building of Area A was exposed, and with it clear stratigraphic proof that it is later than the houses at the base of the slope. Moreover, another grave (Grave 185 in square 5I56) yielded further Early Dynastic I pottery from the very surface of the site. Apart from its date, Grave 185 is interesting because it accommodated at least 5 individuals. The better preserved skeletons seem almost to have been arranged in a large circle with their arms and legs flung out. Two of them were overlapped in this position, but the bodies had not been thrown in for the pottery was quite carefully placed around and among them. No obvious explanation or parallel for this grave is immediately apparent.

Excavation on the West Mound and Uruk Mound

During 1981 we began the investigation of the earliest occupation certainly represented at Abu Salabikh: the Late Uruk period, the time during which writing was first invented in Mesopotamia. In the spring Prof. T. Cuyler Young, Jr., of the Royal Ontario Museum spent three weeks with us, working on the Uruk Mound. The scraping of the surface in 7 10-m strips did not reveal any architecture, in contrast to the success we have had with this technique on the Early Dynastic mounds, but a sounding of 2 × 2 m went down through thick deposits of the Late Uruk period, which Prof. Young considers likely to be associated with a substantial building nearby to the east. Readily accessible sites of the critical Uruk period are not as frequent as might be supposed, and this mound offers an excellent prospect for future work.

In the autumn we returned to the West Mound, having processed and virtually written up the results of the scraping operation, in order to excavate and put our conclusions to the test. A trench was opened in 2G36-46 (20 × 4 m), where we knew that Early Dynastic levels were on the surface, so as to achieve a stratified sequence into the Late Uruk levels presumed to lie beneath, while at the same time defining the stratigraphic relationship between the thick, double enclosure wall and the houses that stand within it. We were particularly interested in the transitional phase between Uruk and Early Dynastic, often called the "Jamdat Nasr" period and best known for its black and red painted pottery.

In 3G81, where we knew Late Uruk pottery was already at the surface, we opened an area of 10 × 4 m, as a control. Near to this trench we also investigated the contents of two more domestic ovens or kilns which had been used for baking bricks or pottery, or both. All these installations were of the Late Uruk period, with the characteristic pottery types of the period, with plentiful ugly handmade beveled-rim bowls, combed greyware jars with handles, and common use of burnishing on bowls and jars. Jars were vegetable-tempered, hand-formed, and finished on the wheel. In addition, there were interesting transitional forms: bowls that were wheel-thrown, like Early Dynastic conical bowls, but with a beveled rim like the Uruk type.

Pottery exactly like that in 3G81, on the surface, was found in 2G36-46 for the lowest 3 m before we reached water, showing that this part of the mound must have been occupied more recently. Above these levels with Uruk pottery the beveled-rim bowls and soft, vegetable-tempered pottery was absent, and instead we found grit-tempered, wheel-thrown jars, often with four tabs at the rim, and typical Early Dynastic I solid-footed goblets—these by the hundred! This change in the style of the pottery coincided with the first construction of the thick enclosure wall already detected in 1977 by surface scraping. The cross section through the double wall revealed that it had been originally only a single, 2-m-wide wall, to which frequent additions were made, culminating with the black brick wall that runs parallel on the south. Thus it became a multiple enclosure wall that has parallels at a later date at Lagash (Al-Hiba) and at contemporary sites in the Hamrin Basin on the Diyala to the northeast.

The abrupt transition just described leaves us with a problem: Did the break in the architectural and ceramic sequence involve a lapse of time or not? And how does it relate to the Jamdat Nasr period? We did encounter occasional rather sad fragments of what must have been splendid polychrome vessels, but they were rare and do not suffice to define an entire period. Few other pottery types are generally recognized to be clear indicators of Jamdat Nasr date, but if the wheel-thrown beveled-rim bowls mentioned above were chronologically as well as stylistically transitional, we may have put our finger on one. In that case the gap in time, if there was one, was slight: But this is an important issue which will require further testing.

REFERENCES

Items marked with an asterisk (*) are preliminary or specialists' reports based on the British expedition's work at the site from 1975 to 1981.

ADAMS, ROBERT McC.
1981. Heartland of cities. University of Chicago Press, Chicago.

ADAMS, ROBERT McC., and NISSEN, HANS J.
1972. The Uruk countryside. University of Chicago Press, Chicago.

BEN-DOR, I.
1950. Nahariya excavation report. Quarterly of the Department of Antiquities of Palestine, vol. 14, p. 19.

BIGGS, ROBERT D.
1967. Semitic names in the Fara period. Orientalia, nova series, vol. 36, pp. 55-66. Pontifical Biblical Institute, Rome.

1974. Inscriptions from Tell Abū Ṣalābīkh. Oriental Institute Publications, vol. 99. University of Chicago Press, Chicago. (The definitive publication of the inscriptions from 1963 and 1965.)

BIGGS, ROBERT D., and POSTGATE, JOHN NICHOLAS
*1978. Inscriptions from Abu Salabikh, 1975. Iraq, vol. 40, pp. 101-118.[1]

CLUTTON-BROCK, JULIET P., and BURLEIGH, RICHARD
*1978. The animal remains from Abu Salabikh: Preliminary report. Iraq, vol. 40, pp. 89-100.[1]

DIAKONOFF, IGOR MIKHAILOVICH
1974. Structure of society and state in Early Dynastic Sumer. Sources and Monographs: Monographs of the Ancient Near East, vol. 1, no. 3. UNDENA publications, Los Angeles.

GELB, I. J.
1972. From freedom to slavery. Pp. 81-92 *in* "Gesellschaftsklassen im alten Zweistromland, XVIII. Rencontre assyriologique internationale," D. O. Edzard, ed. München.

KRECHER, JOACHIM
1978. Sumerische Literatur der Fara-Zeit: Die UD.GAL.NUN-Texte. Pp. 155-160 *in* "Bibliotheca Orientalis" 35. Leiden.

MOON, JANE A.
*1981. Some new Early Dynastic pottery from Abu Salabikh. Iraq, vol. 43, pp. 47-75.[1]

PAYNE, JOAN CROWFOOT
*1980. An Early Dynastic III flint industry from Abu Salabikh. Iraq, vol. 42, pp. 105-119.[1]

POSTGATE, JOHN NICHOLAS
*1977. Excavations at Abu Salabikh, 1976. Iraq, vol. 39, pp. 269-299.[1]
*1978. Excavations at Abu Salabikh, 1977. Iraq, vol. 40, pp. 77-88.[1]
*1980a. Early Dynastic burial practices at Abu Salabikh. Sumer, vol. 36, pp. 65-82.[2]
*1980b. Excavations at Abu Salabikh, 1978-79. Iraq, vol. 42, pp. 87-104.[1]

POSTGATE, JOHN NICHOLAS, and MOOREY, P. ROGER S.
*1976. Excavations at Abu Salabikh, 1975. Iraq, vol. 38, pp. 133-169.[1]

J. N. POSTGATE
J. A. MOON

[1] Publication of the British School of Archaeology in Iraq, London.
[2] Publication of the State Organization for Antiquities and Heritage, Baghdad.

Population Ecology of European Mute Swans in Chesapeake Bay

Grant Recipient: Jan G. Reese, St. Michaels, Maryland.

Grants 1573, 1746, 1902: To study nest success, seasonal movements, and distribution of feral swans.

The European Mute Swan *(Cygnus olor)* has been cherished as a symbol of purity and elegance for centuries. European immigrants perpetuated this belief and practice in North America by bringing European Mute Swans to their parks, zoos, and private estates shortly after the turn of this century. Some of these exotic swans eventually escaped or were purposely released into the wild, where they began nesting. A similar series of events gave rise to the presence of European Mute Swans in Chesapeake Bay. A mated pair of pinioned Mute Swans escaped captivity from an impoundment at a waterfront estate along the Eastern Bay tributary of east-central Chesapeake Bay in March 1962. These swans successfully nested there in the wild that summer, and the flock had increased its numbers to 18 by 1968 and to 151 by 1974 (Reese, 1969, 1975).

By volume, the European Mute Swan is the largest species of bird on the North American continent; males approach a weight of 13.5 kg and have a 2.5-m wingspan. These swans are a territorial species that exhibits aggressive behavior, especially in defense of its territory when nesting. They are sedentary and feed on submerged aquatic vegetation. Several thousand European Mute Swans are now in coastal and estuarine habitats along the Atlantic Coast, from New Hampshire to Virginia, in the Grand Traverse Bay area of Lake Michigan, and on southeastern Vancouver Island, British Columbia.

The Chesapeake Bay is one of the primary waterfowl wintering areas in the Atlantic flyway. A large sedentary population of an aggressive, vegetarian waterfowl of this size could have a detrimental effect on both the ecology of the Chesapeake Bay and the future of native waterfowl. I monitored nest success, population expansion, and distribution of the flock from 1962 through 1975. Associate George Fenwick and I used the 1976-1978 National Geographic Society grants to broaden the study of seasonal movements, life histories, and population dynamics as a prerequisite for future management or control of this potential nuisance species. There is one other North American Mute Swan study (Willey and

Halla, 1972), while several comprehensive studies are available for European swans (Berglund et al., 1963; Minton, 1968; Jenkins et al., 1976).

Auxiliary Markers

Volunteers and I marked 141 swans with aluminum U. S. Fish and Wildlife Service (USFWS) leg bands and auxiliary markers of coded plastic neck and tarsus bands in 1971-1975. All nesting pairs and young were banded in 1971, and the progeny of all successful nests were banded each year thereafter. Unmarked swans over 1 year old were sometimes captured for banding during the mid-1970s; these swans were thought to be young fledged before 1971. It is believed, therefore, that the entire Chesapeake population was banded.

Neckbands 8 cm wide were marked in a contrasting color several times around with a 2.5-cm-tall, vertical code of two letters and two numbers. The tarsus bands were 4 cm wide and had codes 1.5 cm in height. Coded neckbands could be read as far away as 350 m with a 30-40-X spotting scope, and thus permitted recognition of individual swans without recapture.

Most of the data compiled on life histories, social organization, and dynamics of the population prior to 1976 were based on over 2000 resightings of these marked swans. It was imperative that this banding and resighting effort be continued in 1976-1978. This phase of the study, however, required a greater expenditure of time, manpower, and finances each year as a result of the nearly exponential annual growth of the population. In 1976-1978, 191 additional swans were fitted with USFWS bands and auxiliary neck and leg markers, and almost 10,000 resightings compiled. Benjamin Bright and Lawrence Hindman of the Maryland Department of Natural Resources, Wildlife Administration, were instrumental in assisting with manpower, equipment, and auxiliary markers for banding. Volunteers Linda Gibson and family made over 4000 neckband resightings during the period.

Some of the more important facts learned from resighting of the auxiliary-marked swans are as follows: Of the female swans, 4% paired when less than 1 year old and 13% nested as 1-year-olds. Most paired at age 2 and began nesting by their third year. No males paired before their first birthday, and only 1.7% nested as 1-year-olds. Time between pairing and nesting for 87 swans was 1 year for 63%, less than a year for 28%, and 2 years for 9%. Incestuous pairing and nesting were observed six times during the study. Male survivorship from one year to the next averaged 90% during 1971-1978, and females averaged 89%. Swans 2 years old or older constituted 52% of the population in 1971-1978, while only 35% of the population actively engaged in nesting. Males dominated all age classes with their lowest mean ratio of 54% before the first birthday. A comprehensive analysis of the population demography is presented in Reese (1980).

Distribution and Seasonal Movements

Eastern Chesapeake tidal water between lat. 38° 30′N and 39° 10′N was surveyed from an altitude of 300 m in a Cessna 172 approximately every 30 days from March through September during the years 1976-1978, to monitor swan population numbers, seasonal movements, nest territories, and distribution. All Chesapeake tidal water north of lat. 38° 25′N was included in at least two of the surveys each year. Locations of swan flocks and territories were later visited for study by boat. Areas where flocking occurred regularly were surveyed weekly from ground vantage points until the flock disbanded. Each swan nesting territory was visited by boat five or more times during each nesting season. Personal observations of swan nests or flocks were solicited from residents viewing these activities on their property.

European Mute Swans were observed during 1976-1978 in every major Chesapeake Bay tributary north of lat. 38° 30′N except the Elk River. Swan activity was concentrated, however, in the tributaries of the Chester River, Eastern Bay, and Choptank River on the northeastern side of the Chesapeake. Nesting swans were seen only in these three major tributaries.

While molting their remiges, all nonnesting swans joined a single flock at some time between July and September. A brackish tributary 0.9 km long and 0.3 km wide on the north end of Eastern Neck Island National Wildlife Refuge was used by the molting flock. The estuary lies in a northwest-southeast position and contains water over a meter deep at mid-stream during low tide, and a dense bed of Eurasian milfoil *(Myriophyllum spicatum).* Tides are semidiurnal and rise and fall 45 cm. Approximately 28 ha of marsh land, predominantly *Scirpus americanus* grass, lines the tributary, especially the southwest portion where the margin is over 200 m wide. The marsh is deeply dissected by small, irregular natural channels, in which the swans can hide. Water depth is less than 1/2 m off the entrance to the tributary and this serves as a natural deterrent to boats. These conditions and parameters provide food, cover, and protection for the molting flock during the flightless period when they are vulnerable to human harassment. Most individuals remained a part of the molting flock for about 50 days, and a few swans were still present into October. The molting swans had completely dispersed by early November when the native, migrant Whistling Swans *(Olor columbianus)* arrived in the upper Chesapeake Bay.

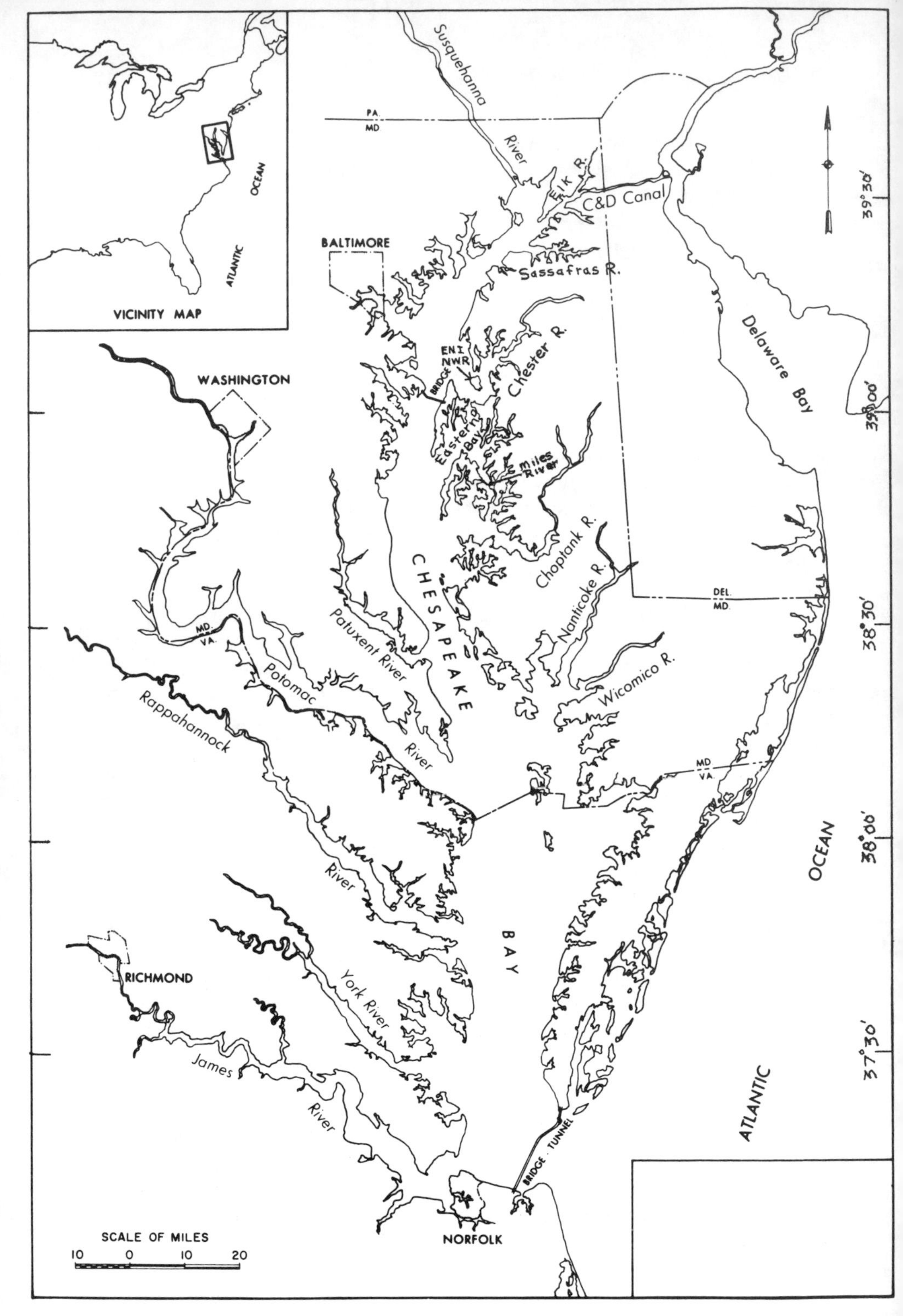

FIGURE 1. Chesapeake Bay study area.

Flocks of up to 40 swans were occasionally seen in tributaries of the east-central Chesapeake Bay in December and January, but most swans gathered in smaller flocks during these months. In February and March, the nonnesting swans were dispersed in pairs or small flocks. During this time there was a stationary flock of 25 to 30 swans at the mouth of Spencers Creek, on Miles River in the Eastern Bay. Observations of auxiliary-marked swans at this location showed that individuals remained a member of the flock for only a few days. The size of the flock remained constant, despite the high rate of turnover in membership. The designation of this location and the purpose of every member of the population visiting there at this time of year was not ascertained. During April through June the nonnesting swans ranged throughout the northern half of Chesapeake Bay in pairs and flocks of less than 10 swans. Sexually mature swans that had previously nested remained all year in their territories or home ranges.

Reproductive Success

European Mute Swan nests were located by aerial and boat surveys of shorelines. Reproductive success was studied by visiting each nest every 12 days during the nesting season. A total of 100 nesting attempts (involving 40 individual pairs) was studied during 1976-1978. Eggs were found in 92% of the nests, eggs hatched in 66%, and young fledged from 55%. A total of 487 eggs was studied; of these, 51% hatched and young fledged from 40%. The percentage of hatchlings that fledged was 78. The average clutch size was 5.3, and the average brood size was 3.7. The average number of young fledged per nest with eggs was 2.1. These reproductive parameters were comparable to those observed in the same area in 1969-1979 (Reese, 1980).

The causes of 242 egg losses were variable. Most notable were 121 eggs that disappeared between nest visits, 33 that were abandoned in nests, 27 that were flooded by high tides, 27 that were found outside the nest, and 19 that were found as fragments. Eggs may have been abandoned because the swan was unable to keep them warm during flooding. Eggs found trapped in marsh vegetation outside nests indicate that some of those that disappeared may have been carried away by tidal action. These factors suggest that flooding of nests by spring tides was responsible for most egg losses. Flooding was the major cause of egg loss in other studies (Perrins and Reynolds, 1967; Willey and Halla, 1972). Additionally, 10 eggs were addled, and someone drilled holes in 5 eggs to counter reproductive success.

A total of 43 young disappeared between nest visits. People daily observing swans near their waterfront estates report young swans being preyed upon by marine turtles *(Chelydra serpentina* and *Malaclemys terrapin)*. Most young swans that disappeared were less than 40 days old; turtles or other predators may be responsible for many of these losses. Six young in several different broods appeared injured or sick before disappearing, and I can offer no explanation for these losses. A terrestrial predator killed 2 young, and a hatchling was found dead in a nest after a chilling rain.

Population Expansion

Annual population numbers were derived from actual counts taken during aerial and ground surveys, observed reproductive success, and life tables compiled from resightings of auxiliary-marked swans in 1971-1978. The Chesapeake population consisted of 203, 274, and 315 swans, respectively, during the years 1976-1978. The mean rate of population increase was 42% annually during the first decade, 27% the first 6 years of the second decade (1972-1978), and 36% for the 16 years since the original swans escaped into the wild.

REFERENCES

BERGLUND, B. E.; CURRY-LINDAHL, K.; LUTHER, H.; OLSSON, V.; RODHE, W.; and SELLERBERG, G.
1963. Ecological studies on the Mute Swan *(Cygnus olor)* in southeastern Sweden. Acta Vert., vol. 2, no. 2, pp. 167-288.

JENKINS, D.; NEWTON, I.; and BROWN, C.
1976. Structure and dynamics of a Mute Swan population. Wildfowl, vol. 27, no. 1, pp. 77-82.

MINTON, C. D.
1968. Pairing and breeding of Mute Swans. Wildfowl, vol. 19, no. 1, pp. 41-60.

PERRINS, C. M., and REYNOLDS, C. M.
1967. A preliminary study of the Mute Swan *(Cygnus olor)*. Wildfowl, vol. 18, no. 1, pp. 74-84.

REESE, J. G.
1969. Mute Swans breeding in Talbot County, Maryland. Maryland Birdlife, vol. 25, no. 1, pp. 14-16.
1975. Productivity and management of feral Mute Swans in Chesapeake Bay. Journ. Wildl. Management, vol. 39, no. 2, pp. 280-286.
1980. Demography of European Mute Swans in Chesapeake Bay. Auk, vol. 97, no. 3, pp. 449-464.

WILLEY, C. H., and HALLA, B. F.
1972. Mute Swans of Rhode Island. Rhode Island Dept. Nat. Res., Div. Fish & Wildl., pamphlet 8.

JAN G. REESE

Evolution of Brachiopods

Grant Recipient: Joyce R. Richardson, New Zealand Oceanographic Institute, Wellington, New Zealand.

Grants 1577, 1944, 2380: For study of the marine environment of Recent brachiopod faunas, of evolutionary mechanisms in living brachiopods, and of the evolution of brachiopods.

Environments of Living Brachiopods

Brachiopods are the only animals now alive that occur in the same apparent form as they did at the beginning of the fossil record (approximately 600 million years ago). These animals are therefore a prime source of information on the earliest fossiliferous periods of the earth's history. Their abundance during most geological eras and their rarity in modern seas means that most information about the phylum has been derived from its fossil representatives.

The aim of the first of the three expeditions was to locate previously reported but unpublished sources in southern New Zealand and from these to record the characteristics of species and the nature of the environments. Although the members of these expeditions found prolific sources of living brachiopods, neither the characteristics of the animals nor the environments they occupied conformed with current concepts of the phylum and the distribution of its members. Therefore, a second expedition was planned to sample and study the faunas in a manner that would establish the validity of our observations.

The dominant impression of all fieldworkers engaged in the project was the opportunism exhibited by some species. Articulate brachiopods have been long considered as a sessile hard-bottom fauna. In our fieldwork we found the same species attached to great varieties of substrate (rock, shells, seaweeds, chitin, ascidian tests) or to be free-lying (without attachment or anchorage) on shell gravel, sand, or mud, from the intertidal zone to depths of 340 m, and in weak or strong currents. Brachiopods are common throughout the study area (Fig. 1) and are the dominant group on the vertical rock walls of the fiords and on the floor of Paterson Inlet, two areas of great environmental contrast. In each of these areas the same brachiopod species are associated with totally different biotic assemblages (Willan, 1981; Grange et al., 1981). One prime aim

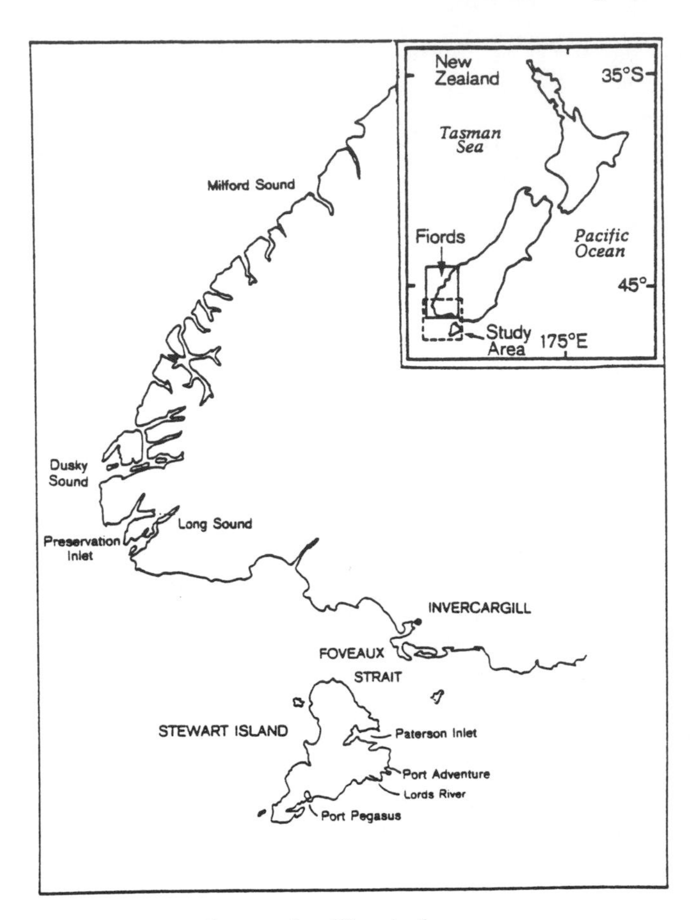

FIGURE 1. The study area.

then (following verification of these observations) was to determine the factors governing such marked environmental tolerances.

PROCEDURE

The first expedition (February 1977) used the private research vessel *Acheron* for eight working days at sea. Six scientific workers and divers sailed from Bluff, the port of Invercargill, to anchor on the first night in Paterson Inlet, Stewart Island. We remained in the inlet for the whole period because large numbers of brachiopods were collected in dredge hauls and further exploration showed that three species were common on intertidal and subtidal rock surfaces and that two of these and one other species comprised the dominant animal group on the floor of the inlet.

Fifty stations were sampled in the inlet. At each of these, water (for salinity and temperature) and sediment samples were collected. Samples of the biota present were collected by scuba from areas of specific size so that estimates of densities in different localities and substrates could be made.

The second expedition (February to March 1979) had two objectives. The first was a closer study of the varied populations occurring in Paterson Inlet. The second was the exploration of other inlets on the east coast of Stewart Island and of neighboring coastal waters—Foveaux Strait and Preservation Inlet at the southwest corner of South Island. The N. Z. Oceanographic Institute's research vessel *Tangaroa* was used for the latter purpose. The Paterson Inlet study was land based (at the island's only motel) and collections were made from boats provided by the N. Z. Forest Service. Fourteen participants in this study represented various institutions and disciplines. We thought it would be profitable if the same collections were studied from the diverse viewpoints of mathematicians, morphologists, geologists, and taxonomists.

Collections by scuba of all the material (biota, living and dead, and sediment) contained within seafloor areas of specific size provided the data from which to establish settlement patterns, population structures, and mortality schedules in benthic populations of the brachiopods. With samples scraped from rock walls, they also provided an estimate of relative densities of brachiopods in relation to other biota and of the substrate preferences of different species. Examination and measurements of individuals provided a record of larval attachment sites and indicated whether any correlations occurred between habitat and shell shape. Some of the material in the collections was used to assess gonad condition and to correlate the soft internal structures with the characters of the shell that enclosed them. Theories of animal movement, orientation, and other aspects of behavior derived from morphological studies were tested by the divers' observations of in situ populations.

Marine Environments

Brachiopods occur in all the inlets along the eastern coast of Stewart Island, in Foveaux Strait, and in all the fiords examined. This whole area is assumed to have been under ice, or dry, during the last ice age: Marine environments in this area of New Zealand arose during the melting of the ice 7000 to 11,000 years ago (Cullen, 1970). Foveaux Strait now separates the relatively shallow drowned river valleys of Stewart Island from the deep, glacier-cut valleys of Fiordland. Thus while the strait, the fiords, and the inlets share the same date of origin as the marine environments, different physiography gives to each segment a different hydrological character.

The contrast in physical conditions in these environments is reflected in the resident biota. The rocky subtidal areas of the inlets contain the algae and molluscs and the sponge-hydroid-ascidian associations found in similar situations throughout New Zealand. The faunas in the fiords are not comparable with those from any other New Zealand area nor have similar subtidal rock wall faunas been described from any other of the world's fiords. The common inhabitants of other subtidal rock surfaces—algae and molluscs—are rare or absent and the walls of the fiords are covered, almost exclusively, by brachiopods, corals, and serpulid polychaetes (Grange et al., 1981). Benthic associations in Foveaux Strait, the inlets, and the fiords show similar contrasts (Willan, 1981).

Results

Nine species, representing three of the five orders of living brachiopods (Acrotretida, Rhynchonellida, Terebratulida) were collected in the study area.

The larval forms of all species examined attach to whatever substrates the environment offers. Vertical rock walls of granite provide the only surfaces for attachment in the fiords and all nine species were found attached to these walls or to the shells of other brachiopods already attached to these surfaces.

In Paterson Inlet granite is again available as outcrops and boulders near the shorelines, but the floor of the inlet provides a large surface area (65 km^2) on which the attachment sites available differ with substrate type. The empty shells of a variety of molluscs together with the shells of living and dead brachiopods are the principal sites of attachment in areas of shell gravel. In muddy sediments the sites of attachment are the shells and shell fragments of the bivalve *Chlamys gemmulata* and the brachiopod *Terebratella sanguinea,* which together comprise the dominant and almost the sole epifauna of muddy sediments in the inlet. Those individuals attached to small shell fragments are effectively free-lying from early growth stages, and larger pieces of shell usually disintegrate before the attached brachiopod grows to maximum adult size. However, pieces of the attachment surface adhere to the tip of the attaching organ (pedicle) and so provide sufficient evidence for later identification. The consequence of the capacity of some brachiopods to use any fragment for settlement means that these species can occur as both attached and free-lying populations.

Four brachiopod species occur in Paterson Inlet and only three of these occur in both attached and free-lying populations. Those species found only as attached populations (in areas where other alternatives are available) possess a pedicle of a type different from that characteristic of species that may occur in virtually any habitat and in which use of the pedicle as an adult attaching device seems unnecessary for growth and survival. The pedicle has always been considered to be uniform in structure and function in articulate brachiopods but these studies have shown that the pedicle and its musculature displays greater variability than other brachiopod systems (Richardson, 1979).

In Paterson Inlet individuals of the same species are found attached to rock walls in areas of strong surge or current and are also found free-lying, at no particular orientation in mud (Richardson, 1981a). The individuals from populations in each of these environments are similar in overall size and in growth increments (Aldridge, 1981).

It appears, therefore, that the physiological requirements of brachiopods are such that they operate effectively in diverse physical conditions. Nor were any differences observed in the nature of the feeding or the digestive organs in individuals from different habitats.

In the species studied, clear-cut morphological differences were not apparent in populations from attached or free-lying habitats (Aldridge, 1981). However, differences in habitat could be identified from histograms constructed from populations occupying either attached intertidal or attached subtidal or free-lying benthic habitats (Stewart, 1981).

Conclusions

The prolific populations studied in the course of these expeditions have provided a great deal of insight into a group whose fossil distribution appeared to be so different from that of its living representatives. The distribution of Paleozoic brachiopods can now be accounted for in terms of present-day faunas. Basic data collected on these expeditions show that maintenance systems are as efficient in depositional environments as they are in rocky habitats.

One key factor in this revision of brachiopod characteristics is the realization that attachment is a larval, but not an adult, need in some species. All species studied require a larval settling surface but no morphological or physiological barriers exist to a free-lying existence on soft substrates.

It is suggested that the individual's capacity to function in a wide range of physical conditions results from the association of unchanging and stable maintenance systems with one variable system (the pedicle). This association accounts for the patterns of distribution observed in dense living faunas in New Zealand waters. Marked differences in the biota of the fiords (Grange et al., 1981) and of the inlets (Willan, 1981) express the contrast in the environments occupied by the brachiopods.

Thus these observations contradict existing concepts of articulate brachiopods as sedentary, immobile forms restricted to hard substrates, a pattern of distribution that has always seemed irreconcilable with the fact that most fossil brachiopods have been recovered from originally soft sediments.

In sum, field observations showed that in New Zealand, at least:

- Brachiopods are found on unconsolidated shelf sediments in addition to rocky shoreline habitats.
- Sedentary or sessile life-styles are characteristic of forms occupying rocky shoreline habitats but not of species that live in mud, sand, or gravel.
- Brachiopods have the capacity for motile behavior; motility is the function of the pedicle system which is variable in structure.
- Life-styles appeared to differ with substrate type.

Evolutionary Mechanisms in Brachiopods

From the results of these two expeditions it was concluded (Richardson and Mineur, in press) that previous observations of living articulate brachiopods have been made from forms occupying one habitat only. That is, the characteristics of brachiopods from all marine habitats have been defined from species that may occupy only one of these habitats (and that could also be specialized for that particular habitat). This error of interpretation has always constituted a biological straitjacket for paleontologists who have had to force all articulate brachiopods into one behavioral mold despite the diversity apparent in the hard structures that house the pedicle system. Thus, although brachiopods provide such an abundant, continuous, and accurate record of life in ancient seas, the absence of basic data on living faunas has been a major constraint in the interpretation of fossil species and their habitats.

Our studies of the living had indicated that associations between morphology and behavior and between behavior and substrate could be defined and that it should be possible to test the validity of these associations against the cold facts of the fossil record. The Waitaki Subdivision includes Middle Eocene to Upper Oligocene deposits (Gage, 1957) with extremely rich brachiopod assemblages found in a variety of greensand and limestone sediments. They contain 15 articulate genera, all assumed to have lived as sessile forms attached to hard substrates. Collections were also made from Miocene deposits in the Waipara District (Wilson, 1963) in Northern Canterbury.

Procedure

The principal aim of the fieldwork was to collect populations with known relations in time, and with sufficient well-preserved specimens to analyze morphologically and statistically.

Statistical design was a major part of the collecting program to ensure that other workers would be able to test conclusions derived from fossil collections. In addition, new methods of measuring morphological variables had been established in preliminary work. Previous methods had proved inadequate because they employed sets of measurements devised for bivalve molluscs. The shape and curvature of the beak needed to be incorporated in any assessment of variables because it is one of the most valuable sources of information on life habit. Measurements of individuals were made by using a simulated digitizing table (overhead projector and graph paper). Several methods of shape analysis were applied to these measurements and it was found that canonical variate analysis highlighted differences in shape (Aldridge, in preparation).

Fieldworkers excavated large blocks of substrate from 16 localities in the Waitaki area. At a working base in Oamaru, specimens were removed from successive layers, then cleaned, sorted, and analyzed to provide information on habitat type and life-style.

Information on habitat type was obtained from sediment analyses and from the population structure of different species—a method established by Stewart (1981) from studies of living species which showed that some habitat types could be determined by a combination of length frequency curves, adult size, and shell growth patterns. Life-style was determined by reconstruction of soft anatomies and comparison with living forms with known behavior patterns.

Results and Conclusions

Two types of faunal assemblage could be recognized within the numerous fossil localities investigated. The members of one of these assemblages possess the morphological characteristics associated with species that occupy rocky shorelines in Recent seas and are found in the relatively rare shell limestones. The second assemblage, which occurs in greensands and fine-grained limestones, shows the morphological (and population) characteristics of species found only in unconsolidated sediments in modern seas. Therefore some deposits contain a group of sedentary cliff-hanging species, others a group of bottom-dwelling species that would have been free-living and motile in life (Mineur and Richardson, in press). Both assemblages are abundant in different types of sediment but the area occupied by the medium- to fine-grained sediments (in which the benthic group occur) far exceeded that of the shell limestones.

Therefore, from brachiopod evidence only, the Oligocene deposits of the Waitaki District (in which brachiopods are the principal faunas) do represent some rocky shoreline habitats but they are derived principally from level bottom, soft, benthic sediments and their contained faunas.

This conclusion is consistent with evidence from other fossil remains such as whale bones (Fleming, 1979).

Comparisons of the two types of brachiopod assemblage throughout long time sequences also showed that sedentary species (from shell limestones) show little change in form throughout the Cenozoic period and they show clear lines of descent. In fact, brachiopod communities found in present-day rocky shoreline habitats consist of similar aggregates of species to those found in Eocene and Oligocene deposits. Moreover free-living species are not found in deposits younger than mid-Miocene and it is assumed that all six genera *(Aetheia, Neobouchardia, Pachymagas, Rhizothyris, Stethothyris, Waiparia)* are extinct.

This marked difference in the continuity of different types of faunal assemblage may be attributed to changes in the substrate type available in different eras. The sedentary genera found in Tertiary deposits occupied the same habitat and substrate type as living forms occupy in Recent seas—the rocky shoreline intertidal and shallow subtidal areas of the New Zealand coast or its offshore islands. However, the Oligocene greensands and their contained faunas do not occur in the post-Oligocene deposits in other parts of New Zealand. Their absence can be attributed to tectonic activity and regressive phases that have taken place during the Tertiary period in New Zealand.

Many free-living species are found in the extensive bryozoan limestones of the Miocene and like their Oligocene counterparts, are not found in later deposits or in Recent seas. In Recent seas, the only free-living forms collected are species of one genus *Neothyris* and they are found on sediments that consist of a thin layer of shell debris overlying mud or muddy sand.

This information has provided insight into factors that lead to extinction and that promote or inhibit change.

Extinction. The disappearance of free-living benthic species during the New Zealand Miocene bears some similarity to worldwide extinction events such as the Permo-Triassic. In both instances, species adapted for life on unconsolidated sediments have become extinct while surviving forms appear to have been sedentary. Species that are pediculate and that can follow both sedentary and free life-styles (modern analogues are species of *Terebratella,* see Richardson, 1981b) may provide the stock from which free-living forms evolve when benthic habitats are available.

Change. Rates of change in populations seem to be related directly to the availability of habitats (i.e., substrates). Change occurs more rapidly with any restriction in the substrates available for settlement in a particular area. For example, in some areas both hard and unconsolidated substrates are available for settlement. The species that occupy these areas and can live as both sedentary and free forms exhibit little change from ancestral species inferred to have occupied similar habitats since the beginning of the Eocene. In areas in which hard substrates only are available for larval settlement (e.g., steep rock walls of fiord basins) populations follow only one life-style and this is evident in their morphology (Aldridge, 1981). Similarly, the availability of extensive areas of unconsolidated sediments (e.g., Chatham Rise, Campbell Plateau) apparently leads to the evolution of free-living forms such as species of *Neothyris*. This evolutionary process culminates in exclusively free-living forms because the morphological features associated with free life on benthic sediments are incompatible with a sedentary adult life-style.

REFERENCES

ALDRIDGE, A. E.
1981. Intraspecific variation of shape and size in 2 Recent New Zealand articulate brachiopods. N.Z. Journ. Zool., vol. 8, pp. 164-169.
____. Systems of measurement for brachiopods. (In preparation.)

CULLEN, D. J.
1970. Radiocarbon analyses of individual molluscan species in relation to postglacial eustatic changes. Palaeogr. Palaeoclim. Palaeoecol., vol. 7, pp. 13-20.

FLEMING, C. A.
1979. The geological history of New Zealand and its life, 141 pp. Oxford University Press.

GAGE, M.
1957. Geology of the Waitaki Subdivision. N.Z. Geol. Surv. Bull., no. 55, new ser.

GRANGE, K. R.; SINGLETON, R. S.; RICHARDSON, J. R.; HILL, P. F.; and MAIN, W.
1981. Shallow rock-wall biological associations of the southern fiords of New Zealand. N.Z. Journ. Zool., vol. 8, pp. 209-228.

MINEUR, R. J. and RICHARDSON, J. R.
____. Free and mobile brachiopods from New Zealand Oligocene deposits and Australian waters. Alcheringa. (In press.)

RICHARDSON, JOYCE R.
1979. The pedicle structure of articulate brachiopods. Journ. Roy. Soc. N.Z., vol. 9, pp. 415-436.
1981a. Distribution and orientation of six articulate brachiopod species from New Zealand. N.Z. Journ. Zool., vol. 8, pp. 189-196.
1981b. Brachiopods in mud—resolution of a dilemma. Science, vol. 221, pp. 1161-1163.
1981c. Brachiopods and pedicles. Paleobiology, vol. 7, pp. 87-95.
1981d. Recent brachiopods from New Zealand—background to the study cruises of 1977-79. N.Z. Journ. Zool., vol. 8, pp. 133-143.
1982. Contribution on brachiopods to the Red Data Book, International Union for the Conservation of Nature.
1983. Brachiopoda. *In* "The New Zealand Biota—What Do We Know After 200 Years," P. J. Brownsey and A. N. Baker, eds. Nat. Mus. N.Z. Misc. Ser. 7.

RICHARDSON, JOYCE R., and MINEUR, R. J.
——. Behavior and survival. Scientific American. (In press.)

STEWARD, I. R.
1981. Population structure of articulate brachiopods from soft and hard substrates. N.Z. Journ. Zool., vol. 8, pp. 190-197.

WILLAN, R. C.
1981. Soft bottom assemblages from Paterson Inlet, Stewart Island. N.Z. Journ. Zool., vol. 8, pp. 210-248.

WILSON, D. D.
1963. Geology of the Waipara Subdivision. N.Z. Geol. Surv. Bull., no. 64, new ser., 122 pp.

JOYCE R. RICHARDSON

Fission-Track Dating of Lower Paleozoic Volcanic Ashes in British Stratotypes

Grant Recipient: R. J. Ross, Jr., U. S. Geological Survey, Denver, Colorado.[1]

Grant 1641: In support of fission-track dating of lower Paleozoic bentonites in British stratotypes.

In order to establish an isotopic, fission-track chronology based on lower Paleozoic British stratotypes, 41 collections of bentonites and other volcanically derived rocks were collected in five main areas of Ordovician and Silurian outcrops in Wales, England, and Scotland in September 1976 (Fig. 1). These are the areas studied by Sedgwick, Murchison, and Lapworth in establishing the lower Paleozoic systems on which our modern work is based (Ross et al., 1977).

Although only 21 of the 41 samples collected have been analyzed, they had provided minimum ages for the lower Arenig, lowest Llandeilo, upper Caradoc, and upper Ashgill Series of the Ordovician System, and for the lower Wenlock, uppermost Wenlock, and middle Ludlow Series of the Silurian System. The project was undertaken under the auspices of the U. S. Geological Survey and the National Geographic Society; fieldwork and shipment of samples were supported by the Society. For a definitive treatment of this work see Ross et al., 1982.

It is our purpose to establish an isotopic geochronology of early Paleozoic time, particularly of the Ordovician, using the fission-track method of dating bentonites and other volcanically derived strata in the British stratotypes, against which all other lower Paleozoic biostratigraphic sections throughout the world ultimately are compared.

About 15 kg of rock constituted each sample, considerably less than we had originally planned; the logistics of gathering samples at the end of fieldwork in southern Scotland for consolidated shipment by air freight from London to Denver dictated a reduction in the size of collections. With a few exceptions, the reduced sample size seems to have been adequate to produce enough zircon crystals for analysis.

To the four main areas of outcrop of the Ordovician System in Wales and England, as shown in Figure 1, we must add a fifth area east of Moffat, Dumfrieshire, Scotland, where bentonites are abundant.

[1] Current address: Department of Geology, Colorado School of Mines, Golden, Colorado.

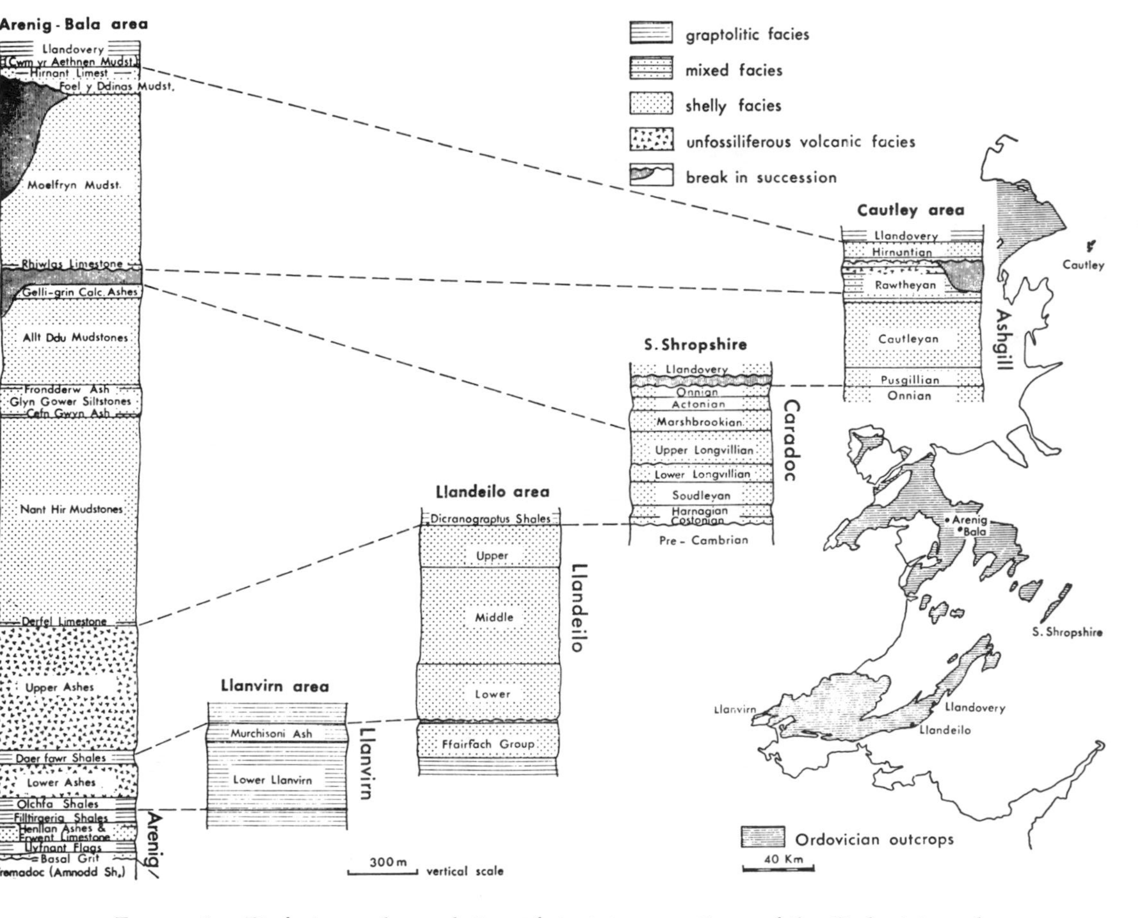

FIGURE 1. Biofacies and correlation of stratotype sections of the Ordovician of England and Wales (from Williams et al., 1972).

Areas of Investigation

BALA DISTRICT AND ARENIG FAWR, NORTHERN WALES

The first area visited was that in which we hoped to collect very old Ordovician rock, from the type section of the Arenig Series (Fig. 1) west of Bala, in northern Wales. Thanks to detailed mapping by Bassett, Whittington, and Williams (1966), and to our good fortune in persuading Prof. Whittington to be a partner in our efforts, collections were made from ashes and tuffs in beds equivalent to strata to the lower Arenig Series, Llanvirn Series, and Caradoc Series.

The oldest sample analyzed (no. 8) came from below the Arenig Henllan ash in the Llyfnant Flags (Fig. 1), from the west side of Arenig Fawr, and is high in the zone of *Didymograptus extensus.* Trilobites from the ash have been described by Whittington (1966). The radiometric age of the sample from the Llyfnant Flags is at least 493 ± 11 m.y. Two samples (no. 1 and 2) from the Gelli Grin ashes, east of Bala Lake, produced dates of 460 ± 14 and 469 ± 12 m.y.; this formation is Longvillian, equivalent to beds in the middle of the Caradoc Series. These ages are reasonable; their very reasonableness indicates that some ashes in the Bala District have not been as drastically heated as originally thought.

POWYS AND DYFED (SOUTHERN WALES)

Twelve collections were made in southern Wales along the belt of outcrop from Llandrindod Wells to St. Davids (Fig. 1). In this large region, C. P. Hughes discovered 19 different localities at which volcanic strata had been described. At 2 localities we were unable to find the reported ashes. At 5 other localities the rock seems so thoroughly indurated that separation of zircon crystals was deemed impractical. The four samples analyzed gave mixed results.

The most rewarding collection of the four (no. 13) was taken from a thin bentonite layer in shales bearing *Glyptograptus teretiusculus,* in a stream section east of Bach-y-graig, near Llandrindod Wells. We obtained an age of 477 ± 11 m.y. from the sample, which comes from the topmost Llanvirn or lowermost Llandeilo Series. Two other samples indicated that the rock had been heated after deposition, which may be significant in delineating Silurian or later tectonism. In the upper reaches of Howey Brook, east of Llandrindod Wells, a bentonite (no. 12), lying beneath shales carrying *Didymograptus murchisoni,* might have given an age for the Llanvirn Series. Regrettably, the fission-track age of 433 m.y. is probably early Silurian. Similarly, rhyolitic ashes (no. 16 and 17) of the Fairfach Group (Llanvirn Series) collected on Coed Duon Hill near Llandovery gave an age close to 400 m.y.; the rhyolite must have been heated secondarily until very latest Silurian or early Devonian time. A collection from the Pwllevog volcanics (Arenig equivalent) at Whitesands Bay, west of St. Davids, produced only three tiny zircon crystals, too few to permit an age determination. A sample from the Llanvirn volcanics (zone of *Didymograptus murchisoni)* at Abereiddi Bay has clearly been heated to give a date of 444 ± 12 m.y.

SHROPSHIRE (CHURCH STRETTON, WENLOCK EDGE, AND LUDLOW)

Initial collecting was mainly from the type sections of the Wenlock and Ludlow Series of the Silurian. In this area we had the great advantage of knowing that none of the bentonites had been heated above 80°C, and that any zircon or apatite crystals should give satisfactory fission-tracks for dating.

From the Buildwas Formation (basal Sheinwoodian), close to the base of the Wenlock Series, a bentonite (no. 23) had an age of 422 ± 10 m.y. Another bentonite, from the Much Wenlock Limestone Formation at the top of the Wenlock Series (no. 26), gave a minimum age of 416 ± 9 m.y. Separate analyses on different fractions of a collection (no. 28) from the top of the Bringewood Beds (Bringewoodian) in Sunnyhill Quarry, near Ludlow, produced ages of 409 ± 9 and 404 ± 12 m.y. The Bringewood Beds are close to the middle of the Ludlow Series. An estimated age of 405 m.y. is therefore not unreasonable for the top of the Ludlow. We might also guess that the time represented by the Ludlow Series was about 10 m.y. in length, and by the Wenlock about 6 m.y. Unfortunately, we have obtained no samples from the type Llandovery Series suitable for fission-track dating.

The original locality in the Acton Scott beds, Caradoc Series, of the Ordovician System, on the south side of the Onny River, was resampled in the company of Dr. W. T. Dean of the Geological Survey of Canada. A collection made by Ross in 1968, with Dean, was shown to have a minimum age of 451 ± 21 m.y. (Ross et al., 1976) based on fission tracks in apatite and using an old decay constant. The result using the new constant and zircon crystals from that early collection is 464 ± 21. The data for the Acton Scott Beds based on 1976 samples from the same locality is 468 ± 12 m.y.

CAUTLEY DISTRICT (SEDBERGH, CUMBRIA)

In the company of Ingham a search was made for Cautley volcanic rocks within the Ashgill Series containing zircon crystals. The search was not successful and the one sample (no. 36) could not be dated.

MOFFAT DISTRICT, DUMFRIESHIRE (MOFFAT WATER, DOBS LINN)

East of the town of Moffat in Dumfrieshire, Scotland, the section at Dobs Linn was made famous by Lapworth in 1878; it exhibits a complete

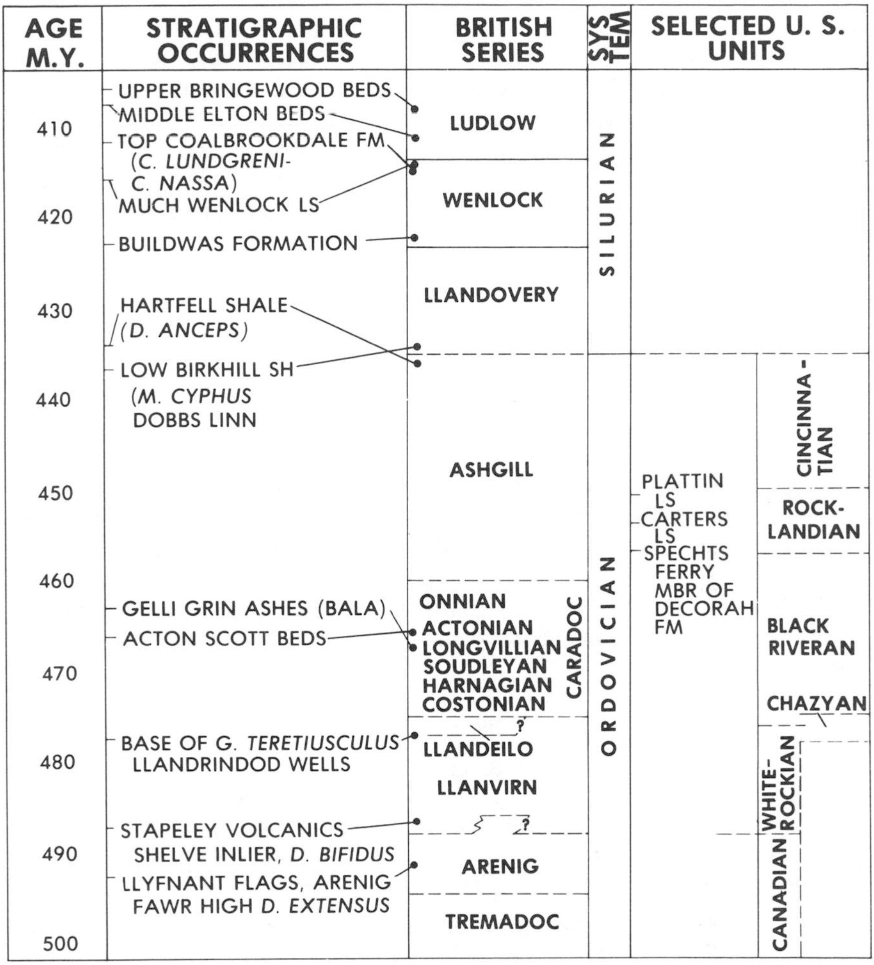

AGE M.Y.	STRATIGRAPHIC OCCURRENCES	BRITISH SERIES	SYSTEM	SELECTED U. S. UNITS	
	UPPER BRINGEWOOD BEDS				
410	MIDDLE ELTON BEDS	LUDLOW	SILURIAN		
	TOP COALBROOKDALE FM (*C. LUNDGRENI-C. NASSA*)				
420	MUCH WENLOCK LS	WENLOCK			
	BUILDWAS FORMATION				
430	HARTFELL SHALE (*D. ANCEPS*)	LLANDOVERY			
	LOW BIRKHILL SH				
440	(*M. CYPHUS* DOBBS LINN	ASHGILL	ORDOVICIAN		CINCINNATIAN
450				PLATTIN LS	ROCKLANDIAN
				CARTERS LS	
460				SPECHTS FERRY MBR OF DECORAH FM	
	GELLI GRIN ASHES (BALA)	ONNIAN (CARADOC)			BLACK RIVERAN
	ACTON SCOTT BEDS	ACTONIAN (CARADOC)			
470		LONGVILLIAN, SOUDLEYAN, HARNAGIAN, COSTONIAN (CARADOC)			CHAZYAN
	BASE OF G. *TERETIUSCULUS*	? LLANDEILO			
480	LLANDRINDOD WELLS	LLANVIRN			WHITEROCKIAN
	STAPELEY VOLCANICS	?			
490	SHELVE INLIER, *D. BIFIDUS*	ARENIG			CANADIAN
	LLYFNANT FLAGS, ARENIG FAWR HIGH *D. EXTENSUS*				
500		TREMADOC			

FIGURE 2. Fission track dates of lower Paleozoic volcanic ashes in British stratotypes, compared with U. S. formations.

stratigraphic succession across the boundary from the topmost Ordovician Hartfell shales (equivalent to Ashgill Series) into the lowermost Silurian Birkhill shales (equivalent to Llandovery Series). Furthermore, the transition from one to the other is interbedded with numerous bentonite layers. Three collections were made with Ingham. One (no. 39) from east of the Linn branch from the zone of *Dicellograptus anceps* has been analyzed by the fission-track method; the resulting age is 434 ± 11 m.y. Another sample (no. 41) was taken west of the Linn branch about 3 m above stream level and above the west fault. Thick bentonite in the lower Silurian Birkhill shale not higher than the zone of *Monograptus cyphus* has an age of 437 ± 11 m.y. This analysis at least indicates that the Ordovician-Silurian boundary is not younger than 437 ± 11 m.y. old.

For the first time isotopic dates have been obtained from bentonites interstratified within the type sections of two lower Paleozoic systems. The ages obtained, using the fission-track method, are mostly in the proper order and of reasonable magnitude.

Our preliminary results are shown graphically (ages in parentheses are estimated) and compared with fission-track dates on three formations in the central and southeastern United States (Fig. 2).

Acknowledgments

I am grateful to the following researchers who also participated in this project: C. W. Naeser and G. A. Izett, U. S. Geological Survey, Denver, Colorado; H. B. Whittington, C. P. Hughes, R. B. Rickards, Jan Zalasiewicz, P. R. Sheldon, and C. J. Jenkins, Cambridge University; L.R.M. Cocks, British Museum (Natural History), London; M. G. Bassett and W. T. Dean, National Museum of Wales, Cardiff; Peter Toghill, University of Birmingham, Church Stretton; and J. K. Ingham, Hunterian Museum, Glasgow.

REFERENCES

BASSETT, D. A.; WHITTINGTON, H. B.; and WILLIAM, ALWYN

1966. The stratigraphy of the Bala District, Merionethshire. The Quarterly Journal of Geology, Geological Society of London, vol. 122, pp. 219-271.

BASSETT, M. G.; COCKS, L.R.M.; HOLLAND, C. H.; RICKARDS, R. B.; and WARREN, P. T.

1975. The type Wenlock Series. Institute of Geological Sciences, Annual Report, no. 75/13, 19 pp.

COCKS, L.R.M.; HOLLAND, C. H.; RICKARDS, R. B.; and STRACHAN, ISLES

1971. A correlation of Silurian rocks in the British Isles: Geological Society of London special report, no. 1. Journal of Geology, vol. 127, pp. 103-136.

LAPWORTH, CHARLES

1878. The Moffat Series. Quarterly Journal, Geological Society of London, vol. 34, pp. 240-346, pls. 11-13.

ROSS, R. J., JR.; NAESER, C. W.; and IZETT, G. A.

1976. Apatite fission-track dating of a sample from the type Caradoc (Middle Ordovician) Series in England. Geological Society of America, Geology, vol. 4, pp. 505-506.

1977. Fission track dating of lower Paleozoic bentonites in British stratotypes. U. S. Geological Survey Open-File Report 77-348, 12 pp.

Ross, R. J., Jr.; Naeser, C. W., et al.
1982. Fission track dating of British Ordovician and Silurian stratotypes. Geological Magazine, (Cambridge), vol. 119, no. 2, pp. 135-152.

Whittington, H. B.
1966. Trilobites of the Henllan Ash, Arenig Series, Merioneth. Bulletin of the British Museum, (Natural History), Geology, vol. 11, no. 10, pp. 489-505, 5 pls.

Williams, Alwyn; Strachan, Isles; Bassett, D. A.; Dean, W. T.; Ingham, J. K.; Wright, A. D.; and Whittington, H. B.
1972. A correlation of Ordovician rocks in the British Isles. Geological Society of London, Special Report No. 3, 74 pp.

R. J. Ross, Jr.

Traditional Palestinian Potters

Grant Recipient: Owen S. Rye, Department of Prehistory, Australian National University, Canberra, Australia.

Grant 1692: Study and recording of the work of Arab potters in Israel.

The fieldwork supported by this grant from the National Geographic Society was completed over 5 months (March through July) in 1977. Previous fieldwork had been conducted in 1973 and 1974 leading up to this final season. The major aim of the project as a whole was to make a written and photographic record of an industry that is almost wholly unmentioned in the literature. Traditional pottery was collected, with which I hoped to reconstruct a history of changes and developments in traditional Palestinian pottery related to the major social upheavals of the past 30 to 40 years. The 1977 field season enabled successful completion of all these aims.

There are two entirely separate traditions of Palestinian pottery-making. In one, village women build pots by hand-forming methods, never using the potter's wheel. They fire vessels in open fires, not kilns. Two different classes of pottery are made by women: cooking vessels, for which the clay is calcite tempered; and storage vessels for water and household commodities, for which the clay is tempered with various additives, crushed pottery being a common one. The storage vessels, which usually have painted decoration, are fired to higher temperatures (up to 900°C) for strength, while the calcite-tempered vessels are fired to lower temperatures because calcite is unstable when fired higher than about 800°C. Different fuels are used for the two classes of firing. The vessels made by women, especially in the past, have been for immediate household use as well as limited trade.

The major traditional industry is a wholly male preserve, and this was the object of our study. In some aspects it can be shown to have origins dating back to the Philistine potters of the Iron Age, so it is a tradition of considerable age. Potters at the center of the modern tradition are Muslims, with almost 100 men working in the region: about 40 in Gaza, 30 in Hebron, and others in small workshops in Jabba, Irtakh, Acco, and Nazareth. There are only 6 Christian potters: 3 in Haifa, 1 in Nazareth, and 2 Armenian workshops in Jerusalem.

The four workshops of Christian potters are distinctly different from the Muslim workshops now, although prior to 1948 the Haifa workshop produced wares similar to those of the Muslim industries. The Haifa and Nazareth potters have now been educated in European ceramic colleges and their concern with sculptural and modern ceramics is outside the Palestinian tradition. The influence of their work is now becoming apparent in the repertoire of some Muslim potters, especially those who cater to the tourist market.

The Armenian potters are a distinct group, never having had any direct connection to the Palestinian tradition. Their families moved from Kutahya, in Turkey, earlier this century, brought in by the British administration to assist with renovations of the Dome of the Rock mosque in Jerusalem. They now carry on production of work essentially in the Kutahya tradition—glazed ware, decorated with brushwork in underglaze colors.

There is no evidence of a continuing tradition of Jewish potters in the region. Israeli potters of the present day are European in outlook and emphasis. They work as artist potters, or are organized in small factories producing ceramics by modern industrial methods. In most cases these industries can be dated to the post-1948 period, with a few dating earlier this century, after the Zionist settlements.

The Muslim workshops were the major focus of study. Characteristically, each workshop has one or two master potters, whose sons work from an early age as assistants or apprentices. Inheritance of the craft is patrilineal. Eldest sons eventually take over the workshop from their fathers, in a system which contributes to stability of the tradition. Outsiders are usually employed only for tasks such as clay preparation, although skilled throwers may be employed temporarily or permanently. In cities or villages, for example, Jabba, where movement of potters has not been extensive, potters are all members of extended families. Gaza has the greatest diversity and over the past 40 years has seen the most extensive movement of potters both into and out of the city.

Workshop location is most often at the edge of the village or town, although, in Gaza, workshops are within the urban area. Each Palestinian workshop has one or two kilns outside, as well as an area for clay preparation. Inside there are three main areas: one for clay storage, one for the potter's wheel on which vessels are formed, and one for storing drying vessels.

The clay used by the potters is rarely obtained in one specific location, but from any accessible outcropping of a particular deposit; for example, the Gaza potters obtain clay from a strata that extends over 30 km. The clay body used by the Gaza potters is based on a single clay, but elsewhere it is more common to use a mixture of two clays. Also, as at Hebron, sand is sometimes added.

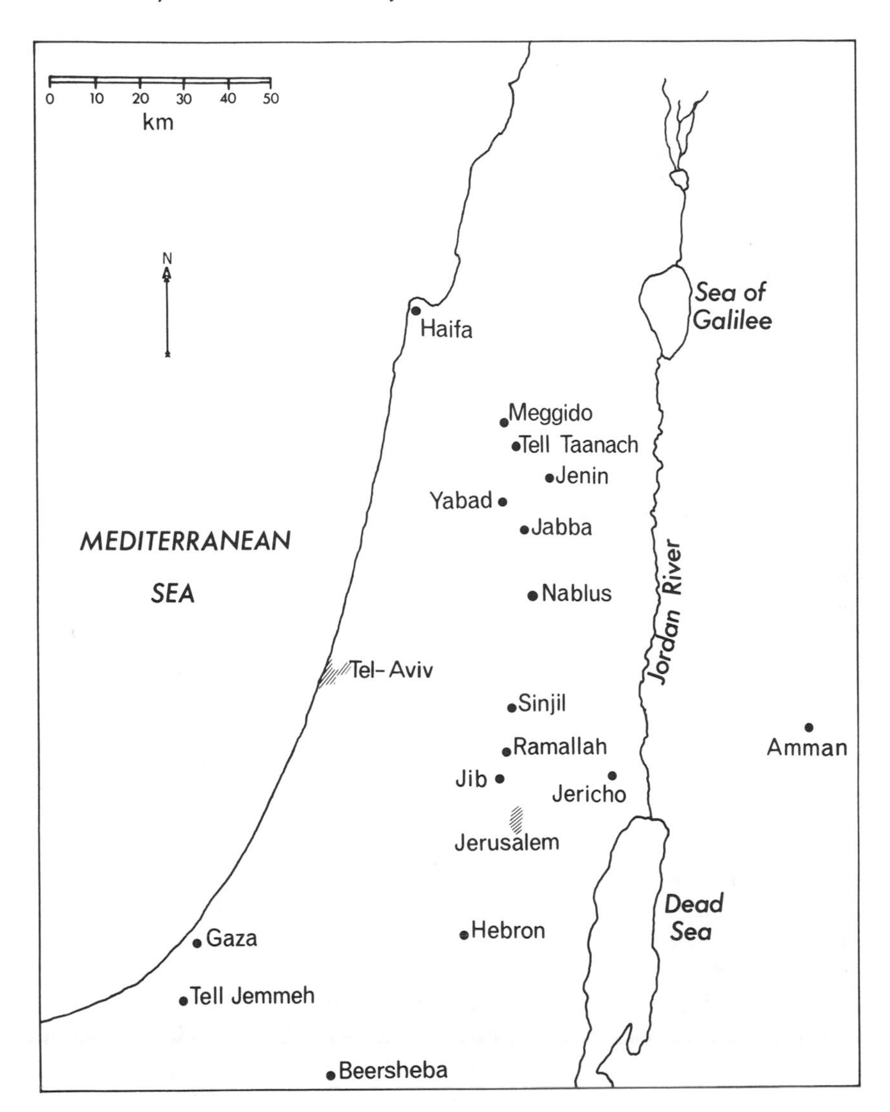

FIGURE 1. Region in which studies of Palestinian potters have been completed.

A technique brought to Haifa from Lebanon about 100 years ago, and now widespread through movement of potters in the region, is the use of seawater to mix the clay. An alternative (used at Hebron which is far from the sea) is to knead salt into the prepared clay. In either case the addition of salt produces a range of fired colors, which vary according to firing temperature, from red to orange, yellow, green and at the highest temperatures (over 1100°C) the surface of the ware becomes white.

At all workshops the clay body is prepared in the same way. The bottom of a clay-preparation pit is sprinkled with sand (and ash from the kiln at Gaza). The mixture of materials is dumped into a deeper pit, the amount of each material being determined by volume measurement. The materials are stirred with water, often by simply tramping up and down in the pit with feet and legs. The slip thus prepared is then allowed to stand for some time so the coarse particles can settle out, and is then run off into the sand-lined drying pit. The sand prevents clay from sticking to the floor of the pit. When the clay has sun-dried to plastic condition it is stored inside the workshop for later use.

The potter's wheel is used for forming all vessels. The traditional wooden wheel is set into the ground and the potter kicks on the top of a flywheel. In some areas a modified version of this wheel is powered by an electric motor.

Palestinian potters use what I believe to be the world's most sophisticated throwing techniques. The *tijlis* technique is apparently limited to the eastern Mediterranean region and is used now mainly by Islamic potters. It involves using several stages of throwing to form vessels, as opposed to turning or trimming off excess clay, as used in other wheel-throwing traditions in Europe, Asia, and many Islamic countries. In the *tijlis* technique, one end of a vessel (say the top) is formed on a solid lump of clay. The completed end is allowed to dry enough to support itself. Then the vessel is placed back on the wheel, dry or completed end down, supported in a chuck. The solid lump of clay now uppermost is opened and used to complete the other end of the vessel (in this example the base).

There is considerable variation in ways of forming a vessel with this technique. All the observed variations have now been classified into eight groups, which can be used for comparison with pottery excavated by archeologists. Because the techniques are so distinctive, the question of their origin has been examined by looking for evidence of the technique in archeological material now in museums. The most useful collection for this purpose is located in the Rockefeller Museum in Jerusalem. The earliest examples of vessels made with this technique date back 3000 years, and there are examples of its use in every period from then onward. Significantly, the earliest examples I have seen formed by this technique are Cypriot and Cypriot-imitation vessels of the Iron Age. So the present evidence suggests that the technique originated in Cyprus.

For firing pottery, the traditional Palestinian kiln is still used by most workshops. The kiln design is related to Islamic kilns used in other Middle Eastern countries as far away as Iran, Pakistan, and India. While there are quite minor variations from one Palestinian center to the next, the overall design is constant. An updraft kiln, it is circular in plan, with a domed crown. Inner walls are built from clay mixed with straw, but some potters have recently tried using modern firebrick for the interior with the result that the kilns cool too slowly after firing. An outer insulating wall, usually of stone, is added. The firebox is built inside the lower part of the chamber, and flame travels upward through holes in the top and sides of the firebox, up through the wares and through a hole in the crown of the kiln. Vessels are stacked on top of each other in the kiln, and no form of shelves or other setting aids is used. The kilns can be up to 3 m high. Fuel for firing is always waste from other industries. Sawdust, banana leaves, olive pressings are examples; more recently wood shavings soaked in used motor oil, and used motor tires have come into use. The choice of fuel is based on availability and lowest cost factors rather than efficiency or cleanliness of combustion.

In some areas, particularly Gaza, black pottery is produced. This is essentially the same as the red pottery except for its treatment at the end of the firing. When full temperature is reached, if red pottery is desired the kiln is simply allowed to cool. If black ware is desired, at full temperature the firebox and chamber of the kiln are stuffed full with organic materials (although motor tires are now commonly used for this purpose). The stokehole and exit flues are then sealed and the kiln allowed to cool. Carbon incorporated in the pores of the ware by this much-reduced cooling produces the black color. The technique as used in Gaza is similar to that used in the Nile Delta, and has considerable antiquity. It has recently been introduced in some other Palestinian workshops, notably at Jabba.

The time taken for firing varies with the particular clay body in use. In Gaza, for example, the clay is prone to firing damage and firings take over a week, with most of this time involving slowly preheating the wares. In contrast, at Hebron the clay body is sandy and open and can be fired quickly; firing starts on the morning of one day and the kiln is cool enough for vessels to be removed the next day.

These kilns fire unevenly, being considerably hotter at the top than at the bottom near the firebox. Temperatures measured in Hebron kilns varied from 900 to 1100°C at the top of the kiln to 750 or 800°C near the firebox.

Despite the existence of an overall tradition of pottery-making in the region, there are differences among wares from different centers. There are local styles which can be distinguished even when vessels have essentially the same size, form, and function. The nature of decoration of unglazed vessels is one aspect of style. Gaza potters tend to use ribbing and ridging created during the throwing process as a primary decorative feature. Hebron potters use rouletting or wavy combed bands, and the Jabba potters use combing as the main form of decoration.

By far the majority of the Palestinian potters' output is unglazed ware. This is true for pottery throughout the Islamic world, past and present, despite the impression given by art historians' emphasis on the study of and publications on glazed ware. Unglazed pottery is the ware of the people. Glazed pottery is produced by some Palestinian potters, as it has been at some stages in the past. The Christian potters of Haifa use glazing techniques recently learned in Europe. The Armenian potters of Jerusalem work in the tradition of Kutahya, in Turkey, but have recently begun to use glazes and other materials imported from Europe. Some Muslim potters of Hebron produced glazed ware for local consumption, but now the only glazed ware made in Hebron is derivative of the Armenian Kutahya tradition and uses imported materials.

Recent Changes and Developments

While the main emphasis of this work has been documentation of the Palestinian pottery tradition as it is, considerable effort has been devoted to documenting recent changes and developments in the work of the Palestinian potters. Of special interest has been the effect of recent wars and occupations on the work of the potters. The major events in the minds of all the potters were the wars of 1948 and 1967; none were unaffected by these events.

As noted above, there has been a decline in the number of potters working in the survey region, from a 1931 census showing 211 potters to our 1977 survey showing less than 100 potters. The reasons are more complex than first expected. Warfare is one: numerous potters have left the region as refugees. Fear of ill treatment by the Israelis is one motivation. Another is that potters need markets and the refugee camps are filled with poor people among whom the potters' wares are in demand. It has not been possible to document where the potters have gone, or how many became refugees, other than by the testimony of the remaining potters. This suggests that a small number moved to Lebanon both in 1948 and 1967, but that the majority of those who left are now in Jordan. Many of these originally came from the large coastal pottery center at Ramle, where in 1931 there were 50 potters; now there are none. Many moved to Jericho in 1948; in 1967 they moved to Jordan.

For those who did not become refugees, another reason for declining numbers has been a gradual change in the status of the profession. Instead of training their sons to be potters, potters have sent their sons to school, and on graduation they work in other professions with higher status.

A less significant factor has been competition from new materials, such as metal or plastic, used for vessels serving functions similar to those of the potters' wares. Whereas in other parts of the world this competition has caused total extinction of traditional pottery-making, the Palestinian potters have been able to change their production to satisfy new markets, where there is both purchasing power and demand. Examples are the production of glazed ware, of miniature vessels and antique reproductions for sale to tourists, and of flower pots for sale to Israelis. These adaptations have been favored in larger centers where contact with the new consumers is greatest.

One major effect of the 1948 and 1967 wars on Palestinian potters was a wide exchange of information. This resulted from movement of potters within the region itself, as well as movement in and out of neighboring countries. Some of this was refugee movement, some was temporary travel in search of work. Most of the potters are illiterate, so direct contact is required for exchange of information. This movement accounts for much of the change in use of materials, and mixing of styles, from one Palestinian center to the next in the past 30 years. Although many potters who have worked in other countries know of styles and techniques used elsewhere, they do not necessarily use this knowledge unless changes in market conditions favor its usage. The information acts as a reserve for adaptation to new conditions.

Some potters who did not move during wars have had to adapt material usage because of territorial changes. One potter had his clay source on land which became part of Israel, to which access was denied. His search for new clay resulted in changes in other aspects of his work, firing being affected because the new clay required different firing treatment.

Other potters who did not move from their traditional homes, as noted above, adapted their production to new markets. The most extreme example is given by the Christian potters of Haifa. Prior to 1948 their production consisted almost entirely of water pots for the Arab market. Most of the Arab population left as refugees in 1948, to be replaced by Israelis. The potters began making flowerpots for this Jewish market. After 1967 cheap pots from Gaza and Hebron were increasingly sold in Haifa, seriously affecting their custom. The Haifa potters then learned to make European-style glazed artistic ware, which is almost entirely sold to Israelis. This has meant a total change in materials, techniques, and the repertoire of wares.

To a lesser extent changes have occurred in other centers also. A study of the complete repertoire of vessels produced in Gaza and Hebron shows how changes occur at different rates in different workshops. Some potters are innovative, some conservative. The success of an innovation encourages other, but not all, potters to adopt it. Thus, the process of change in a tradition, even at a time when change in the region as a whole is extremely rapid, can be relatively slow overall.

Detailed analysis of technological changes in recent times shows that change occurs at different rates for different aspects of the technology. From most likely to change, to least, the order is:

Use of Fuel. This can change from one firing to the next.

Shape of Vessels. This can readily be changed within the limitations of forming techniques available.

Forming Techniques. These may be changed, usually by adopting techniques used elsewhere, but minor changes in technique are the most likely, and these tend to be closely derived from the existing tradition.

Materials. A change in materials, especially clay, usually requires extensive experimentation and a period of nonproduction or heavy losses; and usually results in changes in other parts of the process (drying, firing, productivity, vessel functions, workshop organization).

Kilns. These are long lasting and are viewed as "permanent fixtures" since they represent considerable investment of labor and money. All Palestinian kilns are basically the same, whereas there have been many recent changes in other parts of the tradition. Kilns only change when there is a total change, such as in the introduction of glazed ware production by some potters.

Acknowledgments

This and previous field seasons were aided by airfare subsidies from the Smithsonian Institution; by grants from the Smithsonian Institution, the Concordia Committee for Archaeological Study in the Near East, Birzeit University, and the Tell Taanach Excavation Fund. Special thanks are due Albert Glock, formerly of the Albright Institute for Archaeological Research, and to John Landgraf; without their assistance little would have been achieved. Thanks also to Gus van Beek and William Potts, and to the late Clifford Evans. The Palestinian potters gave hospitality and shared their knowledge generously, especially Abed il Halim of Hebron.

OWEN S. RYE

Biological Investigations in the Pantanal, Mato Grosso, Brazil

Grant Recipient: George B. Schaller, New York Zoological Society, The Zoological Park, Bronx, New York.

Grants 1691, 2202: For study of the ecology and behavior of the jaguar in Mato Grosso, Brazil.

The Pantanal, 100,000 km^2 in size, consists of marshes and seasonally flooded grasslands, sparsely dotted with trees, whose expanses are broken by thickets, stands of palm, and patches of deciduous and semideciduous forest. Many shallow ponds dot the area, and streams meander sluggishly through it before draining into the Paraguay River. The whole area is flat to undulating, seldom more than 100 m above sea level. The climate is seasonal with nearly half of the 1100 mm annual precipitation falling between December and February; temperatures range from as low as 0°C to as high as 41°C during the June to September dry season. Since the Pantanal was little known biologically, we began research there in 1977. In addition to general investigations—such as a census of marsh deer (Schaller and Vasconcelos, 1978b) and botanical studies (Prance and Schaller, 1982)—we concentrated our efforts in three localities, each selected for a particular research opportunity. This report summarizes three periods of study:

(1) From April 1977 to September 1978, we (George B. Schaller and Peter Gransden Crawshaw) worked intermittently on the Acurizal Ranch bordering the Paraguay River (Fig. 1). Our major work on the 137-km^2 ranch consisted of determining the mammalian biomass in different habitats (Schaller, 1983) and in studying the endangered jaguar (Schaller and Vasconcelos, 1978a; Schaller and Crawshaw, 1980). Additional jaguar research was done on the Bela Vista Ranch, a 90-km^2 island just north of Acurizal.

(2) The capybara and Paraguayan caiman *(Caiman crocodilus)* represent potential sources of meat and hides, economically viable alternatives to cattle ranching. From October 1978 to August 1979, we (Schaller and Crawshaw) investigated these species along and near the Transpantanal Highway which bisects the northern Pantanal (Crawshaw and Schaller, 1980; Schaller and Crawshaw, 1981, 1982).

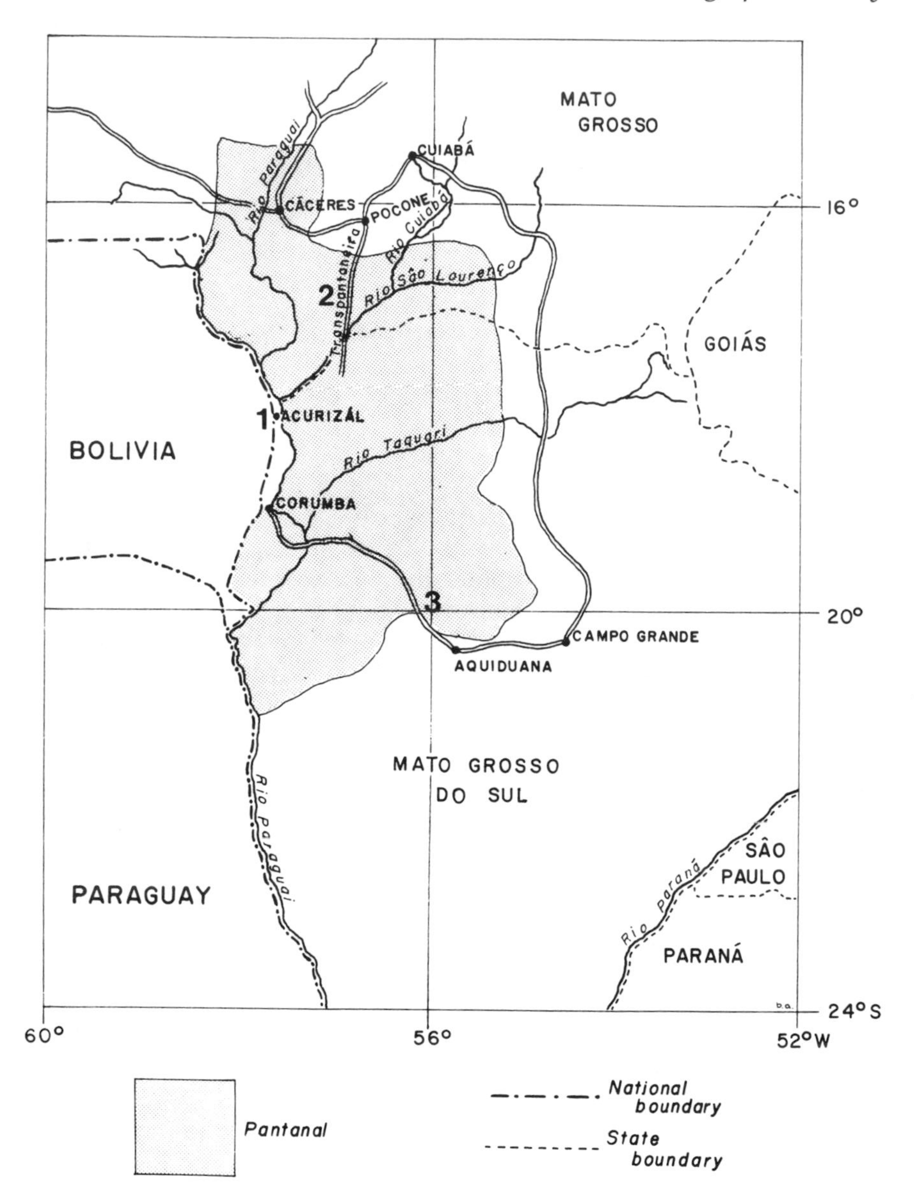

FIGURE 1. The Pantanal region of Mato Grosso, Brazil showing the main study areas: 1, Acurizal; 2, Transpantanal Highway, and 3, Miranda. (Adapted from Prance and Schaller, 1982.)

(3) From August 1981 to November 1982, we (Howard B. Quigley and Crawshaw) studied jaguar, as well as puma and ocelot, intensively on the large Miranda Ranch in the southern Pantanal (Fig. 1).

Since the details of our work are available in several publications, this report summarizes only certain aspects.

Biomass

The Acurizal Ranch is about 24 km long and 5 to 10 km wide, and lies between the Paraguay River and the Serra de Amolar, a ridge rising to an altitude of 900 m. About a third of the ranch consists of floodplain, covered with rafts of water hyacinths *(Eichhornia)*, seasonally flooded pastures covered with shrubs and tall herbs, and stunted gallery forests growing along watercourses. Another third is relatively level and dry at the base of the Serra. A deciduous forest covers some of this area. Trees reach a height of 22 m and the canopy is continuous. In one quadrat of 1 ha there were 279 trees (15+ cm dbh) of 36 species. The *cerrado*, a forest type typical of central Brazil, is found mainly in two valleys that project into the Serra. Most trees are only about 10 m tall and the canopy is discontinuous. There were 190 trees of 22 species on a 1-ha quadrat, and two thirds of the trees belonged to only 6 species. A gallery forest, with some evergreen species, occurs along streams in the valleys. Most habitats have been modified to promote cattle production. Some forests have been turned into pastures, which in some instances have reverted to dense scrub. A final third of the ranch consists of steep, rocky slopes sparsely covered with deciduous forest near the base and *cerrado* higher up.

To census forest mammals, especially small nocturnal ones, is difficult, and we used various techniques. The distribution of monkey groups was plotted after repeated sightings; deer, tapir, peccary, and armadillo were tallied by walking in transect lines for 2282 km and by making fecal counts; jaguar and puma, among others, were estimated on the basis of tracks; capybara were censused visually along shorelines; foxes were trapped, tagged, and released; and small rodents and marsupials were snap-trapped on 1-ha plots in different vegetation types.

At Acurizal 64 species of mammals were recorded, of which 21 species were bats (Table 1). More work on the ranch might also reveal pampas cat *(Felis colocolo)*, oncilla *(Felis tigrina)*, grison *(Galictis vittata)*, and four-eyed opossum *(Philander opossum)*. The giant otter *(Pteronura brasiliensis)* has been exterminated in the area.

In estimating numbers and densities of the species (excluding bats) we confined ourselves to 70 km^2 of terrain, including 37 km^2 of deciduous

TABLE 1. Mammals (Excluding Bats) and Their Biomass at Acurizal
(Adapted from Schaller, 1983.)

Scientific name	*Common name*	*Avg. wt. (kg)*	*Est. no.*	*Biomass (kg)*
MARSUPIALIA				
Monodelphis brevicaudata	Short-tailed opossum	.06	--	--
Marmosa pusilla	Murine opossum	.06	--	--
Didelphis albiventris	White-eared opossum	1.25	?	--
PRIMATES				
Aotus trivirgatus	Night monkey	.80	30	24.0
Callicebus moloch	Titi monkey	.70	70	49.0
Cebus apella	Black-capped capuchin	2.10	225	472.5
Alouatta caraya	Black howler	4.50	180	810.0
Callithrix argentata	Black-tailed marmoset	.32	60	19.0
EDENTATA				
Myrmecophaga tridactyla	Giant anteater	20.00	4	80.0
Tamandua tetradactyla	Collared anteater	5.00	30	150.0
Euphractus sexcinctus	Six-banded armadillo	3.30	400	1320.0
Tolypeutes matacus	Three-banded armadillo	.90	300	270.0
Priodontes maximus	Giant armadillo	55.00	?	--
Dasypus novemcinctus	Nine-banded armadillo	3.00	150	450.0
LAGOMORPHA				
Sylvilagus brasiliensis	Brazilian rabbit	1.15	50	57.5
RODENTIA				
Sciurus langsdorffi	Squirrel	.30	20	6.0
Oryzomys delicatus	Rice rat	.025	--	--
O. concolor	Rice rat	.06	--	--
Akodon varius	Grass mouse	.04	--	--
A. lasiurus	Grass mouse	.04	--	--
Calomys callosus	Vesper mouse	.015	--	--
Thricomys (Cercomys) apereoides	Spiny rat	.20	--	--
Proechimys sp.	Spiny rat	.045	--	--
Coendou prehensilis	Prehensile-tailed porcupine	2.6	?	--
Hydrochoeris hydrochaeris	Capybara	30.00	110	3300.0
Dasyprocta punctata	Agouti	3.00	75	225.0
CARNIVORA				
Cerdocyon thous	Crab-eating fox	5.20	20	104.0
Chrysocyon brachyurus	Maned wolf	23.00	*	--

Scientific name	Common name	Avg. wt. (kg)	Est. no.	Bio-mass (kg)
Nasua nasua	Coati	3.00	150	450.0
Procyon cancrivorus	Crab-eating raccoon	10.00	6	60.0
Eira barbara	Tayra	4.00	6	24.0
Lutra platensis	LaPlata otter	9.00	*	--
Felis pardalis	Ocelot	8.00	4	32.0
F. yagouaroundi	Yagouaroundi	5.00	2	10.0
F. concolor	Puma	48.00	2	96.0
Panthera onca	Jaguar	70.00	4	280.0
PERISSODACTYLA				
Tapirus terrestris	Brazilian tapir	150.00	45	6750.0
ARTIODACTYLA				
Tayassu tajacu	Collared peccary	18.00	55	990.0
T. pecari	White-lipped peccary	28.00	110	3080.0
Mazama gouazoubira	Gray brocket	15.00	120	1800.00
M. rufa	Red brocket	26.00	120	3120.0
Ozotoceros bezoarticus	Pampas deer	40.00	6	240.0
Blastocerus dichotomus	Marsh deer	80.00	8	640.0

*Transient

forest, 18 km² of *cerrado*, 6 km² of gallery forest, 5 km² of pasture, and 4 km² of young secondary forest. The total estimated numbers and the biomass of each species are presented in Table 1, excluding 9 species of small rodents and marsupials with a combined biomass of about 1678 kg. The total biomass was 26,587 kg or 380 kg/km². Ungulates contributed 62.5% to this figure and capybara 12.4%. Next, with 8.5%, were the edentates. Small rodents, rabbits, agoutis, and marsupials comprised 7.4% and arboreal species—primates and squirrels—5.2%. Lowest in terms of biomass were carnivores with 4.0%. The livestock at Acurizal included about 1500 cattle and a few horses, sheep, and pigs with a total biomass of about 3750 kg/km², a figure 10 times greater than that for native mammals. The biomass figure of 380 kg/km² is low when compared, for example, with the 1756 kg/km² in the Chitawan National Park in Nepal which also has 7 ungulate species (Seidensticker, 1976). Several factors are responsible for this low figure, as discussed below.

Habitat Modification

Five times in this century, most recently in 1974, exceptionally high floods inundated large parts of the Pantanal. At such times small terrestrial mammals are eliminated unless they can find refuge on islands of high ground. Intensive cattle management changes a complex habitat to a simple one, in the process eliminating most forest mammals. Fire, which often sweeps through *cerrado* during the dry season, deprives small mammals of cover and food.

Hunting

Capybara, armadillo, and all ungulates are hunted for food by ranch hands and squatters; foxes and small cats are killed because they prey on chickens; and puma and jaguar are shot because they take cattle, and, in addition, jaguar skins are valuable trade items (3 jaguars were killed and 1 was captured on Acurizal in 1974 and 2 more were taken in 1978).

Disease

Capybara were abundant on Acurizal until the 1974 flood. At that time, many died of disease, probably equine trypanosomiasis. The population was still affected in 1977, and this, together with poor reproductive success, caused a continuing decline.

Aerial censuses of marsh deer over large parts of the Pantanal also showed poor production of young: an annual increment of only 4 to 6% is not high enough to maintain the population. The reason for the virtual lack of young remains unknown, but disease appears a likely cause.

Predation

Jaguar subsist on a wide variety of wild mammals in the Pantanal—capybara, marsh deer, tapir, otter, *Aotus* monkey, coati, raccoon, and giant anteater, to name a few—as well as such other vertebrates as curassow *(Crax)*, caiman, and anaconda *(Eunectes)*. Puma also have a diverse diet. The biomass of puma and jaguar at Acurizal was 376 kg and prey biomass, excluding small rodents, 24,533 kg, or 1 kg of predator per 65 kg, seemingly a high predator biomass; however, cattle are not included in these figures.

Our best documented example of the effect of predation on prey concerns capybara. Jaguar killed 20 to 23% of a sample population of 30 to 35 capybara within 2 months in 1977. Disease also affected the animals. The relative impact of the two mortality factors could be deduced from capybara skulls found in the field. Of 70 skulls, 26 comprised definite kills, and a few others, probable ones, suggesting that disease and predation affected the capybara about equally. Table 2 presents the approximate ages of capybara at death. Age structure was similar in animals dead from predation, disease, and poaching. The evidence indicates that predation was rather unselective and that most capybara died young, few exceeding 4 years at death. Apparently disease, coupled with poor reproduction, judging by the few young observed, reduced a large capybara population to a level where jaguar predation could have a significant effect.

TABLE 2. Approximate Age of Capybara Found Dead at Acurizal and in the Northern Pantanal

	Acurizal			*Northern Pantanal*
Approximate age (months)	*Predation*	*Mainly disease*	*Poaching*	*All causes*
Young 0-3	0	2.3	0	10.6
Young 3-12	0	0	11.1	4.1
Yearling 12-18	3.8	2.3	0	4.9
Adult 18-22	7.7	9.0	11.1	20.3
Adult 22-30	26.9	31.8	16.1	26.0
Adult 30+	61.5	54.5	61.1	34.0
Sample size	26	44	18	123

SEASONAL CHANGES IN FOOD ABUNDANCE

Changes in food abundance may influence populations in an environment as seasonal as at Acurizal where, for instance, many trees are leafless in September. The mammals at Acurizal reveal several trends in resource use. One is that terrestrial mixed browsers and grazers—tapir and deer—contribute most to the biomass (47%). Low shrubs and trees are abundant, and grass and some fruits also provide forage. Primary grazers are absent, except for the capybara which can achieve high density and biomass (338 kg/km^2 in our northern study area) if good grazing exists near water. All small rodents at Acurizal appear to be seed-eaters, as shown by stomach content. Grass-eating rats and mice generally occur at higher densities than seed-eaters, whose food supply is dispersed and seasonally erratic. Arboreal leaf-eaters are rare, the howler monkey and porcupine being the only species that have to some degree specialized on this food source. The seasonal availability of most leaves and the rare leaf-killing frost make the Pantanal marginal for arboreal folivores. Nearly two thirds of the nonvolant species subsist on or supplement their diet with seeds and fruits, among them the 6-banded armadillo and several small carnivores. Insects, especially ants and termites, are abundant and a fairly predictable resource, and the edentates, small marsupials, 4 monkey species, as well as fox, raccoon, and coati have specialized on this food source or added it to the diet. In terms of mammalian biomass, probably about 8 to 10% can be attributed to an insect diet.

Eisenberg et al. (1979) studied species diversity and biomass of mammals at two Venezuelan sites. One area, the Guatopo National Park, is hilly and covered with semideciduous and deciduous forest, and the other, Masaguaral in the llanos, is ecologically similar to the floodplains in the Pantanal. In addition, Eisenberg and Thorington (1973) provided data for a rain forest area, the small Barro Colorado Island in Panama. Comparisons of these areas can only be made in general terms, for the study sites not only differ in size, but some species have also been exterminated and tallies may be incomplete. Table 3, however, shows that Acurizal is relatively rich in nonvolant mammals. For example, the Pantanal harbors as many kinds of primates as some rain forest areas, even though trees are only half as tall and half as diverse, and food resources are more seasonal; there are also as many carnivore and ungulate species in the Pantanal as in the rain forest. The Venezuelan study areas are relatively impoverished in number of nonvolant species when compared with the Pantanal; in fact, the figure for the whole llanos is only 42. This may partly be due to vagaries in distributional patterns. The llanos and Pantanal show little mammalian endemism, species being derived from habitats surrounding their respective river basins, and the greater variety in the Pantanal may reflect a greater variety of surrounding habitats.

With regard to biomass, Barro Colorado is four times higher than the other areas. About 60% of this biomass consists of sloths, which do not occur in the Pantanal, and another 9% consists of primates. The low biomass of arboreal folivores at Acurizal is probably related to food availability during the dry season. Masaguaral and Guatopo are similar in that biomass is around 1000 kg/km^2. Once capybara recover and hunting ceases, Acurizal could no doubt support as high a biomass as these areas.

TABLE 3. Number of Nonvolant Mammalian Species and Their Biomass in Several Neotropical Areas

Neotropical area	*No. species*	*Biomass (kg/km^2)*
Masaguaral West	28	479
Masaguaral East		1086
Guatopo	40	946
Barro Colorado	40	4431
Acurizal	43 (+10)*	380

*Figure in parentheses indicates species recorded in Pantanal but not at Acurizal.

Capybara Social Organization

We studied one capybara population along 7 km of the Transpantanal Highway in a mosaic of pasture, scrub, forest, and small ponds. Censuses in 1978 and 1979 indicated a stable population of about 350 animals, with mortality—principally disease (55%), jaguar predation (12%),

TABLE 4. Compositions of Selected Capybara Groups

Adult male	*Adult female*	*Yearling*	*Young*	*Total*
1	1		3	5
1	3		1	5
2	5		7	14
3	10	2	11	26

and human poaching and vandalism (33%)—about equal to the annual increment. The population consisted of 26% adult males, 30% adult females, 5% yearlings (12 to 18 months old), and 39% young. Of the animals observed, 7.4% were alone, 60.6% in groups of 2 to 10, and 32% in groups of 11 or more, with the largest group having 37 members. Females outnumbered males by a ratio of more than 2:1 in groups, whereas the population itself was close to parity. An average of 23% of the males was solitary and another 4% was in male groups with up to 8 members.

Table 4 presents compositions of 4 of the 9 groups we observed repeatedly between July and December 1978. Compositions ranged from a nuclear family with 1 adult male and female to a harem with 1 male and several females to mixed groups with 2 or more adults of each sex. These groups remained stable for extended periods, except for births and deaths, even in the presence of many unaffiliated animals which occasionally joined certain groups temporarily. Solitary males often made contact with groups, sometimes remaining at the periphery of large ones. Groups restricted their movements to specific localities, small ones ranging over 12 to 35 ha and large ones 125 to 200 ha. Range borders overlapped, and, in addition, small groups sometimes resided wholly within the range of a large group. Some grazing areas as well as certain ponds were communal, different groups remaining near each other though seldom making direct contact.

The question arises as to how groups maintained their integrity. Scent and direct aggression appeared to be important spacing mechanisms. Two glands are used in communication, one, a sebaceous gland on the snout, and the other, paired anal glands. Scent from the former is rubbed on vertical objects, such as stems, and deposits from the latter, often mixed with urine, are dragged along stalks which the animal straddles. One animal often covers the scent mark of another with its own. Of 436 observations of marking among sexually inactive adults, males accounted for 90%; of 201 observations during courtship, males accounted for 51%. The sexual condition of the female obviously influences her marking frequency. Mating reached a peak with the onset of rains in October through November. Most aggression involved males, often a group male in pursuit of a peripheral male: of 90 overt acts of aggression observed, 93% occurred between males. Females are as large as males—males in our study area averaged 43 kg and females 40 kg—and they are equally well armed with sharp teeth, yet we seldom observed them in altercations. Once 2 females from different groups reared up on their hind legs, mouths open, when they met; and occasionally a female rushed at a peripheral male. Aggressive interactions were also observed during courtship, and it is possible that at such times, females influence group formation by selecting a mate, usually (in 84% of observations) one as large as or larger than herself. Once a female had accepted a mate she tended to ignore or attack other males.

The most striking aspect of capybara society was the wide spectrum of social systems operating in a small population—pairs, harems, and groups with several adults of both sexes. Such flexibility enables species to adapt to different conditions of food abundance. The capybara is a grazer, and, given the mosaic of habitats in the study area—ranging from open pastures to forest with its sparse grass cover—a variable social system has obvious advantages. The stability of groups was affected by severe stresses, among them a lack of water that forced groups to concentrate around a few ponds during the dry season, and that resulted in a high death rate which disrupted group membership. Yet groups tended to be cohesive, even outside the mating season, indicating strong selection for a stable social existence. One factor promoting such group cohesion may be protection of young. Litters contain up to 7 young, unusually many for a hystricomorph, reflecting high natural mortality. We observed one instance of a peripheral male attacking and killing a young before being driven off by a group male and female, and indirect evidence indicated that this was not an isolated incident. Adults also provide protection against black vultures *(Coragyps)* and other small predators. In addition, group females that have given birth at the same time, as they often do, may suckle each others' young, a further benefit of living in a group.

Nesting and Food Habits of Paraguayan Caiman

Paraguayan caiman are of moderate size. An adult female has a snout-to-vent length of about 80 to 95 cm and an average weight of 18 kg, and an adult male has a length of 110 to 125 cm and weight of 44 kg.

Nesting

A total of 69 nests of *Caiman crocodilus* was found between January and March 1979. Of these, 2 lacked eggs, the female having built a nest without depositing a clutch, and 14 nests had already been destroyed by predators, leaving 53 nests which provided information. Most hatching occurred during March, with a sharp peak March 21-30. Assuming a gestation period of about 70 days, most egg laying occurred during January, at the height of the rainy season.

The main requisites for a nest site were the availability of leaf litter or other vegetation with which the female could construct a mound in which to lay her eggs, and the proximity of water. Nest material was transported for no more than 3.5 m. Average size of nest mounds was 134 cm in length by 117 cm in width at the base and 40.5 cm in height; average egg number in full clutches was 31 (21 to 38), and average egg measurements were 67.7 mm in length, 42.6 mm in width, and 75.3 g in weight. We ascertained the fate of 48 nests. Of these 37 (77%) were wholly destroyed, 36 of them by predators, mainly coati and crab-eating fox, and one by a combination of predation and flooding. Four nests were partially preyed upon but some eggs hatched, and 6 nests (12.5%) hatched successfully. All eggs in one nest were infertile. Of the eggs laid, 6.3% were infertile, 71.9% were taken by predators, 1.5% were destroyed by floods, 2 eggs were inadvertently broken by the female, and 20.1% hatched.

Female caiman showed maternal behavior by guarding the nest, helping to release young from the egg chamber, and protecting hatchlings. Females varied in their attentiveness to nests. Several ceased to protect nests in the daytime after only one visit by us, although they returned at night, indicating that they were extremely sensitive to disturbance. Some females always left nests unguarded, except for sporadic visits at night, perhaps a reflection on previous adverse contacts with man. We spent a total of 21 nights in blinds near nests to observe hatching behavior. Females have two main functions at hatching: They open up the nest, allowing young to escape from the egg chamber, and they crack open unhatched eggs with their jaws, assuring a simultaneous hatch. Young then move to water where the yipping calls of the hatchlings and the grunts of the female serve to maintain contact.

Food Habits

We observed food habits and feeding behavior of about 3000 caiman in small ponds bordering about 14 km of the Transpantanal Highway. Speeding vehicles and vandals killed caiman on occasion and we checked stomachs for food content. Of 31 stomachs examined, 35% were empty. The most important food was fish, followed by snails, crabs, and insects. In addition, caiman occasionally captured and ate birds *(Egretta, Aramus),* other caiman, reptiles *(Dracaena, Eunectes),* and capybara. Caiman characteristically waited for fish to come within snapping distance. One fishing technique was more complicated: Facing land at right angles, a caiman moved almost imperceptibly sideways for 263 m as if herding fish, then arced its body shoreward, gently wiggling its tail while advancing into the shallows and then snapping at fish that tried to escape this seining attempt. Of 5267 observed snaps and lunges at fish, an average of 6.3 were needed to catch a fish, a success rate of 15.9%. In daytime, caiman fished most actively between 0600 and 0900 hours, and least from 1000 to 1500 hours. There was usually little fishing in daytime until for unknown reasons most or all caiman in a pond began to hunt and continued day and night for as long as 13 days. For instance, 85 caiman in one pool fished from July 28 to August 9, capturing an estimated total of 10,208 fish, or 120 fish per caiman, and then most left the pond. Four seine samples contained an average of 575 fish weighing 6.9 kg, showing that the pond had not been fished out.

To determine how far caiman travel, we captured, tagged and released 143 animals, most of them adult. Resightings showed that few animals traveled more than 4 km during the dry season, our longest distance, that of a subadult male, being 9.4 km. Instead, most caiman concentrated in certain ponds. Of 43 suitable ponds available, 54% of the animals crowded into 5 ponds, behavior perhaps related to the breeding season. Dominance and courtship displays by males began in late July and reached a peak during November and December. As these observations show, the intricacies in social responses of crocodilians are not just limited to maternal behavior and courtship but also extend to feeding behavior and movement patterns.

Movement Patterns of Jaguar, Puma, and Ocelot

We conducted research on jaguar and other large cats in the Acurizal area and at Miranda.

Acurizal

At Acurizal an adult female jaguar and her presumed daughter, estimated to be 15 to 18 months old, were resident and another adult female and a male visited the ranch intermittently; a third female, about 3 years old, apparently moved into the area in late 1977 or early 1978 and was then radio-collared by us. At Bela Vista 1 female with a semi-independent young, about 12 to 15 months old, an adult female (radio-collared), and an adult male remained within 90 km^2. These 9 jaguars occupied a total of 227 km^2, or 1 jaguar per 25 km^2. The female and her presumed daughter at Acurizal had identical ranges covering an area of about 38 km^2, and the radioed female there traveled within an area of 25 km^2, their ranges partially overlapping. The male's range at Acurizal included the ranges of all females, covering 21 km^2 within Acurizal, but his total range was probably at least twice as large. The radioed female at Bela Vista roamed over 34 km² within a 2-month period, and the male used the whole island. Although several jaguar may frequent the same area, they remain essentially solitary except during courtship and for interactions between mother and offspring.

Jaguar and puma are sympatric in the Pantanal. The cats overlap in size—weighing about 50 to 55 kg, a male puma is as large as a small female jaguar—and they prey largely on the same species. In some areas they are ecologically somewhat separated, the puma most abundant in dry vegetation types and the jaguar in moist ones, but this was not so at Acurizal; 3 or 4 puma frequented the ranch, none wholly resident. Jaguar and puma often used the same habitats, and indeed used the same trails the same night. However, puma seldom visited the northern part of the ranch where jaguar often hunted, suggesting a degree of spatial separation, of mutual avoidance.

MIRANDA

Most research at Miranda has focused on the jaguar and ocelot (Table 5). There we radio-collared an entire jaguar family group, a mother and 2 offspring—a male and a female—before the young became independent.

TABLE 5. Large Cats Radio-collared at Miranda, September 1981 to October 1982

Species	*Month captured*	*Sex*	*Wt (kg)*	*Est. age*
Jaguar*	Sep. 1981	F	41	14-16 mo
Jaguar*	Dec. 1981	F	85	Adult
Jaguar*	Dec. 1981	M	70	17-19 mo
Jaguar	Oct. 1982	F	67	2-3 yr
Puma	Dec. 1981	F	28	9-12 mo
Ocelot	Feb. 1982	F	5	Young adult
Ocelot	Apr. 1982	F	4	6-8 mo
Ocelot	Apr. 1982	F	8	Adult
Ocelot	May 1982	F	7.5	Adult

*Animals are part of a family group, a mother and two grown cubs.

From late December until late February 1982, the 3 animals remained in the same area and then broke up, dispersion perhaps precipitated by the adult female's approaching heat. The young male moved and settled about 30 km from the range occupied by his mother, whereas the young female has never been located more than 12 km from her mother. When the family was still together, the range of the young female encompassed

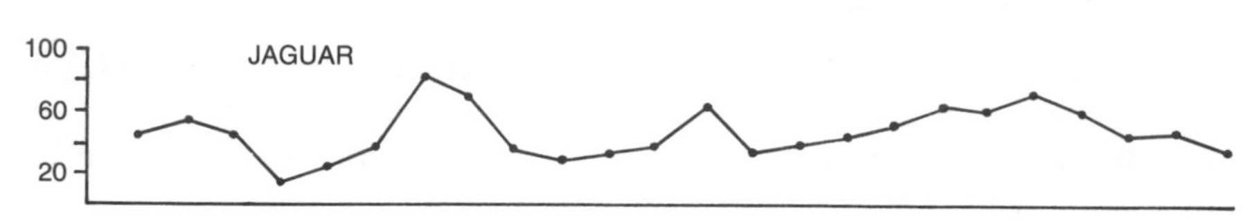

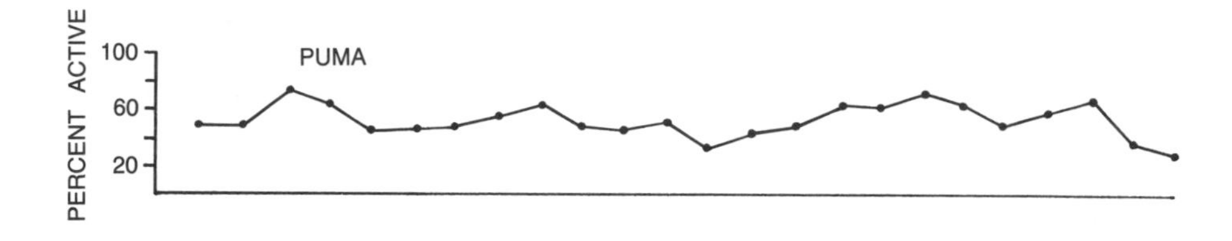

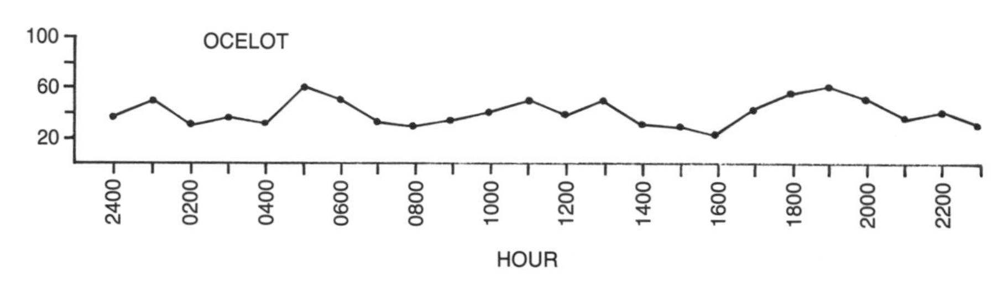

FIGURE 2. Twenty-four–hour activity patterns of jaguar, puma, and ocelot at Miranda, expressed in percent active radiotelemetry readings.

19 km^2; after dispersal her known range enlarged to 50 km^2 during the 10 months she has been radio-tracked. However, from early July to the end of October 1982 her movements have been limited to about 15 km^2, centering around a large forest, where, we suspect, she may have given birth. The young male ranged over about 110 km^2 in 10 months, probably a minimum, since air searches at times failed to locate him. Another female partially inhabited the ranges of the mother and young female.

The collared puma ranged over 82 km^2 in 10 months of tracking. The 2 adult female ocelots had ranges of 0.8 and 0.9 km^2, respectively, and the subadult female, 0.52 km^2.

The radio-collars contain a motion sensor which transmits information whether the animal is active or inactive. Whenever possible, the activity of collared animals was monitored for 24 hours or more, readings being recorded every 15 min. Figure 2, which is based on 1199 activity readings for jaguar, 1318 for puma, and 1022 for ocelot, shows that all 3 cat species have similar patterns: All may be active or inactive at any time of day and night, and all tend to be most active around dawn or dusk.

The jaguar data from Acurizal, Bela Vista, and Miranda show that the ranges of neighboring females overlap, that the range of a male is larger than that of a female, and that a male's range includes the ranges of at least 2 females. Acurizal and Bela Vista had only 1 resident male, suggesting that a male tolerates only females and subadults as residents within his range. Young males appear to disperse from their mother's range, whereas females tend to settle nearby. How jaguar space themselves is unclear, for they vocalize rarely in the Pantanal, and they seldom leave prominent visual and olfactory markings in the environment, in contrast to several other large cat species which advertise themselves conspicuously (Schaller, 1972). However, the land-tenure system of jaguar appears to be similar in most aspects to that of such other solitary cats as puma (Seidensticker et al., 1973) and tiger (Sunquist, 1981).

Acknowledgments

The research team included Howard B. Quigley of the Cooperative Wildlife Research Unit, University of Idaho, Moscow, Idaho, and the New York Zoological Society; and Peter Gransden Crawshaw of the Instituto Brasileira de Desenvolvimento Florestal, Palacio de Desenvolvimento, Brasilia, Brazil.

Our research was supported by the New York Zoological Society, the National Geographic Society, the National Science Foundation, the Instituto Brasileiro de Desenvolvimento Florestal, and the Fundação Brasileira para a Conservação da Natureza. The Conselho Nacional de Desenvolvimento Cientifico e Tecnologico kindly gave permission to do the research. We are especially grateful to the Klabin family for permission to work on the Miranda ranch. Of the many persons who helped us, we are particularly grateful to M. T. Jorge Padua, R. P. Leal, J. M. de Vasconcelos, J. Weaver, J. Schweizer, and G. Prance.

REFERENCES

Crawshaw, P., and Schaller, G.
1980. Nesting of Paraguayan caiman *(Caiman yacare)* in Brazil. Pap. Avulsos de Zoologia, vol. 33, no. 18, pp. 283-292.

Eisenberg, J.; O'Connell, M.; and August, P.
1979. Density, productivity and distribution of mammals in two Venezuelan habitats. Pp. 187-207 *in* "Vertebrate Ecology in the Northern Neotropics," J. Eisenberg, ed. Smithsonian Institution Press, Washington, D. C.

Eisenberg, J., and Thorington, R.
1973. A preliminary analysis of a neotropical mammal fauna. Biotropica, vol. 5, no. 3, pp. 150-161.

PRANCE, G., and SCHALLER, G.
1982. Preliminary study of some vegetation types of the Pantanal, Mato Grosso, Brazil. Brittonia, vol. 34, no. 2, pp. 228-251.
SCHALLER, G.
1972. The Serengeti lion, 480 pp. University of Chicago Press.
1983. Mammals and their biomass on a Brazilian ranch. Arq. Zool. São Paulo, vol. 31, no. 1, pp. 1-36.
SCHALLER, G., and CRAWSHAW, P.
1980. Movement patterns of jaguar. Biotropica, vol. 12, no. 3, pp. 161-168.
1981. Social organization in a capybara population. Säugetierk. Mitt. vol. 29, no. 1, pp. 3-16.
1982. Fishing behavior of Paraguayan caiman *(Caiman crocodilus).* Copeia, pp. 66-72.
SCHALLER, G., and VASCONCELOS, J.
1978a. Jaguar predation on capybara. Zool. Säugetierk., vol. 43, no. 5, pp. 296-301.
1978b. A marsh deer census in Brazil. Oryx, vol. 14, no. 4, pp. 345-351.
SEIDENSTICKER, J.
1976. Ungulate populations in Chitawan Valley, Nepal. Biol. Cons., vol. 10, pp. 183-210.
SEIDENSTICKER, J.; HORNOCKER, M.; WILES, W.; and MESSICK, J.
1973. Mountain lion social organization in the Idaho Primitive Area. Wildl. Monogr., vol. 35, pp. 1-60.
SUNQUIST, M.
1981. The social organization of tigers *(Panthera tigris)* in Royal Chitawan National Park, Nepal. Smithsonian Contr. Zool., no. 336, 98 pp.

GEORGE B. SCHALLER
HOWARD B. QUIGLEY
PETER GRANDSDEN CRAWSHAW

Photoperiodism and Physiological Ecology of a Relict Equatorial Alpine Butterfly

Grant Recipient: Arthur M. Shapiro, Department of Zoology, University of California, Davis, California.

Grant 1614: For a study of *Reliquia santamarta,* an unusual butterfly restricted to the alpine zone of the Sierra Nevada de Santa Marta, Colombia.

Reliquia santamarta is a recently described (Ackery, 1975) pierid butterfly apparently endemic to the high alpine ("superparamo," Van der Hammen, 1974) zone of the Sierra Nevada de Santa Marta, northeastern Colombia. Because of its isolation in this relatively inaccessible and biologically little-known area, the existence of such an animal was unsuspected until 1971 when Michael Adams, then a graduate student at the University of Manchester (United Kingdom), first saw it while doing survey collecting in the southeastern part of the range. He was unable to secure a specimen of this swift-flying animal until the following year, but ultimately a good series was accumulated. The genus *Reliquia* was described as monotypic but closely allied to the widespread Holarctic genus *Pieris.* As Figure 1 shows, the facies of both sexes is remarkably similar to high-altitude and high-latitude populations of Nearctic *Pieris* of the *callidice* species group. Because of the similarity of habitat, the phenotypic resemblance could represent evolutionary parallelism rather than very close phylogenetic relationship. Morphologically *Reliquia* also appears close to the *callidice* group, but decisions as to its affinities must take into account characters of the immature stages, hitherto unknown, and any other relevant data which may become available. In any case, *Reliquia* seems to be rather distantly related to the very distinctive group of Andean endemic genera, the *Tatochila-Phulia* group. It is unique south of Mexico in having the submarginal chevrons pointed *inward* in the interspaces—in all other South American montane and alpine pierines they point *outward.* Only one Old World genus, *Baltia* from the central Asian highlands, resembles them in this regard.

The resemblance to *Pieris* suggested that *Reliquia santamarta* might represent a stranded Nearctic invader in South America, presumably of Pleistocene vintage. The Cruciferae, on which the Pierini feed almost obligately, are viewed by most phytogeographers as invaders from the

FIGURE 1. Dorsal surfaces (left group) and ventral surfaces (right group) of three pairs of pierines from extreme climates (males at left in each pair).

Top pairs: *Reliquia santamarta*, Colombia, 4200 m (lat. 10°44′N). Center pairs: *Pieris occidentalis calyce*, Colorado, 3800 m (lat. 40°01′N). Bottom pairs: *Pieris occidentalis nelsoni*, Alaska (low altitude) (lat. 64°51′N).

north into Plio-Pleistocene South America (Raven and Axelrod, 1974). Mainly a temperate and alpine group, they presumably could not have become established before the Andean orogeny. If this interpretation is correct, *R. santamarta*—localized on the northernmost mountains of the continent—could represent a relict of the original stock from which the large Andean pierine fauna was derived by adaptive radiation (Klots, 1933). The peculiar biogeography of the Sierra Nevada de Santa Marta supports this view. The Sierra is astonishingly insular. It is relatively unrelated faunistically or floristically to the Serrania de Valledupar, only 62 km away across the Cesar and Rancheria Valleys; the Serrania is the northernmost prong of the Andes proper and has a basically Andean biota, but the Sierra is floristically related to highland Costa Rica (A. S. Weston, pers. comm.) and has a large number of endemic plants and insects (M. Adams, pers. comm.) including the intricately branching arborescent frailejons, *Espeletia glossophylla*, the most conspicuous alpine plant. Of its faunal elements only the birds show a conspicuous Andean connection (Todd and Carriker, 1922), but even in this group endemism is marked. After *R. santamarta*, the zoogeographically most intriguing Sierran animal is another pierid butterfly, *Nathalis iole* (Coliadini). Otherwise unknown in South America, this common alpine resident of the Sierra occurs in lowland desert washes and in urban vacant lots from southern California to Georgia, south to Guatemala and the West Indies! The commonest alpine butterfly in the Sierra is a skipper (Hesperiidae) belonging to the large Andean genus *Hylephila*.

For over a decade I have studied the biology of the Nearctic pierines, especially the *Pieris callidice* group in western North America. These animals have invaded a wide variety of climates, including desert, Mediterranean, and high alpine. They show abundant evidence of adaptive radiation in ecophysiological characters, especially those that enable them to cope with seasonality. Many pierines of middle latitudes are multivoltine and have seasonal phenotypes under environmental (photoperiod and temperature) control, which may or may not be physiologically coupled to pupal dormancy (diapause). In middle latitudes photoperiod is a much more reliable predictor of season than is temperature, and hundreds of studies by workers in North America and Europe have shown its importance in regulating seasonal phenomena in plants and animals of all kinds. In addition to multivoltine-polyphenic pierines, numerous pierines are univoltine-monophenic, and I have accumulated substantial evidence showing that they are generally derived from multivoltine-polyphenic ancestors (Shapiro, 1976). That is, generalized, developmentally plastic pierines have over geologic time invaded harsher climates and undergone progressive evolutionary adaptation under directional selection. One obtains such evidence by rearing the animals in ecologically meaningless regimes, such as continuous light. In the real world inhabited by univoltines, selection has pushed alternative phenotypes off the end of the experienced photoperiodic scale. There is, however, no *a priori* reason why they should not still be expressed when the animal grows up in a regime too bizarre to have been experienced in its evolutionary history. The genetic basis for phenotypic plasticity seems very persistent, suggesting that it is connected to a variety of developmentally essential pathways. To date I have not found a univoltine Nearctic pierine that does not show such relict polyphenism under the appropriate rearing regime. This evidence of progressive adaptation to adverse climates bears on the long-smouldering problem of latitudinal gradients in species diversity. Many ecologists contend that glaciated and other recent, severe environments have vacant niches and are undergoing enrichment by colonization and adaptation; this seems to be the history of the Nearctic pierines.

Reliquia santamarta thus offered a unique opportunity for research bearing on biogeography, physiological ecology, and systematics. The seasonal biology of equatorial insects in general is very poorly known. It is frequently, perhaps erroneously, assumed that they breed continuously with no dormant period. At lat. 10 to 11°N, *R. santamarta* has a spread of about 70 min between its longest and shortest days of the year. There is apparently only one photoperiodic study of an insect from such latitudes in the literature. That species did not show any phenotypic response to day length, but some plants, native to higher latitudes, find the photoperiodic difference in Trinidad (at the same latitude as the Sierra) significant, and flower only seasonally. *Poinsettia,* native to Mexico, is an example; it is seasonal in Trinidad but aseasonal at Cali, almost 4°N. This suggests that if *R. santamarta* really were a Pleistocene invader from North America, it could show the same relict polyphenism as its cousins there if reared on the same regimes. The experience of the handful of collectors who have visited the Sierra demonstrated that *R. santamarta* must be multiple-brooded, flying in the relatively dry trade-wind season, or *verano,* in December through March (with perhaps two broods) and again in the shorter, less reliable *veranillo* in July. No phenotypic differences are apparent among animals collected at these different times. Its natural phenotype is, however, adaptive at both seasons. Pierine phenotypes are used in thermoregulation. These butterflies are heliotherms, and raise body temperature to flight-sustaining levels by a series of orientational maneuvers to trap incoming solar radiation on heavily melanized surfaces. As Figure 1 again illustrates, pierines of cold climates are remarkably consistent in pattern. Populations in warm climates, and summer phenotypes of multivoltine populations, lack the heavy dark markings beneath. Parallelisms in phenotype are mirrored in thermoregulatory and other behavior, so much so that knowing the behavior of Nearctic alpine species was a tremendous asset in studying *Reliquia* afield.

The weather at Cambirumeina, the type locality of *R. santamarta,* is rarely favorable for flight for long. In the rainy seasons, when the insect probably does not fly (or at least emerges at much lower density), it is almost continuously cloudy, rainy, or snowy, and too cold for flight. In the two dry seasons, flight activity is usually possible for only a few hours in the morning, since fog and drizzle set in sometime between 10 a.m. and 2 p.m. daily, rendering activity impossible. At daybreak the temperature is usually below freezing, and flight generally begins about 8 a.m. when sunlit areas may have reached 10°C while shaded ones are still frozen. Since feeding and reproduction depend absolutely on flight, which is only possible in sunshine, any adaptation that helps *R. santamarta* raise its body temperature earlier—maximizing the time available for flight—will be rapidly selected, and it is no wonder the wings are always dark. There is no reason why *R. santamarta* might not produce a light phenotype if reared on a long or continuous day—that is, if it were recently descended from an ancestor that produced seasonal phenotypes. Production of such a phenotype would strongly support the Pleistocene-invader hypothesis; failure to produce it would not necessarily rule it out.

An expedition to obtain livestock for experimentation was mounted in January 1977, with funding from the National Geographic Society and the National Science Foundation. It consisted of Mrs. Adrienne R. Shapiro, Dr. Arthur S. Weston (a botanist based in Australia), and myself. We reached the trailhead at San Sebastian de Rabago, Cesar, Colombia, 1900 m, on January 14 and were guided up via Duriameina and Mamancanaca by Elias Gregorio Izquierdo from the settlement of El Pantano. We sighted our first *Reliquias* at midday January 17 on the west side of the pass to Cambirumeina, where we made camp at 3950 m. Through January 22 we made daily behavioral observations of *R. santamarta* on the south slope of Cerro Icachui, up to 4400 m, and throughout the surrounding country. These dramatically demonstrated that behaviorally, *R. santamarta* and *Pieris occidentalis calyce* of the alpine western United States are indistinguishable. This includes their use of hilltops as sexual rendezvous sites (Shapiro, 1977a). Eight females were collected and induced to oviposit in containers in camp, using previously tested methods. We took many photographs and did extensive floristic survey, with particular emphasis on the Cruciferae; this area has received little botanical attention since the Seifriz expedition some 40 years ago. The eggs were transported back to Valledupar, Cesar, on January 26 and thence to Cali, south-central Colombia, where the photoperiod experiments were carried out.

The experiments demonstrate to my satisfaction that *R. santamarta* does *not* have a relict polyphenism like its putative Nearctic relatives. Its phenotype proved refractory to change, even under continuous light and high temperature conditions (Shapiro, 1977b). In the course of rearing I obtained the first photographs and preserved material of the egg, larva, and pupa—all of which have traits bearing on the classification of the beast (Shapiro, 1977c).

The behavioral, physiological, and morphological life-history data are combining to give us a picture of an animal clearly related to, but surprisingly different from, the Nearctic pierines. *R. santamarta* must have undergone very rapid evolution to have diverged so much from its relatives if it is really only of Pleistocene age; this, however, may not be. The very complex tectonic history of the Sierra (Tschanz et al., 1974) allows other interpretations. (See also Van der Hammen, 1974 for the climatic history of the Colombian Andes.) The picture should clarify somewhat as Adams continues to work up the butterfly zoogeography of the ranges along the Caribbean margin (Adams, 1973). *Reliquia* may indeed be a relict of the line ancestral to *Tatochila;* but, if so, it is a much older relict than we had imagined, since evidence that it may antedate the Andean orogeny is accumulating from my work in that genus. The geography of the crucifers is, moreover, much less clear-cut than Raven and Axelrod imply. Studies of the developmental and phenotypic responses of *Tatochila* to environmental conditions may help to give us a picture of how its adaptive radiation took place, and in what geoclimatic context.

REFERENCES

Ackery, P. R.

1975. A new pierine genus and species with notes on the genus *Tatochila* (Lepidoptera: Pieridae). Bull. Allyn Museum, vol. 30, pp. 1-9.

Adams, Michael

1973. Ecological zonation and the butterflies of the Sierra Nevada de Santa Marta, Colombia. Journ. Nat. Hist. vol. 7, pp. 699-718.

Klots, Alexander B.

1933. A generic revision of the Pieridae (Lepidoptera), together with a study of the male genitalia. Entomologica Americana, vol. 12, pp. 139-242.

Raven, Peter H., and Axelrod, Daniel I.

1974. Angiosperm biogeography and past continental movements. Annals Missouri Botanical Garden, vol. 61, pp. 539-673.

Shapiro, Arthur M.

1976. Seasonal polyphenism. Evolutionary Biol., vol. 9, pp. 259-333.

1977a. Notes on the behavior and ecology of *Reliquia santamarta,* an alpine butterfly (Lepidoptera: Pieridae) from the Sierra Nevada de Santa Marta, Colombia, with comparisons to Nearctic alpine Pierini. Beiträge zur Neotropischen Fauna, vol. 14, pp. 161-170.

SHAPIRO, ARTHUR *(continued)*
1977b. Evidence for obligate monophenism in *Reliquia santamarta*, a neotropical alpine pierine butterfly (Lepidoptera: Pieridae). Psyche, vol. 84, pp. 183-190.
1977c. The life history of *Reliquia santamarta*, a neotropical-alpine pierine butterfly (Lepidoptera: Pieridae). Journ. New York Entomol. Soc., vol. 86, pp. 45-50.

TODD, WALTER E. C., and CARRIKER, M. A., JR.
1922. The birds of the Santa Marta region of Colombia: A study in altitudinal distribution. Annals Carnegie Mus., vol. 14, pp. 3-611.

TSCHANZ, C. M.; MARVIN, R. F.; CRUZ, B. J.; MEHNERT, H. H.; and CEBULA, G. T.
1974. Geologic evolution of the Sierra Nevada de Santa Marta, northeastern Colombia. Bull. Geol. Soc. of America, vol. 85, pp. 273-284.

VAN DER HAMMEN, T.
1974. The Pleistocene changes of vegetation and climate in tropical South America. Journ. Biogeography, vol. 1, pp. 3-26.

ARTHUR M. SHAPIRO

Petrology of the Type Area Trondhjemite in the Trondheim Region of the Norwegian Caledonides

Grant Recipient: William B. Size, Emory University, Atlanta, Georgia.

Grant 1696: In support of research on the petrology of igneous intrusions in the Norwegian Caledonides.

Trondhjemites have been called by other names in the literature, including sodagranite, plagiogranite, and leucogranodiorite. They are distinctive rock types and are abundant in continental Archean-age rocks (Arth and Hanson, 1975). The association of trondhjemites with younger mobile belts at continental margins and subduction zones indicates that the production and growth of continental crust may be associated with the genesis of trondhjemitic rocks.

The purpose of this study is to quantify the mineralogic, chemical, and petrologic characteristics of the type area of trondhjemite as first proposed by Goldschmidt (1916) and to provide the data necessary for this area to be used as a standard against which to compare other trondhjemite-bearing areas. Of equal importance in this study is an examination of the different petrogenetic models proposed for the origin of trondhjemite to determine which, if any, are consistent with the data from the type area trondhjemite (Size, 1979).

The general study area is in the Trondheim region (Fig. 1), which is considered to represent the type area of the "eugeosynclinal zone" of the Norwegian Caledonides (Strand and Kulling, 1972). Petrochemistry of the eugeosynclinal magmatic rocks and interpretation of their relationships to the tectonic history of the Trondheim region have been discussed by Gale and Roberts (1972, 1974).

The area reported in this study is located 45 km south of Trondheim near the town of Støren (10°20′E long., 63°N lat.). The major area of interest is 2 km east of Støren at the Follstad Quarry. Duplicate trondhjemite samples were collected from the quarry and from the same intrusive body north and south of the quarry. For comparison, other trondhjemite bodies were sampled from the surrounding area, which will hereafter collectively be called the "Follstad District trondhjemite."

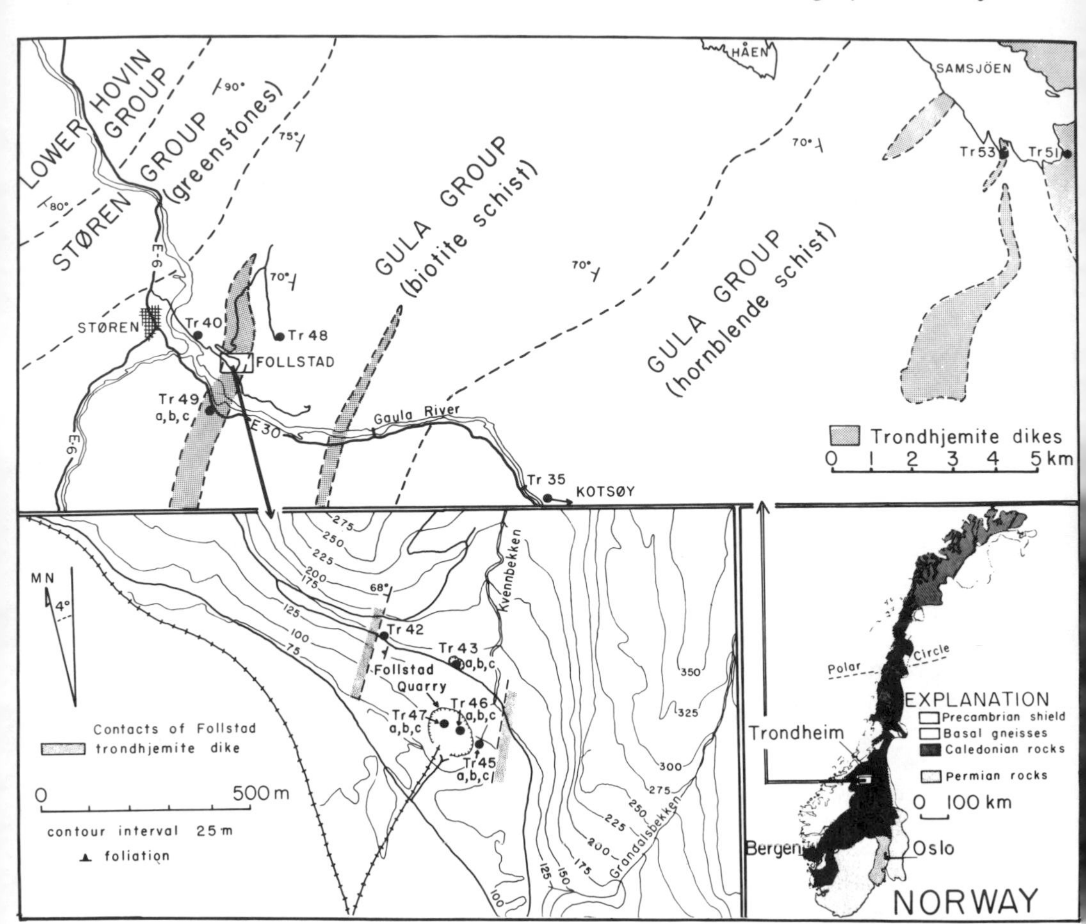

FIGURE 1. General geologic maps and two sample location maps of the study area in the central Norwegian Caledonides, south of the city of Trondheim. Geology after Wolff (1976).

There were three or four periods of trondhjemite intrusive activity in the Follstad District during the Lower Paleozoic. The oldest trondhjemite bodies tend to lie within the regional foliation. Younger trondhjemite intrusions cut across the foliation and tend to be contorted into later, open-type folds. An even younger phase is represented by the Follstad body, which has little mechanical deformation but contains a metamorphic mineral assemblage. The youngest phase of trondhjemite emplacement is represented by the trondhjemite pegmatites. No examples of this last type are found in the study area, but are in the Stjørdalen Valley.

Most of the trondhjemite bodies in the study area are discordant and contain xenoliths of country rock (Fig. 2), as can be seen in the Kvennbekken stream just west of the main Follstad Quarry. At contacts with the country rock, trondhjemite is not chilled and shows a fluxion foliation. Many of the dikes show evidence of being multiple intrusions, judging from the sharp discontinuities in grain size and mineral proportions across the dike (Fig. 2). Most of the dikes in the area are not as wide as the Follstad body, and even the smaller ones do not show any chilling, a good indication that the wall rock was at a reasonably high temperature at the time of intrusion.

The Follstad trondhjemite body is approximately 375 m wide in the vicinity of the main quarry. It has a general strike of N20°E to N25°E and dips approximately 68° to the northwest. Its western contact with the Gula phyllite is very sharp, with slight silicification and hornfelsic texture as the only contact metamorphic effects. Iron-staining and a weakly developed cataclastic zone were observed at the contact.

Sampling and Analytical Methods

Thirty samples of trondhjemite were taken from dikes in the Follstad District. Other trondhjemite intrusives from the surrounding region were also sampled for comparison (no. Tr 35, 40, 42, 48, 51, 53). However, sample Tr 40 was ultimately determined to be a quartz keratophyre, and Tr 51 is a leuco-monzogabbro.

Rock samples for statistical analysis of variance were taken from fresh exposures of trondhjemite in the Follstad District. At each outcrop location, three rock samples, each weighing 2 kg, were taken 5 m from one another in a triangular arrangement. Two thin sections were cut perpendicular to one another from each rock sample. The remainder of the sample was then trimmed to remove any surface alteration and then powdered in an agate mill for chemical analysis. The powders were split for major and minor element analysis.

Chemical analyses of SiO_2, TiO_2, Al_2O_3, and CaO were done by X-ray fluorescence spectrometry (J. Sandvik, analyst); total Fe, MnO, Na_2O, and K_2O were determined by atomic absorption spectrophotometry; FeO by titrimetry; H_2O (total), CO_2, and H_2O by gravimetry; and P_2O_5 by spectrophotometry. Results of the chemical analyses are available from the author upon request.

Trace-element analyses were done by neutron activation at the Nuclear Research Laboratory at Virginia Polytechnic Institute and State University (T. F. Parkinson, analyst). Samples were irradiated in a thermal flux of $1.3 \times 10^{12} n/cm^2/sec$, using high resolution Ge(Li) detectors. U. S. Geological Survey standard rocks BCR-1, AGV-1, G-2, and GSP-1 were used as standards.

FIGURE 2. Multiple trondhjemite dikes in outcrop on the southeast shore of Samsjoen (Tr 51, Fig. 1). Cross-cutting dikes contain xenoliths and are not chilled against the Gula schist country rock. The largest dike represents a composite intrusion.

Petrography

TEXTURE AND STRUCTURE

Follstad trondhjemite is whitish in color, speckled with dark brown biotite. In hand-specimen it is homogeneous and massive, having only a weak foliation which is defined by biotite and muscovite and which strikes N40°E and dips to the northwest. Prominent jointing strikes N5°E to N12°E and dips 45° to 47° to the northwest.

Trondhjemite samples from dikes in the Follstad District are holocrystalline, medium-grained (0.5 to 1.5 mm) and hypidiomorphic-granular in texture. As the degree of alteration increases, the rock texture grades into allotriomorphic-granular. Slightly metamorphosed varieties of trondhjemite have a weakly developed granoblastic texture.

Three different types of mineral clusters are present in the rock: (1) mafic clusters, consisting of epidote, biotite, muscovite, sphene, and zircon; (2) quartz clusters; and (3) clusters of plagioclase laths with small,

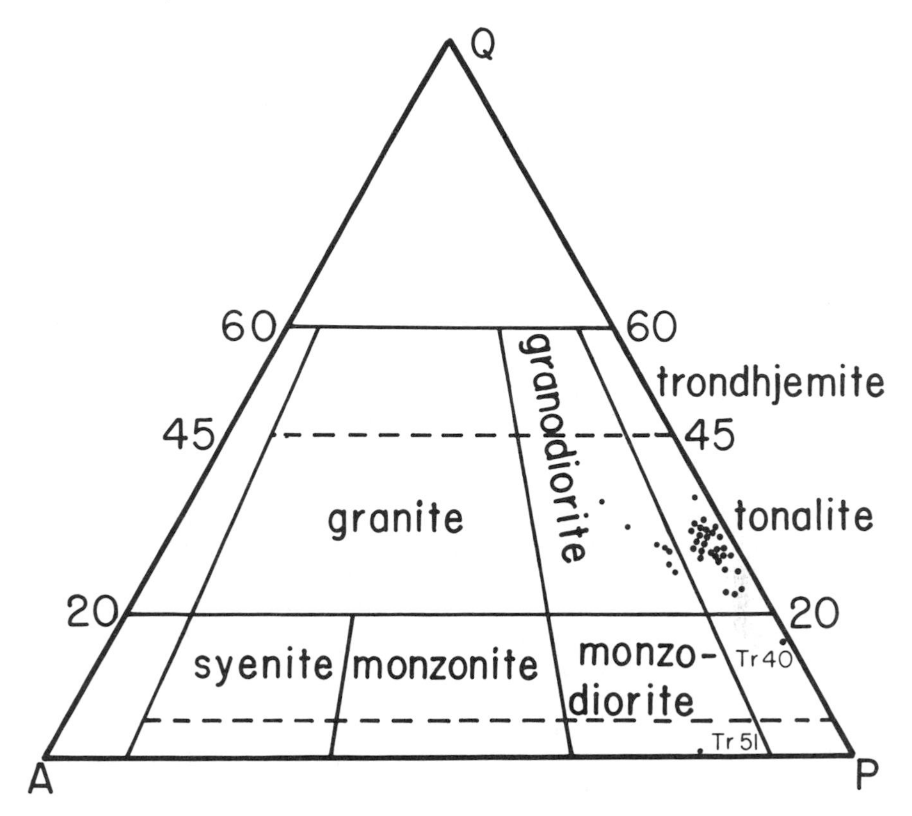

FIGURE 3. Triangular plot of the relative percentages of modal quartz (Q), alkali feldspar (A), and plagioclase (P) for the trondhjemitic rocks in the Follstad District. Rock name field boundaries after Streckeisen (1967).

angular, interstitial spaces filled with albite. These clusters appear more indicative of magmatic synneusis than metamorphic segregation.

In thin section, biotite and muscovite plates are commonly bent and crudely aligned to define a faint foliation. Locally quartz and plagioclase have been microsheared into a mortar structure. Grain boundaries rarely interlock; rather, most are straight to slightly curved, indicating recrystallization. Overgrowths of albite on plagioclase are conspicuous, even in hand-specimens.

MODAL MINERAL DESCRIPTION

Trondhjemites from the Follstad District show a very small degree of modal variation. The composite average for 30 samples can therefore be viewed as representative of the entire intrusion. A triangular plot of the relative modal percentages of quartz, alkali feldspar, and plagioclase (Fig. 3) shows that most samples plot in the tonalite field and none of them in the trondhjemite field. Chemically and mineralogically, however, the rocks from the Follstad District are true trondhjemites; in fact, the quarry at Follstad is viewed as the type-locality of trondhjemite as first proposed by Goldschmidt (1916). The boundary between tonalite and trondhjemite (45% quartz), as shown in the diagram, is not truly representative of the natural system. Most trondhjemitic rocks from other areas would also plot in the tonalite field of Streickeisen (1967). The mafic index of tonalite is higher than that of trondhjemite and the SiO_2 content is lower, so there is actually a real difference between the two rock types.

Major element analyses and CIPW norms for the Follstad District trondhjemite showed relatively high contents of silica and sodium compared with the low content of potassium. The Na_2O/K_2O ratio averages 3.8. The high Na_2O content relative to K_2O is in part due to alteration and metasomatism (sericitization, albitization). Trondhjemite averages 16.2% Al_2O_3, which classifies it as the high alumina type (greater than 15% Al_2O_3) as defined by Barker and Arth (1976). In contrast to trondhjemites worldwide, Follstad District trondhjemite has relatively low amounts of total iron (average 1.36%), and the FeO/Fe_2O_3 ratio is relatively high at 1.34. The total Fe/Mg ratio is also low (average 2.83) in comparison with that in trondhjemites from other regions (Arth and Hanson, 1975). The low Fe/Mg ratio, together with the low potassium content, indicates that these rocks represent a primitive magma type that has not further differentiated to leucogranodiorite or leucomonzonite by the removal of plagioclase.

A comparison of the K_2O content versus SiO_2 shows that Follstad region trondhjemites plot in the continental trondhjemite field of Coleman and Peterman (1975, p. 1105), with more K_2O than the oceanic plagiogranites. There is not enough range in the compositions of these rocks to show any trend in crystallization. The correlation coefficients for major oxides, however, show that as silica and potassium increase, calcium, iron, magnesium, sodium, and aluminum decrease correspondingly.

Trondhjemites plotted on an AFM diagram (Fig. 4) are at the low temperature end of the gabbro-trondhjemite trend (Barker and Arth, 1976), which is a subtrend of the more general calc-alkaline suite. Other eugeosynclinal magmatic rocks from the Trondheim region are represented by the shaded area of Figure 4 (Loeschke, 1976, p. 45). This field also shows a calc-alkaline trend, with Follstad trondhjemite at the most differentiated end. This demonstrates that Follstad District trondhjemite may represent the lowest temperature melt of a basaltic magma.

The triangular plot of normative Qz-Or-Ab (Fig. 5) shows that all of the trondhjemites plot away from the eutectic melting composition in the

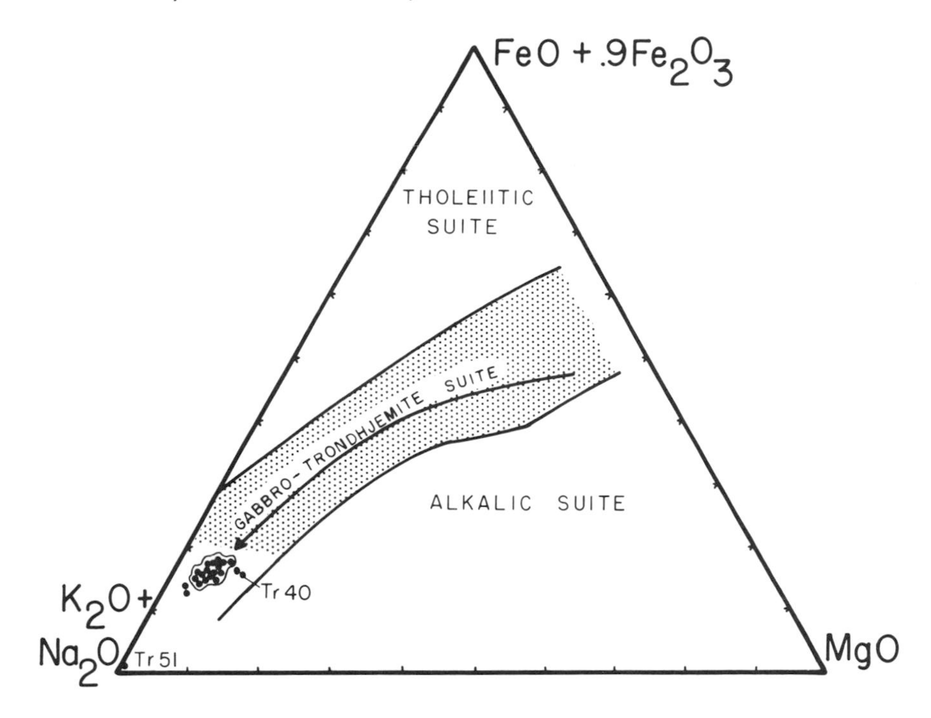

FIGURE 4. AFM plot for the Follstad trondhjemites. Gabbro-trondhjemite trend after Barker and Arth (1976). Shaded area represents locations for the eugeosynclinal magmatic rocks in the Trondheim region (Loeschke, 1976). Group of points outlined represents trondhjemite samples from the Follstad Quarry.

Or-Ab-An-Qz-H_2O system. The trondhjemites, as plotted, show a slight decrease in An content that corresponds with distance away from the minimum melt composition, as would be expected in a fractional crystallization process or a partial melting process. However, rocks so poor in K_2O, yet rich in SiO_2, cannot be easily accounted for unless a low K_2O-bearing parent material is invoked. Also shown in Figure 5 are the eutectic point and cotectic lines for P_{H_2O} = 2kb at an Ab/An ratio of 3.8, which is near the Follstad District trondhjemite ratio of 3.5. If the trondhjemite represented a melt composition, it would have crystallized at approximately 750° to 800°C. The calc-alkaline crystallization trend shows potassium enrichment toward the lower temperatures (Fig. 5), whereas the gabbro-trondhjemite trend does not (Barker and Arth, 1976). Arth and Barker (1978) would identify this as the calc-alkaline trondhjemitic trend. This deviation is explained by differences in parental material (tholeiitic versus alkalic basaltic magma).

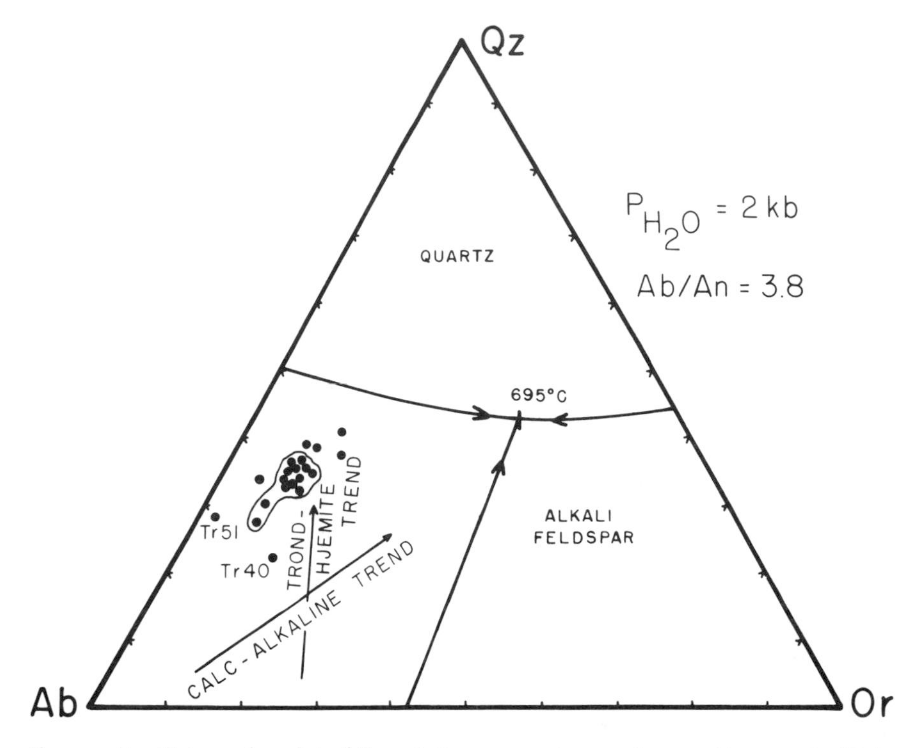

FIGURE 5. Triangular plot of the relative percentages of normative quartz (Qz), orthoclase (Or), and albite (Ab) for the Follstad trondhjemite. Group of points outlined represents trondhjemite samples from the Follstad Quarry.

Conclusions

Models for the origin of trondhjemitic magmas are clearly polygenic, but the model that most closely fits the data for Follstad District trondhjemite is one of equilibrium melting of a low-K_2O tholeiitic basalt during anatexis in an orogenic zone. Helz (1976) performed melting experiments on tholeiites in the low temperature melting range (680° to 1000°C, P_{H_2O} = 5 Kb) and determined that within the hornblende stability field, partial melts of all the starting basalts are strongly quartzo-feldspathic and corundum-normative (the Follstad trondhjemites are also corundum normative). The composition of the low temperature melts are quite consistent and insensitive to differences in starting materials, P_{H_2O} or F_{O_2}. One exception is that the relative abundances of calcium, sodium, and potassium vary directly from the source rock to the magma.

The results of Helz's experiments can be directly related to Follstad District trondhjemite. Støren Group greenstones are similar in composition to the basalts used by Helz (1976) as starting material, except that the K_2O is lower in the greenstones (K_2O = 0.16 to 0.22%) than in the basalts (K_2O = 0.49 to 0.97%). The solidus for the basalts is at about 690°C and the melt compositions are all similar up to the upper stability field of hornblende. The Or is relatively constant as long as hornblende is the only alkali-bearing phase. The melts move out toward the center of the Qz-Or-Ab ternary only when plagioclase begins to separate from the melt. The closest natural analog to the melts derived in the partial melting experiments of the tholeiitic basalts is the trondhjemite suite. At 825° to 850°C and P_{H_2O} = 5 kb, the composition of the partial melts from the 1921 Kilauea tholeiite and the Picture Gorge tholeiite (Helz, 1976) had almost the same bulk composition as Follstad District trondhjemite. The slight difference is that K_2O content is lower in these trondhjemites than in the basaltic melt. This difference could be accounted for by the lower K_2O content of Støren greenstones, if they were comparable to the parent material for the trondhjemite.

Summary

Trondhjemite of the Follstad District intrudes a sequence of associated Lower Paleozoic metasedimentary and metavolcanic rocks of the Caledonide orogen in central Norway. There were four periods of trondhjemite intrusion in this district, with the oldest intrusives the most deformed. Trondhjemite at the Follstad Quarry near Støren is late tectonic, and has an upper greenschist facies mineral assemblage. Follstad District trondhjemite is homogeneous in mineral and chemical composition, and shows little evidence of any earlier or later differentiation. Its composition is at the low temperature minimum of the gabbro-trondhjemite trend, which is a subtrend of the calc-alkaline series. However, distinctive compositional gaps in the trondhjemite compared with other associated magmatic rocks in the Trondheim area are difficult to explain by a simple fractional crystallization model.

Composition of Follstad trondhjemite is characteristic of trondhjemites of other regions associated with mobile belts and greenstones (Shelbourne pluton, Nova Scotia, Albuquerque, 1977; Twillingate pluton, eastern Newfoundland, Strong et al., 1974). Trondhjemites associated with basic volcanic rocks are peraluminous; high in SiO_2, Al_2O_3, and Na_2O, but low in K_2O; usually late tectonic; extremely homogeneous in composition; depleted and show a highly fractionated REE pattern; and have low abundances of Rb compared with Ba.

The petrogenetic interpretation for the origin of Follstad trondhjemite is based on the model of equilibrium melting of a K_2O-poor tholeiitic basalt during anatexis in an orogenic zone. The regional tectonic setting of the Follstad District and the character of the associated rocks support this model. Other models, such as anatexis of continental crust or partial melting of greywacke, would not produce the composition of Follstad trondhjemite.

Composition of Follstad trondhjemite plots away from minimum melting temperatures in the Or-Ab-An-Qz-H_2O system. Melting experiments of Piwinskii (1968) and Wyllie (1977) show that below 2 kb pressure, temperatures necessary to produce an anatectic melt of trondhjemitic composition are too high to be produced during normal regional metamorphism. However, in the range of 5 to 10 kb P_{H_2O}, a trondhjemitic melt can be produced between 760° to 840°C. This work agrees with the work of Helz (1976) on the partial melting of tholeiitic basalts, which produce a trondhjemitic melt at 825° to 850°C at $P_{H_2O} = 5$ kb. Composition of the trondhjemite produced would show major element, trace element, and REE abundances as seen in the Follstad trondhjemite, if hornblende is a residual phase.

Acknowledgments

Support for this research was provided by a Fulbright-Hays Senior Research Award and by a grant from the National Geographic Society. Special thanks are due to Prof. Chr. Oftedahl, Mr. Tøre Prestvik, and to all the other faculty and staff of the Geologisk Institutt at the University of Trondheim. This Institute also provided logistic support, laboratory, and field expenses while I was on sabbatical leave in Trondheim. Thanks also go to State Geologist F. Chr. Wolff of the Norwegian Geological Survey for accompanying me in the field, and for his discussions on the trondhjemite field relations. David Roberts greatly aided me in the understanding of the structural relationships and their tectonic interpretation in the Trondheim region.

REFERENCES

Albuquerque, G.A.R., de
1977. Geochemistry of the tonalitic and granitic rocks of the Nova Scotia southern plutons. Geochim. Cosmochim. Acta, vol. 41, pp. 1-13.

Arth, J. G., and Barker, F.
1978. Geochemistry of the gabbro-tonalite-trondhjemite suite of southwest Finland and its implications for the origin of tonalitic and trondhjemitic magmas. Journ. Petrol., vol. 19, pp. 289-316.

Arth, J. G., and Hanson, G. N.
1975. Geochemistry and origin of the early Precambrian crust of N.E. Minnesota. Geochim. Cosmochim. Acta, vol. 39, pp. 325-362.

Barker, F., and Arth, J. G.
1976. Generation of trondhjemitic-tonalitic liquids and Archean bimodal trondhjemite-basalt suites. Geology, vol. 4, pp. 596-600.

Coleman, R. G., and Peterman, Z. G.
1975. Oceanic plagiogranite. Journ. Geophys. Res., vol. 80, pp. 1099-1108.

Gale, G. H., and Roberts, D.
1972. Paleogeographical implications of greenstone petrochemistry in the southern Norwegian Caledonides. Nature–Physical Science, vol. 238, pp. 60-61.
1974. Trace element geochemistry of Norwegian Lower Paleozoic basic volcanics and its tectonic implications. Earth and Planetary Science Letters, vol. 22, pp. 380-390.

Goldschmidt, V. M.
1916. Geologisch-petrographische studien im hochgebirge des sudlichen Norwegens, IV. Ubersicht der eruptivgesteine im kaledonischen gebirge zwischen Stavanger und Trondhjem, 140 pp. Vidensk. Selsk. Skr. I. Mat. Naturv. Kl. no. 2.

Helz, R. T.
1976. Phase relations of basalt in their melting ranges at PH_2O = 5 Kb. Part II, Melt compositions. Journ. Petrol., vol. 17, pp. 139-193.

Loeschke, J.
1976. Petrochemistry of eugeosynclinal magmatic rocks of the area around Trondheim (central Norwegian Caledonides). Neues. Jahrb. Miner. Abh., vol. 128, pt.1. pp. 41-72.

Piwinskii, A. J.
1968. Experimental studies on igneous rock series, Central Sierra Nevada Batholith, California. Journ. Geology, vol. 76, pp. 548-570.

Size, W. B.
1979. Petrology, geochemistry, and genesis of the type area trondhjemite in the Trondheim region, Central Norwegian Caledonides. Bull. Norges geologiske undersøkelse, Bull. 51, no. 351, pp. 51-76.

Strand, T., and Kulling, O.
1972. Scandinavian Caledonides, 302 pp. Wiley-Interscience, London.

Streckeisen, A.
1967. Classification and nomenclature of igneous rocks. Neues. Jahrb. Miner. Abh., vol. 102, pp. 144-214.

Strong, D. F.; Dickson, W. L.; O'Driscoll, C. F.; and Kean, B. F.
1974. Geochemistry of eastern Newfoundland granitoid rocks, 140 pp. Canada, Dept. of Mines and Energy, Report 74-3.

Wolff, F. C.
1976. Geologiske kart over Norge, berggrunnskart TRONDHEIM 1:250 000. Norges geologiske undersøkelse. (Map.)

Wyllie, P. J.
1977. Crustal anatexis: An experimental review. Tectonophysics, vol. 43, pp. 41-71.

William B. Size

Communication and Reproductive Isolating Mechanisms in Greater Prairie Chickens and Sharp-tailed Grouse

Grant Recipient: Donald W. Sparling, University of North Dakota, Grand Forks, North Dakota.[1]

Grant 1630: In support of a study of behavioral isolating mechanisms between Greater Prairie Chickens and Sharp-tailed Grouse.

Greater Prairie Chickens *(Tympanuchus cupido)* and Sharp-tailed Grouse *(Pedioecetes phasianellus)* share a narrow zone of sympatry in the north central and midwestern United States. Hybridization between these species usually occurs at a rate of 1 to 3% (Johnsgard and Wood, 1968) but even that percentage rate once eliminated an island population of Prairie Chickens in Canada (Lumsden, 1970). Because hybridization is relatively rare between closely related avian species and even more infrequent between genera, the major purpose of this study was to identify mechanisms that maintain species integrity while still permitting limited intermating. Major emphasis was on ethological (communicatory) mechanisms; geographic distribution, breeding seasons and times, and hybrid fertility were also examined.

Methods

Current geographic distributions of the two species were determined from questionnaires sent to conservation agencies of all states and provinces having extinct or extant populations of either species. Responses and accompanying range maps were obtained from all but two provinces.

Field studies were conducted on a 210-km^2 study area in Polk and Red Lake counties, northwestern Minnesota. Legal and floristic descriptions of the area are in Jorgenson (1977). Prairie grouse had been sympatric in the area for approximately 100 years (Partch, 1973).

Daily observations were made from blinds located on display-ground peripheries during the 1975-1978 breeding seasons. Five-minute activity

[1] Now at U. S. Fish and Wildlife Service, Northern Prairie Wildlife Research Center, Jamestown, North Dakota.

samples of focal animals were taken every 20 minutes in 1975 and 1976, and 15- to 60-minute samples were recorded daily during 1977 and 1978. Recordings of vocalizations were made with a Uher 4000 Report-L tape recorder and Uher 540 or Sennheiser 804 ultra-unidirectional microphones and analyzed with a Kay Elemetrics Co. Sonagraph model 7029A set at Hz ranges of 20-2000 or 40-4000 depending on call characteristics. Some interspecific comparisons of homologous calls were made with discriminant analysis and canonical correlation. To supplement field observations, films made with a super-8 movie camera were analyzed with a film editor or stop-action projector.

Playback experiments with the Uher tape recorder and Nagra DH speaker-amplifiers tested intra- and interspecific responses of males to calls. Taxidermist mounts of hens in the copulatory position and observations of focal males when a hen visited a mixed-display ground helped to determine responses of males to con- and heterospecific females. Responses of females to males were determined from field observations and by experiments conducted in captivity. In these experiments hens were ushered into a 15-m × 45-m enclosure in which three males of each species and an F1 hybrid male had established territories. Positions of females were recorded every 10 seconds until they copulated. Female preferences were determined in two ways: Initial preference was the amount of time a female spent in a male's territory in comparison to the size of that territory relative to others; ultimate preference was the choice of mates.

Breeding experiments were conducted in captivity to determine hybrid fertility. In 1976 a Prairie Chicken male and Sharp-tail female were crossed; resulting F1 hybrids were backcrossed or intercrossed in 1977 and 1978. The number of eggs laid, fertilized, and hatched were recorded. Complete procedural details are in Sparling (1979a).

Results and Discussion

Geographic distribution is an important isolating mechanism in these species. About 20% of the Sharp-tail's range is in sympatry, compared to 50% of the Prairie Chicken's (Fig. 1). Moreover, Prairie Chicken populations are discontinuous throughout this area and may be more subject to hybridization than if they were continuous. Major land-use changes, particularly at the prairie-woodland interfaces of Minnesota, Wisconsin, and Michigan may favor Sharp-tails over Prairie Chickens.

Local Distributions and Breeding Activities

Fifteen display grounds, including 7 Prairie Chicken booming grounds, 3 Sharp-tail dancing grounds, and 5 mixed grounds, were

FIGURE 1. Distributions of Greater Prairie Chickens (dotted), Attwater's Prairie Chicken *(T.c. attwateri)* (solid), and Sharp-tailed Grouse (hatched).

found in the study area (Sparling, 1980). Mixed grounds were distributed throughout the area, and there was little difference between species in areas used for displaying. In addition, hens tended to nest in similar habitats. Thus, habitat preferences appeared to be unimportant in maintaining species integrity.

Seven hybrids were identified on the area. Four were F1 hybrid males that defended territories. One of these (Fig. 2) was highly aggressive and held a central territory on a booming ground for 3 years. Two apparent F1

FIGURE 2. F1 hybrid male in 'booming' position. This individual maintained a central territory on a Prairie Chicken booming ground for three years. Many of his postures and displays were intermediate between those of Prairie Chickens and Sharp-tails (e.g., shortened pinnae, slightly elevated wings).

× Sharp-tail backcrosses (as determined by plumage characteristics) held territories on different grounds in 1978. An F1 hybrid female copulated with a Prairie Chicken but no hybrid male was seen to copulate.

Breeding seasons were virtually identical for both species. Males began establishing territories in mid-February to early March, depending on weather, and females started visiting leks in late March. Peaks of hen visitations occurred between April 9-12 for Prairie Chickens and March 30-April 9 for Sharp-tails. Smaller, second peaks occurred around April 17-27 and April 15-20 for the two species, respectively. Peak periods of copulations followed first peaks of hen visitations by 5 to 7 days. Although the two species differed in peak times of visitations and copulations within a year, males remained active throughout a breeding season, and a receptive female could potentially find a mate of either species. Almost all copulations occurred around dawn.

HYBRID FERTILITY

Six female and one male F1 hybrid survived to adulthood from the Prairie Chicken × Sharp-tail cross. Five females were backcrossed to adult males of both species and laid eggs. Hatching success (number of eggs laid/number hatched) was 59% and 67% for Prairie Chicken and Sharp-tail backcrosses, respectively. Sixteen backcross progeny survived to become adults. Although an F1 and a Sharp-tail hen were kept with the F1 male, he was a listless displayer and probably did not copulate. No fertile eggs were laid by either hen. Although hybrids are fertile, the sample size was too small to evaluate fecundity.

ETHOLOGICAL ISOLATING MECHANISMS

Although ethological isolating mechanisms may include several factors such as breeding seasons and habitat preferences, in this paper the term refers only to mechanisms involved in intra- or interspecific communication. Marler (1957) suggested that if communication efficiently maintained species integrity, forms of signals should follow two principles: Signals involved in agonistic behavior should be similar and promote spacing among individuals; and signals involved in epigamic contexts should be different and inhibit communication between potential heterospecific mates. Polyvalency and different rates of evolution associated with sexual selection may confound this simple dichotomy, however.

Prairie grouse share seven homologous visual displays. Face-offs, stand-offs, running parallels, and forward rushes (terminology after Lumsden, 1965 and Hjorth, 1970) are involved in territorial defense and are virtually identical in both species. Males appear capable of understanding heterospecific aggression, for they held mutually exclusive territories on all mixed grounds examined (Sparling, 1979b).

Prairie Chicken booming displays (Fig. 3) are homologous to Sharp-tail cooing displays (Fig. 4). Booming functioned in medium-range advertisement and courtship and was most common when females were present (Sparling, 1981a). Cooing displays, however, served as tonic signals to maintain *status quo* among territorial males and rarely occurred when females visited. Sharp-tail dancing displays (Fig. 5) were similar in function and context to Prairie Chicken booming displays but were very different in form.

Nuptial bows and flutter jumps of both species were involved in epigamic contexts. Sharp-tails kept their wings horizontal in nuptial bows and were silent in flutter jumps; Prairie Chickens held their wings pressed to their sides in bows and uttered whines and cackles while jumping.

FIGURE 3. Male Prairie Chicken in booming display.

Booms and coos, whoops and chilks, whines and cackles are homologous vocalizations. While Prairie Chicken booms and whoops and Sharp-tail chilks were involved in epigamic contexts, coos functioned in medium-range advertisement and in maintenance of *status quo.* Whines and cackles occurred in aggression and alarm in prairie chickens and only in aggression in Sharp-tails. Booms were readily distinguished from coos by note durations (2.7 versus 0.2 seconds) and internote intervals (6.6 versus 3.4 seconds). Whoops were distinguished from chilks by lower frequencies. Prairie Chicken whines tended to have higher frequencies, and their cackles had shorter note durations and internote intervals than corresponding Sharp-tail calls.

Using discriminant analysis and canonical correlation (Sparling, 1983), I found that whoops and chilks were most different between species, whines were more similar, and cackles were most similar; over 10% of the two species' cackles were misclassified as belonging to the other species. Of these calls, only cackles resulted in significant interspecific responses in playback experiments. Thus, these calls supported Marler's (1957) hypotheses. Sharp-tail gobbles and cork notes, however, contradicted his hypotheses, for they elicited significant intra- and interspecific aggressive responses but were not in Prairie Chicken repertoires.

FIGURE 4. Sharp-tail male in cooing display.

FIGURE 5. Sharp-tail male during a dance.

Prairie Chicken males actively courted con- and heterospecific hens, although males whooped and stamped more when conspecific hens were present than when only Sharp-tails were on the lek (Sparling, 1981b). These males also courted and copulated mounts of both species. Sharp-tail males chilked less frequently when only Prairie Chicken hens were present than when conspecific hens were visiting, and did not court or copulate heterospecific mounts.

In captivity, females of both species showed strong initial and ultimate preferences for conspecific mates. Prairie Chicken hens spent 99.8% of their time in Prairie Chicken territories; significantly different ($p<0.005$) from the expected 72.9%. Three of the four hens tested mated with a Prairie Chicken male during the experiment; the other mated with a conspecific after testing. Sharp-tail hens spent only 49.5% of their time in conspecific territories, but this was significantly greater than expected (19.3%, $p<0.005$). Seven of 10 Sharp-tails mated during the experiments, all with conspecifics; the rest also mated with conspecifics after testing.

Hybrid and backcross females showed no clear initial preference as a group. One Prairie Chicken × F1 backcross spent all her time in Prairie Chicken territories; another in those of Sharp-tails. F1 hybrids (3 individuals) spent 93% of their time and Sharp-tail × F1 backcrosses (4 individuals) spent 69.3% of their time in Prairie Chicken territories. No hybrid group differed significantly from expected values. Six hybrid females mated; all except a Prairie Chicken × F1 backcross with Sharp-tails. Two F1's and a Sharp-tail × F1 backcross did not mate. All females avoided the F1 male's territory. This was similar to a situation on a booming ground on which Prairie Chicken females either skirted the central territory of an F1 hybrid or quickened their pace to leave if chased into it.

Although habitat preferences, breeding seasons and times, and hybrid fertility appear insufficient to maintain species integrity between Prairie Chickens and Sharp-tails, geographic distribution appears important in maintaining allopatric populations and communicatory mechanisms are effective in areas of sympatry.

Acknowledgments

Financial support for this research was provided by the National Geographic Society, the Grand Forks Chapter of the North Dakota Wildlife Federation, Sigma XI, the Norman Pankratz Conservation Fund, and the Department of Biology, University of North Dakota. Additional support came from the Agricultural Experiment Station; University of Minnesota, Crookston; Dan Svedarsky; Lew Oring; and my wife, Paulette. John Roseberry critiqued the manuscript.

REFERENCES

HJORTH, I.
1970. Reproductive behavior in Tetraonidae with special reference to males. Viltrevy, vol. 7, pp. 183-596.

JOHNSGARD, P. A. and WOOD, R. E.
1968. Distributional changes and interaction between Prairie Chickens and Sharp-tailed Grouse in the Midwest. Wilson Bull., vol. 80, pp. 173-188.

JORGENSON, J. P.
1977. Pinnated grouse *(Tympanuchus cupido pinnatus)* movements and habitat utilization in the northern Great Plains. M.A. Thesis, Univ. North Dakota, Grand Forks.

LUMSDEN, H. G.
1965. Displays of the Sharp-tailed Grouse. Ontario Dept. Lands Forests Tech. Series Res. Rep. 66.
1970. A hybrid population of prairie grouse on Manitoulin Island, Ontario. Paper presented to 32nd Midwest Fisheries Wildl. Conf., Winnipeg, Manitoba.

MARLER, P.
1957. Specific distinctiveness in the communication signals of birds. Behaviour, vol. 11, pp. 13-39.

PARTCH M.
1973. A history of Minnesota's Prairie Chickens. Pp. 15-29 *in* "The Prairie Chicken in Minnesota," W. D. Svedarsky and T. Wolfe, eds. Univ. Minnesota Tech. College, Crookston.

SPARLING, D. W.
1979a. Reproductive isolating mechanisms and communication in Greater Prairie Chickens *(Tympanuchus cupido)* and Sharp-tailed Grouse *(Pedioecetes phasianellus)*. Ph.D. Dissertation, Univ. North Dakota, Grand Forks.
1979b. Evidence for vocal learning in prairie grouse. Wilson Bull., vol. 91, pp. 618-621.
1980. Hybridization and taxonomic status of Greater Prairie Chickens and Sharp-tailed Grouse. Prairie Natural., vol. 12, pp. 92-102.
1981a. Communication in prairie grouse I. Information content and intraspecific functions of principal vocalizations. Behav. Neural Biol., vol. 32, pp. 463-486.
1981b. Communication in prairie grouse II. Ethological isolating mechanisms. Behav. Neural Biol., vol. 32, pp. 487-503.
1983. Quantitative analysis of prairie grouse vocalizations. Condor, vol. 85, pp. 30-42.

DONALD W. SPARLING

Nonmetric Multidimensional Scaling Analyses of Temporal Variation in the Structure of Limnetic Zooplankton Communities

Grant Recipient: W. Gary Sprules, Department of Zoology, Erindale College, University of Toronto, Mississauga, Ontario, Canada.

Grant 1574: For a study of invertebrate predation and competition, and the structure of crustacean zooplankton communities.

In order to examine seasonal changes in the structure of limnetic zooplankton communities, samples were taken weekly from June through December 1976 from three sites—Blelham Tarn (0.8 km long, 0.10 km^2 surface area, 6.8 m mean depth), English Lake District and two large (about 45.5 m in diameter) cylindrical tubes, anchored in the sediments and buoyed up by inflatable rings (Tubes A and B) therein. The tubes isolated some 18,000 m^3 of water to a depth of 11 m. The data were summarized and analyzed by nonmetric scaling ordination. In Tube B an association comprising principally small zooplankters such as *Chydorus, Ceriodaphnia,* and *Bosmina* as well as *Daphnia* and *Cyclops bicuspidatus* tended to oscillate in composition without showing any definite seasonal cycle. On the other hand, Tube A and the tarn had higher predator densities, including a higher abundance of *Chaoborus, Cyclops leuckarti, Diaphanosoma,* and *Leptodora* which cycled in a more pronounced seasonal pattern. During 1976 Tube B developed a large September bloom of *Microcystis aeruginosa* and maintained an oxygenated hypolimnion, as did Tube A. By contrast the tarn was dominated by nannoplankton and developed an anoxic hypolimnion. Populations of the predator *Chaoborus* and planktivorous fish were greatest in the tarn, least in Tube B, and intermediate in Tube A. Thus differences in species composition of the sites and, more importantly, in their seasonal cycles of change are related to variations in predation intensity, quality of algal food available for herbivorous zooplankters, and chemical stratification and the dynamics of nutrient input. The importance of time variation in lake properties, particularly in assessing responses to stress or in the development of lake types for experimental or management programs is emphasized. Results of this study are published in detail in *Hydrobiologia,* vol. 69, no. 1-2, pp. 139-146 (1980).

W. Gary Sprules

West African Settlement Geography Along a Linguistic and Environmental Transect

Grant Recipient: Reed F. Stewart, Bridgewater State College, Bridgewater, Massachusetts.

Grant 1625: For study of West African settlement geography along a linguistic and environmental transect.

The study was of similarities in traditional ways of life among peoples of a single language family (Mande), extending from the dry savanna to coastal forest. It concentrated on village layout and settlement patterns of the northern group of Mande-speakers (Manding), but included peoples of other Mande groups and of other language families for comparison. The aims were to examine variations in cultural landscapes against the background of differences in the physical environment, primarily bioclimatic, within the framework of linguistic differences.

Fieldwork (supported almost completely by the National Geographic Society) during June, July, and August of 1976 was in Liberia, Sierra Leone, and Mali. Archival research extended the study to Guinea, Ivory Coast, Senegal, and Upper Volta. The aspects of traditional ways of life studied were selected as phenomena that were amenable to mapping and comparison, relatively independent of the environment, and fairly resistant to change.

Manding culture was studied for a variety of reasons. My wife and I had taught for 8 years during the 1950s in Liberia, where she learned the speech and script of Vai, one of the Mande languages, and where I had begun geography as a profession, being particularly interested in the distribution of languages. Liberian colleagues reported that often one could not distinguish communities of Vai from those of the neighboring Gola aside from the very different languages. By contrast, a 1972 conference at London's School of Oriental and African Studies stressed the distinctiveness and unity of the Manding. Further complicating the point, studies by authors such as d'Azevedo (1962), Maquet (1962), and Morgan and Pugh (1969) noted major cultural divisions among the peoples of West Africa, but each drew the boundaries quite differently and used different criteria.

Supporting the idea of substantial differences among the 20 or so Manding peoples—linguists vary in their classification (de Tressan, 1953;

Long, 1972; and Dalby, 1980)—are: the range of occupations, from pastoral to horticultural to riverine to urban; architecture varying from round with thatched roof to rectangular and adobe; differences in the relative strengths of Islam and animism, among other aspects.

On the other hand, Dieterlein (1955) and Goody (1961), among others, report strong links among the Manding and between the Manding and their neighbors. There is, for instance, a septennial gathering of Manding *griots* (poets/musicians/historians) in Mali, with participants coming from surrounding countries to literally rebuild an ancient ceremonial house. Also, people in Mali, Ghana, and Upper Volta, who do not speak Mande, claim at least mythic connections with the Manding; and several of the Mande groups are renowned and far-ranging traders. Finally, many of the ancient kingdoms and empires of West Africa had Manding as extremely important elements in their administrations (Levtzion, 1973). Senegal's former president, Leopold Senghor, is a contemporary example of the political importance of the Manding. The question, then, is the extent to which the Manding are united in culture and the degree of distinctiveness of that culture.

This survey of a wide area with many peoples (Fig. 1) was based on several assumptions: (1) that many aspects of culture, including intangibles such as beliefs, are represented in what can be seen and mapped; (2) that the iconography of a people has observable expression; (3) that useful observations of those expressions could be made in a relatively brief field trip (an assumption based on my 8 years of living in Liberia, on 3 years in Kenya, and on 5 years of community analysis as a geographer in the United States, Canada, and Nicaragua); (4) that communities could be found in 1976 that preserved much of the traditional ways of life as of the early 1900s and that elders in those communities would be willing to talk to an outsider about those ways of life as handed on to them by parents and grandparents; and (5) that several villages in the central part of a people's area could validly serve as representatives of the way of life of the people as a whole.

The gathering of information was organized around "culture complexes," assemblages of tangible and intangible traits. In addition to the layout or plan of each village and to the overall pattern of settlements and farms within each area, the complexes included the role and status of the blacksmith and the smithy, the method of land tenure and allocation, the kind and power of the chieftaincy; and the importance of secret and sacred societies and their effect on the landscape.

That last complex requires elucidation: In almost all traditional communities in Liberia and adjoining countries, almost all adults are members, through a several-months-long initiation, of a dominant secret society. Even an outsider can see the ceremonial houses in a village and may know that there are ceremonial forests which are forbidden to the uninitiated. There are masks of the men's or women's society which may or may not be seen by outsiders but which are commonly known to exist. There are graduation ceremonies and funerals, more or less open to the uninitiated, as well as other manifestations of the societies which can be observed without prying into matters forbidden to the outsider. The general functions of these societies are widely known to encompass formal education, guarding religious practices and community morality, and guiding political life. Ceremonial structures, burial places, sacred forests, and shrines protecting crops, houses, and villages are often observable and therefore can be mapped.

Methods

Field visits began in Liberia where I have many friends who could assist in the task of rapid and sensitive inquiry into the various complexes, in obtaining permission to sketch maps and take photographs, and in evaluating the process and results.

Meetings in each community were primarily with the elders. Since the focus of the study was on the ways of life in the early 1900s, there was little pressure to present a "modern" impression to the outsider. In fact, I was almost overwhelmed by historical information. This was partly because the study was vouched for by people whom the elders trusted, partly because I had a fairly good understanding of the etiquette demanded of the stranger, and partly because of the general good nature of people. Perhaps it was also helpful that I am a greybeard, that my children have Vai or Gola names (useful as ice-breakers in conversation), and that I have a smattering of Vai speech.

After presenting my credentials from the appropriate governmental authority to the chief or his representative, I spent a number of hours explaining, often through an interpreter, the purposes of the study and asking questions. Notes were taken in writing and on tape. Maps were sketched and photos taken. Later, I obtained aerial photographs of the areas visited. These data together with archival material and visits to several settlements in any one language area allowed cross-checking for internal consistency. All the sources came together in the synthesis of the data, even concurring about the several peoples who presented problems of departure from the general cultural patterns.

From Liberia, I went to Sierra Leone where the dominant language is also English, but where I knew few people. The field visits went well due to the refinement of procedures during the Liberian phase. The work in Mali, where French is dominant, went equally well thanks to the previous experience and thanks to the assistance of an accomplished interpreter and scholar, M. Malik Yatarra. It was my good fortune that he was

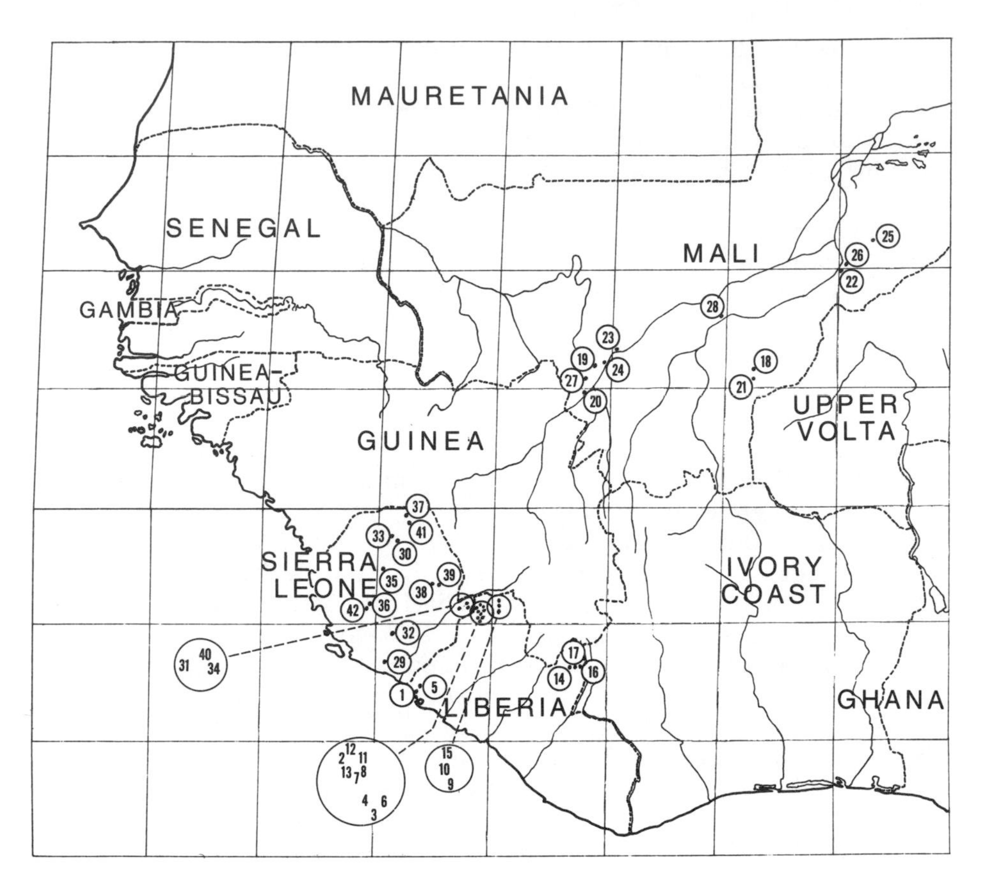

FIGURE 1. Field visits.

	Community	*Language group – Family*
	LIBERIA	
1	Bomi	Vai - Northern Mande
2	Foya Dundu	Kissi - West Atlantic
3	Gbanehima	Gbande - Southwestern Mande
4	Gbawohun	Gbande - Southwestern Mande
5	Gbesse Gambi	Gola - West Atlantic
6	Hailahun	Gbande - Southwestern Mande
7	Kapi	Kissi - West Atlantic
8	Kimbalo	Kissi - West Atlantic
9	Kpademai	Toma - Southwestern Mande
10	Kpakemai	Toma - Southwestern Mande
11	Kpandilo	Kissi - West Atlantic
12	Kpombu	Kissi - West Atlantic

13	Pleyama	Kissi - West Atlantic
14	Sakole	Gyo - Southern Mande
15	Velezala	Toma - Southwestern Mande
16	Yable	Gyo - Southern Mande
17	Yonlu	Gyo - Southern Mande
	MALI	
18	Banamba	Minyanka - Senufo
19	Jelibani	Malinke - Northern Mande
20	Kangaba	Malinke - Northern Mande
21	Karangasso	Minyanka - Senufo
22	Kessedougou	Bambara - Northern Mande
23	Nafadgi	Bambara - Northern Mande
24	Samelbamban	Malinke - Northern Mande
25	Sangha	Dogon - Dogon
26	Somadougou	Bambara - Northern Mande
27	Tigo	Malinke - Northern Mande
28	Wenja	Bambara-Northern Mande
	SIERRA LEONE	
29	Blamah Massaquoi	Vai - Northern Mande
30	Bumban	Limba - Limba
31	Giehun	Mende - Southwestern Mande
32	Johun	Mende - Southwestern Mande
33	Kamabai	Limba - Limba
34	Kpongbondu	Kissi - West Atlantic
35	Mabonkai	Limba - Limba
36	Maseru	Temne - West Atlantic
37	Musaia	Dyalonka - Northern Mande
38	Ngiehun	Kono - Northern Mande
39	Sawoko	Kono - Northern Mande
40	Senehun	Kissi - West Atlantic
41	Yisimaia	Kuranko - Northern Mande
42	Yonibana	Temne - West Atlantic

assigned by the Ministry of Arts and Culture to work with me throughout my stay in Mali. The governments of Liberia and Sierra Leone, as well as of Mali, were all of significant assistance in the fieldwork. The authorities in the Ivory Coast were equally ready to help, but my advance letters had gone astray and there was not time to fit my research into that which had already been approved for the period of my visit. I used the extra time to return to Liberia and visit a people who had representatives living in both countries. Permission was not granted for fieldwork in Guinea.

The data were analyzed by language family, subfamily, and individual peoples, all according to the level of similarity of the several aspects of the cultural landscape. These were examined for the relation between manifestations of culture and the location on the environmental transect of the peoples. A third consideration was the effect of vicinality, that is, of how similar in cultural landscape neighbors might be. The study was in part cartographic (what patterns did the various cultural aspects show when plotted on maps); in part mildly statistical (since the data were not gathered under conditions of meticulous control); and in part subjective, taking into account the "feel" of the various communities, i.e., information that perhaps was not strictly comparable.

To summarize, the field trip took me to several settlements in each of 17 language groups and provided photographs and maps, written and taped notes of interviews with village elders, and "ground-truth" for the interpretation of aerial photographs. That was combined with archival material for those peoples and for the other 11 peoples in the overall study. The aim, and the result, was to survey comparable aspects of culture over a considerable distance rather than to attempt a more complete ethnographic study of 1 or 2.

Study Findings

Enough unity of iconography was found so that the following idealized village plans and settlement pattern sketches and the commentary on them can represent the manifestations of the 6 culture complexes under study remarkably well.

Hamlet

Sketch A in Figure 2 is of a hamlet well enough established to have a sacred society hut and protective shrine, but probably sharing a sacred initiation school forest with the town from which the hamlet founders came. Several houses have protective "medicine" as do fields and paths. The community is not large enough to warrant a palisade. For this first sketch in the series, the kitchen gardens, cooking houses, and bathing places are shown. Omitted are granaries and subsidiary residences for older children. Also omitted is farmland in fallow—only the actively farmed portions of the shifting cultivation cycle are noted.

50-Year-old Hamlet

Sketch B (Fig. 2) shows the same hamlet 50 yr later in its growth. The founding chief is buried in the plaza and the present chief, descended from the first chief, lives in his grandfather's house. Succeeding generations have built their residences near those of their progenitors and there are family divisions within the village known to the residents but almost imperceptible to visitors. In this sketch, kitchens, storage huts, individual shrines, and bathing places have been omitted. The community has grown enough to have a "palaver house" where elders can gather and public trials and discussions can take place. A palisade has been built and has sprouted into a ring of trees which can be joined into an effective defense when needed. The village now has its own blacksmith shop near one of the entrance roads.

100-Year-old Village

The third sketch (C) shows the community another 50 yr later, when its population has tripled. Clansmen of the original settlers occupy wards D and G, with collateral clans in wards E, F, and H. The pattern of houses in those wards is similar to that of sketch B. The people of ward I are of a different language group and are in the "strangers' quarter."

Although family compounds in forest areas are composed of free-standing houses and in the drier savannas of houses joined either by common load-bearing walls or by adobe fences, in the strangers' quarter (I) the houses are set in clearly marked circles and joined by fences of grass-stalks, almost a woven fence, a carryover from the residents' origins in the transitional forest-savanna mosaic zone.

Inside each compound of the community the preparation of food, weaving of cloth, and familial interchanges are distinct from those of neighboring families of the same lineage. Mapping the ward of one lineage as distinct from that of another requires an intimate knowledge of the community, for the divisions are not of distance, but of belonging.

The town chieftainship has moved away from the direct descendents of the original chief, and ward F is politically important enough to have a separate plaza and protective medicine, as does the strangers' quarter. The second ceremonial hut may be for the women's society or for the hunters' society. A town this large would almost certainly have its own sacred forests. It would also have a weekly market, held in a clearing outside the ring of trees, but not indicated on the sketch.

Figure 3 shows town C, founded about 100 yr ago by an important farmer from what is now regarded as the parent community (D), about 7 km away. In turn, town C retains a strong influence on its daughter (village B) and brings those young women to its every-4-year session for Society initiation. The Men's Society in town C recognizes the spiritual and political seniority of town D, even though the chief of the younger settlement, C, was elected as paramount chief of the area in the most recent shift of power among the people of the tribe.

Abundant arable land was the principal reason for the choice of the new settlement's general location, although a good supply of water was considered just about as important, and the possibility of good hunting

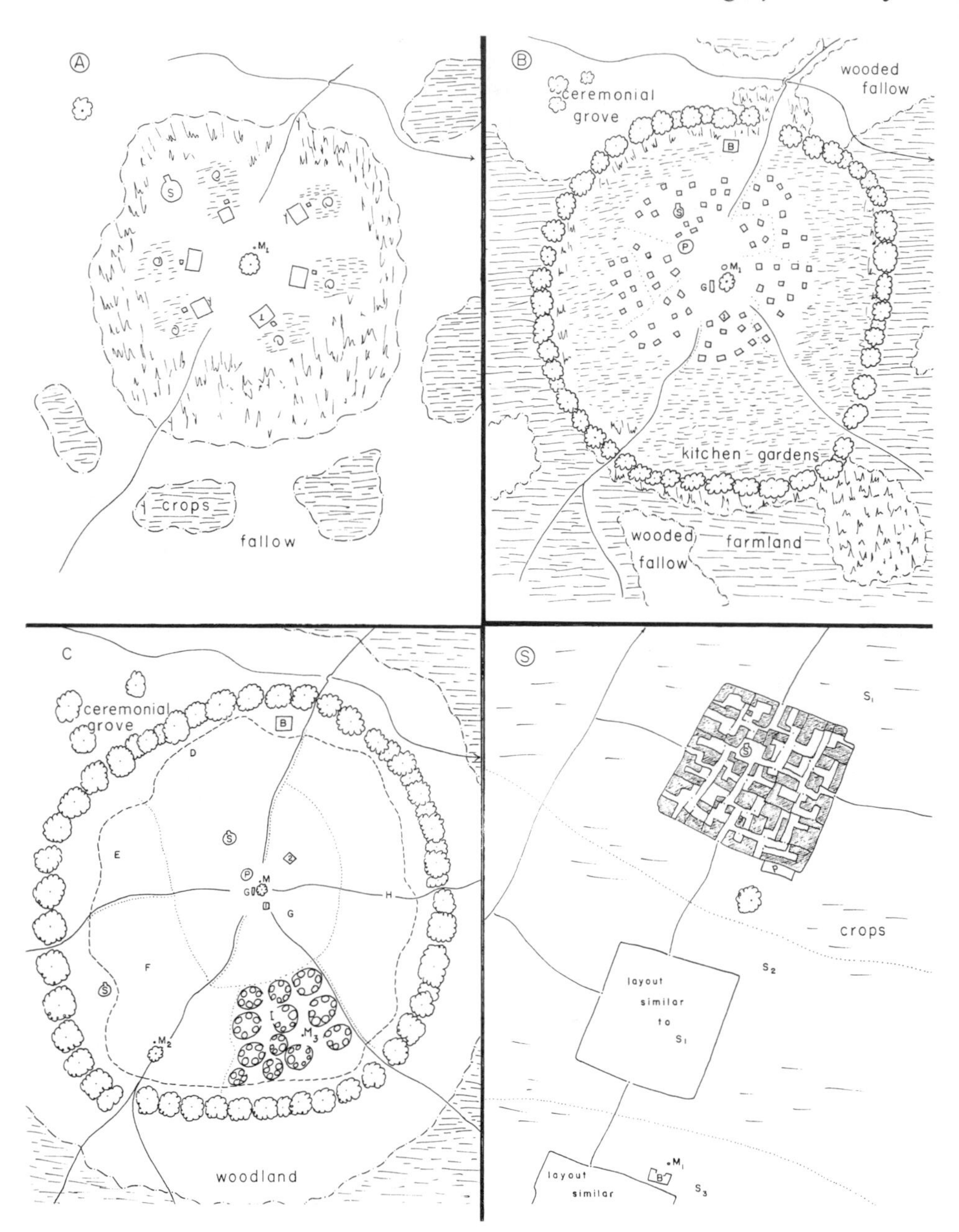

FIGURE 2. (A) Established community; (B) the same community 50 yr later; (C) the same community 100 yr later; (S) Minyanka-type village.

Residence and kitchen

Residence of first chief of village

Residence of second chief of village

Residence with walled compound

Residences with fenced compound

Bathing enclosure

Sacred or ceremonial structure

Blacksmith shop

Deliberately planted tree

Palaver (meeting) house

Village founder's grave

Shrine protecting village

Protective "medicine" for house or field

Doorway or gate in adobe wall

Major pathway

Stream

Boundary of family ward or quarter

Edge of residential area

Kitchen garden

Grass and shrubs

Edge of woodland

Major cropland

was also weighed. The specific site was chosen for strategic purposes, as the traces of the no-longer-needed stockade testify. Part of that protective fence runs through a small patch of high forest in which are buried the bodies of many of the prominent townspeople of the past. That grove, partly because of its function as a cemetery, is the place of periodic religious ceremonies. Other burials are in the compound of the deceased. The bodies of those who die as a result of their own sorcery are buried in unmarked graves well away from town. Leaders of the Society are buried in a secret location, presumably in the high forest away from town, reserved for Society activities.

Leading out from town, beyond the remains of the defense wall, are well marked pathways toward the major nearby communities. Those roads are bordered by trees left standing in the recurring clearing of farmland. For as much as a kilometer from town the roads are a striking part of the landscape.

Within the agricultural area there are wooded precincts devoted to the educational and the most secret aspects of the men's and women's secret societies (see Fig. 3), including the months-long school for adolescents. Masks, mostly seen only by initiates, are prominent representatives of the Society (it/they really deserve capitalization) in community affairs (Harley, 1950).

The influence of the Society extends to details of farming and crafts, as well as to those of birth, education, marriage, death, and the afterlife. The blacksmith, for example, has an honored position in the community and in the oldest sacred Society, being an herbalist and a celebrator of specific rituals, such as circumcision, on behalf of the people. His training and installation as the smith of the town were sanctioned by the Society and he both guides and is regulated by that political and religious committee-of-the-whole.

The office of blacksmith is a family prerogative and responsibility, and the senior wife of the smith is an important member of the women's branch of the Society. The smithy is on the outskirts of the residential area, partly because of the danger of sparks from the forge in a community of thatched roofs. In that smithy, the blacksmith acts as a repository of news and is often the most authoritative adult in the settlement during the working day, all others having gone to the farms.

Islam is influential in the town, though it is not the faith of many of the residents. The external trade of the community is handled by a Mande-speaking Muslim and his advice is sought by the gerontocracy, especially about "external affairs." He even competes with the blacksmith and the midwife (another Society-sanctioned office) as a source of aid in illness and in divination, using the prestige of literacy and of the Koran to give authority to his amulets and predictions. There is a small mosque in

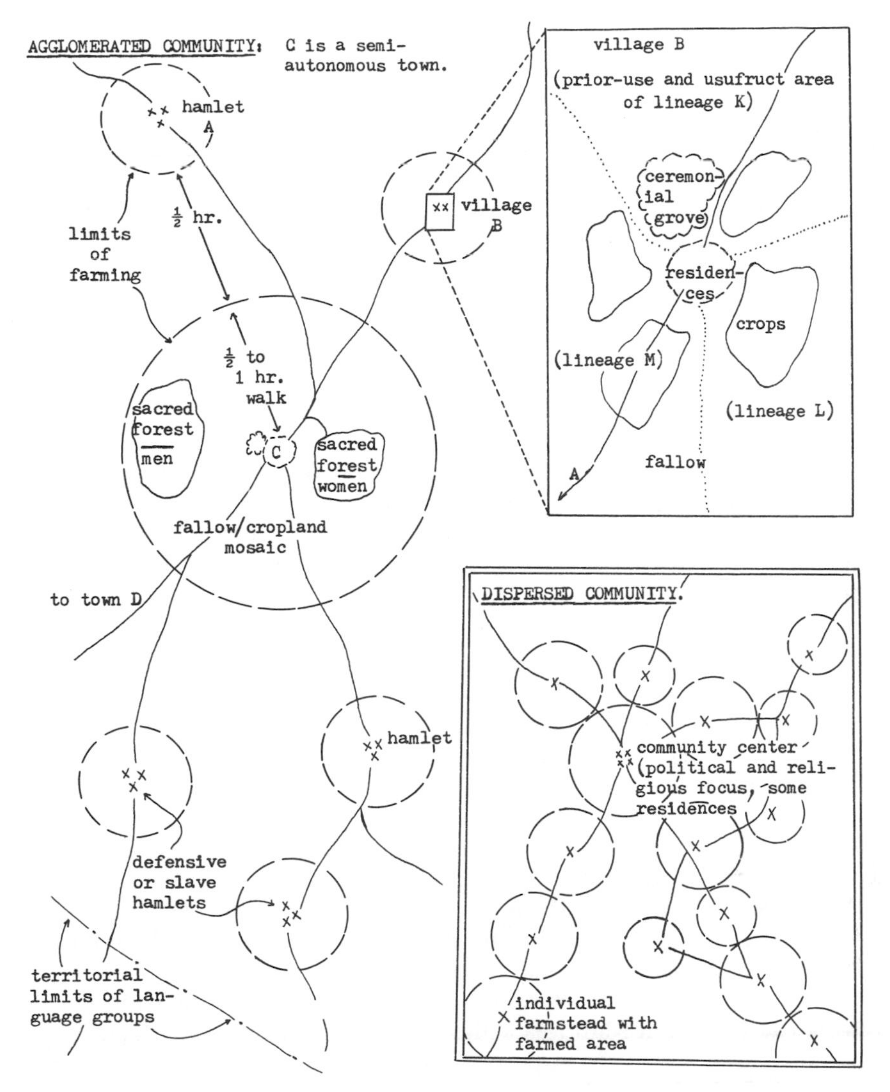

FIGURE 3. Settlement pattern sketches (not scaled).

town, away from the center. In a neighboring community, Islam has become so influential that the Society of the animists has been largely supplanted by the Muslim equivalent, the Bili—primarily a school for the initiation of boys into adulthood. The congregation of the mosque, at least the older men, serves as the behind-the-scenes leadership of that community, paralleling the Society in animist towns.

Minyanka-type Village

Sketch S shows the Minyanka type of village, with each ward, S-1, S-2, and S-3, being for a separate clan or lineage, although the whole community has a single politico-religious system. The village shrine is in the oldest ward, as is the palaver area near the large tree. Ward S-3 is the residence of the blacksmithing lineage and the smithy has a separate ceremonial site associated with it. The Minyanka, of a separate language family, challenge the study's tentative finding of an underlying common West African iconography.

Mossi-type Village

The Mossi of Upper Volta, not included in the fieldwork, depart from the patterns outlined here and are represented by the dispersed community in Figure 3 (lower right). As are the Minyanka, they are of a language family markedly different from that of the Manding. Those two peoples, the Minyanka and the Mossi, are the ones in which major differences in the culture complexes coincide with language divisions to separate them from the rest of the peoples in the study.

Conclusion

Of course, there are numerous minor departures from similarity of the complexes, but aside from the major anomalies of the Minyanka and Mossi, the cultural landscape exhibits a strong degree of unity throughout the study area. There is no evidence of correlation with environmental differences in the data for village layout, settlement pattern, blacksmithing, or political and religious systems. Since the bioclimatic differences affect the length of the shifting-cultivation cycle, there is some difference in the land tenure and allocation complex which correlates with environmental variation.

Since the information was analyzed in relation to lexical differences among the Northern Mande-speakers, a general pattern of decreasing similarity of cultural landscape within the Northern Manding was revealed in concert with a decrease in the proportion of cognates with the Bambara and Maninke, taken as central to the Northern Manding in linguistic terms, using data from Long (1972). Beyond that Northern Mande group, lexical data were insufficient to show more than a trend for the culture complexes between Manding subfamilies to be less similar than those within the Northern Mande. When all 28 peoples of the study were compared with each other, however, even the Northern Mande are distributed along continua of culture-complex similarities. The other groups (Southern Mande, Southwestern Mande, Eastern Mande, West Atlantic,

Limba, Kru, Senufo, Volta-Comoe, Oti-Volta, and Dogon) are interspersed along those continua.

Viewing the data with respect to the correlation between vicinality and similarity of cultural landscape, the effect of closeness or distance seems to be greater than that of language similarity or difference.

One expectation of the study was that the Societies would be found to exert a great influence on the cultural landscape of peoples in and near Liberia and less influence in the grassland areas, making a clear division apparent. In fact, one form or another of quite comparable sacred Society was found throughout the study area, sacred precincts and ceremonial structures being equally important in village layout and settlement plan everywhere, though the Societies might be Islamic rather than animist, or hunters' rather than more generalized Societies.

The fieldwork, archival search, and data analysis strongly suggest an underlying similarity of culture not restricted to any one language or environmental zone, a West African iconography that is reflected in the way peoples order their lives. It may be obscured by environmentally influenced differences in architecture or crops, but it is so pervasive that it seems to date at least to the widespread kingdoms and empires of the last 2000 years. To speculate even more broadly, the commonality of culture may be the result of a common migration pattern into West Africa over the preceding several thousand years. Work on this hypothesis has been sparked by data from this fieldwork (Stewart, 1978).

REFERENCES

DALBY, DAVID

1977. Language map of Africa and the adjacent islands, 63 pp. plus 4-sheet map. International African Institute, London.

D'AZEVEDO, WARREN L.

1962. Some historical problems in the delineation of a central West African region. New York Academy of Sciences, Annals; Anthropology and Africa Today, vol. 96, pp. 512-538.

DIETERLEN, GERMAINE

1955. Mythe et organization social au Soudan française. Journ. Soc. Africanistes, vol. 25, pp. 39-76.

GOODY, JACK

1964. The Mande and the Akan hinterland. Pp. 190-218, *in* "The Historian in Tropical Africa," J. Vansina, R. Mauny, and L. V. Thomas, eds. Oxford University Press, New York.

HARLEY, GEORGE W.

1950. Masks as agents of social control in northeast Liberia. Papers of the Peabody Museum of American Archeology and Ethnology, Harvard University, vol. 32, no. 2, 43 pp., illus.

LEVTZION, NEHEMIA

1973. Ancient Ghana and Mali, 283 pp. Methuen & Co. London.

LONG, RONALD W.
1972. The Northern Mande languages: A statistical retesting of 22 idiolects. Paper presented at a Conference on Manding Studies, School of Oriental and African Studies, University of London.
MAQUET, JACQUES J.
1962. Afrique: Les civilisations noires, 287 pp. Horizons de France, Paris.
MORGAN, W. B., and PUGH, J. C.
1969. West Africa, 788 pp. Methuen & Co., London.
STEWART, REED F.
1978. Nile to Mano migration, 5000 to 10,000 B.P.: Speculations on the historical geography of the Vai language, 9 pp. Paper given at 10th annual Liberian Studies Conference, at Boston University African Studies Center.
TRESSAN, M. DE LAVERGNE
1953. Inventaire linguistique de l'Afrique occidentale et du Togo, 241 pp. plus 9 sheets of maps. Memoires de l'IFAN, no. 30, Dakar.

REED F. STEWART

Fish Poisons in the Sunflower Family

Grant Recipient: Tod F. Stuessy, College of Biological Sciences, Ohio State University, Columbus, Ohio.

Grant 1586: In support of a study of fish poisons in the sunflower family in Panama.

The research trip to Panama in June 1976 was quite successful and resulted in many interesting collections. In addition, it was possible to complete laboratory studies during the year on these collected materials.

Our studies covered three areas of investigation: (1) Use of *Clibadium asperum* for fish poisoning by the Chocó Indians of Darién, Panama; (2) field collections and laboratory studies of *C. asperum* and related species; and (3) general collections made in the little known Cerro Pirré region of southeast Darién.

Clibadium asperum of the sunflower family is referred to as *catalina* or *salvia* by the Chocó Indians of Darién, Panama. Its use as a fish poison or *barbasco* is now banned by the Panamanian government, as it kills small fish as well as large ones. *C. asperum* is often a very common shrub on disturbed stream banks and river margins as well as in secondary growth of abandoned fields. *Catalina* is still used to a limited extent as a fish poison during the dry season. During such periods, fish are trapped in small pools by the receding water, or they may be forced into shallow, partially dammed-off sections of the stream by the natives. Varying quantities of fresh, ground leaves of *Clibadium* are added to the water to stun the fish, which are then collected. According to the Chocó, it is best to allow the ground plant material to stand overnight before use. They also say that if the material is added to water containing urine, the poison is not effective, nor is it effective if a person spits into the mixture (this was not tested).

An experiment was performed to test the effectiveness of *catalina* as a fish poison and to study the methods employed by the Chocó in its use. About 1 kg of fresh leaf material of *C. asperum* was gathered and ground into a thick paste. This was done with the aid of a large mortar and pestle carved from sections of tree trunks or limbs about 40 cm and 8 cm in diameter, respectively. The leaf material was allowed to stand overnight. Since it was the beginning of the wet season and the stream level was high, the leaf material was taken to a small stream of standing water in the jungle lowland. A portion of the stream (ca. 3 m by 1 m with a maximum depth of ca. 25 cm) was dammed at both ends with brush to prevent the fish from escaping. The fish poison was placed in a loosely woven basket, about 30 cm in diameter, which was submerged nearly to the rim. It was agitated back and forth to release the water-soluble poisons. Within about 2 min, several small fish ranging from 3 to 7 cm in length began leaping through the water's surface. This continued for 5 to 10 min. Gradually the fish ceased movement and floated on one side. About 15 fish were stunned in this manner. A few of these were transferred to uncontaminated water, where they revived after 5 to 10 min. Others were collected for species determinations. Identifications of the fish by Dr. Ted Cavender of Ohio State University indicate two species present: *Astyanex fasciatus* ("sardina de montana," family Characidae); and *Thoracocarax* cf. *maculatus* (hatchet-fish; family Gastropelecidae). These specimens are now on deposit in the Zoological Museum of Ohio State.

Many excellent collections of *C. asperum* and related species were obtained in Darién and in other provinces of Panama. In fact, all the relatives of *C. asperum* growing in Panama were collected, and these are (number of populations shown in parentheses): *C. asperum* (10); *C. pittieri* (1); *C. grandifolium* (2); *C. surinamense* (26); *C. leiocarpum* (3); *C. sessile* (1); and *C. pilonicum* (1). These total 44 different populational samples from 7 species. From nearly every population, herbarium vouchers, chromosomal bud material, and fresh leaves, stems, and roots (plus occasional flowers and fruits) were collected. These last plant parts were shipped back from Panama by air mail and promptly frozen for subsequent laboratory studies on the fish-poison compounds. Several large burlap sacks of dried leaf and stem material of *C. asperum* were also obtained for chemical studies. The herbarium vouchers are already mounted and on deposit in the Ohio State University Herbarium, with some of the duplicate material ready for exchange with other institutions. Twenty-three successful chromosomal preparations have been made (about half of the collected populations) and the results of the analyses to date indicate a uniform haploid number of $n = 16$. One live plant of *C. asperum* was also brought back, and after a slow start, it is now becoming successfully established in the Ohio State University greenhouse. This will be very important to the fish-poison bioassay work, when the plant eventually produces more leaves which will be freshly harvested for laboratory tests, because preliminary bioassay tests of goldfish in a laboratory aquarium have shown no fish-poison activity (in fact, no effect at all) when up to 3 gm of dried, crushed leaf material was added to 2 L of distilled water. Work on the detailed chemical investigations by Dr. Fischer in his laboratory at Louisiana State is still in progress.

Because the observations of the use of fish poisons by the Chocó Indians in Darién, Panama, afforded an opportunity to become closely acquainted with these people, the situation presented itself to explore the poorly known Cerro Pirré region of Southeast Darién with Chocó aid, and to make general collections. Only two botanists have been to this area previously, and for very brief periods: Dr. James Duke (one of our associated investigators) and Dr. Alwyn Gentry. We were able to make a collection of over 30 good flowering materials and these are still under study in our laboratory. Duplicates of these specimens will be exchanged with other U. S. botanical institutions.

The grant from the National Geographic Society has helped us make a significant contribution to our understanding of the use and nature of fish poisons in the sunflower family. Further studies on this project, especially those involving detailed chemical and pharmacological work, are continuing.

REFERENCES

Czerson, H.; Bohlmann, F.; Stuessy, T. F.; and Fischer, N. H.
1979. Sesquiterpenoid and acetylenic constituents of seven *Clibadium* species. Phytochem., vol. 18, pp. 257-260.

Bohm, B. A., and Stuessy, T. F.
1981. Flavonol derivatives of the genus *Clibadium* (Compositae). Phytochem., vol. 20, pp. 1053-1055.

Stuessy, T. F., and Liu, H. Y.
1983. Pericarp anatomy in *Clibadium, Desmanthodium* and *Ichthyothere* (Compositae, Heliantheae) and systematic implications. Thodora, vol. 85, pp. 213, 227.

Tod F. Stuessy

Radiotelemetry Study of the Oilbird

Grant Recipient: Bernice Tannenbaum, Department of Zoology, University of Washington, Seattle, Washington.[1,2]

Grant 1644: In support of a radiotelemetry study of the oilbird in Venezuela.

The oilbird *(Steatornis caripensis)* is totally frugivorous, feeding primarily on the large nutritious fruits of the families Lauraceae, Palmae, and Burseraceae (Snow, 1961, 1962). Fruits are swallowed intact and the seeds later regurgitated. Most populations of this species occupy roosts in caves throughout the year, although some populations are known to abandon the nesting cave each year after breeding (Tannenbaum and Wrege, personal observations). The birds' use of cave roosts makes it possible to determine the composition of their diet by collecting seeds regurgitated inside the cave.

Because the birds rely entirely on fruits of forest trees, sometimes in regions where human activities are rapidly destroying forests, conservationists have expressed concern over the future of the species (De Bellard-Pietri, 1977). In addition, poachers remove nestlings from many colonies as a source of food and fat.

The purpose of the present study was to identify environmental factors responsible for regulation of the birds' reproductive cycle, and to recommend conservation measures based on these findings. We pursued two major lines of investigation: We compared the breeding cycle at two oilbird colonies, one protected and the other subject to poachers' visits; and we examined the role of habitat destruction around the colonies in order to determine the influence of local food supply on populations.

Study Sites

Venezuela

The Cueva del Guácharo, 6 km west of Caripe, Estado Monagas, Venezuela (10°10′N, 63°33′W), is located at an altitude of approximately

[1] Present address: USDA Forest Service, Columbia, Missouri.

[2] Co-investigator on this project was Peter H. Wrege, Section of Ecology and Systematics, Cornell University, Ithaca, New York.

1100 m in rugged mountainous terrain. The area within 17 km of the cave has only small patches of the original premontane wet forest, the remainder being primarily coffee plantations. A substantial mountainous area east of Caripe is less disturbed and supports a half-dozen known oilbird colonies.

The cave was decreed Monumento Nacional "Alejandro de Humboldt" in 1949 and the area around it "Parque Nacional del Guácharo" in 1975. Visitors may enter the cave only in the company of official guides, who effectively prevent poaching. The Cueva de El Toro in Estado Falcón, which also contains a large oilbird colony, was created a national park in 1969. These are the only oilbird colonies in Venezuela currently under protection.

The Cueva del Guácharo contains the largest known oilbird colony. Other observers have estimated 10,000 birds in the cave (W. Lowrie, pers. comm.), but our estimate for 1976 was about 5000 adults, based on numbers of active nests and numbers of individuals sitting on the other ledges. The study period was May to November 1976 and January to February 1977.

TRINIDAD

Oropouche Cave, 5.75 km north of Valencia, Trinidad, is located at about 160 m elevation at the edge of premontane forest mixed with lowland trees and small coffee and cacao plantations. We estimated 300 to 350 adults in the colony in 1977. Almost every year between April and June this colony is visited by poachers who harvest larger chicks in accessible nests (B. Tannenbaum, personal observation; R. Muzini, pers. comm.). The study period at the site was April and May 1977.

Methods used in this study and details of rainfall and temperature at study sites are described in another publication (Tannenbaum and Wrege, 1978).

Results and Discussion

NESTING CYCLE

Nesting in the Cueva del Guácharo was fairly synchronized. Of eggs for which hatching dates are precisely known (n = 77), 70% hatched between June 1 and July 1, following a 32- to 35-day incubation period; no eggs were laid after June 6.

Completed clutches of eggs ranged from 1 to 3 eggs ($\bar{x} = 2.25 \pm 0.59$, n = 72 clutches). Chicks in 62 additional nests had already hatched by the time we first censused them, and therefore initial clutch size is unknown. Of the pairs of birds occupying censused nests, 92% initiated broods be-

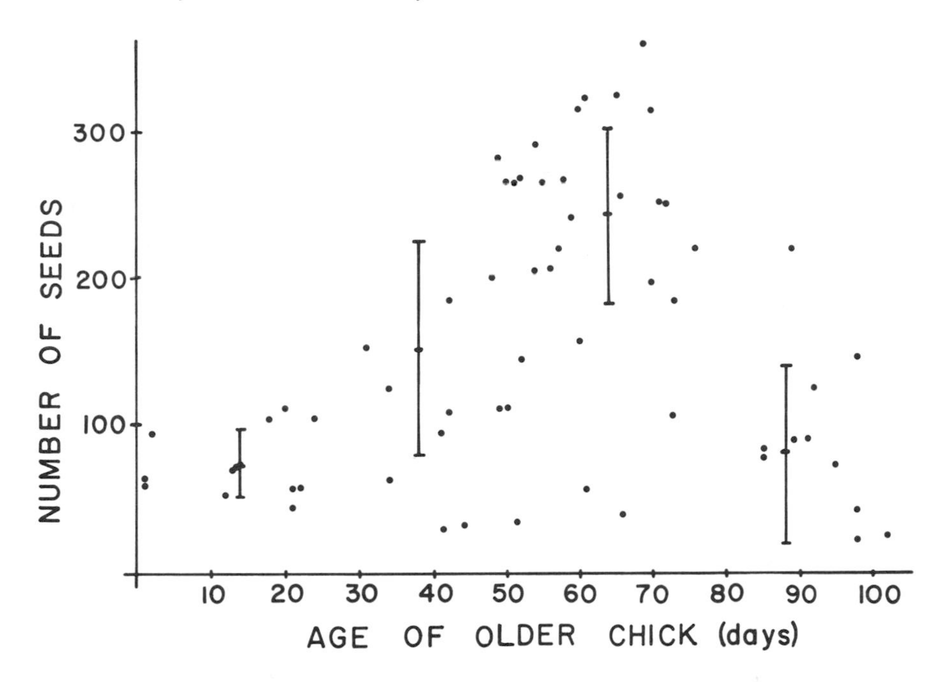

FIGURE 1. Numbers of seeds deposited nightly at nests with 2 chicks as a function of the age of the older chick. Vertical bars indicate 1 standard deviation.

tween April and June 1976. In contrast, the breeding season in two Trinidad colonies (Oropouche Cave and Arima Gorge) was far less synchronized (Snow, 1961; Tannenbaum and Wrege, in press). Disturbance by poachers early in the present study made it impossible to accurately determine clutch size of Oropouche Cave birds.

Oilbird chicks have an unusually long nesting period because nestling growth and development proceed relatively slowly (White, 1975). By 4 weeks of age, chicks were entirely down-covered and had developed a thick deposit of fat in the abdominal region. Flight feathers first appeared at about 5 weeks of age. By 63 days chicks had reached their maximum weight (600 g or more) and were almost 50% heavier than adults, but were still down-covered. Chicks began to lose weight between 65 and 75 days. Collections of regurgitated seeds at nests indicated that chicks were still fed by adults during the following 25 to 30 days that the chicks spent in the nest before fledging, but fruit delivery rates dropped steadily (Fig. 1). Steady weight loss was accompanied by growth of tail and wing feathers, and chicks eventually left the nest with plumage and at adult weight ($\bar{x} = 404.7 \pm 49.9$, $n = 8$).

Reproductive success of Cueva del Guácharo adults with larger clutches or broods was higher than that of adults with single-egg clutches (Table 1). Overall, breeding pairs produced an average of 1.22 fledglings during 1976. Of all pairs known to have attempted breeding, 69% had chicks that reached fledgling age. It was not possible to determine reproductive success in Oropouche Cave during the short study period at that site, but in previous years at another Trinidad colony, nesting success was similar to that of Cueva del Guácharo (Snow, 1962).

TABLE 1. Reproductive Success of Oilbird Pairs in the Cueva del Guácharo During 1976

"Brood" designates chicks in nests for which the initial number of eggs is unknown. "Clutch" refers to the number of eggs originally observed in the nest.

Clutch or brood size	*No. broods or clutches*	*% Hatching success (no. eggs)*	*% Fledging (no. chicks)*	*x̄ Chicks fledged/pair*
1-egg clutches	3	0 (0)	—	—
2-egg clutches	19	66 (25)	48 (12)	.63
3-egg clutches	13	56 (22)	59 (13)	1.00
1-chick broods	3	—	33 (1)	.33
2-chick broods	31	—	89 (55)	1.77
3-chick broods	3	—	78 (7)	2.33
TOTALS x̄	72	59 (47)	82 (88)	1.22

NESTLING MORTALITY

Causes of nestling mortality varied at different colonies. Snow (1962) attributed occasional losses of very young chicks to starvation, predation by crabs, and falling from the nest. During the present study, starvation was a major cause of mortality in Cueva del Guácharo—particularly of chicks more than 60 days old—but not in Oropouche Cave. From June through mid-August, 60 chicks, alive and dead, were found on the floor of Cueva del Guácharo. All chicks aged 3 weeks or older were fat. In the middle of August, however, the number of chicks found on the floor suddenly increased, and in September the number of fledglings found on the cave floor also increased sharply (Fig. 2). These increases coincided with a sharp decline in the number of fruits brought into the cave by adults (Tannenbaum and Wrege, 1978). Most of the chicks found after August 15 were emaciated, in contrast to normal chicks of the same age, which are very fat. Most young chicks found on the cave floor probably died, as adults appeared to feed only the chicks in the nests. Some fledged young could fly and might have survived, but most were in poor condition.

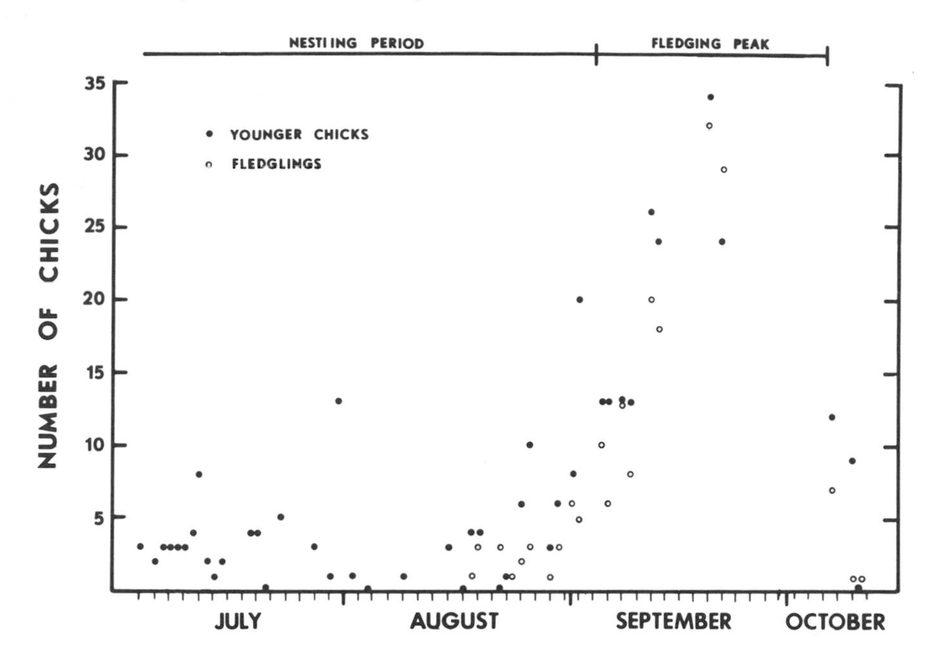

FIGURE 2. Numbers of chicks found nightly on the floor of Cueva del Guácharo, July through October 1976. Small marks on the abcissa indicate 2-day intervals.

In contrast, during 2 months of study at Oropouche Cave, only 2 chicks, both fat, were found on the floor. There was no evidence of starvation in any of the remaining chicks in censused nests. Poachers removed 44% of chicks from censused nests (n = 34 nests) in early April.

DIET OF OILBIRDS

Seeds of almost 30 different species of fruits were deposited by the birds in the Cueva del Guácharo and 16 species at Oropouche Cave (Table 2). These belong primarily to three families of plants: 14 Lauraceae, 8 Palmae, and 4 Burseraceae.

Proportions of different seed types deposited in collecting baskets on the cave floor reflect fruiting peaks of major food trees (Fig. 3). Between the beginning of fieldwork in May and the end of September 1976, fruits of palms and other families were eaten at the Cueva del Guácharo. When we left this site, between October 1976 and February 1977, the palm *Euterpe* accounted for 40 to 72% of the diet, with the remainder contributed by the palm *Geonoma*. The birds' breeding season coincided with the fruiting peaks of the Lauraceae and Burseraceae, but no single species dominated collections through the entire breeding season. Instead, we

TABLE 2. Characteristics of Fruits Collected at Caripe and Oropouche Study Sites

Seeds of all types listed were collected in the caves, but characteristics of some intact fruits were taken from specimens collected from trees.

Name of plant	*(n)*	*Largest dimension (cm)*	*Wet wt (g)*	*Ripe fruit color*	*Fruit odor*	*Toughness of seed coat*
Palmae (8 species)						
Geonoma spp.	60	0.7	0.2	purple, red, blue	no	very
Euterpe spp. *Prestoea* sp.	29	1.3	1.59	purple	no	very
Roystonea sp.	24	1.7	0.8	purple	no	very
Bactris sp.	22	2.1	3.3	orange, red	no	very
Jessenia sp.	10	3.6	14.4	purple	no	very
two unknown[1]		>1.3	?	?	?	very
Lauraceae (14 species)						
Ocotea sp.	3	2.4	2.0	green	yes	soft
O. wachenheimii	5	1.8	5.15	green	yes	soft
O. caracasana	8	3.25	11.4	green-to-brown	yes	soft
O. oblonga	25	1.5	1.0	green	yes	soft
Nectandra kaburiensis	30	1.2	0.5	green	yes	soft
Cinnamomum elongatum	15	1.4	1.0	black	yes	soft

Persea caerulea	10	1.1	0.75	green	yes	soft
Beilschmiedia sp.	7	6.0	14.0	green	yes	soft
Nectandra membranacea	5	1.0	0.6	black	yes	soft
type #11	10	1.5	1.1	green	yes	soft
4 unknown[1]		>1.7	?	green?	yes	soft
Myristicaceae (1 species)						
Virola surinamensis	5	1.6	1.2	brown capsule, red aril	yes	fairly
Burseraceae (4 species)						
Dacryodes sp.	10	2.75	2.7	green	slight	fairly
types #21 and 27 (*Trattinickia* spp?)		>1.3	?	green?	yes	very
one unknown	10	1.5	1.5	green	yes	very
Moraceae (1 species?)						
Ficus sp.[2]		?		green	no	soft
Four others (family unknown)[3]		?		?	no	soft

[1] No intact fruits collected.
[2] Seeds collected in feces (1 sample).
[3] Seeds collected in feces (5 samples).

found distinctive peaks for three major genera *(Dacryodes, Cinnamomum,* and *Persea),* each of which at its peak contributed 50 to 75% of samples. The palms *Euterpe* and *Geonoma* made up the remainder of the diet. Numbers of seeds in nightly samples increased through the breeding season along with chicks' weights; as total numbers of seeds brought into the cave began to decline at the end of August, weights of chicks and numbers of types of seeds also declined (Tannenbaum and Wrege, 1978).

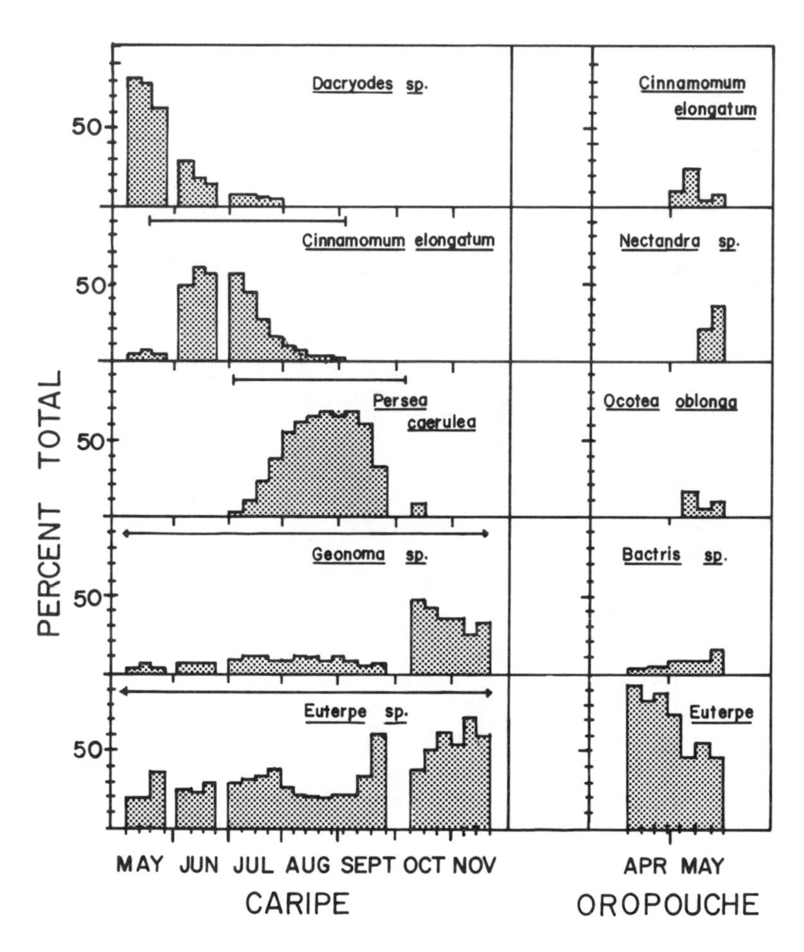

FIGURE 3. Deposition of seeds of the major oilbird food trees in the Cueva del Guácharo (Caripe) and Oropouche Cave. Gaps indicate periods in which no samples were collected. These species comprised at least 92% of all seeds deposited in these caves during the study periods. Small marks on the abcissa indicate 1-week intervals.

Foraging Behavior

We observed groups of up to 20 birds feeding in *Persea, Cinnamomum,* and *Nectandra* trees. Individuals hovered silently for 3 to 4 sec at a tree, in which time fruits were plucked and swallowed. They then flew a short distance, circled, and returned to the tree, hovering at another spot. No group of birds visited a particular tree for longer than 5 min.

In July and August 1976, 6 birds in the Cueva del Guácharo were tagged with 7- to 12-g battery-powered radio transmitters, and, in April and May 1977, 2 Oropouche birds were tagged. At least 5 of the birds had chicks in the nest during the tracking period (maximum 42 days).

Most of the marked birds at both sites made at least two flights from the cave each night, and in a third of all sessions three flights were made. Individuals were most consistent in the time they first left the cave and in their initial direction, while the length of time spent away from the cave varied from one night to the next. Foraging trips for Cueva del Guácharo birds averaged 3 hr, 20 min ± 23 min, and for Oropouche birds, 1 hr, 15 min ± 43 min. The average period between trips for all birds, i.e., time spent inside the cave at night, was 2 hr, 45 min ± 23 min. Plantations surrounding Cueva del Guácharo contained many fruiting trees between April and September 1976. Birds consistently visited these trees, but individuals during this period regularly foraged much farther from the cave, returning with fruits from trees that are rarely found within 8 km of the cave (Tannenbaum and Wrege, 1978).

Initial directions taken by radio-tagged Cueva del Guácharo birds reflected the behavior of the vast majority of birds in the colony as they flew west from the cave into a forested valley. The valley lacks roads and footpaths beyond 2 km, and it was impossible to track tagged individuals farther than 6 km from the cave.

We estimated flight speeds of birds by timing one radio-tagged bird on six occasions from Oropouche Cave to a point $1\frac{1}{2}$ km away where it passed directly overhead. The area it crossed has no food trees, so our estimates of speeds between 20 and 24 kph represent direct flights. Since time actually spent in traveling between trees is brief, most of the foraging trip must be spent in traveling between trees. In a 3-hr trip a bird could fly 20 km to a fruiting tree, with sufficient time to process a stomachload of fruits, based on processing times of large chicks and typical adult stomachloads (Tannenbaum and Wrege, in press).

Availability of Fruit

Examination of the region within 2 km of each cave revealed fruiting trees of 6 of the major species (*Euterpe* spp., *Prestoea* sp., *Geonoma* spp.,

Cinnamomum elongatum, Persea caerulea, and *Dacryodes* sp.) used by the Cueva del Guácharo colony, and 7 of 8 of the major trees used by the Oropouche Cave colony. At least 92% of all seeds deposited in the caves were from these species. Fruiting periods of the important species are indicated in Figure 3.

In general, non-palms were highly seasonal in fruiting, and individuals of the same species were synchronized. Fruits of non-palm species were available between April and September at the Cueva del Guácharo. During the brief study period at Oropouche Cave, both palm and non-palm fruits were available. Palms, except for *Bactris,* produced fruits throughout the year, apparently unsynchronized with conspecifics. In coffee plantations near the Cueva del Guácharo, a few lauraceous species were much more abundant than in nearby undisturbed forest because they have been selectively used as shade trees by local coffee growers, but palms were virtually nonexistent. In undisturbed forest the situation was reversed, and palms outnumbered non-palms. At Oropouche Cave, where an extensive primary forest is adjacent to the cave, palms outnumbered non-palms in the forest, but plantations contained virtually no food trees.

Results of radio-tracking and examination of food-tree distribution within several kilometers of both caves suggest that, although trees with large fruit crops existed near both caves during the breeding season, tagged birds usually traveled much greater distances, even after visiting these nearby food trees. We suspect that depletion of ripe fruits on these trees did not account for long-distance foraging flights in the breeding season. Evidence on individual birds' fruit selection suggests that birds with chicks in the nest may deliberately select a variety of fruits each night in successive flights (Tannenbaum and Wrege, 1978). In order to obtain such a variety, it appears that Cueva del Guácharo birds may visit both forest and plantations in a single night.

Results point out the close dependence of the breeding cycle of Cueva del Guácharo birds on the fruiting season of trees near the cave. Within a reasonable foraging range (ca. 17 km) of the Cueva del Guácharo, apparently few lauraceous or burseraceous species fruit between September and February. The remaining food sources are those species of palm that appear to produce fruit at a low but steady rate throughout the year.

Synchronized breeding and the switch to dependence on palms during the nonbreeding season appear to occur in several other colonies in Venezuela which we visited briefly (Tannenbaum and Wrege, 1978). However, Snow's (1962) results in one Trinidad colony and our brief study of the Oropouche Cave colony (Tannenbaum and Wrege, in press) show that oilbird populations elsewhere do not synchronize the breeding season. Habitat destruction probably accounts in part for the absence of a consistent year-round supply of fruits near some caves like the Cueva del Guácharo, but another reason for the difference between Venezuelan and Trinidad populations may lie in the degree of synchrony of fruiting of non-palm food trees. In Trinidad, at least two non-palm species, plus the palms *Eutrepe* and *Jessenia,* had fruit in every month (Snow, 1962). Synchronized breeding populations in areas with narrower fruiting seasons may be more likely to experience reproductive failure in years when major food trees fail to set fruit. Results of the present study do not yet permit us to distinguish this possible cause of massive starvation of chicks in the Cueva del Guácharo in 1976 from causes associated more directly with deforestation in the vicinity of the cave. Results clearly indicate, however, that deforestation has reduced the number of palms remaining near the cave, and that these are the critical food source during the nonbreeding season. Because certain palms *(Euterpe)* are still being cut in remaining patches of forest to obtain the edible palm heart, reduction of the food supply of the Cueva del Guácharo oilbird population will become more critical in the future.

With respect to the consequences of poaching on populations, evidence of the present study and estimates of the Oropouche Cave population in the past (Snow, 1961; R. ffrench, unpubl. data; Tannenbaum and Wrege, in press) indicate that large stable populations can survive in spite of annual harvesting, provided that some nests are inaccessible and the forest is undisturbed. We conclude that the effect of deforestation at the Cueva del Guácharo is more grave, even though this colony no longer suffers from poachers' visits.

Acknowledgments

We received help from a number of individuals and organizations during the study. In particular we would like to thank the following individuals: Dr. Eugenio de Bellard-Pietri, Dr. Edgardo Mondolfi, and William and Diane Lowrie for their aid in Venezuela; Dr. Julian Steyermark, Dr. David Snow, and Dr. H. E. Moore for technical assistance; Mr. and Mrs. Ralph Muzini for their hospitality at Oropouche Estate; and Marianne Saphra for assistance in fieldwork.

The project was made possible through grants from the World Wildlife Fund-US Appeal, the Harris Fund, the International Council on Bird Preservation, the National Geographic Society, and the Academia Venezolana de Ciencias Físicas, Matemáticas y Naturales.

REFERENCES

De Bellard-Pietri, E.

1977. El guácharo *(Steatornis caripensis)*, especie amenazada. XI Reunion Anual de la Asociación Conservacionista del Caribe, unpublished report.

Snow, D. W.

1961. The natural history of the oilbird, *Steatornis caripensis*, in Trinidad, B.W.I., Part I. Zoologica, vol. 46, pp. 27-48.

1962. Op. cit., Part II. Zoologica, vol. 47, pp. 100-221.

Tannenbaum, B., and Wrege, P. H.

1978. La ecología del guácharo *(Steatornis caripensis)* en Venezuela. Boletín de la Academia Venezolana de Ciencias Físicas, Matemáticas y Naturales, vol. 38, pp. 72-90.

——. Breeding synchrony and nestling mortality in oilbirds breeding in the Cueva del Guácharo. Boletín, Sociedad Venezolana de Ciencias Naturales. (In press.)

White, S. C.

1975. Ecological aspects of growth and nutrition in tropical fruit-eating birds. Ph.D. dissertation. University of Pennsylvania.

Bernice Tannenbaum
Peter H. Wrege

Island Primates of the Western Indian Ocean

Grant Recipients: Ian Tattersall, American Museum of Natural History, New York, New York, and Robert W. Sussman, Washington University, St. Louis, Missouri.

Grant 1679: In support of a study of the behavior and ecology of the lemurs of the Comoro Archipelago.

The original intention of our project was to carry out behavioral and ecological research on the lemurs of the Comoro Islands, an archipelago in the northern Mozambique Channel, western Indian Ocean (Fig. 1) during the months of May through August 1977. However, logistical and political difficulties prevented us from fulfilling this plan, and the research fell instead into two primary parts. During May through June, we both made a preliminary study of the natural history of the crab-eating macaques *(Macaca fascicularis)* of the island of Mauritius (Fig. 1). This study was continued by Sussman through July. In July and August, Tattersall studied the activity patterns of the brown lemur *(Lemur fulvus)* on Mayotte Island of the Comoro Archipelago. Short synopses of both studies are given below. In addition, brief observations were made on *L. mongoz* of Mohéli Island, lemurs in Madagascar were filmed for locomotor studies, and preserved material of *M. fascicularis* was studied in the British Museum (Natural History).

The Crab-eating Macaques of Mauritius

Crab-eating macaques have existed on the Island of Mauritius (720 mi^2) at least since the beginning of the 17th century; they were probably introduced by Portuguese sailors returning home from Java. Since their introduction they have proven to be highly successful colonists, and despite the considerable inroads made by man into the vegetal cover of Mauritius, monkey populations exist today in many parts of the island.

The Study Area. Our study site lies at the western base of Montagne du Rempart, western Mauritius, and forms part of a private reserve owned by Médine Estates Ltd. The site is bordered by fields of sugarcane, and several types of secondary vegetal formation are represented. (See Fig. 2.) Mean annualrainfall in the area is under 50 in.

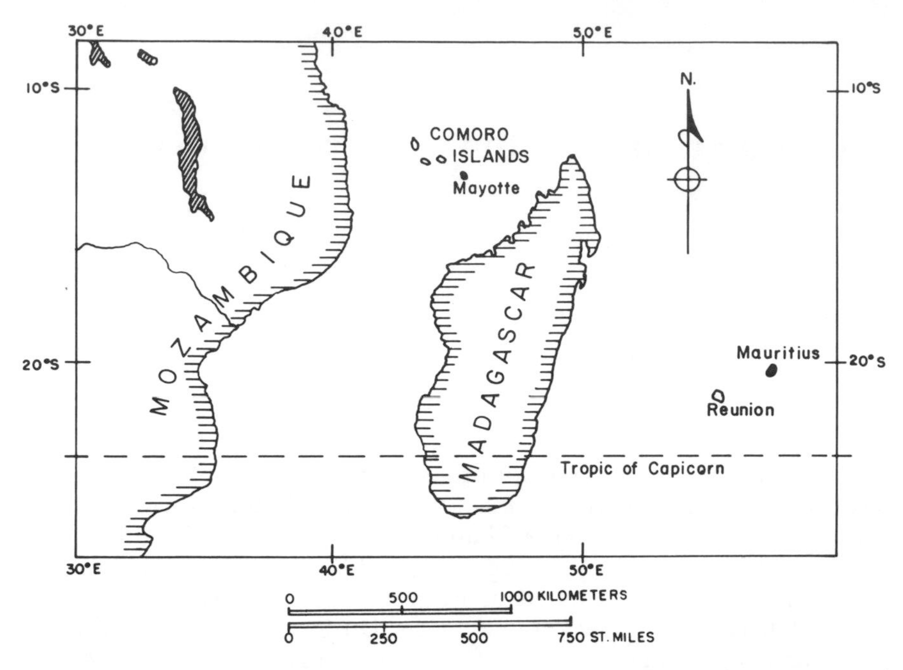

FIGURE 1. Part of the southwestern Indian Ocean, showing the positions of Mauritius and Mayotte.

Methods of Observation. Our observations centered on a single large group of macaques, which we followed between dawn and dusk, for as long as contact could be established, or observed from various vantage points. Habituation of the animals to observation progressed slowly, but after 2 months of study it was well advanced. Our observations were primarily concerned with activity cycles, ranging patterns, foraging behavior, and diet; notes were made of social interactions, but interpretation of these is difficult since the group was large and individuals could not be identified consistently. Quantifiable data were collected as follows: at each 5 min interval it was determined whether any individual was engaged in feeding, grooming, moving, resting, traveling, or "other," and at what level of the forest the activity was taking place. This procedure gave us an idea of what activities the animals were performing at different times of day, and at which levels of the forest they were most often performed. Although these data are quantitative, we regard them as preliminary because of problems arising from the differential visibility of the monkeys in different parts of their habitat and in different activities. Over the 8 wk of intensive observation we accumulated about 125 hr of observation.

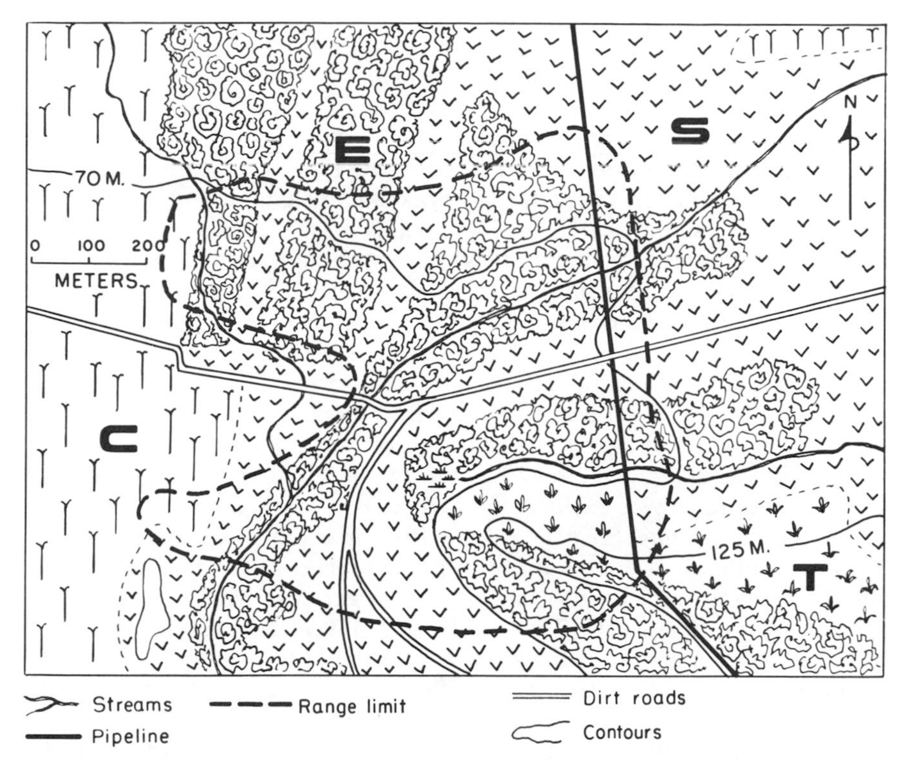

FIGURE 2. Map of the study site at Montagne du Rempart, showing vegetation, landmarks, and range limit of the study group. S: savanna with small trees; T: *Leucaena* and *Furcraea* thicket formation; E: moist riverine forest; C: canefields. Patches of dense thorn scrub (not marked) also occur.

Group Size and Composition. We censused the macaque group at every opportunity, and arrived at a minimum figure of 67 individuals. Clearly, in Mauritius, as elsewhere, the basic social unit is a multi-male group of large size. Most foraging, however, is done by subunits of the group, which independently visit different parts of the home range. The mean size of 10 such subgroups was 18.6 individuals, with a range of 7 to 41.

Use of the Home Range. During the study, our subject animals were never seen outside an area of about 42 ha (Fig. 2), and their movements within this range were closely governed by the distribution of specific resources. The entire group would normally sleep together in a clifflike area at the south of their range. They fed often near this site, but parties of macaques would travel over 1 km to obtain specific foods. Most day ranges, however, were more limited.

Activity Patterns. Activity was almost entirely restricted to the hours of daylight. During this period, a high level of activity was maintained with an activity:rest ratio of 3.5:1. Feeding was the most common activity (32.2% of time), followed by movement (23.2%), resting (21.9%), other (mostly social interactions: 11.7%), grooming (7.1%), and travel (3.8%). The general pattern through the day was one of sustained high levels of feeding, with a slight peak from 1400 to 1700 hr (38 to 41% of time). The consistency of macaque activity was more striking than any tendency of partition activities according to different times of day, and time spent feeding is comparable to that of a variety of other cecopithecoids.

Use of Forest Strata. M. fascicularis appears to be more versatile in its use of the forest in Mauritius than in its homeland of southeastern Asia. The macaques fed at all levels of the forest available to them, although 70% of feeding took place in the canopy or in the tops of low trees. In all other activities, however, over 70% of time was spent on or just above the ground, and travel was exclusively terrestrial.

Diet and Foraging Behavior. Mauritian macaques are very eclectic feeders, exploiting a wide variety of plant species but at the same time showing a very high level of short-term selectivity. Much time is also spent foraging for insects. Tamarind pods *(Tamarindus indica)* made up the greatest proportion of the diet during the study period (33%), followed by the berries of an unidentified native species of *Ficus* (22%). None of the 18 other plant species exploited provided more than 8% of the diet, and the top 5 species together accounted for 75% of the diet. Fruit was overwhelmingly the largest dietary component (70%), followed by stems and bracts (13%), leaves (9%), invertebrates (5%), and flowers (1%).

Seventy-two percent of feeding time was spent in the tree branches, and the macaques displayed much agility and inventiveness in terminal-branch feeding. Insects were discovered by turning over rocks, or were caught on the wing; termite tunnels were broken open, as were the shells of *Achatina* and small river snails. We did not observe predation on birds' nests, but this has been reported from elsewhere on the island (McKelvey, 1976). It seems likely that the macaques are the most effective predator on some of the highly endangered bird species of Mauritius. Sugarcane made up 8% of the diet, and the monkeys would visit plantations at considerable risk to themselves.

Discussion. This preliminary investigation has revealed that *M. fascicularis* (Fig. 3) on Mauritius both shows similarities to (e.g., in being an eclectic omnivore with heavily frugivorous tendencies, and in showing a loose group structure in which a large basic social unit tends to split into subgroups for daily activities), and differences from its Asian conspecifics (e.g., in exhibiting a substantial degree of terrestriality).

FIGURE 3. Subadult male *Macaca fascicularis*.

The Mauritian macaques are of special interest and deserving of further study for a variety of reasons. Mauritius provided its monkeys on their arrival with a wide array of potential habitats, almost all of which seem to have been exploited. Detailed study of the Mauritian macaques in a range of different environments should allow us to better understand how a colonizing monkey species may adapt to a new spectra of ecological opportunities in the absence of the competitors with which it is normally sympatric. On a more general level, it will be interesting to learn whether, or to what extent, social organization varies with habitat differences. In sum, the Mauritius macaques provide a model of high potential significance for the study of a variety of fundamental questions of primate ecology. A more detailed account of our work so far may be found in Sussman and Tattersall (1980, 1981), and we hope to undertake further studies in the near future.

The Brown Lemur of Mayotte

Lemur fulvus is one of only two lemur species with wild-living populations represented outside Madagascar. The subspecies of Mayotte, *L.f. mayottensis*, had previously been the subject of a field study under National Geographic Society auspices (see Tattersall, 1977, and NGS Research Reports, volume 15), which revealed considerable differences in behavior from its close relative *L.f. rufus* in Madagascar (Sussman, 1975).

The July through August 1977 study was undertaken at the same locality, Mavingoni, as the previous one, but included observations made at night. Observation techniques were as described for the earlier study, and were similar to those noted above for the Mauritian study. A total of 204 hr of daytime observation was added during 1977, together with about 50 hr at night. This report summarizes the results obtained on the activity patterns of *L.f. mayottensis*. It should be noted that the earlier study was carried out in the wet season, while that of 1977 was during the dry.

Patterns of Daytime Activity. The most striking difference between the wet and the dry season resides in the proportion of time devoted to resting. Whereas in the wet season the activity:rest ratio was 0.52, in the dry season it dropped to 0.40. Both of these figures are lower than the corresponding ones for *L.f. rufus* (1.0 and 0.79, respectively); but both subspecies exhibited a similar decline in overall activity during the dry season. This drop in activity is associated in the case of the Mayotte lemur with an accentuation of both the peaks and troughs of activity. The tendency of the lemurs to indulge in long periods of midday resting was more pronounced during the dry season than the wet, but so also was early morning and evening activity, especially feeding.

Nocturnal Activity. Although *L. fulvus* has generally been reported to be diurnal, evidence has been accumulating for some time that its activity is not restricted to daylight hours. During the 1977 study I attempted to undertake nocturnal observations, and succeeded in keeping in contact with a group of lemurs from sunset to sunrise on 2 nights; additional nocturnal observations were made on several nights over periods of from 1 to 4 hr. Although nighttime observations, made with the aid of a powerful spot lamp, were recorded in the same manner as those made during daylight, the vast accentuation of visibility bias at night suggests that it would be unwise to make detailed comparisons between the nocturnal and diurnal data. Instead, a broader measure of activity is used.

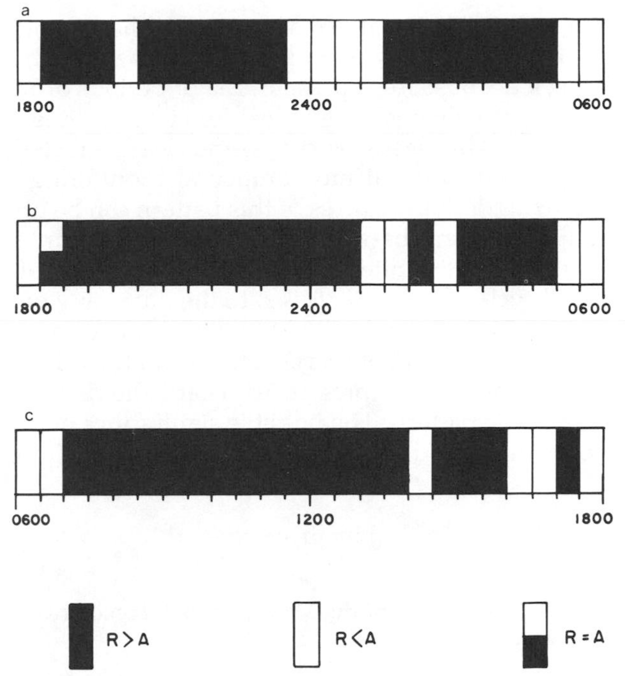

FIGURE 4. Half-hour periods of observation of *Lemur fulvus mayottensis* characterized according to whether observations of resting exceeded those of activity, or vice versa. a, night of July 26-27, 1977; b, night of July 30-31, 1977; c, daytime on July 18, 1977. R, resting; A, activity.

In Figure 4, each 1/2 hr of both nights of continuous observation is characterized according to whether, in summing the 5-min samples, more individuals were recorded to be active than resting or vice versa; the nights are compared with a randomly chosen day treated in the same manner. On both nights the number of such periods where activity is greater than rest (A>R) exceeded that for the sample daytime: 8 and 6.5, as compared with 6 (the mean for 16 days of observation during the dry season was 6.5, the range 4 to 10). On both nights, the periods of activity following 1800 hr and preceding 0600 hr represented major feeding bouts which began before nightfall and continued after sunrise, respectively. Feeding bouts of considerable duration also occurred during the middle of both nights, but there were substantial differences between the nights (as occurred, indeed, between days) in the amount and the timing of the various activities. The food sources exploited at night appeared to be precisely the same as those exploited diurnally.

Discussion. This "diel" pattern of activity in the Mayotte lemur differs distinctly from that of any other primate so far studied, and the factors influencing it are obscure at present. Major periods of activity began and ended without any consistent regard for either light levels or ambient temperature, the two classic *zeitgebers,* and clearly much detailed field study, combined with careful environmental monitoring, will be required before the underlying causes of this pattern can be understood. It is worth noting, however, that within genus *Lemur* a complete spectrum of activity patterns is exhibited, from the nocturnality of *L. mongoz,* through the diel cycle of *L.f. mayottensis,* to the diurnality of *L. catta.* It is possible that the pattern seen in the Mayotte lemur represents a transitional stage between one end of this spectrum and the other, although it would seem most prudent at present to regard the diel activity of *L.f. mayottensis* as a stable pattern. The possible significance of these findings on the Mayotte lemur is discussed at some length by Tattersall (1979, 1982).

REFERENCES

McKelvey, S. D.
1976. A preliminary study of the Mauritian Pink Pigeon *(Nesoenas Meyeri).* Bull. Mauritius Inst., vol. 8, pp. 145-175.

Sussman, R. W.
1975. A preliminary study of the ecology and behavior of *Lemur fulvus rufus* Audebert 1800. Pp. 237-258 *in* "Lemur Biology," I. Tattersall and R. W. Sussman, eds., Plenum, New York.

Sussman, R. W., and Tattersall, I.
1980. A preliminary study of the crab-eating macaque *(Macaca fascicularis)* in Mauritius. Bull. Mauritius Inst., vol. 9, pp. 31-57.
1981. Behavior and ecology of *Macaca fascicularis* in Mauritius: A preliminary study. Primates, vol. 22, pp. 192-205.

Tattersall, I.
1977. Ecology and behavior of *Lemur fulvus mayottensis* (Primates, Lemuriformes). Anthrop. Papers Amer. Mus. Nat. Hist., vol. 54, pp. 421-482.
1979. Patterns of activity in the Mayotte lemur, *Lemur fulvus mayottensis.* Journ. Mammal., vol. 60, pp. 314-323.
1982. The primates of Madagascar. Columbia University Press, New York.

Ian Tattersall
Robert W. Sussman

Principles of Vertebrate Locomotion

Grant Recipient: C. Richard Taylor, Museum of Comparative Zoology, Harvard University, Cambridge, Massachusetts.

Grant 1609: In support of a study to uncover general principles of vertebrate locomotion, using East African animals.

Physiology of Locomotion

Our research goal was to answer the following questions:

- How does an animal's top speed depend on size and build?
- How does the speed, stride, frequency, stride length, and energy consumption when an animal changes from one gait to another (a walk to a trot, or a trot to a gallop) vary with size and build?
- How does the maximum rate at which animals can supply energy to their muscles (both oxidatively and anaerobically) depend on their body size and build?

Additionally, we formulated a fourth question which we tackled in collaboration with Prof. Ewald Weibel and his group in the Department of Anatomy at the University of Bern, Switzerland:

- Do animals build and maintain just the amount of structure they need to meet functional requirements, at all levels of organization?

Important new generalities have emerged from the studies of how animals move across the ground, how much energy they use to move, and how the energy is used by their muscles. The studies carried out in Kenya under this grant from the National Geographic Society were extended and completed in subsequent studies in our lab, resulting in a series of four papers on the energetics and mechanics of terrestrial locomotion published in 1982 in *The Journal of Experimental Biology* (vol. 97). The data collected in the first paper were obtained during the period in Kenya, while the other three papers are extensions of this work carried out subsequently.

Taylor, C. R.; Heglund, N. C.; and Maloiy, G.M.O.
Energetics and mechanics of terrestrial locomotion. I. Metabolic energy consumption as a function of speed and body size in birds and mammals. Journ. Exp. Biol., vol. 97, pp. 1-22 (1982).

New data relating rate of oxygen consumption and speed are reported for 8 species of wild and domestic artiodactyls, 7 species of carnivores,

4 species of primates, and 1 species of rodents. These are combined with previously published data to formulate a new allometric equation relating mass-specific rates of oxygen consumed ($\dot{V}_{O_2}/M_b$) during locomotion at a constant speed to speed and body mass (based on data from 62 avian and mammalian species):

$$\dot{V}_{O_2}/M_b = 0.533 M_b^{-0.316} \cdot v_g + 0.300\, M_b^{-0.303}$$

where $\dot{V}_{O_2}/M_b$ has the units mL $O_2 sec^{-1}\ kg^{-1}$; M_b is in kg; and v_g is in m sec^{-1}. This equation can be expressed in terms of mass-specific rates of energy consumption ($\dot{E}_{metab}/M_b$) using the energetic equivalent of 1 mL O_2 = 20.1 J because the contribution of anaerobic glycolysis was negligible:

$$\dot{E}_{metab}/M_b = 10.7\, M_b^{-0.316} \cdot v_g + 6.03\, M_b^{-0.303}$$

where $\dot{E}_{metab}/M_b$ has the units watts/kg.

This new relationship applies equally well to bipeds and quadrupeds. Of the values calculated from this general equation for the diverse assortment of avian and mammalian species included in this regression, 90% fall within 25% of the observed values at the middle of the speed range where measurements were made. This agreement is impressive when one considers that mass-specific rates of oxygen consumption differ by more than 1400% over this size range of animals.

FEDAK, M. A.; HEGLUND, N. C.; and TAYLOR, C. R.
Energetics and mechanics of terrestrial locomotion. II. Kinetic energy changes of the limbs and body as a function of speed and body size in birds and mammals. Journ. Exp. Biol., vol. 97, pp. 23-40 (1982).

High-speed films (light or x-ray) of 4 species of quadrupeds and 4 species of bipeds running on a treadmill were analyzed to determine mass of the animal ($E_{KE,tot}$). A mass-specific power term ($E_{KE,tot}/M_b$) was calculated by adding all of the increments in E_{KE} during an integral number of strides and dividing by the time interval for the strides and body mass. The equations relating $E_{KE,tot}/M_b$ and speed were similar for all bipeds and quadrupeds regardless of size. One general equation for the rate at which muscles and tendons must supply energy to accelerate the limbs and body relative to the center of mass seems to apply for all of the animals:

$$\dot{E}_{KE,tot}/M_b = 0.478\, v_g^{1.53}$$

where $\dot{E}_{KE,tot}/M_b$ has the units W kg^{-1} and v_g is ground in m sec^{-1}. Therefore $\dot{E}_{KE,tot}/M_b$ does not change in parallel with the mass-specific rate at which animals consume energy ($\dot{E}_{metab}/M_b$), either as a function of speed or as a function of body size.

HEGLUND, N. C.; CAVAGNA, G. A.; and TAYLOR, C. R.
Energetics and mechanics of terrestrial locomotion. III. Energy changes of the centre of mass as a function of speed and body size in birds and mammals. Journ. Exp. Biol., vol. 97, pp. 41-56 (1982).

Measurements of the mechanical work required ($E_{CM,tot}$) to lift and reaccelerate an animal's center of mass within each step as a function of speed and body size during level, constant average speed locomotion was reported. A force platform was used in this study to measure $E_{CM,tot}$ for small bipeds, quadrupeds, and hoppers. We have already published similar data from large animals. The total power required to lift and reaccelerate the center of mass ($\dot{E}_{CM,tot}$) increased nearly linearly with speed for all the animals. Expressed in mass-specific terms, it was independent of body size and could be expressed by a simple equation:

$$\dot{E}_{CM,tot}/M_b = 0.685v_g + 0.072$$

where $\dot{E}_{CM,tot}/M_b$ has the units of W kg^{-1} and v_g is speed in m sec^{-1}.

Walking involves the same pendulumlike mechanism in small animals as has been described in humans and large animals. Also, running, trotting, and hopping produce similar curves of $E_{CM,tot}$ as a function of time during a stride for both the small and large animals. In small animals the front legs are used mainly for braking, while the back legs are used to reaccelerate the center of mass within a stride. In large animals the front and hind legs serve to both brake and reaccelerate the animal; this difference in mechanics is significant in that it does not allow the use of elastic energy in the legs of small animals, but does in the legs of large animals.

HEGLUND, N. C.; FEDAK, M. A.; TAYLOR, C. R.; and CAVAGNA, G. A.
Energetics and mechanics of terrestrial locomotion. IV. Total mechanical energy changes as a function of speed and body size in birds and mammals. Journ. Exp. Biol., vol. 97, pp. 57-66 (1982).

The final paper of the series examined the link between the energetics and mechanics of terrestrial locomotion. In this paper the kinetic energy of the limbs and body relative to the center of mass ($E_{KE,tot}$ of the second paper) is combined with the potential plus kinetic energy of the center of mass ($E_{CM,tot}$ of the third paper) to obtain the total mechanical energy (excluding elastic energy) of an animal during constant average-speed locomotion. The minimum mass-specific power required of the muscles and tendons to maintain the observed oscillations in total energy ($\dot{E}_{tot}/M_b$) can be described by one equation:

$$\dot{E}_{tot}M_b = 0.478.v_g^{1.53} + 0.685.v_g + 0.72$$

where $\dot{E}_{tot}/M_b$ is in W kg^{-1} and v_g is in m sec^{-1}. This equation is independent of body size, applying equally as well to a chipmunk or a quail as to a horse or an ostrich. In marked contrast, the metabolic energy consumed by each gram of an animal as it moves along the ground at a constant speed increases linearly with speed and is proportional to $M_b^{-0.3}$. Thus, we have found that each gram of tissue of a 30-g quail or chipmunk running at 3 m sec^{-1} consumes metabolic energy at a rate about 15 times that of a 100-kg ostrich, horse, or human running at the same speed while their muscles are performing work at the same rate.

Conclusions

Our measurements demonstrate the importance of storage and recovery of elastic energy in larger animals, but they cannot confirm or exclude the possibility of elastic storage or energy in small animals. It seems clear that the rate at which animals consume energy during locomotion cannot be explained by assuming a constant efficiency between the energy consumed and the mechanical work performed by the muscles. It is suggested that the intrinsic velocity of shortening of the active muscle motor units (which is related to the rate of cycling of the cross-bridges between actin and myosin) and the rate at which the muscles are turned on and off are the most important factors in determining the metabolic cost of constant-speed locomotion. Faster motor units are recruited as animals increase speed, and equivalent muscles of small animals have faster fibers than those of larger animals. Also, the muscles are turned on and off more quickly as an animal increases speed, and at the same speed a small animal will be turning muscles on and off at a much higher rate. These suggestions are testable, and future studies should determine if they are correct.

Match Between Structure and Function: Are Animals Built Rationally?

The field study of wild animals in Kenya also provided a unique opportunity to examine the match between structure and function. We combined resources with a group under Prof. Ewald Weibel from the Anatomy Department of the University of Bern in Switzerland. We selected the mammalian respiratory system (from the lung to the mitochondria in the muscles) for study, because it provided a convenient system to test our hypothesis. The results of the study were published in 1981 as a series of nine papers constituting an entire issue (vol. 44, no. 1) of *Respiratory Physiology*.

In this series of papers we examine the question of whether and to what extent structural properties are important determinants of oxygen flow at each level of organization in the respiratory system, except for the heart and circulation (which have been left for future studies). In undertaking this task we were motivated by the firm belief that animals are built reasonably. If this is true, then the muscles should maintain a mitochondrial complement just large enough to provide the adenosine triphosphate (ATP) required for maximal work performance; any superfluous mitochondrial mass would be wasteful. Likewise the size of the pulmonary gas exchange apparatus should be just large enough to afford the conductance required to allow an oxygen flow rate matched to the muscles' oxygen needs during maximal work. The structural design of the respiratory system should thus be matched to the functional requirements.

Clearly, this concept specifies for the special case of the respiratory system the main elements of a rather general principle of regulated economical construction which should apply to all levels of biological organization, from the cells and their organelles to organs and functional systems, and finally to the whole organism. The principle states that no more structure is formed and maintained than is required to satisfy functional needs; this is achieved by regulating morphogenesis during growth and during maintenance of structures. We propose to call this principle *symmorphosis*, defining it as a state of structural design commensurate to functional needs resulting from regulated morphogenesis, whereby the formation (μο ρφωσιζ) of structural elements is regulated to satisfy but not exceed the requirements of the functional system. It is evident that this principle of regulated morphogenesis is akin to *homeostasis* as the principle of regulated function.

From this concept of close structure-function correlation we derived the following hypotheses:

The structural design is a rate-limiting factor for oxygen flow at each level. For example, the maximal oxygen flow rate into the sink depends on the number of respiratory chain units available, and hence on the surface of inner mitochondrial membrane into which they are packed. Likewise, the oxygen transfer rate from air to blood in the lung depends on the air-blood contact area established by the lung's tissue barrier.

The structural design is optimized. That is, there is just enough structure at each level to support the maximal oxygen flow rate, perhaps with some minimal safety factor. This hypothesis derives from the notion that maintaining biological structures with their often high turnover rates is costly. In fact, there are numerous well known examples where structures become quantitatively reduced when they are not required to work.

The structural design is adaptable, at least within certain limits. This hypothesis is clearly a consequence of the two others, because if structure is rate-limiting and optimized to functional demand, then an adaptative change of function must entail an adaptive response of structure. Specifically, if oxygen requirements on the part of muscles are altered, the structural design properties of all parts of the respiratory system should become adapted.

How do we approach the problem of testing these hypotheses? One way would be to modify the oxygen requirements or some of the conditions subserving the maintenance of an oxygen flow rate. But, because we are interested in the entire respiratory system and its integral performance, we chose a comparative approach with a double strategy.

First, we examine animals of about the same body size but adapted for different aerobic performance. Thus, the capacity for aerobic energy conversion is much larger in the horse than in the cow, or in the dog than in the sheep, or—among small animals—in waltzing mice than in laboratory mice. Among the bovids in the African savanna, wild species such as gazelle, gnu, or eland must move long distances to find food, but domesticated species such as sheep, goats, or cows, use minimal effort because man optimizes the food supply; one would expect the oxygen requirements of these groups to differ.

Second, we exploit the size variation in the animal kingdom and the fact that metabolic rate changes nonlinearly with body size. It has been well documented that the size of many organs increases in linear proportion to body mass (M_b). Thus the volume of blood, the mass of the heart, or even the weight of the lung are approximately constant fractions of body mass and increase linearly with M_b. On the other hand, it is known since the pioneering work of Kleiber[1] that resting oxygen consumption or metabolic rate increases with the three-quarters power of body mass. Thus, expressing metabolic rate per unit body mass we find a mouse of 20 g to consume oxygen at about 10 times the rate of a cow of 500 kg. It is evident that this experiment of nature presents us with much larger differences among the metabolic needs of animals of varying size than one could find in any laboratory equipment. It thus appears that this approach affords the necessary material on which to study the question of whether the size of the various structural components interposed in the pathway for oxygen is adapted to the oxygen flow requirement of the system.

The plan for this integrated study was rather complex and required a number of different steps, all linked by the common goal of relating in quantitative terms the structural properties of the respiratory system to the functional requirements of oxygen flow from environmental air to the mitochondrial respiratory chains.

TAYLOR, C. R., and WEIBEL, E. R.
Design of the mammalian respiratory system. I. Problem and strategy. Resp. Physiol., vol. 44, no. 1, pp. 1-10 (1981).

---

[1] Kleiber, M. Body size and metabolism. *Hilgardia*, vol. 6, pp. 315-353 (1932); and Kleiber, M. Pp. 453 *in* "The Fire of Life," John Wiley and Sons (1961).

We selected wild animals over the widest range in body mass that could reach $\dot{V}_{O_2}$ max on our treadmills. In addition, we selected domestic animals of the same body mass, that we believed would have the greatest range of aerobic capacities.

SEEHERMAN, H. J.; TAYLOR, C. R.; MALOIY, G.M.O.; and ARMSTRONG, R. B.
Design of the mammalian respiratory system. I. Measuring maximum aerobic capacity. Resp. Physiol., vol. 44, no. 1, pp. 11-24 (1981).

We developed an accurate and reliable procedure for measuring $\dot{V}_{O_2}$ max that could be applied to all of the animals selected for this study. We also compared it with another commonly used approach to measuring $\dot{V}_{O_2}$max, namely cold exposure. This treadmill procedure is described.

TAYLOR, C. R.; MALOIY, G.M.O.; WEIBEL, E. R.; LANGMAN, V. A.; KAMAU, J.M.Z.; SEEHERMAN, H. J.; and HEGLUND, N. C.
Design of the mammalian respiratory system. III. Scaling maximum aerobic capacity to body mass: Wild and domestic animals. Resp. Physiol., vol. 44, no. 1, pp. 25-38 (1981).

The treadmill procedure for measuring $\dot{V}_{O_2}$ max was applied to a wide size range of wild and domestic animals in Africa and a reliable allometric relationship between $\dot{V}_{O_2}$ max and M_b was determined.

WEIBEL, E. R.; GEHR, P.; CRUZ-ORIVE, L. M.; MÜLLER, A. E.; MWANGI, D. K.; and HAUSSENER, V.
Design of the mammalian respiratory system. IV. Morphometric estimation of pulmonary diffusing capacity; critical evaluation of a new sampling method. Resp. Physiol., vol. 44, pp. 39-60 (1981).

The procedure for measuring the diffusing capacity of the lung was refined so that it could provide more accurate estimates for animals over the wide range of M_b used in the $\dot{V}_{O_2}$ max studies, and so that it could be carried out more efficiently—an important consideration when lungs of so many animals were to be measured. This procedure is described and compared with the previously used methods.

GEHR, P.; MWANGI, D. K.; AMMANN, A.; MALOIY, G.M.O.; TAYLOR, C. R.; and WEIBEL, E. R.
Design of the mammalian respiratory system. V. Scaling morphometric pulmonary diffusing capacity to body mass: Wild and domestic mammals. Resp. Physiol., vol. 44, no. 1, pp. 61-86 (1981).

The modified procedure for estimating DL_{O_2} was applied to the same individual animals for which $\dot{V}_{O_2}$ max had been determined, and allometric relationships between DL_{O_2} and M_b and between DL_{O_2} and $\dot{V}_{O_2}$ max were established. In this way we related the maximum flow rate of oxygen across the lung to the structural components that determine DL_{O_2}, namely alveolar surface area, capillary surface area, capillary blood volume, and air-blood barrier thickness.

HOPPELER, H.; MATHIEU, O.; KRAUER, R.; CLAASSEN, H.; ARMSTRONG, R. B.; and WEIBEL, E. R.

Design of the mammalian respiratory system. VI. Distribution of mitochondria and capillaries in various muscles. Resp. Physiol., vol. 44, no. 1, pp. 87-112 (1981).

Techniques were developed to study the structures that limit oxygen delivery and consumption in the muscle. Two structural elements were considered to be most important: the mitochondria and the capillaries. The heterogeneity of distribution of these elements among different muscles and different types of muscle fibers and how to deal with it, are described.

MATHIEU, O.; KRAUER, R.; HOPPELER, H.; GEHR, P.; LINDSTEDT, S. L.; ALEXANDER, R.McN.; TAYLOR, C. R.; and WEIBEL, E. R.

Design of the mammalian respiratory system. VII. Scaling mitochondrial volume in skeletal muscle to body mass. Resp. Physiol., vol. 44, no. 1, pp. 113-128 (1981).

The procedures developed in the previous paper were used to determine the mitochondrial volume and density in four selected muscles of each of the animals that had been studied. Allometric relationships were established both for volume density and the volume of mitochondria as functions of M_b and $\dot{V}_{O_2}$ max.

HOPPELER, H.; MATHIEU, O.; WEIBEL, E. R.; KRAUER, R.; LINDSTEDT, S. L.; and TAYLOR, C. R.

Design of the mammalian respiratory system. VIII. Capillaries in skeletal muscles. Resp. Physiol., vol. 44, pp. 129-150 (1981).

The techniques developed were used to determine the relationship between mitochondria and capillaries in muscle.

WEIBEL, E. R.; TAYLOR, C. R.; GEHR, P.; HOPPELER, H.; MATHIEU, O.; and MALOIY, G.M.O.

Design of the mammalian respiratory system. IX. Functional and structural limits for oxygen flow. Resp. Physiol., vol. 44, no. 1, pp. 151-164 (1981).

The results obtained in the papers described above were brought together in this final paper, which discusses our general hypothesis that animals are designed economically and that, at each step in the respiratory system, the flow of oxygen at V_{O_2max} is limited by the structures involved: Animals do not build and maintain structures in excess of what they need.

Conclusion

In each of the levels examined—mitochondria, capillaries, lung—it was evident that there should be a close quantitative correlation between the structural parameters that determine the various conductances and the flow rate of oxygen. But in none of these levels did we find an agreement between the scaling factors for maximal oxygen consumption and for the relevant structural parameters. Thus we ended with a number of paradoxes that needed explaining. The clue was to identify additional size-dependent factors that influence the relationship between structure and function and that may well have remained undetected if we had simply compared animals differing in terms of oxygen need but matched in size. Thus one of the important insights we have gained is that the double strategy of varying functional loads on the system, both independently of body size and as a function of body size, is a useful way of checking the conception of models on which we attempt to base the structure-function correlation.

With respect to mitochondria we found that it was the total mitochondrial volume of a muscle that had to be compared with oxygen consumption, rather than mitochondrial volume density. For capillaries we need to look at the total energy supply—oxygen and substrates—rather than only at oxygen flow. And in the lung, a system that at first appeared simple and well worked out, we must now consider boundary conditions that affect gas exchange between air and blood as a function of body mass. There is still hope that the structural parameters influencing the various conductances of the respiratory system are well matched to the oxygen flow requirements, even in mammals of different body size. But the situation is less simple than one would think, and a thorough analysis of scaling relations, when viewed critically, is a very useful tool for improving our understanding of how structural design may affect functional performance.

C. Richard Taylor

Ecology and Behavior of Rain Forest Peccaries in Southeastern Peru

Grant Recipient: John Terborgh and Richard A. Kiltie, Department of Biology, Princeton University, Princeton, New Jersey.[1]

Grant 1612: To study the feeding behavior and ecology of white-lipped and collared peccaries in Peru's Manú National Park.[2]

In tropical rain forests, most ungulates and other terrestrial herbivorous mammals are solitary (Eisenberg and McKay, 1974). The main exceptions to this generalization are found among species of the superfamily Suoidea—the pigs (Suidae) and peccaries (Tayassuidae). In comparison to open-country species, however, most suoids are still not very social, since "sounders" of one or a few adult females and their dependent young are the basic social units and adult males are solitary. The only species whose group sizes rival those of plains species is the white-lipped peccary *(Tayassu pecari)* of Central and South America. In its rain forest habitat, this species is usually reported in herds of at least 50 and often over 100 individuals.

We set out to examine the ecology of "white-lippeds" in hope of discerning the adaptive basis for their distinction as the only rain forest ungulate that lives in large social groups. For comparison, we also studied the smaller collared peccary *(Tayassu tajacu).* Although "collareds" may form groups that include as many as 30 individuals in arid parts of the species' range (Sowls, 1974), in Neotropical rain forests they travel either in small sounders or as solitaires. We hoped that the ecological traits that distinguish white-lippeds would be most clearly discriminated by studying both species simultaneously in the same habitat.

What follows is a summary of our results. Fuller descriptions of our observations and analyses are available in Kiltie (1980a).

---

[1] Present address of Kiltie is Department of Zoology, University of Florida, Gainesville.

[2] Funding for this project was also provided by the U. S. National Science Foundation, Princeton University, and the Scientific Research Society of North America (Sigma Xi). We also gratefully acknowledge the help and encouragement of the Peruvian Ministry of Agriculture, Direction of Forestry and Wildlife.

Study Site

Both peccary species are hunted relentlessly by aboriginal and immigrant residents of Neotropical rain forests (Kiltie, 1980b). Thus it was necessary to study them at a place that was remote from human settlements. Cocha Cashu Biological Station, in Peru's Manú National Park, provided an appropriate site. The difficult journey to this isolated station and the pristine beauty of the spot have been described in a previous report to the National Geographic Society (Terborgh and Janson, 1983). The station itself consists of a thatched-roof house, which is about $\frac{1}{2}$ km from the Manú River on the bank of an oxbow lake (Cocha Cashu). Another lake is about $1\frac{1}{2}$ km east of the house. A trail system bounded by the lakes and the river covers an area of roughly 3 km^2. Most of our observations were confined to this area because the flat terrain and nearly unbroken forest make it dangerous to travel elsewhere without carefully charting one's course.

Peccary Groups and Group Movements

Our main way of gathering information about the peccaries at Cocha Cashu was by a "pig log," in which all biologists at the station were asked to record details of their encounters with either of the peccary species. This record was maintained for a total of 16 mo in 1976, 1977, and 1978. Additional records of white-lipped peccary appearances were made in July and August 1975.

Encounters with Collared Peccaries

There were 132 encounters with collared peccary groups recorded during the study period. The number in any given month varied from 2 to 22, but this variation was attributable to changes in the number of observers resident at the site (which ranged from 1 to 12). The animals were seen at all daylight hours, and they were sometimes heard after dark as well.

More often than not, collareds detected an observer before the observer detected them. In such cases, the encounter consisted simply of a sharp "woof" from the animals or a rapid clacking of their teeth, followed by their unseen flight. Once in a while they were detected by sounds as they foraged, or they were spotted as they crossed a trail. The best (and rarest) opportunities to watch the animals came when an observer was involved in a relatively quiet and motionless activity and the peccaries wandered into view.

The distribution of minimum group sizes reported in encounters with collareds is shown in Figure 1. In most cases, it was only possible to

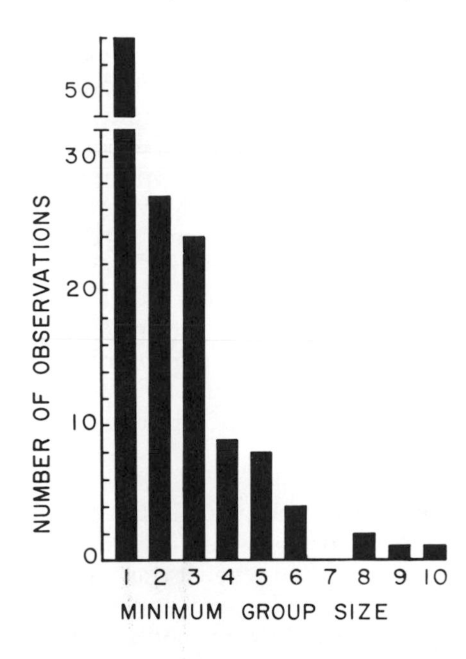

FIGURE 1. Distribution of minimum group sizes recorded from encounters with collared peccary groups.

say that there had been at least one adult present. Undoubtedly the real distribution of collared group sizes is not so dominated by solitaries as the figure suggests, but it is still noteworthy that groups larger than 10 were never observed. No group was observed with more than the maximum number of juveniles that a female can produce in a single litter, which is 3 (Smith and Sowls, 1975).

Invariably, collareds fled as soon as they sensed that they were under observation. It was not possible to follow them because they continued to be alert for pursuers and because the leaf litter that covers most of the forest floor did not retain their tracks. The best that one could do to study their activities under these circumstances was simply to inspect places where the animals, or evidence of them, had been discovered.

Collareds were repeatedly encountered at some places in the study area. These places tended to be in the vicinity of wallows that the animals were known to use, or near trees whose bark they gnawed, or near treefalls in which they appeared to rest in safety from predators. This repeated usage of certain spots suggested that the groups had restricted home areas.

ENCOUNTERS WITH WHITE-LIPPED PECCARIES

Herds of white-lipped peccaries or evidence of herds was discovered on 60 days during the study period. There were no occasions when we knew that more than one herd had entered the study area on the same day, but we did not know if the herds were the same from one encounter to the next. Variation in the monthly number of encounters with white-lippeds was not so clearly related to variation in the number of observers at the site as for collareds; instead, the frequency of their appearances seemed to be related to the seasons. During the dry season (May through September), white-lipped herds appeared at the site once every $4\frac{1}{2}$ days, on average, while in the wet season (October through April) they appeared at average intervals of $14\frac{1}{2}$ days. The range of intervals between appearances was from 1 to 32 days in the dry months and from 2 to 50 days in the wet months. Neither season's distribution of appearance intervals could be distinguished statistically from what would be expected on a random basis, with constant probability of appearance from one day to the next.

More sustained periods of contact were possible with white-lipped herds than with collared groups, but contact did not usually last more than a few hours. There were only two occasions when a herd was known to have spent a night in the study area. Often when it was reported that a herd had been encountered somewhere within or near the study area, subsequent searches on that day or the following morning produced nothing but tracks. This fleeting behavior stemmed in part from the herd's nearly continuous movement (even after dark), and from its tendency not to turn frequently in its marches. Examples of the paths of herds on two occasions are shown in Figure 2. In both of the cases illustrated, and in other cases not shown, the herds radically changed course only after having spent considerable time foraging in zones of high *Iriartea* palm tree density.

Maintenance of contact with white-lipped herds was facilitated by the variety and volume of the animals' noises, which permitted them to be located at a greater distance than that at which they could detect an observer. When foraging undisturbed, adults made low, resonating grunts that could be heard over 100 m away. As a herd drew nearer, strident barks and staccato clacking of teeth signaled squabbles within the herd. Both youngsters and adults also made a raspy bleat, almost reminiscent of a person retching. Still another source of noise was the popping and cracking sounds emitted as the white-lippeds crushed hard nuts and seeds in their powerful jaws.

Maintenance of contact with herds was also aided by the fact that the discovery of an observer by a few individuals on the periphery of a herd was often insufficient to cause a sustained flight by the entire group. Even when the majority fled, the herd often did not go far at first, so that the group could be relocated a short distance away. When the observer was careful not to press too closely, it was often possible to stay at least in

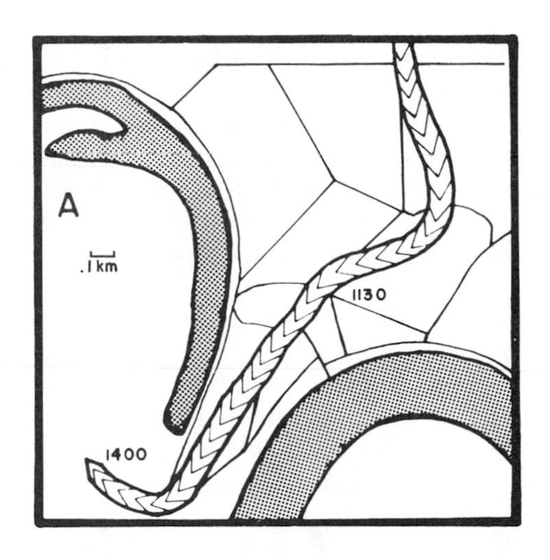

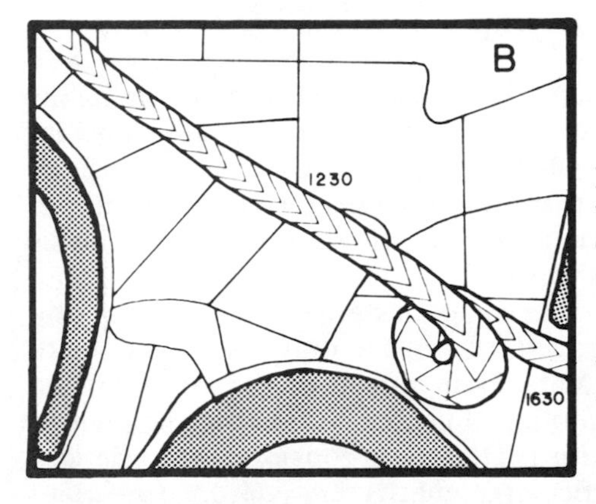

FIGURE 2. Approximate paths of white-lipped herds across the Cocha Cashu study area on two occasions (A, July 27, 1975; B, July 31, 1975). Hatchings point in the direction of the herd's movements; numbers show the approximate times when the herds were located at those points. Light lines are trails and stippled areas are water bodies.

auditory contact with the animals for long periods. Following was usually continued until the animals quickened their pace (sometimes for no apparent reason) and moved far beyond the trail system, or until night fell.

If a herd was repeatedly alarmed, it would eventually break into a fast-paced, sustained retreat. This kind of flight seemed to be elicited when one of the larger members of the herd detected the observer and uttered several deep, sharp barks. The aggressive behavior for which white-lippeds are famed was never observed in the herds at Cocha Cashu.

White-lipped herds typically included a large number of individuals, but there were only a few occasions when groups could be counted. The best opportunities arose when a herd crossed a gap in the forest, such as a trail, a stream bed, or the river. During the 16-mo period of records, there were only 5 such occasions: The counts at these times were 138, 102, 90, 90, and 110; however in each case more individuals were known already to have passed uncounted. Under normal circumstances when precise counts could not be made, the estimated sizes of the groups were between 100 and 200 individuals. On two occasions, smaller groups (about 30 in each case) were reported, but both times larger groups were sighted in the area within the next 24 hours. The small groups may have been "satellites" of the larger ones.

White-lipped herds included individuals of all sex and age classes. No herds were observed in which the proportion of youngsters was great. Usually the estimated number of juveniles was less than 20%. Mating activities were observed in herds in July 1975 and August 1977. If most mating occurs at this time, then young would be born 5 mo later (Root, 1966) in the wet season, when our observations of herds were fewest.

Foraging

We used several lines of evidence to characterize the foraging habits of the two peccary species. These included direct observations and inspection of areas where the animals had been encountered; analysis of stomach contents from peccaries that had been shot by a resident hunter outside the park; feeding experiments with captive animals; and analysis of the mechanics of the peccaries' jaws.

Stomach contents showed that both species are omnivores, but animal parts (mostly from invertebrates) constituted only trace portions of the total volumes of stomach contents. Plant reproductive parts averaged about two thirds of the stomach contents in both species, and plant vegetative parts were the remaining third. There was considerable variation, however, and the contents of particular stomachs ranged from pure plant reproductive parts to pure vegetative parts.

Direct observations indicated differences in the way that individuals of the two species searched for food. White-lippeds bulldozed the litter, skimming through the upper few centimeters of soil. This "rooting" was particularly concentrated along the sides of fallen logs and exposed roots and at the bases of plant stems (from seedlings to tall, buttressed trees). Evidence of their rooting was also often marked beneath lianas and clumps of low, overhanging shrubs. A census of fruit densities indicated that the white-lippeds were finding palm nuts in these places, apparently after the fruits had been "scatterhoarded" there by rodents (Kiltie, 1980b; see also Smythe, 1978; Heaney and Thorington, 1978). Consumption of hard fruits was also indicated by the cracking sounds usually heard from a foraging herd. Inspection of zones, however, where herds had foraged indicated that some kinds of fruits were not eaten, apparently because they were too hard even for white-lippeds to crush.

Collareds appeared to use their snouts more discriminatingly than white-lippeds—more like a shovel than a plow. They were observed sniffing over the litter rather than through it, and their diggings were patchier and deeper than those of the white-lippeds. These excavations were not directed at the bases of lianas, logs, etc., as the excavations of the white-lippeds were, and the object of their interest was often obscure, though it was sometimes apparent that they had chewed on roots (Eddy, 1961, documented the ability of collared peccaries to locate and consume underground plant parts in arid environments). Collareds were also often seen foraging beneath trees that were bearing soft, fleshy fruits. They were observed cracking the hard nuts of *Astrocaryum* palms, and stomach contents indicated that they ate *Jessenia* palm nuts; collareds, however, did not appear to eat some of the harder nuts (e.g., those of the *Iriartea* palm) that white-lippeds consumed.

Indications that there was a difference in the maximum hardnesses of nuts and seeds that the two species could masticate were corroborated by feeding tests with captive peccaries in the Lima (Peru) Zoo. We presented several species of nuts and seeds from Cocha Cashu to the Zoo's groups of collared and white-lipped peccaries. The white-lippeds masticated all the nuts that we knew they could eat from field observations, and they tried but failed to crush the nuts that they did not consume in the field. Collareds failed to crush any of the nuts, in spite of repeated attempts.

We were able to get more concrete measures of masticatory strengths of the peccaries by two further studies. First, we brought specimens of nuts and seeds from Cocha Cashu to labs in the United States and tested their resistances to crushing on "weight-loading" machines. The results are shown in Table 1, along with comparable data by Janzen and Higgins (1979) on the seeds of another tree species *(Enterolobium cyclocarpum)* from Costa Rica. As expected, the items eaten by both peccary species were most easily crushed; those eaten only by white-lippeds were intermediate; and those eaten by neither species were the most resistant.

The second investigation was a theoretical analysis of the peccaries' jaws as levers (assuming that the jaw joint acts as a fulcrum). With measurements of the lever arms of jaw muscles, resistance arms of food placed between the molars, and estimates of the relative forces of the jaw muscles, we calculated that white-lippeds should be able to crush food items at least 1.3 times more resistant than the hardest that collareds can crush. This calculation was consistent with the observed ratio of 1:1.4 between the mean maximum resistance of the hardest seeds crushed intact by white-lippeds *(Iriartea)* and the weakest seeds crushed by them but not by collareds *(Socratea).*

TABLE 1. Crushing Resistance and Other Traits of Some Palm Nuts and Legume Seeds

(Entries are mean ± standard deviation; sample sizes are shown in parentheses after weight.) All species except *E. cyclocarpum* were collected in the Manú National Park, Department of Madre de Dios, Peru. All flesh was removed from the nuts or seeds, and they were air-dried. Some specimens at the extremes of size were included in the samples for each species.

Species	*Load to break (kg)*	*Minimum dimension (mm)*	*Weight (g)*
Phytelephas sp. (Palmae)	1260 ± 390	28 ± 2	28 ± 4 (17)
Dipteryx micrantha (Leguminosae)	610 ± 100	25 ± 2	22 ± 4 (21)
Scheelea sp. (Palmae)	450 ± 120	26 ± 3	28 ± 3 (19)
Mauritia sp. (Palmae)	390 ± 70	27 ± 1	19 ± 2 (7)
Iriartea sp. (Palmae)[a]	350 ± 70	18 ± 1	5 ± 1 (32)
Socratea sp. (Palmae)	250 ± 40	15 ± 1	3 ± 1 (35)
Enterolobium cyclocarpum[b] (Leguminosae)	170 ± 20	8 − 10	1 ± 0 (347)
Astrocaryum sp. (Palmae)	140 ± 30	19 ± 3	9 ± 2 (34)
Jessenia sp. (Palmae)	100 ± 40	21 ± 1	8 ± 1 (20)

[a]Hardest of the tested seeds that is crushed intact by *T. pecari*. All weaker species are known or presumed (in the case of *E. cyclocarpum*) to be eaten by *T. pecari*. *Mauritia* seeds may also be eaten by *T. pecari* after they have been "chipped" to a smaller size.

[b]Data from Janzen and Higgins (1979) for specimens from Costa Rica. This is the hardest of the tested seeds that are eaten by *T. tajacu*. The weaker species are also eaten by *T. tajacu*.

Conclusions

It is a recurrent theme in ecology that closely related species diverge most decisively in their diets and/or foraging habits when the food supply is at critically low levels (e.g., Smythe, 1978; Terborgh and Janson, 1983). In Neotropical forests, the peccaries are only two among many terrestrial, frugivorous mammals. They differ from the rest, however, in having two foraging options that are almost entirely their own. One is the ability to use below-ground plant parts, and the other is the ability to crush very hard nuts and seeds. Collareds appear to be the better rooters, while white-lippeds are the champion nutcrackers.

How might the exceptional abilities of the white-lippeds to crush hard fruits be related to their distinctive social habits? There are at least two ways. The first concerns the manner in which such fruits are most effectively harvested. Some Neotropical palms and other hard-seeded tree species are markedly seasonal in their production of fruits and also may be highly aggregated in certain habitats. Efficient exploitation of such resources would require prior knowledge, by experienced individuals, of their locations and seasonal availability. It might thus pay less-experienced white-lippeds to "parasitize" the knowledge of more experienced ones by traveling with them to good foraging locations. Territorial defense by individuals might not be a viable option for a species dependent on such "patchy" resources, because the individual territories would be too small to contain all the resources needed for a year-round food supply. And highly concentrated resource "patches" capable of accommodating large numbers of individuals could not be defended either.

The second factor concerns the effects of group formation on the white-lippeds' individual risks of predation. Most terrestrial mammalian herbivores in rain forests can take advantage of the forest cover and avoid predators by being inconspicuous. Solitary white-lippeds, however, would be very conspicuous while feeding because the mastication of hard fruits inevitably produces popping or cracking sounds that can be heard 20 to 50 m away. These sounds would make them very vulnerable to detection and attack by their predators (human, jaguar, puma). By forming groups, individuals can combine their "zones of detectability" so that the total detectability per individual is lower than what it would be for solitaries. Furthermore, white-lippeds in groups can benefit from cooperative detection of predators (thereby reducing the need for individual wariness while foraging) and from cooperative defense.

In contrast to white-lippeds, collared peccaries may live in small groups and on small home ranges because they are less specialized as nut eaters and can turn to alternate resources (roots, soft fruits, green plant parts) during periods when nuts that they can eat are locally scarce. Furthermore, since their alternate foods are soft, and hence quiet to consume, collared peccaries will not be so easily detected by predators.

REFERENCES

EDDY, THOMAS A.

1961. Foods and feeding patterns of the collared peccary in southern Arizona. Journ. Wildl. Manage., vol. 25, pp. 248-257.

EISENBERG, JOHN F., and MCKAY, GEORGE M.

1974. Comparison of ungulate adaptations in the New World and the Old World tropical forests with special reference to Ceylon and the rainforests of Central America. Pp. 585-602 *in* "The Behaviour of Ungulates and its Relation to Management," V. Geist and F. Walther, eds. IUCN Publ., new ser., no. 24, vol. 2.

JANZEN, D. H., and HIGGINS, M. L.
——. How hard are *Enterolobium cyclocarpum* (Leguminosae) seeds? Brenesia. (In press.)
HEANEY, LAWRENCE R., and THORINGTON, RICHARD W., JR.
1978. Ecology of Neotropical red-tailed squirrels, *Sciurus granatensis*, in the Panama Canal Zone. Journ. Mammal., vol. 59, pp. 846-851.
KILTIE, RICHARD A.
1980a. Seed predation and group size in rain forest peccaries. Ph.D. Thesis, Princeton University.
——. On the significance of white-lipped peccaries in Amazon cultural ecology. Current Anthropol. (In press.)
——. Distribution of palm fruits on rain forest floor: Why white-lipped peccaries forage near objects. Biotropica. (In press.)
ROOT, CLIVE G.
1966. Notes on the breeding of white-lipped peccaries. Int. Zoo Yearb., vol. 6, pp. 198-199.
SMITH, NORMAN S., and SOWLS, LYLE K.
1975. Fetal development of the collared peccary. Journ. Mammal., vol. 56, pp. 619-625.
SMYTHE, NICHOLAS
1978. The natural history of the Central American agouti *(Dasyprocta punctata)*. Smithsonian Contrib. Zool., no. 257, 52 pp.
SOWLS, LYLE K.
1974. Social behaviour of the collared peccary *Dicotyles tajacu*. Pp. 144-165 *in* "The Behaviour of Ungulates and Its Relation to Management," V. Geist and F. Walther, eds. IUCN Publ., new ser., no. 24, vol. 1.
TERBORGH, JOHN, and JANSON, CHARLES H.
1983. Ecology of primates in southeastern Peru. Nat. Geogr. Soc. Research Reports, vol. 15, pp. 655-662.

RICHARD A. KILTIE
JOHN TERBORGH

Cenozoic Fossil Vertebrate Search: Australian Pilbara and Canning Basin Areas

Grant Recipient: William D. Turnbull, Field Museum of Natural History, Chicago, Illinois.

Grant 1658: In support of a study of Cenozoic fossil vertebrates in Western Australia.

To date, all efforts to gain a Tertiary vertebrate fossil record from the vast northwestern portion of Australia have failed. Given the importance of having such a record to help in deciphering the pathways of marsupial evolution and migrations, the time appears to be right to expect the region to yield results to a persistent search effort. Within the last 12 to 15 years extensive topographic and geologic mapping and geological investigations relating to mineral resource development have been completed, and the road-net improvement has made the country far more accessible than before. Hence, we now know precisely where Tertiary and Pleistocene sediments are to be found, and how they may be reached most efficiently. Some of the basic references are Casey and Wells, 1956; Traves et al., 1957; McWhae et al., 1958; Veevers and Wells, 1961; MacLead, 1966; and Raine, 1972.

The Society supported three months of intense work by me and my assistant Peter Crabb, a graduate student at Monash University, and enabled us to team up with Dr. E. L. Lundelius, Jr., and R. Lundelius to proceed with the prospecting effort with efficiency and relative safety. I have successfully cooperated with E. Lundelius, Jr. in previous similar research efforts that have resulted in significant additions to our knowledge of Australian mammalian evolution (Lundelius and Turnbull, 1967, 1973, 1975, 1978, 1981, 1982; Turnbull et al., 1965; Turnbull and Lundelius, 1967, 1970), and three other reports are well advanced. Although we did not have spectacular success in our primary goal of obtaining a first Tertiary vertebrate record from the north of Western Australia, we did succeed in proving the potential of one locality, Ederga Spring, General Locality (GL) 25. There, two fossil vertebrates (a partial pelvis of a Euro-sized macropod and a questionable tooth that remains indeterminate) were found. A persistent follow-up effort at this locality should be undertaken. It might produce a meaningful faunal record. We also succeeded in several important peripheral aspects related to the main effort, as indicated in the following paragraphs.

1. A series of lithic samples was collected from the Oakover Formation, or its presumed equivalents (see GL 4-19 of Fig. 1), from various fascies. Study of one of these, the siliceous caprock, has begun. Initial interpretation of thin-sections suggests primary, rather than replacement, deposition at one locality, and we expect that more petrologic evidence will come from these rock samples. This will provide understanding of depositional and subsequent conditions that may afford clues to fossil potentials for future work. Of particular interest will be evidence relating to calcium-silica replacement or migrations. Some representative samples were deposited with the Western Australian Museum (WAM).

2. A collection of Recent and subfossil remains representing at least three phascogales, four rodents (identified by A. Baynes as *Mus* sp., *M. musculus*, *Pseudomys hermansbergensis*, and *Notomys* cf. *alexis*), lizards, and birds was made in the remote Rudall River area (GL 15) where few, if any, collections have been made. The sample came from a small owl pellet deposit. It has been divided between the WAM and the Field Museum of Natural History (FM), the larger portion appropriately remaining in Perth in the care of Drs. D. Kitchener and D. Merrilees.

3. An unrecorded Tertiary oolitic deposit was discovered (GL 13) and all voucher specimens and data were turned over to the WAM and the Western Australian Geological Survey through Dr. G. Kendrick.

4. A series of extinct warrens, probably made by colonies of a potoroine, *Bettongia lesuer*, now extinct in the area, but which is known to have occupied it within historic time, was found. The warrens were observed in many places northward from Doologunna (GL 4), all the way to the Rudall River (GL 15). One of the better examples was trenched, and examined in some detail. It may deserve publication.

FIGURE 1. General localities of Pilbara and Canning Basin areas: Monger's Lake (1), Lake Austin (2), Meekatharra (3), Doolgunna Station (4), Newmann and South Flank Opthalmia Range (5), area near junction of Weeli Wolli and Packsaddle Roads (6), Weeli Wolli Spring (7), "Marillana" Station (8), Newman (9), Balfour Downs (10), Bee Hill (11), Skull Springs, Davis-Oakover Junction, Carawine Gorges (12), Oakover River crossing at Braeside Homestead (13), Rudall River (14), area marked (1) on the Rudall 1:250,000 sheet (560185 to 564186 on south to 560190 in north) (15), Ripon Hills manganese mining center (16), Oakover River channel from the Warrawegine-Burramine crossing south to Braeside crossing (17), Hammersley Range (18), Kangaroo Creek (19), creek 11 km west of Giralia homestead (20), Lake McCloud (21), Murchison River (24), Ederga Spring (25), Yarra Yarra Lakes (26), Collie (27), Kojonup (28).

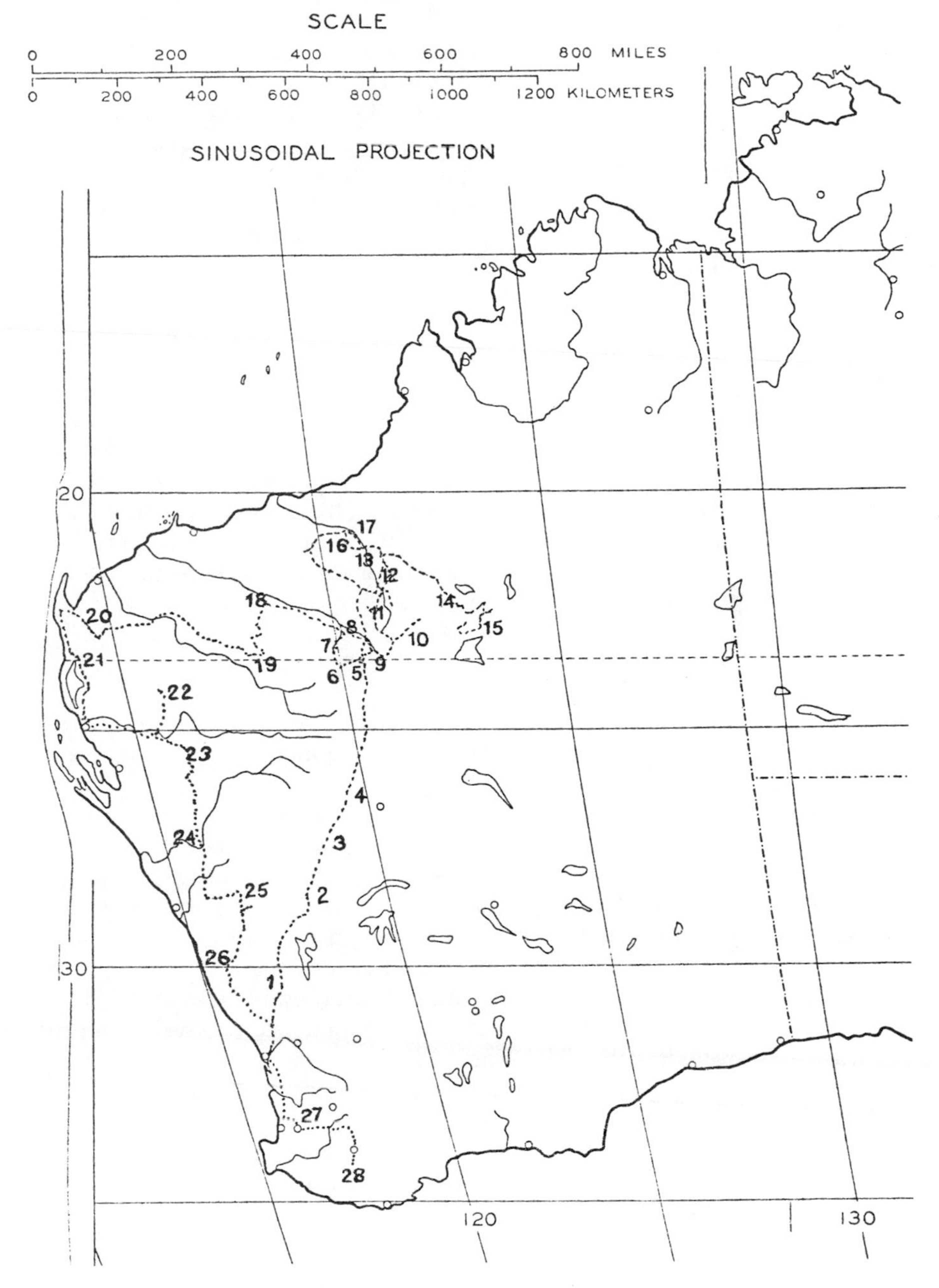

GOODE BASE MAP SERIES
DEPARTMENT OF GEOGRAPHY
THE UNIVERSITY OF CHICAGO
HENRY M. LEPPARD, EDITOR

5. A sampling of dead modern land snails was made for Dr. A. Solem of the FM, whose extensive investigations of Australian land snails were initiated by samples collected by us in 1964. On this latest occasion, operating in areas that Solem could not visit, we were able to expand significantly his geographic coverage. Samples from each of 10 localities (GL 12, 13, 17, 19, 20, 21, and 25) were deposited in the WAM, and all materials have been given to Solem for study, and will be included in part 7 of his Australian land snail monograph. (Parts 1-4 have been published, part 5 is in press, and parts 6 and 7 are in ms.)

6. A collection of fruiting bodies, stems, and leaves of *Banksia*, and some *Araucaria* cones were collected from the Tertiary Merlinleigh Sandstone (GL 22). The locality has been known for some time, but we more than doubled the number of reference specimens available. The collection has been split between the WAM and the FM and recently two taxa have been described (McNamara and Scott, 1983) based largely upon this material, *Banksia archaeocarpa*, and *Banksia* sp. These mark the earliest unequivocal occurrence (Eocene) of this important genus in Australia.

7. A random collection of Recent road-kill kangaroo skulls (and some other vertebrates) was made to augment the FM collections. These represent a degree of geographic diversity (GL 4, 5, 8, 10, 12, 15, 17, 21, 25) for two taxa, *Macropus robustus cervinus* and *M. rufus*, that has not been available here until now.

8. Five occurrences of aboriginal artifacts were discovered and reported to Dr. C. Dortsch of the WAM, and voucher specimens were turned over to him for the record.

Every opportunity to advance our understanding that can be gained from these peripheral aspects of our effort will be explored. We are concentrating at present on the lithic samples. It is important that our failure to find Tertiary vertebrates (and the failure of prior attempts by others) must not be interpreted as signifying that there is no potential left for success: this would be a great mistake. In many places the signs are good, i.e., fossil invertebrates, wood, and other plant remains and root fillings are locally present. Furthermore, the basic reasons given at the beginning of this report remain valid. There are still vast areas to be searched, and even those areas that we prospected may well contain fossils that we missed. Ederga Spring, now a proven locality, is an example of that, it having produced numerous freshwater invertebrates (hydrotiid-type shells), a freshwater snail (Planorbidae) in addition to the macropodid partial pelvis (still undescribed), and a crocodile tooth.

To provide the greatest advantage to future attempts, we must seek to understand the peculiarities of fossilization processes applicable to this huge area. It is hoped that we may be able to contribute insights that will benefit the next search efforts. Our plan now is to do petrologic studies on the full suite of lithic types, based upon the samples we collected. Initially, we will have help from Drs. B. Woodland of the FM and R. Falk of the University of Texas, and will call upon others if, in their opinion, it is warranted to do so.

A final means of aiding future efforts is by documenting the areas that we prospected and our observations at each locality. This will follow, seriatum, under the 28 general locality designations shown on the map (Fig. 1). The listing is too lengthy for inclusion here, but copies may be received on request from either W. D. Turnbull, Department of Geology, Field Museum of Natural History, Chicago, Illinois, 60605; or from E. L. Lundelius, Jr., Department of Geological Sciences, University of Texas, Austin, Texas, 78712.

REFERENCES

CASEY, J. N., and WELLS, A. T.
1956. Annual summary of activities of the Canning Basin party, 16 p. Bureau of Mineral Resources, Australia.

GEOLOGICAL SURVEY of WESTERN AUSTRALIA
1975. The geology of Western Australia, 541 p., 84 figs. Geol. Surv. of Western Australia Mem. 2.

LUNDELIUS, E. L., JR., and TURNBULL, W. D.
1967. Pliocene mammals from Victoria, Australia. P. K9 *in* "Sec. C., Abstr., 39th Congress." Australia and New Zealand Association for the Advancement of Science, Melbourne.
1973. The mammalian fauna of Madura Cave, W. A. Part I. Fieldiana: Geology, vol. 31, no. 1, pp. 1-35, 13 figs.
1975. The mammalian fauna of Madura Cave, W. A. Part II. Fieldiana: Geology, vol. 31, no. 2, pp. 37-117, 21 figs.
1978. The mammalian fauna of Madura Cave, W. A. Part III. Fieldiana: Geology, vol. 38, no. 1, pp. 1-120, 27 figs.
1981. The mammalian fauna of Madura Cave, W. A. Part IV. Fieldiana: Geology, n.s., no. 6, pp. 1-72, 21 figs.
1982. The mammalian fauna of Madura Cave, W. A. Part V. Fieldiana: Geology, n.s., no. 11, pp. 1-32, 10 figs, 4 pls.

MACLEOD, W. N.
1966. The geology and iron deposits of the Hammersley Range area, W. A. Western Geol. Surv. Bull. 117.

MCNAMARA, K. J., and SCOTT, J. K.
1983. A new species of *Banksia* (Proteaceae) from the Eocene Merlinleigh sandstone of the Kennedy Range, Western Australia. Alcheringa, vol. 7, pp. 185-193, 3 figs.

MCWHAE, J.R.H.; PLAYFORD, P. E.; LINDNER, A. W.; GLENISTER, B. F.; and BALME, B. E.
1958. The stratigraphy of Western Australia, 161 pp., 10 figs. Geol. Soc. of Australia.

RAINE, M. J.
1972. Bibliography of the Canning Basin, W. A. Bureau of Mineral Resources, Australia, Rep. 155, pp. 1-50.

TRAVES, D. M.; CASEY, J. N.; and WELLS, A. T.
1957. The geology of the southwestern Canning Basin, Australia. Bureau of Mineral Resources, Australia, Rep. 29, 48 p.

TURNBULL, W. D.; LUNDELIUS, E. L., JR.; and MCDOUGALL, I.
1965. A potassium-argon dated Pliocene marsupial faunaș from Victoria, Australia. Nature, vol. 206, no. 4986, 816 p.

TURNBULL, W. D., and LUNDELIUS, E. L., JR.
1967. Fossil vertebrate potential at Smeaton, Victoria. Pp. K10-11 *in* "Sec. C, Abstr., 39th Congress." Australia and New Zealand Association for the Advancement of Science, Melbourne.
1970. The Hamilton fauna, a late Pliocene mammalian fauna from the Grange Burn, Victoria, Australia. Fieldiana: Geology, vol. 19, no. 11, pp. 1-163, 31 pls.

VEEVERS, J. J., and WELLS, A. T.
1961. The geology of the Canning Basin, Western Australia. Bureau of Mineral Resources, Australia Rep. 60, pp. 1-323, 144 figs, 4 pls.

WILLIAM D. TURNBULL

An Archeological Survey of the Upper Zambesi Valley in Western Zambia

Grant Recipient: Joseph O. Vogel, Northern Illinois University, DeKalb, Illinois.

Grant 1596: For a survey of an Iron Age settlement of the upper Zambesi Valley, Zambia.

The origins and expansion, early in the modern era, of the Bantu-speaking peoples of southern Africa are subjects of some importance to historians, geographers, demographers, and other students of the African continent. The movement of Iron Age peoples into the subcontinent was once conceived as a single moving cultural frontier, but it is now viewed in the more complex terms of two or more independent streams of movement (Phillipson, 1975). The material remains of these prehistoric events are the proper concern of the archeologist, but Iron Age archeology in Africa is still so new a field that large areas of the continent remain unexplored. One such area is the upper Zambesi Valley in western Zambia (Vogel, 1976). Our earlier survey indicated that evidence of early communities in the Kalahari sand country of the upper valley could be found (Vogel, 1973; Vogel and Katanekwa, 1976). This research also indicated that we had evidence of two distinct cultural traditions within the upper valley during the 1st millennium A.D. Evidence of the subsequent Iron Age occupation of western Zambia until quite recent times was totally lacking, and we were unable to posit even a tentative cultural sequence for this portion of the country.

The vast area of western Zambia is dominated by the dual features of a broad, deep expanse of redeposited Kalahari-type sands and the Zambesi River. Centers of population are found along the river's course or upon elevated mounds in the periodically flooded plains of its valley. The sands are usually not very fertile, and the river, though perennial, varies from season to season in its volume. At times of flood a broad sheet of water, miles across, fills parts of the valley. The shifting nature of the river and the transient occupation of much of its valley produce an area in which the investigation of Iron Age activities may proceed only with great difficulty. In an area of limited pottery manufacture the archeological survey attempts to reconstruct conditions conducive to village life and to detect alterations to the soil or vegetation in the place of more traditional indicators of human occupation.

During June and July 1976, archeological reconnaissance of the upper Zambesi Valley from Kalongola to Katima Mulilo was continued. The survey proposed, specifically, to locate areas of Iron Age activity. Although primary concern was the distribution of the Early Iron Age societies, characteristics of subsequent culture were also of interest.

One survey area was centered on the 5th-century site at Sioma Mission (Vogel, 1973). Only one other site, at Kalongola, 50 km to the north, was then known (Vogel and Katanekwa, 1976). It and Sioma possessed pottery of a similar type, which though characteristic of the Early Iron Age differed from the contemporary wares of other areas of Zambia (Vogel, 1976). This survey area, though of more than 500 km was, for reasons made obvious below, not everywhere amenable to Iron Age occupation. Access to water and a deep arable sand were considered primary criteria, followed by the availability of iron or other raw material sources. The survey technique included interviewing local villagers to determine whether fragments of pottery or iron were discovered during plowing or the construction of huts or pits at villages; but the main activity consisted of walking all fields and excavating soundings to determine the depth of surface indications.

The environments of the opposing banks of the Zambesi differ radically. The western bank, which occupied most of our attention, appeared the most likely to contain areas of archeological interest. Although all of the area is characterized by a deep deposit of Kalahari-type sand—loose, finely grained, and unstructured yellowish sediments—the eastern side of the valley has the added appearance of an open, low-lying, and generally flat floodplain. The vegetation is essentially riverine, being of a type characterized as floodplain grassland, containing a number of species—for example, fan-palms (*Raphia* spp.)—not found on the western shore. This plain, which may flood, is periodically marshy and extends 10 km or more back from the main channel. It is occasionally broken by a wooded hillock of deeper sand—remnant of a once more extensive sand cover—but usually the surface soil is a thin deposit overlying a dense gravelly stratum. This portion of the valley appears to be related to older courses of the river, being an obvious erosional surface, overlain by water and windblown redeposition. No sites were found in this zone; the wooded flanks are somewhat distant and too divorced from the river's main channel to support settlements. The nearest present-day villages are some distance away, and access across the floodplain is extremely limited. Our own survey required canoe transport across the river followed by reconnaissance on foot to likely localities. All present-day occupation of the plain seems to take the form of small seasonal fishing villages of grass huts. Such may have been the case for some time, since we found no evidence of other occupation anywhere in our traverses of this zone.

The western bank presents a different aspect. Here the shoreline forms a more obvious relief and the land rises with varying degrees of steepness to the west. Farther west begins the broad, open grassy Siluana Plains, but fringing the river are wooded zones containing *Burkea, Copaifera,* and *Baikiaea* types, broken occasionally by poorly drained zones of *Hyparrhenia* grass and thorny shrubs. The large expanse of the Matabele Plain carries the east-bank floodplain environment across the river, where a number of buried and seasonal channels of the Zambesi produce a marshy plain whose open water is used for fishing. Neither of these plains is suitable for permanent settlement, although temporary fishing encampments appear on the Matabele Plain during the wet season, and surface deposits of ferricrete, suitable for smelting, are to be found on some of the poorly drained areas. Expectation for evidence of Iron Age settlement was restricted therefore to the narrow wooded zones fringing the river. Both Sioma and Kalongola were on deep sandy deposits within the wooded fringes. Both are quite close to the river's shore, and Kalongola is heavily eroded along its eastern edge. Soundings were dug into the various sandy knolls we encountered. Our trenches usually disclosed a layer of gravel, whenever they penetrated the sand. The overlying sand varied in depth from 30 cm to over 2 m (in trenches abandoned at depths below anything of cultural interest). Surface finds of weathered pottery were found at localities approximately 3, 5, 6, and 10 km north of Sioma Mission. Though tested by two or more 1-m^2 trenches at each locality, none disclosed subsurface remains of archeological material of any consequence. The paste and rim forms associated with the surface finds are similar to those from the Sioma site. There is no evidence of further occupation between the Early Iron Age and quite recent times (represented by fragments of Mbunda pottery from near Sioma and Senanga). The present-day villages date from the early 1950s, when people moved south from the Barotse Plain.

Though Early Iron Age people appear to have settled a limited portion of this stretch of river, subsequent erosion has apparently moved the main channel of the river westward, cutting back the west bank and leaving the floodplain to the east. This has reduced the evidence of occupation to scattered and unsubstantial remains along the western shore.

This occupation could not have been a particularly dense one, since favorable localities were very limited. Otherwise one may conclude that the area, though of considerable interest to the archeology of Zambia, possesses little upon which future research could be based.

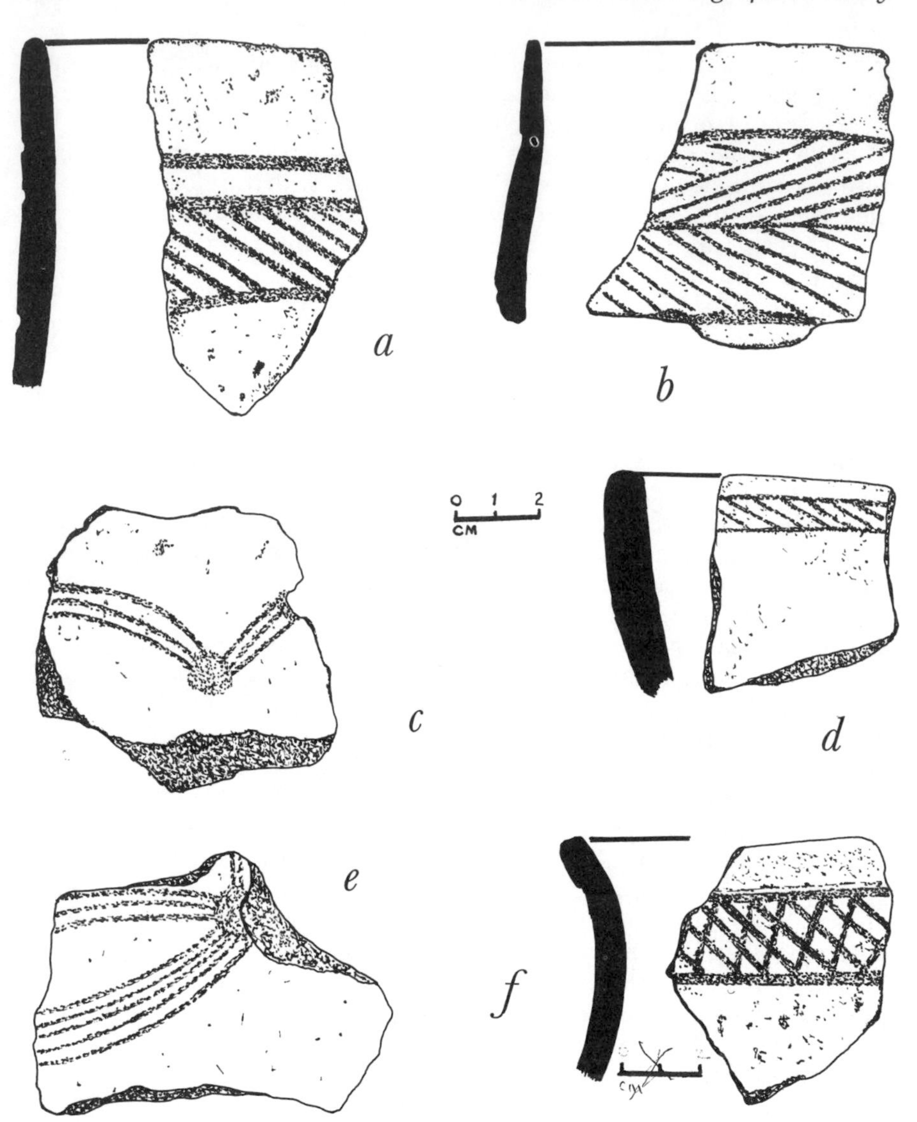

FIGURE 1. Pottery from Mwangambo (a,b), Moomba (c-e), and Kande (f).

In terms of ancient occupation and archeological interest, the nearly 35-km-long stretch of valley centered upon Lusu Hill appears the most significant. The valley here is lined by deciduous woodlands. There is little evidence of floodplain grassland, though there are occasional poorly drained areas covered with grasses. The sides of the valley rise moderately from the river level, for the most part, though there are a number of steep sandy hills. Each of these hills is topped by a present-day village and each village superimposes itself upon an ancient village site. The declivities between the hills are filled with thin gravelly soils, and the hilltops seem the best source of arable land.

Some of the archeological villages (for instance, at Salumano), though smaller than their modern counterparts, seem to cover areas of an acre or more. Pottery fragments similar to those from Salumano were found at the villages of Mutanda and Kawendo, 2 and 3 km south of Salumano. Further evidence of Gokomere-related ceramics are found as far north as Kalobelelwa, approximately 50 km north of Katima Mulilo.

North of Kalobelelwa the soil becomes thin and gravelly again, and we located no evidence of prehistoric occupation. Around Lusu most of the area accessible to us produced archeological evidence. The Early Iron Age settlement seems to have been dense or at least concentrated upon each suitable locality. Potsherds found at Mwangamo (Fig. 1a, b) atop Lusu Hill were heavily weathered, fragmentary, and difficult to characterize. Globular vessels with in-turned rims, and straight-rimmed jars occur; decoration includes incised herringbone motifs. This material resembles that from Naluyoyela (Vogel and Katanekwa, 1976) and is, therefore, probably part of a Gokomere-like assemblage, although there are no well developed or decorated rim bands.

Some sherds collected at the Moomba site (Fig. 1c-e) on the eastern side of the valley appear to belong to a different, possibly later, tradition. One bowl fragment is decorated by a narrow diagonally incised band below the lip, a fragment from an undecorated jar with outturned rim. These outturned rims have been found elsewhere, but in Early Iron Age contexts, in western Zambia. Two other fragments are decorated by sharply incised curvilinear decorations, which include a thumbprint at the points of intersection of the curvilinear elements. This old village is located at the site of the Mkushi Sawmill, approximately 10 km east of Lusu School.

A number of similar sherds (Fig. 1f) were found at Kande, adjacent to the southern end of Salumano. The single diagnostic sherd has an everted rim, decorated with a band of crosshatched incisions in the crook of the neck. It is identical to the type Simbusenga Class 2 of the Victoria Falls region.

A midden on Lusu Island (Fig. 2) produced a collection of pottery related to that from Moomba and Kande. Five diagnostic sherds were recovered: 1 is from an undecorated bowl, 3 from decorated bowls, and 1 from a decorated pot. This last has the remnant of a curvilinear festoon suspended from the crosshatched band. A thumbprint "dimple" occurs

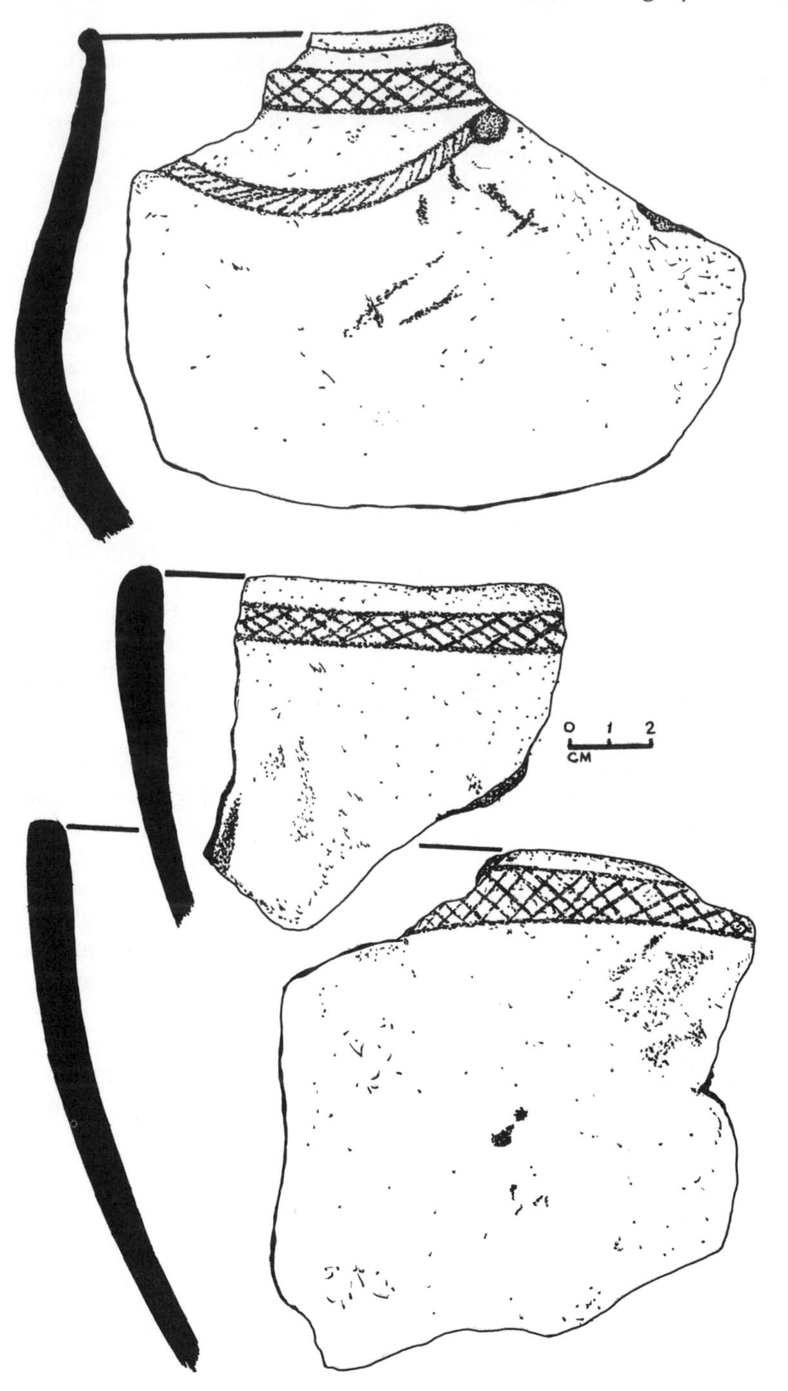

Figure 2. Pottery from Lusu Island.

at the point of juncture of the two elements. This dimple impression reproduces those found at the Moomba site. In each case the decoration takes the form of a narrow band of crosshatched incision.

These last three sites, plus one at Sikosi (on the east bank near the Njoko confluence, which produced a number of undecorated sherds of similar fabric) appear to be evidence of an occupation during the mid-2d millennium. The source of this occupation may still be difficult to determine, but it does appear to be related to a range of materials of the early to mid-2d millennium, which occur throughout Southern Province. Previously they were known from only as far west as Machili. These ceramics are known as the antecedents of ethnographically known varieties. Such is not the case in Western Province. Later ceramics from there are usually described quite differently (Phillipson, 1974).

My survey results suggest that the southern half of the area possesses a cultural sequence that may be divided into three parts. The earliest settlement began in the mid-1st millennium with an Early Iron Age occupation related to the Gokomere tradition. This population occupied the sandy hilltops predominantly along the western bank, in the area from immediately north of Katima Mulilo to Kalobelelwa. Sometime in the early 2d millennium they were succeeded by a different culture, related to those in, and apparently moving from the direction of, the Batoka Highlands through the Machili Forest. This was in turn replaced by the culture of the latest and historically known population of the valley.

None of this proposed sequence has been tested by excavation. This process should produce the numerous details we expect at Iron Age sites. The basic outline is spare but plausible. Farther north we can see only the earliest settlements related to source areas different from those of the Gokomere tradition.

The effects of time and the river have severely limited our present and future investigations. The sequence there appears to be one of an early Iron Age settlement at least as far south as Sioma, followed by a long hiatus until quite recent times. This picture may be oversimplified, but we have very little evidence at this time.

The two Early Iron Age cultures are still to be seen as distinct. The valley was quite definitely settled from two different directions—Sioma people moving south along the valley and Gokomere people moving northward, also along the river. Each appears to have exhausted the possible habitation spots before the frontier was joined in any substantive way.

Acknowledgments

The author thanks the Committee for Research and Exploration of the National Geographic Society and the Graduate School of Northern Illinois University for providing the opportunity to conduct this survey.

My colleagues at Northern Illinois University, R. Provencher and M. J. Hanifi, were particulary helpful in the planning stage. I wish further to thank my former colleagues at the Livingstone Museum for their encouragement and assistance during the time of our visit to Zambia: K. Mubitana, director; N. M. Katanekwa, keeper of prehistory; and J. Banda, prehistory assistant. The Capuchin Fathers of Sioma Mission were particularly helpful, as also was the staff of the Lusu Tsetse Barrier and various other officials of the Zambian Government with whom we came in contact. The assistance of E. J. Hockley was invaluable. The field drawings were produced by Jean Vogel, a resourceful and cheerful safari-companion.

REFERENCES

PHILLIPSON, D. W.
1974. Iron Age history and archaeology in Zambia. Journ. Afr. Hist., vol. 9, pp. 191-211.
1975. The chronology of the Iron Age in Bantu Africa. Journ. Afr. Hist., vol. 16, pp. 321-342.

VOGEL, JOSEPH O.
1973. The Early Iron Age site at Sioma Mission, western Zambia. Zambia Mus. Journ., vol. 4, pp. 153-169.
1976. The Early Iron Age in western Zambia. Curr. Anthrop., vol. 17, pp. 153-154.
1978. Recent archeological survey in western Zambia. Curr. Anthrop., vol. 19, no. 1 (March), 1978, pp. 148-149.

VOGEL, JOSEPH O., and KATANEKWA, N. M.
1976. Notes on Early Iron Age pottery from western Zambia. Azania, vol. 11, pp. 160-167.

JOSEPH O. VOGEL

Acoustic Communication and Behavior of Southern Right Whales, *Eubalaena australis*

Grant Recipient: Charles Walcott, Department of Cellular and Comparative Biology, State University of New York, Stony Brook, New York.[1]

Grants 1602, 1732: For a study of vocalization and behavior of the southern right whale.

The majority of vocal sounds made by animals are generally assumed to serve some communicative function. Demonstration of acoustic communication has relied primarily on the technique of correlating observable changes in the behavior of an animal with the acoustic signals produced or received. The function of sound types is often deduced by an interpretation of these results and the social contexts in which they were made. Sound playback experiments are often used to test these deductions concerning a sound's "meaning" and its dependence on the social context. It is often inferred that the degree of complexity in the signal repertoire is indicative of the complexity of the social system.

Mysticete whales are known to make a variety of sounds (Schevill and Watkins, 1962; Cummings et al., 1971; Payne and McVay, 1971; Thompson et al., 1979) but there is little scientific evidence to demonstrate that these sounds are communicative. This state of affairs is not surprising in light of the obvious difficulties encountered when working with these large, pelagic mammals. It is difficult to observe and follow them, to reidentify them from one day to the next, and very difficult to determine which animal under observation is vocalizing. Recently, through a combination of efforts, solutions to these problems have been found. Roger Payne has developed a technique for accurately tracking the movements of whales with a surveyor's theodolite. This technique has been used by Würsig (1979a, b), Clark and Clark (1980), and Tyack (1981) to determine swimming patterns for cetaceans. Methods for identifying individual whales using photographs of natural markings have now been applied to humpback whales (Katona et al., 1979) and southern

[1] Principal Investigator: Christopher W. Clark, The Rockefeller University, Field Research Center, Milbrook, New York.

right whales (Payne et al., 1983). Acoustic tracking of individuals from the sounds they make has been reported by Walker (1963, though he was not certain that whales were the source), Watkins and Schevill (1972), Watkins (1977), Clark and Clark (1980), and Clark (1982, 1983) using hydrophone array systems.

The data reported here are the results of an 18-month field study on a free-ranging population of southern right whales. The aims were to determine the acoustic repertoire of the whales, to correlate the sounds with other activities, and to demonstrate the possible communicative function of the sounds. The evidence shows that there are correlations between sounds and activities, that the sounds are communicative, and that the function of the sounds can be interpreted from the activities of the whales and the contexts in which the sounds were made.

Materials and Methods

Location

Data are based on the results of observations on free-ranging southern right whales in the Golfo San José, Argentina from July 16, 1976 to December 21, 1977. Observations were made (1450 hr) from a hut situated on the edge of a 46-m cliff overlooking the southeast corner of the gulf. Additional observations (130 hr) were made from other nearby locations when sun glare obscured a group or additional indentifying photographs were needed. No observations were made from boats.

Group

The term "group" refers to 1 or more whales seen within close proximity of one another (approximately 15 m or one adult whale's length). In general, if 2 members of a group could be tracked and the distance between them was greater that 3 or 4 whales' lengths for more than 5 min, they were considered separate groups. The point of separation was defined as the point at which we began tracking both groups separately.

Identification

The head callosity patterns of southern right whales can be used to reliably distinguish individuals and reidentify individuals over long periods of time (Payne et al., 1983). Whales were photographed whenever possible using cameras (Nikon F) with 50- to 1000-mm lenses. Photography concentrated on the head callosity patterns, the white back and belly patches, the back edges of flukes, and the anogenital region. An effort was also made to photographically document behavior, particularly that of active groups.

The sex of right whales can be determined by the morphology of the anogenital region. A whale was determined to be female if it was seen alone with the same calf on at least three different days, or if it had mammary slits on either side of the genital slit, or if no anus was seen separate from the ventral slit during a complete view of the ventral area between the genital slit and the flukes. A whale was determined to be male if a penis or an anus widely separate from the ventral slit was seen.

Observations

Whales were observed on 159 days between May 14 and December 9, 1977. All whale groups seen within approximately 1 km of the hut were observed by ad-lib sampling (Altmann, 1974). A surveyor's theodolite (Kern model DMK 1) was used to record the location of a group with a maximum error of ±1 m at 1 km. A pair of binocular spotting scopes (Bausch and Lomb with X15 eyepieces) mounted on a heavy tripod in the observation hut was used for behavioral observations. The data collected for each group sampled included time, group identification, description of activity, number of animals, compass headings of group members, and location.

Acoustic Sampling

Tape recordings were made during all periods of observation. The receiving system consisted of a hydrophone array (Clark, 1980) and a Sony TC880B tape recorder ($^{15}/_{16}$ ips) or Nagra IV-S stereo tape recorder ($3^{3}/_{4}$ ips). The hydrophones were bottom mounted in relatively shallow water and were not used during low tides. A total of 1102 hr of tape recordings were made during the daylight hours in 1977 for an average of 4.5 ± 1.5 (SD) hr of recordings per day.

Sound Direction Sampling

A portable real-time sound-direction–finding system for underwater sounds (see Clark, 1980, for details) was used for a total of 231 hr during 32 days of observation. This device computed and displayed the direction to the sound source whenever a whale made a sound with a fundamental frequency between 50 and 500 Hz, that was 3 dB above the ambient noise level.

Definitions of Activities

Details of one whale's behavior within a group of active whales were difficult to record. Often a familiar posture or movement would be seen but assigning the behavior to an individual was problematical. In order to avoid defining a large set of behaviors that could not be reliably scored, all references to the behaviors of groups were reduced to a set of five activities: resting, swimming, mild activity, full activity, and sexual activity. These activities are not necessarily mutually exclusive.

Resting. Whales that remained in the same location without any evidence of physical exertion were considered as a resting group. Most resting groups drifted at the surface with their nares and a portion of their backs above the water. Sometimes a resting whale would remain underwater in the same spot, and surface occasionally to breathe.

Swimming. Whales moving from one location to another at a fairly constant speed were considered as a swimming group. In shallow water, whales would swim at the surface or alternate between swimming at and just below the surface. In deeper water, whales would usually swim long distances underwater, surface, take a quick series of breaths, and submerge for another long, underwater swim. Swimming whales that were approaching an active group would typically submerge when 0.5 to 1 km away and then swim the remaining distance to the group entirely underwater.

Mild Activity. A group was mildly active if it disturbed the surface to produce white water, but the activity was frequently interrupted by brief periods of resting or swimming.

Full Activity. A group was fully active if its movements produced constant white water.

Sexual Activity. A group was sexually active if it was known to contain both males and females and a male was seen with his penis extended.

Description of Sound Types

The sounds of southern right whales have been described by Payne and Payne (1971) and Cummings et al. (1971, 1972, 1974). Recently, the author described and classified southern right whale sounds using principal components analysis. The sound sample was based on over 1500 hr of recordings made throughout the 1977 season during all times of day. The sounds were categorized into 3 general classes— blow sounds, slaps, and calls—and each class was subdivided into types. There were 3 types of blow sounds: normal, tonal, and growl blow sounds. There were 4 types of slaps: flipper, breach, lobtail, and underwater slaps. There were 6 types of calls: up-calls, down-calls, constant-calls, high calls, hybrid calls, and pulsive calls. All blow sounds and all slap sounds, except underwater slaps, are audible both in air and underwater. In general, the call repertoire is best described as a continuum with certain types more common than others (Clark, 1982).

Group Data

A total of 187 groups was investigated with the sound-direction-finding equipment when the group responsible for the sounds was not ambiguous and when the groups were not seen with sea lions *(Otaria flavescens)* or porpoises *(Lagenorhynchus obscurus* or *Tursiops truncatus).* Each group was described by the following variables: total number of whales (a single whale considered as a group of size one), number of females, number of males, activity (including its duration), and rates of sound production for blow sounds, slaps, and all 6 call types.

Results

Individual Sighting Data

By comparing whales in over 10,000 photographs taken throughout the 1977 season both with themselves and with the identified whale heads in an identification catalogue (Payne et al., 1983), we were able to identify 135 different whales. Of 75 identified whales 46 were female and 29 were male. Of the 60 whales of unknown sex 48 were relatively small animals (estimated body length <12 m). They were sighted on only one or two days and were rarely seen in fully active or sexually active groups. This suggests that these animals were subadults and sexually immature.

Correlation of Activity, Size, and Sexual Composition with the Sound Rates of Acoustic Groups

Activity vs. Sound Rates. The activity of a group differentially affected rates of sound production (KW, $p<0.01$) for 6 of the 8 sound types: up-calls, high calls, hybrid calls, pulsive calls, blow sounds, and slaps. Significant differences among the sound rates per whale for different activities are noted in Figure 1.

Size vs. Sound Rates. The size of a group differentially affected rates of sound production (KW, $p<0.01$) for 5 of the 8 sound types: up-calls, high calls, hybrid calls, pulsive calls, and blow sounds. In a few cases, the size of the group engaged in a particular activity had significantly different effects on sound rates.

Sexual Composition vs. Sound Rates. The sexual composition of a group differentially affected rates of sound for 4 of the 8 sound types: up-calls, hybrid calls, pulsive calls, and blow sounds. In a few cases, depending on the type of activity, the sexual composition of a group had significantly different effects on the sound rates.

The Contexts in Which Sounds Were Made

One of the major purposes of this study was to correlate the whales' behaviors with the sounds they made. The eventual aim is to understand what, if any, communicative function is served by each of these sounds. The results just presented demonstrate that there are correlations between behaviors and sounds.

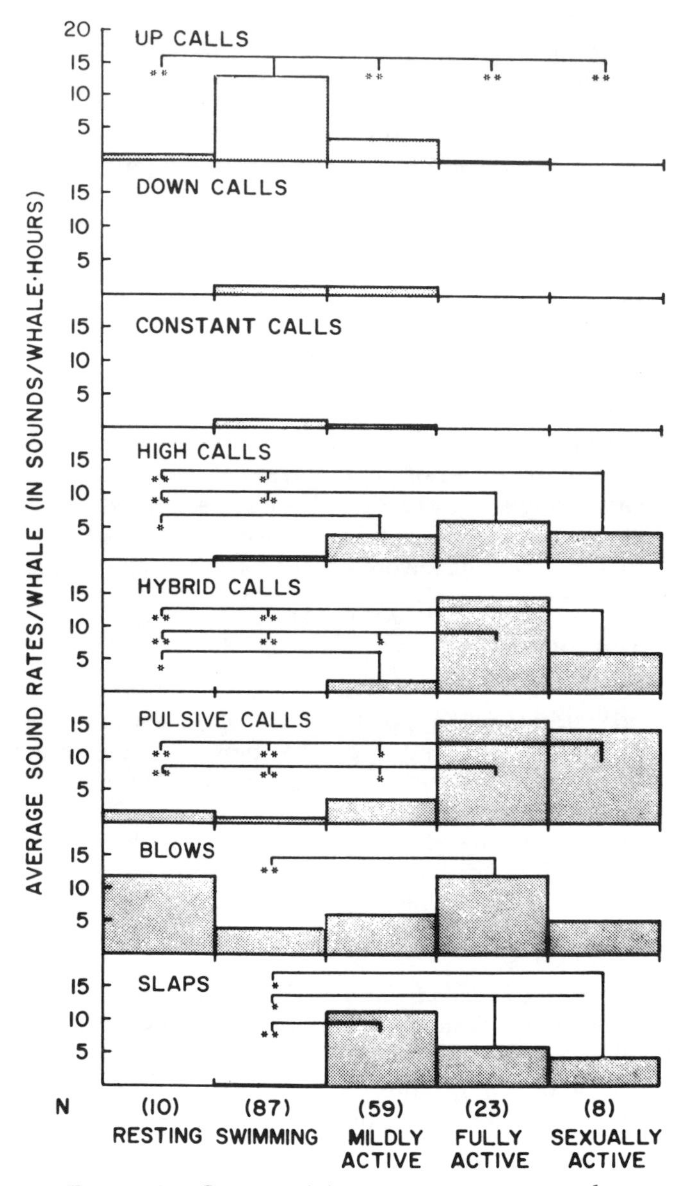

FIGURE 1. Group activity versus average sound rates per whale (in sounds per whale-hour). Asterisks (** for $p<0.01$, * for $p<0.05$) indicate those cases in which groups engaged in different activities differed significantly in their call rates per whale.

Communicative Function

For a fuller discussion of these results, see Clark (1983).

Blow Sound. The author proposes that some blow sounds have a function that is communicative. In general, these sounds are threats that serve to warn other animals that the whale is disturbed. Possibly the level of disturbance is encoded by grading in the intensity and harshness of the sound. If these blow sounds are threats, this would possibly suggest that the long tonal, blow sounds from resting whales indicate that the animal does not want to be disturbed. Another explanation could be that these moans are simply the snores of a sleeping whale (Payne, pers. comm.).

Slap Sound. The sound produced by flipper slapping in the context of an active group of several whales probably functions as a threat with the possible consequence being a physical strike. How the loud, sharp underwater slaps were produced is unknown. The slaps were painful to an unsuspecting listener and might also have been painful to the other whales, porpoises, or sea lions that were closer. The author believes that these underwater slaps are threats and that because of their intensity are stronger threats than flipper slaps. The function of belly slapping by pairs of whales is not clear.

Up-call. The up-call was the most common sound made by the whales. Calves, subadults, adults, males, and females all made this call. Up-calls were usually associated with swimming whales or in a few cases with single resting or single mildly active animals that called just before they started swimming. In about half the cases when a swimmer made an up-call, another whale called back, the two swam to each other as they called and then stopped calling once they were together. This evidence strongly suggests that up-calls are "contact" calls. They function as long-distance signals that aid in bringing the whales together.

Down-call. The down-call was not common. It was made by lone males and lone females when they were swimming or mildly active and when they were in situations similar to those in which up-calls were heard. In fact, if a swimmer did make down-calls it also made up-calls. This evidence suggests that the down-call is a type of "contact" signal made by a whale that is moderately excited. It functions to keep whales in acoustic contact but does not serve to bring whales into physical contact.

Constant-call. The constant-call was quite rare and was made only occasionally by swimming, mildly active, or fully active groups of whales. The two times when a whale made exclusively constant-calls, the animals were both single, pregnant females. Since, in general, constant-calls were made so infrequently and almost always when other call types were prevalent, it is not possible to infer the function of this call type.

High Call. A very few isolated high calls were made by swimming whales but, in general, the high call was made by active groups and the number of calls made by the group increased as the level of activity increased. Groups of 2 or 3 females would make a few high calls and no other calls after joining and becoming mildly active together. Fully active and sexually active whales would make both isolated high calls and high calls arranged in a series with hybrid and pulsive calls. The rate of high calling in these fully active and sexually active groups increased in proportion to the number of whales in the group. Since rates were measured in calls per hour per whale, this would mean that a whale in a group of 4 would tend to make more high calls than a whale in a group of 2 or 3. As a result of this evidence, this author suggests that high calls indicate a general level of excitement, but their true function remains to be determined.

Hybrid Call. The hybrid call was made almost exclusively by active groups and mostly by fully active and sexually active groups containing males and females. Hybrid calls would sometimes be made as isolated calls but usually were produced in a series with high calls and pulsive calls. Groups of 2 whales made fewer hybrid calls per whale than larger groups and the hybrid calls from pairs would usually be isolated while the hybrid calls in the larger groups would almost always be included in a series.

Pulsive Call. The pulsive call, like the hybrid call, was made almost exclusively by active groups containing males and females. The rate of pulsive calling decreased as the number of whales in the group increased, suggesting that group size and a whale's pulsive call rate were negatively correlated. In fact, this is probably not the case: If rates are computed in calls per hour for the various group sizes, there are no differences in rates as group size increases. This would suggest that perhaps most of the pulsive sounds are made by only 1 or 2 individuals in fully active or sexually active groups and not by all members of the group. This suggestion is supported by the observations that two pulsive calls were never produced simultaneously by an active group.

Pulsive calls would either be produced as isolated calls or in a series, and in most cases the series contained both high calls and hybrid calls. The one time that a mildly active group made a series containing only pulsive calls was when a mother was separated from her calf by a pregnant female. The other two times that only pulsive calls were produced occurred when a calf was being jostled and lifted up on the belly of a male and when a male interrupted what appeared to be a courting pair.

There is a general association between hybrid and pulsive calls given in a series, and large, active groups of both sexes. Although the data are still too limited to infer a definite communicative function for these two call types, the author's distinct impression is that hybrid and pulsive calls are aggressive signals directed at other members of the group. A further impression is that the amount of pulsiveness in a call and the number of calls in a series indicate the level of aggression within the group.

Summary

The sounds made by southern right whales are not random but are intimately related to the social context and activity of the animals. A resting whale does not call very often but sometimes makes long moans while exhaling through its nostrils. A swimming whale that is alone and seeking other whales makes up-calls. A whale that is alone and moderately excited makes up-calls, down-calls, flipper slaps, and loud blow sounds. A female that is excited and with other females makes high calls. A whale that is excited and involved in a group of sexually active animals makes high calls, hybrid calls, pulsive calls, flipper slaps, and loud forceful blow sounds. It remains to be determined whether some variable in the contact call encodes for the identity of the caller and whether the more complex associations among variables in the sounds from active whales encode for some subtle parameters of the social context.

Acknowledgments

I am particularly grateful to the people of Chubut, Argentina for their gracious hospitality and support. Specifically I wish to thank the Chubut Department of Tourism, Pepe and Sarah Ferrero, Carlos Garcia, and Juan Carlos and Dianna Lopez. I am also indebted to G. Blaylock, J. M. Clark, J. Crawford III, and A. Mcfarland for their invaluable assistance with the collection of field data; A. Bindman, G. Blaylock, C. Breen, J. M. Clark, S. J. Clark, R. DiOrio, and D. Munafo for their dedicated help with the data reduction. J. M. Clark, J. Perkins, V. Rowntree, and E. M. Dorsey assisted in the process of identifying whales from photographs. Helpful criticism of the manuscript was provided by R. Payne, R. J. Rohlf, W. E. Schevill, D. G. Smith, P. Tyack, C. Walcott, and G. Williams. This work was supported in part by a grant from the National Geographic Society, a U. S. Public Health Service Biomedical Research grant to the State University of New York at Stony Brook, and facilities and equipment from the New York Zoological Society.

REFERENCES

ALTMANN, JEANNE
1974. Observational study of behavior: Sampling methods. Behavior, vol. 44, pp. 227-267.

Clark, Christopher W.
1980. A real-time direction-finding device for determining the bearing to the underwater sounds of southern right whales, *Eubalaena australis.* Journ. Acoust. Soc. Amer., vol. 68, pp. 508-511.
1982. The acoustic repertoire of the southern right whale: A quantitative analysis. Anim. Behav., vol. 30, pp. 1060-1071.
1983. Acoustic communication and behavior of the southern right whale *(Eubalaena australis).* Pp. 163-198 *in* " Communication and Behavior of Whales," R. S. Payne, ed. Westview Press, Boulder.

Clark, Christopher, and Clark, Jane M.
1980. Sound playback experiments with southern right whales *(Eubalaena australis).* Science, vol. 207, pp. 663-665.

Cummings, W. C.; Fish, J. F.; and Thompson, P. O.
1971. Bio-acoustics of marine mammals of Argentina: R/V Hero cruise 71-3. Antarct. Journ. U. S., vol. 6, pp. 266-268.
1972. Sound production and other behavior of southern right whales, *Eubalaena glacialis.* San Diego Nat. Hist. Trans., vol. 17, pp. 1-14.

Cummings, W. C.; Thompson, P. O.; and Fish, J. F.
1974. Behavior of southern right whales: R/V Hero cruise 72-3. Antarct. Journ. U. S., vol. 9, pp. 33-38.

Katona, S.; Baxter, B.; Brazier, O.; Kraus, S.; Perkins, J.; and Whitehead, H.
1979. Identification of humpback whales by fluke photographs. Pp. 33-44 *in* "Behavior of Marine Animals—Current Perspectives in Research, Vol. 3: Cetaceans," H. E. Winn and B. L. Olla, eds. Plenum Press, New York.

Payne, Roger S.; Brazier, O.; Dorsey, E.; Perkins, J.; Rowntree, V.; and Titus, A.
1983. External features in southern right whales *(Eubalaena australis)* and their use in identifying individuals. Pp. 371-445 *in* "Communication and Behavior of Whales," R. S. Payne, ed. Westview Press, Boulder.

Payne, Roger S., and McVay, S.
1971. Songs of humpback whales. Science, vol. 173, pp. 585-597.

Payne, Roger S., and Payne, Katherine
1971. Underwater sounds of southern right whales. Zoologica, vol. 58, pp. 159-165.

Schevill, W. E., and Watkins, W. A.
1962. Whale and porpoise voices, a phonograph record. Woods Hole Oceanogr. Inst., Woods Hole, Mass., 24p

Thompson, T. J.; Winn, H. E.; and Perkins, P. J.
1979. Mysticete sounds. Pp. 403-431 *in* "Behavior of Marine Animals—Current Perspectives in Research," vol. 3, "Cetaceans," H. E. Winn and B. L. Olla, eds. Plenum Press, New York.

Tyack, Peter
1981. Interactions between singing humpback whales and conspecifics nearby. Behav. Ecol. Sociobiol., vol. 8, pp. 105-116.

Walker, R. A.
1963. Some intense, low-frequency, underwater sounds of wide geographic distribution, apparently of biological origin. Journ. Acoust. Soc. Amer., vol. 35, pp. 1816-1824.

WATKINS, W. A.
1977. Acoustic behavior of sperm whales. Oceanus, vol. 20, pp. 50-58.
WATKINS, W. A., and SCHEVILL, W. E.
1972. Sound source location by arrival-time on a non-rigid three-dimensional hydrophone array. Deep-Sea Res., vol. 19, pp. 691-706.
WÜRSIG, B., and WÜRSIG, M.
1979a. Behavior and ecology of the bottlenose dolphin, *Tursiops truncatus,* in the South Atlantic. Fish. Bull. U. S., vol. 77, pp. 399-412.
1979b. Behavior and ecology of the dusky dolphin, *Langenorhynchus obscurus,* in the South Atlantic. Fish. Bull. U. S., vol. 77, pp. 871-890.

CHRISTOPHER W. CLARK

Population Density, Mating Territoriality, and Sex Change in Coral Reef Fishes

Grant Recipient: Robert R. Warner, Marine Science Institute and Department of Biological Sciences, University of California, Santa Barbara, California.

Grant 1621: In support of a study of the behavioral ecology of sex change in tropical reef fishes.

Much attention has been focused on the phenomenon of sex change in tropical reef fishes (e.g., Robertson, 1972; Warner et al., 1975; Robertson and Hoffman, 1977). Most of these fishes change from female to male later in the lifetime of the individual. Current theory in evolutionary ecology suggests that this sort of sex change is an adaptation to mating systems in which older, larger males prevent younger males from breeding. Thus an individual that changes sex can reproduce as a small female early in life and change sex only when it is large enough to compete successfully as a male (Warner, 1975; Warner et al., 1975).

Recently, in research supported by the National Geographic Society, it has been discovered that in many species the situation is more complex than previously supposed. Many wrasses and parrotfishes of the Caribbean consist of two sexual types, one a primary (non–sex-changing) male and the other the "normal" female-to-male sex-changer (Warner and Robertson, 1978; Robertson and Warner, 1978). This poses an intriguing and important problem for evolutionary ecologists: How can two types of males (primary males and sex-changed females) coexist in a population when these males are theoretically in competition with one another for a limited supply of females?

My colleague Steven Hoffman and I attacked this problem in two ways. First, we experimentally demonstrated that increases in local population density can have a detrimental effect on the mating success of large territorial males. Second, we showed that in successively larger local populations the density at the mating site increases and smaller, nonterritorial males mate with an increasing proportion of the available females. Thus the coexistence of the two sexual types can be explained by the fact that each type has a habitat where it does better than the other.

We carried out our experimental density manipulations in the San Blas Islands, off the Caribbean coast of Panama. The species chosen for the study was the ubiquitous bluehead wrasse *Thalassoma bifasciatum.* This species is ideal for this work because adults are restricted to the reefs upon which they settle as juveniles, and mating occurs every day of the year. Spawning takes place on the down-current edges of reefs, where both territorial males and smaller, nonterritorial males gather for about three hours a day. Females spawn once a day, either pairwise with a territorial male or with a group of the smaller males. The smaller males attempt to intercept females en route to the larger males' territories, or they will steal matings by dashing in to deposit sperm at the moment of egg release during a pair-spawn. Larger males spend most of their time courting visiting females and defending their territory against smaller males.

Changes in population density around a territory can have a paradoxical effect, since both the numbers of available mates and potential intruders are altered. We suspected that the daily mating success of a territorial male was limited by the time available for courtship and spawning, and that this in turn was limited by the time remaining after territorial defense. This leads to the prediction that, under most circumstances, territorial mating success will decline as population density increases, reflecting changes in the number of interfering males but independent of increases in the number of available females.

Because the territorial males return to the same site day after day, we could test our prediction by recording the daily mating success of a particular individual over a series of days, then alter the size or composition of the reef population and monitor the subsequent changes in territorial mating success. We performed 14 experiments, including increasing or decreasing the population as a whole (keeping sex ratio constant) and changing only the numbers of males or females. On all but the smallest reef our results indicated that the number of smaller males surrounding the mating territory had a strong negative effect on mating success, while the number of available females had little or no effect. Where population density was raised, for example, the territorial male spent more time in defense and less time in courtship, and was less successful in bringing the courtships through to mating (Warner and Hoffman, 1980a).

How does this relationship help to explain the mixture of sexual types in this species? Since females prefer to release their eggs in a relatively restricted down-current site regardless of reef size, the density of competing males is higher on larger reefs. We found that on smaller reefs, populations of *T. bifasciatum* are small enough that large territorial males can successfully exclude small males from breeding. Although both sexual types can become territorial males, those individuals that reproduce as females until they are large enough to compete as territorial males would be most reproductively successful on smaller reefs. On larger reefs, we found that the density of small males at the prime mating site is sufficiently high that the territories of larger males are located in less desirable up-current locations. On these reefs, the majority of spawnings occur with nonterritorial males. If there is any cost to changing sex in terms of time or energy lost from reproduction, then the primary males would be more reproductively successful than sex-changers on larger reefs.

This suggests that the overall frequency of the two sexual types is maintained by differential natural selection in local populations of different sizes. If reefs were all small, for example, we would expect few primary males in the population as a whole, while sex change should be rare in species where local populations are all large and densely distributed. We tested this idea by comparing *T. bifasciatum* with the closely related rainbow wrasse, *T. lucasanum*, of the eastern tropical Pacific (Warner and Hoffman, 1980b; Warner, 1982).

We studied the rainbow wrasse in the Perlas Islands of the Bay of Panama. This is a much more productive area than the Caribbean, and few small patch reefs are present. Accordingly, the local populations of *T. lucasanum* are larger and more dense than those of *T. bifasciatum*. Our surveys showed that while the mating behaviors of the two species are virtually identical, the rainbow wrasse has a much higher proportion of primary males and a lower rate of sex change than does the bluehead wrasse. The larger territorial males are very rare in this species, and have relatively low mating success. Thus we were able to successfully predict changes in mating system and sexual composition based on an independent measure of local population size distribution, which our hypotheses had suggested was a critical environmental factor.

We are presently continuing our investigations of the bluehead wrasse, testing hypotheses about the costs of reproduction and the dynamics of female mate choice.

REFERENCES

Robertson, D. R.
1972. Social control of sex reversal in a coral-reef fish. Science, vol. 177., pp. 1007-1009.

Robertson, D. R., and Hoffman, S. G.
1977. The roles of female mate choice and predation in the mating systems of some tropical labroid fishes. Zeit. Tierpsychol., vol. 45, pp. 298-320.

Robertson, D. R., and Warner, R. R.
1978. Sexual patterns in the labroid fishes of the western Caribbean, II: The parrotfishes (Scaridae). Smithsonian Contrib. Zool., no. 255, pp. 1-26.

WARNER, R. R.
1975. The adaptive significance of sequential hermaphroditism in animals. Amer. Nat., vol. 109, pp. 61-82.
1982. Mating systems, sex change, and sexual demography in the rainbow wrasse, *Thalassoma lucassanum*. Copeia, vol. 1982, pp. 653-661.
WARNER, R. R., and HOFFMAN, S. G.
1980a. Population density and the economics of territorial defense in a coral reef fish. Ecology, vol. 61, pp. 772-780.
1980b. Local population size as a determinant of mating system and sexual composition in two tropical marine fishes (*Thalassoma* ssp.) Evolution, vol. 34, pp. 508-518.
WARNER, R. R., and ROBERTSON, D. R.
1978. Sexual patterns in the labroid fishes of the western Caribbean, I: The wrasses (Labridae). Smithsonian Contrib. Zool., no. 254, pp. 1-27.
WARNER, R. R.; ROBERTSON, D. R.; and LEIGH, E. G., JR.
1975. Sex change and sexual selection. Science, vol. 190, pp. 633-638.

ROBERT R. WARNER

Geology and Vertebrate Paleontology of the Late Miocene Gracias Formation in Central Honduras

Grant Recipient: S. David Webb, Florida State Museum, University of Florida, Gainesville, Florida.

Grant 1697: For a study of fossil vertebrates of Central America and the "great American interchange."

When the terrestrial biota of the two American continents was abruptly brought together after some 100 million years of isolation, the changes were undoubtedly drastic. The biological and ecological results of this "great American interchange" are understood in outline partly from present distributions of Pan-American species and partly from good records of fossil vertebrates in temperate latitudes (Webb, 1978; Simpson, 1980). But great improvements in the detailed understanding of the interchange are expected from direct study of fossil history in Central America.

The present report focuses on the vertebrates of the Gracias Formation, the richest pre-Pleistocene fauna in Central America. The National Geographic Society-Florida State Museum paleontology expedition, consisting of the author and his associates, Howard H. Converse and Jon A. Baskin, spent nine weeks in February and March 1977 amplifying the record of late Miocene life in central Honduras. Special efforts were made to recover smaller, ecologically more significant specimens by massive screen-washing efforts at previously discovered sites. By and large this effort was unsuccessful; from about 8 tons of prime matrix, only 1 partial frog skull, 1 fish vertebra, and a few freshwater turtle elements were recovered. In addition, this effort produced several larger vertebrate elements, including the only identifiable record of the family Tayassuidae in the fauna. This report summarizes the paleontological findings of this expedition along with discoveries from earlier work in the Gracias Formation.

Childs Frick (1933, p. 527) introduced the Gracias fauna as follows:

> The occurrence of Tertiary mammal remains in the vicinity of Tapasuma, Honduras, was first reported to the [American] Museum by Mr. A. W. Anthony. The latter had visited this area in 1927 during the course of a collecting trip for the Department of Mammals, and had secured four teeth of a small *Hipparion*-like form and a mastodont premolar.

Frick then sent John Blick back for more extensive work during the dry season (winter) in early 1929. The principal results were the two proboscidean mandibles described as *Blickotherium blicki* and *Aybelodon hondurensis* by Frick (1933). In addition, Blick obtained a small collection representing several other species, listed by Frick as: *Hyaenognathus, Pliohippus, Hipparion, Merychippus, Protohippus,* a Teleocerine rhinoceros, and a Procameline. Specimens from this collection are referred to hereafter by the prefix F:AM.

The second series of paleontological expeditions in the Gracias area of Honduras were sent by the Walker Museum of the University of Chicago and were led by Paul O. McGrew, Grayson E. Meade, and Paul C. Miller. Their first effort of two months in the winter of 1937-1938 resulted in the major faunal review by Olson and McGrew (1941). A second expedition, also led by McGrew, with Albert Potter as assistant, was supported by the Field Museum of Natural History in Chicago and extended for three months during the winter of 1941-1942 (McGrew, 1942). On this trip McGrew and the Field Museum crew also "discovered additional members of the Gracias fauna, among which is the dog described below [as *Osteoborus cynoides*]" (McGrew, 1944). These two seasons yielded the large collections that are now housed in the Field Museum. These collections are referred to by the prefixes WM (for Walker Museum) or P (for the Field Museum's paleontology collections).

The most recent paleontological work in the Gracias Formation has been conducted for the Florida State Museum by the author. These trips included one month each in early 1968 and early 1969, the winter of 1970-1971, and the 1977 expedition described above. My collaborators on these earlier trips included Howel Williams of the University of California, John E. Mawby, now of the California State University of Fresno, and my wife, Barbara. The resulting Florida collections are intermediate in size between the F:AM collection in New York and the combined WM collections in Chicago and are referred to by the prefix UF.

Geologic Setting

Honduras, Guatemala, and the Mexican department of Chiapas make up nuclear Central America, a block with a long complex geological history. In northern and eastern Honduras the most widespread pre-Cenozoic

FIGURE 1. The Gracias Formation in the Department of Lempira, western Honduras. Montaña de Celaque to the southwest is the highest mountain in Honduras and was uplifted after deposition of the Gracias Formation. Fossil localities are: X_1—Las Culebras, X_2—Minimo Locality, X_3—Tepusuna Hill, X_4—Camino Locality, X_5—Ultima Locality, X_6—Saddle Locality (plants), X_7—New Year Locality, X_8—Rancho Lobo (includes plants), X_9—Rio Grande Locality. X_1, X_3, X_7 and X_8 were the most productive.

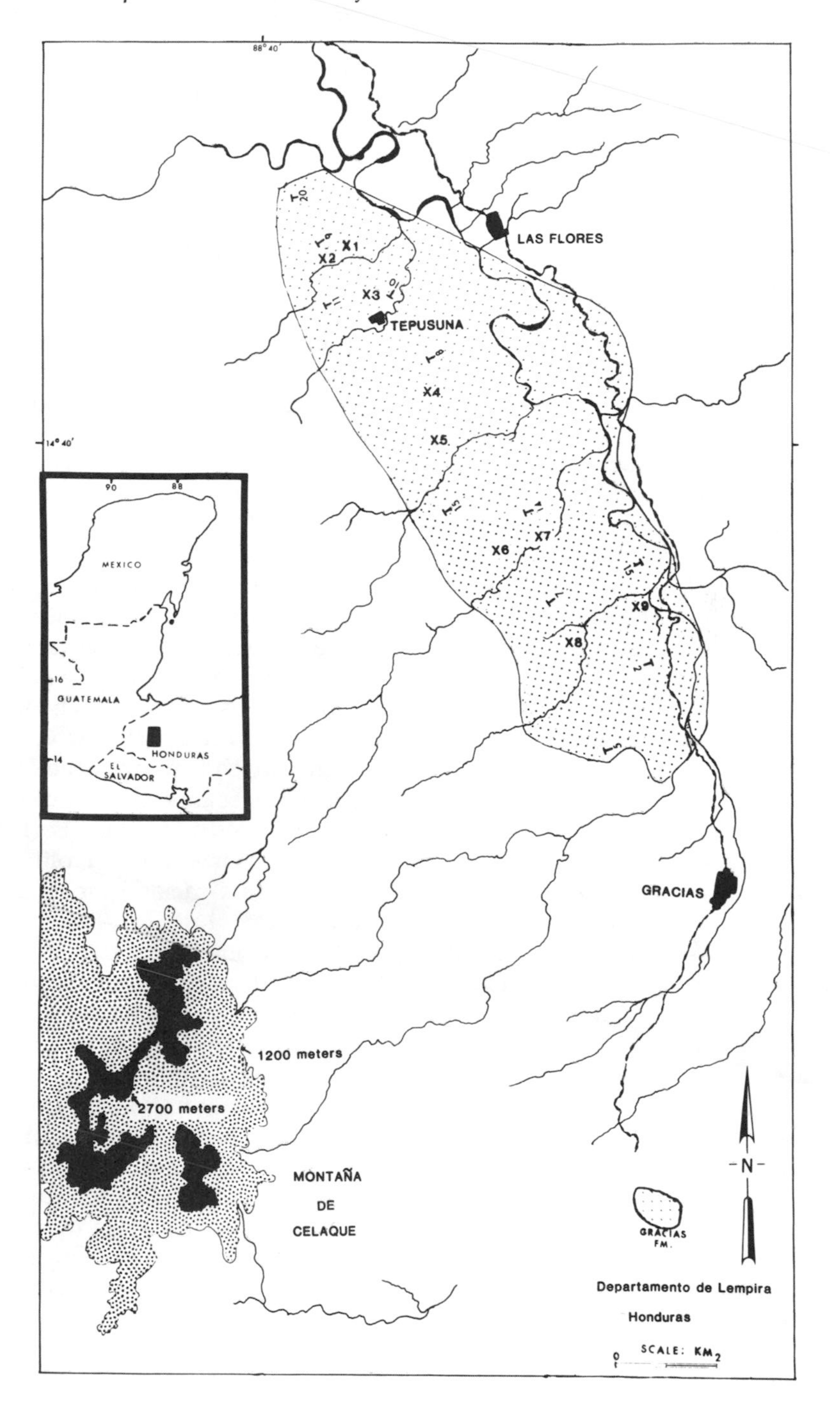
LAS FLORES
X1
X2
X3
TEPUSUNA
X4
X5
MEXICO
GUATEMALA
HONDURAS
EL SALVADOR
X6
X7
X9
X8
GRACIAS
1200 meters
2700 meters
MONTAÑA
DE
CELAQUE
N
GRACIAS FM.
Departamento de Lempira
Honduras
SCALE: KM 2

rocks are limestones and marine red beds of Cretaceous age. Cenozoic rocks are very widespread and are predominantly volcanic. By far the most extensive exposures in Honduras consist of mid-Miocene ignimbrites (ash flows). The southwestern third of the country is wholly dominated by rhyolite ignimbrites which often reach thicknesses of 500 to 1000 m.

Williams and McBirney (1969) mapped the distribution and described the nature of the Miocene ignimbrites in Honduras. They have observed extensive fluviatile and lacustrine beds associated with the ash flows in western Honduras; in some areas the sediments underly the ignimbrites, in other areas they are interbedded with them.

Olson and McGrew (1941) named the Gracias Formation for the fluviatile and lacustrine tuffaceous sediments that accumulated north and west of the town of Gracias. Figure 1 indicates the distribution of the Gracias Formation as mapped by our expedition. It generally resembles the outline provided by Williams and McBirney (1969). The Gracias Formation accumulated in an ovate basin about 15 km long by about 6 km wide at its greatest width. The basin is a graben formed by north-trending faults. The fault along the eastern flank is conspicuous whereas the fault system bounding the western flank is partly obscured by rhyolite boulders from Montaña de Celaque. The Gracias Formation sediments show little deformation except that beds increase dips toward the basin center. The attitudes of the beds range from 5° to about 20°. Clearly the uplift of Montaña de Celaque, the highest mountain in Honduras, at 2700 m, occurred after the Gracias beds had accumulated. The present streams carry boulders and gravel far coarser than the clastic sediments of the Gracias Formation. Uplift of this mountain, composed of crystal-rich welded rhyolite ignimbrites, probably accompanied faulting of the Gracias graben and deformation of the Gracias Formation strata.

The Gracias Formation deposits represent predominantly floodplains and occasionally ponds rich in pumiceous and tuffaceous clastic sediments. The predominant sediments are coarse and tuffaceous sandstones. Even the occasional marl lenses are interbedded within coarse sands or gravels rich in quartz, feldspar, and biotite, indicating derivation from rapid erosion of nearby ignimbrites. North of Tepusuna, near the northern end of the Gracias Formation, the abundant red pumice fragments exactly resemble those exposed in the old ignimbrite hills just north of Las Flores. In general, the siliceous volcanic fragments appear coarser in the northern part of the formation; lenses of clay and marl are much more common in the southern half of the formation near Gracias.

The maximum exposed thickness of the Gracias Formation is about 150 m, measured at Cerro Lobo just south of Locality 9 (Fig. 1). Section 1 of Olson and McGrew (1941) taken at Rancho Lobo (Locality 8) represents

FIGURE 2. Rancho Lobo (Locality 8) looking west. The most fossiliferous stream channel deposits are about 1 m above the author's head in unit 4 of Olson and McGrew (1941). At the top of the photo is a water-laid tuff bed (their unit 5) that is widely traceable.

the lower 60 percent of the section at this hill. The uppermost white ash bed in that section can be traced nearly continuously northward to Locality 6 (the Saddle Locality) and then northward to Tepusuna Hill (Locality 3) where it outcrops about 15 m above the base of the section (Olson and McGrew, 1941). Thus, the northern part of the basin evidently represents in part somewhat younger sediments than the southern part of the basin. Tepusuna Hill is the center of a very large and important collecting area which was the original area worked by Frick parties and later also visited by McGrew and his associates. The latter parties, however, concentrated their efforts at Rancho Lobo to the south (Figs. 2 and 3).

FIGURE 3. Close view of fossiliferous channel sands containing incisor teeth of *Pliohippus hondurensis* and rhyolitic pumice fragments, Olson and McGrew's unit 2 at Rancho Lobo.

In our fieldwork we attempted to intensively prospect all exposures in order to assess microgeographic and paleoecological variation within the Gracias Formation. It is noteworthy that productive sites are almost randomly distributed the length of the graben. Localities are poorly developed on the margins, but this is largely attributable to the shallow erosion on the east flank and the boulder fan cover on the west flank.

We were strongly impressed by apparent paleoecological and sedimentological differences between the northern sites (Sites 1 through 3) around Tepusuna Hill and the southern sites around Rancho Lobo (Sites 6 through 9). (Sites 4 and 5 may be regarded as transitional.) As noted above, coarse sands and gravel lenses are more prevalent in the north whereas marls and clays are more frequent and more persistent in exposures in the southern part of the basin. It is common to find recognizable plant remains in these latter deposits, notably palm stems and leaves. Olson and McGrew (1941) gave the following brief floral listing based on a limited sample of plant remains:

Family Sapindaceae:	*Schmidelia* sp.
Family Cellastraceae:	*Gyminda* sp.
Family Leguminaceae:	genus indeterminate
Family Palmae:	genus indeterminate
Family Gramineaceae:	genus indeterminate

We found numerous similar plants from the southern area. We found no recognizable plant remains in the generally coarser northern sediments. Striking differences also occur in the relative abundances of the vertebrate fossils. In the northern localities *Hipparion* teeth are about as common as *Pliohippus* teeth; whereas they are exceedingly rare in the southern localities. Gomphotheriidae, Rhinocerotidae, and Gelocidae are also considerably more common to the north. A simple hypothesis to explain these observations is that during deposition of the Gracias Formation the sediment source was generally from the north. Fine-grained sediments and more ponded situations predominated in the southern parts of the Gracias basin. There, also, lowland or wetland species would be more abundantly preserved. An upland savanna woodland biota would occur in the coarser detritus deposited by swifter streams entering the ancient Gracias valley from the north. Although the northern sections occur in part stratigraphically higher than the southern sections, the principal differences are probably environmental and paleoecological.

Systematic Paleontology

In the course of studying the new fossil vertebrate collection from Central America, I have also restudied the two previous fossil collections from the Gracias Formation. The revised faunal list includes several new taxa, but it also deletes several mammalian taxa incorrectly listed in earlier studies. The following discussion briefly considers the present status of each taxon in the revised list of vertebrates in the Gracias fauna.

Class Osteichthyes

One small vertebra represents this class at the Las Culebras site. It is remarkable that no other fish scutes, teeth, or bones have been observed in the Gracias Formation.

Class Amphibia

Family Ranidae, *Rana* sp. A partial skull from Las Culebras represents a large ranid frog. The specimen represents the posterolateral portion of a skull, which reveals many details of the occipital and temporal regions.

REVISED FAUNAL LIST

Class Osteichthyes
- Telostean species

Class Amphibia
- Family Ranidae
  - *Rana* sp.

Class Reptilia
- Family Emydidae
  - *Rhinoclemmys* sp.
- Family Testudinidae
  - *Geochelone* sp.

Class Mammalia
- Family Canidae
  - *Osteoborus cynoides* (Martin)
- Family Gomphotheriidae
  - *Rhynchotherium blicki* (Frick)
- Family Equidae
  - *Hipparion plicatile* (Leidy)
  - *Pliohippus hondurensis* Olson and McGrew
- Family Rhinocerotidae
  - *Teleoceras* cf. *fossiger* (Cope)
- Family Tayassuidae
  - *Prosthennops* cf. *serus* Gidley
- Family Camelidae
  - *Protolabis* cf. *heterodontus* (Cope)
  - *Procamelus* cf. *grandis* (Gregory)
- Family Gelocidae
  - *Pseudoceras skinneri* (Frick)

CLASS REPTILIA

Family Emydidae, *Rhinoclemmys* sp. A nuchal bone from a small turtle (UF 46671) is closely comparable to the genus *Rhinoclemmys* presently living in Central America. A number of distinctive features, including the narrow anteromedian scute, the strong midsagittal keel, and the strong posteromedian concavity, combine to make this reference convincing.

Family Testudinidae, *Geochelone* sp. One large shell and a number of shell fragments represent at least one species of tortoise. These samples are presently under study by Walter Auffenberg at the University of Florida.

CLASS MAMMALIA

Family Canidae, *Osteoborus cynoides* (Martin). In a special contribution to the Gracias fauna, McGrew (1944) described and figured an excellent palate that he referred to as the well known hemphillian *Osteoborus cynoides*. Additional collections represent this species, including UF 17771, RM^1 from the New Year Locality; UF 45879, trigonid of RM_1 from Las Culebras; and F:AM 27020, the lower jaw fragment, and F:AM 27021, a left M_{1-2}, from Tapasuma.

The only carnivore taxon originally recognized by Olson and McGrew (1941) was the genus *Amphicyon*, while Frick (1933) listed the genus *"Hyaenognathus."* Further study of both specimens attributed to *Amphicyon* shows that they too represent *Osteoborus*. The broken M^1 from Rancho Lobo, WM 1767, exactly resembles the other first upper molars of *Osteoborus* from the Gracias Formation. *O. cynoides* from the Gracias area is further represented by several postcranial specimens.

Family Gomphotheriidae, *Rhynchotherium blicki* (Frick) (synonyms: *Blickotherium blicki* Frick, 1933; *Aybelodon hondurensis* Frick, 1933). The rich sample of proboscideans from the Gracias Formation provides the oldest evidence of the remarkable genus *Rhynchotherium*. Whereas Frick (1933) described two new genera and species, continued collecting has provided new morphological and statistical evidence that there is but one species. It is possible, as Tobien (1973) has suggested, that *Rhynchotherium* species represent the antecedents of the highly successful Pleistocene neotropical proboscideans such as *Haplomastodon*.

Figure 4 represents a left mandible, P27129 from Tepusuna (Rio Campuca) Locality, which embodies many of the characteristics of *Rhynchotherium*, including the deep, down-turned symphysis with large, lingually flattened lower incisors (here represented by alveoli), the shallow horizontal ramus bearing a broad last molar with four and a half simple lophids. This specimen is very close to the same late ontogenetic stage as the type *"Aybelodon hondurensis"* Frick (1933). Another mandible, UF 17797, represents an even earlier ontogenetic stage than the type of *"Blickotherium" blicki*, for it has the deciduous fourth premolar and the first molar in place with P_4 in the crypt below. These and other specimens provide enough ontogenetic continuity to show that *"Blickotherium"* was based on a very young specimen and *"Aybelodon"* on a fully mature specimen of *Rhynchotherium*.

The correct generic assignment of the Gracias proboscidean depends not only on accurate description of this sample, but also on the phylogenetic framework of New World Gomphotheriidae. Tobien (1973) has done much to bring order to this complex subject. In a careful analysis of the genus *Rhynchotherium*, he found most species of that genus to be transitional to the North American brevirostrine group that includes *Haplomastodon*. However, he regarded the enamel-banded lower incisors found in the type mandibles of *R. edensis* and *R. blicki* as "enigmatic," and to this degree tended to disunite the group. If the genus *Rhynchotherium* is

FIGURE 4. Left mandibular ramus of *Rhynchotherium blicki* (Frick), P27129; lateral view showing downturned symphysis and dorsal views of the symphysis and the third molar.

sustained, as seems reasonable, then there is little doubt that the Gracias proboscidean can be included under that rubric.

The distinctive features of *Rhynchotherium* lower tusks are lateral compression with lingual flattening and development of a broad enamel band on the labial side presumably to facilitate "scissor-like" occlusion with the upper enamel edge. These features are evident in the adolescent-type mandible of *R. blicki* in the Frick Collection at the American Museum of Natural History, as in the "neotype" specimen of *R. edensis* (Frick, 1933). They also tend to be confirmed by isolated tusks of similar character such as UF 18033; although there is no definite association with a mandible, they differ markedly in form from other specimens that are surely upper tusks. Webb and Tessman (1968) showed that the absence of enamel on the lower tusks of *"Aybelodon hondurensis"* is due to old age and breakage.

Family Equidae, *Hipparion plicatile* (Leidy). The new collections from the Gracias Formation considerably enlarge the sample of hipparionine horses referred by Olson and McGrew (1941) to *Neohipparion montezuma* (Leidy). They figured WM 1787, a worn M^1 and also measured a poorly preserved P^2 (WM 1788). The present sample includes about 50 cheek teeth including the first known lower dentitions. This new sample provides at least a modest basis for understanding the ontogenetic and individual variation which is essential to proper systematic study of hypsodont horse dentitions. Some of the slightly worn teeth have been sectioned to provide additional insight into ontogenetic variation.

The 24 upper cheek teeth include associated P^4 and M^1 (UF18034), the lots numbered UF45896-7 all from Tepusuna, UF18125-7 and 46321-5 from Las Culebras, and F:AM 31111 and 27041-3 from the "Lobo" area. The 26 lower cheek teeth include an associated P_2-M_3, UF18036, the lot, UF18036, UF18125-7, and UF45898-900 all from Tepusuna, as well as lot UF18131 and UF46651-3 from Las Culebras. A deciduous third upper premolar, UF18125, and a deciduous third lower premolar, UF18126, were also collected from Las Culebras.

The range of sizes indicated in Table 1 falls well below that typical for *Cormohipparion occidentale* (see for example Webb, 1969) but is not too small to be included in *Hipparion plicatile.* Unfortunately the sample is too incomplete in various wear stages and tooth positions to warrant statistical treatment. The crown height of slightly worn upper cheek teeth in the Gracias sample ranges from about 42 to 48 mm in the range expected for *H. plicatile* and *C. occidentale*, but well below the height found in samples of the *Neohipparion eurystyle* group.

In virtually all features, the hipparionine horse teeth from the Gracias Formation appear to fall within the range of *H. plicatile* (Leidy) originally

TABLE 1. Measurements (in mm) of *Hipparion plicatile* Cheek Teeth

Specimens from Frick collection, American Museum of Natural History (F:AM), University of Florida (UF)

UPPER CHEEK TEETH

Specimen	*UF 45897*	*UF 18034*	*UF 18034*	*UF 46323*	*F:AM 27041*	*F:AM 27042*	*F:AM 27043*	*F:AM 31111*
Tooth	M^3	P^4	M^1	P^2	—	—	—	—
length[a]	16.6	19.0	18.8	23.0	—	—	—	—
width[a]	14.4	19.9	18.2	17.0	—	—	—	—
height[a]	40.8	41.1	38.2	36.0	—	—	—	—
length[b]	—	—	—	—	17.0	19.0	20.3	17.6
width[b]	—	—	—	—	16.9	18.8	19.4	17.2
height[b]	—	—	—	—	46.8	40.0	42.0	41.5

LOWER CHEEK TEETH

Specimen	*UF 18036*	*UF 18036*	*UF 18036*	*UF 18036*	*UF 18036*	*UF 18036*
Tooth	P_2	P_3	P_4	M_1	M_2	M_3
length	19.5	18.0	19.4	18.7	17.5	18.1
width	10.3	10.7	11.2	10.9	11.3	8.7
height	21.5	31.9	40.7	34.5	35.0	37.3

OTHER LOWER CHEEK TEETH

Specimen	*UF 45900*	*UF 18035*	*UF 18035*	*UF 18035*	*UF 18035*	*UF 18131*
Tooth	M_3	M_2	M_1	M_2	M_2	M_3
length	19.0	20.6	18.1	24.2	20.0	20.3
width	9.1	8.3	12.0	11.0	10.6	9.6
height	50.0	ca. 40	36.2	50.0	44.0	31.3

[a] cut at 30 where crown dimensions were measured
[b] cut at 36 where crown dimensions were measured

described from Mixson's Bone Bed in Florida. Since only one or two upper teeth and no lower teeth have been described or figured, these comparisons rely on undescribed material from Mixson's, McGehee Farm, and the Love Bone Bed in Florida (Webb et al., 1980). Comparison with *Hippotherium montezuma* Leidy, suggested by Olson and McGrew (1941), is restricted to the only known specimen, the worn type molar from Lacualtipan near Vera Cruz, Mexico. It seems preferable to leave that taxon as a *nomen dubium* (MacFadden, pers. comm.); and in any case several of its features suggest the *N. eurystyle* group, clearly an inappropriate assignment for the Gracias sample. Thus, it is appropriate to refer this sample to *H. plicatile* on the basis of the following features: About 48-mm crown height, oblique elliptical protocone, moderate stylar cusps, markedly plicated metaloph borders, short labial P^2 parastyle, and, in lower teeth, moderately to deeply penetrating ectoflexid, subcircular metaconid and metastylid, lingually placed circular entoconid, and strong plicaballinid and isthmian plications.

Family Equidae, *Pliohippus hondurensis* Olson and McGrew. This is the most common species in the Gracias Formation. Olson and McGrew (1941) presented an excellent description of the material and a discussion of its affinities. Although extensive new collections have been added, they do not equal the quality of those taken by McGrew's party at Rancho Lobo.

Family Rhinocerotidae, *Teloceras* cf. *fossiger* (Cope). The Gracias Formation provides the southernmost records of Rhinocerotidae in the New World. Frick (1933) listed a "teleocerine rhinoceros" on the basis of F:AM 27023, a jaw fragment with several broken teeth, and Olson and McGrew (1941) assigned an edentulous jaw fragment and a cervical vertebra, P1790 from Tepusuna, to "the general teleocerine group."

The maximum height of the ectoloph of the nearly unworn right P^2—UF46319 from the New Year locality—is 26.5 mm, the anteroposterior length is 27.1 mm, and the maximum width is 23.9 mm. The reduced dimensions and the degree of hypsodonty mark this as a progressive specimen of *Teleoceras*. With respect to such features as incomplete protoloph and the weak anticrochet, this tooth is closely comparable to P^2 in the large *Teleoceras* samples from the Love Bone Bed and Mixson's Bone Bed in Florida.

Other molars including an M_1, UF18103, and several upper molar fragments, UF18015, from the lower part of the Tepusuna Locality, also indicate the presence of a progressive species of *Teleoceras*. The tallest crown measurement from UF18015 was 35 mm, but this was a well worn tooth. A series of four vertebrae and ribs, the distal end of a tibia UF18039, and the fragment of a juvenile phalanx UF18040, were collected about 20 m below the peak of Tepusuna Hill.

Family Tayassuidae, *Prosthennops,* cf. *serus* Gidley. The presence of the peccary family is here documented for the first time in the Tertiary of Central America. The left M^3 from Las Culebras, UF45881, presently provides the best evidence of a tayassiud in the Gracias Formation. It is a fairly well worn molar, 20.6 mm long, 16.9 mm wide across the anterior loph, but only 11.7 mm across the posterior loph. The enamel is remarkably thick and the pattern includes four major cusps, several stout accessory cusps, and abbreviated anterior and posterior cinguli. The measurements and cusp pattern compare well with those of the large species of *Prosthennops, P. graffhami* described as new by Schultz and Martin (1975) from the *Amebelodon fricki* quarry in Nebraska.

Family Camelidae. Olson and McGrew (1941) compared the three postcranial specimens then available to "large specimens of *Procamelus* from the Great Plains of North America." Substantial increases in the camelid sample, including two dentigerous jaw fragments clearly indicate the presence of a second smaller camelid genus in addition to the large *Procamelus.*

Family Camelidae, *Protolabis* cf. *heterodontus* (Cope). Several specimens in the new collections indicate a moderate-sized camelid. The slightly worn M_2, P27127, from the Rancho Lobo locality measures 28.0 mm long and 13.2 mm wide, and has an unworn crown height of about 18 mm. It is proportionally much narrower and less hypsodont than such progressive genera as *Procamelus* or *Hemiauchenia,* but falls within the range of *Protolabis heterodontus* (see for example Webb, 1969, p. 150).

The molar has a simple pattern with angular crescents, with styles, and with no development of a "llama buttress," as might be expected in *Procamelus* or certainly in *Hemiauchenia.* The jaw is remarkably shallow (29 mm below M^2) even for *Protolabis,* but this may be exaggerated by its immature stage of development. The angular region, shown by Honey and Taylor (1978) to be so diagnostic of *Protolabis,* is broken away. Even so, the anterior insertion area of the masseter muscle shows considerable rugosity, as is especially common in *Protolabis.*

A maxillary fragment, UF45882, from the New Year locality, bears a heavy-rooted canine tooth about 5 mm in diameter. Anteriorly the fragment reveals the premaxillary suture and posteriorly the strong lateral concavity or "pinched" rostrum characteristic of *Protolabis.*

Family Camelidae, *Procamelus* cf. *grandis* (Gregory). The record of the large progressive cameline from the Gracias Formation remains unsatisfactory. A few fragmentary specimens are added to those referred to *Procamelus* by Olson and McGrew (1941) (namely two distal ends of a radio-ulnae, one of which was figured, and the proximal end of a radius). The most helpful new specimen is a broken cannon bone composed of fused metacarpals III and IV, UF18042 from the Tepusuna Locality. Near mid-length it measures 49.8 mm in transverse diameter and 35.4 mm in anteroposterior diameter. This compares well with large specimens of *Procamelus grandis* (e.g., Webb, 1969, p. 162). A radio-ulna, presumably the basis for Frick's (1933) recognition of a "procameline," numbered F:AM 27022, is also comparable in size to the largest species of *Procamelus.*

Family Gelocidae, *Pseudoceras skinneri* Frick. Olson and McGrew (1941) figured and discussed at some length a heavily worn M_3 of "a small pecoran, probably a cervid, which was found near Tapasuna." Despite its advanced wear, they noted that it was much more hypsodont than molars of *Mazama*. Fortunately, better and more extensive material now indicates the true affinities of this small ruminant.

A right mandible with a moderately worn molar series, UF18041, from Tepusuna is closely comparable with the type mandible of *Pseudoceras skinneri* Frick 1937. The narrow molars, strong protostylids and entostylids, and especially the simple narrow heel of M_3 are diagnostic. This specimen is slightly larger than the type, which is among the largest representative of the genus. Two other molars, P27090, a LM^2 and P27130, a RM_3, also represent this genus.

Elsewhere, I have shown that *Pseudoceras* cannot belong to the Camelidae as Frick (1937) had supposed, but is a distinctive New World representative of the Gelocidae (Webb, Ms.). The limb elements, unknown to Frick, generally resemble those of gelocids and moschids. Seven postcranial elements can now be recognized from the Gracias Formation, including UF numbers 18132-34, 24997, 45880, and 458933. Evidently these small hornless ruminants were rather common elements of the Gracias fauna, in contrast with their extreme rarity in midcontinental North America.

Age of the Gracias Fauna

Previous views of the age of the Gracias fauna have been equivocal. In their major contribution Olson and McGrew (1941) concluded that "the horses of the Gracias Formation are equivalent to the Clarendonian horses of the United States" and further that ". . . there is no reason to believe that the Gracias fauna is any younger than Clarendonian." An *Osteoborus* palate discovered only a year later, however, suggested to McGrew (1944) "a Hemphillian age for the Gracias fauna." He concluded that final paper by stating that "it is probably best to reserve positive judgment on the age of the Gracias fauna until further facts are available."

One of the principal purposes of the present faunal revision has been to further investigate the age of the Gracias fauna. It is now evident that the Gracias fauna correlates with early Hemphillian faunas in temperate North America. The two most definitive comparisons at the species level are the canid, *Osteoborus cynoides,* best known from the Coffee Ranch Quarry (type section of the Hemphillian stage), and the equid *Hipparion plicatile,* well sampled at its type locality, Mixson's Bone Bed in Florida. The five other, non-endemic large mammal species are compatible with an early Hemphillian age, but also range into the late Clarendonian in midcontinental sites. The previously-known range of the genus *Rhynchotherium* was late Hemphillian and Blancan, but an earlier record in the Gracias fauna does not contradict any other information about its distribution in time and space. Thus, the most parsimonious interpretation of the overlapping large mammal age-ranges in the Gracias fauna is early Hemphillian, some seven or eight million years ago in the late Miocene.

Conclusions

The Gracias fauna is by far the southernmost late Miocene vertebrate fauna in North America. Its importance stems from the fact that it lies some 10 to 20° of latitude south of the classic midcontinental sites. Whereas they occupy temperate latitudes, the Gracias fauna, between 14 and 15° north latitude, clearly falls within the tropics.

The principal result of the present brief revision has been to render the Gracias fauna less exotic than previously supposed. The two formerly endemic proboscidean genera of Frick (1933) have been reduced to synonyms of the familiar genus *Rhynchotherium*. The apparent uniqueness of the indeterminate cervid has vanished with material recognizable as *Pseudoceras*. Only *Rhinoclemmys*, a living genus of Central American turtles, and the fossil mammal species *Rhynchotherium blicki* and *Pliohippus hondurensis*, remain as apparent endemic species. The rest of the Gracias species resemble species familiar in the midcontinent.

Olson and McGrew (1941) stressed the possibly unique tropical features of the Gracias environment and thought it "quite different than those on the great plains to the north at about the same time." In the present study, however, the northern Gracias localities have been shown to represent somewhat less humid settings than the southern Gracias localities. The faunal composition of the northern localities seems more broadly comparable to that of temperate faunas, suggesting a less distinctive suite of environments. In the absence of adequate samples of the microvertebrate fauna and the flora, such a debate is perhaps premature. The present view, still based on limited faunal evidence, is that the large mammal fauna of western Honduras was not greatly different from that at temperate latitudes of North America. Two physical features that surely favored such continuity were the relatively mild climate at all latitudes, with no freezing winters even at temperate latitudes, and the fact that Central America was a southern cul-de-sac with respect to terrestrial fauna. It is not so surprising that the large-mammal fauna of Honduras showed continuity with faunas to the north, if it had no major climatic differences and no other faunal contacts during the late Miocene.

REFERENCES

FRICK, CHILDS
1933. Tooth sequence in certain trilophodont-tetrabelodont mastodons. Am. Mus. Nat. History Bull., vol. 56, pp. 123-178.
1937. Horned ruminants of North America. Bull. Amer. Mus. Nat. Hist., vol. 69, pp. 1-669.

HONEY, JAMES G., and TAYLOR, BERYL E.
1978. A generic revision of the Protolabidini (Mammalia, Camelidae), with a description of two new Protolabidines. Bull. Amer. Mus. Nat. Hist., vol. 161, pp. 367-426.

MCGREW, PAUL O.
1942. Field Museum Paleontological Expedition to Honduras. Science, vol. 96, no. 2482, p. 85.
1944. An *Osteoborus* from Honduras. Geol. Ser. Field Museum of Nat. Hist., vol. 8, no. 12, pp. 75-77.

OLSON, E. C., and MCGREW, P. O.
1941. Mammalian fauna from the Pliocene of Honduras. Geol. Soc. America Bull., vol. 52, pp. 1219-1244.

OSBORN, H. F.
1936. Proboscidea: A monograph of the discovery, evolution, migrations and extinction of the mastodonts and elephants of the world. Vol. 1, Moeritheriodea, Deinotheriodidea, Mastodontoidea. New York, American Museum of Natural History Press.

SCHULTZ, C. BERTRAND, and MARTIN, LARRY D.
1975. Cenozoic mammals from the central Great Plains. Part 3. A new Kimballian peccary from Nebraska. Bull. Univ. Nebraska State, vol. 10, no. 1, pp. 35-46.

SIMPSON, GEORGE C.
1980. Splendid isolation. The curious history of South American mammals, 266 pp. New Haven, Yale University Press.

SKINNER, MORRIS C., and MACFADDEN, BRUCE J.
1977. *Cormohipparion* n. gen. (Mammalia, Equidae) from the North American Miocene (Barstovian-Clarendonian). Journ. Paleontol., vol. 51, no. 5, pp. 912-926.

TOBIEN, HEINZ
1973. On the evolution of Mastodonts (Proboscidea, Mammalia). Part 1. The bunodont Trilophodont groups. Notizblatt des Hessischen Landesamtes für Bodenforschung zu Wiesbaden. Bd. 101, pp. 202-276.

WEBB, S. DAVID
1969. The Burge and Minnechaduza Clarendonian mammalian faunas from north-central Nebraska. University of California Publications, Department of Geological Sciences, no. 78, pp. 1-191.
1978. Evolution of Savanna vertebrates in the New World. Part II. South America and the Great Interchange. Ann. Rev. Ecol. and Syst., vol. 9, pp. 393-426.

WEBB, S. DAVID, and TESSMAN, N.
1968. A Pliocene vertebrate fauna from Manatee County, Florida. Amer. Journ. Sci., vol. 266, pp. 777-811.
WEBB, S. DAVID; MACFADDEN, BRUCE J.; and BASKIN, JON A.
1980. Geology and paleontology of the Love Bone Bed from the late Miocene of Florida. Amer. Journ. Sci., vol. 281, pp. 513-544.
WILLIAMS, HOWEL, and MCBIRNEY, A. R.
1969. Volcanic history of Honduras. Univ. Calif. Pub. Geol. Sci., vol. 85, pp. 1-101.

S. DAVID WEBB

Thermal and Gaseous Conditions of Hornbill Nests

Grant Recipient: Fred N. White, University of California, Los Angeles, California.[1]

Grant 1664: In support of a study of nesting energetics in African hornbills.

This study was undertaken to elucidate the nature of the thermal and gaseous microclimate within the tree-hole nests of hornbills. From such data, deductions concerning the energetic advantages or disadvantages of nesting strategies can be made (see Bartholomew et al., 1976; Kemp, 1976; and White et al., 1976). Many avian species use tree holes as nests. The hornbills offer a particular advantage for such studies because the female, eggs, and young are sealed within the nest for a major portion of the nesting period. Thus, a predictable occupancy characterizes the nest.

Research took place between late November through December 1976, in the vicinity of Nylsvley, South Africa. We headquartered at the South African Ecosystem Field Station, where laboratory facilities and housing were kindly arranged through the offices of Dr. Bryan Huntley (Council for Scientific and Industrial Research, Pretoria). We received every possible assistance from Mr. Ernie Grei (Ecosystem Station Manager). Dr. Warwick Tarboton, Dr. Ian Temby, and Mr. Peter Frost were most helpful in putting us into the field at known nesting sites. Their knowledge of the savanna and the birds of the area saved us many days of searching for appropriate study areas. Mr. Frank Becker (Olympus Corporation of America) arranged for our rental of a fiber-optic scope and camera. This instrument allowed us to inspect the interior of the nest, document its condition, and verify occupancy and stage of development of the young.

[1] Now at Scripps Institution of Oceanography, University of California, San Diego, La Jolla, California.

Methods

Feeding Behavior

Observations on the feeding behavior of male parents were made from hides set up near study nests. In one instance the nest hole was so situated that the male *(Trockus flavirostris)* found it sufficiently difficult to perch so all feeding was done on the wing. This required extremely close coordination between the male and female, who accepted the food at the entrance slit. A loud vocalization by the male always just preceded food presentation. It appears that nest hole selection does not require a perch for the male although most nests observed had such a perching site. We have the impression that feeding frequency increases as the young develop; however, it would require an inordinate number of observations to verify this. Kemp (1976) has obtained data from Kruger National Park which shows feeding frequency to increase with developmental time until the female breaks out of the nest to join in the feeding of the fledglings.

Temperature and Gaseous Environment

We equipped 5 nests *(T. flavirostris,* 4; *T. nasutis,* 1*)* with remote temperature sensors. The units were fabricated in our laboratory and are capable of storing temperature data at preset time intervals in a "memory." We periodically retrieved data from the remote units by displaying it in digital form on the data collection unit. Each storage unit was calibrated against known temperatures. The remote units are approximately 2 × 2 × 3 in. and were attached to trees in wire baskets. The temperature sensors (thermistors) were fed into drill holes at appropriate locations within the nest to record temperatures from the next chamber in the vicinity of the bird(s), above the entrance hole (funk hole), tree surface, and a point roughly midway between tree surface and nest chamber. One unit recorded shaded air temperature near the tree trunk. The fiber-optic scope was used to evaluate internal nest condition, nest occupancy, and precise location of temperature sensors. Characteristic temperature data, recorded from the nest of a Grey Hornbill, is shown in Figures 1 and 2.

Figure 2 illustrates diurnal temperature fluctuations in the nest of *T. nasutis.* The chamber air to which the female is exposed varied between 21 and 31°C, while the tree surface varied between 15 and 44°C. On another day, surface temperature reached 51.5°C while the maximum chamber temperature was 34°C. The peak chamber temperatures were of brief duration because of the cooling trend that occurs late in the day. The tree exhibits sufficient insulative quality and low thermal conductivity that, as shown in Figures 1 and 2, an out-of-phase relationship exists between outside and inside temperatures. The system acts much like an

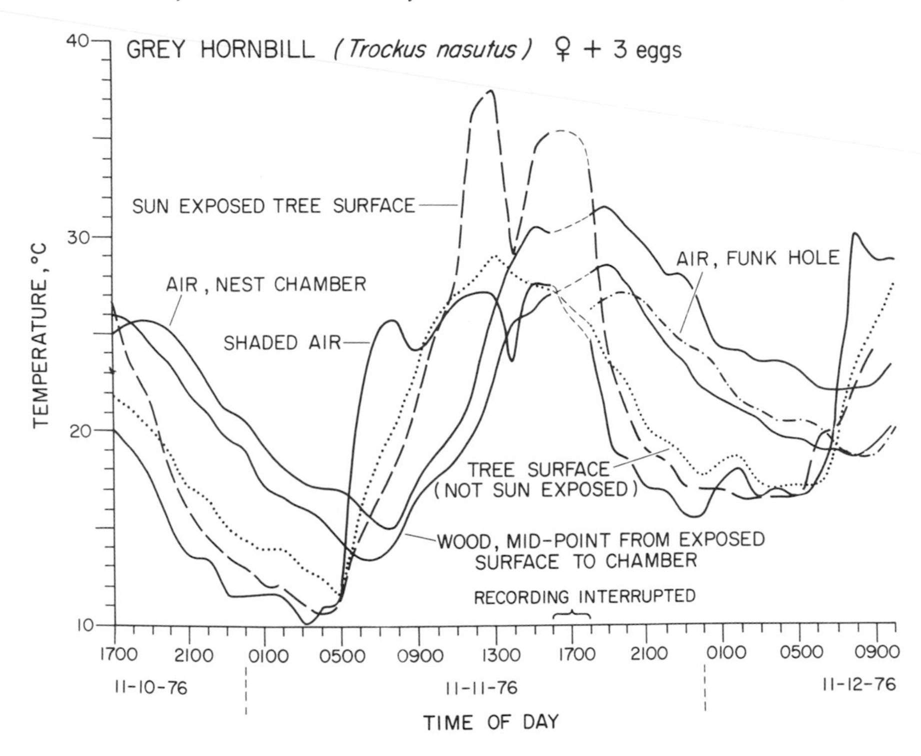

FIGURE 1. Characteristic temperature data recorded from inside nests of the Grey Hornbill, November 1976.

adobe house—the transport of heat through the wall structure is such that, during the cool of night, heat within the wall flows into the structure while the outer structure cools. Thermal lag during the hot period of the day prevents excessive overheating while ambient temperature rises.

Since the birds use the lower portion of the tree cavity, which is situated below the entrance slit, we suspected that convective transport of heat (due to metabolism) may be important in transmitting heat upward from the cavity. If this were true, one must postulate an influx of ambient air over the lower portion of the entrance slit and outflux of warmer air from the top. A number of field measurements show that a gradient of around 0.5°C exists from upper to lower slit. Thus, the birds' heat production, in conjunction with the geometry of the nest chamber, powers ventilation. This was verified in a model nest with a constant heat source in the nest chamber. In the model, this system failed to clear heated air when the heat source was moved above the slit while venting through the funk hole was prevented. The location of the nest chamber below the

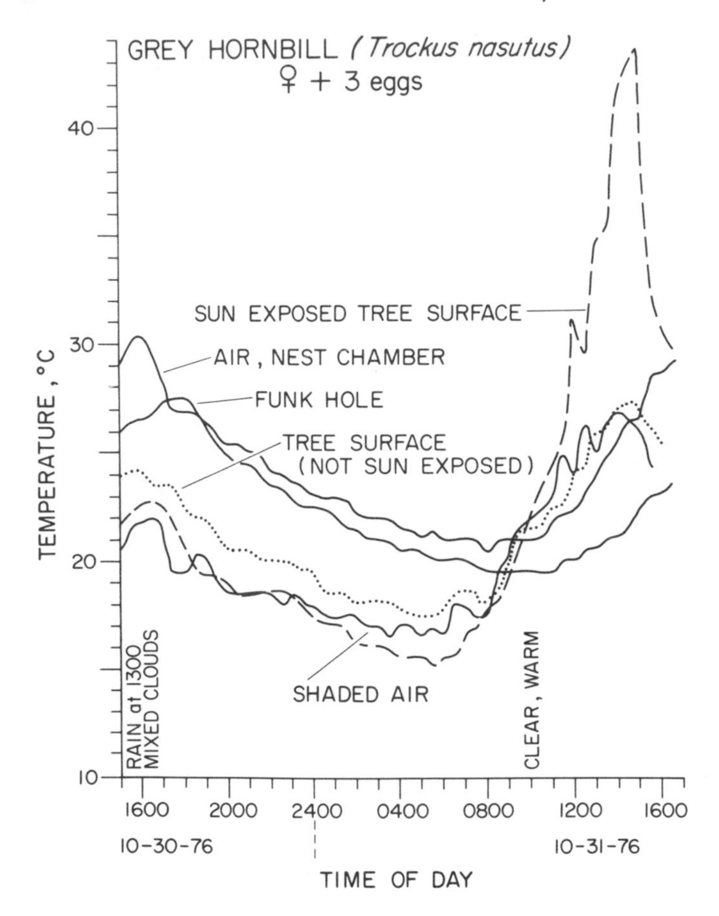

FIGURE 2. Characteristic temperature data recorded from inside nests of the Grey Hornbill, October 1976.

slit is essential unless additional venting is present. This aspect of ventilation, especially in nests that are completely closed, excepting the slit, is an important determinant of nest gas composition as well as thermal environment. Our measurements of chamber O_2 revealed that O_2 levels were seldom more than 5% lower than ambient air. This system also prevents accumulation of CO_2 at levels that might be of physiological concern. We had intended to measure O_2 consumption in situ by a gas dilution method; however, venting through the funk holes was so effective as to make these measures impossible in the study nests. At Nylsvley, such venting, through heart rot channels, characterized over 80% of the nests examined; at Kruger Park 50% of 45 nests were so vented.

The thermoneutral zone (range of environmental temperature over which metabolism is minimal) of small passerine birds, such as the House Sparrow, is between 20 and 32°C. The chamber temperature of hornbills appears to remain in this zone for the vast majority of the time; however, no data exist for O_2 consumption/ambient temperature relations for hornbills or for other birds of their size range. It is clear from this study, however, that the environment of the nest is of energetic advantage as compared with external nesting. During daylight hours shaded air temperatures were always within the presumptive thermoneutral zone. Thus, compared with nesting externally in the shade, it is difficult to assign an energetic advantage to the nest under such circumstances. Nevertheless, it is clear that advantages exist at night since a large proportion of the dark hours are characterized by air temperatures below 20°C and may reach 10°C. (See Fig. 1) Nest air temperature was maintained at 5 to 7°C higher than external air throughout the night. Based on data for other birds, lower critical temperatures are around 20°C. In Figure 1, we note that from 1700 hr, Nov. 10, 1976, to 0600, Nov. 11, 1976, air temperature remained below the presumptive lower critical temperature. It seems likely that during the molt of the female which occurs within the nest (Kemp, 1976), her lower critical temperature will increase owing to her loss of insulation. Thus the nest has a clear nighttime advantage in reducing the effect of thermal environment on the energy requirements necessary for thermoregulation. These advantages, coupled with the predators' lack of access to the nest (Kemp, 1976), convey considerable survival advantages to the occupants during the critical reproductive phase of their life cycle. A stable warm environment may be of particular advantage to chicks as they develop thermoregulatory capabilities during their early development.

The self-correcting effect of metabolism on heat flow and convection of gases prevents depletion of O_2 stores or accumulation of noxious levels of CO_2. We have previously demonstrated, for sociable weaverbirds, very significant consequences of nest structure on energy conservation during the cold winters in the Kalahari Desert (White et al., 1975). For tree-hole nesters, our study of hornbills should provide a general model which extends our appreciation of the biological significance of this widespread nesting habit.

Acknowledgments

Working with me on this project were James Kinney, Scripps Institution of Oceanography; W. Roy Siegfried, Percy Fitzpatrick Institute of African Ornithology, University of Capetown, Rondebosch, South Africa; and A. C. Kemp, The Transvaal Museum, Pretoria, South Africa.

REFERENCES

Bartholomew, G. A.; White, F. N.; and Howell, T. R.
1976. The thermal significance of the nest of the sociable weaver, *Philetairus socius*. Summer observations. Ibis, vol. 118, pp. 402-410.

Kemp, A. C.
1976. A study of the ecology, behaviour and systematics of *Trockus* hornbills (Aves: Bucerotidae). Transvaal Museum Memoir No. 20, pp. 1-125.

White, F. N.; Bartholomew, G. A.; and Howell, T. R.
1975. The thermal significance of the nest of the sociable weaver, *Philetairus socius*. Winter observations. Ibis, vol. 117, pp. 171-179.

White, F. N.; Bartholomew, G. A.; and Kinney, J.
1978. Physiological and ecological correlates of tunnel-nesting in the European Bee-eater, *Merops apiaster*. Physiol. Zool., vol. 51, pp. 140-154.

Fred N. White
James Kinney
W. Roy Siegfried
A. C. Kemp

Physiological Ecology of the Hawaiian Monk Seal *(Monachus schauinslandi)*

Grant Recipient: G. C. Whittow, Kewalo Marine Laboratory, University of Hawaii, Honolulu, Hawaii.

Grant 1580: For a study of the adaptation of seals to the tropics.

The thermal properties of water are such that any mammal that spends a substantial amount of time in the water has to compensate for high rates of heat loss to the water. The thick layer of blubber or fur and the high metabolic heat production of most aquatic mammals testify to the need for these compensations. Some marine mammals, however, have penetrated the tropics and, while it is unlikely that the relatively high temperature of tropical waters gives rise to any problems in the dissipation of body heat (Whittow, 1976), if the animals leave the water, as pinnipeds must, in order to breed, sleep, or molt or for other reasons, they encounter conditions for which they are ill adapted. Their high metabolic rates and effective insulation compound the difficulties that they experience in losing heat to a hot environment. How then do pinnipeds adapt to the tropics? Of all the seals, the Hawaiian monk seal is the most tropical in its distribution (Scheffer, 1958). Yet, for the most part, the physiological and behavioral features of its adaptation have not been identified. The study described in the present report was designed to obtain as much information as possible on the thermoregulatory behavior and heat tolerance of the Hawaiian monk seal, within the constraints imposed by the conservation status of the seals. Hawaiian monk seals are an endangered species, and this precluded all but the simplest measurements and observations.

Procedures

Hawaiian monk seals were studied on Tern and Trig Islands at French Frigate Shoals in the northwestern Hawaiian Islands (Fig. 1). French Frigate Shoals is an atoll consisting of a crescent-shaped reef and approximately 12 sand islands. Tern Island is 900 m long, partly man-made, and at the time of the study was the site of a Coast Guard Loran Station. Seals hauled out on the beaches of Tern Island irregularly and

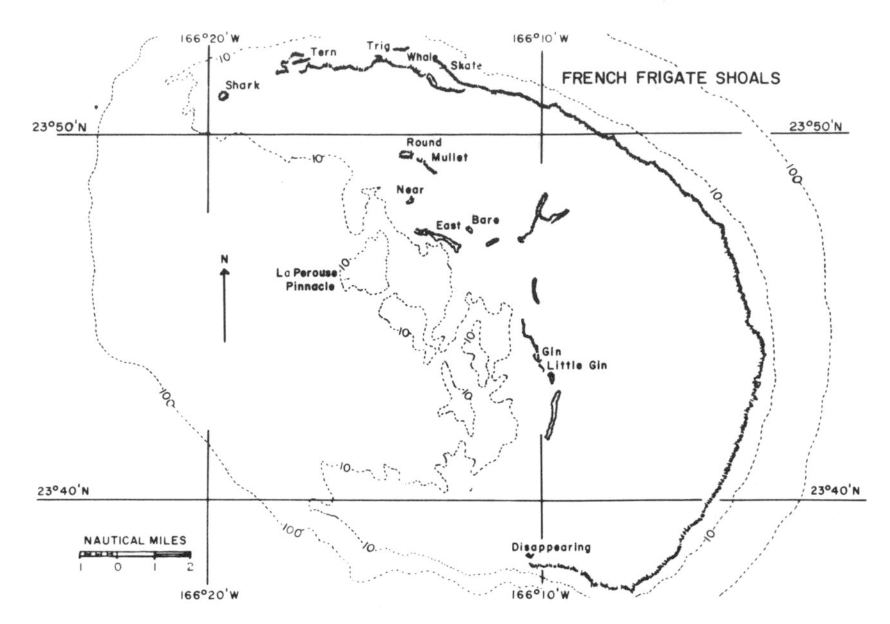

FIGURE 1. French Frigate Shoals showing Tern and Trig Islands. Depths in fathoms.

usually singly; they do not breed there. Trig Island is approximately 351 m long, with a resident population of 30 to 40 seals. Additional observations were made on the 14-year-old captive animal at the Waikiki Aquarium. This was a male seal, kept in a 95,000-gal pool with a central artificial island 6 m long.

On Trig Island a group of seals was under continuous observation from approximately 0830 hr to 1600-1800 hr. Their position and orientation were plotted on simple maps constructed at intervals of 30 min. Records were also kept of the temperature of a 15.2-cm black globe, the temperature of the sand surface, and the magnetic compass bearing of the sun and wind. On some occasions, a single seal was observed, and a complete dossier kept of its movements, behavior, and postural adjustments. On Tern Island and at the Waikiki Aquarium, the latter type of observation was the only one made. The captive animal hauled out regularly on the artificial island, in its pool, following its second feeding period of the day, at 1430 hr. Consequently, records of the behavior of this seal were kept only for part of the day, from 1430 to 1800 hr. Occasional measurements were made of the surface temperature of the Trig Island seals, their heart rate and respiratory frequency. No consistent attempt was made to record the size of the animals observed, other than to note whether they were adult (large) or subadult (small).

FIGURE 2. Seal sleeping in a posture exposing the greater part of the pale ventral and lateral surfaces to the sun.

Results

Movements. The Hawaiian monk seals at French Frigate Shoals characteristically slept on dry sand on the level beach platform at night, and moved down to moist sand on the beach slope during the day. This pattern of movement was observed both in groups of seals on Trig Island and in single seals on Tern Island. The movement seemed to be related to the prevailing climatic conditions. Measurements made on the beach platform and also on the beach slope revealed that, by moving down the beach, the seals were, in effect, attenuating the increase in the temperature of their environment during the course of the day.

Posture. While ashore, Hawaiian monk seals lay prone (on their ventral surface), completely supine (on their back), on either flank (side), or in an intermediate position between the flank and either the supine or the prone positions. Analysis of detailed records of the behavior of seven seals at French Frigate Shoals revealed that during the day, the length of time that the seals lay on their flanks was greater than that for other postures. However, as this included time on both flanks, it was clear that the most favored single posture was the prone position. This posture was obligatory when the animals moved up or down the beach. It was apparent also that, although the prone position was the most favored single posture, the seals lay for most of the time in postures (supine, flank-supine, and flank) that left the greater part of their light-colored ventral surface exposed to the atmosphere (Fig. 2). There was no simple relationship between the posture of the seals on the one hand, and the wetness of the seal and its substrate, on the other. Nor did the posture of the seals seem to be connected with the black-globe and sand temperatures on the beach platform.

The frequency with which the seals changed their posture, on the other hand, appeared to be related to the environmental conditions, as well as to the duration of exposure to these conditons. Thus, as the temperature of the sand and black-globe thermometer increased, the dry seal changed its posture more often. When the seal was wet by rain or sea, however, its rate of change of posture diminished.

Orientation. In order to reveal an orientation of the seals with respect to the sun and wind, relatively long periods of time were needed in which the seals did not change their position on the beach. Because of the movements of the seals between the beach platform and slope, this was not possible. Plots of the bearings of individual seals observed on separate days, together with those of the sun and wind, throughout the day, did not reveal any readily discernible pattern.

Wallows. As reported by Kenyon and Rice (1959), some of the seals lay in depressions (wallows) in the sand. There seemed to be little relationship between the incidence of wallows and the meteorological conditions. The incidence of wallowing during the day was relatively low; in 26 records of groups of seals consisting of 7 to 23 individuals, the mean number of seals in wallows was 10.1%.

Shade. On some of the islands at French Frigate Shoals there is no shade. On others, shade is provided only by one or two low bushes *(Tournefortia argentia).* On Tern Island there is more extensive natural shade, and also the artificial shade provided by seawalls and buildings. In only one instance was a seal observed to seek shade in the middle of the day. However, this animal was wet when it sought shade at 1313 hr, and it was returning to a position that it had occupied overnight.

Other Behavior. Apart from brief moments of alertness when the seals changed their posture, moved down to the beach slope, or executed the other movements described above, the seals were completely inactive when they were ashore, and they slept for the entire time.

Coat Temperatures. The surface temperature of the dark fawn hair on the dorsal surface, and also that of the very light fawn hair on the ventral surface of the seals, was measured in a number of animals, under a variety of conditions. In spite of variations in the length of time that a particular surface had been exposed to solar radiation, in the intensity of radiation, in wind velocity, and other factors, the mean temperature of the dry dorsal surface was significantly higher ($t=4.77$; $p<0.001$) than that of the dry ventral hair (Whittow, 1978).

Breathing Pattern. In none of the seals observed was there any evidence of thermal polypnea or open-mouth panting. On the contrary, in all of the animals studied the pattern of breathing was similar, consisting of periods of apnea (breath holding) alternating with periods of breathing. The duration of the period of breath holding was as long as 453 sec; in general, the periods of breathing were shorter than the periods of apnea.

Heart Rate. The heart rate was relatively easy to count when the seals were holding their breath; the mean heart rate of the seals thus measured was 49.8 beats/min.

Conclusions

Although air temperatures in the northwestern Hawaiian Islands are relatively high, and the levels of solar radiation very high, the overall heat stress imposed by the environment is attenuated by the strong trade winds and the high reflectance of the white coral sand to solar radiation, which result in lower sand surface temperatures than might be expected. Hawaiian monk seals, nevertheless, were unable to tolerate these conditions without behavioral augmentation of conductive and evaporative heat loss, and possibly both behavioral and physiological reduction of heat production. The most important components in the monk seal's heat tolerance were the movements of the seal down the beach slope onto wet sand, an increased frequency of change of posture, and the absence of other activity while ashore. The role of the coat in the attenuation of solar heat gain remains to be elucidated.

REFERENCES

Kenyon, K. W., and Rice, D. W.
1959. Life history of the Hawaiian monk seal. Pacific Sci., vol. 13, pp. 215-252.

Scheffer, V. B.
1958. Seals, sea lions, and walruses, 179 pp. Stanford University Press.

Whittow, G. C.
1976. Temperature regulation in marine mammals. Pp. 88-94 *in* "Progress in Biometeorology," S. W. Tromp, ed. Division B, vol. I, part I. Swets and Zeitlinger, Amsterdam.
1978. Thermoregulatory behavior of the Hawaiian monk seal *(Monachus schauinslandi).* Pacific Sci., vol. 32, pp. 47-60.

G. C. Whittow

Archeology and the Highlands of Southwest Iran

Grant Recipient: Allen Zagarell, Department of Anthropology, Duke University, Durham, North Carolina.

Grant 1603: For an archeological survey of routes through the Bakhtiari Mountains of southwest Iran.

The factors leading to the rise of man's first civilization in "Greater Mesopotamia" have occupied the attention of archeologists, philologists, and historians for well over 100 years. Recently researchers have been moving away from simple artifact descriptions, attempting to understand the processes and mechanisms within the societies producing the artifacts, not only within the centers of civilization but also in the surrounding borderlands. Adams (1974, p. 3) expressed the opinion that the chronic flux and local instability of populations played an important role in the development of state society in Mesopotamia. Others have suggested that highland pastoralists bordering the Susiana Plain played an important role in the late prehistoric-early historic periods (Wright et al., 1975; Lees and Bates, 1974).

In 1974, in order to better understand the role of the highland inhabitants of Greater Mesopotamia, I decided to carry out archeological surveys in the Bakhtiari region of the Zagros Mountains, the region bordering Khuzistan to the northeast. (See Fig. 1.) The region was ideally suited to offer information about the nature of true highland cultures. It borders on one of the alluvial centers of civilization, yet the mountain zone is formed by a series of chains tending northwest to southeast. The peaks occasionally rise to approximately 4000 m. Interspersed among these chains lie valley systems running parallel to them. Communication from valley to valley within a system is relatively easy, but between systems it can be carried out only with difficulty. A limited series of "roads" run through the mountains joining Khuzistan with the Central Plateau (see Sawyer, 1894; Ehmann, 1974). Sections of the Zagros are suitable for cropping or improved pasturage (Dewan, 1968, p. 258). The area receives considerable amounts of precipitation, overwhelmingly concentrated in the winter months, mainly in the form of snow (Ganji,

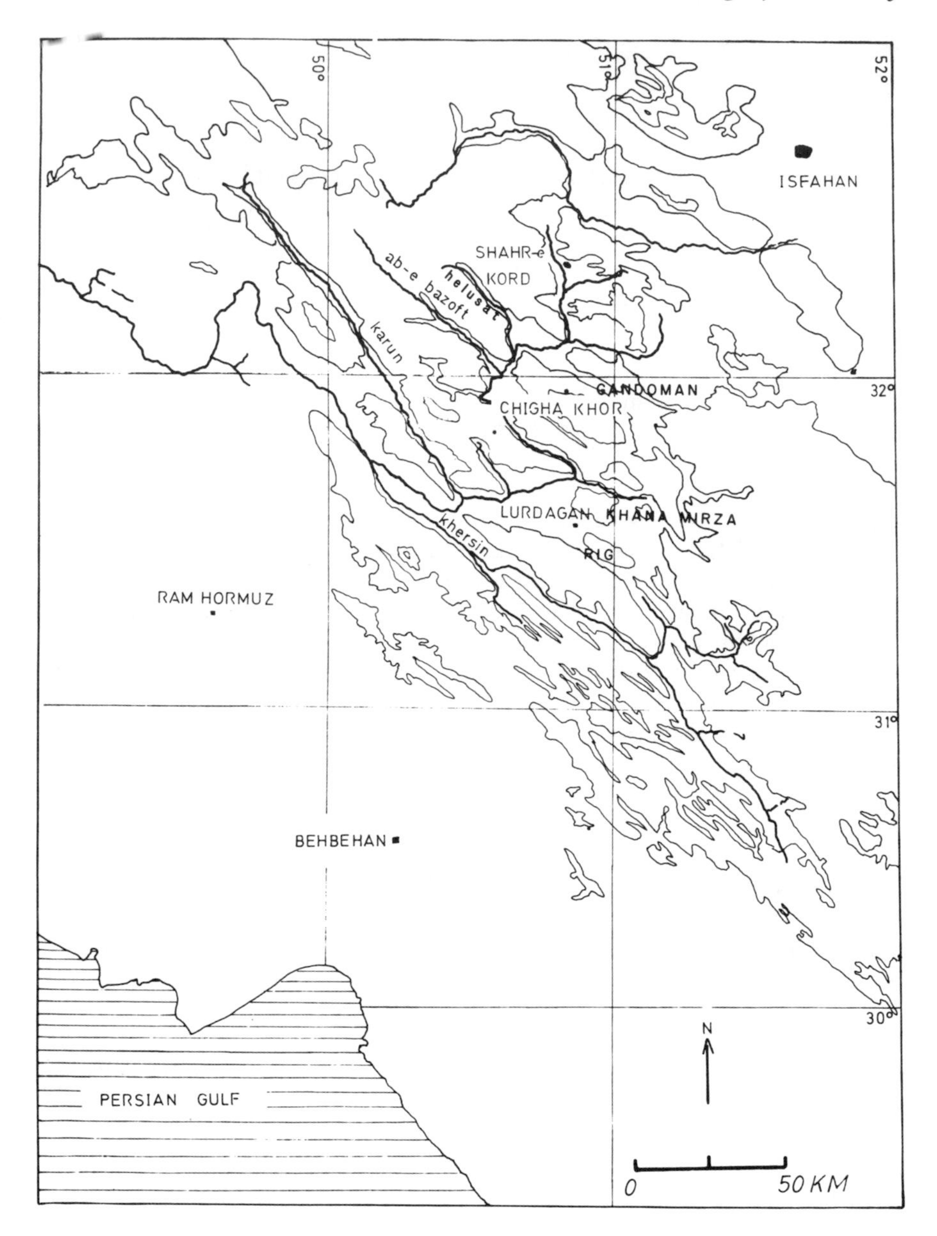

FIGURE 1. Bakhtiari region of the Zagros Mountains.

1968, p. 236). Rainfall may reach above 1000 mm a year; the highland region west of Fars receiving over 400 mm (Ganji, 1968, p. 234, fig. 79). Rainfall may, however, vary as much as 100% from year to year.

The area is drained by an extensive system of rivers cutting through the mountains, emerging as the Karun to the south or the Zayande Rud to the north. The beds, however, are usually too deeply cut to be of use for the mountain dwellers themselves. Much water flows from natural springs bursting forth from hillsides or bubbling up in the midst of valleys. Many valleys are covered by shallow lakes, seasonally changing shape, often close to shrub-oak covered arid steppes.

The inhabitants of these mountains are the Bakhtiari, a confederation of tribal groups which at one time exercised considerable influence over Khuzistan from their mountain strongholds. The Bakhtiari are predominantly a pastoral people; a large majority is involved in some type of seasonal migration. Nevertheless, traveling from valley to valley, one sees considerable cultivation, including rice cultivation, carried on by "settled" and nomad alike. The nomadic sector may move as far afield as north Khuzistan in winter, to Shahr-e Kord, far to the north, in summer; but shorter migrations are much more common, frequently involving no more than valley-to-mountain movements. The people themselves stem from several ethnic groups—Lurs, Turks, Arabs, among others—and have adapted themselves to various niches within the mountains. These adaptions vary from fully nomadic pastoralism to buffalo herding in swamp areas in the high mountains.

Archeological Survey

In 1974 work began in the Bakhtiari region with an intensive archeological survey of the Khana Mirza Plain and less intensive surveys of the Rig and Lurdagan Plains. In 1975, several soundings were carried out, and the more northerly valleys of Gandoman, Chigha Khor, and Imam Qais were surveyed. In 1977, sections of the road leading from Isfahan through Lurdagan to Shushtar, and from Isfahan through Ardal to Shushtar were surveyed. In 1978 the Shahr-e Kord Plain was surveyed and a small sounding was undertaken at Qal'e Geli in the Lurdagan Plain (Zagarell, 1982). Very limited amounts of work had been undertaken in the region before these surveys, particularly in reference to the earlier periods of occupation.

Only rare finds point to an early paleolithic occupation of the high mountain region. At the cave site of Sangiyan, in the Shahr-e Kord plain, there was an epi-paleolithic or proto-neolithic occupation (Zagarell, 1982, pp. 18-20). There are also indications of an aceramic neolithic occupation of this section of the highlands—at the rock shelter of S4 and perhaps at the open air site of Qal'e Rostam (Zagarell, 1982, pp. 18-20; Nissen and Zagarell, 1976, p. 162). With the ceramic neolithic, relatively abundant evidence of highland occupation becomes available. The best known of these village sites is Qal'e Rostam, tested in 1975 (Nissen and Zagarell, 1976), but sites appear in several areas of the northeast section of the Bakhtiari Mountains; for example, Choledan in the Helusat River valley (Zagarell, 1982, p. 22) and the heavy concentration in the Shahr-e Kord Plain (Zagarell, 1982, pp. 23-25). These ceramic neolithic village and cave sites represent a hitherto unknown neolithic "culture." Presently, this assemblage is only known from the Bakhtiari region. Although the bone samples still have not been examined and only preliminary studies of the soil samples have been carried out, it is quite probable, based on the settlement distribution and tool types, that these people were engaged in a mixed economic strategy, consisting of hunting, gathering, herding (?), and agriculture. The pottery wares characterizing the neolithic may be divided into three successive stages. The earliest group is a handmade, crude, heavily chaff-tempered, undecorated pottery (Qal'e Rostam Phase III). It is followed by a handmade, chaff-tempered, highly polished red ware (Phase II). The final stage is represented by a handmade, chaff-tempered, buff-slipped ware, painted below the carination on the external surface, and internally, with a shiny red paint, but painted black along the rim (Phase I).

The next identifiable phase is the Early Chalcolithic (Eskandari phase); at two or possibly three sites in the Khana Mirza and Rig Valleys and at several Shahr-e Kord sites, there appears early black-on-buff pottery which has close ties to the lowlands of southwest Iran (Zagarell, 1982, pp. 27-29). This complex seems to be intrusive, emanating from the southerly alluvial region. Sites continue to represent rather tiny villages. The settlement distribution essentially corresponds to the pattern detected in the earlier phase. Interestingly, similar to the later ceramic neolithic pattern, few sites seem to have been occupied during the Early Chalcolithic.

The next phase, the Middle Chalcolithic, represents a serious break with earlier developments. The number of sites increases dramatically, as does site size. Sites appear in the plains. Many sites concentrate around areas suitable for limited irrigation, around central mud flats or swamps, seasonally expanding and contracting. Other sites occupy areas where sizable natural springs make limited irrigation possible. In one case, at L 1, Qal'e Geli, in the Lurdagan Plain, a significant part of the plain seems to have been irrigable. Thus it would seem that to some extent use was being made of naturally irrigable areas of the mountains.

Not only does site size increase in the Middle Chalcolithic period, but size-difference among contemporary sites seems to have undergone some change. At least three of the sites of the Lurdagan/Rig/Khana Mirza region appear to have attained relatively large dimensions. One must reckon with the possibility that some of the villages were exercising a degree of authority which is reflected in site size. This conclusion also refers to conditions in the Shahr-e Kord Plain but there is significant local variation in the Gandoman Imam Qais Chigha Khor region; only tiny villages sitting along streams or in naturally irrigable zones occur in this period.

Pastoral activities also seem to have played some role. Apparently caves were in use, as reflected in the finds at the cave Eshkaft-e Rigo, k 63, in the Khana Mirza Plain. Caves in other regions seem to have come increasingly into use during this period (Zagarell, 1982, pp. 83-85). In this regard the site of Chiga Khor, in the plain of the same name, may be of some interest. The Middle Chalcolithic settlement is a rather tiny hamlet, sitting on the extreme northern tip of the mound. The site faces a shallow natural lake to the north. The plain surrounding the site is muddy and difficult to cross even in late summer. In winter and spring the site apparently is surrounded by water. Even if one assumes that the water level was approximately that of the present—and there is reason to believe that actually it was higher—it appears that this settlement may have been a seasonal or special-purpose site. We know that in the recent past it has been used only seasonally.

The pottery of the period shows close relationships to the so-called Bakun late B and A_{1-4} group known from Fars Province to the east and Behbehan to the south. Although the group itself broadly relates to the black-on-buff tradition common throughout much of the contemporary Near East, it is considerably different from the pottery of the Khuzistan Plain. I have divided the Middle Chalcolithic into two subphases, naming them after local sites, respectively, Chellegah and Afghan. One may surmise that a true highland culture, based on that more mobile mixture of pastoralism and cultivation typical of the more recent dwellers, began to differentiate itself from the lowlands—which were becoming more irrigation-oriented.

In the Late Chalcolithic phase, the number of sites decrease precipitately. Moreover, a number of subphases are combined under this heading, including a Bakun A_5, red-ware (Berjui aspect) group, one comparable to the late Uruk of Mesopotamia (Sharah buff ware), and a Godin VI, late Sialk III-related group. Unfortunately the entire pottery complex remains largely unidentified. This casts uncertainty on the settlement pattern of this phase. Nevertheless, it seems quite probable that the village-dwelling population of the highlands decreased dramatically.

Of special interest is the Godin VI, late Sialk III-related group. Small numbers of sherds were found in the Khana Mirza Plain in 1974 and 1977. This pottery tradition does not develop out of the local pottery tradition;

rather it is intrusive. How the pottery was brought into this section of the mountains and what activities it represents are uncertain. To the north, at the site of Sharak, near Shahr-e Kord (a site dominating one of the main roadways through the Bakhtiari Mountains) this pottery group is common. I have argued elsewhere that this pottery group may represent a 4th-millennium trade network going through this section of the Zagros (Zagarell, 1979, and in press, a).

In the time-period following that represented by the Late Chalcolithic pottery, the centers of civilization entered the light of history, establishing state-organized societies. The lack of a controlled chronological pottery sequence makes it impossible to establish a definite settlement pattern. What is certain is that the centralizing tendencies of the lowlands were reflected in the mountains. The pottery continued to have its closest links to the eastern highlands, but retained ties to the lowlands.

Work in the highlands is still in a very early stage; only a minute section of the Bakhtiari Mountains has been examined, and new methods corresponding to the difficulties of highland surveys have yet to be developed. Still, it is becoming increasingly clear that sizable populations inhabited the region, and that these populations apparently had considerable "autonomy," although, except for the neolithic period, they cannot be considered to have been isolated, insofar as we can see from their pottery. They were certainly a force to be reckoned with in their day, and those interested in understanding the cultures of the lowlands must reckon with them once again.

Acknowledgments

The 1974 season was supported by the Freie Universität of Berlin. The 1975 season was carried out under the leadership of Prof. Hans J. Nissen, with funds supplied by the Deutsche Forschungsgemeinschaft. The 1977 season was supported by the National Geographic Society of America. A 1978 season was supported by the Deutsche Forschungsgemeinschaft.

REFERENCES

ADAMS, ROBERT MCCORMICK
1974. The Mesopotamian social landscape: A view from the frontier. Pp. 1-12 *in* "Reconstructing Complex Societies," 170 pp., C. B. Moore, ed. Supplement to the Bulletin of the American Schools of Oriental Research no. 20, Cambridge, Massachusetts.

DEWAN, M. L.
1968. Soils. Pp. 250-263 *in* "Cambridge History of Iran I. The Land of Iran," 784 pp., W. B. Fisher, ed. Cambridge University Press, Cambridge, England.

EHMAN, DIETER
1974. Verkehrsentwicklung und Kulturlandschaftswandel in Bakhtiyari (Mittlerer Zagros). Sociologus, vol. 24, pp. 137-147.
GANJI, M. H.
1968. Climate. Pp. 212-249 *in* "Cambridge History of Iran I. The Land of Iran," 784 pp., W. B. Fisher, ed. Cambridge University Press, Cambridge, England.
LEES, SUSAN H., and BATES, DANIEL G.
1974. The origin of specialized nomadic pastoralism: A systemic model. American Antiquity, vol. 39, pp. 188-193.
NISSEN, HANS J., and ZAGARELL, ALLEN
1976. The 1975 expedition to the Zagros Mountains. Pp. 159-189 *in* "The Proceedings of the IVth Annual Symposium of Archaeological Research in Iran," F. Bagherzadeh, ed. Iranian Centre for Archaeological Research, Tehran.
SAWYER, H. A.
1894. The Bakhtiari Mountains and Upper Elam. The Geographic Journal, vol. 4, pp. 481-505.
VANDEN BERGHE, LOUIS
1968. Die Erkundung der Zivilisationen des Alten Iran. Informationsbericht, vol. 33-34, pp. 1-70.
ZAGARELL, ALLEN
1975a. An archeological survey in the northeast Baxtiari Mountains. Pp. 145-156 *in* "The Proceedings of the IIIrd Annual Symposium on Archaeological Research in Iran," F. Bagherzadeh, ed. Iranian Centre for Archaeological Research, Tehran.
1975b. Nomad and settled in the Bakhtiari Mountains. Sociologus, vol. 25, pp. 125-138.
1977. The role of highland pastoralism in the development of Iranian civilization (proto and prehistoric Iran). 305 pp., illus. Ph.D. thesis, Freie Universität of Berlin.
1979. The mountain zone of south-west Iran—meeting point of lowland and the central plateau in the late prehistoric period. *In* "Akten des VII. Internationalen Kongresses für Kunst and Archäologie. Archäologische Mitteilungen aus Iran. Ergänzungsband." Dietrich Reimer Verlag, Berlin.
1982. Bahtiyārī Mountains, Iran. Beihefte zum Tübinger Atlas des Vorderen Orients Reiche B (Geisteswissenschaften), no. 42, 204 pp., illus. In Kommissionen bei Dr Ludwig Reichert Verlag, Wiesbaden.
____a. Baxtiari Mountain survey 1977. *In* "The Proceedings of the VI Annual Symposium on Archeological Research Iran," Iranian Centre for Archaeological Research, Tehran. (In press.)
____b. The first millennium in the Bakhtiari Mountains. Archäologische Mitteilungen aus Iran. (In press).
____c. Indigenous development and external integration: The Baxtiari Mountains. *In* "The Proceedings of the First USA/USSR Archaeological Exchange." Harvard, Nov. 9-23, 1981. (In press.)

ALLEN ZAGARELL

APPENDIX

Grants for Research and Exploration Made by the National Geographic Society in 1983

2590: To William S. Brown, Skidmore College, to study population ecology of the timber rattlesnake in New York.
2591: To Joel Berger, University of California, Davis, for research on wild horses in Nevada: reproduction, mortality, and social biology.
2592: To Rodney M. Jackson, California Institute of Environmental Studies, to study radio-tracking snow leopards in the Himalayas.
2593: To William G. Johnston, Saskatchewan Energy and Mines, for a survey of the glacial indicator fan from the Deep Bay, Cretaceous Shale, Reindeer Lake.
2594: To Richard C. Fox, University of Alberta, for a study of the Upper Devonian Tetrapods from New South Wales, Australia.
2595: To John A. Gifford, University of Miami, to research the continuation of underwater coring off Franchthi Cave, Greece.
2596: To Edward M. Schortman, Kenyon College, for the Santa Barbara archeological project in Honduras.
2597: To Pedro I. Porras G., La Pontificia University, for archeological investigations at Sangay A. Site, Morona Santiago, Ecuador.
2598: To William G. Dever, University of Arizona, to develop the Tell el-Hayyat project in Jordan.
2599: To William R. Biers, University of Missouri, for research on the Mirobriga project in Portugal.
2600: To Steven D. Busack, University of California, Berkeley, for the empirical testing of vicariance biogeography.
2601: To Richard E. MacMillen, University of California, Irvine, for the ecological energetics study of Australian honeyeater birds (Passeriformes: Meliphagidae).
2602: To Alwyn H. Gentry, Missouri Botanical Garden, to study the tree species diversity in upper Amazonia.
2603: To Gordon D. McPherson, Missouri Botanical Garden, for Euphorbiaceae research in New Caledonia.
2604: To Gary S. Chafetz, Harvard University, to study ground-penetrating radar survey to locate the lost army of Cambyses.
2605: To Alasdair J. Edwards, University of Newcastle upon Tyne, to research the fishes of Saint Helena Island.
2606: To Michael J. Ryan, University of California, Berkeley, for research on the environmental influences on the evolution of frog vocalizations in Panama.
2607: To Thomas J. Cade, Cornell University, to survey population ecology of the Gyrfalcon in Iceland.

2608: To Thomas B. Haviland, Australian National University, for the Flowering of Man Project—nature and daily life in Zinacantan, Mexico.
2609: To Thomas R. Hester, University of Texas at San Antonio, for investigations in rescue archeology at the main pyramidal mound, in Colha, Belize.
2610: To J. Richard Steffy, Texas A&M University, to study conservation and reconstruction of the boat at Herculaneum, Italy.
2611: To Leonard B. Thien, Tulane University, to research pollination mechanisms of primitive angiosperms.
2612: To Mason E. Hale, Smithsonian Institution, to survey rain forest lichens in Queensland, Australia.
2613: To Maurice G. Hornocker, University of Idaho, to study the ecology of the bobcat in the River of No Return Wilderness in Idaho.
2614: To Dian Fossey, Karisoke Research Center, to study the behavior and ecology of the mountain gorilla in Rwanda.
2615: To Christopher Uhl, University of Georgia, to research the rehabilitation of damaged ecosystems in the Amazon Basin.
2616: To Siim Sööt, University of Illinois at Chicago, for the study of urban transportation and urban structure in a planned society in Estonia.
2617: To Michael E. Brookfield, University of Guelph, for research in radiometric dating of rocks of the Karakorum, northern Pakistan.
2618: To Robert D. Ballard, Woods Hole Oceanographic Institution, to explore the mid-ocean with ARGO/JASON vehicle.
2619: To Ed Landing, New York State Geological Survey, to study the biostratigraphy and depositional tectonics of the Lower Cambrian, Avalon Region, eastern Newfoundland.
2620: To Sankar Chatterjee, Texas Tech University, to explore Triassic vertebrates in west Texas.
2621: To David J. Duvall, University of Wyoming, to analyze the ethology and movements of free-ranging *Crotalus viridis viridis* in Wyoming.
2622: To Charles J. Cole, American Museum of Natural History, to study the unisexual clones of shiny lizards, *Gymnophthalmus underwoodi*, of West Indian origin.
2623: To Calogero M. Santoro, University of Tarapaca, Chile, for the research of cave and rockshelter art of northern Chile.
2624: To Gary O. Rollefson, Yarmouk University, Jordan, for excavations at Ain Ghazal, a pre-pottery Neolithic village in highland Jordan.
2625: To David P. Crews, University of Texas at Austin, to study behavioral ecology of the parthenogenetic mourning gecko *(Lepidodactylus lugubris)* in Hawaii.
2626: To Thomas J. Givnish, Harvard University, to research carnivory in the bromeliad genus *Brocchinia* of the Guyana highlands.
2627: To Andrew T. Smith, Arizona State University, to study the behavioral ecology of the Asian pika (genus *Ochotona)*.

2628: To Norman Hammond, Rutgers University, for the Nohmul project: the emergence of a Classic Maya regional center.

2629: To Barry C. Bishop, National Geographic staff, for the east-west alpine zone research project.

2630: To Kenan T. Erim, New York University, for study, research, and restoration activities at Aphrodisias in Turkey.

2631: To Alan C. Walker, Johns Hopkins University School of Medicine, to support excavations at the Miocene hominoid site of Buluk, Kenya.

2632: To Mary D. Leakey, for field work at present-day salt works in Kenya for comparison with pits in Bed III; and for preparation of a report on the Kakesio–Makau expedition.

2633: To Ross D. E. MacPhee, Duke University Medical Center, to support a study of pre-Holocene mammalian paleontology of Madagascar: the absent record.

2634: To J. Malcolm Shick, University of Maine, to research defense against photosynthetic oxygen toxicity in animals with algal endosystems.

2635: To David B. Weissman, California Academy of Sciences, to study zoogeography, systematics, and bionomics of the Orthoptera of Baja California Islands.

2636: To Abbot S. Gaunt, Ohio State University, for the study of coiled tracheae in cranes—bizarre structures of undetermined function.

2637: To Frances C. James, Florida State University, to support his analysis of clinal variation with transplant experiments with Red-winged Blackbirds.

2638: To Joshua R. Ginsberg, Princeton University, to research behavioral ecology of the Grevy's zebra *(Equus grevyi)*.

2639: To William A. Watkins, Woods Hole Oceanographic Institution, for the identification of sperm whales by their underwater pulse patterns.

2640: To Carol L. Jenkins, Papua New Guinea Institute of Medical Research, to study nutritional adaptation of foragers, Western Schrader Mountains, Papua New Guinea.

2641: To Cynthia M. Beall, Case Western University, to survey lifelong high physical activity levels and biological aging in Nepal.

2642: To Stanley J. Olsen, University of Arizona, to research early camel domestication in China.

2643: To Jeffrey S. Soles, University of North Carolina at Greensboro, for the Mochlos Field Survey in eastern Crete.

2644: To Hiro Kurashina, University of Guam, for the study of the origins of human settlement in Micronesia.

2645: To Gary A. Haynes, Smithsonian Institution, for taphonomic studies of Zimbabwe elephants—perspectives on Pleistocene death assemblages.

2646: To Marc Bekoff, University of Colorado, for research on social behavior and organization of Evening Grosbeaks.

2647: To Ann L. Rypstra, Miami University, Ohio, to study prey consumption and aggregate behavior in the spider *Nephila clavipes* (L.).

2648: To Robert E. Ricklefs, University of Pennsylvania, to investigate energetics and reproduction of Midway Island seabirds.
2649: To Alfred H. Siemens, University of British Columbia, to study pre-Hispanic wetland agriculture in Veracruz, Mexico.
2650: To Wilbur Zelinsky, Pennsylvania State University, to research the emergency evacuation of cities: a comparative, cross-national study.
2651: To Sara Clark Bisel, Smithsonian Institution, for the salvage and study of ancient Roman population at Herculaneum, Italy.
2652: To Richard A. Tedford, American Museum of Natural History, to study the stratigraphy and vertebrate paleontology in eastern lake basin, South Australia.
2653: To Harm de Blij, University of Miami, for the South African viticulture project.
2654: To Farish A. Jenkins, Harvard University, to support the earliest mammal fauna in the New World project.
2655: To David W. Krause, State University of New York at Stony Brook, to study the early Cenozoic mammalian faunas of the Crazy Mountain Basin, Montana.
2656: To Howard Topoff, Hunter College of CUNY, for research in slave-making behavior in the ant *Ployergus breviceps.*
2657: To Ralph W. Schreiber, Natural History Museum of Los Angeles County, to research seabird recovery from population failure, 1982, Christmas Island, Pacific Ocean.
2658: To Richard D. Snow, State University of New York at Albany, for the Mohawk Valley project.
2659: To Livingston V. Watrous, State University of New York at Buffalo, to support the Cretan exploration project.
2660: To Robert L. Hohlfelder, University of Colorado, Boulder, for excavations in the ancient harbors of Caesarea Maritima, Israel.
2661: To Izumi Shimada, Princeton University, for the development and organization of Sican metallurgy in ancient Peru.
2662: To Peter S. Wells, Harvard University, to study the economic basis of later prehistoric Europe by excavating settlements in West Germany.
2663: To Gerrit Davidse, Missouri Botanical Garden, for the botanical exploration of Cerro Kamuk and adjoining Costa Rican massifs.
2664: To Bruce M. Bartholomew, California Academy of Sciences, for the botanical expedition to Sichuan Province in the People's Republic of China.
2665: To William A. Calder, University of Arizona, to research migration and population dynamics of hummingbirds in Colorado and Montana.
2666: To Michael Greenfield, University of Los Angeles, to study alternative reproductive behaviors of desert grasshoppers in California.
2667: To Victoria L. Sork, University of Missouri, St. Louis, for studies in population ecology of *Gustavia superba* (Lecythidaceae), a Neotropical tree species in Panama.

2668: To Thomas R. Vale, University of Wisconsin, to study views along U. S. 89—reflections on the interior west.
2669: To Forrest Pitts, University of Hawaii at Manoa, to research three decades of change in two rural Japanese townships.
2670: To John Eyre, University of North Carolina at Chapel Hill, for a study of the urban growth centers in Micronesian economic development.
2671: To Mario Hiraoka, Millersville State College, to support the flood plain mestizo subsistence study in the Peruvian Amazon.
2672: To William C. Mahaney, York University, to research the Quaternary history of Mount Kenya, East Africa.
2673: To Frances C. James, Florida State University, for his analysis of clinal variation: transplant experiments with Red-winged Blackbirds (supplemental).
2674: To Melvin L. Fowler, University of Wisconsin-Milwaukee, to research formative (pre-Classic) water distribution systems at Amalucan, Puebla, Mexico and vicinity.
2675: To Douglas D. Anderson, Brown University, to study prehistoric archeology in southern Thailand.
2676: To George E. Stuart, National Geographic Society, to research ancient Maya writing in Mexico.
2677: To Christopher B. Donnan, University of California, Los Angeles, for the multidisciplinary study of the ancient Peruvian city, Pacatnamu.
2678: To Thomas E. Levy, Albright Institute of Archaeological Research, Jerusalem, to support prehistoric investigations of early farming societies in the Negev Desert.
2679: To Donald H. Keith, Texas A&M University, excavation of a 16th-century shipwreck at Molasses Reef.
2680: To Dennis J. Stanford, Smithsonian Institution, in support of the Blackwater Draw archeology and paleoecology program.
2681: To David R. Brauner, Oregon State University, for the Pilcher Creek archeological project.
2682: To Howard C. Gerhardt, University of Missouri, to study the evolution of acoustic communication in Australian treefrogs.
2683: To Leslie D. Garrick, Seton Hall University, to research the ecology of American crocodiles in Jamaica, West Indies.
2684: To John C. Ogden, Fairleigh Dickinson University, to study the foraging ecology of the green turtle.
2685: To Stanley N. Williams, Dartmouth College, for geochemical monitoring of magma migration at Long Valley Caldera, California, radon and mercury detection.
2686: To Paul C. Sereno, Columbia University, to study phylogeny and comparative morphology of the dinosaurian family Psittacosauridae.
2687: To Peter Dodson, University of Pennsylvania, for the paleoecology study of the Judith River (Oldman) Formation in Dinosaur Park, Alberta, Canada.

2688: To Zheng Bao Lai, Kunming Institute of Zoology, for research on birds of southern China.
2689: To Monique Borgerhoff-Mulder, Northwestern University, to study the polygyny threshold and its application to a Kipsigis case study.
2690: To Peter I. Kuniholm, Cornell University, for the Aegean dendrochronology project in Turkey.
2691: To Elizabeth C. Stone and Paul E. Zimansky, State University of New York at Stony Brook, for excavations on the lower mound at 'Ain Dara, Syria.
2692: To James L. Gould, Princeton University, to study the use of the earth's magnetic field by honeybees.
2693: To Lon L. McClanahan, California State University, Fullerton, to study the physiological ecology of amphibians in the chaco boreal of Paraguay.
2694: To Duncan W. Thomas, Missouri Botanical Garden, for botanical exploration of the evergreen forests of southwest Cameroon.
2695: To Carl F. Vondra, Iowa State University, for a depositional analysis of Morrison and Cloverly Formations, Bighorn Basin, Wyoming.
2696: To William C. Livingston, Kitt Peak National Observatory, for the exploration of the landscape in the ultraviolet ($\lambda < 340$ nm) in Arizona.
2697: To Tim W. Clark, Idaho State University, for the meeteetse black-footed ferret conservation studies in the western United States.
2698: To John T. Polhemus, University of Colorado Museum, Boulder, to support zoogeographical studies of tropical Saldidae and other aquatic Hemiptera.
2699: To Michael Archer, University of New South Wales, to study relationships of the enigmatic mammals from the New Guinean highlands.
2700: To Biruté M. F. Galdikas, Tanjung Puting Reserve, for long-term orangutan research at Tanjung Puting Reserve in Indonesia.
2701: To Patrick J. Dugan, University of Durham, to research the distribution of wetland birds within the Senegal Valley, West Africa.
2702: To Naguib Kanawati, Macquarie University, for excavations at Akhmim in upper Egypt.
2703: To William S. Ayres, University of Oregon, to support archeological research on Ponape, Micronesia.
2704: To James C. Kemp, University of Oregon, to study the polarimetry of the extraordinary eclipsing star system Epsilon Aurigae in Oregon.
2705: To Eldon E. Ball, Australian National University, to research biological colonization of a recently formed volcanic island in Papua New Guinea.
2706: To Michael O. Dillon, Field Museum of Natural History, Chicago, to study the botanical response of Andean Desert Loma Formations to the 1982-1983 El Niño meteorological perturbation in Peru.

2707: To Antonio Hussey, University of Hawaii, to research resources for development: tourism and small-scale, indigenous enterprise in Bali.
2708: To Timothy G. Bromage, University of Toronto, for a field survey of Plio-Pleistocene deposits in Malawi's hominid corridor.
2709: To Larry D. Martin, University of Kansas, to investigate the Sangamon interglacial fossil deposits in Natural Trap Cave in Wyoming.
2710: To James E. Martin, South Dakota School of Mines and Technology, to study taphonomy of the Miocene Flint Hill locality in Bennet County, South Dakota.
2711: To Paul S. Martin, University of Arizona at Tucson, to study a unique deposit of extinct Pleistocene megafauna in Bechan Cave, Utah.
2712: To Robin W. Woods, Devon Social Services Department, for the Falkland Islands avian ecology expedition.
2713: To Merlin D. Tuttle, University of Wisconsin at Milwaukee, for studying the evolutionary impact of sound responsive bat predators on African frogs.
2714: To Thomas W. Sherry, Dartmouth College, and Tracey K. Werner, University of Massachusetts, to research foraging behavior and natural history of the Cocos Island finch *(Pinaroloxias inornata)* in Costa Rica.
2715: To James G. Morin, University of Los Angeles, for studies of bioluminescent communication in marine ostracods in Panama.
2716: To Jonathan Copeland, University of Wisconsin at Milwaukee, for neuroethological studies of bioluminescence in *Dyakia striata,* a terrestrial mollusc in Singapore.
2717: To Ian D. Hume, University of New England, Australia, to study nutritional physiology of the rufous rat-kangaroo.
2718: To Randall W. Davis, Scripps Institution of Oceanography, to research bioenergetics of Gentoo and Macaroni Penguins on South Georgia Island.
2719: To R. E. Magill, Missouri Botanical Garden, to study the bryophytes of the afro-alpine region of southern Africa.
2720: To J. D. Chapman, Chancellor College, for vegetation studies of the Mt. Mulanje massif in Malawi.
2721: To Robert R. Humphrey, University of Arizona, to research 90 years of change along the U. S.–Mexico boundary.
2722: To Howard B. Quigley, University of Idaho, to study jaguar ecology in the Pantanal region of Brazil.
2723: To Thomas T. Veblen, University of Colorado at Boulder, to investigate gap dynamics in the Valdivian rain forest in Chile.
2724: To Colin E. Thorn, University of Illinois at Champaign, to support the geomorphic model of periglacial landscapes project in Norway.
2725: To Rodey Batiza, Washington University, for a geological and biological study of Cocos Island.
2726: To J. F. Bonaparte, Universidad Nacional de Tucumán, to research Jurassic and Cretaceous terrestrial vertebrates of South America.

2727: To Rae Natalie P. Goodall, Centro Argentino Austral de Investigación Científica (CADIC), to support research on cetaceans of southern South America.
2728: To Payson D. Sheets, University of Colorado at Boulder, to study settlement and volcanism in the Arenal area in Costa Rica.
2729: To Thomas B. Croat, Missouri Botanical Garden, to investigate the flora of Cerro de la Neblina in Venezuela.
2730: To David Kuczynski, Moron University, to research the rotifer fauna of the Argentine's Patagonia as limnological indicator.
2731: To Peter G. H. Evans, University of Oxford, for studies of the conservation biology of Dominican rain forest birds.
2732: To Frans B. M. de Waal, University of Wisconsin at Madison, for a comparative study of the ethogram of the bonobo *(Pan paniscus)* and the common chimpanzee.
2733: To Rolf O. Peterson, Michigan Technological University, to research predator-prey relationships between wolves and moose on Isle Royale in Michigan.
2734: To John W. Sheets, Central Missouri State University, Warrensburg, for studying the historical demography of Colonsay and Jura (the Inner Hebrides), 1892-1975.
2735: To Luis Abel Orquera, University of Comahue, for the Tunel site archeological excavation in Argentina.
2736: To Gary J. Samuels, Department of Scientific and Industrial Research, New Zealand, for taxonomic and biologic studies of fungi in Brazil.
2737: To François Vuilleumier, American Museum of Natural History, New York, for research on niche shifts and double invasions during speciation of Patagonian birds.
2738: To Tom Gehrels, University of Arizona, for studying a microwave data link for the space-watch camera.
2739: To Judith E. Winston, American Museum of Natural History, to study life histories of lunulitiform bryozoans.
2740: To Melvin E. Sunquist, University of Florida, to research ecology and behavior of ocelot in Venezuela.
2741: To Martin F. J. Flower, University of Illinois at Chicago, for volcanologic studies in the Azores: evidence for mantle upwelling.
2742: To Thomas E. Miller, Western Washington University, to study the karst development and associated archeology of the Chiquibul, Belize.
2743: To Stephen J. Culver, Old Dominion University, for the sedimentologic study of late Precambrian glacigenic deposits in West Africa.
2744: To Noel T. Boaz, New York University, for paleoanthropological research in the Semliki Valley in Zaire.
2745: To Patricia V. Rich, Monash University, Victoria, Australia, to study the Ghastly Blank, 2.
2746: To Timothy M. Caro, University of Cambridge, England, for research on the cheetah male coalitions in Tanzania.

2747: To Deborah R. Smith, University of Tennessee at Knoxville, to study population genetics of *Anelosimus eximus,* a cooperative Neotropical spider.
2748: To R. J. McIntosh, Rice University, for archeological reconnaissance in the region of Timbuktu, Mali.
2749: To Arthur G. Miller, University of Maryland, to study pre-Hispanic murals of Oaxaca in their archeological contexts.
2750: To Richard L. Radtke, University of Hawaii, to research the ecology of the giant clam, *Tridacna maxima,* at Rose Atoll, Samoa.
2751: To Robert R. Hessler, Scripps Institution of Oceanography, for the project on photographic documentation of deep-sea hydrothermal vent fauna in the Pacific.
2752: To Biruté M. F. Galdikas, Tanjung Puting Reserve, for long-term orangutan research at Tanjung Puting Reserve in Indonesia (supplemental).
2753: To Nancy M. Farriss, University of Pennsylvania, for research on food in the ecology and cosmology of Mesoamerica.
2754: To Thomas A. Demere, San Diego Natural History Museum, to study late Pliocene marine vertebrate fossils, a bone bed quarry.
2755: To Bruce J. MacFadden, University of Florida, for research on the Pleistocene vertebrates and chronology of the Tarija Basin in southern Bolivia.
2756: To Phyllis C. Lee, University of Cambridge, for studying immaturity and social integration in the wild African elephant.
2757: To Martin Daly, McMaster University, Ontario, Canada, for a radiotelemetry study of kangaroo rat behavior.
2758: To Emmanuel K. Agorsah, University of Ghana, for settlement pattern analysis in the northern Volta Basin of Ghana.
2759: To Amini A. Mturi, Tanzania Government, to support the Lake Ndutu archeological research project.
2760: To Barbara A. Purdy, University of Florida, for research on the identification of woods from an archeological wet site in Florida.
2761: To Charles E. Lincoln, Harvard University, for new archeological research at Chichen Itza in the Yucatán, Mexico.
2762: To David Oates, University of London, for the London Institute of Archaeology expedition to northeastern Syria.
2763: To Richard E. W. Adams, University of Texas at San Antonio, to support the Río Azul archeological project.
2764: To Ralph W. Brauer, University of North Carolina at Wilmington, for the live retrieval of deep sea crustaceans for physiological study.
2765: To Kirk O. Winemiller, University of Texas at Austin, for studying the community structure and convergent ecomorphological trends among Neotropical stream fishes.
2766: To Sheila M. O'Connor, University of Cambridge, to research the ecology, conservation, and management of lemurs in undisturbed forest patches in Madagascar.

2767: To Harold B. Rollins, University of Pittsburgh, to study the effect of 1982-1983 El Niño upon Peruvian molluscs and the paleoecologic and archeologic significance.

2768: To Marvin J. Allison, Universidad de Tarapaća, to study pre-Columbian American disease.

Index